MW00620728

No Place Like Nebraska

Anatomy of an Era

Volume 1

By Paul Koch

Copyright © Paul Koch, 2013
All rights reserved.

THERMOPYLAE PRESS
No Place Like Nebraska: Anatomy of an Era Volume 1
Paul Koch

Copyright 2013 by Paul Koch
All Rights Reserved

Copy Editor: Paul Koch
Cover Design: Randy Shamoun
Cover Photograph: Merle Henkenius/John D. Young
Interior Design: Paul Koch

All rights reserved. This book was self-published by author Paul Koch under Thermopylae Press. No part of this book may be reproduced in any form by any means without the express permission of the author. This includes reprints, excerpts, photocopying, recording, or any future means of reproducing text.

If you wish to do any of the above, please seek permission first by contacting npln.info or huskerpowerpaul@yahoo.com

Published in the United States by Thermopylae Press

ISBN 978-0-9896070-9-4

About the Author:

Paul Koch earned a BS in Education from the University of Nebraska-Lincoln. He served as a strength & conditioning specialist for the Nebraska Athletic Department from 1987 to 1995 before transitioning to the entertainment and housing business. He now resides in Southern California where he enjoys family, surfing & poker while anxiously awaiting each Cornhusker Football season's arrival.

Dedication:

To my parents Marv & Kathy Koch, that you might know what busied me so.

To my beautiful bride Daynelle, for her support, and also my little Husker Holly, that you might know of the company your father kept.

Acknowledgements

Don't take a passing glance at this Acknowledgements section before swiftly moving on to the body of work, because once you fully comprehend the nature of the endeavor you'll come away with an understanding that any great feat, success or accomplishment was achieved because teamwork occurred. In this case, so many people assisted in putting this book together that I fear in some way or fashion someone will be left out. If this person is you, please accept my deepest apologies and pin it all on a freakish lapse of memory.

Of those I can recall, many wonderful friends contributed: there was my primary test reader Chad Stanley along with Tom Wald, Monte Kratzenstein, Virginia Goedeken and Byron Peterson, photographers Merle Henkenius & John D. Young, graphic artist Randy Shamoun, Randy Gobel for lending me his ring collection, and valued friends & Husker fans who urged me on when it all seemed too big a feat to pull off. A very special kind of gratitude goes out to the players, coaches, staffers, media personalities and fans who allowed me to mine the recesses of their memories while piecing together a historicity of that era, including Anne Hackbart's kind assistance in corresponding with Tom Osborne and Michael Stephens, Nebraska's Assistant AD for Marketing, Licensing and Concessions. I owe a heartfelt apology to Steve Volin (whose interview was somehow erased) and to Henry Cordes of the Omaha World-Herald (for withholding some info contained in this project while trying to assist him with his own). There was Doak Ostergard too, who helped get the ball rolling since everyone has scattered throughout the earth, plus Eric Wicherski & Lance Knapp for giving me a sounding board on Huskerboard.com and David Max & Joe Hudson via HuskerMax.com, a site that proved enormously invaluable.

I also have a soft spot in my heart for Vicki Capazo of Nebraska Sports Information for her help in acquiring archival photos, plus Keith Mann, Jennifer Miles, Debbie McBride, Bryan Pruitt, John Reece, Bob Hammons, Jon Pedersen, John Livingston, Joel Wilks, Lu Pavelka, Tony Veland, Aaron Penland, Mike Roberts, Dave Ellis, Tony Ortiz, Jill Deets and others for providing some great snapshots from the old college days. Then there was Mike VanCleve with his inspirational 'Dominate' pencil drawing: Mike, you give daVinci's Vitruvian Man a run for his money. Even though the combined volumes of this work total over eight hundred eighty-five thousand words, your photographs & art embellished the story. Thank you to everyone. I hope you are proud of your contributions, as I'm very grateful for you. GBR!

Contents

Some books are to be tasted, others to be swallowed, and some few to be chewed and digested.

Francis Bacon, *Of Studies*

There is no place like Nebraska,

Dear old Nebraska U.

Where the girls are the fairest,

The boys are the squarest,

Of any old school that I knew.

There is no place like Nebraska,

Where they're all true blue.

We'll all stick together,

In all kinds of weather,

For dear old Nebraska U.

Dear Old Nebraska U (School Fight Song),
Harry Pecha, Nebraska Class of 1924

Foreword

Brass Tacks with Charlie McBride

Let me put it to you straight: I absolutely hate surprises, both in life as well as on the playing field. When they happen things often end in disappointment, and then a man's left to pick up the pieces and quickly put something back together just to keep his rear-end out of hot water. Not very fun stuff.

That being said, on rare occasions the pendulum swings in the opposite direction and you're left with a real pleasant kind of surprise. Now, those I can handle. And mark my words, what Paul Koch has put together here with his analysis & tale about one of the finest five-year stretches in college football history is one of them. What we had during that 1993 to 1997 stretch of Cornhusker Football was the treat of a lifetime, because it was the kids and what they accomplished that made all our efforts worthwhile. The book you hold in your hands is a treasure trove of insight about how that era came to be, and if you miss even one page of it you've missed the point entirely. It may not the first, but I can vouch that it's the best of its kind. It made an old man laugh, instructed and reminded him of some things he'd always known but had yet forgotten, and even made him get all watery-eyed once or twice. I'm not gonna tell you who that old man is; you'll have to figure that out for yourself.

I've known the author since he was a greenhorn on Boyd Epley's weight staff and about as wet behind the ears as a goldfish. But like many Nebraska boys Paul had a work ethic, was a quick learner, and was relentless in his pursuit of building up a better student-athlete. I've always been grateful for the product that Husker Power strength staff churned out, because they allowed me to do my thing as Defensive Coordinator with greater effect. And believe it or not, almost twenty years later Paul now has something else to hang his hat on, because he took those same intangibles into his investigative writing and came up with a story of Husker Football -or any college football program, for that matter- to rival all others. He honored me with a request to write a foreword and it's been a pleasure to oblige him, because I imagine this book will be passed on from generation to generation, from locker room to locker room, and maybe even help to settle some chat room arguments and bar bets. It's voluminous, concise and loaded to the barrel with vignettes, anecdotes & incidents that piece together an incredibly accurate and entertaining narrative of that time in history.

What you hold here is a historical treasure about a state, a university and, most importantly, a team on a quest for greatness. So don't drop the ball: Read it! Then return to it often for good measure. This old man is glad that he did.

Charlie McBride, Nebraska Defensive Line Coach/Defensive Coordinator (1977-/1982-1999)

Prelude to a Miss
(Or "A Providential and Fortuitous Confluence of Events")

Place-kickers aren't normally prone to run this fast. "Yeee-haaw! Shit-fire, you sonsabitches! Shit-fire!!" Adrenaline coursing, tongue cursing and legs furiously back-pedaling across the grass, Byron Bennett crosses the 30, the 35, now to the 40, he's to midfield. Hands drawn as mock gunslinger's pistols, he blazes the broad span of the Florida State Seminoles' far sideline with imaginary fire, "Yeah baby! Woo-hoooooooo…!" His orgasmic celebration swiftly concludes as a horde of teammates in red, white and grass-stained regalia consume him in a brutal yet joyous embrace, his having split the uprights with a screaming 27-yarder bound for the Keys; the go-ahead field goal serving as a fine exclamation point to a Texas kid's Nebraska football career on a gridiron in south Florida's urban armpit.

Our wristwatch reads 11:13 p.m. on a muggy and maniacal January 1st, 1994 in the middle of Miami's Little Havana District. The shifty air is moist and heavy, rain having fallen for a brief spell earlier this afternoon. The turf –or, more appropriately, the swatches of Bermuda Grass sod intermingled with the loose, painted, teal-colored sand of the old Orange Bowl- looks as if a massive herd of elephants crossed an African savanna on their jaunt to a watering-hole. Wait. Let me re-phrase that: A herd of elephants actually *did* cross the turf earlier that evening, albeit as part of the famed "Red, Hot and Orange Halftime Extravaganza" for the 81,536 fanatics in attendance and the millions of Americans transfixed to their television tubes. All eyes awaited the crowning of a new king: it would be either the University of Nebraska's Tom Osborne or Florida State University's Bobby Bowden, each man relishing an opportunity to finally knock a King Kong-sized monkey off his back after careers full of wide-rights, out-of-bounds receptions and tipped two-pointers. College football-lovers keyed-in on the event this night also yearned -perhaps subconsciously- to find who would be on the winning end of an ideological, organizational, geographic and even demographic waging of a modern day civil war, more or less. Much hangs in the balance as this war-like scrum is played out in the sweep of a sixty-minute span.

Byron's imaginary Colt .45's were the only firearms unholstered this dark night, although a seemingly unending fusillade of body-shots resounded in bloody, sweaty, spit-filled & bruising series of volleys, each consisting of botched assignments, missed calls, spine-jarring collisions and vulgar jawing for a better part of the evening. And now? Byron's kick resulted in a scorekeeper's tally of 16 to 15, with the game's lead and decisive edge going to the farm-state Cornshuckers. The victorious end was near! Oh, so near. Triumph, finally! After more than two painful decades of Husker heartbreak, elusive victory was in the grasp. Almost. Can you feel it coming in the air tonight?

Only one minute and sixteen seconds remained on the end zone scoreboard's clock: 01:16. Let's think about that for a moment. Let it sink in. A minute-sixteen: a span of time such as this normally passes without the blink of an eye. But in this situation? *This* situation? It's an eternity. Because –to borrow a line from Tom Petty- because sometimes the waiting is the hardest part.

To understand the context of this historic spectacle, recall that the State of Nebraska's beloved and top-ranked Cornhuskers entered the game a disgustingly disrespected 17-point underdog by the odds-makers in Vegas; this despite being undefeated, unbroken and untied since August of 1993. Rarely one to comment on anything outside the rubric of family and football at the time (much less the shadier aspects of sports society) Doctor & Nebraska Head Coach Tom Osborne replied in response to a reporter's question about the contest's larger-than-proper point-spread,

"The gamblers bet with their dollars and not with their hearts. And you play the game with your heart… so we'll see who's right and who's wrong."

It was no sure bet, this much is true. For a Husker team approaching so near the pinnacle, the mountaintop, the Everest of college football, to suddenly and swiftly bow out in defeat after such a grueling and hard fought contest would seem unfathomable, unbelievable, pure fiction. The road here had been too long, too arduous, too taxing for most human bodies and mortal spirits. The mountainous trail to this New Year's Day 1994 was a full twenty-two years of trudging, of painfully plodding uphill, tweaking and massaging the University's program here and there, an ever-evolving team of young men yearning, burning, striving for an existence as the elite of the sport. The Scarlet Brotherhood's once tanned but now ruddy and weather-beaten faces –simple, red N's on their helmets signifying this unique tribe– they had ventured much too far on this annual journey to the temperate climes of southeast Florida's bowl venue to return home with another black eye, to once again hang their heads in defeat until memory fades with springtime's renewal. Even more, the mood and tenor of an entire state's inhabitants rested on these boys' shoulders and their push to victory as it always had for years long before. Springtime seems a lifetime away, the sharp sting of death so near the front door's exterior in the snow and the ice and a bone's frigid, winter chill. A full season's dreams and aspirations have steadily built to a crescendo in this football championship game. Much is at stake as the collective cabin fever of a long Nebraska winter arrives at a dark, Januarial head. Because -as we all know- the bitter winters remain historically steadfast in their refusal to surrender a grip on the freshly birthed pages of newly hung calendars. But now? But now the fog has lifted. Sunlight gleams on the eastern horizon. A victory celebration is only seconds away, this tenuous one point lead firmly in hand as a result of Byron's kick.

But then? It happened: The Unthinkable. With only 1:16 on the clock and against false hope, all fears were realized. And it wasn't one bit pretty. The team summarily shot itself in the foot when the ensuing kickoff rolled out of bounds: "Fifteen yards," said the official. Near game's end there wasn't much gas left in the tank for these boys, for a defensive pass rush was mustered but brought low by waning legs. Then there was a "Dead Ball. Personal foul. Late hit out of bounds..," shouted the official, the result of a Barron Miles' nudge on freshman Seminole running back Warrick Dunn as he scooted into the sideline morass, "Fifteen yards and first down, Florida State." And then –unbelievably- an overthrown ball resulted in a sketchy pass interference penalty against defender Toby Wright."Half the distance to the goal," rang the referee's voice over the soon-to-be-demolished old stadium's bicentennial era sound system.

Now the ball -this oblong, brown, leather spheroid- sits on the Nebraska three yard line. Surely a quick dive play off center will end the battle once and for all for the young men from Tallahassee, giving them the win they so desire. But it was thwarted! The gritty

Blackshirt defense stuffed the run play for a one yard loss at the 4! Denied entrance to the end zone's no-man's land by the fleetest defense afoot, perhaps a kick could undo the Scarlet and Cream once and for all, saving the odds-makers, plungers and bettors some small, slight face. An impending field goal try would be a veritable chip-shot. Gift-wrapped, in a word. Like shooting fish in a barrel. With a shotgun. Big fish at that.

So out trots a cherubic freshman kicker, a Sports Illustrated coverboy from the recent yet long gone summer of 1993, crowned a possible savior for Coach Bowden's heretofore frustrated title aspirations. His teammates shut out of the end zone by Cornhusker Defensive Coordinator Charlie McBride's cunningly barbaric, brisk and brash defense, he'd converted three field goals already tonight, only missing a first quarter try from all of 47 yards out. And now came this. This? A piece of cake. He could pull this one off with both eyes closed, were he so inclined.

And he did it. The kid absolutely nailed it for three easy points. The score now? 18 to 16, the decisive edge now going to the Seminoles! Sunshine State hysteria fills the bowl's floor with the Florida State players swarming the field, engulfing the slight-framed kicker, the weight of them bearing down and pressing him and his holder firmly to the midfield turf. A rear-assaulting Gatorade bath envelopes Coach Bowden, his eyeglasses fogging into a semi-blind haze of jubilation concurrently mixed with disgust, as he suddenly realizes time remains on the clock: *"The celebration can wait! Get back here on the sidelines, you dummies! Get back here!"*

Now it's Bobby who's put on the defensive for his coaching chops and a triumphal conquest. His magic number? 00:22. Twenty-two seconds remain. Nothing to bear much cause for concern -it's no minute-sixteen, mind you- but still nothing to scoff at considering the genius on the far sideline and his assorted generals up in the press box. And, oh yes, Coach Bowden respectfully shakes his head, "Those dang Nebraska boys! Osborne's gritty bunch out there just don't know the meaning of the word 'quit,' do they?"

Could Coach Bowden's bunch hold on and hold out for a mere twenty-two ticks of the Timex? "That rascal Tom," Bobby mutters to his conscience, "…what does he have hidden up his dad-gum sleeve?" For a split-second, the coach rues the dispatch of two defensive assistants to his good friend and adversary's Lincoln offices the previous spring to teach them the finer points of this 'speed defense' commonly known as The Four-Three. But they've been friends and admirers for years, coexisting as leaders and educators of some of America's most talented young gridiron greats, so this contest means all the more. Braggin' rights, you know. Off-season dinner banquets are heck of a lot more enjoyable when you've finally got a shiny new national championship ring to wear on that long-empty right ring finger. But he forgets all of that in a moment, turning his attention back to the field of play…

And suddenly, in an 'it-ain't-over-'til-it's-over' display of bravado and balls flying, sophomore Cornhusker quarterback Tommie Frazier floats arms-length from the pocket's scrum and heaves a perfect, frozen-rope spiral downfield to tight end Trumane Bell who's thirty-four yards removed, as he contorts his arms and lanky 6 foot 3 inch frame at the out-of-bounds mark. It tickles his fingertips, but a garnet & gold Seminole shadow foils the pass attempt, the ball falling earthbound and incomplete. Now only 8 seconds remain on the clock."Quick! Call the next play!" Coaches Frank Solich and Milt Tenopir bark play-call options down from the stadium's spartan little sweatbox upstairs to T.O., Ron Brown, Turner Gill and Dan Young on the sideline below, "Okay, this one has to do the trick…" We see slotted receivers wide out right, shotgun formation, one running back in the backfield."We only have ten guys out there!" a voice fretfully bellows."Bell?! Trumane! Get out there!" On a moment's notice Trumane bolts onto the field to make it an even eleven versus eleven once again. He's motionless in his stance for a slender sliver of time.

The ball is snapped. The speedy receivers set out blazing downfield like a shotgun blast on full-choke. Seminole Linebacker Derrick Brooks hesitates for a split-second and turns a shoulder toward the left flat. Trumane, seeing this, cuts a straight path downfield, making a running lane of the hash marks. Suddenly the ball is airborne and number 80 catches it mid-stride! Now time -and yards- are in a race to the finish: "Can't... run ...fast enough!..." Trumane's world becomes slow motion, "or... far enough!" The lunging swipe of an outstretched linebacker's arm results in a shoestring tackle. Trumane's body, like the downward death-spiral of a gunned-down quail, alights accrumpled on the 29. Two seconds precariously hang on the clock as his knee impacts the ground and, for all intents and purposes, stops the clock. But wait! "The clock is still ticking!," Husker Nation blurts in horrified disbelief. It counts down to triple zeros."Is it over? Is it really *over*?!" Was this last gasp for naught? "It *can't* be! It just can't! No freaking way! There was still some time left on the clock!"

Again, the hysterics. A mob of Seminoles again pours onto the field, the stands erupt, and Referee John Soffey and his team of Big East officials are caught with their figurative pants down: "Was he tackled with time remaining? Are there one or two seconds left? Get these cameramen off the field! Where was he tackled? The 35 yard line? The 27? Can't these Florida State Troopers help out a little here? Get these damned kids off the field! Holy crap! What to do?! Oh no, Osborne is shouting this way and pointing a finger to the turf. What's he saying? "One second left? Twenty-nine yard line?""

Tom Osborne and Nebraska Receivers Coach Ron Brown are beckoning a full fifteen yards out of their sideline coaching box & sharing their spot-on recall with the addled officiating crew. *"Get the fuck off the field, old man!",* a hulking FSU offender bellows at the stately Osborne. But Coach is deliberately oblivious to the remark, busy with more pressing matters of breathing life into this drive, this game of a lifetime, this last lunge for victory by gaining one more offensive snap. Just... one... more... snap of the ball. Offensive tackle Zach Weigert, though, is nonplussed at hearing the coarse comment, helmet in hand and threatening to dismember the jerk's head right on the spot, *"Don't you ever talk to Coach that way! I'll fucking kill you! No one talks to Coach that way! No one!"* T.O. swiftly extends a hand and urges Zach to calm himself and make haste to the sideline before an unsportsmanlike penalty makes it all but finished, this last gasp for the win, for hard-fought glory, for a championship. For what seems a swirling eternity, chaos rules.

Then, after a time, anarchy slowly regresses. Pandemonium recedes. Calmer heads prevail. The sidelines are filled once again. What is the call? Ears are on edge, tingling in anticipation. The referee strikes a pose and clicks his microphone... it's announced over the tinny Orange Bowl loudspeakers, *"There is one second remaining on the clock."* A cry promptly goes up from the Nebraska ranks: "Field goal! Field Goal unit! Get out there! Go, go, go!" This is where we encounter our man Byron Bennett once again.

Poor Byron. Number 13 was not expecting this encore. In his mind he'd already won the whole damned ball of wax a minute and fifteen seconds ago."Ho-leeee shit!", he thinks to himself, "...what kinda mess have I gotten myself into?" It's gonna test his abilities: he must now boot the ball 45 yards and then some through the yellow stanchions on the dim and ever-thickening Orange Bowl horizon. Quarterback Tommie Frazier attempts an abrupt motivational session, grabbing Byron by the jersey lapel and urging, "Just do it," before an official sends him scurrying to the sideline. Byron leaves the huddle and sets up. "Hey-sooos Cripes!" he holds convention with himself, "So this is how it all ends, huh?

National Champs or Bust?…a hero or a zero? Well, alright then, dammit. Let's give it a shot. Gonna need a lot of leg. The wind's been all over the place tonight. Shit fire." Shit-fire, indeed.

We close in tightly now for one microscopic biologic moment in time: it's the lactic acid, adenosine tri-phosphate and phospho-creatine stores of cellular bodies bulging, it's norepinephrine surging, it's a million nerve synapses heaving, pulsating, slowly and ever so surely coming undone in the pit of one's gut. It's a time he'll always remember, a time he'd love to forget."Man, it's sooo loud in this place," whispers a small silent voice deep in the belly of Byron's brain."Focus, now. Focus…" as he attempts to zero-in on the task. He can't hear holder David Seizys calling out the snap count from a mere 3 yards away. He wonders how the hell long-snapper Aaron Graham, twice the distance removed, can even pick up David's voice barking out the call. He likely can't. There's no way! Hopefully the guy reads lips, because it's gonna take something extra to pull this thing off without a hitch. "Well," summoning all his courage, "here goes…"

The ball is suddenly snapped! The line of scrimmage flexes and yaws… footholds give… grunts abound as sand and turf scatters along the trench… arms tangle and furiously slap, elbows jerking out a frantic tango… a lone defender in the Florida State backfield takes to a stratospheric air, arms stretched overhead in an attempt to block the field goal attempt… and Byron? What about our man Byron?

He hears nor sees none of it, eyes instead fixated on this little patch of grass at #22, his holder David Seizys' foot. Byron's world suddenly becomes it's own small, vacuum-like, muted kind of dream sequence. "The ball will soon be here…" He lunges forward and plants his foot. "Head down", he reminds himself, his leg whipping fiercely, forcefully forward toward the ball, "Follow through, now…" And then… Contact!! It's airborne. Now comes the hardest part: the waiting, the watching. "Where will it go?" A slicing defender suddenly crashes in off the line's outer edge and knocks our holder David Seizys from his crouch, sending him sprawling wildly onto his backside. "That should draw a penalty flag," thinks the kicker."Move the ball forward and re-try? The game can't end on a defensive penalty. That's the rule…" But there's no flag. Not yet. Not a yellow hankie anywhere to be seen. Another millionth of a second passes. *Still* no flag? None? "Are these officials blind?! Crooked!? Or just plain incompetent?! Who the hell are these clowns, anyway!?"

Oh, the ball, you say? Did it perfectly and forcefully split the uprights? Is victory finally ours? Has the jinx been lifted? The pox extinguished? Is there finally, eventually, the long-awaited glory, the emphatic triumph, the elation of conquest, the emotional release? Well…?

We know all too well how this scene ends. In the aftermath, 1,800 miles away on the North American Plains more than a few quite worthy television sets have been quickly reduced to tomorrow's trash heap. Many a radio has played its last Kent Pavelka broadcast, its last country song, its last weather forecast, its last commodities report. Hearts are in throats. Countenances fall. Mouths are agape. Grown men clench their fists, eyes welling up with anger and tears. Women weep. Even more so the youngsters, sobbing uncontrollably, their faces buried deep in couch pillows. This ugly moment is seared into their short memory for a lifetime. Shocked. Jilted. Crestfallen. Flummoxed. Anguished. Nauseated. Mere words cannot properly articulate this pain, this empathic suffering, this cosmic sucker-punch another "how-many-bowl-games in a row, now?" Wide lefts can do that to a person. Just ask Bobby.

While the television shot -flickering- goes down to NBC Sideline Reporter O.J. Simpson stalking a drenched, convivial Coach Bowden for a live post-game victory remark, a middle-aged man in a red t-shirt storms angrily out of the house -screen door banging- and into the frigid, deathly, biting Midwestern night air of his farm's front porch. From the icy railing he screams out a most profane litany of profanities at the surrounding snowbanks, questioning his Creator's sense of fair play."This beer tastes like shit!" he mutters bitterly, settling into a sulk and crudely heaving the can and its contents far, far, far into a vast, dense, blue, moonlit Nebraska darkness.

But take heart, dear reader, that's not how the story ends. Not so sadly. Not by a long shot.

Truth be told, it's not how the story begins either. This exasperating, drama-filled, seventy-six second snippet in history actually fell '*in media res*', smack-dab in the middle of it all, to be precise. Because, as the old saying goes, the sun actually *did* come up the next day over the Nebraska plains and, well, life *did* go on. Sort of, anyhow.

Let's just say it was a long winter until the spring's thaw finally arrived, that contest's resultant score perpetuating a private, ever-building, and heretofore untold bounty of tenacity and self-determination that would eventually go down in the annals of history as a most victorious of eras, the residue of that team's resolve begetting a change from sacrosanct darkness to blinding light, coming on in a flash. It was excellence communally personified, and it was glorious.

Some might describe what came later as a providential and fortuitous confluence of events, an assemblage of persons, efforts, premises & presumptions hitting their climax, a harmonic convergence of characters on a hidden quest among the golden fields of corn, far away from the limelight, from the prying eyes, from the calls that heads must roll. Far, far away from most everything, really. Others might call it a hoarding of talents, a type and shadow of the epidemic proportions soon to arrive on the college football landscape, a last gasp at an ever-elusive grasping for greatness in the waning twilight of a coaching lifetime, a fleeting anecdote making a compelling case for seizing and securing a semblance of superiority in mankind's often otherwise droll existence.

It just may have been all of those things rolled up into one, truth be told. The question is, how and why and in what way did the Husker Football team's magnificent rebound from that contest's disappointment come about? What propelled them to repeated conquests of every foe long thereafter?

Well, if you must know? I have the answer. You see, I've learned a few things, I've talked to a few people, I have the inside track. So let me ask a question: Do you want to see, to hear, to find out some secrets? Do you wish to participate in something special? Something grand? Something wholly set apart? Make a choice and make it now! For just this once, be bold. "Yes", you say? Then drop everything and come along. I hold the key. This is where we find ourselves: unlocking and opening the door and boldly, curiously, conspicuously drawing back the dark, forbidden curtain for a taste, a glimpse, to see with our own eyes how it all came to be. Take my hand and hold tight. Firmly now, as the scene slowly comes into focus. This should be a grand sporting adventure. Read on, my friend, to hear an epic saga of greatness and beauty, of pluck and plight and perseverance. Of championships. Of football glories. Read on.

Introduction

The Great 60 & 3 Why? and How?

So very difficult a matter is it to trace and find out the truth of anything by history, when, on the one hand, those who write it find long periods of time intercepting their view, and, on the other hand, the contemporary records of any actions and lives, partly through envy and ill-will, partly through favour and flattery, pervert and distort truth.

Plutarch, *Lives of the Noble Greeks*

Why and How. To be perfectly frank, the two words -at first blush- don't amount to much. But these small & simple three-letter words have long been my favorites. Directed with discernment, Why and How hold within them the power to obtain a vast world of detailed information. Information which, if applied correctly and in the appropriate context, can accomplish a great many things. Profound and astounding things, I tell you. They can: save a life, improve a life, end a life, extend a life, even create a life. This means a great deal if you value life. They can build empires, too. And also tear them down. It all depends upon who does the asking, who the answering, and whether the revelatory data creates a stronger bond of mutual understanding or rends a last remaining, slender thread of hope asunder.

Over the span of four recent years I found myself engaged in a grand passion. It was a passion involving a madly stultifying use of those two simple words: 'Why?' and 'How?'. Doing so opened up a new world to me, a world which I had already experienced closely and thought I knew greatly of. But I was proven wrong, for in my asking Why and How and throwing their derivative cousins about I came to a greater appreciation for a page in history that, in retrospect, has proven itself a bedrock of this man's life's experience. I'm speaking of a time involving great upheaval: of sorrowful setbacks, of grand accomplishment, of personal, physical, emotional and spiritual growth that took place in a university setting on the Midwestern plains at the turn of the twenty-first century.

Witnessing Greatness

I was a young and naïve undergraduate earning a bachelors degree when it all began in 1987 and by the time my run ended in early 1996 I found myself participating as an able professional in the same setting, catching a rare glimpse of a drive to greatness from my unique, rare and intimate front row seat. I was very moved during that time as its witness, and am even more so in these latter days. That era sometimes seems as if it were a dream because it was near perfect. And in this fallen world that's a mighty damned tough thing to achieve: perfection.

More precisely, as a Strength & Conditioning Coach on the University of Nebraska campus in the Star City of Lincoln, Nebraska from the 1987 through 1995 seasons, I participated in the genesis of a spectacular run of unparalleled college football dominance by the famed Cornhusker Football squads. Among those were the 1995 Cornhuskers, widely hailed as possibly the greatest college football team of all time, the result of a nuanced re-organization begun in early 1990 that produced an astounding won-loss record of 60 wins and 3 losses in a five year span from 1993 to 1997 for Coach Tom Osborne's teams. That 60 & 3 record computes to a 95.2% success rate, an unheard of accomplishment in the modern era (since 1970) and what I consider an underappreciated achievement in the annals of history, particularly considering today's sport-obsessed society.

To wit, since 1970 only five other Division 1 football programs have dared to even approach the level of that 95.2% proficiency: Alabama's 2008-2012 teams (61-7, 89.7%), Boise State's 2007-2011 teams (60-6, 90.9%), USC's 2004-2008 teams (59-6, 90.7%), Oklahoma's 1971-1975 teams (54-4, 93.1%) and Miami's 1987-1991 teams (56-4, 93.3%). Yet, for all the media hoopla and ESPN love-ins, none can touch the 1993-1997 Cornhuskers. These teams found themselves in five Big 8/Big 12 Conference Championship-determinant games and four NCAA National Championship games in which they earned a record of 7 and 2 for an amazing 77.8% success rate. Again, it's worth noting these contests pitted the Scarlet & Cream against each season's best-of-the-best and not some proverbial tomato can, to borrow a boxing metaphor. To add, a 95.2% success rate is absolutely profound considering -unlike most organizations, be they sporting, business, or social- it's a rare numerical feat from a purely mathematical standpoint in and of itself.

But what makes these numbers all the more impressive is the mandated rate of astounding 'turnover in the workforce,' per se, because a Division 1 college athlete had only five years to complete his four years of eligibility. Note this, because I challenge you to show me any endeavor on a grand scale able to train and produce such sustained results with an annual minimum workforce turnover of 20 percent, for I can think of no other. Then again, I think much about Nebraska Football and not a lot else.

Now, that last statement (though somewhat facetious) may cause you to perceive me as a rather shallow human being, but in the course of marrying & divorcing, raising children, career advancement, churchgoing, and other participatory activities & social norms of the modern era, I derive great satisfaction in immersing myself in this grand obsession known as Nebraska Cornhusker Football. Why? (There's that little word.) I'll tell you why.

The Power of 'Why?'

This is my one great Why?: because on late summer, autumn and predominantly early winter Saturday afternoons I'm able to emotionally -and oftentimes physically- join alongside and vicariously struggle through an hours-long battle against foes fairly matched in equal ability while yearning to arrive at the top in victory. Why? Because the game inspires. Because it gives me hope for the future. Because I see a true-to-life metaphor in the sixty-minute struggle. Because I observe an epic battle that I, too, experience in daily life, i.e. burdensome government regulations, penurious taxation, sickness & death of loved ones, career challenges & setbacks, hostile climates, personal disappointments, conundrums and the like. It oftentimes seems as if the Universe's forces are arrayed against me and me alone, but despite these hurdles I still find a way to come out a winner & alive (or at least even in the game) and hold my head high that I survived to fight another day, eternal hope reigning.

I believe there are also a multitude of lessons to cull from these shared experiences from football Saturdays. Parallels both inspiring and instructive can often be drawn. Analogies abound: False start in a game? Get moved back 5 yards? Let's dial up a play to attack the weakness of an obstructionist defense and gain that first down yardage anyhow. A full work-week's efforts erased by a computer glitch and I'm knocked back to square one? No problem, let's dial up a new gameplan to take all-comers head-on and achieve a profit anyway. That's the essence of business, my friend, something consuming at least five days of our week. Destiny favors the bold and perseverant.

Sure, there are other Why's for this love of all things Husker, Cornhusker, Bugeater, Big Red, Scarlet & Cream or however you want to label Nebraska Football, but that is my overriding reason, other Why's answered as a subset of the one, great, basic Why as a fanatic of the team and the sport. Then there are the smaller Why's, too: Why the University of Nebraska? Why this institution in this locale? All things both conference-wide and nationwide being equal, why did these Huskers achieve excellence while contemporaries of that era fell short? I just had to know the answer to all the 'Why's?'

The Entertaining Nature of 'How?'

A more apt word, then, getting past Why?, is How? -and this is where things get really interesting. So much so that you are now, at this very moment in history, consuming the final result of my one, great, personal 'How?' as it relates to Nebraska Football greatness: 'How did all of this come about? How were methods tweaked? How were minds changed? How were bodies built? Were I to find answers to all these How's?, could there be such a thing as a flowchart for fortune, a prescription for prosperity, a recipe for reward?' And if so, could I possibly possess the ability to adequately articulate a template for sharing these springboards to success? I'll be completely honest with you in saying that I entered the journey with some self-doubt and trepidation, to say the least.

Listen, I'm no professional writer, no seasoned journalist, no highly trained wordsmith. Trust me, dear brother/sister. But guess what? Any dullard can do it. Really. I'm a prime example, believe me. I implore you, there's absolutely nothing outstanding about Paul Koch as an intellectual, a man, a father, a son, a friend, a businessman, a person of faith. I simply refused to stop asking 'How?' until I felt I had a reasonable grasp of the respective replies, that's all. And the great 'How?' in this case? Please practice patience, as some backstory will enrich the experience and give you a firmer grasp of the nature of our endeavor. My one great How? all started with a book, a beauty, and a belief. Let me explain.

Laying the Groundwork

A Book: It was November 2008 and I was living in San Diego, California as a dozen-years removed, transplanted Nebraskan involved in the residential real estate market as it was turning from boom-to-bust amid a worldwide financial crisis. As a Realtor representing primarily first time home-buyers due to my fondness for teaching, engaging and assisting my clients in obtaining the American Dream, my business was drying up. Big time. With a hefty mortgage, stay-at-home wife and infant child, and an extremely elusive supply of lending capital available to my clients during a financial meltdown, I had to branch out and move with the times or be left 'picking up after the last pony in the parade,' if you catch my drift.

To make ends meet I accepted a position as Asset Manager for a local non-profit housing developer and management entity. There was great satisfaction in this move, mind you, serving more vulnerable segments of our society via provision of affordable rental housing in a very unaffordable American city. It was personally gratifying and morally satisfying, but it came with a caveat: I was to function as a hub of communication between various facets of the organization and the outside business world. From Property Management to the President & Board of Directors to Banking & Lending Institutions to General Contractors to Building Maintenance to regulatory governmental agencies and even the residents themselves, I saw both astounding levels of professionalism and proficiency as well as frustratingly inefficient uses of people and resources. As an individual who fancies himself a mover & shaker, a team player and a policy-maker, I asked myself, 'How can we achieve and operate at peak organizational performance in this niche market segment?' (That must be the old strength coach in me, always looking to identify areas of weakness and potential improvement.)

Looking for an answer in my off-hours studies, I came upon an astounding business book: Jim Collins' *Good to Great* (2001). His tome set out to divvy up the champions from the also-rans in America's corporate world, distilling the axioms gained from an intensified, prolonged study of these corporate winners into a few basic tenets of applicable insight. The book was an inspiring and eye-opening read, both confirming and simultaneously dispelling some beliefs I had held about success in American business enterprise.

But then -much to my surprise- there was a larger, more unexpected epiphany: It made me hearken back to my days as an Athletic Department employee on the Nebraska campus, helping me to sense amazing parallels not only in the way these corporate titans achieved business results, but also how Head Coach Tom Osborne and his staff conducted their business of educating young men while attaining Herculean status as college football titans. At first I thought it was my memory playing tricks on me, waxing nostalgic about the good old days and recalling the positive experiences while subconsciously negating the rough patches. But the more I reflected on that time as it related to the book it was eventually affirmed in my mind that there was, indeed, something incredibly unique and earth-shattering in the way the organism known as Nebraska Football succeeded in the latter span of my years there in the 1990's. The question was: How?: 'Just how did those Cornhusker teams do it?' That was my big 'How?' 'In what way did the Cornhusker elevens succeed beyond incredible odds and expectations?' My curiosity grew. And then it grew some more. It began to eat at me.

Then there was:

A Beauty: this is the ugly part. It's an oxymoronic statement, I get that. But it's true. Six years previous I married a young woman who couldn't have been more different than myself: She being raised in a single-parent home in a relatively un-churched, large, urban, Latino environment in the American Southwest, whereas I had grown under the nurture of a father and mother in a tiny, rural, Christian, European-American environment in the Midwest. We nicknamed our union Chips and Salsa. Chips, due to my cornfed ethics, values, and upbringing, and Salsa, corresponding to the often spicy, mixed, and refreshingly dissimilar ingredients she brought to the proverbial table. What at first seemed a case of opposites attracting and complementing each other, over the course of years it began to slowly unravel, a union becoming disunion, worldviews diverging, beliefs dividing, hopes shriveling and dying, and fears real or imagined driving a wedge beyond the point of rapprochement. I wondered how this came to be, because I'd seen teammates of equally dissimilar demographics become lifelong friends and blood brothers while at the University of Nebraska during those happy 90's.'Was the difference, then, a matter of her female and my male orientation?,' I speculated.'Or was it something else?' There seemed such harmony among the teammates and staff at Nebraska consisting of the better part of almost three hundred individuals, so why couldn't a measly two people find a way work things out? How could we do it? Again, there's that word: How.

And finally, there was:

A Belief: I believe Malcolm Gladwell's book *The Tipping Point* touched on it best when he wrote, "We need to prepare ourselves for the possibility that sometimes big changes follow from small events, and that sometimes these changes can happen very quickly." You may be thinking the aforementioned chapter's drama involving that 1993 11 win and 1 loss Husker team and Byron's final, wide-left field goal attempt played a large role in later seasons' accomplishments, and you would be rightly so in thinking such. But only to a point, you see. And this is why 'Belief' brought me back to the word 'How?', for belief can get you out of a tough spot time and again. Of primary note, let's go back to 1990/1991:

The '90 season was a rough one. By Nebraska football standards it was rougher than most, because a team that was traditionally strong year in and year out had somehow lost its gusto, its moxie, its mojo, and faltered to a nine and three record by year's end. Now, don't get me wrong, nine and three is a tremendous accomplishment in its own right, but not in the way it transpired. This was Tom Osborne's Nebraska Football, built on Bob Devaney's decades-old blueprint for championships and the premise that a team well-prepared and well-versed in the schemes and attitudes that it took to succeed could stand a fighting chance versus any and all foes in any and all arenas, lucky twists of fate notwithstanding. But it was the *way* in which those three losses transpired that mattered most, grinding at the collective conscious, for it seemed much of the crew of student-athletes were content with a nine win season and a New Year's trip to a bowl game much nearer the equator… and little else. There was a noticeable lack of cohesion, of focus, of discipline, of yearning for higher ideals and expending ultimate efforts, especially the type of effort considered greatest of all: not the effort necessary to win, but the effort to *prepare* to win.

Not that there were slouches or a lack of talent in that '90 grouping. Oh no, this team was plenty talented, with as many as eight future NFL contributors in that year's ranks of upperclassmen and those turning pro early. So the lack of success wasn't about the prevailing talent or lack thereof. What was it then? Well, at the time there seethed a shallow undercurrent of racial tension, traces of black liberation theology and subtle race issues both real and imagined being levied via a small contingent of campus educators and student-athletes. Navel-gazing, finger-pointing and charges of most subtle bias were whispered whenever a perceived slight or injustice appeared. William Shakespeare once penned that there was, "something rotten in the state of Denmark." Well, in this case Nebraska Football wasn't far behind, because by the 1990 season's end an eight win run turned into a one and three slide. Those three losses were by a combined 43 points to the opponent's 117, averaging to a 39-14 score in favor of the other guys: most definitely un-Nebraska-like. And the result? In the national media the team became a paper tiger no less, a Doberman without teeth, a cop without a gun, a switchblade dull as Grandma's old butter knife. Nebraska was a 'name team' that you passed through on your way to a National Championship, as the Colorado Buffaloes and Georgia Tech Yellow Jackets both did that 1990 season.

But something even more profound was amiss, because for the first time in who-knows-when Nebraska football almost fell from the ranks of the ranked."Unfathomable! Blasphemy!," you might say. But in early 1991 this was the present reality, and something had to be done. The questions emanating from the second floor Coaches' offices of South Memorial Stadium were, "*Can* something be done? What could be lacking?" If the answers could be determined, then "How can the needed changes be best affected?" (There it is again, that word: How?)

There was a belief that things could turn. And belief is a strong emotion, a driving force, an impenetrable notion. Belief alone has carried man across desserts, across an ocean's vast expanse, to the moon and back. To paraphrase an old Henry Ford quote, "If you believe you can do a thing or can't do a thing, you're right." In the pages that follow you'll find just how proper and powerful and cataclysmic a belief can be.

Making it Worth Our While

But before moving on to the answers in the forthcoming pages I first set a few ground rules prior to embarking on this endeavor, my journey back to the great Why and How of those 60 & 3 teams. First and foremost it was this: Relentlessly seek authenticity. Why authenticity? Because without fully, wholly and unsparingly splaying open any object for inspection and fact-finding the resulting content and conclusions are too often found unoriginal and wanting, dull and uninspiring, lacking. So I yearned to be true to the truth, to flesh out all leads, covering all the grounds, approaching from all angles. I guess one could say that my respect for you, dear reader, was such that I would hold nothing back, even if it meant that this book may occasionally offend. It's a fine line to walk, I know, but you're owed nothing less. In the final analysis, it's my hope that your sensibilities are not alarmed by what you read in the coming pages. (I might add, I was in the midst of a bitter and drawn out divorce & custody battle while conducting a majority of these coming interviews and looking for some much-desired happiness and a little more laughter in an otherwise somber life. So please forgive if I seem at times flippant or condescending or a grand wise-ass, as this wasn't my intent.)

Lastly, I want to share with you an old Indian tale I'd once heard, about four blind men who wanted to learn of the animal known as the elephant. The story goes that a great ruler had gathered the blind quartet all round this mighty & kingly beast, whereupon they were given a brief moment of self-directed discovery. So, while one blind man intently caressed and beheld and never strayed from the elephant's ear, another remained fixated only on the beast's trunk, whereas the third only the behemoth's tusk, and the last only its hind leg. After a moment the elephant was then led away from the sightless crew.

Shortly thereafter a great argument ensued, for the blind man who only caressed the massive creature's ear said, "I now know by experience that an elephant is flat and pliable." "That is incorrect!" said the one who fondled the trunk, "an elephant is long, tubular and flexible!" The third man disagreed all the more, stating, "You are amiss, the elephant is thick and round and immovable!", because he had beheld the leg. The fourth and final tusk-beholder replied, "I disagree fully and in all ways with all of you! This I know: the elephant is smooth and hard, with a sharp, pointed tip!"

The moral of the story? It's a healthy reminder to always cast a sizeable net when gathering information, necessarily maintaining a widened focus though not at the expense of fine & equal detail. So that's just what I did. This anecdote in mind, I resolved to contact as many of my former Nebraska Football Staff confidants, peers, and players of that era to gain a complete answer as to the Why and the How of their 60 & 3 greatness. Who would answer me back and how many conversations would that entail? I figured I would know when I got there.

Prepare for Kickoff

And ultimately -after conducting over one hundred interviews with the people who lived out this era in the flesh- I believe I've arrived at my great Why and How destination with many -if not all- the answers, plus some ideas and axioms you might find useful for whatever you endeavor in life. This pending chronicle provides you, dear reader, the rare experience as an all-hearing, all-seeing fly-on-the-wall, transporting you back in time with the benefit of present day perspective and understanding. What follows is a deeply personal journey to my Great 60 & 3 Nebraska Football Why and How. You may at times become shocked and taken aback, be turned to giggling fits of laughter, or even glean some inspiration. In any regard I hope you enjoy the trip, because I sure as heck did.

'We Refuse to Lose'

PHIL JOHNSON/THE WORLD-HERALD

HAVING A BALL: Nebraska's David Seizys, a senior from Seward, Neb., celebrates his fumble recovery on a kickoff return by Oklahoma's Darrius Johnson with 13:13 left. Also pictured are Nebraska's Lorenzo Brinkley and John Reece, No. 6. The fumble set up the Huskers' second touchdown in 13 seconds, a 20-yard run by Calvin Jones.

To kick this thing off in proper fashion I sent former athletic trainer and present day NU player-liaison Doak Ostergard an e-mail requesting contact info for a number of people. He was kind enough to mass-mail it out to the players from that era to get me started, and David Seizys was the first person who replied. And what a great subject to begin with: a smallish Nebraska kid, a walk-on, a guy who made his mark on special teams and the most of his God-given abilities on the way to earning a scholarship. It's a modern-day retelling of the infamous Rudy-story, exhibited numerous times over at the University of Nebraska from the 60's to present day. Let's get this party started…

Notable quote #1:
"Coach Osborne had his priorities that were the high standard of God first, family second, and for us it was school third and football fourth."

David Seizys

Walk-on, Wingback, Seward, Neb. (Ft. Calhoun)
Where are they now? Lincoln, Neb., Teacher/Coach

Question: So David, your last year playing was..?

David Seizys: My last bowl game was the Florida State Orange Bowl where we lost by the field goal at the end there.

Q: You played offense and special teams, right?

DS: Kickoff, punt teams, and I actually held for extra points and field goals.

Q: So you were the holder for Byron on the infamous last second field goal attempt…

DS: Yeah.

Q: Can you walk me through what happened there? I'm sure you were on the sidelines as Trumane Bell caught that last pass, correct?

DS: We were just concerned about time at that point. We didn't really feel like we were going to have the opportunity to kick that field goal, and all aspects of the game seemed like the clock had run out on us, you know? The officials, for some reason - they called a bad game - really had been calling a bad game the whole time. There were some bogus penalties, the touchdown that William Floyd scored - he had fumbled before he went into the end zone and I believe John Reece recovered the fumble - but they said he'd already crossed the plane. So anyways, they put time back on the clock, and without hesitation they sent us out there. Florida State had called a timeout, so it just kind of iced the whole situation. We got in the huddle, I just said something to the fact that this was one of those storybook endings that you always dream about, 'Let's go get this one.' Byron marked off his steps, I got the snap and put that hold down.

It took me two years to realize that it was actually a good hold, because I couldn't watch the game. Finally, two years later I realized it was a good hold. As soon as he kicked it it looked like it was heading straight down the middle and as I was looking up a Florida State guy just came up and whacked me. And as I was kind of going down into the ground the ball kind of went with me and it went left. It was heartbreaking; a heartbreaking ending to an awesome career and an awesome time at Nebraska. You know, Osborne's response -I saw it later- he just kind of put his head down, then looked up and said, "Okay, let's go." It was just the way he always preached, you know? It was all about how you play, and he said that all the time. And he lived it at that moment.

Q: What else did you do on special teams?

DS: I was the 'outside contain' on the left side on the kickoffs.

Q: So you're the guy getting 'mugged' as you go down the field?

DS: Oh, a couple times, but you kind of learn to swim around after a while, make sure your head's on a swivel. And on the punt team I was on the left side, again, responsible for blocking two guys and outside contain.

The punt team -the way it was designed on the bullet punt- the way it was designed, I was supposed to protect the left side by myself and then the personal protector would always be on the right as a second guy, he would always go to the right. So I was kind of always on an island. It's actually a funny story, the first time I was ever given that responsibility was against Middle Tennessee State my junior year and we were inside the ten yard line…

Q: No pressure there, huh?

DS: Yeah, right. And Coach Dan Young, I'd been doing it here and there in practice, and Trumane Bell -not to discredit him, but he wasn't getting the job done- and I was standing there not doing a whole lot, not even on the kickoff team yet, and Coach Young grabs me and says, "Get in there." I'm running in there just going, 'Oh man, this is my one chance. Don't blow it.' Coach Young came up to me on Monday and said, "You're starting on the punt team," and I was, 'Cool!' From that point on it was a whirlwind. It was my dream to contribute any way I could, it just came to fruition and I made the most of the opportunities I was given.

Q: Were you recruited much out of high school?

DS: Just the smaller in-state schools: Doane, Midland, Dana. And I just kept saying the same thing, 'I want to play for Nebraska.' I think word got out that I wanted to do that so nobody else recruited me.

Q: Scholarship or Walk-on?

DS: Walked on and eventually earned a scholarship. I wanna say it was the summer before my senior year.

Q: How did that happen? How did it feel?

DS: Well, we were in the midst of two-a-days and Coach Brown had called me out of a big meeting. He called me out and said, "You've been doing great things for us," and I said, 'Thanks.' I thought that was all he was gonna say so I turned back to return to the meeting room and he said, "Hey, wait." I said, 'What's that?' He said, "We want to give you a scholarship." And it was just kind of one of those, 'Am I hearing correctly what he was saying?' He said, "Don't you have anything to say?" I said, 'Yeah, I'll definitely take the scholarship!' and then proceeded to have one of the worst practices I'd ever had. (laughs) I was ecstatic.

You know, there was a pay phone underneath the stadium at the time, and right after the meeting I ran out under the stadium and gave my parents a call, and it was one of those emotional moments where I told them I earned a scholarship.

Q: Going through that process: a talented walk-on who came to NU and worked your way up the ranks and earned that scholarship... what did that do for you?

DS: It set me up for life, you know? You always have those 'what if' moments in life: 'What if I'd done this or what if I'd done that,' I think I would have always questioned if I could

have played at Nebraska had I not gone there. You know, some people live vicariously with those what-if's. I joke with my wife Kim all the time and I tell her, 'Gosh, you know if I was 6'2" I would still be playing...' We just get a big laugh out of that. Every now and then when it's the end of the month and the bills aren't quite matching up to what we're making, she just says, "Gosh, if you were only 6'2"." (laughs) We have some fun with that.

But all jests aside, it's one of those deals where you're going, 'Of course, I could have played 3, maybe 4 years at a smaller school, but I would always have in the back of my mind, 'Did I sell myself short? Did I make the most of the abilities God had given me and sell that short?" Like I said, I'm one of those kids who lived the dream for 5 years of his life and everything that came my way was just a blessing from God.

Q: Did you redshirt, David?

DS: Yeah, when I was there they still had the freshman team, so I'm kind of dating myself a little bit. Shane Thorell was the coach then.

Q: So you were there when the Unity Council got started?

DS: The first year we had the Unity Council was my junior year. I was actually part of that my senior year, one of the receiver representatives. From when I came in, I wasn't with the varsity much, but that redshirt year and then my sophomore year it seemed like we were on the cusp of something. We just didn't have too much of a direction, but it seemed the Unity Council was more of, "Let's take this out of the coaches' hands. Let's do this from within." From that point on, process was being made toward that 4-5 year great run of things, where it was no more of the coaches really having to be the disciplinarians. Obviously, there were some situations: the Lawrence Phillips-kind of thing where it was taken out of the Council's hands. But as far as the school, getting to class, making sure you go to the study table, hooking up with tutors, that was being taken care of within.

The coaches were then free to be coaches and work with us on that level where we could take care of other things. And I think the relationships with the coaches were a little different then, and although they were authoritative figures, it wasn't seen as a discipline figure, it was more a coach, "Let's give him the just due he deserves, because he was coach." For lack of a better term, it was less babysitting.

Q: Were there any negatives to the Unity Council? Did it create hard feelings within the team?

DS: It was kind of a natural thing that happened. That first year, obviously there was a little bit of conflict there, where some guys would be, "Who put you guys in charge?", but it was something voted on by the position players. You know, the receivers voted me on -and here I am a walk-on and this is quite an honor, first of all- and the guys on the council really started to take it seriously. The idea of it, Jack Stark was at the forefront of that and just really put the presence of the players in there, and after awhile the resentment was gone and they understood what we were trying to do. We were trying to clean house and go in the right direction. We were at a roadblock and needed something else to get us over the top, kind of bring it over the edge.

Q: Were some guys actually kicked off the team?

DS: If there was ever any kicking-off happened, that was in Coach Osborne's hands.

Q: Did we have some 'problem children', for lack of a better term?

DS: Yeah, there were. Absolutely, there were some repeat offenders. Once it got to that point of making that decision of whether they stay or go we made our recommendations, then that was in Coach Osborne's hands. There actually were some recommendations, some that were followed through. Specific players, I don't remember kicking off, but there were some we sent to Osborne, and those kind of held up.

Q: It created a sense of ownership through the democratic process, then?

DS: It wasn't one of those things where this was set up and the coaches would take it out of our hands. They kept it in our laps and on the table and they let us run with it.

Q: That was quite an awesome responsibility…

DS: Yes. We'd meet weekly or when something would arise. Sometimes it was nothing new, "Old business, any new business?" You know, it was really interesting, the players were on a point system, when they got two points they had to come up in front of us. It was "Yes sir, no sir, I'll get to class," I thought, "Holy smokes, this is pretty awesome!"

Q: You think it played a part...

DS: It was one of those things that was needed. It was player-directed, player-led, and there was always a coach there so it didn't get out of hand. They were there just kind of monitoring and they let us do our thing. I don't want people to think it was the driving force that led to the turnaround, but it was key. It can't be discounted.

Q: Were you good friends with Byron Bennett?

DS: Oh yeah, obviously we'd spend an awful lot of time together: I'm holding and he's kicking. It was just for that year, 1993. Just being a kicker and being on special teams you're kind of aware who those guys are. He was a great guy to be around.

Q: Do you keep in touch with him?

DS: No. I think of him often, but it's one of those things where life kind of happens and you just lose touch. If you ever get ahold of him just tell him I miss him.

Q: By the way, your wife wasn't a walk-on, was she?

DS: No, she was scholarship. She doesn't rub it in my face, though. But she does remind me now and then that she was two-time Volleyball Lifter of the Year. (laughs)

Q: Boy! She must have had one awesome strength coach…

DS: (laughing) She did!

Q: I loved working with both of you guys. I remember the Volleyball girls would come in and lift, and then the baseball guys would just be in awe of the volleyball players' intensity in working out: just as much dedication, intensity & resolve as you guys on the football team. So tell me, do you have a favorite play from your time in uniform?

DS: Oh gosh, yeah. Absolutely. It was the Oklahoma game my senior year, we had just scored -Abdul Muhammad had just scored- extra point good, we go up 14-7. The ensuing kickoff Mike Minter kind of races down ahead and hits the ball carrier's hand, (he actually over-pursued), and I'm coming down from the left side. It's in slow motion. You know, one of those slow motion things? I can see him, where he's just kind of juggling the ball. And as he turns around he slips and the ball's on the carpet. I come up over the top of him, reach up underneath him and scoop the ball up, grab the ball. And then we're on the 20 and Calvin Jones scores on a 49 Pitch and we go up 21-7. Seals the deal. It's like I'm still there. A little bit heavier and a little bit slower, but I'm still there in my mind. (laughing)

Q: Anything you wish you could do over again?

DS: It would have to be that field goal.

Q: Let me ask you now: you said two years later you realized it was a good hold?

DS: Yes.

Q: So do you wish 1)the play could be done over or 2)you wish there were something you yourself could do over?

DS: It was a good hold. But it was one of those things where your kicker is getting ready to kick… and I wish I would have said something to help him to relax. I don't think either of us were nervous at that point 'cause a few minutes earlier we thought we'd kicked what was the winning field goal. It was a minute-sixteen. That one?

That was a chip shot. I was really nervous for that one 'cause it was one of those things where, 'people are gonna know if I screw up on this one,' because it was a chip shot. Not really that it was planted in my mind, but -you know- you want to do well. That one goes through and we're ecstatic. And then the next one you go, "Hey, we were just here. This is just a repeat."

Q: Obviously, you were able to get in the huddle because Florida State had called a timeout, right? Can you remember the huddle?

DS: That was interesting, too, 'cause here I am, the walk-on and I'm in charge of the huddle. We're in the huddle and it's just one of those moods where you're saying, 'Hey guys, we just did this. Let's do it again.' I don't remember anything too crazy in that huddle at that time. It was just the same call as I always made, 'Fullback, double bump. Let's get this thing done.'

Q: Do you recall Zach Weigert saying something to the FSU players for telling T.O. to, "Get the fuck off the field!"

DS: I'm glad you brought that up. I do remember that. And that was in response to, "Did we get the timeout?" Tom Osborne went out there, "Was the timeout called?" Then he was arguing the spot. They didn't have replay then, so they spotted it where they spotted it.

Q: Do you think Byron is ever haunted by that final attempt?

DS: I'm sure it did, or probably does. I hate to say it that way, but it would have to. I mean, I was the holder and it took me two years to watch it. I remember the next bowl game and I was with my folks in Wyoming at the time, watching with my folks, and the winning touchdown going in was such a release of emotion. I was just weeping at the fact that Nebraska had won. I remember saying -I'm crying and looking at my Dad- and saying, 'The monkey's off our back! We won, we won!' It was nighttime in Wyoming and I started lighting off fireworks. It was awesome. And the national championship celebration after that, I felt like I was a huge part of that, being a former player.

Q: Was Coach Ron Brown your position coach?

DS: He was an incredible spiritual mentor to me. My mom and my dad are neat Christian people. And if you were to ask me who my hero was, without hesitation I would say my dad, and a close second would definitely be Coach Brown. Every day, just by his mere presence, he demanded excellence. And it wasn't that stereotypical, 'hard-nosed coach excellence,' it was excellence because you have God-given ability and you have to give it all up to Him. It was that kind of presence.

Q: Any one person under the radar who meant something special to you? Someone behind the scenes for you or your teammates?

DS: Oh, man. There's so many. If it was a friendship thing it was quarterback Joel Cornwell. We were pretty good friends. He was my roommate on road trips. But as far as the whole scope of things, Tommie Frazier comes to my mind because of the fact that he's one of those guys when he first walked on campus, that expectation of him. And he started his freshman year. There's something special about him.

Another guy who took me under his wing was Nate Turner. Absolutely just kind of a big brother. And he looked out for me and talked me through some things. I know every athlete goes through the thought of, 'This is just way too much,' and can't handle it anymore and you want to quit. He was there at those times when you wonder if it's worth the effort, getting beat. You're practicing and standing in the stands during the games, and in practice you just get pounded on. He just reminded me, "You've just got to go through it. You'll get there."

Q: And what was it like to finish a punishing practice and then you have to go straight to the weight room for lifting?

DS: Oh, man, it was brutal. (laughs) After awhile you just get into that mentality, 'This is one way of making myself better.' For me, I knew I was a walk-on and couldn't cut corners. For me it was kind of a release, 'cause I knew the weights weren't going to beat on me. I just kind of bought into the bigger, faster, stronger thing, but there were days you walked off the field after a 100 degree practice and the weight room is the last place you wanna be. But you knew it was for a greater purpose.

Q: What went through your mind on performance testing day, when you ran the ten and forty yard dash, the vertical jump, the pro agility run?

DS: It was one of those dreams where I always did the best I could. I never wanted to look back and wonder if I could have pushed a little harder. I was just one of those kids who grew up giving 100%, and the coaches would say, "This is a 50% practice." I always wanted to go hard, and it's the only speed that I knew.

Q: What do you do now?

DS: I'm a 6th grade teacher. I coach high school football and track. Leffler. I teach math and science.

Q: Tell me, what kind of attitude was instilled by Coach Brown? Not being the prototypical prima donna receivers, how did he instill the attitude? You guys were some nasty little cusses out there, weren't you?

DM: Yeah, we were always cutting their legs out. That was something we learned early on. If you weren't going to be diving down on every play you weren't going to play. He'd tell us, "You're swinging and punching the inside of their thigh (and your shoulder would go there, too), and you follow through."

Q: You actually punched the inside of the defensive backs' thighs?

DS: Oh yeah, it was just brutal. And toward the end of the game when you've got walk-ons going in there, you still had to do it. And those defensive backs -you could only take 60 or so many guys to travel on road trips in the Big 8- there are still 1st and 2nd string defensive backs still in there at the end of the game and they're just cussing us out and saying, "Come on man, the game is over! What are you doing?!"

Q: And your response would be?

DS: 'I don't want a zero on the grade card! Sorry!' So we're cutting these guys down at the end of the game and they're running for their life. The ones and twos had been cutting

them down, too. We're just trying to get our little piece of the pie. Some of these guys, toward the end of the game, they're just cutting and running from us. They don't want anything to do with us fresh guys just coming in. We're diving at air, because they're running a 4.4 the other way. We'd get turf burns all the time. Sometimes it's just a beautiful piece of work and he's ready to hit you, and you clobber him and his feet are straight up in the air. It was great. Those were great times.

That was kind of funny, because they opened up spring practice one time recently, and me and Riley Washington and Abdul came back and we're just yucking it up on the sidelines because those receivers out there, they had no clue on how to block. It was kind of funny, because we were heckling them a little bit. A lot of those guys were just having a hard time getting off of jams and were trying to block. It was something that just wasn't instilled during the previous four years, but they were working hard. So it's coming around.

Q: Any peculiar practice stories from the 90's?

DS: When we were getting ready for the '94 Orange Bowl they were piping in the tomahawk chop song like Florida State would do, and I'm standing next to Coach Osborne and I say, 'I bet you have this on CD playing in your house?'And he said, "Man, I hate this song!" It was such dry humor. And then one time in practice he pours Gatorade all over Kevin Raemakers. Just those dry moments where you go, 'This is Coach Osborne doing this?' It was a full jug of Gatorade. A couple of guys held Raemakers down and Coach Osborne got him, just unloaded on him. You just say to yourself, 'Did I just see Coach Osborne doing this?'

Q: Any locker room guys that really stand out from those days as far as leadership?

DS: Trev (Alberts) was, and Kevin Raemakers was, and (John) Parrella. They were awesome guys there that literally were huge, figuratively were huge in their leadership. And you know, I've heard horror stories of hazing in the Callahan era and even the Solich era, but in our time it was flat out, 'we were a family, that didn't happen.' But as far as leaders, those were three huge leaders right there.

Q: Any summation of things that we haven't touched on? Innerworkings? Special significance?

DS: I don't know if anybody else would go this direction, but I truly think God had his hand in that era. You look at Coach Osborne. Look at him. He's not one of those huge rah-rah guys, but spiritually he had it together, and there was something about him and his spiritual life that attracted others and held others intact. And in the day and age of running off to the highest paying positions, we had continuity and we had bible study together in the mornings. They were doing the work of God, and I know that had something to do with it. There's a whole lot of people out there that don't want to hear that or disclaim that but I don't know how you can, because Coach Osborne had his priorities that were the high standard of God first, family second, and for us it was school third and football fourth. He lived it. It wasn't just lip service. The thing that was a huge thing there was not only did coaches and players have loyalty to him, but he had loyalty to them. That doesn't happen very often anymore.

To this day -it still blows me away- he knew exactly who I was the first year of practice. He knew who my parents were, and here is this god-like figure and he's thanking me for being on the team. And to this day he's still, "Hey David, how are you and your family?" To this day he'll stand there and have a conversation with you and actually talk. It's the untold things, the absolutely spiritual nature of what was going on there, God's hand was on that team from the get go. The loyalty both ways, being reciprocated both ways with the coaches and the players, it was just absolutely incredible.

End conversation.

If you didn't pick up on David's warmness of character and forthright manner from this conversation, maybe this vignette will give you an idea of what kind of young men were around in those years:

You'd be hard-pressed to keep me away from each season's home opener. Well, I was once in Lincoln for the season opener against Western Kentucky (which was a bit of a yawner), but it was great to experience the old juices flowing again in Memorial Stadium on a late summer afternoon nonetheless. My seat is situated in the East Stadium behind the team about four rows up at about the thirty-five yard line, and in the middle of the game who comes and taps me on the shoulder? David Seizys and his wife (former Husker volleyballer) Kim. I turned from the game's action to look for whoever it was tapped my shoulder as he said, "I knew it! We were sitting in our seats (about 30 rows up) and I said to Kim, 'Doesn't that look like the back of Paul Koch's head?' Well, sure enough, it is you!"(laughing) For a guy to leave his seat mid-game and make a special trek to visit a guy on the mere whim that the backside of his noggin looks historically familiar speaks volumes about the kind of guy David was, and is, and once more brought home the lyric, "There is no place like Nebraska," because it's people that often make a place what it is.

A few things danced around my head as I hung up the phone on this conversation, and number one was the fact that this rough and tumble game of football leaves an indelible mark on the young men playing it. It took the span of an entire two years for him to distance himself from the pain of being a part of that missed, last second field goal attempt for an elusive national championship. Two years! I can only imagine what it meant for him to hold the tip of the pigskin to his index finger before Byron gave it a swift boot, dreams and last chances and the end of a boyhood dream summarily becoming crushed in the aftermath.

The second and most profound statement I latched onto was when he spoke of the Almighty's hand in things. I don't want to get too spiritual here, because I'm seeking tangible, physical, codified reasons for why those teams were so great, but I have to conclude that a sense of providence - something, or *Someone*- had a hand in all of that success. Perhaps a Diety and its outgrowths will show themselves in this journey, but for now I want to keep on searching as we track down and converse with the varied individuals who played their respective part.

One last thing stayed with me, and it was David's mentioning the rocky start-up of the player-represented group named The Unity Council. We'll hear more about it as we go on, but the inherent seriousness and sense of duty it created must have crossed a crucial bridge for the players, with the coaching staff handing off minor policing of their peers to do as they felt proper. I recall a point made in Jim Collins' Good to Great, where he speaks of having 'the right people on the bus.' The Unity Council separated the right people from the wrong and a line was crossed into greater accountability, focus, and respect for the goal of the institution known as Nebraska Football. With a mention of the outstanding leadership by previous years' defensive linemen John Parrella ('92), Kevin Raemakers ('93) and Trev Alberts ('93), the genesis of the Unity Council was definitely a bold and bright move by Coach Osborne and staff.

Notable quote #2:

David Seizys on The Unity Council: "Let's take this out of the coaches' hands. Let's do this from within."

"We were that close to going out forever. But there was one man who taught us to fight, to storm the wire of the camps, to smash those metal motherfuckers into junk. He turned it around. He brought us back from the brink."
The Terminator, James Cameron, Gale Anne Hurd, Harlan Ellison, William Wisher, Jr.

Two of the more famous individuals borne out of little Wahoo, Nebraska were "Wahoo Sam" Crawford (1880-1968), all-time triples leader (312) and Baseball Hall of Famer, and Darryl F. Zanuck (1902-1979), co-founder of the 20th Century-Fox movie studio and producer of the first ever talking film, "The Jazz Singer." A third person -tying them together with both a movie and a sports connection- would have to be Matt 'The Turmanator' Turman, bursting onto the scene in 1994 as the national media all but wrote off the Cornhuskers chances at holding their number one ranking due to the failing health of its number one and two quarterbacks.

Mr. Zanuck's biography states that he was "undoubtedly one of the most remarkable men ever to become a Hollywood mogul. He rose through the ranks of the studio hierarchy *on sheer will*, overcoming every obstacle that confronted him." (IMDB.com) (emphasis mine) Matt Turman wasn't far removed from this description, possessing a drive and a Coach's son's acumen for the game, using every and all options available to make something of himself and the sparse opportunities provided. It ain't everyday a person gets to talk one-on-one with the Turmanator.

Notable quote #1:
"…the way Nebraska ran practice was so much more efficient than any other school I've ever seen."

Matt Turman

Walk-on, Quarterback, Wahoo, Neb. (Neumann)
Where are they now? Omaha, Neb., Coach

Question: Hey Matt, what are you doing these days?

Matt Turman: I'm a teacher and the Head Football Coach at Skutt Catholic High School in Omaha. I started there in 2002. We've been pretty successful, 3 years ago winning the state championship and been in the semifinals two years since then.

Q: Any guys go on to play at the U?

MT: Just one thus far. A couple of others have been asked to walk on and that was during the Callahan time period, so they went elsewhere- NW Missouri, and started there. Two brothers started at UNO on the O-Line.

Q: These schools need a Turmanator to take 'em over the top! (laughs) So do you recall your first day on campus?

MT: My first year was '92. I graduated in May of '92 and I grew up in a town 30 miles from Lincoln, in Wahoo. I didn't live in Lincoln that summer, I just lived at home. So they asked me to drive in and work out with the team. I was just walking on, so I would do that.

I didn't know anybody. Walking on from a small town in Nebraska, the only person I knew was the coaches and players I'd seen on TV. A little intimidating. I guess one of the first things I realized -'cause most of the players, even the walk-ons, they were used to being the big fish in a small pond- we ended up being the minnow in the ocean. But one of the things

I remember, about two weeks into the deal -you know how we had lifting and the conditioning stuff out on the field during the summers along with the passing league? Well, a bunch of the guys decided they were going to the Student Rec Center and play some pickup basketball, and I was a defensive back there at first, they recruited me as a defensive back. Anyway, I started to play a little defensive back and few of the guys said, "Hey, we need a couple guys to play," and I didn't even know 'em, but ended up going with them. So we're playing and -do you remember Will Shields, "Big Will"? So Will's coming down once we're playing a game (and I was an All-State basketball kid), but Will's coming down and he gets the ball on a fast break and I run down there and maybe try to get in front of him. Now, Will's like what, 6'1" 300 lbs? And so I'm running down there and I'm thinking, 'Do I get in front of him?' And I do it. And all of a sudden he just elevates... and dunks it! And I thought to myself, 'I'm in a different league here. What am I getting myself into here? Six foot, 300 lb. guys who are two-hand dunking it?!' I'm like, 'I'm a little out of my league here.'

Q: (snickering) Do you recall any of the other guys you played with that day?

MT: Yeah, John Reece, a few other guys. Barron Miles, he was a good basketball player, but Will really stands out from that day. It wasn't even like they asked me to play, they just asked me to play because they needed more people, to fill the quota. Later on I got to know Barron really well over on the defensive side of the ball, he was just really one of the great defensive guys. He kind of took me under his wing. And then they moved me to receiver after summer. All summer I do stuff at defensive back, then they move me to receiver. Then we had all those quarterbacks get hurt, so they moved me to quarterback. By the time the bowl game was over that first season I was a quarterback.

Q: Were you willing to take that on?

MT: When they recruited me I told them I wanted to play quarterback. They told me they didn't need any more, they were loaded. You know Tony Veland was there, Mike Grant. There was a senior -I don't remember his name, I'd have to look at a roster- but he was 4th string, though he knew everything. In my freshman class was Tommie Frazier and Ben Rutz, who came in with me. There were so many. Tony Veland tore his patellar tendon, Tommie was starting about 4 games in as a true freshman, Ben Rutz thought he was never going to get a chance so he transferred to Kansas, and then we lost Mike Grant. We were real short on quarterbacks, so they asked me before Spring Ball if I would move to quarterback and I jumped at it.

Q: Was your dad a coach, too?

MT: Yeah, he was a high school coach. He was an offensive guy. All-American quarterback at Chadron State. He got a bunch of pro letters to go free agent, but just got married and decided not to go. That's one of the reasons I ended up going to Nebraska and walking-on, because he always told me that he always wondered if he could have played at Nebraska. That's basically what my dad said and it really influenced me at taking a shot.

Q: Did you think you had a legitimate shot?

MT: You know, I was coming out of high school at 165 lbs. Now, granted, I was -my junior and senior year- I was one of the fastest guys on team. I could always run, but I knew size was always going to be a hurdle to overcome. But you know, I just figured I've always had to work real hard for everything I'd gotten, and that's what I did. And the hard work ended up paying off when I got the opportunities.

And I tell my kids that all the time, 'You don't know when the opportunity is going to come, but you have to take advantage of it when you get it.' That was always my motivator.'If you get a chance, take advantage of it.' Growing up in a small town, you always wanted to play at Nebraska. Having a jersey and helmet was already big, but you always wanted to play and start. When I got the opportunities, that was what I was most proud of, looking back on things.

Q: When you where thrust into the starting role, when was that?

MT: My redshirt sophomore year. And that was interesting, when I moved to quarterback after one season as a receiver. And here's kind of a funny story about Nebraska and me playing: at my high school we ran the triple option and we would read the defensive end, and at that point and time Iowa State was doing the same thing, so when we got to that game –again, I was a summer DB, fall receiver, and when we got to ISU week the coaches knew I had run that type of option- so they moved me to quarterback for that week. It was an absolute nightmare. You know that option stuff, when they do it like Georgia Tech does now and people don't know their assignments and are just kind of running free? So at practice we have all these people screwing up, and the coaches? McBride is just yelling at them, Steele just ripping on them. So they're getting mad and they just pound on us. The coaches get mad and say, "Do it again!" (laughs) "Do it again." I tell you, those three words were just the bane of your existence.'Cause you just got *pounded* on. The defensive guys now know what's coming, too."Do it again!"

Q: So you were pretty motivated to pitch that ball instead of keep it and turn up field?

MT: They'd just tee off on you. But, oh well.

Q: When you joined the quarterbacks you spent more time with Turner Gill and T.O.?

MT: Every meeting. It was kind of intimidating. Coach Osborne kind of grills you. When you watch film he's not just gonna sit back. He's pointing things out and he's grilling you with questions and "what coverage is this" and "where are we long," and "who's the hot read" and "what front is that", and "do we audible?" It's just over and over again. There was no real time to rest. Practice was physically demanding, but the film room was mentally demanding. It wasn't like you just go in there and relax.

Q: Would everyone get grilled in equal measure?

MT: Not as much, but everyone got grilled some. That was the interesting thing. And I'm fourth string just like that, because there wasn't anybody else. And we're getting ready to go out to UCLA and the Rose Bowl and they can expand the traveling roster, the non-conference roster. So they said, "We're taking four quarterbacks." So I was traveling to the Rose Bowl to play UCLA in the middle of all the game prep and everything, that was kind of cool. That was the first trip I was really eligible to go to, not being a redshirt.

Q: Was that UCLA game Lawrence Phillips' coming out party?

MT: Yes, it was.

Q: Did you get to know him very well?

MT: I knew Lawrence. He wasn't, I guess, a guy that I was hanging out with on the weekends, but I knew him pretty well. To me, the whole situation was kind of unfortunate. I'll say this -and I know a lot of my teammates I've played with would say the same- but he was the best football player I ever saw put on pads.

Q: More so than Tommie?

MT: Yeah, not even close. I don't know of hardly anybody that would say otherwise, except Tommie. (laughs) You know the year he got in trouble, the two games before that he had rushed for something like 600 yards. And you know, he worked as hard or harder than… he was one of the top 5 guys at putting in work on the team. He was a great teammate.

Q: So what was it like? Were you very nervous during the week leading up to the Kansas State game?

MT: I really wasn't all that nervous because first of all Coach Osborne and Coach (Turner) Gill just do a great job of getting you ready. I wasn't as nervous as I thought I was, because I knew what was going to happen. And the week before I played most of the game against Oklahoma State, and the week before that I played most of the Wyoming game. Brook (Berringer) played until halftime and I played most of the second half; about a minute into the second quarter of the Oklahoma State game I was put in. So the time I'd put in previous to then wasn't just mop-up duty, I'd put some time in. It wasn't like it was the first time stepping on the field, you know?

But it was a little bit different because Oklahoma State and Wyoming weren't as good as K-State then. But looking back on it I was surprisingly calm. We were playing down at K-State and I think that actually made it easier. It was a rainy, cold day. I think I only threw like 8 passes. 5 for 8 for not very many yards, although Eric Alford dropped like a 30 yard pass that should have scored. (laughs) That was like the only pass we threw down the field. All the other passes were short ones: swing passes, short, little curl patterns, just enough to keep them honest. Coach Osborne told us before that we were, "Just gonna go in and we're gonna use our linemen…" like Brenden Stai, Zach Weigert, Aaron Graham, Rob Zatechka, Joel Wilks. 4 of those 5 guys were pro lineman, and then Cory Schlesinger, a 12-13 year veteran in the pros at fullback, and Lawrence, a top 5 pick in the NFL draft, "…we're gonna use those guys and we're just gonna pound on them." We knew going in that that was going to be the game plan.

Q: Did Kansas State know it, also?

MT: They had to. You've got a 3rd string walk-on who doesn't have a whole lot of experience starting. I think what they were saying was, "When they run the option, let him run." (laughs) I mean, do you want Schlesinger or do you want Phillips running around on the corner, or do you want Turman cutting up the middle into your linebackers? That would be my thought. And we never really threw the ball a whole lot, so they didn't have to change that. It wasn't like when Tommie was playing we were throwing 50 times a game or anything.

Q: Did T.O. or Turner teach an attitude or mindset as far as the quarterback position?

MT: There were a few different things that would be interesting for you. For instance, Osborne was really big on, "We couldn't run out of bounds and we couldn't slide," so we were always supposed to lower our shoulder and get extra yards. But if we did just run out of bounds he wasn't a yeller or screamer. He did things differently, like you let him down. You knew his expectations -what he expected of you- and when you didn't meet them he didn't really have to say much. He'd just say, "Matt, why did you run out of bounds?" And you just go, 'Coach, I'm really, really, really sorry.' It was just the way about him, his demeanor, his stature, his reputation, his aura.

Q: What do you think created that aura?

MT: Well, it's hard to pinpoint and articulate. But to me, he's such a genuine person. His answers are genuine, he doesn't beat around the bush, right? There's no gray, it's just black

& white. And you can tell by the way he does things that he cares about you. The best way I can put that is this little story: Okay, we've won a state championship and he's in the middle of some political race running for, I think, Governor, and extremely busy, right? And he takes the time out -first of all he knows I'm the coach there, he knows that we won a state championship- and he sends me a handwritten letter saying congratulations. And he calls me on the phone and it says on the caller ID, "Osborne for Governor," and I'm thinking, 'Hey, they're calling me to vote for him. Well, that's already a done deal, you don't need to try to convince me to do that.' So I'm not gonna answer. But then I pick it up… and it's him! And that's the kind of person he was; he cared about you so much, and you knew that. And because of that, this 'aura' around him was -when he expected you to do something or asked you to do something and you didn't get it done- it made you feel worse. It made you try harder. It made you give everything you could because he cared so much about you that you wanted to return to him the trust and caring he put into you. You cared about doing things the way he wanted and needed it to be and took care of him.

Q: Sounds like he appealed to your conscience?

MT: That would be a good way to put it.

Q: Do you find yourself modeling much of your coaching after any of the coaches at Nebraska?

MT: Interestingly, my dad and him, they were very similar. I'm not a yeller and screamer, I don't get mad very much. Basically it's about telling them what my expectations are. And if they don't meet them I'm not gonna yell at 'em and scream at 'em and call them names, but I'm gonna say, 'Hey, you're better than that, our program has become better than that. And if that's what I'm gonna get, I'm gonna find somebody else to represent our school and our program in a better light.' And that's what's expected.

Q: What year did you graduate?

MT:'96. And after the '94 season was over, in January of '95 they did give me a scholarship.

Q: I thought you'd ended up earning one. So, do you ever wear your championship rings?

MT: Never. And the rationale behind that? I'm not much of one to brag about past accomplishments. I don't know. I heard an interesting thing on the radio today. They were talking about the Pittsburgh Steelers and how they won the Super Bowl, and they were talking to Hines Ward and they asked him about his Super Bowl ring, asking if he wanted to get another one. And he said, "Of course I want to get another one." Then they said, "So you can wear them both at the same time?" And he said, "Well, I never wear the ring." And they asked why? And he said, "As soon as you wear that first one it becomes about what you've done in the past and not about what you want to accomplish in the future." And I'm not playing football anymore, but that's the interesting thing: people ask me about the National Championships -and I'm very proud of them- but the state championship we've won at the high school is a close second. It's a state championship compared to a national championship, but as you go on and you continue on with what you love to do, you're always hungry for the next challenge, and when you get to that next challenge and you're successful, you're proud of it. But I don't know …. I probably should wear 'em. (laughs)

Q: Turner Gill: what did you pick up from Turner? Anything different from Coach Osborne?

MT: Their demeanors were very similar. And Gill, just because he played for Coach Osborne and coached with him, the thing that struck me about him was his professionalism and, again, he was the same way: he treated his players in a way you knew he cared about you. Even though I was a former defensive back and receiver, within two weeks of moving to quarterback he knew who my parents were, and my brother and my sister. They just find things about you and they were concerned more about you than just what's on the football field. Sometimes they'd just say, "How's your dad doing? Is his team gonna be any good?" They just talked to you."I see you have a little brother playing, I see him on film a little bit...so do you have any other brothers?" And I'd say, "No, I have 4 sisters," and they just remember that.'Cause even Coach Osborne, when he called about the state championship he asked how my two boys were doing. And I'm like, "How does he even remember that I have kids?" He just keeps up with all that stuff, you know. And I have a girl on the way now.

Q: Matt, what are you most proud of as a player?

MT: It's hard for me to have anything besides the game I got to start versus Kansas State. That was a lifelong dream. If you're not talking about that type of stuff, it was just growing up in Nebraska, just winning the national title was something that was extremely satisfying. Just knowing that you were a part of that and how important it was to not just the football program, but to the state as a whole. That's probably what I would say just really sticks out the most. Just the fact that year '94 we were undefeated and the win versus KSU, and then we were able to go forward and win the national title. It was the whole thing.

Q: Any instance you are least proud of or wish you could do over again?

MT: That's hard for me. Everything for me down there, it seemed it was just kind of sugar-coated. The first game I ever suit up for I'm headed to the Rose Bowl, the first game I play in was against Pacific and I scored a touchdown and threw for a touchdown! Now, Pacific wasn't very good, but we were beating them pretty bad and they put me in the game, and we run an option and I run in for touchdown. And then we call a short pass play and we convert it to a fade because they were up in press coverage, so I threw a touchdown.

So, Paul, I don't know. I guess if I had to do it all over again, I would have liked another opportunity to start. My senior year Tommie and Brook were both graduated... and that was something: Brook Berringer was my roommate on away trips, from the UCLA game - which was my first to go on- we roomed for every game we had together. Even home games. I guess if there were anything I would do over, it would be to tell him not to get on that airplane.

Q: Anything you look back on today and get a chuckle over?

MT: Well, there was, I don't know if you were familiar with the big meeting room in the auditorium where we would meet together as a group. It was pretty funny. There was time they were re-doing some of the chairs in the meeting room, and they were kind of like the seats in an old theatre where you could lean back on some of the chairs and recline back a little bit. Well, Coach Osborne sat in the same spot every day, and they removed the back off of his chair. So we're sitting in a meeting and he's standing up and talking to everybody, and then he turns the lights off and goes to take seat so we could watch special teams film as a group -offense and defense together- and he goes and sits in his chair and leans back and falls with his head straight over his ass, straight back onto his back and his feet are in the air! (laughs) You know, a lot of people probably would have cussed, "Oh, shit!" or something, and he just was like, "Whaoooaaaa"…and somebody flicks on the lights, and his feet were sticking up right to the ceiling. It was one of the funniest things I remember. I wouldn't believe it if I hadn't seen it for myself.

Q: Gives you a real idea of his character and self-discipline in a moment of surprise, eh? Any idea of who removed the chairback?

MT: You know, I think it was just them working on the chairs. I don't know. It wasn't like they did it to him on purpose. A lot of the chairs were missing backs, and he was surely not paying any attention to the chair he was going to sit in. He turned off the lights and, you know, he's probably so focused and can't see….he probably didn't even know the chair back wasn't on there. The same chair he's been sitting in for 23 years is missing a back. (laughs)

Q: Any other insights into the organization? What made it so successful?

MT: There is a lot we could talk about. One of the things to me that really stuck out -and talking to other people and other teams with other kids that walked on down there- one of the things that was real neat was the walk-on program under Osborne was really amazing. Besides some getting a scholarship check, you couldn't have told the difference between the walk-on and the scholarship player. You couldn't have told the difference between Tommie Frazier and myself those first two years by the way we were treated. From the academic support we got to the way the strength staff treated us, there was no difference! So that endeared a lot of people, and it really caused the walk-ons to work hard because they knew they were gonna be treated right, that if they rose up the depth chart they were gonna be given a chance. I've talked to people now, and they say the walk-ons during the Callahan era didn't get all the gear that they gave the scholarship kids, and just the attitude in the strength training staff, they didn't get the attention that they normally would.

Speaking of, I wasn't real happy with the Callahan regime. For example, he sent me a form letter when we won the state championship, and Osborne -who was gone- sends a handwritten letter and also calls. Callahan sends me a form letter, and it isn't even signed, it's stamped. And on the top of the letter it says, "Dear Fred." Interestingly enough, it was the first name of the coach in a different class who won a championship. They couldn't even change the name on the form letters. It was just wrong.

And when I went down there for one of the football clinics I was introduced to Callahan by Dave Cassidy, Head of Football Operations, who was a nice guy. His kid was a high school kid and I'm a high school coach, so he knows my dad and he introduces me to Callahan and he says, "This guy here was a former quarterback here at Nebraska who started during the national championship years." So Callahan kind of looks me up and down, gives me kind of a squint with his eyes and says, (incredulous)"You *really* started?" I just wanted to say, 'Well, *yeah*, I started! And I've got more rings than *you've* got.' And that's just how he was. But I'm a high school coach in the state and a former player, and he won't let me come watch practice. Stupid stuff. I'm glad it's not that way anymore.

So anyway, the walk-on thing was a huge deal, the way you were treated. And then the second thing that was really unique -and you don't know it's unique while you're playing there- but when you're in the coaching ranks? Well, I've seen a bunch of schools, colleges who were successful programs, and I went out and watched Virginia's practices, Missouri and more, but the way Nebraska ran practice was so much more efficient than any other school I've ever seen. And what I mean by that is most teams would divide up offense and defense, okay? And half the field would be offense and half would be defense. And basically you'd have scout team offense against first team defense, and scout team defense versus first team offense on different sides of the field. So those guys would get 70% of the snaps and the two's, the second teamers, would get 30 percent the snaps, okay?

Well, at Nebraska it was different. They ran 4 stations. So you had a first team offense run and a pass station and the first team defense run and a pass station. Now, those stations were done at the 50 yard line going in toward the endzone, and the pass station we ran from the goal line out to about the 40. So instead of having just your first team and second team get 70% and 30 % of the reps, the first team would get about 70% of the run station, the second team would get 70% of the pass station, and they'd have 3rd and 4th stringers getting 30-40% of the reps! So you had -for me when I was 3rd string quarterback in 1994- if that would have been now, I wouldn't have taken a snap until the week of my first game when I was moved up to second string when Tommie got hurt. But I had been taking reps running Nebraska plays from the first week of practice. Granted, I wasn't getting as many reps as Tommie was or as Brook was, I shouldn't be. I shouldn't have been maybe only a third of the time, but I was still getting reps of what we were doing.

And so, people always said that Nebraska always ran up the score, but I don't think we did. They were good athletes, first of all, then they had been practicing this stuff. It wasn't like it was brand new and a scout team kid hadn't run 19 Sprint Option since spring ball of last. They got the reps and they knew what they were doing, and the mental part of it was all there. And I think that's another reason they were so successful: so many kids were getting prepared. When you do that you feel like you're engaged, you don't have third team kids saying, "This sucks, I'm not even getting to practice." You feel involved! And it keeps morale up.

Q: And speaking of team-wide morale -where you couldn't slide or run out of bounds...

MT: He actually lifted that rule for me. (laughs) Because Tommie was hurt, Brook was hurt, and we didn't have anybody else after me. Here we had Clester Johnson, a wingback taking reps in practice at quarterback because we didn't have enough guys at quarterback. Coach Osborne told me, "If you need to get out of bounds, I'm giving you permission." (laughs) Another funny rule he had? It didn't matter how cold it was -like just the other day it was minus 15 here in Omaha- even days like that, if you had any chance of carrying the football such as quarterback, running back, receiver, you could not wear anything on your arms, you could not wear any long sleeves. He said that that caused fumbles. You know how people liked to wear that Under Armor-type stuff back then? He said that wouldn't give you the same tactile grip or feeling like football on bare skin. So if you go back and look, none of us guys had anything on our arms no matter how cold it was.

Q: The opponents thought you were just trying to look like tough guys, huh?

MT: Yeah, but it wasn't. It was his deal and I kind of agree with it, I actually do. I told him a couple of times, 'Coach, I'm the 3rd string quarterback, if I get in I'm probably gonna be okay. Can I just wear some long sleeve stuff while I'm standing on the sideline?' And he's, "Nope."

Q: With the no-sliding, no running out of bounds rule, I theorize that one of the reasons there was such team unity was because the quarterback wasn't some elevated prima donna - like some precious, gentle egg- that he was a tough guy taking shots just like everyone else. Would you buy into that line of thought?

MT: I would definitely agree with that. If you're a quarterback you'll obviously be called a pretty boy, that just goes along with being a quarterback. But I agree, and that's part of the reason where I told you everybody was treated the same. In that sense, he didn't want his running backs running out of bounds and he didn't want his quarterbacks running out of bounds, either. It was the same expectation for everybody. And as you know, it changed.

And they changed it for me, basically, because he understood we were kind of in dire straits, we didn't have a whole lot of other options at quarterback.

Q: So if you would have gone down it would have been Clester Johnson?

MT: Yes. And you wanna hear a funny story? There was a student manager who played on the team -who had played quarterback in high school- and they actually asked him to walk-on in the middle of the season. Adam Kucera, from Seward, maybe. I mean, he never got to play but he was practicing and taking some reps. And I don't even know if it was so much that he would even get to play. And then Clester, our starting wingback, he wasn't getting any reps because he was running practice reps at quarterback. We didn't even have anybody to hand the ball off in practice! It was kind of crazy that you had a Division 1 school and so many players on the team and we didn't have any quarterbacks left, with all the injuries and transfers.

Q: Ever keep in touch with the guys?

MT: Most of the guys from around here I see fairly regularly. I keep in touch with Darin Erstad.

Q: You know, when I moved early '96 to San Diego as the Famous Chicken's Producer and Road Manager, I recall running into Darin in Vancouver, British Columbia when he was in Triple A ball playing for the Canadiens. I'll never forget running into him in this little ballpark at the edge of Canada and talking Husker football in the dugout before the game. The Chicken thought we were absolute football nuts because that's all we seemed to talk about when I met up with guys...

MT: Yeah, we talk or e-mail every three months or so. He married a friend of my wife's. And my wife was an athlete in Lincoln, too. Kim DeHahn, she was an All-American gymnast.

Q: And now you've got a family, eh? And speaking of family, what would you say about the Husker closeness?

MT: You know, it would be the family atmosphere. People tell me this all the time, how strange it is, because it's a whole remarkable family thing. Even my wife commented on it. We were back in Nebraska here and she's working for an orthopedic group and we're at a Halloween party, and there's this kid name Chad Sievers, he's from Valley, Nebraska. Didn't play when I played. I knew he played, he knows I played, he's selling medical orthopedic stuff. Maybe I've seen him once or twice. Anyway, we see each other at this party and the first thing we do is come up and give each other a hug. And you're like, 'It's just weird, I don't really know him but I know he played football and he knows I played football, and you're just automatically welcomed.' It's like that with players. Dave Rimington, he's around here some times, first thing you do is shake hands and give 'em that one-arm guy-hug and 'How you doing?' It's just like you're automatically in this big, huge, extended family. Guys you don't know or haven't played with or seen in years, it's just like you fall back into step and those 4 or 5 years had initiated you into 'The Club.' It's really kind of cool.

Q: A fraternity without the hazing?

MT: Exactly. And other people make comments, "You don't even know him." And I'm like, 'Yeah, I do know the guy.' You know he went through the same stuff I did. You don't 'know him' know him, but you've warmed-up on the same grass outside old Buck Beltzer field on the practice grass, walked along the same pathway to the training room and lifted the same weights.

Q: Anybody behind the scenes who was a real important cog in the whole family or someone special to you who stands out? Anybody who had a major impact behind the scenes?

MT: I didn't have him as a coach, but the reverence you always hear the guys talk about for Coach Osborne? Well, the defensive guys, they had the same type of respect and admiration for Coach Charlie McBride. And again, I don't know him as well because I was never in meetings with him except for the team meeting as a group, but I would say he'd be up there at the top.

Other guys? Well, two guys in the training room I could not have lived without...Jerry Weber was awesome. And Doak Ostergard. Those two would be probably stick out a little bit. For me, particularly, it's Jerry, 'cause I kind of endeared people to me because of my underdog role and worked hard. Jerry kind of took a personal interest in me. After I was hurt or dinged-up he was always there to assist me. It was kind of like he was my personal trainer. You know how they made every kid tape up to prevent ankle injuries and sprains, how they made every single kid tape up for every game and every practice? Well, I absolutely despised it. I can't stand 'tight' anything. Even now. I wore my helmet loose, I wore my shoulder pads loose, I hated it. But whenever you didn't have your ankles taped they'd send you running up the stadium stairs. So I talked to Jerry and said, 'Jerry, I've never sprained an ankle in my life.' So Jerry would just basically put on enough tape so it looked like my ankles were taped, but they weren't taped at all; it wasn't like they were supporting anything. And he'd do that for me every day. I wouldn't let anyone else do it. He taped my ankles every day for 4 years!

Q: Cosmetic tape job, eh? And the Kansas State game you started, you still didn't get your ankles taped, just to be safe?

MT: Nope.(laughs) I just couldn't. It bugged me.

Q: Where were you for the '94 Orange Bowl versus FSU? In the stands or on the sideline?

MT: I was standing on the sideline. My redshirt freshman year. My redshirt year we played Florida State, too, but they beat us bad. And then the Orange Bowl, we should have beat them when Charlie Ward was playing for them.

Q: We did beat them, Matt. We did. They only had a higher score when time ran out. We outplayed them.

MT: I agree. You're right. That, and I can honestly say, the first year we played in the Big 12 championship and lost to Texas. I wasn't sick that week.

And you know what, when you asked earlier if I could change things? It would have been a chance to play more my senior year. I still played a lot, but I never started again. Scott Frost came in and he did a good job, he won the national title the next year. But that Texas game Mike Minter was sick, Terrell Farley, Jason Peter...it was just kind of a bug hit and we had five or six who were all 1st teamers.

Q: Did that contribute greatly to the loss, or is that looking for excuses?

MT: That's one thing I took from my dad and my coaches is that 'you don't make excuses.' And my kids know that. I don't like excuses. They'll say, "Well, they're doing this out there to me, Coach," and I say, 'Hey, you either do or you don't get the job done.' That's all there is to it. They're 5 minutes late to a meeting and I say, 'Where were you?' and they'll say, "Coach, I'd tell you, but it would be an excuse." (laughs) 'Alright, well you'll just get some running.' They just know there are no excuses.

Q: Any other character-building or revealing bits you've picked up over the years?

MT: Well, there was the Unity Council. I was a part of that. Players could meet with the coaches if they had concerns, and sometimes guys would be intimidated to go see Coach Osborne. But here were two defensive backs, two defensive lineman, two o-lineman, two receivers, two quarterbacks/offensive backs. They were kind of the liaison. And sometimes if the coaches had something they were thinking of trying, they ran it by us first to see what our response would be. Sometimes we'd do it before the bowl game and they'd ask if we should do anything differently for the bowl game. We'd say, "We go to practice at 7, but you'd wake us up at 6 a.m. to bus over there and there isn't anything to eat for breakfast, so were all up early for nothing." So they'd have fruit out before we'd leave and stuff like that. Again, it brought morale up... we were being heard. And sometimes some of the freshmen or redshirts, it was easier for them to come to a player and say if something was bugging them. Sometimes it was just dumb and we'd tell them to shut up."I don't think we should have to lift before practice", and I'm like, 'Well, that's not going to change.' But it was good, it was neat. And it wasn't always just things that needed changed, but also if there were morale issues or "What should we do to make sure guys aren't drinking too much alcohol during the season?" There were all kinds of stuff like that to deal with. The coaches would come up and say, "Hey, what should we do to try and curb the guys drinking during the week?" or "How do we stop the underage kids from drinking?" or "Should we bring in a speaker to talk to us about it or give us ideas?", or ask some of the leaders of the team to talk about the dangers of getting caught up in, you know, whatever. It was a good medium to talk about some things you just normally don't talk about during a team meeting.

Q: And I've got to ask you about your senior year and the Arizona State game. That loss: What's going through your mind? Can you relate any thought or experience from that game?

MT: Well, that was a hard game for me. Not long before that, maybe the second game, Scott Frost and me were battling for the starting job -and he started both games previous- but I was getting reps. And we went down there and things weren't going well -I was told that I was gonna be inserted in the first possession of the second quarter- and they end up punting the ball and it's downed at our 1 yard line. They come to me, "Where the ball is at, we don't want to risk the new quarterback and center exchange going bad", so I never got in. And the opportunities never really came for me that game. I think we set an NCAA record for safeties that game. It was just a weird game. And part of it was we were maybe a little too overconfident. I think we just thought we could waltz in there. We'd won how many games in a row -we'd won like 26, 27 games in a row- and just never thought ever about us not winning a game.

Q: Anything else you keyed in on that was inspirational for you?

MT: The one thing I liked was that saying in '93, the 'We Refuse To Lose.' That was my favorite.

Say, do you remember the prayer we used to say before the game? That was always something that the team was pretty inspired by, too. Here's another funny story about that: I can't even remember who we picked to do it, but we always picked a guy to say it in the lockerroom beforehand. We picked a guy who wasn't going to get to play much that year, but he worked really hard. I can't remember his name, but he had to say it. And if you remember, they'd say it, "Dear Lord, in the battles we go through in life…", well, he gets about halfway through and he forgets the words. And the he's like, "Uuuugh, uuumm.." and then we're like, "It's okay, it's okay..." and a guy next to him says, "Let's just start over." So he starts over again and he gets to the same spot, again, and forgets the words. And don't forget, this is a prayer, right? And he just swears. He yells out, "Shit!" And now everybody's laughing, it was hilarious! So then he has to go through it again and gets stuck again (laughs)..and then one of the other guys just takes over for him. I'll never forget it. We were all laughing so hard. It was the first game of our senior year. I don't even remember who we were playing, but it was a good way to take the edge off the first game nervousness for some guys, I'm sure.

Q: Well, Matt, I appreciate your time and it really means a lot…

MT: Oh, and I have to say the weight room was very important to us. I spent a lot of time in there. I liked to lift. The progress I made was light years! (Bryan) Bailey would push me harder than anyone. And the other thing he was way good at for me -I hurt my shoulder once- he was great at the rehab stuff. He kind of, again, took a liking to me, took a personal interest in me. Maybe it was that underdog role. I think he kind of did, too. Bryan Bailey worked a lot with my wife, too. She had a back injury from gymnastics. My wife and I both are really big Bryan Bailey fans. Tell him I said 'hello.' He's worked with a lot of big-leaguers, he might not remember me. (laughs)
And if you've got to know, my favorite part of the weight room was the fact that that was where I met my wife. You know, those gymnasts didn't lift much, but she was in there doing rehab for her back, and that's when I met her and started talking to her. It was really corny, too. The Olympics were on and gymnastics was on the TV in the weight room and I went up and asked her some stupid question about some cheesy gymnastic thing to start a conversation. She makes fun of me for it to this day. I say, 'Well, it worked!' (laughs)

End conversation.

 The first golden nugget of information was Matt's mention of the coaching staff's unique ability to give practice repetitions to twice as many players than most. Through an ingenious method of simultaneously compressing the equivalent of four scrimmages onto one football field, vast gains were achieved. The least of which meant less watching and more doing by the younger members who were not only able to cut their Division 1 football teeth via the daily beatings from the top two teams on the depth chart, but who also were able to, as Matt stated, "(get) the reps…You feel involved! And it keeps morale up." As a result, the youngsters were quite constantly reminded of how far short they fell in the pecking order, forcing them to either improve their games or leave the squad. The resultant morale made for greater competition, which I believe can only help a group of young men on their way to proficiency in most any skill or regard. It also drove them to relentlessly make up for physical deficiencies through use of the strength and conditioning program, which we'll get to shortly.

 The second item that caught my ear was his mention of Coach Osborne and how his manner of communication, "made you try harder, it made you give everything you could because he cared so much about you that you wanted to return to him the trust and caring he put into you. You cared about doing things the way he wanted and needed it to be and *took care of him.*" (emphasis mine) How often do you hear a college football player speak so protectively of his coach? *"Took care* of him"?! 'Did Matt really just *say* that?!,' I thought to myself. That's almost unheard of! For a guy from a top-ranked college football program to mention a fondness beyond measure for one of football's legends makes me wish I had touched on the subject more.

Last of all, I was touched after posing the question 'What would you do over?' I was expecting to hear something about keeping the ball on an option to score a touchdown instead of pitching it or something like that, but after some genuine thought on his part Matt summed it up as more than a game when he said of deceased quarterback Brook Berringer, "I guess if there were anything I would do over, it would be to tell him not to get on that airplane." Brook was a great kid, and his passing was a great loss. My eyes get a little wet just thinking about the kid. I still miss him.

Notable quote #2:
Matt Turman on Head Coach/Offensive Coordinator/Quarterbacks Coach Tom Osborne, "He's such a genuine person. His answers are genuine, he doesn't beat around the bush, right? There's no gray, it's just black & white. You can tell by the way he does things that he cares about you."

Chicago Police Officer Jim Malone: You wanna know how to get Capone? They pull a knife? You pull a gun. He sends one of yours to the hospital? You send one of his to the morgue. That's the "Chicago Way"! And that's how you get Capone! Now, do you want to do that? Are you ready to do that?

Federal Agent Eliot Ness: I have sworn to capture this man with all legal powers at my disposal and I will do so.

Chicago Police Officer Jim Malone: Well, the Lord hates a coward.

- David Mamet, *The Untouchables*

One thing I recall about Bryan Pruitt was his gritty, honest, tell-it-like-it-is Chicago style, as well as his nose-to-the-grindstone work ethic. The first guy I contacted via the new social media known as facebook, he's our third Husker Football walk-on in a row. Although never in the starting lineup, he nevertheless had a profound influence on his teammates both by his drive to contribute as well as his driven attitude. This may be a poor attempt at stereotyping, but deep in his heart Bryan was and always will be a scrapper/underdog. His present day job on the SWAT Team seems the perfect fit. I'm glad he's the guy kicking down doors and pointing the gun at all the bad guys in my stead.

Notable quote #1:
"We were (huddled up only) 3 yards from the ball. We couldn't wait to get the snap off."

Bryan Pruitt

Walk-on, Offensive Guard, Midlothian, Illinois (St. Laurence)
Where are they now? Springfield, Illinois, Law Enforcement

Bryan Pruitt: Let me ask you about your book… that was nothing but blue-collar athletes going to work every day -nothing flashy- and we just went to work. Is that the approach the other guys are giving you?

Question: I've only begun, Bryan, but I just recall all the guys came to the practice field with the notion that they were going to show up and bring the full load every day, punch the other guy in the mouth hard enough to make him think about quitting, and then hang around to find if Saturday proved any tougher.

BP: My senior year in '94, Coach Osborne decided that it was time to increase the number of plays we were running. I don't know if you remember in the '80's and the early '90's: the big thing for offense was that they used to huddle up 10-15 yards off the ball… well, look at the '94 team. Nobody may have noticed this or paid attention on the game film, but we were 3 yards from the ball. We couldn't wait to get the snap off.

Q: Were you part of the original 'Pipeline'?

BP: Some people, being away from it in Illinois, they only want to know if you started. I was second team, so to them it's no big deal. But getting back to the question, it was just wanting to go out and it not mattering who lined up in front of us…I kind of think that ties into with when we were huddling up 3 yards off the ball. It was the kind of ', "Hey, we're gonna run the football, and we don't care if you know were gonna run the football…we're gonna run it there."

We didn't try to cover up audibles and stuff like that.'Two opposite' was our big audible. Like Peyton Manning does, trying to cover up audibles and stuff like that? No, Tommie Frazier just basically said 'two opposite,' which meant the run was just going the other way, or he'd call the play at the line. The other team knew what the play was, but we just went ahead and ran it and dared 'em to stop us.'Two opposite' was like this: say we were going to run a counter sweep -Tom's big running plays were the inside traps, options, counter sweeps. Say we were gonna run a 48 Counter Sweep, which means our left guard and tackle are pulling around the left end. We would just call 'two opposite,' so as soon as you heard two opposite you just knew the play was going the other way. It was just the reverse of what you heard in the huddle. Coach Osborne did such a great job of simplifying things for everybody and not making it so complicated that you couldn't think of what you were doing. It doesn't get any simpler than 'two opposite.'

Q: And the opposing defenses knew what it meant?

BP: Yeah, and I don't ever remember changing it at all throughout the year. Like I said, we weren't really trying to hide anything.

Q: Do you remember a defining 'Nebraska moment' that stands out to you as far as the championships go?

BP: My first exposure to it was right after Nebraska lost to Georgia Tech in the Citrus Bowl. I remember Georgia Tech just kicked our tail, and my first meeting with them was right before spring ball and weightlifting and all of that. But the biggest thing I remember is some coaches talked, and then Boyd Epley stood up in front of everybody. And for whatever reason, the thing that stuck out to me was, he said, "The biggest problem we have right now in this room is we have the "Have to be's" and the "Want to be's." I don't know if you remember that speech, Paul, but he was basically calling everybody out and saying that there were guys who went to do their lifting because they 'have to be' there. And what he wanted to do was get rid of those guys and just have guys that 'wanted to be' there. That was something. I've always kept that in my head. For whatever reason, that just stuck out to me, because how true was that? Even with work or whatever, as you go on, there's a guy that has to be there and doesn't want to be there -and there are guys who *want* to be there- and it makes a difference.

Q: I remember a week or two after that Georgia Tech game. It was actually the first time in what -20 years?- we finished out of the top 20 in one of the polls? And Boyd -you've got to know this- Boyd loved holding meetings. I remember he walked into our strength staff meeting and he was just livid. He's red in the face and pounding the table with his fists, letting out a few swear words, and even his hair is getting messed up! In his mind you could see that he made the distinction that we had to somehow become a team of 'Want to be's' if we ever expected to live up to the hopes that Nebraska football wanted to reach, you know? We were never gonna let it get this bad again, right? I considered that the low point of the organization. Would you agree?

BP: Yes. And if you remember, everybody was calling for Tom's head. They said he couldn't win the big one and it was time for a change. They wanted his head. And I've gotta be honest -I don't remember any specific names now- there were some guys who worked, but they didn't work nearly as hard as some of the guys on the '93-and-after teams worked.

Q: And the Unity Council?

BP: I think it helped weed out some guys. It made everyone accountable.

Q: Was there a mindset being changed? Was there anything done comparing '94 to '90 that you recall?

BP: I don't know if I can put my finger on it. But I think the guys on the team started to learn how to do things better. They started to learn how to prepare to do some work. Then (sports psychologist) Jack Stark came in, and then (nutritionist) Dave Ellis came in, and it was just a complete mindset across the board with Keith Zimmer and Dennis Leblanc in academics. The whole program just did a 360. They said, "This is how we did things in the past, but those didn't exactly work, so we're going to change things." I remember academics, going to class and Keith and Dennis are outside the room with a roster making sure guys are going to class; with Dave Ellis, guys working harder; Boyd pushing guys harder. I don't think Boyd gets enough credit for what he did. I think Boyd -correct me if I'm wrong- but what he and his staff put together for the guys was something.

Q: Do you remember specific strength coaches working with particular segments of the team?

BP: You know, it was you or Bryan Bailey or Randy Gobel, I don't remember. Bryan, you know, he was one of my favorites. I don't think he gets any credit. He was always there working with guys on the O-line or guys who were injured. He was around all the time and the guys had a really good relationship with him where you could talk with him and get along with him. And when Bryan said it was time to do something, guys would do it. I think the guys had a lot of respect for Bryan.

And as far as what you said earlier, seeing things change, the '94 Orange Bowl where we lost to Florida State? The next year -the morning of the '95 Orange Bowl with Miami- I woke up about 6 in the morning and couldn't sleep. And I remember going downstairs to the lobby to try and find something to eat, and Coach Osborne was sitting downstairs by himself, in our meeting room by himself, watching film at 6 in the morning. That sticks in my mind. I remember that like yesterday. Just sitting down there all by himself the morning of the game.

Q: Tell me about Coach Milt Tenopir or Coach Dan Young.

BP: Milt, he's a tough cookie, a tough guy to crack. I remember the first two years there, the guy didn't know my name. Probably didn't even care if I ever showed up again. I mean, he cared for the guys, but he just didn't have the time for the new guys. He expected you - when you came in there- that you knew what you were doing. He was a coach without being a coach, I guess, is what I'm trying to say. He expected you to learn the stuff. He'd show you one time and he expected you to pick it up. And if you didn't, well, that was on you. You had to figure it out.

Q: How was that communicated or passed on to you?

BP: If you remember, the alignment was stretched base. That was our big line technique: stretched base. If you're covered, stretch double; if you were uncovered, there was a certain footwork that's involved in that. And I played defensive line mostly throughout high school, and coming in trying to play offensive line was a technique I'd never seen before and I had a heck of a time grasping it. And he would get on your case and he'd finally just, "I don't have the time to teach you anymore. I have to get the older guys ready." He's was a real son of a bitch, sometimes, (laughs) trying to know.

And the best thing about Milt was, I always knew what kind of attitude he was in, because we'd always start practice off with our 2 o'clock film sessions. We'd always meet and do a team briefing with Coach Osborne and all the coaches, and then we'd split up and do our breakout sessions and the O-linemen would go into Milt's office. And when you walked in he'd be calling the guys by their names. If he called me 'Pruitt' he was pissed off. If he called me 'Pru' he was in a pretty good mood, and if he called me 'Bryan' he was in a real good mood.

Q: What would determine these moods?

BP: Either how you practiced or how you played or how the team did. But you always knew what kind of mood he was gonna be in. He's a helluva guy, he'll do anything for you.

Q: And what about those post-Spring Game gatherings Milt would hold for you guys?

BP: It was just great to see him in his home. I guess growing up and playing for him, he was such a perfectionist: he expected perfection from us every game, every practice. Everything we did was filmed, watched and graded, over and over. That's the way you'd see him all the time. You didn't understand Milt Tenopir and what he was about until he invited you over, and we did it every spring. It was a few days before the Spring Game -I could be wrong- or it was a couple days after. But either way, he would go out and buy the best steaks, he would have some pretty good drinks, and I don't remember anything more than just sitting in his garage: just sitting there and kicking back and having a good time with everyone. His wife was always there, and if it was one thing that really brought it together for me, he was a different person at home. Definitely more laid back. And I guess he used to own a bar in a town outside Grand Island in the 80's and he had some guys over one time and kind of got in trouble for it, had to miss a bowl game or something. I think when he got away from the field he just loosened up. And away from campus and Coach Osborne it was nice to see him let his hair down and relax some more.

Q: And Coach Young?

BP: Coach Young. I was still working with the kickers and he wasn't around that much. And you know, Milt was always up in the press box during games and Dan worked the sidelines. If you remember Dan's speech, he was like "Pruuuu-ittttttttttttttt, get innnnnn!" I think the guys had more fun imitating him more than anything else. He was a character.

Q: How did you end up coming to Nebraska, anyway?

BP: Well, growing up in Chicago, all the Big 10 schools, Purdue, Michigan State, I went to the Notre Dame spring game, went to Michigan's football camp. Michigan State was where I really wanted to go to. It's where I thought I was going. When the school found out I was gonna be a Prop 48 they essentially just turned their heads away from me and didn't want to have anything to do with me. They said to go to a junior college. I was basically just forgotten.

Q: How did you end up in Nebraska, then?

BP: I don't know if you remember Joel Gesky. He was a High School All–American offensive tackle and Charlie McBride recruited him heavily. I lived three blocks from Joel: we went to school together, we always hung out together, went to the same Catholic school together; I always thought I was just as good as him, if not better. I was basically a dummy in high school. I was a Prop 48. I passed my ACT and I didn't have the GPA to get a scholarship and I was being recruited by everyone just like he was. So one day Charlie was at Joel's house and I just happened to be there (laughs), and the meeting was done and I let Charlie know what was going on and the fact I was having troubles with my grades. He said, "Here's what you do: Apply and see what happens." And I apply and I think it was Agricultural, which was over on East Campus. And I got in! I got a letter saying I was being accepted.'Cause I was looking at junior colleges until I got accepted by Nebraska. And Joel got a scholarship to Nebraska, and it helped out to know someone going there. And he ended up not being as strong or as fast as Zach and Brenden and was 2nd string, but he graduated early and then went home to work. I mean, if I had gotten my degree early? I'm thinking I'd stay around to play a part on the team, but he took off. I guess that was his choice, but there were some really good guys there, and when he was gone I don't think he was really missed. Nothing against Joel, but if you weren't 100% focused on getting the job done and maybe thinking about leaving and calling other schools, we just didn't miss you much in the end, you know?

Q: Bryan, you saw the -relatively speaking- worst to the best. You bridged the gap smack dab in the middle of this dynamic change. Anything else stick out to you about that period?

BP: Correct me if I'm wrong, but at the beginning of the nineties the defense was a 5-2 and then we changed it up to the 4-3, the Colorado or Missouri game.

Q: Prior to that, was it a work in progress? You were seeing it in practice?

BP: I'm sure it was Coach Steele's and Coach McBride's baby. I'm pretty sure I was on the scout team then. I remember Coach Steele always took me and Joel Wilks and some other guys, had us run against linebackers Mike Anderson and (Mike) Petko and Ed Stewart and he'd just tear us down, beating each other. I played against Eddie Stewart in high school in Chicago. And Eddie was a little guy, he wasn't very big at all, and he ended up playing SAM linebacker for us. Essentially a safety or a corner playing linebacker, and that was done specifically to compete against the Florida schools, the Florida State's and Miami's.

Q: Do you recall the guys making shirts up one time that said, "Hey, my name is Ed, too!"

BP: Yeah, I recall that. I can't pinpoint it, but they were all defensive guys that did that. I think they were feeling left out because Steele would always focus on Ed and forget them sometimes.

And I've gotta tell you, I'm not a huge Kevin Steele fan. If you remember, he was from the South and he had a real bond with the black athletes, and I remember walking by him one day and said, 'Hey Coach, how are you doing?' And he was looking right at me as he walked by me and he didn't say one word as I said 'Hi' to him. But then Eddie Stewart or somebody else was right behind me and he goes, "Hey Eddie, what's going on?", put his arm around him and hugged him and all that. And that kind of rubbed me the wrong way, you know? And a few years later, I remember he was roughed up by Kevin Greene who went after him on the sidelines in Carolina, in the NFL. I remember seeing it and it stuck in my head, and I thought to myself, 'He probably deserved to get his butt kicked.' It just didn't sit well with me when a guy would treat you like that, when you're trying to work your way up the depth chart and you're a walk-on, and guys like that treat you like that. It just wasn't the way things were supposed to be.

Q: Let's do a 180. Tell me about Coach Osborne...

BP: The biggest thing about Coach that I'll always remember: he didn't tolerate anybody swearing at all. I mean, I never one time heard the guy cuss. And we knew he was mad when he said, "Gosh doggit" or something like that. He just didn't care for it. Sometimes you'd try to make a name for yourself and you'd get into a fight with Jason or Christian Peter and he wouldn't tolerate that. He'd send you to running the stadium stairs. He always said, "If you can't control yourself in practice, how are you going to do it in a game?" The other thing was that old commercial, "When E.F. Hutton talks, people listen." Whenever he would walk into a room everyone would shut up, and no one would disrespect him by talking. Whenever he was in your presence you were on your toes. Guys wanted to hear what he had to say.

You'd come in on Monday morning and he'd have the game film broken down already, what our goals were, what we did last week. We had at least 25 goals that we were trying to achieve each week. I think he got a bad rap -especially after Lawrence Phillips- you heard people say that all he wanted to do was win and that Lawrence came back for that. Well, I think it was just the opposite. The only thing he cared about were his guys -the guys in the room- making sure they were going to school, making sure they were taking care of their family and just getting better. I think the winning for him was secondary.

And if you remember, we had about 200 guys around on the team then. In '90 they had freshman ball, and then '91 we still played a couple of JV games. I'm thinking there were 90 freshmen on the freshman team, 75 to 90, if I recall. My sophomore year I started a couple of JV games, I picked up a fumble against Air Force and went about 40 yards. I don't even remember half those teams, I'd have to look at a schedule or something. But I think there were something like 150 guys on the varsity while we were over there at the North Stadium locker rooms.

Q: When did you move over to the South Stadium locker room with the varsity?

BP: I'm thinking that was probably spring of '92 or '93 was when I moved over. I remember when I first got on, I think we were 7 deep at each position on the offensive line.

Q: No wonder Milt didn't have much time to spend with you, huh?

BP: He just had to get the guys ready. That was a big part of it.

Q: Do you think the coaches used that environment to look for the self-starters, the leaders, instead of lazier guys, the followers?

BP: Well, with that many guys, my opinion was that sometimes the scholarship guys were actually treated a little differently than the walk-ons. You may hear differently from some guys, but that was my experience. They were sometimes treated just a little bit better.

Q: Did you earn a scholarship? And how did you find out, if so?

BP: Yes, '94, my senior year. We were getting ready for the bowl game and Coach Osborne came up to me & Brady Caskey and said that unless something changed, they were going to hold two for us guys. And something happened so that they ended up only having one. And I remember Brady said, "You know what, you need it more than I do. I'll give it to you." Brady ended up giving his scholarship, his childhood dream, to me. He's my best friend, lives now in North Platte. We talk a couple times a month. I love him. He'd tear his back off for you.

Q: Do you ever wear your championship rings?

BP: I don't very much. When I was a Nebraska Trooper I was looked down upon. There were a lot of guys in that organization that were very upset that I was even there. A lot had to do with Lawrence Phillips and Christian Peter and Tyrone Williams, just all those idiots getting in trouble. And the Nebraska State Patrol was really concerned that I was one of those guys. And especially since I was from Chicago, they were concerned I'd bring some of that same kind of attitude into the department, and that was obviously something that you can't have. And I find out afterwards -talking to some of the guys who did my background check- I went through their process that first year and they kicked me out after my polygraph test. And it wasn't because I lied or anything on the polygraph test, it was just that I admitted to being in several fights when I was in college. Obviously, a lot of them were the result of drinking alcohol, which Coach Osborne always talked about not doing. He would always say, "There's nothing good that happens after drinking alcohol." And their impression, when I'd tell them I got into these fights? They felt I didn't learn from that experience, that I didn't really have very much remorse for it. That was the reason for bumping me the first time through.

Q: But you persevered…

BP: Absolutely. I went through the process again and I got on. And I've gotta say, I poke a lot of fun at Boyd, but I remember after Florida State, I believe there was a minute-sixteen or so on the clock. Well, in the summertime -every day we had our summer workouts- when we thought we were done or we went through and completed every drill, Boyd or his staff would put an extra 1:16 on the clock and we'd do drills until that last minute-sixteen was finished. It was basically him saying, "Listen, the game ain't finished until the clock reads zero." It was driven home to us.

Q: Do you think any of the guys thought that was hokey or corny?

BP: I don't recall anybody ever saying that. They really bought into it. And talking about the years, I remember my first year there that summer, we had about 70 guys who would show up for summer conditioning, but my senior year we had about 150 guys there. There was nobody going home. It was almost expected that you would be there working out. And it wasn't from the coaching staff, it was from the players. As far as O-Line goes, I'd say Rob Zatechka, he was kind of the big ring leader on that. Zach Weigert, he was a clown but he was there at practice. He was clown, but he was there. Brenden Stai, he was another leader of that group.

Q: If I recall, the strength staff actually reached a point where we decided some of the guys were working too long in the weightroom, so we'd kick everybody out and lock the doors early in the summer evening…

BP: Yeah, they went to Gold's, and Christian Peter and Jared Tomich and Brendan Stai would all go there and do even more. Looking back on it, I don't know if they were doing it to get better for Nebraska Football or for the future, but they were pushing hard to get so much better.

Q: You talked earlier about Coach Osborne having 25 goals you wanted to achieve. How often did you achieve those goals?

BP: Right around 15 was the average. One of them, I don't remember them all, it was something like 'so many offensive plays over 25 yards', it might have been five. For Tommie, he wanted 55% completion percentage, and comparing to some other programs, I don't think it was really that high, (laughs) but for us running the option and what we did that was pretty good.

Q: Did you think those goals were realistic. Did you expect to meet them?

BP: I tell you this, I think everybody bought into everything Coach Osborne said to us. I can't tell you why, but we did. And a great example goes back to that video of the National Championship game in the locker room at halftime in Miami, where they show him saying, "Hey, you guys are in better shape and all." And we believed that, because I think we did everything to be in that position. And my senior year, Coach came in and talked to us after we played Oklahoma and said, "Okay guys, we run the option. I can't force you guys to do this -and option football is about timing- and we need to practice to keep our timing. I have you scheduled for your first practice on December 17th or we can start earlier, but I'm leaving it up to you guys." And he left the room. And all the guys voted to continue practicing. I think after the OU game in prior years they'd take a week or two weeks off and then they came back and started practice. He realized that we needed to keep practicing, so all the guys had maybe two or three days off but we were still practicing.

And we were down in Miami before the game getting ready and there were a bunch of pre-game events, and all the guys from Miami were running their mouths (and that was the same thing with the Florida State guys, they were running their mouths). And when we were down there we were practicing like there was no tomorrow. Sure, we wanted to have some fun, too. When we were down there we were practicing hard, but we were seeing the other guys partying and having a great time. They were all so arrogant, thinking they were going to walk all over us. So when he said that, reminded us of that, we knew. And especially in the middle of the game and we're playing them and they're down on one knee and they're bent over at the waist 'cause they don't have any air... and us guys are all, "Come on, let's go!" For that game, it was definitely the conditioning thing that Coach talked about and we bought into it. He said it and we knew we did it, did the work. The Florida State game was the fact that nobody gave us any respect, that was a motivator in that game.

Q: What about the field conditions at Miami?

BP: Very sandy. I was a wedge breaker. That's where I played the bowl games. But yeah, it was a very sandy, very different kind of field. Nothing I don't think we'd ever seen before. The year before I was on the kickoff and the PAT field goal team. My senior year, I played quite a bit in the first 6 games or so, probably 10 or so snaps a game to give Brenden Stai a break. And then as the games starting getting tighter and it wasn't as hot anymore Coach wasn't giving breaks as much anymore. And I was pissed. I remember one day sitting in team meetings. It was Coach Steele, McBride, up there just chewing the defensive guys' asses because they didn't have anybody running down hard on the kickoff team, guys weren't selling out. And I walked in to see Coach Tenopir and said, 'Coach, this is my senior year. I've gotta play. You gotta get me out there, this is killing me. Can you talk to the coaches about giving me a chance as a wedge-breaker?' He kinda looked at me like, "You're nuts, you know that?" He says, "I'll mention it", and sure thing he did. So they gave me a shot.

One day we were out there and they didn't think nothing of it, Coach Steele yells my name and says, "We're gonna give you a chance and see what you can do." This was right before the Missouri game of my senior year. So we get a couple of practices in and they sent me out there on kickoff. And everybody went nuts on the sidelines. The linemen thought it was awesome. All the little guys were jacked up, and first time down... and it's real simple, the wedge breaker lines up right next to the kicker, Darin Erstad. I think you had R1 and L1, the numbers go out bigger as you go out to the sides. The primary responsibility is breaking the wall. You don't even have to tackle, really, it's just about breaking the wall of guys. It means you gotta haul ass down there and you gotta get around that first block. Those guys are running back ten yards and then trying to take you out. And then when you get past that first wave you're trying to find that wall -which is usually about 4 guys- and you're doing everything you can do get down there and try to take out two or three guys with one hit. You had to sell out, you had to be a little bit crazy, there's no other way to explain it. You're running full speed and trying to make a big impact for those guys. Sometimes when you did you stopped the ball-carrier or made them change directions, and then you set them up for some other guys to come in and make a tackle. Cool thing about that, for me, is the

Oklahoma game I had two tackles. Blew through the first guy, blew through the second, and lo and behold, I had two tackles. So I had Special Teams Player of the Week for two tackles versus Oklahoma, which was pretty cool. And I know that Miami game, the first time I got to run down on the kickoff, I don't even remember who the deep back was, but as soon as he caught the ball he just took off, and I remember thinking, "Holy smokes!" I couldn't believe how fast the kid was. This wasn't like a regular Big 8 team, you know? But the thing for me was that I got to get back out on the field. That was important to me.

Q: You could tell a difference in the speed of those guys?

BP: Absolutely. Absolutely. I think with our guys, our group of seniors, we weren't afraid of anybody. We just had one thing in mind: beat them down and win it. You know? We just knew we were better.

Q: Obviously the other guys wanted to do the same…so how did it end up that we did the beating instead of being the beaten?

BP: That's a good question. Well, I think through all those years of practices we had a system down. All the repetitions, and the fact that the guys knew how the coaches called the plays, they just felt or knew it was the right combination, you know? It was definitely a pride thing for the O-line. My senior year, we led the nation in rushing again. We just knew we were going to run them over. And if it wasn't the first string guys who were doing it, it was the second string guys who would come in and get the job done. I think the offensive line really put the team, offensively, on our backs, and offensively carried the team.

After that Florida State game right away we -almost immediately- we talked about it. We were so close, we had that game. And then they scored right away after that call on Barron out of bounds. And then Tommie hits Trumane Bell -who was also from Chicago- who had a great catch. And then they dump Gatorade on Bowden already. And like I said, Byron, we knew he was at his limit as far as distance. The funny thing for me was, I remember being out there and then I go straight to thinking, "Oh God, please don't let me be the guy who jumps offsides!" Because you couldn't hear anything. You couldn't have heard 17 fighter jets go over, it was that loud. Anyway, Zach Weigert was out there, too, and the Florida State guys were just running their mouths like crazy. They were saying things mostly directed at Coach Osborne, if I recall. Stuff like, "Get the fuck off the field!" I don't remember anything else, but Zach was jawing back at them. Zach was the big shit-talker for us, as far as offensive linemen go. And he could back it up, too. I don't even remember if it was ball placement or time remaining or what the issue was, but they were telling him to get off the field. I remember thinking, "Who the hell are these guys? Nobody talks to Coach like that!" So, like I said, I remember lining up for the ball, couldn't hear anything, just giving it our best shot…and Byron kicked it left.

Q: You usually played PATs and FG attempts?

BP: The whole year I was. And David Seizys was the holder on that. I couldn't hear anything. Anything! I just remember thinking to myself, 'Don't be the guy who jumps offsides or moves and pushes us back 5 more yards.' Because you could go down in history. And, unfortunately, Byron has. Because of the field goal.

Q: You know, I wanna get a hold of that guy, because most people forget that 1:15 before that try he nailed a three-pointer. I hope he's not too scarred from the experience, you know?

BP: If you do talk to him, try to see if he still says the phrase -what was it?- his big phrase was "shit-fire!"

Q: Shit-fire? In what context?

BP: Yeah, obviously, being from Texas, he was a big Texas guy. He always ended a sentence with "shit-fire." (laughs)

Q: (laughing) Do you have a favorite play or recollection above all others?

BP: I tell you this, probably one of the coolest moments was being in the South end zone in the locker room: the very first time walking into the locker room and walking up to the locker and seeing a jersey hanging there with your name on it. And some guys, you hear about the tunnel walk and running out onto the field? Well I never even saw those people when I walked out of the tunnel. I never even saw or heard those people when I came out of the tunnel. Maybe it was focus or tunnel vision, I don't know, but it was never the biggest thing for me. It wasn't that exciting. It was seeing that jersey with your name on it. Kind of more of like, 'Alright, I've made it. All that work has finally paid off. You're somebody now.'

Q: What kind of emotions? Was it relief, was it inspiration, getting a tear in your eye?

BP: Probably for me, it was grabbing a jersey and holding it in my hand, looking at it and thinking, 'I can't believe I've done it.' Not that you're done, but it was a first step, the first reality check that, 'Hey, you're here. This is for real.' For me, that was one of the coolest things.

Q: If you had one moment or thing to do over, what would it be?

BP: (Long silence) (laughs) I'm pretty happy the way things turned out. When I came in, I kinda got lost in the shuffle. There were so many guys. They were kinda like, "Hey, if you wanna play offensive line, you can play offensive line." I only weighed 265 lbs. I should have played another position. Maybe I could have been a linebacker, maybe I should have played fullback. I probably should have thought more of playing in the NFL. A lot of people ask me, "Why didn't you play in the NFL or try it?" For me, the goal was just to make it to Nebraska and play college football and make the team. With some of these other guys Nebraska was just a rung in the ladder for their ultimate goal of the NFL. But it wasn't like that for me, I just wanted to make the team and make it the best I could, and get on the field. And make the traveling squad. It was more of the short term goals. So yeah, thinking back, I would have liked to tried a different position.

Q: You thought you could've given Cory Schlesinger a run for his money at fullback, huh?

BP: I think I could've. (laughs) I think I could have. I mean, I love Cory, he's a great guy. (laughs) But it would have been fun.

Q: Any good practice stories?

BP: Let's see, every Friday we had our 30 minute practice the day before the game. Of course, the linemen, we usually had everything done. There was nothing that we could do, so Coach Tenopir would get the guys and line all the guys up single file and he'd have the guys run pass routes. Even throw the football for 'em. That was Milt's big thing, on Friday before the game, was throwing routes for the guys.

Q: No pulled hamstrings or other injuries?

BP: Oh, I'm sure they did, but most of the time it was from laughing at the other guys so hard. Your linemen are linemen not because they're so big, it's because they don't have hands. (laughs) And there were some guys, like the Zach Weigerts who tried to show off their skills, that was pretty funny.

And of course, some of the fights. I don't know if you remember the pits, down in the pits, that was our home away from home. Osborne didn't come down there very much, and we didn't slack off, but that's where we had our wars: offense versus defensive line, down in the pits. Guys got nasty down there, punching each other. I got punched in the balls one day. I remember Bill Humphrey, blocked him and knocked him on his ass (this was before he switched over from defensive line to O-line for his senior year). So I knocked Bill down and maybe laid on him or something and stood up and was watching the running backs, and the next thing you know I'm just bent over at the knees cause Bill punched me in the balls. I'm like, 'Who does that to another guy?!' (laughs) All those stories about Christian Peter, some of those guys spitting, I don't know if you remember that quarterback from Kansas State?

Q: Chad May?

BP: Chad May! All those stories about our guys punching him in the balls, spitting in his face, gouging him in the eyes? All true! But of course, Coach Osborne never knew about all that stuff. He would have been furious if he found out that type of stuff was going on.

Q: How do you think he never knew?

BP: I don't know. I'm not real sure! Quick football story: I was a dirty offensive lineman. I was basically a defensive lineman playing offensive line. I hate to say this without really saying it -and I hate to sugarcoat it- but we could get pretty dirty. For offensive linemen, we'd 'cut' like crazy, we blew guys knees out and ankles all the time. One play we're doing an 18 Option, I was out there working with Brady Caskey. It was against Colorado State, I believe, and the tackle's gonna try to get off the guy and the guard is going to pick him up, a technique called 'pull and overtake.' So we're basically working 2 on 1 on the option, so Brady reaches his guy and he takes off for the linebacker (there was a technique you could use if you planted your helmet down on the other side of the guy's foot, and then you plant your shoulder down on the guy's foot you could tear his ankle or knee out). And, of course, I did that because he had no idea I was coming, and the guy's holding his knee. And I remember we were 20 yards downfield and Brady said, "Did you get the guy?" I turned to him and said, 'He's laying back there.' Of course, they carted him off. And it's terrible to say, but we got pretty nasty.

Q: Any remorse for something like that happening?

BP: No, it was just part of it. That's the way we were taught. It would happen. We got down low on the guys, that's the way we did business. Not that guys were afraid to play us, but they were very emotional playing against us. They, the defensive linemen, didn't like us going down low. But that's part of what made us pretty good, was that fear that we would mix things up. That was important to our success. They were pissed, yelling at the refs, yelling at us, calling us cheap, you name it. They just hated it. They were just verbally upset. Of course, they'd try to get their shots in when they could. But you're wearing pads, so it never really did anything.

Q: Anybody behind the scenes play a large role in your development?

BP: From an academic standpoint, I'll be the first one to say Dennis Leblanc. That guy was instrumental in getting me developed. For me? I can't give him enough credit, what he did behind the scenes. Here's an example: we played Florida State in the '92 Orange Bowl. I didn't do so hot in school that semester. Dennis probably came to me during practice and said something like, "Wait until after the game." I remember on the plane going back to Lincoln he walks up to me on the plane and says, "Hey Bryan, what happened to your grades last semester?" And I remember playing dumb like, 'What do you mean?' "Well, you got an F in this and you didn't pass this and you got an F in this. Unless you pass 16 hours next semester you're gonna be ineligible." How's that for a flight home, having all that on your mind? To me it was just the way Dennis would motivate the guys. He would pick the right time to do it. And then he would pick the right time and say, "Hey, you screwed up. You gotta get your ass in gear." And it took me enough time, I had a tough time. It took me 5 ½ years to get my degree. So I graduated and I go up and get my diploma. I walk back to my seat and open it up, and there's a card in there from Dennis and Keith Zimmer. It says, "Congratulations! We knew you could do it." That will always stick in my mind. I know there was nobody else had a card in their diploma, but I did. They didn't have to push you, but they did. Especially if you were a walk-on. They could have focused all their time on the scholarship guys, but they didn't. They pushed everybody. Like I said, I owe a lot to those guys.

Q: You're not the first guy to say that, Bryan. Many sing the praises of Dennis and Keith…

BP: And you know, the biggest thing for me was when Coach Osborne took the negative rap for some of those guys who went out and did dumb stuff. It just pissed me off when some of the guys went out there and gave the team a bad name. There were enough guys out there doing good and nobody ever gave them much credit. People ask me all the time, they asked me what Lawrence was like. I remember he grew up in a foster home, I remember Coach saying he's probably never had a family before. He's probably never had anybody that would guide him. His freshman year, that's the only thing I remember about him, his freshman year he got into a fight with another guy in the locker room. I'm sure he beat the kid up, if I remember. But he was fine, all the years I was there, to my knowledge I never ever seen him have any problems. Always talked to him, say "Hi" to him, he was just like everybody else. But in those later years, the trouble he ran into? It was shame, just a shame. He was a truck, he had it all. He had the size, the power, the speed. He should still be playing in the NFL. He was that good.

Q: Any of the other guys stand out to you?

BP: I'll be the first one to tell you, I'm not a huge fan of Tommie Frazier. He was put on a pedestal when he got there. He was good. Coach held him up there on that pedestal and took care of him. He knew he was gonna take the team pretty far. I mean, that was his boy. I remember Coach coming into the team meetings, everybody was quiet. Except Tommie. He was always kind of joking with him, and Tommie had a different relationship with him, because he was working with him all the time. Tommie would be the guy always playing pranks on Coach Osborne. He didn't treat the guys like they needed to be treated. Jared Tomich one day asked him to sign a helmet, autograph a helmet for somebody, and he wouldn't do it. Jared said, "If you don't sign this helmet, I'm gonna kick your ass." He had to threaten the guy to get him to sign the autograph. And it was pretty common, guys would circulate stuff around the locker room to be signed, and everybody did it. But he wouldn't do it, he was too good for that stuff. He wouldn't give you the time of day.

Q: And Brook?

BP: Brook was a big quail and pheasant hunter, I'm sure you know that. As far as Brook, he was a hard working guy, he came in and put his time in. I don't have anything but good things to say about Brook. And when Matt Turman was running the show, all the guys did everything they could to protect him. A little guy coming out of nowhere, we did our best to take care of him. And when he played, like I said, it was the offensive linemen's attitude, it didn't matter if the other team heard the play or not, or who the quarterback was, we were gonna run the ball over you. That was the mindset that Milt instilled in us.

Q: How did you know if Milt was unhappy with you during the game, with him being up in the box?

BP: He came down at halftime. But he had a pretty good feel for the guys, and he'd get on you as you were right there. And sometimes he'd get Dan (Young) to try to get on you, but that never really worked. Dan wasn't a real motivator. That just wasn't his style, you know. (laughs)

And another story: the year we played Florida State and we were 17 point underdogs, Lance Lundberg -there was a kid from Bradenton, Florida, he went to the same school as Tommie, a little defensive back– Lumpy (Lundberg) ended up blocking him one day, we were just wearing helmets. Anyway, this little guy ended up punching Lumpy. He sucker-punched Lumpy in the locker room. It was big deal and they ended up sending the kid home from the bowl game. But what they ended up doing, some of the black guys thought it was racially motivated, that they sent the kid home. And talk about the Unity Council, the team got together without any coaches and talked about it, and that was one of the big things that brought us back together. This was down in Miami getting ready for Florida State. Lumpy had a black eye for that game. I apologize for not remembering the kid's name, but that was something that really stands out to me.

Q: One more question. Any strange routines or superstitions?

BP: I remember for me, my senior year, the Pipeline. All the starters, where they'd pull the white socks up over their calves? Aaron Graham started that, the O-line. And my senior year I'm not the starter, I had to rebel -my thing being the second string guy- I had to do just the opposite of that. So I wore little ankle socks with the hightops, but you can't see them in the high tops. I took my shoes, wiped the little Converse sign off it, and it looked like I wasn't wearing any socks at all. So, being different, I wore 'em down all the time. It was a spirit-filled group, that's for sure.

Q: And you said Milt would get on you pretty good?

BP: Like I said, when we were down in the pits he would definitely get on the guys. He let you know you weren't in high school anymore.

Q: And what about Charlie McBride?

BP: Oh yeah, absolutely. I had a really good bond with him. Because I went to Morgan Park Academy, and I think he was over in Beverly on the South Side of Chicago. He always kind of had a special thing, being from Chicago. He would always come over and talk to me and ask how things were going. I always got the impression he looked out for me. And he was nuts! (laughs) He wasn't like any other coaches. I guess, being a defensive coordinator/defensive line coach, he had to be that way, and having the defensive linemen that he had -Raemakers, Parrella, the Peters- you're just living with a bunch of goofballs, guys that weren't all there, you know? He was definitely the right one to be leading that group. What an awesome guy, though. I don't have anything but good things to say about Charlie. He would definitely get in guy's face and let him know what he's thinking. Grab them by the facemask and spit, whatever. He got on guy's asses. He worked the defense like no other coach. He put his guys through the paces, every day, intense. The offensive linemen, you can be intense, but you can't be intense the whole time. Being O-line, there's a lot of thinking involved, they're just a different breed. I think so. You had your defensive linemen for a reason: it's not because they were really good at doing something. Some guys are offensive linemen and some guys are defensive linemen, there's a lot of thought process going on. With defense they're just reacting to what's happening.

Q: And your mindset going into a game? Game prep? When it came time to play? Was it confidence, cockiness?

BP: Coach would always stress -for the second and third string guys, when you got in- they could handle mistakes, but they couldn't take mental mistakes, 'cause if a quarterback got hurt because you screwed up mentally, it wasn't good, they wouldn't have it. And they wouldn't put you back on the field because they'd lose all confidence in you. For me, we'd come in on Friday and we'd take a game test. We'd actually... Coach would have however many plays on a piece of paper, he'd have 7 or 8 different defensive plays on the paper, and you had to draw not only what you were doing, but know all 6 offensive line positions, including tight end. And that was for each play.

And Nebraska Football during those years, there was no way you could come into that system and play right away in two years. It took 3 years to actually learn it, to be able to do all 6 offensive line positions. As far as transitioning to the game it wasn't the physical aspect, it was the mental aspect. That's what was expected from you, and once you did know what you were doing that's when you could excel, because you weren't thinking anymore. You just went out and did it. Because you'd seen it in practice so many times.

That's where the coaches really got good at getting guys ready for the next team, showing them the defenses and what they'd seen in film. Basically, what I do for work now? We practice it and rehearse, and then sure enough, come game time we've seen it before; we do the same thing we've done a thousand times before.

Q: Being on a SWAT team, you've seen some pretty intense situations, huh? Dodged a few bullets?

BP: I have. Yes, I have. Basically what I do now is what I was doing playing football at NU. It's like playing football: there's 10 other guys on the team with you. We're basically a fine-tuned orchestra and were counting on the other guys to know what they're doing. A lot is at stake: your lives. I don't worry about the guys next to me. I know they're doing what they're supposed to be doing. I'm not spending my time looking around to check on the other guys. I'm able to focus and just react. For me, a lot of that comes from football, that's where I developed all of that. I think that's why I'm so good at what I do now, is because of football.

Q: Matt Turman said the quarterbacks were told they could never run out of bounds. Do you think that helped create some unity among the team? That even those guys were always taking and giving shots out there?

BP: Yeah, it could have had a part. I know that for us it was 'pancakes.' They were a big thing: Pancake blocks. Milt always had a big board up there in his office where he tracked the most pancake blocks. That was taking the opponent and 'flat-backing' him. And you know, I think a lot of those teams, they pitch the option and things like that, they pitch the ball and then they just jog the other way? Well, with Matt and Tommie and Brook, they were out there trying to make blocks. I think that had a lot to do with it, that those guys were out there busting their ass, too. They weren't prima donnas. Absolutely. And I always remember those receivers practicing, Ron Brown and those guys worked harder than you'd believe. They learned to block hard before anything else.

Q: David Seizys talked about getting in there at the end of games and punching guys in the thigh and getting cussed out by the opposing DB's...

BP: You've got to remember, it was like throwing meat to the wolves. Our second and third string guys would bust their ass all week in practice, and now was their chance in the spotlight. They'd finally have their chance to perform and get after it. It was chance to make a name for themselves. It was a good group of guys. I remember a lot of times the other team was like, "What the hell is going on here?" They're frustrated, they couldn't believe that here comes another crew of guys on the field to kick their ass! (laughs)

Q: Do you ever remember any team or any game where they essentially said, "Please, let up on us!?"

BP: UCLA a little bit, when we played 'em at home in '94. I was on the team when we went out to UCLA when they had J.J. Stokes, the big receiver. Those guys pretty much gave up a little bit, I remember. Most teams, when they were playing Nebraska, were like, "Hey, this is our big chance. Our chance to shine," even when they were getting beat, they were still playing us tough. I was talking to somebody the other day, too, and Utah always seemed to give us a good fight. That was before Urban Meyer passed through there. I remember when they came out, they really played us tough.

Q: Anyone take you under their wing and help you along when you first got rolling there?

BP: No doubt, it was Brenden Stai. Brenden learned from Will Shields, and those were the two guys I backed up, Will and Brenden. I think it was just taking care of the guys underneath you. I remember sitting with Brenden at the locker and just talking, and when I didn't understand something I'd explain it to him and he'd explain it to me, or whatever. He always took care of me and made sure I knew what I was doing and that everything worked the way it was supposed to. And the funny thing is, we were essentially about the same age, but for whatever reason he was always a good guy and looked out for me.

Q: Brenden was a pretty good guy, wasn't he?

BP: I don't know if you remember, but it was our big, top-secret thing for the '94 Orange Bowl: Brenden was right guard, and as soon as we got home from the OU game they switched Brenden to left and put Joel Wilks at right guard. They didn't want anybody to see that until the game.

Q: How did you guys, as linemen, take that move? Were you all sold out for it?

BP: Oh, absolutely. Joel did it for the team. Basically Coach came in and said, "(Warren Sapp is) gonna be a problem for us, and the best matchup right now is gonna be Brenden there over the top of him, taking him on." You know, I don't think anybody had a problem with it. You know that's pretty uncommon, after about 10 or 11 games to take a guy and move him, practice him a couple of weeks and basically switching his position, because everything is completely different. I think what he accomplished that game was huge. And being a part of the system for so long probably helped him do that, for sure.

Q: How did you guys grade out in that Miami game?

BP: You know, Paul, I don't think I ever saw grades on that game. That's a question you'd have to ask Milt. I'm not sure.

Q: And the Florida State game the previous year?

BP: Oh, I'll be honest with you: I've seen the kick, but I don't think I've watched the game. Ever. I have the game downstairs, but I've never watched it. If you break that tape out again, I was the left tackle on the kick. I remember that field, planting my left foot against one of those Alexanders for FSU. He played a few years for the Minnesota Vikings, that's who I wound up blocking. I stepped and my feet gave out on me, and you can see I end up on the ground. And he got a pretty good push and someone comes up, over the left side of him and gets really high. I don't know the kid's name. I always wondered, because I gave up a little ground on my block, 'Did that screw up Byron and affect him and his kick?', you know? I always wonder if that may have contributed at all, you know? I sure hope not, but you think about it sometimes.

Q: You know, sometimes us Husker fans on the West Coast get together in the offseason and watch an old game to get the juices flowing for the upcoming season. And call me sick, but I love watching that '94 FSU Orange bowl game. It was a great struggle and you guys gave the most tremendous effort that I ever recall. It was a war. I remember being so proud of you guys. It seemed the team crossed a threshold that game, and you knew that it was yours for the taking. Too bad 1:15 later it was to be otherwise, though. It was yours. And the next year you guys, as a team, made sure that you went out and proved to the rest of the world that you were as good as you knew you were. Would you agree or am I full of it?

BP: I agree with that 100%. The other thing about that, too -and correct me if I'm wrong- but I don't remember the guys complaining or whining about it too much, either. That's a blow we were dealt, and it was up to us to make sure there would be no doubt the next year. And I was talking to T.J. Slansky at the Spring Game this past year and I asked him that question. I said, 'Hey, let me ask you how you felt about missing the national championship on that kick, and then watching your team the next year go out and win it. Were you pissed?' He said, "No, man. All of the guys were proud of what you guys did." That was pretty cool. We felt that way, too, it wasn't just for us guys but for all those guys before us, too.

End conversation.

Wow, how rich was that? We touched on so many issues here, it's difficult to focus on simply one or two. But in the course of my great Why and How I must make some choices, and the first issue that clamors for attention was his mention of Team Psychologist Dr. Jack Stark and Nutritionist Dave Ellis joining on, as well as, "This is how we did things in the past, but those didn't exactly work, so we're going to change things." It brought to mind Mr. Collins' book where he made the point that, ""Stop Doing" lists are more important than "to do" lists." What did Nebraska Football stop doing? If memory serves, they stopped going after so many of the blue chippers for a specific position, per se, in recruiting and instead looked for "Nebraska guys," student/athletes who had speed to burn and the capacity to move closer to the line of scrimmage on the defense, in particular. Plus, instead of the assistant coaches only recruiting their assigned regions of America, they were allowed to personally target the players they coveted no matter their geographic location. The result was athletes' greater familiarity with their primary mentors in the early stages of recruitment rather than mere acquaintance-ships until they arrived on campus in the fall. The bonds between coach & athlete were then closer, and this as a result led to better communication, more effective teaching, and often more proficient play at an earlier stage in their careers.

One could argue that Bryan stated just the opposite too, though, for he mentioned the lack of mollycoddling and ongoing personal attention at the outset by Offensive Line Coach Milt Tenopir. At first glance one would suppose there was a conflict within the system, but in thinking about it further I've come to the conclusion that it was designed, it was for a purpose and, moreover, it was proper. I say that because it separated the men from the boys, the leaders from the laggards, the "Want To Be's" from the "Have To Be's", as Bryan mentioned about Boyd Epley's line drawn in the sand that early January meeting of 1991.

Many books have been written on the concept of motivation and what roles both intrinsic and extrinsic motivation play in the workplace environment, and all signs point to intrinsic motivation (that derived from within a person) as being the prime driver of a majority of successful people and organizations, with extrinsic motivators such as compensation or perks playing a close but noteworthy second fiddle. Bryan began his playing career as a Prop 48 walk-on, so one can see how that ordering played out in true-to-life form.

Two other items of note: One was his mention that, "..if you weren't 100% focused on getting the job done and maybe thinking about leaving and calling other schools, we just didn't miss you much in the end." This further convinces me that the "Get the right people on the bus and the wrong people off the bus" axiom was coming into being as a part of the team culture. I find it reminiscent of the "If you're not for me, then you're against me" line of thought. And with the ample number of volunteer walk-ons from both in-state and out, I can see how this was a comfortably fashionable mindset. Also, in speaking of the 'right people,' my hat goes off to Brady Caskey, his offensive line mate, who chose to forgo his Nebraska schoolboy dream of a scholarship just so this Chicago-area friend and his family could have life a little easier on the fiscal side of the family ledger. If that isn't a fine example of love, of brotherhood, of sacrifice, of unity and cohesion, I don't know what is. God bless you, Brady Caskey, wherever you are.

Notable quote #2:
Bryan Pruitt on Coach Tom Osborne: "The only thing he cared about were his guys, the guys in the room, making sure they were going to school, making sure they were taking care of their family and just getting better. I think the winning for him was secondary."

"Courage; Generosity; Fairness; Honor; In these are the true awards of manly sport."
Inscription on the Northwest Corner of Memorial Stadium,
Hartley Burr Alexander, former UNL Professor of Philosophy

Mama HuskerPower: that's Linda Ybarra. Though surrounded by alpha males in the confines of the West Stadium Strength Complex for the better part of twenty years, Linda ruled the roost and was a guardian of the gate to those passing through the doors of the monstrous strength training facility located under West Stadium's bleacher seats. Keeping the staff's young guns in check, coordinating the Husker Power Booster Club and just about everything else happening to take place on that end of the campus, she saw and heard everything. Big brown eyes and a friendly -yet at times stern- manner, you knew who was boss whenever seated at her massive, wrap-around desk facing the visitor's nook and weight room entrance. I was interested in what she had to share.

Notable Quote #1:
"With athletes, integrity should be your number one focus. With Coach Osborne around you always knew where you stood."

Linda Ybarra

Question: Linda, you just never seem to slow down…

Linda Ybarra: It seems that way.

Q: You're working with Randy Gobel, John Ingram & crew at Nebraska Facilities now?

LY: Well, Boyd was kind of overseeing everything at first. And then Steve Pederson came around and reorganized the whole department. They were going to initially put me in with Bob Burton in the business office. Boyd had a fit, saying, "There's no way you're going to take her away from me." So he didn't. But things changed when Steve came around - especially at the end of his time there it got kind of weird- he was really kind of a different type of person. He did some good things for athletics. He did. But he just picked up this one guy, and things seemed to go downhill after that.

Q: When did you join Nebraska Athletics?

LY: August of 1985. I started working for Boyd as the Office Manager for the strength and conditioning program and making the Husker Power Club better. We went from 500 to over one thousand members in the group, pretty much setting a standard for the booster clubs, and they were really able to help the program.

I think it was Boyd and his vision for the strength program that changed a lot of things, especially how the rest of the athletic department saw what these groups could do. And you know, Boyd had a vision. And I think because of that vision he was able to promote the program. (A lot of strength coaches around the nation had molded their programs after it.) He was a great boss, he expected loyalty. But then, also, he pretty much let me do what I wanted to do. Some people saw that as being pretty spoiled. (laughs)

And like I said, Steve Pederson did some good things for athletics: he helped build our new, beautiful complex, and he expected perfection and he expected loyalty, but after a time he got to thinking -and this is my opinion- he was expecting everyone to be 'perfect', you know? And not everyone is perfect. There was some micro-managing. And I liked Steve as a person, but you can't have a successful program if you're operating out of fear. You can't run a business like that. With athletics that's your number one focus, and it ended being like a dysfunctional corporation. With athletes, integrity should be your number one focus. With Coach Osborne around, you always knew where you stood. You weren't concerned about who was watching or if someone was going to 'tell on you.'

Q: You say Boyd had a vision. Was that vision ever fully realized? Was it fully concluded?

LY: Well, I think his legacy is this awesome program he created. He did have a vision, and he expected things to turn out the way he had planned. Unfortunately, some things didn't work out that way.

Q: I remember those meetings around '91 or '92 where he was beginning to sketch out what the new North stadium complex would look like. This was, what, 12 years before it was finalized?

LY: Ah, yes, he liked those meetings. (laughs) And yes, it all started with Boyd. He'd planned a long time ago to build the new complex. It was only realized when Steve came on board. Even former athletes come around nowadays and they say, "Where are all the old people? I'm lost here!"

Q: So you arrived in '85 and we went through that rough year in '90, finishing out of the top 20 for the first time in years. Do you remember that time?

LY: That was a long time ago, Paul. I just know that when we had that many losses, things changed a bit. It was hard, hard work from that point on. I remember when I first started working for Boyd in '85 it was like: you had an in-season from August through the Football season, and then winter conditioning, and then summertime the athletes would go home and return in August. Well, because Boyd had this vision of how a program should be, things became year-round. There was no summer vacation, they'd go from winter conditioning to spring ball, and then they were encouraged to stay around and keep working over the summer to get better. That's what I think turned the program around, he gave them the desire to get better. And those athletes, they realized that and worked that much harder. And when Charlie McBride was around those Blackshirts worked really hard and earned that name.

Q: Do you recall any special people?

LY: I remember Charlie and Milt and Ron Brown, those guys were all good coaches. They had a good vision -not to discount our present day coaches- but those guys and so many athletes would pass by the front desk every day and you got to know them and they became part of a family. It was like I know Trev Alberts, and he'd pass by and you'd say hi.

Q: I remember a lot of times walking through the front door of the old strength complex, Linda, and all I'd see were big old rear-ends in red gym shorts because they were always leaning through the reception window talking to you for a spell before exiting the weightroom. It was like you were a 'Weight Room Mom', a 'Den Mother' kind of thing.

LY: A lot of former athletes walk in nowadays and they remember who you are. That's what sets them apart and set us apart. We took the time to know them personally, and they realized it. We weren't just interested in them because they were an athlete, but because they were a person. You know, there were so many guys from Chris Caliendo to Mike Murray, Kent Wells… all the wild guys. (laughs) Grant Wistrom and John Parrella. I really got close to John Parrella. He took the time to really get to know who you were. And he'd even come back in the offseason to say 'Hi', maybe not specifically to me, but he was friends with Mike Arthur and Randy Gobel and Boyd. So many of those guys would come back during the

NFL offseason and they'd workout and say 'Hi'. It meant a lot. And Grant Wistrom, his hair! (laughs) He did have a head of hair. They ended up shaving their heads, shaved it all off.

Tom had always allowed former athletes to come back, and even if some had to come back to finish their degree, he let them do that. The athletes just loved him.

Q: Any good Coach Osborne stories?

LY: When I first started working there I noticed that people would call him 'Coach', and one day I just happened to be in the football office -and I'd always called him 'Tom.' I never called him 'Coach', and somebody asked me one time, "Why are you calling him 'Tom'?", and I said, 'Well, that's his name. Why would I call him 'Coach'?' (laughs) And I've always called him Tom, but some people thought that was disrespectful, and I've never ever changed. Even with him being Athletic Director, I still call him Tom.

Q: Did he ever bring up the topic with your calling him by his first name?

LY: No. Every time I'd see him he'd always take the time to ask how you were doing, and he was very interested in how you were doing. He'd always take the time with you and have a conversation with you. He was never too busy to do that.

Q: What stands out about those championship years?

LY: I remember when we won the National Championship in Tempe, when Tommie ran down the sidelines with the football and scored at the end. I remember that one. That was great one. And of course in Miami when Cory Schlesinger rolled into the end zone. And I think what set us apart was our team was so dominant in the 4th quarter. I think that's what Boyd's legacy was. We'd train our athletes to be dominant in the 4th quarter. And that earned us a lot of respect.

Q: I've gotta ask you Linda. Were you around the day that Coach Osborne blew a gasket about the rap music playing on the weight room's overhead speakers?

LY: Oh, yes. He didn't like that. He did not like rap. Especially when rap first came out, there was a lot of vulgarity in the rap, and that was one of the things that he did not accept.

Q: I heard he walked into the weight room, heard the music's lyrics and then walked straight back into the Strength office and exclaimed, "Judas' Priest, Boyd! Do you hear that?!" From that day forward I believe rap was off the playlist. (laughs) And I believe previous to that, because of the Unity Council, various groups of players petitioned for their favorite types of music to be playing on specific days.'Equal time', so to speak. Do you remember that? There was country music one day, classic rock another day, rap another, and so on. But much to a segment of the team's chagrin, rap music was no longer in the rotation after that.

LY: (laughs) You're right.

Q: Anything else about those years that stands out to you?

LY: Well, I remember all the staff working so hard together in late December loading up the semi-trailer with all the weights to take down to those bowl games. You guys would spend all day tearing apart the weight room and placing it into the semi-trailer, and then Randy Gobel even got his commercial driver's license so he could help take the weights down to Miami and Arizona and such for all of those bowl trips. So whenever we'd go to the bowl trip, we'd go set up our own weight room down there. Either Randy or Boyd would set up a location to rebuild our weight room so the players would have the familiarity with their same equipment they were used to using, so it felt like their home weight room.

Q: Another little thing that made a great difference to the players, yes?

LY: Yes. So many people put a lot of hours in: from the trainers to you strength coaches, to Dave Ellis and nutrition. And we'd have the Open Houses on game day for some people to come in and see what we were all about, and I know a lot of people tried to copy what we were doing. Also, we had so many boosters who contributed to the Husker Power Club, and that gave rise to a lot of other support groups sprouting up for various causes and programs within the athletic department, almost too many to mention.

Q: Is the Husker Power Club alive to this day?

LY: It's still going on. They've combined it into the Husker Athletic Fund, and I believe in some respect it's still alive today.

Q: Anything else worth mentioning about those years, Linda?

LY: We'll, if you recall, Boyd was the one that started the strength program ever since he got out of college. But the facilities have always stood out to me. We started with the West Stadium, then we moved our office out into a trailer in the parking lot outside the Baseball offices when we made it even bigger in the early 90's. (And one time a student was backing out of their parking stall and they backed into the trailer! (laughs) That was a nice surprise.) There were so many people, just like a family. Like you, for instance. We became just like family, with Kelvin Clark and Jon Jost and so many guys. When you became part of the strength staff and spent so much time together we became just like family. I believe Kelvin (Clark) is down in Dallas now and I know Jon (Jost)is down at Florida State. And John Archer was at Nevada, but he's down in Houston now. Kevin Coleman and Courtney are married now. Curt Thompson, he's here in Lincoln. I saw him one day a few months ago, he'd been out running. He's married with triplets!

Q: You're something like 'Grandma Husker Power,' Linda! (laughs)

LY: You can never have enough grandkids. (laughs) I have five of my own.

Q: I remember some parties you and your husband Angel would have. What were those about again?

LY: They were Mexican food parties. Tacos, enchiladas, margaritas and Coronas. I remember a few times when you, Bryan, and Arturo Garcia were still in my yard at one in the morning.

Q: That's all off the record, Linda. Off the record. (laughs) And do you still keep in touch with Turo?

LY: I can't say that I have. I do remember him having a saying, "A lumberjack never takes a day off!" He wore those flannel shirts and boots and looked like a stocky Mexican lumberjack. (laughs)

Q: I remember the poor girls outside the Lincoln bars on weekend nights. Out of nowhere he'd go up to some unsuspecting gal and say, "Tickle your ass with a feather?" They'd go, "What did you say to me!?" And he'd reply, "Typical Nebraska weather."

LY: It doesn't surprise me. (laughs) You guys worked hard and then blew off some steam now and then. For Boyd it was golf, and Bryan (Bailey) was always working out.

But Boyd, I must say, was instrumental in presenting a vision and making it come alive for people. To the point to where it is now. And Frank Solich? I liked Frank. I thought he was a good coach. All those coaches who worked with Tom those years were just great guys. You'd get to know them on a one-on-one basis. They were good guys. And when you had leadership within the coaches, you had leadership among the athletes.

Q: Any parting thoughts?

LY: Well, I think we had an awesome staff in those years. We had you of course, and Randy (Gobel) -who I still work with- and then Boyd and Mike Arthur and Bryan Bailey. I've seen some coaches come and go, but you guys were very good at teaching technique, at teaching a vision of where you'd want to go and how a strength program should be run, and I think that says a lot. And the next time when you come up to Lincoln, bring your parents by. I haven't seen them in awhile. It would be nice to say 'Hi' to them.

End Conversation.

An exemplary ambassador for anyone having anything to do with Nebraska Football and Memorial Stadium, it's evident Linda maintains profound respect for former Head Strength Coach and Master Innovator Boyd Epley. From the vision of future Memorial Stadium expansion to advances in strength & conditioning to his sense of purpose in maintaining Nebraska's foothold in the college football pantheon, Boyd was a maverick. Like most Husker fans, I shudder somewhat when the name Steve Pederson is mentioned, so we'll just skim over that unpleasantry and its Cliff Notes-sized lesson in trash-canning almost forty years of excellence in pursuit of God-knows-what. (For the record, I twice requested an interview Steve Pederson but received no reply.)

Linda mentioned those cold, Saturday winter mornings between Finals Week and Christmas Break when the Husker Power staff would gather to disassemble 3/4 of the weightroom, packing everything into a loaner semi-trailer for a cross-country trek down to the bowl site where a miniature version of the same weight room would magically appear for the pre-game strength maintenance of the players. These seemingly small and inconsequential attempts at player comfort and familiarity were a prime example of Boyd & the crew's attempt at leaving no stone unturned in pursuit of bowl victory. Don't for once think the players didn't take notice.

*Side note: You've no idea how depressing it was unloading the semi-trailer upon its return to Lincoln and piecing the whole place back together again after another crushing bowl loss. There were seven straight from the time I joined the staff in '87 to the Florida State/Orange Bowl loss after the 1993 season. But there was a belief in a better future, so let's keep moving on to find out why...

Notable Quote #2:
Linda Ybarra on staff relations: "There were so many people, just like a family. We became just like family."

Towering genius disdains a beaten path. It seeks regions hitherto unexplored. It thirsts and burns for distinction; and if possible, it will have it...

Abraham Lincoln

It's a common misconception that Omaha's airport was named after Boyd Epley, godfather of collegiate strength training. That honor actually goes to former Omahan Eugene C. Eppley (1884-1958) (no relation), who was at one time the world's largest individual hotel operator and something of a philanthropist. One wouldn't be far off, though, in stating that without Boyd's biceps, brains and barbells Nebraska football may never have gotten off the ground a mere 56 days after America placed the world's first man on the moon.

Taking flight like a Saturn rocket, the college football landscape was forever altered through this man's unique blend of marketing chutzpah and hell-bent curiosity in finding the secrets to athletic performance perfection. A true alchemist, over the years Coaches Devaney and Osborne handed spitfire underclassmen straight off the farm over to him and his staff, expecting and often receiving future Blackshirts and All-Americans semesters later. If results were what you wanted, Boyd was the man to deliver.

As a young assistant I asked him one day what the secret to success was. He said, "Paul, it's simple. First, you do a good job. Second, you tell everyone in the world about the good job you did." Who could argue against such logic?

Notable quote #1:
"The great ones adjust."

Boyd Epley

Question: Knowing you, Boyd, you're still in superior fitness these many years later...

Boyd Epley: I'm doing pretty well. Still work out 4 days per week. I squatted 405 lbs. on my sixtieth birthday, so I'm trying to hang in there.

Q: Colorado Springs treating you well?

BE: I don't really take advantage of Colorado. Since coming here August of 2006 I've put together 4 books and started a corporation with my wife. It's basically Husker Power Inc. recreated in Colorado under EpicIndex.com.

What Jane and I are trying to do is take what we started there at Nebraska and reach out to the high schools here and help them. So I'm trying to get this stuff worked into the high schools. Every school, every kid will know what their rating is and they can compare one kid to another. It's creating momentum. The second thing I'm doing is, I took our index points and created an international index championship where in July we had athletes from Japan and Ireland and England and the United States -and this year we'll add China and Canada- and we'll have an Index Championship in Las Vegas. So I've been a busy boy.

Q: I can't see you slowing down, Boyd. You have too much drive…

BE: You're probably right. It's all good, you know? The US Olympic Committee called and they're talking about ways to identify talent for future Olympians. I have a proposal to go China to test 4,000 students that are 8 to 11 year olds.

Q: A good way to standardize performance testing, making apples-to-apples comparisons throughout the world, eh?

BE: That's what we found, and if you can remember at Nebraska we tested vertical jump, pro agility and 10 yard dash in the fall and then we'd test the 40 yard dash in the offseason. Coach Osborne was pretty smart, he didn't allow us to measure the 40 yd. dash in the fall because someone might have a hamstring pull. And I didn't think much about that until I came to the NSCA, and I went back and had Dr. Chris Eskridge compare the 3 tests versus the 4 tests, and we found almost 100% correlation between the two, which means we can identify talent with just the three tests. So we don't have to run 40 yards. So now if a kid scores over 1,000 on the three tests combined I'll honor them with a certificate and make a big deal out of it. So it think I've got a niche. Testing has become a big deal. What I'm doing is, I've got permission from Mike Devaney, Bob Devaney's son, and I'm using his quote, "If anybody gets slower, you're fired." (laughs) Because that's what he told me back in September of 1969 when he hired me.

Q: Let me ask you, Boyd, was there any way of him concretely measuring their times in 1969 to find if any players got slower?

BE: Well, when he told me that, it put the fear into me, and I came up with the pre-test and the post-test timing. That led to our four-step philosophy of 1) testing first, 2)evaluating, then 3) setting goals, then 4)following the program. It was all because of Bob giving us an ultimatum. Because if anyone got slower I wouldn't have a job, you know?

Q: Did anyone get slower?

BE: Oh yeah. Along the way, once in awhile someone with an injury, someone would get slower. But overall we dominated so early. You know, he hired me in 1969, and in 1970 and 1971 we were national champs, so he thought that was a pretty good deal, pretty direct cause & effect.

Coach Devaney hired me on September 15th, 1969. We didn't go to a bowl game in '67 or '68, but in '69 we had good success and won 9 games and went to the Sun Bowl. We beat Georgia, got some momentum and then won the national championship the next year.

Q: How long were you there at Nebraska, Boyd?

BE: 37 years, 35 of them overseeing the strength program. The last couple of years the athletic director asked me to oversee the design and construction of a $56 million building, The Tom Osborne Complex.

Q: I remember sitting in a staff meeting in '91 or '92 and you shared this grand vision of building on the site over there at the North Stadium. Did that all start with you?

BE: No, what happened was, I was asked to serve on a committee -a planning committee- a Master Planning Committee. Joe Selig was in charge of facilities at the time and Bill Byrne was the athletic director and we looked into what our needs were, and we came up with a master plan that was a little more expensive than what we could afford, really. It couldn't get done because it was like a $109 million dollar project. And then when Steve Pederson - actually, Steve asked me to go to Pittsburg with him as his #2 guy- I said, 'No, I want to stay at Nebraska and build this building.' Well, it never got done, it just kept getting bigger and more expensive. So when Steve came back as athletic director he chopped it and made some priorites and cut it down to about $50 million. Well, it ended up being $56 million when it was all done and said. And it turned out pretty nice, though. Have you been back to see it?

Q: Last time I was back Dave Kennedy was in charge, and I've never been a big Dave Kennedy fan, so I just kind of stayed away. No, I haven't been there thus far. (Author has since visited the impressive complex)

BE: Dave probably wasn't the right person for Nebraska. He was a good strength coach, but his philosophy was so different from what we had in place that it absolutely destroyed Nebraska's Husker Power program.

Q: You know I don't like to badmouth people, Boyd, but I recall watching a game some years and thinking, 'These guys are folding down the stretch in game after game. They don't have the power to finish off a game like we used to. These guys remind of the old Ohio State teams when Dave Kennedy and John Cooper were there, where at the end of the season -when it came time to face Michigan- they would just peter out.' They seemed to run out of gas…

BE: Well, with all respect to Dave, we made a philosophical switch just after he'd left the program in 1988. We made a video to show the football staff in about 1988, and right after that we quit running long distances and we got real powerful. And the recovery was in the body's correct energy system. Well, Dave Kennedy had left the program by then and didn't get the memo. So when he came back as the Head Strength Coach, he went back to the 1988 philosophy that he knew best and it was a disaster. He was running the players two miles for the linemen and three miles for the backs and ends in comparison to a time when we weren't running any more than 40 yards. And so to give you a good comparison, it was a real stark contrast -like black and white- next to each other, what he brought in there. But the important thing to note was the 1991 winter conditioning program when we went 6,000 workouts without an absence, and the players really, really focused. We had 78 school records broken at the end of the winter conditioning program in one day.

Q: What was the buildup to the team becoming super-successful? Was it player accountability, focus?

BE: Well, the season before that was 1990, and we lost three games in a kind of shocking way. You can find out the scores, it was like 45-10 to OU, to Colorado, and the Georgia Tech bowl game. So we lost to both national champs -which doesn't sound like a real bad thing- but for Nebraska the effort wasn't there. We had some talent, players like Bruce Pickens on the team that got drafted real high, but Bruce Pickens had a lot of absences in the strength program.

It was just sort of an attitude where the players would just as soon get punished for missing the workout than for doing the workout. It was just that mindset, not where you think it should have been. So when we got together after the season was over -you would think that after losing the bowl game that badly that there would be some fight from the athletes, that they would like to get going into the winter conditioning program in a positive way- but when I entered the room and saw the athletes were sitting with their feet up in the chairs and their caps on… Dennis LeBlanc was the first one to have to address them -and that was typical- and then we got on with the conditioning program. Well, when Dennis was done talking…. and they hadn't really paid him much attention and given him the respect he deserved; they weren't quiet, you know what I mean? They were still talking and they were disrespectful -it just wasn't right- and so what I did, I had a ring. In fact, I'm sitting in my house right now and I'm looking at that ring. It was a paperweight.

Q: I remember that humongous thing! That massive, gold championship ring about the size of a man's fist, right?

BE: Well, someone gave it to me, and I've had it on my desk for years. It's a great big paperweight that looks like a championship ring, but it's way too big for someone to wear.

So anyway, I put it in my pocket before I got over there to the South Stadium to talk to them, and after Dennis was done talking I held that ring up and I didn't say a word.... I just held it up. And you know, there's 200 guys in the room, they think it's a ring -because it's real large- but it looks like a real ring. I tell them, I said, 'Gentlemen, this is a national championship ring.' (It really wasn't, but they didn't know because they'd never seen one around there for so many years, and it got their attention.) But before I said a word, I just stood there holding the ring, and the room got quiet. At first there was still guys talking and being disrespectful. I'm not sure how long, exactly, but the players eventually caught on that I wasn't talking and was just standing there holding this ring. And then, it got so quiet, it actually scared me. It's like, 'Wow, now I've got their attention. Now what am I gonna do?', you know? (laughs)

And so then I told them, 'This is a national championship ring, and I have a plan to get each of you one of these. But we're gonna have to make some changes, and the changes are gonna have to come today.' Then I proceeded to tell them what the plan was:

It had to do with 3 steps. I told them that every team that I know of, regardless of the sport, was made up of three groups: 'You have players that are there because they want to be', (fortunately Nebraska is blessed with a lot of those type of players.) They do what you ask them to: the squats, the leg presses, they do the exercises they know are gonna help them regardless of how hard it is, if the coaches ask them to watch what they are eating they watch what they are eating, they do everything the coaches ask. We were blessed with a lot of those type of guys.'The second group is here because they have to be, not because they want to be.' (But maybe their dad or their uncle or grandfather or mother told them, somebody told them they had to play for Nebraska.) The kid maybe wasn't there because he wanted to be, but because he had to be. I said to them, 'The third group that a team has…', and for lack of a better term, I called them, "jerks." 'Now,' I said, 'the first step' - actually it was a two step plan- the first step was to '…eliminate the jerks.'

So I drew up on the chalkboard in the Auditorium, the Nebraska football meeting room, and there were a couple coaches in there, too. Dave Gillespie was. Coach Osborne was not, he was out recruiting. (It was my job to take it over on the first day of the winter conditioning program.) So anyway, I'm up there in front and I draw a big round pie-chart with a major portion of the circle containing the words 'Want to be', a good portion of the circle covering up the 'Have to be', and just a little sliver were 'The Jerks.' I said, 'The first step here -if we want to win the national championship in the future- is to eliminate the jerks from this program. So,' I said, 'what I'm gonna do, I realize that some of our athletes have chosen to miss their workouts rather than come and do what we ask them to do' -and we decided to punish them when they did this. (Now, punishment is a negative thing, punishment doesn't work.) 'And so from this day on, we're not going to punish you for missing the workout. You're gonna have a choice: you're either going to come and do the program and the things we're asking you to do, or your done. You either come to the workouts or don't, it's your choice to not be on this team anymore.' And that kind of shocked them a little bit. I explained to them that we were going to give them one absence. One of the guys raised his hand and said, "You mean if I miss once I'll be off the team?" I said, 'It's your choice every day whether you are on this team or not. There won't be any punishment, it will be your choice. Every day you come do the program and you'll benefit. The program works. You come, you do it, you'll make progress. If you decide not to be on the team, that's your choice. It's your choice every day.'

I said, 'Now, right now anyone who does not want to be on this team, I want to you to leave now. I want you to get up and leave. You're done. You're no longer a part of Nebraska Football. Leave right now.' (pregnant pause) Nobody left. So I went to the chalkboard and I erased the word 'Jerks' completely. And I said, 'Okay, we've accomplished number 1, we have no more jerks in the program. You're here because you're gonna do this program.' Now, step two is to motivate the 'Have to' group to be 'Want to' guys. So I went into kind of a long speech there on what the difference was between willpower and doing things right and what they're asked to do and all that. It was probably a little longer than they wanted to hear, but I wanted to get it clear that we were going to commit to doing the program right. So when I got done with that part of it I handed out a red mesh jersey that they would use in winter conditioning practice. (I went to the equipment managers beforehand and got 200 of these jerseys) I handed them out and said, 'If you are going to commit to what we just discussed…,' and we went over goals and what it was going to take to win. I said, 'if you're going to commit to the plan, I want you to put this red jersey on right now.' And every single one of them put the jersey on. I said, 'Alright, every day I want to you to wear this jersey to winter conditioning. And when you put this over your head -when your neck passes through this jersey- I want to you to remember you've commited to these goals. If you show up over there without the red jersey, you're done. If you're gonna commit to these goals, put the jersey on.' And they put it on.

And then I said, 'I want you to stand if you're committed.' (It was all about getting them to commit to doing all of this, right?) So 200 guys stood up. And I got chills running down my spine, because these guys were jacked up- and it was a very motivating moment. I said, 'Alright, now we're one team. I eliminated that other group altogether. We have one circle, one team, committed to doing the program, committed to doing what's right.' I said, 'Now, let's go run.'

We went to run and then we went and lifted. We had two workouts: a running workout and a lifitng workout. And every day we counted how many workouts we accumulated, and we went 200 workouts until we lost our starting middle guard and our starting I-back. They were no longer on the team, they chose not to come.

So on a day toward the end of the 6 week winter conditioning program (it was a Monday and we were going to test on Wednesday so we gave them Tuesday off to recover), so on Monday I got them all back together and I got them in the auditorium again and said, 'You guys have gone 6,200 workouts and have lost two guys. You've made tremendous progress because you applied yourselves. So we'll expect you to break at least 50 school records on Wednesday. The most we've ever broken before is 17, and I expect 50 new school records on Wednesday.' They kind of looked at each other, "Is he kidding?" Paul, they went out and broke 78.

Q: Wow! And how did you come up with the '50' number, Boyd?

BE: I was just guessing! (laughs) Watching them work out and looking at the physical development, you could tell they were much better. I knew of one athlete who had 140 absences in his career. That's like missing a whole year of your 4 year career. So anyway, we had 200 guys without a single absence. So when you apply yourself, it's like watering a plant: it grows stronger and sturdier.

It's incredible the progress they made. Coach Osborne called me in when we lost the two players. He explained, he said, "We recruited these young men. We were in their house, the homes with the parents, their families, and you kind of run these kids off." I said, 'That's not the case. They committed to doing the program. They committed to doing it and it's their choice.' He said, "Well, I'll be really disappointed if we lose any more kids." So I was in kind of a tough spot there. Nobody was trying to run anybody off of the program, but the end result was Coach Osborne really got back a football team. He got a disciplined group of athletes who worked their tails off and made great progress.

So when the program was over they went into spring football and they kind of reverted back to their own ways. (They didn't have the same rules. The rules were only for the winter program.) So somewhere along the line in the spring Coach Osborne called me into the meeting room with all the football coaches and said to me, "How do we get that discipline back? You really had this thing going in the winter and we recognize that this is a great thing, but we kind of slipped back a little bit here." I said, 'The punishment didn't do them any good all those years.' I was the guy who gave the punishment all those years as the strength coach to Osborne, and before him, Devaney.'Punishment is a negative thing and it just doesn't.. it's not effective.' And he said, "Alright, what do you have in mind?" I said, 'You know on your drivers license that you have a point system? And you have a little bit of flexibility, and if you do well and get some points back on occasion? You could probably have a traffic ticket or something, but you can overcome that if you have good driving record and get some of those points back. See, you can accumulate some points, but it doesn't end your career.' That was maybe, probably a little drastic, where if you were off the team if you missed more than once, you know?

So I came up with this -right off the drivers license concept- if you miss a workout you forfeited a point, if you miss a practice you get two points, or a meeting or anything that might possibly come up, a class you're supposed to go to, a certain number of points. So we came up with this point system right on the spot. So Coach Osborne then went around the room to each coach, if they wanted to implement this system, and he went one by one and asked each one of them. He didn't just say, "Let's give this a try." He looked at each one of them right in the eye. So they agreed to give this a try.

The punishment? We didn't get that quite right. The punishment was if you got a certain number of points you had to go before Coach Osborne. Well, if you recall, Coach Osborne was a legend in the state of Nebraska and across the country, and getting to go into his office and talk to him one-on-one was not real punishment -it was more of an honor, to be honest, you know? So that didn't work as well as I thought it would. So the first year we tried to do it that way, but it didn't have quite the effect I wanted it to.

So the next year I got together with Jack Stark and we created the Unity Council. The Unity Council was set up to look at who has the points. If you got enough points you had to go before the Unity Council and explain yourself. And the Unity Council was made up of players at different positions on the team, they were considered leaders on the team. They had other purposes, too, they entertained ideas that might be good for the team, if someone had a gripe about the music in the lockerroom they would bring it before the Unity Council. So Jack Stark was kind of in charge of the Unity Council, but he was from Omaha so he couldn't be there all the time. So I took the meetings' minutes and I presented the minutes to the coaching staff the next day.

The meetings were like on Monday nights or whatever. Between Jack Stark and I we kept it together. I presented the points and kept the points, and Jack would have the larger part of the meeting when he was there. The Unity Council had a good impact on the team, and athletes who had some frustrations that might normally build up into more than it should be were able to get it off their chest and get it resolved right away. Coach Osborne would listen very carefully to what they would bring up, and their concerns. And he made sure - now, he was a players coach- he made sure their concerns were heard and dealt with. It was a good thing. He treated it with respect and they treated it with respect, and Dr. Stark did a good job, too. It helped with the point system and gave the point system a strong impact rather than just going to Coach Osborne by himself, you know. It worked out real well.

Q: I remember when that was being implemented, there were a few hiccups, some guys weren't buying into it a lot of whining and complaining, but they came around and really bought into it...

BE: What I liked about it -and I was on both sides of this- I was in charge of the discipline when I saw it wasn't working and then I was in charge of the winter program where there was incredible discipline. But it was too intense, they couldn't carry it on for a long period of time. It worked great for six weeks. So what I liked about the point system is that it gave the athletes a little bit of flexibility, where they could miss a workout or miss a class and they wouldn't miss a football game, but if they missed 3 or 4 things it added up real fast, and pretty soon we had players that actually were held out of games. And it was really their responsibility.

What it did, it really treated them like adults. You know, if you have two or three speeding tickets, pretty soon you weren't going to have a drivers license. It worked just the same, the same concept. It didn't matter who recruited you, it didn't matter if you were black or white or whatever. It was fair. And for all those reasons, it worked.

Q: Before that big commitment meeting, when you went in there to call them out, where did you get that from? Did you already consult with the coaches, with Coach Osborne?

BE: Well, when I realized in 1990 -this one player who ended up being drafted number one, in the first round- had 140 absences, where we were averaging 30 absences a day. We were averaging 30 players missing a workout a day, and I knew that without discipline the program was not working. We tried making them run stadium steps, we tried gassers, we tried them rolling so many yards down the field, we made them throw up doing things like that. One punishment we had was doing hang cleans with dumbbells. We tried any type of discipline that every other school has ever tried. And you had to be safe when you do something like that, it couldn't be ridiculous. But that type of thing wouldn't work; some would rather do the punishment than the workout.

It's all a matter of attitude. So during the course of all that I was looking at all different kinds of options, and I got to thinking about the drivers license and how fair it was. And Coach Osborne was accused once in a while of favoring a player or another, those kind of comments can turn into racial tension if you look at it that way. Coach Osborne was always fair, very fair. If someone got disgruntled, they could accuse the head coach of playing favoritism: "That guy, he only got punished and had to run two laps. I did the same thing and I had to run 4 laps!" You hear those kind of things. So we were looking for something that was fair no matter who you were: black or white, what part of the country you were from, whether you were a Nebraska guy or not, a senior, a freshman, a walk-on, a star player, an All-American, a Heisman player, it didn't matter. This system was fair. That's what he needed. He needed something like that that would have a little bit of teeth in it. Not so much that we were running players off, but a system that was fair, equitable, gave the players a little bit of flexibility, treated them as adults, and made it be their choice to do the right thing. And I think it really hit a home run.

I had a plan, I drew it up over in the West Stadium conference room. I had Mike Arthur come in and look at it and then I went over to the football team meeting. And when Osborne asked me what I had in mind I went to the board and I wrote it up there. I don't remember the change that we made, but there was only one change. It might have been two points for missing something rather than one, but out of twelve things there was only one change. It didn't change after that for many years.

Q: So you brought it in and the staff bought into it and the rest was history?

BE: And then the next year Jack Stark got involved in creating a Unity Council, so we had somewhere we could send these players who accumulated points. (To be honest, Coach Osborne was almost too nice to them. He was a very considerate man, and what they really needed -instead of having a father figure that was real considerate like he was- they needed someone that's kind of gonna give them a little firmer tone, like Christian Peter or a Jason Peter or someone like that, who'd say, "What the heck are you thinking here!?") So the players on the Unity Council were pretty tough on these kids who accumulated too many points, who weren't doing their job, who were letting the team down. And they were much firmer, much tougher than the coach was, if you get my point.

Q: Studies have shown that to be true. Have you ever read the book 'Influence: The Psychology of Persuasion' by Robert Cialdini, a professor at Arizona State University? He wrote a wonderful little book on human thought tendencies and motivation, why people do what they do, and even how to persuade them to do what you want them to do…

BE: Haven't heard of it. But one thing: the freshman that were in that meeting on January 17th, 1991? Those freshmen ended up winning the national championship in '94. The offensive linemen: Brenden Stai, Rob Zatechka, Zach Weigert, those guys were all freshmen in the meeting that day.

So what happened, they made all the progress in 1991, but they weren't quite good enough to win the national title when they played Miami and Florida State and so forth, it took them a couple years to put it all together. But as those freshmen carried on this discipline they got almost unbeatable, they really were a talented group of kids through '97 there.

Q: Let me ask you: being a college athlete yourself, what was your first impression of the University of Nebraska?

BE: My first impression was from when I came to visit Frank Sevigne, the head track coach, with my parents. My parents actually lived in Nebraska and I was in Arizona. We moved to Arizona and I lived there 10 years, but toward the end of that ten year period my dad got a job putting roofs on the housing for the Air Force folks. He had this roofing contract, so he was up there 2 or 3 years doing this big project. When I got the scholarship offer to Nebraska my parents were already living there, so I came up and stayed with them that summer. So when it came time to come down to the school they brought me down because they wanted to look around, and we went up the track office and met Frank Sevigne. Of course, I met him one time when he recruited me. He came to Arizona State for a track meet and he knew I was a junior college pole vaulter in town, and invited me over to ASU to do a workout so he could look at me. So I just happened to have really good day that day. I jumped higher than the ASU pole vaulters did that day, and Nebraska didn't have much of a school record; their school record was 13' 7" at the time, and I was jumping 15' 1¼", which was the national junior college record. And so I jumped over 15 that day, and he walked up and says, "Are you interested in Nebraska?" I said 'Yes.' He said, "I'll send you the papers". I wasn't sure what he really meant, but later a scholarship offer came in the mail, so I signed it and sent it in.

Then I went with my parents to visit him and he gave us a little tour, walked around. You knew Nebraska was a big school. I came from a junior college where they didn't have the big stadium, the big buildings like Nebraska does. I was impressed with the campus. And I went over and they introduced me to George Sullivan, and George said something like, "How high are you doing?" And I said 'Oh, around 15 foot', and he said, "Don't worry, Coach Sevigne will have you down to 14 foot in no time." (laughs) So I could see they got along pretty well and it was a nice, family environment.

George wasn't the head trainer at the moment, it was a guy named Paul Schneider. George had a friendship with Frank Sevigne, so he went to the away track meets and had a special interest in the track athletes. So when I'd have to get my ankles taped, George would be the one to do that. George is a special guy. I'm not sure how to describe it, but when he grabbed ahold of your ankle it would just make you feel like you were in good hands. And he'd tape that ankle up, he just did it in a way that you felt comfortable that he did a great job every day. Very comforting, you know? So, I remember that very well, meeting him and having a little tour around the facilities.

Track was exciting, pole vault was exciting, but I really had a disappointing career because I got hurt. I went out and set the Nebraska school record right away, the first meet. I went 14' 6" or something the first meet. They had to put the standards up on some straw bales because the standards they had wouldn't go to 14 foot. They had some old ones, so when Coach Sevigne saw that he ordered some new ones that went to 19 feet. The world record at the time was only like 17, and so he got these real fancy standards, so the sky was the limit. (We tried to pyschce out the visiting pole vaulters by setting it as high as we could, so when they'd walk in and see the bar up there and go, "Wow, I've never seen anything like that!" But it didn't do much good.

Q: What about the people of Nebraska?

BE: Well, I had a lot of visitors when I was overseeing the strength program, and the visiting coaches would always marvel at the work ethic of our athletes. And they came to try to copy the Nebraska program -the Tennessee State coach visited 3 times, and Virginia Tech, you name the school- they came to study what Nebraska did and why we were so successful, but they weren't able to duplicate it when they went back home because the Nebraska athletes had this tremendous work ethic.

And a lot of it had to do with Coach Osborne's philosophy. He had a running attack, so he recruited athletes that would be aggressive and physical in the running game. If I had a strength program at another school -let's say BYU, known for its passing game- if I would have been at a school like that then I wouldn't have had the success or the recognition like the Nebraska strength program, because the head coach wouldn't have needed it as much. In Coach Osborne's case, my philosophy blended right in with his philosophy, because when we got strong it enhanced his ability to run. And he relied on that strength, and he told those players that in the fourth quarter, "..those times you'd only get 2 or 3 yards in the first quarter, by the 4th quarter you're gonna dominate and we're gonna get 7 and 8 yards, you're going to dominate and were gonna control the game." And that's exactly what happened.

Q: Like the halftime speech against Miami in the Orange Bowl in '95?

BE: Exactly. And his greatest speech I ever heard was before a game versus Illinois. Nobody writes those things down. You're in the locker room and he's just talking, and years later I asked him about that speech, and he really didn't even remember the details of it. But I heard him speak many, many times and he was my head coach for 25 years, so I heard him address the team many, many times in different ways. But I think the Illinois game (they had played in the Rose Bowl the year before and they were Big 10 champions, maybe co-champion or something), they had a great year the year before. They had a good coach, too -Mike White, I believe- so they were gonna give us a run for the money. So we went there to play and Coach Osborne told them -I can't quote him exactly, I wish I would have written it down- but he says, "When you get out there, the first few plays you're going to experience a kind of nervousness and you're going to feel like you're kind of exhausted. But that's just nerves, you're really not exhausted. You're one of the best conditioned football teams to ever take the field, and you work through that. It's just kind of a nervous thing. You are physically prepared to dominate this game, you are gonna go out there and control this, make those tackles, you're gonna make them feel every tackle. They're gonna know you're out there on every play, and after the first quarter we're gonna have a lead and we're gonna keep the lead..," and just kept telling them what was going to happen and how physical they were going to be. We were ahead 28 to nothing after the first quarter.

He was just impressive, and you listened to him. And basically, what he was doing, he saw the kids and how hard they had worked during the summer. He knew they were prepared, he knew it. And he just kind of told them what he saw and he gave them the confidence, and they wanted to go out there and just dominate. I remember that as a very motivating event.

And what you recalled was recorded by Jeff Schmall during the Orange Bowl game, but he gave many speeches like that that weren't recorded. Nobody else was around but the players and the coaches, he was tremendous at just kind of telling them what was going to happen to them out there.

Q: I know this might seem as coming from out of the blue, but did you play high school football?

BE: I played high school football and was a pole vaulter. When I went to Nebraska I really intended to try out for football but I broke my leg. I broke it out there in Memorial Stadium. It used to be grass instead of Astorturf and it had the pole vault runways and the box where you put the pole -they had the box in the ground- I came down and landed in that box and didn't get far enough into the pit and broke my leg.

And then my senior year I hurt my back and the doctors said, "We're not going to let you pole vault anymore," so they asked me if I'd be interested in supervising the weight room to kind of make up for using the scholarship. And that changed my life. It ended up costing Nebraska a lot of money, because I asked to spend a lot of money on weight rooms over the years. (laughs)

Q: How did you feel about that, when they asked you to do that?

BE: Well, as an athlete, you have to realize: here I am on the pole vault and I'm hurt and trying to rehab this back injury, and I had 5 or 6 football players following me around. Joe Orduna was one of the players, and he'd had a knee surgery. And you've got to think back at this time, if you had knee surgery your career was over. And I worked with him and I didn't realize I was doing anything special; I was just in the weightroom, he was in the weightroom. He was just working out with me, and he went back and ended up getting drafted in the 2nd or 3rd round by San Francisco and had a successful career. And that was unheard of for an athlete to come back after a knee surgery.

And he wasn't the only one, there were other players that went back, so pretty soon I had like 10 or 12 guys waiting for me when I'd come to the weightroom, you know? And this weightroom was just this small, little room off of the training room, and you had to kind of go through the training room to get to it, go up over these stairs and go down into this little space. And all it had was this little Universal gym and about 5 dumbbells, one bar, 300 lbs.

and one bench and that was it. And it was about 900 square feet. And one day I'm in there with the guys, only these injured football players and I. No one else was lifting. (They were told not to, told that it hurt their performance.) One day the trainer comes up over the stairs, says,"Epley, you've got a phone call." I say, 'Who could that be?' Nobody knows me, I'm just a pole vaulter between my junior and senior year and I had my back injured. Nobody knew me, you know? And he says, "Get in here! It's Tom Osborne!" So I go and pick up the phone and sure enough it's Tom Osborne, and he says, "Are you the guy that's been showing these players how to lift weights?" And it kind of got quiet. I thought I was in trouble. And I said, 'Yes.' And he said "Well, could you come over to my office?" And I thought, 'Oh no, this sounds bad. I'm really in trouble.'

So I went over to his office and he explained that these injured players were coming back out to practice and they were doing real well, that they were actually stronger than they were before they were hurt. And he says, "Can you help us do that for the whole team?" And I said, 'Coach I'm just an athlete. I'm a pole vaulter.' And he says, "Can you help us or not!?" And I said, 'Well, sure I can help you, but you don't have a big enough space. We can only get about 30 people in the room at one time and that's it.' And he said, "How about we knock that wall down so we can open up the room next door where the classroom is next door, where we can use that space, also?" And I said,'Well, we could do that, but then you're gonna need more equipment,' and he said, "Well, can you help us with that?", and I said,'Yes.' And he said,"How soon?" I said, 'Well, if I bring you a list tomorrow..,' and he said, "You can?", and I said,'Yeah.'

So I made up a list of squat racks and benches and things I thought they'd need, just the basic stuff. I brought it over to him and he was standing outside the office area there and he said, "Alright, let me give this to the secretary," and he doesn't even really read it that closely, and he says "This is what we need?" And I said, 'Yup.' And he hands it over to the secretary and he says, "Order this." And I say, 'Coach, I forgot the second page.' (laughs) And he looked at me -you know how smart he is,(laughs) he knew what I was up to- and anyway, he looked at me and laughed and said, "Alright, bring me the second page tomorrow." And I said 'Okay,' and I went home and added dumbbells and some pulleys and other stuff to the list. I was just afraid the first time because I thought that 'they're never gonna approve all this.' So I really made a nice list up and brought it back to him and he says, "Alright, this is it, right?" (Little did he know I'd always be bringing him lists later on.) (laughs) And he said, "Alright, Boyd, we need to go in and see the boss." And I go, 'What do you mean?' He said,"We need to go in and see Bob Devaney and get permission to do all of this." So we go around the corner into Bob Devaney's office there in the Coliseum, located up on the second floor -that office is now John Cook's office- there was a big seal, the Nebraska State Seal on the wall above Devaney's desk, and Devaney's at his desk and he's sitting there in his red, leather chair. I remember it like yesterday, I remember where I stood and where Osborne stood, and where Devaney was sitting, and Coach Osborne explained to Devaney, the athletic director and head coach, who I was.

Bob said, "I've seen Boyd when he's in the weightroom. You're a pole vaulter, right?" I said I was. He said Tom told him that I was helping the injured players get stronger and that Tom thought it would be a good idea if the entire team lifted weights and if I'd be willing to help teach them. And Bob says,"Why would you want to do that?" So I was faced with the prospect of having to defend my program, and I'd never had to do that before. So here I was trying to explain to him that it would make the players stronger and faster, and it would help them win more games, and he said, "Well, if Tom thinks this is important, we'll give it a try." And then he looked me right in the eye and pointed at me and says, "But if anybody gets slower, you're fired." But I wasn't really hired yet! (laughs) I was still an athlete, but it was during that time period that I had injured my back. And I don't know if it was Devaney or the trainers or what, but they kind of told me I couldn't pole vault anymore because Devaney wanted me to be the strength coach. And magically I started getting paid $2 an hour to watch the weightroom instead of having my scholarship. They saw to it that I got paid for supervising instead of being on scholarship and being on pole vault, they said it was too great of a risk.

Then after the first year Coach Devaney called me in and said, "You're the best value we have in this department," and he gave me a raise that made me feel pretty good. Of course I was making two dollars an hour, so it didn't have to be much. (laughs)

Q: If you had a chance to do anything over again, would you?

BE: Oh, I'm sure I would do a few things differently. But nothing comes to mind. I was there a long time, and I'd like to take the opportunity to thank all the people that helped me when I started out who didn't get much credit. I worked hard but no one really recognized the effort, and later in my career it was just the opposite. Whenever we'd win a national championship I'd get credit for that, but I probably got more credit than I deserved. There were a lot of people that helped me along the way. You were one of them, Mike Arthur certainly was one of the most significant to make an impact in the program -he was with me 25 years- Randy Gobel, Bryan Bailey, Dave Kennedy, Jerry Schmidt. There were 64 of my assistants -I made a list of their names- 64 guys that contributed to that program and they're the ones that did the work, they're the ones that should get the credit. And you know, later on I had a strength coach for every position on the team.

Q: When was that? '92 or so?

BE: Well, what happened was, we weren't beating the Florida States. We weren't quite good enough, mad at what was happening, Florida State was putting linebackers in the defensive line and putting defensive backs up playing linebacker, and as a result everybody was quicker than us. And here we were with these big linemen that were slow as compared to these Florida athletes. It wasn't that we were really slow, it was just that they were moving people into positions that made them much faster. So we had to catch onto that.

Charlie McBride figured it out. Remember Ed Stewart? He was actually a defensive back and he was physical enough, strong enough, fast enough, but they moved him forward to play linebacker, like Miami was doing, so he was much quicker than a normal linebacker instead of a Jerry Murtaugh-type guy who would come over and knock your head off. He was a quicker, more agile guy, so Coach Osborne did as much as he could of that and started recruiting more players like that, and he came to me.

You know Coach Osborne never asked me to do much -he let me run the program for the most part all those years- but he came to me and asked me to improve our agility, we needed to work on our agilty. So we made a major change in the program, we went from the 'county fair' where athletes would go from one station to the next to the next (actually that was part of the original program that Cletus Fischeer came back with from Texas) and over the years I changed some of those stations, but we kept the county fair concept where everybody would go from one station to the next until we completed the winter program. Well, when Coach Osborne asked for more agilty, we changed to more of a position-specific deal where the defensive backs would stay in one area of the field, those linemen on the offense would stay in one corner, the defensive line would stay in another, the running backs in another corner. The team was divided into 4 stations, so the drills were created to provide for agility in each of the 4 corners. And they were different. The O-line didn't do the same drill as the D-line did, so I needed specialists at each of those corners. So I had my staff become specialists on what the people needed in that corner, and each one of my strength coaches had an assistant (in case one wasn't there the other could handle it). It was great for the team, but it was difficult for me not being able to work with each player individually so much, so I kind of lost that personal contact. So each of those players had their own strength coach that they learned to relate to, and then those strength coaches got to be their personal friends, and I kind of got more distant over time. It was in the early '90's there, but it contributed to us becoming much more agile as a team, much faster.

The other concern, though, that ended up showing up years later was that we had to go back and look at that change. The drills that we were doing in the winter, the football coaches then would do the same drills in the spring and then we would do the same drills in the summer, and the coaches would do the same drills in the fall. As a result we started having overuse injuries…

Q: The symphysis pubis-type of things?

BE: Yes, and we found out we were training certain drills 254 days a year. And that ended up being too much for some athletes, and they broke down and started having osteitis pubis injuries. And at one time we ended up having more osteitis pubis injuries than anybody else in the country that I'm aware of.

So that became a concern. And some people in the program blamed the squat exercise for that. It was ridiculous. It wasn't the squat, but that's what some people thought. It was actually overuse. So we had to kind of change our summer program and get away from those position-specific agility drills and go back to some of the county fair exercises where it was less intense and get away from that overuse syndrome we'd gotten into.

Q: Too much of a good thing, eh? So what what was it like standing on the sidelines, knowing you did everything you could? Until we got over the bowl/Florida teams hump, what was going through your mind when we were losing to the Miami's and Florida States in those bowl games down there in Florida?

BE: Well, there's not too much you could do, but standing on the sideline is exciting because you're part of the team and you can feel the pulse on the team. If you just watch TV and see the expression of a team, winning or losing, you could tell by the expression. But when you're on the sidelines you're part of that and it's exciting.

One of those frustrating times for me was when we played Florida State and 1:16 was left in the game and we were ahead, and it looked like we were gonna win the game. So I went up to the seats where my son was seated with my wife and my daughter. Well, I went up to get my son so he could be on the sideline when we would celebrate the national championship, and so by the time I got back down a minute sixteen had expired and we'd lost the game. Florida State had driven down the field and kicked a field goal and beat us. So I didn't really get to see what happened there, because I was fighting the crowd to get up there.

That was another one of the things -you were still around then- during the winter conditioning we really didn't do anything special after that game, but during the summer time we did. I asked Randy Gobel if we could turn the stadium's scoreboard on for the summer. Nobody had ever really turned it on during the offeseason like that before. So he had to go up into the press box to do it. I had him put 1:16 on the clock above the north stadium, on the scoreboard. So it was the first day of summer conditioning and I told a couple of the seniors what I was about to do, so I had their support. We did our first workout that summer, and then we'd usually come together after the workout for announcements or whatever. So we got them together and I said, 'Alright guys, last January

1st (or whatever it was), we lost to Florida State with 1:16 left in the game, and you just throw in the controversy with the officiating this and that, but we're gonna add 1:16 every day to the workout all summer long.' And then I had them look at the scoreboard. They looked up there, and I said,'We're gonna run an extra 1:16 every day to remind you, no matter how tired you are, or how bad the officiating is, you'll be able to overcome anything that happens when you get that close to winning the national championship again. There will be nothing to stop you from winning it.' One of the first guys said , "I ain't running no extra whatever..," and one of the seniors just elbowed the guy right in the chest -thump!- and everybody else understood that this was already agreed to and that was the way it was gonna be.

Q: Who first came up with the 1:16?

BE: It was my deal, we discussed it in the staff meeting and Randy Gobel had to go figure out how to do it. And Randy had to do it everyday the whole summer. It was a pain in the neck for him. It wasn't easy for him to get up into the press box everyday, it was locked. But it had a tremendous impact.

You know how the energy systems work: you don't run for more than 5 seconds as a football player. So we weren't going to just go run continuously for 1:16. What we did was came up with 10 hurdles from the track team, and the players went in and around the hurdles; we created an obstacle course with the hurdles and the players all lined up and went in and out of these hurdles and finished up, and then turned around and came right back through it. And we did it every day after the workout and it became a mental thing. They knew they had prepared for the 4th quarter if they did this extra drill.

And when it came time for the season to begin, when they got to the 4th quarter, you see when teams raise their hand and put 4 fingers up? Well, our team meant it. When our team got to the 4th quarter they put those fingers up and they knew they were prepared for anything in the 4th quarter. What happened was, they became unbeatable and they ended up going into the 4th quarter -and of course Schlesingner scored two touchdowns in the 4th quarter while Miami was on oxygen on the sideline. And Miami couldn't get a first down on seven series in a row in the 4th quarter. 7 series in a row, we dominate them in the 4th quarter. They got no first downs, and we scored two touchdowns and won the game. Well, it worked so well.

And football is a mental game, it's willpower. And these kids really responded to where the next year, in 1995, there was no game where we were even behind in the 4th quarter, it was like a runaway. We finished up Florida 62-24.

Q: It seems the only hurdle was dealing with the Lawrence Phillips issue...

BE: Lawrence got kind of a bad rap in that situation. He didn't actually... well, that's water under the bridge. He may not have been worth all the effort with his actions after that thing. But that's kind of a sad thing. Lawrence was the leader in the Heisman Trophy race at that point. We beat Michichan State 50-10 that day and he sprained his ankle and he went home that night after we got home from Michigan, and someone called him and said his girlfriend was over at Scott Frost's house. So he got out of bed and went but the the door was locked, and he climbed over the trellis, and he went in. He didn't hit Scott and he didn't hit her.

You know that's pretty good restraint from someone considering the situation, but he pulled her down the steps and she kind of banged her head on the steps. But he pulled her and she banged her head coming down the steps and cut her head open, and I believe she had 5 or 6 stitches in the back of her head. He never did hit her. And for that he lost millions and millions of dollars. Because she was a woman's basketball athlete he was told he was not able to go the training table anymore, because she might be there. He was not allowed to go the the weightroom because she might be there. He wasn't allowed to to go to the athletic training room to get his ankle worked on because she might be there. So all those games before the bowl game, he wasn't able to get treatment on his ankle. Somewhere along the line in about November Coach Osborne told me some things were cleared up now and he could resume practice. So the first day we could get him started he couldn't run, because his ankle was still hurting and he wasn't able to get treatment on it. He was months without doing any rehab on it at all.

So it took us awhile to get him to where he could run and cut on that ankle, but he worked so hard that by game time Coach Osborne decided that he had earned the right to start the game, and he did and had a tremendous game and just ran all over Florida and had a great game. To be honest, we could have won that game without Lawrence Phillips. But it was nice to see him get the reward for the work he had put in, because a month before he could hardly run.

Q: Anything else about those years that made them special, stand apart from others?

BE: I think one of the advantages we had was the nutrition program. George Sullivan had overseen it for a number of years, overseeing the training table, and as he got older Bill Byrne asked me to oversee the training table. For 9 years I oversaw that, and I hired Dave Ellis to be the nutritionist. I think he did a tremendous job giving Nebraska an advantage that they didn't have prior to that.

And a lot of the things that he wanted to do cost money, and we got Bill Byrne to support that and we were able to provide supplements, not only for football, but all sports. Byrne was really a good athletic director, he didn't want us to focus on football only. If we were gonna do something he wanted it across the board, so I went to him and said, 'We'd like to start a supplement program.' And he says,"How much, will it cost?" I said,'$25,000.' He says, "Just for football? How much for all sports?" I said, '$45,000.' He said, "Let's do it." That's the kind of attitude he had. It took me a couple tries to catch on to what a great athletic director he was. It didn't take me all that long before I realized that if I was going to try to implement something, he wanted it done for all sports. He was very supportive, he was very equitable, he wanted me to hire a female strength coach at that time, he kind of got things started that way. He came to me one day and said,"What do you think of hiring a female strength coach?" I said, 'Well, we have one in training who's almost ready to assume that type of position, and right now Danny Noonan is ahead of her as far as readiness, so he would be in line ahead of her.' And he said, "Well, can't we hire both?" I said, 'Well, certainly.' He said, "Well, let's do it." So he got what he wanted and I got two more tremendous strength coaches. He was just an amazing A.D., he really was. He had a vision, and when George retired they needed someone to oversee the training table. It gave me the opportunity to present a concept to him, and that was the Performance Team. We knew we were going to add nutrition to the team, so we added Jack Stark for Psychology to it. So we had the psychologist, the nutritionist, I think both of those guys, Jack Stark and Dave Ellis, really did contribute to the success of Nebraska football there in the '90's. There is a need for those roles, and those guys did a good job in those roles.

Q: Just let the coaches coach and then others will fill in the gaps?

BE: Yes, our Performance Team did a really good job there in the '90's. It was tremendous. You know we only had 1.7 million people in the entire state, so it just kind of shows when you really focus, like 1991 in that winter program. Champions really are made when no one is watching. I believe that's actually a Steve Pederson quote. (laughs)

Q: Let me ask you, Boyd, what was your motiviation as a strength coach. What drove you?

BE: Early on my role was a strength coach and I worked out with the players and I wasn't much older than them. I was stronger than them, for about 19 years I was stronger than them. Then it changed and the guys like Dave Rimington were stronger than me and I couldn't keep up with the workouts. For many, many years I would do winter conditioning with them, I wanted to do the drills right along with them so I'd know what kind of intensity they were working at. I had a certain respect from them because I could do it with them, and then as I got older that changed and I became more of an older coach, and you don't relate to the younger players as well when you get older, and so my role kind of changed. The guys like Mike Arthur and Randy Gobel, they didn't leave the program, they stayed there and were loyal. All these staff members gave me their entire career and the Husker Power Club was realy helpful in allowing me to keep my staff and serve my staff, because the staff had their responsibilities with the athletes. So as you get older things evolved.

Q: Do you have a favorite play or favorite moment in your time there?

BE: Well, I have a play that I remember like it was yesterday, but it wasn't my favorite. I was standing on the sideline in Miami and we looked like we were going to lose, Irving Fryar dropped a pass in the endzone. But then on 4th down and 12 we gave the ball to Jeff Smith and he ran for a touchdown, and all we had to do was kick a field goal and tie. And Coach Osborne decided to go for two, which created a tremendous reputation for him in having high character. It was a tremendous thing that he did. I remember shaking Mike Arthur's hand at that moment, because we were going to make that that two point play and we were going to win, we were going to be national champions. I remember we shook hands and we watched the play, then the ball hit Jeff's shoulder. It bounced off and we didn't win. I remember that play about as well as any. Wasn't my favorite, but is one that I certainly remember, and it made Coach Osborne a legend in the game of football. A tie would have ended up giving us the national championship because we were undeafeated and would have become number one, but that wasn't what we went there to do. And that meant an awful lot to us who were real impressed with what Coach Osborne did there.

Q: A favorite game?

BE: I have two. The one against Miami where we were trained in the correct energy systems and they were exhausted and on oxygen. We found out later that Miami had been training in the wrong energy system, they were running 220's and 440's. But there are a lot of coaches and trainers still don't get that right, don't understand what the energy systems are and how they work. They train athletes in the wrong way. Unfortunately, we have some athletes dying as a result.

The Miami game where we came back in the 4th quarter was the best example of a team that has been conditioned properly versus one who wasn't. Although they might have had better talent, in the 4th quarter they just couldn't keep up with us. If there had been a fifth quarter, they would have had to take the Hurricanes to the hospital.

The other game was the Florida championship game; beating Steve Spurrier and beating them that badly when they were ranked #2 in the nation, I think they were #2 and we were #1. What happened there, I think there was so much attention on the Lawwrence Phillips issue, nobody realized that we had a pretty good football team. I remember being on the football field in warmups. You know how Nebraska would go on the football field to warm up in three groups: you had the people that handled the ball would come out first, then the linebacker-types would come out second, then the linemen would come out last. They didn't quite do much to warmup, so they came out last. So I'm out there and the first two groups are on the field, and the assistant coach, Ron Zook -he was with Florida at the time- he was a friend of mine and he came over and said "My, you guys are big!" And I said, 'Ron, what do you mean?' And he said, "Look at your guys, they're huge!" And I said, 'Ron, the linemen aren't out there yet.' And he said, "What do you mean?" I said, 'The big guys aren't out there yet.' He looked around and said "What do you mean, Boyd?" And I said, 'Here they come!' And about that time the linemen come running out, and he looked at them and said, "Oh, my God!" (laughs) They just weren't prepared for Nebraska that night.

Q: Any funny moments with Coach Osborne or anyone else?

BE: Mike Rozier. Mike Rozier was great guy, funny guy. But he was also a valuable person on the team and we couldn't afford to get him hurt. One day at testing he wanted to run another 40 yard dash time. Well, he'd already run twice but he wasn't happy with his time and he wanted to run an additional one, and I told him, 'No.' So we were putting the equipment away. And we were all finished up and I look back, and here he's running stark naked down the field in the 40 yard dash! (laughs) But he didn't run any faster…

End conversation.

Nebraska's strength staff once employed a young graduate student assistant out of Brownsville, Texas who was quite a motivational fellow. Arturo Garcia was his name and he possessed a variety of quirky witticisms. One of them summarized Boyd Epley to a 'T', and went something like this: "You can't stop the man with a plan, because there's not a plan to stop the man." Catchy, don't you think? Also very true.

Boyd was a planner, a dreamer, a visionary, and until now has never gotten his due for his ability to elicit development in a college kid's most important muscle of all, the one right up there between the ears. I overheard ESPN's Scott Van Pelt once make this statement about strength coaches, "Their only role is to act like the biggest dickhead ever… all the time." Well, Boyd was cut from a different kind of fabric altogether, bringing science, marketing and facilities together to aid development of full physical potential via the Husker Power program.

Of course, the University of Nebraska weightroom was a spectacle and a marvel in itself, but merely *possessing* the nation's largest weightroom and knowing how to *properly use* the nation's largest weightroom are two different animals, and Boyd used it to maximum extent. Employing multiple assistants with diverse talents and peppering the rafters and walls with catchy slogans such as, "Combine running, stretching and lifting if you dare to be great," and "The great ones adjust," it took the better part of twenty-two years to finally perfect the physical development of the post-adolescent human male for total football dominance.

Rather than training players for only improved health and general fitness -which was the bellwether of the time- Boyd and Husker Power staffers set the bar multiple notches higher and ahead of many programs you'll still find today. Testing every player's vertical jump, the direction-changing Pro Agility Drill, and both the 10 & 40 yard dash multiple times per year and then tying those test results and the student/athlete's body weight, height, and muscle mass into complex mathematical algorithms, he (along with assistant Mike Arthur and, most notably, University Professor Chris Eskridge) found a simple way to compare the performance parameters of all athletic positions and body-types in order to separate the corn from the cobs. (Please pardon the pun) The result was not merely a self-assessment tool to note an athlete's physical development, but a method of assessing each athlete's weakness, aiding one to devise a plan to improve upon those weak links through future training regimens.

The result of this merging of science and mathematics was called the Performance Index, which was also tied into something known as a Strength Index: using the Hang Clean, Squat and Bench Press Exercises (Bench Press was later eliminated due to its almost total inability to predict athletic prowess). The result was an across-the-board measuring stick for each athlete to use as personal- and team-wide competition for every training & testing period thereafter. Were a player to achieve an Index Score of 500 points on each Index variable, the athlete was not only allowed to lift at his discretion on the hallowed Record Platform sitting center stage in the colossal weight facility, but his name was -for all intents and purposes- etched into a statue at the base of the raised platform for all of Nebraska Athletics' eternity. (These indexes were also a great predictor of All-American worthiness and the potential to excel in the perceived ultimate realm: professional football)

Combining both 1) a full understanding of how the human body best recovers to full power from one football play to another with 2) an obsessive focus on physical domination, it all came together in those glorious 60 & 3 teams. Building a sense of community, dedication and accountability through the Unity Council at the time, each player knew that simply pouring his full effort into 'the system,' —especially the Husker Power training system- improvement and success were only a matter of time. If not? Well, then one had only himself to blame for failing to reach the human performance heights dreamed of as a young recruit.

Notable quote #2:
Boyd Epley on the the 357 days per year Memorial Stadium's bleacher seats are empty: "Champions are made when no one is watching."

Butch Coolidge: (beating up Marsellus Wallace) You feel that sting, big boy, huh? That's pride fuckin' with you! You gotta fight through that shit!"

Quentin Tarantino, *Pulp Fiction*

Do you remember those old Jiffy-brand peanut butter ads? To loosely paraphrase, "Choosy mothers choose Biff!" Jokes aside, Mike "Biff" Roberts was one tough & persevering hombre. If you saw him in street clothes you'd never have guessed he played football for the University of Nebraska. I'm sure now and then he'd be at some campus house party and a couple buddies would try -laughably and unsuccessfully- to convince a pretty young coed that he truly was a member of the Cornhusker football team.

Now, that's not a put-down of Biff, but rather my way of paying respects to a guy who - despite lacking an overly physically imposing stature at the time- made hay every day on the practice field as a member of the scout team. Like the old saying goes, "What matters most is not the size of the dog in the fight, it's the size of the fight in the dog." Let's reacquaint ourselves with Biff…

Notable quote #1:

"I can remember it was tough to even *walk* after some practices. Of course, you never showed it…every player feeds off of that. It builds chemistry. It's that hard work ethic."

Mike "Biff" Roberts

Walk-on, Rover, Omaha, Neb. (Central)
Where are they now? Council Bluffs, Iowa, Law Enforcement

Question: So Biff, where did you grow up?

Mike Roberts: Originally from Omaha. I attended Omaha Central, what they called 'I-Back High.' We had Leodis Flowers, we had Curtis Cotton. I came to Nebraska in 1992 and redshirted my freshman year..and I finished with the '97 Orange Bowl game, the end of the '96 season.

Q: Hey, Calvin Jones was from Central, too, right?

MR: Yeah, he was two years ahead of me. He didn't know me too well. I was just a skinny little beanpole on the sophomore team when he was a senior making the state records for yards and all that stuff, being recruited all around the nation.

Q: What position did you play in high school?

MR: I played safety and receiver, and was recruited as a receiver. And Central was a real top-notch school when it came to recruiting, and they were looking for blocking receivers that could also catch well. The only reason the university knew about me was when I went to the football camp and had the greatest three days of my life! (laughs)

Q: In what respect?

MR: With everything: testing, catching. I caught everything with my eyes closed just about, with one hand, I don't know how I did it. My testing was decent, no blazing speed where the eyes would pop open, but it was a 4.7 electronic time, which is pretty decent for a young high school kid. And they were probably thinking, "By the time he gets to Nebraska and develops he'll be running 4.5 or 4.6 electronic."

Q: Sure, "Let Boyd get ahold of him and he'll really make some progress," right?

MR: Exactly. And that never happened. I don't know if I'd peaked or what. (laughs) What happened was, I had a bad high school senior year. Nebraska didn't have enough scholarships and I wasn't scholarship material for that level, so they asked, "We'd love for you to walk on", and the walk-on program was huge at that time. And I had a few scholarship offers to Northwest Missouri State, Wayne State. I was part of a great walk-on group that year with Adam Treu, Brian Schuster, Jon Vedral. All those guys became starters, so I had a great class I joined in that year.

Then every summer I had to go back home and work, stuff the Husker Football staff set me up with at the time. And the jobs sucked. (laughs) I was like, 'Hey, I'm supposed to have the easy job,' like watch other guys do work. (laughs) They found me a job at Pamida, like a small Kmart in smaller towns. They put me in the warehouse so I had to load up all the merchandise that they were going to ship out. So we'd go and load like a hundred boxes of Tide that weighed 30 lbs. and then 100 boxes of Duracell batteries that weighed 50 lbs. And it was high speed, you had to do it quick. And the warehouse was 100 degree heat and almost 100% humidity and no breeze or wind at all. After 8 hours of just throwing boxes it was bad.

Q: Nowadays they call that a great 'core workout!'

MR: (laughs) When I went home it made it all the more difficult to workout with the guys, too. Maybe only twice a week I'd make it to the stadium to workout. And I didn't hit it hard until August before fall camp, as far as getting back in shape. I was like, 'I'm losing a step every year, losing 5 lbs. of muscle every year instead of gaining 5 or 10 lbs of muscle every year.' It kind of froze me as far as progressing at Nebraska. I could compete, but not at a first string level.

Q: And what was the highest you ever found yourself on the depth chart?

MR: It was my redshirt sophomore year, they had me rotating with the first team. I got back from the summer and they were, "Hey, you made it back. I'm glad you're still on the team!" But they had me rotating in and out with the Blackshirts. I think they were giving me that opportunity to earn some playing time and I'm thinking, 'What the hell? Did they not get the message that I wasn't really here this summer?' And then that fall camp I blew out a flexor tendon in my finger and they were like, "Well, we can either tape it to your middle finger," -you know, 'cause it was my ring finger- "..and play with it for the rest of the season and it'll be like that forever. When you make a fist, that finger will stay straight" - 'cause the tendon connects to the bone that causes it to flex- "or," they said, "you can get it fixed and you'll be out two and a half months, which is more than half the season." So, I'm like, 'Well, shit, I'm not some dynamic, All-American Blackshirt so I'll get it fixed.'

Q: Did you ever see any special teams play?

MR: They really wanted me to start on punt returns because I was a pretty aggressive, decent hitter. I didn't have the weight behind me as far as going against the 250 lb. guys. I did punt returns for a couple of weeks and they had me blocking this like 250 lb. fullback, and I was a buck-eighty! And that didn't turn out too well. (laughs) Then I was on kickoff team off and on throughout my career and I was able to letter my last two years, which was something like 10, 11, or twelve quarters to letter.

Q: What was the biggest game you were involved in?

MR: Oh, Michigan State in the '96 year, I think it was. I played pretty much a whole quarter and then half of another.

Q: Coming from a big high school program, what was your first impression when you first joined the team?

MR: As far as the athletes putting out effort, in high school you'd see someone being lazy and slacking when it was practice and training. You know, people goofing off. At Nebraska there was no goofing off in practice time, it was 100% full bore training and practice. I was, "Man, these guys are serious!" They were going full speed. In high school you didn't see guys going all out. So that was a big surprise, which was good, because that tells me, "You've got to go all out every play, every drill. Backpedal drills, you do it as fast as you can, the wet turf drill."

Q: The wet turf drill?

MR: It was when you're backpedalling, you chop your feet in really small steps. And if you chopped your feet you wouldn't slip. If you planted your feet and tried to cut you might lose your balance. But every drill was just super intense. No laziness.

Q: Do you have a time or play you wish you could do over?

MR: Yeah, my redshirt freshman year they put me in the last couple series. And here I was like 8th string or something, you know, and here I'm getting put in. It was either Pacific or North Texas, I can't remember, but they threw a bomb on me, knowing that I was a rookie and stuff, and the ball was coming down and I'm like, 'Here's my chance to get an interception,' and we both jump up and our feet get tangled coming down, and I'm lying on the ground and looking up and he's got the ball in his hands, falling out of bounds. If not for that he would have walked into the end zone. I wish I could've gotten that ball. I think that was my first time ever being in, too.

Q: That being a home game, what was the first game you recall traveling with the squad?

MR: It was either K-State or Missouri, one of them. It was Missouri. I remember we stopped for lunch at some park and I'm like, 'What the heck?' We stopped and hopped out of the bus and had brown bag lunches. I don't know where it was at, had no clue. It was always the bus, it was just that distance where it made sense to take a bus. I don't remember too much about it, for some reason they wanted to keep the starters in pretty much the whole time. The home games were where you really had the chance to get in.

Q: So what's happening on the sideline during these games?

MR: Even as a backup it's intense. The tunnel walk, it's intense. And you remember the Unity Prayer? We had great leaders, and when I went to the Varsity locker room it was kind of like an initiation. They had this little fun thing where they beat on you. (laughs) Like a gang-beating, you know? You're one for life once you're in. After they knock you out and beat you. (laughs) Oh, it was brutal, me and Aaron Davis got it the worst. Ask him about the initiation. It was me, him, a few other guys when we moved from the north locker room to the south.

My redshirt year I was in the north, my freshman year I still stayed in the north locker room, and then I moved over the next year. They end up telling you, "You're South" when fall camp starts, and your name is on the locker and all that good stuff. And I think they first started this -I don't think it was tradition- they pretty much dragged you out to the center of the room. They'd just surround you with about 50 guys and you're just curled up in the fetal position (laughs) and then after they throw and dump a bunch of water bottles on you, it's pretty much done. (laughs) They had guys watching the door, 'cause Osborne would never allow that. And a couple guys, they'd get you when you just walked out of the shower, so you were butt naked. (laughs) You might not want to put this in the book and get us investigated by the NCAA. (laughs) But it was all good.

Q: Any particular teammates really stand out to you?

MR: Lawrence Phillips. He was just the nicest guy in the world. He was just a workhorse! Some guys, being that good, they'd usually slack off sometimes. But not Lawrence. He was a really hard worker. I never saw it and he never told me, but I think Ahman Green got his work ethic from watching Lawrence Phillips. In practice it was 100%. The option drill, he'd always be going 100%. But for some reason, as fast as he could run, he would push the envelope. What a work ethic. He already had blazing speed for his size.

We even got into a couple of fights, you know? We always had fights in practice. On the field he was business, and I remember we got into a couple of tiffs back and forth. No punches flying, but as far as, "I'm gonna f** you up," he'd talk a bunch of smack and stuff. But off the field, he was just the nicest guy, would buy you a pop. But it was when he was drinking he got into the silliness and in trouble with the law and stuff. I mainly fought with Damon Benning. We got into a couple of fights where Osborne made us both run the South Stadium stairs. All we would do was punch each other and scar up our knuckles, hitting ourselves in the helmet, you know? That was when we wouldn't try to grab each other's facemasks and try to twist each other's heads off. (laughs)

Other than that, there was one time the entire Blackshirts -I was with the 2's and 3's- the Blackshirts were on the other end, and we were going light scrimmage on both sides, and all of us got into a huge fight with the first string offense. We were all just, "What the hell's going on down there? Man!" Someone had lost their helmet. And Christian Peter had his helmet off, and someone blasted Christian with their helmet over his head. I don't know if it cut him or what, but Christian just went nuts. The offensive linemen looked like they wanted to kill him, and it seemed to go on for a full 5 minutes.

Q: Obviously, Coach Osborne was around, right?

MR: Yeah, and the coaches just stayed out of the way. Someone told me it occurred because they were all pissed off because they were thinking they were going to go home for Christmas break, and instead the coaching staff decided to stay and keep on practicing through December. Anyway, that's just what I heard from a guy or two.

Q: What created most fights?

MR: I don't know if it was that they wanted not to show they were giving in to the other players or, "You're not going to get the best of me." To a degree, the coaches would force it. One of Coach Solich's fullbacks went at it with a middle linebacker and the fullback lost the fight. Well, Solich grabbed his helmet - which was torn off during the fight- and said to the player, "If you're gonna go...GO!" Then he took the guy's helmet and tossed it over to the sideline. (laughs) I was like, 'Man!'

The practices, that's where I think we became great, and the chemistry was so good. It was just blood, sweat and tears in those practices. But it got us all closer when it came to the games. And do you remember 'The Circuit'?

Q: The old Metabolic Power Circuit in the weight room?

MR: Yeah. I tell you what, that was just brutal!

Q: Funny you say that, Biff, I've been working out in my garage doing that circuit recently.

MR: Are you kidding me!?

Q: Well, being an old strength coach, you go with what works, right? (laughs) Getting a super high intensity set of lifts in with exactly and only one minute of rest in between each set…

MR: Man, you're nuts. That was horrible. You know how many people puked after that? Well, I was one of them! That was terrible. And then, of course, the sprints we'd do, too. Then the guys started pulling some muscles, so then we switched it up to running later down in the Cook Pavilion. And then we'd have to do the circuit afterwards. Well, I could hardly do the sprints before the circuit, I don't know how I was going to do them afterwards. I mean, you needed like a two hour rest after that circuit to do anything, much less run.

Q: And then the circuit would always end up with biceps and triceps at the end. I recall not many guys wanted to hang around and just work their arms all day during that part of the lifting season.

MR: Arms wasn't too bad, but it was nothing compared to those squats! I remember the first thing we started with was squats, and for some reason it just killed! Octavious McFarlin, me and him were about same age and played the same position. I remember him one time, he was in pain and laying out on one of those carpet benches out by the entrance to the weight room and academic center after that circuit. And he was just like, "Don't talk to me… or I'm gonna puke!" It was hilarious, he was trying not to puke for about a half hour. He was just rolling around. Man, I tell you, that circuit was just brutal.

Q: So who was your position coach?

MR: Darlington. Coach D. I was good friends with Dave Alderman and Chad Blahak, and we'd always call him Dad, like, "Hey, where's your Dad today?" It was our way of making fun of him. And I'm not sure if he ever did play football. Rutgers, I think he was from. He was a big x's and o's guy. He was the old guy. We'd always make fun of him and talk about how he was around for the Louisiana Purchase and stuff like that. He always took it well, he was a joker. He'd always say -if you tripped or fell down in the process of turning your feet- he'd say, "The sniper up there got 'ya." He'd always make funny sounds while we were watching film.

He was always big on recovering first before you looked back at the ball. That was a big issue for Nebraska fans, "Why don't they turn around and look for the ball?!" Coach D said you had to be 100% recovered to turn around and look for the ball, you had to be elbows to elbows. And if you were just a half-step behind he didn't want you looking back for the ball. I don't know if it was from his experience -if he saw too many cornerbacks get burned because of that- but you couldn't be behind the receiver if you wanted to look for the ball. Sometimes it depends on the arc of the ball and all that, but that was the issue. And his technique was that you waited for the ball to hit the receiver's hands, then you would bring that arm down and knock it out. Of course, 9 times out of 10 we would fall and the receiver would walk in.

We also had a technique of punching at the ball, from underneath instead of on the top. We'd do the fumble drill, too, scooping up fumbles would be a drill, too. I was like, "Fumbles? We're just going to fall on it, right?" Believe it or not, there was a technique for scooping up a fumble and we'd practice that. I think his drills as far as technique were very good.

Q: He was a pretty cerebral guy?

MR: I'd say that. When I came in I wasn't even aware of some of the terminology that he had. It was like, 'What's 'technique'?,' you know? He'd always say, "Play your technique," and you'd progress and learn and eventually pick it up. He was very good at explaining, "This is the reason we go man to man", or "This is the reason we play the receiver soft," things like that.

Q: It seems Coach Osborne would always remind the coaching staff as a whole to 'coach positive' and be encouraging. Do you recall anything like that?

MR: Yeah, he would point out what you did wrong, but he would never chew on you. Now, Coach (Kevin) Steele was a whole different type of coach. But a couple of the other guys, they respected him, but they couldn't stand him. You'd have to ask the linebackers. They'd know more. He was a more of the 'get in your face, criticize you-kind of guy", that was his nature. He got in my face one time and he was like, "What the f**k are you doing?" He said it real low, in almost a whisper, so Coach Osborne wouldn't hear him, you know?

Q: Did you answer him?

MR: Well, I was a back-up on specials, second string. It wasn't kickoffs, it was punt returns. And they were yelling my name. And I'm never in this drill, and I'm on the other end of the field. They must have been screaming my name for like 5 minutes, and finally I run over there and Coach Steele comes up and grabs my facemask and pulls my head into his and whispers that, and then says, "Get out there." And I'm like, 'Hey, I didn't hear 'ya.'

Q: Any of your teammates stick out to you from those days?

MR: Oh, Christian Peter by far, is one. As far as leadership. His speeches prior to the game were tremendous. Just the way he acted and how he felt about the team we were playing, you could hear him breathe heavy, how he would show his emotion, it was how he could hardly control himself. You saw how intense he was into the team we were going to play, and it would go through all the other players. He would really pump us up. When he became captain he'd always get the pregame speech in -like when we went to Michigan State- they had a Christmas tree up in the corner and there were Christmas bulbs, all green. Well he's freaking out during his speech and he grabs an ornament off the tree and smashes it into his face! And there's just blood all over. He cut himself, and the players are all just ready to go out there and kill Michigan State, you know? His intensity in practice, he would get in fights all the time. He'd just always go 100% against the offensive lineman, and that was typically against the ones (first team).

That's how it was, usually the ones versus ones, two versus twos, threes against threes, and so on. Rarely did they pit the ones versus 4's and so on. Maybe Coach Osborne, the first week of fall camp practice would pit the rookies against the ones, maybe that was just to toughen them up or show 'em what it's like, you know? And I heard about this -I never saw it- but the rookies were in and the seniors and everyone else came in a few days later, and Christian was going against some redshirt right out of high school. Supposedly the freshman was intimidated and didn't go hard against Christian. Well, Christian goes and just wallops him right upside the helmet, "Don't you ever go half-assed against me, or I'll kill you!" That's what it took, you know? That's what brought it together as a team, you know? It was huge, walk-ons, everyone…

Q: "If you're not going to bring it, get out of here," eh?

MR: Exactly, and Christian had no idea who this kid was, just that he didn't go 100%. That set the tone, you know?

Q: Any of the National Championship games stick out to you?

MR: Miami by far. For some reason, I don't know if I'd say we had a better team than the '95 team, but those guys with Ray Lewis and Warren Sapp were good. I think that Miami team was a lot better than the Florida team.

And here we're going down there kind of beat up because we were beating each other up, we just killed each other in practice. I think he gave us a good 4 or 5 days of rest when we got down there. And those first two weeks we just killed each other down there, too. We go in there and we're down at first and it looks like another Miami/Nebraska year, you know? But we finally came out and did it, whether it was due to our working hard or from losing the year before.

Q: You were on the sideline for the 2 point loss to Florida State the year before

MR: Oh yeah, that was brutal. Of course the 'clip,' then when we stopped them at the 1 yard line and they called it a touchdown and the ball never got across. That would have changed the game.

Q: Any moments stick out to you from that game?

MR: Just all business. We were serious, we wanted to win. It was what they were thinking: they had the right technique, the right plays, the right responsibility. I remember we did a lot of rotating, just like we did the year before. I know we had a lot of guys in, especially on the front, the D-line. Other than that, it was watching every play hoping it goes our way. And then, of course, the bad calls, but it was quite an experience.

Q: Any of you guys ever talk about that phantom clip on Corey Dixon's 77 yard punt return?

MR: No one knows about it but the players. All the players would talk about it, you know, bring it up every once in a while. But no one else knows about the phantom clip. Of course, it was Corey Dixon who ran it back. At one time it was, who was it, a fullback? I think he went on to play special teams for the Vikings. He was a long-haired fullback. A California boy? And they thought it was him, he was a great special teams player. No one was really sure. Everybody was, "No, I didn't clip." But after the bowl game, I don't' think anybody ever went over the film on that one.

Q: So the bowl game film wasn't gone over?

MR: Nope, that was done, it was over. You just let it go.

Q: Is it true that all of a sudden things would come to a screeching halt in practice to work on special teams?

MR: Oh yeah, special teams was its own little time during practice. It was warm-up drills first, then position drills, then we'd go to the run station, then pass station, then we'd break and go specials, then we'd go do option drills. I think they'd go full field punts and kickoffs. But they were never 'live', you just made sure you'd go down the field and find the guy and know who you were going to block on the kickoff return. Kickoff team? After all the work we'd done on the previous drills, they weren't too concerned with us tackling. They would make sure the kicker got the ball off and the return guy would be able to catch it. Those were the two big things.

Q: What made those teams special, Biff?

MR: Well, coming in a freshman, the seniors would show what it takes to play at this level. Like Tyrone Byrd and Steve Carmer, and those guys were seniors when I was a freshman. They showed the effort it took to train at this level, the blood, sweat and tears."This is what it's gonna take", you know? It was brutal, brutal training in practices. I can remember it was tough to even walk after some practices. Of course, you never showed it. But you spent some time in the hot showers. I was just beat up and sore every practice. I'm sure other players were, too. But you know, you see another player and you're thinking, "They can take it. They're doing it. He's fine, so I'll act fine." So every player feeds off of that. It builds chemistry. It's that hard work ethic.

And we're talking about an intensity that's just out of this world. I can remember some of the starters would say, "It's worse to go against the starters of our team than the other teams." The scrimmages were worst, playing against each other than against the other teams, you know? The blood, sweat and tears, with the circuit and then the sprints. And then going into spring ball we had two live scrimmages every week.

Q: It was a crucible, a gauntlet, it took some manhood to survive?

MR: Oh, by far, there were some guys. Like Sedric Collins, he had an injury, came back well. And I don't know if it was the physical-ness coming in or some personal issues, but he quit. And then some of the walk-ons. I remember about 11 guys I came in with, and I think about 5 or 6 finished: me, Turman, Chad Blahak, David Alderman, Adam Treu, Kory Mikos, and Schuster and Vedral. I think those were the only ones left.

Q: And what have you taken into adulthood, good or bad?

MR: It's all good. Knowing that in life you've got to work your butt off to be successful. Unless you're lucky somehow and some way. Me, being a police officer, you have a lot of down time, and there were times I was lazy and patrolling and just driving around, not being proactive. If you're not being a proactive, hard working police officer, other people look at you and it affects your future. I've been turned down before, not going to certain schools. So I always have to be putting forth my best effort.

And fellow officers on the force? It's kind of like you're brothers. You're brutal toward them because you love them, you know? I tell you what, they love to hear the stories of the Nebraska locker rooms..

Q: Like Christian?

MR: Exactly! I can remember one day at Nebraska one of the guys said, "Hey, can you grab that towel for me?" And I lean over, and I feel somebody's stuff on my shoulder...and it wasn't a hand! I knew something felt different. And all the guys started laughing, so I knew I'd been had. I jumped back and was like, 'Get your stuff off me!' (laughs) Goofy stuff like that.

And after the practices and the wars, everybody left it on the field, you know? And there was Lumpy, Lance Lundberg, he got into a fight during one of the bowl game preparations. It was a kid from Florida, a skinny kid, a cornerback, he was a starter at one time but then got hurt. I forgot his name. Anyway, he got pancaked by Lumpy in practice. And the other guys made fun of him, "Man, you got jacked up there!" And he didn't take it well, being a freshman, his ego was kind of hurt, and he goes up to Lumpy in the locker room, taps him on the shoulder and then punches him right in the eye. Lumpy just looks at him and says, "Dude, what is your problem?!" Coaches sent him home for the game, though, of course.

The next day. And Lumpy had this big, huge black shiner for the game. That sucker was nasty. Thank God he didn't have any broken bone or anything from that punch. That kid came back on the team after the bowl game, but he was gone, they sent him home for the rest of the time there.

Q: Was there any particular background figure who stood out to you?

MR: Of course, the big names: Sully. George Sullivan. We'd give him some shit, joke with him. There was Doak. I'm trying to think of the Graduate Assistants, most of them would only get two years there to get experience. The defensive back assistant, he wasn't has intense as Bill Busch. Clayton Carlin, his dad was involved in big time football. Very calm guy, wouldn't get heated up over anything. Wouldn't yell too much, very collected and Osborne-like. I liked him because he didn't yell at me! (laughs) And of course, Bailey. Bryan Bailey. I loved Bailey, I hear he's out on USC's staff now. They gotta be loving him. Then there's Keith Zimmer and Dennis Leblanc. Of course, they're roles got bigger as I left, they would always help you out if you needed a tutor or advice.

Q: Anything about the training table?

MR: I remember they had a study hall for all freshman for two hours, Monday through Thursday, 7pm to 9 pm. Me, I was not a Brainiac by far, so I had to buckle down and do my assignments. Some guys, of course, they'd goof off and play dice in the bathroom, play craps. They'd get caught and in trouble, of course. (laughs)

Q: What was your major

MR: Criminal Justice!

Q: So you knew what you were getting into?

MR: No, not a clue. (laughs) Going in, I wanted to coach. I'd been in sports my whole life, thought I could relate to athletes pretty good. So I go to the Teachers College, and I thought, 'Man, this is not for me.' So I got into business: business is in just about everything. Tried a few of those classes, accounting and stuff, and it didn't really turn out to be my liking, either. And then I take an intro criminal justice course and had Professor Eskridge. Probably the best professor I ever had.

Q: Chris Eskridge?!

MR: Yeah, and he ended up working with Boyd Epley in the weight program on coming up with the weight formulas and stuff like that. So Chris Eskridge was an awesome professor, and I was like, "This is really interesting. I love this sh*t!" So I switched majors three times until I got into criminal justice. So here I am.

Q: You've probably heard it a few times, "You football players have it easy, Everything is given to you. You guys are so pampered, not like the regular students?" What would you say to that?

MR: Oh, if they only knew how beat up I was every night, how sore I was, how tired I was. I would get home at 8 o'clock at night after pretty much weightlifting, eating dinner, showering, all that, 7:30 or 8 I'd get home. I'd have to take a power nap from 8 to 9 just to rest up to study from 9 to 11. Just for my body to rest, that's what it took to get by. I needed that rest to heal my body.

You see all the fame and glory on game day. The fans, they don't see behind the scenes how hard we worked, how much we studied, the blood, sweat and tears, what it takes to get the job done.

Q: Did you ever go in front of the Unity Council?

MR: No, its role was to make sure everyone was on the right track if you messed up. It was pretty closed-door stuff. I guess you might get called in and things were taken care of or you were admonished or things like that, but it usually never got past the closed doors, unless there was a major problem, which there rarely ever was. It was pretty discreet. There were some good leaders. Christian, you have to talk to, he was a great leader. You could hear him screaming in the weight room lifting the weights, and he had his troubles off the field. But the main point was, did you learn from the experience and grow from it, you know?

Q: Anything about Coach Osborne stand out to you?

MR: The one moment for me? I made him laugh one time, which was hard to do. He didn't laugh very much. It was during practice, Jeff Makovicka came out to the flat, like a 5 yard 'out' in the flat, and I was just waiting for him. It was my coverage and he had his back turned to me and I thought, 'What are they thinking?! I could take his head off!' I could have killed Jeff, literally killed him. That would have been a terrible cheap shot. It wasn't a live scrimmage either, just wrap-up, so as soon as he caught the ball and turned around it was a split-second deal. I smacked him with my helmet and wrapped him up, and as I was doing that I just screamed. I went, "POWWWWW!" His eyes popped open and it scared the living shit out of him. And Osborne knew Jeff just about pissed his pants, so he had some giggles on that. That was my own personal thing with Coach Osborne. I don't know if Jeff remembers that, but he'll remember my name. We had some little tiffs, some run-ins. (laughs)

End conversation.

Biff's comments brought to light just about every successful workplace example of role-finding, or 'fitting in.' From his journey of finding where his personality and talents fit in when choosing a major to finding his place on the team depth chart, he was always in his quest to determine his role, as all were, and to excel in it for the good of the team. Sure, he would have loved to be a first-teamer. Who wouldn't? But he —like so many others- was always very in tune with his standing in relation to other student-athletes at his position and knew that banging heads in the middle-of-the-week practices would surely pay off in a game-time victory at the end of that week. The only thing worse than a guy who always complains about 'getting the shaft' from a coach who wouldn't play him is the guy who thinks he was better than that All-American starter in the first place. Biff displayed none of that prevalent attitude, instead functioning the best he knew how with the tools given him.

The longer I've lived the more this outlook amazes me, because most individuals seem to take care of Number One at all costs, often to the disruption and in many cases the destruction of team chemistry. I was once told that the term 'University' was actually a compound word meaning 'Unity among diversity." From his high schooling at Omaha Central, I can guess that Biff was ahead of the curve on the concept of diversity and how it could relate to success. Perhaps humility lies somewhere in the mix, too. The gist I'm getting so far indicates there was great humility in the ranks, this despite the fact that most of these high-performers on a top ranked football team are generally predisposed to higher levels of self-esteem due to performance mastery and resultant confidence. The hard part is finding that confidence while getting your butt handed to you every day as a scout-teamer.

Along with that thought, did you get the notion that anything less than a person's greatest effort was unacceptable? Not only in games, but even in practice and training situations? I loved the vignette about Christian Peter's chastisement of a frosh who only tepidly stepped into the fray, "Don't you *ever* go half-assed against me, or I'll kill you?!" This mindset wrought astonishing ramifications to the entirety of the team, oftentimes producing insurmountable leads built up early in the game. Those scoreboard leads and the ensuing comfort levels among the coaching staff then allowed the starters rest from a whole game's action, their removal thus saving them from potential injury and providing a preservative effect on the starters' season-long efficacy. Secondarily, many of the third and fourth and even fifth teamer's were then allowed a chance at game action in front of the Husker home crowd: a players dream. What a motivational loop they had going there! It all started with a dedication to full effort at every turn.

Notable quote #2:
Mike "Biff" Roberts on weekday practice work effort, "Every drill was just super intense. No laziness."

Don't forget us, but don't mope. Make lots of new friends. You'll never be twenty again.
Take a chorus girl out to supper – a pretty one, mind!

Nebraska author & Pulitzer Prize winner Willa Cather, *A Lost Lady*,
Courtesy of the Willa Cather Trust

It took a major pair of cajones -especially if you were a Michigan kid- to turn your back on Bo in those days. Coach Bo Schembechler, that is. Topping it off, doing so to walk-on at the University of Nebraska was enough to get you committed to a pysch ward. But that's exactly what Mark "Zeke" Cisco did, and you'd be hard-pressed to find a story as timely and unique as my conversation with him reveals here. Another coach's son who broke the mold of the old B1G10 region and instead followed the chorus line, "Go West young man..." he grew in stature and found his football heart's delight at Nebraska, as well as a cute little Husker cheerleader to call his bride. Zeke's playing days came to a close at the very beginning of the great 60 & 3 era, so I was interested in his opinions and experiences just as that grand crescendo began to find its footings.

Notable quote #1:
"You couldn't take a break, because there was always somebody standing there waiting. And I took a lot of pride in always being the guy standing there waiting."

Mark "Zeke" Cisco

Walk-on, Strong Safety, Monroe, Michigan (Jefferson)
Where are they now? Byron Center, Michigan, Coach

Question: Hey, Zeke. How's that little cheerleader of yours treating you these days?

MC: Yeah, I started dating Angie in April of '93. About that time David Noonan made the fateful phone call for me. (laughs) He called her up and said, "I know somebody who wants to meet you." Tell you what, I wanted to put the phone right through his face, but it worked out alright. (laughs) I even tried to duck out of a date one night and said, 'We have a recruit in town. I can't go.' And my roommate -who was a local yokel from Pawnee City- he said, "That's' okay, I know her. She's a nice gal. You're not getting any help on this one." I even asked him to take her to the country bar Guitars & Cadillacs, a place where no one from Michigan would ever be caught dead.

Q: Come on now, Zeke, I used to go to that place!

MC: Never would I go there. I said, 'Look, you go there and I'll scholarship you the whole night. I'll take care of whatever it costs you.' He said, "Nope." (laughing)

Q: All's well that ends well? (laughing) So you're coaching now?

MC: Yeah, I'm the head football coach at Byron Center, Michigan, which is about nine miles south of Grand Rapids. I grew up in Monroe, Michigan, the east side between Detroit and Toledo. Factory heaven.

Q: For six years I traveled America as the Road Manager and Producer for the San Diego Chicken, Zeke, so I've crossed many of those same roads: Toledo for the Mudhens, Grand Rapids for the Whitecaps, Muskegon, South Bend, Lansing, you name it...

MC: Oh yeah, and after I was done playing I coached at Nebraska Wesleyan for Steve Stanard, coaching with Morgan Gregory and Bruce Moore. That was kind of our connection there. And then I left Nebraska and came back to Michigan. I didn't want to move every four years for the rest of my life. I came back to Michigan where my dad is still a high school coach here, and it wasn't such a bad deal.

Three years later I became a head coach at a school in Battle Creek, and then it was, 'Well, my wife was either going to leave me and head back to Nebraska or we we're going to move to a more conservative area,' because -I mean, you've been between Toledo and Grand Rapids- that's like driving from New York City to Des Moines as far as the people go. So that was the big push. And I knew some guys up in the Grand Rapids area, so I resigned as the head coach and I took a teaching job up here and became an assistant. And now I'm 20 miles from huge sand beaches, I'm 27 miles from skiing, and I'm 3 hours from Chicago and 3 hours from home.

Q: When was your first fall at NU?

MC: It was the fall of 89'. You know, my first impression was that I'd landed in church, to be honest with you. Coming from a Rust Belt city where it was, you did what you were told to do and you didn't question it, it was tough. And your parents had tough jobs, and the last thing they wanted to hear was how mean your coach was. So, right, wrong or indifferent, where I grew up was, 'you just shut up and listen and you do what he asks you to do.' It didn't matter why the coach asked you to do something, you just did it that way.

So when I first got out to Nebraska and Coach Osborne it was a culture shock, because it was just so, I don't know, friendly, to be honest. There was just quieter expectations that were asked of you and you were still held accountable for that. That was the first thing, it just really shocked me. That was the opposite of the type of environment I'd grown up in athletically.

Q: And when you say 'quiet expectations', how did you come to pick up on those expectations?

MC: Living in the home of a head coach and knowing Coach Bo Schembechler personally, and being in the Woody Hayes and Bo Schembechler area, that's what I understood college football to be like. It was fire and brimstone. But Nebraska was the Midwest. The *true* Midwest, not the 'Midwest' I grew up in. Being around Coach Osborne and the staff, Coach McBride was more of a rust belt guy, but just the whole atmosphere shocked me. How could you be good like this, you know?

Q: It was 'passively' good?

MC: Yeah, but the expectation was the same and the results were the same. Without question, it was good players with great resolve who represented the university appropriately. For the most part, it was far and few between where some players got into trouble.

Q: Who was the first coach you had a lot of interaction with?

MC: The first guy I had a lot of interaction with was probably Dave Schramm, and I think he's the recruiting coordinator and running backs coach at Utah now. He was a guy who played with my brother at Cornell of Iowa, of all places.

That's what really started the ball rolling for me. I was already signed, sealed and delivered to Michigan. I had my roommate and had my tutor and the whole deal. And Coach Osborne called and my mom answered, and she read him the riot act not knowing who he was. (laughs) He called my dad the next morning at 5:45 eastern time and we were in Lincoln the next week. I did have a little bit of a connection -Coach McBride had recruited Lawrence Cooley out of my home town, and the guy who I coach with right now, his younger brother played for Tony Samuel at Western Michigan. He was nose guard and a boxer, so he piqued Tony's interest. So Coach Schramm and Coach Samuel knew where I was from, knew the area and obviously Coach McBride and Lawrence Cooley, so we had that connection.

Q: You were really set to attend Michigan?

MC: Yes. I had my roommate set up and I had my tutor and the whole deal.

Q: What turned you?

MC: Just the visit alone. We made it in the spring time, it was early spring. The whole atmosphere, it was a family-oriented atmosphere. It was so different than what I was used to, and it was still a historic program I didn't know much about. People here in Michigan still don't know about it. I don't know, I can't put a finger on it, but the general interest was, "You're going to come here, you're going to get a fair opportunity, and we're gonna take care of you." That was enough.

Q: Was a certain player your chaperone?

MC: I met Matt Penland on my visit. He was visiting there, and then he stayed for that summer as a walk-on out of Florida. And I thought to myself, 'Hoy cow, this is a walk-on out of Florida?' He'd skipped his own all-star game and stayed in Lincoln to work out, and he was the first guy I met in the weight room. And the first guys that I roomed with were Will Shields and Roderick Washington for fall camp. So that was a little bit of a culture shock for me, too.

And then Thanksgiving of my freshman year, we're still in freshman football and I really wanted to go home -but the dorms close at noon and my flight didn't leave 'til 4pm, so I didn't have anywhere to go. So I dug through the phone book and I called David Noonan, because I knew he lived in town, and I stayed there for awhile, and his parents really became my parents. They ended up giving me keys to their home and they really took care of me out there. It was my home away from home. They took me out on my birthday, they took me out on his dad's birthday. I became part of their family. I visit him every time I go back. I was in his wedding. I talk to him on the phone quite often.

Q: What was your parents' first impression of Nebraska? I'm sure your father was probably a lifelong Michigan fan?

MC: My dad played at Michigan State, got hurt, and played at Toledo. He played for Coach Devaney, actually, at Michigan State. He said, "You've got to go meet him. He'll know who you are." And I'm thinking there's no way. So we walk in to meet him and Bob Devaney says, "Am I gonna have to take you to class like I had to take your father to class?" And we all just started laughing. So that was part of that first visit. And just to see a guy who my dad played for in 1954, I thought, 'Man, this is a special place.'

Q: Did the facilities stand out to you?

MC: You know, Memorial Stadium was nice. It was a lot like Ohio State's stadium is, but wasn't as big as it was. I wasn't blown away by all that stuff just because I was around it since my dad was a coach. I knew Lloyd Carr since I was 6 years old, so I was always around those type of people and places a lot. So the facilities weren't shocking, but what blew me away was how nice the people were: the people in the grocery store, the people who waved at you, the people who held doors open for you. Either I was an immature guy or just somebody who wasn't very nice. (laughs)

Q: You played defense, so you were probably nasty to begin with…(laughing)

MC: I was a quarterback in high school! I walked-on. I was a walk-on at Michigan, too. It was just that I wanted to take a shot. I knew if it didn't work out I could always go home.

Q: What did your friends and family members say about your going to Nebraska? That was probably the furthest thing from their mind, no?

MC: Oh, definitely. They were, "You're going where?!" My dad was really excited because he knew about the tradition and the history, and thought it was neat that I was at least gonna take a chance. My friends said, "You can't make it. You're not gonna make it. You'll come home with your tail between your legs." And to be quite honest, that was probably part of the reason I stayed. I remember sitting in my dorm room on my birthday, on August 23rd my freshman year. I came back from practice and there were no gifts at my door, no phone calls waiting for me. The State Fair was going on and I remember sitting there looking out the window of my dorm room in Schramm Hall. And I remember thinking, 'Well, either I'm going home now or I'm staying here right now.' And you know, they took an interest in some crappy walk-on from Michigan.

Q: You were a defensive back from the get go?

MC: From the get go. I played free safety on the freshman team. I was actually captain the first game there. We had a bunch of guys like Chad Hunter out of Texas, Marvin Callies out of Houston was a quarterback, Vernon Powell out of East St. Louis. But the thing that helped me out was nobody could catch punts but David Seizys and I. It was, "Hey, did you do any of this in high school?" And I was, 'Yeah', so, "Would you like to do it?" and I'm, 'Sure. What the heck,' and doors kind of opened.

And Matt Penland and I, when we first got to camp, we both made a deal that no matter what happened, that we would finish. If we could finish, if we could still walk… we shook hands and made a deal right there on the spot, that we were going to finish our careers at Nebraska no matter what. Unfortunately, his injuries stopped him, but he's the Nebraska Team Chaplain now.

Q: When it came time to move from the freshman team and over to South Stadium, what role did you play on the team?

MC: At the end of that freshman season I practiced two weeks with the varsity. There was, I think, six of us: Mike Heins, Matt Penland, Lance Grey, and I believe Greg Fletcher, and Kevin Raemakers. Those are the guys that I knew, and then that spring I moved to strong safety and Reggie Cooper was banged up -like a forty-year old guy with bad knees in a 22-year old body- and then Curtis Cotton got injured, so here I stood after 5 games of spring practice I got an opportunity to play. And Pat Tyrance kind of talked me through the whole deal, "You'll be okay, you'll survive."

To be honest, things really fell my way. There were a lot better players there that left, there were better players there, athletically, that played in front of me, and I didn't play in front of anybody who was better than me. I played behind a lot of great people, without question, but things just fell my way. I didn't officially redshirt until the Friday night before we played Baylor that next fall, so I never spent a lot of time on the scout team. Maybe a couple of practices here or there. I was always just kind of a gold shirt. Just wavering in that area the whole time. So I never had to really suffer through the beatings with Richard Bell and Nate Turner and Morgan Gregory beating the crap out of me for a couple of weeks.

Q: Let me ask you, Zeke, for the uninitiated, what was a 'gold shirt'?

MC: We were backups but we weren't scout teamers. We were the second group. You know the Blackshirts? Well, we were the guys behind them, and the Goldshirts were like the threes and fours. And somehow I managed to stay in that void.

Q: So I'm thinking your position coach was Coach Darlington. Tell me about Coach D.

MC: History. He told stories. He used to say things like, "Back in 1983 we played Auburn and we did this to Bo Jackson." And of course, being around guys like Marvin Sanders and Tyrone Byrd, well, as soon as he said that we would go dig the videotape out. And sure enough it was 8 minutes left in the 3rd quarter, and sure enough that play would happen, exactly.

Q: He wasn't just pulling your leg?

MC: Oh no, he was a true historian of the game, without question. So yeah, that was the biggest thing that stuck me about him. Every time we tried to call his bluff he had the answer. You might want to call him now, because after signing day that's when he'll really get busy. When you're not with the big boys, after signing day is when you pick up the scraps. That's when you pick up guys like us who wander around. (laughs)

Q: What was your main contribution?

MC: Boy, I don't know. I was lucky enough to hang around and letter for three years. The guy I ended up living with was Troy Branch -who had no white guys in his high school- living with a white guy who had no black guys in his high school, from opposite ends of the world. But the one thing he used to say -and we've talked about this many times- it was just that you couldn't ever take a break from going hard, because there was always somebody standing there waiting. And I took a lot of pride in always being the guy standing there waiting. There was Tyrone Byrd and Reggie and Steve Carmer, and we were there and we were ready and we were treated great.

And the things you guys did for us in the weight room? You took time with us. That's how I knew I could compete, that's how I knew I could get out on the field. So I got a chance to return punts, a guy who could do this or that. I was always waving my hand to go out there, even if it was just to be in a tackle on the field. And you know, maybe that was the coach's son in me, but I knew my role. I knew where I belonged. I wasn't bitter about it. I was really happy with the opportunity I got. I was pretty happy, to be honest with you.

Q: What would you say you were the most proud of?

MC: Surviving? (laughs) Lettering. You know, when I first got the notice that I'd lettered I about cried, to be honest with you. It just blew me away. There was just so many good people there athletically. I remember walking from the athletic office over to the bookstore, thinking, "Geez, I can't believe this. This is really something." To be able to do that for three years was huge for me, to step across that big, fat, white line on the field. Like most people inside the Berlin Wall at that time, you had to get across that sucker, you had to find a way to get out. And I just absolutely refused to give in. And it never went my way, but that was okay. All these people were just, "Hey, just keep doing this, keep doing that," and that was awesome.

I participated in three championship teams, I went to bowl games, I traveled to Japan, I made 150 great friends that if something happened to me and I picked up the phone? I could call anyone and they'd pick up the phone and they'd say, "What can I do to help?"

Q: Who do you keep in touch with?

MC: With Troy Branch, with David Noonan, Mike Heins, Ken Mehlin, both stars from out of state and walk-ons from in-state. Guys whose families, like the Heins family -when I couldn't go home for spring break they made me work on the farm, but they fed me and they took care of me- and the Roger Anderson's did the same thing. Those are people I've remained relatively close to. I talk to Gerald Armstrong, Doug Colman, who's coaching again.

Q: After that '90 season ended on a sour note, it seemed like things started turning around. Do you recall a vibe?

MC: I remember winter conditioning that year. It was pretty rough, winter conditioning was, and right before spring practice we had a full team meeting and we had a players-only meeting where you could stand up and say what you had to say. And I think that turned out to be about 3 hours long, and there were a lot of people speaking from the heart, whether it was good or bad, saying what they had to say, challenging some things that happened. We had some great players on that team, we really did. Look at all the guys that got drafted off that defense, guys who took me in that were great guys. We just fell apart at the end of that previous year.

And that was when the development of the Unity Council that came about. And I think that was really Coach Osborne and the rest of them: Coach Tenopir, Coach Brown, Coach Samuel, Coach McBride, putting it in our hands. They were like, "Okay, you complained, now here's your opportunity. Well, now we're giving you a voice." And I really think that created a sense of trust, maybe, between players and coaches, a sense of ownership and a little bit of trust. It wasn't something that was a drastic change, it wasn't anything that you were going to see, but I think that started the ball rolling a little bit.

You know John Parrella, Kevin Raemakers in that group, the thing they said was, "Hey, give us a little ownership. Give us a little control, we won't let you down." And they did a great job with it. And players held players accountable. You know, I read Jason Peter's book last spring and he talked a lot about players holding players accountable. And you didn't dare give up on those guys and you didn't dare get in trouble at that point. Nobody wanted to go sit in front of Coach Osborne. Whether you were 18 or 23, no one wanted to go sit there and say, 'Geez, Coach, I let you down. I'm sorry.' He just had the ultimate trust in you that you were going to do the right thing. And I don't know if that group in '90 felt that way. But that was a big impetus for the whole deal.

Q: What kind of interaction did you have with Coach McBride?

MC: You know, him screaming at me most of the time."You freaking DB's, you can't catch a damn ball!" Chasing me back to the huddle when he got a chance. But I remember talking to Adrian Karsten from ESPN before we played Colorado and it was just freezing in the stadium. And he said, "Wow, you guys are pretty tough out here in half-shirts." And I said, 'Yeah, but now we're going inside in 15 minutes while the offense has to come out here and handle the ball.' And he says, "Well, how come"?" I said, 'So Coach McBride can have his way with us while Coach Osborne is occupied out on the field.' (laughs)

Then, of course, getting better players helped as we went along. You didn't come to Lincoln to lay out in the sun or have girls all around. I remember when Troy Branch hosted Kevin Carter -who ended up playing for the Rams- on his recruiting visit, and I think the temperature was minus 13, and he was just at Florida State the week before. And what were we gonna tell the guy, "It's great here"? It's so cold the snot in your nose freezes! It just got to the point that those teammates of mine were the kind of guys we were going to find.

And Coach McBride's favorite comment was, "Does your heart pump blood or Kool-aid?" He used to always ask that. Sometimes you questioned yourself. It was a whole mindset.

Say, here's a little story: My brother lived in Phoenix, so we went out to the game that year and spent a week in '96. And we flew back and got stuck in Cincinnatti in a snowstorm, and Coach Ron Brown got stuck in the same little airport with us -in that same little part of the airport- and he's the one that saw me. Here's a guy I never played for and he grabs me and says, "Hey, what are you doing here?" and I said, 'We just got back from Phoenix.' And he said, "You know, you guys were really responsible for all this. You may not think that, but you were a part of it. You guys like Troy Branch, Mike Anderson and the other guys involved really rolled that over and changed the mindset a little bit, became more servant-oriented." Those are just defensive guys that come to mind. The other guys like Terry Conneally, Christian Peter -I mean, he grew up 10 years in the 5 years he was there- Ryan Terwilliger, Mike Minter, Tyrone Williams, all those guys. And then on offense it was the same scheme but different names, they just took ownership of it.

Q: I'm sure you mixed it up with Ed Stewart and the guys, too?

MC: Sure, sure, since I was a DB. I remember Kevin Steele came to the meeting room one day and he said, "We need a WILL linebacker. We're running low. We're running out of bodies. Does anybody want to come?" All of us were like, "I don't want to play for that guy." And Ed, he was a tweener athletically at that point, so it was a good move for him.

Q: Ed didn't come along very willingly though, did he?

MC: No, but I think people said, "Look, you're not going to play in the secondary, now. You're not good enough. But you can play here, we think you can play."

Q: I remember one time a bunch of guys on the defense made up some shirts that said, "Hey, my name is Ed, too!" Do you remember that? What was that about?

MC: That's right, that was the linebackers. Oh yeah, I remember. And I had the inside scoop, because I used to go bowling with Troy and Phil Ellis and Mike Anderson, those guys were my closest friends. That was a shot at Kevin Steele. I know he had to smile a little bit, but I'm sure it stung. They all came in the first day of practice wearing those shirts. It was just Coach Steele. We're talking about Coach Steele, a guy so neat that he wrote boilerplate on the chalkboard that looked like he typed it. He was so anal it wasn't funny. He probably still is, I don't know. He was a great technician. I mean, a lot of guys didn't like him, but to a man if you want to teach somebody how to play linebacker he was the man. I'm not sure Doug Colman might have him on speed dial. Steele'd be the right guy to call to teach a kid how to play.

Q: Why wouldn't some guys like him?

MC: He just wasn't a real friendly guy. I mean, if you passed him in the hallway he wouldn't even acknowledge your existence. But it's funny, me being a special teams guy? We'd argue with him. I was hard-headed enough to actually argue with him, which got me nowhere. (laughs) I can remember him chasing me off the field at UCLA, screaming at me, "That's your block!" and I'm like, 'Yeah, I know that, as well as 60,000 people here and everybody else on TV.' Here I am, some scrubby walk-on and he's chasing me. We had a lot of times like that. He was just an interesting guy. He was a neat fellow first and then a good coach, very good at that part of the game. I played on the punt return team, a little on the kickoff team, enough to travel here and there. Some weeks I did, some weeks I didn't.

Q: Any one play stick out more than other?

MC: Probably the first time I got to play in the UCLA game, just because being from Big 10 country that field was the Mecca, that was the Rose Bowl. I remember running around the field like a little kid that Friday when we got there, just like a knuckle-head. I remember the first play I played in that game. I almost threw up, I was so excited. And I had family there in L.A. That, to me, was something really special. It was a punt return. I was on the punt return team. I think I even lined up wrong. I remember Matt Turman making that road trip, because we were short at quarterback and they were asking guys, "Could anybody play QB?" 'Cause he was a receiver.

Q: That was Lawrence Phillips' coming out party?

MC: Right, 'cause Calvin Jones had been beaten up in the first game against North Texas, and then I think we played Texas Tech next, maybe we went out there to play UCLA the next week. That was something to remember. He was the man. There's something to be said for playing guys in their hometown. Lou Holtz was the master at it. He played all the guys when he was at South Carolina who were from Ohio. So when they played Ohio State in the bowl game they had a great game.

Q: Any memorable off-field occurrences?

MC: Boy, I tell you, I was part of the Teammates Program. That was special now that I look back on it. At the time I did it because Coach Osborne was just asking, "Who wants to do this?" And being in a home where my dad was kind of a mentor, players kind of lived with us, so I thought that was kind of cool and I got involved with it. And I got paired up with a kid named Sean Applegate, who ended up playing there at Nebraska and played very well. He went to Peru State and they tested him out when he visited because you could do that at Division 2 schools, and he told me his vertical jump and 40 time and I said, 'You know what, we're going to call Coach Osborne. We're gonna go in there and sit and talk to him about this.' And I remember looking at him and he was like, "Are you nuts?!" and I said, 'You are a receiver and you can play here. And if you knew who Coach Brown was you'd know that he'll find a place for you if you want to play.' At the time I think we were doing a commercial for the Teammates Program and we were sitting in Coach Osborne's office and I said, 'What do you think about this kid coming here?' and he said, "Well, it's up to him." That really struck me, and Sean took the ball and came and played and scored touchdowns and the whole deal.

He was my mentee. We'd take him up to East Campus and shoot pool or go bowling with Troy, be over at the house and just hang out and talk with him, call him once in awhile, play Frisbee with him in the summer time -not a whole lot, not as much as I could or should have done- but it was a door for him. His mom was a great lady, fantastic, but she was single lady with a son and a daughter, his younger sister, and I'm sure it was a struggle for her. That was, now that I look back on it, was really something special. I was glad to be a part of it. It probably made me grow up a little bit out there, what little I did. To me that was really cool.

And obviously, the academic awards we got there, I remember Coach Osborne saying, "The team GPA is 2.77" and some guys would roll their eyes. But the average GPA of the university is 2.6, and some of the guys were like, 'That's right. That's us.' And then meeting Gale Sayers, shaking his hand and having him hand me a medal, that was pretty huge. You know, they always had somebody who administered the medals at those academic banquets. I think Dick Enberg did one time and Gale Sayers one time. To me that was gold. Growing up knowing about 'Brian's Song', you know? And I have it framed in my house right now, the program from that banquet with his signature on it. I didn't have a major until they told me I had to finally pick one. I became an education major. And I swore I'd never do it since my parents were teachers.

Q: Did you picked up anything useful from your time at Nebraska to make you a better coach?

MC: There are a few days I can hear Coach Brown's voice, Coach Tenopir's voice, and I didn't even play on offense. But I heard all these things and I think, 'How would they handle that? How would they handle this, how would they do that? If I had a Lawrence Phillips how would I handle that?' And even at my last interview, I got asked about Lawrence Phillips, you know, "Why would they keep him? Why did they do that?" And I said, 'I'm going to tell you. Honestly, because Coach Osborne really thought that if he was given another chance that he would figure it out. He thought if he were given another chance he would help the kid.' Coach Osborne knew our family, our parents, he really knew everything about us. And I really think he thought he could make a difference for this kid. And when it was time, it was time. He said, "This is enough, you need to go." And I'm so excited that Coach Brown is back. He really had an impact on me, and I never even played for the guy.

And Marvin Sanders, when I was a freshman he was a senior, and you always knew if you didn't know anything you could go see this guy. And one time in the weight room I went up to ask him a question, and said, 'Hey, you don't even know me, but I'm a freshman and I have a couple questions for you. Can you help me out?' And he sat me down there and gave me clinic.

Q: So he was 'Coach' Sanders before he was Coach Sanders?

MC: Yeah, so there was a lot of treatment like that. Probably undeserved.

Q: Any good practice stories?

MC: All kinds. (laughs) I know the steps out there at South Stadium pretty well. (laughs) I guess I got a little chippy out there, just to be survivor. That was part of my role, I guess. I just wasn't fast, wasn't big, wasn't this or that like some people were, so that was my survival instinct. And Coach Osborne would be like, "Dadgummit! What's wrong with you? What's going on out there?" So I knew when I heard that I'd be running some stairs, you know? So off I went.

I remember yelling at the referees at the scrimmage one time, 'cause Corey Dixon was cutting me. And I remember just cursing and kicking him in the head and cursing the ref out. And I come to find they were the guys who blew the Colorado State/Air Force game that year. And I don't know how I found out -maybe Greg Fletcher let me in on that- but I found out during the scrimmage. I remember some call they made that game essentially cost the game for one of those teams, it was on the news. And of course, I had to tell them I knew about that. And I remember a hand on the back of my jersey, and here was Coach Osborne. And I shrink and I'm like, 'Oh no, I'm done. He's sending me home. Here I go.' And maybe being a coach's son, being around that stuff, I just couldn't resist, because I thought I was getting short-changed.

Q: So you'd be banging heads with the receivers every day in practice. Any guys stand out there?

MC: I was banging heads with anybody who was willing! You know, receiver-wise, I remember Richard Bell and Morgan Gregory beating the crap out of me and giggling.

They'd laugh at each other. But then as I got older it got better. Nobody knew how good those receivers were because we ran the ball.

Cory Schlesinger and I became pretty close friends because I knew he'd never make a cut and I was just gonna have to bite my mouthpiece a little harder when the hit came. (laughs) I think I have a picture, I remember from a scrimmage, of him running through me, me hanging onto this leg, my chinstrap hooked to my nose. Sports Information sends a triplicate copy to both of us. I walked in the locker room and Cory reaches into a manila folder and grabs one out and says, "Swwwwwweeeeeeeet!" And of course, Cory, being a joker, stands there and spins in a circle for everyone to see. And of course, Trev Alberts standing there announces it and says, "Oh, that's great picture of you, Cisco! That's really awesome!" 'Thanks, man. Thanks.' (laughs)

Q: So your last game was the Florida State 18-16 game?

MC: Yeah, 18-16 game.

Q: Can you bring me back there?

MC: I broke my hand before the game. I shattered it on a helmet in practice the day before we left. A day before we left. And I remember having George Sullivan near me and I said, 'Hey, I can't get my glove off. Will you cut it off?' and he said, "Well, you broke your hand", and I said, 'Oh, come on! I did not! You're crazy.' I can't hang on to the ball while we're playing catch. And you know Sully, he was ready to beat me. I said, 'I did not break my hand. You're crazy.' And he said, "I'll see you at 7 in the morning." So 7 o'clock the next morning I went there and he took an x-ray and he put it up in the old, crude x-ray room down there in south east corner of the stadium. And he stuck that x-ray up there and showed me what happened and I go, 'Oooh, that's bad.' And he said, "That is bad. Well, do you want to get it operated on?" I said, 'No, no, no, no. I'm going now.' So I practiced all week with a broken hand with a splint on it. Which was dumb. It hurt, and Mike Heins and I were road roommates. And I remember telling him, "Don't set the alarm clock, 'cause after I take this pain pill I'll be up at six, guaranteed. And we didn't set it the whole week. And we were never late.

And I remember talking to a reporter from Monroe, Michigan and he kept asking, "Do you think you have a chance?", and I kept going, "Yeah, of course we have a chance! What are you talking about?!" And I remember how good Charlie Ward was, watching film of him, all of them games. And it was a game we should have won. A missed kick? Yeah, but there were some other things that happened that we should have done a little better. It was a little disappointing, but now you look back and you think, 'We could have been the only team to win 3 in a row.'

I remember the smell that night. Everything about it. I remember the first year in '91, when we were down there, I was stretching on the field the night before the game. The top 70 went out there and stretched. And I remember sitting on the field thinking, 'Man, I wish my friends could be here,' you know? I just wanted them to be part of that. It was pretty cool.

I remember at 6 in the morning we woke up to a roaring noise and I'm like, "What in the hell is that?" Look out the window and we're staying at the Hotel Sophie, and it was right across the street from the stupid airport. That was our 'move off the beach' as a way to protect us, so we could be next to the airport and wake up at 6 a.m. for a 9 p.m. game. (laughs)

Q: So obviously you're on the sideline. Were you suited up or in street clothes because of the broken hand?

MC: Oh no, I practiced all week and suited up. I was a backup on all the special teams that I had played on. So I could play. I didn't, but I could have. And the guy I would have had to block on punt returns was Ken Alexander, who's about 260. And I'm thinking, 'There's no way in hell I'm gonna be able to do this. With a broken hand I've got no chance, because I can't hold him.' And it was a great college football game. It's forgotten in lore down there, but there were some great players on the field for that game. There were some great plays that were just unreal.

The funniest thing was, we played those guys so much that we were so much alike, the coaching staffs were such good friends. It was like playing against ourselves, to be quite honest. A little bit different offensively. Coach Osborne and Coach Bowden, such good friends. Coach Bowden spoke at Coach Osborne's 200th victory deal that year. It was really like we were playing ourselves.

Q: And obviously, we fashioned some of what we did after them so we could play with them?

MC: Oh, definitely. I remember the spring practice conversations between both schools. I remember the '91 Miami game, thinking, 'Oh crap, these guys are incredible.' You know, in '91 it was the only time ever in my life I thought we would lose a game. When their defense took the field I remember thinking, 'Whoa!' I remember those three guys came out: Armstead, Barrow and Smith and they did their whole thing. I remember looking over at Troy Branch and thinking, 'Oh boy, we're in trouble.' It was a 22-0 game. And they split with Washington. We had lost to Washington, too. But Miami was pretty good.

Q: Anything else as far as the turnaround? Creating a new mindset?

MC: The 'Unity, Belief, Respect' thing. Remember John Calipari at UMass stole that from us? 'Play Like Champions' & 'We Refuse to Lose.' That was '93 when we had those black shirts during winter conditioning, and that was the year we got red tanktops. And then that summer we got black t-shirts that said, 'Unity, Belief, Respect' on it. I still have that around somewhere. It was 'enough is enough.' It really was, and we had the right people to do that.

And I remember Cory and I sitting on the beach that morning waiting for the sun to come up on Miami Beach after the Florida State loss. And it was cloudy that morning and the stupid son didn't come up. It was behind all those clouds, and I'm thinking like, 'Are you kidding me!? How fitting!' And I remember saying to Cory, 'You better freaking win next year.' And he said, "We will." Sure enough, they did.

Q: Anyone behind the scenes play a big part for you? Unsung people?

MC: There were a lot of people. And I think that makes the difference. You talk about good to great, building momentum, all the little nudges that don't necessarily move the wheel but they make it spin a little faster? All that academic stuff, we were light years ahead of it. People that took a special interest in you like Keith Zimmer. The whole strength staff there was just unreal. Bryan Bailey saying, "You can do this, you're gonna play. Try this, do this." It was just all the time, little nudges. They were a community of people like that. Like I said, the Nebraska families that took me into their house, took me out on my birthday, had dinners with, celebrated Easter? It just made it different than any other place in the country. I don't care where you're at, something they have that no one else has. No one else.

And that was the main difference, the people just took such an interest. The gosh darn news media was at the Dental College when we got fitted for mouthpieces as freshmen! They were! And we were freshman, but it didn't matter. People were treated the same, for the most part, more than any other place in the country. Just the fact -with Trev and the Butkus, Will Shields- there was no separation. There was separation on the field talent-wise, but there wasn't anywhere else. We were all treated the same. And I remember people saying, "You know Trev?!" and I'm like, 'Sure I do, he's just a regular guy.' And I remember trying to cry my way out of study table, saying, 'Hey, I'm getting good grades.' And they were like, "No, you have to come to this." Things like that, and that's why I go back and visit those guys and we just talk.

It wasn't easy, but it's so much different than people you talk to from other places. There were some haves and have-nots. I know a lot of people who played at Michigan: there was the Demo Squad, which was the scout team, and then there were the other people. And the Demo Squad hardly ever got to dress, didn't ever. You just didn't have that expectation there: you just went to get the goody bag from the Rose Bowl and stand on the sidelines in front of 100,000 quiet people. In Nebraska? If that would have happened we wouldn't have been very good and the scout teamer would have played. Other players would have run you out of the locker room if you had that kind of attitude. I know a guy it happened to. They just ran you off, they just beat the crap out of you until you relented and said, "Okay, I just quit," you know? On the field they didn't go out of their way to do it, but they just made it known that they weren't going to tolerate laziness. And off the field, in the locker room, they weren't afraid to say, "Hey, you can't just stand around all day. You're not helping." There were a lot of those talks that went on, and that doesn't happen in a lot of places.

Without question, there was a legacy you had to uphold. And at Nebraska it didn't matter who you were, guys would come back. Guys would say something to you. Neil Smith would say something if he came back, it didn't matter who you were or where you were from, what color you were. He'd say something if he didn't think you were holding up your end.

And quite honestly, Bryan Bailey was a guy who was real instrumental to me. Here was a guy who would go out and run 33 miles on his 33rd birthday and then he did a squat workout. And I'm like, 'Why the hell would you do that?' And he would say, "I just wanted to see if I could do it. I rode to Nebraska City and back on my bike," and I'm like, 'Are you stupid? What's wrong with you?' Here was a guy who was down the line in the hierarchy of the strength staff, but was still given a part and had to, was expected to hold up the guys. Even you. You guys were given responsibilities and I know you were held to them. We all were. Jack Stark, there was no place to hide there. Even academically, there was no place to hide. You were given chances, but if you fooled them that was it, it didn't matter who you were. And Doak, there's another guy. And George Sullivan, he gave us the most beautiful wedding present ever. He just blew me away. All the times I got busted for wearing a cap in the training room and got slapped on the neck. And all those times I get back to Nebraska and Doak gives me a hard time about not stopping in the training room when I visit my wife's family, he said, "Hey man, why didn't you stop by?" And I'm like, 'Why would you want to see me stop by,' you know?

Q: Any last insights to share before we go?

MC: Oh, I just… I owe that area a lot. I've changed a lot. Immaturity? There's a lot of people that gave me second chances there. And it's funny, like you said, there's not a day goes by that I don't think of something that happened there. Geez, it's amazing. I'm all so thankful, I could never spend enough time with all the people, enough for all the opportunities they gave me.

And Troy Branch, you've got to talk to him. He's got a great story. I remember going back to Camden for his mother's funeral a couple of years ago and spent about a week there, and

I said, 'I know we've had this conversation before, but how the hell did you ever get out of here?!' I got back home to the wife and I felt like I'd been in a bad dream. That place is unbelievable. And I've been in bad places in Detroit and Chicago and Dallas, and nothing compares to the things I saw in Camden. He stayed in Lincoln, didn't go back. Troy never went home and I never went home, so we ended up living together. We played a lot of pool together, were over at Noonan's house. We actually worked at a bicycle shop together. That was our thing, we rode a lot. I think we rode every stretch of Lincoln.

Q: I used to live over by the Children's Zoo and used to love biking that stretch down Normal Boulevard to my office at Memorial Stadium.

MC: Oh yeah, I remember biking that stretch. We used to live not too far from where you were over on 26th and J for awhile, but then we were at 36th and U. Plus we couldn't afford to pay parking tickets. (laughs)

Q: Anything else?

MC: Oh, I get a lot of questions about Lawrence Phillips. He was the best, man. I remember Coach Tony Samuel saying that. "He's the best, Chief." The best one we've had. He was awesome. I remember when he was a freshman and they wanted to redshirt him and he was, "I'm not gonna redshirt." And I'm like, 'What the hell's wrong with you? Why don't you want to redshirt?' And we had a scrimmage the following day and were going to teach him a lesson. And we didn't!

He was good, he was unreal. And he was a nice guy, but he was also a guy you said "hi" to every day, 'Hey L.P. how's it going? How you doing?' Just because he was a mean SOB, there's no question about it. I supposed if your parents dropped you off at the steps of a boys home when you were 10, that's a whole different story. Not having one parent, rather than even two, that's a little different. He was something else. He was good, I know you know that, but people don't know how good he really was. And he never shied away from anybody in practice, that's for sure. He was tough.

Q: Anything else?

MC: Just the whole staff at Nebraska: a lot of different personalities, very different personalities. It goes back to the staff there at Nebraska like Coach Solich, Coach McBride, laid back Coach Samuel, Coach Young. I mean, there was fire & ice in that crew. If you can't get along with one of 'em you've got a problem. (laughs)

End conversation.

In his book *Finding a Way to Win*, Hall of Fame coach Bill Parcells wrote, "If they don't bite when they're puppies, they usually don't bite." Now a big dog in the Michigan high school coaching ranks, Zeke still radiates the same brand of gumption and verve as always. Can you sense from both his and the previous conversations why it's so enjoyable for me to reconnect with these guys after all these years? I know this is good for a man's soul, because I find myself shaking my head and laughing long after hanging up the telephone.

You might imagine how entertaining it was spending a good two or three minutes in the strength complex chatting with the players between each set of lifts two to four days per week. As a strength coach one always encouraged them while they performed their lifts, always seeking the best, safest display of proper lifting form in order to avoid injury. Most conversations were much like you just read here, and very tight bonds were developed. What a job. Can you believe that I actually got *paid* for it?

Did you notice that there was a semblance of elitism going on in the program? If a situation arose to where the collective 'team' got the feeling that a student/athlete wasn't 'all in' and fully dedicated to the team goals, "they just ran you off, they just beat the crap out of you until you relented and said, "Okay, I just quit." Sounds rough, I know. Maybe even unfair to some. But it, too, was another testing ground, a crucible through which one had to pass to call yourself a Cornhusker Football player. With great privileges came great responsibilities and oftentimes greater trials to endure still.

Zeke also mentioned a great legacy to uphold. To some that may sound a bit hokey and overdramatic, but every single day these boys were constantly reminded that they were merely the most recent version of a long line of Cornhusker squads. Framed & mounted photos, old team records, awards, and paintings of past Husker heroes on the walls served as a link to the past and a subtle hint of a tradition of excellence to maintain. He spoke of 'quiet expectations.' It was as if the Ghosts of Football Past were constantly watching, constantly vigilant –possibly even judgemental to a point- silently cajoling these boys onward and upward in their quest to fulfill their friends' & teammates', their coaches', their University's and the entire state's quest for a perfect season and that elusive national championship. Most every player of the day had not yet been born the last time the Cornhuskers could truly pronounce at season's end, "We're Number 1!" That last happened in early January of 1972, but a plan to change all of that was afoot.

Another parallel that caught my attention was the mention of, "It was just all the time, little nudges." I am beginning to believe Mr. Collins was spot on in his "Good to Great" when spoke of the 'flywheel' metaphor in his book, using a word-picture of this massive, heavy wheel needing constant, gentle nudges over the course of time to finally get the thing turning and functioning, brought to a speed suitable for success, for meaningful and lasting work.

Lastly, Zeke spoke of Lincoln's citizenry and of the state's friendliness. I have conflicted views of that characterization, for I believe there is a marked contrast between the term 'friendly' and the term 'kind.' I believe, as a general rule, that Nebraskans are some of the kindest people you will ever meet. Friendly? I'm not so sure, because many possess a rather private nature, while stereotypically maintaining an inner disposition of friendliness. That being said, if memory serves, this neighborliness seems always eager to burst forth whenever encountering a friend or stranger in need. Then again, maybe I'm parsing words and not giving the populace its due. I'm attempting authenticity here, calling a spade a spade, and suggest that the fans themselves may have played an important role in this story of 60 & 3 greatness. We'll see if that's revealed as we continue on in my great Why and How.

Notable quote #2:
Mark "Zeke" Cisco on the culture: "My first impression was that I'd landed in church, to be honest with you."

It's often said that a picture is worth a thousand words. Take a quick look at the pencil drawing you see on the next page, compliments of former Husker offensive lineman Mike VanCleave. Back now? Quick: what descriptive terms come to mind? Hulking? Powerful? Annihilating & muscular? Dominant, perhaps? How about tenacious, overpowering, violent, sinister, grotesque? Omnipotent even? These terms and more quite aptly describe Milt Tenopir and Dan Young's offensive lines of the day. Read on as we cover my hour spent with Brenden Stai and you'll get an idea why the words written printed above are very fitting…and then maybe you'll come up with a few choice descriptives of your own. Here's the California Kid, a.k.a. Brenden 'Socks Up' Stai…

Notable quote #1:
"I came into the weightroom one day and I pulled my socks all the way up, and I go, "Socks-up Tuesday!" "

Brenden Stai

Scholarship recruit, Offensive Guard, Yorba Linda, California (Anaheim Esperanza) Where are they now? Lincoln, Nebraska, Coach

Question: You always were a pretty hard lifter, weren't you Brenden?

Brenden Stai: Oh yeah, I took a lot of pride in that, for sure. I came from a great high school program, Esperanza. You've probably heard of that there in San Diego, but there in Yorba Linda, California, Orange County, Esperanza High School is well known for its weightlifting program.

Q: Was that a major draw that took you to Nebraska?

BS: I think so, yeah. The Esperanza Aztecs, they built their whole football program around strength and conditioning. And the guy that ran it out there, he later became the head coach. He's an amazing guy who grew up in the same kind of mindset, who grew up with strength condiitong and flexibility and everything. He was a big weightlifter guy, and I remember his kid who we used to mess around with. He's no longer a kid. He recently graduated from West Point. He had that kid doing the clean and jerk when he was 5 yrs. old, so you can never start too young.

Q: Oh, and before I forget, I think it was Zeke Cisco who said I had to pass this on: he said you were the best 300 lb. white man that he's ever seen dance.(laughs)

BS: (laughs) Oh, wow! I just saw his wife not too long ago, a couple of days ago, matter of fact.

Q: I heard you were originally an Arizona State commit, right? And in some way Tom Osborne made a visit and encouraged you to take a visit to Lincoln?

BS: Exactly. You know, George Darlington was the one who recruited me. He just happened to be in the weightroom at Esperanza and was looking at another guy who was one of the top rated defensive tackles in the nation, Keith Vitti, who was my workout buddy, as well. And when George came in to take a look he asked my coach, "Well, who in the heck is this kid next to him?" And my coach said, "As a matter of fact, a lot of schools on the west coast are looking at him. You might want to take some time and look at his film and see what you think." And before you knew it, I was getting letters from Nebraska and asking me to take a visit. At the time I was pretty much everything but signed to

Arizona State. Their offensive line coach there, I absolutely loved. He was always around, he was always making an effort to really win me over, and he did. And it wasn't that hard because a lot of my heart was in that area, my mom's family was from Phoenix. And looking back at that now, thank God I didn't go, because a few things happened a year after I went to Nebraska, and the whole coaching staff was fired. So it was great I stayed away from there.

Now, Tom Osborne, he ended up coming out. It was a cool day, sitting out in one of these -out in California the population has really affected some of the facilities, so they have these what they call 'portables,' like a mobile home, they use as a cloassroom, and you see them everywhere- well, I was out in one of these portables and Coach comes knocking on the door, peeks his head in and says, "Hey, I need Brenden to step outside for a minute." And the teacher was like, "That's okay." So I walk outside and here's Coach Osborne standing there in his red blazer and gray slacks, looking at me kinda with that one eye half-open, the other eye with that squint, you know? And he has his hands crossed and he's just himself. And of course, I knew who he was -I really didn't kind of take in the whole moment- here was this legend who took the time to come to my high school and sit down and watch film with me and ask me to take a visit to Nebraska officially. And I was like, 'Yeah, I'm in.' And I ended up taking a visit out to Nebraska and I ended up recommitting myself.

And it's kind of ironic, because my dad this spring called me and gave me the actual years and hours and days for however long ago it was in 1990 when I committed to Nebraska. Because today is National Signing Day, you know?

Q: How about that. You're right. So Terris Chorney was there for you very first visit, and you said it was pretty cold then?

BS: Yeah, it was.

Q: So can you describe your first fall camp? What stood out to you?

BS: Well, I made the trip across country with my mom and my girlfriend, who's now my wife. I was obviously in love with my girlfriend and there was a lot going on. I remember the day they dropped me off, I stayed a couple days at Coach Darlington's house. He lived out south of town out on Yankee Hill on a big, nice, old acreage. And when they left, I remember feeling this overwhelming feeling of being abandoned.

All of a sudden I didn't know if I was in the wrong place, not knowing anybody, 'Did I make the wrong decision?' And it didn't take long once I transferred from George's house to down at the University to get ready for fall camp. I think it was about two weeks before the varsity squad, and obviously, at this time they had the freshman football squad. I think I stayed in Schramm dorm for camp and ended up transferring to Abel Hall. You had that feeling of being abandoned and being lonely and missing everything, literally. But the coaches, the trainers -I didn't really know a whole lot of players- but the sense of family when I first got there to Nebraska was amazing. Not only that, but outside of that, the people instantly gave me a feeling of, 'Hey, I'm in the right place.' It was a huge turning point in my life.

So here I was, 18 years old, I had direction and knew what I wanted to do -but had to make a commitment to actually going about it on my own, and not a lot of people do that- and not a lot of people understand what goes into that, there's a psychological rollercoaster ride when you do that. There's a the feeling of loneliness and wanting to go back to what you're used to, and I remember thinking about when I made my decision and what I wanted to do: and I wanted to get away. I wanted to experience something completely different than my whole life previous to that, and Nebraska was definitely the road to take. And looking back on it now, it was the best decision I ever made.

Q: Do you recall the first person on the team you befriended?

BS: Yeah, I have good memories. The first was walking into the training room, the south endzone training room where the varsity would get taped, where the varsity locker room was. I didn't know anybody except Jerry Weber and Jack Nickolite and Doak, as far as trainers go. I didn't know anybody, and I look over and here's this guy up on the tables getting his ankles taped, and I hear "Brenden!" And I turned around and look at this guy, and he said "How are you doing?" My first, initial thought was, 'This guy… this guy is gigantic! I can't believe how big he is!' And for whatever reason I just blurted out, 'Hey, are you Mike Petko?' He says, "No, I'm Rob Zatechka. I'm a freshman like you. I'm playing in the All-Star game here at the stadium." I was like, 'What?! Are you kidding me?!' I'm looking at this guy and he's 285 lbs. –and I'm 240 lbs. soaking wet. Wet behind the ears coming in -and I look at Rob and he's got a full-on beard, looks like he's been in the program 4 to 5 years. So that was really my first memory, was meeting Rob.

And then, of course, getting a chance to watch those guys play: Cory Schlesinger played in that game, Terry Conneally played in that game, some other guys, Zach Weigert played in that game. So there was a lot -Calvin Jones played in that game- so I got a good idea what to expect as far as becoming friends goes, and that was great. I just couldn't believe Rob. I remember reading about him in Huskers Illiustrated. They did a feature on me and also a feature on Rob. They did a feature about his academic as well as his athletic prowess, as well.

Q: Did he know your name from the same Huskers Illustrated article?

BS: All Rob had to to do was take one look at it, one time -he probably had a photographic memory- and knew everything about me."You're from Yorba Linda…." He's like giving me all my stats, "You were lineman of the year, you were 246 lbs…" I'm like 'What?!' Little did I know. (laughs) Little did I know.

Q: So '90 was your first fall. Did you redshirt, Brenden?

BS: I did. It was a little bit of a different deal there. Ed Stewart, myself, Connealy, Rob, Zach, who else? Calvin Jones, I think that was it for that class. We all redshirted. Everybody else, except Cory, we played on that freshman team. Obviously, it created a great opportunity for guys to play at an early age, and you got to play the freshman squad of schools like BYU, Air Force, they came in and played us. And that was the last year, I think, Nebraska was the last one to participate in the freshman football program at a Division 1 level. So for me and the guys, we didn't have to play on that team, but still had to practice with them every now and then, and we were put into a position where we were above the 8 ball, because most of those guys playing on the freshman team would pretty much have to redshirt and start over the next year and really have 3 years of trying to compete and start for Nebraska. On one hand we really got great time playing the game right out of high school. And you crave for it. Now, I didn't play really until my junior year, so I didn't start and play for Nebraska until my junior year.

Q: Was that frustrating?

BS: It was. It was for me. I think it was my second year, I had a little bit of a chip on my shoulder when I came out of high school, I thought I was better than I really was. It took a lot of humbling that happened on my part, and I look back on that and I'm very grateful for a lot of people who intervened in my thought process. And there was a lot that had to do with it: I was missing home, I was missing my girlfriend, I was not getting the opportunity to prove myself day in and day out. It was sporadic here and there, struggling with that, overcoming the fact that I had one of the best linemen ever play at Nebraska and probably an NFL Hall of Famer, Will Shields, sitting right in front of me. So it was a long haul that I had to look at.

And I'll never forget Coach Kevin Steele, somebody spread a rumor that I wasn't happy with my situation and I wanted to transfer. And it was during one of our practices -now, we gave everyting we had every day and that's what really made us the team that we were in '94 and carried it on to '95– anyway, one day in practice we were going against the defense and beating the snot out of each other, and Zach and I are on the right side. Coach Steele, Coach Kevin Steele comes up to me in the huddle, grabs me by the facemask right in front of everybody, and basically gives me the riot act, essentially gives me the "I love you. You're wanted. We need you. You're gonna be a great, huge part of what we have going on here. Don't think about leaving," you know? It was one of those things, just a shot of adrenaline, and it really made me take a look in the mirror and say, 'What am I doing?' And I sat back and I looked at what I was and set goals for myself.

And that next spring after Spring Camp and I sat down with Coach Tenopir -where we would go over all of our goals going into fall camp- and he asked me, "What are your goals Brenden, what are you shooting for this summer?" I said, 'Coach, I'm gonna come in here and I want to be the best offensive lineman in the country.' And he said, "What?" And I said, 'I want to be the strongest guy on the team. I want to be the fastest offensive linemen. I want to be the best guard in the country.' The whole time he's looking at me like, "This guy is full of crap." He looks at me and he says, "Well, those are great goals you have there. They're a little lofty, but I like them." And so I did everything I could to get to that level of obviously committing myself not only physically, but mentally in the classroom with my schoolwork, and every time I stepped out on the field it was not only about improving myself, but doing everything I could to improve my teammates in every level.

Q: I remember whenever you'd come into the weightroom you seemed super-intense. There were some days where you wouldn't even laugh or joke, so you really seemed dialed in...

BS: Yeah, and even to this day I don't go there to socialize. I was, 'Hey, I'm gonna get some work done here. Focus in on what you've got to do and get out.' I don't know what year you left, but when I'd leave, the impression I left with everybody was that I was the last guy there...

Q: I remember booting you out of the weightroom!

BS: And there were a lot of guys who weren't very happy with me staying there longer than they wanted me, Boyd Epley being one. And turning the lights out on me, and me yelling at them, "Go away!"

Q: And then you guys would go sneak off to another gym, wouldn't you?

BS: Yeah. Now Paul, there were games, Paul, like Pacific, and after the game we'd be in the weightroom working out. Over at the Rec Center we'd workout. We'd workout at Goodyear, where I do now.

Q: I remember being in a staff meeting and Mike Arthur was, "They can't stay longer than 45 minutes. We don't want them working out any longer." And I'd say, 'They're going over to Goodyear, what good is it going to do kicking them out?'

BS: Oh yeah, anywhere and everywhere we could get our lift in, and that was kind of where we felt the most comfortable. If we didn't get our work in we'd get this guilty conscience. And believe me, there were times -I wasn't stupid when it came to working out- I tried many different workouts, and that was really where Boyd and I kind of butted heads. He had his philosophy and it worked and it was great, but there were some things he and I didn't see eye to eye on, like defensive backs shouldn't be doing the same weight training that offensive linemen should be doing. And over the years we had our discussions about it, and obviously how I felt that it kind of represented what I did out on the field. And everybody has their own way of doing things, and one thing I didn't want to do was step on his toes too much, but it got to the point where he was ready to kick me out of the gym. And it got to the point where Coach Milt Tenopir found out about it and he said to Boyd, "Hey, listen Boyd, if Brenden's out of there, we're all out of there." And it's one of those things Boyd understood, that, "Hey, listen, we're all in this together, and we need to get along, and we have to make sure we're not stepping on anybody's toes here. And if it's working for Brenden, let's let him do it." And I think Boyd kind of had the same feeling with Rob, who did his own thing, and Joel Wilks and Matt Shaw, and there were some other guys who just loved working out. We loved working hard, and I think a lot of what we did was to reset the culture as far as the work ethic and what it took to put your time in the weightroom, out on the field, whether it was winter conditioning, summer conditioning, in practice when it came to the season, where you were giving everything 100%, and that's what we did.

Q: If I recall, did you and Rob put together a special 6-day routine?

BS: Yeah, in the offseason we had some different things we did. What we found later on in our careers, really, in the NFL, was that there's a lot of muscle memory that happens. And you being a strength coach -you know this- but it's about trying to trick your body into thinking that you haven't worked that same body part and making sure you shock it every time. Getting into that mindset that 'every time I come in here I don't just want to maintain, I want to get stronger.' And over the years I figured out a way to do it, and for me it was working one muscle part as hard as I could once a week. Three days later I still had lactic acid in there and it still hurt me.

In the NFL I would still do it. And like squatting, I still do it, and sometimes we'd know when we'd overdo it because we got too tight. And some guys in the NFL would eliminate squats altogether because we were getting too tight in the hips. But a lot of body movement weightlifting as far as lunges and side lunges and jumps and box jumps and all the other things that shock the system, that philosophy that Rob and I had, I think we probably went back and forth between 32 or 33 workouts, but the offseason was basically our experimental time.

Q: And you gusy changed the culture with your ethic, I tell you that…

BS: I have to tell you the truth, Paul, when I first came into Nebraska I was -besides looking at Rob- when I looked around at the team, I wasn't impressed. I didn't see guys that impressed. When I was working out in my high school gym there was a poster on the wall of Nebraska's weightroom. Back then the NCAA would allow you to advertise your university with posters and stuff like that, and so I remember squatting in the squat rack looking up at the Nebraska weightroom and then there was a little bubble on the left side with Boyd with his nice little suit coat and the fake hairdo and all this, and I remember having this vision of what Nebraska Football was all about. And I remember seeing pictures of Danny Noonan and Dave Rimington and some of these guys thinking, 'Man, this is what Nebraska football is all about!' Some of the guys were just dominators, you know?

And I get there, and there were some guys who couldn't even bench their own weight. And it was like, 'Holy cow, what is this all about?' And I tell you this, I remember, collectively, the Pipeline, all the guys would hang out after we'd workout, we'd all get in the locker room and we'd sit around. I remember one time sitting around and it was, "What can we do to change the atmosphere around here? We need to get over the hump." And it really fell on us, once we got the reigns, my junior and senior year, a goal we had was, "We're going all the way, we have to take this team to the next level. How do we do it? We have to change the culture. We have to change the mindset of the players around there. We have to get used to winning. We can't just be satisfied with going to a bowl game, we have to win a bowl game! How do we do that? How do we put that together?" And so there were a lot of things that came together for us, and fortunately we had a lot of success, because we didn't have a lot of injuries. We had some obstacles to overcome; Tommie, my senior year, getting the blood clots and everything, that's another story, but obviously every season every team has its ups and downs. But we didn't have too many valleys. We had a few peaks.

My junior year going into that Florida State game we had a really -I thought we had probably one of the best years at Nebraska that '93 season at that bowl game- and then the next year we had to overcome a ton of adversity, we were down to our 4th string quarterback, go into a volatile environment there in Manhattan and playing Chad May and the offense they had there, and we were really ripe for a beating, and we ended up overcoming. How did we do that? With our defense! Those guys stepped up, and we ran the ball something like 80 times up the middle. That's all we could do, and there's a lot of things that kind of played into that, being fortunate and not having a whole lot of injuries, but keeping those guys together and keeping that core, especially up front. Every game is won up front. It all comes down to that.

And looking at those things we tried to instill, that whole environment in the weightroom and out on the field, one day I said, 'What was it that made those '70's teams great?' And I was thinking about it and thinking about it and thinking about it. And one day I come in and say, I came into the weightroom one day and I pulled my socks all the way up and I go, 'Socks-up Tuesday! Socks-up Tuesday!' Everybody said,"What's that all about?" And I said, 'That's how they wore them in the '70's and that's how they won the national championship.' And I swear to you, Paul, everybody on the team was like, "That's it!" And boom, the next year everybody was wearing their socks up.

And then in college football, it was weird! In college football, everybody went from wearing the low socks to socks up. It was everywhere. It was great. It was great!

Q: And you started it, huh? You brought back 'old school.' And I don't know if you remember, but Bryan Pruitt told me that he left his socks down just because he was little bit of a rebel. (laughs)

BS: (laughs) Oh yeah, totally yeah! And you know, the thing with Bryan, here's a guy that - this is kind of behind the scenes- he's a guy who really made the team what it was. Bryan Pruitt on your team is invaluable, because he's the guy that brings it a thousand miles per hour every day. He's gonna make you better. He's the guy you have to have. Here was a core. Those guys who were the walk-ons, the guys who are fighting to get one snap out there? You know, those are the guys who make the team what it is. John Parrella hit on it the other day. He said, "With those guys, you had to strap it on every day or they'd make you look foolish."

Q: And Bryan ended up volunteering to do kickoffs, too?

BS: Oh, yeah. Brian was a nutball. (laughs) He was one of those kamikaze guys who got on kickoff teams, oh yeah. In all sincerity, you've got to be crazy. Number one, to be on that team… but to *volunteer* for it? It points to what he does now, he's got that 'not quite right in the head' thing! (laughs) He's an adrenaline junkie, that's for sure. To walk into a place not knowing what lies behind that doorway, guns and bullets all…

Q: And where did the Pipeline-thing start? Do you know?

BS: I do. You know the thing about it was that we once again –collectively- all of us sat around and every day we'd talk about stuff, and what we really wanted to do was really put a label on what we were doing up front, across the board for all the offensive linemen. And we were getting so much attention up front because we were putting up some great numbers. And once again, it just kind of fell down to me and someone said, "What do we do?" And actually, Rob and I used to talk about this all the time when we were younger, because we'd always get in that back room in the weightroom and kind of work on our 'guns.' Remember that back room, with the mirrors? We'd sit around going, "Hey, wouldn't it be cool if we had this huge poster, and it would say, 'Pipeline,' and it would have our guns, our pipes?" It was so weird how everything came to fruition, everything we talked about, from the pancakes to the pipeline.

And you know "The Pipeline" really took effect when Colorado got off the plane with pipe-cutters. And we knew exactly what that meant, because they were going to bust the pipe in half, right? Yeah, sure, they came in here and we whooped up on 'em. It was great.

Q: And how did you come up with the 'Pipeline?'

BS: Just the arms, you know, 'the pipes'. One day we just said it would be cool if we were known as the 'Pipeline', and boom, there it is. They had a poster with us on it and there was culverts, they got us around a bunch of culvert pipes for the picture, and I'm not sure if they ran away with the Pipeline thing, it think that was just us. And after the season we had some shirts made. Aaron Graham couldn't do it because he was still eligible to play NCAA-wise, so he couldn't do it, but Zach, Rob, Joel and I made sure it said on the front, 'The Pipeline' and 'When it's on the line' on the back. I still have a couple of those shirts that haven't been taken out of the wrapper.

And what was great was that it got into Sports Illustrated. And I remember talking to reporters back then, it was, "What's that all about?" I said, 'You know, it's more about putting the offensive linemen on the map. You always hear about the running backs and skill position guys, and linebackers, making plays all the time, getting their face in front of the camera. And the only time you heard about offensive linemen was when it was a penalty.' I said, 'It really puts us on the map,' and it really did. What happened was, it shone a little more light on what really makes an offensive team work. If you don't have the unity, the cohesiveness, the attitude and the ability, controlled aggression and smart guys up front that were athletic, you're gonna be a subpar team unless you had all those ingredients, and it starts up front. And the defensive side of the ball, unless you have those defensive linemen slowing those guys coming off the ball for those guys on the second level, what kind of defensive line are they, really? And at least those guys get the stats and notoriety for getting sacks and all that attention, but for linemen on the offense, the only thing you can do is get a pancake. And really, who monitors that, you know?

So we monitored pancakes, how many times can we get guys on their backs. We started that, and when I talk about that Sports Illustrated article it was about putting offensive linemen, period, on the map, and especially the offensive linemen at Nebraska.

Q: And you talk about controlled aggression, where did that come from? Coach Tenopir, Young? Yourselves?

BS: I think the attitude came from us collectively as offensive linemen. We just decided that we were going to be just dominators. It started off with Mike VanCleve, who was a tremendous artist, and he said, "Brenden, can you see something that has the word 'Dominate' and have a picture of two offensive linemen just bending guys over backwards, and their pipes just flaring up, the left and the right?" I still have that picture he drew, and if you a want a copy of that to put in the book I can get a copy for you. And I went up to Coach Tenopir and I said, 'Listen, you've gotta take a look at this picture.' It literally took him no more than 5 seconds to go, "It's going up on the wall!" And he had somebody superimpose that on the wall of the offensive line meeting room. And when Callahan came into power they took it down.

Q: Pretty cool stuff. And you talked about unity. What I'm understanding is that the coaches obviously did their jobs, but you guys were very proactive and took charge of a lot of stuff yourselves.

BS: Absolutely. The one thing we developed was -it really came from a lot of guidance and counseling from Coach Osborne and some other coaches- but it was, "You guys have to take on this as a team." And it's one thing to sit there as a coach and say, "Hey, you've got to understand: if you do this, that you make sure you understand there's consequences for every action, good or bad. And so, we don't want to sit up here and act as the police. If something happens within this team, you have to figure out a way to deal with it. And obviously, if it is that much more serious, then we'll step in." But with the captains that we had and everybody collaborating on what should happen, that just created that Unity Council, which was put in place to create an atmosphere of family, and at the same time, hold anybody accountable for any action that had to be addressed. And what happened, it really stemmed from all the players coming together and figuring out what was keeping us together, but at the same time acted as a deterrent for guys going out and doing their own thing.

Q: Unity, belief, respect?

BS: Absolutely. A lot of that happened in the PR Department, but I think a lot of it had to deal with Jack Stark, the psychologist. Jack, he had a lot to do with helping the guys formulate some sort of -from a psychological aspect- formulating some of the stuff. I wasn't on the board for the Unity Council, those were the Captains. It was always Rob, Zach, Ed Stewart, Terry Connealy, Trev Alberts, those were the guys that really headed it up, and there was an agenda there and everybody had to vote on it."Refuse to Lose", "Unfinished Business", the guys absolutely bought into that. With those words, I should go back and restate, the "Unfinished Business" obviously came from that loss to Florida State, but it was something that was ingrained in us after that game. It was, "Man, if we had just two more plays! One more play! You know, we'd have won that game." We didn't leave it all out on the field there, and we had some unfinished business to do. A lot of it had to do with Coach Osborne's talk after that game and the next summer the 1:16 up on the scoreboard. There was a definite focus there for everybody, and we got right back to where we wanted to be and we finished it.

Q: Do you recall Coach Osborne's talk after that Florida State game?

BS: It's hard to. With those kind of losses you're just kind of ...it was hard. I think back and try to wrestle away a lot of what coaches say after a game, losses and wins. For example, I listened to Coach Bill Cowher give a speech after the AFC Championship in Pittsburgh and

I totally forgot how emotional it was for him, being a young coach and getting to that point where he promised he would take that team. And I totally forgot how Greg Lloyd got up there and started talking about the defense and dropped an F-bomb -it got on TV- so they went right back to the studio and Joe Montana. He mentioned the offensive line, and he mentions my name… but I totally forgot about those talks for whatever reason. I just remember the overall feeing of being so close but still so far away, just having so much to do, you know? But very inspiring. And one thing I do remember at halftime of that '95 championship game where Coach Osborne's speech talks about a few things that are gonna happen here, from here on out, that are gonna decide this game, "We're gonna make a big play. They're gonna make a mistake and we're gonna get a huge turnover." It was amazing how those things, the penalty that happened, there was the turnover which I call the safety, of course the huge play at the end of that game, scoring with Cory and wearing them down. That's one thing he said, "We were gonna wear them down", and of course, all those things happened. It was great. It was almost like he was prophet up there, he just kind of laid it out and it happened.

Q: Recalling that Miami game, you and Joel Wilks did the switch, right? Can you give me some insight as to what was going on in your mind?

BS: Well, Coach Tenopir asked me to stay behind one of those meetings. We were doing bowl preparation. It was actually right after that last game and they gave us about a week off to take our tests, take our finals, let us relax a little bit before we get back into it. And it was after a meeting and he goes, "Listen, Coach Osborne wants to meet with you, and when you're done meeting with him I want you to come back in here." So I went in there and sat down with Coach Osborne and he basically laid it out for me, "They've got a guy, Warren Sapp, he's a huge cog in the middle of their defense. He's a very disruptive player. He's probably the best defensive lineman you've ever faced, will ever face. So what we want to do is kind of focus a lot of the attention on that matchup between you and him. So we want to move you over to the left and Joel over to the right and then create a strategy of plays that will basically take his strength and use it against him." And, of course, what we're talking about -I had to either sink or swim on this, with every pass, whenever we run the ball- I had to dominate and I had to wear him down. I couldn't let him get the best of me. And I said, 'Coach, I'll do anything, anything for this team to get us to that championship. I'll do it.' And, of course, he was very thankful and he said, "It's gonna take a lot of work, a lot of focus on your part." And I went into Coach Tenopir's office and he said, "Well, what do you think?" I said, 'I think we can do it. Let's get after it.'

So we started talking about some plays, you know that quick draw that we ran a couple of times. And if you look at that last touchdown, on that play there was really only two people that blocked anybody, it was me and Aaron Graham. (laughs) If you look at right tackle, Zach Weigert comes down and totally misses his cut, when Joel pulls to the left to trap Warren, and Warren's like 10 yards up the field, so he doesn't have to touch him. Then you've got me: the whole play was, I head-bob Warren and get him to go up the field, and then go straight after the middle linebacker -I think Ray Lewis- on that play. Rob came across and just basically got in the way, it seemed. Basically what happens is the left guard and left tackle would ultimately meet at the linebacker position, but Rob didn't meet anybody, and the next guy over was Matt Shaw, who -really, if you think about Matt, he cut off somebody, which was critical, cut off the legs to penetrate that inside gap there- and then Abdul Muhammad on the outside, he had the best part of what created that touchdown because he sprinted and got in front of this guy and didn't block him, just kind of cut him off, and then Cory scored. So really, when you look at that play, it was kind of designed to utilize our ability to have Cory run the ball on a quick trap/draw play and utilize their strengths against them and it's exactly what we did, scored twice on it. It was definitely a challenge for me.

And the funny thing about it, Joel, when he heard about it, he was pumped up. He was like, "Yes." Once it went public, in the media, it became a war of words with Warren and I. I told him I was going to wear him out and he said he was going to "rip out my larynx" and this and that. You look back at those newspaper articles, it was funnier than heck, and the attention was there. And it was such a smart game plan by Coach Osborne. And Warren, the guy was good. He was probably one of the best defensive tackles to come out of college, maybe besides Cortez Kennedy or a Bryant Young. Those guys are so quick and fast and strong. And of course, Warren had all that together, and I played against him every year in the pros. And every year he gradually got heavier and heavier and heavier and less and less effective, but those early years he was just dominant.

So, it was fun, because once we got back into the swing of things I graduated. It was my graduation ceremony and it was right before we left for down to Miami, and I'd practiced for about a week after we left graduation. And right after graduation I was just overwhelmed all day long, you know: just graduated from college and my Mom is here, it was very, very emotional for me. So we get to practice, and I think I screwed up about 10 plays at the left guard position, and all the coaches were like, "What the heck is going on?!" And I think after maybe a couple of plays, but it seemed like ten plays, and Coach Osborne was like, "Maybe we should have let you have the whole day off, Brenden." (laughs) But from that point on I was very focused and went into that game just completely determined to get after Warren and their whole defense and wear them down.

And looking back on that game and the first play, you know, it's an interesting insight when you talk about offensive lineman; your first series -you more or less see them on film, you mentally prepared yourself for all the plays that you've got, all the defensive looks you could possibly have- but now it's time once you get in that game, you understand the speed of it and you've got to try to convert yourself and conform yourself around the situation. And it takes some getting used to, a couple of plays. And Warren Sapp was one of the better pass rushers, and for an offensive linemen in the NCAA there's a lot on my plate there -not that I lost sleep or anything- but I knew I had to be very focused on my technique. That first play we come out I took a little three-step drop and what I was gonna do was sit on Warren a little wider. One of those moves he did was a rip and a slap at the same time, and I was expecting him to come back inside. So Aaron, our center -no one was helping on that, because Aaron was sliding to the right- it was just Rob and I sliding out taking care of man versus man on the left and so I had to really protect that inside. Well, he did exactly the opposite. The first thing he's gonna do it root-hog and bull-rush me, and not a lot of guys could do that to me. He bull rushes me, pushes me back about 3 or 4 yards. So the plays over, it's a three-step drop, and we completed it. And I go back to the huddle and look at Aaron and he goes, "Gee-eez!" I said, 'Did you just see that?' Warren got up underneath me, and he was so fast and so quick into me and I was like, 'Holy crap!,' and Aaron looked at me and goes, "Oh, my God!" and I go, 'How'd you see that?' And he goes, "Well, they didn't need any help, and I looked over at where you were getting drilled back." And I said, 'That's the last time that's gonna happen, too.' And it sure was.

Warren made some plays that game, that play we designed strictly for him we had to kind of adjust a little bit, because the timing wasn't right for our one back position. The fullback position was great because it was a quick, little trap, but if we ran that draw with Warren, I remember one time he was so quick up the field he was around me before whoever the running back was -maybe it was a shuffle pass- but I remember it being a little draw or something inside, and he got all the way around that super-quick. So when we got to the sideline it was, "Hey, we cannot delay or stall any sort of action in the backfield with this, guys. I am set on the guy, and if he goes inside I'm drilling him inside. And if he goes outside I wanna get him out and go try to run and get somebody else.' And he was around me so fast, the ball hadn't even gotten handed off or shuffled forward.

Q: I think I recall that backfield horse-collar tackle on Lawrence on one of those...

BS: That was the one. That's where he went over by the sideline in front of Coach Osborne and all that stuff. After that it wasn't a piece of cake, but I tell you what, we wore 'em out. And that doesn't mean I wasn't worn out. I remember going up to the room after we won and everybody was so excited down there at Bel Harbor and everybody was jumping up and down. And I remember some sound clips of the game -and Aaron and I were roommates- it was after the game and we were laying there and my whole body is cramping up, I'm so exhausted. And my wife calling up -my girlfriend at the time- she was saying, "Where are you?! We're down here in the lobby! Everybody wants to talk to you, everybody wants to see you!" And I'm like, 'I'll be down in fifteen minutes.' So tired, you know? Not only was I physically tired, but emotionally. It was just a tremendous experience we'd been through, and to just climax at the very end there and win it all.

There was no doubt in my mind if they were going to give it to us. Penn State was kind of on the bubble whether or not they would have a split title, they kind of struggled with the Oregon offense. Going in we were #1 and they were #2, and it's something I'll never forget. I can close my eyes and remember everything. Just the smell and the air of competition. It was just tremendous.

Q: Somebody else just the other day, they remembered the smell of that night...

BS: The smell. That, I remember, it was not only that humidity, but if you remember they had a circus, with elephants out there on the field. There was the smell of elephant poop out on the field, too. It was weird.

Q: (laughs) Did you ever get the chance to talk to Warren Sapp about that game?

BS: All the time. I shouldn't say 'all' the time. You know, when I was playing against him he'd always jab at me here and I'd jab at him there. Funny, it was about 4 years ago and I was sitting outside the L.A. Convention Center while taking my real estate licensing exam right after I retired, and I was sitting at a little Starbucks Coffee stand, and he was actually standing in line. Somebody goes, "Isn't that Warren Sapp?" And I turned around and said, 'No way.' So I get up and go over and started talking to him, and turns out he was there for some adult entertainment convention or something (laughs) giving autographs, and I say 'What!?' And it was about the time Nebraska baseball was in the College World Series the year we were playing Miami, so I basically told him, 'You know, it's Miami versus Nebraska. And you know what's gonna happen?' And he says,"What does that mean?" And I say, 'Well, of course, Nebraska is gonna win,' and he says, "Only if they cheat!" or something like that, and then he says, "Stai, you hold!" I said, 'Hey, did I ever get called holding on you? No! It's only holding if you get called for it.' (laughs)

Q: Hey, I don't know if you're aware of it, but you were paid a huge compliment by Warren Sapp a few months ago on Showtime's NFL show. Did you hear about it?

BS: No, what was it?

Q: Well, there was former Giants quarterback Phil Simms and the crew. It was mid-season and Warren was harping about some guys taking a play off here or there and about getting dominated too easily, and Phil Simms say something to the effect of, "Come on, Warren. You had to have taken a play off now and then." And Warren was like," Nope, I never took a play off or toned it down or gotten dominated or anything like that. I was a force." And Phil Simms was like, "Oh, really?" So the next week's show rolls around and, sure enough, Phil Simms had the production crew get some old game clips out. And one of them might have been when you were playing for Carolina -I don't remember- but one of the clips had him rushing the pass and you just smack him on the side of the head and on the shoulder and you just drove him to the turf. And Warren Sapp says, with a bit of exasperation, "Yeah, but that was *BRENDEN STAI!*"

BS: (laughs) He never beat me once. Well, actually there was one time we were playing Tampa Bay and the guy I was playing next to -it was a revolving door at that right tackle after my third year. It was just so frustrating- but a guy named Jamain Stephens was playing right tackle and he got beat, and it was on a pass play and I was blocking Warren and kind of flushed him out of the pocket… and the next thing I know, he keeps going. The play is about 5 seconds into it and I'm like, 'Where are you going?' And I turn around and our quarterback's right there and he ends up fumbling. Our quarterback gives up the ball and then Warren jumps on the ball, gets the ball. And I'm right there, so it looks like I gave it up or something like that, you know? But I never gave it up. Never gave up a sack to Warren. Going up against a guy like that, that's saying something, because he obviously was a great pass rusher, probably one of the quickest guys I've ever played in my life. He was the fastest thing I'd ever seen. And then you've got some guys like Rob Burnett, a lot of people don't even know who he is, but he played for the Browns and then ended up transferring to the Ravens and won the Super Bowl. There's a guy, I gave up two sacks to that guy in my career. I went against him 5 straight years and gave up two sacks. And you remember how quick and how fast they are. They can make you look foolish.

Q: I'd love to speak to Warren Sapp. Any idea what he'd say about that game?

BS: I think he'd tell you at the end of the game they got worn out, but he'll say they were the better team. He's always going to defend his position, if I know Warren. I think he's got a tremendous amount of respect for me, as well as the offensive line. They had Ray Lewis, Rohan Marley back there, Dwayne Johnson, Kennard Lang, all those guys had the #1 defense that year, and for us guys to go down there on their home field and take control in the fourth quarter when we were maybe getting our butts kicked, while never giving up, and wearing them out and having them on their knees while we're ready to do our next play says a lot. I think he'll speak to that. But you'll never be able to get him to admit they got dominated.

Q: Were you on the field blocking for Byron's last second kick versus Florida State the previous year?

BS: No. What happened was, normally whenever you started at Nebraska you normally weren't in on the field goal protection. For example, when I was coming up through the ranks, the only time I got on the field was for field goals. And it was exciting, obviously, and the games we were blowing guys out we got on the field.

It's interesting you asked this, because when we scored that touchdown to go up, I went off to the sidelines. And Zach and I went over to the sidelines and there at the very end was O.J. Simpson, who's standing there with his NBC microphone, and we both looked at him and go, "What is this!? Is this a fluke!?" Before that game in the papers and on TV and on NBC, he said the only way Nebraska would win would be by fluke. And, if I recall, he had his Bruno Magli's on. (laughs)

Q: Do you keep in touch with Zach at all?

BS: Yeah, I see him every now and then. He's a busy guy here. I think he lives in Omaha and every now and then we have these get-togethers. I see more of Joel Wilks, who lives in Oregon. He lives in Portland, Oregon and he just had a baby boy.

Q: The Fall of '92 when we switched to the 4-3 defense. Do you recall that?

BS: Yes, it was more or less the bubble defense that we ran. It was more or less a borrowing of what Arizona was running, and a lot of people went to that. Oh, absolutely, I recall the switch. It made a huge difference for us, because it reminds me -defenses that run it today, it's an unconventionalnl defense when you look at it, because it can have a resemblance of a 3-4- but what happens is you have a guy who can float around. New England runs it a lot. And what it does, it creates confusion up front for your offensive line, because if you're going against a conventional defense you've got a Mike Linebacker, a Will, a Buck, a Sam, whatever you want to call it. And basically, what you are doing is, you're trying to recognize the strength of the defense, and from that Middle Linebacker you go either left or right depending on the play and the strength of the defense. And what that defense will do is not only give the linebacker the ability to come up and "Green Dog" a little bit or play back and then come late, but also gives the ability to kind of disguise a lot of what you're doing as far as blitz packages and gives someone the ability to put their hand down and walk around a little bit and create confusion up front.

Q: And how long did you see that in practice until they broke it out for the Colorado game?

BS: Oh, I don't know. The thing about it was, when you're talking about some of the bigger games that we played, we would mix different days here and there. If we had extra days we'd mix in a little Colorado here and there. And we saw it for quite some time. And obviously, I didn't play on that side of the ball, but I knew with the type of guys we had - especially the defensive backfield and the linebackers we had, very athletic types- we had guys who could cover a guy coming out of the backfield and then go against the big guys when rushing, trying to penetrate that line. And in one shape or form, Coach McBride would implement a defense that would obviously create a lot of confusion and havoc and then just literally dominate the game. The Blackshirts really came to fruition that '92 season and all the way up until the recent revival.

Q: And let me ask you, do you have a favorite or most memorable play?

BS: Man, let me just start by play. I'm gonna go one step further, let me go with most memorable picture. The picture I remember -and I still have it to this day- Calvin Jones, we were playing, (it might have been the Colorado State Rams) we were playing them at home and I think it was pretty much an inside zone play, but what you see in the picture is: there's five defenders on the ground, maybe 4 defenders on the ground, and there's me and Aaron that are on top of them all, and basically they're just flattened on the ground, and I'm looking up at Calvin. We're in the background and Calvin is literally 25-30 yards down the field. And in the background with me you see Aaron on top of his guy, basically with his hand in his face, bending him backwards, just driving him into the ground, like he'd killed his mother. It was just a great picture.

And some of the moments that I remember, it was just offensive line play. And a lot of people don't know this, but we played Oklahoma State, it was on TV, and one of their linebackers was an All-American and he was chirping in the paper all week long about how he was going to let us have it and this and that. And we were watching film the night before the game at the hotel and Coach Tenopir, he's got film of the Oklahoma State defense up there and he makes reference to this player, and he goes, "We can't let this guy do this to us. You guys up front, Brenden, you make sure he doesn't this and that.." And Aaron looks over at me -and Aaron tells the story better than I do- he looks over at me and says, "What are you thinking?" And he says that I looked at him with the most intense, psychotic look and said, 'I'm gonna knock… him… out!,'right? First play of the game, Paul, first play of the game I come off the ball and I hit this guy so hard upside the head, he goes just like a freaking bean bag, like a sack of potatoes, just goes limp and, boom, just drops. I knocked him out! I couldn't believe I'd knocked him out, you know?! I went back to the huddle and I looked at Aaron and he goes, "We freaking knocked him out!"(laughs) You didn't hear from him the whole game, he was out. I gave him a concussion. And he pretty much vanished from the national scene after that play. Of course, that was Coach Osborne's 200th victory, maybe? I pretty much went in there and smacked him upside the head.

And there were other things. We used to come off the ball and do some crazy stuff. We'd get up underneath guys. And if you understand offensive line play, it's all about leverage. And what you try to do is start off low, and you get high, and a lot of times when I would get into guys -all of us really- we'd do this: we'd grab guys up underneath the shoulder pads and with our free hand we'd take the backside of their leg and flip them over. You just didn't see that, you know? Just killing guys, driving them 10-15 yards down the field and just annihilating them. Those are the type of things you take pride in as an offensive line. We just dominated that way. We set the tone for those guys afterward. That's what I'm most proud of, when we look back on what we did, we set the table for the success for everybody across the board, the whole team. The guys I came in with and graduated with, we all put a lot of effort into trying to establish a different culture as far as a team: Nebraska dominating. Wearing them out and dominating. And every time you walk out and line up on that line and those other guys are just, "Oh no, here they come again." That's the mindset that we wanted, you know? And that's the biggest thing I take away from playing for Nebraska, just creating that atmosphere there.

And every time I watch teams now, I'm very active with the radio show and I see these guys and I wish they could feel that. And it seems to me that it's coming back, and I think Barney Cotton is doing a great job of instilling that tradition of nastiness and dominance. You look back on some other games, of course, one of the games obviously was the National Championship game, there's nothing that can beat that. That was a culmination of 4 1/2 years of hard work, blood, sweat and tears. That all came together and that was something special. The stories go on and on and on, but when you talk about some of my memories and the most wonderful things I took away from it, it was the guys and just the relationships with the guys that you take away was special. It was awesome.

Q: Any favorite practice stories or recollections?

BS: Well, two of the best recollections I can give you are these… I used to love goal line plays. We would have one of our drills -the drill was on the goal line, 1's versus 1's- two shots at getting into the end zone. And Coach Osborne, he'd stand on the sidelines and he'd be the official giving us the touchdown or not. And what was great about those moments was, it was at the end of practice and everybody was fired up. It was just crazy. The defense was fired up, defensive coaches were fired up, you had Coach McBride yelling, spitting and screaming. All the guys on the defensive side of the ball hooting and hollering, trying to get us to jump offsides. All the offensive coaches fired us up, giving us the play, "Get after it!" And just getting two shots to go after the best and get into the end zone, you know? That was great.

And, of course, those goal line situations we would just run in practice, driving down the field in practice, Aaron and I and everybody would look over and we'd say, "National Championship, here we go. Last drive. Here we go. Come on, National Championship." And we'd do that all year long, for two years.

And of course we're in the game, Paul, and we're driving the field. We're driving down the field, here we are, we're getting to ready to win the National Championship. (Before all this happens, in the beginning of the game, I think Aaron steps on my feet 4 or 5 times and he's wearing, I think, inch and a half spikes, ok? I don't know if you've ever had a 300 lb. human being step right on top of your foot, right on top with one of those spikes. It hurts. Literally, I couldn't walk for like a month. I was limping, it hurt so bad -of course, not that night- but I was getting sick of him stepping on my feet, right?) So here we are, we're getting ready, we're driving down the field, we're doing it for the National Championship, we're doing our thing, we're getting close to the red zone, we're getting in there and Aaron looks at me and says, "Let's go! National Championship! Here we go! " And I look at him and I go, "Quit stepping on my feet!" (laughs) It was one of those stories you never forget. As far as all the preparation that we put in, it was something else.

Q: Anybody behind the scenes as far as staff that sticks out to you, who meant something special?

BS: Well, as far as behind the scenes: everybody. You can't leave one person out. Jerry Weber, Doak, all those guys, it was a family atmosphere. There was a cohesiveness and chemistry that was there. And I remember Coach Ron Brown talking about it. Here's a bunch of these coaches that had been there forever and just understood not only Coach Osborne's philosophy, but each other. And you know those final years, where the cylinders, everything was going at 100 miles an hour? Everything was working like a perfectly oiled machine.

That being said, you not only had a family atmosphere with Coach Osborne allowing those coaches to have a family life, but also instilling that family atmosphere with the team. The unity we had, there was a couple guys you've really got to throw some props to behind the scenes that worked with me, each and every day behind the scenes, on the sideline. And to this day -I did a camp out at USC, a Nike camp- and here I was in the USC weightroom and I'm overseeing the Bench Press part of the Combine Camp, and Bryan Bailey comes walking out of the office and he's standing there with Mark Sanchez and Matt Leinert. And he points to me and he says, "This is the guy!" He starts going off about the work ethic and all that stuff, the weightroom, and what we did out on the field."This is the guy..." Bryan? There wasn't one time I couldn't say, 'Bryan, I need you today,' and he was always there for me.

And some of the other guys? Ed Stewart, great leader. A guy that sacrificed a lot trying to convert from a safety to a linebacker, and ended up being one of the better linebackers in the nation. And guys like Terry Connealy, there was a guy who was mild-mannered off the field, just a good gentleman, came from a great family, one of our captains, just great leadership from our captains. Every week a captain would get in front of our team, and he started off as a low rumble in his speech just before we went out on the field, but at the end of that speech, I don't know how he could talk after this, but his face was bright red, purple almost, he was just screaming at the top of his voice, banging into guys, just sweatin' and spittin' and getting everybody riled up and then, BOOM!, we'd hit the field. But Terry, you know, those type of guys who had just a complete and utter passion, for not only football, but Nebraska Football? Those are the guys you want leading your team. And the list goes on and on, but it was a great experience.

And it's weird, you know, your best friend you had as a kid or in high school, you know? You see them twenty years down the road and it's like you just saw 'em yesterday, and I think that's really the best way to capture the friendship and those relationships we had on that team. It's something that you never forget. We did something for the state that really was never done, and of course those guys after us had a chance to do it, but this state went twenty-some odd years after the last National Championship and we brought it back, you know? And it was something else. I remember Zach Weigert and I talking one day about it, he said, "Do you understand if we won the national championship, what this will do for the State of Nebraska, but also for us?" I mean, just leaving a legacy of this team that came in here from '90 to '94, what we did." And it was true. He spoke nothing but truth with that statement. It was an amazing thing, and a lot of things were spurred after that championship season, that whole 'Eye in the Sky' and the tunnel walk, that all started. I remember the first time I heard it, it was on the radio and they were talking about the possibility of us going on a National Championship run, and everything that came together at the end there, it was all just very special.

Q: And you met those goals that Coach Tenopir thought were kind of lofty?

BS: Yeah, yeah, you know I wasn't quite the best, but I had a chance to play next to the best with Zach Weigert winning the Outland Trophy there. The thing I'm prideful of, for playing next to him, was that not only was he a great player, but he made me a great player, and it's infectious. Zach and I were the fourth pair of All-American guard and tackles ever in the NCAA's history. To achieve something like that is pretty cool. You know Zach, when he won that -and this is what epitomizes the type of team that we had- when he won the Outland Trophy the first thing he did was, he paid respect to not only his teammates, but in particular the offensive line. He went right down the line and named all of us. And that's just like the kind of man Coach Osborne was, the young men who came in as kids, he wanted to obviously mature them into great football players and great men. Good stuff!

End conversation.

You may recall Boyd Epley's interview a few pages earlier, especially the place where he mentioned how the freshman offensive linemen of the time reaped the benefits of the team's newfound commitment. Brenden Stai was one of the freshman linemen in attendance that historic day and what he said in this conversation about creating a new order, a new way of thinking, of acting, of foregoing all but complete dedication to the endeavor, speaks volumes about the direction Nebraska Football began aiming. In Boyd's interview I brought up the title of what I find to be an absolutely fascinating book, *Influence: The Psychology of Persuasion* by Robert B Cialdini, Ph.D. In it he writes about innate human longing to be perceived as consistent, and goes on to say this about the power of commitment, "If I can get you to make a commitment (that is, to take a stand, go on record), I will have set the stage for your automatic(..) consistency with that earlier commitment. Once a stand is taken, there is a natural tendency to behave in ways that are stubbornly consistent with that stand." Read that again."Once a stand is taken…" The terms stubborn and consistent exemplify many individuals of that 60 & 3 era.

And take a stand is exactly what Brenden did. Much more than a mere drone going about his business and doing only as he was coached, Brenden played a large part in turning the fortunes of the Nebraska offense's bread & butter -the offensive line- into an unstoppable fighting force. Can you imagine the letdown he felt upon his first few weeks in the Nebraska weight room? Here he was, a high school kid with visions of joining the big boys, lifting alongside the hulking brutes of the Varsity O-line, only to find that it was all mostly in his imagination. Now, this isn't a blanket statement or full-scale indictment of the entire offensive line of the earlier time, but it was a fairly apt generalization: these kids just weren't hard-core weightlifters. (Also, I might add, this fact should lend valuable reverence for Offensive Line Coaches' Milt Tenopir and Dan Young's ability to turn out quality O-line performances despite the lack of physically dominating kids at the time.) But Brenden and his buddies helped to change all of that, and once the '6 weeks of Accountability' of that 1991 Winter Conditioning session hit, the young guns' attitude about moving some weightroom iron around spread like prairie wildfire to the rest of the bunch. Fanned by those earlier flames, the Unity Council was simply a rational next step.

Now, if you were to ask me to place a label on what came out of those brainstorming sessions between Brenden and his linemates, I would call it "The N Factor." Why? Because their focus was not merely on raising their own level of performance, but that of the eNtire organization. (grammatical error mine) They were interested in collectively, more than individually, finding the magic elixir that would propel them to greatness. Brenden mentioned the metaphor of the 'reset button' and reaching back to the legacy of the last national championship teams of the 70's for clues, i.e. Socks-up Tuesday. I loved that part. At a young age they already possessed 'the 10,000 foot vision,' considering and evaluating an issue from an executive point of view, a mature and educated one at that. Some folks call it 'big picture' thinking, and the final result was an artful piece of work.

I will begin to label the facts, findings and distinctions of 'The N Factor' as we go on, because I'm beginning to notice golden nuggets are piling up and feel that doing so will help manage the points gathered along our journey. Thus far The N Factor consists of: commitment, accountability, repetition, reciprocation, sacrifice, family, role, humility, vision, legacy & community support. I think we're off to a good start, anyway.

Notable quote #2:
Brenden Stai on the Pipeline's role, "…we all put a lot of effort into trying to establish a different culture as far as a team: Nebraska dominating. Wearing them out and dominating. And every time you walk out and line up on that line and those other guys are just, "Oh no, here they come again." That's the mindset that we wanted…"

em·i·nence: high station, rank, or repute.

out·li·er: a person or thing that lies outside.

I've chosen to label a few select individuals a term I recently coined: Eminence Outliers. An Eminence Outlier –EO for short- is a person of supremely high competence who appears on the scene from elsewhere and functions primarily out of the public view, but has a markedly & excessively profound impact on the organization in their employ. In other words, these people are desired not only their unique skillsets, but for their secondary intangibles as well. Though functioning most often behind the scenes, to miss their effect is to miss the mark entirely. To wit, I've heard tales of supposed big name coaches who were trumpeted as splash hires in the hopes of leading their new employer to football's Promised Land only to fail miserably and fall short of expectations. A primary reason for many of those failings is an exhorbitant ego mixed with an inability to acquire or retain eminence outliers (and inliers, for that matter) to their staff. Nebraska Football suffered mightily from this very curse in the following years during management/coach turnover, though it was quite fortunate to concurrently possess more than one of these EO's during the 60 & 3 years. A few names have been hinted at in previous conversations, and it was my fortune to catch up with Dave Ellis, our first Nebraska Football Eminence Outlier.

On any particular day of the year you'll find the former Omahan in the offices of a Foxborough, Massachusetts football stadium, an Ann Arbor, Michigan hockey rink, a San Diego, California baseball diamond, an Oklahoma City basketball arena, or any variety of locales (undisclosed due to reasons of National Security). A gregarious and affable personality with penetrating insight into athletic performance nutrition, Dave arrived on the Lincoln campus after a short stay at the University of Wisconsin with former Husker Linebacker and Head Badger Coach Barry Alvarez. Fresh from an historic Rose Bowl appearance and victory after that institution's 31 year bowl drought, you can bet your cheese & broccoli that Dave had a large hand in making that success happen by way of the training table.

Notable quote #1:
"So when you work around coaches that have job stability, sooner or later they get around to the little things, you know. That's sports psychology, nutrition…"

Dave Ellis

Question: So you're now a Colorado-based sports nutritionist serving the world, Dave?

Dave Ellis: Yeah, It's been a leap of faith, but it's gotten to be more of a -how shall we say it?- a very diverse practice. It's been very challenging, a lot of growth. Along with my collegiate exposure, my exposure's been very diverse: NASCAR, NHL, NFL, you name it, NBA, MLB, Olympic. I still have a hell of a college stable. It really caught me off guard; when I left Nebraska I didn't think they would ever pay to have somebody come in on a daily-charged basis like I do. Oklahoma hired me the day I left Nebraska, and it's just kind of kept going from there.

Q: How did they find out that you'd left Nebraska?

DE: Their strength coach Jerry Schmidt was my old roommate at Nebraska. Anyway, Schmitty snagged me right way, and then I just kept picking up colleges. I'm still working for Frank Solich at Ohio U. Anyway, I started the practice in March of '01 and it's really blossomed.

Q: Do you ever hook up with Dr. Jack Stark anymore, with NASCAR?

DE: Yeah, Jack is the guy that initially introduced me to some contacts at Hendrick Motors, and he's since gone on to work with Toyota. It's interesting. I enjoy going to it periodically, it's a 10 month season. Those guys are a bunch of nomads and live out of a bus. It's amazing.

Q: So Dave, your first year returning to Nebraska was the summer of '94, right?

DE: Yeah, I left Barry Alvarez's staff right before the Kickoff Classic against West Virginia. I was still with Wisconsin when we won our first Rose Bowl, the same time Nebraska played Florida State. I was starting to get some contact from Nebraska, they were finally going to be creating a nutrition position. So I came back. There was a committee: Turner Gill was on it, Mike Arthur, Rhonda Revelle the softball coach. They interviewed some people.

George Sullivan had the nutrition responsibilities under his wing for… historically, the trainers always had that. And Boyd got a shot at it in regards to having control of nutrition support services, and that would involve me coming back and handling body composition assessment and tracking things over the long haul, setting some realistic goals for the athletes, monitoring their frame size and growth, figuring out how much weight they could carry, managing the training table, managing the travel feeding, supplementation, just creating a full-fledged support service.

Of course, I was suddenly being pulled into recruiting, too: every sport wanted me to help them recruit. On your day off they still wanted you to come in and help recruit. It was a lot of fun. Those were good years. In total, I think I worked 16 years at Nebraska & 4 at Wisconsin, in the collegiate ranks. So I did my 20 years in the collegiate ranks before going private.

It was just time to step out and get some different exposures. And believe me, they're still stretching me. There isn't a week that goes by that I'm not standing in a Major League dugout or in the pits of NASCAR, the sideline of the Super Bowl or whatever, up in the mountains with our Special Forces. It's just such a diverse mix.

Q: Incredible. You were a freshman at the University of Nebraska in 1982, right?

DE: I went to Omaha Burke and came down to Lincoln in January of 82'. It's when I came to campus as a student. Then I got a job from Boyd. I ought to send you this letter. I actually found a letter I wrote Boyd, kind of begging my way into working for him. It was the summer of '82. He let me on board because I was studying nutrition. He had plenty of strength guys, andf he didn't really have control of nutrition back then. He knew the value of it. Osborne obviously knew the value of it, as far as a few head coaches who saw fueling as one of those percentage benefits that was worth having plugged in.

So when you work around coaches that have job stability, sooner or later they get around to the little things, you know. That's sports psychology, nutrition….some pieces that when a coach is still trying to put together a coaching staff and recruiting the caliber of athletes they want, they are really lost. Then they come around to button things up when they are past that "Am I gonna get fired?"-stage and have some stability, you know? It's interesting, because rarely do you find a guy right out of the gates, who from day one, is worrying about sports psychology and nutrition. We're kind of the more advanced practices, if you want to think of it like that.

Q: Didn't you initially work in some shape or form for the University before you left for Wisconsin?

DE: When I left for Wisconsin I was over working for Mike Arthur and Boyd Epley at Body Enterprises (a private company). I was still coming to campus on a regular basis and doing stuff, whenever they needed help. But it only took a couple of years of that for me to know that that's not what I was gonna want to do. I wanted to work for an athletic department and athletic setting, the strength and conditioning/nutrition side, when Alvarez got his job there.

I had 4 really good years there at Wisconsin and I literally had head strength coaching responsibilities. And they finally gave me nutrition responsibilities on a full-time basis there my last year. I think that's kind of what got Nebraska's attention. They had success and suddenly I was full-time on the nutrition side, so that got them spurred to start taking some actions and getting me back.

It was a no-brainer, going to Wisconsin, which was still in the developmental stages back then. Wisconsin very much resembles Nebraska now, but not back then. And going back to a very highly developed infrastructure with a very secure head coach and coaching staff in football wasn't something I wasn't going to pass up.

Officially, I rejoined Nebraska football after you guys left for the Kickoff Classic in '94. I joined the staff the day or so after the team left for that game, but I had already done the menus for the Kickoff Classic. The classic story is that it was the first time Sully (Head Trainer George Sullivan) had not been in control of the pregame meal. So I put together an entire new pregame meal format that wasn't really supervised (because I was in the middle of moving back to town), and I remember (Steve) Pederson (the Director of Football Operations) calling me from the Meadowlands and saying what a great success the new pregame format had been… but how traumatized Sully was upon going up to it, when he saw all that food was sitting out there. He was afraid everyone was going to overeat and cramp up.(laughs) It wasn't like the old pre-plated 'eat a piece of steak and the broccoli/potato/whatever' they had traditionally offered the players.

Q: Instead of a TV Dinner-type setup, you had more of a buffet?

DE: Yeah, I mean the kids just kind of have to paint a picture of the way they want the diversity of food on their plate. But the selections were all appropriate in nature -and you usually get half of your group- because there's a lot of idiosyncracies that go on on game day with guys and their appetites and their attitudes and the things they like to eat. It's also a matter of not sticking the wrong things out so all the guys are burping it up at game time.

The fact is -long story short- had we lost that game and the guys had went out and cramped, God only knows if I would even be in the business. (laughs) It would have been over! Sully would have snatched the responsiblities back. And I've gotta tell you, I'm a big fan of Sully, because back on my first go around with the Athletic Department Sully was one of those guys that invested in me. He got me trained in body composition assessment, he introduced me to the American College of Sports Medicine meetings, some regional meetings. So Sully and Boyd, together, both saw something they wanted to invest in, and they did.

But, you know, change comes really slow. Programs having success? A lot of them validate *not* making changes based on the fact that they've had success: "Well, we won back then, and we ate this way, so why are we gonna change?" That second go-around after I came back from Wisconsin we made a lot of innovations in the way we fed them during two-a-days. Not just feeding traditional breakfast, lunch and dinner (knowing the kids were absolutely not going to have the appetite after that second practice in the heat), and maybe we needed to think about sending them to meetings after supplementing them with some appropriate foods and then bringing them back a couple hours later and then feeding them a hot meal. It was just one of those deals where we made a lot of changes. Within the first year and a half to two years coming back they just let me have free run of it, to be honest with you, and to have to take the helm on all these issues: supplementation, feeding, body composition assessment, all these different roles.

We had a very established school where we won the National Championship the first year, so it was kind of one of those fairytale deals. So change -along with success- is why you're hearing things from those guys (you're talking to). It was the commingling of the two, where Tom got over the hump and won his first National Championship in a very hostile environment in Miami -an extraordinarily hostile environment- almost unthinkable to go in there and jerk one out of their teeth on their turf in that cesspool. Miami was about as hostile a crowd as you'll ever be around, really. I've run into some beauties along the way, but it's right up there. That was huge. And then for that team, that staff and those athletes to go on the kind of run that went on there where we won 3 National Championships in 4 years? To have that kind of percentage of winning was just extraordinary. To this day those are great, great memories. The early, formative years before I went to Wisconsin -great growth years all along the way- but until you really get that responsibility, people have the confidence in you and give you the responsibility? I was really fortunate along the way.

Q: When you did return to Nebraska were there any differences between this newer crop of athletes and the Nebraska players of old? Talent levels?

DE: Well, they got some skill kids in there. The days of corners and safeties having marginal speed were kind of over. Tom had kind of brought in a caliber of athlete that could run; that could run with any skilled team in the country.

I think he learned a tough lesson when he lost to Schnellenberger at Miami. He had tough kids and we could match up in some spots on the field -where people covered a little less space on the line- but we had a tough time matching up in some skill spots. It's not like we had a bunch of slowpokes; we had Mike Rozier back then, Irving Fryar, Turner Gill. But in the end, we didn't have probably what we needed at wide receiver, safety and defensive backs in particular. They were great kids, don't get me wrong, but they just weren't the kind of kids you'd routinely find around the state of Florida, you know? I thought Tom and his staff had learned some valuable lessons on what they needed to strengthen and take care of from a personnel standpoint.

And Tom's introduction of me to the team was, "Hey, we're bringing Dave back. He used to work for us. He's a guy that will roll up his sleeves and will get down in the trenches and work for you. He's gonna figure out how to make a difference and how to teach you guys the value of nutrition and food," you know? That's my forte, applied sports nutrition. I'm not a clinician sitting in the office -not a 'bring me sick kids, shake a rubber porkchop-educator,' I'm a 'roll up your sleeves, let's impact the quality of the food supply, let's get the athletes trained to know how to use it on the days we're training and the days we're not training' kind of guy. That's the attitude I come in with, still today.

What I do is go in and take the food in play –the food you've got- and create a system so they understand how to use the fuel. A lot of people eat and it's just based on an impulse, alright? They're hungry, and they go out and solve the hunger and they do it as cheap as they can and it's not healthy and it's a bit of a disaster. Training tables are a commitment to having a superior food supply, staying open later, and creating some type of a system so the athletes can truly understand how to 'paint the picture' on their plate the way it should be painted. Literally everything I did at Nebraska, I still get paid to do today….because so many people are still not caught up to what we were doing back then. It's crazy! Fifteen years later -what we were doing for our athletes?- I'm still getting paid to go implement with Super Bowl champions, World Series champions in Major League Baseball, and it's the first time they're hearing it! The first time they've done anything. And the whole time I'm just kind of giggling to myself thinking, 'Geez, I guess we were kind of a little bit ahead of the curve.' But it was Tom's commitment to nutrition that we were ahead of the curve, because of his own health issues that he'd dealt with.

And he knew he could push the troops harder. I think anybody who's ever had a brigade of warriors in any kind of battle -with the right rest and the right fuel you can march a little further and harder. Tom got it. Tom got it a long time ago, as did Boyd and Mike Arthur and the strength and conditioning coaches. They got it."I guess we don't recover from our workouts very fast when our kids aren't fed and fueled. And we have only so many weeks to work out, and it seems if we recover faster we can kind of out-work the competition." It was a great environment because there wasn't much that you learned in your collegiate curriculum of studies that we weren't already living out. It was, 'you turn around and everything that you ever learned in any physiology, and biology, and nutrition or exercise class, you were already living it.' We were already doing it in day-to-day practice. It was kind of like, "Oh, that makes sense. We see that all the time." It was an extraordinarily valuable but taxing experience working full-time for Boyd. And as you know too, Paul, it was all done while turning around and simultaneously going to school.

Q: I remember pushing the envelope and falling asleep in the books at night. So you were doing both, too?

DE: Yeah, I did my undergraduate work and graduate work at Nebraska, and at all phases I was working for the Athletic Department in some capacity. And as you know, you went to work when Boyd needed you to work and school came second. So it took you a little longer to get through it all, through school.

But my point is that the paradigms that you were in, those types of settings, were very concrete, because you were applying them. Obviously, it's a great education model because you're not just learning by rote, grinding on information. So it's not just in one ear and out the other. Until you get through the test of burning the candle at both ends… it might take longer, but the applied settings really and truly helped with understanding what you were learning.

Q: I recall sometimes wanting to correct some of my professors because it seemed they were teaching some pretty archaic stuff. (laughs) But some of those 70-80 hour weeks paid off in the learning department, I agree with you. Upon taking the reins at Nebraska, were there any differences in team philosophy, unity, mindset, or attitude that stuck out to you when you came back in mid-'94?

DE: I think Jack Stark had gotten involved when I came back and entered the scene at Nebraska with the Unity Council. I don't think I knew Jack before I left, but I got to know him and we became fast friends upon my re-arrival at Nebraska. He was very well-connected with the kids and I knew he was having an impact and he was wired to the kids, and they talked. He had their attention, so Jack and I have done a lot together over the years. We don't talk too much anymore since I moved to Colorado.

Jack had done a good job of bringing the Unity Council into existence, and you know, what you learned there is this: when there is an element of self-governance with the athletes managing themselves, setting some rules for the team, doling out punishment for those who step over the line, quite often they're harder on themselves than the coaches would have been for the same infractions. So there is a lot of value to modeling by the upperclassmen who not only are leaders in the locker room and on the field, but off the field, also. It was really good for leadership development all around. And what Jack was doing with these kids, at the time when I came back, there were just some absolute warriors, the kind of leaders you run into once in a lifetime. The Zach Weigerts: Zach was the kind of guy who could get it done on the field and march up and down the sidelines when our backs were against the wall and get everybody to play over their head and play tougher than they could have ever played and mustered up on their own.

So when you see athletes pulling that kind of performance and digging down, trying to get the hard stuff out of their peers, and then you see them governing themselves to some degree with the Unity Council, it was just wonderful to see. And there were just legions of leaders that came through: Jared Tomich, Mike Brown, the Ralph Brown's, you could go on and on and on. The Peter brothers, these guys were just tougher than nails. And pain, discomfort, hot, cold? It didn't matter, they giggled at it all, laughing in the face of it all. On the road? It didn't matter. These guys were the kind of warriors that are not so easy to find. It's a tough deal nowadays to identify kids like that, who can back it up on and off the field, you know? They're not ever going to be selfish, not going to 'check out' on you, they're not going to back down, and have so much pride in what they do that they're gonna contribute no matter how adverse the circumstances. There was such a special group of people. Tom brought skill in, governance and unity issues, and self management that was great.

And Tom, some of the best speeches he gave in that locker room that I was privy to, he could literally look the kids in the eye -like before his first national championship victory in that hot hell-hole of a locker room in the old Orange Bowl, where there was like 'no air', they were pumping air in there with fans, everybody was sweating buckets, jammed in there like sardines- when your head coach looks at you and says, "There's gonna be a time when momentum is just gonna shift. One minute they're gonna have it, then we're gonna have it. Don't worry about it. It's gonna come right back to you. And the reason it's going to come right back to you is because you are better prepared. You guys have outworked these guys. I can promise you they've never ever tried working as hard as you have on and off the field." And the kids could literally look at each other, and they'd say, "Yeah, he's right!" And when things go wrong, you're not worried."No matter how adverse this gets, we're gonna battle through and we're gonna be the champion in the end." And it had teeth. And it really meant something. Tom finally had everything in place: how we trained and how we fueled and how we had managed ourselves on and off the field with our leadership elements. And for a long time he was 'the guy that couldn't win the big one.' It was very consistent, but he didn't have the formula to win the big ones early on. Those were good years, Paul. Those were excellent years.

Q: 60 & 3, Dave. No one's touched that in modern day college football...

DE: One of the strongest eras ever. Those were teams that ran the tables and won with style points, literally. And it comes up in every discussion about the best team in the history of college football. I feel very fortunate to have been given those responsibilities and be around during those years, and have an extraordinarily soft spot in my heart for the people who gave me those opportunities, the mentors in my life who had a positive influence there. And the relationships with those athletes and coaches? It was very special.

It was a tough day when we moved away in 2001. I think it was July 2001. Then when we moved out here in 2003 to Colorado. It was very, very hard to not work for that athletic department and still live in Lincoln. It was something that I cared for deeply, but to look at it in the newspaper and TV and radio every minute of every day was very hard, because I kind of knew the handwriting on the wall with regards to what was going down there for Frank. He didn't deserve it and it was tough to watch.

Q: So you left before Frank was let go?

DE: I left before Frank. I worked for him for a few years, from the time he took the helm to the end of his campaign in the 2001 season.

Q: What led you to leave after 2001?

DE: You know, Darin Erstad, in particular, came back for a game and said, "Hey, I'd love to have you work with me on my nutrition issues." He was with the Anaheim Angels at the time and I couldn't do it, just completely booked with my responsibilities at Nebraska, doing some clinical work with the hospitals around town, getting my R.D. at the time. I had never gotten my R.D. so I still had to get that done. And I was just blown away when he told me how much he was willing to pay… and it was half my salary. And I was completely flabbergasted. Here I am, a state employee putting in 12-14 hour workdays, six, seven days a week, for geez….

When I left, I was probably on top of the sports nutrition industry, say 50 grand a year. So here a guy offers me 25 grand to do his nutrition. And I'm just doing the math, right? And going, 'Geez, I could probably see my family more, maybe make more, won't stretch myself so thin…' And, quite honestly, I was seeing some bad things in regard to the commitment that was going to keep football on top at Nebraska, as far as priorities in the athletic department. Had Tom been the athletic director I'm sure there would have been a more harmonious transition to Frank, an evolution of things at Nebraska to where the dip they went through never would have happened. But there was time there where priorities were not straight, and when Tom was there Tom was suffering through some of that, too, his last couple of years. So it was awkward. I was watching a good thing start to unravel a little bit, a lot of it was out of the control of what traditionally had been the football staff's control.

Q: As far as priorities?

DE: Well, it's one thing to build the skyboxes, but in the end, you know, it was things that directly impact the ability for football to practice appropriately in the cold months. Maybe things that Tom would have liked to evolve, that Frank would have liked to evolve, they were then being reprioritized to fund a banking track out at the Devaney Center. I mean, who knows, football was still paying for everything but football wasn't getting much of a say as far as those revenues, had they been able to make some of those calls…

Q: Sounds like the typical American taxpayer (laughs)…

DE: Yeah! A lot of what we're all experiencing right now. I think a good partnership of - what I've experienced in athletics- is that an A.D. isn't an autonomous figure over football or the revenue sports. They're partners where they say, "Look, if you don't succeed and I don't succeed we're both gonna be out of here." Those are the really good dynamics versus the 'mystery manager' over the coach, and the coach's wishes are lost in other priorities or misappropriated priorities.

It's no secret that Tom and Bill Byrne didn't see eye to eye on the priorities that were impacting football. When Tom left, I don't think Frank had as much political capital to work with as Tom, obviously. It was a real sad day when Tom Osborne was not handed the reigns as the A.D. when the opportunity came first pass. I'm glad he's back right now, because I'm sure there's nobody cared more about that state than Tom Osborne.

Q: If you were to identify the greatest team need when you first got there in 1994, what sticks out in your mind?

DE: There was a food supply but the kids didn't know how to use it. So we partitioned food into three steps: 1) food that keeps you from getting sick, 2) foods that we use for energy, and 3) food that help us resolve muscle soreness. We took the foods and we partitioned the three steps so the athletes could then be educated on how to get something from each of those three steps.

Q: What was it, again?

DE: It was the antioxidants. The first thing the kids come in and see is the fresh produce, whether fresh fruits and fresh vegetables or other great antioxidants like nuts and seeds and olives. We had all those types of foods, and the key was very simple: get some color on your plate. It's the biggest weakness of a student/athlete's diet. A lot of them grew up eating meat and starches and they didn't understand the short-term immune benefits to being committed to those antioxidants in the long term, to disease prevention benefits, that just continued to grow and grow and grow. As far as the peer review research, these concepts are sound.

But when it was all said and done, we made them pick their fresh produce, tried to get away from being just a bunch of meat-and-potato eaters and really sold that into the kids as to why that is important, strengthened the variety there. And of course, there were always carbs around. Carbs are cheap: bread, pasta, rice, potatoes, sugars from beverages, and even some desserts for the athletes. But that wasn't new, there was plenty of that going on when I got there.

And of course, protein sources, one thing I did was make sure there were more lean options for the kids so on off days when they were injured or sick they were less prone to stumble into a medium- to high-fat source of protein when they could've or should've been using a leaner source.

So there was a commitment immediately to evolving our food supply, merchandising it using these three steps, and then changing the way we were feeding incidental to competition on the road, during two-a-days. And, of course, also coming up with a cost effective supplement program where we literally made our own version of Gatorade, our own version of GatorPro, a post workout recovery shake. We brought in more sophisticated programs for connective tissue remodeling, brought in some work- and weight gain-advantages with creatine for individuals who were candidates, who wanted to gain weight in the offseason by taking on more reps in the weightroom where we were focused on adding muscle, you name it. We had implemented a lot of big things there, but none bigger than our commitment to feeding these athletes at home and on the road. And when we couldn't use solid foodstuff we'd be using a liquid-soluble form of calories that was well-timed, incidental to training and recovery purposes.

And all that together was quite new. There was just a lot going on. And when the coaches started to say, "Look, we've thrown every rep at 'em in practice that we've ever thrown and more, and the kids are standing there looking at us like, "What next?"" (laughs) Those were the kind of feedback I was getting from Milt Tenopir or whomever. They were throwing everything they've got at these kids in practice and these kids are taking it and looking for more, not even on their knees. I got that feedback by the end of the first season. So it was a deal where it didn't take long for our coaches to come around, because they liked to win.

And if Nebraska was anything, it was a 'rep factory' where our walk-on program allowed our Ones and Twos to go live on the Threes and Fours, minimize the chances the Ones and Twos were going to hurt each other because they were beating up on the Threes and Fours. And we out-repped the country on the football field like no other. So really, all Boyd and you guys had to do was get the guys bigger and stronger, and then the football coaches finished them off with a very sport-specific conditioning program called reps… and a lot of them.

Q: High intensity reps, too…

DE: Yeah. Nobody could touch us with regards to our practice reps in the week because of our ability to rep on Threes and Fours. So we didn't have to be horribly sophisticated with our speed and agility and conditioning activities, because Osborne had the ability to get a lot of that done for us. We just had to have them in the ballpark. If we had them 80% of the way, believe me, the coaches were going to finish them off the second they put pads on these guys. And hey, Tom is a gentleman and a scholar and a leader, but man, and I will tell you, nobody took a pound of flesh harder in practice than that staff. They weren't afraid to rep these kids.

Q: Do you have a favorite team from those years that stands out more than another?

DE: I think winning in Miami the first year was a real accomplishment, it really was. The Fiesta Bowl against Florida was a fashionable win like no other, an ass-kicking. And it was against my old roommate Schmitty, who was working as the strength coach for Spurrier at the time, and it goes down as one of the biggest polish-up jobs that I've ever been involved in, to where we went undefeated and won with the kind of style-points where everybody was going, "Holy smokes!" So those two stick out to me the most, but the kids were special on all three of those teams. And there was an element of luck, as you saw, in every one of those seasons.

But I think the first one –'94- was not as skilled a group of kids as the last two national championships: they won a little bit more on guts and toughness. But man, they were all great groups. What I recognize about Midwest kids is that there's nothing that scares them. Wherever those kids came from -in the entire country of ours- they learned how to practice in the heat, they learned how to practice in the cold, they worked themselves from that old, crappy locker room in that north stadium into the south stadium and, believe me, they didn't want to go back there. The whole thing worked, it really did. To this day I still counsel teams that design the new palaces and to-die-for locker rooms. I tell them to have some old, crappy locker room, somewhere that every once in awhile you can send somebody back to if they get a little selfish and forget what it takes to contribute to their team. That there wouldn't be a bad place for everybody to start at, because those were some humbling months and years for some of those guys down in that old locker room, with a grumpy guy like Walt (Johnson) washing your jock once a week. (laughs) That model -and it wasn't by design- it was just that they couldn't fit them all into that one place. But it was actually a hell of a model.

And there are a lot of problems now with selfish kids who are all style and all flash, that progress from one level to the next based on their skills, but they're really not tough, they're really not big-time competitors, they really don't know what to do with their backs against the wall. They succeeded because they had exemplary skills, but they didn't have the backbone with it. And that's become a huge problem in athletics now. And those type of teams that get assembled with all that flash, when their back's against the wall they can't look each other in the eye with credibility and say, "Hey, we've had worse. Not a problem. Let's go! We've dealt with worse than this. We're prepared for this. No problem." They're instead saying, "Well, I guess this is my last game in college. I don't want to get hurt. My agent's waiting for me in a limo outside. I'm going pro. Let's see if I can just fake an injury and get out of this game." That's the kind of crap that's going on now. None of that crap went on when we were dealing with those three national championships. Every one of those kids was committed to being a contributor, succeeding and finishing, and doing something extraordinary for their team and their families and the alumni of that school so that they would remember.

Q: And if you took a play off in practice somebody would beat the living crap out of you, right? (laughs)

DE: There was somebody that would challenge you out on the field, and when that locker room door shut there was someone man enough to make sure they'd get the message out there. They got that message in the locker room. And I knew when that stopped happening, because Nebraska made a change for the worse. Remember that one game where Eric Crouch almost got his head torn off at that game against Kansas State?

Q: I've got that picture in my office.

DE: It might have been that K-State game where (Equipment Manager) Glenn Abbot packed like only 20 freaking capes. It was ridiculous. Here we are in a sleet storm and we have just enough capes to cover the 11 starters on offense and the 11 starters on defense. And it's freezing. It's literally raining sleet, and we're standing there ill-equipped to cope with this as a team. It was a bad day: the officials aren't calling anything, everybody was in on it, you know? (It was one of those classic K-State deals, having somebody rifling through the garbage cans at the hotel, had somebody rifling through the bags in our locker rooms, everybody in that whole town was in on that deal. They were gonna get us that trip. The reason I know? Mike Stoops. It was because Mike Stoops was on that team, so I got the lowdown on it later when he was at Oklahoma with his brother.) And the bottom line is, I'm standing on the sidelines and we're trying to get a cape for the starters who came off that field hot and sweaty so they could kind of stay warm without going back out there and pulling up lame on us or get sick. And I found myself in a battle to get capes away from guys who were not gonna play that day but were on the roadtrip and who didn't care enough about their own teammates to give that cape up. And I'd never experienced that from the day I arrived at Nebraska, had never experienced selfishness before, because on game day everybody in that locker room and on that sideline was dedicated to doing whatever it took to get a win. Now, as trivial as that sounds, I knew right there on the spot, 'This is not good. I've never seen this. I've never seen somebody not sacrifice and contribute to this team's whole potential to win a game because they were too selfish, because they wanted something more than considering the needs of the starters.' It was just weird, just like an iron anvil hitting you on the head, it wasn't good.

I know the number one job of being a head coach in athletics is to spot selfishness, break it down before it infected anybody else, because this was truly the cancer and the nemesis and the start of the unraveling of the fabric that I really thought characterized Nebraska, okay?

They had each other's backs all those years. We had the kids who were getting the rings, going to the bowl games and getting things, going right to the good locker room. And guess what, they didn't have any clue what it really took to go out there and have all that success, who just wanted all the benefits and had never learned along the way what the 'sacrifice' piece was all about, what the 'paying your dues' piece was all about, having to humble yourselves to anything. And I think we still had the north locker room at that time, but it was just something along the way that some kids were slipping through some cracks, they were being cow-towed to. You think about Charlie McBride; It was probably not a kid Charlie McBride ever brought in, no matter how highly recruited they were, how big a stud they were, that Charlie didn't make them earn his respect and work their way up through the trenches. That's why those guys played so hard for Charlie. You couldn't understand a word he was saying at halftime when his teeth were coming out and he was spitting bubbles, but I promise you, every guy in that locker room would have run through a wall for that guy, because by the time you were a starter for him you had earned it. We were missing some of that, and that might have been my last year, that Kansas State game. Do your homework on that. I think that might have been the last year. That might have been when I knew, where I said, 'It ain't good.'

Q: The ship's going down. Jump off?

DE: It wasn't so much 'the ships going down and jump off', so much. It was, 'Okay, things are gonna be harder to succeed here based on the dynamic between the administration and football and the kind of kids that were coming up through the ranks, the selfishness.' I could tell we had seen some better days, and knowing what was waiting for me out there, I was intrigued to test the waters, you know?

Q: Do you have a favorite kid who blossomed right in front of your eyes?

DE: Grant Wistrom was one of the case studies that I always showed recruits. Certainly any kind of rush end/outside linebacker recruit, I'd show 'em a 212 lb. to 265 lb. metamorphosis, a combination of maturity and training adaptations that occurred. And these parents and young athletes came in wanting to know how their bodies might change over the course of their 4 to 5 year exposure. And the reason I liked Grant's data along with many, many other great documents & body composition histories was because of what kind of warrior he was. He was just a kid whose motor ran no matter how healthy or how sick he was; you couldn't tell the difference. So Grant will go down as one of my favorites. He was no less a 'baller' than Mike Brown or the Peter brothers, or Zach Weigert, or X, or Y, or Z -and I know the purpose of your book, you're always looking for the favorite thing or interesting story or episode- but I guess in the end, it would be a disservice to say that Grant was typical of the kind of leader that we had, that made that program a success. I got to work with Grant during his pro years so I had some follow-up with Grant after I left Nebraska -on behalf of his agent when I was asked to work with him- and worked with the teams he was on. And he was just as big a factor on the next level. And that's why I bring him up here, because Grant was a force not just in college. He was kind of a light Defensive End/Outside Linebacker guy at the pro level, but he was just as big a force.

Now, *those* were men. This is a different gig. These aren't just a bunch of big-hearted kids with wet noses, these are the best of the best. These are men who are in their prime who could break just about every college kid in half, you know? And to go have that kind of impact at the next level? Watch Zach Weigert, Mike Brown play as long as they did at the next level, it was easy to see they were special kids, they were difference makers on every team they were on. They were the same kind of leaders in the pro ranks as they were in college. They were all extraordinary kids, making it easy to go put in a 12-14 hour day when you're working with those kind of kids, to make sacrifices, you know that they're sacrificing and you're right there with them. Really easy to put in a 12-14 hour day when Tom Osborne was getting there to the Stadium before you and then leaving there after you. We were really all just trying to serve the caliber of people that were there, that Tom had recruited, that staff and himself. These guys were... it wasn't a put up or shut up deal, it was 'put up because you didn't want to let them down.' A 'You came to work every day and you did what you could because you just didn't want to let them down'-kind of a deal. And we were all bleeding for that program.

So anyway, it was all good stuff. It's really hard to find that kind of heart in the pro ranks. It's a very different deal: you have players with agents in their ear, contempt between players & coaches, and coaches & management, it's just this circle of distrust and, you know, "What's in it for me?" And, "I'm gonna make my money now before I get hurt"-kind of deal. Everybody is kind of for themselves on these things. I was with the New England Patriots on their last Super Bowl championship season and hired their sports dietitian for them, who's there now full-time. So I was with them, and through that whole season on the sidelines for the games I was 'The Cramp Guy.' And, oh yeah, do you remember I started that Cramp Program? Do you remember that?

Q: No, tell me about it...

DE: Well, when I was at Nebraska I had a game day role beyond feeding, which was an additional hydrating factor on the sidelines. The focus was on interventions that minimized conditions of cramping, so I did a lot of homework on what was really going on in a muscle that would cause it to cramp. There was something going on that was more than just dehydration and sodium loss. There are many ways to cramp, and one that we typically see in football is very regional. It's going on in a muscle bundle that's overworked. It's certainly hot, acidic, the ph is very low, tremendous free radical production, compromised antioxidants, the fluid status in that tissue may also be compromised. It's a little hard to say, the whole story on exercise related muscle cramping is yet to be pieced out. Anecdotally, we learned that introducing some very water soluble buffers in a bottle for defensive guys stuck out there on the field when the offense was struggling -to keep them on the field even when they start to grab and catch a cramp, stretching and icing that hot muscle and then literally force feeding water laden with various buffers orally- we could keep that kid on the field. And that was my role, and it went beyond doing their feeding. So, in addition to the feeding and such, I was 'Game Day Cramp Guy.'

Q: I do recall some guys on a Monday or Tuesday, saying "Man, every time I came off the field Dave was right there in my face with water!"(laughs)

DE: (laughs) Right. It was a force feeding, because when athletes are unhappy and something goes wrong they quit drinking. So it's my job to furnish them no matter how good or bad things were on the field, to stay on pace and proactively get ahead of the high-rep, emotional leaders who are more prone to cramp, especially early in the season when environmental conditions affect us, and also on fields where there is a sloppy field and more destabilization and fatigue going on there. So cramping is something that I studied a great deal when the game day intervention role was introduced at Nebraska, and it's something I still use today in the pro ranks.

Hey, if I can keep a Rodney Harrison on the field in a Super Bowl while Donovan McNabb's barfing and everybody's cramping on the other sideline, that's a three point game, you know? That's a big deal. So it was good to be able to go to the pro ranks where you have some credibility, that they listen to you. In the pro ranks they're almost scared to have somebody stand in front of their team, because if you go in there and you can't hold the kid's attention with some credibility, it makes whoever brought them in to look like a dope, whether it's management, coaching staff, whomever. Then they start with, "What next? What kind of junk are you gonna bring in next and waste my time?"

Q: Voodoo? Witch Doctor?

DE: Exactly. Right. In the pro ranks you survive on credibility. Messaging has to be on-point. And if you can help a guy stay in the league longer, lining his pocket, he'll listen to you, believe me. And when you can go in front of a crowd and not lose a team and make the coaching staff and management look good, you're on your way. College sports has a lot of heart, okay? That's hard to find in the pro ranks. But I tell you, on that Super Bowl team there were 'Grant Wistroms' on both sides of the ball that I thought made the diference. It was a neat year. And it was the year we moved to Colorado and they asked me to move out there and work for them full-time, and I couldn't do it. Literally, I'd just finished moving the family to Colorado. We finished that season and I just ended up getting somebody hired full-time for them to doing a great job for them. That's fun stuff. It's great to have been a part of it and see elements in the pro ranks that resemble what was going on in our heyday at Nebraska.

And how do I say this? There's no 'chance happening.' This is why teams succeed: You always have guys who take control in that locker room, and then have a presence on the field or the court that eliminates the most selfish, self-centered, 'what's-in-it-for-me' guys, and makes them champions. It was no different with the Pats, and you can tell from one championship team to the next, those elements are there. I can understand why Tom succeeded.

Q: Did anyone on those pro teams or latter college clients try to pick your brain on other things relating to those Nebraska teams?

DE: They all respect Tom and his staff's achievements. Yet, you learn pretty quickly that you can't name-drop 'Nebraska' all the time. It's been the experiences that I've had since going private, into the pro ranks, that have allowed me to diversify my experiences. Yeah, I still talk about Nebraska all the time, but it's more intermittent when it's appropriate, because now I have so many other experiences to draw upon, too.

Funny, I was just watching some video clips and seeing some pictures tonight from my years when we were at Nebraska and we'd go to bowl games and have the big Christmas meal, and one of the players would dress up as Santa and my kids are sitting on his knee. Well, one of my kids needed some pictures for his high school graduation, so when I was going through them I was finding all kinds of Nebraska–days stuff. We spent a lot of holidays in the Fiesta Bowl and the Orange Bowl. A lot of good memories of Christmas in Miami. But Pederson and Callahan and those guys cut back. That was tough. It really was.

Q: Do you have a favorite sideline moment?

DE: A lot of good ones, man. But I'll tell you kind of a funny one: we were at Kansas -and this was when Frank was the head coach- and the mascot, the Jayhawk's marching around behind our sideline. I think they had a track around the field there. Well, all of a sudden the coaches' headsets went out. The Jayhawk *unplugged* them! He was kind of standing by the sideline in front of the student section to get them going, you know? And Frank came smoking around to the source of the headsets and the crime and see what was going on, and literally tracked down what happened. I just knew this Jayhawk was up to something because he was standing right there as I was dishing out the fluids and stuff. He was banging on stuff, being a jerk, and I wanted to kill him. It was just one of those funny moments where we're on the road and almost got beat at Kansas and pulled it out of our rear-ends, but the mascot had almost been our undoing in regards to our ability to communicate.

That's the kind of chaos you get on the sidelines. People throwing stuff at you, like at Missouri when they threw corncobs at you. It was surreal, literally thousands of corncobs hurling at us. That was the kick-in-the-air Wiggins-Davison deal.

Q: Corncobs?!

DE: They threw corncobs at us. All of a sudden the student trainers that are on loan to you from the hosting school when you are on the road, after they scored I saw them literally running... *running* away from the sideline. And as I saw them running away I look up and here come the corncobs. It was a premeditated deal. The beautiful thing was, not only did we tie that game in a crazy fashion and go on, and then Scott Frost runs the two minute drill like Dan Marino and goes in there, and we went in. And their fans, they're standing on the edges of the field, the fans just bull-rushed the field. So after all those corncobs we ended up going in there and pulling one out of the 'jaws of death' and then to go on and win the championship.

It was that kind of crazy stuff that you experienced on the sidelines with unruly fans. Going into Oklahoma one time, with Frank as the head coach when we lost down there -I think Eric Crouch's junior year- we got trapped on the field. The cops had us surrounded because the fans were trying to get to us. They were pepper-spraying people. It was bedlam. We got off the field with a police escort, fans were taking swipes at us. It's just every one of those big games on that sideline level, with all those achievements going on with the kids overcoming adversity, coaches overcoming adversity, a win or even a tough loss, you've got fans to deal with, you've got TV people to deal with, you have all these distractions, so many things that go on.

It all comes with experience, Paul. So, like these wily old veterans that stay in sports forever, they kind of see it all and have a remedy for all the B.S., they learned the hard way what to do, what not to do, and get through all the B.S. I'm sure I could come up with more stuff if you gave me enough time.

Q: I'm used to hearing about the snowballs and iceballs and beer bottles from the drunks at Colorado, but never corncobs at Missouri...

DE: Colorado: drunks standing there, you're tying your shoes and they're right there standing there cussing you out with a bottle in their hands, a security guy looking right at them. Colorado? We stole so many games away from them. I know why they hate us, no doubt about it. You know, I'm trying to think of a good one at the pro level. The Super Bowl, Eugene -what was his name?- one of our safeties breaks his freakin' arm at the Super Bowl, Rodney Harrison is a middle linebacker back there playing safety. You know, a big-time warrior -should have been the MVP of that whole game- and he starts to cramp in the 4th quarter."We can't lose this guy!" He comes off the field, I start force-feeding him the buffering stuff to keep him on the field while Philly and Donovan McNabb is freakin' barfing and puking and cramping on their sideline, and we win that game by a frog hair. And I can guarantee you, how we handled ourselves leading up to that game? How we watched the food supply we had in the locker room to accomodate the crazy schedule that comes with showing up so early for a game because of the traffic and the festivities? We had a better plan, and I know; I walked to the Philly locker and saw what they did and what they didn't have. It's great when you have a guy like Belichick look you in the eye and say, "You made a difference." So that's cool. It's fun to go and make a difference, and that's what I get paid to do, make a difference. And if you don't make a difference you won't be around very long.

Q: Any final thoughts on those championship years? Anything behind the scenes you thought made a difference?

DE: Well, you know, Steve Pederson, I'll give him some props. I know he didn't go out on a great note with the fans of Nebraska. They would have probably preferred to see Tom as the A.D. on the first go around, but Steve was really strong at taking care of off-the-field football business as a Football Operations guy back in his day, and he and Boyd were juggernauts when it came to recruiting. So if the coaches could just tell them who to get in there for a visit, they would make sure from the time that visit started until the time it ended that it was a really well-oiled machine and the kid got some exposure and the kid would really remember it after all of those visits, "Man, Nebraska really had their act together."

And time and time again, nutrition was the differentiating factor. The fact that we even had a system, a training table, even had a supplement program, that we even tried body composition assessment, that we even knew what frame assessment was in predicting weight gain, all these things were differentiating factors. So our off-field organization, with Steve and Boyd as far as the recruiting piece, was great. And the innovation Jack Stark brought to the table was great. Tom once said, "Nutrition could make a 2, 3, even 4% difference in the highest levels of sport. Even a ½ % will make a difference." We were just part of a pretty well-oiled machine.

Q: You mentioned 'frame assessment.' I remember you getting into that. What does that entail, for the average fan's curiosity?

DE: It deals with lot of measurements of skeletal structure beyond height that have big impacts on somebody's individual capacity to carry body mass in the form of muscle. For example, a Chris Dishman -not the tallest cat in the world- but he had the trunk of somebody who is 7'2", you know? Short legs, but this mass of humanity and this very long trunk. If someone has a long trunk relative to their height they carry more weight, so 'wide shoulders, deep chest, wide hips, deep pelvis,' they have a very robust frame, like you find on the big Czechs, Polacks, and Dutch–types you find there in the upper-Midwest.

I used to measure athletes all over the country, now -literally- so it's kind of interesting. Starting in the Dakotas and all the way into upstate New York there are some huge human beings. There are some big Clydesdales and they are… they're getting bigger. It's not uncommon to run into the 350-400 pounders now who are 24-25% body fat or less. That's the typical body fat of a lineman who can move. In my lifetime kids have gotten bigger, and a way to determine who can carry more weight for their height is based on trunk length and the more robust characteristics of their frame. It's something I almost published for a thesis, actually, but I ended up not doing it because so many teams pay me to come in and do that. It may be the only thing I do for some teams, monitor body composition and frame. It's a differentiating factor for my private practice and it's totally proprietary, I don't give the formula away.

Bo brought me back in to come and measure frames up for him, it's the only thing I've been back to Nebraska to do since Bo got the job. I got to know Bo when he was at Oklahoma, actually. And so that helped their staff, who didn't know that group of athletes, to be able to look at them and say, "Defensive end or defensive linemen? Tight end or guard?" Help them know what's going on…

Q: So you're helping find the correct placement on the field for these guys as far as position & body type?

DE: I do that a lot now. I turn around and tell a team when they've got a player who can't get any bigger, who's really stacked for their frame or who has room for additional mass, I can think of them playing in a couple different spots. I've got a formula depending on what your needs are: you can keep them light and mobile or could accrue more mass and play in a smaller space where more body mass is required. So yeah, I do a lot of helping any sport figure out what is appropriate on an individual basis in sorting out what spot they play in that sport.

You've got all kinds of little fullback types and noseguard types and sawed-off guards and center-types that carry a ton of weight for guys of a very short stature. So it's a big part of my practice. It's what brings me back in for these teams. Major League Baseball and NBA? A lot of young kids, these cats aren't done growing, so we can see even when the vertical growth slows, Paul. A late-bloomer may not be done growing until his sophomore or junior year of college, but once they are done growing vertically they still stretch out: their shoulders get wider, their chest gets deeper, their hip and pelvis gets wider 'til their mid- to late-20's. So we're monitoring frames to see when they quiet down, when the vertical piece is over, when the dimensional changes are over, that's who they are. Then their frames stay quiet… and then they start shrinking! At about age 35 they start *losing* bone mass. You know, bone is just like muscle, frames actually start getting smaller. It's in a constant state of flux. It's just a little harder to see the changes because they happen in smaller increments.

Q: You're a pioneer, Dave. You are the very first human being I ever saw wearing Rollerbades. In what, '87? You used to rollerblade around the old track around the football field when the band was practicing at about 6 in the morning.

DE: (laughs) Yeah, that's going way back! Until the bread truck almost took me out one day! Seriously, I hit a few funny spots around that field. It wasn't the best place to do that. Rollerblades, I might have had one of the first pairs of those. I remember a cop pulling me over in Lincoln once just so he could see what I was doing. I was rollerblading from my house out on about 48th Street down to the University at the crack of dawn and this guy was like, "Buddy, I don't know what you're doing, but you need to get out of the street. What the hell have you got on your feet?" Good old Lincoln, Nebraska. (laughs) But I tell you what, Tom's and Charlie's were big sets of shoes to stand in, and there's not a dollar value you can put on leadership that is time-tested. And those coaches were comfortable in their own skin and they had nothing to prove. They could go out there and emit a totally different kind of persona than a person who's trying to prove that they can do the job.

But in the end, I do stay in touch with Tom. We do stay in touch. It's mostly me calling him. But I've always tried to communicate with him over the years because he's a big enough man to stand in there and talk about things to a football team, "Why it's important to love the guy playing next to you", and he can come off in a very meaningful and credible fashion. I was in every one of his team meetings his last year when I was there. I tried to make every one the whole time I worked there. I was in every one of them. I didn't know, I wasn't sure…'What if this is Tom's last year? I'm gonna make every one I can make.' And it was truly his best year of messaging to the athletes that I had ever seen.

Q: In what regard?

DE: You know, just in that he always put thought into what he was gonna say. But I think he went out of his way that last year to try to message to them in a level that maybe any other year he could have said, "Nah, we can make it through this year without a lecture on why it's important to love your fellow teammate." Love.. you don't hear a lot of coaches lecturing about that.'Man Love', you know? That's what I'm saying. That was just one of the principle-laden lectures where the kids in the room, maybe they didn't have any clue of the message they were hearing. They showed up like any kid running from class to class, kind of getting ready for football practice. They had no idea the caliber of messaging that was coming from Tom, messaging that most coaches would never attempt. So that's my kind of respect for Tom. I'm the kind of guy who defends him over Lawrence Phillips. I say, 'Tom is the kind of guy who keeps Lawrence close for Lawrence's benefit, not the program's benefit. He cares whether the kid is gonna go back to the streets or come back and potentially become a citizen.' Of course, he got burned on that one, but in the end I know he did it for the right reasons, not the way the media tried to portray it. That's the kind of guy he is.

He obviously had some juice in him when he got done coaching or he wouldn't have become a Congressman. My point is: he's a leader. He can do anything he wants to be a leader in. My respect for him? I can't really measure. Like the Lute Olson's of the world. I worked for Lute at Arizona. Lute and Tom, in my estimation, are the same kind of cats. Comfortable in their own skin, confident, there's nothing they haven't experienced or gone through, and were just as concerned about the development of their athletes as good citizens and potential leaders off the field as they were about the wins on the court or on the field. There are a very select group of people out there, and Tom is in a very elite class, so I just stay in touch with him out of respect for the man.

Q: Well Buck…. I don't know if anybody calls you 'Buck' anymore…

DE: Yeah, that name really stuck, I tell you. Dave Kennedy gave me that name. I showed up to work one time in an old flatbed International truck that I had. I must have been wearing some junky boots -I must have been working in my yard or something- and he says, "You look like Buck of the Wilderness." I looked like I'd just come from some hayseed farm. Kennedy still calls me Buck. Guy's from that era, that staff, still call me that. The guys I still keep in touch with from those days are the strength coaches from those days. Kennedy's at A&M, Schmitty's at Oklahoma. I run into Tony Samuel and Gene Huey now and then at the NFL Combine in Indianapolis, Frank Solich, I used to keep track of Charlie in Arizona. I don't even know if I have his number anymore, though. You've *got to* talk to Charlie.

And I tell you, Matt Turman, you remember when Tommie and Brook were down? Guess who was out there running that offense down there at Kansas State?

Q: I wish I could have seen that one, but I was helping some Nutritionist's wife move the family to a different house in Lincoln that day while he was down in Manhattan, Kansas. (laughs)

DE: (laughs) Well, I saw a few of 'em, and I tell you something. Termie? We were three and out, three and out, three and out, and it was that defense that won that first national championship for us. There were a lot of hard-headed, tough kids on offense and they held their end up at the end, too. There were a lot of games where the offense was a little disabled that year, but there were some badasses on the defense. I tell you what, the Peter brothers? If you went back to Viking days and one of the longboats pulled up on shore and they came out with swords and the freaking horn-heads, it would have been the two Peter brothers off first. They were like warriors that I've never met. And I've meet some badasses. These were two of the baddest dudes I've ever met. They were, along with Wistrom, the real deal.

Q: Do you think Jersey made them that way or what?

DE: Maybe, yeah. Well, when Alvarez turned his program around, he went to Chicago. There's some badasses from Chicago, some kids didn't mind going out in bad weather. Certainly they'd been in a lot of tussles growing up in life, in tough schools, their backs to the wall and being in a bar fight was just a weekly deal for these guys. They were just tough kids. Pain? No big deal. Broken finger? Tape it, no big deal. Big, bloody, fat lip? No big deal. Warriors, Paulie. Warriors….

End conversation.

Well, if you at all doubted me earlier, are you now a believer? Maybe you thought that whole 'Eminence Outlier' stuff at the beginning was a bunch of new-agey management nomenclature and high-minded, ivory tower-like hogwash, but a person would be hard pressed to walk away from any encounter with Dave Ellis and not have something to place in your pocket for at least one extra victory per year. He mentioned Coach Osborne's reference to the 2, 3, or 4% difference proper nutrition and game-time hydration management could make in a season and couldn't have been more correct.

Look at his later Super Bowl experience and the difference his one defender/client made in securing a victory in the ultimate game. Let's be honest, network television isn't too keen on showing players puking on the sideline while trying to sell you potato chips and soft drinks during the commercial breaks, so you'd likely have had no idea what really happens down there on the sidelines without some input from a man who was there, who lived it. And he's got the rings to show for it, too.

In a word, Dave was invaluable. Plus, he got along fantastically with the student/athletes. And in case you haven't put two and two together, the season Dave showed up was the season Nebraska earned its first national championship of that era, stated as only Dave could: "..and (Tom) won his first National Championship in a very hostile environment in Miami, an extraordinarily hostile environment, almost unthinkable to go in there and jerk one out of their teeth on their turf in that cesspool. About as hostile a crowd as you'll ever be around."

In author Jim Collins' book a portion was dedicated the role technology played in those stellar companies' rise, which, from his perspective didn't really amount to much. On this point I would differ, because Dave and the whole organization were working with the oldest technology out there: the human body. And through better strength training, better nutrition and better recovery methods, Nebraska Football took the old school technology of the human body and had them all humming like Porsches on the Autobahn with the RPM needle tickling the red.

I'll mention two other things from the vast multitude of directions one could go with the info garnered from this interview, and they would be his mention of selfishness -or lack thereof- on those teams, as well as the drive and purpose for which the whole organization strove for. There is a term called 'success disease' and it's been known to infect even the best of organizations, resulting in less than best efforts, a decrease in motivation, and a few extra taps on the snooze button instead of 'up-&-at 'em' energy to start the training day. (You may have even seen a small outbreak in early 1996 versus Arizona State, but that bug was quickly driven out of the ranks by that loss.) Dave has work alongside the best of the best in the professional ranks in recent years, and I know he takes profound pride in being around those athletes from the 60 & 3 years. This pride is not only due to the victory tallies, mind you, but for the team's toughness and indomitable spirit. There were some warriors out there, and they were the terror of their foes."Warriors, Paulie. Warriors….," as Buck stated. Match up a group of warriors with a few Eminence Outliers and you've got yourself one hell of a force to be reckoned with.

Notable quote #2:
Dave Ellis on team culture: "There's no 'chance happening.' This is why teams succeed: You always have guys who take control in that locker room, and then have a presence on the field or the court that eliminates the most selfish, self-centered, 'what's-in-it-for-me' guys, and makes them champions."

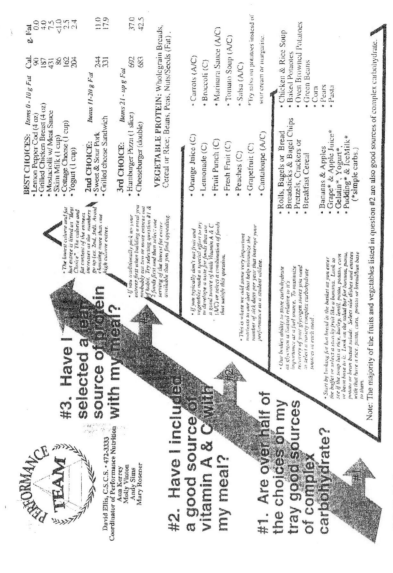

PERFORMANCE TEAM

David Ellis, C.S.C.S. - 472-3333
Coordinator of Performance Nutrition
Ann Kerrey
Molly Vinton
Andy Sims
Mary Rosener

BEST CHOICES: *Items 0 - 10 g Fat*

	Cal.	g. Fat
Lemon Pepper Cod (4 oz)	90	0.0
Grilled Chicken Breast (4 oz)	187	4.0
Mostaciolli w/ Meat Sauce	431	7.5
Skim Milk (1 cup)	86	<1.0
Cottage Cheese (1 cup)	162	2.5
Yogurt (1 cup)	204	2.4

2nd CHOICE: *Items 11-20 g Fat*

	Cal.	g. Fat
Sweet & Sour Pork	244	11.0
Grilled cheese Sandwich	331	17.9

3rd CHOICE: *Items 21 - up g Fat*

	Cal.	g. Fat
Hamburger Pizza (1 slice)	692	37.0
Cheeseburger (double)	683	42.5

VEGETABLE PROTEIN: Wholegrain Breads, Cereal or Rice; Beans, Peas, Nuts/Seeds (Fat).

- Orange Juice (C)
- Lemonade (C)
- Fruit Punch (C)
- Fresh Fruit (C)
- Peaches (C)
- Grapefruit (C)
- Cantaloupe (A/C)

- Carrots (A/C)
- Broccoli (C)
- Marinara Sauce (A/C)
- Tomato Soup (A/C)
- Salsa (A/C)

*Try salsa on potatoes instead of sour cream or margarine.

- Rolls, Bagels or Bread
- Breadsticks & Bagel Chips
- Pretzels, Crackers or Breakfast Cereal

- Chicken & Rice Soup
- Baked Potatoes
- Oven Browned Potatoes
- Green Beans
- Corn
- Pears
- Pasta

- Bananas & Apples
- Grape* & Apple Juice*
- Gelatin*, Yogurt*
- Pudding* & IceMilk*
(*simple carbs.)

#3. Have I selected a lean source of protein with my meal?

The lowest calorie and fat but entree is listed as "Best Choice". The calorie and fat content of the entrees increases as the numbers go up (ex. 2nd, 3rd). Avoid choosing more than one high calorie entree.

If you traditionally pick up two entrees first when building a meal you probably eat two or more entrees out of habit. Try selecting question #1 & 2 foods first and then select one serving of the lowest fat entree available than you find appealing.

#2. Have I included a good source of vitamin A & C with my meal?

If you typically don't eat fruits and vegetables make a special effort to try to develop a taste for foods that are a good source of build Vitamin A & C (A/C) or select a combination of foods that satisfy this question.

This is where we add some very important nutrients to our diet that help minimize the number of sick days per year that interrupt your performance as a student athlete.

#1. Are over half of the choices on my tray good sources of complex carbohydrate?

Our bodies ability to store carbohydrate as energy is listed relative to it's importance as a fuel source. To maximize recovery of your glycogen stores you need to select a twenty complex carbohydrate sources in each meal.

Start by looking for hot bread as you enter the buffet or select a starchy fruit like a banana. Look to see if the soup has a rice, barley, lentil, pasta, potato, corn or bean base to it. Look on the salad bar for bananas, pasta, protein or bean based salads. Select side dishes and entrees with that have a rice, pasta, corn, potato or bread/bun base to them.

Note: The majority of the fruits and vegetables listed in question #2 are also good sources of complex carbohydrate.

ASK YOURSELF THREE QUESTIONS WHEN BUILDING YOUR MEAL

No great thing is created suddenly, any more than a bunch of grapes or a fig...
I answer you that there must be time. Let it first blossom, then bear fruit, then ripen.

Epictetus, circa A.D. 60

Born in Fremont, Nebraska in 1903, Harold E. Edgerton studied to become an electrical engineer and later invented the stroboscopic (strobe) light. Only a curiosity to some, the strobe has been used to give the illusion of slow motion action, catching a series of movements as singular moments-in-time. Zach Weigert, for one moment in time in 1994, was considered the best lineman in all of college football.

Playing on the strobe theme, its most notable common day application is its use on aircraft wings to act as anti-collision devices. Think of the U.S. Navy's precision aviation team the Blue Angels, and you get the idea of what kind of oneness of mind and interplay among team members it took the Nebraska Offensive Line to turn the X's & O's into touchdowns rather than crashing & burning for constant three and outs. Let's hear from Red Husker group leader Zach Weigert, call sign: 'The Slug', on his impressions of that era...

Notable quote #1:
"Everything was a competition with us. Everything there. There was always a competition there to see who could do things the best."

Zach Weigert

Scholarship recruit, Offensive Tackle, Fremont, Nebraska (Bergan)
Where are they now? Omaha, Nebraska, Entrepreneur

Question: Hey Zach, I was talking to Dave Ellis the other day about leadership and he happened to bring your name up.

Zach Weigert: Wow, that was nice of him to do that.

Q: Now, I know you followed your brother Eric to Nebraska. Did that connection help you?

ZW: Oh yeah, we lived together in college, and obviously I had a chance to meet Coach Tenopir and Coach Young and Coach Osborne a few times before I'd gotten to campus there. I met all those guys before I even got down there, so I think Nebraska had a huge advantage of me wanting to go there rather than somewhere else.

Q: Were you really getting pushed by a lot of other schools to leave the state?

ZW: You know, it wasn't for football, because my senior year in football I got mono, so I only played five football games. So I had a ton of universities that were watching me play basketball, because I was a better basketball player in high school than I was a football player. So once basketball season started I wasn't getting much recruiting calls for football, but then they all started calling me to play basketball.

Q: Incredible. Because of your older brother Eric's influence, did you feel like you had a leg up on some other guys who were just coming onto the scene?

ZW: Well, just being close to home and knowing a lot of the guys who were already offensive linemen on the team, as far as relationships. I knew a lot of people who were already there, but I don't think anything can really prepare you to go from a Class C school to the University of Nebraska and playing Division 1 ball, physically, but it just helped to see how some of the other guys you already knew were playing.

Q: Sure. And do you recall anything about your first day on campus, strapping them on? Anything stand out to you as far as surprising you?

ZW: The thing that stood out to me the most was that I was playing better than I thought I would be able to at that level. Because you come from a small school in Nebraska and then you watch Nebraska play on TV growing up and you think, 'I got a scholarship and now I have to get so much stronger and bigger' and all that. And at the time they still had freshman football, so a week into fall camp they decide not to play Brenden Stai and Rob Zatechka and myself in freshman football, but to redshirt us instead. So right there you could see they thought, "Hey, these guys can play already. In a year they could be ready to play." Before that you were usually on the freshman team and then redshirted your second year and then played.

Q: What year was your freshman year?

ZW: That was 1990.

Q: So your experience that year was where we ended on a bit of a sour note and finished with that loss to Georgia Tech in the Citrus Bowl. Is there anything from that year that stands out to you compared to your national championship senior year?

ZW: I just think that you went from having leadership positions on the team —and obviously we were fortunate to have some classes who had a lot of talent and a lot of those guys developed that talent when they were there- but I think you went from having a lot of the leadership from the skill position guys, the running backs and quarterbacks, the linebackers and DB's, but my junior and senior year and even a couple of years after that - we had skill players- but the leadership came from the offensive line and the defensive line. Not that we were in the press the most or talked about the most, but when it came time in the game we could rely on the offensive and defensive line to shut the other team down and do what it takes to win. We were physical up front and that's what made us leaders of our team. I think if you ask any coach, that's where they'd want the leaders as far as positions.

Q: I can't remember who it was told me recently, but they said that after the two point loss to Florida State a bunch of you guys got together and made a pact that you'd never ever let the outcome of a game be that close again, that you'd never leave it up to a kicker's round foot hitting a round football to determine the difference between a win and a loss. Do you remember that?

ZW: Yeah, it was right after the game. (laughs) Guys were depressed, and later that night we were all hanging out and saying that it should never come down to a field goal, that we want to be the ones on the field controlling our destiny and not on somebody kicking a ball.

Q: Can you bring me back to that conversation? Who was there? Where did it take place?

ZW: You know, I think Trev Alberts was part of that conversation, him being a senior, and Kevin Raemakers was around. And those guys were a year older than us —and you felt terrible for them, because we totally out-played Florida State in that game, and everyone who watched it knows that they deserved to win the national championship their last game of their senior year- I think we were sitting round the Sheraton Bell Harbour, our hotel there in Miami. We were sitting around and going over the plays and we said, "You know what, next year we're working our way back here and were gonna be undefeated and we're not going to leave it up to some field goal kicker. We want to be on the field with a lead at the end of the game running the clock out." It was a mix of guys like Terry Connealy and Christian Peter -but you just kind of got that feeling looking at those guys who should have won the national championship and felt sorry for those guys- and it was taken away from them on a field goal. And it shouldn't even have come down to that. To see them lose? We didn't want our senior year to end like that.

Q: Bryan Pruitt said he was in on that last second kick by Byron and that beforehand the Florida State players were cursing at Coach Osborne and hurling f-bombs at him to get off the field and all. If I recall, you really took umbrage to that. Do you remember that scene?

ZW: Yeah, I was actually talking to Coach Osborne about that the other day. (laughs) For me, being a kid from Nebraska and always looking at Osborne as a kid and kind of idolizing him —and my grandfather was actually one of Coach Osborne's coaches at Hasting College…

Q: Really?

ZW: Yeah, so I know how good of a person he is. Not just as a football coach, but just a good person. And the fact that we're on the field and it's a high pressure situation, everybody wants to win, and I'm standing next to Coach Osborne and he's telling the refs, "The ball should be here and there's this much time left on the clock." And of course, he's right. You can go back and watch the film. He spotted the ball correctly and the time on the clock was correct. Well, all the Florida State players had run onto the field thinking the game was over, but we called a timeout so it was all legitimate. Well, a few of their players started f-bombing Coach Osborne and calling him names and stuff, and I totally forgot about the football game when I heard them saying this stuff -and I'm glad I didn't get thrown out of the game. Lesser things have gotten guys thrown out of football games before -but just the fact that he's like a father figure to you when you're playing for him? So them saying something is like somebody saying those things to my mother, you know? (laughs)

Q: Exactly.

ZW: And I pretty much told them what I thought about it. And then, of course, Coach is mad at me for saying that stuff back at them. Of course, I didn't always listen so well.

Q: Well, obviously, we know your senior year was a year to remember in '94, but what other contribution would you say you brought to the teams those years?

ZW: Boy, contributions other than comedy relief? (laughs) You know, I guess I really enjoyed playing there. I've told people, 'If they would've paid my rent and gave me as much food and beer that I wanted I would have played there until I couldn't play anymore.' I really enjoyed being there playing. You know, one of the best and worst days at Nebraska is your senior year there at Nebraska. And I think when I played there -and it wasn't just me, but a lot of guys, most of the guys in my class- but everything was a competition with us. Everything there. There was always a competition there to see who could do things the best.

Q: Were there any rewards for winning these competitions? Any punishments for not doing so?

ZW: It was just pride. I mean, you could have done a running drill for those that lost, but by being the first guy then you had bragging rights all the time. And then, when you have guys with talent there's egos that are involved. And I think what made us different was that guys did it just because we loved playing the game. I mean, we used to get kicked out of the weight room: "You did enough, you got all your stuff done. Get out of the weight room."

Q: You guys would just go to another gym then, wouldn't you?

ZW: Oh yeah, we'd just go to another place. It didn't matter. It was just the competition, and everyone who played there truly loved the school and loved the team, and that wouldn't change for anything. And it's hard to find that: where everyone on the team is on the same page and can be that happy.

Q: I'm sure the pros was a different kind of experience.

ZW: You know, it took me two or three years of playing pro football to come to grips with, 'Hey, you know, the coaches really don't care about me here.' It was a weird feeling to come from Nebraska. And I'd get back to Nebraska and call up Coach Tenopir and say, 'Let's go to the recruiting banquet.' So we go to the recruiting banquet and then we get together and go on fishing trips. There's the money thing when you talk about pro football, but what they don't get is when you have that bond of friendship among the players and staff. And it's not like I never got yelled at by Coach Tenopir for messing up on a play because he's my buddy. I mean, work's work, but to think that you have to completely separate it and make it like, 'Okay, this is work and there's where you can enjoy yourself.' But you look at the teams who win the Super Bowl and they're the teams who were having the most fun.

Q: What do you think set these teams of yours apart from others of that time? The Miami team you played, even?

ZW: I think it was mostly just believing in the guy next to you and the belief in your system. Everyone in that era before the bowl game was always, "Oh, a Nebraska team with corn-fed, big, strong guys just doesn't have enough speed to compete with these Florida teams. The option is obsolete. You can't win with the option anymore. It's an old offense that doesn't have any place." Well, we proved that wrong because Osborne won the next couple national championships with the exact same offense. I just think that everyone believed in what they were coached. When Coach Osborne told you the gameplan you had no doubt that he knew what he was talking about. The assistant coaches all knew what they were talking about. And more than anything, you could say, 'Hey, the guy next to me worked hard and put in as much time as I have and he'll do his job. So all I've got to do is worry about mine.'

Q: Trust was a huge factor?

ZW: Oh, yeah. I mean, in the pros you've got a guy next to you that you knew was out drinking the night before and you're sitting next to him at the line and you're thinking, 'Is this guy gonna get beat and get me killed or make me look bad?,' you know?

Q: And then you're the guy they're spotlighting on the TV camera instead of him?

ZW: Exactly. No one knows it was his guy they're showing on the camera who made you look bad.

Q: What are you the most proud of, Zach?

ZW: I'm probably the most proud of the games we won that year when we didn't have Tommie or Brook. The next year they won the national championship and they killed Florida and didn't have a lot of really close games, but we played a season without Tommie Frazier. We had Brook Berringer, who was hurt for most of the season, and we played some games against top ten teams without either of them. Kansas State? Lawrence Philips had a cast on his hand and we had the Turmanator at quarterback. I'm not taking away anything from the Turmanator, but he's not Tommie Frazier.

Q: I've spoken to him and he's said about the same, mentioning that he wasn't nervous for that game because of the supporting cast around him, with you guys on the line and the running backs, not to mention the Blackshirts.

ZW: The other team knew what we were going to do. And Stai and us, we'd go up to the defensive line and say, "We're running it right here again. Try to stop it." They knew exactly what we were running. Ask Coach Tenopir. I think we ran like 24 ISO's in that game.

Q: Was that the same play that sprung Cory Schlesinger in the Miami game?

ZW: No, that was a trap. An inside trap. That was set up for Warren Sapp. He was so fast up the field all the time, we said, "You know what? Let's not even block him." He ran himself right out of the play and never even got touched.

Q: That's beautiful.

ZW: Yeah, he ran right up the field and we ran right underneath him and he didn't even get touched.

Q: Bryan Pruitt was saying that you guys were so sure of yourselves that you'd huddle up only three yards from the line of scrimmage?

ZW: Oh yeah, our whole thing was to snap the ball with as much time on the time clock as we possibly could. So we just decided to call all of our plays only three yards from the line of scrimmage, and if they heard it, "So what?" It didn't matter. I mean, there were games where we'd have three or four guys stacked right over where the ball was going, and we'd still get a few yards.

Q: As an aside, as the game went on, would most defenses crumble or keep fighting the good fight?

ZW: I don't think people gave up, I just think there were times when they just physically ran out of gas. I mean, we're running plays, averaging fifteen more plays a game than our competition. You just add that up over a game. Plus, the guys that we had hitting them were all pretty tough guys, so it was just a survival factor. I mean, you'd get into a game and they'd have their hands on their knees.

You talk about that Miami game: in a timeout we're all standing there looking at the guys and they're all standing there with their hands on their knees trying to catch a breath. I mean, we're down there in their weather where we supposedly couldn't play because it was too hot.

Q: And trying to snap the ball with as much time left on the clock; was it so they couldn't get a defensive call in, so they couldn't substitute players, tire them out, or all of the above?

ZW: It keeps them from rotating personnel. Because it keeps them from running off the field when you're hitting them, and then it also doesn't let them make adjustments to what you're doing, plus they don't get any breath.

Q: In other words, Coach Osborne's halftime prophesy was all a part of his master plan to wear them down?

ZW: Yep, exactly.

Q: It's great that somebody got that on film.

ZW: You just look at that halftime tape, everything he said came true, "They're going to get a penalty sometime for swinging at someone. Just don't retaliate…" Everything he said happened.

Q: What about that game stands out to you the most?

ZW: You wanna know what stands out to me the most? It's when Brook threw that interception in the end zone. It was getting a little bit late in the game and we're a couple yards from scoring a touchdown, and we threw a pass. We hadn't hardly thrown the ball the whole game and we decide to throw a pass… and we throw a pick. And at that point you could have gone either way: you could have been like, "Oh crap, here we go again. We're going to give it up in the end," but we were on the sideline and every single person on the offense was going up to the defense and saying, "Don't worry about it. We've got it won. Don't worry about it." Not one guy was sitting there and negatively thinking about it. At that point I was, 'No matter what happens, we're going to win this game.' It was crazy. You would have thought that one person would have been like, "Oh man, I can't believe we threw a pick!" The defense was all fired up to go back out there, and they were loving it because they were killing Miami's offensive line. To a man, every guy on the offense was saying, "Don't worry. We'll get this done." We couldn't wait to get back out on the field after that pick. And I've never watched the film. I have no need to watch it. The memories are so much better than the film.

Q: I can only imagine. Film only captures a miniscule portion of what's really going on out there.

ZW: Yeah, and that's the thing that really sticks out to me, was our reaction to a negative thing that happened in the game. Just the attitude.

And another thing that happened -that I remember from playing at Nebraska- was the Washington game my sophomore year where we played at Washington and got beat. We got back to Lincoln at about four in the morning and there's like 150 to 200 fans at the airport cheering for us, saying, "Hey, you guys fought hard." You know, it's easy to get people cheering for you when you're winning all the time, but to have these people there cheering for us? Those are the kind of things I remember. You can't get that somewhere else. It's easy for people to be out there cheering when you just won the national championship, but where are the guys cheering for you when you lost?

Q: That's huge, Zach. We know the success started up front with you guys on the Pipeline; you guys had a bit of a nasty attitude…

ZW: A little bit. (laughs)

Q: Was that self-instilled? Was that instilled in you by Coaches Tenopir and/or Coach Young?

ZW: You know, it's partially that. I think Coach Tenopir and those guys really took pride in teaching us, "Hey, this is how we play here. If you don't want to play mean and play tough, you shouldn't be playing at Nebraska. That's how we play." You know, part of it was the style of football that we played. If you don't play that way running the option, then nothing happens.

So that was a part of it, but another part was that we just had too many guys who liked playing that way. We had Brenden Stai, me, Graham, all those guys. Not that we played dirty, but if we'd bend the rules as much as possible and have a great time, we were all for it. (laughs) I don't think people enjoyed playing against us.

Q: Because of the sheer physicality? The brutality?

ZW: Yeah, the speed at which we played. All day with 300 pound guys going full speed, and we all knew what we were doing. And if it came down to running down a guy and chopping him at full speed, we just didn't hesitate. Whatever you had to do to get it done. To the coaches we'd almost be like, "You ran left a bunch. Why don't you run right?" Because guys wanted the ball to be behind them, you know? Guys wanted to be the guy who made the block.

Q: Any memorable off-field stuff?

ZW: I don't know if there's any I should say. (laughs) Hmmm, can't talk about that one... (laughs) I think I'll probably keep those to myself. Some probably weren't legal, so I don't want to get anybody in trouble. (laughs) I don't think the statute of limitations has run out on me yet.

Q: Any good practice recollections that you'll never forget?

ZW: The best practice we ever had was when Christian Peter got knocked over the head with his own helmet down in 'The Pit.' That was a pretty memorable one.

That one, and when Joel Wilks got into a fight with a guy. The guy was hanging onto his back and Wilks is trying to run around and slam the guy against a wall to get him off his back. That was pretty funny.

The overall funny one was my sophomore or junior year. We had this rule that if you'd gotten into a fight during practice you had to go into the locker room. That was Coach Osborne's rule, "Hey, if you get into a fight, you're out of here." Of course, he makes the rule and the first week there's like twenty fights with guys trying to get out of practice. (laughing) So after we all got into a few fights he decides, "Well, now if you get into a fight you're going to have to run stadium stairs." I don't remember being in another fight after that. (laughs) Of course, the ones in the pit didn't count. He actually had to see you get into a fight, so the stuff that took place in the pit was its own deal...that was just between McBride and Tenopir. But the ones on the field? As soon as he made that rule that you had to run there was never another fight on the field, I think. (laughing) Running stairs in your football pads is not a good thing.

Q: Many say that practice was much harder than the games. Who did you go up against most frequently in practice?

ZW: It depended, you know? A lot of times in the regular practices you'd end up going against Donta Jones and Dwayne Harris and Christian and guys like that. A lot of the practices were against scout team guys, too. So we did both. You pretty much went against everyone on the team who played on defense. Jared Tomich was a younger guy I used to go against quite a bit at practice. There was a lot of competition. Our D-Line still thinks they were tougher, but we got the best of them.

Q: Do you recall when the defense made the switch to the 4-3?

ZW: Yeah, my freshman year and sophomore year they ran the 5-2 and they went to the 4-3. They played so much faster. Instead of being a two-gap team where you took guys head on and you had to get rid of your block and make a play, it changed to where they were just in gaps shooting upfield -guys like Tomich and Wistrom and Donta Jones and all those guys- they were such good athletes that if you put them out on the end and just let them chase the quarterback around it was such a faster, more aggressive team. Instead of a team that read and reacted they were in your face making you react to what they were doing. And you could do that with a 5-2 defense, but that wasn't the style we played. Our defense just got so much more faster each year. And they just kept recruiting guys who were faster and faster, too, it seemed like.

Q: Do you recall your first winter conditioning team meeting after your freshman season in '90? Some have talked about the 'buy in' during that meeting. Does that stand out to you?

ZW: Yeah, when you're young you don't know how things were before that meeting, but I think there was definitely a perception that some of the guys there before weren't the most 'effort' guys. I don't know that, but I just think that a real interesting thing was that we obviously had talented guys, but we also had guys who worked really hard at the same time.

So we didn't just have guys who relied on their God-given ability, we all tried to get better every year. And as you saw these things happen, I think you not only saw a better level of player on the field, but you also saw a guy who worked harder. You saw both.

Q: No stone was left unturned?

ZW: Yeah, my sophomore year was Will Shields' senior year and that's when I really started seeing a difference. I could really tell between my sophomore and junior year that the intensity just really got turned up as far as offseason conditioning and competition. You could just see it. Every year the level of intensity in those offseason workouts just got higher and higher and higher.

Q: Other than the guys up front that you faced daily, who stood out to you as making some real strides on the defensive side of things?

ZW: Oh, you had Barron Miles and Ed Stewart… we had so many good players. All those front seven guys were just phenomenal. Doug Colman, he had a rock head. Then you had Cory Schlesinger who played twelve years in the pros as a fullback, which is unheard of. Abdul Muhammad on offense; he caught more balls than anybody, but he was 170 pounds soaking wet and you'd just see some of the blocks he'd throw in games. It was like our receivers were in some mad race to get downfield and see who could knock down the backside safety and stuff. You wouldn't believe the stuff that we'd see on film. It just came down to the fact that we had guys who loved to play and they were all pretty talented.

Q: I had a conversation with Coach Osborne about the fact that he didn't like our quarterbacks running out of bounds, saying, in essence, "We aren't going to play you ten versus eleven, we're going to play you eleven versus eleven." Do you recall hearing something like that?

ZW: Yeah, you mean as far as the quarterback? Yeah, the quarterback -when I played at Nebraska- was just like another running back…who would occasionally throw. I mean, Tommie was the toughest running back in the country. He was such a good runner.

Q: I'm deviating here, but any other guys from that backfield you could talk about?

ZW: You know, Lawrence was probably, to this day, the most naturally talented football player I ever played with. I'd tell guys in the pro's that all the time and they'd be like, "No way." And I'd tell them, 'The guy could do everything. He could run over you. He could run around you. He'd catch.' And when I was at Nebraska you never heard a peep out of the guy. I mean, the guy was quiet, very respectful to the older guys on the team, just an all-around great person to be around. You know, after we left he had a few problems the next year. And we were together in St. Louis for two years, also.

Q: Oh, yeah...

ZW: Things just went downhill. Here was a guy that if the agents and the people with the money would have just left him alone, he would have been the best player ever. When you get that money and that posse hanging around you who want to spend that money for you it's a bad deal. But I have nothing but good things to say about Lawrence Phillips.

Q: Thinking back, what have you taken from these experiences almost fifteen years removed? What do you hold most close?

ZW: I think being one of the fortunate ones, being able to play pro ball like I did, realizing that you really did have it that good while you were there. There's no place to play football like Nebraska. I've heard some horror stories, a ton of stories from guys who played at other colleges and just hated their college experience.

And you'd hear all this talk of how pro coaches were better than college coaches, but I'd put the Nebraska football coaches up against any of them as far as knowledge and as far as being a good person. I wouldn't trade any player I played with at Nebraska or any coach with another from the pros.

Q: Saying that, can you give me any insight into Coach Tenopir and his methods, how he taught you?

ZW: One thing he was great at teaching guys was the fact that you had to depend on the guy next to you, because offensive line is a group deal. If one guy's not pulling his weight the whole deal doesn't work. And so he kind of taught that approach. And he wasn't a yeller. I've been with so many coaches who swear and yell and this and that, but he would basically say, "This is the way we do things: You play fast and you play physical. It doesn't matter who's across from you if you keep with these fundamentals: play low and keep attacking all the time, and you'll do fine." I remember little Kenny Mehlen one time playing Dana Stubblefield and just eating his lunch. And then Jim Scott, he probably weighed two-sixty and he was one of the better guys I ever played next to. He just got the most out of his players.

And here's another guy like Coach Osborne -like a father figure to you- and I think just taking the approach that if you do this, this and this -and you might not get to play here because of your God-given ability- but you can make the most out of what you are given. That's the approach he took to coaching and I think it's the only approach. At least it's the approach that worked the best with me.

Q: And Coach Dan Young?

ZW: Oh yeah, Coach Young did a lot of work with the tackles. He's another guy. It's so funny how all the coaches were all on the same page. You never had one coach saying one thing and another coach saying another thing. They all had a system and they all believed in that system, and there was no deviation from your coach. If you do one pass set or one run-block step, it didn't matter if it was Coach Young or Coach Tenopir standing behind you, they'd both give you the same response, "You did this wrong" or "You did this right." They all worked together so well and so long and believed in what they were teaching that they all had the same response for you. The assistants, especially with the offensive linemen, I can't think of a word that described the offense line more than the word 'consistent.'

End conversation.

Peer leadership, to borrow from a 1950's media franchise, is a many splendored thing. It's an often ambiguous term encompassing myriad styles and concepts and personalities: from Moses to Meir to McArthur to Martin Luther King, Jr. I had an epiphany of sorts when

Zach mentioned, "the leadership came from the offensive line and the defensive line" of that time. We've heard the ages old saying, "It all starts up front in the trenches" a thousand times from radio and television talking heads, but it was not only the actions of the boys in the trenches that made an indelible mark on those Husker teams, it was their leadership in both word and action. You may have gotten that same impression from our earlier sit-down with Brenden Stai, but like any good pulling guard/tackle combo, Zach drove home the final blow and helped me to turn the corner on grasping a unique bit of insight. Because the offensive line opened up the holes and provided backfield protection, too, one can see how their onfield actions no doubt lent validity to their words in the locker room. I'm fairly certain we'll hear of leadership concepts as we go further in my quest to answer the great Why and How of Cornhusker Football's Golden era, and I hope to delineate the many facets of that leadership, also.

Another bit I found remarkable was the mindset later displayed by the offensive line in their quest for dominance, the notion that, "it should never come down to a field goal, that we want to be the ones on the field controlling our destiny and not on somebody kicking a ball." No offense to Byron Bennett and the whole covey of kickers out there, but if you can dominate, control, beat down and dismantle a team the way these guys purposed, the only use for place-kickers would be point afters and kickoffs rather than nail-biting game winners with everything on the line. And I can appreciate their point, for who truly wants to expend such grandiose efforts toward a game's endeavor only for success to hinge on a rounded shoe connecting with a round ball in the hopes it will travel a straight path? Not me. And not for the offensive line of those days, either.

Notable quote #2:
Zach Weigert on his college experience: "You really did have it that good while you were there. There's no place to play football like Nebraska."

I am a border ruffian from the State of Missouri... In me you have Missouri morals, Connecticut culture; this, gentlemen, is the combination which makes the perfect man.

Mark Twain

World War I's General of the Armies John J. Pershing was born in 1860 in a tiny Missouri farm shanty about 150 miles northwest of St. Louis as the crow flies. First teaching schoolchildren of former slaves, he won entrance to West Point Military Academy and later fought as a Cavalryman against the American Apache & Sioux, then alongside future President Teddy Roosevelt in Cuba at the Battle of San Juan Hill."Black Jack," as he came to be known, was cited for gallantry, extraordinary marksmanship, and his severe coolness under fire. Soon thereafter in 1891, Pershing began his Professorship of Military Science and Tactics at the University of Nebraska. Spending four years in Lincoln (and earning a law degree on the side), he formed the elite drill company later known as the Pershing Rifles. (A sign commemorating this World War I hero stands just 100 yards to the east of Memorial Stadium at the corner of 14th and Vine Street today) History shows that he first earned the (derisive) nickname "Nigger Jack" - subsequently becoming "Black Jack"- because of his service with the 'colored' Army's 10th Cavalry, and brought a distinct measure of discipline, foresight and leadership to the Nebraska campus (much to the chagrin of the pacifist atmosphere of the day). A mentor to America's greatest World War II Generals, this Missourian of humble beginnings was just a first of many to make a name at Nebraska, where the culture he instilled lives on.

But other Missourians of note also played a role on the Lincoln campus, including a great part of those 60 & 3 teams: players like Mike Rucker, Grant Wistrom, Ed Morrow and Jacques Allen, among others. Which brings us to Husker roommates/teammates Kenny Wilhite and Lorenzo Brinkley.

Both hailing from St. Louis, Missouri, at the time of this interview they were both college football coaches on Tony Samuel's staff at Southeast Missouri State University. Looking back, 'Lo' had the unfortunate experience of a nasty, teeth-grinding broken arm in the waning moments of the historic 18-16 Orange Bowl Florida State loss, and if not for that abbreviated gameday his presence on the midway just may have swung the tide in preventing Florida State's final, successful drive. (Again, it's one of those 'woulda, coulda', shoulda's,' but I have a feeling the '93 Husker team would have held Charlie Ward and Warrick Dunn's heroics in check on that drive had he still been in there knocking heads.) Kenny, on the other hand, had played out his college career a year earlier and was watching that game as a pro in the Canadian Football League. Though off the roster, he'd played his part in bringing the team to that point, too.

Let's get ready, hyped and amped for a few bits of insight from two guys who know a thing or two about the Husker's transformation to dynastic status. This one hits from every angle, converging on the subject as the two Husker cornerbacks often did.

Notable quote #1:
Lorenzo Brinkley: "When we got Toby Wright, I think that changed the whole mental state of our defense, because he'd knock the shit out of you, to put it plainly. So it started to be the game where everybody was trying to knock the living shit out of somebody."

Notable quote #2:

Kenny Wilhite: "For the most part, you wanted to win it for the coaches, for the hard work they put in. Especially Coach Osborne, you wanted to win for him. You wanted to win for yourself, but you wanted to win it for him."

Lorenzo Brinkley & Kenny Wilhite

Scholarship recruit, Cornerback, St. Louis, Missouri (Hazelwood Central)
Where are they now? Cape Girardeau, Missouri, Coach

Scholarship recruit, Cornerback, St. Louis, Missouri (Oakville)
Where are they now? Conway, AR, Coach

Question: Hey guys, it's neat to see that the both of you, as well as Troy Dumas and Chris Norris, are now with Tony Samuel at SEMO. That's pretty cool.

Lorenzo Brinkley: It's quite the crew here, that's for sure. A real Nebraska flavor.

Q: So how did you guys end up on the Nebraska campus as young players?

Kenny Wilhite: I actually went to a junior college out of high school, and then the recruiting process started all over again. I narrowed it down to two schools: The University of Pacific and the University of Nebraska. And the reason for the University of Pacific was because John Gruden was one of the assistant coaches on the staff and was the one recruiting me (he actually did great job). When it came down to making my decision I had to ask Gruden, I said, 'Hey, you've been here to Dodge (Kansas) a couple times to see me. If you can get the head man to come down and visit me at Dodge City and then go sit in my living room - in my living room in my neighborhood where I grew up- you've got a great chance of getting me to commit to the University of Pacific.' Ron Brown was recruiting me to the University of Nebraska and I told him the exact same thing.

Well, needless to say, Coach Osborne showed up on a Thursday morning, we went and had lunch (and he signed about 200 autographs in the cafeteria with no complaints), then flew to St. Louis. He called me when he got seated in my Grandmother's living room and I said, 'Coach, I'm going to the University of Nebraska!' (laughs)

Now, once Coach Osborne saw where I grew up, he said he was gonna do whatever he could to make sure I graduated, and that made my decision a lot easier, also. So it was just a matter of whether I could fit in with the guys there and get a good education.

Q: Did that experience affect how you recruit now, Kenny?

KW: Those three -meaning Coach Gruden, Coach Brown and Coach Osborne- were upfront and they weren't just trying to sell me a dream. That's the way I approach it, also, and that's what I tell the kids straight up. I say, 'Hey, this is what I expect. This is what I'm gonna do. You need to be honest with me, also, I'm not gonna give you some B.S. I can't promise you this or that, but I can promise you I'll take care of you the 4-5 years you're with me, get you an education and make you a better person. I'm there for you if you ever need anything, someone to talk to or a shoulder to lean on,' you know? And I learned that from Coach Osborne. Being with Coach Samuel for a few years, he's the same way, too.

Q: When was your first fall on campus at Nebraska, Lorenzo?

LB: It was '89. We were both there when everything went through a change.

The level of professionalism really stood out to me. At that time high schools weren't structured like college programs were. It was an amazing deal as far as the organization and the regimenting of time. In high school you just played -you know?- to put it in a nutshell. We weren't big on the small things in high school, you know? You just showed up and went for the ball. Then it seems like you come to this 'factory,' and everything is so technical, it comes down to the discipline and other factors, that was the case.

Q: What was your biggest challenge to overcome?

LB: My biggest challenge was to get over my own ego and try to buy into the system. I think the light started coming on for me when it was finally my third season, actually. I had some injuries and stuff, you know. I broke my wrist my second year there, so I had to wear a cast for awhile and I think it kind of slowed my progress. But during my time with the injury I started to pay attention a whole lot more, because I wanted to play. You start getting that competitive thing, and athletically you look at other people in the room and you wonder, 'Why's that other guy playing and I'm not?' You start checking yourself.

Q: A little more self-evaluation in addition to the coaching evaluation going on?

LB: Right, because as a young player I had to side against the coach all the time instead of listening to what he'd tell me.

Q: Did you and Coach Darlington butt heads a lot?

LB: Oh yeah, probably more than we should have. (laughs) I was immature, I'll admit that. It was a two-headed thing, too, due to the fact that he didn't really ask to us to buy into the system, to reel us in, because we had so much depth. Initially I was against reaching out for a little guidance at that point in life, and he argued against it.

KW: Coach Darlington was very, very high strung, and I know you know that. And for me, when I first got to Nebraska I was utilized as a quarterback and redshirted and I was on the scout team offense, mostly. (That was in the fall of '90) So I played a little quarterback during Colorado week, receiver sometimes, quarterback during Oklahoma week. Then because of some injuries they were short on the defensive side, and they said, "Hey, if you want to have a better chance to play at the next level you might want to switch to cornerback", and that's what I did.

I only played cornerback sparingly in high school, so it was a learning process. And I tell you what, he stuck by me. He was willing to give me an opportunity to switch over. And Coach D. could be challenging at times, but he's a very, very good coach. He knows his football.

Q: Challenging in what way, Kenny?

KW: He wanted you to be perfect, and if it's not perfect he'd let you know.

Q: In what ways would he let you know?

KW: If only you knew. (laughs) You could hear him from one end of the stadium to the other end of the old grass practice field. You could hear Coach D. But he was a good one, he pushed us a lot in practice and I think he pushed us for the best. He wanted us to be the best -not only in the Big 8 Conference- but in the country. He made sure that every step was right, every technique was right, he was a perfectionist.

And when I first got there, my first year it was Shane Thorell, he was the Graduate Assistant in the secondary. He was just getting started, he was working with Coach D. He was a good one and it was like 'Good Cop, Bad Cop.' He was the one that would give you a pat on the back. Coach D. would let you have it and Coach Thorell was there to pat you on the back and tell you "It's gonna be okay" and everything.

Q: Interesting. Do you guys recall the Unity Council coming into being at that time?

LB: Yeah, I remember it. I'm trying to recall, I'm not even sure if I was on the Unity Council or not. But for some reason it seems at that time that I thought I had a whole lot to say. (laughs) It was good, because we did have a void in the communications between the players and coaches. I think it was the start of the change because the players started to feel a lot more ownership.

Q: Things became less adversarial after that?
LB: To a degree. But we also knew at that point that everything was going to get to Coach Osborne instead of just stopping at a position coach. I don't know how many times they went to Coach with something that maybe they didn't think he needed to hear or maybe he was too busy for.

KW: I was there when they started the Council. I know for myself I never had to go in front of them. Now, I wasn't a saint by any means, but I wasn't going to do anything that crazy to have to go in front of the Unity Council. Either the Unity Council or Coach Osborne or the police? I was like, 'I don't want to deal with *none* of those guys!' (laughs) You know, you were put in situations. Now, the bars? We did our thing, but we took care of each other for the most part. So if you went with somebody and there were other players there it was like, 'Hey, Ernie Beler, I'm getting ready to go, it's getting late. Nothing good happens after 1 o'clock,' you know?

And I remember that time, that team meeting, too. The workouts in January of '91, it changed from having guys trying to skip workouts and looking toward the next level -not wanting to become a team- instead of working out as a team. Guys like Dante Jones and Ed Stewart and Dwayne Harris, they were young guys up and coming, took it upon themselves because they knew what they had. I think after my senior year in '92 (that first Florida State bowl game), they knew what they had and that's why they were able to make it to the National Championship game the next year and almost make it with that field goal.

We were like this family, man. To put that 'N' on your helmet -not only to put that 'N' on your helmet- but once you got that Blackshirt you were part of a fraternity for a long time.

Q: Do you recall anything else making a big difference for your teammates?

LB: I would say one of the things that helped was the fact that we went from the traditional, big defense to more of a speed defense, and they started to move guys like myself and Ernie Beler from safety to linebacker. Ed Stewart was another guy. And I think that allowed us to play at the same level as the other teams, like the Florida schools. I think it became more fun, because we were flying around.

Q: Did you buy into that change? Or did you fight it like Ed did?

LB: I was probably more receptive to it, trying to get on the field. I didn't mind moving closer to the line. They had a plan for me, I guess. The funny part about it, obviously Coach Darlington -he may not remember- we had our differences at that time, but I didn't care what my position on the depth chart was, I felt I could cover anybody.

Then Coach Samuel told me we were looking at moving some guys up to SAM back, so I made my mind up that I wanted to play offense. Then after that Coach Osborne called me in to talk. And if he was calling you in to talk, you already knew what the outcome was going to be. (laughs) I pretty much told him, 'Do I have a choice?' And he said, "Well, we think this would be great for the team." So I said, 'Alright.'

Q: So it took his presenting a vision to really make the deal go down, huh?

LB: You know, when you come in you have your own vision. I had my vision, so I really didn't care about what anyone else said. Until that meeting with Coach Osborne.
I continued with that belief, but I started thinking that I needed to be a lot stronger. I was a quarterback in high school, too, so I thought like an offensive guy. So it took -for me, and this is the honest truth- this is what did it for me one day my freshman year: I saw Jeff Mills, Reggie Cooper, Pat Tyrance and Kenny Walker all together coming out of the North locker room. I saw them guys and I'm like, 'Damn! All you dudes play defense?!' They looked so physical and imposing. They were all chiseled.

Q: They were like the Fantastic Four. Superhero-type physiques?

LB: Exactly! At that point I understood I needed to become a little more built, but athletically I didn't feel like nobody there was that much better of an athlete. You had guys like Curtis Cotton and guys like that, but I never felt I couldn't stop anybody.

KW: (laughing) I remember for the first day of camp, when they'd have freshmen and newcomers report early, I was playing a little wingback, a lot of route running. (Now you want to talk about a perfectionist? Coach Ron Brown was the best, now. He was one of the best coaches with running, blocking, pass catching, the drills we did as receivers, oh my goodness. He was a very, very good coach). So anyway, I played a lot of receiver as one of the wingbacks. You had Nate Turner and Tyrone Hughes, Danny Pleasant, and then myself, we were all wingbacks at the time, so my first four days it was tough, trying to get used to that style of football.

It was very demanding. It was an eye opener. You've got guys that were just as fast and a lot stronger than I was, so it made me realize that I wasn't as good, wasn't as great as I thought I was. Coming from a junior college in Kansas, being a first team All–American player in the Jayhawk Conference, Player of the Year unanimous, I thought I'd be ready once I got to the next level. But I tell you what, it was an eye opener. Just very demanding, and there were some big guys out there. I was but 5'8" and 170-175 lbs. You've gotta go in there and try to block Pat Tyrance at linebacker? Reggie Cooper at free safety? There wasn't any turning anything down. I wasn't scared, but you had to do it. So I had to get in the weight room and get stronger.

Q: And being converted over to the defense, did it take awhile to accustom yourself to delivering the hits instead of receiving them?

LB: In the latter part of my career I did. I think when we got Toby Wright on the team, I think that changed the whole mental state of our defense. Because he'd knock the shit out of you, to put it plainly. So it started to be the game where everybody was trying to knock the living shit out of somebody, and when he came on it showed us it was possible. So those last couple years I became more of a physical guy.

Q: Where do you think Toby's physicality came from?

LB: Do you know where I think it was instilled? It was his personality and his journey, I'd say, because he had an ACL tear in his knee out of high school and had to go to junior college. And then he had a couple brothers ahead of him who played, too,(the youngest of four brothers who played college ball) so I think he had an idea of how to bring it, you know?

Q: And what about you guys? Were you the first in your family to play college ball?

LB: No, my father was drafted by the Steelers and he played Canadian ball for a time.

Q: Tell me, was there a change from the first day you were on campus to the last, as far as a team mindset? Anything come to mind?

KW: Well, the thing that comes to mind was the first day I got there: I think a lot of guys -I don't want to say this the wrong way- but a lot of guys were worried about the next level instead of playing as a team. They were more about their own selves and stats.

Then my last days you had guys like Toby Wright, Troy Dumas, Ernie Beler, Lorenzo & Trev Alberts on the defensive side of the ball, along with Tommie (Frazier), Abdul (Muhammad), Corey Dixon. And those offensive linemen? You can't say enough about them. That last year after the bowl game, that team knew what they had and I think that started the first day of the offseason program. They knew what they had and they worked a lot harder than previous years and they became a team. I don't think anybody was looking forward to the next level. They had 'the team' in mind now. You had the skill guys that would challenge Florida State and Miami: you had Calvin (Jones) at running back, Lawrence Phillips as a freshman, Damon Benning and Clinton Childs, Tommie, Corey Dixon, and I think the coaching staff and the strength coaches putting it all together. I think it was just the guys knowing what they had and deciding it was time.

Q: If I recall, your last game was the 18-16 Florida State game. You broke your arm in that game, right Lorenzo?

LB: Broke my humerus. There was like 7 minutes left in the 4th quarter.

Q: Man, that was crunch time! That had to hurt. In my mind, you should have a National Champ ring on your finger from that game.

LB: I agree.

Q: Nonetheless, can you take me back to that game and what stands out to you, other than the broken arm?

LB: As a defense, that's all I can speak for: we were as geared up and prepared for that team than any other game I've been prepared for. I knew everybody around me was ready for anything that could happen. We were so prepared for that game.

I guess you'd have to give credit to Coach McBride because he was the Defensive Coordinator, but also I think it plays into the fact that we were more of a team at that time. If you remember, we played KU and we won at the end of the game when they missed the two point conversion. I think we knew we were the underdogs for that Orange Bowl, so that also played into it, too, like we had something to prove. The whole year was crazy, and we had to prove that we could finally get to the championship game and be competitive. So it was kind of like, "Are we gonna be the same team or are we gonna try to make a difference?"

Another thing that I think Coach Osborne did back then that helped us was when we started taking the bowl trips a lot more serious.'Cause my freshman year we played Florida State in the Fiesta Bowl and that was kinda out of control…

Q: Partying & staying up late?

LB: It was a fun time instead of taking care of the business at hand. From then on it started being a whole lot more structured, I would say. I just remember guys like Mike Anderson and Trev Alberts, who else? Raemakers and Cory Dixon (who I thought was a good leader), Donta Jones, (a hard working guy…)

Q: He was Lifter of the Year…

LB: Yeah, and we had Barron Miles, too.

Q: That's quite a lineup, with Barron Miles, John Reece, Toby Wright, guys like that…

KW: Actually, my junior year I tore my ACL, when Barron was a younger guy. I knew how good he was gonna be, so that summer I worked out three times a day just to get back and ready for my senior year, because if I wasn't ready to play Barron was going to take my job.

Q: What's your favorite moment as a player?

LB: I guess it would be in the Orange Bowl game playing Florida State when we ran that punt, when Corey ran that punt back. After that, I think we were proving ourselves right that we could beat them, you know? That stuff with the refs didn't even matter, it didn't matter at that point in the game. We'd played like that the entire year, like we knew we had what it took.

Q: Weren't you on the punt return team for that game?

LB: Yeah, I was actually on Corey's punt return. I've seen it on film a couple of times. I remember a lot of plays, you know, the plays that I made, and how it was to play against Charlie Ward and his ability. To see one of his passes go whiz by your head before you could even react to it was really special.

Q: He could put the mustard on it, eh?

LB: Yeah, oh my God. Just looking at his demeanor and all, you just didn't think the kid had it, but he was the real deal. All he would do was just look to the sideline, he never got rattled. I tried to get in his head a little bit and talk shit to him, but he never paid any attention to me. (laughs)

Q: And if you wanted to talk smack to him, what would you say?

LB: Stuff like, 'We're coming to get you', 'I'm gonna knock your block off,' things like that, called him 'soft' and things like that, nothing vicious or anything. Trying to get him to respond, but he'd never respond.

Q: Any recollections of taking other guys out of their game by getting in their head?

LB: Kordell Stewart, we used to get him rattled. And we used to rattle Chad May from Kansas State.

Q: I remember Trev Alberts one year, first play of the game, sacked Kordell Stewart in the backfield right at the first snap. And then I noticed Trev had a little something to say to him. So on Monday he's in the weight room and I say, 'Hey Trev, I noticed you said something to Kordell after that first sack. What did you tell him?' And Trev said, "You better get used to this, because I'm gonna be back here all… day… long."

LB: (laughs) You know where we got that from? From watching old tapes of Broderick Thomas playing UCLA -and it might have been Troy Aikman in the backfield- and you could hear him say like, "I'm gonna be on your ass like this *all night!*" So we'd always say that kind of thing. All game. How much did we blitz back then? Every down.

KW: About those bowl practices… they were like going to training camp all over again. It was very, very structured. You had your free time, but when the coaches had you it was very structured, you knew where you had to be. Like growing up, my ultimate goal was to play in one of those games. And the preparation before that game was… it was crazy intense. Because you knew what you were going up against.

And for the most part, you wanted to win it for the coaches, for the hard work they put in. Especially Coach Osborne, you wanted to win for him. You wanted to win for yourself, but you wanted to win it for him.

Q: That always seemed to be a major goal, didn't it? Being the first ones to win the big one for T.O? Now Lorenzo, with Florida State being your last game, were you able to get over the loss quickly or did it take a while to recover?

LB: Truthfully, I wasn't out there for the last 4 minutes of the game, so it's kind of like a void there for me. You know, after the fact, it just didn't feel like it ended for me. It was depressing, because here it was my senior year and I was off to a good start, I bought into the system and everything, I did everything I was supposed to, and ultimately it affected my draft status. It was a long process for me, actually.

Q: Did you ever deal with Jack Stark?

LB: A little bit. He was around a lot. For some reason I recall him being on the Unity Council sometimes, and being around for a lot of those talks.

Q: So the next year vs. Miami for the championship, do you recall that game? Where were you watching the game?

LB: I want to say I was in St. Louis at that time, and just recognizing and calling out a lot of the defenses that we ran, just being involved in it. But the thing that stuck out the most from that game was the run by Cory Schlesinger, the last back-breaking run.

Q: Anything you wish you could have done over?

LB: Boy, that's a tough one. I guess just the fact that I was so headstrong. I probably should have listened a whole lot more. There was people around there that would talk to me about certain things, like Bryan Bailey, he would say a lot of things to me the later years there that made sense to me. He would always tell me that, athletically, I was just as good as anybody else, as far as being in the weight room and getting better, how he would help me.

Q: Anyone else play a major role as somebody special?

LB: Two people that stuck out to me were probably Doak Ostergard and Coach Osborne.

Q: Can you expound on them?

LB: Coach Osborne, I knew where he stood. I knew that if we had rules, he didn't expect you to go beyond that point. And he'd stick by you as long as he could. The prime example of that would be Lawrence Phillips. If he said it, he stood by his word. And I respected that, because you'd always get into situations where you could take it one way or another. He also stood by what he said and was a great man, in my opinion.

KW: You ever hear that saying, "You don't know what you got 'til it's gone"? Well, my three years under Coach Osborne I *knew* what I had and what kind of person he was. Matter of fact, I went to the convention this past year; he spoke at the convention and he gave me goosebumps listening to him.

And to gain some knowledge from him I try to call him at least once or twice a year. I actually called him about 3 weeks ago and left a message. He called me right back. That guy, there's not enough words to explain the respect, the love, the gratitude that I have for him.

He gave me a chance and he believed in me, he was there in good times and bad. He always told me if I ever need anything not to hesitate to call him and he'd do whatever he could do. And he's a man of his word, I tell you.

LB: And Doak was a laid back guy, but also a straight shooter. He was in a different capacity because he was in the training room, so because of injuries I got to know him a little better, and he would also tell me some of the stuff that I needed to hear and some of the stuff I didn't want to hear. But I trusted him. He was a good guy. A good guy to trust.

KW: I tell you what -when I hurt my knee- if it wasn't for Bryan Bailey and Doak I probably would've had to give up football.

Q: Really?

KW: You've gotta know, from the age of 5 years old I wanted to make it to pro football; it just looms where you try to make it to the NFL, the ultimate goal. When I tore my knee I thought it was all over and actually walked away one day and said, 'I'm done.' And I called my grandmother -and my grandmother was my rock at the time- and my grandmother said, "Tell you what, you make sure and get that degree, because they can't take that away from you." And I just looked in the mirror and said, 'Do I want to be known as a quitter?' There were a lot of guys in the neighborhood said I wasn't gonna make it, said I was too small, so that was my ultimate driving point. And like I said, Barron Miles was behind me and I didn't want to lose my job as a senior to the guy. But if it wasn't for Bryan Bailey and Doak I would have given up. I keep in touch with Doak. I talk to him at least once a month. He was a good one, now. He was very, very good at his craft.

Q: How so?

KW: There aren't words to explain that guy. He was young at that time, one of the youngest staff members on that training staff. So him and Bailey. If Doak knew you could play and he knew you were tough, he'd take care of you. And he knew what I had ahead of me, he pushed me. He knew which buttons to push. It was like him and Bryan took turns.

Q: Bad cop, bad cop?

KW: (laughs) No, it wasn't bad cop. Although I can remember one time Doak was cranking on my knee and he was telling me, "If you don't do this you won't be playing next year….." And I finally told Doak, 'If you don't get your hands off of me, I'm done!' That's it, I walked off. I left, went home, called my grandmother. I came back the next day and apologized to Doak, and he said, "Hey, I'm doing this for *you*. I'm not doing this for myself. Don't think I'm taking a liking to it. I'm doing this to get you back on the field." After that it all was good. I tell you, that guy's one of the best. The way they gave the staff the leeway, it was good.

Q: Knowing where you guys stood after practices and games, plus the setting of goals, what was a big thing for you?

LB: I watched film a whole heck of a lot, and Coach Tony Samuel really knew how to relate to me, too.

Q: Was he the one who recruited you, Lorenzo?

LB: Coach McBride and Coach Brown did. But Coach Samuel, personality–wise, we were a whole lot alike, very competitive but laid back in a sense. He showed me that you can get a message across to a person in more than one way. And Coach Darlington, as far as being a technician, demanding proper footwork? Coach D for sure. Coach Samuel fashions himself after Coach Osborne. He played for him and worked for him for 12 years. He's a man of integrity, a family man, and Coach Osborne is the same.

It's about the players. Once it stops being about the players then you have to get out of the game. Coach Osborne made it about us; it wasn't about his wins and losses, it was about his players and how he cared about them as people. Tony is the same way, and I am the same way myself. Growing up in the neighborhood I grew up in, I always said if I ever find a way of helping the youth of today I'm gonna do it. That's what I'm trying to do. Once I lose the love of teaching and helping them to become men -not only football players, but young men- then I've gotta get out of it.

LB: Coach Samuel solidified to me (ever since my first coaching job), that there was a place for my personality. I'm a lot calmer in situations, something I learned when I was a kid. One guy was my baseball coach, a very good coach, and he always talked about being able to perform in crunch time and not getting rattled, about taking yourself to another place, so I learned that from him a long time ago. I never felt like I would lose. Even now, we're going into all the games thinking we've always got a chance. I mean, what are you even doing out there if you don't think you've got a chance?

Q: What led to that belief?

LB: On those teams at Nebraska I just think that we befriended each other, we genuinely cared for each other, and we competed with each other every day. And you understood that if you didn't compete someone was gonna take your spot away.

Q: Were there any cliques? Walk-ons vs. scholarship guys? Black vs. white? Anything like that?
LB: That was something that Coach Osborne can hang his hat on, because he never treated anybody any different than the rest. I never saw anybody else treat anybody differently. I don't think any of the coaches shunned you. If you asked 'em something you'd get a straight answer.

Q: Coach Osborne had a good, sarcastic sense of humor too, didn't he?

LB: Yeah, he did. (laughs) He did. And the great thing about it was that you never saw it coming, either.

And I have to mention, I liked the fact that sometimes former players would come back. One of the guys that helped me out tremendously was Brian Washington. The thing about him was that I played ball against him in the rec center and things like that, Lorenzo Hicks was around some times, Morgan Gregory was still around for some basketball games, Tyrone Legette.
And if you remember, Brian Washington was drafted by the Browns and then got picked up by the Jets later. And I don't know if he made it to a Pro Bowl or not, but he was really productive, and during those years I would see him working out. He would go out and have a great time at night and then the next morning would be up before anybody and he would bust his tail. And I thought, 'Man, if he can sit out a year from the NFL and then come back and be productive, then I need to be working out with this guy.'

Q: A good role model for you?

LB: Yeah, in that aspect. (laughs) He was a hell of an athlete. Those were some great basketball games we used to play.

Q: What about changes, things you'd implement today if you were starting from scratch in building a championship team?

LB: Just making everybody accountable and then making everybody feel like they are responsible, that was something new and really important, too. The whole team has to be accountable as individuals, but they also have to feel ownership together, too. To put it in a nutshell -you know how it is- if you feel you have a bunch of talent but your whole thought process was about pro football, you won't make much happen. I think that as some of that mindset started to graduate and leave we just started getting a different attitude. We decided, "Hey, it's time to stop doing this and doing that, it's time to make things happen and become accountable to each other." If not, you'll come up short. And the worst thing in the world was getting your asses kicked in front of the world in January. (laughs)

Q: Sure, everyone is watching: your old neighborhood buddies, people who said you wouldn't make it, family, old girlfriends, you name it?

LB: Exactly, you want to prove to everyone that we had what it took. All the shit we used to hear about losing to the Florida teams? We had to prove everyone wrong.

Q: Tell me more about Charlie McBride...

KW: Very, very intense. Yeah, we talk about him all the time. Something we remember the most when we all talk about him are his pregame speeches. Oh yeah, he was the guy, you know? He walks around practice and he's yelling and screaming and he's got chew all down his shirt. But his pregame speeches? Oh my goodness, by the time he'd gotten done with his pregame speech we *ran* down that back stairway to get on that field! How intense his speeches were!

Q: Any particular speech come to mind? What did he say or how did he go about it? What was the method to his madness?

KW: He wanted tough football players, he wanted guys who would lay it on the line. It was love. That whole staff, I can say they genuinely loved every player. He told us he loved us, he knew we were gonna play well, and his last words would be, "Now go out there and kick their fuckin' you know what!" And we'd be jumping up and down and we'd run down that back hallway, that back stairway, and we wanted to go play, man.

And you know, you can have good football players who are nice, you know what I mean? I don't like to use the words 'mean and nasty' too often, but those earlier teams I don't think we had enough nasty guys. The younger guys that were coming up were more nasty than the guys that were a little older.

Q: Was that something that was taught or did it come natural to them, Kenny?

KW: You are born with it. You can try to teach kids to be nasty, be physical, be tough, but I think you're born with it. And teams can bring it out in you.

Like I said, from the age of 5 I wanted to play in the NFL and I was tough and brave and would not back down from anything, from no challenge whatsoever.

Q: It probably didn't help being a little guy, right? I'm exactly your size, so I know what you're talking about.

KW: You know, a lot of guys think 'cause your small they can dominate you or they can beat you at this. I was always the one to make believers out of everybody.

Q: Do you guys keep in touch with many other old teammates?

LB: I used to be around Lawrence Phillips when he was in St. Louis with the Rams. I was around him and Toby (Wright) a little bit.

Q: Do you ever keep in touch with L.P.?

LB: It's a little hard now, the last time I talked to him was '99 or so. At times he could be impulsive, but honestly he wasn't like a guy who would beat people up. He was the most talented guy. I remember his freshman year, there were two situations: one time in practice I was coming up on an angle to wrap him up… and he changed a gear and (you know how some guys on the sidelines can make some catcalls like, "Woooo!"? I turned around and said, "Man, he's gonna be something special!") he made a move on me, he was special!

And then another time against UCLA when he came in and helped us with that game. It was a close one.

Q: How often would you guys keep in touch in St. Louis?

LB: We were closer. I had a job, so sometimes I'd just hang out with the guy. Lawrence was just a young kid from L.A. with a whole damn lot of money! You know? He just needed an older person to be with him, kind of point out things -I wouldn't say to guide him, as most young men aren't liking to be led anymore- but just to point stuff out to him. He probably needed someone like that he could trust, and maybe he would have had a different outcome. Everybody's trying to get you to sign up for this and show up for that, whatever. Help someone start up something, all kind of stuff.

Q: Everyone wanted a piece of him?

LB: Yeah, all kind of stuff. He was a good dude. If you talk to him tell him he's always got a friend in me.

KW: Oh, and before you go, do you remember how Coach Osborne didn't like quarterbacks to turn down contact? It goes without saying that that had an effect on the team, too. He told his quarterbacks they could not run out of bounds, he told you what he wanted and what he expected.

Q: Matt Turman said the same. Well, before we go is there a game that stands out as the shining point of your career as Nebraska Blackshirts?

KW: I wouldn't say a game, in particular. (Though the craziest was Colorado in '91 and we tied them. It was cold and they were throwing snowballs at us. That was the craziest.)I would say walking across that stage midway through my senior year in December for that diploma. Because football, yeah, you know you have your moments and you have your highlights, but the thing I remember the most, the biggest moment that I will always cherish is walking across that stage with my diploma. After being told I wasn't gonna graduate: I was never the smartest, I wasn't big enough, I wasn't this, I wasn't that, the biggest moment was walking across that stage and getting that diploma in December of '92.

End conversation.

Well, I guess we all know who I have to get in contact with after this conversation: Toby Wright. I find it peculiar how a small contingent were able to inspire such a number of their peers. I want to contact those guys -Kevin Raemakers, Trev Alberts, John Parrella & Toby Wright- to get an idea of what made them tick, what ingredients of their personalities and their attitudes made them lightning rods for future Husker success.

Don't ask me why, but I don't suppose the average fan comprehends the mental acuity, communication and interpersonal skills needed to play great defensive football. When a coaching staff prepares the unit to operate at ultra-proficient degrees the game seems to flow that much easier, enabling them to throw a massive wrench in the opposing team's engineworks. That being said, it's taken up a notch even further when it caters to the mindset, the innate sensibilities of those playing their positions. The switch to the 4-3 defense coupled with the arrival of Toby Wright seems to have struck a chord in the defensive backfields of those days, because instead of reading and reacting to what the offense was showing they instead became proactive to an extravagant degree and unleashed the inner Blackshirt. As Lorenzo said, "I think it became more fun, because we were flying around." That must have been pure bliss to operate on the edge of abandon and yet maintain solidarity in quashing opponent's offensive dreams.

Both Kenny and Lorenzo touched on the fact that many of the players began to forgo their future professional aspirations and instead live 'in the moment,' focusing on attainment of the Nebraska's team goals instead of self-preservation at the expense of unity. Trust me, those kids knew if someone was dogging it or 'pussy-footing' around and not giving their full effort. If so, they either came around quickly or were, as was stated earlier, 'forced' off the team. With this 'high tides lift all boats' mentality the change in the general player mindset of the day contributed greatly to their success.

Then Lorenzo added, "the worst thing in the world was getting your asses kicked in front of the world in January." Remember that? Kenny also touched on 'negative motivation' with his, "There were a lot of guys in the neighborhood said I wasn't gonna make it, said I was too small. So that was my ultimate driving point." To add, I was the strength coach for the Nebraska Basketball team for a number of years and one of the more memorable pregame speeches given by Head Coach Danny Nee in that era started with: "Boys, one of the greatest feelings in life is proving people wrong." (The Huskers knocked off #1 Kansas that night despite the Vegas bookies saying it couldn't be done.) Returning to the old neighborhood to confront the naysayers and the Negative Nelly's played a part in many sub-plots, acting as a source of inspiration instead of throwing in the towel when the going seemed too tough to bear. So it appears there was (and is) a place for negative motivation. Kenny also had the negative motivation of losing a starting job caused by competition with the up and comers, "And like I said, Barron Miles was behind me, and I didn't want to lose my job as a senior to the guy." Whether you look at it as a boon or a thorn, negative motivation played its part, and the 'here & now' attitude combined with a team-wide aversion of future embarrassments on national television played a decisive role in the buildup to those 60 & 3 years.

Notable quotes #3:
Lorenzo Brinkley on team motivation: "…the worst thing in the world was getting your asses kicked in front of the world in January."

Notable quote #4:
Kenny Wilhite on his greatest achievement: "The biggest moment that I will always cherish is walking across that stage with my diploma. After being told I wasn't gonna graduate: I was never the smartest, I wasn't big enough, I wasn't this, I wasn't that."

When things don't go your way, never give up. Play the next play with all you have, from the time the ball is snapped until the whistle is blown. Play from sideline to sideline. Once your block is made, look downfield for someone else to block.
Michael Arthur & Bryan Bailey, *Complete Conditioning for Football*

The 1995 Cornhusker team achieved four wins over teams ranked in that season's final AP Top Ten poll. It shares this dubious honor with only four others, the most recent of which were Oklahoma in 2000 and Notre Dame in 1988. For those out there who may have questioned the validity of the 'greatest ever' tag mentioned at the start of this book, know that 1995's was not a schedule consisting of cupcakes from start to finish. The non-conference schedule was: Big 10's Michigan State, Pac 10's Arizona State, Big West Conference's University of the Pacific (okay, you've got me there. *One* cupcake.), and Pac 10's Washington State. As for the conference schedule, on the date of each respective game day Kansas State was ranked #8, a week later was Colorado at #7, followed by Kansas at #10 and then Florida at #2.

Also, take note of the margins of victory. For the entire season's slate they averaged 53 to the opponents' 14.5 points, with one of the more egregious shellackings being the #1 vs. #2 national championship game in Tempe, Arizona versus the University of Florida Gators.

After a challenging season's off-field issues many a sportswriter and pundit piled on while predicting a Gator victory that night. Some examples:

"Nebraska can't spell Wuerffel much less stop him."
Brian Landman, St. Petersburg Times

"Nebraska's running game won't be as effective as when they are chased by the cops."
Bruce Lowitt, St. Petersburg Times

Yet others - tempering their venom- lacked faith in the team's ability to overcome Florida and then-Head Coach Steve Spurrier's prolific Fun & Gun offense:

"The Cornhuskers aren't playing Kansas anymore."
Ron Kaspriske, Tampa Tribune.

"So why are we picking the Gators? One reason: Nebraska won't be able to put enough pressure on Wuerffel. No pressure, no second consecutive national championship."
Gene Wojciechowski, The Sporting News

Let it be noted that the Husker Blackshirts tallied seven sacks and three interceptions that night, Mr. Wojo. The historic 62 to 24 beatdown ended with an act of true sportsmanship by Tom Osborne: Nebraska began with the ball on its own 11 yard line and drove the length of the field for the umpteenth time this evening while amassing 631 total yards, only to finish with quarterback Matt Turman mercifully kneeling for a 2 yard loss on the Gator 3 yard line to end the game on downs.

Now, don't think for one minute that some third or fourth or fifth team running back wouldn't have loved to put one more across that goal line. Such a running back started the season in shoulder pads but was relegated to a coaching capacity and sideline sweat suit by the time the last game rolled around. His name was Chris Norris, and this fullback would have gambled the use of his legs for one more rushing attempt such as this. Let's hear him out...

Notable Quote #1:
"Everybody knew their purpose. It wasn't a deal where anybody was put down or cussed at. When you screwed up they might attack your actions, but not the person."

Chris Norris

Walk-on, Fullback, Papillion, Nebraska (Papillion-LaVista)
Where are they now? Cape Girardeau, Missouri, Coach

Question: So you're Running Backs Coach at SEMU, huh?

Chris Norris: Yeah, Running Backs and Special Teams coordinator. Yeah, it's not too bad. Beats getting a real job, anyway. (laughs)

Q: A quick look at your coaching roster seems like it's the University of Nebraska-Missouri there…

CN: Yeah, I believe we have seven former Huskers on the staff here. (laughs) I tell you, being on the coaching staff and also on the playing side, we do a lot of emulating the way we used to do things at Nebraska. And Tony Samuel being the head coach has some really good insights, as well.

Q: So you were from Nebraska, born and bred, right?

CN: I played at Papillion–La Vista High School and then I got hurt 5 games into my senior year at the University of Nebraska. Broke a bone in my neck. Had a bone chip that put me out of it, so I flipped over to the other side as a student assistant for the rest of that season, for spring ball, and then for summer. Then I got a high school job at Papillion–La Vista for two years.

Q: So I take it you always wanted to play for the Huskers?

CN: I don't know if you'll want this in the book. (laughs) Actually, I was an Oklahoma fan for a long time. More of a Barry Switzer fan, really. I had a little bit of a wild side going through high school, and watching all those Nebraska–Oklahoma wars on TV and the hype surrounding it. I'd go down there to Lincoln on to summer camps, though, and finally took my personal visit there just to see for myself how the coaches coached, how the players reacted to the players, the team in general. I visited Colorado, Iowa State, Kansas, and Kansas State, too.

Q: The Big 8 tour, huh? How would you compare Nebraska's recruiting style versus the others?

CN: Frank Solich was a lot more honest, when it came to Nebraska. They weren't trying to pull a lot of B.S. I ended up being a walk-on down there, and it turned out to be between myselfand… and I guess it ended up being Aaron Graham as far as who got the last scholarship. And I don't know if I'd call the other school's actions 'shady', Nebraska was just a lot more upfront when it came to that; you knew exactly where you stood. When Osborne came to the house you could definitely say that turned it around for me, that I was going there, scholarship or no scholarship.

Q: So when was your first fall there?

CN: Fall of '91. My first practice when it was just freshman because the older guys hadn't reported yet, I figured I could definitely play here, no problem. Then the upperclassmen arrived about 5 or 6 days later and I remember going through our first set of drills as running backs and I found myself on my back the first 5 or 6 reps, laying on the sideline looking up at the skybox. There was Omar Soto, Lance Lewis, Cory Schlesinger, Scotty Baldwin. After that it gets a little hazy. You could tell when a guy's having a bad day, they would just tell me, "Hey, that's okay. Things are going to get better. Hang in there. It's gonna be okay, you're here for a reason, don't give up on us." I was getting knocked down and counting lights that first year, but I just stuck with it.

Q: Anything from the organizational aspect stand out?

CN: We talk about that all the time, especially on the staff I'm with and the other staffs I've been on: they ask how things were at Nebraska. Especially since the success lasted so late into the ballgames, people ask, "How was it? What was it? Why were you so successful?"

We had an enormous team. We had 130 -140 guys on the field at one time, it was probably the most well-oiled machine I've ever been around my entire life. It was so structured, so organized from them doing it for so many years. Everybody knew what was going on as far as the coaching staff, everybody knew their purpose. It wasn't a deal where anybody was put down or cussed at. When you screwed up they might attack your actions, but not the person. But even then the worst yelling and screaming was kept to a minimum, because they would just talk to you and teach you the game of football. It was that teaching aspect, explaining what you did wrong, explaining it to where you never felt scared to make mistakes. There were some times you'd get ripped, but you had the full gamut of coaches. Some were calmer and never yelled, and others yelled and screamed and cussed a little bit, but in the end everybody would explain what to do. It was a real friendly environment.

Coach Solich, my position coach, he was fiery with his actions, but I don't ever remember him once cussing me or getting after me. Whether it was on the field or off the field making dumb mistakes, but he never ripped 'em up and then down one end of the field to the other. But he was a tough one.

Q: Any screamers?

CN: I would say it was the defensive coaches. More intense guys. Coach Steele. Coach McBride was pretty intense. Coach Darlington, who I actually had a chance to work with a few years ago.

Q: How was that experience?

CN: It definitely is a little different to work with a guy who was one of your coaches at one time. Certain guys like him have forgotten more about football than I'll ever know. They have a lot of insight and you learned quite a bit in that short period.

Q: Your own coaching style, did you gather a lot from them?

CN: I'm quite a bit like Coach Solich, growing up and seeing how effective it was. I'm not gonna yell and scream when it comes to the running backs, but special teams is a different story. (laughs) Often I have to deal with that mess, so generally I 'lose it' a little bit. I kind of get in trouble for a generous use of certain language now and again. (laughs) I'm not gonna attack somebody personally. I might cuss them out and use some fresh language to make a point, but it's not to a point where you degrade a player. You still want to be teaching them and not cuss & yell just to cuss & yell. Eventually I'm gonna calm down and figure it out and take that guy aside and teach him what to do, otherwise it doesn't do him any good if you can't get him to understand it, teach them what you want and how you want them to do it. That's what I learned at Nebraska.

Q: That's funny, I remember Coach Solich in the early 90's found a unique brand of sunglasses that appeared on market, and they had a very bendable, unbreakable, rubbery nature about them, whereas all the shades used to be the hard, rigid, and easily breakable sort. Well, Coach Solich walks into the weightroom one day and he says with a smirk, "I just love these sunglasses!" I say, 'Why Coach?' And he says, "Because if you want to act like you're really angry at a player, you can take them off and just throw them down on the turf! The kids will get the idea that I'm blowing my top, but these things *won't* break! They're great!" (laughing)

CN: (laughs) Whenever you saw Frank get frustrated, that's when you avoided eye contact!

Q: So you only played 5 games into your last season?

CN: Yeah. I partially tore my MCL (which put me out the first game), rehabbed and braced that up, then came back 3 or 4 games into it. And then we had a scrimmage on an off week and that's when I finally hurt my neck, and it put me out for good. That was in '95, the Fiesta Bowl year.

Q: Could you sense a change in the team from the first day to your last?

CN: It felt like a continuation, to me. It was really intense, team oriented. Everybody just had a great sense of confidence: we knew we were good because we were gonna outwork you, we had the best coaches in the country, the best program, great history, and that's a lot of responsibility to let everyone down.

I was a walk-on the entire time. I was never a starter, but whenever I did get in I contributed. Special teams and the fullback spot. I was just a team player. We had quite a few, I think 17 walk-ons in that recruiting class: Jeff Makovicka, Steve Volin, Brain Nunns, Wayne Mehlin was actually my roommate and he was the best man in my wedding. He ended up finishing up at Wyoming.

Q: Oh, when did he leave for Wyoming?

CN: Right before his junior year. And he came back after he'd finished his senior year there, he came back again and we roomed together again.

I never thought about leaving, ever. I felt like I was contributing. My senior year, myself and Jeff Makovicka were in a pretty close running that year, then I had my injuries. I never got into much trouble, I just went to school and focused on football.

Q: You always seemed very focused, all business. Would that be a proper characterization?

CN: I guess you could say that. Well, you always look back and say, "I could have done this more or that better", especially as a coach. When I went to Nebraska, that really helped me to be coach. To really understand what's going through a player's head, a guy who's struggling and how to deal with it, a guy who thinks he's a better player than where you have him at, that experience provides me some insight where I can help him get to where he needs to be.

Q: What stands out as your shining moment?

CN: I wouldn't say shining moment, but a memorable one would just have been my getting injured, because if not for that, I might not be coaching. Had I stayed healthy and finished out my senior year, who knows what would have happened or what I would have done. So that was an important thing to me, something I won't ever forget.

Q: So tell me more about the neck injury. How did it happen?

CN: It happened, actually, during the spring. I had a couple bone chips that broke free, around C-3, C-4, and took the normal x-rays and they couldn't tell with the x-rays, but I could feel tingling from my neck down. And then I got my feeling back and everything came back normal.

And then it happened in the fall -two more times during fall camp- and then the last one put me down for about half an hour, and I took an MRI and actually found 5 or 6 bone chips sticking into my spinal cord. It turns out I was actually suffering paralysis with the bone chips pressing against my spinal cord but it didn't cut the cord. And the last shot I took moved them and actually pinched it, so I was paralyzed for a half hour. Then I gained my feeling and my mobility again and they decided to take a different look and that pretty much ended it.

Q: Who ended up breaking the news to you?

CN: Honestly, I don't recall. I was in a haze when it was happening, the disbelief when they told me I was done. Meanwhile, I would walk around and felt good, and didn't want to believe it. I tried doing the old 'player deal' where I asked them to let me sign a waiver and take all the responsibility and keep playing and finish up my senior year, but that didn't happen.

Basically, they placed me up in the office doing G.A. (Graduate Assistant) work, doing scouting and breakdown in the booth during games, and seeing everything from the other side of it and recruiting and that kind of stuff. I figured, 'Hey, this isn't a bad gig. I'm having a good time and they're actually paying me to do this.'

Q: Being in the Coaches' meeting room, anything stand out to you when you joined that side?

CN: A lot more things made sense to me. I could see where I had maybe screwed up a couple times and what I could have done better. You get a better sense of when the coach is right and what he's looking for.

Now, most players are not lacking in confidence; most are really confident but sometimes don't see the big picture and the small things that coaches see, especially in college. You have a lot riding on a bunch of 18 to 23 year olds, and when you find yourself on the other side of that door a lot more things make sense and a lot more details stand out that most players don't see. You get a better feel for what's really happening and what goes on.

Q: Little things like what?

CN: Just the fact that showing up on time for meetings, on time for classes, that little things in life all add up. Now, if a guy's not showing up for class, doing the simple things you ask them to do, how can you count on the guy when the game is on the line? It's the small things about being where he needs to be, their life transferring into the game.

And you can also see where the game transfers in life, into your personal life. Again, I got to see that first hand at Nebraska as far as, "Hey, we're trying to raise young men into adults so they have a life after football." I think that was unique, that they didn't put football above everything else. It was definitely an important aspect of it, that they actually cared about you outside of football.

Q: How would you know this?

CN: Like I said, I was a walk-on, wasn't a household name, and never started at fullback, but I knew I could call Coach Osborne to this day if I need some help with something or I just want to say Hi. He's always there for you. My first full-time job at Tennessee State, he helped me get that. He ended up calling the head coach for me and said, "I think he can do a real good job there for you." He knew my sister's and my mom's name, and when he was in town he'd stop and say Hi to her. It was pretty awesome, the little things.

Q: So you were playing for what what may be known as the greatest college football team of all time and then you're forced over to the coaching side of it. Was there a grieving period of sorts?

CN: Pretty much the next day they made me do it. I pretty much blew them off and went to my locker to get the pads and everything for practice and I saw my helmet was gone, and there was a note telling me where the staff meeting was and what was expected of me up in the office. It was a deal that they wanted me to be a part of. And being there for four years, I decided I wanted to finish the thing off.

Q: Do you recall the first game after that?

CN: No, not really. It was just the work of trying to get some things straightened out: from getting the tapes ready to getting things ready for the rest of the running backs and scout teams, drawing up scout cards, watching the starters and scout team do drills, all of that. Clayton Carlin and Mike Grant were the actual GA's, the three of us were helping out with the cards and scouting and breakdown, and also a few other guys who got hurt. Another was Darren -or Damon- Schmadeke and someone else, I can't remember their name.

Q: What was it like being a student assistant?

CN: Coach Solich let you cut your teeth. He'd give you stuff to get done, put a lot of faith in us at that time, giving us quite a bit of responsibility. He expected something to get done and he just took it for granted that we'd get it done, and I made sure to meet the occasion. And I used to help review a lot of recruiting tapes and do administrative stuff, so I was the first line of defense in recruiting. He somehow believed I could tell a bum from a ballplayer. (laughs)

Q: Tell me more about Coach Solich?

CN: He wanted tough, hard-nosed running backs. He treated running backs and fullbacks the same. He wasn't going to give you a break at all. We'd be in practice and have a few backs on the first team, a few on the second team and a few on the third team, and he expected the fullbacks to know the tailback role so we could always fill in in practice. And I spent a lot of time splitting time with the ones and twos, especially my redshirt year. When tailbacks went down he expected you to jump into the tailback spot and run that option and not say anything about it. He definitely didn't coddle us, but he taught us to be really physical, tough, hard-nosed running backs.

Q: Being a Nebraska fullback carried with it some history. What would you say most distinguished Nebraska fullbacks?

CN: It was an attitude. Pardon my French, but we had to believe we were the baddest motherfuckers on that team. We knew we were gonna get hit on every play, we were expected to look for shots on every single play. It didn't matter what play it was; you went in and got that job done because someone was willing to take your place if you couldn't get it done. That job was never safe.

So you went in there and it was an attitude, and I don't think there was a lot of ego. That's something that shows, too. In the end, the guys who are playing are the guys who are supposed to be playing, and you'll get your snaps. And anybody could get called up on any given day, so the expectation was the same for the starter, for every guy (and I think there were 14 fullbacks). The expectations never wavered, it wasn't, "You are just a freshman or just a sophomore," it didn't matter. You were expected to 'bring it' no matter who you were. You learned to play with pain and sometimes you'd get injured, but you had to know the difference between injury and pain. Everybody gets a little banged up and sore, and it was kind of a badge of honor to make it through a practice that most people in the country couldn't make it through. I mean, every day in practice we were playing against the best defense in the country! (laughs) That's definitely something worth hanging your hat on, too: how many All-Americans you went against. And on game days you knew you had already faced better rush ends, better linebackers, better safeties than any guys in the country.

Q: Any names stick out from those practices?

CN: Phil Ellis: probably one of the hardest hitting guys, pound for pound. In fact, I played against him in the state championship game when we played Grand Island. He beat us my junior year and we came back and whooped their ass pretty good my senior year.

Q: Was there some bragging, some smack talking throughout your college career because of that?

CN: He won one at our expense and I won one at his. He had one ring and I had another ring, so we were even. And our championship rings? I wear them for recruiting, otherwise they're usually in a little box I had made up. They're usually in the box all season, but when recruiting comes around, that's when the rings come out. (laughs)

Q: Which is your favorite ring: 94's or '95's?

CN: Both, for different reasons. I got one as a player and I got one to signify my start of my coaching career, so they have different meaning for me.

Q: What was it like on the sidelines for those games?

CN: That Florida State game was heartbreaker. Everybody who loses a tight one, there's always gonna be a reason why you got robbed. A lot of us believed that one got taken away from us; the 'phantom clip', not crossing the goal line.

Now, as a coach, you see that anything's gonna happen. But that one definitely stings. In fact, I had the chance when I was down in Jacksonville, Florida State was playing in a bowl game in Jacksonville and they used our facilities. And my wife is actually a big Bobby Bowden fan and she wanted to go up and meet him. So she made me walk over with her because she had something she wanted to get signed and there he was wearing this national championship ring. I joked with him, 'Hey, you're wearing my ring.' (laughs) He kind of laughed about it and said, "Yeah, that's how that goes sometimes."

Q: He had his own fair share of missed field goals over the years, huh?

CN: That's for sure.

Q: Do you recall when they put the Unity Council into effect?

CN: That was probably one of the neatest things I've ever seen, doing that. A lot of people try to do something like that after hearing about it and try to emulate it, but that's tough to do. The coaches have to have a lot of faith in the team, trusting players to take care of it. And the coaching staff there? The continuity of that staff? I think it helped to have that kind of stability to put something like that together.

And everyone had to pay their dues, they didn't start right away. Some will eventually play, and some guys don't even get to play come their senior year -quite a few players who didn't play until their senior year- and they were just happy as all get-out when they played.

Q: And then you had guys like Tommie and Grant Wistrom who played right away…

CN: If you have a great program like we did, you get those guys now and then, but nowadays most players don't want to put their time in and wait a few years to play, they want to play now. So I have a better chance at getting some of those guys at our school now because they want to play right way.

Q: Anything stand out as far as the Miami game?

CN: Oh, that one. It was kind of weird, because we were down a little bit and things weren't going 100% our way, but Coach Osborne was so calm and collected, you just knew that something was going to happen if we hung around that game long enough. They had all those phenomenal players -those name players who get all the press- but we just calmly went about our business and in the end we outlasted them and made some other good plays.

Q: Were you on special teams that game?

CN: I was on punt unit and backup on kickoffs and kickoff returns.

Q: What was your position there?

CN: I was one of the up-backs and personal protector on those teams, usually. We saw more consistency and balance and physicality in practice, to tell you the truth, but those guys you had to watch out for. It was fast. (laughs) There were some matchups out there, that's for sure.

Q: In differentiating the Florida teams of those years, in what ways were the Huskers different?

CN: Those Florida teams would definitely talk a whole lot more. Truthfully, I never ever paid much attention to it, though, as I had too many other things to think about.

I think we were a disciplined team. Personal fouls, even a fight in practice? You know that went on, but it wasn't the type of thing really celebrated when a fight got started in practice. There are some places where fights are celebrated from coaches as building a tough and aggressive team, but the coaching staff didn't measure that as a sign of toughness. We were a disciplined team, we're gonna keep running the plays we're gonna run and you're gonna stop us, but eventually the dam is gotta break.

The Florida game was different; we jumped on them pretty quick. It was kind of a foregone conclusion that we would come out on top of that one.

Q: Can you believe we were underdogs in that game?

CN: Yeah, it's that scary speed, that athlete. They have a bunch of players, a lot of talent, thoroughbreds down there in that state and they recruit it, but a more disciplined, more physical team is definitely going to take care of an athletic team. Making a mistake at full speed is still making a mistake.

Q: If you had a chance to do anything differently, would you?

CN: Mostly little things, like spending more time on footwork. Things I see as a coach now? Little things that affected me as a player: eating better, not realizing how short that career really is, that was something. I never took that into account. One day I'm a player and one day I'm not. For me it ended in all of 5 seconds.

Q: Did that affect your psyche or concept of who you were?

CN: It screwed me up for a little while, a lot of 'what if's' and wondering what I could have done differently, you know? In essence I'd already had that injury, so it was just a matter of when I was going to take the shot that ended it.

Q: Do you recall who made that last hit on you? I'm sure you remember…

CN: (laughs) It was Luther Hardin.

Q: Luther always had that killer look. Like a smiling assassin…

CN: It was actually just a run up the middle, a little shot. And I had to let him know it wasn't anything he did. It was going to happen eventually, and he just happened to do it.

Q: Anybody behind the scenes who meant a lot?

CN: Probably, between Doak (Ostergard) and Sully (George Sullivan), those guys did an amazing job keeping us on the field.

Q: Any good stories?

CN: Probably a hundred of them. Sully being that stereotypical gruff, old, grumpy, 'you-can- play, rub-some-dirt-on-it kind of guy,' and Doak was the guy who would get you on the field by hook or crook. Those guys always got you ready for practice and really took care of you.

Q: Any examples of what made them special?

CN: It was just the jolly demeanor. Like I said, Sully was the guy that you couldn't bullshit him. He'd heard it all and you couldn't fool him. He could tell by the way you were looking at him if you had anything wrong or if you were trying to pull something on him. Doak just always had a way to get you out there.

Another guy, Bryan Bailey, a lot of people don't realize what he did. There was no one like Bryan. He was just a little, mean bastard, that's for sure. (laughs) Greatest guy, but as small as he was and everybody kind of looking at him and kind of, "Are you really a strength coach?" He's actually one that helped me out quite a bit. I ended up weighing upward from 260 lbs. and I was just getting to big and too thick for my own good until he finally started stretching me along with the lifting and running and stretching out and getting more flexible and getting my time down to where I was able to get to play at the 250, 255 mark.

Q: Oh my gosh, you let Bryan stretch you?! You were a glutton for punishment…

CN: Oh Jesus, he beat the shit out of me. And he kept calling me 'fatty' because I kept doing that ab workout. If you could only catch that quick little bastard! And him and Doak would find ways to push your buttons, where you sometimes felt like you wanted to take a swing at them. (laughs)

Q: And what was your experience with some of your fellow running backs?

CN: Well, everyone wants to know about Lawrence. Honestly, I liked Lawrence. He was misunderstood on a lot of things he did. I definitely can't speak for his mindset later on with the incident out in L.A. and whatnot, but he just, he never really thought too far ahead as to what consequences were gonna be. But as far as working with him, playing with him and being around him, it was always 'friends first, teammates first ahead of me', he would always take care of others instead of thinking about himself. He just never thought ahead, it's a shame he never thought of the consequences. And I tell you, he is one of the best running backs I've ever been around. Oh, he was a freak! The fact that he came into that national championship game after the long layoff he had, when he was suspended, and then did what he had to do. Got that all cleared up, and then on the biggest stage in college football he brought it. His timing should have been off, he shouldn't have been in game shape, but he was monster. Oh god, he was a freak, his work ethic.

He took the game part serious, did not hold back emotions on the field. If he was pissed off at you, you were gonna know about it. I think that later got him into trouble in the NFL: speaking his mind, not shutting up when he had the chance. He just said what he felt and what was on his mind came out and he got into some trouble. But as far as my personal feeling, I thought he was good guy. What you saw was what you got, on a good day or bad day. And he didn't apologize for anything, either.

Q: What about Coach Osborne?

CN: He was perhaps the most honest person in this profession. He talked to you straight, he didn't lie to you. If he said he cared about you, you would believe that. He cared about the players. He cared about them. It was not all about football. We went there for football, but you got a lot more from him than just football. He did a lot for the community. Just the kind of role model he was, you learned a whole bunch about football from him, too, but you learned a lot about being a man than from just about anybody I can think of.

Q: What about the goals you guys would set?

CN: He started at the bottom and we'd work our way up to the top. Definitely National Champions was always one of our goals. We set that to attain that. And each game we'd set the goals to have that win. We were always setting goals to make them attainable. He expected the best out of us and he gave us tools to be successful.

In the end, I think him and his staff did a real good job of giving each man a role on that team. And if that role meant you did your part, it meant you were going to win. If that meant you were just on scout team that week, if you did your job and each guy did his, that pretty much meant you were going to win. Part of my freshman year and part of my redshirt year, you know, our scout team probably could have beaten some of the Big 8 teams of that time. (laughs) It was a ball-buster practice. We went after it. We went after those guys more than they went after us. We gave them a good look, and they knew they were gonna get it from us.

And I never ever heard Coach Osborne cuss. He had that type of personality where you wouldn't ever want to let the man down. If you let him down he could make you feel so small… with a look or with a few soft-spoken words to you, he'd let you know if you let him down, if you let the team down. That's a feeling that most people did not want to go through again.

Q: What about other coaches on staff?

CN: I would say every coach on that staff was genuine in his own way. Coach Darlington was definitely fired up and opinionated, didn't care what he said around anybody and wasn't going to apologize for anything he said. Anytime he got on guys nothing was ever said with malice or anything that might come off that way. It was an honest staff. You had some guys who would get fired up and definitely get a kick, Coach Tenopir getting fired up, Coach McBride.

Charlie was definitely a character. I was scared to death of that man my whole first year. I didn't want to go anywhere near him. You didn't even want to have any conversations with him. (Or at least I'll call them conversations.) (laughs) One year I was on the scout team, freshman year, we were up at the stadium and Kevin Raemakers kept getting extra shots at you as you walked back to the huddle, on the back of your helmet. And we finally had enough of taking that stuff, and I ended up taking a swing and ended up punching Parrella! And he snatched me up and started running me toward the sideline fence. It was just a matter of which seating row I was going to land on, and then the whistle blew… he just stopped, put me down, and walked away. And that's just an example of how disciplined it was. When the whistle blew it was over and nothing else was thought of it. You either handled it before the whistle blew or it was over. It was never a fact that guys were going to hunt you down after the practice, fights in the locker room, none of that stuff ever got past the field. There was going to be some disagreements and hard feelings, but in the end we were still a team. In my mind, we were still teammates and it wouldn't have a lingering effect.

Q: Any comments about Jack Stark or Dave Ellis?

CN: Jack Stark, he was great guy, really approachable guy. He knew when to keep things to himself, and other times he acted as a conduit with position coaches or Coach Osborne. He could let the coaches know if something was going on in a player's life, their playing, their studying. But he definitely was a help.

I went through a small patch there where I was actually shot in Lincoln my junior year at a party. (We had a birthday party for a buddy and it was one of those deals where a couple guys came over and started some trouble and pulled a gun out and fired some shots.) And that same weekend my cousin had killed himself, so all in all that was kind of a shitty weekend. My mom got a hold of me and told me my cousin killed himself, and then I had to tell her what happened to me. Jack was a great conduit between the coaches and helped get things settled and figured out.

Q: Did they ever catch the guy who shot you?

CN: Yeah, they did. I got shot in the arm. It was a little .22 caliber. I have a little scar on both sides.

Q: And the team mottos. Did those mean a lot?

CN: I think we bought right into it, the 'We Refuse To Lose,' that stuck with most of us. It was so explanatory. We just weren't going to lose that year, and we just made up our minds that we weren't going to lose. Especially that Florida State game. That was something we all felt.

Q: Chris, in my mind, we never lost that game. We simply ran out of time…

CN: (laughs) Exactly! Good way of looking at it.

Q: Any last things that you feel we haven't touched upon?

CN: I think part of it was -as you talk about the parallels between successful teams and whatnot- the countdown to those years was the consistency. The kind of players Nebraska got in those days were hard-nosed, tough players at that time; the fact that guys were turning down scholarships to walk-on at Nebraska, walking away from money. A lot of guys had the opportunity to play for the Kansases and the Iowa States, but I wanted to play for that National Championship, I wanted to play for those coaches, to be part of that program. It was kind of a no-brainer that I'd come down there and do that, and find a way to get it done.

Q: Ever talk to Coach Solich?

CN: Yeah, I see him at the conventions. My wife and I always send out Christmas cards and stay in touch. Sometimes it's hard to just call up and shoot the crap because as a head coach there's always a lot of things going on. It's kind of that same 'ol, Once a Husker, always a Husker. Coach Samuel preaches keeping it in the family. That's why he hired some of us. And that definitely breeds success. Most of the time you have the Nebraska influence, the Nebraska connection when you do your hiring. When you run our program, it's how Coach Osborne did it, without all the flair, without the attitude and all of that. You do it right, take your time, take the calmer approach to ballgames, and you get it done. That's how it was back there and it was a business-like approach. You just went out and did your job. We were just better prepared, had better strength, better toughness, were better conditioned, and as a consequence, the athleticism against the Florida teams, we felt like we could play them.

Q: Do you think it was ever a hurdle in some guys' minds that we would always have to play those Florida teams down there in Florida instead of some other team for the big ones?

CN: No, not really. I think it was a point of pride to try to go down there and kick their ass. (laughs) To this day, as a coach, I enjoy away games as much as I enjoy home games. In some respects it's good to try to ruin some guy's party. (laughs)

Q: Last question, Chris: Let's say I'm a brand new running back on the team and it's my first day of practice, what are you going to preach to me?

CN: Oh, it's going to be 'high and tight, rolling forward.' High and tight, rolling forward. Hold that ball tight over your breastplate. If you fumble that ball, don't look at me, just head over to the sideline and stay about a good 15 feet way from me for the next two or three plays, because the next guy is already on his way in. (laughs) High and tight, rolling forward until you get out in the open field, then you can swing that thing down tight.

And if Coach Solich ever saw a football photograph of us backs with bad backs with bad ball-technique -holding it out and away from the body, with daylight showing between the ball and the body?- you owed a dozen donuts if he found a picture with bad ball-technique.

Q: What kind of doughnuts did Coach Solich like you to bring?

CN: You know, I think it was just player's choice. Whatever you got. I don't think he even ate any. He just left them in the staff room.

Q: He let Coach Darlington and Coach Young eat them, huh?

CN: (laughs) Exactly! And I do it the same way. If you fumble in practice you owe me 20 up-downs right away. And when you get done with that and the ball's on the ground one more time, the next guy's automatically going in. I don't have to say anything. The next guy on the depth chart automatically goes in, whether it's a game or practice. There ain't no running back worth two fumbles. So if you fumble twice, just have a seat.

End conversation.

Listening to this direct disciple of Nebraska Running Backs Coach Frank Solich brought me back to a level of focused, white-hot intensity that a person saw in all of the running backs of the day. A unique mix of personalities and dispositions off the field, there was no hemming or hawing on it because these guys were tough as concrete jawbreakers and put the hurt on many a defender looking to score highlight reel-hits. Starting spots were tenuous, carries were precious, and daily competition was fierce. Like Chris said, "There ain't no running back worth two fumbles."

The coaching style on the offensive side of the ball was very much a study in styles. Notice how Chris made the distinction between attacking a student/athlete's actions rather than the person himself? Think about it: these young men were at an institution of higher learning to challenge themselves, to engage, to grow, to expand their horizons and mature both mentally and physically by way of classrooms both indoors and out. Mistakes were expected but soon corrected, and healthy coach/athlete relationships resulted.

I've always held highest regard for Tom Osborne's Nebraska Football program because of the promulgated vision that education was the key -the main gist of the grand student/athlete experience- and that poor player performances were more often to be blamed on the coach (not the student) for failing to properly convey a point and more effectively instruct. Fortunately, poor performances were a rarity during that era, so finger pointing was kept to a minimum.

Notable quote #2:
Chris Norris on discipline and football/life transferability: "If a guy's not showing up for class, doing the simple things you ask them to do, how can you count on the guy when the game is on the line? It's the small things about being where he needs to be, their life transferring into the game. And you can also see where the game transfers in life, into your personal life."

Nothing is little to him that feels it with great sensibility.
                    Samuel Johnson, *Boswell's Life of Dr. Johnson*

I had a great week of interviews. Why? Because I corralled not one, but both Eminence Outliers, the first of which was Performance Nutritionist Dave Ellis. The other, Dr. Jack Stark, has already been mentioned by a player or two, and if not for his keen and kindhearted insight, his direct, yet calm and patient speaking manner mixed with a fiery competitive streak, I verily believe that 60 & 3 era would have become more like 56 & 7.

The good doctor plied his wares in the Athletic Department's hallways, nooks and players' crannies with an astounding caseload. I recall many a day when -seemingly out of the blue- he would appear after a practice or before a game to sidle up to a player and share a notion, an encouraging word, place a vision of the success in a kid's mind's eye in anticipation of a payoff when the stress was high and clock was running down.

Still in demand by a variety of high profile suitors, I caught him on a bad phone connection with a terribly sore throat and cutting headache that night. Trying to make our conversation quick for his health's sake, I ended the interview far earlier than I would have wished. But then again, a little medicine from the Doc is better than none at all, wouldn't you agree?

Notable Quote #1:
"There were times we'd be in the meeting rooms talking about some of the (players) and there would almost be tears."

Jack Stark

Question: Hey Doc, what are you up to these days?

Dr. Jack Stark: Keeping busy. Doing some consulting work, doing some volunteer work, doing some things with NASCAR right now. So its keeps me out of trouble.

Q: Well, I must say, it's great hearing your voice again. So take me back to '91, before you started working with the team.

JS: I actually started in the '89 season: Spring of 1989. The first two years it was just trying to get them to know me and trust me. And as you know, there were a lot of confidentiality issues and stuff that goes on, a lot of people not really knowing me, trust issues. So it really took me all of '89 and '90 to get to know people. There were some people there before me and, honestly, the players didn't trust one of the guys; so that really took some work.'90 was a really difficult year, and I started doing a lot more work in '91. With Coach Osborne it was wonderful to be and work with a guy who knew what I wanted and trusted me to let me do my thing.

Q: Where were you working with prior to '89?

JS: I was working with the medical school here in Omaha and I was also working in my private practice in town. I went to school at Nebraska and received a degree in Psychology and graduated in '73. In '89 I was working full-time and then came down and put in about 25 hrs. a week at Nebraska.

Q: Were you involved in Sports Psychology before joining the team?

JS: Yeah, I'd been working with UNO in the 70's and worked with everything from golfers to teams for high school, college kids, some pros. Individual stuff, mostly. Then there was an organization in Florida, and I had been down there giving some talks and they recommended me, so in January of '89 I met Coach Osborne and started doing what was supposed to be 10 hours a week. But after that I realized there was a lot of work to be done, so we moved it up to 25 hours a week. I was commuting from Omaha and would come down on Tuesdays and Thursdays and Saturdays.

And that continued all summer long, and then it just worked into being all year-round. There were no formal workouts, but I still hung around after their workouts and talked to them one on one. It was a great time because they weren't so busy, so I was able to get to know them and who they were and build a relationship with them.

Q: Who connected you with Coach Osborne?

JS: It was the National Sports Psychology Forum. I still work with them a little bit. They had a national conference and I think Dave Gillespie called them up and they recommended me to him, and it just kind of took off from there.

Q: So can you place me -as a fly on the wall- in your first meetings with Coach Osborne?

JS: Well, I made a presentation to all the coaches in a meeting there, and afterwards just spoke to Coach one on one. I didn't know how to engage them, but from the meeting and my presentation they found that I was very competitive, that I had some fire. And Coach Osborne had always had somebody he'd used...he'd used a female psychologist on campus in the past, too. (And I don't know if you know it, but Coach Osborne has his own PhD in Psychology, so he always appreciated that, the personal side of psychology.) So I was fortunate and a little different than most people in that I had a number of experiences in educational psychology, sports psychology, clinical psychology, team building and organizational psychology, so I had all those experiences I could use.

Q: How many college football teams had a sports psychologist at that time?

JS: Oh, probably less than 3 or 4, and they were only part-time. And at that time it was really hard to work with teams, because so many people had little regard for sports psychologists. The old model didn't work very well because they thought of us as 'head doctors,' they thought it was a little hokey. So what I tried to do was spend some time getting to know everybody other than getting to be known as 'the guy who you went to when it came to dealing with problems.' I was also the guy who dealt with the sports psychology and that was a big difference.

Q: Hmmmm. Can you differentiate that statement for me?

JS: There were a lot of psychologists out there who liked to present themselves as sports psychologists. And first of all, it's a very tough field; there's a lot of fakes in my field, a lot of pretenders. They might have a PhD in an area, and most who say they are in sports psychology came out of some exercise physiology or physical education department, so they're not a psychologist, but an exercise physiologist who comes at it from the mental side. What I found was that the job was mostly dealing with issues and problems.

Q: You once said that as many as 40% of college students are dealing with psychological issues. Would that figure still apply today?

JS: Oh, yes. And not just athletes, that's all students. And some people think that many athletes have mental health issues and don't deal with stress well, but these players are just like any other college student; it's just that when a typical student has an issue of some sort it doesn't make the newspaper.

Q: I got this from your website, and it says, "It's fascinating, but the team culture almost always seems to overcome any irrational behavior…."

JS: Yeah, that's why team peer pressure is so critical. That's where team leaders have to exhibit leadership. Senior leadership is always so critical. If you don't have that nucleus - because coaches can't always be around- it's important to have that peer pressure in the locker room.

Q: And if memory serves, was the Unity Council your brainchild?

JS: What happened was, I was getting to know the players and noticed that they just weren't getting along. And I talked to one kid who was really helpful with this thing: It was Kevin Raemakers and he was from Nebraska. And we got to talking and I said, "We really need some unity here. You guys need to care about each other, and we need some leaders here who have to care about everybody else." And he went to Coach Osborne and said, "Hey, we need to listen to this project that Dr. Stark is talking about. We need something dealing with unity, Coach." And Coach Osborne asked me if it would work, and I said, 'Well, it may not work the first year, but it could work better after 3 or 4. I think we could become a force and win the national championship, Coach.' And he looked at me and he said, "That's too long. We need it to work now." So I swallowed my estimate and said 'Okay. Well, let's get going on this if we want to get the job done.'

So we started meeting and kept working at it and it was great, just a lot of fun. Boyd Epley had an idea of some points. We used that for awhile, for missing classes and stuff like that. We didn't always use it, but it was a great way of keeping track of things, though we didn't need it after a while.

Q: You said players weren't getting along. What was the primary cause of that? Was it a race issue? Competition? What?

JS: No. I mean, you could have that. You had offense versus defense, in-state versus out-of-state, black versus white, walk-on versus scholarship, you could have all sorts of things that can divide a team. But the good thing was that we got it all organized. The kids just said, "Hey, we've gotta stop this thing", and it took 4 years to get it under control.

Q: Boyd said he thought a great start was the team meeting in early '91 before winter conditioning, and I've also read where you felt halftime of the Citrus Bowl after the '90 season -when Kenny Walker gave Coach Osborne a big hug- maybe that was a huge turning point for the team. What do you say to that?

JS: Well, it was halftime and Coach had talked to the team. And he just had had it: we were playing terrible, we weren't ranked. And I have to give it to Coach, when it came to that next summer he didn't take any vacation. He just cranked it up and basically looked at me and said, "It's going to work now. Right now." He went in there and had some meetings and basically said, "This better work. If you don't, we're not doing it anymore." Essentially saying that,"If it doesn't, you're fired." (laughs) That was early in '91.

Q: So let's go back to that span of time…

JS: I think it peaked in those years all the way up to '97. That's when we had the best leaders we've ever had. You had Jason Peter and Grant Wistrom. Just the greatest, two at the same time. You also had Christian Peter before that, who was a great leader in the locker room in '94 and '95, but in the final two years, those two guys really continued it. And it ran in a progression in further years with other guys. And when I had my heart surgery I didn't work the last two months of that year and just kind of slept in. I had to make some changes, wasn't quite as involved. And of course I left after the Colorado game in 2003 when they got rid of Frank, I didn't want to have anything to do with it.

Q: Any other leaders come to mind from those teams?

JS: Well, each year you had people who became great leaders. All the way through the '90's it seemed each year there would be 2-3 guys out of 16-17 guys were great leaders, and they were the ones that really carried it. Terry Conneally, Chad Kelsay, Aaron Graham were natural leaders. Over the years -I'm trying to think- it seemed like we always had good leaders.

Q: From the way you describe it, they were just guys who rose up regardless of position on the field. Were these leaders created or did they already have it, that leadership factor?

JS: I think these were guys who had some qualities, they already had it. And I had to spend a lot of time, I would speak to them about how to lead and worked with them a little bit. They came in different packages: some guys wanted to beat others up and were tough and wanted to lead from that physical standpoint whereas other guys were more shy, so you had leaders who weren't vocal, and they could identify with some role in a different nature, like your Kyle VandenBosch and that type of player. So they came in all types.

Q: How did you identify these leaders when you spoke to them? Did the coaches tell you to talk to them?

JS: I just had to figure out who had it, who the players respected and listened to. It's interesting, because the players choose who they are sometimes. Sometimes the leaders are the great players and sometimes it just seemed like these were guys who the others listened to. And so I would go to them and say, 'Hey, you better step it up, because the other guys are listening to you. You can't start mouthing off or doing stupid stuff or not keeping your role or be going out on Thursday nights, 'cause we're a team. We need you to do it, and here's how to do it....'

And I ended up spending a lot of time with those teams, because it seemed oftentimes that there were weeks I spoke with every single player. That took a lot of time, but everyone was worth it. I sure enjoyed working with Coach Osborne and the players and built a lot of great friendships.

Q: Any special friendships, guys you keep in contact with to this day?

JS: Oh boy, I probably have 50 to 60 guys that I keep in contact with all the time. There were so many of them, Paul, that were just great. More than a whole decade of guys who were really special, who grew up in front of your eyes and matured and brought that leadership out into the world & their lives outside of football after it was over. Just a special group of people that Coach Osborne and his staff brought in to play. Those classes, you had your Tommie Frazier, your Lawrence Phillips, Damon Benning, Clinton Childs to Grant Wistrom, to.... gosh, there are so many guys come to mind. They were all good kids -and some had some detours in life- in the case of Jason Peter and his life and book that he came out with recently.

Q: Let me ask: were there any distinctions or differences in mindset or attitude from the very outset that you really had to work on?

JS: There was a lot of individual stuff, and guys were focused on what they could do individually to make it to the pros. It wasn't going badly, it was just, instead of the $60,000 or $80,000 a year job they wanted to go to the next level of earning and the $2 million dollars-a-year job, and everybody was focusing on that.

And just more getting along and stuff? It wasn't bad, but it wasn't right where it could have been, and those next few years we had something that was really special.

Q: Was there a greater emphasis on getting to the national championship game, or was that goal always realisitically there? I seemed that in the late 80's and early 90's they were just happy to make it to a bowl game and to party, maybe didn't take it as seriously?

JS: Yeah, and we also ended up getting better players, and they were more serious: the coaches and the players became more accountable and they concentrated on goals and the focus of having a championship team.

Q: What was the most challenging aspect of your job?

JS: I think the most challenging aspect for any coach or anyone working with the players is trust. Once you get that trust, once they know that you are all the way there for them and they can feel free to call you at 2 in the morning, at 4 in the morning and aren't in it only for yourself or just to make money? Having the relationship and having their trust, that was one of the key things.

Q: It took some buildup and time to get to that place?

JS: It takes awhile for guys to know you. They knew the coaches because they sw them about every day, but I tried to spend as much time as I could with them. When they're freshman to the time they're seniors you get to know them a lot better. And by the 2nd, 3rd year there you've already had a bit of time with them, so it's not quite as difficult.

Q: Obviously, there was probably a staff dynamic going on there, too. Any recollections of the coaching staff in general?

JS: Well, we really tried to focus on how the kids interacted with coaches and how to give them feedback, what the likes & dislikes were and how the kids reacted to the feedback that the coaches gave them. And I got really close to the coaches, too, and spent a lot of time just knowing how to give the players feedback, how they worked together, and how to better share the feedback, too. So we got close. Charlie McBride and I were very, very close. It was a tremendous relationship, and the players really benefited from all of that, you know.

Q: You were able to alter their coaching philosophies or methods along the way?

JS: I think it was just knowing how to relate better to kids. There were just multiple kinds of things you could do for a kid on any particular day. For example, let's say you had one of the tougher coaches and I could say, 'How is so and so doing?', and he'd say, "He's doing alright, what do you think?" And I might say, 'Well, I think so and so could use a real pat on the back today.' And the coach would look at me and say, "Okay, I understand Doc. I know you can't tell me everything, but I get the message that maybe the kid's having a rough time elsewhere in life." Maybe the kid's bummed out and feeling down, so sometimes it was just a matter of telling the coaches to deal with a player a certain way that day.

Q: Jack, I know from those years when I was working with the Nebraska basketball team that you had a lot of interaction with a number of other sports, too. In relating to those '93-'97 teams, were the footballers different in comparison to other sports & other teams of the day?

JS: Yeah, their mental toughness was incredible. That's because of the way Osborne ran his program. And I have to tell you, the basketball was there, too. As you know, Danny Nee was one of my best friends, and I worked with football and basketball and spent a lot of time with them, so it was quite an exhausting year, that first year in '90-91. We had some good basketball teams, too, huh?

Q: Indeed. Those were great years. So how would you categorize that mental toughness?

JS: Well, in the 4th quarter we wore people down, and Coach would know how to run practice better than anybody in the nation. He taught physicality; he would emphasize that every day in practice. (And then, in contrast, you would have (Bill) Callahan where you would run a pro-style practice where they hardly ever wore pads, so they never got physical in practice, and that's why they couldn't tackle in a game.)

Q: Please don't go there. I might need some time on a couch with you to get over those years, Jack. (laughs) Now, you were on the sidelines for those games, right?

JS: Oh yeah, I was in the locker room and on the sidelines. I saw everything, I heard everything. A lot of times it was just me and the players in the locker room, so I saw a lot of things and I could keep it to myself. And then they could trust me and share things with me, so it was a very secure relationship.

Q: Anything really stand out from some of those times in the locker room?

JS: What stood out was their incredible love for Tom Osborne. They really, really cared for him. There were times before the team prayer on game day where some guys would have something special to say about him, why they were playing for him. They just cared about Coach. They would do anything for him. It was amazing how these incredibly tough guys talked about how much they cared about Tom.

Q: How do you think that came about, Jack?

JS: It was just because he was always there for them. There were times we'd be in the coach's meeting rooms talking about some of them and there would almost be tears. And he would always call on them and see how they were doing, ask them about their family. He was just a great guy.

It also had something to do with his spirituality, and it was to the point where the players respected his character and just didn't want to let him down. These guys felt like he was a father to them (and some guys didn't have dads), so it was a really special relationship.

Q: Some of the guys who didn't have fathers growing up, were they more taxing on your time?

JS: Not so much taxing, it was just oftentimes that you spent more time with them. Because they needed a mentor, and sometimes it just happened that there were a lot of the black players I became very close to. Sometimes it was merely the fact that the players felt that I understood them. And I'm close to them today and have gone to their weddings and baptisms and family events. So if they didn't have a father I just spent a little more time with them trying to understand them.

Q: Doc, one thing I've always found incredibly inspirational was the team prayer. Did you come up with the team prayer that was shared before the games?

JS: Yeah, there was one of the guys -and I can't remember who it was, who came from the East Coast- he had something kind of ¾ of what we came up with. I tweaked and tweaked and tweaked it, and it became the team prayer and the guys loved it, and I still use it today. I would definitely like to give credit to the guy who came up with it, I just can't remember who it was. (laughs)

Q: Did you present it to Coach Osborne first?

JS: I presented it to the Unity Council. We then used it every game thereafter and it became very sacred; it was the last thing we did before we left the locker room. It was kind of a mantra of sorts, and was done very well. They got into a routine and loved it, so that worked out well.

Q: It seems to me that you and Coach Osborne were quite often of the same mind on a great number of things. Was there anything else you ever brought to him, anything of interesting note that we could share?

JS: Well, there was one time that I recall an idea having quite a profound impact. I believe it was the 1994 season and I went to Tom this one day and said, 'Coach, I would like to have a few minutes to talk with the team –the whole team- in the team meeting today.' And Tom took a little step back and gave me an astonished look and said, "The whole team? There must be something extremely important for you to want to do that…" And I told him that I felt it was something that needed to be shared with everyone and that they would all benefit greatly.

Q: You've got my attention…

JS: So I got up in front of the entire team and the coaches and I told them, 'Listen guys, I've got something you need to hear. I've gone back for ten years or so and looked at all of the scores and schedules from each season. And I've found something that stands out to me, something that screams out to me for attention. This is the 9th week of the season, and every year we have our toughest game -our closest scores and biggest scares, our greatest chance to stumble- on the 9th week…

Q: Iowa State, 1992…

JS: Right! A team we should never have lost to. So I went on, '..I know you guys have mid-terms and papers -it's that time of the semester- so you need to buckle down and be prepared. Get it done early and do it right. No pulling any over-nighters. Get your sleep. And not just Friday night, but Tuesday night, Wednesday and Thursday, too. No parties, no drinking or staying up late. If we stumble just once our dream, our goal, it's gone. This is the week to take care of your business and take care of your bodies.'

Q: The "9th Week Syndrome"?

JS: The 9th week. The season is a grind and kids can lose focus. And it really made me feel good when, at the meeting's end, Coach Osborne reiterated everything I'd shared and said, "Guys, Doctor Stark is right," -I think even he was surprised that I'd come up with that- "..you take care of yourselves and be sure to get all your rest like he says and prepare for your exams." It really validated some of the things that I'd been thinking about and prevented a slip-up going forward. I really believe that.

Q: That's magnificent insight! And Jack, can you tell me a little about the pre-game speeches by coaches, do you have any opinion of those?

JS: (laughs) Charlie used to do one on Friday night and they'd be so jacked up they couldn't sleep. So we changed that, started going to a format on game day where Charlie would talk to the defensive players and the offensive coaches would speak to the offense, and after they'd be done talking we'd watch a video psych-up tape I put together that week. And after the psych-up tapes we'd have the Captains talk, and then right before they ran out to the field they'd say that prayer.

Q: Do you still have copies of the psych-up tapes?

JS: I might have some in the basement. I'm not even sure. They're pretty scattered. They were mostly highlights from the previous game set to music.

Q: Anything ever backfire on you?

JS: One time on tape one of the guys predicted we'd beat Kansas by 40 points, and some of the coaches thought that wasn't a good thing to put in there. And 99% of the time they were right.

Q: Do you recall the score of that game? Did we win by 40?

JS: Oh, it was something like 30 for that game. (laughs)

Q: Any highlights that stand out to you from a particular game or moment?

JS: I think… to me it was Osborne's winning the bowl game after the '94 season: we ended up alone in the elevator and he was thanking me for all I'd done, and to me that was pretty special. Those '94 and '95 bowl games, there were so many people at the airport, it was single file coming off the plane. That was kind of nice, too.

Q: What would you say you're most proud of, Jack?

JS: Well, I've never said it in public, but the thing I'm most proud of was that nobody in my 14 years had ever once attempted suicide. Never attempted it or did it. Given the stress and pressure of 150 players a year for 14 years, that's a lot of players. I went to great lengths to make sure nobody felt like that was the option. We usually stayed on top of it, and if it ever became an issue we were there to stop it soon enough.

Q: If I recall, a player had committed suicide prior to the 1983 or 1984 season.

JS: You know, I think there was sometime around there. I'm not sure of the year.

Q: Can you give me an idea of the pressures these young men were going through?

JS: Well, the biggest pressure, too, is that some of these kids come from homes that have nothing. And they know if they can make it through and get drafted and have a shot at it, it's just huge. Financially, identity-wise, the dedication of everything they've done since they were 6-7 years of age, if they don't make it? It's just crushing to them. So I always tried to have them make sure to have a dream, a backup plan. If they played pro ball, great, but if it didn't happen they could always go on to something else.

Q: Did the players read the papers much? It's easy to say that they don't, but are they affected much by what they read?

JS: Well, they read the internet and blogs and everything else. And you try not to let it, but it impacts them. Some of those people are crazy, it's crazy what you see online these days.

Q: What advice would you give those fans? Any positive, constructive advice from the Good Doctor?

JS: Well, I'd just remind them to remember what it's like to be 18, 19, or 20 years old. You know, if you're forty that's one thing, but if you're a young man and you're trying and you make mistakes, some people say an awful lot of things that create a lot of stress, a lot of hurt.

Q: Speaking of, so many guys talk about Lawrence. How would you sum up your experience with him?

JS: Probably one of the most talented players, and such a tragedy for all that talent to go to waste. He should have been the #1 draft pick, wound up the 8th, 9th, 10th, somewhere. He just wasted it all, it was incredible.

Q: Do you keep in touch with him at all?

JS: I hear he's in isolation. And I hear he has quite a few more years to go.

Q: If you could do the whole thing over, Doc, what would you do differently?

JS: Probably not a lot. I'd probably try to take care of my health a little better. Because it ended up with the surgery and a couple of issues, so I wish that could have worked out better.

Q: What drove you, what inspired you to play such a heavy part in this thing called Nebraska Football?

JS: Well, I had a very active private practice and I was pretty intense, and I decided I wanted to do something for some young people and I thought it was the thing to do. And once you get in there, there are so many needs that you can't say no, so you find yourself being there 10 hours a day, easily. And I'd find myself working an extra 15 hours a week there for free, (laughs) because kids responded and appreciated it and need it. And what we did with Danny Nee and the basketball team was unprecedented, too, going to the NCAA Tournament all those years in a row. We had some good teams.

Q: Behind the scenes, if you were to place a spotlight on somebody in the background who played a large role, do any names stick out?

JS: I think someone who never got full credit, who left before all this really paid off, it was Dr. Ursula Walsh, an ex-nun who got a PhD and became the first director of the academic program, and she was like a Tom to those kids. She ended up doing more counseling for those kids and I kind of saw myself trying to pick up where she left off. But all the academic stuff, that was so solid. She deserves some credit for that. She is the one who, through academics, helped a lot of kids out with the structure she set up. And Bryan Bailey, I forgot about him. Those guys just loved Bryan Bailey.

Q: Tell me more about Strength Coach Bryan Bailey? Why do you think that was?

JS: Because Bryan was a very caring guy. He made no money, hardly, but he could relate to the players and did a lot of individual stuff with them, and he helped them. And a lot of them didn't like Boyd. They hated Boyd, they just didn't like the guy. There were a couple of them, the bigger guys, would probably like to have beat him up. (laughs) He wouldn't come down to the floor very often and spend much time with them, so they didn't get along with Boyd too well. But Bryan was always there for them.

The thing about those players: you can't fool those guys. You can't BS them and you can't fool them. They see what's going on and who's doing what and they know. It was pretty unanimous, the word got around that they didn't like a coach or staff member, it was pretty black and white. If they liked you -like Bryan Bailey- they really liked you. I think he did an awful good job for them. And Keith Zimmer, I saw him do an awful lot of good for those guys, too.

Q: Is there anything we haven't touched upon that differentiated those teams from others of their era? That set them apart?

JS: Obviously, you'll never have another Tom Osborne, not in your lifetime. His skills, leadership, talents, how he did things, I think he's gotta be one of the top three or four coaches in all sports for all time. Your John Woodens, you know? What he did in 25 years was unapproachable. I don't care who you are or what sport you coached, good year or bad year, you'd have injuries, you'd have something, and to do what he did is beyond the norm. It will never happen again.

Q: From one Doctorate in Psychology to another, what made him tick? Any insights the average person wouldn't know about?

JS: I think his grandfather was very special to him. I think it was his spirituality and character that separates him. Let me ask you Paul, did you ever see him disrespect anybody, put anybody down, swear at anybody? Never. I can't even get to Omaha without getting road rage and cursing at someone. (laughs) But he's the most unique man I ever met in my life, and if you don't have Tom Osborne you don't win. You just don't.

End conversation.

Trust, proficiency and open communication are essential to any successful endeavor, and just about any business management textbook will tell you the same. With as large a roster as Nebraska had at the time (160-180 kids) Dr. Jack Stark had his work cut out for him. And with an ultimatum and a timetable set by Coach Osborne, he appeared to be a short-timer and a dreamer, having champagne tastes on only a beer budget. But with a forward lean, a strong shoulder, an open ear, and many trips up and down I-80, he eventually ingratiated himself into the team's inner sanctuaries: their hearts and minds. This Eminence Outlier made it all come together, and I fear my words cannot do the man and his work justice.

Much has been made of the Unity Council (and there will be more), but I just now learned that it was co-birthed as Defensive Lineman Kevin Ramaeker's brainchild during this conversation. (Note to self: I've got to get a hold of Kevin) The famed Unity Council appeared on campus shortly following the appearance of its namesake term: Unity. I recall every Memorial Stadium office door and hallway wall early in the winter of 1991, where just about everywhere you turned there was a Scotch-taped, horizontal 8 ½ by 11 sheet of paper with one, simple word etched in block letters: UNITY. While the barriers were being brought down by an 'intermediary' in Jack Stark, if you will, between the players themselves and between the players and coaches and support staff, a subliminal message was being whispered in all directions: "We are one. We will prevail as one. We hold the key to success if we function as one." Perpetuating the collective 'We', there was also the sentiment that, "We will make it to the top and, in the process, be forever known as the team of legend to give Coach Osborne his first national title." It was a dream of every season's team to be the one to do so.

UNITY, UNITY, UNITY. It was on t-shirts, too. Everybody got one. The next year there arose more t-shirts and signs plastered about with a newer, expanded version: Unity, Belief, Respect. From these basic building blocks grew greater team harmony and trusting, an approach to understanding and appreciating each individual no matter the environment one came from, and a positive mindset that the resultant bonding would produce outstanding results on the field of play.

Particularly telling, too, was Dr. Stark's method of identifying and upping the ante for future team leaders, setting the stage for positive peer pressure. Funny, but when a person typically hears the term 'peer pressure' it is usually in a negative connotation and speaks of keeping a child away from unsavory friends and their influences, choices, and poor leadership examples. Equally telling was the varied mix of leadership styles, from the punch-you-in-the-head types to the watch-what-I-do-and-not-what-I-say types. Theirs was a very interesting, multi-faceted mix.

If it wasn't apparent, you can see that Dr. Jack Stark poured his heart and soul into that team of young men as well as the coaches. For the coaching staff, there was the way he alleviated generational communication gaps and 'tuned the coaches in' to their student's psyches, alerting them to times of vulnerability and the need for a hug some days rather than a swift kick in the rear. For some of these players there was a crucial support system and a father/brother figure whom you could confide in and trust implicitly, oftentimes helping to bear the stress of the unique, pressure-cooker lifestyle of a high profile student/athlete.

I find the manner in which Jack left Nebraska Football both curiously amusing and somewhat tragic, for his heart was literally broken in the way the Frank Solich firing transpired. It takes a man of character to properly esteem another's character, and for Jack it was the end of the road soon thereafter, his unwillingness to remain among lesser leadership coming to bear. Jack's leaving the campus was a Nebraska Football loss that does not appear in any of the record books. For history's sake it should, because it signaled the beginning of a fall from football grace.

Notable quote #2:
Dr. Jack Stark on peer leadership: "They came in different packages. Some guys wanted to beat others up and were tough and wanted to lead from that physical standpoint, whereas other guys were more shy, so you had leaders who weren't vocal."

The man of the prairie is ready for action at home or abroad, balanced by a reasonable culture and poised by an experience whose lessons he does not leave to be learned by his grandsons.

Albert P. Brigham, *Geographic Influences In American History*, 1904

I happened to luck into another conversation with the rarest of birds, this one being none other than Gerry Gdwoski. A native Nebraskan who not only served as the Husker's starting quarterback in years earlier, he also played second fiddle to Coach Osborne as a QB Coach at the genesis of the splendid 60 & 3 run. His was the connection before Turner Gill's arrival on campus amid the NCAA's lopping off of allowable coaching staff numbers. Now the Co-Offensive Coordinator with Frank Solich's Ohio University Bobcats, he's putting his education to good use. I was interested to hear his insights from those early days.

Notable quote #1:
"Trev was senior on that team. Him and Connealy, Raemakers, just defensively it was that crew that probably really started the mindset that you hear a lot about later."

Gerry Gdowski

Question: Hey Gerry, you likely have great insight because you were both a player and then a coach at Nebraska during that renaissance.

Gerry Gdowski: Yeah, I don't know about all that, but I'll try. (laughs)

Q: I remember that in '89 you were All-Big 8, set some passing records, game records for touchdowns. And then what happened?

GG: You know, I had a tryout with the Saints and then got cut. Then I actually worked for an accounting firm up in Minneapolis for close to a year before I went back in the fall of '91 to work as a Graduate Assistant.

Q: When you joined the team again in 91', what time of year was that?

GG: In the fall, just at the start of two–a-days. I guess when I left I didn't anticipate coaching or think about it at that time, but once I'd gotten out and done accounting for a little while I wasn't really happy doing it. I had the opportunity and was actually back for bowl practice for the holidays, talked to Coach Solich and Coach Young. They asked me how it was going and at that time they kind of brought up, "Hey, are you're interested in the fall? In coaching?" That's how I got back in.

Q: So I take it your last game as a Graduate Assistant was the Florida State, 18-16 game?

GG: That was it.

Q: Can you give me some of insight into the duties of your G.A. position those '91-'93 years?

GG: The first year I was mainly with the quarterbacks. As a G.A. I was with the QB's that first year, and then the couple years after that I was with the tight ends and wide receivers. I think that was the first year that they didn't have any sort of freshman team at all, in '91. In the past all the G.A.'s would kind of coach the freshman team.

And you know, either that year or the year before, they decided we needed to basically redshirt everybody. There was an occasional guy who played; Tommie played as a true freshman, there was the rare guy. But speaking for myself, I kind of got caught up with a few other guys in my class who played freshman ball, didn't redshirt and became backups. And all of a sudden our fifth year came up and some of us found we 'wasted' a year playing freshman football, for lack of a better term. That was maybe, perhaps a big factor in what they did later. But I'm sure there were a few guys the coaches ended up getting for a fifth year that maybe they wouldn't have in the past.

Q: A lot of the G.A.'s were former Nebraska players, who I likened to the third arm of a position coach. Would that be a good generalization?

GG: I would agree with that. And you know, it was a lot of behind-the-scenes film breakdown-stuff, too. A lot of times the G.A.'s were working a week ahead as far as the breakdowns, so when you're done with the game on Saturday the coaches want to have that ready as far as preparation. So what they want to watch and what they want to look at is done already, so you've kind of got to both focus on that game that week, but you're also getting ready one game ahead on the schedule.

Q: You were looking ahead as a multi-tasker?

GG: Exactly. And it was a growing experience. Most guys who play, they don't quite understand all that goes into the preparation, how the plan is put together and that kind of thing. So, obviously, it was a good experience.

Q: So when you came back, did you find the offense had changed much from when you were starting and playing?

GG: At that time I think it had started to change a little bit: A few more one-back type of sets, spreading it out a little bit more. You know, when I played it was pretty much a fullback in the game every play, and then as time passed it might be two tight ends and one back in the game, then maybe three or four wide receivers in the game at a time. Not a lot, but things were definitely moving a bit more in that direction.

Q: Any idea what spurred that type of change? That type of thinking?

GG: I'm not sure. Coach Osborne would have the best answer for that. But I think during the late 80's and my time there -even the early 90's- you went to bowl games and you played the Miami's and the Florida States and those type of people, and I think you know that's how they hurt us, also, spreading their great athletes out in space and getting them the ball. So I think any time you see something or play against something that, "Man, that's hard to defend or hard to handle," when somebody does that there's (especially in the coaching profession), there's a lot of copy-catting, you know? And so, I'm sure maybe that had a lot to do with it, the struggles that we had against some of those teams that maybe were a little bit faster than our team, overall. A little more athletic overall. You say, 'Man, what are they doing, how are they getting it done while we're having such a hard time?' I'm sure that on both sides of the ball, playing those teams and having the coaching staffs prepare for those teams you realized the speed factor and the benefit of getting people spread out. You'd definitely take a good look at that type of stuff.

Q: Were you involved in recruiting?

GG: Well, G.A.'s couldn't leave campus, but once guys got on campus we did tours and took them around campus to different professors and whoever they were meeting with and that kind of stuff.

Q: Do you recall being in meetings where the focus of the recruiting was talked about?

GG: I think speed definitely became a factor."How fast is he? Is he a track guy? What are his track times?" Certainly, at that time, you could get a guy into summer camp and time him. So, I think that certainly was a factor in recruiting. In thinking back, you can't really say it was a turning point, but for sure, I think we got faster. How exactly that happened, I'm not sure.

One other thing I can remember during that time was maybe a guy like -the names popping into my head for some reason are Ernie Beler and Ed Stewart, guys that really were recruited as safeties and really wanted to be safeties- they became linebackers. Trev Alberts was originally recruited as a linebacker and ended up being a defensive lineman when they switched from the 3-4 to the 4-3.

Q: It reminds me of Gary Pepin with Nebraska Track. Seems he always recruited the 220 meter runner and then tried to make him into a 440 meter runner…

GG: Yup, sure. Yes, you're right.

Q: And if I recall, you were pretty good in track, too…

GG: Oh, I got around there okay. I wouldn't say I was a blazer…(laughs)

Q: I remember you taking off on a few runs…

GG: I didn't get caught very often. (laughs) And the first year I was back was actually the last year they were allowed 5 GA's. And then they went to 2. And you know, the guy I worked with the whole time there was Bill Busch, who was actually on Callahan's staff. The other guys, Bryan Carpenter I was with, and Brian Mohnsen. When they went to 2 GA's, they stuck around and kind of became the video guys.

Q: Gerry, do you think having Carp & Moose as the video guys made much of a difference at that time?

GG: Yeah, they did. I'd have a hard time saying what other schools did at that time, but today it's kind of pretty much universal. And at that time there were limits to what you could do as far as keeping track of defense and plays they were running, down and distance-wise, what they were blitzing, that sort of thing. You were kind of limited -technology-wise-with what you could do.

Q: So first you're a player and then you're on the other side sitting in the coaches meetings. What stuck out to you most the way their business was conducted?

GG: You know, the one thing that really sticks out to me was -it must have been the '93 season, that loss to Florida State- was the "Refuse to Lose". I don't know who came up with it exactly, but I do remember being in a staff meeting. I remember needing somebody to come up with that, and it became kind of an important slogan for the year. Somebody in the staff room, I don't know if there were strength coaches there at the time, but in the staff meeting it was discussed. And it started to appear on t-shirts shortly thereafter. And I'm not 100% sure, but I'm almost 80% sure it was Turner Gill came up with that. I'm not sure, but that might have been the case.

Obviously, for a long time winning 9 games, 10 games, but when you still struggled at times with certain teams in certain situations it was just about creating a different mindset, as far as, "We're not gonna lose." And I think you look at that Florida State game, there were obviously some breaks went against us, but still everybody kept fighting until literally 1 second left. And we almost got it done.

Q: I remember seeing you on the sideline from the video of that game. What sticks out about that game to you?

GG: I really think that strong-willed attitude was there at that point. I think some people had probably talked about it for a long time, "Uh oh, we're playing Miami again, we're playing Florida State again." I think that feeling around the country, around the state, was that we couldn't compete with those teams. But that was probably the game where there was a change of the attitude, where the guys believed that they could compete and beat them, and that was certainly the catalyst of what happened the next couple years.

And this team had read it and heard it all. It was no different as to what the rest of the country thought about that game, too. I can't remember, but weren't we like 2 touchdown underdogs in that game? But for whatever reason the attitude and the mindset was different. It really stands out to me. Even being on the sideline late in the game you felt like something was going to happen, that we were going to win that game.

Q: Anything else that contributed to that mindset throughout the year.

GG: You can probably point to a few guys that started it. Tommie, obviously, came in and was probably one of the most competitive guys that I've been around. It's hard to quantify, but just the way he played. He was just one of those guys that you kind of believed he was going to figure out a way to get something done to win. And then Trev was a senior on that team. Him and Connealy, Raemakers, just defensively it was that crew that probably really started the mindset that you hear a lot about later with the Peters and Wistroms. Those type of guys, I think they really kind of started that whole mindset that, "Hey, we're gonna get it done."

Q: It was just you and Coach Osborne working with the QB's your first year?

GG: Yes, and then the next year was when Turner Gill came back. That's when we went from 5 GA's to 2. The way they had the staff divided, I went to the receivers the next year, helping Ron Brown.

Q: What was it like coaching along with Coach Osborne? Any bits of wisdom you picked up?

GG: The biggest thing to me (and I think people complained about it at times), was just the way he approached every game. It really didn't matter who you were playing, he got ready the same way, approached the game the same way, did the same things in meetings, in practice. Obviously, as a player you do, you knew the difference...

Q: In what way?

GG: For a #1 vs. #2 game. At the time in the Big 8 the other teams weren't very good for awhile. I mean, Oklahoma's good years were when I was playing, but the other teams weren't very good. Colorado started to come up there toward the end of the 80's. But the way Coach Osborne approached it in meetings and at practice, it was the same, it was very even-keeled, "This is what we have to get done, this is our approach, this is what we're gonna do." And that's the way it was done.

Q: Was there an emphasis on being very positive with the kids?

GG: Yeah, for the most part it was very positive. Different coaches had their different styles. Now Charlie had a little different style. (laughs) I think Coach Osborne's approach was positive in how he approached things, and really it just carried over. I worked for Tony

Samuel for a long time and I work for Frank now, and I think it's really carried over to their approach and it's affected my approach, too.

Q: Your time as a player, as well as G.A., were there any precepts that stand out to this day?

GG: That was probably the main one: just in your everyday approach, you try to be the same. And to be positive -not beat the kids down- try to be as positive as you can and really try to teach as much as anything. Take your role as a teacher and not a drill sergeant–type of approach.

Q: Do you have a moment you're probably most proud of as a G.A.?

GG: You know, I think we won 3 Big 8 championships. To do that 3 times in a row, plus the trips to South Beach, you know, that's probably the big thing. Because obviously, especially at Nebraska at the time, you want to win them all and win the national championships, but you've got to win your conference, and that was always the number one goal, and so to get that done was wonderful.

Q: Was that focus on a National Championship new or was it always there?

GG: I think it was always there. I don't know after the Florida State game, if things changed for the next few years, but we always had that focus while I was there, that we were going to win the Big 8 and we'll see what happens from there.

Q: Anything stick out about the culture or organization itself as being extra special or significant?

GG: It's hard, but going back to it, again, I think something changed in that leading up to that Florida State loss. Again, it's hard to put your finger on exactly what it was, but all of a sudden there were a lot better players, too. (laughs) That was definitely a part of it, probably a very big part of it, but I think there was maybe a little bit of a different attitude during that season, they began to think that, "Hey, we can beat anybody."

Q: Do you think that ending the freshman program made any difference at all?

GG: Very little. You know, the coaches didn't have that much to do with the freshman team at the time. There were some guys who maybe would have played some freshman ball, but they ended up having them for the '94 and '95 teams where maybe they wouldn't have had them in previous years, you know? You might be able to get a roster and figure that out.

Q: Any memorable sideline moments from those years?

GG: Not really, because I was up in the box. At the time the Offensive GA's would go up in the end zone and we'd draw up the defense on cards and send them down to Osborne after each series. I do remember that first game and how fast it was going, how hard it was trying to get all 11 guys drawn on the card at the time. It was a challenge. I'm sure Coach Osborne -those first few series- was trying to decipher what the heck we were writing. (laughs)

End conversation.

Gerry got me to thinking about the old Freshman team and how the new recruits would get some serious reps and "coaching up" by the young bucks on staff, but I can see how its falling by the wayside may have bought the team an extra year of seasoned talent for the '95 year, especially. With the NCAA mandating that coaching staffs be more limited in number (an absolute shame when you look at it from an opportunity standpoint for young, up-and-coming coaches), those freshman were abruptly thrown into the fire against the varsity group and made to sink or swim after the daily poundings they would receive. (I haven't found any evidence that there was a higher attrition rate due to this change.) In other words, throwing them onto the scout team depth chart matured them at a much faster rate than in the past, the speed of the college game being what it is. I don't think the loss of the Freshman Team can be discounted as to its effect in future years, another confirmation that Nebraska Football began to 'stop doing' some things, willingly or not.

As experienced a Husker signal-caller as you could find in those days, Gerry also made note of the subtle changes coming about from a philosophical standpoint with the new looks That T.O. and his offensive coaching staff began to dream up. These shifts left many a defensive coordinator scratching his head, for not only did the opposing team typically have only one week to prepare for the Huskers option game but they now had to find a way to deal with the multiplicity of sets by which Huskers would run the plays out of. It was a simply numbers game. The volume of possibilities and variety of attacks enabled by these new spread-like offensive sets meant the greater one's chances of springing a big play when a defender was out of position, even by a mere yard . This was a case of doing one thing and doing it so well (the option game) that Offensive Coordinator Tom Osborne felt comfortable adding new wrinkles without concern for a drop in execution.

Finally, he mentioned Turner Gill's coming up with the '93 team slogan, 'We Refuse To Lose.' (Soon thereafter college basketball coach John Calipari of the University of Massachusetts copyrighted "Refuse to Lose" and has earned over six figures as a result). It was when he mentioned the t-shirts, though, that made me laugh. As was stated in the last interview, t-shirts were the equivalent of subliminal, indoctrinal bumper stickers for the players. Worn for workouts or just lounging around the study hall or dorm room, every single player every single day was inundated with the Unity, Belief, Respect & We Refuse to Lose message. Even while doing their laundry the players were reminded of the new positive thinkin' in Lincoln.

Notable quote #2:
Gerry Gdowski on Head Coach Tom Osborne's game preparation: "It really didn't matter who you were playing, he got ready the same way, approached the game the same way, did the same things in meetings, in practice."

These were my people. This was where I came from. They knew about hard work, bad harvests, and low prices. But they also knew about the importance of sticking together when times were tough.

Shane Osborne with Malcolm McConnell, *Born To Fly*

Kenneth C. Davis, in his 2003 book *Don't Know Much About History* had an amusing anecdote about General George Washington preparing to cross the Delaware River on a dangerous, revolutionary night raid: "Stepping into his boat, Washington -the plain-spoken frontiersman, not the marbleized demigod– nudged 280-pound General Henry "Ox" Knox with the tip of his boot and said, "Shift that fat ass, Harry. But slowly, or you'll swamp the damned boat." In this day and age of political correctness and side-stepping doublespeak, it's refreshing to hear the truth, the whole truth and nothing but the truth.

That's why this interview with Coach George Darlington makes its mark from a number of perspectives. Always frank and unafraid to offer an opinion, he at times offended some. But everyone knew it was simply a case of "George being George", and that's one of the reasons I find the man so endearing.

I was fortunate to join him on the beautiful University of San Diego campus for a deck-top lunch overlooking the Pacific Ocean on the western horizon. That school's Defensive Coordinator at the time, the mood was relaxed as we shared this informative exchange. It was a fun one. Listen intently, as you'll get an earful on a variety of topics, by George.

Notable Quote #1:
"Our whole thing and Tom's whole thing was "You've got to play better than you did last week, and play to the best of your ability," and that's all that you can be accountable for."

George Darlington

Question: Now George, before we get started I've gotta know: how did you find time to teach that Football 101 class all those years?

George Darlington: It was Thursday night, and the hay is really in the barn by Thursday night as far as preparation. And I recruited California, so I couldn't call until well after 9 o'clock Central Time. So it didn't interfere with recruiting and I just got going with it. The way it got started is, Jim Huge -who had been a quarterback at Nebraska- was a principal at East High School when I first got to Nebraska, and he first taught that class through Southeast Community College. And I would provide him the 16mm film. I handled the film exchange at the time. And then his wife had respiratory problems so they moved to Wyoming and he said, "Well, why don't you teach the class?" So I started teaching it through SE Community, then KLIN heard about it and they made me a real good deal. They said, "Look, we'll sponsor you. You can keep all the money for the class and we'll sponsor it on radio. And it really grew. We even had a waiting list. One year it had 150 people in the class and it went for 6 weeks in the fall. And there were ladies that would take it every year, that were kind of groupies in a good way. Mostly older. One lady just passed away at 105 this past year. She took it until she was 96.

Q: Taking it every year, did they just want to see game film or what?

GD: Part of it was the game film, another part was they'd get an essence, a preview of what was going to happen the next ballgame. When it wasn't too dark we went onto the field and walked through the plays. So besides the video and all that, then we would have a banquet the ladies would sponsor and they would invite one or two players to be their guest. So we would have players that would come, and that was a big hit. The most bizarre thing, probably (and there were a lot of bizarre things), one lady took the class and she commuted from Chicago. She hardly missed a class. She had relatives in Omaha, so if we were playing at home she'd come and stay for the game. Wouldn't fly back to Chicago until Sunday. I remember when registration was going on, somebody said, "Look where this lady is coming from for the class!" And I'm thinking maybe York or Grand Island or something like that, so I said, 'Where's she from?' and she says "Chicago!" (laughs) It was a good deal. I really enjoyed it.

Q: How does the old saying go: "If you want to learn, teach"?

GD: Well, it was fun because of the use of video and stuff like that. It worked out very nice. I taught that for 23 years.

Q: Did you find yourself going through a metamorphosis of sorts in your coaching techniques and doctrine? When we went from the 5-2 to the 4-3 defense, was that a huge thing for you?

GD: Well, I'd kept statistics on our base package as opposed to the 4-3 because the guys didn't want to do it. I was able to show after the year that we were actually more productive with the 4-3. The big thing was, we beat Oklahoma in Norman and played the 3-4. (Of course, they didn't call it that at the time.) But Oklahoma took the ball and drove down the field against our base 5-2 defense, and then we put in the substitution package and stopped them: they kicked a field goal. Next series, same thing. Finally, after that second drive we put the substitution package in the whole time.

And then we played Miami in the Orange Bowl and we lost 22-0 or something like that, and yet we played well on defense against them. It was all 4-3. And what we did, we didn't have very good defensive tackles and we couldn't come up with 5 kids. Of course, you had two tackles and a noseguard and at least a couple subs. Well, we couldn't do that, but we had better linebacker-type kids and we went to the 4-3 and worked with the people we had.

Q: So you're saying it was the confluence of your keeping track of statistics & tendencies as well as a manpower thing? Simply working with what you had…

GD: It was both. Because guys -they could give up their comfort zone, and we'd been successful defensively down through the years- but the 4-3 (with how we played it) fit our personnel better than what people now call a 3-4. 5-2 defense is what we used to say. It was exactly like people are playing today, with 3 down linemen and 4 linebackers. And the substitution package was essentially the 4-3.

Q: How long was that defensive package part of the program?

GD: It was always there in some way, basically on passing downs in the early 90's. But once we committed to it we played it all the time. And we were able to play with some of the smaller kids who were faster, and we improved the speed of our defense with those people.

Q: Was it purposeful that we had more of the smaller, faster guys or did it just happen that way?

GD: Well, we always tried to recruit speed, but it was probably as much as anything the fact that defensive tackles are hard to recruit. We just didn't have a wealth of them. If we would have had a lot of really good defensive tackles we never would have changed. It's very, very difficult to find good, athletic, big people. More like offensive guys.

Q: Now, at one time you were the rush end coach, right? Defensive ends?

GD: Right, defensive ends were really outside linebackers. That was why I say what we call the 50 defense was really the 3-4; it was more nomenclature than anything. We had the Bob Martins, Scott Strassberger, all those kids were outside linebackers, undersized.

Q: I remember there was a big to-do about, "Now we're calling them 'outside linebackers.'" Was there an award or something that we changed that for? Otherwise they were known as rush ends, right?

GD: Exactly. Hey, what do you think of this salmon?

Q: Pretty decent. And I have to tell you, George, I grew up playing 8-man football, so I wasn't as aware of all the intricacies of the game when I came to Lincoln…

GD: I'll tell you, 8-man is fun to watch! What town?

Q: Petersburg. Near Albion. It had the big, white dome at the intersection of highways 32 and 19. My father, Marv Koch, built it to hold fertilizer for his agricultural supply business. We had guys like Kelly Prater in our conference, and the Schmadeke boys grew up 13 miles away, in Albion.

GD: Oh yeah, I remember those guys. I've been through that town a couple of times. What did you major in, again?

Q: Exercise Science, physiology. Though I'd like to think that I actually majored in building champions. I learned so much from time spent in the weightroom, the meetings with Boyd and the crew talking about how to make the strength program better, the whole football staff you were a part of, and working under and alongside Bryan Bailey. I still keep in touch with him every few weeks now that he's up the road at USC.

GD: He really landed on his feet well. He did a really good job. Tell him I said 'Hello' the next time you talk to him, will you?

Q: Will do. And I have to tell you, George, he sometimes says this to the USC players' faces, he says, "You guys have some talent, but you know what? You couldn't touch our teams at Nebraska. You couldn't touch those guys. They had unity, they had work ethic, they were tough, they were fast. You wouldn't stand a chance against those Nebraska teams of the 90's."

GD: Well, I really, sincerely think the '95 team is the best team that's ever played college football. People don't realize that we had horrendous scores against people and took it easy on them. And then you beat Florida 62-24 and knelt down on the one yard line? We had guys who didn't even practice on defense in the game for the kickoff team…

Q: Any names you recall?

GD: No, not exactly, because we were just clearing the benches at that point in the game, you know? Their last touchdown was a kickoff return and I don't think anybody but the kicker had ever covered a kickoff in the game, so they ran it back for a touchdown. Our quarterback, Matt Turman, knelt down on the goal line to keep us from going to 69 points. And the next year that team, Florida, won the National Championship 'cause we stupidly didn't give our players flu shots and ended up losing to Texas in the Big 12 Championship game.

Q: Which reminds me: in your book 'Football 101' you were talking about rare occurrences of crooked officiating…

GD: Well, we had —one most notably, which costed us the most- was the Penn State game in '82 when the kid caught the ball close to a yard out of bounds. The thing I relate to was if they would have had instant replay like they had now; we would have won that game and we would have won the '83 Orange Bowl and the National Championship. (And the close one to that was the William Floyd fumble that we recovered was called a touchdown versus Florida State in '94.) And what the Penn State people don't realize was that the very next play (which was a touchdown play) the ball had bounced, but the out-of-bounds play should have ended it.

South Carolina was probably one of the worst. It was a split crew and we had some Big 8 officials and some southern league and it was absolutely fraudulent. They did everything they could to win. I was on the radio after the game -for some reason that was my turn or that year I was on after every game or something- and I blasted the officials. (Today I would be fined even for telling the truth.) So anyway, on about Tuesday the Big 8 Head of Officials called Tom. And they were trying to have fun with me and they got me out of the defensive meeting and said, "The Commissioner is on the phone. He is really upset." So I get on the phone with him. He said, "Everything you said was exactly right, and I talked to our officials who were there." Everything was out-and-out cheating. And if I recall, Tom or somebody said, "Well, if they were doing that, why didn't you try to even things up and call them the other way? If you see an obvious call is fraudulent?", you know? And our guys didn't do that. We won right at the end of the game. They ran a play they shouldn't have run and they fumbled the ball; they should have just taken a knee.

What was funny about that was that Nebraska Wesleyan, in Lincoln, was dedicating their stadium at halftime. They're dedicating the stadium at halftime, the Nebraska/South Carolina game is right at the end of the game, and a lot of Nebraska fans are there listening to the radio. My wife and daughter were there listening to the radio with their heads down because someone was leading the prayer at the middle of the field, and we recovered that fumble and they just screamed, "Yaaaaaaaaay!" right in the middle of the prayer! (laughs) That was bad.

And then the Clemson game in '82, when Tom went to the Official's meeting before the game -you usually go a couple of days before- he came into our staff meeting after that and said, "We're in trouble." Because every one of those officials knew Danny Ford and were hugging him and all this stuff. And we had so many 15 yard penalties that game. Every time we'd do something a flag would come out.

Q: Like calling Dave Rimington offsides? An *offensive Center* offsides, for crying out loud!

GD: Yes, there was a whole bunch of stuff. It was too bad. And they were good. Clemson was a good football team, but they got an awful lot of help.

Q: So tell me, you were from New Jersey?

GD: No, I'm from Charleston, West Virginia, but I played college ball at Rutgers. And then after going to Stanford I went back and started coaching in New Jersey. I went to Stanford for graduate work and got a double major Masters in PE and History.

I knew I wanted to be a coach when I was 6 years old. I never outgrew it. I was a little kid and I lived 2 blocks from the football field at Stonewall Jackson High School and they were very good when I was in grade school, and my parents would take me to the games. And then I would go over every day and we would play tackle football next to the field or occasionally watch the high school team practice. That's what got me interested.

Q: What position did you play in college?

GD: Defensive end and offensive end. We had to play both ways. It was two-platoon at that time.

Q: You played some lacrosse, too, right?

GD: Yeah, the reason for that was that they had no spring practice at Rutgers at that time, and so they encouraged us to go out for sports in the spring at that time: either track or baseball or lacrosse. So I went out for lacrosse. The first lacrosse game I ever saw, I played in.

Q: Weren't you an All-American?

GD: Yeah, I was third team All-American, primarily as a defensive player. I played for three years. At that time the attack players and midfielders were usually from Long Island or Baltimore where they had lacrosse in grade school and junior high. They were more skilled at throwing the ball and all that.

Q: Like Canadian kids and hockey?

GD: Yes, great correlation.

Q: How did you end up coaching at Nebraska?

GD: I was coaching up here at San Jose State and the head coach got fired. And he had been at a Fellowship of Christian Athletes conference with Tom, and he tried to get on with Tom himself and make me a part of the package. Anyway, Tom called me up and convinced me at the convention in Chicago. I was literally sleeping on the floor between two beds in the Astroturf salesmen's room -because at San Jose there was no money and we had to almost threaten their lives to get money to fly to Chicago- and he interviewed me the next morning after the FCA breakfast.

And then it was really funny, because I didn't have a job and he said, "Well, I'll get back to you. I don't want you to take another job until I get back to you," and all that. And I'm thinking, 'I'll never hear back from this guy again,' So I didn't say anything to my wife when I called her. And then a night or two later Tom called her to encourage her to make sure I didn't take another job. And so when I call she's jumping through the phone! And of course, I had no real opportunities for any other jobs. The Lord really opens a lot of doors and that's a great example of it.

Q: You were Coach Osborne's very first staff member hire?

GD: Yeah, exactly. He'd only been a few days removed from the Orange Bowl when they'd beaten Notre Dame, and there were three coaches that left. One was Coach Devaney retiring, of course, and then there was Jimmy Walden, and another fella who went on to coach at Miami, Florida. Quite frankly, he and Tom -from what I understand- didn't get along well, because basically it looked like he should have gotten the head job. Then he coached in later years as a defensive coach at Kansas State, and I think he may have retired to Omaha. It's silly that I don't remember his name, but anyway, Rick Duvall and Jerry Moore and myself were the new hires. And he retained, of course, everybody else.

Q: What was your impression of the meeting with Coach Osborne?

GD: Well, it was a very short and brief interview because the FCA breakfast went on to the speakers, but we talked for maybe 5 minutes. And at the breakfast he said, "I'd appreciate you not taking another job until I get back. I may have a job for you…", something or other.

Q: Did you ever ask him why he picked you?

GD: No, but I think one of the issues was recruiting. And Rick Duvall and I were both recruiting California, so that might have had something to do with it. Tom used to recruit California, you know, and he had to go all over. I think the head coach I worked for at San Jose gave me a pretty good recommendation, too, so that might have sealed the deal. And like, when I interviewed at Dartmouth prior to that -an example of the contrasts- I was flown up there and was on the chalkboard for three or four hours with the whole staff and all that. It was a completely different interview process. (laughs)

Q: Do you think it was a 'gut' decision for Coach Osborne?

GD: Well, I'm not sure. I think it was the situation where he knew what he wanted and Dewey's recommendation carried a lot of weight because he knew him from the FCA. And I think that was a real help, as he knew where I was coming from. I even paid my taxes (laughs), meager as they were.

Q: So, from '73 until when? Your last year at Nebraska was 2003?

GD: Actually, 2002 was my last season. Frank fired three of the four defensive coaches the day after the Colorado game, so technically we were paid until January 1st of 2003, and I went from there to Marshall.

Q: I'm sure there were some ill feelings after that.

GD: Well, there were ill feelings as far as the family was concerned, but I think the Lord opens doors and he closes some doors. Frank firing six or 7 guys that year didn't help him, because in one year he loses his job. And I don't know whether he would have kept his job if he kept his old staff or not. I don't know how Steve (Pederson) would have responded, if Steve would have worked with all of us.

I knew something was strange that whole year. I mean, it didn't come as a shock at all. There were too many meetings going on, too many backdoor things that, instead of focusing on coaching and getting ready… it was not a shock. The saddest thing, in a way, about the whole deal was Coach Nelson Barnes. That morning his dad had died and then he went to the office and got fired.

Q: Man, you'd better have a foundation of faith, a real 'rock' to lean on that day…

GD: Yeah, Frank knew he was fired the week before because he'd confronted Steve. I didn't. But I knew, because you could tell things weren't right. What was strange about the 2001 season when we lost to Miami, it was probably as good a job of coaching that we'd ever done because it wasn't that talented a team. And to get them into the National Championship game? People lose sight of the fact because, "Well, they got beat badly by Miami." Yeah, but maybe two players on that team would have started in '95. And Miami had a very good team, but my point is that our 2002 team had Fonoti and Crouch and all that, but really it was a pretty average team. But they played hard and they played well. They were -I don't like to use the word 'overachievers' because I think you can achieve up to your ability- but they achieved up to their ability, so that year we probably did about as fine a job of coaching as ever had been done at the school in my 30 years.

But somewhere along the line -whether Monte Kiffin had something to do with that?- I've never asked Frank. I had a 5 minute conversation when I got fired, and that was it. As a matter of fact, Frank was talking to our head coach here the other day because he was trying to help a young fellow he knew get the receivers coach job here, and he mentioned to say hello to me. Which is fine. I don't really have any ill feelings towards him about the thing, because I don't think man has control over those things. I think God has control over them, and I've always felt the head coach has the right to do whatever he wants to do.

In fairness, I expected to finish my coaching career there. I didn't anticipate going anywhere else because I had recruited, well, a number of kids and we'd had good success on defense. We'd all had our different personalities -which a coach may or may not like- but you all know each other, so you work around the strengths and weaknesses.

But going back home to Marshall was kind of interesting in a way, since I was from West Virginia. And it's interesting, the head coach who hired me at Marshall had been the Defensive Coordinator at Florida when we'd mauled them. And I'd done private clinics for them after that year, for two years in a row. Because we beat Florida so bad, some schools would pay for 2-day clinics and you'd go in individually to clinic their staff. And I'd been to Kentucky, so I drove from Lexington to Huntington, which was an hour and half away or so. So I'd met Bobby and saw Bobby there a couple of times, too. So it all came together there.

Q: What was the staff dynamic? What was it like with the different personalities among the group?

GD: Well, one of the things that I think my wife says a lot and is true: the football staff (and I think any athletic staff) has an awful lot of egos. Well, our staff was definitely under the control and under the influence of Tom, and Tom was a tremendous person to work for: a very consistent individual, the most consistent person I'd ever been around. So his leadership blended together people with all different kinds of personalities, some people who weren't particularly buddy-buddy and all that, but he still made it work.

One of the things that was helpful: we'd have a 10 minute chapel every morning for a number of years for the whole staff and you could come or not come -it was your choice- but there was a biblical theme we'd always focus on, which I think was a key factor.

And then Tom was always looking at developing people rather than firing people. As an example, there were situations with secretaries -one particular secretary I remember- when she first came there she was really raw as far as being a secretary and she was really dropping the ball as far as being a good secretary. And some people would say, "Oh no, she's not getting the job done. She just doesn't have the skills or whatever. Let's let her go." And instead of Tom saying, "She's not going to work," he worked with her and she became a tremendous secretary, a tremendous person.

His approach was that way, and it was in football, too. He could look at a guy and project what he could become, not what he is right now. So he could take a guy -a kid on the team- and maybe some of us would be more judgmental and say the kid would never play, but Tom would look at him and say, "Well, if he improves here and if he improves there he might have a chance to play." And Tom was very good that way. Tom wanted stability on the staff and he worked extremely hard, and to my knowledge ever had to fire only two coaches. And he would work very hard to keep people together; so there were different personalities or whatever. We worked around it and blended them together.

I think there is a lot of merit, a lot of benefit to having multiple personalities on staff. If it's all one way I don't think that's good. For example, with Tom you knew he was the steady influence, he'd more than likely talk and coach in a civil manner, whereas others of us at times would get angry and yell sometimes like that. I think there was really a need for both types of personalities. If the whole staff was the same -not pushers and grinders- I don't think you'd be successful, and vice versa. I've visited staffs where everybody's yelling and screaming and I don't think that they can be successful, either, because there isn't a balance there. Almost to the point where I think if you join a staff and if everybody is pretty mellow you better not be, and vice versa.

Q: That being said, where do you think George Darlington fit in?

GD: I was the yeller at times. I would yell at kids. I would never cuss at them, but I would get on them pretty hard verbally. I was the pusher. Anyways, I was contrary to Tom as far as personalities. Same was with Charlie: a very caring guy, really very much a player's coach. But you know, he would go off on guys. And they knew, "That's Charlie. He's gonna blow off steam, but he really cares for me," and stuff like that.

And the big thing, a key for our success -with the number of players and the number of reps- was the scout team and the development of scout team players. And the fact that as coaches (contrary to what the kids perceived), we were very happy for the scout team to do well. We wanted them to do the best they could because it would expose weaknesses, it would expose to a guy, "Hey, I've got to go harder here. I see what the coach is saying. I can't let that tackle hook me, because if I do there's an open lane." I don't know that Nebraska will ever get back to the use of scout team players like we did for development. I think if they ever want to be very successful they're gonna have to, because year in and year out I don't think you're gonna out-recruit the Oklahoma's and the Texas's and the USC's, whereas we used to either evaluate better than them and get some really good players. Well, what is the difference? We had the Jimmy Williamses of the world who were 6', 190 and ran a 4.9, and 4 years later went as a first round draft choice because they grew and they took a growth spurt and they developed.

Plus the repetition of plays: you have two full scout teams going against your defense, 4 stations on the field at one time. We used to have coaches come in the spring and their mouths would be wide open because they couldn't believe it. And since I've left I've tried to emulate it as much as I can, but there is so much opposition. At Marshall they just wanted the scholarship guys and they didn't want to mess with any more of them, not as much as I would have liked. My focus would have been for everybody to get reps no matter who you were in the spring, that way they could learn, they could develop. They'll be a better scout team in the future if they're relegated to scout team in the fall, because they'll give a better look for the starters instead of standing on the sideline watching practice.

Q: When did practicing with those 4 stations begin?

GD: That had to begin in the 60's. I never knew that ever being different from the first day I got there. I assume it was from Coach Devaney, I'm almost sure it was. And I always felt it was crucial, in the spring, that the poorest player on the football team got the same number of reps as the first player on the football team. Sure, he might be a scout team player, but he was better because he had to learn the defense, he had to learn the offense. So, consequently, he gave us so much of a better picture in the fall. And then it speeded up the number of reps that you could get.

You didn't always have to draw cards of every play. If a team was an I-formation team you just called out the terminology, and I think the whole key to the stability of Nebraska to do what they did was the large number of players, the scout teamers: some who walked-on and developed and started, some who became All-Americans. So that allowed Nebraska to have a record that most people really might not even have thought about.

And what is most amazing is that for 30 years we only had one loss to a team with a losing record: Iowa State. After we had won two big games against Colorado and Kansas and got tight ends hurt and all that, we went over there flat and got beat. We still tried to run the offense and, bottom line, they were a terrible team and we lost to them. But that's the only time ever a team with a losing record beat Nebraska. I think that's a bigger accomplishment than the National Championships.

Q: Can you tell me a little about the goal setting? Did the goals change from week-to week or team to team?

GD: Sometimes it did. Although the big thing is a matter of evaluating where your team is in the summer, and then, "Hey, this is a realistic goal considering the different elements for being successful." A lot of the goals were to be "Top 5 in the nation in this category." There were other times the goals would change some because of the strength of your opponent. Maybe we would be playing Oklahoma and our normal goal was giving up 13 points a game, but they were a very powerful offensive team so this game 16 points is a realistic goal. So we would modify stuff.

Q: Do you think the players bought into these goals every week?

GD: Yeah, in fact they would come in on Monday and really want to know, "How many goals did we accomplish Saturday night or Saturday afternoon?"

Q: How many goals would you typically set per game?

GD: I'd say 15 to 17 through the years. We had a goal for interceptions per pass attempt, for turnovers, how many times did we give the ball to the offense?, get our offense inside of their fifty, third down efficiency, first down efficiency, no foolish penalties, penalty yardage, two or less big plays for the opponent. So we had certain goals like that."These elements will allow you to be successful if you accomplish a percentage of them."

Q: When did the goal-setting take place? Who birthed the setting of goals in the first place?

GD: Two different places: motivational speakers, and you'd read about it in books about the importance of goals. We couldn't beat Oklahoma in the 70's and we invited a guy from Edge Incorporated in Phoenix, and he really sold us on goals. He said, "Goals give drive and energy." So we really bought into the goal-setting after he came in sometime in the 70's, probably '77 or somewhere in there.

Then we beat Oklahoma in 78'. Jeff Hansen from Sacramento was the one that made the big hit. That was another example of the officials being crooked, because prior to that last drive we had kicked off and John Ruud ran down the field on the kickoff and hit Kelly Phelps. I think he broke his face or his collar bone and he fumbled with both feet on the ground, but the official said he was down. And there was no way on earth he was down. That was Oklahoma's best team. Then Hansen hit Billy Simms and he fumbled. They were good.

Q: George, the first Husker game I ever went to was that next week versus Missouri....

GD: We had nothing left for that. Completely spent. And they were very good. Missouri was very good, and we still had chances to win the game. And then we didn't lose to Missouri again until 2003 with that staff when Pelini was there. We almost, obviously, should have lost in '97.

Q: Speaking of close losses, any recollections about the '94 Orange Bowl with Florida State and the two points?

GD: Oh yeah, I think about that a lot. The big thing relating to that game was that they were the heavy favorite, 17 point favorites, and the officials didn't prepare because they thought it was going to be an easy game. Crazy Lee Corso, a Florida State grad, was dogging our guys in interviews, and Dick Enberg came and he was really bored that he had to come to a game instead of being out here at home in San Diego.

But the big thing was related to Lawrence Phillips on that one, because Lawrence was a freshman who never missed a practice and everything was fine, and then one December practice on a Saturday morning he didn't show. Tom sent a student manager to the dorm to find out where he was and he wasn't there. Well, it turned out his mother had gotten beaten up by her boyfriend in Omaha. (She had moved from Arkansas and just gotten a bachelor's degree in computers) But anyway, we were dogged so much by everyone that Trev Alberts and the captains went in to see Tom and said, "Will you let Lawrence play? If our top two I-backs get hurt, will you let him play?" And he agreed. Their rationale was, "Coach, they're giving us no chance, they're dogging us every day on TV: blah, blah, blah." And Lawrence had continued to practice and -though he had been suspended for the game- he got in in the second half and he played and he ripped 'em. So I remember that.

I also remember the foul called on Barron Miles at the end of the game. It really was a ticky-tack thing, he hit him over by the sidelines. And then missing the field goal? That fumble on the one yard line? Then we're about to score on the runback for a touchdown and they throw the flag on the phantom clip? To the point, when Bobby Bowden came to Lincoln in the spring to speak at the FCA banquet he was very, you know, admitting that we outplayed them.

And the thing I remember about that game was the way Tom handled it after the game, because we felt our kids played as hard as they could, that's the only focus. See, the biggest thing about Tom was he didn't talk about or focus on winning or losing, it was always a focus on getting better this week than we were the week before.'Cause he would say (and first we could reflect back on some of those games, like Clemson and games like that), was that we had no control over the outcome of the game. The only thing you had control over was, "How well did you play?" And so, we spent very, very little time talking about winning and losing, but he did talk a lot on playing better than we played last week and continuing to improve.

And a lot of coaches get tied into winning, winning, winning: "We've got to win this game." Our whole thing and Tom's whole thing was you've got to play better than you did last week and play to the best of your ability, and that's all that you can be accountable for. If you have that focus, I think that helps you. You've got to play to play, that's what you're focused on. Not, "What's the score?" and stuff like that.

Q: The '93 to the '97 years, was there one year the staff did a better job than others?

GD: Well, I think we just coached like we always coached. Like I mentioned, the '95 team was the best that ever played college football; second team guys went on and became NFL players. The other year that was tough was the '99 year. Because we were the best team in the country in '99, arguably, and we fumbled more than any team in the country and we lost one game because we fumbled all the time. It was just that we had a bunch of fumblers. (laughs) That big I-back was so muscular, Dan Alexander, and Buckhalter tried to put the ball over the goal line and he fumbled against Texas. And we had a couple games where the first play of the game we fumbled, against A&M and we shut them out, and VandenBosch blocked a field goal, and the very next week against Kansas State we fumbled on the first play of the game, and again blocked a field goal. I mean, our defensive guys didn't even get upset. (laughs) They just looked at it and said, "Hey, our offense is our offense: they're gonna fumble it all the time, so we've got to be good enough." We were very good in '99, and it was a team that we should have competed for the national championship. We beat Texas in the Big 12 championship game, and their only score was when they picked up a fumble and ran it in.

Q: Let me ask you, Coach, looking at your statistics comparing the 5-2 to the 4-3, was that something you normally would have done? Or was it a freakish pet project of yours from out of the blue?

GD: No. When I became the secondary coach I always kept statistics of run and pass on all of our fronts and coverages, so I just carried that through with the 4-3 stuff as a contrast to the 3-4 stuff.

Q: So the Oklahoma game was when we went to the substitution package full-time, the 4-3?

GD: We had played the 4-3 during the year some, mostly passing situations. If we had third down and long we'd put in the 4-3.

Q: I keep going back to Ed Stewart, was he the younger player?

GD: He was a younger player, and it's good you mention Eddie. Because of the 4-3 he got to start, and we used him as an example: "Here we have Ed Stewart sitting on his butt. And he's a very good player, and we need to get him on the field."

Q: He was kind of a tweener, right?

GD: Yeah, he was very upset when we moved him from the secondary to linebacker, but he didn't have great foot speed compared to the secondary guys…

Q: The Barron Miles's, the Toby Wright's, the John Reece's…

GD: Exactly. We had some kids who were simply more athletic. Consequently he was the guy, the poster boy. He was so much faster and more athletic than the middle guard would have been.

Q: Any comments about the Unity Council?

GD: I think it was a tremendous tool. Like Tom verbalized it, the players got to know the skinny on what had happened so that you didn't have the problems which you normally would have. Whereas, let's say you and I both get into trouble a week apart and you're a starter and I'm a scrub, and you get off and I get punished. Well, the logical thing was, "Well, if you're the starter, obviously they're going to cut you slack. And if I'm the scrub…?" and so, "Screw him."" Well, with the Unity Council some kid would come in and they would know exactly what he was in there for. And later on somebody would say, "Well, why did he get that punishment?" The Unity Representative would say, "Well, he got that because he did this, this and this. And the other guy got off because of this, which is very minor." Consequently -and more positively- it helped the team become more like owners of a football team. Because they would come up with suggestions and they could go to Tom and say, "We think we need to do this and that." So there were positives to the players having ownership and it developed more and more, because the Unity Council were our leaders. And it kept you from having to put out a bunch of fires with intra-team squabbling. And if you went before the Unity Council you had a chance to say what you had to say. Plus, players were usually harder on their peers than we would be, too.

Q: Did that free you up to do more coaching, then?

GD: Yes, it was very helpful. If a guy missed four classes and we told him, "Hey, you've got to go to class." So if he got dinged or was about ready to lose a game it was cut and dried.

Here was a rule (we didn't have a whole bunch of them), but it was black and white, "You're not supposed to skip class. If you skipped class that's a point (you've earned)."

Q: Any other changes or ways to distill what created that 60-3 record over the course of those awesome 5 years?

GD: Well, I think it was the talent we recruited. We were fortunate to get people who could run. We always tried to emphasize speed, but we did a better job of recruiting speed.

Q: Like getting a guy like Lawrence Phillips? Everyone knows that's a tragic story, and yet many of the former teammates said he was the nicest guy, the hardest working, a great teammate…

GD: The situation started with his mother kicking him out of the house when he was in junior high school. He got home one day, the story goes, and she's all beaten up. Her boyfriend had beat her up. Lawrence attacks the boyfriend and his mother throws him out of the house. That's how he ended up in a youth home.

Q: So he loved his mother -the only parent he knows- and in defending her he ends up getting the short end of the stick? Penalized for defending her? That has to play horrible tricks with a kid's head…

GD: He has about a year and a half before getting out of jail. I've testified for him. I'm trying to think when it was. It was the final sentencing, to try and get him off the three strike thing. It was sad. He's done some things he shouldn't have, and he hasn't handled his temper well.

But if you talked to the coaches who coached him at Barcelona they would tell you exactly what you just said. They were friends of mine and they called me before drafting him, asking what I thought. I said, 'Well, if he hasn't been drinking ('cause I'd heard he'd been drinking) he'll be the best player you guys have. The hardest worker and all that.' Well, 6-7 weeks later they call me after he'd scored three touchdowns in the second half and said "Everything you said is true. He's the hardest worker." In fact, one of the people who testified at his hearing was a teammate from Barcelona who flew all the way down to San Diego from Seattle to testify for him.

Q: You recruited him, didn't you?

GD: Yeah, and I called him and just got a letter from him the other day. I've tried in the last year or so to write every week, but I've missed a time or two. But it's a tough deal.

Yeah, he and Roger Craig were two of the hardest working backs we ever had. Lawrence was extremely unselfish as a player. It never came out of his mouth that he demanded the ball, not once. Whether you handed him the ball once or thirty times, it didn't make any difference. He had a lot of positive qualities. The thing that happened this last incident? I won't bore you with the story, but it was a tough deal.

Q: I think it was a huge credit to the coaching staff that you guys didn't just kick him off the team…

GD: Yeah, and he was home in bed the night he got in trouble. A girl supposedly called and said, "Do you know where your ex-girlfriend is?" Somebody came and drove him over to Scott Frost's apartment. They got into it. She, I think, slapped him and he drug her down the stairs. It was obviously a bad scene but it didn't have to happen. I mean, if a girl doesn't call then he's still just in bed sleeping. He didn't go out that night, he just got back from the Michigan State game, so it didn't have to happen had that girl not called him.

Q: Any other guys stand out that you coached or recruited?

GD: Geez, I was blessed with so many good players. I could start rattling off names… and you're gonna miss some people. There were a number of good leaders: Mike Brown a little bit later, was a really good leader. Mike Minter was an excellent leader, Barron Miles was well respected. Obviously the Peters'. Jason Peter and Grant Wistrom were the epitome of leadership during that time. They had a lot of the fringe players who weren't hard workers and they would either -through fear or whatever- make them work harder. (laughs)

I'm not real good at keeping in touch and that's a negative for me. I run into guys sometimes while traveling. But I don't have a good, continual relationship with a lot of players, which I really am sorry about in some respects, because it would be nice to get together with them and all that. The ones that I get together with most are my first high school kids from the '60's. Toby Wright's over in Arizona and I've helped him coach some guys that he's training. John Reece was real good kid, and Michael Booker.

Q: Anybody behind the scenes who made a big impact?

GD: Well, the FCA guys, I'm trying to think who there was. Matt Penland was one of the guys who counseled some of the guys. We were blessed to have a lot of good people that had certain talents that lent to our success. So many different people who made a difference…

Q: Do you still get approached by Husker fans?

GD: Oh yeah, in the airports all the time. Nebraska fans are a unique group of people. They'll sometimes recognize me and come up and thank me, go out of their way to say nice things, you know? You appreciate it -you're a little ways embarrassed by it- but the passion of the people for Nebraska football is pretty evident. Last year when they sold out for the Spring Game and they were scalping tickets? That shows you the tremendous number of people that singularly care about the football program at Nebraska. That's just awesome. It's one thing to pay 5 or 10 bucks for a ticket, but it's another to be selling a practice game ticket on e-bay for $100 bucks. That's just ridiculous. (laughs)

Q: Do you recall your first incident in moving to Nebraska, as far as grasping the culture… the people?

GD: One of the things was, in San Jose there was a newspaper man. He was working at one of the small papers in the Bay Area up there and he was a died-in-the-wool Nebraska fan. He'd gone to all of the games and the National Championships, so I learned more about Nebraska from him before I ever set foot in Omaha or Lincoln. His was the first "Big Red Room" I ever saw. He had stuff everywhere. I'd seen them play on television, of course, with the earlier National Championships and all that stuff.

Q: It probably never occurred to you that you'd be coaching there a year or two later?

GD: Oh yeah, 'cause after laying on my couch watching the Notre Dame–Nebraska game - in fact, out on a day like this in San Jose, I took my son and we hiked and came back and watched the game- and I remember vaguely when they interviewed a tall, red-headed guy who was going to be the new coach. And I find a few weeks later I was working for him.(laughs) We were blessed.

Tom has gotten tremendous accolades and he deserved them. And the players? The program? Once it got going, I think the biggest thing for us was that we'd probably have won one more championship earlier had we jumped on the bandwagon by recruiting by position and being accountable. By that I mean, I had a lot more influence on what defensive backs were recruited the later years than the way it was before at other positions. You know, you might have an area of the country that you recruit and I might have an area… and you might recruit a pretty good player regardless of position. But maybe we missed players had we evaluated them by position to a greater extent. And once we started doing that we started getting a little bit better players and turned 9 wins into twelve wins.

Q: Was there anyone behind that movement or did it just happen out of the blue?

GD: Well, I think it was probably discussions and arguments about it that kind of got it to be that way.

Q: And speaking of, in your book you mention that some staffs install the game plan together while others rely only on the head coach making the decisions. Did everyone have input at Nebraska? Was it a Brain Trust?

GD: Yeah, our staff? Everyone had input. Offense? I don't know. Tom maybe had more, but everyone had input. Defense? Very much. It was a lot of input by everyone.

Q: Would you do anything differently if you had a chance to do it all over?

GD: Oh, I think you always would have liked to spend more individual time with players. Sometimes you couldn't because of all the rules, recruiting and stuff like that.

Q: That, and flu shots in '96, right?

GD: Oh yeah. Here you have a wealthy, successful program, and for want of a flu shot, arguably, you lose the National Championship.

Q: How many guys were sick that week of the first Big 12 Championship game?

GD: I think about 30. A lot of starters. That previous game against Colorado it was about 32 degrees & damp, and we had kids that day who played two or three plays against Texas and hardly remember playing. They were really gone. Because Texas was not a great team at that time. I mean, they were okay, but nobody was saying that we weren't better than Texas. It was too bad, because I've often said that if we had it to do over we should have taken them and put them in the health center and not even practiced them until Thursday.

Q: Quarantined 'em, huh?

GD: Well, just try to get well. Because we'd already had all these games. And yes, your game plan may not have been quite as sophisticated, but at least you'd have a chance to have guys to play. It was sad. Makes me want to get a flu shot…

End conversation.

Nothing to sneeze at, this interview was a real eye-opener for me. George Darlington was a mad-scientist of sorts, always tinkering outside the box from a defensive standpoint. His and Defensive Coordinator Charlie McBride's meetings and greaseboard 'chat sessions' are of legend, and George's nefariously creative schemes were oftentimes too convoluted and intricate for his young defensive backs to absorb. Even so, it makes perfect sense that he would have been the one to 'crack the code' and push for a switch to the 4-3 defense as the fashion trend in future Blackshirt successes.

As I drove away from the campus interview it hit home just how thin a line the difference between victory and defeat is at this level. Can you imagine how a few $10 flu shots could have turned the course of history? For all intents and purposes, it would not be a far stretch to say that the great 60 & 3 could have been an astounding, mind-boggling, & heretofore undreamed-of 61 & 2, with 4 national championships in 5 years. Would more books have been written about these teams as a result? We'll never know. But at least we have this one, in your hands, to tell the tale. I hope you're enjoying it.

There were so many issues he touched on, but I found it telling how the staff would secretly root for the scout team to 'bring it' to the top teams in every week's practices. In doing so, avenues for correction, for feedback, for teachable moments consistently arose. Touching upon the use of negative motivation once more, you can be sure that 'getting owned' by a scout teamer had serious ramification's on a starter's psyche and drove him to seek constant improvement in technique as well as effort. Much as the Oklahoma matchups of old made Nebraska a better football program and gave them a goal of proficiency to shoot for, the scout teamers were mini-Sooners in so many respects, serving as a whetstone for sharpening the Husker saw.

Then George addressed the oft-misused term 'overachievers.' "I don't like to use the word 'overachievers' because I think you can achieve up to your ability." I've often thought this myself, for who can truly know what a person is capable of achieving? Even the billion-dollar business of the NFL -with their expansive hierarchy of accumulated football knowledge and assorted draftniks- rarely gets things 100 percent right. When it comes to talent evaluation and predicting future upside of a high school kid, Lord only knows. I can see how a lifelong collegiate football coach would have that point of view, for he'd witnessed time and again the stellar High School All-American with a promising future sputter out like a dud firecracker whereas a walk-on out of Page or Papillion or a tweener out of Pasadena bloomed into gameday brilliance. It's a difficult task to measure the heart behind the heft, and a good measure of heart was required to attain the coveted Blackshirt designation of those times, much less George's approval.

Notable quote #2:
George Darlington on Tom Osborne's messaging to the players: "We spent very, very little time talking about winning and losing, but he did talk a lot on playing better than we played last week and continuing to improve."

Andy Dufresne: [in a farewell letter] *Remember Red, hope is a good thing, maybe the best of things, and no good thing ever dies.*

Stephen King & Frank Darabont, *The Shawshank Redemption*

Peter Richmond, in his best-selling book *Baddasses: The Legend of Snake, Foo, Dr. Death and John Madden's Oakland Raiders*, shares a tidbit about Monte Johnson, a former Husker Linebacker from the '70 & '71 National Championship teams: "Like most of the Raiders at the time, his arrival in the loose fraternity was a tad eye-opening."Coming in from Nebraska, Bob Devaney was my coach, Tom Osborne was an assistant," he told me."We were disciplined and structured. You said "Yessir" to the coaches.""

Some things never change, which brings us to Adam Treu. More than 20 years after Johnson anchored the Raider defense in the 1976 Super Bowl, 10-year Raider Adam Treu was the starting Raider center for Super Bowl XXXVII against Tampa Bay (playing in over 150 career NFL games). Arriving on campus as changes were beginning to take shape, he should be able to give us a good idea of the tenor of the squad and the atmosphere around Memorial Stadium from his unique, homegrown perspective.

Notable Quote #1:

"We won some AFC West titles, lost to Baltimore that year in the Championship game, and the next year we win it and go to the Super Bowl. I can relate those three years to those years at Nebraska, where we had enough character guys who loved the game and played it for the right reasons, to where it would wash away or cancel out the guys who didn't have it."

Adam Treu

Walk-on, Offensive Tackle, Lincoln, Nebraska (Pius X)
Where are they now? Bend, Oregon, Coach

Question: When was your last game as a Husker, Adam?

Adam Treu: That would have been the Orange Bowl against Virginia Tech, I believe. Orange Bowl '97, following the '96 season.

Q: Which had the Texas game where they slopped out on us and got the win?

AT: Yeah, that was it.

Q: So your freshman year was…

AT: '92, I redshirted my freshman year.

Q: So you weren't arriving at school from halfway across the country like some guys, but instead grew up in Lincoln. Can you recall anything special about that first day?

AT: I think it was too early for me. I just happened to be at the right place at the right time, you know? I remember dressing up in the North Fieldhouse, making sure I had enough time to get ready for practice.

I was actually a defensive lineman my redshirt year, so working with Coach McBride and Parrella and Raemakers and those guys, I didn't know what I was getting into. Christian was a young Christian, so he was pretty impressionable on some of those guys, some of those antics.

And Paul, my dad worked as a carpenter in the Maintenance Department over there on North 17th over by the Devaney Center, and him and Bill Shepard and Tom Novak would always be in Shep's shop. And he'd often stop by there on his way home, during the season he'd stop by the concession stand on Mondays for the leftover popcorn, he would bring that home. And as soon as I was old enough, I would go down there with my dad and his other co-workers on Saturday mornings and meet in Shep's office and eat donuts, hear dirty stories, get to play with Shep's grandson, Matt, and we'd go up and play in the handball courts or go down in the Schulte Fieldhouse and kick the ball around. I'd help put out the folding chairs back when Memorial Stadium's box seats had folding chairs, and the end zone pylons, and then the pads on the goal posts and the American flags on the four corners of the stadium and the press box. And then I'd get to stay and watch the game up there, up in the four corners where the policemen would stand up there. We'd sit up there and watch the game.

It was a dream come true, even more so than any other kid from Nebraska. I lived it. And when I got there, I walked-on my first year. Milt and Coach Osborne said I wasn't quite big enough yet, so they drafted a letter and sent it to me saying I was going to have a scholarship after the first year. I remember my Dad running off copies of it and putting it in a file and carrying one around in his pocket to show people. And he and my Mom -being an employee ticket holder since the Devaney years and basketball when they played over in the Coliseum- I didn't realize until it was all said and done, but it was quite an experience. To live it and enjoy the success that we had was awesome.

Q: Didn't Shep always have a special cap that he wore?

AT: Yeah, it was a red and white cap, with red polka dots.

Q: That's it! So let me ask you, your position coach was Milt Tenopir after your freshman year?

AT: Yeah, they decided to move me to offense after my freshman year.

Q: What do you think drove them to make that move?

AT: I don't know. Maybe I wasn't mean enough. (laughs) I don't know.

Q: Your first year hanging around all those D-Line meatheads and Charlie, what was that experience like?

AT: It was an eye opener. I never saw anybody that intense and crazy before.

Q: In what way?

AT: In practice if you weren't where you were supposed to be, you would hear about it. I was running scout team so I didn't hear a whole lot about it, but the way Charlie McBride worked his guys until they were about ready to fall over, then he was ready to love on them all the same. He was like a father figure.

Q: In what way did he go about it?

AT: He'd take you aside, away from everybody and say, "I was just kidding" or "If I didn't care, I wouldn't get on you", those type of things….

Q: Then you jumped over to the offensive side with Milt and Coach Dan Young. How was that?

AT: Well, Milt was along the same lines. I think back in the day him and Charlie used to laugh and do one-on-ones against each other, in front of the offense and defensive linemen.

Milt, he didn't have a lot of rules; but the couple he had, boy, you had to adhere to them. And Dan, he was kind of the passing game coach, I guess you would say. He'd throw his two cents in there every once in awhile. Two really great guys, you could tell their love for one another, all the time they'd spent together. They were brothers in a sense. You could talk about the reasons for success: it was like one big family. That staff had been together for so long that they knew what the other one was thinking, and it was just unbelievable.

Q: You said Coach Tenopir didn't have many rules. Can you recall the few he did have?

AT: "Just don't screw up your assignment" and "Don't sleep in the meetings." (laughs) The cot over in the corner of the office was his… and we looked forward to the fish fry at his house after the Spring Game every year. That was a good time.

Q: What would happen at the fish fry?

AT: Just reminiscing and making new stories, shooting pool, drinking a few sodas. (laughs) All my other classmates, the same age as me, we all stuck together outside of football, and there are guys I still talk to often throughout the year: Matt Vrzal, Korey Mikos, Chris Dishman I still keep in touch with.

Q: How did Milt always turn out those great groups of offensive linemen?

AT: It was the trust factor and the fear of letting one another down. And with the tradition being what it was, you didn't want to be that team that didn't win 9 games a year. It was like Wahoo basketball, where they won 115 straight or something like that. Milt's scheme wasn't that difficult and easy to learn. It was simple, so you could just play.

Think about how many guys we had out there: we had 4 stations running (with both scout teams and substitutes), so the number of plays you could run in a practice -the offensive running set was over on the left side, the offensive pass was over in the south end zone- you knew without communicating what the guy next to you was going to do against certain looks. I mean, you didn't have to worry about where you were going.

Q: So once Saturday came around you were operating as a team rather than a bunch of individuals. Was it ever like that in the pros for you?

AT: We did. We had a good line there for about three years, Gruden's last two years and Callahan's Super Bowl year. We had good 'character guys' in starting positions that influenced the rest of the team. They weren't afraid to say what they were thinking, they made sure everybody toed the line, they didn't care how much this guy made or that guy made, they were gonna let it be known what they thought. We were pretty good for about 3 or 4 years, we won some AFC West titles, lost to Baltimore that year in the Championship game, and the next year we win it and go to the Super Bowl. I can relate those three years to those years at Nebraska, where we had enough character guys who loved the game and played it for the right reasons, to where it would wash away or cancel out the guys who didn't have it, who were doing it just for the money or whatever.

Looking back -Rich Gannon, a good friend of mine- Gruden had him get up in front of the team and talk, and he said, "It's no secret: Russell Maryland played for ten years, Tim Brown played for ten years, Jerry Rice played for ten years, Steve Wisnewski, too, all they ever did was what was asked of them." Then he said to the lazier guys, "Hey, if you were working for IBM you'd be out on your ass looking for work." Al (Davis) didn't have a lot of rules. His coaches didn't have a lot of rules and sometimes it would get taken advantage of, so that was the hardest thing my last few years, a lot of them guys were done playing and the younger guys would come in, and the yahoos started acting like they weren't supposed to, that's what they were. It was still hard. I had a few close friends on the team, but it was the putting up with a lot of the B.S. that was pretty hard on me.

Q: And as far as Nebraska goes, do you have a particular game or moment that stands out to you as a favorite?

AT: I think it was the game against Florida in the Fiesta Bowl when I was a junior. I think we were considered underdogs in that game and we'd been lighting it up all year: our defense, our special teams, and just that look on Spurrier's face over there, the disgust was just unforgettable.

I remember just trying to get out of Lawrence Phillips' way that game. I was the swing tackle, so (Eric) Anderson and (Chris) Dishman would start and then I'd come in. I'd go in after a series or two and then take one series at left and then another series at right tackle. It was just making sure we were all fresh.

Q: That was part of the method to the madness?

AT: I think that just through the conditioning program that you guys put on, the number of reps we would take during practice, that was even more conditioning than we ever knew. Running all those plays throughout the practice was very beneficial. And it was as live as could be, except for the scout team. And you had guys on the scout team, they were waiting their turn, they wanted to show what they had, so they were all busting their humps to impress, too.

Q: Who did you run up against in practice the most, made you a better player?

AT: Probably John Parrella or Raemakers, going against them when I was young; getting that eye-opener.

Q: What made the teams special?

AT: Just the way the whole thing was run, top of the line, first class everything. Weight room, training table, having practice in the afternoon and -not being catered to- but giving everybody a chance to succeed was big. And then, of course, Osborne was such an even-keeled guy, you didn't want to disappoint him. But you knew if you did that he understood that you were human and he would talk to you. He could have a pleasant conversation with you.

Q: As far as motivation, how did you guys get motivated? Was it personal, was it the coaches?

AT: It started with the coaches, and I think through the recruiting and the homework they did, making sure that they got the right guys in there, there weren't many who didn't have the right frame of mind.

Coach Osborne, if he said "Darnit!" you knew he was mad, that was a motivation. And his assistants were the motivators; he didn't have to do a lot. That fear, that brotherhood, of not letting one another down, that was motivation for sure, too. The older guys on the team, they were the police, watching their own, grabbing a guy around the neck if they had to and setting them straight. (laughs)

Q: Where would that usually happen?

AT: Maybe over in the Hewitt Center, in the locker room, in a one-on-one basis where you didn't have to embarrass anybody. You were in awe of those older guys and you had to feel them out and act the right way. You were afraid to upset them because you didn't know what they would do. After you earned your stripes, so to speak, then they would welcome you with open arms.

Q: Anybody behind the scenes who you feel was a huge asset to the team?

AT: There's a handful of guys. Dennis (Leblanc) and Keith (Zimmer) in the Academic Center worked their knuckles to the bone helping guys out and making sure they were doing what Coach Osborne told their parents they would be doing. And obviously you guys -like Mike and Bryan Bailey and Randy Gobel- those guys in the weight room, where you could be a sounding board and have conversations with. It was a family, you know? You make nice with everybody, you know? I remember the strength coach in Oakland once said, "It's nice to be important, but it's more important to be nice." So that's one thing that I kind of live by, and a 'thank you' goes a long way to those people behind the scenes.

When you're in a position to have success and actually do it? Well damn it, you better be smart enough to know how you were given that opportunity and understand there's a lot that goes into it. Even Norma Knobel (who used to give scholarship checks), Chris Anderson, Don Bryant, everybody had one common goal and they knew it, they did everything they could to achieve it.

Q: Any special moments with Coach Osborne stick out to you?

AT: Not really. I guess I never had to go to his office because I stayed out of trouble. (laughs)

And people always talk about his dry sense of humor. I was good friends with Doak. He and I played on the Hoop it Up tournament there in the summer, and we played on the Intramural team a couple of years there at the Rec Center. And Doak was another guy that was instrumental, liked to have a good time, play jokes on Coach Osborne and vice versa. Oh yeah, sometimes you'd be getting in the elevator and there would be Mary Lynn (Coach Osborne's Secretary) coming out. And you'd look up on the wall of the elevator and there would be some old picture of Doak that was photocopied from his old high school yearbook or something like that, things of that nature.

And I'd go in the training room in the mornings and I'd work on the Daily Nebraskan crossword puzzle and just talk about things with trainers Jack Nickolite and Jerry Weber.

Q: You talked about "just getting out of the way of Lawrence". What are your recollections of him?

AT: Just a gifted human being. I don't know if he ever got his lifting card signed in the weight room, but he was a monster, years ahead of his development level physically.

Q: What was it like blocking for a guy like that?

AT: Not like we were bent on winning him the Heisman, but you had to make sure we were up there leading the nation in rushing. It was just absurd the amount of yards we were rushing for back then, and just to have him you wanted to make him look good.

Q: Then you'd look good in the process, also, right?

AT: Exactly, that meant you were doing your job. The offensive line doesn't want to be in the paper because that meant you weren't doing something right. (laughs)

Q: What were the favorite methods of feedback you guys received?

AT: The daily film sessions, correcting things that needed correcting. We'd watch all the practices on film and take notes and talk through issues if there was any of that, about certain plays. By the end of the week we'd have a test that Milt and Dan would give us for that week's opponent. (A lot of the time we were all circled around Matt Vrzal, he had all the answers.) (laughs) The x's and o's were drawn in and you just had to draw the assignments of where you were going. There must have been twenty plays and probably four looks against them, so you had about a hundred little boxes to do that. We'd take it Friday afternoon and hand it in, and Friday night we'd stay at the Kellogg Center until Saturday morning. And then we'd eat breakfast and talk about things before the game.

Q: Adam, anything else that I haven't touched upon that set those teams apart?

AT: Some guys learned 'nastiness' a little bit. Milt talked about being nasty. He kept track of knockdowns, pancakes, something that was recorded week to week.

And Coach would recognize Players of The Game: they'd put little plaques in the hallway from the locker room to the training room down there. And there was the Scout Team Players of the Week Award, too, and that plaque on the wall there.

And then walking underneath the old horseshoe there, and seeing the big, red signs that had the record of every season and every bowl game -obviously it started before Coach Osborne and it was Devaney's era, even- and Coach Osborne built it even more and we wanted to keep it rolling.

Q: Did you know Bob Devaney very well?

AT: I didn't. I'd see him down in the training room in the mornings riding the stationary bike and he liked to watch Kiana Tom and her workout show on ESPN there. (laughs) Other times you'd see his secretary come down to the training room after lunch to get a bag of ice, and I don't think it was for rehab purposes. It was time to relax, you know? (laughs)

Q: Any lasting remarks the Husker fans should know about, from your perspective?

AT: You've got to tip your hat to the average Nebraska fan because they know what it takes. Between you and I, when Callahan called and asked me to put in a good word for him to Steve Pederson, I told him before he went there (and I knew he coached under Barry Alvarez at the University of Wisconsin, and Barry's a Nebraska guy), I told Bill, 'Make sure you understand the special tradition.' And he said "Oh, I understand it." He didn't understand it. I said, 'You need to go to through the state and sit in the Legion club in Kimball, Nebraska, or Scottsbluff or Minden or Niobrara. You need to go to these watering holes and meet the state.' He didn't, and I don't think he understood that aspect of it.

And Coach Osborne, growing up there, he 'got' it. And Coach Pelini, he's the right guy who also has the right guy upstairs. He's not too proud to talk to him and take his advice, and it's great to have Doak be back on there again, too. Doak, he was a lot more than a trainer, he had a feel for the shit that was being flung around the training room, and if he felt something was pertinent he'd go share it with Coach Osborne. He was great at keeping a finger on the pulse of the team.

Q: So who did you used to hang around with during those days?

AT: Joel Wilks, I used to hang out with that group. It was Stai and Seiler and Wilks and Mark Gilman. Seiler and Gilman and Stai were roommates and we used to go out together, when I was a sophomore, I guess. And they accepted me, so that was good for my psyche.

Q: Bryan Pruitt was talking me about a certain battle between T.J. Slanksy and Christian Peter when you first joined the team…

AT: Oh yeah, I think Bryan was a year older than me. I remember they were doing a one on one in the Fieldhouse Pit there and Christian got T.J.'s helmet off and hit him across the head with his own helmet. That's Christian for you. (laughs)

Then we played Michigan State my junior year in East Lansing and he's talking to the team in the locker room before the game along with the other captains -Phil Ellis and Aaron Graham and Ed Stewart- and he grabs a clock off the wall, and he punted it! And then he had a 4 inch Christmas ornament and he just smashed it against his face... and after about 2 seconds he had about 40 lacerations on his face from the glass, there was blood just running down his face. (laughs) I remember looking around and thinking to myself, 'Holy cow, what is wrong with this guy?' And Pruitt, did he tell you about his dance moves down in South Beach?

Q: No, (laughs) give me some dirt, man..

AT: We all got false ID's before those Orange Bowl trips, and somebody had a friend that had a lamination machine and had their artist-friend draw the state of Nebraska on a poster board and cut the corner out of it so we could stand there and take our picture with a Polaroid. (laughs) And half of us, our heads were tilted to the side on the ID's because our shoulders were too big to fit in the cut-out. And if we were too far behind the cut-out it would cast a shadow on your forehead! (laughs) We had fun. Everybody stayed out of the papers, so it was good. The bars were open until 5 a.m., so it was like, 'Are you kidding me?' If you were dumb enough or brave enough the first couple nights when we didn't have a curfew down there, until practice started the next day we had a little fun.

Q: So it wasn't entirely all business?

AT: Oh no. You have a bunch of twenty year old kids, it's amazing there wasn't more stuff with all those guys. If you took those ID's we had made back to Lincoln they'd get taken. They'd look at 'em and just laugh at you.

I can't believe Pruitt didn't tell you about his dancing skills in the clubs down there. (laughs) I remember how he used to run. His arms would be going 100 miles per hour sideways. He was a tough son of a gun, that guy. I think he was a wedgebuster on kickoffs. He had no fear.

Q: Well Adam, I can't thank you enough for your time. I ask so many questions because back in those days I was often working with the other teams when you guys were doing your thing. Like the volleyball girls...

AT: We were all jealous of you because you got to work with volleyball. That's when they started wearing those spandex shorts, too. (laughs) We were sitting over there behind the training table window and Rolan, the training table guy, he would keep plates of food aside for us guys, because sometimes we'd be late to eat because we spent too much time sitting by the bench over there watching you do your work with those girls. (laughs)

End Conversation.

Do you remember the earlier conversation with Brenden Stai and my introduction of the N Factor? How some small, seemingly minor detail played a large role in making those teams into what they were? Well, Adam brought up the name of a location that was known in football circles by the simple name of 'The Pit'. The Pit was in the former Schulte Fieldhouse, an indoor facility encased in the North Stadium behind the old scoreboard past the old north endzone. The present day Tom and Nancy Osborne Complex sits atop that site, now serving as its foundation, so it's impossible to visit anymore, banished hereafter to sweat-stained, bruised, and fading memories.

The place was a lower level, basement-kind of room about 25 feet by 40 feet in dimension and covered wall to wall with old, green Astroturf. This was where all the blocking dummies and assorted knick-knacks were stored until the student managers removed them for practice time. It was a 'man cave' in some respects: not much air flow, dark (save for a few naked lightbulbs dripping from naked conduit in the low-slung concrete ceiling), with a few scattered spider webs collecting dirt here and there for maximum testosterone-boosting effect. It was the perfect training grounds for trench warfare.

This was where epic battles were waged: offensive linemen versus defensive linemen. Every day. Out of Coach Tom Osborne's eyesight and earshot, Charlie and Milt's boys waged hell on each other, relentless in their attacks, cajoling and spitting and cursing, with occasional fists flying. This was the place you lost your high school football cherry and stepped into manhood. The weekly combat among the Clydesdales eliminated a miniscule touch of their 'piss n' vinegar,' assisting with alleviating the edginess that comes with the anxiousness of an impending game. Those hand-to-hand encounters left them spent just enough to not retaliate or physically lash out at an opponent during the course of a game, thus limiting penalties of aggression. It turned boys into men and men into warriors.

Adam said it perfectly when he stated, "Some guys learned 'nastiness' a little bit." Case in point was the story that a freshman lineman in those years had experienced his very first practice down in the Pit when a player ripped his opponent's helmet clean off and proceeded to bash his adversary over the head with it, an open gash and bloody mess resulting. Aghast and still reeling from the barbary, the greenhorn telephoned his father from his dormitory room later that night and said, "Dad, I don't think I'm gonna make it. I'm not man enough to play here." His father convinced him otherwise, and the youngster went on to have a nice career in professional football after fruitful Husker seasons.

Adam also mentioned another N Factor, (which was by no means unique to the University, but helped by providing consistent, little nudges all the same) and that was the weekly recognition of Players of The Game both on offense and defense, as well as special teams. There was even recognition for that previous week's practices with the Scout Team Players of the Week Award. Let's face it, human nature desires public recognition for our efforts along with the sense of pride that comes with contributing to something larger than yourself. Unlike the Ohio States and many like-programs, the University of Nebraska never awarded helmet stickers as outward displays of accomplishment (calling attention to yourself apart from the team), but inside the troupe everyone knew who was stepping up on a consistent basis, constantly setting the bar for future peer performance. Unity, Belief, Respect: that's what it was all about. Just know that respect was earned rather than given.

Notable quote #2:
Adam Treu on maintaining the legacy: "With the tradition being what it was, you didn't want to be that team that didn't win 9 games a year."

Is it or is it not a matter of importance that a young man starts out in life with an ability to shut his jaw hard and say "I will," or "I will not," and mean it?

John Heisman

Perhaps the most unsung member of the '94 crew known simply as The Pipeline, Joel Wilks literally scratched and clawed his way to a starting position on the pancaking, steam-rolling, relentlessly hostile offensive line. Picking up the nickname 'Buddha' somewhere along the way, he was extremely good-natured and embraced his Nebraska born and bred underdog status, reaching the apex of every walk-on kid's dream to become a starter. Despite that friendly social demeanor, though, around gametime he would metamorphous from this kindly Buddhan spirit into a snarling, eyes dark as death, frothing-at-the-mouth pitbull. His mean streak intact, Joel and many of the student/athletes of that era were into the heavy- and thrash metal music of Metallica, Slayer, Pantera and the like. This was hard-core head-banging and not for the faint of hearing nor heart. The lyrics of these groups' verse testify to some of that, and were regularly on Joel's pre-game psyche-up playlist. Let's hear now from Joel Wilks, the Pancake King himself...

Notable Quote #1:
"Brenden and I had this thing where we would put a piece of tape across our helmets and we wrote 'PMA' on it. And other guys would go, "What the heck does PMA stand for?!"...it was PMA: Positive Mental Attitude. And that got us through a lot of bad times, just motivated us, you know. Through bad practices and stuff. We always said, "PMA."

Joel Wilks

Walk-on, Offensive Guard, Hastings, Nebraska (Hastings High)
Where are they now? Portland, Oregon, Firefighter

Question: So you were from Hastings, right?

Joel Wilks: No, actually I was born in Omaha. My Dad was a high school principal, so we moved around. We lived in West Point, Nebraska, Red Cloud, and then we ended up in Hastings just for my high school career, for four freshman through senior years.

Q: When it came time to think about college, were you heavily recruited?

JW: You know, I got a lot of interest letters, but as far as actually getting scholarships I was only offered Division 1 scholarships by a couple of schools, Northern Illinois being one. I could have gone to Army, West Point Military Academy. But then I got a bunch of other offers from smaller schools. And when I went to visit West Point Military Academy, I really debated that. That was a really hard decision. What an opportunity that was.

Then what happened was, I deep down always wanted to go to Nebraska. I had so many ties there and grew up wanting to be a Husker. My Dad played there in the 60's (he was in Devaney's first recruiting class). Deep down I really wanted to do that, but it was an ego thing that I didn't want to sit there and just be a walk-on. Actually, I accepted the scholarship offer from Northern Illinois, then it kind of sunk in -and one night I couldn't articulate it, but it was just kind of a bad feeling- I knew I should go to Nebraska and see if I was good enough. I remember getting up in the middle of the night and going into my parents' room and telling them, 'I've changed my mind. I can't go to Northern Illinois. I have to go to Nebraska.' My mom was so happy, she didn't want me to go there, anyway. So they were happy I changed my mind and were very supportive.

Q: That's cool. You know, Army was recruiting me out of high school, and sometimes I wonder what might have happened had I gone there...

JW: Me too.

Q: So you were extremely knowledgeable about Nebraska football coming in?

JW: Oh yeah, I remember every big loss we ever had growing up. We lived it, man. Sooner Magic, horrible.

Q: The '84 Orange bowl two-point attempt?

JW: Oh, I'll never forget that for the rest of my life! I cried for like a week after that. I was devastated, man. Actually, my biggest disappointment in my life was that game. That's what made it so good to get the '95 win over Miami when we did that.

Q: I'm building up to that, Joel. But to start, any memories of the first few days on campus?

JW: Yeah, I remember just being kind of in awe at first, pinching myself and saying, 'Man, I'm really here', after dreaming about this for so long; definitely looking around at the big house and having the 'deer in the headlights' look at first.

But then I had a little chip on my shoulder because I just barely missed out on getting a scholarship (and I think they actually gave the last scholarship to Brenden Stai). But it worked out alright, because otherwise we never would have gotten Brenden, so I was glad about that. But I kind of had a chip on my shoulder when I came in and wanted to prove that I could play, too. I had that look in my eye, thinking, 'I'm as good as these guys.' I wanted to make an impression right away, so they wouldn't forget about me. My plan was not to get pushed around and to get in fights -if that's what it took- so they wouldn't forget who I was. Show them I was tough enough to play. That was my mindset.

Q: How long until you got into your first fight?

JW: I think it was my first day. (laughs) You ask Brenden and those guys. That first year I got into a fight every practice.

Q: Do you remember with whom?

JW: No, I don't remember my first one. Especially my freshman year and my redshirt year. If you remember, my first year I was on that last freshman team, but that second year I was going against guys like Raemakers and Parrella, those guys. If you ask Brenden, those guys, they'll tell you it was an everyday kind of thing.

I remember Coach Osborne, after a while, he was getting tired of it. I remember him sitting me down one time and it was like, "Joel, if you ever want to get on the field we have to know you won't lose your cool out there and get into a fight. We know that you've been fighting for a year now and we know you're tough enough to play." So my plan worked. (laughs)

Q: Any impressions of the program from your earliest days there?

JW: You know, it was a little different, where we were freshmen and we had our own little team and everything. Ever since the first day, just feeling out the guys and seeing how it was gonna be like, it was a deal of having a separate group, ust the anticipation of seeing the scholarship guys, feeling them out, seeing who's a good guy and all. I don't remember much else about the first practices, though.

I noticed right away the scholarship linemen, Brenden stuck out right away for sure, and I knew Rob Zatechka pretty well in high school. Rob was so huge coming out of high school, he was around 290. When I came in I was about 235, which was after a buffet. And Rob is like 290 as a freshman. I wasn't sure if I could play here because of the size and everything. Brenden was like 250 or so, and I wasn't sure if I could play.

Q: First friends you made?

JW: Actually, another kid from my high school team walked on as a kicker, and he lasted like two days. So we roomed together. Three practices and I came back to my dorm room and everything of his was gone, he just bailed.

I became pretty good friends with Matt Shaw right away, we both walked on and played against each other in football and basketball in high school. He was a good friend right away, and then him and kicker Tim Seiler were good friends, so we became friends, too. And then I noticed that Brenden was the strongest freshman in the weightroom, so I kind of hung around him because I wanted to play. I knew I had to get bigger to play and I kind of befriended him and worked out with him. And then we became really good friends and lifted together all the time in college,became lifting partners.

Q: Who's the first Husker staff member you remember getting to know?

JW: Of course, you're in awe of Coach Osborne, but Kevin Steele, you got to know him pretty well. George Sullivan, of course, he was a trainer when my Dad played. When I was in 10th grade or so we had some issues with my lower back so he took me in to see Sully, so I got to know him. He was always giving me a hard time. And maybe not initially, but Doak and I became good friends, too. We'd always mess around with each other.

Q: So your first fall season was 1990. What was the culture of the team compared to when you left 5 years later?

JW: Yeah, it was 1990, and the first couple of years I didn't see the work ethic. I don't remember what the record was in '90 and '91, but I remember getting spanked by Oklahoma and then losing the bowl game. They had the talent, but the work ethic just wasn't there. Even the linemen would be the first guys out of the weightroom. I remember just not being impressed with some guys and their work ethic.

And then here we were getting kicked out of the weightroom by Boyd and his shutting the lights out on us and stuff. We just worked harder than those guys did. I didn't really see the camaraderie and brotherhood that we had, the five of us on the line, for sure. The whole team too, but the five of us on that line were so close, we would do anything for each other. I didn't sense that as much among the group when I first came in.

Q: What fostered that closeness?

JW: We had a lot of things in common. We were tough guys, we had a drive about us, we all wanted to make something really special and knew we had to rely on each other to do that. The time spent together having that same mission, Brenden and all the guys had that push to stay in the weightroom. We never wanted to leave. I didn't want to ever be the first guy out. And we were competitive, so that helped.

Q: Did the coaches preach intensity or attitude?

JW: Intensity was talked about, for sure. Specifically, there was just kind of a thing where Coach Osborne didn't like to see the scrappy ones and fights, you know? But Coach Tenopir and McBride, they loved that stuff. They loved it. Downstairs in the pit doing one on ones, if a fight broke out there you would let it go on for a few minutes. The intensity, just getting fired up, they allowed that. They didn't ever say it specifically; you just knew that's what they wanted, because they let it go when it happened.

Q: It seems like the coaches mainly focused on the technique and the process, depending on you guys to provide your own motivation…

JW: Quite a bit. Milt would jump your butt now and then, but it was more technique. If you weren't doing your job and getting it done, Coach Tenopir could cheat you out of playing time.

But Coach Tenopir, he wouldn't really have to. Some days my senior year, if you were a little sick and didn't feel like practicing, Graham and Stai both would be getting in my face in the huddle, telling me to pick it up and bring it up. So Coach Tenopir didn't have to, because those guys would. They didn't let you have an off day and slack off. It was about all of us being on the same page. They were like, "Man, you've gotta suck it up. I don't care if you are sick or not." A lot of the coaches let the guys do it themselves.

Q: What about Coach Tenopir? Tell me about him.

JW: He's kind of a good 'ol boy. Nice personality, nice guy. But he definitely was intimidating at first, gruff and growly at first, you kind of had to earn his respect. But he loved all his guys, for sure, he's got a heart. Love Coach Tenopir. I remember your first couple of years he wouldn't buddy up to you, you had to earn it. When you were a senior he treated you like more of a friend than anything, but he was pretty hard core at the beginning. I remember him chewing me out a couple of times, but my senior year was great. Had a really great relationship with him.

Q: What did he chew you out for?

JW: Just technique and stuff. I mean, you're coming out of high school, and the difference in technique from college and high school is just ridiculous. In high school you just came off the ball and hit people, but in college it was a matter of, "Your step with your right foot being two inches or an inch shorter than where it has to be." So much technique, it was really hard at first. It takes you a couple of years just to understand the offense and have my technique to where I could even play. So when you're young, on every play there was always something to get chewed out for your first couple of years, (laughs) something you could do better. He would ride me pretty good. Also, he respected me, that I was tough enough to play, and he wouldn't have done it if he didn't care.

Q: Did Coach Young work with you much?

JW: Yeah, he did a lot of the pass stuff. He recruited me, too. He was more quiet. A pretty quiet guy, more so than Coach Tenopir. I guess his low-key personality, I don't think I became as close to him as I did with Coach Tenopir. He kind of took a little crap behind the scenes from the guys because he had a quirky personality. (laughs) He would coach us up in practice and have a funny way of talking and we'd joke with him. So many guys would imitate his voice. It was all in fun. He was a good guy.

Q: So Milt focused on the run game and Coach Young had the pass protection, huh?

JW: Yeah, that's how they split it up, for sure.

Q: So the typical week, what percentage of time would each of them spend with you guys?

JW: I don't remember us passing a ton. Tommie Frazier, a lot of that was play action stuff. We didn't do a lot of one-on-one stuff, but we did a group thing where we spent 15 or 20 minutes each practice doing it, it was pretty short. As far as technique, it was pretty short. Majority of the time was with Tenopir working on the reps most of the time.

Q: The reason I ask was that I saw some of Tommie's stats and I couldn't believe how many touchdown passes he had. I didn't recall him throwing that much.

JW: What he did was big plays -play action stuff where a guy was wide open- like Mark Gilman and those guys.

Q: What about Coach Osborne? Any special conversations or memories?

JW: Obviously, that one about the fighting, for sure. I remember when he called me and told me I was going to be on scholarship. After two years he told me I was going to be on scholarship, which was pretty neat, told me what a good job I was doing. It was great.

Q: Do you recall much about that day?

JW: I remember sitting in his office and the conversation. I remember just being fired up and calling my Dad right away. I think it was spring or summer going into my third year, I was on scholarship that fall. I was really excited and it was a feeling of accomplishment, knowing you earned it, that he really respected you, that you earned it. Validated it, you know?

Q: All those fights paid off?

JW: (laughs) Exactly!

Q: Did he possess any peculiar mannerisms?

JW: You just respect him with everything he did, a great guy with his values and morals, such a top notch guy with everything. I feel so fortunate to have been there and played for him when he was there. Everybody just put it on the line for that guy, such a father figure. He's trustworthy, he didn't lie to you, just did everything the right way. It was an honor to know him and play for him.

Q: Your last year was the '94 team, what do you think set the team apart from others in those years?

JW: Definitely, it starts from the top. Coach Osborne was a different breed. Coaches go about things in different ways, and he went about it the right way, and that pays off over time. It starts with him and what he built, having the right coaches underneath him. He wasn't the rah-rah, kind of guy, but he had guys underneath him who did. You have to have those guys. He didn't micromanage them and just let them do their thing. He had Coach Steele and Coach McBride, he knew what he was doing.

Q: Tell me about Charlie…

JW: The guy, he was intense, man. He was always intimidating. You never really got to know him, being on the offensive side. He would just chew those guys out and intimidate them, but by the time they were juniors and seniors they would put their life on the line for that guy, you know? Just an intimidating guy. Like he had that switch on him where you wonder if someday he might go crazy. He'd look at you like he was gonna kill you, you know? I didn't say much to him at first, not until I got a little older. He'd get fired up, doing one-on-ones down in the pit he would get those guys so amped up. He would get them in a circle and just yell at them. He got so intense down there, we had so many intense battles down there, fights. There was some crazy stuff down there. All of that comes from McBride. Some guys would get their helmets ripped off, and people swinging helmets. You could kill somebody, getting that intensity up. The most intense it ever was down in that pit, Christian and Jason Peter and John Parrella; they didn't get any meaner than that. It made everything else you encountered seem pretty easy, you know?

Q: And when you say 'the pit', we're talking about the lower room down in the old North Fieldhouse, right? Where they used to store the blocking dummies?

JW: Yeah, we used to live down there!

Q: I'm sure you can still hear Charlie yelling to this day?

JW: Oh, he was just screaming. Us O-linemen, we were pretty much chilled, you know? But the D-linemen, they were in there screaming and hollering about how they were gonna get after us, and when they came in there it would get heated. Coach Tenopir definitely wanted to get after it, but he didn't do all the screaming like the defense did.

Q: Do you recall some choice words Charlie used?

JW: He wasn't afraid to cuss. (laughs) Maybe that's why we were down in the pit, I think, because that way Coach Osborne wouldn't get to or have to hear them cuss. I never heard him say a swear word for five years.

Q: Charlie made up for it?

JW: Oh, yeah. (Laughs) Coach Steele was intense, too. I remember one day when I was a redshirt, he pulled me over to work with the linebackers and we had to do a one-on-one drill. He had us 10 yards apart and he had us come off the ball and go full speed, taking on the linebackers. And I'm the only guy over there and I had to take on 10 linebackers by myself, just getting my bell rung. And I remember him just screaming, "Come on, Wilks!" I'm like, 'Dude, are you kidding me?' All these guys were getting rest and I'm the only one.

And we were on scout team going against the defense and if we were slacking he'd come into the huddle and grab our facemasks and shake us around, bumping up against us and pushing us around. That guy was catch, yeah. I never became really tight with him. He was pretty intense. I just remember always being kind of intimidated, he had that crazy thing going for him, too, where he could snap.

Q: Any memorable games stand out to you?

JW: Of course, that Orange Bowl is the one I'll always remember the most. There's two games that I played the best in. When we played Colorado my senior year and we beat them at home, I had a good game there, had a few pancakes on Ted Johnson, he ended up being in the pros. And we were always competing for the most pancakes, that was a big deal, seeing at the end of the year who had the most pancake blocks. And against Oklahoma State I had 19 pancake blocks, the most ever, so I remember that game. But definitely the Orange Bowl against Miami was a game that sticks out.

Q: What about that game?

JW: Just the guys we were going against: we had Ray Lewis on my side, Warren Sapp on the other side. Also, the year before against Florida State -me personally- I didn't have my best game and didn't play that well, so the next year coming back I wanted to do better. And Coach Tenopir said I had a really good game there, so that really was great to hear, and that sticks out.

Q: You switched from your normal left guard position to the right side for that game, right?

JW: Yeah, that was a coaching decision, Coach Tenopir and Coach Osborne. At the time I was pretty pissed about it, because they wanted Brenden against Warren Sapp, and he'd been tearing people up all season. Brenden and Zach over there, our two All-Americans, it kind of pissed me off at first and it was kind of an insult, but looking back -weeks after making that decision- I respected that. It was probably more embarrassing more than anything for a short while, more of an ego thing, having to tell people why we did it when they would ask me, you know? Like I wasn't good enough or something. Sapp was a good player, and if they wanted to put a good player like Brenden on him, I respected that. But I wanted to prove myself, so that motivated me for that game, too, and I wanted to show them that I could take him on, too, and I chop blocked him a few times and smacked him around pretty good, so I had my three or four traps on him. Actually that last touchdown by Cory, I trapped him. And that was my only game on the right side.

Q: So you were dealing with a lot of things. What or who else were you dealing with that game? Was Dwayne Johnson, "The Rock" over there?

JW: Yeah, I got into a fight with Dwayne Johnson during that game. We got our facemasks tied up, he called me a bitch and all this stuff, talking smack. I ended up giving him a hip toss and throwing him on his back. It was awesome. Working with the firefighters, whenever I see Dwayne Johnson on TV I always tell them I smacked him around. (laughs)

Q: Pancaked him, eh?

JW: Yeah, they had some big names on that defense, so it was pretty cool.

Q: What about interaction with some of the other guys? A lot of banter back and forth?

JW: Yeah, there was a lot. I thought the year before, Florida State was the team that talked the most at that point, but Miami was even more so. Warren Sapp, for sure, he talked the whole time. Ray Lewis, too. Those guys for sure, also Marley, little Marley. Oh God, he talked so much. He was so tiny, but he talked so much!

Q: What would he say?

JW: I couldn't even understand him, to tell you the truth, so much chatter. The best was toward the end there when we were driving, they were so tired they couldn't even talk, it was awesome. And Zach (Weigert) was kind of our talker, our big talker, he started yelling over there during the timeout at Warren and those guys, asking them what was up, why they weren't talking now? It was hilarious. I'll never forget it, even now, they were so tired they couldn't say a word. (laughs)

Q: So the '94 Orange Bowl, the Florida State game, how much did you play during that game?

JW: I rotated in that game. Rob Zatechka and I rotated in and we'd alternate. We'd go two series and alternate. I played left side and played half of that game. I was injured early my junior year so I didn't play until halfway through the season, so that was really the biggest game I'd ever been in, for sure. I was pretty nervous, played alright, but I made mistakes and stuff. It was kind of tough to take at the time.

Q: Was there a different intensity that game compared to a regular season game?

JW: Oh, definitely.

Q: Could you give us a scale of magnitude in comparing that one?

JW: It was a ten. That and the Miami game were the most intense games I ever played in. That year we played Pacific, and I would give that a minus 2. I played half the game and remember eating a hotdog on the sideline during the game. (laughs) We were eating on the sidelines and Coach Osborne didn't think that was too cool, so we got in trouble for that. It was Zach Weigert's idea, so we blamed Zach.

Q: Do you recall that Florida State game with Zach at the end there giving the Florida State guy a hard time for cursing at Coach Osborne?

JW: The last series I wasn't in for the kick, I was on the sidelines. I remember more of Byron Bennett and how nervous he was on the sidelines. I wasn't very confident seeing his body language there on the sidelines. He was kind of saying, "I don't think I can make it. I don't think I can make it." And I was like, 'Are you kidding me? What are you talking about?' He was pretty negative, you know, so I didn't think we had much of a chance after seeing that. It was too bad, but that's what I remember about that last part of the game.

Q: Any one significant play stand out to you. A matchup?

JW: The biggest play my senior year was that pancake on Ted Johnson. I'll never forget that play pancaking him. Coach Tenopir put in a special play -we hadn't run it at all the entire season- for me to pull around. Everybody was gonna wash everything down and I was gonna pull around, and the last second I saw his eyes get all big and just got underneath and drove him, picked him up and slammed him on his back. Executed the perfect pancake you dream about. One of those kind of deals. It was the first touchdown. Schlesinger scored the first touchdown.

Q: I'll have to go back and look for that. Any other funny stories worth sharing?

JW: A lot of them. Just a lot of horsing around. For me, we were living in the dorms for a couple of years. I remember one time Matt Shaw and Tom Seiler (I had one of those Suzuki Samurais that didn't have the top on it), Shaw and Seiler stole that thing off the top of my rig and it started to rain, and I was freaking out trying to find where it was. They had me running around all day long searching for it, giving me hints about where it was, running all over campus trying to find this thing. I was freaking out, worried I was going to ruin my interior and everything.

So finally I called Shaw at his home. I'm just pissed and I'm just cussing and yelling at him, and he says "Hey Joel, say hello to my Mom. You're on speakerphone right now." He had it on speaker phone and his whole family was having dinner over there. And his Mom is a real nice, religious lady, very proper, and she says "Hi Joel." And I'm just like, 'Awwww!' I couldn't believe it! I was so embarrassed, man. We'd be cracking jokes like that, always doing stuff like that.

Q: Any good practice stories?

JW: The things I remember most from practice is the fights. Some were pretty funny. Like one time I was on scout team -and again, that's when I was getting in all those fights– well, they set this thing up with Parrella and Raemakers, they were just tired of me getting in fights and stuff. So they grab me -and this was a bowl game practice- right at the end of the play everybody was watching, and they were just pounding on me, swinging, both of them just swinging and I'm just covering up and they're pounding on me and they're just laughing. Giggling and laughing while they're doing it! And I remember looking over at the scout team and those guys aren't helping me. I'm thinking, 'What the heck are you guys doing?! Aren't you gonna help?!' (laughs) I was pissed.

That, and I got into fight once with Christian Peter in practice and Coach Osborne pulled us aside and made us run stairs for about 45 minutes in South Stadium for that. Christian and I are running looking over at each other and Christian is dropping f-bombs, calling me an eff-ing pig, saying that and chewing me out, in a fun way. It was funny.

And that one time I was so sick and Brenden and Aaron getting in my face that day and chewing me out that day. I remember that, It was awesome.

Q: And Joel, what kind of feedback did you guys get? Next day?

JW: Yeah, next day we would go over the previous day's practice and go play-by-play, position-by-position, every play every practice. For games they grade you: zero, one and two. A number, then you get a score and then pancakes. You were always getting graded, always getting looked at, always getting coaching. It was huge.

Q: Do you recall who led that senior year in pancakes?

JW: I did. Yeah, one hundred and forty -two.

Q: Do you recall who the closest guy was to you?

JW: I think it was (depending who you ask), Brenden would say it was him and Graham and Weigert would probably say it was them. (laughs) I think it was Weigert, but the three of us were right there, it came down to the last game. We were all probably within 5 to 10 pancakes from the top. I ended up getting 142, so that's kind of bragging rights, you know? 'You guys got your All-American trophy, but I got the Pancake Title.' (laughs)

Q: What did the Pancake King get? Was there a prize?

JW: No, it was bragging rights, is all. We all really wanted it bad, though. We did take a picture. I remember, at the training table where all of us were sitting at a table eating pancakes, and they put me right in the middle, in the center with this big stack of pancakes in front of me, so I guess since I was the champ I got to sit right in front of the huge stack. (laughs) Best seat at the table.

Q: What would you say you were most proud of?

JW: I was just proud of, I guess, the path I had to come up: to get there and how it finished. The story couldn't be written any better, it was a dream come true. How it turned out for me, to walk on and come up through the ranks and end up starting and then winning the national championship. Every day, one day at a time, it was how I approached it, my work ethic and being consistent every day. And being only 230 lbs. when I came in, it took everything I had to get to that weight and that level. Just the consistency every day, coming in and doing the work. Getting to that level was a dream come true.

Q: The process of becoming the player you wanted to be?

JW: Sure. Coach Osborne always stressed the process and the journey, you know? It was just doing the right thing every day, and it paid off.

Q: Wish you could do anything over?

JW: I've never really thought about that before. Wow, that's a good question. You know, not really. Like I said, I felt I did everything I could, maybe I wished I could have been an All-American. I never had a dream to play in the NFL, but it would have been nice to have a chance, at least. You know, I did everything I could every single day and it wasn't in the cards. It wasn't like I came out of the womb a 13 lb. baby like Brenden. (laughs) I wasn't as naturally gifted, as far as my frame and that kind of thing. I think I got everything out of my career and my body. I'm pretty satisfied with how everything turned out for me. I don't really have any regrets.

Q: And If I recall, was the CFL after you?

JW: Yeah, they were. I told them I was gonna come up there, but a week or two before camp, I just didn't have it in my heart. I felt like the days were over, I played my best game and we one the national championship. And I didn't want to linger on and play in all these different leagues and get injured. And I felt pretty satisfied with where I was, and I realized that if I wasn't gonna get any chance in the NFL I was gonna call it a career. The same thing like my college choice, if I wasn't going to play at Nebraska I wasn't going to play anywhere else. I wanted to give it a chance to play at the ultimate place, if it wasn't there then I didn't want to play. Same with the NFL. So I changed my mind and started up the diet plan, dropping weight. So here I am.

Q: How heavy did you get?

JW: My heaviest was about 285, I usually played during the season at about 275. I always wanted to get to 300. I would sit there at the training table, you can ask those guys, they'll tell you. I would be sitting there for two and one half hours, trying to eat. I'd go through like 3 or 4 groups of guys sitting at my table. (laughs) They'd keep rotating by as I sat there and ate. That was surely my way of trying to get to 300, I guess.

Q: Sounds like you were a table centerpiece. Everything moved but you. (laughs) You were a fixture.

JW: Oh, I was. Those guys would make fun of me so much. They were like, "You're still here?!"

Q: Any personal thing, a saying or something that you could stick to on a bad day to get you through?

JW: Oh yeah, Brenden and I had this thing where we would put a piece of tape across our helmets, and we wrote 'PMA' on it. And other guys would go, "What the heck does PMA stand for?!" We used to have deep and meaningful talks about stuff, about life and practice and that type of thing, and Brenden came up with it. Like one time, when my girlfriend and I broke up during college, I was talking to him and he kind of helped me through that. And it was PMA, Positive Mental Attitude. And that got us through a lot of bad times, just motivated us, you know. Through bad practices and stuff. We always said, "PMA." Even though the tape came off the helmet, we'd still say 'PMA'. Look at each other and say 'PMA', it would get us fired up, you know.

Q: Were there any PMA's going around on that final drive for Cory's last touchdown drive against Miami?

JW: Oh yeah, one thing we also did, kind of a thing that would bring each other up. Whenever we were in the huddle and really needed a big play, really needed to come together and get something done, Aaron Graham would always lean over and reach down and grab us by our shins, our calves, the front of our legs, and all of a sudden it became a big deal where we always called it the 'calf grab.' All the times we needed a big play, for big games, he always would reach down and do that. And it kind of reenergized us and got us so jacked up. I remember him doing that on the final drive, on that last play where Cory scored there in the Orange Bowl. He didn't grab them the year before and we didn't get it done, so he did that and we ended up scoring on the next play. To this day, every now and they we'll be talking and if you sense a guy is down or something you say, "Hey man, do you need a calf grab or what?" It's kind of special what we all had there.

Q: Nice. Anybody else in your group stand out to you from those days?

JW: One guy, Bryan Pruitt, he had a really intense personality and intense work ethic on the field. He was the kind of guy that definitely fit in with all of us, the same mentality, and he was so undersized. I think that kind of hurt him initially, but he had that tough, Chicago mentality, a really tough guy. I think he fit in and rubbed off on everybody, I would definitely say him. He really sticks out to me.

Q: Any staff members you think were really helpful to you?

JW: Oh yeah, one guy who really was great and I keep in touch with to this day was Keith Zimmer. Whenever I get back I try to see him. He made a really big impression on all of us. Really cares about the athletes there and does a great job.

Q: What did he bring to the table?

JW: He's just a real good personality, and great sense of humor. We could go joke around with him. And he'd always help you out. He cared about you, not just in football, but with academics, trying to decide my major and what career to choose. He was always there for you, always had an open door, always had time for you, was never too busy. So, he was just a great guy.

Q: When most fans hear something like that about an academic advisor, they probably think that he ended up writing papers for you. In what ways did he help out?

JW: Oh no, (laughs) it was just academic resources. If you had a question about a career he would get a hold of a former player or somebody in the community and you could to talk to them and ask questions. You could always count on him with little questions or help, but it was nothing like papers or anything like that.

Q: Nothing like Florida State? (laughs)

JW: Yeah, (laughs) he'd help you find a tutor. He was just kind of an ear, too. If you had a tough day, you could just sit in his office and talk to him a lot.

Q: Does Jack Stark stick out to you at all?

JW: Yeah, I had some good times with Jack. He did a lot of visualization stuff, he'd make tapes and do that kind of stuff. Spent a bit of time with him too, he was helping me out when I was there for graduate school, too, so we had a good relationship.

Q: And you were on the strength staff after '94, right?

JW: Yeah, just one semester, when I was taking grad classes. It was mainly over at the Devaney Center helping out with track and that kind of stuff.

Q: So were you under me for awhile doing that?

JW: Yeah, I was. I started off in the stadium and then I ended up doing track stuff, so yeah, I was under you for a while.

Q: You knew your way around the weight room so I didn't have to keep too close of an eye on you. (laughs) And let me ask you, what did you take away from the whole experience? Things you learned and use to this day?

JW: I relate a lot of what I do to my football experience: it's the team thing. There are eight of us in our station and we're a tight knit group, maybe it's at the level of the Pipeline, it's a unique experience. With these guys you have to have unity and go into a burning house together and know you can rely on each other. There's a lot of similarities, that closeness, that teamwork we had with football. So I rely on how to get along with guys, build that camaraderie together, stuff like that. And just like Coach Osborne always said, "Doing the right stuff and (knowing) how to treat people and be an asset to the group," and I feel that that I'm always looking out for the team, not an individual thing, I don't need to stand out or anything. It's about getting the job done and working together to do things. You get more satisfaction out of the team thing rather than the individual accolades, you know? I was so happy for those guys to get All-American, not jealous or anything. At all. I was so happy for them.

Q: I heard Zach mentioned everybody's name when he received the Outland...

JW: I remember when he did that. It was awesome, we were pumped about that. He deserved it, he was a great player.

Q: So Zach was the only smack-talker on the O-line?

JW: Oh yeah, he was the biggest talker, for sure. I remember so many times in the huddle, you'd look over, he wasn't even listening to the play being called! He'd be pointing over at guys, talking smack to them. It was like, 'Are you even listening to Tommie calling the play?'(laughs)'Do you even know the play?' He'd just be chatting it up.

Q: What would he be saying?

JW: Oh, just how he was going to get after the guys, just how he was gonna kill 'em, stuff like that. Gonna show 'em what's up. I don't know how he said it, it was all about how he was gonna dominate the guy, you know? He was funny. He was hilarious to listen to. He'd start laughing in the huddle and it was like, 'Are you serious?'

Another story: I remember one time I told Adam Treu to pass the salt at the training table - and Treu had a great arm, and Matt Shaw challenged him to hit something way up near the ceiling of the Training Table- and Adam just heaved it up there and hit the thing! And the plastic salt shaker just exploded and rained salt down all over me. Showered me with salt, just covered me. It was funny. Treu and I have some good stories.

There were so many guys from those days. And Lawrence Phillips, he was a great teammate. I remember the Pipeline was on the sidelines in a huddle getting fired up before the game for the Orange Bowl and he just exploded into our group, jumped right in there. And he jumped through the middle and he was crying, full tears, telling us how hard he was going to run for us, how all we had to do was make a couple of holes and he was gonna run, how emotional he was, how he just cared so much and wanted to do such a good job. I never partied with him or saw him much outside the stadium -I never knew that side of him- but from a personal experience he was such a great guy. I loved that emotion and passion that he had.

Q: What did that do for linemen like you, blocking for a guy of his caliber behind you? Did it spur you on even more?

JW: It definitely motivates you. Having him and Tommie (and Brook was a great guy and a great player and I had confidence in him, too), but there was a little something extra when Tommie was in there, maybe it was the cockiness he had. He was obviously such a great player, but he had something about him. And Lawrence, they made you play better and gave you confidence, it was incredible having those guys in there.

Q: Knowing if you just gave 'em an inch they'd make a yard?

JW: Oh yeah, you just had to make a little hole, just hold them for a second and it was over.

Q: You held?

JW: On every play! I'd never admit to it to a defensive lineman, though! (laughs)

Q: What would you say about Tommie?

JW: At the time he got so much attention so quickly when he came on campus. He was a little cocky, you know. But you got to know him and spend a lot of time with him, outside he's a different guy. A great teammate, same thing, real passionate.

He did have his moments where he had the cockiness about him. I remember one time at the training table a little kid came up to him and asked him for an autograph and he said no, and the little kid ran off crying. I don't know what was going on there, what the situation was. Maybe he had a bad day. And I remember one time, when I was a sophomore, asking him to sign a football for me and he wouldn't do it. It was like, 'I'm your teammate, you know? And you won't autograph a football for me?' So I was kind of pissed. He was kind of immature, grew up a lot, and later on he was a junior when I was a senior and he grew up a lot. So it was different. I remember he just had that air about him, that confidence when he came into the huddle.

Q: What about the Turmanator?

JW: I just remember that the Kansas State game, he was handing off to Lawrence every play, I remember the Kansas State guys were joking around and laughing at how small he was, but what a great job he did. A lot of teams would have folded, having their third or fourth string QB in there and all, how small he was, but he rose to the occasion. I can't say enough about him. He had a lot of poise and he kept our magic season rolling. He did a great job.

I remember we ran Lawrence Phillips on an ISO up the middle about 40 times. We started telling Kansas State what side we were going to, "It's goin' to the right this time, boys. Let's see what you can do!" (laughs) We'd get 7 or 8 yards every time. That's what I recall about that game.

Q: Well, before I let you go Joel, anything we didn't cover that you feel made us so successful during those years?

JW: Well, if I were to go back to one thing, it was just that bond, that chemistry of playing with the guys those years. I don't know if it was by chance or what, but we had a lot of similar guys with a lot of motivation and lot of passion about it. We just had a tight group and were such good friends, and that was the key for me. And that's what I miss the most, too, just the love of the guys and being around them, all the guys. What I remember most was the good times with those guys and just putting everything on the line for them.

Q: Do you want me to pass on any word to the guys down the line when I talk to them?

JW: Who did you say you were talking to next, Troy Dumas? Tell him "Bhudda said Hi". And have you talked to Donte Jones, yet? Tell him the same. Donte and I had a lot of fun times together. Donte always acted like he liked me a little more than he should have, you know? (laughs) Like he always had a crush on me, joking around. Tell all the guys, "Bhudda says Hi."

End conversation.

PMA: Positive Mental Attitude. How about that for a personal mantra to get you through a few lean, rough spots in life? I enjoyed talking to Joel again, and almost forgot that he was under my supervision for a short while as a student assistant Strength Staffer after his last bowl game. In the course of my great Why and How I am finding it refreshingly and insightfully peculiar how some kids would create a slogan, a motto, a catchword to spur them on when the enthusiasm waned, when their bodies were are less than prime due to study load, sickness, fatigue, whatever. Most of these kids were already high-achievers, part the top 5% of high school players in the country. I'm led to believe this percentile figure isn't due to talent alone, but also the ability to process self-motivation tricks and techniques, assisting them "through bad practices and stuff." That's what I've garnered from dissecting some of these conversations.

I've held off mentioning it yet, but it should be acknowledged that talented running back Lawrence Phillips by and large appeared to be quite a respected and well-loved teammate. In attempting to contact the figures of the day for future conversations I'll refrain from expounding on him for now, but he's definitely on my radar for the part he played on the those teams, controversial figure or no. Quarterback Tommie Frazier's name has also come up, too, though not necessarily in the light that I've expected as it compares to Lawrence. Whereas Lawrence was noted for his poetic ball-carries and the tragic episode of teen heartbreak and its resulting domestic altercation, Tommie, rather, has always been known for his incredibly successful win/loss ratio as well as the health issues he had to battle through. It's probably a little too early to point out, but I have feeling that there was a brotherly love for Lawrence while there was more of a respect for Tommie. Surely we'll hear more as we go on.

Joel also mentioned the coaching staff's unique dynamic and how Tom Osborne was able to (purposefully perhaps?) assemble a team of varying contrasts in personalities, some completely dissimilar to himself. I've arrived at the impression that the team looked to its head coach for displays of calm, self-assured, undoubting leadership while in the meantime sought the quite unique assistant/position coaches for closer bonds of not only a coach/player or mentor/mentee relationships, but even friendships. This contributed to a form of 'participatory management,' meaning that everyone had input, collective 'skin in the game,' and found their role boundaries oftentimes blurring, especially when communicating up and down the leadership hierarchy in times of heated competition. There was also Joel's, "You were always getting graded. Always getting looked at. Always getting coaching." The communication and learning never ceased.

Finally, Joel revealed something about the concept of vengeance and what a motivator it, too, can be. Speaking of the undefeated 1983 team's loss at the hands of the University of Miami Hurricanes in the 1984 Orange Bowl, "I'll never forget that for the rest of my life! I cried for like a week after that. I was devastated, man. Actually, my biggest disappointment in my life was that game." That may sound like hyperbole to an outsider, but I'm pretty sure you, too, have a vivid memory of that last second two-point pass attempt from Turner Gill to Jeff Smith and the crushing, last second tip of the ball by 'Canes Strong Safety Ken Calhoun. It extinguished a perfect season and a surefire first national championship for Tom Osborne. It still pains me to think about it. In my mind's eye I'm still a high school sophomore sitting on the edge of the sofa, hands prayerfully clenched and feet rapidly tip-tapping non-stop, nervous as a whore in church, hoping, praying, waiting for the successful conversion. Then in a split-second: heartbreak. I can empathize with Joel, because it was like having your heart ripped out and stomped on. Revenge was sweet, and the calf grabs plus a little PMA sure did help for good measure.

Notable quote #2:
Joel Wilks on growing up a Husker fan: "I remember every big loss we ever had growing up. We lived it, man. Sooner Magic, horrible."

People, I just want to say, you know, can we all get along?

Rodney King, 1992

On campus and around America, 1993 was a year of turbulence and change. January began rather calmly, ushering in a new U.S. President: Hope, Arkansas' William Jefferson Clinton. February, on the other hand, got messy real quick. Dredging up memories of the 1992 L.A. Riots, it began with the Federal trial of four Los Angeles police officers accused of beating parolee Rodney King after his infamous high speed freeway chase. Only days later Tim Berners-Lee (a researcher at the European High-Energy Particle Physics lab in Geneva, Switzerland) unleashed the World Wide Web upon us. Then, only days later, New York City witnessed a group of Islamic radicals try to fell its World Trade Center with garage-laden cyanide explosives.

Concurrent with these events, the Nebraska teams were putting their finishing touches on their third straight Winter Conditioning program with a renewed sense of purpose and commitment, further building to big changes on that fall's horizon. The Huskers were being forged into men, into warriors just as the great wheels of the 60 & 3 were set in motion. Which brings us to Troy Dumas, a young warrior from the edges of Wyoming ready to knock the snot out someone, anyone. It was pretty rare for a kid in those days to forgo some type of redshirt experience, but Troy pulled it off with aplomb. In looking back on old game film from that era you'll not find another athlete who could make a tackle and quickly spring to his feet, only to leave one opposing player after another injured and writhing on the turf in pain. Troy could 'bring the wood,' as former Husker outside linebacker Broderick Thomas used to say. And the neat thing was, he was such a calm, quiet and easy-going guy off the field.

Notable quote #1:
"We had conversations about goals that we made that game. And we always talked about the ones we didn't and tried to get that figured out."

Troy Dumas

Scholarship recruit, Linebacker, Cheyenne, Wyoming (East)
Where are they now? Cape Girardeau, Missouri, Coach

Question: So let me ask you, Troy, when was your first fall camp?

Troy Dumas: '91. I played in four years and didn't redshirt. It was kind of unique for that time.

Q: Did you notice a profound change in attitude during that time?

TD: Yeah, that's one of the things that got better over the years. It just came down to, "Let's see if we can pour everything into it and see where it takes us." Knocking on the door and seeing if someone's home, you either have to put up or shut up at some point.

Truly, the biggest thing that stuck out to me was just going into the locker room and getting your helmet with the red N on it. You start thinking: it comes with so much tradition and so many good players that played here and it was just an absolute honor at that time. And I wasn't the only one in awe at that moment. There were a couple of the freshman, there was Abdul Muhammad just sitting there on the locker room bench and staring at it, and he couldn't believe it, it was such an honor. Those were such sincere feelings. We were about to embark on something special. You could just feel it that first day.

Q: How so?

TD: The simple fact that we're gonna be Nebraska Cornhuskers and there is tradition here to be upheld, and we wanted to prove coming in as freshman that we could play and wanted to win a championship by the time we left here.

Q: Your class had that collectively in mind from the start?

TD: I'd like to think our class was special because we had that in mind. Not only that, but we were more close-knit off the field as well. My class and the '92 class bonded so well, gelled so well together that it contributed to that, too. It's not something that happens for everybody and every team.

For the most part everybody was on the same page as far as what we wanted to accomplish and how we were going to get it done. It was just like everybody found something in common with everybody. It didn't really matter what kind of lifestyle you came from or what state you came from, but you had that common bond going in as freshman at this prestigious powerhouse. But on top of that we just found a lot of ways to get along with each other. There wasn't a whole lot of shit going on.

Now, obviously, I could bring up certain incidents that happened when we were freshman, you know. It was actually 'the fight' that broke out; I think it was the weekend right before school started, all the freshmen were down at Harper-Schramm-Smith dorms.

Q: I've never heard of this. Tell me more.

TD: A big fight broke out with all of us freshman and the local thugs, so to speak, or whatever you'd call them. That night all of us freshman came together and had each other's back, and we didn't know each other from Adam. That was our first bonding moment, and you can ask any freshman that came in that '91 class, everybody could speak to that. Every freshman football player was involved in that in some way. They were either throwing blows or breaking up fights or what have you, and you can ask anybody who came in that class. They can talk to you about it. But it was a bonding moment. It took place in the parking lot outside the dorms. I was there along with Clester Johnson, Dwayne Harris, Ken Bello, Christian Peter, Abdul Muhammad was there, Jacques Allen was there.

Q: What precipitated the fight? Who started it?

TD: From what I understood, at the time it was something every new freshman class had to go through with these individuals. But after that day -the whole vibe of that freshman class that came in?- they just really stuck together and took it to those guys. Those guys had never had a butt-whooping like that, so we kind of set the stage at that moment. We didn't take too much crap.

Q: Were the individuals you fought fellow students or just kids showing up on campus?

TD: Just kids. It seemed every year they would try to pick a fight. I think they called them "The Lincolnites" or something like that. And we'd only been in Lincoln like a week and a half, two weeks.

Q: Funny you say that. I recall back in about '87 there was this one bar fight. We had a big O-lineman -the kid was a rangy 6'8", 315 or something like that- well, another one of the guys got into a scrub-up at an 'O' Street watering hole and this guy supposedly went running out of the bar, didn't back his buddy up. He lost a lot of guys' respect for his lack of unity and you can bet money it affected the team on down the line. But this story of yours sounds just the opposite…

TD: Yeah, totally opposite. We get together to this day and that incident will always come up in some shape or fashion. It was pretty significant. The coaches probably wouldn't count that sort of thing, but we bonded and gelled from that day on. We had our closest relationships since then.

Q: Every street fight I've ever been in (and they haven't been many) holds one image that sticks out. Do you have anything like that?

TD: (Laughs) Well, Dwayne Harris, he was a pretty tough, strong guy. And taking on one was enough for most guys, but he took on two at a time. Dwayne swung some pretty big fists. (laughs) I'll leave it at that...

Q: He didn't mind getting double-teamed, so to speak?

TD: He was a one-man wrecking crew. (laughs) But as for me, it wasn't a culture shock moving to Lincoln at all. I showed up pretty hell-bent on showing people I could play and didn't want to redshirt. I wasn't really intimidated by anything or anybody. The only thing I was really tentative about was learning about the game and the scheme, but physically I was okay.

Q: So your position coach... you did a position switch, didn't you?

TD: Yeah, I was with Coach Darlington for a few years then I switched over to linebacker because of injury. But it wasn't something that just came out of the blue, because we were changing the defense. And that nickel position was actually a strongside linebacker position, so it wasn't a really big switch because that defense we ran was basically a third down defense in '91 (and it eventually became our every down defense). Ernie Beler was hurt, Lorenzo Brinkley was hurt. It put me up closer to the line of scrimmage and let me be more aggressive, better than being patient and playing free safety. I was physical, so I'd come up and hit people, getting sucked in sometimes, but it was a different mindset for sure.

Q: What made Coach Darlington stand out?

TD: Well, he really knew a lot. Because he'd coached so long, he stood out, pretty intense. In the way of knowing what you are doing and how you line up and make sure you can make the right adjustments and calls and everything like that. His biggest pet peeve was, "You have to know what was going on back there with the secondary." It's a cerebral game for him. You had to know what you were doing back there. It's upsetting when you make a mistake back there, because that could cost you the game.

Q: So then Coach Samuel became your position coach when you moved up to linebacker/outside linebacker?

TD: Coach Samuel was more laid back, and technique-wise it was more footwork that anything. So I could make adjustments or calls pretty easily. It wasn't a matter of learning the defense, but more technique and learning how to shed blockers and things like that.

Q: What can you tell me about Coach Osborne?

TD: Spring ball my senior year, we were doing a scrimmage and I tattooed Tommie coming down the line on an option. And the next day I was walking down the hallway to the field and Coach Osborne came up to me and put his arm around me and kind of said, "Hey, take it easy on the quarterbacks."

Q: Kind of like, "I appreciate your effort, Troy, but kind of back off on our QB's", eh? (laughs)

TD: Exactly. I caught Tommie on the chin pretty good. (laughs) As a defense, it was everybody -not just one person- that everybody rallied around. We rallied around the fact that we were all good, felt like we were the best and "everybody here is important, not just one person." It was a team defense.

But if I were to say one person who really had some effect, it was Tommie. He had that glow, that leadership quality. With his junior year and blood clots and what not, everybody thought our national championship run was over, and we took that personally as a defense, that elevated our game there. At the time people weren't really looking at the defense as the identity of the team, it was pretty much offense this, offense that. So when Tommie went down? It got personal. People had to realize that we were more than just an explosive offense. It was blue collar and we would do anything we had to get the job done.

Q: Not a lot of pretty boys out there?

TD: Not on the field. In the between the sidelines we strapped it on and got the job done.

Q: What differentiated us from the other great teams of the time?

TD: Well, we talked it, so we were gonna walk it. That was huge. I'll be frank about it: if you're gonna put it out there, you're gonna have to back it up, too. We sincerely believed that.

Q: Speaking of, there was the Unity, Belief, Respect, the We Refuse to Lose, and Unfinished Business slogans. Did you guys buy into that stuff?

TD: When the coaches came out with that it was something that we agreed upon, wanting to become of the same mind. I remember how Unfinished Business was, everybody wore that on their sleeve for the whole year and felt it and believed it. After coming up so short with the Florida State fiasco, how could they not buy into it?

Q: Florida State, you were on the special teams that game, right? What did you take away from that game?

TD: The biggest thing was that we were the underdog and came in and basically beat them – despite a couple of plays- and we came in there and played with them. Face it, it wasn't the best game that was called: crucial calls in that game didn't go our way, they were questionable. They didn't have instant replay those days, and it's unfortunate how it worked out. But we left there with the confidence to be able to sustain that level of play and compete with the Florida schools.

Q: This is a big 'what if', but if we had won it, do you think we would have repeated the next year?

TD: That's kind of tough. It could have went either way.

We had gotten to that point where we were a victim of our own success at that point, but we didn't know what to expect. Playing them so close, there's no question afterwards that we could play with these guys, so coming back next year we knew what to expect, what the standard was, so it was just a matter of taking all the steps to get there.

I'm not sure that if we'd have won that Florida State game if we would have won those back-to-back seasons. That '95 team was just a whole other ball of wax, there, too. (laughs) We were the epitome of college football, we had the best defense in the world, the fastest defense. We won like it was nobody's business.

Q: Makes you wish you would have redshirted!

TD: Absolutely, (laughs) we were knocking the crap out of people. It was just a work in progress, you know?

Q: What was it about that team? Was it effort, unity, talent?

TD: I would have to say effort and unity. We weren't the most talented team out there or the fastest, but we went 100% every play, we were gonna practice our tails off in the process, and we were gonna win. There was never a question before the game if we were gonna win. It was just, "How much are we gonna win by?" We were gonna hang in there and find a way to do it. It takes a lot to have 11 people on offense and defense on the same page.

Q: Everybody pulling the rope in the same direction gets a lot more accomplished?

TD: Absolutely, then when you add a little aggression to it, that 'I'm not gonna take any crap from you'-kind of thing. It made us tough to beat.

Q: Who gave us the best fight, if you recall?

TD: It would have to be those Miami teams. That was part of their whole deal, talking trash and whatnot. You never ran into a more mouthy group. That was their deal.

Q: Even on offense, they were talking smack?

TD: Their receivers, it was pretty typical.

Q: Verbiage that's repeatable?

TD: None of it's repeatable. (laughs) We'd be getting into race relations and all that...

Q: A favorite play from your college career?

TD: Well, it would be my first start as a sophomore at free safety against Arizona State, and I could have picked the ball off at the 5 yard line... and it just sailed through my arms. It would have been 95 yards smooth sailing.

Another one, my senior year, I returned one 54 yards or something like that, and then I got pushed out of bounds by a lineman. I caught a lot of crap about that, but we ended up close to the red zone, so that was okay.

Q: What about practices?

TD: I do remember Lawrence (Phillips). I had a clean shot on him (I was kind of off to the side), to blindside him. Most people, I'd be in that position and they were going down off their feet, you know? I remember hitting Lawrence...and it kind of threw me for a loop, because he kept running! (laughs) I mean, most running backs would have been eating the turf, but he was an incredible talent. He had a center of gravity that was low. I remember hitting him with everything I had and he kept going. It was like, 'Wow! Okay, I guess I'll have to knock him off his feet and wrap him up.' And Lawrence was really good. He obviously had some issues and whatnot, but he was one of those guys, he got along with his teammates. Outside that circle might have been a different deal, but he was fun to be around and it was friendship.

Q: Any other good practice stories?

TD: Not really. As far as defense was concerned, we had it in our mind that we were going to kick the offense's butt every day. We looked forward to doing that. I mean, we believed in our mind that we were the best defense in the nation. And they were facing our defense every day, and there were times they couldn't move the ball on us. I think they started to believe we were pretty damn good, too. They thought they had the best offense, so there were some battles. And everybody took pride in what they were doing, no question about that.

Q: What would you tell people about Coach McBride?

TD: He had a way of motivating his players, especially the day before or moments before the game. He had a way of talking to and letting us know, always keeping in mind the tradition of the school, playing for your family and the people that loved you, that was preached to us every weekend. It was never just screaming, everything in the meeting was one tone. But when he was done talking he had you wanting to eat gunpowder. He always made you want to give 110%.

Q: Do you find yourself borrowing from Charlie now that you're a coach?

TD: Oh yes, you can't help but not. You kind of model yourself after them. All of them you picked something up from: Coach Samuel, Coach Osborne, Coach Mike Shanahan, Guenther Cunningham (the K.C. Chiefs' defensive coordinator), it's an interesting mix to pick things up from as far as getting your guys ready to play and motivated. I'd have to say I'm pretty intense and get them after it. As a player I wasn't all that vocal, (my roommates would always call me the 'Silent Assassin') but when I'm out there I want to go 110 miles an hour and knock your head off.

Q: One of my childhood heroes was Oakland Raider Jack Tatum, and they called him 'The Assassin'. (laughs) What about that mindset and attitude? Was it preached or was it coming from each player individually?

TD: It was pretty etched in stone when you get there. We were self-motivated as a team - the coaches kind of knew that- but for the most part were self-motivators and knew the kind of attitude you had to have to get the job done. It was basically already there, the coaches just had to fuel the fire. I just remember from the first day of practice, there was a practice tempo that required you to have a high motor. If you didn't have that you'd have a hard time adjusting.

Q: And other than that big fight when you were freshman, any other off-field stuff from those days?

TD: Well, that was the biggest, most significant one the whole time we were there.

I remember Clester Johnson put on the greatest parties ever, they were just classic. I don't know what it was, but Clester was good at the communication skills and he always made his place the party to be at. He would only have two per semester but they were special.

Q: What about the defensive goals every week?

TD: We'd actually make them up. We'd all come up with our own individual goals, and it was something to go out there and try to meet them. And if we did, it meant we'd win. We'd always go 105 miles per hour and not worry about it, but they were set at a high level and we were going out there determined to play at a high level every game.

Q: What was the main, overriding goal?

TD: No touchdowns! We always felt that the offense only had to score 7 points per game. If they could do that we felt we could win.

Q: What about the grading process after each game?

TD: We had conversations about the goals we accomplished that game and we always talked about the ones we didn't, and tried to get that figured out. We had goals for scoring, passing yardage, running yardage, turnovers, those were the biggest ones. We'd usually hit most of them, too. Some of the passing teams would be a little higher, but we usually made our goals.

Q: Where would those goals be set?

TD: They were lofty, but we were thinking we could realistically attain them, too.

Q: What are most proud of?

TD: Just playing with the guys I had the opportunity to play with; such a unique bunch. You don't run into that very much these days. That's a hard thing to find. Kids are different these days and you have to think of ways to motivate them. I talk to them from time to time about how it was when I was a player and how close we were as a team. I preach that kind of stuff to them.

Q: Is there one shining moment in your career that really stands out as a favorite?

TD: It would probably have to be beating Kansas State my senior year, because we were down to our third string quarterback and we were supposed to have our doomsday as a defense with Chad May. And we pretty much shot Chad May down that day. It was on national TV, an early morning game, and we had a chance to show the whole nation that our defense was no joke.

Q: That was even greater than the National Championship, the Miami game?

TD: Absolutely! If we don't win that game we don't even get in the national championship game.

It was the way Coach Osborne wanted things done. We were a family, man, that's the bottom line. Most people don't understand how close-knit we were as a team, almost freakish. There was something there that was truly unique. We had our team prayer, so we all had a lot of faith and bought into that. It was our staple before every game, and it got pretty emotional from time to time. That prayer evoked emotions, no question.

Q: Anybody behind the scenes who made a difference?

TD: I would just have to say it was the tradition rather than just one person. It wasn't anything that was really vocalized, you just knew when you got there, you knew that the position you played came with some responsibilities you had to live up to. There was lots of pressure, and we realized along the way that we had to compete. It wasn't the kind of pressure that we didn't want, we were looking for it.

Q: It seemed we had a whole lot of proactive, unified, self-motivated team members…

TD: Yeah, when it came to football. (laughs) With other things it was a little different. But the football part was no question. (laughs) I just go back to that team prayer all the time, and focusing on my little world. Right after the team movie the night before I really started to focus.

Q: What do you draw from those experiences and apply to your present life?

TD: You're champions! (laughs) You know, you sacrifice to get that. You're always gonna learn something from that and incorporate those type of things into your later life: going about doing things the right way, creating expectations that things are going to happen.

Q: Kind of like, "The right thing may not be the easiest thing to get you over the top, but you do the right thing, anyway?"

TD: Exactly. Go the long route. The Nebraska program was built on hard work and the dedication of its people, and if I had a chance to do it over again I wouldn't change it in a heartbeat. Nebraska is a special place.

End conversation.

Troy mentioned 'The Prayer.' Just moments before they gathered hand-in-hand and stormed the field via the famed Tunnel Walk, they huddled in a massive circle at the center of their locker room and spoke this collective Husker pre-game prayer:

"Dear Lord, in the battles we go through in life we ask for a chance that's fair, a chance to equal all your stripes, a chance to do or dare. If we shall win let it be by the code, with our faith and honor held high. If we shall lose let us stand by the road and cheer the winners as they go by. Day by day, getting better and better, a team that can't be beat... won't be beat!"

The words reflect on concepts of humility before a great God, of giving a worthwhile witness to His glory, of sportsmanship, of holding steadfastly to integrity amid the course of battle, and the idea that, in the final tally, effort matters even more than victory."Go the long route," Troy said. It echoes famed sportswriter Grantland Rice's glorious poetic summation:

For when the One Great Scorer comes
To write against your name,
He marks -not that you won or lost-
But how you played the game.

-"Alumunus Football," Only the Brave and Other Poems

So we have The Prayer, which Dr. Jack Stark and others have spoken of, but this is the first I've heard of 'The Fight.' This may or may not be news to you, but at that time existed a street gang of sorts who went by the name of 'The Lincolnites': punks, troublemakers, drug dealers and thugs who used forced fights with Nebraska Football players as an initiation rite to their membership. Rather than separating themselves from potential brush-ups by remaining on the right side of the tracks for the entirety of their Nebraska college experience, I think it speaks volumes about the self-assurance and moxie of the 1991 recruiting class who drew a line in the sand and then proceeded to pound those hoodlums into it. The historic scrum bonded these boys for life, because after the carnage they knew they could depend on their teammates come Hell or high water. Who would have guessed that one special encounter with delinquents would play a crucial part in future on-field success? Not me. But there it is, nonetheless.

In the final summary of this endeavor, if you find my writing capabilities have fallen short of conveying an accurate portrayal of the solidarity and fellowship of that era, I then ask you to lean heavily on Troy's words, instead. They cannot be better stated: "We were a family, man. That's the bottom line. Most people don't understand how close-knit we were as a team, almost freakish. There was something there that was truly unique."

Notable quote #2:
Troy Dumas on Defensive Coordinator Charlie McBride's pre-game speeches: "When he was done he had you wanting to eat gunpowder. He always made you want to give 110%."

Coaches have to watch for what they don't want to see and listen to what they don't want to hear.

John Madden

The second man from the coaching staff to respond to my query, I corralled Tony Samuel on his home phone early one offseason morning in Cape Girardeau, Missouri. This was prior to his leading the Southeast Missouri State University Redhawks to its first winning season and playoff appearance in a decade and being honored as winner of the prestigious Eddie Robinson Award as the Football Championship Subdivision National Coach of the Year. A former Nebraska player himself, the man known for his coolness and confidence has taken many of the 90's lessons and applies them in the present day. I'm excited to hear what he has to share. Buckle up and listen up, you're about to get an education.

Notable quote #1:
"I always thought our edge had a lot to do with special teams, which had a lot to do with depth, which, to me, went directly back to the walk-on program."

Tony Samuel

Question: What do you recall about the first day you stepped on campus as a student, Tony? Any lasting impressions?

Tony Samuel: It was cold. It was a recruiting trip. And then the first time I came back was early August for fall camp that first year, and then it was very hot. Out at the old airport where you walk off the plane into the outdoors you felt the air blowing hot, and that was the first time I ever felt hot air blowing on me. (laughs)

It was very different coming out of that environment where I grew up in Jersey City. As far as the original culture there? First you had the fact that I'd never lived in a dorm before, that was different. Doing things with the whole team and eating at the training table, that was unique. It was all completely different. Life was a little slower paced, a lot of family-type people. Coming out of high school living in one world and all of a sudden you show up and its entirely different. And then you show up for camp, and then you realize how big some of these guys really were. Back in the 70's you wore tight-fighting clothes, so you could tell when a guy was pretty well put-together. (laughs)

Q: So you returned as a full-time coach in '86. What role did you play on the staff, rush ends from the start?

TS: Well, we called it (that's the part that really became confusing to a lot of people), we called it a Defensive End back then, but they were really, truly Outside Linebackers. Because we ran a 50 defense and an Eagle defense, and later we switched to the 4-3, then they were truly Rush Ends/Defensive Ends.

Q: If I recall, did they change the name to Outside Linebacker when the Butkus Award first started?

TS: Well, we had Rush Ends, and I coached Rush Ends and outside SAM backers, which was the Outside Linebacker. We went from, if I remember correctly, from Defensive End to Outside Linebacker, then we switched to Rush End.

Q: Different names but the same position, regardless?

TS: No, when I first got there it was a different defense. The Travis Hills', the Trev Alberts', they were right in the transition period. They were true Outside Linebackers.

When I played, I never put my hand on the ground, I was a standup-type football player. And so was Broderick Thomas in the late 80's, for the most part. After that transition we put the hand on the ground when we played our nickel defense, which started to become popular, if you remember, around the country. That started getting popular and we put our nickel defense with a four man front with all four of the men's hands on the ground. Those guys were then playing both Outside Linebacker and Defensive End depending on what package we had on the field.

Q: I bet that kept some offenses guessing.

TS: It was our nickel defense where on passing situations we'd put that in, and after the years it finally just became our 4-3 defense (after we had a run against the University of Washington, because they had a real similar defense that we started to run). And you know coaches are copycats, and we went to the 4-3. And then we went to what we called a Bubble Defense, which was another way of attacking, which got its start at the University of Arizona. More and more, as the years go on, it's very multiple defenses, you know? Like right now you see people talk about the 3-4 defense; in my head that's the 50 defense.

Q: Old wine in new bottles?

TS: Yeah, a few differences, of course, depending on how you look at it. 34 has 3 down lineman, and the 50 defense has 3 down lineman, depends on the terminology.

Q: What was the coaching staff dynamic?

TS: Charlie (McBride) had gotten there in about '77, my senior year. He coached me, and George (Darlington) was my position coach.

Q: Did you always see yourself getting into coaching?

TS: When I was done playing I was actually thinking of teaching. I knew I could do it, and then I found out I had a chance to be pretty good at it. I really liked working with players, helping them overcome the speed bumps and the hurdles that you have to go through. I hadn't planned on being a coach, but once I started doing it I knew that's what I wanted to do.

Q: Now Tony, you've coached some great players. What might those hurdles be?

TS: First and foremost, you get to the university and you have the differences, some people say 'culture' and all of that, you're in the dorm and all of that, the freedom, responsibility, dealing with being a public figure, going to school, and just the general issues of needing someone to talk to. So many things before you even start talking about understanding how important it is to learn and fine tune all these different football techniques. Some of these kids coming out of high school, they're so good they can rely on those physical attributes and gifts.

Q: Who sticks out most among those under your tutelage? Who made the biggest strides?

TS: I think they all did. I remember when I came back in '86 in the spring, Broderick was a sophomore (because he never redshirted) and he was very, very willing, but he needed to…he was a defensive lineman in high school in the interior, but he was a guy where we worked together and he was very willing to learn.

Q: He had a good motor?

TS: He had a great motor, but by far there were others. The only guy that came close to being ready to play in my career there was (Grant) Wistrom, as far as being ready to play from the start. Trev was a guy that played every single spot on the football field in high school, so he was never able to lock in on any position. You know, a lot of great teams do that, and Trev and Travis were in that same boat. Travis Hill, I remember watching his high school film: he was returning kickoffs, he was playing linebacker one minute, he was playing defensive line the next, he was all over the place, you know?

Q: I bet that was interesting… watching some of that film.

TS: We had the benefit of doing that at Nebraska. We had the opportunity to look at them and determine the type of motor they had. And if they could play hard every play in the game, they stood out to me. It was only a matter of teaching them.

Q: Can you define a player who has a 'good motor?'

TS: One, they had to be playmakers. This is my definition, now. I was looking for playmakers, which means they've got to play hard every single play. And then two, did they make plays? Some guys play hard, but when you watch the tape they don't make plays. And for that position, number three, I want to see how fast they can get to top speed. Is it two steps, one step, three steps? Some guys have a better initial burst from start to top speed, so I was looking for that sudden burst.

Q: How did you differentiate the great motor guy from an average motor guy? Any differences as far as mindset?

TS: Well, they're typically guys that are very, very intense competitors, and for one reason or another they either don't want to lose or let people down around them. You've got to go have great ability, too, but the ability is not always the most determining factor. You might watch them on film and they might make two phenomenal plays, but then when a play goes away from them they just jog over there. Those are the guys you can develop, but if they already have it in them that they go hard all the time -it could be from great high school coaching, it could be from parents, it could be from a brother when they were young and told they always had to go hard- if it's already ingrained that's one less thing you have to worry about.

But you've gotta go back and remember this is not an exact science, so you've got to pick a guy to come to your school who pretty much feels they can make it. Because if you pick a guy and spend a whole year developing him and he doesn't make it competing at the highest level you've lost that whole year.

Q: Take me into a typical staff meeting…

TS: We started in a full staff meeting -not every day- but for the most part we'd start out with staff meetings. Of course, certain people would come in and give a report: an academic person would come in and give a report, or you might have Boyd or another strength staff member come in and give a report, or the training staff give a report, you always had something going. Most of the meeting time, especially in-season, we'd separate into offense and defense.

Q: Let's say you're putting together a game plan vs. Florida State or Miami. Did everybody have input? What was that dynamic?

TS: We really were together for such a long time, and I was a part of that system for so long, Charlie was there before I even left and I was GA for those guys. And, of course, I played for George and all those guys were there, John Melton was there, everybody was there. We all knew each other 100 years, you know what I mean? And everybody would sit down and kind of look at the film and talk over things we wanted to do, and then we'd go out to practice.

Q: Some coaches are notorious as career vagabonds. What kept you guys together in Lincoln for so long?

TS: For me, I was there 11 years. A good part of it was the way the thing was set up, the lifestyle. It was really a great place to live, raise the kids, the public school system was like most private schools around the country, the quality of living was good. And, of course, you look at the program and you hit it on the head, we were all able to be a part of the system for years and there is a loyalty that had built up there that was incredible.

Q: At that time did you assistants pay much attention to the pay at other schools?

TS: To be quite honest, I never did, but I can't speak for anybody else. I didn't know what other schools were paying. I honestly couldn't tell you. (laughs) Coach Osborne didn't ever come close to the money you see going on out there now. To be quite honest with you, I was just happy to have the opportunity to come back and take a shot at the national championship. We missed a few shots at those things over the years…

Q: What was it that finally took you away to New Mexico State?

TS: For me, it was the opportunity to be the head football coach. I knew I was going into a tough situation, trying to win down there. Matter of fact, I had a team that went 1-10 the year before and all of that, but I just wanted to get an opportunity to see what I was capable of doing. I went down there thinking I could put together a pretty good staff of guys. I had watched them –personally- as GA's at Nebraska, guys who had moved on, so I believed I was gonna go down there and, not that I was a great guru, but felt that the staff I put together was really a great bunch of coaches. And I figured we'd have a great bunch of coaches and we could all get it done, you know?

Q: You had Barney Cotton, Jeff Jamrog…

TS: And we had Gerry Gdowski, and Steve Stanard who's the Defensive Coordinator at Tulane, Clayton Carlin at Cornell as Defensive Coordinator, Rich Glover at Defensive Line, Kendall Blackburn who was at Nebraska for a short stint as GA who helped bring Derek Brown to Nebraska, and Bill Busch, who was a GA at one time.

Q: If I recall, you did a pretty good job of turning things around there.

TS: The overall record? If you know, it usually takes about 3 years to get yourself on par (and we basically had to start over from scratch), but we had a great running back down there. You look at most programs, the third or fourth year you finally make your hay, you know? We had a great staff, had kept one guy from that prior staff. And everybody else going in, they all had Nebraska ties. I felt it was important to have a lot of guys who didn't have to discuss a whole lot of things so we could hit the ground running. It prevented a lot of arguments about every little thing. Same philosophy on a lot of things, which helps.

Q: So you've taken that same mindset to Southeast Missouri State University?

TS: Yes, because I felt we made it work at NMSU. And the same mindset, the personal dynamics. And you look at it now, yeah, Maguire is our Defensive Coordinator (who played at Nebraska and Creighton Prep), and of course Troy Dumas and Kenny Wilhite, Lorenzo Brinkley and Chris Norris, and Brian Boerboom, our Offensive Coordinator. And the guys who left NMSU went on to bigger and better things: Marvin Sanders was on that staff,

Kevin Lightner (who replaced Barney at the time), Mark Mauer replaced Clayton when he went to Cornell...

Q: Wasn't Clayton the high school coach of Miami quarterback Frank Costa, who we met in the national champ game?

TS: Yes, he was. He was the high school coach at St. Joe's Prep in Philly. And when we played Miami he was on our sideline, instead.

Q: Was Clayton able to impart some special insight about how to attack the guy?

TS: He helped me as the defensive ends coach and with the defensive line. I mean, you can still pick up things from watching film, but anybody who is that close to a guy and knows him that well, you can't help but pick up something that can help you, you know? Sometimes you could tell just by reading his body language when he set up to throw, and we learned watching film that he wasn't a good scrambler. Sometimes, you know, you more or less make calls with the things you find from the film, but if there is somebody there with special knowledge they can really help you cut through the red tape. (laughs)

Q: So take me back to the '90 season, where we ended on a rather low point...

TS: We got beat by OU and then we went down and we got beat by Georgia Tech in the Citrus Bowl. In my mind? That was the turning point in my mind. For Nebraska it was still decent -we still won 9 games and all those kind of things- but in my mind (again, I can't speak for anybody else) that was an all-time low for me as a part of the Nebraska system. Getting beat by Georgia Tech the way we did, I had no idea why. We'd had worse losses, like that Iowa State loss in Ames in '92 -I would rank that as a low- but for some reason for me the Georgia Tech loss really ranks high. I don't know why, but that was a turning point.

It was tough, because one, we were in a bowl game but we didn't have any chips on the table to play for other than to play for pride, and as you know, being part of that program, how big that was. If you go back and take a good look, that was really tough.

Q: What was the most impactful change to come from that low point?

TS: I think we started really thinking and deciding to go to the 4-3 look.

If there were any other real pragmatic changes, I know I made an effort to spend more time talking to other players other than just my position, trying to get inside their head. I always talked to all the fellas, I always saw myself as a guy who could notice the freshmen or guys struggling and tried to get them to see different things and give them a couple words of encouragement to keep going. I spend much of my time doing that now.

Q: Was that something you did on your own or was it encouraged for the whole staff?

TS: I think I did it, anyway. Coach Osborne always gave us freedom to be ourselves. If you look at all the staff -you've been around them- we were our own personalities. We weren't any clones. Everybody was themselves, you know? We had a tradition to pass it on, you know. There was somebody there, back when I was a freshman, who looked out for me. Whether it was something the coaches encouraged or what, that's just the way it was.

I don't remember how that all developed, but it was rare. I think it was just a matter of looking around a little more, instead of just my position. And it might just be a couple words to a guy, sometimes that's all it takes is sharing a couple words here and there with a guy. It wasn't anything fancy where we sat down and created all these fancy speeches for the guys. (laughs)

Q: You said we had some tremendous talent in those years. Anything else stand out to you as far as separating us from other teams?

TS: I felt when we switched the defense it really got things up and running. Obviously, I remember our offensive line going from good to great. That really jumped out at me, too. There was a stretch there where we were a dominant offensive line, going back to that game. And I thought, of course, when Tommie Frazier showed up. He was made for our type of offense.

There were so many combinations of things. It was about our recruiting. If you look at our recruiting, we were never ranked really high in the nation my whole time being there. We'd watch film sometimes and turn down guys and say, "Well, he's got this 'All-American this and that,' but he just doesn't fit what we want to do."

Q: I think that discombobulated a lot of people over the years because of our recruiting class rankings of #19, #31, that type of thing. Then those same guys are wearing National Championship rings a few years later. Did you know what you were looking for precisely?

TS: Back in those days there were different people around the country where everybody had their area. I had Texas, myself and Jack Pierce had that area split. You'd get on the phone and call people. You still had people that gave you lists of names, and sometimes you had people who'd give you their ranking, but we would get those lists and start either calling them, checking on them, watching film on them. Recruiting was very different than it is today.

Q: What would you say the greatest difference was?

TS: Timing. Nowadays you get juniors. A lot of kids are already set at that time, going into their senior year. In our day, it was a very, very, very rare occasion where you didn't have time to evaluate a kid's situation and then have them make a decision. It was different that way, for sure. But we still had a lot of things going, it just wasn't as fancy as it is now. It's a full-blown business now, where you have some people making decent money on it. With changes brought on by the computer, it's really changed it.

Q: Was there a certain mindset you taught along with the techniques? Infused into the guys?

TS: Well, we were the 'difference makers' in my mind. We could ruin games, in my mind. That's what they all had to know coming in. 'If you're in this room, you've gotta win. You can change games from this position. Every Saturday, every guy who throws the ball, you sack him. On every throw you need to bother them. Sacks happen. You bother a guy. Sometimes you only sack a guy one play a game, but when you touch him and touch him and touch him, he starts to feel your presence. He'll force some bad throws' and things like that.

Q: Sounds like the Miami game to a 'T', with their quarterback Costa…

TS: Yeah. That, to me, was the ultimate showcase for, in particular, the Defensive Ends. Because you had a quarterback who wasn't mobile. And we weren't worried about taking chances because we didn't have to worry about the 'contain.' They left us one-on-one a lot of times with their tackles and ends, and we were able to come underneath and counter and do some things. And don't forget now, we were able to get good pressure from the inside as well, the 'push' at the front where Costa wasn't able to step up and throw, so then the ends would scream off the edges and go outside and in.

Q: It became something like throwing a football in a coat closet for the guy…

TS: Exactly. You want them to throw off the back foot, make them have an off-day.

Q: In prepping for the 94' Florida State game, was your approach different with Charlie Ward at all?

TS: I don't think so. I thought we were gonna be coming back down there having a great chance to win. And when I walked into the locker room after the Florida State loss, there was Trev and some of those seniors already telling those guys to come back down and win it. The mindset was changed that night.

Q: In what ways, Tony?

TS: One, we felt we won that game…

Q: I agree…

TS: And so having that feeling, if you go back and remember we went down there many years and were getting beat. And if you remember, one year we got shut out by Miami. But, no matter how you cut it, your guys starting getting to wondering if they can. And the Florida State game, I think, told us that we can come down here and do something.

I know that might sound strange for a team that's winning 10-11 games at a click, but you show up at the Orange Bowl and get beat 3 or 4 years in a row, that gets a little tough, you know? You play the Florida schools that are already acclimated and basically own the place. I thought that game was a combination of confidence and more determination to realize, "You know what, we can beat these guys. We can get it done." It turned it into a really great atmosphere for the players to prepare to come back down. That was the ultimate goal from day one. I remember when the phrase was coined: Unfinished Business. The team, and pretty much the state, that became a state motto in my mind, not just a team motto. (laughs) That Florida State game was a full-blown war, a full blown toe-to-toe heavyweight fight, blows coming from all angles. That was as physically taxing a game as I've ever been around. The intensity? Wow! I was in the press box back in those days, and you could still get that feeling all the way up there.

Q: Anything really stand out about that game in particular?

TS: One, I remember Corey Dixon returning the punt that gets called back, and then I also remember Florida State taking a timeout late in the game when they were on defense and they looked beat, they looked tired. I remember thinking, 'You know what? We finally got 'em.' I wouldn't say it out loud, but it looked to me like we broke them. They were looking fatigued and they were just a very tough, physical team, and that's where I thought that we'd got 'em, you know?

And I also remember they came back and scored late in the game and then we came back and had that final field goal opportunity. Those are the things that stand out for me. That was a tough ballgame. I was more looking at the situation where I thought we 'broke' them. We were notorious for breaking teams, along those lines, either fatigue factor or spirit factor. You've seen it, you've been around many years where all of a sudden, it's like a full court press. And if you remember we were a very high tempo offense, ran a lot of plays, we got that ball snapped anywhere from 11 to 14 seconds left on the clock, and we were a high pressure defense. It reminds me kind of like those basketball teams that just keeps running waves of people at you until you break. And eventually, when I say break, there is a point there where you can sneak in a few quick scores while they're on their heels, and all of a sudden you flip the game. Like a punt return. Or you have them tired and one play that maybe was a two yard gain in the first half, now it's 7-8 yards, where their back finally breaks.

Q: What are you the most proud of?

TS: It's hard not to be proud of beating Miami. That was my favorite game being there. More than anything, as a player I stood on the sidelines in '78 when we beat Oklahoma. But being inside the system and working it? Miami. There's no question. You've gotta understand, one of the reasons I chose Nebraska was they won those National Championships in the early '70's and I went there in '73. I figured that I'd just go there, since I'd just come off a high school team that went undefeated for the first time in that school's history, and I figured I'd go to Nebraska and win a National Championship. And here we had to wait 21 years.

Q: Worth the wait, though?

TS: Oh yeah. That game sticks out, that's the key for me. That's my favorite game. Like you, I thought that Florida State may have been the most pivotal game in that era's history, but I really liked the Miami game. And if you looked at it, we won in Nebraska-style. We broke them, I thought.

Q: Any favorite or memorable events stick out to you?

TS: Probably one of my memories was my last year: we go back down to the Orange Bowl, we didn't play for the National Championship. That was the year we lost to Texas in the Big 12 Championship game…

Q: The infamous 'Flu Game'?

TS: Yeah, remember that? Never anything like that, so many guys getting sick. That last couple of practices, never anyone in particular, but I remember looking around and Wistrom and Tomich were my starting ends, and you had some of the other guys following up. If you remember, we always had two starters and two pretty good guys developing into the rotation, so we had anywhere from a 3 to 4-man rotation at the ends. And just knowing that I was leaving, I wouldn't say it was tough, but it was special. The year before when we won the National Championship, Dante (Jones) and Dwayne (Harris) were starters, and (Grant) Wistrom and (Jared) Tomich were in the rotation.

Q: Your cup overfloweth?

TS: Right. It was nice to develop it and get it to a point where they were all part of the system, you know? Typically you get a couple of them that had been there a little longer and they were more ready than the other ones. The other ones were damn good, but they weren't ready to go, so to speak, yet. They might have been ready, not 'all the way ready,' but we always had them on track.

Q: Any memorable player interaction that stands out from those years?

TS: I always enjoyed my meeting with my guys, I totally enjoyed those guys. To me, going to a meeting where we got to coach by position was the highlight of my day, sometimes. There was one in particular, I don't know if you've ever heard the story, but it was a little different. We'd always have a team meeting first and then break into our individual meetings. Well, I always gave the fellas -there's no magical number, two minutes or something like that- before I'd walk in. They'd get their little time to cut loose and joke, whatever, but one time in practice Tom just got blindsided. You remember how we used to practice on the field? Well, Tom had his back to the receivers and he flat-out got wiped out.

It was scary, it was so bad. I was glad when he bounced up. He got up, but it could have been really bad, ambulance and all of that. Well obviously, it was on film, and I remember hearing them laughing louder than normal. And I go into the room there and they're running that play back, over and over and over..cracking up laughing. Now of course, Coach Osborne hears the commotion and peeks his head in there too, you know, and Dwayne Harris in particular, he just couldn't stop laughing. I had to give them another 5 minutes so they'd finally stop laughing.(laughs) You had Dwayne and Dante and Grant and Chad Kelsay. Chad: I always thought he made unbelievable strides from where I saw him in high school, from where he showed up as a freshman to the time he showed up for his junior year. He was a special guy, how he developed.

Q: What would you say about Charlie McBride?

TS: Well, Charlie, to me, is one of the best motivators I've ever been around. I learned an awful lot from Charlie, a very unique guy. Charlie basically let me do my thing. He didn't bother me with technique. He wasn't a hands-on Defensive Coordinator, he let you figure it out. I thought he was very special. A great motivator.

Q: How would he motivate?

TS: He had his ways. He talked to 'em. I remember him giving some great speeches on Friday night or Saturday morning. He used to always give his speeches on Friday night, and a couple of players asked him not to give it on Friday night because they ended up getting so wound up they couldn't sleep. He was the guy that knew every little thing. I learned so many of the fine point techniques from him. To this day he's one of the best guys in the country.

Q: What about Coach Osborne?

TS: I always felt that I could trust him. There's nothing better than knowing that you can trust your boss, you know? I always knew I could trust him. I always thought I never wanted to let him down.

Q: So many of the players say that, too, Tony. They didn't want to get that look...not even hear him speak, but just let him down and get 'the look'…

TS: Exactly.

Q: Anything else you think played a huge part in the last few years you were there on those championship runs, Coach?

TS: Well, not really. It was just the overall system. We had, for what we did, the ultimate system. I know one thing that we haven't mentioned, but I always thought our edge had a lot to do with special teams, which had a lot to do with depth, which to me went directly back to the walk-on program.

If you remember, when you go look around (I liked to do that for my own liking sometimes), I'd just fiddle and go through the roster in my head and say, 'How many of these guys playing a lot now were walk-ons that earned scholarships? And whatever?' You go back and look now, and there were some large numbers of guys we developed. Because in Nebraska, if you came out of that state and went to another school, that was unheard of. If you were from Nebraska that's where you went. We always lost one or two, you know what I mean?

But if you remember, how many people in Nebraska remember Lance Gray? Lance Gray was a great special teams player for us. He set the mindset, he got other teams to understand the Nebraska mentality just by his play. He was a walk-on coming all the way from New York. He wasn't even a Nebraska guy.

Q: Any guys you still keep in touch with, stay close with?

TS: You'd be surprised how they call. Two weeks ago -and I don't hear from Barron Miles in forever- and just the other day I get an e-mail from him. He was one of my favorite guys. That guy had the biggest heart and spirit than anybody around. I remember him in particular, he won the Oklahoma State game for us. The blocked punt and recovery in the end zone, because they were giving us the what for, he scored that touchdown and we pulled it out. And you have guys like Travis Hill, and Broderick comes out to my golf tournament, and Jamie Williams is out at San Francisco Academy of Art, Athletic Director (and my son played basketball out there). I went back last year for a good friend's funeral in Omaha and ran into Neil Smith and Lawrence Pete and those guys. I keep up with the family, a lot of them. My old teammates, you know? Guys like Tim Wurth and Derrie Nelson. I'd been there a lot of years man, and all of a sudden they pop out of nowhere on you. (laughs) And the situation with technology, you know, they go on the website and find my e-mail address.

Q: That's how I found you. (laughs) Last question: anyone behind the scenes you feel had a large influence on success?

TS: George Sullivan! No question. George was everybody's father, you know? He was everybody's Daddy. Old George, he kept the rules straight, "No hats in the house"...grabbing them off guy's heads at the training table, slapping them in the back of the head. He was the trainer, but you didn't show up in there being soft in the training room, "If you're hurt, you're hurt. Let's get that thing fixed." A "We're not here to pamper you"-kind of guy.

Q: That so funny you bring that up, Tony. I remember so many kids would sit down to eat at the Training Table and forget they had a cap on, and then George would come around the corner and smack 'em up the backside of the head. And then everyone else's head was on a swivel! (laughing) In a millisecond they would snatch their own caps and throw them to the floor before he had a chance to catch them! (laughs) Old school-hilarious!

TS: You said it, Paul. He was a great guy.

End conversation.

Tony's conversation was jam-packed with insight, am I right? I'll surely attempt to get a hold of both George Sullivan and Lance Gray, hereafter. I'd forgotten about ol' Bullethead (Gray) until Tony refreshed my memory, and have decided from here on out to make every possible effort to contact the people whose names are mentioned in these interviews. I guess it's more organic this way, unplanned and coming about by providence rather than some pre-planned order or methodology. Doing so may seem a little disjointed, but the ride might be all the more exciting as a result. I hope you won't mind the randomness.

Tony talked about 'The Motor,' a quasi-objective way of evaluating a player's effort through a wise coach's eye, and gave me a little hint as to how unique the recruiting methods were, as well as how foundational an 'inner drive' was to the incredibly effective Rush Ends of that era. He seemed to indicate that it was something that may not be teachable, that you either possessed 'drive' or you didn't, and that he simply inserted the techniques of the 'difference maker' position on top of the foundational template of 'The Motor.' If you are a student of the study of psychology and the whole Nature versus Nurture debate, you'd likely have something to think about for awhile with this one.

Another item that caught my attention was his mention of working for Coach Osborne and, "I always thought I never wanted to let him down." Didn't we hear the same thing from Quarterback Matt Turman? So it appears that not only did the players of the day hold profound reverence and respect for T.O., but his staff did, also. Fascinating, to say the least. Refreshing too.

Then he went on to talk about something that I've always been extremely proud of, the fact that the Cornhuskers, "won in Nebraska-style. We broke them… We were notorious for breaking teams, along those lines, either fatigue factor or spirit factor." It's one thing to be the team who last has the ball in a score-fest before time runs out to secure a victory, but it's a whole other ball of wax to actually break another team's spirit. That statement of ideology, to me, is a huge part of what made the 60 & 3 teams special. Not only did it result in victories, but was possibly a method whereby bad experiences were buried deep inside opposing team's heads, setting the stage for future meetings via psychological warfare and imprinting. If you don't think this is a valid point, I ask you, "Have you ever seen the movie Jaws?" The next time you have an opportunity to take a dip in the ocean you'll probably think twice about it, won't you? It's imprinting at its finest, and it works. Just ask Madison Avenue.

Lastly, Coach Samuel pointed out something that I feel is often lost on many a fan, and that is the fact that these players are, to be perfectly blunt, really just a bunch of young kids. Somewhat scared and confused and still trying to figure out who they are, where they fit in the world, and what direction they are heading in life, the load of full-time student and a Division 1 athlete in an environment as football-obsessed as the state of Nebraska is not and was not for the faint of heart. Just something to keep in mind.

Notable quote #2:
Tony Samuel on recruiting student/athletes to Nebraska: "There were so many combinations of things. If you look at our recruiting, we were never ranked really high in the nation my whole time being there."

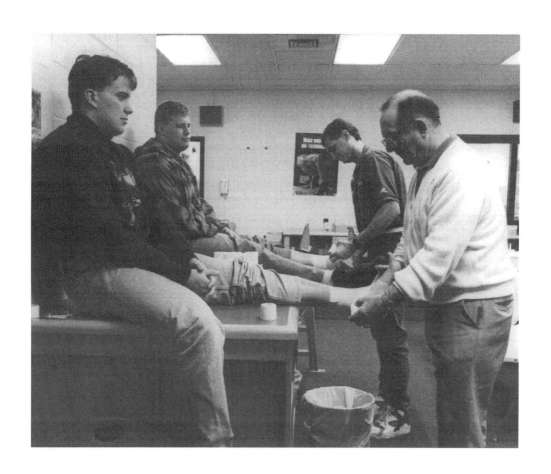

Prevalent agriculture and the absence of mountains do not mean sordid purpose or narrow vision. The prairies have their own expansiveness and may lure the eye to the horizon when older countries are looking at their own garden patch.
Albert P. Brigham, Geographic Influences In American History, 1904

"You're the Tape Guy!" I once witnessed a Certified Athletic Trainer attempting to explain his vocation's essence to a member of the public in the airplane seat adjacent his. It was comical and went like this: "So, you're an Athletic Trainer, huh? Is that something like a doctor?," she asked."Well, no, but kind of," he replied."Is that something like a weight guy, then?" "Well, no, but kind of." "Is that something like a coach, then?" "Well, not really, but kind of." "Oh, I get it. You're the Tape Guy!" she joyously surmised."Yeah, that's it," he answered, with a besmirched roll of the eyes, "Tape Guy…"

Unbeknownst, the blonde in seat 24D was factually describing the multitude of roles Nebraska's athletic trainers fulfilled throughout the course of a day. (Although she did forget to mention the roles of counselor, surrogate father, messenger, and all-around indispensible healer) Doak Ostergard was that kind of a man. The youngest of the full-time staff, he was a bridge between the college kids and the coaches, alternately acting the bothersome juvenile & sage elder when with the kids, then as a point of contact in bridging the player/coach chasm with the staff. Doak, for lack of a better word, was 'the finger,' constantly taking the pulse of the athletic department at the place where the rubber meets the road: the athletes. He built strong bonds with the kids and had an uncanny ability to know what went on behind closed, off-campus doors, the shenanigans happening long after the bars closed on "O" Street. Let's hear now from Doak Ostergard, Certified Tape Guy.

Notable quote #1:
"That's the difference between fear and love. It's very simple. You can't be afraid to get close enough to the athletes, to show you care about them. Being genuine is part of showing that you care."

Doak Ostergard

Question: Hey Doak, thanks for participating in this…

Doak Ostergard: I hope I have something to add.

Q: Well, I have to tell you that a lot of players bring your name up a whole lot as somebody who stands out to them…

DO: I must have fooled a lot of people. (laughs)

Q: They mention your name often, which must mean that you were developing great relationships with them…

DO: Well, as a trainer you got to see a completely different side of them. To me, the training room, weight room, equipment room, you're in the trenches, the front line. The dynamics of the relationship are completely different and you get to know them a lot better, they're gonna be more comfortable coming and sitting down in the training room and just talking like you normally would, as opposed to putting up a little bit of a front.

The coaches oftentimes have something to 'hold over their head' with playing time, so they're gonna act differently with them. Coach/Player relationships is always an interesting deal, and there's so many different ways coaches handle that: some are gonna be the real authoritarian, some the warm & fuzzy, but the dynamics with people on the ground level are more than a 'friend.' At least it ends up being that. To me, if you're a coach or trainer, teacher, parent, it doesn't matter, the first thing you have to have with your student-athletes, kids, is respect, otherwise it doesn't matter what you know. You have to have that, so I guess I'd become friends with them as soon as the dynamic, the respect was in place. They knew they were gonna get treated with respect, and in turn, they had to treat us with respect. Then you could usually just proceed into friendship.

Q: And from your perspective, how was that first step -respect- earned in your particular situation?

DO: I think I probably tried -I shouldn't even say 'try'- but so many other people who grew up in Nebraska, who used to work in the program, they reflected the state's values. One of the things you learn by growing up in Nebraska -you don't realize that you learn it, you just think that's the way it is everywhere- you're genuine and fairly transparent. So if an athlete comes in, they don't necessarily have expectations, "Hey, you've got to be a buddy to me," but it's fairly reasonable to have expectations to be genuine and honest when dealing with them. So I think that as long as they knew that, that's a big cornerstone to building good relationships with them.

Q: When did you become a full-time trainer?

DO: '89. That's when Jack Nickolite decided he was going to go to Physician's Assistant school. We only had the training room down at South Stadium there with Jack, Jerry Weber and George Sullivan as full-time trainers. That year was crazy, that's how you got to know so many guys, too, because you'd be working with so many sports. So Jack decided we'd need a two-year assignment while he was gone, and I figured it would be pretty good on the resume for those two years then, working both Nebraska Basketball and Football.

Q: I remember you coming over to basketball…

DO: Those were long, long days. Those two years were a grind. I don't know if you remember, but you know, you do the two-a-days for football, then you get things settled down with the beginning of the season into a groove doing the football thing, then October 15th comes around and you start basketball practice and still have the football stuff. And in '89 Danny Nee wanted to do two-a-days for basketball starting on October 15th. So you did two-a-days in the fall for football, two-a-days for the start of basketball, and then over the Christmas vacation Danny decided he wanted to do two-a-days again. (laughs) So then you just finish basketball, you'd be done about Mid-March, and then you'd have spring football start. And then at that time they had basketball camps starting in May, and the last one (they had 7 camps, long team camps that lasted 5 days) and the last one was a long one that finished right before football two-a-days started. They got their money's worth out of me, I tell you. (laughs)

Q: That's how you stayed in such great shape, Doak. You never had time to eat!

DO: Yeah! Exactly.

Q: And you talk about the different coaching styles, the dynamic. Any certain coaches' styles stand out to you?

DO: Well, yeah, of course I'm getting off on these tangents and I think the point of your book, you're trying to identify what separated Nebraska from other places, right? Let me back up a little bit and start with the broader scope why Nebraska was separating itself from other teams of the time. I may have mentioned this to you the last time we talked, but there's two different schools of thought out there. One, people will say that the football program helped define the characteristics, the personality, what have you, of the state of Nebraska. The other school of thought has it that the State of Nebraska helped shape the football program. I firmly believe that the state shaped the football program. If you think about it, there's a lot of similarities to the guy that's in Nebraska trying to improve his farm. He's gonna take what he's got and improve that farm year after year, getting a little bit better as far as yields, what have you. It's the same type of cycle with football, where you have a staff that's stayed intact for a long time, you can make those adjustments and improve. You don't have to make a big gain all at once. Luckily, we were good and stayed good for a long time, but to me that's what you're doing in football. Every year you have a new crop, you're trying to yield the most bushels out of it. And you know, the farmer-type people of Nebraska, they're modest, hardworking people. Just like the football team, they're not going "it's hard work," executing, getting a little bit better than the next guy, and that totaled up to become something pretty extraordinary. So I really think that's been the affection of the state of Nebraska for the football program. They could see some of the same values they grew up believing in reflected in the football program.

Q: 6 or 7 home game Saturdays were reflected back to them every fall …

DO: And also showing the rest of the nation, "Hey, you might think we're backwards out here or whatever, we don't have all the fancy, schmancy whatever...but we know what's important." You take care of what's important, you do a good job at it, and you're successful. So I think that's been the real affection for the state, and then of course that's the very foundation, I believe, for the success of the program.

And then you brought those outsiders in that didn't understand that and did not reflect the same values, and that's what started some real cracks in that foundation. These same people out in Nebraska who'd been supportive for so many years, all of a sudden what's out on the field was not reflective of what they believed in, that's when you started to see people leaving games early, at halftime, for a game or two.

Q: Would you say the walk-on program was the 'head of the spear'?

DO: The walk-on program was like the mortar in the bricks. You may not get a walk-on to be one of those big, solid stars, but it would bind them together. So you've got full support from everybody in the state, and usually somebody would know somebody that's on the team or part of the team; it might have been somebody in Gothenburg knows somebody in Lexington, so it just made you feel that connection. So then these walk-ons, all they were here for was to play for Nebraska. It wasn't to get to the NFL or anything like that, their goal was to play at Nebraska or at least be on the team and run out on the field, do whatever.

Well, that's the type of people you need to have this mortar to hold it all together, to make the other bricks stronger. That's the linking factor of all the towns in the state to support the program, and it's also the linking factor within the team. Because then those work ethics (which are kind of hard to find except in the Midwest) are built into the other components and into the football team.

Q: That's a good take, Doak.

DO: And to backup an even broader perspective, you grow up here and you don't go to a lot of other places, you just think the rest of the world is like here. And then you go out there in the world and experience some things and you realize, 'Hey, the world is not like it is here.'

Q: No wonder the world's so screwed up, right?

DO: Yeah, and then you have to think about it and say to yourself, 'Why is that so unique to the Midwest?' And I think it comes down to the fact that those values are protected in these small towns. Think about it, things change slowly in small towns and it acts as a kind of preservative.

And you think, before people settled here, you have yourself thinking, 'What kind of person stops here and settles here in this state?' I mean, you have your gold rush going on, people coming from these beautiful states on the east coast and they go to the west coast, and who's stopping here? And the dust bowl, who stays? Well, it's the people who've got that 'stick to it' character. More 'long term result' people. It's just that type of person who ended up here.

Q: You could say they were a very persevering people, or maybe you could say they were just really hardheaded? (laughs)

DO: Well, I'm half-Dane, and they're known for being really hardheaded. (laughs) Maybe that's why the few things I have accomplished is just because I am hardheaded…it causes you problems. (laughs)

Q: One thing I think makes the Midwest, and Nebraska, really special, is the winters. It toughens you up. It sells you on the point that you don't have all year to get some things done that you have to do, you have a small timeframe within which to do your work before the weather turns against you and shuts you out, so you better not lollygag and be lazy about life. Otherwise you're behind the 8-ball and you're gonna end up paying for it, you know?

DO: It goes back to that type of person. How many people do you know, "It's cold, winter. I'm heading out for the sunny states or whatever." A Nebraskan is the kind of person who doesn't mind tolerating the inconveniences, because it is harder to live here than it is in Texas, the extremes are a lot greater. It just comes down to that type of person, what kind of person wants to settle and stake out land in Nebraska? It would be real interesting to do a profile, to find what type of person was willing to settle and stake out land in Nebraska.

So that's a little bit of a broader stroke, but to get back to your question, Coach Osborne stood out to me. He would take all those characteristics in the state (and to me they were even magnified, and part of it is because of his faith). Nebraska's a pretty conservative, religious people. But he would take it to the extreme a bit. He was smart enough to recognize the resources he had to work with.

It's like anything, no matter where you're located, you have to know what your resources are. It's a pretty short-term solution you're looking at if you don't take into consideration the resources you have to play with.

Q: Sounds like he was a man who didn't make excuses for what he didn't have?

DO: Exactly. Another thing we've taken for granted here for a long time was the ability to have the same people at the helm. Take somebody who has all the tools but only give them a few years, they only have a chance to learn from their mistakes. Without that, you're gonna have to hit it right the first time. That's the deal with today's college athletics, you only have so much time to do well. You wouldn't be able to find out the 'Nebraska Way', who's gonna be able to persevere, make adjustments, and be better for the long term. That ability, I think, was pretty darn important.

And one thing that was unique, Coach Osborne kind of sheltered us from the rest of the world, because he had seen other places were like. There were a lot of people who never had to worry about getting fired, having radical changes, you know, having that long-term stability. And his values of evaluating people? No matter what your input into the team was, he valued you. For that process to work, it takes time. It's a bit inhuman to do otherwise. I mean, human nature wants quick results, and if you do something that I don't like, human nature is to get mad and tell you to leave or whatever. So it was a characteristic of his to be very tolerant of a lot of things, and just trying to get you to do your best, a lot of multiples that come into play.

Q: You always had a great relationship with Coach Osborne.

DO: Yes. Well, I think. Maybe you'd have to ask him. When I started in the 80's and he'd walk into the training room there was this uncomfortable feeling, and I think he knew he made people feel uncomfortable because they'd be so intimidated. He'd go into the sauna and then people would come running out of the sauna. (laughs) I couldn't figure out why, because he's a nice enough guy and everything. Maybe this was my hardheadedness, but I couldn't figure out why people were that way.

And I said to myself, 'I'm not gonna have this guy intimidate me.' And so I just kind of set out to treat him like anybody else. And anybody who knows me is gonna find out that I'll start off by poking a little fun at you and trying to break down the shell a little bit…

Q: Soften him up a little?

DO: Right! I remember the time when I first got to talk to him very much, he'd had his knee 'scoped'. And I just kind of observed from a distance because he was dealing with George Sullivan. I can remember thinking, 'We need to get this guy going, he's not doing much to rehab the knee.' George went and put Coach in the whirlpool one day, and he's sitting in the whirlpool. And George went in to sit at his desk and fell asleep. (George would take a mid-afternoon nap every once in awhile, and he was kind of long in there) And after I watched the clock for awhile, I noticed nobody's going to talk to this guy and he's been in the whirlpool for too long, now.'I'll just go get him out of there. I'll start doing some things with him.' (laughs) And even with some of the athletes, they make you feel like, "Don't bend my knee like that," because sometimes, even scopes, you can lose that range-of-motion and it hurts trying to get that back. I thought, 'This is what I do with an athlete. And if it's good for the athlete, it'll be good for Coach.' And I started doing those things with him.

So that's how we started communicating a little bit. And I think he really appreciated the fact that I would treat him like anybody else. And I think directly then, which was helpful - these other guys in the late 80's and 90's- we had these characters, these personalities, that fit in pretty well, they could also see that he's on the ground level with them, just considered him one of them. There was somebody that Coach would make fun of or tease (and of course they thought that was funny, because I'm ordinarily teasing them), so it showed them a different side of Coach, that "Hey, he can have fun!" I would just guess - and this is just an observation- but I would guess that the guys in the 90's would feel closer to Coach than the guys in the 70's or 80's. I don't know if there's an average age, where there's a separation of age where automatically they're going to respect you. Maybe in the 70's he was young enough and the dynamics were different, or maybe it's just that they didn't understand that he could be fun guy to be around and joke with. I really think the guys who came through, those personalities like Kevin Raemakers, Christian Peter, even Tommie (who let it be known that he wasn't going to be intimidated by Coach), I think that changed the dynamics of the relationship a bit.

But back to your original question, Coach obviously stands out, but I think everybody else and the stability just kind of evolved, and they became better coaches. And there wasn't as much elbowing of other people to create your own space-type of thing, where they were happy where they were at. Of course, Charlie McBride would be the polar opposite of Coach, where you had your sweet and sour. (laughs)

Q: How would you describe Charlie?

DO: Bipolar. (laughs) Charlie, you didn't know where he was coming from or what he was gonna say. Coach Osborne described him one time, "Charlie is either all hot or all cold." (laughs) So anytime you're going to approach Charlie or be in the same room, you're going to want to guage his temperature before you say anything to him. His players really loved him, those D linemen.

Q: I heard nobody could motivate them like Charlie, getting them fired up. Were you ever around for any of those sessions?

DO: Here's a difference, too, between motivating with that old staff and how I saw Callahan and that group do it. And this is something, even if you're a team captain and stuff, but to get up and give a motivational speech, most people just think that you get up and do a lot of yelling and rah-rah stuff and that fires people up. Well, Charlie seemed to me like his method was he was gonna tug at you emotionally, and he's gonna start off and try to touch your heart, and it's not gonna be yelling and stuff. It's gonna be trying to get inside you, then maybe you'll build where there may be some yelling or whatnot. (Of course, if it's halftime there might be some yelling and such, but you've got to develop a rapport with the guys to have much effect on them) Charlie giving his speeches? To yell, the kids just block it out after awhile, but if they feel like you're talking to them directly and they know you care about them, it's gonna carry so much more weight.

Q: Out of love rather than treating them as tools to get the desired result?

DO: Yes. And Coach Osborne, when he would give motivational-type speeches, he always –it's so simple I don't know why people just can't do it- but he was really, really good at not yelling. Because it prevents somebody from getting anxious, prevents them from making mental errors, it promotes performing at your top level by breaking things down to their most simplistic level."Here, if we just execute this", or "Here, if we attain this goal, no turnovers," give very objective measures that they can see and they can get focused on, then you're only dealing with what you can control and you're not worrying about what the fans are doing, etc. He was really good at that. To me, that's a no-brainer, you can't just stand up and yell at somebody."We've got to be able to run the ball!" What does that tell them? In his mind, it was like, "We need to be able to run the ball. If we need to be able to run the ball, what has to happen? We're gonna need Joel Wilks to have a really good game. And these blocking schemes here are going to work best for him, so if we can just get him coached up on how to take this step, and get things broken down to where he just has to perform this simple function, right here." And it just takes all the static away. It's just so much easier for kids to understand and perform out there.

Q: Would Coach point people out like that, a certain person?

DO: Not necessarily. You know, he came back and talked to one of Frank's teams after he was done coaching. It was going to be a big game with all these distractions and they could have been wide-eyed and worrying about things they had no control over, and he just said, "Guys, today's game is going to be determined in a space of about this wide." And he held his hands about three feet apart. Now, young guys are going into this game thinking all these big ideas in their head that you really can't put your hands on, and he breaks it down for them: "This space, three feet deep, the line of scrimmage," he said, "on each play, you're either going to go this much forward or this much backward. Whoever goes forward most times is going to win the game. Now you know why every play is important, why it's so important to put to so much effort forth on each play. You can't take a play off." He just broke it down that simply.

And then, it was interesting because Coach, he was a great example of teaching from the proper aspect. This is an opposite example: Bill Callahan shows up here and Matt Penland wanted to be the Team Chaplain, so he was trying to meet with Bill Callahan. And talking to me, he wanted to know different things. I kind of coached him up on what I would see, what I thought, and he eventually starts meeting with him, and here is the #1 question he asked Matt: "What is the #1 form of motivation?" Matt was reluctant at first, "Why would he ask that?" He eventually asked, and Callahan said, "Fear. Fear is the biggest motivator." That's what he used. And I don't know if that's Lombardi, and maybe even Charlie at times, too. But just to use fear? You saw the difference. Callahan used fear, and Coach Osborne used love.

Here is the prime example of why love is better(and I don't know if Matt Penland ever got around to telling Callahan that): say, "Paul, you're standing outside your house and it's on fire and you've got the Chief or Captain of the fire department standing there yelling in your ear, ""Paul, go in there and see if there's anybody left in the house!"" You're laying there, you may be worn out, burned up, lungs full of smoke already, and he's gonna hold your job over your head to get you to go into the house. Is he gonna get you to do it? Maybe. Every time? Probably not. Now picture yourself standing outside there, same situation, but your children are still in there. Nobody's gonna have to ask you or tell you, you're not gonna just go through the motions, you're gonna search and seek like no other. That's the difference between fear and love. It's very simple. Pretty easy to figure what you should do in the coaching profession. So you can't be afraid to get close enough to the athletes, to show you care about them. Being genuine is part of showing that you care.

Q: And kids can see right through it if you aren't genuine in the first place, right?

DO: Yes. And an interesting thing, the January before I got fired, this is after we'd been to the Cotton Bowl. And we had an okay season, but Running Backs Coach Randy Jordan comes down to the training room shooting the breeze with me every once in awhile -and he went to my parent's house one time while we were golfing and eating some hamburgers, that kind of thing- and he said, "Man, I just want to win! We've got to win! What do we have to do to win, Doak?" And I said, 'Well, it's not the trainer's position to be saying, but you asked. So I'll tell you my thoughts...' I said, 'Three things that Callahan and the team can do to really make a difference: 1) Coach Callahan has to act like he really cares for the guys. He can't get up every few months and just say "I love you guys." It has to be demonstrated on a daily basis by every one of you guys. 2) I said 'Our defense is terrible. We've got to get back to where we want to hit people. And we've got linebackers who are stepping around blocks. That's got to change.' And 3) I said, 'On offense we really don't have an identity. We need to just get something that's our bread and butter, so narrow down the playbook to where we can really get good at that part of it, and then add more later.' And Randy said, "We'll, that's not gonna happen." (The narrowing down of the playbook) You know the ironic thing of it is? It happened in January, one month before I get fired. And they hang around one more year. And the funny thing about that, if he would have listened to what I had told the running backs coach, he probably would have been more successful.

Another thing: I had to meet with Callahan after the Oklahoma game and he was acting like such a little baby. Acting like he was the only one that was upset that we lost the Big 12 Championship game to Oklahoma. It was like, "Be a bigger man. Realize that your players are maybe upset, too. Mo Purify was the last one in the locker room sitting there in tears because he'd fumbled the opening play and feeling bad. You're so worried about yourself you can't even see that." Anyway, I go up the next day to meet with him after giving treatments and I can't believe what a big baby he's acting like. And I try and lighten him up. (Sometimes that's what a trainer has to do for coach: get him out of his funk) Well, he wouldn't have it. So I finished going through the injury report, letting him vent a little bit, hearing him tell me how, "We're never going to beat Oklahoma." He said, "Now I know why you used to just run the ball for three yards at a crack. Lesser teams can beat better teams doing that." And I'm thinking, 'Well, if you know that and you want to win, don't you think maybe that that is something we should work on?'

Q: 'Physician, heal thyself'?

DO: Yeah. And so anyhow, it was time to leave and I'm debating, and I figured, 'Well, I've gotta say this: "Coach, don't forget what they say, 'If you lose, don't lose the lesson.'" He was missing it. He was missing the opportunity to learn from it. He was just sitting around pouting. Part of it was the fact that he never wanted to be at Nebraska, and I think if he was successful he'd be looking onward and upward and get other offers somewhere else. That's why I think he was so upset. And the Head Coach, you should held to a higher standard in the way you act, you need to look at the whole picture and think, "How are we going to make this better?" I'm getting off on tangents here, but that's a major difference in coaching styles and what's truly successful.

Q: Thanks for that. Tell me, what kind of schedules did you guys keep?

DO: Well, an average day you'd get there at 7 a.m. and have a coaches meeting. Coach would need the report, the general discussion for the day, you know. The discussion could be, "How do we wanna set up our practice over Thanksgiving break?" or it would be, "Alright, we're gonna have a life skills lesson, some general things." Then you go down and do treatments 'til the noon hour, do whatever things you need to take care of in the morning, return phone calls, then you've got certain athletes needing to go to clinics, hospitals, dentist, get them to the different places. You do your treatments again, go to lunch, then you've got practice preparation, bracing, all that stuff, then you go to practice and take care of anything that occurs on the practice field, afterward you do more treatments, then after that doctors come in and go over things with the athlete, and then get ready for the next day. Coach Osborne had enough trust in me, I did a few other things. If there was a kid supposedly laid up in the dorm room I'd go check on him. Or if he was down in the dumps. Or if somebody was needing to go to the independent center because of a positive drug test or something. There was a lot of stuff there that was my duty. I think it was kind of by design, they wanted me to have some 'alone time' with them.

Q: Kind of a mentor/mentee–type relationship?

DO: Yeah, it probably helped that I already had a relationship with them already. Kind of a back-handed compliment was Lawrence Phillips, after he'd left here and finished his first year in the pros with the Rams he still needed to come back and serve some time out in Airpark, minimum security. And he'd had his knee operated on and he needed physical therapy. Well, the Rams were concerned that he wouldn't be able to get to the therapist (they would release him for that). So anyway, I get a call from his agent and from the Rams and they tell me that they need somebody who can be trustworthy and all, and Lawrence said I was the only one that he would go with. So I ended up driving him from Airpark to therapy at 70th & Van Dorn. So, you know, Lawrence had a lot of good characteristics that people don't know about. Sometimes as a trainer that was something you had to take as a compliment, sometimes. It was, 'Hey, I know at least I made a connection with someone.'

Q: A year later they could have called Santa Claus or the Easter Bunny, but you were the man he knew and trusted. That's quite a compliment. What else about your relationship with Lawrence?

DO: I remember the first day Lawrence walked into the training room. Coach Darlington walked him in. You could just tell by the look, he was a cut above. Pat Englebert, the old D Lineman, would call me every year and want to know who my sleepers were. And I said, 'You know what, this Lawrence Phillips guy, I haven't seen him do anything, but he sure does look like a player.' And Pat said, "I doubt he'll be as good as Derek Brown or Calvin Jones." (laughs)

So the next thing that happens is we go over to testing and I watch Lawrence run his 40, a watched him and Riley Washington run it. And Riley was running a 4.7, and that's all he could do. He couldn't figure out that timing system that well. So Lawrence ran his first one in 4.74, and watching him walk back to the start, he was mad! So I watch him, and he gets ready to start the second one, and he was so mad, that on his start he tries so hard that he stumbles his first few steps… stumble, stumble, stumble. But then he gets his feet back under him, and it's like he's shot out of a cannon! And after the stumble out of his start he still ends up running a 4.64 40. So I'm in the training room and I call up Pat again and tell him, 'Well, if you saw what I saw today, you'd have a pretty good feeling. I still haven't seen him on the field or in pads, but I've got a pretty good feeling about him.' And Pat was like, "No way. No way." (Pat's and my relationship is where we always argue, just to have fun, you know?) I said, 'Well, we'll see when he puts the pads on.'

So fall camp starts and Lawrence puts the pads on and he's running with the scout team against the Blackshirts. He runs and breaks one a little bit, goes 7, 8, 9 yards down the field and there's a big collision. You hear the pads 'POP!' And you say to yourself, 'Okay, we're gonna find out a little something about him.' Some young guys, they get hit like that and shy away. And he turns around and starts coming back, and he's got a big ol' smile on his face. (laughs) I call Pat back and say, 'He's gonna be better that Derek and Calvin. You watch.' (laughs) But my relationship with Lawrence started out like any of the other guys. You just treat 'em right and you kind of warm up to each other and get to know one another. I knew he had quite a temper. His temper and his hardheadedness was his downfall. I'd heard about him getting into some fights. But somehow we got to a certain level where he would trust me and respect me and we got along well.

And one thing I remember, one of the running backs, a fullback, maybe it was Brian Schuster, a white guy from Nebraska was gonna get married: and all the running backs decided they were going to meet at the stadium on Saturday and decided they were going to go to the wedding. And all the guys show up except the black guys, and Lawrence was the only one to show up. He was the only black guy, right? So they're sitting there thinking it's going to be an uncomfortable deal for Lawrence and they're giving him subtle opportunities to get out of it, "Hey, do you want to call someone or go look for 'em?", you know, give him opportunities to get out of it. And Lawrence was just, "Well, they aren't here. Let's go." So he goes. And to me, that's a sign of character. You say you're going to do something, and you do it.

The deal with Kate McEwen was really overblown. It sure got a lot of publicity. It wasn't like he was beating her head against a mailbox and all that. That didn't happen. That whole night is a whole other story. I don't know the name of the girl who called him up and started it all. Lawrence was the one that told me that some girl called him, and didn't say who it was. But yeah, she was as much to blame for the whole thing as he was. Like I said, Lawrence had a very hard head and a temper. You'd see that sometimes, he didn't really trust a lot of people. He was in a group home since he was thirteen and both parents probably had left him, and he wasn't that bad of a guy unless you make him mad. You didn't want to make him mad. The one thing that people never quite understood, but Coach Osborne's approach to these guys was, he would come to your house and say, "Paul, I want to recruit your son." And he wanted you to feel like he would treat your son the way you'd want your son to be treated, so he's gonna do everything he can for him, just like you'd expect. Not just use him up and throw him out if he's not producing, football-wise. Everybody has value. So anyhow, when it comes to the Lawrence issue? Working from that angle? He'd want the parents to approve of how the kid was being treated. And he also knew the only way to get Lawrence to do the right things was through football. If he didn't have football out in front of him, he was likely destined to do bad things. Coach knew that, but he knew he was going to be criticized heavily by letting him back on the team. For Lawrence's sake and allowing him back, he could make him go to anger management, alcohol counseling, whatever it might be. But if he gets kicked off the team he doesn't have to do anything. Then you've got a chance to go on to play pro football and make some money.

He didn't want to take that opportunity away from him. That line of thinking had worked on numerous people, and there's more success stories, but you don't hear about them. You only hear about this because it didn't work out. That's what's hard for people to understand. They can't understand Coach Osborne and that he would actually do something for the greater good than for himself, to win the game or whatever. That's not the truth.

And a couple broader things people should know about the 90's, unless people were here and viewed it and experienced it during that time, they can't understand how physical practices were. Just like conditioning yourself to run a mile or whatever, you condition yourself to play physical. That's the big difference. You see so many teams now, and hardly anybody likes to play that way. But you condition them and they'll do it. There's a greater price to pay for that, but you get in a game and the other team pays a greater price as the end result, and it results in wins.

Q: And deep down, that's what you trainers are for, anyway. Getting them healed up, right? (laughs)

DO: Yup, (laughs) by the time they got to the game, that was going to be easier than practice. And even if you write three pages about that, people still aren't going to understand how physical practices were.

And the other thing was that everybody clicked, where it was all moving in the right direction. In any organization you're gonna have 10-20 % at both ends, the good and the bad. Let's say 20% are good and you're not gonna have to worry about them. The bottom end, you're gonna have 10-20% that you're going to have to deal with on issues. The key is to get that 60% in the middle to follow the good and go that way, then you start to get a few of the bad going the right way, too. It was unreal there, the run that Coach had, that run where I didn't really remember having to push hardly anybody, push them out to practice. They'd show up at the stadium and just expected to go out to practice. So there was a lot of 'buy in.' Remember that 'Respect', and early morning practice during two-a-days? Guys didn't care. They thought they were paying a greater price and they were gonna do it.

I remember after that '93 Orange Bowl against Florida State. I was sitting next to Terry Conneally on the bus, and everybody... you could just feel it. They couldn't wait for Spring Football and the next fall to start. Usually you get done with the bowl game and you were like, "Ughh. I need a rest." But everybody was convinced they could be national champions and it played out that way the next few years.

Q: I know you have a 9:30 a.m. meeting coming up, so I'll try to get you on your way quickly. From your perspective, did the average player feel much pressure to perform, any undue pressure?

DO: I don't think so. I think there was just expectations. You walked out on the field and I think you just expected to beat the snot out of somebody. I don't think there was ever pressure. There was a lot of confidence, and that turn, that night after the Orange Bowl after we got beat by Florida State? That was a turning point. Anxiety and all that stuff? The way Coach Osborne would just break it down and you just execute. That took off a lot of pressure.

Q: In '92 Turner Gill came back on staff. Did that make a huge difference? Do you think it opened up Coach Osborne for other things?

DO: Not that I thought, so much. I thought that Turner was pretty limited in his involvement because Coach Osborne still coached the quarterbacks. Turner spent a bit more time with those guys. It wasn't until probably Coach left that Turner got more responsibility and, of course, when Frank left he was really thrown into it. But I didn't see that.

Q: What did Turner primarily do when he joined that seasoned staff?

DO: Well, just Turner, himself, he commands respect, and has a lot of dignity. So aside from his personal attributes, of course you'd have to sit in all the coach's meetings to find if he was adding things to the offense or what not, but I didn't get that sense.

Q: In your time as a trainer, Doak, what are you most proud of?

DO: Hmm, probably all the friendships that I made and continue to have. Just the sheer numbers, because there are so many. You could create friendships. But if you're not in the trenches you don't get the opportunity to really make those kind of friendships. I hardly even get the opportunity to meet them these days.

Q: Any one shining moment stick out to you?

DO: Well, if I had to pick one, probably that first national championship, since I'd been there on the sideline when Miami beat us in '84, and ten years later to go back to that same place and beat them. A little satisfaction there.

And then the other time -I mean, some of these moments became commonplace- but another time it was pretty impressive when we walked up to the Fiesta Bowl to play Florida. That site, just at dusk, there was just enough sunlight you could see all the Nebraska fans that were down lining up for the team, and up and down the ramps in the stadium, and you had that chant, "Gooo Biiiiigg Ree-eeddddddd!!!" That chant. There were so many people. But walking in there, we walked by -there must have been 10 or 12 redshirts from Florida- they were all tall, athletic looking kids. I remember thinking, 'Man, if these are the guys that aren't even playing, we're in trouble.' (laughs) Physically, just off the hoof, they were impressive. That's the way it was when we walked out onto the field versus Tennessee in '97, too. It was, 'How are we gonna beat these guys? They physically looked so much better!' But I guess that's why we beat teams that probably did have more physical talent, just the way we did things. And that Fiesta Bowl, you know how they have those hills in the background out there, just the Nebraska fans packing the place. The image was amazing…

Q: Anything you personally wish you could do over?

DO: There's always things you could do better, isn't there? There's always times you're in the grind and you're short on rest and maybe you don't treat somebody quite the way you wish you would have, you're kind of short with them. There are always some regrets and you wished you would have handled some of those things better. Everybody had a sense that maybe that run would last forever, but during the time you're thinking, 'Shoot, we're gonna go on doing this for a long time.' You wish you would have soaked it up a little bit more.

Q: Smell the roses a bit more?

DO: Yeah, I wish somebody could have talked Chancellor Graham Spanier into naming Al Papik the Athletic Director. That was the start of the demise, right there. It wasn't Steve Pederson firing Frank Solich, as much as everything was put in motion earlier. Bill Byrne brought extra pressure to Coach. He really felt like he had to win every game after they hired Bill, but what it would have done was assured some continuity for the program. The thinking was Al Papik would do it until Osborne was ready to step down, so Coach Osborne would never have left the program. Just think what that would have been like: In '99 we were the best team in the country and Frank was the coach, but would Coach Osborne's presence have made a difference somewhat? I don't know. A lot of people miss the big picture and don't realize that's what put so many things in motion.

Q: Anybody else's contributions behind the scenes mean anything special to you?

DO: That's hard to say. There were so many people. And it likely varies so much from person to person, who you have contact with more on a day to day basis. I mentioned Coach Osborne's way of doing things, and everybody was important. So it could be the Student Manager or Student Trainer spending time with one particular person who they felt like they have some value to put in, and would take the time to do that. You just don't know the ripple effect, then, who it affected.

Q: Anything about that inaugural Big 12 Championship game versus Texas? That very first one?

DO: Coach Osborne wasn't a big believer in flu shots until that game. It became mandatory after that, that everybody got flu shots. We had so many people sick, and some people might think, 'Loser's limp,' making excuses. But honestly, that week we had close to forty people with the flu. And this is the real flu, not just a silent flu that comes and goes. It's the respiratory flu. They didn't have the most extreme case possible, but it still affects you.

Q: Weren't we missing linebacker Terrell Farley for that game, too?

DO: Yeah, He got kicked off the team before that. He just couldn't stay away from the sauce.

Q: Any parting shots? Any other lasting impression made on you from the experience?

DO: Well, the simplest description would be the example of Coach Osborne. You just followed his example and you just worked hard with what's right in front of you, what you can control. I don't like to regurgitate too may quotes, like in the book the Nebraska Way, but I think he magnified what he learned growing up in the state, boiled it down to the purest form, and then you'd try to reflect him. You take the very ordinary and make it extraordinary. It's the thing that made Nebraska great, the ordinary attributes of the state. It's what we do. It's a very condensed, really solid version of it.

Q: Did you ever get the chance to go fishing with Coach Osborne?

DO: I don't like to fish. But I've been golfing with him. (laughs)

Q: How would you describe that experience?

DO: The guy's got a pretty ugly swing, but somehow gets the ball where it needs to go.

Q: He breaks it down and simply does the little things, huh?

DO: Yep.

End conversation.

You've likely noticed that the role of the trainer was much more than making ice bags and taping ankles. In many ways the training staff members were surrogate parents/big brothers/coaches, because at the time there was an NCAA-mandated limit to the amount of time a football coach could spend with an athlete each week: a paltry 20 hours per week. Who better to promulgate institutional norms and values in their stead than the athletic trainers, as close relationships were developed between staff and athlete during those long training room hours on the padded tables, in the ice bath, or during breaks in rehabilitation? The bonds last to this day and are a testament to the camaraderie and unity of those times.

One diamond I gleaned from this gravel pile was that of simplification, of 'reducing to the ridiculous,'or 'breaking it down Barney-style.' Remember, kids are very much atwitter in the moments leading up to a big game: there are so many concerns and tasks and neuroses tossing around their heads and stomachs that sometimes it's difficult for a post-adolescent to gain a focus. But on these occasions Coach Osborne would quite succinctly reduce the game down to its most simple of components, like blocking and tackling. Surely the players were able to catch a breath of fresh perspective, as a result, and have one up on an opponent who may have failed to do the same.

It hasn't been touched on overtly, but I hypothesize that the gaps in age between the coaches and players played a part, too. Having a seasoned staff with an average tenure of almost 13 years each at the institution, the situation could have gone either one of two ways: the communication could have suffered because of coaches being out of touch with the kids, or it could have thrived because the players respected these mens' experience and gave their words greater credence. To be honest, I think it was about 80% the latter from what I've heard (and from what my feeble memory recalls). To add, it didn't hurt that every now and again the grownups acted exactly like kids and joined in some of the hijinks. Those rare situations can bring a group together, no joke.

Doak also made point about Nebraskans and their school spirit in general. I've always wondered exactly what role the fans may have played in all of this, and in all honesty would have initially argued against his comment of, "I firmly believe that the state of Nebraska shaped the football program." But then, as if on cue, he directly mentioned the storied walk-on program of Nebraska's homegrown players and their place in the mix, the "the mortar in the bricks," so to speak. Who can argue with that? Not I. Doak has thought long and hard about these issues and he's about as qualified a person as any to comment upon them, so I find myself being dragged, somewhat, in that direction of thought, despite my own predilections. He also mentioned that he was a hard-headed gent of Danish descent, and to that I wholeheartedly concur without a moment's hesitation. I say this in kindness, but also truthfulness, for the last thing you wanted to do was get on Doak's 'Shit List.' He in the training room and Reconditioning Specialist/Strength Coach Bryan Bailey in the weight room were seemingly always engaged in a tug of war over when and who would oversee an athlete's return to full strength and the field of play. Let's be refreshingly honest here, this was no utopia in Memorial Stadium's offices, because it made for some tense, uncomfortable situations between the strength staff and the training staff. But after all was said and done everyone benefited, as steel sharpened steel.

Notable quote #2:
Doak Ostergard on the singular importance of each individual: "I mentioned Coach Osborne's way of doing things, and everybody was important. So it could be the Student Manager or Student Trainer spending time with one particular person who they felt like they have some value to put in, and would take the time to do that. You just don't know the ripple effect, then, who it affected."

Across the river from Iowa is Nebraska, and Omaha ... the second tier of states beyond the Mississippi, prairie on the east and arid on the west. It is like its eastern neighbor in its soil – fine, deep, level, and easily tilled... She found to her sorrow that corn could not regularly be grown west of the middle of the state, and hence adjusted herself to the environment, by pasturing the west and plowing the east; Typical of the progress of this young and physically monotonous state, her state University gathers at Lincoln two thousand of her sons and daughters, and takes no place inferior to cattle or corn in the hearts of the citizen of the plains.

Albert P. Brigham, *Geographic Influences In American History*, 1904

Born in Sioux City and raised in Polk City, Iowa, business management guru W. Edwards Deming once replied to an underling's challenge while guiding Japan's post-nuclear, World War II economic recovery, "It is not *necessary* to change. Survival is not *mandatory*."(emphasis mine) Whether spoken tongue in cheek or pointedly sarcastic, he made a valid point by any measure. Change is inevitable, and one man who experienced much during and since those 60 & 3 days is Trev Alberts. Never one to shirk responsibility, defer accountability or shun the glare of probing eyes and lights, his peer leadership was notable and noteworthy while a Nebraska student/athlete.

Our conversation took place early in this process of my great Why and How, and much has changed in the short span of time after our chat, as he now presides as the University of Nebraska-Omaha's Director of Athletics. Survival is not mandatory? Ask Trev and I guarantee you'll get a contrarian answer. Let's catch up with the man in life's mid-stream.

Notable quote #1:
"There was real leadership, a real understanding of what was important, that Coach O really understood the bigger picture of collegiate athletics. It wasn't just about wins and losses, but about developing young men."

Trev Alberts

Scholarship Recruit, Outside Linebacker, Cedar Falls, Iowa
Where are they now? Omaha, NE, Administrator

Question: Thanks for your time, Trev. Do you recall your first day on campus as a freshman?

Trev Alberts: I certainly can. It was the summer of 1989. And you know football was always very important in my life, but I have to tell you, I felt like I was a fairly well-rounded student-athlete. I liked football, but school was important to me as well, and I think the thing that really struck me immediately when walking on campus was how important football was to the state of Nebraska: the culture of the football team, that group of guys that the state could really take some pride in. I understood it just wasn't necessarily playing football with my buddies. Now, it would turn into that -because I would make some lifelong friendships and relationships- but I think it was really an understanding of how important football was and what was expected. And of course, my four years, it never diminished, because it was very important to the university, to the state. It was the unifier, the common cause Nebraskans could feel good about or mourn together over. It was a real link and it was important to our state -not that I felt a burden or anything like that as a young student/athlete- but I certainly understood my responsibility and my part in the game.

Q: Growing up in Cedar Falls, Iowa, and home of University of Northern Iowa, what was your favorite team as a kid?

TA: By far it would have been the Iowa Hawkeyes. We were inundated with Iowa coverage, so it was Chuck Long, Gordie Bohannon, Larry Station, I knew 'em all. Guys I really admired, knowing about them all.

Q: So how the heck did you end up at Nebraska?

TA: I really intended to go to Iowa. It was a place that I admired and in Hayden Fry's hands, who'd really turned the program around. The Hawkeyes had recently fallen on hard times (though we were all well aware of what Coach Fry had done), but we really took a trip out to Lincoln to 'enjoy a free weekend', get to know the little state to the west.

We had no idea what we were about to experience. My parents were obviously very integral in the decision making process. We had a chance to go out and meet the coaching staff and meet the people in the athletic department, and there was this real sense of family. You know, Nebraska was just competing at a different level at that point. There was a standard of excellence, we could really tell the community was largely driven by not only the university, but the football team's success. In the short time with Coach Osborne and learning a little bit about his values and his expectations, it was a real drawing point. There was real leadership, a real understanding of what was important, that Coach O really understood the bigger picture of collegiate athletics. It wasn't just about wins and losses, but about developing young men. Obviously it was something I was drawn to immediately.

Q: Was it a game day you visited?

TA: No, it wasn't. It was actually quite late in the recruiting process. I wasn't a highly recruited player, I wasn't actually recruited much at all. I gather, and I'm not for sure, but I think they probably missed out on a few big-name linebackers and sort of went down the list a bit and came across this rather gangly kid from northeast Iowa. But it was a natural fit. I had the same values as the coach and the Athletic Department, so it was a nice fit.

Q: Were you a farm- or city-kid?

TA: I was actually a bit of both. It was a unique upbringing in the sense that I was the farm kid but I lived in town. My father grew up a farm kid, and so did my mother, but my mom didn't want to live on the farm. So my dad went to University of Northern Iowa and got a business degree and he actually worked at the Cedar Falls utility company as the general manager, but also bought a farm from his father -my grandfather, who died early in life- so we farmed about 300 acres of corn and soybeans in Allison, Iowa, which was about 35 miles northwest of Cedar Falls. So I spent most of my evenings and Saturdays on the farm, but I never did actually sleep there. So you got to enjoy the benefits of living in town, but you also learned how to work on the farm.

Q: Sounds a lot like my upbringing. There was never anything lacking on the to-do list, no?

TA: That's right. Never had much time to sit around. My mom and dad never really played sports, but my older brother did. And then I thought I'd be real smart and go out for every sport so I'd get out of having to work, but all that happened was my dad would wait for me to get home from practice and then we took off. So as soon as I got home from practice we had to work, it didn't work out too well for me. (laughs)

Q: Any differences between Iowans and Nebraskans? Or would you lump them together as Midwesterners?

TA: You know what, I really would. I'd lump them together. I still really respect the people of Iowa, the Iowa people. I'm still a fan of Iowa football, I love the Iowa people. I watched the people of Cedar Rapids with great pride when the flood came through, it was remarkable to watch -through tears- the people dealing with that tragedy. You never heard any complaints, you saw neighbors pick up and go help a fellow citizen. It's what Iowans were about, it really brought back a lot of pride for me. And I tell you, the same thing would happen if it were to occur in Nebraska. Midwestern people, that's just how we're raised, there's a sense of accomplishment beyond self and a sense of responsibility beyond self. So I'd lump the two together as far as what they believe in.

Q: So when you arrived, where you a rush end or outside linebacker from the get-go?

TA: Actually I was a middle linebacker. All 6'4", 210 lbs of me!(laughs) Kevin Steele was the middle linebacker coach and I played middle linebacker. Being a small-town kid, you usually played running back and linebacker, that's really what my background was. They tried me out, and after about the third day they figured out I wasn't gonna fit there. In fact, when Coach Osborne announced he needed to speak to about 4 or 5 guys and asked if one of us would move to outside linebacker I had be the brown-noser -just so happy that he didn't send me back home because I wasn't good enough- and said 'I'll move!' So the quest began and I moved from middle linebacker to outside linebacker, and it was probably a good move for me. I was kind of tall and just think my body frame fit that outside linebacker position rather than that middle linebacker stuff, just going north and south instead of all that east and west stuff.

Q: And speaking of, it must have been your senior year, the Colorado game when we played them there, if I recall, one of the first plays of the game I remember you got into the backfield and you sacked Kordell Stewart. And when you got up from the turf you said something to Kordell. A few days later in the weightroom I asked what you had said to him. Do you remember what that was?

TA: Geez, I don't want to misquote myself. (laughs) It wasn't something that will embarrass me now, is it?

Q: Oh, no, Trev. As I remember, you simply told him, "You better get used to this, because I'm going to be back here all ....day.... long." (laughs)

TA: Yeah, that's probably right along the lines of what I was thinking. Generally, the message I always wanted to send was that "for 4 quarters we were going to be playing with that energy, that sort of effort, and we're not going to let up. So it wasn't going to be getting any better than right now." That's what we were trying to accomplish. Whether on offense of defense, we wanted to our opponents to know at the end of the game that if they were in the ball game that we were planning on playing every single play to the utmost.

Q: So you had Coach Samuel as a position coach. Would the coaches encourage that type of psychological warfare or was it mainly just teaching technique?

TA: I certainly don't want to paint a picture that there wasn't impact from a psychological standpoint, as the coaches had us prepared for the game. I think that stuff's probably more internal. You either want it or not.

I cared deeply for Coach Osborne, for Tony Samuel, and deeply for Charlie McBride... I like to win, and I'm a poor sport when it comes to losing, and we put so much into it. For instance, if you fly all the way to Boulder, put up with that nonsense, we might as well win, you know? (laughs) I don't recall ever, ever putting on my uniform at Nebraska and even walking out to the field and thinking 'We're gonna probably lose.' And I have to credit the coaches for that.

Q: How would you say they built upon that culture? How was it instilled?

TA: It was just how you went to work. It was the expectation from the day you walked on campus, there was level of excellence that was just kind of understood, it wasn't hoped for or aspired to, it was expected and it's just what we did, it's who we are, it's the way we worked and cared for each other. I'd assume that was put in place by Coach Osborne and the coaching staff. And we met it and tried to exceed it.

Q: And Coach Samuel, how would you describe Coach Samuel?

TA: I think what made him special was the fact that he played the game and it was his credibility from that perspective, he started as an outside linebacker and we knew he'd been through the wars. And probably the thing he'd benefited from was because he understood the wars and the culture, he knew exactly what we were going through, what it was like at the end of the day, as a freshman or as a senior, the responsibility that position entailed. I think he understood people and his great gift was having a great ability to read people, to understand what motivated them. Some kids needed more, some needed less. Some needed a pat on the back and some needed yelled at. He never treated every single guy the same. He had that ability to assess what our needs were and he tried to fill those.

Q: What would you say your need was?

TA: I was probably more the guy who needed to be encouraged. I didn't need to be yelled at, I needed to be coached. I was going to give you all of my effort that I had. If I made a mistake it was not because of effort, it was generally because I didn't know what I was doing or was confused. He simply taught me, he coached me, he did what he was supposed to do. He didn't yell and scream and try to protect himself from the defensive coordinator or the head coach. He had a very, very effective style and I would have run through a wall for him.

Q: What about Coach McBride?

TA: Different style. Of course, he coached the defensive line, so my interaction with him was less. But no less the same, a motivator, a tough guy, he would tear your heart out but be the first guy there if you ever had a need. There was never any misunderstanding that he didn't care for you, because you always knew he did. He was also the Defensive Coordinator, so he had a different role. There had to be little bit different style, you can't have everybody on the staff being your buddy. You needed some enforcers. He was a general, a guy that would command action out of you, but he would also get down in the trenches with you and go to battle with you, so I have a great, great deal of respect for that man.

Q: In one sense, was Charlie maybe the alter ego of Coach Osborne?

TA: I think a little bit, I think you better have a Defensive Coordinator that engenders aggressiveness. I can't imagine a passive personality in that role playing real well. I just think it was a really nice balance, a nice chemistry on the staff. Coach Osborne understood when building the staff that it didn't make a lot of sense to have the same personality, you know? We were the Blackshirts, we were the aggressors; it would only make sense the leader of the Blackshirts be a little of a Blackshirt himself.

Q: What can you tell me about the feedback, the grading process, the film study?

TA: A good coach understands that during the week is a time to teach and coach, during the week is a time to get after people. The game is a game. During the game is not a time to embarrass a player, not the time to single out a player, not the time to have the player completely walking on eggshells because he's concerned about making a mistake. Game time is about time to play, time to release, time to play with energy, you know what I'm saying? Play with freedom.

I think our coaches did a great job of that. Coach Osborne had no tolerance for coaches who undressed players on the sideline. I'm not saying that a coach didn't get after you (I had my fair share of Charlie McBride grabbing my facemask and chewing tobacco spit in my face as he was yelling at me),(laughs) but I was a young player and they were mental mistakes, mental-type things. I think they did a great of job of teaching during the week and then just letting us perform during the games.

Q: Somebody said that January of '91 was a major turning point leading into the success of your senior year, where all of the guys stopped making excuses and really dedicated themselves to the program. Do you remember that?

TA: I do. And I think the reality was that we weren't a very good football team, we weren't a very tough football team.

I always thought about being a champion: First, you have to have the courage to win. Second, then you have to have the talent to win. And part of having the courage to win was being willing to pay the price. I will tell you -early in my career?- that we didn't have the courage to win. I think we were pretty good, we were alright. We won 9 games but we didn't have the courage to win, we didn't pay the price to win. But then as my career progressed I believe that we finally -come my senior year- had the courage to win. But I think we were still missing some players as far as the talent.

But then that next year some of that talent started to grow up and show up, we were beginning to turn the corner. But certainly early in my career I don't believe the football team wanted it enough. I say this tentatively, because I respect deeply the leaders that came before me: I think there was great leadership, individually, on those teams when I was a young player. There were guys like Pat Tyrance, great individual leaders, but as a whole the leadership wasn't where it needed to be, nor was the courage to win.

Q: How was that courage then developed?

TA: I just think there was a determination and desire to say "enough is enough." Part of it was that meeting, part of it was that message, part of it was, "enough of this nonsense," you know? We got embarrassed in the Citrus Bowl against Georgia Tech, we got embarrassed in bowl games. It was just getting tiring being embarrassed against top competition. We beat all the teams were supposed to beat, like Missouri and Iowa State and Kansas and Kansas State. We beat all of them but no one cared about that. We were relevant locally, we weren't relevant nationally. I think there was a concerted effort from everybody. There was the strength staff, the athletic staff, the trainers. We needed to turn the corner and do what we needed to do to win. Everybody was encouraged to go the extra mile, and it was a concerted effort from the top. And we paid a bigger price.

Q: In what ways would you quantify that price being paid?

TA: I think unity was very important. I think Dr. Jack Stark had something to do with that, the Unity Council, better communication from the coaching staff about, "This is your team, not ours. Seniors need to step up." There was better leadership, guys were more committed. Guys quit going out and drinking Wednesday and Thursday nights. I think when I was a young player some of the older kids I knew were out downtown, they weren't as committed as they needed to be. They weren't as committed in bowl games.

The advantage, the sad fact was that we were Nebraska and we were going to win games, but then something changed. I certainly think there were a lot of people in the program who just got tired, were the kind of people who, when challenged, weren't going to go cower in the corner and give up. We were the kind of people who say, "Alright, enough of this crap. Were gonna find a way," and we found a way to out-work people.

We out-worked them, and then the coaches out-recruited where we got some people like the Peters' and Tommie Frazier and Grant Wistrom. We started getting some players. It was a concerted, collaborative effort. That's who we were: "The only chance we have to be successful was being on the same page, going the same direction."

And I think the coaching staff went to more speed and started putting it on the field. They realized having speed was very important. My junior year we went through a stretch where we played Colorado at home and they were ranked highly, and we beat them 52-7. And the next week we played Kansas. They were a top 10 team and we blew them out, too. We largely played nickel the entire game, so we played a 4-3 defense with the outside linebackers with a hand down -235 lb. guys with speed- and think they realized that speed kills. And they studied Florida State a little bit more and what they were doing, and made changes schematically, as well.

Q: You were at the next year's National Championship game on the sidelines, right?

TA: I was standing there with Doak! I just remember this team having the courage, having paid a bigger price than us. I felt good about that fact. It wasn't just me, but my class. I felt our class positioned the future, as being good stewards of Nebraska football. If you approach it that way, the class after us was positioned for success, we taught them how to work. Their leadership built off of ours. They had the courage to win, but I think some of that talent was beginning to mature, and they were pretty good, man. I just remember going into the locker room after the game to congratulate Coach Osborne and I remember him saying that he wished I have won the championship, that our class deserved it. And I thought that was pretty telling.

Once again, it was his humility. It wasn't about him, it was about the program and how he cared about his players. That was pretty cool.

Q: From your last game as a Husker, that 18-16 Florida State game, what stands out to you?

TA: Well, just the back and forth, playing against Charlie Ward. I respected him greatly. I thought he was a warrior, thought he played with a champion's heart.

The last drive I felt terrible. I made some big plays, our defense made some big plays, but you measure champions by whether or not they get it done in the crucial times. And, quite frankly, we -and specifically, I- didn't make a play on the last drive, and well...I lost, we lost. It doesn't make me happy. If you keep asking me about it I might hang up the phone. (laughs)

Q: Were you spent by that time?

TA: I didn't have anything left. The only consolation I felt was in walking back subsequent to the game, I didn't have anything left. I probably could have been in a bit better shape, I went on a tour -you know, with academics and the Butkus Awards and All-American stuff- but I didn't have anything left. I literally was emotionally, physically -and I'd even say spiritually- I was spent. I didn't have anything left. I gave it everything I had. It wasn't enough. But Coach Osborne told us that we played like champions. And that was the thing that was important. I put some solace in that.

Q: You essentially played with only one arm in that game, didn't you?

TA: Well, a lot has been made of that. I had two arms and I had a functioning right elbow. I wouldn't say it was quite as strong. I wouldn't say it held me back. I watched the film maybe once or twice after that game and there was probably 3 more plays that I left out there on the field, three more sacks that I should have had. But I can't say that I'm some sort of hero because I played with one arm. I was able to do all I could do.

Q: So your rookie year you're in Indianapolis with the Colts the whole time. Was that Miami U. game then the first time you'd seen the '94 team live all year?

TA: Yeah, I came back for that Orange Bowl game.

Q: Did you sense a change in the vibe at all?

TA: A sense of urgency. I could sense it was a team that was destined to win, and I just remember looking at the offensive line and thinking I was glad I didn't have to play against them every week. I remember it was just the focus. I remember during the week Miami had a few things to say, and I could see a football team motivated to get the win for Coach Osborne.

Q: Any other memorable games stand out to you from those playing days?

TA: I always enjoyed playing against Iowa State because I was from there, other than the fact that we lost to Iowa State in Ames. That was pretty embarrassing. They deserved a lot of credit, with a 3rd string quarterback in Marv Seiler. They switched to the option -the same option we'd been playing against for 20 years- and we just couldn't stop them.

I remember that game, but you know, not any others in particular. Every game was an incredible environment full of fans who were passionate. Every game was just a pleasure, a joy, a privilege. I know a lot of guys wait until after they're done to realize it, but I knew that I was pretty privileged to get to play there. I knew that.

Q: Any favorite or most memorable play?

TA: I remember a play against Kansas, my junior year. I believe Chip Hilleary was at quarterback, I remember a pretty good left tackle and we were really concerned about the sweep play to June Henley the running back. The left tackle had a real good first step, and Coach Samuel was really drilling it into us to make sure were weren't getting hooked. And I just remember getting into my stance, and everything Coach Samuel taught me just came to fruition and I saw the first step, and I just explode! And it was kind of like the culmination of everything Nebraska did for me, because in one sense I had Coach Samuel teaching me that play, it was the explosion from the strength staff and you all, and getting my helmet ...here's a guy who's 320 lbs…. and I drove the guy! Just drove him back like twelve yards, right into my arms was June Henley for a 16 yard loss. It was such a good feeling because I dominated the block, then obliterated Henley on the tackle. And I have a picture of it. I just swallowed him up. It really wasn't against a 'name' team, a big deal, but that one play really symbolized everything for me. I remember that.

Another one I really remember was playing against a guy named Barrett Brooks. He was a left tackle at Kansas State, and I needed one sack to break Jim Skow's all-time single season record for sacks. Of course, the guy's coaches had gotten him prepared and for the first three quarters this guy was kicking my butt. I couldn't get my hands on the quarterback to save my life. And he talked more smack! And you know, the end of the third quarter we're walking down to the other end of the field and he's in my ear, "You ain't nothing, Alberts. You suck! You're so overrated!" (And I generally tried to save all my energy, generally, to play) And finally this guy was in my ear so much I said, 'You know what, Barrett? You're right. You're the best left tackle I've ever played against.' And he said, "Really?!!" And I say, 'I'm serious! I've never....', and I could just see him starting to feel real good about himself. And of course, the second play of the 4th quarter I went right around him because he relaxed, and I got my sack. And I walked past him on the way back and said, 'Well, you're *almost* the best left tackle I've ever played against.' (laughs) I remember that play.

Q: (laughing) Any memorable practice events from those days?

TA: You know, most of my memories are from the days of my redshirt year going against Doug Glaser and the late Jake Young, going against the first team. Those guys would just toss me to the ground and laugh at me. It made me really question whether I was tough enough or man enough to ever even play at Nebraska. You know, when you've got Tom Punt, 6'8", 320, and those guy's like Doug Glaser, it was really intimidating lining up against those guys. But you realized shortly that if you could hang and if you got through this and persevered, you could get through anything. Some of the stuff that I endured and went through, it made you unafraid of anything or anybody. If I survived fall camp at Nebraska with the seniors when I was 4 or 5 years younger, there isn't anything else I can't accomplish.

Q: Any extra-curricular, off-field occurrences from those days worth sharing?

TA: Not really. Nothing I can comment on.(laughs) Nothing like Jason Peter. You know, we were typical college kids and a typical college team, but for the most part we were a pretty focused group. We cared for one another and we wanted to win. My focus was getting my degree in 4 years, getting the best grade point I could and winning as many games as I could, being the best player I could be, along with being a good leader. I could say I had my share of fun. I hear other guys telling some stories and I wonder, 'Where was I during some of that?' (laughs)

Q: Any good stories about Christian when he first came in?

TA: Christian, the whole thing with him was that he pretty much sat down at the training table… and he never really got up! (laughs) He just kept eating! And it would be like 2 o'clock and he'd still be sitting there. And I remember Charlie McBride used to get real upset at him because for like three plays he'd be just dominant, but then he got tired fast. (laughs) But then he lost some weight and got in shape and he was as dominating as any player I played with. It was a lot of fun.

And I'm sure you might know, but Christian, his life is remarkable. He's not anything close to what you remember of him as a player. He's happily married, a loving father and husband. I believe his time here really made an impact on his life, as well. And his brother, too, for fighting through what he went through.

Q: Who did you have for a roommate?

TA: My first year I roomed with Troy Branch, a terrific roommate. Deep admiration for Troy. Brilliant young man and a terrific football player. And for one year I roomed with Matt Penland and Greg Fletcher. And then Coach Samuel asked me if I would room with Travis Hill. Travis had some difficulties with some old roommates and he thought I could be a good influence, so Travis lived with me. And then I lived with Rick Schwieger, a track athlete, for awhile. And then I finally ended up with Byron Bennett at the end, a kicker. So I lived with linebackers, I lived with kickers, and I lived with track athletes. Needless to say the kicker and the decathlete were a little different than linebackers. (laughs) It was a learning experience. I keep in touch with Byron, he's doing a great job coaching high school football and being a schoolteacher.

Q: Is there anyone behind the scenes who you feel played a huge part in your development there?

TA: You know I'd really hate to single out just one person. I just tell you that since I left I've paid a little bit more attention to other athletic departments. And I have to tell you, there are so many people -and as a player you have no idea- whether it's the Chief Financial Officer or Norma Knobel, who made sure you got a little money on the plane, it was just so many people working so hard for the football program's success: whether it's an intern, whether it's recruiting or the Head of Football Operations.

The thing is, there are so many people who should get all the credit, and rightfully so. And there are so many people working under them doing the day-to-day dirty work, and those are the people who never get a 'thank you', that nobody knows about. And without them we're not winning national championships. So those people unselfishly are doing something, not because they need the individual accolades, but because they care enough about the program and the student-athletes to do that. Those are the people, looking back, you had deep admiration and respect for, because they weren't making tons of money. Some of them were making peanuts, but they really cared. And those are the people I really respect.

Take a guy like Keith Zimmer. I'm 18 years old and I miss my mom and dad and all of a sudden Keith says, "What's wrong, Trev?" And the next thing you know, there's catharsis going on. The difference makers: Keith, Dennis Leblanc, Jerry Weber, Doak, these guys, all of them. Bryan Bailey used to… I remember one time he said "What's wrong?" and I quoted a bible verse and said, 'The spirit is indeed willing, but the flesh is weak.' And he actually had that printed on all of our workout sheets,"The spirit is indeed willing, but the flesh is weak." (laughs) "I want to do (the workout), but I'm dead." Boyd, Mike Arthur, he's banging away on some computer coming up with new, creative ways to be successful. Randy Gobel trying to creatively come up with another machine for us to try. It's non-stop. Butch Hug with the facilities. I don't know who brought all the tackling dummies down to Schulte Fieldhouse when we did the one-on-ones, you know what I mean? So many people. And you know there were some people in the Development Office soliciting funds allowing us to have the facilities we had. Folks like Lee Sapp, the big name donor people, the Cook family. Those are the people, anytime I get a chance to, I let them know that as a student/athlete I was the beneficiary of that."I want you to know that you just didn't give money blindly, it didn't go nowhere." We directly benefited from the Hewitt Center. I had a chance to study very comfortably and earn a degree because of somebody's unselfishness. The unselfishness across the board, across the state, made us so successful.

Q: What makes you most proud of your time there, Trev?

TA: I don't think it was any wins or losses or any individual thing like that. I'm just most proud of the fact that I had a chance to be a part of the Husker family. I find myself talking to my kids, (and my parents raised me with a moral compass, they did everything they could while I was with them and they did everything they could until I left the nest), and I felt the University of Nebraska, I felt everything my parents taught me was then sort of picked up by Coach Osborne and the University of Nebraska and it was taken to the next level. It was remarkable, well chronicled. I had the greatest experience a student-athlete could possibly have. I couldn't possibly, in my dreams, have said, 'Okay, this is what will happen.'

And the thing I see, is that they do everything in their power to make sure that subsequent student-athletes have that kind of experience that I had. And to the best of their ability, they do. Some guys, for whatever reason, get hurt, but there is a standard at Nebraska to create some really productive citizens, great members of society. I could never pay, give any amount of money, for what they did for me. The fans, everybody associated with it. I'm not one of those kind of people who live in the past, it's not 1993 for me. It's 2009, but at the same time I look at those experiences and memories as flat-out being the best. It didn't get any better than that. And I didn't even win a national championship.

Q: Well, the scoreboard never showed it, but you were a champion, Trev. I don't know how it happened, but they ended up having two more points on the board when the clock showed zeroes. Last question: Anything else play a part in the organization coming together, from your perspective, that I haven't touched on in our time here?

TA: Like said a little bit earlier, I really believe that there was a concerted effort from everybody involved, starting at the top, a compete evaluation of what we were doing. Remember, we changed defenses from a 5-2 to a 4-3, we made some changes in the weight program, it was across the board. It was a general, "We're not going to go out and let this happen again. Enough is enough. We're going to finish the drill. We're going to be a champion. We're going to practice like champions, we're going to pay the price -whatever that price is- to achieve the highest levels." When you get everybody (as you know, there can be actual issues between the Strength Staff and Athletic Medicine), but everybody decided to get on the same page and say, "Let's finish the deal here." It was across the board and everybody paid that price. At the end of the day, no matter how talented you are, the team that's willing to pay the highest price is going to win.

Sure, talent had to be part of it, but I've seen a lot of teams with less talent win, seen a lot of coaches with less football coaching ability be good coaches because they worked for it. I think it was just a unique time when you had a combination of people willing to pay a price with a group of young men who were extraordinary. Guys like Tommie Frazier, who had some extraordinary natural abilities, it was convergence.

Everybody had a part, but somebody had to lead it, and that person was Tom Osborne. I love Coach Osborne, how each week, I relied on the fact that each week he had a theme, whether it be perseverance, toughness, et cetera. He always had a quote from maybe Tom Landry or Roger Staubach, and the Player Of The Game got that plaque. And I've got a lot of those plaques. And I've got to tell you, I wouldn't say that any one is my favorite, but they were all well-accomplished people and it was really important. There was whole bunch of them Coach presented to us on a weekly basis.

End conversation

"We could really tell the community was largely driven by not only the university, but the football team's success." Trev touched on a number of issues here, the first being his almost immediate recognition of the importance football played in Nebraskan's lives. Growing up in Iowa, I suspect the Nebraska Football team's familial cohesiveness on a grand scale engendered a blessed hope in both him and his parents during their visit to Lincoln. (And to think that it was on more or less a whim?) Of course, it goes without saying that Coach Osborne's being a figurehead of integrity, a reservoir of character, a possessor of true leadership attributes were the straw that broke the camel's back as far as the Hawkeyes' chances were concerned. Scoreboard: Nebraska 1, Iowa 0.

Secondarily, Trev made me harken back and try to recall to any occurrence of ugly sideline moments or incidents of player beration by a coach. Funny, but I just can't recall any, which makes me realize that Trev was right: the coaches verily did all their coaching during the week and then let the players turn it loose on Saturday."The hay is in the barn," was a popular phrase come Friday afternoon, and with a willingness to fully prepare during the week, it made for much pleasurable game days…and victories. Unless a player exhibited a gross lack of discipline on gameday, you never heard of the kind of butt-chewing that one would expect during the sideline moments in the heat of the battle. But then again, Nebraska football always did their best to recruit character kids, so the chances of any disciplinary lapses were potentially less prevalent than some to begin with. Trev was a high motor guy and one of the 'character kids' among so, so many of the day.

Another lasting item of note was the change in his old teammates over a year's time, when he spoke of visiting on the sideline for the '95 Orange Bowl versus Miami. 365 days, 5 hours, and 48 minutes removed from the exhaustion and heartbreak of the 18-16 final, he noticed a palpable sense of urgency, of destiny, of resolve in their eyes. Remember, this was one year removed from the 1:16 and the Unfinished Business of the offseason."Enough is enough. We're going to finish the drill. We're going to be a champion. We're going to get the win for Coach Osborne."

This perfect scenario of vengeance contained only one anomaly, though, being that the foe was to be the University of Miami rather than the one everyone really wanted to face again: Florida State. Payback was diverted to the Canes -Goliaths in their own right- and the stakes were upped even one notch higher for this one: Top defense in the nation, their tropical climate, their home locker room, their raucus home crowd, with 62 wins in the last 63 games on this home field (a 98.4% home field winning percentage). For the Nebraskans on the squad who could recall crying their eyes out over the Canes' monumental upset of their Huskers on the same sandy, spotty, divotted and cigarette-butted Orange Bowl turf a decade before, this was an extremely close second option. Enough is enough? In some of those player's minds, what was a puny minute-sixteen of a year ago compared to 11 year quest for vengeance on behalf of the '83 team? It turns out that enough was enough on that January 1st of 1995.

Notable quote #2:
Trev Alberts on the thought process that turned it around: "We're not going to go out and let this happen again. We're going to practice like champions. We're going to pay the price -whatever that price is- to achieve the highest levels."

But one day, when across the Field of Fame the goal seemed dim,
The wise old coach, Experience, came up and spoke to him.
"Oh Boy," he said, "the main point now before you win your bout
Is keep on bucking Failure till you've worn the piker out!
                                    Grantland Rice, *Alumnus Football*

"Failure is not an option." Best known as the inspirational motif surrounding 1970's famed Apollo 13 NASA mission to the moon and its perilous return back home, the motto could also serve as an apt metaphor for the Academic & Life Skills Counseling Department at the old Hewitt Center. With Keith Zimmer and Dennis Leblanc playing the role of Coach Experience in Grantland Rice's poetic verse above, they daily strove for student success from their office locations in the bowels under West Memorial Stadium's 50 yard line.

Equal parts drill sergeant/social worker/Cub Scout Den Mother, Keith served the student/athletes as a guiding light in preparing and transitioning into life after college, readying them for the strange and eerie day of leaving the nest to make hay in the real world of cubicles, commutes and budgets rather than cornerbacks, coursework and blitzes. Let's now transition to Keith, a man deftly focused on warding off failure in life's future endeavors.

Notable quote #1:
"If you pay attention to people, if you work consistently with people, if you are there for them day after day, if you pledge your support to them, usually they engage with you and they appreciate that and they will work hard for you. And, ultimately, people are succeeding and achieving their goals."

Keith Zimmer

Question: Keith, so many of the guys said that you meant a lot to them as student-athletes, and I'm really pleased that you'd take the time for a little interview.

Keith Zimmer: Anything I can do to help. It sounds like a great project.

Q: Well, let me start. You helped write a few books, most notably the one with Grant Wistrom and Jason Peter, how did you get involved in that?

KZ: Well, those were things where the players wanted to do a book, and basically wanted to go to somebody they could trust and to have someone help structure the book and organize it and put it all together. It was really their book, but I was just the behind-the-scenes guy that helped organize it and make sure that it got done and in a timely manner and reflect positively on the players, as well as the university and the athletic department. It's basically what you're doing, interviewing the athletes. So many of these fans, they recognize the student/athlete for the athlete and the player and the uniform and helmet and jersey number, and they don't understand all that goes in to representing Nebraska football, all the behind-the-scenes and the day-to-day efforts. So putting the human interest of the student/athlete out there is something people enjoy reading about. And it does justice to the players that way, as well.

Q: So then you did the 'Heart and Soul' book, right?

KZ: Yes, that was Grant (Wistrom) and Jason(Peter). They were high profile players who wanted to do something and they approached me, trusted me, and I think first of all they thought it would be a neat keepsake to have regarding their career. And they wanted to be able to tell their story. They felt such pride playing in the program for Coach Osborne. They were two just very determined, relentless guys. They really were the heart and soul. They were fun to work with. I did a little editing with those guys, Paul. A little editing. (laughs) I had to tone it down a little bit. If you looked at Jason's recent book (Hero of the Underground), you might get the idea. That was the unedited version. Very raw. (laughs)

Q: So where are you from originally?

KZ: Wayne, Nebraska. Northeast Nebraska. My Mom worked in education. She was a peer educator. My father worked in real estate: farm real estate, agricultural real estate. I had one brother, he's almost two years older than me. So it was a good upbringing. Good values reinforced to me. Athletics was a big part of my life. That's one reason I got drawn into working in college athletics; always enjoyed helping people and counseling and guiding people. That, along with my passion for athletics. So it led me to the perfect career of student/athlete counseling.

Q: Were you a Husker fan as a kid?

KZ: Oh, come on, Paul. Come on, Paul! (smiles) No comment. You know the answer to that.

Q: Well, you had Wayne State there. Sometimes the local affinities take hold, you know?

KZ: If you're a Nebraska kid you grew up idolizing the program. That's why it's such an honor every day for the people who work there every day. When you walk through the front doors of Memorial Stadium every day, that's just something you hope people don't take for granted. They should feel very honored and have a lot of pride to not only help the students there, but really, you're kind of an extension of the entire state. And just a feeling that a lot of people would like to have, just to be able to walk through Memorial Stadium for not just 6 or 7 days throughout the year, but something you do every day. And you're not just supporting the team, but you're developing men and women every day. And that's the biggest part of what we do here at Nebraska.

I came here to Nebraska to complete my Masters Degree and finish up doing my internship. So in 1987 I just showed up at the university looking to get practical experience and get some internship credit for it, and was lucky enough at the time that Roger Grooters gave me the opportunity to volunteer and accumulate some hours toward my degree completion. I did that for a little over a year basically as a volunteer, doing academic counseling with students on a daily basis. And after that year I felt like I needed to put my Masters Degree to work and hopefully get a paid position. I started to apply to a number of positions around the country and got a few offers, and luckily at that point Coach Osborne was able to convince Coach Devaney to create an additional academic counseling position. He saw value in some of the things I was doing with student- athletes, and another academic position was created in 1988. and I became full time with the athletic department.

Q: What was the value that Coach Osborne saw? How was he tipped off to that?

KZ: One of the new things that I brought with me was the emphasis on career counseling and life after sports, so that was something that was really emphasized in my graduate program and something I tried to get started in my first year here, doing some things with career development and exploration, resume writing and internships. I think Coach Osborne saw the importance of that and the value in getting athletes prepared for realistic career opportunities and life after football at some point. That was something that made our program, at the time, unique, and you knew that that would serve the program well and serve the players well. I think he liked that piece of it, and it got some attention and motivation to get the position created.

Q: I'll bet 25 years earlier when he was leaving pro football, it was something he would have liked....

KZ: Well, you know the good thing about Coach Osborne, he has always been education-oriented; that's a big part of him, who he is. And having his Doctorate degree and being in education and teaching like he has, to have a guy like that as your football coach and then as your Athletic Director speaks well for people in academic and life skills, because you know you're going to have his instant support.

Q: Let me ask you, Keith, a lot of folks probably don't have a solid idea of what the academic advisors do. Some may even think that you write the papers for them. (laughs) Can you give me a little insight?

KZ: Well, right now, Paul, I'm not doing any academic counseling, but for about 20 years I was doing the day-to-day counseling. And basically you're making sure the incoming athletes transition well into the 4 year college setting, so you try to prepare them for the academic survival and study skills so they can earn a college degree. There is the teaching of study skills and time management, making sure there is a passion for their academics and connecting them with their degree of choice, and just making sure they have the day-to-day support for a balanced division of academics with athletics, be that tutorial support, a mentor, study hall supervision, helping create communication between the student-athlete and faculty members -appropriate communication- so that they are monitoring and taking an active role in the process. And also the things alluded to earlier: the basics of making sure that they understand the importance of class attendance every day, being active and attentive when attending class, because all things contribute to their success academically.

Q: What is the typical transition like for the kids?

KZ: I would say that it's a balance, a time management issue, just the study skills, that it's a lot more intense. What you've done in high school or junior college isn't going to get you fully prepared, and it's a little different ballgame. Just like it is on the field, everything is accelerated and the expectations are a lot higher, and what you did in high school athletically or academically won't be enough to have you achieve at a high level at the collegiate level.

Q: You helped them learn a healthier respect for regimentation, setting and following a set schedule?

KZ: Yeah, the consistency, the accountability, and really just having a good attitude, being respectful to everybody that you work with, and taking advantage of the unlimited support available on campus and in the athletic department. Because part of that comes from having a realistic perspective and value of where athletics is going to take you; not just putting all your efforts and energies into becoming a professional player, but recognizing at the same time that you have to place equal effort into your schoolwork and your career outside of athletics. If you have that well-rounded perspective typically things work out pretty well for you.

Q: Let's say you have a Parade All-American coming in and they feel they're on the fast track to the pros. How do you engage them to also take their studies seriously?

KZ: Well, I think the first thing you have to do is support their goals athletically, you'd never want to discourage somebody's dream if they want to play in the NFL. You tell them,

'You know what, that's a great goal. We're going to support that and help you become the best player you can. But in combination with that, in order to continue as a collegiate athletically you have to perform academically. And Nebraska's #1 goal is to see you earn a college degree and graduate, and hopefully that's a goal that you have and that your family has. Nebraska would not be doing you justice in following through on how we recruited you if we didn't work tirelessly to help you earn your college diploma.' Again, you have to support their athletic ambitions, because if you squelch that and discourage it you're going to create some tension in your working relationship and that wouldn't be real positive. And, of course, the football coaches aren't wanting you to do that either; they want you to support athletic aspirations. So certainly the joint end of those goals is to encourage them to be balanced with other goals and also to be realistic. We use statistics, show what the statistics are with the NFL: even if they do advance and beat the odds it's not going to be more than 3 to 4 years on average. So you just try to give them some numbers and be encouraging and be as positive as you can.

Q: Harkening back to those mid-90's, what stands out to you about those athletes?

KZ: There were a lot of great players in those years, those were some of our best years. And you look at some of those rosters: you have Barron Miles, a pretty small guy at cornerback who to this day is still playing up I Canada. Some of these guys were just high achievers in everything they did. I guess what I learned in working with all those guys was to never underestimate them, no matter what their status was athletically, and respect the unity and support you saw within the team, the chemistry. It didn't seem to matter if a guy seldom played or was a high profile guy, there was a brotherhood among all those teams. You still see that today: they stay in contact, they're supportive and have ongoing relationships.

That's one thing when you talk to all these former athletes, when you talk to them it's 'relationships'. You hear that word come up over and over again. Those special relationships that were formed came about because of athletics. The lifelong relationships, that's what we were able to play a part in. It's a lot of fun.

Q: Plus an awesome responsibility, yes? In the recruiting process when you have a coach in the living room telling them that Nebraska is going to give their son a quality education, you're where the rubber meets the road as far as that's concerned, no?

KZ: Ultimately, the student athlete has to do the work. We're more like an offensive or defensive coordinator, we try to put the athletes in the right position and give them good advice; but obviously there's a lot of scrutiny, a lot of integrity, a lot of compliance. The student has to do the work, they earn the degree; we just direct them and navigate them and encourage them along the way. The college graduation, as you remember for yourself, that's the crowning moment. Some of these young men maybe didn't think that was possible when they came here. But when that day comes and they walk across the stage, that's like the national championship.

Q: Keith, some guys have told me that the diploma meant more to them than the national championship…

KZ: That very well could be, because athletics came a little easier for them. They may not have seen graduation as something that could or would happen, so I can see where a lot of them say that. It's just a life-changing moment that opens a lot of doors and opportunities for them, which they're going to need for the next 35-40 years of their lives. Maybe they underestimate it on the way in, but as their college experience unfolds and maybe nothing happens athletically, -injuries, playing time, whatever that may be- I think eventually they all start seeing the significance of a college diploma.

Q: I suppose you keep in touch with a lot of those guys over the years?

KZ: You know, I talk to a lot of them. And a lot of them call me if they're going through a career change or need some advice on a number of things, and that's a proud moment when those former athletes still have a lot of confidence, 15 years later, and call you and ask you for some direction and some support.

I think that's what makes Nebraska special, because when your playing days are over Nebraska doesn't just discard you and move on to the next group, but tries to maintain that relationship and pledges that ongoing support forever. I think that's why there is such long-term affection for the University of Nebraska among former athletes: not just football, but all of them. And whether it's me in Life Skills, or Dennis LeBlanc in Academics, or the trainers like Doak Ostergard or the strength coaches, I think that's really everybody's approach and philosophy. That's the way it should be, you just don't start to forget about these people once they're done winning the national championships for you, but use their expertise to benefit the program, and that's what we're trying to do.

Q: Any memorable experiences with coaches or staff members of that time?

KZ: They were really all memorable, growing up as a kid like you, you're a fan of the Nebraska program, to think that 10-15 years later you're sitting in a meeting with Tom Osborne or Bob Devaney. Those first few times interacting with those people, that was a little different, you're in awe. But later, after awhile, you understand you all have the same goal to develop student athletes and be successful on and off the field. Just to play a part in that with all the coaches and the support staff, you start to not really pay attention to who you're interacting with, but who you're dealing with in the shared vision of what we're trying to accomplish. So at the beginning it's little awe inspiring, but after awhile you tend to forget you're working with some of these legendary figures and you start to look at them as co-workers who have the same goals and vision in mind for the program.

Q: Speaking of the goal and vision, do you recall Coach Osborne setting out a road map, working on creating a vision?

KZ: I think the big thing that Dennis and myself tried to do (which came from Coach Osborne), was to make sure that everybody you deal with be treated equally. It didn't matter if you were the starting player or low-impact player who maybe didn't contribute for three or four years, the important thing was to be attentive to every student, every person. And that was kind of the philosophy of Coach Osborne, how the Nebraska program has flourished, with the walk-on program and tradition and treating everybody well. You don't really hear a lot of disgruntled athletes coming out of the Nebraska program because of the way they were treated. That's something still to this day, you make time for everybody. What matters is their effort and their goals and how you can help them achieve them.

Q: Speaking of, any stories close to your heart about your ability to play a big part in someone's life?

KZ: Well, one guy who had a lot of impact on me was Brook Berringer. He was very community-minded -and obviously, the tragedy when he died in the plane crash- Brook was a guy who did a lot for the entire state. And I have always been the guy who's done a lot of community programs with the athletes and coordinated a lot of the outreach efforts, so it's been kind of exciting to see the impact from the efforts of Brook and the people like Will Shields. Those guys created such a legacy that I still try to carry on with the present players.

We have the Berringer Citizenship Award to honor players who do a great job in the community every year, so it's been great to be a part in some of these guys' lives, so they can emulate and encourage other players to model the positive actions of those guys that have gone before them.

Brook's mom, too, she's still is very involved here at the University. Some people just looked at him as the ultimate team player who was a great quarterback when we had one of the nation's best quarterbacks, so I think a lot of people tend to overlook how gifted he was athletically and how he had a great chance to play in the NFL. But he was the complete person, great student, very community-minded. And that's why, when he passed tragically, it really shook the entire state. People felt like they knew Brook Berringer because he was such a physical guy, not just on the field, but in the community and the schools in outreach programs across the state. You'd see the memorials outside the stadium for weeks afterwards, and to this day there is the statue of him and Coach Osborne outside the stadium. Here we are over 14- 15 years after his death and he's still a prominent person in a lot of people's lives.

Q: Last questions, Keith. Any unique constraints, from your perspective, that made things more difficult for the players?

KZ: Honestly, whether they play softball or tennis for football or golf, I wouldn't say they have any constraints within their sport. One of the things I try to teach all of them is the value of athletics, of how you can take those transferable qualities that you develop day after day, month after month, year after year for sports, and how those can benefit you in life to leadership, to teamwork, to being competitive, to being driven, to perform under pressure -no matter what their sport- to apply it to life, because it gives them a huge advantage. And as their career unfolds, it helps them to apply those things and be very successful well into the future.

Q: Ties it all together, Keith?

KZ: That's how we roll, Paul. (laughs)

Q: So where did you gain the skills to build the Life Skills segment?

KZ: Well, a lot of it is just the counseling skills and how you work with people and how you treat people. I was taught that with my undergrad and graduate educational work. I also had a position before I did my graduate work, Paul, where I worked in social work for the Department of Social Services when I was fairly young. I did some abuse investigations, worked with at-risk children, a lot of different families and parents. And through those positions and through the education, the big thing that I learned was how to work with people, how to listen to people, counsel people, direct them, advise them, how to follow up with them. Really, that's at the heart of what I do. If you pay attention to people, if you work consistently with people, if you are there for them day after day, if you pledge your support to them, usually they engage with you and they appreciate that, and they will work hard for you. And ultimately people are succeeding and achieving their goals.

In all honesty, there's nothing sophisticated to what I do. It's just those core values of being consistent, paying attention, listening, working hard, and I think that's the way a lot of Nebraskans work. A lot of Nebraskans in the state and a lot of people in the athletic department do that, and the student athletes and their families then begin to perceive you in a pretty positive light.

End conversation.

It's hard not to be a fan of a guy like Keith Zimmer. I'm sure some might even be a little envious of what he's able to bring to the student/athlete's fore. I, too, was a student/staffer on campus back in the day but was never able to capitalize on this man's services. As a result, I now feel that the experience was somewhat lacking. (Perhaps that's just envy talking)

From our brief conversation one can sense a measure of virtue and servanthood in the man, don't you think? He's one of those folks who never ever forgets what the Nebraska Football team means to its fan base, and in many respects you could say that Keith still is a fan of the boys in scarlet & cream, only now he's in a position to shape and form and mold them to some extent. What a fulfilling vocation.

I'd never heard it phrased that way before, but his statement rings true: "When your playing days are over Nebraska doesn't just discard you and move on to the next group, but tries to maintain that relationship and pledges that ongoing support forever." So true. Even for the boys from back in the 90's, they know to this day that they can call Keith for some direction, insight, or work connections and have his full dedication and attention. That's pretty rare, and quite frankly goes against human nature. I know why Coach Osborne would want to create a position for Keith Zimmer, because he was of like mind. And that's a good man to have around.

Notable quote #2:
Keith Zimmer on his mission and priorities: "You make time for everybody. What matters is their effort and their goals and how you can help them achieve them."

You may my glories and my state depose,
But not my griefs; still am I king of those.

William Shakespeare, *King Richard II*

English Theologian John of Salisbury wrote in 1159's *Metalogicon*, "We are like dwarfs sitting on the shoulders of giants. We see more, and things that are more distant, than they did, not because our sight is superior or because we are taller than they, but because they raise us up, and by their great stature add to ours." A lasting memory I'll always have of Spartanburg, South Carolina native Kareem Moss is of him raising up Tom Osborne on a shoulder (aided by Gregory, South Dakota teammate Jon Vedral) for a National Championship victory ride after the '95 Orange Bowl. Helmet and pads discarded, Kareem brandishes a million dollar smile along with a sweat-soaked gray t-shirt and a wrist bound with athletic tape. The jubilation began with his last second interception of Miami quarterback Frank Costa and all but ended the contest, and it's a fitting paradox that the man whose shoulders bore a 22-year national championship void was finally elevated to his rightful air. Let's hear from Kareem Moss, a high-stepper who, like Trev Alberts earlier, had also experienced enough of the same old same old, it seems.

Notable Quote #1:
"We used to walk around singing a little tune, "We're tired of being stepped on", like a song, a little chant. And that kind of brought us together even more, along with "Unity, Belief, Respect", "Unfinished Business" and so forth."

Kareem Moss

Scholarship Recruit, Strong Safety, Spartanburg, South Carolina (Garden City CC)
Where are they now? Spartanburg, South Carolina, Business Executive

Question: So Kareem, when year was your first fall camp at Nebraska?

Kareem Moss: '92. And I was previously at Garden City, Kansas. I had a choice to go to junior college 30 minutes from home or 14-15 hours from home, and I'd been around there all my life and I wanted to get out and see what the world has to offer, see what God had in store for me. So I went out to Kansas on a wing and a prayer, and that's how I ended up there, to see what the world had to offer. At that time I had to go through junior college because of academic reasons.

Q: Were the Huskers on the radar from the start?

KM: Not at all. I went to junior college to go back to Clemson. But unfortunately Danny Ford left Clemson when it was time for me to come out of junior college. (He went to Arkansas) I was going to go there, but it wasn't really official. So I'm in Garden City and I redshirt my first year, so I had 5 years to play 4. And the next year I came back and I ended up starting. I would have made All-Conference but I ended up breaking my leg. I played 5 games: the first four and then the bowl game. I played in the bowl game with a cast on my leg, playing at outside linebacker. (laughs)

Q: With a cast on your leg?!

KM: I played in the game. I wanted to get on the field, Paul! It was tough after waiting a year and being so far away from home. I'd started to question whether or not football was my calling. But like I said, I played those 5 games and I still ended up getting recruited by all the Big 8 schools. The Big 8 at the time: OU, Kansas, Kansas State, I was real enthused by

Kansas State, how they treated me on my visit. I also looked at Georgia while I was back home on my break and set up Arkansas. But between Arkansas and Kansas State there was this school called Nebraska that talked to me. Coach Ron Brown first contacted me, then Coach Osborne and Coach Samuel and Coach Darlington, they flew down in a private plane to Garden City to visit me, and I sat in the airport and talked to them and set up a visit.

And once I visited Nebraska and found out the tradition - not only for sports and winning, but academics and the graduation rate- I was on board after that. There was something about Nebraska I couldn't deny. I had a wonderful time on my visit there. Derek Brown was my host. I met all the guys and we had a good time. We also went to a couple recruiting parties. I was sold on Nebraska once I visited, with Derek showing me around, the ins and outs of Nebraska. Also, Tyrone Legette, and Doug Waddell.

Q: Good 'ol "Twinkie" Waddell?!

KM: Yep, Twink. I sat down and talked with them on my visit, and they just made me feel more comfortable. I ended up not even taking my visit to Arkansas because that next week I went and committed and signed the papers to Nebraska.

And in junior college not only did I redshirt and go through all that, but I lost my stepfather, too, so that really disrupted my family. So to overcome all of that and still have the options that I did, it made me realize that there really was something about football that I could partake in and get something out of.

Q: You had a lot of adversity before you even set foot on campus?

KM: Before I even came to Nebraska. Yes, not to mention a few odds and ends once I got there: the adjustment to not being a star player, a face in the crowd, and then working my way up to a starting position.

Q: What was the biggest adjustment?

KM: Becoming a leader at such a prestigious school; it wasn't that I couldn't handle it, but there were times I couldn't do some things that I needed to do. But before I graduated I was called on to help lead Nebraska to success.

Q: As far as leadership, what was the biggest contribution you made?

KM: Working in the outreach program, being a role model with the young kids. But also having the vision to being able to take care of my family at some point in time, all the things that we'd gone through before I even got there. I was really the man of the house. There were all the kids at home with the family: I had one sister and two step-brothers at the time, and all this was going on when I was 18-19 years old. I had to grow up faster than I probably wanted to, but by the grace of God I don't think I fared too bad. I didn't do a lot of things I really wanted to do, but I didn't fare too badly.

Q: You have some specific goals you wanted to achieve?

KM: Oh yeah, I couldn't wait for the day I'd be able to sign that pro contract, looking forward to the day I had something to give, do what I'm doing now, help build schools and go back in the communities that are less fortunate than some. Build them up to give them the resources both academically and athletically, as well.

Q: Do you recall your first few days on campus? Anything stand out?

KM: Just the support from the community. And the coaches, as well. There's a certain respect you attain when you put on that Husker red. I hadn't even played yet, and people knew who I was. I was forewarned that I'd get that type of respect. At some point in time how could you not succeed without that kind of support, you know? Sooner or later, you have to succeed with that much support. And it was somewhat similar to home, because we didn't have a pro team in South Carolina. We took to Clemson and South Carolina at the time. But the Cornhuskers, you know, Memorial Stadium being the 3rd largest city in Nebraska, that really sticks out a lot.

And Coach Osborne, I can't say enough about him. Over the years, he's a remarkable guy. When us guys talk now, we talk about how special Coach Osborne was when we came through Nebraska.

Q: Who do you keep in touch with the most from those days?

KM: I talk to John Reece and Lorenzo Brinkley, Toby Wright every now and again. I just recently started speaking with Twink again. I still have a lot of people I want to go through and reach out to them again.

Q: Tell Twink I said Hello, will you? He spent a lot of time on the Schwinn Airdynes. He should be riding the Tour de France by now, with all the hours he logged on those things!

KM: Yeah, he did!

Q: And who were your best friends?

KM: Donta Jones and Ed Stewart and Doug Waddell. I was roommates with Donta and Twink, when I first got there they kind of took me in and showed me around. Then I hung around with Lo Brinkley a lot, and then I ended up being roommates with Ed Stewart.

Q: So your position coach from the start was Coach Darlington?

KM: Coach Darlington, we didn't hit it off too well when I first got there. Just our communication and me understanding the game a little better than he thought I should have. We bumped heads. For a short amount of time there I was way immature and it started to get a little personal. Once I started to grow up a little bit and mature and I started to play more, we became more successful once we became a unit.

Q: Did he require something special of you guys?

KM: I just think of all the coaches I had previous to that, they always allowed me to play my game. At Nebraska with Coach Darlington there were some other things that we had to get through so we could understand each other, at first it was communication. Me, personally, it was the communication process. I was a little bit more of a young man than he thought I was, it was hard for me to understand where he was coming from. But like I said, once I matured and got my priorities in the right place I understood where he was coming from.

Q: Sort of bringing you up to speed?

KM: Pretty much. I never doubted I could play the game -I always knew I could play the game- because I was always the leader or a character on some teams I played on. It was just an adjustment to play Nebraska football and be successful.

Q: It's never as easy as it looks on Saturday, is it?

KM: No, it's not. No, it's not. (laughs) You don't just go out there and throw the football and catch it. We did accomplish a lot when I was there, though, and that felt good because I never liked for things not to be achieved on 'my watch,' you know? As a team or as an individual.

Q: Were you always a pretty goal-oriented guy?

KM: Yeah, somewhat. I set goals and worked my way toward them. There's always certain goals I set for myself, you know. I think once you do that success will come.

Q: Any other coaches you grew close with?

KM: Yeah, Coach Ron Brown. I got real close with Coach Brown because I wanted to switch positions. Because of the communication problems Coach Darlington and myself had, I wanted to go play receiver. (A couple of other guys did, too.) Coach Brown recruited me, he was my point of contact at Nebraska. I got closer to Coach Gill after I graduated. He gave me an opportunity to play some football after I graduated. I went to British Columbia, the BC Lions. I went up there for a mini-camp. I didn't make the team, but after sitting out a year it let me know that I could still play the game. I had a daughter at home that I had to be around and be supportive of growing up, so I didn't attack it like I wanted to. Sometimes I still wonder if I could have done a little bit more in that arena, but I'm still glad I had the opportunity that I did.

But sometimes it still haunts me, Paul, it's the question of, 'Why didn't I even get invited to the combine?' We had a Pro Day there at Nebraska and I ran a sub-4.4 40 yards for the pro scouts. And I knew they were interested and I still didn't get invited to the combine, to show some more skills on a higher level. That question, still today, kind of plagues me and bothers me. If I wasn't working with kids like I do I would probably go insane trying to figure out why. I just put my energy into the kids, help them understand that even though they may be gifted at some things, nothing is a sure thing. How do you make it through adversity, how can you make it through adversity, you know? How are you going to deal with it?

Q: Any special recollections of Coach Osborne?

KM: He was stellar guy, man. You know, one of the reasons I could run to him after we won the national championship and take him up and put him on my shoulder was because of the guy he was even before that, before he won the national championship. I always thought he was a classy, cool, laid-back kind of guy, because when he spoke he really and truly meant what he was saying. Through that, it not only helped him be successful in a lot of areas, but a lot of guys around him learned how to be successful. I, myself, being one. Coach Osborne had a lot to do with my growing up from a boy to a man, realizing the changes I had to make when I got there.

Coach Tenopir, Coach Solich, those guys, although they were coaching other positions they were laid back and straight forward as well. That staff there was very supportive in meeting my goals and achieving them.

Q: What stands out in your memory? Something you'll never forget?

KM: I think it was my second year, having the opportunity to play Florida State for the national championship. And when we went down to Miami we spoke to some kids there. That really stands out because a lot of those kids were, they needed some type of leadership, some type of role models. Myself, Mike Minter, Tyrone Williams, we all went and had a chance to talk to the kids. They had a BBQ for us, and I remember we had to hurry up and eat so we could talk to these kids. I was apprehensive at first, but when I got up to speak I started to realize that this is probably something outside of football that was going to have a grip on me for the rest of my life.

And then there was the loss when there was the 1:16 seconds left, where we had Florida State beaten. And knowing that we actually had them beat? That next season we were dedicated after that. The next year after every practice we had 1:16 put on the clock and went that much longer, after every practice, where we dedicated ourselves to finishing our Unfinished Business: "We've got unfinished business here, folks." That really sticks out, because that extra work we put in made all the difference in winning the national championship against Miami in Miami.

Q: You know Kareem, I was watching a tape of that game last night and it seemed you were everywhere during that game…

KM: You were right, Paul. My senior year, I played so much that 'How could you not know who Kareem Moss was?'

Q: You were on defense, you were on the punt team, the punt return team as the return man, right? You took some hits!

KM: Yeah, kickoff team. They tried to take me off a couple of the special teams because I would be strong safety. But we had a young guy as the backup and I felt that -even though he had the talent- that we might be shooting ourselves in the foot without my experience back there. He had the skills, but he was a young guy.

I had to play just about every down that year. It was just something I had to do. Earlier they did take me off those special teams, but when they did the opponents' stats started going up. So that had to change, and I couldn't not be on those teams that I had before. So I begged them to put me back on special teams. I just had a knack for the ball. A lot of times it may seem like I was out of position, but I was blessed with a little quickness, a little speed, to be where I needed to be before the ball got there.

Q: I remember one of those punt returns, it seemed like you were outnumbered by about 4 Miami guys yet still managed to squeeze out an extra ten yards of return. Do you remember that?

KM: Yeah, I remember breaking Ray Lewis' tackle. He was a sophomore at the time, but I think he was still second team All-American that year.

Q: Any major recollections of the Florida State game, Kareem?

KM: I didn't play much that year. That's the year I was going through a lot of things, not only at home, but at school. I was wondering if I could even play football at that level. I was standing on the sidelines but I was growing up. That year was really a learning year for me, because going into the fall of my junior year I was projected as a starting corner. I had to really earn that position in spring ball. I was having a good time out there, Paul. And the next fall I rested on my laurels a little bit, and a guy by the name of Tyrone Williams kinda snuck in there and did what he had to do and became the starter, so I had to do some more learning, you know. I don't like to say I lost my starting position, but I made sure to stay focused and the next year I came back and played every down and never came off the field. I was second team All-Conference AP and Coaches Poll my senior year, third on the team in tackles, second or third in interceptions. It just baffles me how I didn't get invited to the combine or Senior Bowl game, you know?

Q: If I recall, you made the final interception of the national championship game versus Miami, right? Jumping around like a madman, celebrating…

KM: Oh yeah, Miami talked so much trash in the press, in the paper and all that stuff. Before the game they were telling us how slow we were at defensive back and how we couldn't stick with them. And it kind of looked like that at the beginning, but once we buckled down and got into the flow of things we were the team to beat that night. We were in the top five in about every defensive category, so that night once we got in the flow there was nothing we felt that we couldn't do. Once I caught that interception (which I probably could have knocked down because they had the ball on like the 5 yard line), we could have gotten the ball back on the 5 yard line and probably scored again. (laughs) But I couldn't take a chance on somebody else catching it, so I just had to make that interception and make sure that nobody would take that ball from me until I got up. With some of the receivers running around out there, there was some pride involved there.

Q: They were talking a lot of smack out there, weren't they?

KM: Oh yeah, until they realized we were serious. After a while we earned their respect and they started calling us by our first names, as if we grew up together and we were childhood friends or something. It was like, 'Okay, now they're starting to respect us here.'

Q: Until then, I supposed they were calling you unrepeatable names? Saying impolite things about your mother?

KM: Oh yeah, unrepeatable stuff. That's right. All that.

Q: Now Kareem, you say your first fall was '92, right? Did you ever really buy into the slogans, "Unity, Belief, Respect", "Refuse to Lose"? Did you buy into that?

KM: Oh yeah, we did. And we also came up with a sub-slogan, too. We were walking around saying that we were "Tired of being stepped on." Because by us going to quite a few championship games we didn't feel we were getting the respect we deserved. So we used to walk around singing a little tune, "We're tired of being stepped on", like a song, a little chant. And that kind of brought us together even more, along with "Unity, Belief, Respect", "Unfinished Business" and so forth.

Q: No national media respect?

KM: Nobody respected us. It was like, "Hey, if we play Nebraska in the bowl game we'll win the national championship." That label was placed on us. I know Georgia Tech shared the national championship with Colorado one year. Another year we lost to Miami 22 to nothing. That was the year I committed to Nebraska. And I was sitting there watching the TV and scratching my head, thinking, 'That's the school I'm going to? Maybe that's what I'm going for, to help us win.'

Q: What do you think set those teams apart at the time?

KM: I think it was focusing on winning. Really focusing on winning. Coming together and doing it every game. One game at a time, of course, but winning every game. Because like I said, we had been successful in so many areas: academics, graduation rate, 9-10 games a season, going to a bowl game… all that was set up for us, so now what? "What do we need to do? We need to win the national championship game." I think we won the Big 8 4-5 years in a row. The only thing left to do now was win the national championship.

I think as a team -coaches and players- we broke it down and came together and really focused on how to do that. Some people in growing up and in business say, "I want to be successful", the question then is, "How do you become successful? How do you achieve what you set out to achieve?" We really focused in winning every game, one game at a time, and before you know it we played for the national championship. Two out of the three years I was there we played for a national championship. I think in my 3 years there we lost 4 games. And not to mention the dominance they carried on after I graduated, '97 and continuing on all those years.

One thing that factored into that was Coach Osborne and how he trusted in his staff to get the job done. One of my guys, to this day I love, is Coach McBride. A really hard-nosed, straight forward coach. I just really looked up to him. I don't think he knew it at the time, but I really latched onto him. Although we may have bumped heads a couple of times, I really saw him as a great male figure at the time.

Q: What was it like to bump heads with Charlie McBride?

KM: Oh, it was something else. If you're gonna step in the fire, you better be ready to put it out, because he's gonna keep you going.

Q: I've been told Charlie was a unique motivator. How did he do that?

KM: Yeah, man, he was. He'd get you ready for a game. Some of the speeches he would give us? Some of the things he would tell us, how "We have an opportunity to make history here, why don't we go out and do it?" And he had the chew in his mouth and he'd turn red and throw his arms down to his sides and scream at the top of his lungs. You just had to feel it. You just had to feel it. He was the Defensive Coordinator and he'd get us prepared early in the week. He was really good at getting us prepared early in the week, defensively. You knew you were gonna be ready that week. You'd be ready.

Q: Was there a specific mindset communicated?

KM: Basically, just handle your responsibilities, at full speed. If you mess up, just make sure you do it at full speed. You might be where you need to be even though you made a mistake. And really, just be a man about things.

And we used to get together and hang out with the guys all the time. I was the barber, I cut hair. So a lot of guys would come over to my house and get a haircut and we'd hang together and kind of got focusing on one common goal and make sure we could achieve it. Some of the guys who were there, like Calvin Jones and Toby Wright, Trev Alberts, Travis Hill, Kevin Raemakers? Some of those guys, I wish we could have won the national championship for those guys, and it wouldn't be Nebraska football without those guys. I hate that we didn't get them a ring. The least that we could do as a team, myself, Mike Minter, Barron Miles, Tyrone Williams, Tommie Frazier, Lawrence Phillips, all these guys, Ed Stewart, Terry Conneally, the least we could do is win it for all those past players. We really were playing for them because they set the tone for us in that era of the 90's, the dominance. Those guys had a lot to do with us dominating the 1990's.

Q: And Kareem, before you spoke about the focus of winning every game. I'm of the opinion that it's very difficult for a bunch of college kids to maintain focus for 11-12 consecutive weeks. There is usually a little bit of a letdown somewhere along the line. What would you say about that, and how would you say you kept your focus?

KM: Well, I would say the group of us would just hang out and really kind of create a small, off-field game plan to get over the obstacles. You know, at one time I got in trouble. I don't want to get into it, but a couple of my teammates were always around, and once we made up our minds it all of a sudden became a unit. There was a oneness. Nobody disrespected anybody for who they were, where they came from. We just kind of reached above all of that and really enjoyed where we were. We were all here for a reason. I can't stress that enough, the importance that God had played in our lives, me personally in overcoming so much adversity. And still going through it, I just had to kind of give it all up and let God help me figure out what was going on with me personally. I did the best that I could. I couldn't shy away from that. That's how I was raised. My mother did a good job of teaching me the importance of being spiritually grounded. And with all the adversity that was going on, that helped me understand a lot of things that were happening. And some of the things that didn't happen, too. It kept me grounded.

And we, as a team, resolved to party less and work more. Twinkie had me going to church quite a bit while he was there, Doug Waddell continued that on. It was a home away from home, being how he was from South Carolina, too. He helped me to understand how, as a young man, to be spiritually grounded.

Q: How did you become the team barber?

KM: Oh man, I picked that up in junior college. I was kind of picky, and all the guys in Kansas weren't very good barbers. And the ones that were around? I thought, 'I could cut my hair just as good.' So I cut it myself, cut my own hair. I messed it up a time or two, (laughs) but I caught on. Then I got a lot of practice and guys started knocking on my door.

Then by the time I got to Nebraska I had it all figured out, and both me and Toby Wright were doing it. Toby, that's how we ended up living together and came in together. He had two years and I had three to play. We still stay close. I learned a lot about football and a lot about life from him, he's a good friend.

Q: One of the guys told me that Toby really brought a physical, hitting mindset to the team…

KM: Yeah, we kind of fed off of Toby. I was kind of like that -a physical corner in high school and junior college, and I played safety from time to time, because of my physical attributes- but Toby came in and took it to another level. You know when you had the ball in Toby's vicinity that you were really gonna get hit, and might get hit very hard. We really fed off of that. That came natural to him. He went on and did the same thing at the next level. A lot of NFL guys may have learned some things from his being aggressive and so physical.

Q: Any games stand out to you, Kareem?

KM: Oh, my first interception in Lincoln was at Memorial Stadium and I wasn't yet a starter. I was a sophomore, I caught my first interception and they couldn't tackle me for some reason. I kept running into opposing players and they couldn't tackle me, all those people and all that energy, that sea of red, just energized me and it really sticks out.

Also, my first moment walking thorough the tunnel. I never knew that that many people could be at one place at one time. And I never knew what it sounded like. Gamecocks, you could get a couple ten thousand for a game. High school, junior college? But Nebraska is Nebraska. That's a different level. Nothing was comparable to that first time walking out of the tunnel. In fact, me and Toby were walking next to each other, walking two by two, it was me and Toby Wright. He said, "Hey, this is what we're here for." And we both even started crying a little bit. We'd realized that we were on the way to achieving our goals, going through that tunnel for the first time. It was an amazing feeling. It was something else. And as a visiting player, when you see that first guy coming out wearing the red? Well, it don't stop. We'd just keep it coming until the end of the fourth quarter, we'd never let up.

Q: Getting into your mind, how did you feed off the energy of the crowd?

KM: Well, it let me know how committed they were to Nebraska football. To make a long story short, how could we let our supporters, our fan base, down? They showed up every time we played. At the end of the day we're playing for ourselves, but with the support from the fan base, you just can't let the fans down. They looked up to us so much that it's a great responsibility, they supported us and we played the best that we can.

Q: Did you ever feel they expected too much?

KM: Once I learned the game of college football I never looked at it that way; I thought it just went hand in hand. And going back to that first interception, it was like playing that first game on TV. That was something else.

Q: Some folks back home might be watching?

KM: Oh yeah, the phone was blowing of the hook, Paul. Then I'd go home and you'd thought I'd made a movie or something, like I was from Hollywood or something. People would come up to me and say "You're Kareem Moss! You played on TV for Nebraska!" We'd had a couple of people came out of South Carolina and did a few things, but at that time it was something that I had never experienced in my life, and getting attention for doing something positive.

Q: Any memorable practice story?

KM: I think it was my first legitimate practice as a Blackshirt. That was something special. Because I had always heard of the Blackshirts and I was, 'Where did that come from? We're red and white, where did that come from?' Once I learned that Blackshirts were not only the starters, but the main source of the defense that the people were depending on to stand up and be counted. My world had just started. I was there three years, Paul, and I didn't get a Blackshirt until my senior year. I think when you finally step up and be a leader like I knew I could be, the coaches understood that I had matured, they didn't have to really worry about me as a player, for a young man that made a difference.

I just know that I had it on at practice, and the whole time before I got it I was like, 'I've gotta get a Blackshirt. I've gotta get a Blackshirt.' I'd never asked for anything, I wanted to feel as though I'd earned it. I never wanted anyone to give me anything. Anything but an opportunity. Then I'd earn it.

Q: Anything else that stands out that made a difference in your life?

KM: The bad was the incident that gained national attention for me and Tyrone (Williams), and I think Tyrone bore the brunt of that situation more than anybody else. I felt like I had a lot to do with it happening, but things just kind of got out of hand and we were kind of in the wrong place a the wrong time, and we all reacted the way we know how to react, the way we were somewhat raised on, how to protect and defend ourselves. Then the media account blew it way out of proportion. We just had to own up to it.

Like I said, by the grace of God Tyrone wasn't affected by it, to prevent him from being as successful as he wanted to be. I think it had to do with pride, with girls, with some of the guys, the Lincolnites. They had a problem with us coming into their community. Their girls liked us and so on and so forth, and when we'd go out there would always be a confrontation between us and some Lincolnites. It was unfortunate, you know, but those are some of the things you go through growing up. Being a young man and successful, there's a lot going on with being a player now in the communities that surrounds them, good and bad. Not everybody liked Nebraska football... (laughs)

Q: Especially if you're drawing all the good-looking girls away from them...

KM: That's something we didn't seek out. It just kind of happened, Paul! (laughs)

Q: And what were the perks, the privileges, of being a player?

KM: The attention you would get academically. Just walking around campus in your sweats, not to mention going back home. And like I said, not a lot of people from Spartanburg, S.C. played at Nebraska. And the tradition that Nebraska had, that ranked up there as one of the best colleges and universities in academics and athletics than anybody in the country. That N on your sweatsuit or your jacket or your helmet was really something special.

Q: What would you say you are most proud of?

KM: Really and truly, it was getting my degree. Had I not gotten my degree I don't know where I would be right now. Like I said, I didn't get the opportunity to make a few dollars and take care of my family like I wanted to. But being as I got my communications degree I still have so many more options and can be a leader and know I can achieve what I want.

Q: Anybody behind the scenes who mean a lot to you?

KM: There was a situation that happened, remember Scott Baldwin? Scott Baldwin. I had a chance to sit down with him and talk to him a few times. I didn't really know the details of what happened in his situation and how he ended up like he did, which was unfortunate, but seeing Scott walk around and run around like he did before this situation happened, it was the reason I went back to wearing the number 29. It was because of Scott Baldwin. Just being able to do the things that I could do, run around and compete, and then compare my situation to Scott Baldwin's was a major component inspiring me to do the things that I did, as far as success goes.

My first year I was number 29, then I wanted to wear the number I wore in high school, number 1. Mike Grant graduated, so I got my number 1 to kind of go back to, but then we had this freshman running back come in, a young man named Lawrence Phillips who was supposed to redshirt but we had a number of injuries at I-back so he didn't get to redshirt, so he had to play. And I decided to go back to my number 29 in honor of Scotty, and that number worked just fine for me. I said, 'Lawrence, you can have number one. Scotty's number is calling.'

And I wish I could have been a little closer to him and helped him through some of his issues he was dealing with, you know? Sometimes you take things from your past and you're thrown into situations where you don't know how to deal with things. I wish I could have been there to help him more. Had he been able to handle some of the adversity he'd been through, I think he would have been much better off. I love Lawrence and I always wish him well and keep him in my prayers.

And then Tommie Frazier, there's another guy who overcomes adversity. Tommie almost died, and to see him in that hospital in that bed with those tubes going through him and into his heart, it was all so impossible. It was a reminder of just how good I had things, of how you never know when you may go down. It was simple blood clot in his leg -which almost caused his life to end- and in that same year having him come back and contribute to winning that national championship? I have to call him a super man for God. I've gotta give it to him. And then to come back and keep a level head and win another after that when they beat Florida? To come back after that happened?! I mean, I broke my leg and came back, but to almost die? He looked so helpless, but then he bounced back that same year and contributed to us winning. It was really hard to look at him. From being used to seeing him running up and down the field, then seeing him so motionless and immobile was scary. It was a scary moment for me, for one of my teammates. I was scared for him, but I never doubted he'd really be alright. I did doubt whether he'd be able to play football again. But that proved it right there when he came back to play another season.

And you can't forget Matt Turman, after Brook Berringer got hurt. Brook was a wonderful guy as well, I can't end without saying a few things about Brook, how beautiful he was helping us win the national championship. I can say that of all the years seeing Nebraska football and following it, that we were one of the teams that touched on pretty much every aspect of life to overcome and win a national championship. I would say that '94 team was the best, just being able to deal with life and do what it did.

Q: Anything you wish you could do over, better, differently?

KM: I would say it happened just like it was supposed to, because now I'm the man who knows that I am where God wants me to be. Yes and No, Paul, (laughs) but I worked hard and continue to work hard to make something better for someone else.

Q: Last question. Anything we haven't touched on that played a huge part in the success you guys had?

KM: Let me think about that. (pregnant pause) I think it was the confidence we developed and the tradition that we had to sustain before we even won the national championship. All the years before us were a major component in us being successful. I want to give credit to all the guys who came before us, even as far back as those '70 and '71 teams who won those championships. They were my role models at Nebraska because they had accomplished a feat that nobody else had done.

I remember having quite few conversations with Johnny Rodgers. There was a time when I was there and he was working on a degree, too. He was my mentor. We'd sit down quite a few times and talk about past, present and future endeavors. That, and just wanting to be the first team to win the national championship with Coach Osborne.

End conversation.

That settles it. I don't care if I have to hop a railcar to Hoboken, I promise you that I must and I will search out and locate Toby Wright for this project. It amazes me the difference his positive peer influence had on these guys. You've heard it before: in some way, somehow, Toby Wright brought a uniquely savage art to his Rover position and found ways to make actions speak louder than any words. Also, there was Kareem's mention of his friendship with former Husker Running Back Scotty Baldwin, a sad and tragic story in its own right, and the sway that relationship held. Evoking the age-old dramatic arc of securing victory in memory of a fallen teammate —think "win one for the Gipper" here - seeing a paralyzed Scotty in his wheelchair or the immobilized Tommie Frazier confined to his hospital bed likely had a profound effect on most of those young men, because the vision of an impaired peer etched into their young, impressionable minds served as a glaring reminder of how limited a time they had to shine in the spotlight of football Saturdays. It created a personal and a collective sense of purpose and urgency, engendering the notion of redeeming the time. Then you add the shared life lessons of Johnny Rodgers, a former Nebraska Heisman Trophy winner one score-removed from the college game, and it's highly likely these brushes with legacy had a unique ability to rouse the passions.

I guess another term that stuck out to me would be the word 'community.' Maybe even 'family.' Can you imagine these guys hanging around an apartment or dorm room receiving haircuts, watching Sports Center on TV, talking about their goals, their focus, next Saturday's opponent, encouraging and exhorting one another, maybe even critiquing that day's practice? Surely there was a lot of joking going around, too, but it's become apparent to me that these guys had reached the edge of the map as far as what Nebraska Football had achieved. And in doing so, their pride and their consciences were pricked, for they could either continue to coast along and meet the standard of recent 9-win teams, just falling short of the gold ring, or they could push the envelope and grasp, even embrace, "the opportunity to make history." The holy scriptures state that "He has also set eternity in the hearts of men," and the result of this divine knowledge is the notion that deeds and accomplishments live on in our stead long after we have passed. This was an interplay of tradition and legacy.

Finally, I think Kareem's maturation process, like so many others', was pivotal. For all the recruitniks' ballyhoo and bluster, there is the somewhat immeasurable factor in every kid at every school playing every position, which is the ability to sacrifice ego and 'get with the program.' It was not an easy nor a pleasurable exercise to be under the tutelage of George Darlington, as others have already attested. George had a 'my way or the highway' mentality, and unless you were traveling on his bus you might as well be on the roadside thumbing it. Many student/athletes in the defensive backfield gave the thought of jumping onto another bus -i.e. Ron Brown's and his receivers- serious consideration. But in the end, with one more year of seasoning, of adjusting, of learning, of contorting themselves and readjusting their mental image and how they fit in the scheme of things, their perseverance finally paid off. In spades.

Notable quote #2:
Kareem Moss on fan support in Memorial Stadium: "Nothing was comparable to that first time walking out of the tunnel. In fact, me and Toby were walking next to each other, walking two by two, it was me and Toby Wright. He said, "Hey, this is what we're here for." And we both even started crying a little bit."

Remember when life's path is steep to keep your mind even.

Horace, *Odes. Book II*

Matt Vrzal knows a little something about possessing the 'right mix', whether that mix be associated with barstool patrons or pizza pies... or even football, for that matter. A character with sly wit and personality in spades, I had a blast tracking him down for a look into the Husker kitchen of old. Joining the Nebraska squad as it was breaking out of its 1990 bear market, his prudent investment of time, money, sweat and blood at the age of 18 years paid off handsomely in the student-athlete experience, and he now continues as an entrepreneur with Piezan's Pizzeria at 15619 West Center Road in Omaha.

'Verz', as he is often affectionately called, brought the qualities of energy, discipline, integrity, and instinct –not to mention humor- to the Cornhusker squads back in the day. And let's face it, the more varied the toppings, the better the eating. Let's feast upon his reminiscences as he puts the tomato sauce where his mouth is.

Notable Quote#1:
"(Bryan) Bailey said, "Well, you're no longer national champs." And we're like, "What do you mean? Yes we are." And he's like, "Nope. It's over. Now you're trying to *defend* your national championship. This is a new deal." It may not have registered as much as the time-on-the-clock thing, but we thought at that moment, "Hey, he's *right!* We're *not* anymore. He's right!""

Matt Vrzal

Walk-on, Center, Grand Island, Nebraska
Where are they now? Omaha, Nebraska, Entrepreneur

Question: Let me ask you, Matt: when was your first fall camp?

Matt Vrzal: Fall of '92.

Q: What was your first impression of those first days?

MV: Well, I walked-on. And it's actually documented in my high school yearbook where a friend wrote, "I don't know why someone would go to college and pay to play football." (laughs) It was probably one of the best, most initially intimidating things I'd ever been a part of, because for all my life, it was all I knew: from Saturdays to that really long stretch of bowl heartbreaks.
I remember my father and watching the '84 Orange Bowl game at a friend's house. Everybody was having a good time and my old man went to grab an adult beverage. He sat down without opening it and they were getting ready to go for two, and he said, "We got this, we're gonna win. All these years of hard work is gonna pay off." Then Turner Gill rolls out and throws the ball and it gets tipped and gets knocked down. And an unopened can of beer -my father, in his hand- crushed it! There was beer shooting out, and at the time I was sitting there and thought, 'Wow!' Then later on when I was in high school and I thought I was really strong I tried doing it with a can of Coke, and I couldn't do it! I thought, 'If it means that much to people, it must really be special. I want to be a part of that and play whatever role I can play.' It was, at the beginning, unbelievably intimidating, but by the end I could say it will be like my home for the rest of my life.

Q: Any of the coaches make an impression on you right away?

MV: I had gone to the football camps so I had met a lot of the coaches and knew them. And maybe it's my smart aleck nature, but Boyd (Epley) was always a trip to me. Because he was always worried about Boyd. I don't know how he was to work with, but he was always like Jimmy Johnson: not a hair out of place. (laughs) And he was always flexing. I walked by him one day in the weightroom and said 'Do you ever breathe? Do you ever fully exhale and just let it out?' He just smiled and said, "Verz, when you're in as good a shape as I am, it never goes out." I was like 'O-kayyy....' (laughs)

And Coach Osborne, it took me probably a year. I knew what color his shoes were, but finally after about a year I could tell you what color his eyes were. We would meet while coming down the same hallway and I'd just look at his feet. And the guy was amazing: he knows your name, he knows everybody's name. He's like "Verz?" and I'm like, 'Adidas size 11, how are you doing?' (laughs) It was just nice to be in the presence of him.

Q: Any teammates you befriended right away?

MV: You know, for some reason, everybody for the most part -and I mean nothing bad, because we knew Tommie was kind of on a different level- but everybody in our recruiting class kind of clicked. Ben Rutz was a great buddy of mine right out of the gate, (Chris) Dishman, (Kory) Mikos, (Adam) Treu, (Jeff) Ogard, (Scott) Saltsman, we kind of had that bond. We knew by looking at each other that we weren't the most athletic guys around, but were gonna have some fun and beat some people and win some games. It was just great camaraderie.

And I was lucky I had Phil Ellis, who I played with at Grand Island, he kind of showed me the ropes. The first time I met Aaron Graham I thought he was as dick. He was just Graham. But once you get to know him, he's fine. I still talk to a lot of those guys. I often block out an hour a day and just talk to those guys: Clinton Childs, Damon Benning, Johnny Vedral.

Q: So you show up in '92 and there was no more freshman team. Were you working with Milt from the get go?

MV: Yep. Him and Coach Young, yeah.

Q: Can you describe that experience? Your impressions of the coaches?

MV: Well, when I came in I got to know Ogard pretty well, and Dishman and Mikos, (because we played together in the Shrine Bowl), and when we came in we had freshman two-a-days before all the older guys came in. And for some reason the system Milt had devised just clicked with me. We'd put three or four plays in every day, and I would have them ready to go before the practice started. And he'd ask what the center does and I'd know. And then he'd ask what the guard does and I'd know. So that made me feel good. The system wasn't gonna be so confusing to me that I couldn't keep up, but his style and his demeanor about things, it was just what I was used to coming from high school where Ken Fischer was my high school coach. So I knew it was discipline, it was "Yes, Sir. No Sir.", it was "hustle to everything and do the best you can all the time." So in that aspect it worked out well. And having a great group of guys made it all that more fun.

Q: What about Coach Tenopir's coaching style?

MV: He was intense. You would go through some classroom stuff and you would find out what you were going over that day in practice, what plays you were gonna install, and it was just technique. And every day you knew what you were gonna do. In the end, that footwork, it really paid off. I go on (Matt) Hoskinson and (Joel) Makovicka's radio show every now and then, and one week a guy called in and said "No offense, but you guys were never in that really great of shape." And I said, "I was in shape!" (laughs) He was saying we were fat, and I was, "Hey, we were fat, but we had really good feet, we were strong, and we could move. At the end of the day an offensive lineman only has to be fast for 10 yards. If we're having to run 30, 40, 50 yards we've gone way too far, other than to celebrate. (laughs) You better be high-fiving somebody." You learned technique and the technique translated into the games.

The whole staff was just so great at preparing for the game. You'd get to a game and there wouldn't be anything that you hadn't seen multiple times in practice. The amount of preparation that the coaches put in, we just had supreme confidence going into the games, especially the '95 team. I was a second teamer, but there were games where we were pretty sure and said, "Hey, let's start the second team and go at it. We can win."

Q: I heard there was a time where the second string started the second half while a bunch of the starting offensive linemen bought some hotdogs and were eating them on the sideline?

MV: Yeah, that was Weigert. That was against Pacific. That was a Zach-ism, they played in the first series of the second half. But yes, he was trying to buy hotdogs. (laughs)

Q: What about Coach Young?

MV: If ever there were two polar opposites from a personal demeanor standpoint, there was Coach Tenopir and Coach Young. Coach Young was just so laid back and talked so slow and quiet. You know, if you got him fired up you knew something was really, really wrong. But again, another guy -with the passing schemes that we ran?- he knew them inside and out. It was good because with lineman, you have so many linemen, you try to get everybody reps, and it was nice to have a pass station and a run station, even in your individual sessions. So half would go with both coaches and you would learn both sides. Just the attention to detail: new blitz packages, new personnel, Coach Young probably knew personnel better than anybody. Coach Young was just so laid back (laughs) and had that slow way of talking. Despite those mannerisms he was a great coach.

Q: Were you a town kid or farm kid?

MV: I lived in town in Grand Island. My grandma owned farm up by Norfolk, in fact she still does.

Q: What about the grading, the feedback process?

MV: Okay, there was 1 point for the mental aspect of the game, "Did you do your assignment correctly?" There was one point for the physical part, "Did you execute the block as determined?" And that was it. A 2 point grading scale. If you didn't do any of them you got a zero, if you knew where you were going but didn't get there you got a one, if you did them both well you got a two. That's how it went. Then you have an average. And an average for the game was a 1.98, something close to that. Then he'd (Tenopir) tally pancakes in another column. Those were a separate monster.

Q: Sort of like a cherry on top?

MV: Yeah, you had your overall score, then you had your pancake total.

Q: Were there any particular types of motivational methods? Rah-rah? Or just job focused?

MV: Usually they'd do that when you went through your warm ups, they'd bring you up and Coach would say, "I love all of 'ya." Then the last thing they'd say was, "The hay's in the barn." Essentially, "Let's go to work now. Let's just go do it." With that group of guys it was just a mentality, a mindset. We knew what we did in practice, we knew we probably worked harder than anybody else we played against. You could sit there and worry about it, and 'Oh gosh, did we do everything to get ready?' But with our staff, to have that piece of mind, you knew your position, you knew they didn't outwork us, they didn't out-game plan us. They might have more talent than us, but they wouldn't beat us.

Q: Any other motivations for you or for your teammates of the time? I know its hard staying 'up' for a whole season, week after week...

MV: For me, being a Nebraska kid and getting a chance to kind of know, just to maybe look at it instead of, "Hey, we won. We one the game again." I'd always talk to the guys from Indiana, Oklahoma, Texas, wherever. I'd say, 'Hey, look at the people, look at the fans...' I remember my parents and Wistrom's parents tailgated together, and we'd walk over to the tailgate and I'd say, 'Look at the people. Look what it's done for these people. Look outside yourself and just think about it: This is Nebraska, this is important to the people. This is all we have. We don't have pro teams, we don't have major metropolises. We have this, and you guys are part of the reason this state has so much pride in itself.' At the end of the day we hang our hat on a few things, and one is Nebraska football. And I think a lot of the Nebraska guys had the same mentality, just that sense of pride."We're winning, people feel pretty good about themselves." Sometimes you'd have 40,000 people at an away game, like at Kansas one time. 80% of the people were Nebraska people. That was part of the reason we were able to win so many games, that pride factor it brought to the people.

Q: So Matt, what was your last game?

MV: Virginia Tech, Orange Bowl.'97 Orange Bowl to the '96 season.

Q: Had it not been for the flu virus versus Texas for the Big 12 Championship game, how would you have rated that '96 team compared to the previous two?

MV: I think the one thing that my class probably did lack was a vocal leader. You had a lot of guys like Jared Tomich, who would always lead by example. He was gonna go out and he knew, we knew that he was gonna get double-teamed, but we also knew it was gonna free up Wistrom, it was gonna free up Kelsay, it was gonna free up Jason Peter. So maybe that one vocal leader, that one guy you could look at. (And I'm not calling out Jared or anything like that, don't get me wrong. That wasn't his demeanor.) But we just didn't have that Christian Peter who was going to get up and give a rah-rah speech before the game. You know, maybe that. That would have been what was lacking.

Q: Anything about developing team unity? What stands out to you?

MV: You know, the big thing for me that at times gets overlooked? You had a lot of Nebraska guys. And maybe not even that, but Nebraska fans. You can get guys from out of state and you'd ask them, 'Why did you come here?', and they'd say, "We had a great tradition, great history." I'd say, 'But did you ever cheer for the team?' "Uh-uh, no, it's not my area." But you had those Midwestern guys. The majority of the Pipeline -outside of Stai- were Nebraska/Midwestern kids. (And you pretty much imported your skill positions, something Nebraska just has to do because Nebraska high school just doesn't have that speed yet.) But the guys in the machine were Nebraska kids. On the defensive side you had Phil Ellis at linebacker, and Mike Anderson before him.

It was almost a mentality for us where we just said, "That's enough," for those 7 or 8 years we'd watch our team's butts get kicked in the bowl games, "We're gonna win the thing." It was just that mentality. As I said before, everybody was on that page. It was just that feeling like we all said, "Hey, that's enough. We have the best staff, we have the best work ethic, we have the best fans. Let's do it. No more being scared." And the very scary part about it was the '93 Orange Bowl against Florida State, there are a lot of things that should have turned out differently in that game. And then the transition in '96, with Scott Frost taking over at quarterback? We had a couple of freak things happen that really prevented us from just dominating. But the guys that got it all started, the Mike Andersons, the John Parrellas, the Kevin Raemakers, we owe a lot to those guys. They taught us how it needed to happen.

Q: Were those guys vocal about it?

MV: Oh yeah. Raemakers and Parrella, at some point in my life I hope I'm able to financially do it, I want to get those guys a ring made. Because those guys are the ones that really, really laid the groundwork. Of course, Nebraska has had the tradition forever, but they were focused on getting to that title game, and then, "Hey, we're gonna win them. We're going to make everyone pay on these teams, and they're gonna know that they played a football game." And that was a great thing for me. We had a bunch of guys who bought in, and we were dumb enough to be dangerous, was about it. (laughs) You just went about your business, and then you brought in your 'freak' talent. Guys like Wistrom and the Peter brothers, and Chris Dishman (a phenomenal college player), and Aaron Graham showed up, Stai, Weigert (a homegrown kid), Joel Wilks (a kid that probably shouldn't have been playing but worked his way into it). He'd eat 7,000 calories a day to get up to 275 lbs. If he told you he weighed an ounce more than that he was lying. (laughs) You had that where it was just right for us, it all kind of blended. You had your Alpha as Coach Osborne and everybody bought into that.

Q: Tell me more about Coach Osborne. You get older and you get more comfortable talking to him, what stands out now?

MV: I'm still not comfortable talking to him. (laughs) Coach is Coach. At the end of the day, what makes him the man that he is? He's happy for us, that we had success on the field. And he's proud of us for the success we had off the field.

I owned some bars in Lincoln for awhile, then I got out of the business and ran into Coach. I was barely a week out of it and he said, "Verz, that's a good move. I'm sure that you're gonna pursue a respectable line of work." (laughs) And I said, 'Coach, restaurants are fun, but people like to go to bars and enjoy themselves. And it's not all just breaking up knock-down, drunken brawls. It's an exciting atmosphere.' And he said, "It's just good to see you move on in your life." (laughs)

Q: So you owned a few bars?

MV: Yeah, I had Lazzari's Pizza. And remember Herm's?

Q: "Coldest Beer In Town"?

MV: Yeah, we renamed that one "The Bar." And the Lizard Lounge? Bought that one and renamed it "Downtown." And then we had Sidetracks. (The two in the middle were more just fun and games for us.) Kids would be in the bar and they would call their friends and try to tell them where they were. They'd say, "Where are you at?," and they'd say, "The Bar!" And you could hear them say, "Yeah, I know that, but which one?" And they'd say "I'm at The Bar!" (laughs) As you know "O" Street is referred to as downtown, so you'd hear conversations about that, too. "Where are you?" "Downtown." "I know, but what bar?" "That's what I'm saying, I'm at Downtown!" (laughs) Those were just funny names that when it was 12:30 at night and I was grouchy and tired, I could just laugh.

Q: (laughing) Getting back to the teams, what do you think separated the teams from others of their time?

MV: Every team kind of had their special players. You know, we were lucky enough to have Tommie, Lawrence, Ahman. Everybody had that… it was just the "it" factor. The '83 team, they had it, but it just wasn't in the cards for them, there was something wrong with the universe that year. But for us everything just clicked.

More than anything it was respect for everybody. It wasn't like everybody liked everyone, but there was respect, kind of like big brother, little brother. You know, "I can pick on them, but you can't pick on them." And it didn't matter, black, white, purple, yellow.

Q: Any particular recollections of that brotherhood, that unity?

MV: Here's one for you. For the holidays -my redshirt year, Thanksgiving- some of the guys, because they closed the dorms they sometimes put the guys in hotels. One year I took the Peter boys, Scotty Saltsman, Ben Rutz, and (Ryan) Twig (Terwilliger) (because he lived way out west) they became a part of my family. (Christmases, too, when we could, because we had an early Christmas. Oh yeah, and Larry Townsend. Big Larry Townsend! When he showed up my grandma looked at him and said, "Uh Oh, we're gonna need more food.") (laughs) But yeah, stuff like that was a great example of what kind of family we had. The great bonds, the buddies that you cared about, you don't want them by themselves. As we moved on in college we rented houses, and all the guys came over to the house for early Christmas and Thanksgiving and my Mom and Grandma and my Aunt would come over to our house and cook. Those are the things outside the game that bond you. All the blood, sweat and tears on the field really bond you as a team, but those off the field things are sometimes just as important, the friendships and brotherhood and stuff like that. Clint Finley still calls me every Thanksgiving and asks -us bohonks (Bohemian's) call them rolls, but they're really biscuits- he says, "Hey, can I get some of your Grandma's biscuits?" (laughs)

Q: Any memorable play stand out for you, Matt?

MV: You really want me to do this, Paul? From a team aspect, the '94 triple zeros on the scoreboard was unbelievable for me. From the gut wrenching year before that we had in '93 when that clock went to zero? Wow, what a feeling! And that Miami team ended up having 7 or 8 Pro-Bowlers from that team that we beat that year, but the next year when that clock read triple zero and we were ahead and won the national championship, that was probably the moment of all moments.

From a personal aspect, for me it was when we were playing Arizona State and I was (Aaron) Graham's backup. It's second, third quarter -and I didn't play a whole bunch, enough to say I was a player and that made me proud- but not enough to say that I really made that much of a difference, really. Well, Graham comes sprinting off the field screaming, "My helmet's broke! My helmet's broke!" So Coach Young sends me in the game. And we had worked this freaking play every time in practice and it was Shotgun 36 Trap. What happened was, the center snaps the ball directly to the running back and the quarterback misses it. (And I had this bad habit of launching the ball over the quarterback's head and the running back's head, okay?) So I'm in and Tommie doesn't know I'm in, and he calls the play and looks down and sees it's me and says, "Verz, you got this?" And I'm, 'I got it.' He goes, "I can call timeout." And I'm like, 'No, don't call timeout! I've got it.' So I get in my stance and I'm like, 'Okay…' (Now, I've got to keep my rear end low for this snap. You had to keep your butt low to keep the ball low.) So it looks on the field that my rear end is so low that it's only an inch above the heals of my shoes. It looks like I'm on the toilet, and if that's not the truth, Paul, I'll kiss your rear end and like it. (laughs) Anyway, I snap this thing and it's just a little bit high, but Ahman grabs it. And they blitz right into it, somehow. I took my step –really, the fastest block I've ever had- I pick the noseguard off and knock him into the blitzing linebacker and Ahman goes for 70-something yards for a touchdown.

And on the field, (we had to watch it on film about 800 times) but Ahman takes off and he's going (and I had my block, and the defensive lineman is down and the linebacker's down), and then I take off. I started chasing him. I was running and celebrating and having a great time, and we get into the endzone and I can't believe he caught it. And later, with Coach Tenopir in the film room, he goes "Verz, you are really kind of fast! (laughs) If you look here, Ahman is ten yards ahead of you and you haven't even started running yet. (And we watched this so many times) You're giving him a 10 yard lead. Ahman is 20 yards ahead of you, and then you take off." Then as the film goes on, now it's only 18 yards, now it's only 15 yards, now it's only twelve yards from catching him. And he's like "You are actually catching Ahman Green!" (laughs) Everybody is laughing and hooting and hollering. So I'm laughing, too. It was funny. Well, I get into the endzone and Coach is like, "Now, here's where it gets scary." And I'm thinking, 'Oh no,' (because I knew what I did). So Ahman literally gets to the endzone and turns around and I'm like right there! He turns around and jumps up and I catch him. And I didn't think he was going to jump up, and he kind of almost knocks me over.

It ended up on the cover of Huskers Illustrated that week. We beat them like 77 to 14. Then Lance Brown did that backflip. They were all mad because they thought we ran up the score. Matt Turman did his job: he checked out of an audible that he saw. Lance Brown saw it too and ran the right route and Turman hit him on a post route and he scored. Then like a doofus Lance Brown does a backflip.

Q: After that game, I think I saw a T-shirt in the Nebraska Bookstore saying, "If you don't like us running up the score…get a defense."

MV: Yeah. And Graham was always gone on Friday, which was prep practice, and I had to run with all the ones. It was raining and we had to hurry up and Brook was the quarterback, and I just launched it over his head. And Brook's like 6'5" -it's impossible to launch it over his head. But I did it. Coach Tenopir was gone, so the film session the next day we went to watch with Coach Osborne… and the clock just couldn't go fast enough. I was like "Come on, clock! Just keep going. Go fast so we can get out of here before we get to that play!" Well, we didn't. And we get to that clip and I'm thinking, 'I am so screwed.' So it's paused right at the height of Brook's jump and the ball is just sailing over his head and his reach and Coach Osborne goes "Verz, what happened there?" I was like, 'Coach, it was my fault. Nobody to blame, I didn't do everything correctly. I got excited when I saw the blitz I had to pick up. I didn't panic, and I just wanted to get over there fast enough. But I didn't take care of my first responsibility to get the ball to the quarterback. There's nobody else to blame but me.' And then he stopped the film. He didn't just pause it. He stopped it.

And Tommie turns around to me and says, "Oh, you're done." So I was like 'Oh man, they're gonna kick me off the team….I am outta here.' And Coach Osborne says, "Verz, I've been coaching for a long time…" and I was like 'Oh, my God, please let this slide…?', and he goes, "I have never had anyone give me an answer to a question like that." And I look at Aaron Taylor and I'm thinking, 'This could be good or this could be bad.' Coach Osborne goes, "You could have blamed that on the wet ball, on the nose guard (who'd jumped offsides on the play, but he got back), you could have blamed it on any number of things, but you didn't. You just admitted what you did wrong," and then he just stopped…

and went on to the next play on the film. I look over at Dishman and I ask, 'What the hell was that? Was it good or bad?' And Dishman says, "I think that's good, but I'd ask him later." (laughs) But then Coach did say, 'Vrzal, that's probably one of the best answers I've had in my coaching career.'

Q: And is there anything you wish you could do over, better, differently?

MV: Um, this is just more a psychoanalysis of myself, but for me it would be to realize that, being a lot healthier now instead of being just a real big, strong guy, to maybe realize that I was good enough to be there. Because there's always the doubt in your mind, 'Are you good enough to be here? Are you good enough to play?' In my situation, you've got guys with a scholarship in front of you, but you get your shot and try to work your way up.

And me? I was a walk-on for a reason. And I should have realized that I did have the talent, but I think that year in '96, my senior year, I should have been starting. I still have that in my own mind. I realize the situation, if I had more confidence in myself I could have been the starter. Let me retract, I should have been the starter. I knew the system, I knew I had to be in better shape, and when I got into camp I realized I wasn't. That maybe might have alleviated some of the panic, because we had so many great linemen. And was I better than Chris Dishman? No. Was I better than John Zatechka? No. Was I better than Aaron Taylor? No. Was I better than Adam Treu? No. But you know, maybe you don't have that knee-jerk reaction where you move Taylor to center and Dish to guard, and then you've got everybody out of position. But if I do better for myself, then you have a three tackle rotation, three guard rotation, and a two center rotation. And that was my thing, I was battling some inferiority stuff in my own mind. We started spring ball and it was, "Let's move Taylor to center." I don't hold anything against anybody, it was just that I let myself down in that aspect, and that's so hard to deal with most days. I should have been more prepared. We shouldn't have needed that option.

Q: What would you pin that on? The weightroom & staff?

MV: No, not the weightroom. I was always in there and did well. If it wasn't for a broken strap on the hang clean I would have been a winner on the Performance Index Platform.

Q: Aw, really?!

MV: Yeah, I broke a strap on my last rep. I had one side racked and the other side was on the ground. Dave looked at me and he goes, "Dude, I am so sorry. That was the one that would have put you at 500 points for the Performance Index." Maybe I'm not looking at it correctly, either, though. I wasn't the fastest guy. I thought I had decent feet, but man, we just had so much talent.

Q: Any thoughts on those slogans? What did you guys think about those? Did you buy into them or think they were hokey?

MV: It wasn't something that you woke up every morning and go like, "Unfinished Business, let's get it going." But it helped. The thing I liked the most was when summer conditioning from '93 going into '94, the amount of time being put on the clock. That was a good one. I liked that one.

But you know, Bryan Bailey, when we won '94 and were in summer conditioning going into '95, we always liked to flip him crap and give each other a hard time. Well, Bailey said, "Well, you're no longer national champs." And we're like, "What do you mean? Yes we are." And he's like, "Nope. It's over. Now you're trying to defend your national championship. This is a new deal." It may not have registered as much as the time on the clock thing, but we thought at that moment, "Hey, he's right! We're not anymore. He's right. Now it's time to go..." That wasn't necessarily a motivating factor, but a lot of guys, it registered with them.

And those '95 guys -I think there were a lot of them- they won't say it, but they wanted to show everyone that "Hey, there's a lot of that '94 team that's gone, but a lot of the parts that made that work are still here." And anybody, anywhere, I will come out and tell anybody, that '95 team would have just pounded any team that USC had, any OU team from back in the day, any Notre Dame team that ever existed. You were looking at a team whose closest game they had was a 14 point game, and that was due to the fact that Washington State, I believe, scoring a touchdown with their first team offense on our third team defense. That turned it into a 14 point game. Other than that, nobody was close. That Florida team had so much speed, so much talent.

I remember them after that game. They did their share of running their mouth before: "We're so good, we shouldn't even be on the same field with Nebraska. Why are we even here? They should just give us the national title," blah, blah, blah down the line. Well, if you poke a bear with a stick long enough, that bear's gonna come up and bite you. I tell you what, after that game there was a different tone. Walking off the field they were like, "Hey, you guys are the real deal. You are as advertised. We don't belong on your field."

Q: Anything else about the process, team building, that stands out that drove the team. You said Bailey made that comment. Wasn't he in charge of working with the O line at that time? Was he you guys' personal trainer?

MV: He just floated around. He was such a great guy. All you guys in the weightroom were such great guys. Mike Arthur, too. And Boyd was flexing and never breathing, though he just got under everybody's skin. (laughs) But you kind of have to have that figure. You'd be working out and here would come Boyd, and you'd be like, 'Boyd, just go back to your office.' (laughs) We'd test out and he'd come over and act like he was the one that trained you all the time, then he'd go back in his office. We knew who really did it. (laughs) That was more of the linemens' view of Boyd. (laughs)

And another thing: fighting in practice, to me, always brought everyone together. Remember, for a fight to happen you have to have two people who deeply care about the situation or the circumstance of what has happened. They have that passion about that. If you have somebody come to blows there is a reason: You're either getting beat or beating the other guy. And one, he doesn't like getting beat, and two, he doesn't think it should happen.

And there were times when it was just miserable: that time after the final exams and before you left for the bowl game, when there was nothing going on except practice. And you'd see those fucking MUSCO lighting trucks come in. Then you were like, 'Crap!' and you know since they've got lights out there you're gonna be practicing 'til like 6, 7 o'clock.

And I recall the times we went to live one-on-ones, it was my sophomore year. I'm Aaron Graham's backup, and away we go... "Goal line! Ones against ones!" And I'm thinking, 'This is a bad idea, there is some tension in the air. It's palpable. This is not good.' So here we go. Somebody had to come out, and Steve Volin comes in. Now, when you pit Christian Peter against Steve Volin, it's a defensive win. But the more you get into offensive line play the more you realize one thing: the beauty of the 'cut block'. It's an unwritten rule when you're going one-on-one's, you don't 'cut' people. So they toss the ball and, well, Volin cut's Christian. And I'm watching this as a backup and I'm saying, 'Uh oh, this is not good. Volin is not going to like the repercussions of this.' So Christian shoves his head in the ground.

(That's the thing about Christian, if you do it one time he'll let you get a way with it, but if you do it again, "We're gonna have a problem.") So he shoves his head in the ground, "You fat SOB, don't you cut me!" Bow, wow, wow, and so on. So we got back to the huddle and Coach Tenopir, with his ornery demeanor, has his dander up because the toss didn't work too well. And he says, "We're gonna run that again." So here comes Volin up to the line, and I'm like, 'Volin, don't do it. Don't do it…'

And he did it. He cuts Christian again. Christian, for as big as he was, was so ungodly quick. So as Volin cuts him Christian already has him shoved into the turf, his hand on his facemask, lifting his helmet up on his head so he can get the proper punching angle. He starts firing jabs into Volin's face! Well, Graham sees this and he goes and hits Christian! Well, then Jason's radar goes off and says, "My brother is being hit. I've got to go help.", and here comes Jason into the mess! And then Stai sees this and jumps in! Then Tomich and Wistrom see the Peter brothers getting picked on, and they go psycho! So this thing is literally squared off! Linebackers have running backs, corners have wide receivers, safeties have tight ends, a couple of guys that are backups are pushing each other. (laughs) It was just bedlam. There was a fight everywhere. And Coach Osborne is blowing his whistle as loud as he can to save his life and nothing is happening. (laughs) You usually hear the whistle and you stop it, you know? Well, he keeps blowing that whistle and nothing is happening, so he finally lets out a "Dadgummit!"

And out of all the whistle blowing and commotion, the 'dadgummit' stopped it. It's over. He's so mad and his face is so red, and he just pointed a finger and it's shaking and he yells out "Christian!" and he points to the South Stadium stairs. Then he goes, "Volin!" and he pointed. And I'm like, 'That sucks!' ('Cause he'd already gotten punished.) And Christian says, "How many?" And Osborne goes, "Until we start gassers!"

So these two dudes start running stadium steps. Now, Coach Osborne: a faithful, holy, upright man, but there's a devious side to him. They're up at the top of the stairs of the South Stadium and Christian is trying to play the game: he's trying to time it so that when that final whistle blows and gassers start, he just has to come down. Coach Osborne and him are squaring off, and neither one will acknowledge they're squaring off. So Christian finally decides to turn around and run down, and when he gets to the bottom he takes one last look back. And Coach Osborne goes, "Huddle up. Run one more play." Christian takes off. And he's about a quarter of the way up, and Osborne blows the whistle for time to run gassers. (Now, if you know Christian, he's not going to go only a quarter of the way up and turn around, he's going to go all the way up to the top and then run all the way back down.) So we get done and we're all on the gasser line anticipating when his whistle is gonna blow and how I'm gonna cheat so I don't have to touch all the lines. And we're standing there, and finally someone on the defense says, "Hey, are we gonna *go*?" And Coach Osborne says, "We're gonna wait for those two." And they were about three quarter of the way up now. They had to finish that last one, so he got an extra South Stadium stairs out of them, ninety six rows. And they come down, and they are just gassed, huffing and puffing. And Coach goes, "Alright, defensive linemen first!" (Defensive line *never* went first!) He lined them up and ran 'em. And by that time, the lactic acid had built up so much -and Christian ran with wide elbows, anyway, when he wasn't tired- but man, now he was swimming. (laughs)

Q: For the sake of educating the uninitiated, define what a gasser was…

MV: Oh, it was lining up on the sideline and then sprinting across the field to the other sideline and back, then across and back. So two times across and back the width of the football field was a gasser. Sideline to sideline.

Q: And being a former player, what would your response be to the person who said, "You players have it easy, you get everything."

MV: There's a whole gamut of things that come into my mind when you say that. The first one, initially was, 'Hey, come live my life. Do that for a couple days and then tell me what you think.' Did we get special treatment? To an extent, yeah. The real difference back then was that the food was prepared off-site and then shipped out to the dormitories whereas our food was made right there. Now, I won't say that was fact, as I got that from a second hand source. Computer lab? At the time every sorority had them, every fraternity had them, the residence halls had them. Tutoring? If you go to the Union there are tutors available everywhere. And then I would also say, 'Ok, if you don't want us to get special treatment, then let's not play football. We'll see what happens to your university.' Your computer lab is not there, your Love Library remodel doesn't happen, you don't have a Physics Department. The revenue we get, it's a necessary part of the game.

I got into it once, just jiving with an athlete from one of the other sports, and they were saying "You football players…you get so much more of this and that." And I responded, 'That's great. Any point in time if you guys want to pay for your own sport, have at it. You have fun with that four game season. (laughs) Golf? You can go hit range balls. Awesome. Have fun with that range ball competition.' For those sports it was, 'Hey, let's keep it in perspective. Yes, we do play a revenue-producing sport. We're more than happy to do that. Do we get a couple extra perks? Yes, we do. So we can go watch our buddies play baseball and play basketball and have you guys get this experience, too. Don't forget that.'

Q: Great response. And I have to ask, any special talents or personalities that stand out to you from those days?

MV: Well, speaking of Lawrence Phillips, he was just a great guy. I had a lot of fun with him, joking around the locker room with him. And when he got to the NFL, you could see if he ever had an issue come up it would usually be a mixture of alcohol in the situation. And maybe it's just me (I'm kind of a bleeding heart), but try to understand the situation he came from, where he was left on somebody's doorstep, saying, "Hey, take care of my kid." I may be wrong on that, but that's kind of the way I understood it. That's got to do some damage to you as a person. Just dealing with that feeling of abandonment, I suppose.

Locker room Lawrence? I loved him to death. He was funny. A great sense of humor. A great teammate. But he had a short fuse and he needed to take care of it. That just really hurts my heart. And when he got picked up by St Louis I went and told him, 'Listen, I don't want anything from you. I'll pay rent. I'll go get a job in St. Louis and I'll just come with you and be your support staff, see what you can do to the NFL. I've seen Walter Payton play in person, seen Tony Dorsett play in person. And you're better. You're better than both of them.' And he looked at me and said, "You would do that, wouldn't you Verz?" I was like, 'I'd do it in a second, buddy. I'd move down there and, like I said, get a job. I don't want to be paid by you, I just want to make sure you don't get in harm's way.' He just laughed it off. That guy was so unbelievably talented. Just gifted. He had everything: power, finesse, moves, speed, ughh! Just as a fan of the game of football, that one hurts my heart.

Q: I feel much the same, Verz. Tell me, anyone behind the scenes play a huge role in those teams? Anybody stand out to you?

MV: The entire support staff: managers, strength staff, secretaries, sports information. All those people. Those are the people for me. The trainers, they don't get enough credit. You guys will be the first ones to acknowledge that we weren't easy to work with. (laughs) There was a lot of bobbing and weaving and trying to get us to work some days when we didn't feel like it, but you guys got us to do it. The folks up in the office handling staff schedules, all those people. They were all part of it. All those people did such a great job, they allowed the coaches just to focus on the coaching and teaching. Those student managers, we put those guys through hell. They were always there if you needed anything. They were great. The behind the scenes guys. If you'd like me to mention some of them you've got Mike Mason in the equipment room…

Q: I'll have to get a hold of Mike. That's a great idea. Well, thanks for your time talking about the memories, Matt. It was fun.

MV: No problem.

End conversation.

Proper planning prevents piss-poor performance. Though I never once heard that phrase uttered in the halls of Memorial Stadium, the 6P axiom was the unspoken mantra of the players and staff in that 60 & 3 era. Maybe a sanitized, more politically correct way of conveying the point would be to 'leave no stone unturned,' because the rocks were constantly rolling from Sunday through Saturday in Lincoln. At that time in the early 1990's the collusion of computers and videotape was still just a vague dream, but Nebraska led the way with a new-fangled way of working with game film and practice film: it was called digital format. This was way, way, wayyyyy before YouTube and podcasts and video streaming the like, and the simplicity with which film could now be sliced and diced and repackaged lent to a super-efficient use of opponent's game film (as well as a rehashing of the previous day's practice film). What this new technology did was speed up film study to uber-efficient blocks of coach/player interaction as well as provide a virtual non-stop feedback loop in the preparation for next Saturday's contest. While the opponent was most likely fumbling with scratchy VHS recorders or Super 8 film projectors, Nebraska's coaching staff could -with a click of the mouse- go exactly where they wished and pinpoint a play, a maneuver, a technique or tendency, and make the most of every teachable moment. With that came players' renewed confidence that they had not only seen everything that the opponent could possibly throw at them, but it also provided an opportunity to view how they reacted to game-like simulations on the practice field in the days leading up. In essence, it removed necessity of a whole first quarter of the game to explore and surmise opponent's moves and strategies, thus allowing the game plan to move forward at warp speed. Resultantly, the Husker squads often jumped out to early leads, which led to larger leads as the game moved along. The hay was in the barn at an earlier stage than most contests of that era, playing a vital role in getting ahead, turning up the heat, and staying ahead.

Another item that stood out was Matt's mention of the '96 team's absence of a vocal leader. To drive home a point -in case you may not have paid much notice- he did not say that there was a leadership vacuum, but that there was no vocal leadership. If I could deduce anything from that '96 year it would be the absolute necessity for a team to possess at least one outwardly rambunctious, gregarious, over-the-top verbal leader to complement those quiet leaders all around. I think of Christian Peter and Kevin Raemakers when I make that statement, and I look forward to what they might add to the conversation as we go forward.

Another item touched upon was Matt's mention of the bonding experiences apart from the campus team activities. Can't you just imagine some of these beefy brutes sitting down to a holiday feast and scarfing down massive quantities of food in no time flat? If you'd ever seen Larry Townsend in person, you would know exactly why Matt's grandmother shuddered, as 'Bohonks' are pretty well-versed in churning out good quantities of holiday food. And too wit, did you notice just a little glint of a difference between the group of '92 guys in relation to Tommie Frazier? I did. It seems to me that his peers respected perhaps the greatest college quarterback of all time, but they didn't necessarily become fast friends. Interesting.

Lastly, Matt mentioned how the 1:16 on the clock during the summer workouts of '94 were a huge motivator. As longtime Husker fans, we've likely heard it more than we have the Pledge of Allegiance, but I find it peculiar from a psychological point of view that the constant reminder a negative memory repeated over and over was actually turned into a positive. Think about that paradox for a brief second: what would you think of seeing a photo, every single day, of your Ex or an IRS Auditor or the thug who mugged you last year? I don't suppose it would give me the warm fuzzies, if you get my drift. Nonetheless, it's a testament to the fortitude of those kids and acts as Exhibit A for the concept of taking a frown and turning it upside down. Making hay? Indeed!

Notable quote #2:
Matt Vrzal on being a Nebraska Football fan turned player: "If it means that much to people, it must really be special. I want to be a part of that and play whatever role I can play."

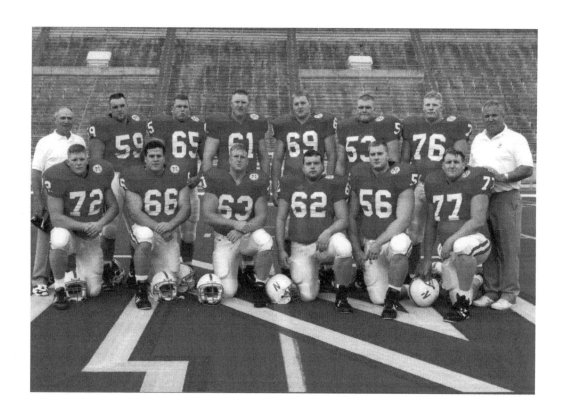

There is no great genius without some touch of madness.

Seneca, *Moral Essays. On Tranquility*

This interview had me catching up with a notoriously evasive man: my good friend Bryan Bailey. It's hard to not like 'Beetle' Bailey, as many players came to call him during that 60 & 3 era. His working relationships and numerous accomplishments have earned him the label of Eminence Inlier, in my book. But Bryan Bailey had once been an outsider, too, even by strength staff standards going back as late as 1990.

Do you remember the movie *Good Morning Vietnam*? Near the end Sgt. Major Dickerson is informed that he'll be sent to the island of Guam to serve out his remaining enlistment, to which he moanfully replies, "Guam, sir? There's nothing going on in Guam! Why *Guam*?!" Beginning his tenure blocks away at the Devaney Sports Center weightroom (the Guam-esque equivalent of a thousand miles removed from Nebraska Football) he found his 'in' by way of a few Husker stars reaching out for miracle cures, and for history's sake we can thank the likes of Steve Taylor, Von Sheppard, Richard Bell, Ken Clark, Reggie Cooper and Mike Croel. These young men could be found discreetly sneaking over to the Sports Center to rehab their injuries with this skinny, freckled, little red-headed guy who Boyd had somehow kept hidden out of sight.

But kids will talk. And he was just too good to be kept a secret. Even in hushed tones, word got out, finding their way to the big man at the top. And just as Tom Osborne spotted a talent in Boyd Epley twenty years previous, the intuitive and fearless leader knew he had something special in Bryan when he brought him over from the crackerjack box of a weightroom over at the Devaney Sports Center to West Stadium's massive confines. No longer wiling away at the purgatory of a sports-performance outpost, Memorial Stadium's strength complex was now his playground.

And oh boy, could he get an injured athlete back into the mix, many times faster and stronger than even before. In the Steve Pederson/Bill Callahan shakeup he was shamelessly told to pack his bags and head back to 'Guam' in order to make way for a Pederson crony. But a pretty sharp fellow by the name of Pete Carroll -who knew a thing or two about talent – speedily coaxed him away to southern California, much to USC's great gain and pleasure. You would frequently see Bryan roaming the sidelines during USC's greatest years, and be sure that Bryan Bailey and football success for both programs was a strong cause & effect relationship. Why? Because simply put, Bryan developed champions. Period. Let's get a little taste for what Bryan "Beetle" Bailey, the pride of Arnold, Nebraska, was cooking up in his laboratory of pain during that great era…

Notable quote #1:
"It became that strength coach had one group -a position that you worked with- and you became *their* strength coach. It made it very competitive for all of us, which was a neat thing to do. Like the rest of them, I don't want to lose. That's what it's all about. Everything was about competition."

Bryan Bailey

Question: What brought you to Nebraska Football?

Bryan Bailey: I heard there was a job Boyd Epley had in strength and conditioning, where I could work with the other sports. I figured it was a good opportunity. (Back then you either worked with football or you worked with the other sports. You had five people that worked with football and then you had one guy working with the other sports.) (laughs) You've been there, you know what kind of challenge that is. I was working on my PhD in Exercise Physiology. It didn't seem like anything was opening up, so that's what I decided to do. I worked 40 hrs. per week and tried to go to school.

Then I got hired on and there was this football player named Steve Taylor: he'd hurt his thigh and was afraid he wasn't going to be able to play in the Oklahoma game. So he came over to the Devaney Sports Center and we did some work in the swimming pool. Somehow we got hooked up and worked together. He said I helped make it so he could play in the Oklahoma game, and he told Tom Osborne after that. So Tom Osborne made me a part of the football program and the rest is history.

Q: Was Von Sheppard in there somewhere, too?

BB: Von Sheppard. He was there. Steve Taylor and Von Sheppard. Von had torn his ACL- one of the best athletes they'd seen in a long time back then. Last I heard he was a teacher in Minnesota up there. They were all really good friends; the relationships are more important than anything, an inspiration in that they want to be something. And you can help them reach for it. To potentially help them meet their goals? That's something that was important to me.

Q: Bryan, I know this is excruciating because you don't necessarily like to talk about yourself.....

BB: It is. But Steve Taylor and Von Sheppard, they were the key to getting me in because they came and found me. Remember we had the Reel Runner machine over there in that little Devaney Center weightroom?

Q: The Reel Runner! A great piece of machinery…

BB: That's how it all started. Steve Taylor and Von Sheppard came over, and that's how I got found.

Q: So they brought you over to football and created a special position for you, the title of 'Reconditioning Specialist" or something like that?

BB: Yeah, they knew I was a little odd. (laughs) The (organizational) flow chart they had did not contain the kind of things that I did. Instead of just following the mainstream I used to look at things that could possibly happen to put a person in a successful situation so they'd feel better about themselves. It's a nice way to do things –going with the current- but to get somebody, to get into the gray area between their ears and get them inspired toward moving in a positive direction is more important that just following the status quo. It's nice to have more to offer than that, and if you can get their brains going in a positive way of working and looking at things, they heal a lot faster. I still believe that.

Q: It's equally important for the athletes to know how you're doing something and why you're doing something that actually doing something?

BB: Yeah, not "Just follow what they tell me to do." I think it's about a more important concept: it's called cooperation. I call it 'tapping in.' When they are tapped in everything else going on in their life is 'tapped out,' and if you can get them focused on that, they can get better. Some people say, "I really can't do that." Well, that's part of the problem. There's a lot more to a person's make-up than what they can't do, because it's more important to focus on what they can do. Once you make up your mind to work on the things you can do, it opens up things and you make the progress.

Q: How did you get them to focus, to 'tap in' on the things that one can do?

BB: Just by using my position, the place that I held in the weightroom. And they trusted me, that I had a personal interest in them. It just wasn't, 'What can I get out of this?' They knew I really cared about their well-being and wanted them to get better.

And part of the process is getting them to reach their potential, it's not just, "Okay, I've got this potential." You might see a person with a lot of God-given ability and everything is fine and dandy when things are going right, but once things go wrong and they have an injury, they don't know the proper way to work and they don't know where to start. And that's where somebody else has to intervene and show them how to put themselves back together, because they've never been there. Once they can figure those things out, when they get to feel what it's like to be an average person, you've got to slow things down for them until they get back to speed.

Q: It seemed to me you were part strength coach/mad-scientist/motivational guru, and maybe even part sadist. Where do you feel you fit in the whole scope of the program?

BB: Looking at a dartboard, I was that bulls-eye. (laughs) Probably all of those things you mentioned, where they loved to hate me. I didn't want to be loved by everybody, known as somebody who just goes along with things. I didn't always get my own way, but anytime you can challenge everybody in the system and make somebody become the best they can be (and they won't like it at the time), but when they look back on it they'll say, "That person helped me become the person I am." Other people may say I was a real asshole…

Q: That was just me saying that, Bryan…

BB: (laughs) Other people might say I was the mad scientist. But at the end of the day, I had to look at myself in the mirror. And was I doing it to be a selfish person or a selfless person? I tried to do what I thought was right, tried to do the best with what I knew at that time. Many times I've had to apologize for doing things that haven't been helpful to an athlete. I've probably made more mistakes than any other strength coach out there. But if you can never say that, then you've never worked with great athletes. I've been very, very blessed. I've trained the best, I've worked with some of the biggest names in athletics. That's a blessing.

When they show up to get better, what will you say you've accomplished with that person? You sometimes want to piss them off… and if you piss them off they become aggravated, and they'll come back the next day and try to get better. Some might say, "Never put them in a position to look bad." Well, I want to make them look bad in a good way, because if they can handle that, when it comes to going out into the real world then they're not as scared of being ridiculed for what they do on the field.

Q: You were my mentor in many respects, Bryan, and there were so many days you would cajole an athlete and push him and make him want to quit. And when they arrived at that point of weakness and vulnerability you would find a way to get an extra rep or an extra set out of them. But then the next day they'd come back and be thankful that you'd done it! They seemed genuinely thankful that you'd pushed them to an uncomfortable place to make them better…

BB: Yes, I agree with you. I just think there is a lot we leave in that reserve gas tank, because the 'unknown' is uncomfortable: "If you put too much out there, I might get hurt." But if they trust you enough, they put it out there and they give it back to you.

That's what was great about being a little piece of machinery in that great big clockworks that was headed by Tom Osborne. It was about the process. If you give it up -if you sincerely give it up?- if you work with kids and they trust you, they'll walk on water for you, show a great trust. And then you'll see greatness.

Listen. I have no greatness, but I get to work with greatness. And you stroke that greatness. (You can either stroke it or inhibit it with ridicule.) And many times you have to stroke that greatness and allow it to grow and make it struggle and go through all that, help them figure out that they have more to give than they thought they had to give. I think one key is to see greatness in them before even they can see it. I just think that's a key to life, if you care about people.

Q: You were simply exposing them to realizing their full potential?

BB: It's about exposing them to who they want to be. Let's face it, it's a very scary world. What people don't realize -and I understand this a lot better than most, doing this as long as I have and seeing some great athletic performances- yet at the same time I've seen how fragile some of those people are. What these athletes do is very unique, and once you get to talk to them behind the scenes and know them, you understand that they can be really scared of a lot of things, how they can be ridiculed for who they are, for what they do out there. And that's just one aspect.

And that's probably one of my biggest aggravations, because they bring so much more to the table than just their athletic talent. I've known more people who've been Academic All-Americans, I've known more people that have gone on in life... Troy Branch, for example. He didn't make it in the NFL, but he's a great lawyer. I came back to Lincoln one time and he introduced me to his wife and his kids. He said "Bryan, I'd like you to meet my family." That means a lot, because it tells you that somewhere along the line we became family, it wasn't one of those dysfunctional families that we all belong to. Nebraska was one of those places -where if you show up and you let your barriers down and put it out there, "and even if I'm not very good, I'm going to work myself as hard as I can"- and they did. That's why it worked. We were family.

Q: What stands out to you as far as turning the corner? I'm sure you remember the meeting a week or two after the Citrus Bowl when Boyd walked into our Strength Staff meeting, screamed out some four-letter words and pounded on the table with his fists, "No more, no more! We're going in a different direction! This is Nebraska!" Do you remember that, and the subsequent reevaluation process?

BB: Vaguely. When I first came on board, the biggest thing was to get to a bowl game. That was what everybody wanted to do, "We've got to get to a bowl game." It wasn't about winning a bowl game.

And also it was, "We've got to get that ring." It was always about 'getting' something. That's where we were: "We've got to get there, we've got to win the Big 8, we've got to go to the bowl game." There wasn't a master plan to win it all. It wasn't about getting to the Orange Bowl and winning it all, it was about how much fun it was to go to the bowl game.

I remember that Citrus Bowl, and there were some really talented guys on that team, guys like Will Shields. Yeah, we had a really good time: we got to go to Universal Studios, I ate the biggest baked potato in my life, I thought it was a mutant. I had a really good time, but at the end of the day when we came back home I was very empty inside. That's my opinion. You had worked so hard, and then at the end of the whole process what did you accomplish?

You expected to win. You expected to win, but you didn't want to win. You expected it, but you didn't put forth the effort at the end of the season. And Boyd had gotten tired of that, too. You know, you put that hard work in, worked harder than anybody else, and it seemed we just couldn't get over the hump. Why? Because the emphasis was just to get there. And the players who won those national championships hadn't felt the same way. Now this was about, "Hey, we're not just the wood-chuckers of the Midwest here. We're the Cornhuskers and we want to take on the whole world." I think the players made up their minds to not just be content with getting to bowl games anymore, but in winning them. They said, "Let's go show everyone who the Cornhuskers really are, the whole world who we really are."

There is a difference between wanting and needing and believing. When they started believing they were contenders to be the national champions, the players -more than anybody else- they did it. They were willing to go through the process. It wasn't, "You need to do this, you need to do that." They were player-coaches. Certain players at each position, they said, "The problem stops here." If you have a certain group of players at each position who say, "Hey, we're all in this together. If one person messes up, we all mess up." Certain players said, "Hey, we're going to make a commitment to follow this to the end. And it starts in January."

And people may not realize how many times -278 days out of the year- you're going to be training. And then you realize how many times you're going to play: 14 times? 14 games is what you get, you're chance to shine, maybe. 14 times to show who you really are in public. That's it. That's the magic number.

Q: Going back to the player/coach thing. Any names stick out?

BB: I'm spoiled. I was spoiled. There was a whole group. I can look at the whole team in 1994, I can look at all the offensive linemen and the defensive lineman. People go look at that '94 and '95 team. We had Mike Rucker (at the time Mike Rucker was behind Grant Wistrom), Michael Booker and Mike Minter. Go all across the offensive line, go three deep. See all the guys we had, that could have and did play in the NFL. They got drafted. The offensive line: Aaron Graham, Brenden Stai, Zach Weigert, Mark Gilman, all those guys… I hate to say it, but they were like my best friends. Defensively, you had Christian, Jared Tomich, Jason, Grant Wistrom, Terry Connealy. The whole group, they took a genuine interest in getting this done. There was an energy, "If we do this, we deserve to win." They had some energy and started to believe it, and when everybody believes the same thing, watch out.

Talk to one of my best friends, Cory Schlesinger. Rockhead. When they'd go out there and do drills they didn't just do them haphazardly. They said, "Hey, I'm going through and everybody else behind me is going to go through it hard, or were gonna do it over again." It wasn't just about going through the motions. They took a genuine interest and became detail-oriented. They wanted to be crisp, not make a marathon out of it. "Let's do the work and let's go home." That's my perspective of it.

Q: So they had a very 'Midwestern work ethic' kind of attitude? Get the job done and go have fun?

BB: Yep, just 'tap in and tap out.' Coaches were like that. The players were like that. The players took it personally, they wanted it. Phil Collins sings that song, "In the Air Tonight." It reminded me of that.

Q: Great song! It reeks of comeuppance, of vengeance. Of correcting slights, righting wrongs, exposing things to the light. And Bryan, you were notorious for put in so many hours, because you pretty much seemed to live in Memorial Stadium. Of course you went home to sleep, but I remember mornings waking up at 5:30 to work out with Jack Nickolite -before any athletes showed up- and you would already be there sometimes. What was your typical schedule?

BB: Notorious, huh? (laughs) I'd get there sometimes at 5 in the morning and maybe leave 8 or 9 at night. I believed in WIT: Whatever It Takes. For me, I wanted to get in as much work as I could, because I didn't think I could get it all in. That was who I was. And like I told you before, that was my family. Those kids were my kids. Some people won't like that, but it is what it is. When you see somebody out there and they give you everything they've got (and it's a dream when they do that), and you know when they come to Nebraska to be football player they deserve to receive the best you can give to them. I wasn't gonna sit down in my office at the time they're in the weight room there, I'd do that on my own time when they weren't there, like early in the morning or late at night. A lot of people didn't like that, but I'm one of those who feels that if you don't spend time with the kids somebody else will.

Q: Make hay while the sun's shining?

BB: Yeah, making hay. Some days I felt like I'd slept in the hay. (laughs)

Q: In '93 during the offseason, a different way of coaching the players appeared, didn't it? Where every strength coach was given a position to oversee, a specific group of players, I think…

BB: It became that strength coach had one group -a position that you worked with- and you became *their* strength coach during the winter conditioning period. It made it very competitive for all of us, which was a neat thing to do. Like the rest of them, I don't want to lose. So at the end of the day, at the end of winter conditioning at the testing, you wanted to see which group had the most improvement.

That's what it's all about. Everything was about competition. Look, I'm redheaded, I'm short, I've got freckles, I've been competing all my life. (author laughs) I'm glad you got a big joke out of that.

And you asked, "Why did I stay so late?", there were walk-ons and guys like the Joel Wilks', the Cory Schlesingers', they wanted an opportunity. Coach Osborne said they would get an opportunity, so I wanted to give them that opportunity through the weight room

Q: (laughing) "I'm sick and tired, and I'm not going to take it anymore!?"-kind of thinking, huh? So here's Bryan Bailey, about 5' 9", about 150 lbs soaking wet after a dip in Branched Oak. So how did little Bryan Bailey end up with, of all people, the Pipeline, the big offensive linemen?

BB: It was mutual. Because I had done my work. I had a plan and I was going to work my plan. I worked really hard to get educated as much as anybody else around about strength & conditioning and sport specificity. You'd worked with me. I never ran marathons (and everybody said that I must have trained to do that), but I only ran to get my head straight when other things were going on. When I went for a run it let my mind work and allowed me to clearly think about other things.

And the Pipeline? They were really good friends of mine, very good friends. They were like my sons, and they trusted me and I trusted them. And they asked for me. So Boyd let me have them. They made me who I am. Each person might have had a position they worked exclusively with: the defensive line, the linebackers, the defensive backs, the running backs. I could probably mention all of them. Brook Berringer was a really good friend of mine, Tommie Frazier was a really good friend of mine, they all knew what they meant to me. They were all my special people.

And those people -each one knew, the Pipeline- that they would make everybody else work harder. The lines on both sides, we all knew that the game was won in the trenches. The running backs and quarterbacks? All the time, I'd tell them, 'If you want to make a lot of dollars someday, you go up to that line up there and give them credit every time you're in front of a microphone.' If you want a good crop, you better have a big tractor.

Q: Tell me about your relationships with some of the coaches...

BB: I'd say the one I was closest with was Tom Osborne. Each day during the time Coach Osborne had that 20 minute period when he'd come in and lift weights, we'd talk about leadership, how you get people to go in the direction of what your vision is. I watched him and how he handled himself. He always gave me the time of day if I had any questions - because I always strived and wanted to be successful- so I always looked at how he was successful, how he treated people.

You know, some people didn't like the way he treated Lawrence Phillips and started calling him a bad person. Tom Osborne had a vision that "each person is unique" and had something to offer. And Tom Osborne helped me to become a humble person and teach me about the process. That's one person I've looked up to all the time. He simplified things and showed you what life was all about. So Tom Osborne really meant something special to me.

Q: When you talk about leadership, does anyone comment or observation stand out to you?

BB: Yeah, 'walk the talk.' If you're gonna talk it, then walk it. And Coach Osborne didn't have to say that, he lived it. The best lessons I learned from Coach Osborne was when he didn't say anything.

I'll never forget the time he came in and worked out much later in the day, while there were two janitors cleaning up the weight room there. And he stopped his whole workout, his little squat routine, and asked both of them how they were doing, how their families were doing. Then afterwards I asked him how he was doing, and he said, "I'm doing great. But I better hurry up, because one of our guys is gonna have knee surgery and I want to go see him tonight yet." So there wasn't a time that guy didn't make time for somebody else, and I thought, 'If he can do it, why can't I do it?'

I was grateful to be a part of that family and to carry his message to the players. Because it's not about getting the most out of them for four years and throwing them out, it's about what they become later on. You come back and look at them ten years later and you ask, 'What did they become?' Hopefully everybody that you meet along the way in life, hopefully you've brought something positive that will make them better. The process.

Q: Any other coaches, special relationships, recollections?

BB: Turner Gill. Turner was a protégé of Coach Osborne as a player, a coach. His coaching style was real direct. Some of us, we have to be real dramatic and all, but others will just say, "This is what needs to be done in this situation." You might bring somebody down, but you must also tell them what they need to do right.

All the coaches. Charlie McBride had a gift, you had better be kind of a hell-raiser with him. And on offense? You better be nice but you've gotta be nasty: and the offensive line was nasty. You don't get paid to be nice."We're humble, but we're gonna win." That's why they called them the Pipeline, "If you get in our way, we'll roll over you." Ron Brown, Frank Solich, those were guys that I related to, also. While I was there, a lot of people didn't like my quirkiness, my nerdiness, they thought I was way out there, but that was what I knew.

I wasn't really a party person, I just wanted to know what the truth was. Now that I've done it for 47 years it seems I have more questions than answers, but I truly cared about the players I worked with.

Q: Have you sensed a change in the youth since your days at Nebraska?

BB: Yeah, we've evolved into more entitled-minded programs. Kids are more entitled because we made them that way. Other people work very hard to get them into situations and now they don't have to work very hard. It helps to have an organization, from Tom Osborne to Pete Carroll, where everybody is going to work.

If you don't want to get better you're going to have a tough time. Because it's all about competition. And when you realize that: everything you do is about competition? Then you'll go places. Kids like me because they know I'm a competitor and I'm going to put them in a position where I'm not only gonna make them better, I'm gonna make them the best.

Q: The kids had so much respect for you because you were willing to push the envelope, push the limits. Every birthday you used to run your age in miles, right? When did that start?

BB: When I was 24 years old.

Q: What drove you to do that?

BB: Because I wanted to do what nobody else had ever done, I wanted to be my own person. I said, 'I've lived this long and I've been very fortunate, and I'm going to do something special to celebrate.' I tell you what, when you turn 40 years old and you put those miles in, the last thing you're gonna want to do after that is drink a lot of beers. (laughs) Now I'm at an age where I ought to start thinking about drinking 50 beers, instead. I might feel better about myself. (laughs) Anyway, I guess I just started running my age.

Q: Does one birthday stand out as harder than another?

BB: Yeah, 40: because it was freezing outside. November 24th. I had to stop at 42 because I had hip problems and I couldn't run anymore, so I started doing it on the bike. And I had to stop doing the bike about 7 years ago. Now I make sure I go surfing on that day, instead. Longboard.

Q: You were always on the sidelines. Any particular sideline situation stand out to you as momentous?

BB: Yeah, I don't know which game it was, but it was on national television and we were the 'Get-back Coaches'....

Q: Explain what a 'Get-back Coach' is.

BB: The 'Get-back Coach', what they do is, there's players on the sidelines, and you're supposed to stay so many yards off the field for the coaches and the referees, so the coaches and players don't get on the field and run into the referees and get them pissed off.

So you'd tell the players, 'Get back! Stay back!' The coaches wanted to keep the players back (and sometimes we had to keep the coaches back. Some of those coaches are just a little bit insane, they lose their brain most of the time).

Anyway, we're in the middle of this game -I think we were playing Oklahoma at home- and everybody's uptight. And I'm trying to keep the players back. Mike Arthur, myself, Randy Gobel, Boyd, John Archer or Jon Jost, we're standing there and I'm supposed to be standing behind Charlie McBride. Anyway, the players keep getting up and across out of bounds line there, and we got a penalty. And that was not good.

So they said, "Who was that on?" and the official said, "Charlie McBride." And Charlie turns around and grabs me by my shirt and he says, "What is your job?!" I said 'Getting people back.' And he says, "Why don't you do it?!" And I pointed at Mike Arthur and say, 'I'm just doing what he told me to do.' And Charlie takes me by the shirt -on national TV- and takes me all the way down to Mike Arthur, where he's standing and he says, "What is you guys's job?!" And Mike says, 'I don't know what you're talking about.' (laughs) He looks at both of us and says, "You're Get-back Coaches! Do your job!" (laughs)

Q: He's got two little red-headed strength coaches by the shirt collars…(laughs)

BB: Mike says, "What was that all about?" I go, 'I think he's a little uptight.' (laughs) So it was one of my more comical moments.

Q: Any other special moments?

BB: The best one was away from the game. It's Phoenix, Arizona and we won our second national championship in a row. I get up the next morning, we're staying at some resort, I forget the name of it. I'd go running every morning, getting up just to enjoy being alive (this is the day after spanking Florida)and I run like 500 yards. And lo and behold, I'm out there at 5 in the morning and there is Tom Osborne with his grandson. I said, 'What are you doing?' And he said, "Ah, Bryan, this is the best part of my day." And I said, 'What about the national championship?' And he says, "Well, you know, I get up today and it's over: today's just another day. And this guy here needs all the help he can get." That's one of the greatest things I've ever seen or heard. Because most people think you get up the next day thinking you're invincible, you've won the national championship, but it's just another day and you have to do it all again. To this day I carry that with me, because I look at that and say, 'That's what life's all about.' He still had enough time to spend with all the people.

He wore so many hats. And it sounds like I'm putting him up on a "God level," but how he carried himself and what he did, it made me do the things I chose to do. That man deserves everything he gets, because for that little guy hanging onto his hand for dear life, that was greatness.

Q: Very interesting answer, Bryan.

BB: And the thing about that game - you ask Christian Peter, you ask Aaron Graham - we knew we were going to win that game. There was no question going down there whether we would win or not. It was just the question of 'How much were we going to win by?' It was as different attitude, a different outlook. And you saw what happened.

Lawrence Phillips never even worked out the whole time until he got to the game, and then he ran wild. He was a man-child. He and I became really good friends, always good friends. His story, to me, I still have problems that he did all those things, but behind all of that, if people really got to sit down with him and he trusted them, he's a gentle person. If he got to know you and he trusted you, boy, if I'm going into a dark alley that's the guy I'm taking with me. And I guarantee I'd be coming out of there, too. (laughs)

Q: (Quoting) "Yea, though I walk through the valley of the shadow of death, I shall fear no evil, for Lawrence Phillips has my back?" (laughs)

BB: That's right! (laughs)

Q: Any one game stand out to you?

BB: They all do, because they all counted. Everybody will probably talk about the time when we went to Miami and Coach Osborne gave his halftime speech. It happened like everybody says, what he said was going to happen. But to me, every game - every game that we were a part of - they were all important. They all had something meaningful to it.

If you ask me what the most momentous game is? Probably the most momentous? We go to Colorado. And this was one to save somebody's job. Yeah, we were all there. And there were a lot of people who had counted us out. And there's a football team that put a lot of trust - 105, 125 guys got ready to go to this game versus Colorado - they knew it, we knew it, and certain people didn't say it, but other people told us, "We have to win this one for our coach." And we did! And when you win a game -and we know it, we've all been kids- we left it all on the field that day and then some. And in that locker room they thought they had done something that nobody else could do.

And on Sunday afternoon they found out that it was not enough. Momentous? Yes. Because I watched for the next 48 hours: a bunch of kids who had given everything, trusted the system, and then it was like a part of their body was just cut off. I don't understand that diplomacy, don't understand those politics, but I do understand kids.

End conversation.

Bryan is a fairly philosophical fellow and I hope you got the gist, just one iota, of his mad, multitudinous methods when it came to training the student/athletes. Never the flashiest, most physically imposing or social-minded guy, he instead excelled at getting an athlete one-on-one and finding their trigger points, mental blocks and physical inequalities to strengthen up and smooth over. A master motivator in his own right and a quasi-team player/rebel, Bryan lunged, sprinted and marched to the beat of his own drum… bongos, even. I say that in jest, because we all know that every jest contains a modicum of truth. And truth is what he was always in search of: the truth about human beings and their reaction to various mental stimuli and distresses, not to mention bodily ones. I recall the old John Cougar Mellencamp song, Hurts So Good, when it comes to Bryan and the footballers, because he could bring on the hurt, yet they knew it was eventually for their good.

We heard how Bryan was a fellow apostle with Coach Tom Osborne in his care for the student/athletes, as well as his belief in the process of collegiate athletics. In speaking to Bryan and the other Eminence Outliers I have come to notice that, despite career specialty, it all boiled down to having the utmost care for the athlete's welfare in mind, not their own personal egos. (Maybe I should rename the term EEO's: Ego-less Eminence Outliers) Kids can spot a phony from a mile away, and one could sense the gravitational pull these types of individuals –like Bryan- had on them. The beauty of it was that the Athletic Department was burgeoning with these kind of people, some in every department for every student/athlete and not just the football team. Talk about sharing the wealth.

And speaking of wealth, I think it's important to remember some crucial numbers, or more appropriately, the ratio 278:14. If your team makes it to a conference championship and then to a bowl game, this is the top end: 278 training days:14 gamedays. Back in the great 60 & 3 era no conference championship game existed, so it was more like a 278:12 or 13 ratio. To think that 278 days of training and preparation all boiled down to only a dozen to thirteen opportunities for the average college football player to show what he is made of in competition, it further evidences the sense of urgency and seriousness with which they all took their tasks. In building and/or maintaining a legacy, a tradition, the stakes sure were high. They still are. Maybe even more so.

The last thing I'll mention is something I touched on much earlier, which pertains to the weakness, the fragility of the common student/athlete's psyche. Bryan's remark, "you understand that they can be really scared of a lot of things, that they can be ridiculed for who they are, for what they do" makes me much less apt to rage at the TV when a kid misses a block or drops a pass or muffs a tackle. It's not as if they are professionals with just that week's game as their one and only focus, but these young adults are also juggling class attendance, homework assignments, paper-writing, lab sessions and tests at a non-stop pace. It's a pressure cooker to be sure, and thinking back to the period when I was that age I'm not sure if I would have been comfortable with a national television audience observing my every move.

Notable quote #2:
Bryan Bailey on peer leadership: "They were player-coaches, certain players at each position, and they said, "The problem stops here." If you have a certain group of players at each position who say, "Hey, we're all in this together. If one person messes up, we all mess up.""

Football is the ballet of the masses.
Dmitri Shostkovich

Starting from 1682 to 1763 and again from 1800 to 1803, France owned the Louisiana Territory. In the process of traversing the great, watery divide to the New World that country's great sailing ships carried within them a horse named the Camargue, an animal native to their harshly climatic southern marshes. The gardiens (French for cowboy) eventually headed westward, taming wild horses (originally carried from Spain) on the southern American plains. So, in a sense, the first American cowboys were actually Frenchmen.

Why the strange lead-in, you might ask? Well, the world is full of interesting, odd and often surprising turns. Which brings us to Brett Popplewell, Nebraska's wide receiver from half a world away in Australia. How did that come about and what role did this addition from south of the equator play in that era of 60 & 3 greatness? Read on, mate…

Notable quote #1:
"They just got the people in the right positions at the right time. The people were wonderful, and that's what makes it."

Brett Popplewell

Scholarship recruit, Split End, Melbourne, Australia
Where are they now? Melbourne, Australia, Management

Question: So I hear you're pretty busy these days?

Brett Popplewell: (heavy Australian accent…you don't hear most of the r's pronounced) Work's been pretty crazy. I'm living in Melbourne now, and I've been spending a lot of time in Sydney lately. I got back last night about 10:30 p.m. and then I'll go back tomorrow night on a late flight for two more weeks. A lot of up and back at the present, but I won't complain. The travel wears you out, but it's good to keep moving and have a job in this present economy. (laughs) I spend time going from Japan to heaven knows where half the time. By the way, I was actually back to the states, in Nebraska for two days last Memorial Day weekend and I got to stay with Jon Bostick. I spoke to Nate Turner, who's in Chicago, and we keep in touch, too. He came over here to play rugby one time in Australia. I think he struggled for a time getting used to the game without shoulder pads and all. (laughs) I turned on the TV one morning and he's on Australian TV hosting a big Rugby tournament out of Sydney. And we ended up meeting up again, and it was also the same time the Super Bowl was on. That was the year Calvin Jones was playing for Green Bay. We keep in touch a lot over the miles through facebook.

Q: That's how I found you!

BP: Oh yes, trainer Bob Hammonds and all sorts of guys. It's amazing how easy it is to keep in touch with people now.

Q: You've got that right, and now I'm here spanning the globe and talking to Australian Brett Popplewell about Nebraska football. Go figure…

BP: It's hysterical. I tell you what happened to me: one day I was just walking along the beach about few years ago and this guy walks up to me. It was a hot day, January, with my dog and this guy says, "That's a good looking dog. Do you mind if I pet him?" And I say 'Sure,' and I noticed he has an American accent. And he's wearing a t-shirt that says

'Omaha, Nebraska.' And I say, 'Are you from Omaha?' And he says, "Yes, I am." I said, 'That's funny, I went to school there and played football there back in Nebraska in the early 90's.' And he goes, "Your name's Brett isn't it?" (laughs) 'Yeah,' I said. And anyhow, his name is Jim Meier, and he says, "I've met you before." (I was Calvin Jones' roommate back then) And it turns out I met him through Calvin and his family. And he gave me his business card. So I get home and I end up showing it to my old man, and it turns out my father sat next to this guy on a flight back in '92 or '93 as he was going there to watch one of my games. And he pulled out this business card that the man had given him, and it's the exact same business card of 11-12 years before! They'd sat next to each other on a flight from Sydney to Los Angeles. And talk about how bizarre, how small is the world, for something like that to happen? It's insane. A very small world. Halfway across the world you still bump into people who have that connection to Nebraska football.

Q: Let me ask you, Brett, how did you end up playing football at Nebraska?

BP: I'd played in a local league here in Australia. It was then the VFL in Australia, the Victorian Football League, and then it became the Australian Football League, the AFL. And one of the teams was the Victoria Lions. Anyhow, I signed with them. From there I played American football in a local league, which was 16 years of age here. It was like your average high school team. And then some people suggested, "Why don't you go to the States?" I was in my last year of high school and I took recruiting trips to Nebraska, Tennessee, and NC State, too.

I was at Nebraska for 4 ½ years there, and I ended up signing with the Scotland Claymores in the NFL Europe at the time and then I'd had a fractured skull. I was actually doing quite well, and I had a non-contact drill and fractured my skull. So I wasn't able to play for three months, and that was about it. I had a great time. I absolutely loved it.

For me, coming from Australia, my expectations were a little different. Because you don't grow up there, with high school sports and seeing it in the newspaper, that just didn't happen in Australia. Over there in the U.S., you've even got TV shows and movies about high school football, but here you just never heard of it much. To me, I was just going to play and see how that went. And I was fortunate enough to do that, but I never had any expectations that I was going to be a superstar or anything like that, like so many American high school guys come in thinking. The memories you look back on and the people are what make it special, though.

And a funny thing about Nebraska Football, we get a lot of the games on TV here in Australia. A good friend of mine from high school, she's now working at SportsCenter for Asia-Pacific ESPN, who does programming for Australia, and she said, "If you want certain games on, just send me an e-mail of who you want to put on." So I did, and she's put a good number of Nebraska games on ESPN Australia. (laughs) So it's been fantastic.

So I see those games on TV, which is awesome. And for the first time in awhile I watched the National Championship game, and I thought about the National Championship games against Florida State and Miami the year where we won. And playing in those two games, it's amazing thinking back at the jump that we made to end up playing in those two games, you know? The memories are really, reflecting back on, to sit back and say 'Wow, to think of those guys we played with and what they did and as successful as we became..,' it's pretty amazing to look back on that. Personally, what I did -and looking back as a team, what we did- it's quite a thing to achieve. I'd like to get back and see a game, which I'm sure I'll do in the next couple of years.

Q: So you went to a high school in the United States for your senior year?

BP: I was in year twelve here in Australia. I left halfway through year twelve in Australia and entered year twelve in the United States. And high school was a lot more rigorous in Australia compared to the United States, so the transition was pretty easy. It wasn't like going from high school to college and all the changes one goes through, so it was pretty effortless to make that change. It was dumb luck, and when we checked into the dorms for the first time, I was living with Tony Veland and Charles Green, a safety from Louisiana, who I think ended up going back home to play for Louisiana Tech. And I remember sitting there in the bloody dorm room making up names, stupid names for the plays we would run, just laughing our butts off. And to think that we're here 17 years later, you think 'Holy Cow, where did the time go?' It's nuts when you think of how long it's been.

Anyhow, they'd seen some film on me and decided to take a chance. And it was the summer before my freshman year in passing league, and Nate Turner was really good to me, Bostick was really good to me. Some of the chaps that we used to get along with and how well they accepted me, especially the African –American athletes, was absolutely fantastic. At the time, Clinton Childs, he used to call me "The Australian Nigga." (laughs) That was the biggest level of acceptance, where they accepted you for what you did on the field by bestowing a nickname on you, and the small things ended up meaning something to you. Here I was in a different country and playing a sport I wasn't that experienced with (at that time I'd essentially played 11 games of American football by the time I got to the University). I was able to travel pretty much when I was there and start a few games. You look back on it and it kind of means something to you, all the people you met. And we remain friends to this day. That nickname, it was the ultimate level of acceptance and funny to look back on. We got a lot of laughs over that one.

And the internet is so great, because I keep up with a lot of the guys now. I keep track of Lawrence, what's happening with that, and I guess they locked him up last fall? There was someone -when he was with you - he was the loveliest person in the world when he was playing football, and when he got away from football was when he got involved in all that other stuff. It's a shame, it was such a waste of talent. And some of the crap I've been reading, it's a shame. That guy had the world at his feet, and the alcohol and his personal demons - it's funny when you're with these people and they go on to a the level of stardom and celebrity- when you're with them they're not any different than anybody else. Whether you win the national championship or a Super Bowl or local football or tennis competition or something like that, the feeling of winning is the same for us. The only thing that's different is how everybody else reacts to it. We win the national championship, and there's something like 10,000 people in the hotel lobby, you know? But the feeling of success and achievement is no different. I've been around some of the guys who had trouble with that and how others react to them. And for Lawrence, he ran into some of that.

Q: What year was you first join Nebraska?

BP: It was '91.'91 through '94, when we beat Miami for the national championship. I remember going down to do passing league that first summer, there were some really lovely blokes. So that was my first real memory doing that, coming down and sort of floating around with some of the guys like Keithen McCant, Mike Grant, Mickey Joseph. Those guys were all really good to me. I think they just liked to poke fun at me because I was from Australia.

And I remember Calvin -Calvin Jones- he had that dog he named Heisman, that Viszla. Anyhow, I remember one day we were living in the townhouse out there in Lincoln and we came home, and the dog had gotten a jar of my vegemite (and vegemite is really salty), and the dog had sat there and eaten this bloody jar of vegemite and had gotten itself sick!

(laughs) It's those little things that you look back on now, those silly things. And all those relationships that came out of it. Unfortunately, I haven't spoken to Calvin in ten years. I know he's in Lincoln, I've heard. Have him give me a call if you get in touch with him, will you?

Q: Absolutely. And let me ask you, when you first moved to Nebraska was there anything about the people that stood out to you?

BP: They were all lovely. It was a much slower pace considering where I'm from, because Melbourne is essentially 3.5 million people. And to move to a town that had 250,000 people, that was a bit of a shock I must admit, getting used to it. I found the people really lovely. People were really lovely in terms of being very welcoming, taking me in. I remember Calvin took us back to his Grandmother's place for Easter one year, and I tell you what, it was one of the best experiences I ever had. There were about 45 people there, and I was the only white person. And the chitlins I can't quite get over -I didn't find those good- but it was one of those moments where they were so welcoming to me. In a time when there were so many racial troubles going on - to experience something like that?- there was nothing to do with the color of your skin, the people were just really open and lovely. Now, I don't know if it was because I was from Australia, but they were especially nice to me. Black, white, everyone was so lovely to me going over there. They always wanted to help out. I was really fortunate from that point of view.

Q: And Brett, your position coach was Ron Brown?

BP: Yes, I know he's back to coaching again. It was a great experience that I really enjoyed and felt very fortunate, with all those guys: Reggie Baul, Corey Dixon, Trumane Bell. I was pretty lucky to have relationships with those guys.

Q: What would you say about Coach Brown's methods? What about the man?

BP: Look, he and I didn't always see eye to eye. I think in terms of respect and the coaching side of things, he was fantastic. We didn't always see eye to eye on a personal nature. But there was always a level of respect there, I think. If I saw him tomorrow I'd shake his hand and give him a hug.

I remember one guy who always stuck out was Mike Vedral. I remember one time he dropped from first string tight end to third string tight end, just like that. And I recall Vedral saying, "Coach Brown said to me, "Well, I've prayed about it and this is what the Lord's told me…", and I remember Mike saying, "Yeah, but I've prayed I'll be a first round draft pick," as a way of being a little bit sarcastic. Now, that's not the message you want to send to a player when you move him down a depth chart, you know? I must admit, I did get a little bit frustrated at times, when some of the players -and I realize and think it's great that there was a forum to express their religious beliefs- but sometimes found it a little bit self-serving when they said "I'd like to thank God to allow me to win this football game." Because I'd like to think God has more to worry about than a football game, with all that's going on in the world right now, and I just found it a little self-serving, you know? I appreciated the message, but society's going into the crapper at the moment. The moral culture of people now is awful, so I just get a little bit taken at times when it becomes, "God helped us with this game." I just think to myself, 'What about the poor sap on the other side of the line? Did God tell him, "Well, just tough luck, guys?" ' But that's just me. There are many ways to go about it.

Q: What did you not see eye to eye about?

BP: Just some of the ways decisions were being made. A lot of it came down to player relationships. All the guys think they should be playing, you know? Some guys get the chance, and some guys do and they don't. My biggest mistake, from a personal standpoint, was that Nebraska probably wasn't the best place to develop as a wide receiver. I remember playing with a guy from UCLA who held a lot of their records, he was down in Atlanta in a training camp and then he went to play for Scotland. Before I got hurt we spent six weeks in Atlanta for a training camp, and three days before we flew to Scotland I fractured my skull and they didn't take me. But just being there in the pro style offense, there were some things I'd learned from Coach Brown that flew directly in the face of what I'd learned.

But everybody's different. And you have to be careful when you talk about stuff like this, because it's such a small part of the entire experience. It's such a small thing, but it's one of those things that makes for a talking point. Like I said, if I walked up to him today I'd give him a hug. Because there's no doubt he cared for his players and took the time, it's just whether you always agreed or not.

And there are so many different personalities. Let's be honest, coaching is no longer what it was like 40 years ago, where it was one message. Now it's pretty much a, 'me, me, me' thing where everyone's about themselves. It's such a selfish society, where everybody gets a time-out instead of a good crack on the ass, you know? (laughs) It's those hard times, that's where you learn the lessons, not being told to go sit in the corner for a timeout. (laughs) Anyhow, that's just a personal thing. You're still gonna have those good and bad experiences, they develop you. Otherwise you get a bunch of spoiled brats. It's not always, "Your fantastic, you're fantastic." The real world doesn't work that way. And I think it's a good way to learn how to handle rejection. Life isn't always a bed of roses, you know? And from a coaching standpoint, it's very difficult, because there are so many different personalities. Coach Brown's intentions were always about finding the best way that he could improve you and make a difference. I look back very fondly, though, on the experience. I'm very proud of it. I'm grateful to say I played at a school that was so successful, but more importantly it was the people I met, the relationships. Like playing that game in Japan my sophomore year; going over there and sharing it with those guys, it was a great experience. And then we get in the fight with the wrestlers in the bloody stairwell the night after the game. (laughs)

Q: With the wrestlers?

BP: I believe it was David White, an outside linebacker from Louisiana. There were the Wrestling World Championship Tag Teams competition going on there in Tokyo and we were in this bar (and it was funny because there were these three bartenders. Two of them, I'd played against them while playing Australian Rules Football in Australia), so we went there. But what happened was there were these guys running down into the stairwell. I guess somebody had said something, and then all this commotion was happening, but it was funny. It was these two Wrestling Federation champions. Remember when we all came back to Lincoln, T.O. locked us in a room in the auditorium, because they said some of the boosters had paid for this bar for all these guys to go to and they were trying to figure out who it was for and who it was? But it was the last night in Japan, and the game was on at twelve o'clock Tokyo time so it was on primetime here, and we didn't have a lot of time to go out. And we ended up getting to bed at 3 o'clock in the morning and having to get up and get our bags ready at 5 o'clock for the flight out. It was a rough night.

Q: What about Coach Osborne?

BP: Everybody respected him and wanted to play for him. He was such a revered person in terms of his influence, his talent about his business, what he stood for. With him it was always "You got what you saw and what you saw, you got." He was always playing it straight, up front, very honest with me. Fantastic, a great coach, such an honor to say you played for someone like that. You've got Bear Bryant, Joe Paterno, Bobby Bowden. With the greats. I played for one of the great coaches. At the time it doesn't mean that much to you, but as you ask me now and you get to reflect on it now, there's no doubt it was a big honor to say I played for him.

Now, it doesn't mean as much here as it does in the States, because here in Australia nobody really knows much about him. But some of the people around here I've shown my ring to or shown some of the games to, they have some appreciation for it. They're blown away by the magnitude of it all. But for the most part, there's no doubt that they only really 'get it' when they see the size of the crowds.

Remember that photo of Memorial Stadium with the sunset? Well, I had all the guys sign it. When people see that, they're amazed at all the guys who were part of those teams. And if you walked into my house you'd have no idea that I played for the University of Nebraska. But my father has all my stuff from those days: the jerseys, the rings, the poster, the game tapes, all that stuff. Obviously, as a father he's obviously very proud. The only thing, to me, that I've really cherished, are the names of those guys and all the relationships, the guys from that '93 team.

Q: Any other coaches stand out?

BP: I got along really well with Coach Solich, Tony Samuel. Charlie McBride, I thought was a real character. Funny guy. Kevin Steele, I got along with real well. Even George Darlington. You know I returned punts and kickoffs, I can roll through those guys, I haven't forgotten any of them. All the coaches and the positions they coached, Milt Tenopir, all those guys. Just great relationships.

And who knows, maybe I was a novelty for them, too, to teach football to a guy from the other side of the world, you know? Everybody's got a view and a different way of looking at things. And that's part of the experience. And once you start winning that makes it all that much more fun. I remember my first year, when we were 14th or 15th in the country to where we became dominant. Those last two seasons where we shanked a bloody field goal, in all honesty, from 43 yards. Byron would probably make that kick 8 out of 10 times. And Darin Erstad, he was clutch. (laughs) One time when he was playing -and I actually saw the Houston Astros in San Francisco and wanted to say hello to him- but I know how focused he was pregame in batting practice and all that.

Q: Do you recall the first game you played in?

BP: Cripes, I want to say it was North Texas or something like that. One of those taxi games. The fondest, specific games, I remember are the two big ones when Kansas was really good (the year we lost to Florida State), where be beat them something like 52-10. And then Colorado and Westbrook and Rashan Salaam and we beat them, as well. I have really fond memories -even though we lost- of the Florida State game. Just because we were given no chance, and I remember the whole buildup to that week, with Charlie Ward and those guys. I think we were 17 1/2 point underdogs, there had never been a spread, a point spread like that, and here we lost 18-16 by a missed field goal. And they had a couple of lucky penalties: Corey Dixon's punt return is not allowed, they called a cheap penalty call, and William Floyd's fumble for Florida State and they called it a touchdown.

And then, obviously, that national championship game we won versus Miami, I remember we just knew it in the huddle that we were gonna stick that ball down their throat. And Tommie was such a leader, no-nonsense and getting everyone pulled together. Phenomenal from that standpoint. There's a game you remember.

That '93 season was the greatest season, even though we didn't win. And then the next year we were so convinced we were going to win, the mindset was so different from the year before. In the end we'd gotten a little bit of luck, I feel. I remember they had Trumane Bell on one side and Reggie and Abdul running down the other side. And Tommie hit Trumane and got him going down the middle. If there were 30 more seconds in the game we probably would have won it, but unfortunately there are only 60 minutes in the game, and not 60 minutes and thirty seconds! (laughs)

Q: Florida State or Miami, in which game did you play the most?

BP: I played more in the Florida State one. The Miami one, my finger was broken. The Florida State game we lost, that was a hard one, it was pretty special for those guys who were seniors that year. Those blokes were great.

Q: What position did you play that game?

BP: I played split end and wingback. I played on one punt, too, I believe. We went to shotgun a lot, and it depended on personnel, and I went to slot to read the defense and run the hot route. The Florida State game was the one where Abdul cracked his ribs, too, I guess. So I ended up playing something like 40 odd plays in that game. And to sit down an hour like this and think about those games, and it comes back to you how it was so much fun and you remember all those guys you played with. Those were great times.

Q: Do you have a favorite play that stands out to you?

BP: No, it wasn't about that. Though, the '93 year we did play Kansas on the road, and they were going for two points, and they'd driven down the field, and Lorenzo Brinkley and Ed Stewart both lined up on the same side, and they were both meant to be on the opposite side and they ran the tight end away from them. And I can't remember what the final score was, but to this day I recall standing on the sideline and Abdul Muhammed jumping on my back and just screaming. The elation, the relief, little things like that, you know?

I saw a lot of great plays and some of the runs Lawrence used to make were spectacular, some of the stuff Tommie used to do. But to me, I look at it more than the plays, it's the people and what I got out of it. That was what I took away from it. To be honest with you, the games, all they did was facilitate the relationships you ended up making. Those guys, if I didn't play football they probably wouldn't speak to me. They're no different than anybody else in the world, but they did have superior athletic ability and were in the right place at the right time, because I really do believe it's such a game of opportunity.

Certainly, the offense was a great matching of ability of those guys with what they ran, and that is certainly one thing that Coach Osborne was born to do. He could really swap people in there and did such a good job. With the exception of 2, maybe 3 games per year, we knew we were going to win because we had more talent. It really always came down to Colorado, because Oklahoma was really terrible when I was there, and a bowl game or the UCLA or Washington every year. Those type of things there, ultimately I think it facilitated relationships and that's what I've gotten out of it. Good people and good times, very fortunate, no doubt about it. What an opportunity I had.

And the first football game I saw was Dwight Clark making that catch against the Cowboys. My brother decided the 49ers would be his favorite team and he wanted a red jersey like those guys, and then he noticed that Nebraska had red in their uniforms, too, so he decided that was the football team he was going to support, something like 7 years before I even went there to University. (laughs) Who would've known? And then 10 years later, it's ironic that I ended up playing at Nebraska and winning a national title as a part of the team.

Q: Is there anyone that stands out to you as someone who meant a lot to you?

BP: I was lucky to have great relationships with a bunch of those guys: Bryan Bailey, Jerry Weber. I was very fortunate to be around those people. And for me, the biggest thing was my parents. On three weeks notice they were willing to send me half the way around the world. That was a big call for them to do. They had to fund all that, so I was very fortunate to be given the opportunity to go and do it.

It was one of those things where everyone just does their thing. It wasn't just one individual. Of course you had Tommie Frazier in there and he took that thing to the next level, but the reason we were so successful was because it was such a team environment and everyone was playing for each other. Look, the superstars the fans will remember, but every guy had a part in it. You have some of the guys on the offensive line who some of the fans probably won't remember, but that's where it all starts. And the defense? Some of those guys did such a good job at stopping people. Overall, it was such a team environment, a team concept And the type of offense we ran to be successful -the option at the time?- when the West Coast Offense was really taking off. They just got the people in the right positions at the right time. The people were wonderful, and that's what makes it.

Q: Last question, Brett. Do you ever wear your national championship ring?

BP: No, if I wore that thing out here they'd look at me like I was lunatic. They'd think I was Liberace. (laughs) My God. Those things are at home in mom and dad's safe. I've pulled them out a couple of times, I reckon, in the past ten years. More just to make sure they were still in existence, that the old man hadn't pawned them off on Ebay. (laughs) He's got a complete set of championship rings through the years. All that stuff, the rings and clothes, once it was done, now it's just memories. Like I said, pretty much the only thing I have around the house is that picture that all my teammates signed. That's what is most important to me. It was all good. It was a good time.

End conversation.

Holy crikeys, every team should contain at least one Australian, if you ask me. Jokes aside, Brett was a very lovely bloke in his own right, and I nearly dropped the phone when he mentioned the 'Australian Nigga' moniker. Now, I typically cringe at every mention of the N-word, though in this particular case I couldn't help but laugh and embrace it due to the fact that it served as a sign of acceptance and affection, a unique bond of brotherhood, just as he did. (Later on we'll hear from Sonya Varnell, Coordinator of Multi-Cultural Programs, on how she attempted to enrich the black athlete experience on the Lincoln campus), but you can see here that the student/athletes themselves had no problems breaking down barriers that only years earlier had cast a dark pall over the team. Chalk one up for unity among diversity: university.

Now, in keeping things really real and not trying to make this some rose-colored, over-nostalgic walk down memory lane, did you also, as I did, happen to hone in on Brett's mention of Ron Brown's "Well, I've prayed about it and this is what the Lord's told me..." as a response about a player's demotion on the depth chart? Such a statement presupposes extra-biblical revelation and should hold no place in our churches, much less our locker rooms. I know it's somewhat popular to be a Christian-basher these days but there is a fine line to walk in properly living out the Christian life. That line seems to me to have been crossed, and in truth sends a bad message, a bad witness, of the Lord and Savior Jesus Christ. (In full disclosure, I hold an extremely high view God, of scripture, and the message of the bloody cross, but imputing the Almighty's nod in matters relating to judgment of an athlete's performance capabilities seems a far stretch.) God bless his heart, for Ron Brown and Turner Gill both helped lead me to Christ through shared meals together at the training table, but I can see how this type of witness can turn to be both a blessing and a curse, depending on the situation. (I'll withdraw from my bully-pulpit now)

Lastly, the story of another fight -this one in Tokyo, Japan- caught my ear. I want to find out more about this, because if it's anything like the earlier brouhaha we heard of, it too may hold a special key to the bonds of the Scarlet Brotherhood. Be it the Lincolnite punks in the dormitory parking lot or some professional wrestlers outside a Japanese bar, boys would be boys. And if their manhood or sense of dignity were ever called into question they had no qualms about letting their fists do the talking. If you are one of those who automatically defer to the 'caveman as footballer' camp, you might be nodding your head and thinking, "Aha, the truth finally comes out! They were really all just a bunch of dumb, rapaciously thuggish jocks!" But if you look at it from a 'team' viewpoint, these kids had the backs of each and every one of their own, and it was a cold day in hell if they'd ever turned theirs away from another in straits. We'll continue to let the facts roll in how they may. In the meantime, let's keep rolling with the punches.

Notable quote #2:
Brett Popplewell on the team concept: "Everyone was playing for each other…. Look, the superstars the fans will remember, but every guy had a part in it."

If fate means you to lose, give him a good fight anyhow.

William McFee, *Casuals of the Sea*

Making its way to Japan over the vastness of the Pacific Ocean in 1945, the battleship USS Pennsylvania carried one particular soldier among others tasked with decoding encrypted enemy messages. Though fully up to the challenge, his true talents lied in performing magic tricks and an engaging, witty, conversational banter. His name? Johnny Carson, Norfolk, Nebraska's most famous son. Were it not for Fat Man and Little Boy's timely visits to Hiroshima and Nagasaki as he and his shipmates ventured toward the proposed Asian combat zone, the world may have never enjoyed Johnny's long running Tonight Show antics. A 1949 University of Nebraska graduate with a bachelor of arts degree in radio and speech with a minor in physics, Johnny brought people together. And with his sidekick Ed McMahon they were a unifying factor for much of late-night America from the 60's to the early 90's.

But just as Johnny was hanging up his clubs in 1992, another unifying Norfolker was just getting into full-swing. His name was Kevin Raemakers, and I'll call him the 'Mad Uniter' here. Why? Because his outgoing personality, his eventual maturation, and his desire for Nebraska Football greatness lit a match that soon catapulted to a raging inferno. Hold on folks, this should be one helluva interview. Without further ado, heeeeerrre's Kevin!

Notable quote #1:
"That's when I felt things clicked. When we changed our defense and they said "Okay, you're not 320 lbs. anymore, you need to play 285-290 lbs. And it's all speed, pin your ears back and just go.""

Kevin Raemakers

Scholarship Recruit, Defensive Tackle, Norfolk, Nebraska (Norfolk Catholic)
Where are they now? Atlanta, Georgia, Management

Question: What year was your first fall camp, Kevin?

Kevin Raemakers: First camp was '90. I played freshman ball and after three games got moved up to varsity. I redshirted my second year because Kenny Walker was there at the time and I wasn't going to beat him out, and then I started the next three years.

Q: What was it like for you being around Kenny?

KR: Kenny was awesome, because here was guy that was obviously deaf, and just ultimately led by example and couldn't say a thing. So his actions spoke volumes more than words, and you saw the way the guy worked out and the way he played.

And every play was 120%. I don't care if we were in helmets or full pads, versus the scout team or the starting offense, he was full bore. So he was a great guy to look up to. As a young guy coming in it was like, 'If I'm gonna play at this level I've got to be as good, if not better, than this guy.' I was in awe. He was so intimidating. If the guy took his shirt off you're just in awe of him. Here I am wearing a freakin' training bra and a fat roll, and this guy doesn't have an ounce of fat on him.(laughs)

Q: Did you ever see Kenny play basketball?

KR: Yeah, at the Rec Center. The guy could have played basketball at Nebraska if he wanted to...

Q: Kevin, this one time I saw him with one foot planted out by the three point arc, right? He then pivoted, took one step, elevated and just tomahawked the freaking basketball! Danny Nee saw it and just about crapped his pants! (laughs) So tell me, what stood out to you when you first stepped on campus?

KR: At the time, in high school you're All-Everything. Right? You won football titles, wrestling titles, track titles… and when I got to Nebraska I was basically a man-child. I was basically a big fish in a small pond in Norfolk, Nebraska, Class C ranked. So I thought I was all that and a box of peanuts. And one thing that really stood out to me was one, my ego, and two, how immature I really was, because I was an extremely selfish, immature kid coming into Nebraska. At the end of the day, it was like, 'I'm gonna come in, start, be this All-American everything.'

I don't know if you remember offensive lineman Jeff Cheney, he wasn't the greatest player and kind of was the butt of a lot of jokes, but the first practice I lined up at nose guard and he's playing guard, and I'm thinking, 'I'm gonna be eating this guy's lunch every play.' And the first play from scrimmage he gets up under me and just puts me on my back! That was my wake-up call, and it took a year for people to forget about that play. Here's this high school All-American, Nebraska Athlete of the Year, and I'm just going to come in and dominate people, and he just absolutely physically kicked my butt. It was a wake-up call that I needed to step it up and tell me I wasn't as good as I thought.

Q: Anything organizationally stick out to you?

KR: I think the biggest thing was -you know, you grow up in Nebraska: I was going to games as a freshman and sophomore in high school, and then I was recruited my junior and senior year, so I was basically there every weekend at home games- but when you walk on campus and you're there and you see how it's run, it's so professional and it's so serious. The minute they blew the whistle it was intense. It didn't take you very long to figure out that you needed to focus, stay intense, and the speed was so much greater than what I'd ever experienced. My hardest practice in high school would have been my easiest practice at Nebraska. It just stepped things up a whole other notch. Everyone is flying around 100 miles an hour. It was awesome.

Q: Any good friendships you had going in? Any new guys you met?

KR: What was really weird was, I was recruited as an offensive guard. A lot of people don't know that. I was a pulling guard in high school and could move and was used to that position, and after testing out at Nebraska Charlie McBride walks up to me as we make our way out of the fieldhouse and says, "You need to come to Defensive Line meetings tomorrow." I never took one snap at Nebraska on offense: I immediately was plugged into the D-Line. Right off the bat Kent Wells, Mike Murray, Lawrence Pete, those guys took me under their wing. They treated me like one of their own. It was just amazing, because I hadn't proven anything at Nebraska.

And you look back in hindsight and when Christian came in, they asked me to take him under my wing. So I'm assuming that's what they did with Mike Murray, Lawrence Pete & Kent Wells. These guys would work out and I was invited to work out with them in the weightroom, just to push you. You learned the good things from them, because all of us learned a lot of bad things away from football. But when you got onto campus there, they were great mentors and they passed the baton on to you, and then you passed it on to others when you left there. There were always good relationships, good support. You know, some people tell you that I was one of those guys that was supportive, but here I was 18, 19 years old and these guys are treating me as if I'm one of their own.

Q: That's quite a group, too: Wells, Murray, Pete?

KR: Oh yeah, they were nuts. People thought we were nuts. Russ Hochstein was an offensive lineman who played at Nebraska long after I was gone and now plays in the pros, and there was an article that was sent to me where a reporter asked him, "Who was the craziest player you ever knew?" (And I never played with the guy, okay?) And he said, "Kevin Raemakers." And I'm like, 'What?!' (laughs) I don't even know the kid! Don't think I ever met him! But I guess them just seeing us and hearing about the things we did... and a lot of it's embarrassing. I'll even run into people nowadays and I'll be like, 'Gosh, I apologize for being such an ass!' (laughs) And they go, "No! You were great because of how hard you pushed us."

Q: What people would say that?

KR: I'm good friends with Zach Weigert now, and Jason Peter, and they said, "You guys basically paved the way and the foundation for the way things went." It's just kind of a role you got into. At the time you don't really think about it. And your confidence level is up and it works for you and it works for the team. It just is real weird. It's flattering, its humbling that people bring my name up and John Parrella's name up. You really don't think about the impact you've had on guys until you're gone.

Q: Does that come out of the blue for you?

KR: Well, I heard it the year after we'd left and missed the field goal versus Florida State. Connealy had said it the next year after the Miami win. And then Osborne was really cool: he sends me a hand-written letter with a national championship t-shirt and hat and it said, "We finished what you started." A lot of guys started bring my name up and all of a sudden I start getting these calls from all these writers, saying, "Do you know what they're saying about you?" It was just humbling.

And now I go back and the guys I played with start getting inducted into the Hall of Fame now. They invite you back because you played with them. So they invite you back and they're up there giving their speech and they go, "I owe a lot to Kevin Raemakers." And I go, 'I used to just pound on you in practice...' and I wouldn't even think the guy would want to talk to me.

But at the same time there are guys there who still hate my guts, guys like Aaron Graham, as an example. Him and I to this day won't talk to each other. I went against him every day and called him every name in the book, never thought he was any good. And I always let him know he wasn't any good. Our egos just won't let it go. (laughs)

Q: I have to say, Murray and Wells -as role models- those guys did some absolutely crazy, gross and nasty stuff, didn't they?

KR: Well, they did. But it was our group. When Pat Englebert was a senior and I was a sophomore, we were the ones that started what we called "the Girthing."

Q: The Girthing? (laughs)

KR: What we would do -and it was only done strictly on your birthday, it had to be your birthday- what I did was, it would be after practice and I'd lift my shirt up and people would spit on my belly, wipe snot on it, and then I would lay on your face while they held you down. As that went on, it got more and more disgusting, people crapping in a bag and bringing it out to practice and wiping it on my belly and me laying on someone's face. We had Jason Pesterfield (got a turd in the face), he's puking on the turf. I'm on my knees getting up, and George Sullivan, he kicks me in the ass and smacks me on the back of the head. And the shit's all over the field. It was bad.

And then my senior year, we "Girth" Charlie! (laughs) Charlie (McBride) took his teeth out and he freaking bit me in the gut and punctured my freakin' fat roll! It was out of control. (laughs) We were nasty. I remember Christian crapping in his hand and wiping it on my gut, it was just nasty. And Charlie knew it was coming, during the week we were talking about it. And he said, "Don't you even think of it," and the guys brought him down to the ground - not too hard- but he spit his teeth out and bit me in the gut!

Q: So Charlie was your position coach the entire time?

KR: Charlie was my position coach my whole time. And you know, Charlie was like a father. He always took care of his guys. He was very hard on you, but away from the field he was like your dad. The whole time at Nebraska he was awesome. I could talk to him about anything. After my parents got killed my first call was from my brother, and the first call from a non-family member was Charlie McBride. He could barely even talk, he was just, kept saying how sorry he was, how much he loved me.

You know, when I had my knee surgery after I blew my knee out in the Orange Bowl my sophomore year, he was the last person I saw before I went under, and when I woke up he was standing there with my mom and dad. That's just the type of guy he was. And that's kind of how the whole program was. I never once felt at any point during that time that I wasn't part of the program. And I would say the intensity and support that they showed during that rehab time actually picked up, all calling me on the phone and "Are you still working out? School? Training room?" They were checking up on me. You know how it is, that's probably the most depressing time at Nebraska that I experienced. Even losing my Blackshirt for awhile to Jamie Liewer, who's a great guy. And that's humbling in itself, and frustrating, but at the end of the day it's my fault and nobody else's. And when you blow your knee, you're thinking, 'I'm never gonna play again. I'm starting as a sophomore, I'm gonna play pro ball,' and then boom! It's over.

Q: That's pretty tough for a 19 year old…

KR: Yeah, a 19 year old kid who thinks he's all this and a box of peanuts, and here I am hobbling around.

And I have to say, Charlie is the kind of guy -back when I was playing- he's the type of guy who could have put on the pads and played. He was that intense. That guy would go from zero to one thousand in a second. But the details? He was a master at motivating people and pushing you beyond your limits. You thought, 'I can't do this,' and he'd show you how to do it and he'd push you to do it. As rough and tough as he was, he always made me feel like I could walk through a brick wall, that there was nobody better than me, that there wasn't an opponent who I didn't feel I couldn't kick his ass.

The things he said, you couldn't put in writing, "I can't believe we gave you a f***king scholarship. This is a joke, you should be playing at Wayne State." But then you go in the film room and he goes, "This is a great job. Step here with your foot, reach with your left hand here… " He'd show you ways to beat your opponent. He was a great teacher of the game and an unbelievable motivator. And different techniques? The motor never stopped with that guy. If you had a tank that was half full you were not going to play for Charlie. You had to be half nuts.

And I think the greatest compliment we got, when we went back for the alumni thing, Debbie -his wife, she came up and said to me, Christian, & Connealy- she said, "You have no idea how much Charlie misses you guys. It's not the same. He talks about you guys all the time." And that group was a very, very special group. You've got to understand, that group from Pat Englebert all the way to Jason Peter, we were together 6-7 days a week. Even when football was over on Saturdays we would hook up and eat together on Sundays. We were always together.

Q: Was that encouraged by the staff, the coaches?

KR: No, it was just something you did. And you always looked out for each other, whether it be on campus or at the local watering hole or wherever you were, it was just a very tight-knit group. I can't explain it, the bond and unity that we had was absolutely unbelievable. To get that group of those different personalities together? We came from all over the country, and to get that close? It was like you knew each other since you were in the first grade. Charlie would talk to us in team meetings, "You eleven on the field are like brothers. Every one behind you is a brother to you. You have to look out for each other, take care of each other." And they'd practice that daily.

And Osborne, in writing our goals up at the beginning of the year, and even if you look at our Championship rings that they had, it said, "Unity, Belief, Respect." So, unity was #1, you've got to believe in each other, and you've got to respect each other to be one cohesive unit. And we totally were. Absolutely were. Never did you see or hear guys fighting in the huddle. If we were up or we were down, never were people fighting in the huddle. Now, you'd have people come back to the huddle, Trev Alberts or Pat Englebert, or Conneally or Parrella, and say, "Pick it up, Raemakers, that guy was yours. C'mon, that guy got through your hole." That was it, but it was encouraging. And I don't know about you, but it hurts a lot more coming from a player than from a coach.

Q: Oh yeah...

KR: When you've got Trev Alberts, "That was your guy," or Mike Anderson or Mike Petko, those linebackers, "You've got to squeeze that guard down, he's all over me." Then I'm not doing my job. You don't want to let your guys down. Absolutely not.

Q: And what about Coach Osborne?

KR: You know, one thing about Coach Osborne... it was like I said, I came to Nebraska very immature, highly touted and made some really, really immature, bad decisions: got into some fights, got into some trouble downtown, the police and some local students. And Osborne called my parents and I into a meeting on a Sunday morning after I'd been arrested downtown and he basically said, "I'm taking Kevin's scholarship away. He can't continue to do this. We've given him chances, he keeps messing up.." and he looked at me and he apologized to me. He said, "I've failed you. But I promise you one thing, you will graduate from this university and you will be an asset to this community. But I'm telling you right now, you'll never play on that field again." I literally sit there -at the time, 290 lbs., 6' 4"- I'm literally just sobbing in his office. It was the absolute, ultimate wake up call. It was like, 'I'm done. I can't keep doing what I'm doing.' He telephones me to this day, I get a Christmas card every year, I got a phone call after my parents died, had dinner with him in Chattanooga when he was in town. Just a great guy, just a great guy.

Q: How did you get back on the team after that, Kev?

KR: Well, just proving to him: my grades obviously got better. I worked out hard, came back better, faster from my knee surgery, and just proved to him that 'I can do it.' I personally went back to him two or three weeks later and I begged him. I apologized, and he said, "I'm taking your scholarship away."

And he called me back a month or two later and asked how committed I was, said he liked what he was seeing, liked what he heard from Boyd and your staff, liked what they were seeing. And he said, "This is your last chance." And I never, never got called back to his office again (unless there was a player he wanted me to talk to or something came up in Unity Council that he wanted to be aware of).

Q: What effect did the Unity Council have?

KR: It was incredible. Now, when I got in trouble -you remember the Unity Council, there were players selected from every position. There were 8 to 10 guys. We'd meet up in the stadium every Tuesday night after practice and dinner- and I got called in. And I'd get called in normally as a member of the Council, but then I got called in to sit in "the chair." Basically it's a circle of guys and you sit in the chair and you tell the teammates what happened. It was like, 'I was downtown in a bar. Some guys were ribbing this girl. I told 'em to leave her alone, they started giving me shit. I told them to leave it alone, they didn't leave 'em alone. The guy pushed me, and I just went off on him. And that's how it happened.' Pat Englebert said, "Listen, I love you to death. We've been friends since high school," (since I used to compete against him in track and stuff), and he said, "I'm telling you right now, if you don't grow up and focus on your schoolwork and focus on the task at hand, they're gonna let you go. You're gonna be gone." Not a lot of guys said anything, because you had Eric Weigert, you had Mike Croel, but when it came from Pat it was just devastating, because I'd started with the guy the year before! And here I am sitting: I'm a member of the Unity Council, but now I'm in the chair. It was embarrassing.

The deal is, no Unity Council member should ever be in the chair. Those are the guys the coaching staff looks up to, the ones they and the team picked. So it was extremely humbling, but at the same time it was a blessing in disguise. And I think Coach Osborne obviously knew I had potential. But Paul -at the end of the day?- my problem wasn't that I was a dumb kid, it was the problem that my ego and my maturity was so far behind everybody else at that age. Because I was so used to being 'It', I was the man. It was like, 'I've arrived, I'm here.' But it was really, "You've arrived, but you haven't even started yet." I was a nobody.

Q: Any thoughts about any of the other coaches stick out to you, Kevin?

KR: Well, Milt Tenopir and Dan Young had recruited me as an offensive lineman. And Milt Tenopir would always come up to me after a practice or a game and made it a point to tell me how I did or shared things that I could work on after he saw film the following Monday. He'd say, "Do this" or "You had a great game," just constantly encouraging me. I didn't even play for the guy. Just always encouraging me. And he was busy enough. He had All-American Jake Young and the guys on the line, and when I redshirted that year I played my ass off against Eric Weigert and those guys, pushing them. And he'd come up and thank me. He'd tell me, "The guys we faced Saturday afternoon weren't as good as you. You have a bright future ahead of you." Even the players would tell me that, "Shit, you're a lot better than the guy I went against Saturday." So that was huge compliment, you know? You don't know intentionally if they were trying to build your confidence up, but just them telling you helped so much.

Q: So now you're an upperclassman and you've gotten past all that immaturity and assumed more of a leadership role on the team. How did you exert your influence on the younger guys?

KR: My deal was, I was constantly a bit of a free spirit, if you'd say that. I was very talkative, very aggressive, very physical, constantly pushing the guys in the weightroom, in summer conditioning. If someone didn't show up the next time we'd sit there and bust their balls, really get on them, tried to lead by example. And it's weird, it was nothing that you practiced or rehearsed for, it would just happen: the work ethic and the aggressiveness on the field.

Now, I would talk shit on the field, you ask anybody. I was an ass on the field and would try to get in guy's heads, but after practice or in the showers I'd always compliment them, 'Hey, you had a great practice,' or 'You did a good job,' constantly encouraging the guys around me. The deal is, if I was having fun and I had guys pushing me, it made me work harder. If I felt someone moving up on the depth chart (and I knew how good, you know, Christian Peter was and Jason Peter was), I figured the harder I pushed them the harder it's gonna make me work, because I don't want to lose my spot, I don't want to lose my Blackshirt. And then it was a competition. I wanted to be like Pat Englebert, I wanted to be like John Parrella, and Christian wanted to be like me, and Jason wanted to be like Christian. It was a constant cycle, you know?

Q: So what was your first thought that first day when Charlie said, "You're joining me on defense"?

KR: I was –honestly?- extremely concerned. Nervous. Because I wasn't a big fan of defense in high school due to the fact that a lot of times I was double- and triple-teamed, so I wasn't a standout on defense. But if you're taking three guys to block someone, that alone is going to leave two guys free or open, so I was just really concerned: 'I don't know how to play defense. I know offense. I know how to pull, I know how to pass block.' But once I got over there and I realized the mentality -and it fit my mentality, the way I was- because when I played the light was on but not everybody was home all the time, you know? (laughs) So I had to play… the best way I could describe it was, "You had to play nuts under control." You had to play just out of your mind, but you had to control yourself.

Q: That's a fine line to walk…

KR: Yeah, it was hard. And that's why I struggled so much early on, because I couldn't separate leaving the field from walking into The Rail or some other local watering hole.

And that's really where I struggled. I wanted everyone to know me and know who I was, and I was gonna make a name for myself both on the field and at the local tavern. But one thing -when I got in trouble?- Dennis LeBlanc told me after I got in trouble, he said, "Listen, I don't want to see you ever wear another Nebraska t-shirt to class. I don't want to ever see you wear another sweatshirt to class. You are student." Because I wanted the attention I'd wear all my Nebraska shit to class, wear a Nebraska sweatshirt to the bars. And if I wasn't getting attention academically, getting attention playing, physically? I was going to get attention in the bar. Like, how stupid is that, you know?

Q: Was it a little difficult to go incognito thereafter? Actually finding something to wear that didn't have the Nebraska script on it?

KR: I would basically just go into Christian's closet or steal Connealy's clothes. (laughs) That was the joke. Connealy's mom would tell you, I would go to their house and I'd grab a shirt. I'd take a shirt and wear their clothes. I was your stereotypical dumb jock. I always wore Nebraska shit, and once I was through the transition and put the ego on the back shelf, then I only wore the Nebraska stuff on the field where 80,000 people will see me instead of 100 people at a bar. That made sense.

Q: What about Charlie being a great motivator? What did he say to motivate you?

KR: With Charlie, he was basically all verbal. Very verbal. Now and then he'd grab a couple props, sometimes he'd bring a board with a nail in it to practice. He'd say "If you don't get off the ball I'm gonna ram this in your ass." Or he'd take his chewing tobacco (he always chewed Copenhagen), he'd throw it in your face. Charlie was the type of guy, you'd be watching film in meetings and he'd go, "Oh, hell! Look at this!" And it would be a play of me getting hook-blocked. Some guy from Missouri was hooking me and he was like, "You look like a dancing bear! Can you believe it guys, that we gave a scholarship to a dancing bear?!" And he would just keep going and going and going, to the point where it would be, "Hey Coach, enough. I got it. Enough." He knew how to motivate each kid differently.

And with me, I responded really well to the nasty, vulgar, verbal abuse. And I wouldn't even call it verbal abuse. I mean, if we talked to our kids that way, sure, but I knew exactly what his intentions were. I knew after the game, in the locker room he'd come over and give me a hug and kiss me, I just knew that. But Monday through Friday that guy was so far up my ass that you couldn't even breathe.

Q: So it wasn't necessarily negative, it was more goading than anything?

KR: Yeah, exactly. He would point it out and let you know, "Hey, you getting 'hooked' is unacceptable. You're better than that." He'd let you know in front of your teammates so they'd push you too, you know?

And I tell people, 'When we won, practices were hell the following week.' When we lost, it was different. It was just kind of the reverse psychology. You would think that when you lose, when you got beat, they'd just tear you down, but they didn't. They'd still push you - but when we were winning?- they'd be harder on us when we were winning than when we were losing. And we didn't lose that much, we really didn't.

Q: What, only the Iowa State game your junior year and Florida State game your junior & senior years…

KR: Yeah, we lost that bowl game.

Q: Here's what I've been hearing, Kevin: it seems in '89, '90, '91 there was a little more individualism, not as much closeness in the team?

KR: Yeah, you could see that, too. Guys weren't as cohesive. You could see that. You remember the training table? It was the same group of guys there at the training table for three years together there. It got to the point where Coach Brown and some of the other coaches said, "Guys, break it up a little bit. Go sit with the freshmen, go sit with the diverse guys." It was always a group of white guys, so we had to mix it up a little bit. We started doing that and bringing more guys into the circle, and pretty soon it was 6 every week, and then it turned into 8, and then it turned into, hell, we had a whole, huge table of 15-20 guys sitting together eating, you know?

Q: Dr. Stark once mentioned a big moment may have been halftime of the Citrus Bowl, where Kenny Walker got up and gave Coach Osborne a big hug and begged him not to retire. Another one was what Boyd said in January of '91, the team meeting right before winter conditioning, where he pointed out the 'Wanna be's,' the 'Have to be's' and 'The Jerks.' Do you remember that at all? Were any of these the impetus to some changes?

KR: I think the big thing was after my sophomore year where we got beat by Gino Toretta and Miami, 22-0. We came back and the coaches had a meeting and just said, "Listen, we're gonna change up our defense: we're gonna play like a bunch of crazy bandits. You guys have got to do this together, because if we do this we're not gonna have individuals." That's when it was pointed out, that's what Boyd was talking about: "There were guys that wanted to do it, guys that had to do it, and some guys that just aren't gonna do it... and they're not gonna be around here." I don't know if he called them jerks, they just weren't going to be around here.

And it became a point of "Do I wanna do it or do I have to do it?" You found out real quick who was out there because daddy wanted them to play at Nebraska and they got a scholarship and they weren't happy and didn't get the playing time and weren't willing to push themselves to get a starting spot. And I think that turning point that Boyd mentioned, was going into that winter conditioning after the Miami loss. Pat Englebert had graduated, John Parrella was a senior, I was the junior, so on and so forth. That's when I felt things clicked. When we changed our defense and they said "Okay, you're not 320 lbs. anymore, you need to play 285-290 lbs....and it's all speed, pin your ears back and just go." And I felt like that was the style, the character we had on the team and the athletes we had on the team, that was when things started changing. And then we had a good '92 season and then in '93 go undefeated and play for the national championship.

Q: It seems to me that national championship game was huge turning point, also. It wasn't a victory on the scoreboard, but you knew in your heart that you actually played well enough to win it. I hate to bring up a potentially sore subject, but what about that game stands out for you?

KR: Well, first of all, we were seventeen to twenty point underdogs and that game should've been over at halftime. But we had a great, great two weeks of practice down there; guys weren't getting drunk and chasing cat. It was just very focused. It felt like we had played just as well as their team. They were fast and athletic, but we realized right away we had a chance. And I remember thinking, 'Hey, we're gonna beat these guys.' And I never in my mind, not for one minute did I doubt that we weren't gonna win. Even when Byron was kicking that field goal I still thought we were gonna win the game.

And I don't know if you remember, but William Floyd, Florida States' Fullback, scored that one touchdown that wasn't even close. And that just fired me up even more, you know? It fired me up so much that I got a late hit on Charlie Ward, which really helped, you know?

Q: I remember that!

KR: It was your emotions taking over, and the officials kept protecting him. They would tell us on the field, "Stay away from the quarterback." And they were like, "Balls gone! Ball's gone!" It was to the point where the guy hadn't even thrown the ball yet and the refs were yelling, "Balls gone! Ball's gone!" It was just bullshit.

And this year... this year (and I'm getting off the subject) for the first time I watched that game. On the Classic channel one Sunday they're playing classic games: it was that game and it was narrated by William Floyd. They talked about a couple things that stood out, and he said, "When we got into this game we definitely took them (Nebraska) for granted. We knew they were big and physical, but we didn't realize how athletic they were and how they didn't stop. How every one of those guy's had a motor, and it never stopped!"

I got that penalty four or five plays before Floyd supposedly scored that touchdown, and he even said, "There were some frustrations going on on the field. Would I throw a flag on that? No." And the announcer even said, "That was a real questionable call," and Floyd said, "But I'm glad they called it, because it set us up for that touchdown." And I'm like, 'Oh, great! I blew the Orange Bowl for us.'

Q: No, no, no...

KR: But when Floyd jumps for the endzone, the announcer said that it was a real questionable touchdown. And Floyd said, "Listen, we won the game. I'm not gonna say I was in the end zone or not. The scoreboard says I scored." (But he never came out and said, "I scored a touchdown.") People -to this day- will come up and say, "You guys got screwed in that game." To this day! And that was like 15-16 years ago?

Q: A lot of the younger players said that after that game they knew in their heart of hearts that they could play with anybody...

KR: Right. And I tell you what, I work out with Garrison Hearst. He and I train together at a local gym. He played at San Francisco with William Floyd, and once Garrison found out I played football at Nebraska he said, "William told me you were the best team they'd ever played." That's huge.

Q: Wow, that's something to hang your hat on. And Kevin, I've watched that game in preparation for talking to some of you guys; you barely touched Charlie Ward on that penalty call, didn't you?

KR: Yeah, I touched him on the shoulder, just kind of pushed him. He didn't fall down. I just kind of pushed him and they threw the flag.

Q: Well, I remember Charlie McBride on the sideline said something to you, and he seemed kind of conflicted, because it's a ricky-ticky call. But then again, you were trained to go 100% on every play, so how can they expect you to hold back now?

KR: When I went to the sideline Charlie just yelled at me, "Use your fuckin' head!," but then he said, "But don't let up." So again, being nuts but being under control."Use your fucking head, but don't let up. Be smart." That's what he said to me. I thought I'd never play another snap again.(laughs)

Q: And I've got to ask you, Kevin, would the f-bombs fly out of Charlie's mouth within earshot of Coach Osborne?

KR: Oh yeah! With Charlie, what you saw was what you got. He never changed, because Charlie was the type of guy that would just break you down. That was his whole deal, when you came in to him you were just a big chunk of clay; he would mold us and form us the way he wanted. Charlie was intense, spit in your face, his eyes bulging out of his head. And Coach Osborne would put his arm around you, analytically, "Let's talk about this." I felt like I was going to confession in church, you know? (laughs)

Q: Good cop, bad cop? Coach Osborne knew what he was doing when he pulled that staff together?

KR: Absolutely. He knew the guys that would pull his strengths up and help him out with his weaknesses. That staff, I'm telling you -and I said it in my Hall of Fame speech- you had Coach Brown, Coach Samuel, Darlington, Dan Young, all those guys, Kevin Steele. It was an unbelievable staff that was always on the same page. I don't know what happened behind the scenes, if they got along or hung out together, but to us guys there was nothing that could get in their way.

Q: Any other thoughts or recollections from that Florida State game stands out in your mind?

KR: I mean, the whole game was awesome. I didn't have a great game individually, but the play of the Trev Alberts'es? The play of Tommie Frazier, Lance Lundberg and our offensive line moving them back? Terry Connealy, Toby Wright, Mike Anderson? I miss a tackle and, boom, here's Mike cleaning up. It was just like we were flying. Everything seemed so fast. Guys were just flying around. By far one of the fastest games ever. The game flew by time-wise, but the speed on the field?

One thing in my mind: after the game I'm sitting in the hotel room with my dad, crying, and just saying, 'It was just so fast!' I was exhausted after that game, but the speed of the game was incredible.

Q: Any other favorite practice story?

KR: There were so many. My experiences at Nebraska were everything and more than I could ever dream of. There were so many good practices, so many good memories, it was a great experience. Making a decision to go there was the best thing I did.

Q: Where else where you recruited to?

KR: I went to UCLA, Notre Dame, Tennessee and Iowa, because I was going to wrestle and play football. So Hayden Fry and then Dan Gable -because I'd gone to Dan Gable's wrestling camp the year before- they said I could play football and wrestle.

Q: And once you stepped foot on campus you realized that it's hard enough to play football alone, much less football plus wrestle?

KR: Exactly. I would go down and wrestle with Tolly Thompson, who was the heavyweight, and Rulon Gardner. I would just go down there to roll around with them because I was big and strong, and Coach Manning asked, "Can you come work out these guys?" So I would come down there and work out with them every now and then. They were superior wrestlers.

Q: That's' pretty heady company, Kevin. Here you had Tolly, who became the NCAA heavyweight Champion, and then you have Rulon, who became the Olympic champion...that's pretty huge. You were a sparring-partner equivalent of that great Russian, Alexander Karelin, in training Rulon?(laughs)

KR: Yeah, right. That dude would rip my head off. (laughs)

Q: Let me ask you, was there anyone behind the scenes, the inner workings, who meant a lot to you?

KR: There is. I think there's three departments that do not get enough credit. One's gonna be the training staff: Doak, George, Jerry. You've got to understand, those guys kept us on the field for 4 years. I don't know if you're gonna talk to anybody who didn't have an injury and those guys got you back and were on the cutting edge in rehabilitation, the nicest equipment, ice baths after practice, tubs before, stretching, just taking care of you. They were awesome. They were there 7 days a week. People don't understand that. Sunday morning's after the game they were giving treatment again.

And the strength staff, I was a huge Randy Gobel fan and Boyd Epley fan. Those guys were constantly monitoring you, talking to you, come up at lunch and see what you were eating, just constantly on you.

And then at the end of the day, Keith Zimmer and Dennis Leblanc, those guys taught you how to be a student. A lot of people forget that. If you go to Nebraska and think you're just gonna play football, you are mistaken. You are gonna go, you're gonna get an education, they're gonna push you and they're gonna monitor you. The deal at Nebraska -if you're fortunate enough to get a scholarship to play there- they will produce outstanding citizens. If you come to the program you will succeed. There's no doubt in my mind, you will succeed. If you commit. But if you wanna do your own thing you're not gonna graduate, you're not gonna play football. You might go to the pros, and what percentage comes back and finishes school? I'm not sure.

Q: Well, anything I haven't touched on that you feel had a big effect on creating this unbelievable, unstoppable run during Coach Osborne's end of tenure?

KR: There are two things that really stand out in my mind. From your position all the way to the trainers to the coaching staff, everybody was all on the same page. We had the same common goals, the same theme. And every department had the same intensity, whether it be weightlifting and conditioning, when you went to study table you had to buckle down for two hours and just focus on your schoolwork, when you went in to get treatment you'd walk out of there soaking wet because of rehab, you're getting your body stronger, healing from your injuries, to the training table. Everybody was on the same page, we had the common theme.

And you hear this all the time, "Nebraska has the greatest fans in the world." And I will tell you, our fans are amazing. Down here -you know I've lived in Tennessee, I've lived in Louisiana, I've lived in Georgia- and even the Clemson fans from the recent game we had at the Gator Bowl, they've talked to me and said, "Your fans are incredible! Good people." They live for Nebraska football, and the way they treated us is phenomenal.

And win or lose, they were just so awesome, so supportive.

The letters you would get? When I got hurt -when I blew my knee- I get this big freakin' stack of mail! The mailman brings me this big honkin' stack of letters! I don't know how the hell they got my address, but he must have brought a stack of something like 75 letters. People I don't even know. Don't even know! Just, "We hope you're doing well, we're thinking of you. We can't wait to see you get better and get on the field again." Just totally encouraging.

Q: That does a lot for a kid knowing he's gonna be out of commission for awhile…

KR: Yeah! When you feel you're not gonna be a part of the program, here these people reach out even further and draw me into the family more than when I was playing.

Q: Any special perks or privileges as far as being a Nebraska football player?

KR: I think just putting that helmet on alone is the biggest privilege and honor, to say I wore the Blackshirt. I wore the N and I played on that field. That in itself is an honor.

Q: Do you still have your Blackshirt?

KR: Oh yeah, I've got my Blackshirt down in my basement, framed; my Orange Bowl jersey framed; and my helmet from my senior year downstairs. My wife calls it 'My Shrine to Myself.' (laughs)

Q: Any parting shots, Kevin?

KR: Hopefully, I think if you were to interview guys from the '90 to the 2000 class, I think you would hear a lot of the same answers, I think. It would show you that everyone was always on the same page. And I think after Coach Osborne's departure and Coach Solich's departure, a lot of things changed. I think a lot of tradition, a lot of things we used to do, maybe the athletes weren't given, weren't empowered to do some of the things we did when we were there together. They basically gave us all a leash, and they knew player by player how long that leash could be. And they let you take that leash to the last inch. But then if you got a little outside that line they'd rein you back in. There's no way without

Boyd and Bryan and Keith and Doak and George and Jerry and Dennis, there's no way I'd have graduated or even played after I got in trouble my sophomore year. There's no way. I mean Osborne, I thanked him at my Hall of Fame banquet and said, 'This guy never gave up on me. And he had every right to. Because you know what? I would have. If I were him, I would've.'

Q: Which probably, for the average person out there, sheds some light on his treatment of Lawrence Phillips…

KR: Exactly.

Q: And hey, I swore I heard somewhere at a banquet or something that someone thought your name was Rainmakers. Do you remember that?

KR: Yeah, they thought I was Indian. I'm Dutch, man. Just because I've got a big, fat, wide head and a big, wide nose doesn't automatically mean I'm Indian. (laughs)

When I went to Iowa the first time I met Hayden Fry. My brother and I went on the recruiting trip. We were walking around and they had a place where they meet the recruits and are shaking hands, and a lieutenant there said to Coach Fry, "Hey, this is Kevin Raemakers and his brother Mike." And Hayden Fry looks at me and he says, "Rainmakers? You know, you sure don't look Indian." And I thought, 'What?!' My brother looked at me and mumbled, "Who is *this* asshole?" (laughs) Hilarious.

End conversation.

Well, what did you think? I've known Kevin since he was a rotund little toad of junior high age, as many of his relatives lived in my little hometown of Petersburg in Boone County, Nebraska. And though he's matured and become a successful, responsible businessman, husband and father, his personality remains unchanged: refreshingly honest & open, funny, and bluntly outspoken as ever. You've gotta love guys like that. They're not so tightly wound, and they bring a degree of levity to a team who just might be. Yet still, when you see the fire in their eyes as situations get down to brass tacks, it steels your focus even more. Kevin was an original. Coach Osborne recently referred to him as a 'free spirit.' Well said, Tom. Well said.

You know, human nature for the most part is resistant to change: just about any and all change. Yet, did you sense the joy and passion in Kevin's speech when he talked about the switch from the read & react 5-0 to the attacking 4-3 defense? "Listen we're gonna change up our defense, we're gonna play like a bunch of crazy bandits." What 18 year old can't get excited about that kind of talk? Heck, I'm in my forties and this kind of stuff still fires me up and makes me want to strap 'em on one more time.'Unleashed' may be a good term for what that defensive switch accomplished: "Okay, you're not 320 lbs. anymore, you need to play at 285-290 lbs. And it's all speed, pin your ears back and just go." I can't wait to talk to Charlie McBride and some more Blackshirts to get their slant due to a loosing of the fetters because, in the final analysis, I'm of the belief that it was the defense who may have been the crucial link to those championships. I say this because Coach Osborne's offense had already been nudging the periphery of a powerful and perpetual proficiency.

Kevin also reminded us of the never-ending quest for improvement. There was no resting on one's laurels, like when he said, "When we won, practices were hell the following week. When we lost, it was different. It was just kind of the reverse psychology." Along with that came his mention of competition, as well as the daisy-chain of peer leadership and goal setting, of wanting to measure up to the upperclassman who preceded you: "I wanted to be like Pat Englebert, I wanted to be like John Parrella, and Christian wanted to be like me, and Jason wanted to be like Christian." There was the Kenny Walker effect, too. It was as if one didn't have to reach too far back in Husker history for a reminder of the ethic and the legacy to strive for, because your role models were right there in the flesh setting an example in daily drills, how they approached their tasks, pushing you along and mentoring you via both word and action. You just had to be sure nobody knew it was your birthday on that particular day, because, let's be honest, who ever really wants to be Girthed? Joyce C. Hall, another famous former Norfolker, was the founder of Hallmark Cards, which tells you that birthday greetings come in all sizes and types.

Notable quote #2:
Kevin Raemakers on the defensive change: "Listen, we're gonna change up our defense: we're gonna play like a bunch of crazy bandits."

Sweet are the dreams of college life, before our faith is nicked-
The world is but a cherry tree that's waiting to be picked;
The world is but an open road-until we find, one day,
How far away the goal posts are that called us to the play.

Grantland Rice, *Alumunus Football*

Before introducing our next individual I think we ought to take a seat and collect our thoughts -to surmise where we've been thus far- and organize the points made. I suppose you're beginning to get a reasonable understanding of the tenor of the Nebraska campus in the early to mid-1990's, but if we're going to make this trip worthwhile we should grab our bag and think about readjusting & repositioning its contents for the remainder of the journey. In doing so, I surmise that we still have only a shallow, vague grasp of concepts that could bear more fleshing out, so we'll continue to delve even further into those nuances as we proceed forward with the interviews. Some aspects of our inventory have me wanting more, plus I'm really enjoying finding the answers to each individual "Where are they now?"

In my head it's becoming apparent that the N Factor consists of four principle components: 1) persons, 2) places, 3) things, and 4) the ethereal/metaphysical/ untouchable things which may only exist in theory or ideology in our minds, that are merely concepts. Maybe we should call them ideas and thoughts. Abstractions, even? In any case, here's what we've gathered thus far:

Persons:
Coaches, Athletic Department support staff, community support, fan support, a diversity of mentors, Eminence Outliers, warriors, the 'difference makers', character kids, a vocal & non-vocal leader mix, free spirits, family, The Lincolnites, opponents.

Places:
The North Field House locker room, South Stadium locker room, The Pit, Grass Practice Fields, Memorial Stadium, Weight room, Hewitt Academic Center, Training Room, Training Table, Dormitory Parking Lot, Downtown on 'O' Street, Tokyo, Japan.

Things:
Offensive multiplicity, competent communication, the joy of playing the spoiler, task simplification, negative motivation, The Motor, the walk-on program, positive peer influence/leadership, preparation, new technology, off-campus bonding, breaking others' will, defensive scheme change, friendly picking on others, nicknames of acceptance, lack of excessive ego's, fights on and off the field, maturation, lasting servanthood, the Girthing, repetition.

Ideas/Thoughts/Concepts:
Commitment, accountability, reciprocation of respect, sacrifice,
roles, humility, vision, legacy/tradition, belief, competition, dominance, family, Positive Mental Attitude, present-day focus, recognition, revenge, role awareness, sacrifice, trust, unity, vision, a sense of urgency, resolve, a sense of destiny.

I like this list and look forward to embellishing it with what we come upon in later chapters.

We now come to Al Papik, Senior Associate Athletic Director and Head of Compliance. Though that title sounds about as exciting as watching toenails grow, I think you'll find an individual with a very interesting past and a keen awareness of the Nebraska program in that era of 60 & 3 greatness. Here's a man I greatly respect and admire: Mr. Al Papik...

Notable quote #1:
"Tom Osborne had a major, major role by his ability to see the big picture of what needs to be done, to get the program to that level and keep it at that level, be it his staff, the facilities, the recruitment, and to instill that into a program where everybody was trying to achieve these same goals."

Al Papik

Question: Al, I really appreciate your taking some time to share with me some of the ways you were able to facilitate Nebraska Football becoming what it was and still is…

Al Papik: No problem at all.

Q: So where did you grow up?

AP: I'm from Nebraska. I attended Crete High School and went the service and had two years of military duty, and enrolled at Doane College and played 4 years of football there. Leaving Doane College, I started out teaching and coaching at Laurel, Nebraska, then went to my hometown, which was Crete, Nebraska and coached the football team there for two years. Then went to Doane College and was the athletic director, head football coach, and head track coach for 17 years. Then I went into administration at Doane College for one year, was Director of Admissions and Administrative Assistant to the President. The following year, the fall of 1974, I took a position at the University of Nebraska as Director of Admissions.

Q: How was the transition from coaching to administration?

AP: Well, it was an easy move. It was an easy transition because my years of coaching at Doane College. Working for a small college, the head coach does the large majority of the recruiting, so I was quite involved with admission activities and actually assisted the department in the general recruiting and the processing of students. So it was a smooth and easy move.

Q: How did you come upon making the move to the University? What precipitated that?

AP: Through the work I was doing at Doane I got to know the people that were on the road representing the university and became well acquainted with Bob Devaney and his staff. (And even before him, with Bill Jennings and his staff, too) And they're coaching 25 miles away, so our paths crossed quite a bit.

The Nebraska admissions office had an opening, and I found that a number of people in the admissions office were involved in athletics as far as determining eligibility requirements, working with the Big 8 Conference on initial eligibility and continuing eligibility and that sort of thing.

They called and recruited me, so to speak, and wanted to know if I would be interested in an interview, and I went up there and accepted the job. And for 12 years I served as Director of Admissions before I went over to the Athletic Department.

Q: Earlier you spoke of paths crossing. Speaking of that, I heard you had the opportunity to coach against a certain football-playing redhead for Hastings College back in the day…

AP: That's right. Tom Osborne was an outstanding small college athlete in the state of Nebraska. He played at Hastings High School, stayed in Hastings and played at Hastings College. Doane and Hastings were traditionally rivals, and he, of course, had 4 years that he was an outstanding athlete there. We had them on our schedule each and every year.

Q: Did you try recruiting him to Doane?

AP: No, I think it was a pretty well done deal already. (laughs) His father was very involved in Hastings College as a supporter of the institution and everyone knew that Tom was going to go to Hastings College in the later part of his high school career.

Q: This might be a little off track, but I once heard that Bill Parcells had his first coaching job at Hastings College...

AP: I'm not sure it was his first coaching job, but I think you're right. Bill was an assistant coach and a line coach at Hastings College when I was coaching at Doane. He came from something like South Dakota, I'm not sure. But yes, he did serve for some short period of time, and I'm not sure of his length of service, but much more than one season.

Q: Was there anything about Tom Osborne as a college player stood out to you?

AP: Other than the fact that Doane was on the short end a majority of the time in the outcome of the contest? (laughs)

He was the quarterback. Tom McLaughlin was his head coach and used him very effectively. He had that ability to throw the ball and throw the ball deep. But he was also a running quarterback, so they utilized his athletic ability to a great extent. They had some good years when Tom was playing for them.

Q: A lot of play-action stuff, in other words?

AP: Yes, that's right.

Q: So you were in Admissions at Nebraska, what brought you to the athletic side?

AP: I think it was the relationship I'd developed with Bob Devaney. The Shrine Bowl game there in Lincoln… every year Doane College was the South Shrine camp's site for about two weeks of training for that particular game. Well, I was the camp director for it, and Bob would always have his assistant coaches around. So there was a lot of give and take between the University and myself, and I knew the staff and a number of assistant coaches. And of course, Tom Osborne became a part of Bob Devaney's staff, though we had established a relationship there prior to his involvement with the football program.

When I took the Admissions job the administration decided the Admissions Office would be responsible for initial eligibility for the Athletic Department: what the University requirements were, what the Big 8 Conference requirements were, what the NCAA requirements were, and if students qualified, et cetera. And as soon as I came aboard as Admissions Director Tom asked and wanted me to be involved when recruits came on campus. (Many times the coaches were busy with coaching football in practice or the game, so Tom felt the recruits needed an opportunity to see the institution as a whole, rather than just come to visit the football coaches and the football facilities.)

Q: That fall of 1974 was when you joined the University was Coach Osborne's second year as a head coach. Any recollections of seeing him as a player first and then years later as a head coach? Any impressions of his maturation?

AP: Well, Tom was doing his graduate work at the University of Nebraska while he was assisting Bob Devaney. And Tom and a number of university athletes who went to grad school and were undergraduates had a basketball team; they'd travel around and they came down to Doane College on occasion, so I had an opportunity to visit with him when he was a student.

And, of course, Tom approached Bob about being on the coaching staff, and Bob saw a lot of potential in him and gave him the responsibility of working with student athletes from an academic point of view: if athletes were having academic problems, to prevent any academic problems, to be sure they received academic advising, to be enrolled in the proper program.

And out of that grew an academic advising program at the university that was second to none in the late '70's and through the decade of the 80's, where a program headed up by Ursula Walsh started to get a lot of national recognition for having large numbers of students graduate, having a high grade point average and a large number of Academic All-Americans. The impetus started there, of course.

And Tom, when he was named head coach he put a great deal of emphasis on having a program that was solid and had the facilities and support and worked within the confines of rules and regulations of the NCAA. I think that Nebraska took a leadership role in the kind of emphasis they were putting in academic support for the student-athlete, and that was shown in the facilities, the Hewitt Academic Center, and the number of staff that were involved in the entire program for all sports, men and women.

And when the Unity Council was established, that was also one of the issues that maybe led the country at that time. I think Nebraska was doing more than a vast majority of colleges in that area. (I thought that it wasn't just Jack Stark that created the Unity Council, but Tom had a Unity Council going before that.) He also did a great deal with psychological counseling, to get sports psychologists to assist the coaching staff, working with the coaching staff and with the student-athletes in the roles they would play. He felt those would be a significant contribution to performance on a Saturday afternoon.

Tom was able to get so many staff areas to support his goals: to recruit a good number of football players (the kind who would stay with us for the 4-5 year period), the kind of staff who would be able to coach them up to where they could compete for conference championships. He had a vision that took a great deal of support. He had to make sure he had the business office, the strength training complex, the food service, the sports information, the academic support, the ticket office, that everybody was involved in this. And each year to start off the season there would be a meeting with all the appendages the student/athlete would touch or who would have an affect on the football program, emphasizing that we were "all in this together and we need to think alike and support each other and have a role in the culture of this program as to what we're trying to accomplish." Tom had that kind of ability.

Of course, Bob Devaney had a real sense of collecting a very diverse, but a very effective staff, too, whether it was coaches or support staff. And initially Tom was able to, of course, keep some of those people, the majority. And then Tom was able to surround himself with the people who stayed with him a long time and were very capable and bought into the system. He really developed things behind the scenes. That was very easy to spot, how and what Tom was doing and what his objectives were, how he went about ensuring what was to be accomplished.

Q: So from the beginning he seemed to have a wonderful organizational mindset? A grand vision?

AP: Yes, well said.

Q: Looking back and witnessing how the program operated under Coach Osborne's vision, was there anything you wish you would have done during your stretch Doane? Anything you wish you'd implemented those earlier days?

AP: Well, those are two different creatures: coaching at a small college and coaching at the University of Nebraska. We did have an opportunity at Doane during my last few years of coaching where we were very successful. We actually, toward the end of my tenure, went four straight years without losing a contest.

Q: Really, Al?!

AP: The first year, 1968 -I'm not even sure of the exact year now- maybe it was '66, we had an undefeated season. And I wasn't aware of that, but it was the only undefeated season ever in the history of the institution. And we then had 4 consecutive seasons of being undefeated. So they allowed us, a small college, allowed me at least to leave the state and do a lot of recruiting in the Chicago area and a spot in Texas where I had some contacts, and Pittsburgh, so it was quite obvious that you could win football games if you can recruit talent.

But I got out of the coaching business when Tom became the head football coach, so I became a Sunday morning quarterback. (laughs)

Q: I'm sure you knew better than most what was going on every Saturday, Al! I wasn't even aware of your coaching exploits. What was your career record?

AP: I don't really have that. I was there 18 years and I was selected on three different occasions as the College Coach of the Year in the state of Nebraska and was in the Nebraska Football Hall of Fame after that, of course. That was not the objective, but it was nice.

Q: Does any one particular Husker game stand out to you more than others?

AP: Probably the one Husker game that's stood out as much as any, was how dominant Nebraska was in the National Championship game when they defeated Florida in the Fiesta Bowl for the National Championship. Not necessarily Tommie Frazier's outstanding run (which is shown over and over again), but the game as a whole: where Nebraska was the underdog going into that contest and yet emerged as totally dominant in every phase of the game. As to that particular day? How superior Nebraska was in every part of the game? It wasn't a close ballgame in the way great contests are judged (like the Game of the Century that Nebraska had with Oklahoma and some of our other contests), but that would be the one from my point of view.

Q: Did anything stand out to you as far as the mindset of the athletes of that time? A culture, a mood that made those teams special?

AP: Well, I think it was Tom's organizational structure with recruiting, with the actual practice sessions, and the fact that he recruited a large number of walk-ons.

The walk-on program was one of the major factors that enabled him to do what he wanted to do as long as he had enough people. He could have several stations going on at the same time (because everybody knows that a lot of coaching is repetition). And to go through the drills and go through those activities and to repeat them day after day after day? With a large number of people you could get this done. So his squads, the number of people that we had out for football, were much larger than the average institution had, and it allowed him to have a greater number of drills and activities going on at the same time.

Nebraska was fortunate that in our state there's no other division one school that's going to recruit the athletes. There is no professional football in the state, either (you have to go Chicago, Denver, or Kansas City), so the fan base was more supportive of the college program. And it assisted in the product that Tom and Bob were able to produce. Tom did an excellent job in recruiting and keeping this staff and having quite a bit of diversity, and they related extremely well to the student-athlete. You could see the program that he was building and compare it as we'd go to the games on Saturday, whether it's the Oklahomas, Kansas States, Iowa State's.

And even the outcome at the end of the year with the bowl games? The situation aided and allowed him to be able to carry out what he thought needed to be done to be competitive on a national basis.

Q: Any idea what kind of numbers other schools would have had at that time?

AP: I don't know the exact year, but earlier in Tom's career and in Bobs career we didn't have the strict limit on the number of scholarships that could be granted, and Nebraska had larger squads than many of the schools do today. So as a result some of the other schools weren't able to recruit the top athletes, because the schools like Oklahoma, Nebraska, Alabama, Michigan, Ohio State, they had more quality student-athletes coming out of high school, junior colleges. (And of course, there's a completely different situation today, because the numbers are smaller as dictated by the NCAA, the number of people on scholarship.) Rules and regulations sometimes will change the opportunity that schools had to one time recruit their share or more than their share of student-athletes, making them unavailable to other schools.

Q: Stockpiling, so to speak? Defensive recruiting?

AP: Exactly.

Q: During your term there in the 90's, what was the greatest challenge you encountered?

AP: The challenge, I think, was the issue of how competitive the recruiting was and how complex the rules & regulations for the NCAA or the respective conferences certain institutions belonged to; how complex those rules and regulations are, and how easy an institution can violate some of those rules and regulations and possibly not even be aware of it.

And yet, the pressure to recruit? There needs to be some kind of program on campus whereby people could make sure their coaches were informed, were well aware of what's permissible and what's not permissible, what the impact might be. Because if a school was in violation they could lose scholarships or in some other way be punished, and that would be a blow to the institution where they could be contender one year and then the bottom of their league the next few years. There was a heavy price to pay if an institution or coaching staff or a program stumbled, so I was a critical part of keeping the program at the high level and yet being within the rules and regulations of the governance, whether it's the institution's, the conference's, or the NCAA's.

Q: And the whole Big 8 to Big 12 switch- is there anything you think Nebraska could have or should have done differently in setting that up?

AP: I think the Big 8 was a great conference. There was a congeniality among those 8 schools that maybe was a little stronger than it might have been in the Big 12.

Bringing the Texas schools from the Southwest Conference to form a conference of 12 was basically done for monetary reasons. There's no question that nationally they would have a greater opportunity to get to the major bowl games, have the national rankings to increase attendance, do a more effective job recruiting nationally, but it changed the culture a little bit, the relationship between the institutions, I think. You can see that today: there's a lot of money in the state of Texas where they're able to do things because of financial reasons and support that they have from boosters, to make the competition even greater in the athletic arena.

For example, I was talking to Tom Osborne after he accepted the Athletic Director's position here recently, about what problems he sees that are different from when he was here as a coach. And he said the emphasis was on the budget and funding, that every one of the respective sports in the program has a budget problem that is real, and that improving and maintaining facilities is an ongoing situation. So that's a big issue. And it's not the most favorable for some people who don't have the resources to tend to those sort of things, no question.

Q: Sounds like a typical farmer/rancher. You give it your best shot and you make do with what you can? Take what rain the storm clouds give you?

AP: That's right. I was born and raised on a farm, but my parents moved when I was in high school, so my early days were on a farm, yes.

Q: Good football training, a farm or ranch is. No?

AP: No question. (laughs)

Q: You were in the service for World War Two, right Al? Any special travels or experiences?

AP: I was in the US Army. When I graduated from high school the draft was still on for World War II. I thought I could beat that draft so I enlisted before I was drafted. (So I wouldn't be assigned to the US Army Infantry. That's where most of the people were being drafted into) And lo and behold, I still went into the service as an infantry replacement and did training in Camp Fannon, Texas, right out of high school for 17 weeks, and then shipped to Fort Meade, Maryland because everything was hot and heavy in Europe in World War II at that time.

The day we arrived in Maryland, VE Day was declared and the war was over in Europe. So there was a little problem with a number of several thousand of us that were on our way to Europe, so we took a little additional training in Washington, DC and then we shipped across the country and left Seattle to go to the Pacific(because quite a bit of action was still anticipated at that time.) We stopped at the Hawaiian Islands to do amphibious training and be issued our M-1's on the rifle range and to get ready to go to Iwo Jima or Guadalcanal or some of the islands at the time being seized and held by Japan, and they looked at my record and saw that I had taken a typing class in high school and pulled me out to work at a separation center in Hawaii. And I stayed there for 2 years to finish my enlistment.

So I was blessed by what I took in high school and spent my time in the Hawaiian Islands until I was discharged from the service. And I was discharged in August and enrolled that same month in 1946 into Doane College.

Q: Who could have thought that one high school typing class would have such a profound effect on your life?

AP: Exactly, and I probably took it to get out of some tough science class or something, (laughs) I'm not sure.

Q: There was probably a good looking girl or two in the typing class, I'd guess....

AP: Or the instructor was. (laughs)

Q: What was your greatest accomplishment, owning the tools and skills you brought to the program?

AP: The ability to work with a variety of publics, whether it was the administrative people in an academic setting, or the instructors in the department's and the various disciplines in the institution, or whether it was the coaching arena or whether it was the students. I always made an attempt to relate appropriately to a variety of publics and to be able to see the big picture as to what our real objective was, and find the appropriate way to accomplish our goals and objectives.

Q: And the real objective would be to create an educated citizenry?

AP: In general, that would be the best way to put it.

Q: And the personalities of the coaching staff, who stands out to you?

AP: Well, Bob Devaney, of course, was a unique individual. Bob Devaney could have been the CEO of General Motors or any major corporation. A lot of people didn't feel that Bob was that astute, but he had that kind of ability and insight and organizational mind, so he was a great person to observe and be around. I recall when the University received the edict to establish a compliance program, and although Bob definitely wanted me to accept that position, he did tell me, "Hey, we don't need a compliance program, we won the national championship without one." And someone said, "Bob, that's why you won the national championship, because you didn't have any compliance program." (laughs) So that's the kind of individual that he was.

And I think Tom Osborne had a way of getting a large number of people to support his objectives. He was able to -in his own mind, to develop and plan what the culture should be, what the goals and objectives should be- and later attain those and to see the difference in the individuals or how they would accomplish that.

But the kind of relationship that we were able to have? Although I was Director of Compliance during the time that Bob Devaney was the Athletic Director, I reported directly to the Chancellor. (And that was not the best working relationship. There aren't very many people who would accept a position like that: where the Athletic Department pays your salary, you work for them and you work with them, yet you don't report to them.) But we knew each other well enough and were blessed to have a great working relationship when Tom Osborne was the football coach and when Bob was Athletic Director.

Then I had a couple of years with Bill Byrne coming in as the new Athletic Director when Bob retired as AD. Bill was very supportive of myself and even wanted to expand the work, administratively, that I would be doing within the entire department. It was a positive experience and I was able to have a good relationship with a practically all sports that were offered within the Department of Athletics.

Q: I'm sure that setup created some tension now and then, what with you reporting to one entity, but being employed by the other?

AP: If the Chancellor's Office would issue an edict that said, "Get this done, but don't inform Bob about it," those were some rough waters to work through, (laughs) but they worked out.

Q: Any recollections of the position coaches? McBride, Darlington, Turner Gill and the others?

AP: Yes, the last two years of Tom's coaching career I served as Director of Operations. Every morning we would have our football meetings, so Tom put me in a position at this large football table with all the assistants and strength people and medical people. I had Charlie McBride sitting on one side and George Darlington sitting on another side, and invariably Tom would encourage this considerable conversation between coaches where they would support or disapprove or present their own way to accomplish what the day's objectives might be, planning the program for that day or that week or that contest, et cetera. So, not being on the football staff as a coach but only being on the football staff as an administrator was a different position and made for an interesting day. (laughs)

Q: I'm sure you say that a little tongue in cheek, Al. Any particular moments stand out as worthy of remembrance?

AP: Charlie McBride, of course, tried to portray the 'tough guy' role, you know? "I'm the guy who can chew an athlete out if it needs to be done," coming at it from the 'tough guy' point of view. Ron Brown or Turner Gill were maybe from the other side. George Darlington would like to get on the chalkboard, and no one was better. No one could ever outdo George if he got on the board and explained what would work and what would not work, et cetera. There was just a continuing conversation, which ended up being very positive -because everything would be brought out- and before we would leave the meeting we were all to agree on a certain position and support it. So without going into any specifics, we had a multitude of personalities that complemented the entire program, because it was so diverse.

Q: Coach Osborne was a real consensus-builder, then. Was he instrumental in plotting a direction for the upcoming game or did the assistant coaches help do that week by week?

AP: I think Tom drew out what he'd like to see accomplished in sort of a general way, and the coaches needed to get together to decide in a specific way how to meet or attain those objectives. He would, in most cases, have the majority be the rule. But he certainly provided the leadership and determined what the topics would be for the day.

Q: Oh, to be a fly on the wall in those meetings!

AP: Right! I'm glad that they're not on record. (laughs)

Q: Did you ever find yourself raising your hand and saying, "Hey, guys, time out. I've got an idea here," being a former coach.

AP: Oh, no. (laughs) I can recall the last two years at Nebraska with Frank Solich as head coach. Tom came to me and said, "I'm going to make it official tomorrow, but I want you to stay and serve in this position with Frank for a year," and I stated I would. But it surprised a lot of people, because Tom wasn't quite ready to quit coaching yet (probably should have made that decision to be an athletic director and coach like some people were in that day and age, and then give up coaching later), but he did promise this position to Frank Solich and he felt that it was time to do it. And it followed a championship game and the bowl game and so forth, so it was sort of the opportune time.

I don't think one could ever say that the coaching staffs that Bob Devaney and Tom both had weren't diverse. They had a great deal of loyalty, stayed a long time, were very capable and very much responsible for the outcome and success that was put toward Bob and for Tom -whoever was the head coach- in the final accomplishments.

Q: Just to insert my opinion here, Al: I was kind of hoping that you would have served as Athletic Director for awhile.

AP: Well, there was a move internally, though at that stage I was talking about retirement two years before.

I stayed longer. That, I did, because the timing wasn't right, and the Chancellor at that time wanted to be sure that the administration -according to the bylaws and so forth- made sure that we ran the athletic department, not Bob Devaney or Tom Osborne. So the situation wasn't an ideal situation, but it would have worked out -could have worked out- that if Tom wanted to coach a couple more years he could have and then become Athletic Director, but for whatever reason he didn't want to pursue the issue of doing both. It wasn't that uncommon in athletic administration in those days, but it certainly was moving in another direction with more emphasis on administration, more emphasis on business, rather than a former coach being the director of athletics, subsequently. Like Bob Devaney, for example.

Q: Was Graham Spanier the Chancellor at the time?

AP: Yes.

Q: Did you have any major challenges with the guys who would walk-on out of nowhere: the I.M. Hipps', the Toby and Jimmy Williams'? Any quirky compliance issues you had to deal with?

AP: Oh, I think that we had an issue with Lawrence Phillips, who was one of our outstanding football players, as you know. Some other problems surfaced that were great.

We had an issue where he arrived on campus with an automobile, and we had a program that we'd just put in place where all the athletes had to register their automobile, which he did -he reported the automobile was given to him by a booster. Well, actually the automobile was provided for him by his group-home mother. (And all of that was documented, and we got the necessary information from the group-home mother, that that was her title.) She was the one who owned and ran the group-home in California, and many people in the group home were young men and women who, maybe for whatever reason, had a problem with their home life and had to be housed in the home. And sometimes they would go there under the direction of a court system, and of course the group home was supported by state funds. It was a business that somebody ran in the state of California, in this particular case.

Well, the NCAA had a special program where it said the foster parent could provide monetary support for a student like a regular parent would, but there was nothing ever decided about what role a group-home parent played in this factor. And then they gave us an interpretation that said if the group-home parent did this kind of thing for other people who lived in the area that it would be permissible, otherwise Lawrence would be in violation and we'd have problems and probably have some penalty. So I spent a week in California at the group-home working with her and discovered that there were other students -young men and women that she supported- who'd gone to colleges, gone to a junior college, whether it was the regular support like clothing, etc. Shelter, of course, was provided by the group home and was paid for by the state, and because of that we were able to get out of a situation that didn't penalize us for that particular situation.

Q: And Lawrence's car, was it a rather pedestrian car or an upper-crust model?

AP: It was just a regular car that provided transportation for him, not any fancy Mercedes or whatever. (laughs)

Q: (laughs) In spending the time in California at the group home, were any impressions made on you as to the situation Lawrence came from?

AP: Yes, very much so. Me? Very much so. I think that we knew he was in a couple of different situations at times... had support from someone like an assistant principal or academic counselor/ advisor, somebody in his high school at one time. I think he attended two different high schools, but there were some problems at home where he didn't have the typical parental support that an average athlete would have. (I was not familiar with the way the group-homes worked in the state of California, and I found out on my visit that many individuals were assigned by the courts.) Many times the student wasn't able to function within that family unit, and the student had difficulty keeping in school or keeping them on the right track if they're going to school. In some cases the courts would determine and assign them to a group home and the state of California pays for that young man's room and board and clothing and so forth... and they can still be attending a high school, but that structure would fill in for the lack of parental support that normally does exist.

Q: In summation -from your perspective- are there any other nuances of the 90's teams that made them stand out?

AP: I would just probably say that Tom Osborne had a major, major role through his ability to see the big picture of what needs to be done, to get the program to that level and keep it at that level, be it his staff, the facilities, the recruitment, and to instill that into everybody these same goals, the same objectives.

And the situation was right at that time, also: Nebraska was very supportive of his program. We didn't get the kind of national recognition he would have received if he was in a metropolitan area rather than Lincoln, but a majority of the credit would have to go there, with Tom.

End conversation.

Mr. Papik talked about Tom Osborne's vision -the big picture and how it came about- and Al was certainly one of those visionary people himself. I really enjoyed this conversation, and to be real honest with you, it was the longest we've ever shared. Rarely did I have much to do with him and his work in the compliance office, but still we were of the same unified mind and sense of purpose in our respective departments. That speaks a lot to Coach Osborne's and, to an extent, Athletic Director Bill Byrne's leadership qualities and their constant striving to enhance and increase the tools at the Athletic Department staffs' disposal. It was as if twenty years of collecting the proper people to his coaching staff, creating or adding particular elements of support staff, and the right athletic talent with the proper sense of urgency and destiny finally was realized.

Al specifically addressed the greatest inherent value of the walk-on program, which wasn't necessarily about the talent, but the numbers. It's pretty easy to get all caught up in the "Undersized, under-recruited & inferior to All-American, Cinderella-type stories (which are tremendously inspiring in their own right, don't get me wrong), but the walk-on program's greatest contribution was spreading out the collisions and availing the coaching staff repetition after repetition after repetition. Those reps took a physical toll on the young bodies, but the multiple reps contributed greatly to muscle memory, so it was a great trade-off. What is that, you say? The concept of muscle memory essentially means the play calls, schemes, techniques and skills eventually become second nature: the system and the player eventually merging and becoming one, reaching a the point of involuntary operation. And when you can place eleven individuals at one with their roles & position skill-sets and then merge those eleven into one cohesive, functioning unit, you've got yourself the ingredients for success, for domination, for the capacity to wear on a foe and maybe even break their will.

Notable quote #2:
Al Papik on Nebraska recruiting student/athletes: "Tom felt the recruits needed an opportunity to see the institution as a whole rather than just come to visit the football coaches and the football facilities."

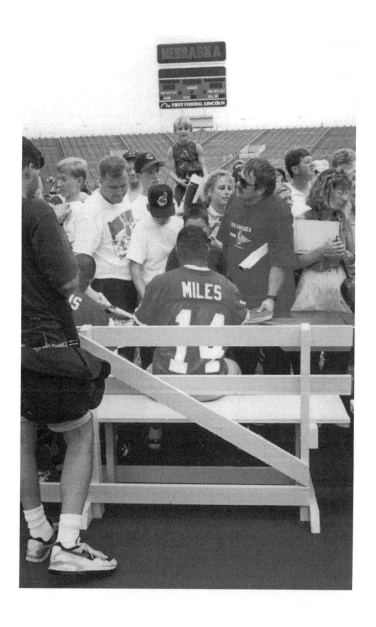

The more we love our friends, the less we flatter them; it is by excusing nothing that pure love shows itself.

Jean Baptiste Moliere, *Le Misanthrope*

If you're the least bit familiar with the U.S. Armed Forces' elite special ops Navy S.E.A.L.s team you may also have heard about the final training crucible which every prospective member must outlast and endure. It's called 'Hell Week,' and reasonably so. Physically draining and mentally straining, this ungodly inhumane test comes to an end when the trainee either crumbles and quits under the duress or remains resolute until that moment when a final bell is rung, signalling to all survivors that they have withstood the full brunt of the gauntlet. To do so engenders an extraordinary fortitude and undying spirit, a profound sense of destiny and perseverance. This attitude, this mindset, this purposeful striving is summed up by two noteworthy slogans among those able to join the unique Seal Team cadre: "The only easy day was yesterday" and "It pays to be a winner." I know a few SEAL-team operators myself and can vouch for their veracity. Which brings us to Barron Miles.

A small kid with a bum ankle, a bloodied nose and swollen eyes, Barron had the verve, the "It Factor", that had a recruiting Frank Solich demanding Barron take a look westward to the oddly mis-shapen state half a world away from Roselle, New Jersey. Though greatly undersized, he brought some pluck to the team by counting the cost, paying the price, and reaping the reward. If the axiom "It pays to be a winner" holds true, let's listen to his counting of that cost as well as the method to achieving the rewards of that great era…

Notable quote #1:
"If I play like I'm supposed to play you're not going to take my job, anyway. That's how I feel. So my objective is to help you. If I can make you better that's gonna make our team better…"

Barron Miles

Scholarship recruit, Cornerback, Roselle, New Jersey (Abraham Clark)
Where are they now? Regina, Saskatchewan, Canada, Coach

Question: So you're with CFL's B.C. Lions, Barron?

Barron Miles: Yep, this is going on my fifth year with them. And I was in Montreal with the Allouettes for 7 years before that.

Q: Turner Gill used to play for the Allouettes, didn't he?

BM: Yes, and Tommie. Tommie played a little bit.

Q: Were you there when Tommie was there?

BM: No, I was in Pittsburgh for the Steelers when he was there.

Q: Forgive me, Barron, I kind of lost track of some of you guys at that time. So tell me, where did you all go to play?

BM: I got drafted by Pittsburgh and I was there off and on for three years. From there I went to Montreal. After the time with Montreal it was on to British Columbia.

Q: How are those Canucks treating you up there? Are you picking up any French?

BM: Actually, I've lost it since I've been in B.C., but when I was in Montreal I was a lot better. Like, if you speak it then I could understand you, but if I don't think about it I could talk back to you. (laughs) Right now my oldest is bilingual. She's fluent in French, and my other two are almost, just starting out. They go to a French emergence school now.

Q: So what do you see yourself doing once the playing days are over?

BM: Coaching. I like to coach.

Q: Where are you thinking?

BM: My ultimate goal, my fantasy job, would be a high school coach. Just because I've had a lot of experience in college and as a professional, and it starts with high school. And if I can get to them in high school and influence them the right way and get them started right, then that can give them a better shot. If they go to college, they'll have a better understanding of what to expect in college and the professional ranks, if it goes that far. I see a lot of kids now, that they don't have a clue. They are so far out there that they aren't prepared to do anything.

Q: So it's just a dream for those kids, but it's not a plan?

BM: Exactly. That's exactly what it is."This is what I want to do." And I say, 'Okay, how are you getting there? Are you preparing yourself? How do you plan on getting there?' They'll be like, "I got time. Don't worry." (laughs)

Q: Was somebody there for you like that in junior high and high school?

BM: I had a lot of coaches who were around, but I was that odd kid. I was that odd kid: I knew what I wanted to do. I knew I wanted to be a pro football player. I knew from day one that this is what I wanted to do and I did everything possible to do it.

Q: Who were your heroes?

BM: My mom is number one, and Marcus Allen. When I was growing up, it was Marcus Allen.

Q: Marcus Allen? Really? All the way out in Jersey you were a Raider fan?

BM: I'd read something about Marcus Allen. He played quarterback in high school and he was an all-around athlete and he just did everything, and that inspired me. I watched him play and I was like like, 'Yeah, that's me.' And the ironic part is, I played against his brother. It's kind of funny how it turned out.

Q: That's something. You know he and his brother, as well as former Nebraska quarterback Steve Taylor, went to school at Lincoln High here in San Diego. Did you ever get a chance to meet him?

BM: No. Nope, never did.

Q: Well, maybe you're the lucky one. Some folks say that you should never meet your childhood heroes. (laughs)

BM: (laughs) I am too busy. I have three kids. They are into sports and everything, especially the offseason here, it's their time. I don't get too much time to spend, too much time with them during the season, so I run around and we both have to go to their a sporting events, and I can't miss it. If I'm not working I'm gonna go. I love it. We always show each other support.

Q: And hey, I heard your interview on Jerry Murtaugh's Legends Radio Show, what's this I hear that you are now #3 all-time in the Canadian football league in interceptions?

BM: I think so. I'm up there. I'm trying to get second.

Q: Obviously longevity plays a part. What do you attribute to your success?

BM: I think I know the game, number one. I understand the game. It's just knowing what they're trying to do. Because in this league once the quarterback knows you can catch, as a defensive back, they don't throw into your area too often, because they know you're looking for the ball. I've been very fortunate. There are only about two or three good quarterbacks who would throw to a receiver who's not open, so where everybody else sees them covered, they'll put it in a spot where the reciever is still running and it's an open area, whereas other young quarterbacks, they have to wait for the guy to be open, then they throw it. Then it's too late and I've got 'em then.

Q: So what year was your first fall camp at Nebraska?

BM: 1992.

Q: So that means your last game as a Husker was against Miami in the national championship game. And you were from Roselle, New Jersey?

BM: Yes, Frank Solich recruited me. At that point my high school was turning around. We had three great years and recruiters started coming in, and my junior year we won state and all these schools started coming out looking at us like, "Okay, what's going on here?" We had great years, and then my senior year we continued the process, we made it all the way to state and ran across a real big team, and we were kind of nicked-up and hurt. We got beat by about two touchdowns, but I think that game alone was probably what got me into Nebraska, because Coach Frank Solich was at the game alone. I had an injured ankle –I'd hurt it right before the playoffs- and they had two guys on breakaways and I ran both of them down. Came out of nowhere and ran both of them down and saved the touchdowns. They ended up scoring. We were down and we were losing, but yet I didn't give up and I ran these guys down…

Q: And with a bad wheel, to boot…

BM: With a bad wheel. I got hit in the nose and my eyes were swollen and everything, too. And after the game Frank Solich drove to my home and sat down with me and invited me to come out for visit.

Q: Who else recruited you at the time?

BM: Syracuse, Kansas, the Carolina schools, UMass, they wanted me to come play quarterback. That was a close one, because I wanted to play quarterback. Northwestern, that's when they turned around and had a great year. There were some good schools at the time. I thought about going to Northwestern and making a name for myself, but Nebraska played out.

Q: What made the difference? Was it visiting the campus?

BM: The main reason I went to Nebraska was because out of the majority of the schools I visited, I spent a whole day in the educational department at Nebraska. When I was on my recruiting trip I had a whole day going over that stuff: "This is where you'll study at, this is how you apply for your tutors," everything like that. I was like, 'Wow, okay.' It was boring and everything, but I knew if I was ever in trouble in school I had an opportunity to better my grades and have someone there to help me and have support, that was huge. That was a no-brainer. That's why I did it.

Q: Did your Mom come along with you on the visit?

BM: No, I was all alone. The biggest thing was, I have three older brothers and two of them were Husker fans. We would watch the Oklahoma and Nebraska game every Thanksgiving. I had one brother who was a Miami fan and I was the Oklahoma fan. I was Jamelle Holloway and running the option. I waited for them to send me a letter, and it never came.

And when I came to Nebraska for the visit, everybody seemed to know about me, they were going crazy. It was already in the air about me visiting Nebraska. I visited in the offseason, it was in the winter.

Q: Do you recall anything from the trip?

BM: Scott Baldwin was from my same high school. He took me around and took me under his wing. The do's and the don'ts. He told me the truth about it. That was real good for them and I knew he wasn't going to steer me in the wrong direction.

Q: So it's mid-summer: you finally make the big trek to the Midwest, and instead of freezing your butt off like your first visit it's probably hotter and more humid than a sauna. Any recollection of your first days on campus as a student-athlete?

BM: It went so fast. So fast. I just remember meeting Troy Dumas, Abdul Muhammad, all these freshman guys. They were very competitive. I was like, 'Hey, I've got my work cut out for me.' I met the defensive backs, Tyrone Legette and all these boys, and I was like, 'Man, these are some huge dudes! They want me to play corner?' You know, Reggie Cooper, Tyrone Byrd, Steve Carmer, and I was like, 'Are you kidding me?!' and they were, "It's okay, you'll be fine. You'll be fine." And then these big freshman guys turn to me and they say, "What position do you play? Are you a receiver, slot, what?" I go, 'I'm a corner.' And they say, "What!?" (laughs) They were all about 200 lbs. I'm probably 5'9" 150 lbs., if that. And they were looking at me like, "Oh man, you don't stand a chance."

Q: Did they say that or was it just a look?

BM: It was just a look. And at that point I already had the notion when I arrived that, 'I don't have any friends. I am here to compete, to be a player. Not just be a body on the team.' I already had it in my mind that, 'I'm gonna be somebody. And that's okay with me.'

And Scott Baldwin was a real help, because he got me positioned in the right direction. He'd tell me, "Hey, when you're supposed to be somewhere, be there early. If you're not there early you're considered late. Just be on time. Do what you're supposed to do. Leave the girls alone, they'll come later. If a girl's trying to take you away from your studies, she's not the right girl for you." He just took me on down the line and told me the do's and the don'ts, and that kept me on track. I was focused. I was like, 'I'm here for a job.' And that's what I did. Most of the guys had seen me play basketball and they were like, "Hey, if he can play football like he plays basketball, he might be alright. He might be okay, I don't know."

Q: And how much older was Scott than you?

BM: Three, four years

Q: Were you around trying to help him with his troubles later on? Was that hard for you, too?

BM: That was very hard. I knew Scott before he left New Jersey. Our families hang out in our hometown. When it happened it was tough, because when he wanted to talk to somebody he would come over and hang out with me because I was pretty much a loner, anyway. And when the problems hit, it was me and him, and I was, 'Okay, what can I do? I don't know.' It was tough. It made me grow up and understand that life is not promised. You don't know what's going to happen. You learned it very quick.

I know he moved and keep in touch with him now and then. We always had a bet. When I arrived that freshman year we made a bet between us about who was gonna make it to the NFL first. And he called me one day and was like, "Okay, I've gotta pay you. You won." After that accident thing I kind of forgot about it, so it was kind of funny how he brought it up. He's doing great. A lot of bad things happened, but with his accident and being in the wheelchair he's accomplished a lot more than he may ever have done had it not been for the wheelchair. He's tried scuba diving, things like that. You put someone in a different situation and they look at life differently.

Q: Speaking of differences, did anything about the people of Nebraska stand out to you as compared to back home?

BM: Yeah, everyone was white. (laughs) That was the biggest difference, just dealing with people that aren't like you. And different language, different speech patterns, and you have to adapt to it. A lot of people don't understand that when you come from an all-black neighborhood, an all-Spanish neighborhood, Asian, whatever it is, and then you get put into another culture, another environment, you have to adapt. And the quicker you adapt the better off you're gonna be. And some people adapt and some don't.

And that was another reason why I had to get away from home, because I wanted to grow up. If I ran into a problem in Nebraska I could write, 'Mom send me a plane ticket, I'm sick of this place. I want to come home.' She would have been like, "Boy, I don't have that money to get you a plane ticket. You'd have to wait awhile or you might have to figure it out." Whereas, if I went to Rutgers or somewhere close to home I'd have been like, 'I'm going home, and just hopping a bus or a train and I'm home.' It was some big growing pains.

Q: Sounds like Cortez's Spanish explorers, forced to burn their ships before taking on the New World. No option of turning back?

BM: Exactly.

Q: Any tensions, tough moments with the local population?

BM: Well, you'd get your tough moments every now and then, because I don't look like a football player. The only thing that makes me a football player is the color of my skin, because most black-skinned people in Nebraska are pretty much athletes (laughs) so if you're at the university and black, for the most part you're on the football team, basketball team, track team. So just to be safe, they say, "Hey, how are you doing?" and try to learn something about you, to find more about you. Overall, I had a great experience in Nebraska.

Q: Do you recall your first ties with the football organization-part of things? Anything stand out as to the way they ran things?

BM: Like I said, I was different. I was so ready to go, it didn't matter what you threw at me, I didn't think it was hard. I was so prepared and ready to do it, it didn't bother me. The only thing that kind of threw me for a loop was when I was running a punt return or had an interception and I was trying to run it back, and the O-linemen were running right with me. And I was thinking, 'What in the world?! Am I that slow? I'm not gonna make it.' But the offensive lineman was Will Shields, and I wasn't accustomed to the speed of the game.

They said, "You'll get used to the speed. Don't worry about it, you'll get used to that. And that's Will Shields, anyway." (laughs)

Q: Matt Turman has a great story about Will Shields and discovering a totally different level of athleticism there at the university. As a matter of fact, Matt gave you an incredible amount of props for being a wonderful friend and mentor to him.

BM: Oh? Nobody ever told me that. I appreciate it. But I know, when guys get on campus upperclassmen normally shun them a little bit, "They're taking my job, coming in for my job-whatever." I wasn't ever like that. If I play like I'm supposed to play, you're not going to take my job, anyway. That's how I feel. So my objective is to help you. If I can make you better that's gonna make our team better, and you're gonna push me and I'm gonna push you. That's the way it goes, whether you play receiver or offensive guard.

What it was, I was going to challenge you. And then I'll help you in the process, and say, 'No, you're giving me a "tell." Do this.' Or 'Don't stand that way, it makes things easy for me. If you drop your hands before the break I already know which way you're going. So don't do that, so you have to come out of your stance a little bit different.' You're just communicating with your teammates. That's just being a good teammate. That's what it is. Just being a teammate. And I was being myself and being true. You can't be phony because after awhile the truth gets in the way. That's the way I always approached it: I'll tell you the truth. I'm competitive, I know that. They tell me that now, my old teammates, now. I don't know how that can be, so I must have been worse when I was in college. (laughs)

Q: Did you arrive with that mindset?

BM: I did. That was me. That's why it was unbelievable. To this day, I still help my safeties. I know that they still all try to come take my job. I tell them, 'Hey, if you can take my job, we'll have a great team.' They look at me like I'm crazy."What are you talking about?" I say, 'If someone asks you if you plan on taking Barron's job, don't say, "Uh, I don't know," like you're going to hurt my feelings…say, "Yeah! I'm here to take his job." " Otherwise, you're selling yourself short.

Q: Did you come with that mindset yourself, was it instilled in high school? Where did you get that from?

BM: Honestly, I don't know. I think, because you're small. I'm the smallest player when I play football. They say I have the "little man complex," I don't know. I'm always hungry. I knew the game, if I could help somebody else and it's gonna make our team better, regardless. It doesn't matter if I'm better than everybody if I don't make everyone else better. What's the use? You need 11 guys to win.

Q: It seems back in the early 90's there was a bit of 'me-ism', but then somewhere along the way the unity, respect and belief came about…

BM: Yes, you're right. I think we had a unique set of guys, because back then they were taking Prop. 48 guys, too. I was one of those Prop. 48 guys, we had maybe 5 or 6 Prop 48 guys my year, Troy Dumas and Abdul Mohammed, they played as freshmen, and the 'Props' that we had were so hungry and so determined to make an impact on the Nebraska team that once we got the opportunity it was like, 'Ok, I'm not letting this go.' It carried over. It was like, 'You just wait and see' what happens when I get the chance to play. The work ethic was building, it was unbelievable. Because we all hung together.

Q: That first year of sitting out really 'killed' you guys?

BM: Yeah, it killed me so bad. I'm like, 'Look at this. This is awful. I should be playing,' you know?

Q: Could you even practice with the team that year?

BM: No, couldn't even practice. We had Dwayne Harris, Charles Randolph, and a few other guys. The upperclassmen would say, "You can't play. We'll see you next year."

Q: As a coach you're not supposed to play favorites, but Barron, I was always rooting for you because you're my size. At least you were blessed with the speed! So I think it always meant I tried to push you a little harder when you came in the weightroom…

BM: Yeah, and I don't see it as much, being as competitive as I am. Back then I was just, there was no way you could tell me I couldn't do something. It was like, 'You say I can't do what? Okay, even if I someway can't do it, I was gonna find a place to do it somewhere until I perfected it.'

And the same thing kind of happened this year. I'd never played racquetball before until I got to British Columbia. They showed me the game and the guy beat me. So I played it every single day and now nobody will play me because they can't beat me. No one will play me. It's pretty bad. They're like, "Don't play him now. Don't. Just don't play him…just let him be." (laughs)

Q: So your position was Coach George Darlington. Memories and recollections of Coach D?

BM: Coach D? Tons! Awww! Coach D: "Follow your feet", every day, every meeting. Him trying to show us how to backpedal was hilarious. (laughs) You know, he'd be, "Don't backpedal like this..and then he'd trip over something." (laughs) We had a ball, we'd go up to his house every year and just hang out, us DB's. Hang out on the farm and he kept us together. He was pretty fair. If you could play he'd give you the opportunities. And even then, we knew the younger guys needed some playing time, so every now and then we'd share playing time with Leslie Dennis, Eric Stokes and those guys. If I'd have been, like, a senior, I would have been, 'Hey, I'm playing. I'm a senior, I'm playing.' If I'd have done that, if others had done that, we wouldn't have been as good as we were. Tyrone Williams did the same thing. If a game got tight, we'd go back in the game and we'd finish the game, but for the most part we'd sneak them in and they got playing time. That was a testament to Tom Osborne in getting the guys in, and George Darlington, and letting the guys play and getting comfortable, getting in the game.

Q: How would you, as players, let the guys come in?

BM: The coach would come to you and say, "Okay, next series Leslie is going to take the left corner." And you'd be like 'Alright,' or 'Hey Coach, I'm in a groove, I want to play.' Then for the most part, if Coach Osborne overrides it then nobody's going in, it doesn't matter what we say. (laughs) That happened one game against K-State. Coach Osborne walks down to me on the sideline while Leslie Dennis was in and says, "You should be in the game." And I was, 'Okay, I guess I should be in the game.' (laughs) I ran back in the game and took Leslie out and that was the end of it. I think Kevin Lockett started catching some balls on Leslie and he said, "No Barron, get back in the game." I felt bad for Leslie, because when a receiver catches a ball you don't want to be taken out of the game. You want to redeem yourself. It was kind of bad for him, but it was one of those games we didn't want to lose and give them any momentum in Manhattan.

Q: Any other coaches stand out to you?

BM: Not too much, I'd just converse every now and then just to understand the defense and making sure everybody understood the big picture. If it was confusing for me I knew half the guys didn't get it on defense. I was kind of the measuring stick for everybody.

Q: Who would you tell that to?

BM: Either Coach McBride or Coach Samuel. Because the linebackers and DB's, we'd work hand in hand, especially in some games like Iowa State. They were running that Wing-T option set, where the corner and linebackers switch jobs on different sets, so we had to be on the same page. If it was confusing and we went to the same person at the same time, it would be kind of messed up, so we had to make sure that was straight. You didn't want too much conversation with Coach McBride, because McBride, every year he'd get on somebody. You didn't want to get yelled at by Coach McBride. He was going to get you, anyway, but I don't think there was anybody he missed. You could go from one of the top superstars all the way down to the bottom guy, you were gonna get yelled at some time. Hands in the facemask, whatever. He'd be yelling and spitting all over you. Yeah, it was incredible, but he was fair. And he didn't yell at the guy that was the fourth team guy, he yelled at the superstar, the All-American, so nobody can complain. He yelled at everybody. We were like, "Don't worry, he yells at everybody."

Q: And what about Coach Osborne?

BM: Great guy, great guy. A very trustworthy man. He came to my high school and flew back with me on my recruiting trip. That was a big step, that was huge. Little town of Roselle, and Tom Osborne the legend is showing up at your school and people just going crazy. That was very fun. That was interesting.

Q: Do you recall the first game you played in?

BM: First game I played in was against Missouri. It was probably one of my worst games ever.'Cause they were like -I forgot who their receiver was, All-American, wore 32- he was easy to cover, but it was my first game and I'm like, 'Okay, don't freeze, don't freeze.' And I saw the whole play the whole way, I saw everything. He was running the corner route, and my feet wouldn't move and he ran by me and I'm talking to myself like, 'What are you doing?' I was like, 'Go!,' and I ran after him and he caught the ball. And I was just mad. They take me out of the game just because of that play, just like the Leslie Dennis thing. And I was, 'Why did you take me out?' "Well, we need to give you some more time. Don't worry about it." And after that it was smooth sailing. And I remember him doing his Tom Osborne Show and they showed that play and he was like, "Well, we're hoping for a lot better things from this guy here." That stuck in my head, like, 'It will be alright.'

Q: Did all the players watch the T.O. Show?

BM: Yeah, everybody watched it, especially after the game, because you got Coach Osborne's opinion of different plays and how he viewed it, and it might be totally different from how you viewed it. So yeah, you've got to watch it. You've got to watch the show, now.

Q: Did you have a most memorable play or game?

BM: Yes, I actually have two. That would be the national championship game that we won against Miami, but the other one was the Thursday night game against Oklahoma State and I blocked a punt. I was having a great game defensively, too, but blocking that punt was the momentum switcher. It was neck and neck and then me blocking the punt might have tied it. And after that it was downhill for Oklahoma State and we ended up winning the game for Tom Osborne's 200th victory.

Q: If I recall, the punter was in the end zone, wasn't he?

BM: He was in the end zone, I caught it in my chest, and that was it. I landed on it and got my touchdown, and the game was history.

Q: Barron, for some reason you were always the fastest guy off the corner and you got to that guy. What would you attribute to the capability of doing that since so many try and fail?

BM: It took some patience to "get off". They call it "get off" now. But I'd been doing that for awhile, and it was just a knack for it, some got it and some people don't. Just get by the first guy, and if you get up on the guy so fast he doesn't know how to react and what to do. Then you go against the first fake and you get a good picture, and then it's just up to you to put your hands on the ball.

Q: I read somewhere that recently you jumped over the long snapper to block an extra point in the CFL?

BM: Yep, I got that last year against Montreal. It should be somewhere, a video clip of it, somebody has it. It was on our local station that promotes our games.

Q: Can you take me back to that Florida State national championship game, what stands out to you about that close loss to end your junior season?

BM: The one that keeps popping up for me was hitting that guy out of bounds and getting the late hit penalty.

Q: Hitting Warrick Dunn out of bounds on their last drive?

BM: Yeah, everybody, my teammates now see that play and they go, "Man, why did you hit that guy out of bounds?" I didn't hit him, it was just me running, protecting myself, and we ran into each other, so that's how I saw it. They're like, "No, no, no. You gave him a little extra hit and everything else."But that game it was penalties; that was it. We were hungry then and we knew we could play with anybody, but for some reason every break went for FSU. And at the end of it we still had an opportunity to win the game. That was just a good game played by everybody and they won.

Q: Did you ever have the opportunity to talk to any of the FSU players about that game?

BM: Actually, Toledo Wall -who went to my high school- was in that game for Florida State. We talked a little bit and the conversation went something like, 'I know you guys should have lost.' And he was like, "Yeah, you played pretty good, but we won. So live with it." And that was it. (laughs) The biggest thing from that game was that you knew we won - even though the score didn't show it, that you knew we won- was when you walked to the bus and all the fans from Florida State were like, "Hey man, way to go. That was a great game. Good job." Deep down inside, they knew, "We got lucky. Good thing the big plays that happened went in our favor." Many years we'd been going down to Miami and playing Florida State or Miami. It was all, "You country boys go back home and play, you're too slow," and all that. You didn't hear none of that after the game. None of that. All you heard was, "Great game. Way to play. Keep your heads up. Awesome game." That was it. This was coming from the fans. The fans of Florida State in Miami. Never heard that before. Never. And that's what it was.

Q: So your old teammates still give you a hard time about that out of bounds tap?

BM: Not my old teammates, my current teammates. They see it on ESPN Classic. They call me up and say, "Hey Barron, you're playing on TV! What number are you?!" And I'm like, 'Oh man….' And I tell 'em and they go watch the game. And the next day they'll walk in and go, "Man, you hit the dude out of bounds! Why did you …?" And you know, I say, 'At least I'm on the Classic.' (laughs)

Q: I spoke with Kevin Raemakers and he, too, spoke of getting that chincy call for tapping Charlie Ward on the shoulder…

BM: Exactly! You see. I mean, hey, sometimes it happens, you know?

Q: Seems to me that was a huge turning point?

BM: It was a turning point. But it was the younger guys, my class and up, when we got the opportunity to step into the limelight of playing in the big games we said we weren't going to be scared or just give the game up. All those years we'd been told that we can't run with them or can't play with them, things like that? We said, "We can play with anybody, so were just gonna go play." And that's what we did. And we showed it and would, could have won, because we knew everything about Florida State.'Good job' goes for the coaches because we knew everything.

We had the game, but it just didn't work out. So we said, "You know what, we want to play Florida State next year." We got back to work after we had our week off. If anybody took attendance -I don't know if they did- but we probably had 100% attendance for summer conditioning.

Q: I had lunch with Coach Darlington recently, and he thought the officials were't prepared for that type of game...

BM: I agree. I agree 100%. Exactly.

Q: I've always wanted to ask you about that little love-tap on Warrick Dunn out of bounds…

BM: Yeah, I still get it to this day. Do you know how long ago that was? They give it to me. And to tell the truth, I have not seen it yet. I have not seen it yet. To this day I am living by what I said, until I see. It was like, 'He shouldn't have called that.' But, hey, that's the way it goes.

Q: I actually taped that entire game on VHS straight from the TV, not the Nebraska voice-over version. I've got everything, if you need it, let me know…

BM: No, I don't need it. I'll believe the fantasy in my head. (laughs)

Q: Obviously, a period of intense focus thereafter the next year and then all of a sudden it's Miami who you're up against instead. Can you take me back to that game and what stands out?

BM: The speech before the game.

But even before the game: it was a business trip. This was our fourth year going to Miami. We'd seen everything, we'd done everything, it was business. We didn't need to go to the functions, "we don't need to do all that other stuff": stay in the hotel room, go to practice, lift weights, watch film."Alright, let's get to the game." But they wanted us to go to all these places and see Miami and sit in a room with them, and we didn't want to do that. We said, "Okay, we'll see you out on the field. You just have your little vacations, but we're gonna see you out on the field and we'll have a game." And no one understood that, the reporters talking about "How are the DB's gonna stay with their receivers? How are they gonna stay with their speed?" and things like that. It was like, 'Oh, we see, you don't think us guys can run with them either, huh?' We got tired of it and just said, "Alright, let 'em talk. We ain't got to do nothing. Let's just play the game." And that was down the line, everybody, the way we felt.

And the day of the game T.O. came in and he told us exactly what was going to happen, and everything he said came true. And you're sitting there after the game and you go, 'Man! Okay, we had adversity, we had a penalty, we overcame it, we had success, then we had drama again, and then we had more success, and then they got tired.' That's exactly what happened, to a T.

Q: If I recall Costa went your way quite a few times, didn't he?

BM: They did. They came. And in the beginning Coach Darlington was like, "Just play off," and listened to the hype of their speed. Darlington said, "First couple of plays, back up and give them some room and see what they do, and we'll go from there." So I'm playing off and they hit a couple of slants and, 'Who can't hit a slant if I'm ten yards off,' you know? That was so simple. But after a couple catches I was, 'That's it. I'm going to play!' And that's when we started moving up and playing defense, playing what we were supposed to play, and that was it. Either you're gonna sink or swim.

Q: What was the rationale for playing off right away?

BM: Just in case."Hey, they're at home, they want to make a big play, you're uptight and you slip or fall or, you know, anything can happen, and they could get a big play right from the jump." Just in case they'd get the momentum and everything. Instead, you play off and you let 'em catch it, tackle them. You know? You let them live but it ain't gonna kill you, nothing too serious.

Q: And if I recall, was that your birthday?

BM: Yep, that was my birthday. All three years.

Q: Wow, all three years, and then you win a national championship on your birthday. You must have really celebrated that night…

BM: I didn't celebrate at all. I just hung out. It was the next step. Once that celebration was over it was, 'Hey, I won the championship, the next step is to get drafted.' That's how it went.

Q: All business?

BM: All business. I say -sooner or later when I stop playing– 'I'm gonna have to enjoy this.' Sooner or later, you know? (laughs)

Q: What do you think set Nebraska apart from some of the other teams of that time?

BM: I think, by far, that state of Nebraska, period, is what set us apart. The fans' commitment to Nebraska football set us apart from everybody. Nobody does it like that. It's unreal, because listening to guys coming from Utah State, from Pacific, you name it, they were like, "Man, this is crazy." The fans, everything is so wild, so enriched with tradition. That was Nebraska, the history with the OU–Nebraska game after Thanksgiving, you had to live up to the standard the upperclassmen set for you. If there was no standard, what do you live up to?

Q: What reminders of the traditions made an impression on you, or what "duty" per se? How was it impressed on you?

BM: It wasn't ever the organization, it was pretty much the players. Like Tyrone Legette, he would come around every now and then and mess with me and stuff like that. He had played corner before me so I was, 'I'm gonna break everything you do. I'm gonna break all your records and everything.' And he took me to the weight room wall where his picture was, and he pointed out his vertical jump record or agility run record or 40 yard record or something like that, and he was like, "Okay, you call me when you break these records. And then I'll come back and see you." That's what it was. The older guys there competing with the younger guys. It was, "Hey, when you see these records, you take them off the wall. You break them." And I only got one of them. The 10 yard dash record or agility, I think. He had the pro agility and something else like the 10 yard dash, but I got the pro agility record. That was it.

Q: Any memorable practice experiences stand out to you from those days?

BM: The best ones, our practice roster guys would dress up into the team colors of the team we were playing that week. Colorado, they'd put the black pants on and they'd come out and they'd act crazy. They would act so crazy. It would be so intense that you're thinking it was a game. But it prepared us so much, the coaches let it go. The coaches were, "I don't care. They're so excited, I hope they do beat you all." Because that's gonna get you prepared for the game. They came out in all black and painted up. It was game day, it was exciting.

You came to practice and it was exciting. They came out Oklahoma's day and they were all dressed in OU colors. It was fun. It was fun, and that's what practice is all about, competing. Because on the odd occasion we'd go against the ones, but for the most part we were going against the practice guys, the freshmen, the sophomores. And it was fun, because they would bring it every week.

Q: Any licks laid by you, or somebody else lay a lick on you that you'll never forget?

BM: I'll never forget, the only person that I couldn't tackle was Damon Benning. Damon Benning would run me over every single time. It was so pathetic. It didn't matter who else would come up, I would hit 'em and make a good tackle. But Damon Benning would come through the hole and I'd hit him, and I'd be on my back and he'd still be running. Darlington would crack a joke, "Hey, did anybody get the license plate number on that truck?" It was like, for some reason, I couldn't tackle him. Yeah.

Q: Any recollections of L.P.?

BM: Lawrence Phillips? Great guy, special guy. He lived with me for a little bit his first year when he first got there. He came up early and he stayed with me a little bit. A specimen, at 195-200 lbs., I think he'd be comparable to any running back, NFL or wherever, that's how talented he was. He came up to Canada and I played with him in Montreal. Same guy, an awesome freak of nature. It was ironic.

Q: Wow! So you guys were on the same team again…

BM: Yeah, Lawrence was always a great teammate, he'd give you his shirt, anything. He was a great guy, but unfortunately things happened, chemical imbalance or whatever it may be. But as a teammate he was a great guy.

Q: Any memorable off-field occurrences?

BM: I think the funniest one was watching Tyrone Williams and Tommie Frazier trying to become firemen, trying to put a fire out at a neighbor's house. We were coming home from somewhere, the three of us, and we get out of the car and Tommie was, "Man, you see that smoke?" and I was like, 'Nah, somebody's burning or grilling something,' And he was like, "No, that's a fire. That's a fire!" So he jumps over the fence and he goes, "That's a fire! The house is on fire! I'm gonna put it out!" And then Tyrone hops over the fence, too.

Now, it wasn't like one of those chainlink fences where you just put your foot in and hop over it. It was a wooden fence. I don't know how he got over the fence, first of all, but he got over the fence and he turned on the garden hose and he started wetting things down with the hose, and then I go in and called the fire department and I go back out and they're still standing there with the water hose. And then the fire truck comes and they just break the fence. They just run the fence completely over. I'm like, 'They just done hopped the fence, and then you guys just run right over it?!' (laughs) And I think they said that those two saved the house, wetting it down and all. I still, to this day, don't know what kind of fire it was. I don't know where the kitchen was, but they just saw smoke and said, "We're gonna put the fire out!" I was like, 'Okay. I'm just gonna go in and call the fire department.' And there was only one hose, so those two could only do so much.

Q: What are you the most proud of?

BM: Getting my degree. Early Childhood Development.

Q: And how in the heck did you pick that major?

BM: That was simple. I first started out in computer programming, and they said I had to take some kind of math. I would have got it if it was calculus, I didn't know what it was, but I knew it had something to do with math and said, 'There was no way I'm passing that class… (laughs) 'there's no way in the world.' Technical analysis, statistics! That was it!

Q: Competitive Barron Miles backing down from a challenge?! Really?!

BM: Yeah, but you gotta know: put yourself in good situations to accomplish our goals. I was like, 'Hmmm, I think we need to look somewhere else.' And the counselor was, "Okay, what do you plan on doing?" And I said, 'I plan on working with kids and coaching or something like that.' So they were, "Okay, let's go this route."

Q: Tell me about meeting your wife. A Nebraska girl from …?

BM: Schuyler. She was from Schuyler. I met her the first day of my math class my freshman year at 8 o'clock in the morning. My freshman year. She sat right next to me and I'd just talk to her every now and then. We were just friends and just showed up at class, and I'd see her and talk to her every now and then. And the middle of my sophomore year I had my own place and she was a DG -a Delta Gamma- and she stayed up the street about two blocks from me, and she just happened to be driving down the street and she saw me at the mailbox and she stopped. And from that point on it was history.

Q: I'm delving into a bit of a touchy subject here, but I remember when she joined the strength staff as a student assistant. Now, most folks reading this might not have known it, but Boyd had a rule that as student assistants we couldn't date student/athletes. How was that for you, that whole situation?

BM: We were dating before she joined, I'm pretty sure. But I was so focused on what I had to do, it didn't matter if she was there or not. Because no one knew, no one had a clue we were dating in the first place. To tell you the truth, no one had clue, even when she was there it wasn't like I was hitting on her or talking to her or anything. It was, 'I was there to work.' And to this day I still don't know how they knew, how it came out. I don't know, but before that point no one knew, and you could tell when she was doing her job. It wasn't a conflict.

Q: I know. To tell you the truth, that's always been kind of a sore spot for me. I remember when she came on staff I was actually advising her in my office and tried to take her under my wing, so to speak, and I said, "Jen, this might sound like I'm your big brother, but you're probably gonna have a lot of guys hitting on you. These guys really take a liking to pretty girls like you, like hungry sharks, and they're probably not going to be too worried about weightlifting. So you be careful and professional and don't get yourself in trouble, okay?' And she was like "Yeah, okay, I understand." And after the whole issue came to light (laughing) I felt so stupid because had I known you two were dating I could have saved my breath, you know? And then she had to leave the strength staff after it came to light, so that left a bad taste in my mouth.

BM: Yeah, and I'm trying to figure out how it happened. She may have even been honest and said something. And it was like a couple years that passed -one or two years- but the way it came out it was kind of wrong because Boyd knew me and knew who I was and what I was about: like if I was a goof-off in everything I did it could have been different. But when I came into the weight room I came in to workout, and when we did conditioning it was to work, you know? I wasn't there to do anything else. Plus, we'd met before she even joined, so that was the kicker, you know?

Q: I hear you. It was great to have Jen on staff for the time she was. Now tell me, is there someone behind the scenes who played a large role for you?

BM: Bailey. Yeah, Bryan Bailey and Randy Gobel. They came up with drills that fit us on the field. Those drills were so new, nobody else was doing them and they were coming up with these drills to perfect our craft. And no one else had a clue. I mean, the stuff we were doing, people are doing them now like they invented it, and Bryan and them were in there saying, "Let's do this. This is what you do when you're making a cut. This is what you do when you get hit and start to stumble. This is the position you're gonna be in, so you have to be strong in this area." Just crazy stuff, but yet, they showed video replays with us actually in those positions. It was so crazy. I don't think they got enough credit. They were the nuts and bolts to that strength and conditioning staff.

Q: Anything you wish you could do over, Barron?

BM: Honestly, nope. I don't think so. It was awesome, it was a great experience going to Nebraska. Meeting my wife, giving me three beautiful children, why would you want to change that? But the funniest thing, going back to Boyd and them, this is how bad I was: coming out of Roselle, New Jersey I didn't lift weights. I only did curls and tricep pushdowns, because I was a quarterback and wanted to be able to throw. So I get there and test out, and I'm not just below average, but below the average of the average. It was bad. And Boyd was sitting there looking at me and he said, "This is terrible. You need to improve this, you need to improve that, you need to gain weight." Then they send the report to Darlington and he sits me down in the office and he says, "You need to improve in this and that."

And the next year it was the same thing, "You need to gain weight. You improved in this and you improved in that, but you need to gain weight." And finally after the third year, they finally stopped and said, "You know what, you're playing good. Just keep it up. Just keep doing what you're doing. Don't worry about it." (laughs) I tell people to this day that I've been hearing it my whole life, "You're too small, you're too small. You need to get stronger, you need to do this." It's only natural, I couldn't help it. I just couldn't gain much weight. And some kids these days are like, "I need to gain some weight, get this big for them to look at me." And I tell them, 'No you don't. You just need to be fast, be explosive, be smart, and just be able to play the game. They can work with everything else.' I tell them, 'If you're that size and you can't run now, how will you be able to run when you get bigger?' And they say, "Yeah, but you got lucky. You went to a big school and all that." I say, 'So you thought it was easy for me? Hey, I went through it. I was 140 lbs. coming out of high school. What was so magical about that?' (laughs) They just thought it was handed to me or something. It was, 'No, you've got to work for it.'

Q: Any other descriptions of the culture?

BM: It's hard to explain. If you weren't there, it's hard to explain it. If you called a meeting for 3 o'clock, everybody knew that by 2:30 you were supposed to be there. Everyone knew come game time you were going to win. You didn't have to say it, everybody knew it already, it was just by how many points."How many points are we gonna win by?" We prepared hard enough, we stayed together, we played for each other. We could be down, losing in some game, but we'd be calm on the sidelines, knowing sooner or later we were going to blow these guys out. We didn't panic. We just knew that we'd win and then go back to Lincoln and relax. It was never spoken, but everyone knew their job and their place, everybody knew their role and what they had to do. It was our time and we ran with it.

Q: What about the slogans?

BM: That was started right after the Florida State game...Unfinished Business. We left something on the field, we weren't ready yet. Florida State was lucky we didn't play them that next year. Miami, we still wanted to win and everything, but we wanted Florida State. They had to go lose to Miami or Boston College and messed it up that year, otherwise we'd have been playing Florida State. They got lucky. Redemption. That was the problem we had to fix.

Q: Do you recall going against any of the Florida State or Miami receivers?

BM: Kevin Knox tried to run his mouth, "You're messing up my draft year. I'm about to get drafted on you." He's yapping at the mouth and I'm like, 'You ain't even gonna catch a ball. What are you talking about?' He's like, "I'm gonna school you all day." And I'm saying, 'Okay, we'll see.' And then he goes over to Tyrone Williams' side and catches one or two and then comes back to me and says, "I'm killing your boy over there!" And I go, 'Man, you haven't even scored yet. What are you talking about?' But other than that, Kez McCorvey, he was quiet, he didn't do too much. The other Florida State guys didn't say too much. The Miami guys were quiet, they were more tired than anything. They were subbing back and forth, and they were tired for the big game like that. Chris T. Jones, just nonchalant, run their routes and go. They relied on their defense. That was it. Everybody else was quiet.

Q: What was it like standing on the sidelines watching Miami's defense get gassed?

BM: Actually, we really didn't focus on their defense, it was just fun watching and expecting our offense to beat them, you know? Actually, I think their offense had negative yardage in the 4th quarter. It was like, "Alright, let's just do our job and go. Let's get the ball back." And I'm trying to figure out, "Why are they so tired? We didn't really sub that much. Why are they so tired?" But that's why we won and they didn't. That was the sign.

Q: You wanted it more?

BM: Exactly! All of us guys, even the receivers, 'The Itty Bitty Committee.' Us guys always had to fight.

End conversation.

"If there is no standard, what do you live up to?" Sometimes a person takes for granted the role tradition can play. At least I'm finding that out for myself in this quest for an answer to my great Why and How. Maybe because I'd grown up a Nebraska kid and just assumed every school, every state had its own provincial traditions and glories. The fact that this isn't necessarily so is finally now beginning to strike a chord with me. By now we've heard a few times how important a role the traditionally televised Oklahoma/Nebraska game played in positioning Husker Football in the minds of so many kids nationwide, too. In those young minds was begotten the fact that Nebraska was a big time program who played in big time games. (Peculiar, but it seems it's never mentioned whether Nebraska won or lost those OU games, only that they were a participant.) Maybe it didn't matter to the fans whose existence lay outside the state boundaries of 'The Good Life.'

And speaking of fans, I think it's important to make the distinction between fan attendance and fan support."The fans' commitment to Nebraska football set us apart from everybody. Nobody does it like that." You could fill Memorial Stadium to overflowing, as many of these guys attest to their amazement, but what I believe is inferred is that these same fans contributed by their actual lack of negativism via booing, belligerence and other bawdy behaviors. Sure, there was a sourpuss here and there and a spare drunk now and then blowing his top and spewing forth verbal sewage, but for the most part Nebraska fans in that period were respectful regarding the home team as well as the visitors. In their eyes, the gameday experience seemed to be more about the action, the effort, the goal rather than an opportunity to abuse their collective voice and demean, degrade or disparage. Memorial Stadium was full of cheer and good will for the most part, which made every Saturday seem a bit like Christmas. Especially with all those big guys wearing red.

A part of that standard, the tradition being passed down from one year to the next, was Barron's mention of defensive back Tyrone Legette from Columbia, South Carolina, a few years older than he. To have an upperclassman bound for the pros thrust forward a challenge, a dare of sorts, to break his own personal athletic performance records, that speaks to the role that legacy played for these guys. You always hear the term 'took me under their wings,' an idiom meaning care and nurture of someone less experienced, and that brotherly oversight and goodwill grew exponentially under the like-kind leadership of Coach/Coordinators Tom Osborne and Charlie McBride and all of the other position coaches, even the aforementioned LB Coach Kevin Steele, to a certain degree. (We'll hear more about Coach Steele when we talk to the linebackers later on)

Barron then mentioned the word 'redemption.' Perhaps that ties in to the concept of revenge, but it appears that winning that first national championship was about more than just winning that first national championship for these guys. Instead it was about proving to both themselves and the naysayers that the previous year was an anomaly, a mistake, and that they had come to right some wrongs and change perceptions, almost to the point of making the crowning of the new kings of college football an afterthought.

To finish here, I was surprised by the mention of the scout team's suiting up in the coming week's opposition's colors. Even I didn't know about that. As the season plods along practices can often become monotonous and perfunctory, so someone somewhere along the line decided to spice things up by providing a true visual representation of the 'bad guys' via decidedly un-Husker practice garb. I wonder if doing so might have given the top teams on the depth chart a mental edge and a sense of familiarity come Saturday, somehow lessening inhibitions and mental blocks because of the newfound normality of the presence of opponents' uniforms in their midst. Maybe that's me reaching for something above and beyond the intent of this practice ploy, but then again, perfect records would appear to back up my theory as having a potential cause and effect relationship during that period. It's hard to argue against 60 & 3.

Notable quote #2:

Barron Miles on the shared mentality of Nebraska Football: "Everyone knew come game time you were going to win. You didn't have to say it, everybody knew it already. It was just by how many points."

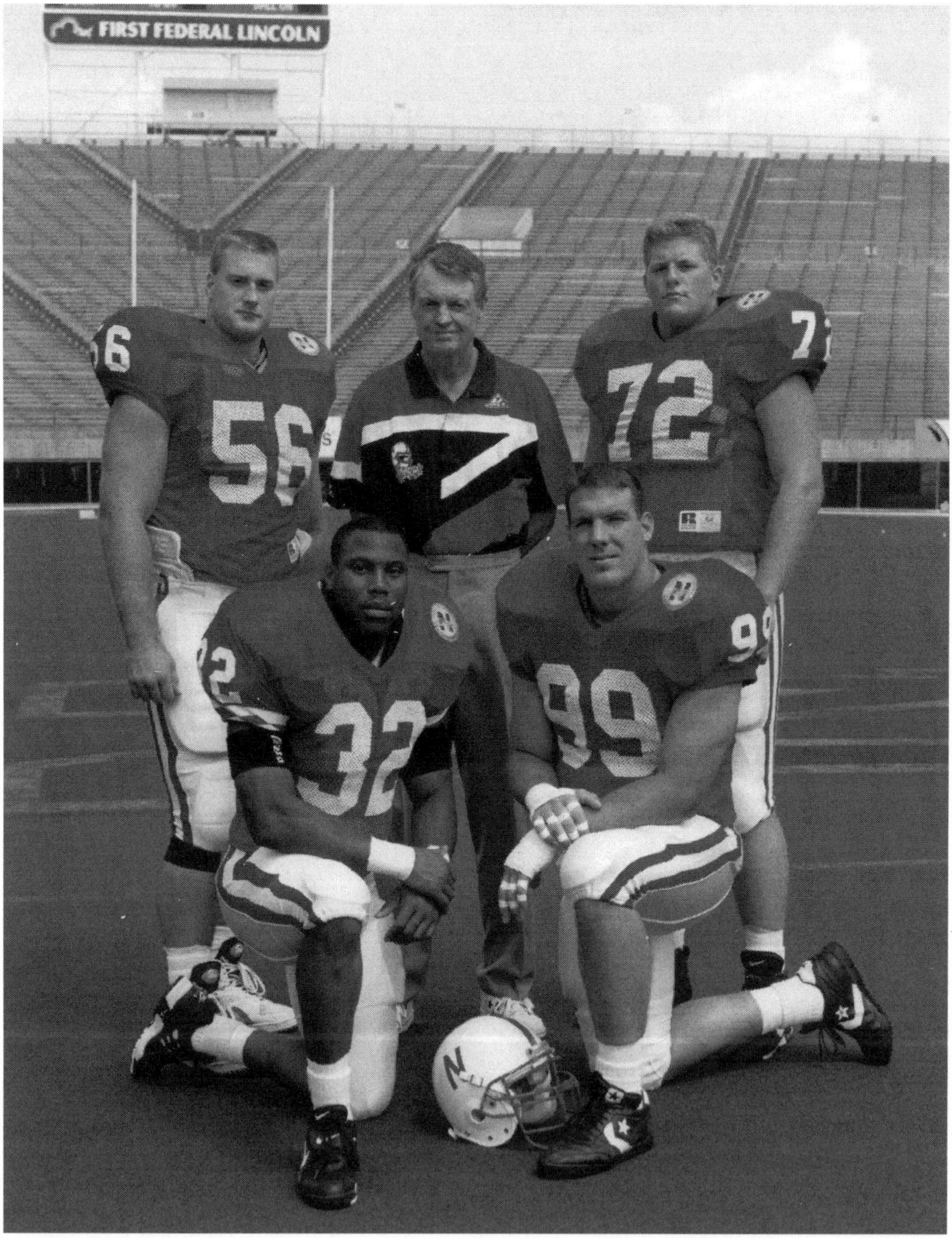
FIRST FEDERAL LINCOLN

Equidistant from the atoms and the stars, we are expanding our exploratory horizons to embrace both the very small and the very large.

Carl Sagan, Introduction to Stephen W. Hawking's *A Brief History of Time*

As man stumbles through the domain of time, the scientific community has been ever involved in discovering the answers to both the microscopic and macroscopic traits of our universe of existence. In a quest for Beginning's answers as well as Tomorrow's direction, the greatest thinkers of our day have most recently toyed with quantum mechanics and the general theory of relativity as they address the two spheres. While the atom is being split in two and the farthest star simultaneously limps further from our telescopic view, answers don't come easy, if at all. The newborn String Theory notwithstanding, brilliant minds have wrestled significant lifetimes and arrived at only partial understandings. Yet everyone has contributed to some small progression of our accumulated knowledge and a firmer grasp of the truth. Which brings us to Rob Zatechka: I think Rob has some answers for us.

Wrestling academia while alternately pancaking opposing D-linemen and linebackers, Rob excelled at both. He was, and perhaps is yet, the Ockham's razor in my quest for answers and revelations to the great 60 & 3. The term "Ockham's razor" refers to a logician's shaving away, a peeling back of, a throwing off of the inconsequential facts in pursuit of an accurate, more pristine, truer way of thinking and knowing. It sets one's head to spinning, to be quite honest. So -with all the brainy mumbo-jumbo aside- I think you'll find a few answers and surprises in what our thinker Rob Zatechka has to share as we further travel on our quest of my great Why and How.

Notable quote #1:

"There was an honest-to-God love between the coaches and the players. And when you can foster that across a team it's gonna be nearly impossible to defeat. And we had that all through the 90's when I was there. I loved the guys I played with, on both sides of the ball."

Rob Zatechka

Scholarship recruit, Offensive Tackle, Lincoln, Nebraska (East)
Where are they now? Omaha, Nebraska, Anesthesiologist

Question: Hey Rob, to begin I've gotta tell you that Brenden Stai recalled the very first day on campus, when you called him out as he entered the training room...

Rob Zatechka: I remember that, and that was like 19 years ago. A bunch of us would look things up on guys through the internet that summer, a few of us guys hung out that summer before our freshman year. Weigert had moved in with his brother, so Zach and I would work out together 4-5 days a week that summer. And it was like, 'I wonder what this guy's going to be like?' We couldn't wait for everybody to come to Lincoln. And it's funny now that you look at it: Weigert grew up here and still lives here, Graham came from Texas and now he lives here in Nebraska, Stai moved here from California and he lives here in Nebraska, and then you have Joel Wilks who grew up here, and then he goes and moves to Portland, Oregon! Funny.

Q: So when was your first fall camp?

RZ: It would have been the fall of '90. Right off the bat I redshirted that year. I took Poli Sci 100 during the summer, so it was a good way to get acclimated. And I was working out with the team during summer conditioning and stuff so that was a good way to get in shape and started getting used to the atmosphere and system down there.

Q: Anything take you by surprise?

RZ: Number one was just the sheer number of guys. A huge number of guys. And even with the volume of guys with the coaching staff (and when I say 'coaching staff' I'm talking about the football coaches, the strength coaches, the athletic trainers, all the way across the board), how systematic it was, how organized it was. Everybody kind of had a feel for what everybody else was doing. Everybody was really knowledgeable with what everybody else was doing and for as many guys as you had to deal with, and at that time the walk-on program was probably one of the strongest ever there.

That was also before most of the scholarship cuts had happened, too. Now it's something like 85 scholarships, but it was still 95 and might have been more, even, than that. I remember they did one scholarship cut when I was in college, and then they cut to 85 scholarships right after I'd left, if I recall. So you had these huge 95-plus scholarship players and then you had nearly that same number of guys who were walk-ons. And then during fall camp you always had your guys who came to the realization that, "Hey this just isn't for me," and they'd leave, so you'd always end up with something like 160-180 guys. Just the fact that everything stayed so structured and organized, that was probably the biggest thing.

The other was the first time I ever had to go against Kenny Walker. You want a 'slap in the face' introduction that you were at the next level? That was it right there. I had to go against Kenny every day, because that first fall I redshirted and was on the scout team. So I went against him every day in practice. There's few human beings on the planet who were just better people than Kenny. He's a great guy, friendly guy, loving, huge-hearted person, but every once in awhile you'd get kind of a wild hair up your backside and see how hard you could hit Kenny, or dare I say, actually block him. And I remember once in awhile doing that, 'I'm just gonna give it everything I've got and see if I can block this guy,' and he wouldn't be expecting it and you'd come off the ball and just drill him and put a pretty good lick on him. But if you did that you better be darn sure and darn ready for that next play, because he was gonna waylay you that next play. And there was nothing you'd be able to do to stop it. (laughs)

Q: Let me ask you: was Kenny and his deafness kind of an inspiration to you guys?

RZ: Well, there were a lot of guys who were really good role models. And Nebraska has always had that. Now, you can have a lot of good role models and a lot of good leaders. I think the things that kind of hurt us early on -and I say 'hurting' and you have to put that into perspective: a subpar year at Nebraska was 9-2, 9-3, and that was considered a sub-par year. A good but not great year was winning the Big 8 Championship. And I think about that time period and we won the conference championship every year I played, except for my redshirt year. But we had that run in the '90's where it became almost mundane to win the conference championship, and you think about the 1980's where you're always battling and in some years come up short to Oklahoma, you had basically '82, '83, '84, '85, 86, '87, '88, winning the conference championship. Winning the conference championship was the goal, but in the '90's it was assumed it was something you should do. The higher expectation was winning the national championship - during the '90's there- I think the growth that you saw was a lot of the increased emphasis on team unity. I'm sure guys have mentioned that before.

One of the things I remember (now, I use this as an example of sort of a general lack of unity): I don't think there was a racial divide on the team, really, but there might have been a mild undercurrent of one. But one of the first team meetings -they actually held it in the old weightroom- and I remember all the backs and receivers were on one side of the room, offensively and defensively, and most of the linemen were on the other side of the room. And I just remembered looking at it, 'You know, you've got two groups of people here. They get along, but nobody's definitely going to be asking anybody from the other side of the room over for dinner.' It wasn't unfriendly, but conversely, you had two groups of people who weren't unified and on great terms with each other. I think there was a bigger emphasis after that 1990 year, to focus on bringing people together.

And they created the Unity Council that was jointly the coaches and jointly with Jack stark, the team psychologist. The thing the Unity Council did was foster a lot of unity, getting people to work together, understand each other, and just have an increased cohesiveness within the team itself. At the same time, when you take a group of people, from kids across the board on the team -the Unity Council was freshman through seniors, it was linemen, it was backs, it was white guys, it was black guys, it was a mix of everybody- it forced guys to see things from other viewpoints. It helped bring the team together. The other thing that it really helped, it felt like it gave the players themselves a little bit of a stake, a little bit of ownership in the team. So all of a sudden team rules and regulations, punishment for breaking those rules, a lot of that ended up being decided by the Unity Council.

So now if there is a team rule, it's the guys you're lining up next to that accept those rules, who set those rules for you. If you break those rules it's that teammate of yours who's gonna have to punish you, that teammate of yours who decides what that punishment is going to be. All of a sudden there's a huge emphasis that everybody is beholden to everybody else on the team, and when that happened it really did a great job of bringing everybody together: "I'm out here and everything I do, I'm doing it for the guy who's lining up next to me. When I'm on offense, everything I do is trying to make it easier for the guys on the defense, because he's out there trying to watch my back, as well." All of a sudden, I think that really changed things in terms of common goals, having sort of a common attitude among guys on the team.

Q: Brotherly-centered focus?

RZ: Hugely so. If there was any selfishness before that -I don't think there was a lot, but probably a little bit of that- it really got pushed aside. And I think the guys were out there with an increased effort to try and win it for that guy who was wearing that same jersey lining up next to you.

Q: Do you recall anything from the coaches, preaching the unity aspect to you?

RZ: You know, they did. And I think it was an issue that Coach Osborne had always tried to preach in terms of common principles: principles that successful people, successful organizations follow. I think Osborne always had a set of rules and principles that he did things by, and he always had a very -and I hate using the term 'game plan', but it is football and it is a game plan, and Osborne always did- he always had a very focused goal in mind with everything he did, and he always had a very focused plan to achieve that goal.

And I think the unity within the team was something that he always preached, but there was a process to go through to find the best way to do things. And I think working with Jack Stark and implementing the Unity Council, I think that's where you started having that final piece of placing that plan into place. It's one of those things where if Osborne had not retired after the '97 season, that run of success he had from the early '90's onward, I firmly believed he would have continued. It might have taken 20 years, and as good as Osborne was it took him 20 years to figure out the exact formula to win a championship nearly every year. And he found that.

Now, I don't think Osborne's goal, ultimately, was to win championships, I think his goal was to do the best job he could, creating good football players and helping people become the best people that he could. And in the '90's he found out his best formula.'99, 2000 they would have won and been in the running for the national championship and been a top 5 team. That trend would have continued there.

Q: Any recollections of your interactions with him? What made him unique, from your perspective?

RZ: I think he was. It was a combination of things: number one, you've got a guy from Nebraska, who when you meet the guy and get to know him a little bit (there are very few people who know him very well) he's a frighteningly down to earth guy. Very, very down to earth guy. That's the way he was brought up, I'm sure. Yet, at the same time just hugely, hugely intelligent. I firmly believe the guy's a genius.

The other thing, more strongly than that, though? Number two, he's hugely principled. He's got a very strong spiritual sense and a very strong moral sense, and I truly don't think he's gonna bend those for anything. Now there's specific instances –say, the Lawrence Phillips affair- and you'd hear people say, "Why didn't Osborne just boot that guy off the team never to see him ever again?" And then you hear people say, "He just used that as an excuse for him to play." I think Coach Osborne truly felt that if he just completely cut all ties with Lawrence it would have been the worst thing possible because you're just unleashing a loose cannon out into the world. I think Osborne's take was, "If we can manage to keep him in a somewhat structured environment, it's the best option we might have to help him succeed, make him a better person." I truly think that he was thinking, "If we can change this guy, make him a better person…." And Lawrence has hurt more people since then, but if we were able to keep him in counseling, get a better education, we'd not only make his life better, but make it better for the whole world. I just don't think he was keeping him around to win a national championship.

Number three, you've got Ahman Green, you've got Damon Benning, you've got Clinton Childs, you've got James Sims. That guy's one of the most spectacular athletic specimens I'd ever seen and he was like a 5th string running back. Nice guy, too. I always thought he was a nice guy. But anyway, you've got a slew of NFL-caliber running backs backing up Lawrence Phillips, so it was like, 'No, he did not need Lawrence to come back and help with a national championship.' Of course, you've got Tommie Frazier and All-Americans on the offensive line, and you've got the defense. They would have annihilated Florida without Lawrence Philips. That was merely icing on the cake…. that's not even icing, that's like a little floral print around the top of the icing on the cake.(laughs)

Q: What about Milt Tenopir and his methods?

RZ: (Laughs) You know, great guy. I truly believe that Tenopir was one of the few guys on that coaching staff who truly -honest to goodness- was one of the few guys outside of Osborne who completely understood Osborne's offensive system inside and out. One of the few guys who really could just sit down -you could remove Osborne from the equation and from a purely offensive system standpoint, game planning, play-calling standpoint- Tenopir was one of the few guys who could do it as well as Osborne, because he knew Osborne's system as well.

Very principled, too. He had a system of how he wanted you to play as an offensive lineman. The big difference -it's not that big of a difference- is Osborne says, "Dadgummit," and fifth year seniors would say "Geez, he hasn't said that for three years." Well, Tenopir was one of those guys where you'd get an occasional cursing a blue streak. At the same time, he was one of those few guys who could kind of tread that thin line between being sort of the firm disciplinarian who was running the show and at the same time be a bit of a player's coach as well. And it's hard to do that. There's not a lot of guys who could do that, and Tenopir was one of the few guys who could do that and do it pretty well, I always thought.

Q: And what about Coach Young?

RZ: You know, kind of same thing as Tenopir. Unfortunately for Coach Young, he was the passing game coordinator for the offensive line, and at Nebraska during that time period - and granted, it really opened up, and in my mind was the birth of the spread options Osborne started putting in there in the early 90's- and even though that offensive system really did open up in the passing sense, in '93, '94, '95 you're running maybe 20% of your running plays out of the shotgun. It was still a run-based offense, if we were going to beat you it was gonna be the running game, and unfortunately Young's teaching took a back seat.

But the thing about Young, though, he was one of those closet geniuses. And you get a guy who was mathematics instructor as a high school teacher and coach, one of those guys where you sit and talk with him and you get half a sentence out and, literally, three thoughts would come flying out of his head and out of his mouth. And before he got halfway through he'd be off on some other tangent before you knew what was going on. It was one of those things where you had to keep up with him, because he was basically about three thoughts ahead of where the conversation was going. Conversely, just a great guy, a wonderful guy.

It's always funny, because on one hand you have guys like Tenopir who knows the system that he's coaching, but at the same time if you screw up he's gonna rip you a new one, though you still loved the guy. There was a common theme with a lot of the coaches at the time when you look at Young, Tenopir, Charlie McBride, you had these guys who were gonna rip you if you screwed up in practice -absolutely rip you a new one- but at the end of the practice they were still the guy you wanted to go up and give a hug to. Like I said, it's hard to find guys like that.

Here's a story for you, mildly off the record: We're at practice, maybe my freshman or sophomore year, and there's this young rising star on the defensive line who screws up in practice. It was some mental mistake he made a couple of times and had just gotten McBride hot under the collar, and I just remember practice stops. And all of a sudden McBride explodes from across the field with just this cursing, screaming and yelling of every four-letter word known to man (some that I think he came up with on the spot) ripping this guy a new one. And basically the gist of it was, "Don't ever do this again or I'll actually kill you." So sure enough, five minutes later, what does the kid do? He makes the exact same mistake again. And you didn't really hear McBride -like I said, they were 30 yards away from us guys doing offensive line drills over by the old Ed Weir track- you didn't really hear McBride not so much as you felt this sonic boom shockwave come across the field when he exploded. (giggles) And I remember he was standing in front of this guy and the kid is staring back at him with kind of a sheepish look on his face, just absorbing this bomb-blast from McBride. And McBride is so stupefied, I don't even have words for it. He ran out of words to say to him, with the reddish, most angriest face I've ever seen from anyone in my life. Speechless, McBride reaches into his mouth and pulls out the largest wad of Copenhagen tobacco and just -he's literally standing two feet away from the guy. Two feet- and with everything he's got McBride flings it right into the guy's face. And it hits his facemask (he's still got his helmet on), and it just explodes and completely coats this guy's face. Black, brown Copenhagen. And all you see when you look at his face is -if you remember that old Al Jolson movie 'The Jazz Singer'?- is the black-face. You just saw white eyes, and the rest of his face was just black from this nasty Copenhagen. (laughing) Now here, the key point of all of this is, at the end of that day -and any day since- you know what? That same player would take a bullet for McBride and he would love McBride for allowing him to do so. Those two guys, to this day, are still tight as can be, best friends, and have an honest to God love for each other. When you have a situation like that, where a guy loves your coach and the coach is abusive (and the coach wasn't abusive), but it's an example of where you have a coach where he can basically, absolutely rip you a new one, and at the end of the day the coach and player still love each other and that player is still willing to run through a brick wall for that coach. You know what, that's a football team that is gonna be nearly impossible to beat.

And it was like that across the board with the offensive line and Tenopir, and the QB's with Osborne, the linebackers with Steele. (Then again, it might have been more of a fear thing with the linebackers and Steele) (laughs) But there was an honest-to-God love between the coaches and the players, and when you can foster that across a team, it's gonna be nearly impossible to defeat. And we had that all through the 90's when I was there. I loved the guys I played with, on both sides of the ball. That was kind of the goal with the huge push towards unity in the early 90's with the Unity Council, Osborne starting the TeamMates Program, and I think the success we had on the field was a big part of that.

And at the same time, you have to give credit to the schemes the coaches came up with. The fact that Osborne went from a pure power option running game to his sort of hard-to-define shotgun forerunner of the spread option that nobody had any clue how to defend, literally a decade before Urban Meyer or Rich Rodriguez or any of these other guys out in the field. And he still doesn't get any credit for it. I'm absolutely convinced Osborne came up with it. We were running fullback traps out of the shotgun, were running QB option keeper, QB passes, like a play where the QB could hand it off, run it himself, pitch it to the running back or throw it to the tight end. All on one play! And we're running it out of the shotgun, how do you defend that? Osborne came up with stuff. But how? We were running the old counter trap out of shotgun, and Osborne came up with all this stuff. I remember back around '92, '93 when he started it, we were, "What is he thinking?" Now, like I said, you've got all these so-called gurus running the spread option that Osborne pioneered a decade and a half ago, and at the time everybody said he was 'archaic'. Back then they were calling this stuff obsolete and archaic, and he was literally 20 years ahead of his time.

The same thing with the defense, the switch from the 5-2 to the 4-3 look and the push for speed, I think everybody nationally was kind of moving that way. I remember that 4-3 initially started as our nickel and dime package to defend against the pass. And all of a sudden they noticed teams had trouble running against it, too. Here you had these pro-style, shotgun passing offenses and they just said, "Hey, let's just leave them in there for that and the running plays, too." It was peachy keen.

Q: Plan B became Plan A?

RZ: Exactly. And you saw a lot of that success just came out of the coaching schemes themselves. The coaches did such a phenomenal job of recognizing the schemes that were going to get the job done and implemented them. Football coaches, historically, tend to be a rather stubborn lot. Well, it's true. They'll have system and if the system doesn't work it's not because there's something wrong with the system, it has to be something else, another problem. It's never the system. Osborne, McBride and all the coaches were smart enough to change as times changed. Not a lot of football coaches do that, and do that effectively. It takes some humility and willingness to see something that isn't working and do something different. And it's not just football, it's business, and they try and plug people into the system instead of bending the system to fit the people. Osborne, and McBride as well, basically said, "Here's what we have to work with. How can we change this system to work within that?"

You think about my senior year in '94: Tommie goes down with the blood clot issues and is out a portion of the year, and you have a guy in Brook Berringer who doesn't have the shifty, elusive quickness that Frazier had, but he's got a true NFL-caliber arm. An honest to goodness NFL-size, NFL-caliber arm. He's a 6'4", 210 lb. guy and he had a 40 yard dash time that was actually faster than Frazier's. He wasn't shifty, but he was fast and smart, and a real nice guy, I always thought. So Osborne was, "Lets take the offensive system and let's fit it to Brook's talents." And all of a sudden we were running so many plays out of shotgun that year. It was literally the QB option keeper to the sideline, just take the ball and read that angle to the sideline. And a guy with Brook's speed is gonna get you 4 yards a pop every single time, which if you do that 3 plays in a row, that's 12 yards and another first down, and then 80 yards later you've got a defense that's sucking wind. Then, of course, you've got a QB with a punctured lung, too, to even things out. (laughs) But Osborne, which impressed me, was always willing to bend the system to the talent he had. And so many other coaches always seem to want to bend the talent to fit their system. And Callahan, when he was at Nebraska, was a 'system' guy: "Here's my system, and if it's not working it's because the players don't fit the system. The system is not wrong. The system is 100% functional." But you saw the first year he came in to implement that system, Nebraska had its first losing record since 1961 because Callahan insisted upon turning a group of players talent-wise who were completely, wholly built for a run-based offense and tried turning them into a West Coast-style passing offense.

The other knock against Callahan was that he tried to call plays. And his system wasn't that bad. It wasn't great, but it wasn't that bad. One of his weaknesses, though, was that he wasn't that good of a play caller and game manager, which happened to be another strong suit for Osborne, just making adjustments during the course of the game. He was very, very good at that. Callahan, not so much. And you tend to see more of that in the NFL. You come out with a game plan in the first half and if the other team makes adjustments at halftime (in the NFL so often you don't see guys making the halftime adjustments to counter-adjust) and in college it was one of those things where even if the game plan was working stupendously during the first half, we'd come out of that halftime with a game plan that was completely backwards from what we did in the first half. Even if things were going right! Because Osborne would anticipate them working on the film clips and the still shots and make adjustments. Well, we'd come out and not do exactly what we did the first half. He wouldn't do a wholesale switch-around, but he'd change things up enough that the opponent had a whole new set of things to deal with that he hadn't seen yet. I think Osborne was always good in the first half -and you never really saw it as a player or a fan- but every few plays was a "test the water" play that he'd throw in there, something that maybe the guys won't be able to deal with. Not really try to gash them with it, make hay with it, but test the waters and see if they're gonna be able to react to this or not. And if you'd do that and the opponent did not react to it in an appropriate fashion, you can bet

Osborne would come out in the second half and just hammer you with those plays. And Callahan, here you had someone so in love with their system where instead of making changes you just ended up losing games.

And you talk about that book you read, with many organizations and many systems? The successful ones are the ones that look at who they have and what they have to work with and say, "How do we become successful with what we have here?" instead of "bending everybody's will" to the system. Osborne was so good at identifying and maximizing talent and then both at long term and short term adjustments -late second quarter, mid-third quarter- and change it if it was working okay, but could have been done better, and implementing those changes in the immediate here and now. Osborne was just a genius when looking at his system over the long term. People called him an offensive genius when he was Devaney's offensive coordinator, and the system he ran with Devaney was a typical pro-style offense with a lot of passers: Ferragamo, Tom Sorely, David Humm, Van Bronson, Bruce Mathison. It was a passing offense, and then the whole running game, option thing didn't come along until basically Turner Gill hit the door in '80 or '81 and he switched to the running game: "Maybe Barry Switzer has something going on over there," you know?

Q: Is there anybody the average fan should know about because of the contributions they made to the team?

RZ: I think Jack Stark is a big one, just in terms of the work he did with the players. And it's one of those things where sports psychology, it was around and it was in use before Jack Stark hit the door down in Lincoln, but he was a guy who revolutionized it, at least for Nebraska, and took it to a whole other level. In terms of a behind-the-scenes guy working with players and keeping some guy's heads on straight, keeping the unity and working toward the common goals, Jack did a solid job. He's one guy.

I think the strength staff: hugely instrumental, but at the same time I think that's something most football fans have a good grasp of. Everybody knew who Boyd Epley was, with the strength program growing up in the '70's and in the '80's.

One of the big things that's been instrumental (and Osborne made the reference in a conversation I had with him over a year ago now and as Athletic Director), I remember Osborne making the point to me to make a big effort to re-establish Nebraska ties, like the walk-on program that got severely restricted under Callahan. Osborne said he wanted to make a big push for that. And Osborne made reference to that, how all three of the National Championship teams (and I haven't checked his numbers, because Osborne is kind of like God: you don't test the guy) (laughs), but Coach Osborne said, "You go back and look at both National Championship teams and approximately 70% of those guys were local guys, from Nebraska and the surrounding states." Osborne said what that did, not that 70% of the starters were local, but 70% of the team were local. Some of those guys were big name recruits from Florida, California, New Jersey, of course, but he said, "You don't have to have all the starters be local, but whatever team it is it definitely helps if you have a majority of the guys on the whole who are local. And what it ends up doing is that it gives the team a vested interest in the University and the state and in the program itself." And so, 70% of the team grew up living and breathing and dying to wear Nebraska Red. And if you do that, the guys from California, Florida, Texas will do the same, as well. Tommie still lives in Nebraska, Stai lives in Nebraska. All those guys not from Nebraska still live here and work here now. Lawrence Pete is not from Nebraska, he lives and works here in Omaha. These guys who go off and play in the NFL, why do they move back to Lincoln or Omaha? You just get the entire team as a whole invested in it all.

I remember the 2007 season, Nebraska plays Oklahoma State and just gets absolutely routed at home by a fairly mediocre Oklahoma State team. Talented, but mediocre as a whole, and Steve Pederson gets fired the Monday after the game, and the TV cameras pan the crowd and before halftime fans are just running out of Memorial Stadium. Paul, it was sad. People weren't angry anymore, they were sad. It was the straw that broke the camel's back. Anyway, a World-Herald Reporter manages to snag a fan at a post-game tailgate right after the game and asks him his thoughts. And it was a very simple comment and simple observation, but it was profound, too. He said, "All these players the coaches brought in to play here, and the coaches themselves, they came to play at Nebraska and not for Nebraska." I remember reading that in the paper and I got chills reading that. I was, 'Oh my gosh, he's right.' Then I got really depressed, because I remember that in college we played for Nebraska. It was for Coach Osborne. You didn't come here because it was your stepping stone to the NFL.

Q: Speaking of stepping stones, the Florida State game when you were a junior, any recollections of that game?

RZ: We don't talk about that, Paul. (laughs) You know what, it was one of those things where a lot of people really want to look at that game and make it a turning point. I don't think it was. I truly think it was just the next step in the progression. Not even that: what you saw in the Florida State game was really the talent, the system and the coaching that we had in place that time, on display. It was one of the few times you saw Nebraska demonstrate what they had done on a truly national level, because you had a #1 vs. #2 matchup for the National Championship, and it was a true 1 vs. 2 because it was a flip-flop in the polls. Whoever won that game was gonna be the national champ, hands down, and so it was the same team we had all year long.

And I've got to be honest with you, most of the pieces for that team were in place the year before when we played Florida State and they beat us by a bit of a larger margin, and I think that was nothing more than player maturity. Instead of a true freshman at QB we had a sophomore at QB in '93. Instead of sophomore and a freshman running back in Calvin Jones and Lawrence Phillips we had a junior and a sophomore running back in Calvin and Lawrence Philips. Everybody was a year older, more seasoned. Trev Alberts, Donta Jones, everybody was a year older in maturity. But that Florida State team in '92 was essentially the same group of guys we played in '93, maybe one defensive end was different. Those Florida State teams in '92 and '93, and those Nebraska teams in '92, '93, a few changes here and there, but it was essentially the same teams. It was like we were a solid team from August through December of '93 and then January 1st we flipped a switch and went on a tear that took us into '94. What you saw January 1st in '94 was what we were doing all year long, you just never saw it on a real good, big national stage until that Orange Bowl of '94.

That was why I don't think it's a turning point, it was just the same thing we'd been all year, but on a national stage against an opponent people didn't expect us to match up with, didn't think we'd remotely be able to beat. And we coulda, woulda, shoulda beat 'em. And with even more maturity the next year in '94, you put us two scores down to one of the greatest defenses in college football history with Ray Lewis and Warren Sapp on one team and then beat them in their own house by wearing them out, having the maturity to hang in there and not cave, stay with the system and stick with the game plan, gonna listen to Osborne, and it worked.

If you even go back to that '92 team (two of the most lopsided victories against good opponents in Nebraska football history), I mean you can talk about that bowl game versus Florida after that '95 season all you want, but that '92 season when we beat Colorado at home Halloween night, October 31st and just shellacked them like 52-7? It was just a runaway victory over a Top 10 Colorado team, and it wasn't even close. And usually when that happens it's when one of the coaches puts together a really good game plan and the other one inadvertently thought the game plan was gonna work, and it didn't. You know, sometimes you're the baseball and sometimes you're the bat (laughs) And then the very next week we had 7th ranked Kansas and they had Stubblefield, Gilbert Brown and Kwame Lassiter and all these studs on defense. They came into Lincoln the very next Saturday and we beat them 49-7. So that '92 team had the ability to go out and take a top 10 team and absolutely dismantle it. What it lacked was just the wherewithal and the mental toughness and the maturity to go out and do that on a week-in and week-out basis. So even in '92 the talent and this system and the ability to go do those great things. It was there, because we did it in '92 and we took some absolutely phenomenal football teams, that's when Oklahoma was still good, a top 25 team. In Norman we tagged 32 points on Oklahoma in Norman, Oklahoma that year. The most lopsided victory over Oklahoma when I was in college came during that 1992 season. They were still a very solid football team. Gary Gibbs was Switzer's Defensive Coordinator. Gibbs' defenses were always top notch, they were always very good. But that '92 season we annihilated Top 10 Colorado, Top 10 Kansas, Top 20 Oklahoma. It was just the mental toughness and maturity issue and the focus, we just didn't have that collectively as a team yet. You saw that in between that Kansas game and that Oklahoma game we went to Ames, Iowa and we lose to arguably one of the worst teams in college football in Iowa State that year. God bless 'em -my dad grew up 30 miles from Ames, Iowa over there in Marshalltown- but as a team we didn't have that mental toughness and that maturity and focus to maintain that kind of productivity week to week to week throughout the full season. That was the difference between '92 and '93.

All of a sudden in '93 that team was there. And it took us from an 11-0 regular season to the bowl game versus Florida State, and Vegas had us as almost 3 touchdown underdogs. That's insane for a #1 versus #2 matchup. That was insane. I understand in Vegas they were trying to generate betting, but still, over 19 point 'dogs? That's ridiculous. But that's my take, I still don't look at the '93 game as a turning point. It was just the same guys playing the same style. Honestly, Florida State was the only team nationally that matched up well enough with us that they could beat us. That game could have gone either way. Florida State, it was a Who's Who of NFL and NBA drafts, here Charlie Ward carves out a 10 or so year NBA career for himself. That was a hugely, hugely talented collection of athletes on both sides of the ball.

Q: We just ran out of time that night...

RZ: We did. And conversely, they had too much time. That was a great Florida State team.

Q: I think that was one of the greatest games ever in college football...

RZ: It was. And you watch ESPN Classic and they still have it as one of their Top 10 football games list.

Q: Flashes of the game stand out to you?

RZ: No. The thing I remember is that everybody you played against -because here you had Derrick Brooks, Derrick Alexander, one of their big defensive linemen- the amount of talent you had playing against every single play, but the fact that we were going out there just punishing them. I remember Derrick Alexander, who played a bunch of years for the Minnesota Vikings, a big stud D-lineman for the Vikings, but he was a senior that year in '93 and I remember blocking the crap out of him and him getting pissed. Because we were flying off the ball and just knocking them backwards in that game. And I'd met him a couple times before, a really good guy, but I remember him just being pissed as hell the whole game because it was one of the few times all year that people had been able to effectively block their defense. There was just a swarm of future NFL guys on that defense.

Then again, the next year with Warren Sapp and Ray Lewis and C.J. Richardson, and the two defensive ends Miami had in Kenard Lang and Kenny Holmes were NFL first round draft picks, too.

Q: And they had the Rock!

RZ: They did. That guy never stepped on the field, and I watch this 'True Hollywood Story with Dwayne Johnson' on TV and I was, 'Dude, that guy never got on the field. He was backing up Warren Sapp!' (laughs) He made it onto the field, and at the time you were like, 'Dude, this guy's a chump. Put in your ones.' (laughs)

Q: Anything more about the Miami game, Rob?

RZ: Well, when I mentioned earlier how hard it was to maintain the focus, that mental toughness from week to week to week. It's hard to do. And sometimes you think you're doing it, but maybe you're not, you haven't done it as effectively as you think you did. From a mental preparation standpoint, I remember going into that Florida State game a year earlier and we could not have been better prepared mentally. The amount of focus and mental fortitude we had going into that Florida State game, I'm actually surprised we didn't win. And the Miami game, in hindsight, that was one of the few games where, by the end of the game, I don't want to say we didn't show up ready to play, but I still feel that somewhere we missed something in a little bit of the game planning, which happens. And you hope talent makes up for it, but it was one of the few games where after going into it, 'Oh, I guess were not as ready to play as I thought we were,' because I thought we definitely had the ability to hang with those guys from the opening gun. It wasn't like we got into that Miami game and, 'Oh my gosh, it's Warren Sapp. He's so tough. I hope he tires out!' (laughs) That was not the case. From moment one it was like, 'I can totally block these guys. Stai and I can take Waren Sapp.' (Because you know they flip-flopped Joel Wilks and Stai, and during the game I remember thinking, 'Dude, Wilks can block this guy.' He was perfectly capable of blocking Sapp) For some reason it was one of the few games that year where we may not have been as focused as we should have been, but it wasn't for a lack of trying.

Like I said, occasionally it slips, whether you want it to or not. Everybody has an off-night, and that was one of the few games that season where we collectively kind of had an off-night. Now, at the same time we also had the wherewithal from the coaching standpoint to make adjustments to the guys pulling things together, and in my mind it takes a fair amount of maturity and focus to -mid-stride, say it was late third quarter– "we should probably start playing some real football." And we did. Thank goodness, from a football standpoint, that we had that ability to pull it together and do that to win the game. The coaches, I thought, made some very good calls and made some good adjustments.

The other game where we might not have had the focus we should have, the Wyoming game earlier in the year. They came out guns-blazing, because half their roster was Nebraska high school kids. They had a 14 or 17 point lead on us at some points in the game, and finally we got our crap together after halftime and went out and just basically just blew them out of the water the second half. We basically tied 30 points on them in the second half. I guess that's kind of my take on the whole rut that we had making the switch from winning conference championships to national championships. I think the coaches had all the pieces in place as early as '91 or '92 in terms of the schemes, the players, the system, the ability to make adjustments and change the system as you went from game to game, year to year, season to season, which was in place earlier on. And the only place that I would say was a real turning point would be in the sense of how we were viewed nationally. It was a turning point in that sense, but not necessarily in the team itself. All of a sudden after that game, from a national perception, I guess it was, "Oh, I guess we can rank Nebraska number one early next season since they can hang with a talented team like Florida State."

And in terms of who you're picking for opponents, we were rooting hard for Miami to make it to the Orange Bowl. Penn State still claims we stole their national championship that year because we bumped them from #1 in the polls. Nebraska was #1, but we got bumped from the #1 spot when both of our top QB's went down.

Q: They were betting against the Turmanator...

RZ: Yeah, that's the point. They figured we lost our top two guys, "They won't be winning the national title now." We didn't even lose a game and we got bumped out of the #1 spot, so don't give me that stuff about how we stole it from Penn State. We just moved back in after we'd been there originally.

Q: Sounds like you've had this conversation before with Penn State fans...

RZ: You've no idea how often I run into them.(laughs) But then we end up beating Colorado late in the season, and there was a Who's Who of NFL lineups: quarterback Kordell Stewart, Rashann Salaam the Heisman Trophy winner, on their line you had Stoltenberg and a few guys, you had Ted Johnson who had a few Super Bowl Rings with the Patriots, Christian Fauria at tight end for like 12 years or so. But we dominated them and they were ranked like #2 at the time, and we leapfrogged Penn State again into the # 1 spot a week after that, late in the season. (Osborne nine times out of ten could always out-game plan McCartney. And McCartney was a darn good coach, he was very good, but nobody was as good as Osborne) But we got that number one spot after shellacking Colorado and we still had Penn State breathing down our necks. Because, if you remember, this was the era of the polls still, not BCS, so it was just polls. So to have a shot at the national championship you had to be #1 and win your bowl game, or hope to God that if you're number two that you win your bowl game and the #1 team loses.

Q: Style points meant everything...

RZ: Exactly. And so, boy, by the end of the year we had the best chance to win the National Championship and make sure Penn State doesn't win the National Championship. Who would be the toughest matchup in any bowl game?

Q: The home team on their home field, of course...

RZ: Home team on its home field! Go to the Rose Bowl and play a good UCLA or USC team, go the Sugar Bowl and play a good LSU team, go to Miami and play them on their home field. That would be like going to the Dallas and the Cotton Bowl and playing Texas. It was literally, "Okay, let's go to Miami to play Miami in the Orange Bowl, which happens to be their home stadium."

Which, I've got to be honest with you, do you know the thing that still surprises me to this day about that game? They were gassed! Everybody talks about Warren Sapp sucking wind and the rest of the defense sucking wind. Paul, those guys were tired. I remember the end of that game I was tired. I played a football game in 85 degree heat and massive humidity, but I'm not that bad. But after that Miami game those Miami players were just dead. They had nothing left in the tank. Those last two offensive drives we had, they had nothing left in the tank at all.

Q: Like pushing around big old Jello molds, huh?

RZ: It was. And you'd hit your blocks and they had nothing left to go after them. Our QB's and running backs would just run right through them, and they didn't have the energy to pursue.

I have a photo here at home, it's taken from the end zone angle and it's taken during a timeout, and we're standing in our huddle (and I think Weigert's maybe got his helmet off, because he always took his helmet off. He could talk smack better that way. (laughs) His line was always, "I want to let Sapp know who's talking smack to him."), so we're standing there because we weren't that tired, and the four Miami D-linemen and one of the linebackers, every one of them has their helmets off and they're taking a knee. The photo shows past the Miami players taking a knee and us just standing there looking at them. And I remember talking about it in the huddle, 'Look how tired those guys are! We don't have that much time left, but we can kill these guys because they have nothing left.' If you ever watch replays of those two Schlesinger traps, take a look at it when you look at the pursuit: we blocked the shit out of Ray Lewis, and there was tiny but fast, little Rohan Marley, and he couldn't catch up to Schlesinger, and you can just see his body language where he goes, "Fuck it. I'm tired." I swear to God, go watch it. You can literally see it in his head, where he comes to that idea. I'll be the first to say Schlesinger's a great athlete, but still you're telling me you're so tired that you can't catch a 240 lb. fullback from Nebraska? That showed how tired those guys were. You can literally see him go, "Oh, forget it."

Q: And it seems to me, watching one of those replays, Abdul Muhammad knocked that guy out..

RZ: Yeah, "Let's take that 120 lb. wingback and block him." (laughs) They just literally cashed it in. They seemed to know they were gonna lose that game and couldn't help it.

Q: Rob, do you remember the first game you played in?

RZ: It was the opening game of the '91 season. I'd have to go look it up. One of those mildly non-descript -and I hate saying that- non-conference opponents. We always had some good teams: we had Arizona State twice, Washington twice, Texas Tech, West Virginia, UCLA, we played Utah. I want to say it was Utah, or Utah State was the opening game. We played Colorado State a couple times, and when Sonny Lubick was there they were solid, actually. It was a pretty good team.

I've got to be honest with you, after butting heads with Kenny Walker for a year and then after Kenny left, guys like Parrella, David Noonan, Raemakers, Jamie Liewer, practice didn't get a heck of a lot easier. Some of the best guys I played against were the guys I was hitting heads with in practice.

Q: Any good practice memories?

RZ: (laughs) There's always little things, stuff that makes you laugh when you remember. For example: the Scout team defense always wore gray jerseys and on offense we always wore the red mesh over our gray t-shirts. And I remember one day in practice, I don't know why, I just decided I wasn't wearing my red mesh over my gray t-shirt.

And it was Thursday practice and it was light contact, and it took Osborne until like the middle of watching practice film… and he looks at me on film at the team meeting after practice and I'm wearing a gray shirt. And then he takes his little laser pointer and circles me, and it looks like I'm this big defensive player who's out of position, but at the same time there's no offensive player blocking him. And Osborne starts circling him with the laser pointer and he says, "Hey! Hey! Hey! Who's got this guy!? Why isn't anybody blocking him!?" (laughs) And I remember going -in the middle of the team meeting- going, 'Oh, that's me, Coach!' And there was like that big pause from Osborne, and he reversed the tape and runs it backward a couple of times, and he sees me going up and blocking the linebackers. And he looks at me and he turns and goes, "Why aren't you wearing a red jersey?" And I don't know what I was thinking, but without pause, without batting an eye, I tell Osborne, 'Oh, you can't see me Coach. I'm in 'stealth mode.''(laughs) I remember, it was one of those comments where Coach Osborne was speechless, didn't know what to say. And a little bit more, he didn't want any further explanation. (laughs) He was basically, "I don't even want to broach the subject further than it already is." He was like, "Well, okay Rob." Maybe once a month for the next few years after that somebody on the offensive line would just not wear the red jersey and he'd be, "What are you doing?" And it would be, "I'm in 'stealth mode' today, Coach." (laughs) There'd always be that big, long pause. (laughs) It was always performed deadpan. And it was always goofy stuff like that.

Remember Larry Townsend? Big defensive tackle out of California? I always remember him wearing his parka under his pads to practice. The California guy was so adverse to cold, he actually wore his full-on full length North Face parka under his pads. Stuff like that, those are the kinds of the little tidbits that you always remember from back then. It's always crap like that makes you laugh from those days.

Q: Any off-field shenanigans for you?

RZ: I was a pretty clean-living guy for the most part. But the off-field stuff, I just remember the fact that everybody always kind of hung around with each other from my freshman year on, and it was one of those things where you'd always end up that a bunch of the brothers on the team would have a house party and you're hanging out with them or they'd hang out with you. Everybody got along well and hung out with everybody else around the team.

Like my sophomore year on we started having rules, like "No parties after Wednesday night." Which always killed me, because then you had all the guys going out drinking on Wednesday night. (laughs) Half the time after the game you were too tired to really raise much of a ruckus and it seemed everybody had a steady girlfriend, so you usually went with her to eat after the game, anyway. Still, everybody was such a nice, close-knit group of guys. It wasn't so much the specific instances, it was just the fact that all the guys really got along.

Q: The opposite of that one early meeting in the weightroom you were talking about?

RZ: Yeah, half the team on one side and half on the other side of the room. But it seemed after that you never ever saw that type of thing anymore. It would have been interesting in the Callahan years, I imagine there was like ten different groups split apart. And like I said, in general the O-line hangs out together, the D-line hangs out together, the defensive backs hang out together, but as a whole we really got along well together.

Q: Any special relationships for you?

RZ: The big thing, for the O-line, obviously, we still keep in touch. We keep up on who's doing what and where, but at the same time you go to an alumni event, the spring game, a game in the fall, and the guy who's a third string safety as a senior when you were sophomore, you run into that guy at the game in the fall and you just strike up a conversation and it's like it was 15-20 years ago hanging out and B.S.-ing with them. That relationship's always there. That's the thing. It's a really good, common bond to have. It's one of those things where everybody gets together and we just really keep in good touch with each other. I still run into guys I literally haven't seen in 15 years, and you just strike up that conversation and it's the instantaneous relationship with that person again.

Amongst the players (granted, Steve Pederson kind of started the tradition), a lot of guys make an effort to show up in the fall to the games, the tailgate events. And I've got to tell you, there's a lot of guys I've reconnected with over the last 3-4 years. There always seems to be a guy or two where you wonder what the heck happened to them, and I've run into them, so that's a great thing. From the alumni standpoint, they've done a really great job, getting the guys to really show up again and show their face.

Ben Kingston, a former fullback from the Solich era, his dad is a surgeon. I do anesthesia with him every now and then. Ben started a website for former players to log onto as a networking site, so that is good, too. And I trade e-mails with Boyd every so often, too, so that's nice.

Q: Rob, one of my most fond memories of those days was our old dumbbell incline press contests, just you and me. Remember those? At least it was a contest for me...

RZ: Oh my God, Paul, I have to tell you: at the tail end of the Callahan era I went to a game, and one of the Sheriff's Deputies who does security for the games took me back into the weightroom after the game, he took me back to that area and I went and found those dumbbells. They're still there! They're pretty dusty. Doesn't look like they've been used extensively. Do you remember those one-fifties's? The one hundred-fifty pounders? Then Boyd bought that new set and got them up to 175 lbs. God, yeah, I remember. We used to pound them out. And I'd get to those 175's. And then I went to the Giants. The (New York) Giants had 180's! I was like the only guy on the team who did 'em.

Q: I remember always trying, thinking, 'Okay, I weigh about half as much as Rob, but I'm gonna push this guy.' Remember that one day I had the 150's and did two or three reps, and then you picked 'em up and repped out about 9 or 10 of them? I went, 'Damn!'(laughs)

RZ: (laughs) That would crush me now. The gym I work out at now, they have 110's. For my first set I rep them out at like 20 reps. It's still fun.

Q: And hey, I have to tell you, there's a high school kid from my church who I had over to my garage gym last night and we did the old Metabolic Power Circuit...

RZ: Oh, you wanna know what kills me? Now that's the kind of lifting I do, the circuit, the high reps...and hey, you wanna know a cool workout I've been doing lately? I got this workout from a bunch of SWAT Team guys in Omaha. They're a bunch of mixed martial arts guys. I work out with them, too. They'd have tears rolling down their face. It's the worst lactic acid burn I've ever felt in my entire life. It's like hitting yourself in the head with a baseball bat and then you're done, then the next day you're a little bit sore, and then it's two days later -like Bryan Bailey's DOMS, the delayed onset muscle soreness. Then it hits you. I thought, 'Holy crap, what did I do to my chest?' (laughs)

Q: And what's your little brother doing nowadays?

RZ: He's here in Omaha, a pharmaceutical sales rep with Merckk. He's a drug pusher. Give him a holler. And if you ever need anything just give me call, I'll likely either be in the operating room or changing a diaper or something, (laughs) but I'll get back to you somehow.

End conversation.

Rob, as was evidenced in this interview, has always been about two steps ahead of the pack and continues to be a blast to converse with. You've no idea how much fun it was in those days for me (weighing about 165-170 lbs.) to take on a 315 lb. Rob in a dumbbell incline press contest. He would, of course, always win, but I'd like to think that my competitive spunk would somehow rub off on him. The other strength staff seemed to have the same modus operandi, and I think it paid off in some small sense for these guys that a full, relentless effort was the key, results coming what may. I remember Rob one day entering the Strength Complex where we sat down on the weight benches and he told me, rather sullenly, how offended he'd been earlier that day, "You wouldn't believe what some guy called me… the guy takes a look at me," goes Rob, "and says, "Holy crap, dude, you're like a Coke machine with arms!"" I nearly fell off the bench laughing! Not because the metaphor wasn't somewhat accurate, but that this big guy was so offended by it and allowed it to ruin his day, exposing the fall in his countenance to me. It was that kind of relationship all around the place with these guys, where facades were few and far between, where many of the people were quite open and exposed to each other with a pervasive sharing, trusting and oneness. These kids could be themselves, and this kind of environment kept the tendency to project false images of strength and invincibility at a minimum. As a result, they were freed up to boldly pursue failure: on the practice field, in the weightroom, in summer and winter conditioning. This limitless pursuit of failure allowed them to mature and, I believe, paradoxically produced their success. It allowed them to go 'stealth mode' quite often, to use Rob's words.

Rob also brought up the growing experience and maturity level of those teams, as well as a college kid's inability to maintain focus and effort throughout an entire season. Despite the human body's inability to maintain more than 8 weeks of peak performance capabilities before it loses its edge, you also had the mental aspect which, truth be told, played a far more major role for the youngsters. I can see how those Wednesday night beer sessions may have been a way for some guys to blow off some steam and relax from the toil, the grind, the pressure, the glare, but I also wonder whether the drinking was more of a performance deterrent or a performance enhancer. Would the fact that the barley-pops were last consumed 60 hours pre-game on a Wednesday night rather than 36 hours pre-game on a Thursday night make a difference? Call me crazy, but I think it did. Why? Because alcohol, as most of us know, acts as a diuretic, essentially dehydrating a person. And if you know much about muscle tissue (a primary success component in physical activities like football) you realize that muscle consists of approximately 75% water. Allowing their bodies an extra day, an extra 24 hours to recover from an acute bout of dehydration could have made all the difference in performance capabilities as it compared to their foes (who likely threw some beers down on the usual Thursdays at their respective campus watering holes). The average college student consumes about 34 gallons of alcohol per year, but Nutritionist Dave Ellis pushed enough water into the players on Thursdays and Fridays knowing they would be more than recovered for the Saturday contests. (In a perfect world the kids wouldn't have drank at all, but this was Nebraska, not Utopia.)

Lastly, of the number of golden nuggets Rob revealed in this interview, I think it's important to note that schemes did play a major role. Now, I won't go overboard with a treatise on play-calls or blocking schemes and the like here. Why? Mostly, because I don't feel sufficiently knowledgeable to do so, but also because we have witnessed many schemes and techniques used over the years to reach championship status -and I don't wish to get into a self-induced argument of one kind being better than another. Suffice to say, no scheme or philosophy is worth a bushel of beans if you don't have the proper individuals to make it work, so my focus will remain on the individuals and the intangibles behind that 60 & 3 success.

Saying that, Tom Osborne was a maverick of proportions in the way he placed defenses in quandaries by forcing them into making split-second decisions (after only a week's preparation) and then exploited those many poor decisions for touchdowns: "We were running fullback traps out of the shotgun, were running QB option keeper, QB passes, like a play where the QB could hand it off, run it himself, pitch it to the running back or throw it to the tight end. All on one play. And we're running it out of the shotgun. How do you defend that? Osborne came up with stuff…. and at the time everybody said he was 'archaic'. Then they were calling this stuff obsolete and archaic, and he was literally 20 years ahead of his time." Well said, Rob. Futuristic stuff indeed.

Notable quote #2:
Rob Zatechka on the offense/defense dynamic: "I'm out here; everything I do, I'm doing it for the guy who's lining up next to me. When I'm on offense, everything I do is trying to make it easier for the guys on the defense, because he's out there trying to watch my back, as well."

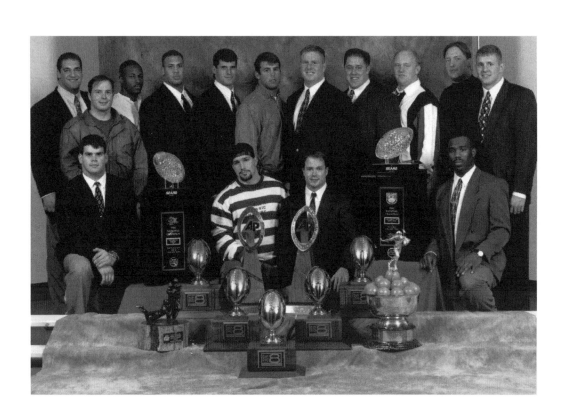

Look at a football field. It looks like a big movie screen. This is theatre.

Steve Sabol

Any writer worth his salt will tell you that the greatest dramatic literary arches rely not in the accurate telling of the protagonist's highest highs, but instead in the grandest portrayal of the story's lowest lows… and how he manages to fight his way out of life's dark valleys. Like any great movie or best-selling book can attest, it's not where you start but where you end that matters most.

Which brings us to Tony Veland. The Benson Bunny's diary will make you cry from triumphal joy as well as tragic heartbreak. A quiet leader, not even the most creative of literary types could have dreamed up the path Tony traveled, because 'The next Turner Gill' had no way of knowing what was to befall him. Let's hear of his beautiful, painful, promising tale and the lessons he learned…with a little encouragement along the way.

Notable quote #1:
"Sometimes it was pretty difficult to make sure we weren't gonna let the inner turmoil stop us from accomplishing our goal. Because it's one thing if you're a unified group of people and others from the outside are shooting arrows at you: you'll still be fine. But if you have people trying to break you down from the interior? That's gonna be the easiest way for stopping a team or organization from succeeding."

Tony Veland

Scholarship recruit, Free Safety, Omaha, Nebraska (Benson)
Where are they now? Omaha, Nebraska, Coach/Financial Advisor

Question: So what year was your first fall camp, Tony? Any first memories, impressions?

Tony Veland: 1991. Man, you're making me go all the way back. (laughs) I think I was just kind of overwhelmed by how many guys were at practice, how big some of those guys were. I don't think I had real grasp as to what I was really getting myself into. And I see all these huge guys like Darren Williams, Mike Petko and John Parrella and I was thinking, 'Oh my God, I better get in shape because I'm gonna be doing a lot of running away from these guys.' (laughs)

Q: Who was the first friend you made?

TV: It was probably Popplewell. Brett Popplewell was the first friend I made. We were roommates and just kind of connected. He was a receiver and I was a quarterback. And I hadn't ever met anybody from Australia and his accent was funny, and we connected and we've been friends ever since. Same old Brett.

Q: Anything stand out from your first practice experience?

TV: I was a quarterback and I think I was still a little, so overwhelmed, 'Here I am at Nebraska playing quarterback here.' I was glad I wasn't on defense at that time, (laughs) and I remember Kevin Steele and Charlie McBride letting a couple of guys have it. I remember we were just starting practice and I was happy I wasn't on that side of the ball, they were pretty animated.

And then I saw Coach Solich go crazy, too, a couple of days later. He'd get on people, too. It was definitely interesting. And you could also feel the energy from Coach Brown with how animated he was. It was just so surreal being in that situation. It was a dream of mine to be playing football at the University of Nebraska. And I didn't know if I'd actually play collegiate football or where at, but to be there at Nebraska and actually know that I was on the field at the time was pretty big.

Q: You grew up a Cornhusker fan, no?

TV: Well, I did, but I was kind of a closet Nebraska fan, (laughs) the reason being was my dad was a huge Oklahoma fan. A *huge* Oklahoma fan. So I hardly ever watched a lot of Nebraska football when I grew up. And when Oklahoma would play Nebraska I was always secretly cheering them on. (laughs) It was a little crazy and a little conflicted, because I hated to go against my dad at that point, but I think that was where I started the whole Nebraska kick. I remember watching Switzer and Osborne back in the day, you know - Steve Taylor and Turner Gill- and I knew that's where I wanted to be. It was all messed up.

Q: So was it a little intimidating at first? I mean, here you are working with "The Man," Coach Osborne?

TV: You know, I think I was just kind of in awe, originally, because we all knew what he'd accomplished at the University. And for him to be spending as much time as he was with the quarterbacks? Because even before I really got a chance to know him I knew he was about more than football. He had that presence about him. It's kind of hard to explain, but some people, after they've accomplished so much and have so much respect from other people, you just kind of felt it.

Q: Did Coach Osborne visit you at your home during the recruiting process?

TV: He actually did. I remember we had a basketball game one night, and I remember him coming into the gym (because it was all kind of hushed)(laughs)and I definitely tried to pick up my play a little bit. And by the time I got home he was there. And he was, "Hey Tony, how are you doing? You know, we're interested in you playing." And I have to tell you, the thing that stood out to me: I didn't realize how tall he was. So here is this skinny giant, you know, (laughs) standing in your doorway. It's kind of intimidating, but at that time it was pretty validating to me, because in high school football we hadn't won very many games. I knew I was an okay athlete but I didn't have crazy stats. But for him to be there interested in me, I was pretty flattered.

Q: What did your Dad think of that whole thing?

TV: Well, unfortunately he didn't get a chance to take part in that. My dad passed when I was a junior in high school and he didn't get to see that. But my Mom thought it was great because her baby was going to college, and I was going to be the first one in the family to do that and we knew it was big-time football. So I knew I was getting ready to do something and I was pretty happy about it.

Q: Your father's passing at that early age… did that affect you as a player down the road?

TV: I think so. It taught me that in life some things happen that you don't expect to happen, and even though they may hurt or it may feel better to just shut down and sit there and grieve and let life go on, you don't do that. It's a situation of 'life goes on' regardless of what happens. That started me on the whole kind of me just focusing on accomplishing my goals regardless of what happened, to keep my mother happy and proud of me, especially since she was really taking care of us and making sure she could do all she could to make us successful. So I did all I could to make sure I was doing everything to be successful.

Q: You were the oldest?

TV: I was the oldest child. I had a brother 4 years younger than me and a little sister about 7 years younger than me.

Q: I'm sure they were proud of you…

TV: I think so. (laughs)

Q: Well, I talked to Bryan Bailey a few days ago, and it seemed that the word around town was that you were going to be the next great Nebraska quarterback. But you ran into some injuries…

TV: Yeah, a little bit. Just a little bit.(laughs) It was really interesting, because they wanted me to play defensive back when I first got there. They recruited me as an athlete but they really wanted me to play defensive back, and I was really determined to prove myself as a quarterback. I thought with their style of football that I had the running thing down as an option quarterback and I had to learn the passing and the defenses and this and that a little more, gain a little more confidence in myself to have a chance.

But I think more than anything it was my inner me saying, 'They are saying you can't do this. Go prove them wrong.' So I think I took that whole attitude to learn as much as I can and make sure I do a good job. And it was difficult because I wasn't the highly touted quarterback prospect: it was Clester Johnson at that time. And we had battled back and forth in high school, and here's this guy who's coming out of high school highly touted, all these stats, he can throw the ball, he can bench 400 lbs., it was just a little intimidating. Not to mention you had the guys already there: the Keithen McCants, the Mike Grants, Mickey Joseph and all those guys. I just knew that I had to get in there and try to take the initiative and make sure that I was going to put myself in the best situation. I tried to become a student of the game and keep Osborne and Gill happy.

Q: Did your doing so make you a better defender in the end?

TV: I know it did. Because when you really become a student of the game it makes you such a better player. I can see that now as a football coach. If I took that attitude that I have now and look at what each individual was doing, what their tendencies were? If I would have studied like that in my prime I would have been a lot more effective. (laughs)

Q: When did you make the switch over to defense?

TV: That was actually in '93. It had been two years and some things had transpired. The first year I redshirt and I learned everything that I could, and the second year I had a chance to actually compete and when I went into fall camp me and Mike Grant were kind of neck and neck, so there was a legitimate chance that I was going to be getting some playing time. And what ended up happening was the last play of the last scrimmage before our first game I end up breaking my collarbone.

So when I broke my collarbone, then obviously Mike Grant was the starting guy. And then we had some guy named Tommie Frazier who, halfway through the season, took over there, and history was written after that. But I came back that year and I was determined to play quarterback and not let the injury stop me. And I still had a lot of other things going on, like a pulled hamstring, rolled ankle, still a lot of minor stuff, and then I still came back.

Then that next year Tommie was looking good, and Brook and me were battling for number two. It was the second or third game of the season and I was running the option, and I went to plant & run and somebody grabbed me and my knee twisted a certain way and it tore my patellar tendon. And once I tore that I went through some changes, and I felt I did everything I could to be successful on the football field but it seemed things kept stopping me, and I didn't really understand why. Because at the time I was a young kid and I felt I was doing everything right: I didn't get in trouble, I was doing pretty well in school, trying to be an example for some of the younger players out there. And here it was: every time I turned around it seemed some type of injury was stopping me from accomplishing what I wanted to do. And I kind of went into a little bit of a funk there and got down on myself and had a little pity party for myself for a few months.

But then I spoke with someone who was from out of town… I didn't even know this lady and she wrote me a letter. She was just encouraging me and giving me words of comfort, and for some reason the words she said really touched me and opened my eyes as to what was going on. Her name was Diane Yeutter. She was teaching in Lexington, Nebraska, and we've been friends ever since.

It was crazy, but she actually used to write Nebraska football players when they were going through things: she'd been writing for two or three years, every week, and she'd write just to encourage them. And she told me that there were times where she, herself, would become discouraged and thought of not writing…. and she told me that I was the first person to respond back to her. So it really filled her day and made her feel pretty good with what she was doing, because I know she was reaching a lot of people even though they weren't getting back to her.

But she reached me. And the words she had for me changed my life. The words were unreal. She was really a beacon for the Lord trying to reach me, and it kind of opened my eyes to why I was going through what I was going through. I started having a dialogue back and forth with her and it was just amazing how my whole outlook turned around. I stopped having my pity party and stopped thinking about me and my injuries, the whole 'woe is me' situation. And I just turned around and said, 'I've got a goal I want to accomplish, and I'm either gonna let this stuff stop me or I'm gonna go after it.'

At that time I figured I was still gonna come back from that knee injury, but I figured, 'Maybe I'll stop getting hurt if I start hitting people,' so I started to try the whole defensive back thing and that's what happened from that point on. It was not an easy switch by any means, because you have to have a certain attitude to play defense. I was used to avoiding people, and now I had to try to run through them… and you have to have this mean disposition. You have to have a little bit of attitude to play defense, and I was really one of those laid back, quiet people.

Q: That's always the impression I had of you…

TV: Yeah, (laughs) very laid back and quiet. And even when I played I was laid back and quietter, but on the field -when I had to get excited?- I did. It was not an easy switch but, at the same time, knowing the quarterback position and knowing the defenses we were running made it a little bit easier. And in high school I played cornerback and safety so I was pretty familiar with it, but it was just getting back to learning the footwork and the constant reps that were going to make me a better player. I made the switch and it worked out.

Q: So before the switch, any impressions of Coach Turner Gill?

TV: Old T.G. (laughs) Coach Gill was just a great individual. There were lots of people on that coaching staff who really left an impression. Just the fact that they were all really good men. I think Coach Osborne, Gill and Coach Brown really stand out in that category. They showed that they cared more about you than just your performance on the field. They wanted you to become a better man, be respectable, to succeed outside of football. And you could see that with the way they coached you and the way they spoke to you. They showed you a certain respect that some coaches don't necessarily show. And not that they held your hand or anything like that, but they just put you in situations so you could be successful.

For Coach Osborne and Coach Gill, they were actually friends. I felt I could talk to those guys about anything. Especially Turner Gill, since he was a little bit closer to my age, but just knowing what he'd accomplished and know what he'd encountered as a player. Because, if I can remember correctly, he was kind of a quiet guy, too, a quiet leader. Did pretty well in school, too, didn't get into trouble, so I related to him well. We had a great relationship.

Q: Any defining moments with those guys stand out to you?

TV: More than anything it meant a lot to me the day Coach Osborne came to the hospital when I tore my knee up. He told me, "Hang in there. I know you're a good kid. You'll battle back from this." He was pretty much telling me to stay on the path and things will work out. That meant a lot to me. He'd seen a lot of football and a lot of football players, so for him, with his insight, to say that to me was pretty special.

And about Coach Gill, I remember I was having a problem with a certain class at a time when I was just coming back from my knee and it was during one of those rehabs when I was in a valley, and he & his wife had me out and we just talked. We just talked and he told me about some of the things he had gone through in his life. And he stated that whenever I needed him I could always call him and he would be a resource to lean on, too.

Q: So then you're on the defensive side of things now, with Coach Darlington?

TV: (Laughs) Coach D. I just love him. He's funny. He's one of those guys who, you look at him and you think, "He can't know anything about football." (laughs) He's kind of clumsy sometimes and his whole demeanor is so matter-of-fact. You just figure, "He can't know anything about football." (laughs) But he's a very, very smart man and well-respected in the NFL defensive community and he was easy to get along with. And one thing that was great about him was he liked me. (laughs) I was one of his guys and I knew he was looking for a certain kind of player, and I felt like I had a decent intelligence and he liked me as a thinker out there.

He was just really a funny guy, but very thorough in the way he had us prepare for games with the film-watching, the scouting material he would give us. I think if there was one thing that would drive us crazy and would be frustrating: we would practice about 15 different kinds of defense each week, and then we'd only use three. (laughs) But he put us in good situations where we could make plays on the ball and be a supporting cast for the defensive line at that time, which was awesome.

Q: A few guys said they'd butted heads with Coach D.

TV: Trust me, I know. I'm trying to be good here. (laughs) I never had any problems with Coach D., but trust me, I saw it. There were definitely a few players who thought a little less of Coach D than I did, but that's just football. (laughs)

Q: And let me ask you, there seems to me a certain progression happened within the team from your freshman year in '91 to your senior year in '95. Can you recall any steps taken or changes that came about?

TV: It's funny that you say that, because I really believe the formation of the Unity Council propelled us to that next level. When you talked the other day about that book, Good to

Great, to run a company the right way one of the ways to make the employees perform a little bit better or take a little more pride in what they're doing is making it their own, and I think that's what the Unity Council did for us. Coach was saying, "Listen, I don't want to be the guy with the iron gavel putting judgment on people all the time. You need to police your team and run this team the way it's supposed to be run." I think we took more ownership of what we were trying to accomplish, not just doing good in school and staying out of trouble, so we tried to do whatever we could to get that monkey off Tom Osborne's shoulders, as far as winning the big game. I think it definitely helped that.

The freshman classes that arrived in '91 and '92 took it upon themselves to do whatever they could to compete with some of those Florida teams, but I really the think the Unity Council was the start of that. And we really realized that, "If this is ours, we need to make sure we have a product out there that we can be proud of. We need to be sure we're representing the University the way we're supposed to." That was really the start of us trying to change the face of our team.

Q: Were you a member of the Unity Council?

TV: I was on Unity Council the last couple of years.

Q: What was that like for you?

TV: It was interesting. (laughs) It was interesting. I don't know if you remember, but '94 and '95 we definitely had some things going on.

Q: It was no walk in the park being on Unity Council…

TV: No, it was not easy. Not easy by any means. But that was part of the challenge. You needed to do what it took to make sure the team stays successful, and if that meant not letting a player do this or that or disciplining some guys that got into trouble, that's what you had to do. I don't remember any specific instances where a certain individual did something and we let it slide. That never happened, but at the same time it was not an easy job.

Q: It wasn't easy judging your peers and teammates, was it?

TV: Not easy. Sometimes it was pretty difficult to make sure we weren't gonna let the inner turmoil stop us from accomplishing our goal. Because it's one thing if you're a unified group of people and others from the outside are shooting arrows at you: you'll still be fine. But if you have people trying to break you down from the interior? That's gonna be the easiest way for stopping a team or organization from succeeding. So I think we did a very good job of managing it and making sure we were a tight-fitting unit.

Q: Any thoughts about other coaches who stand out to you?

TV: Coach McBride. Man, I'll tell you what, that guy there? A great guy, funny guy, but he was intense. He was intense, and I think to deal with the Peter brothers you had to be somewhat intense. (laughs) But when you first got there you knew he was about football and he wasn't going to take any crap from anybody. He had a certain standard of play, and if you didn't meet those standards you weren't going to be on the field, you weren't going to be playing.

There was one particular practice, I remember, where he hurt my feelings a little bit. (laughs) There was a practice, my senior year, and it was wet outside, and there was a particular play and they ran a draw, and James Simms was the running back and he gave me a little move and I missed the tackle. And I think we even made a mistake left to right, and

Coach McBride just let me have it, "What the heck are you doing? I don't know why the heck we brought you here. We're just wasting a scholarship.." He's going off like this, just killing my pride, (laughing) and then they ran the same play again, and the same thing happened!(laughs) And you talk about somebody feeling lower than low. I mean he gave me a look like, "What the hell did we do bringing you here?", and just walked away.

I tell you, I felt bad for two days because of that, but at the same time I respected him for what he said. Because honestly, this is a performance sport and you've got to perform. He was just letting you know it wasn't about your feelings. I learned from that, I tell you that much. After the tears, I learned from it.

Q: Now, afterward you went on to play with the Broncos, didn't you?

TV: I spent three years in the NFL: two years in Denver and one in Carolina.

Q: What do you think set Nebraska apart from other teams of that time?

TV: I think one thing we kind of hit on, the Unity Council definitely set us apart, but number two, and I could be wrong, but I think we just had a serious work ethic. With our weightlifting program and with our offseason program, that really put us in the position to be the juggernaut we became. Football is an "in your face, hard hitting, just grind for 4 quarters"-type of a game, and I don't think there were too many teams in the nation who could compete with us because we were so well-conditioned. The reason we were able to beat that Miami team was because we were so well conditioned. They had Warren Sapp and Ray Lewis, defensive MVP's, so it wasn't like we had greater talent than them. But we were more physically fit, we were a stronger team, I think we had a 'do or die' mentality, a real blue-collar mentality, that was about, "We're not out here to be pretty, we're here to win games." I think that translated well and was something that couldn't be stopped for awhile.

Q: Did the walk-on program do anything for you as far as a motivation?

TV: I don't think motivation, but the walk-on program was very fundamental to the success that we had, because other than a McDonalds All-American type, just about everybody generally knew that first year that they weren't gonna play. Either you were gonna be redshirting or walking-on, whatever the case may be, and you were gonna use that year to learn about the system and develop your body. And there were some of us thinking there was a chance we weren't going to play our second year, either. And that mentality helped us out a little bit, because it actually held true: those first couple years we really grew with the system, really saw what the collegiate football system was about. By the time we got on the field we wouldn't be making the same rookie mistakes that you'd typically make coming in as a freshman, be a little more developed, so we were able to compete with some of those guys by then. Plus, we'd had two or three years with the coaches in the program knowing what to expect and make sure we're performing, so I think the walk-on and redshirt program really made us successful.

Q: Let me ask you, was there anyone behind the scenes who played a big part in those teams?

TV: There were actually two people: Bryan Bailey -when you talk about our weightlifting program, the first person you think about is Boyd Epley, and Boyd was genius to put that team together, there's no doubt about that- but I think Bailey was the guy who really took it to the next level from a relationship standpoint. He really got to know a lot of the players and did what he could to make us better, not just the players who were out there every day, but the players who were rehabbing injuries and had to spend a lot of time in the weight room. He was one of those guys who, when you saw coming (like earlier when I said that about Darlington), you'd think, 'Why the heck is he here? What does this skinny little redhead know about football? What is he doing here?' (laughs) He would come up with the most unorthodox things for you to do. Everybody usually had you benching or squatting or sprinting, and he's got you doing some crazy thing you've never done in your life. But once you're done you're stronger and you just go, 'Where in the hell did he get that from?' But he definitely had a big impact on a lot of us.

And then another guy who really got along well with most of the players was Doak Ostergard, trainer. He was just a really good guy: he understood us, he'd talk to us, and he made being in the training room fun sometimes, but at the same time he was also a guy who was really for the program, and he wanted to make sure we were doing everything we could to represent it well. Between those two guys, they played a big part in our success.

Q: What are you most proud of?

TV: Graduating? (laughs) That's a big thing. I'm most proud of beating all the adversity that came my way. Because here's a guy who had a lot of talent and probably could have been a starting quarterback, but he probably spent more time in the training room than anybody there, always rehabbing or getting something done. And just getting past that and not actually caving in to all the crap that was happening? Because if that would have happened I never would have experienced the national championships. I think we still would have won those, but just being a part of that on the field and then going on to the pros. And then the coaches were such a great support system in going through that.

Q: Anything you wish you could do over or done better?

TV: Oh man, everything! Everything! I wish I would have been a little better student of the game back then. I felt like I put in a good amount at the time, but I probably could have done a little more. I wish I could have spent some more time with some of our guys who were more successful, just kind of pick their brain and how they played. I played with three very, very good players: Barron Miles, he was the best corner I ever played with. Just to pick his mind for what had made him successful, what he looked for. Tyrone Williams, he was one of those guys that just got out there and played. He was never intimidated by anybody, I wish I would have learned a little bit more from him. And one other guy was Mike Minter, and at that time I really stepped in because he got hurt, but I wish I would have talked to him a little more. I wished I'd had his confidence and swagger that would have made me a better player.

But that's all 'what if' and that kind of stuff. I wanted to be the next Turner Gill when I came in, but I had to change my goals. But as long as I was playing football I was happy. I probably would have changed the way I finished school because I had to come back a year after I was done playing to finish my studies. I spent a little too much time on PlayStation. (laughs)

Q: Madden '94?

TV: Yeah, exactly. Exactly! Madden '94 was my downfall! (laughs)

Q: It made you a better coach in the long run!

Tony: Right! But at the same time, some really, really good things happened to all of us, and I'm just very proud to be a part of it.

Q: Do you remember your first game, Tony?

TV: Honestly, I really don't. Oh, I'll tell you the game that stood out for me. The first game playing defense was West Virginia the year we went undefeated. The first or second series they put me in and I made like three tackles and two big hits. That was it for me. I felt like, 'Okay, maybe this safety thing is going to work out for me.' That was kind of it. I made a big hit and I looked up at the Jumbo-Tron at the Meadowlands thinking, 'Yes, I've arrived!' (laughs) That was really kind of it for me, because I hadn't realized what I wanted after not playing quarterback. But when that happened, when we were in New York, that really stands out to me.

Q: Do you have a favorite game?

TV: Oh, it would be the Miami game, no doubt. Because it's amazing: when you see big competition, most people always inwardly root for the underdog. So we were that underdog, we were the guys who'd been there all week, we were being talked down by the fans, by the media, how we didn't have a chance. We knew this was our chance to really seal all that talk, to really build that confidence and show the world what Nebraska football was all about.

From the first play on defense, I made the first tackle on the running back. That just started it. And we knew it was gonna be a slug-fest, that they had a good quarterback, good receivers, a crazy-dominant defense, but we felt like, "Here it is: Our opportunity to shine. We're gonna make it happen," and obviously, as the game goes on they're up and then we're up, and then at halftime Osborne gives that prophetic speech. It was great. We made some good plays, we made some bad plays, but when it was all said and done, what he said was true, they were sucking wind. It was easier for our defensive line to get to their quarterback, his passes weren't as crisp, those 4-5 yard gains turned into 7-8 yard gains on offense, and you could see this thing happening, just building inside of us and energizing us, I tell you. I don't think I've ever felt as good as I did when Kareem Moss caught that last pass, because I knew it was over. I knew that was it and we'd finally done it. And I tell you, I've had a Super Bowl Championship and this and that, but that was the best feeling that I've ever had as a football player.

Q: Take me back. Does the turf stand out to you? The smell, the sounds? What stands out in your memory?

TV: You know, probably all the orange and green that you saw in the stadium, because we're used to the Sea of Red, how when you go there and see that it's a little intimidating. But at the same time, I don't know how everybody else feels, but that kind of charged me, kind of revved me up a little bit: 'We're against all odds, they've been talking stuff about us all week, and it was, "We're in the ring now. Let's do this." '

Q: Any memorable off-field occurrence?

TV: I think one thing that was kind of interesting, we were supposed to go to a professional football game the week of that Miami game and we almost got into fights with some of the fans who were there, because that's how crazy they were, just in our face, talking all this trash. And it was, "Are you serious? Do you wanna put the pads on? Because we can do that." That's what stands out for me at that particular time, to drum up one. Plus, I don't want to implicate anybody. (laughs)

Q: Any memorable practice story?

TV: The most memorable practice I can think of was, I can't remember if it was before or after the Oklahoma game in '95 and we were getting ready to play the Florida team, and there was one practice that was more spirited than any practice we ever had. I can remember going up on the goal line and just banging heads, and I can remember Christian (Peter) and Aaron Graham getting into it.

And this is kind of crazy, because here Christian is our big guy on defense and Aaron is the big guy for the offense and, "What is gonna happen here?" And I hate to say this, because A.G. is my guy… but Christian tossed him like a baby. (laughs) I was like, 'Wow!' (laughs) I may be exaggerating a little bit, but we had 3 or 4 fights happened that particular day. It just showed that we were actually ready to play a game versus this particular Florida team, we were tired of being disrespected and showed that everybody was on the same page.

Q: Well, anything else we haven't touched on that really set those teams apart?

TV: You know, I don't know if this necessarily separated us, but I felt there was one particular time that showed that we were all banded as one and we were going to make this thing happen: Tommie goes down and then Brook goes down, and here's little five foot nothing (laughs) Matt Turman comes in and saves the day and doesn't skip a beat. You could just see on his face before the game first started, he was a little wide-eyed at the start, but during practice that week the coaches had gotten him prepared and we were going up against a highly ranked Kansas State team at Kansas State with Chad May and all those guys, and we knew we had to step up as a defense, and the other players on offense knew they had to step up. For that to happen, after a third string quarterback to come in and us not skip a beat? It meant that what we were trying to go after was real, and after that game happened we knew we were destined to win a championship that year.

Q: And it seemed like a secure, quiet confidence. Not necessarily a cocky confidence, no?

TV: Well, it was a little scary. If you remember that year, we struggled with Wyoming, a team we were supposed to blow out by 70. (laughs) I think we made it easy for the skeptics to believe the team wasn't for real, but at the same time we still did whatever it took to make that thing happen when it was all said and done, to come up with the W. Then after we beat Miami that next year we were just ridiculous, the confidence was sky high.

Q: Nobody could stop you but yourselves?

TV: Exactly. And there's one thing that stood out to me: that particular year in '95 Coach Osborne was a little bit more frank with us and told us that we were the best team in the nation, that we were going to win this national championship as long as we did the things we were supposed to. And I can remember in years prior where I think he had that confidence, but he wasn't as upfront as saying, "You guys are gonna win this championship." I think what we accomplished in '94 really built our confidence, but hearing him be somewhat bold and say we were probably the best team in the nation and win the whole thing, it was like Coach Osborne 'talking stuff,' you know? (laughs) Coach Osborne 'talking stuff,' that really lit a fire underneath us. That's when we really knew. And that was at the beginning of the season, so we knew we had something special there.

Q: Do you think it was the best college football team of all time?

TV: I really do. At the time I don't think we felt that way, but the way we played, with the way nobody really came close, the closest game was like 14 points. The unity, the way we dominated? I think we were the best team ever.

Q: And being on defense, was there a mindset of the Blackshirts that set you guys apart?

TV: Hey, all you had to do was look at the defensive line, and they were leading us. And they were about as mean and nasty as you probably get. If you're not following suit after that? After those guys? You might as well go sit down somewhere. We just had that blue-collar mentality where we were going to be in your face all day. I was very happy to have those guys in front of me because they made my job a heck of a lot easier.

But it was one of those things that when the ball was in the air we were gonna try to get to it, and when that ball was in somebody's hands we were gonna try to get there and not be 'happy' when we got there. So we knew we were pretty decent, and I'm very happy just to be a part of a team that had that many athletes all going in the same direction.

Q: What was it like being a quarterback when Tommie first came in?

TV: Honestly, I knew when he came in and was highly touted and they were saying he was gonna come in and take over -and I didn't have anything personal against him- but I was thinking, 'Hold on, I'm still here. I haven't gone yet.' (laughs) But I was one of those guys - not that others were necessarily disrespecting me- but it always seemed others were writing me off because I was from the Midwest. I wasn't one of those guys from California or Florida or Texas, I wasn't this highly touted quarterback, so I always felt I had something to prove when I was out there. So I had to elevate my game to make sure that all the hype about this guy didn't just take over.

Yet, at the same time, when he first got there I knew he was a good player. He was still young and making mistakes. I think it was as the year progressed and I looked at this guy I thought, 'This guy's a freshman and he's in the huddle telling people what to do, telling them to shut up?' You could see that even as a freshman he was a leader and he was one of those guys who was gonna elevate the other players by the way he played. That kind of showed when he took over against Missouri.

And I can't say enough great things about the guy, because I don't know if my game would have been as good as his, if I would have had the type of effect on the team that he had. So I'm very thankful that things transpired the way they did, because I played on the greatest teams ever. I had two national championships. I can't complain.

Q: Last question, Tony. And Tommie might not like this (laughs) but so many guys have told me that Lawrence was the best player. What do you think?

TV: Lawrence Phillips? Yes, I would say the best player from a talent perspective. There's no doubt about it: Lawrence. I've been in the league and played with some good players, and in my opinion he was the best running back I played with. I think he had everything you needed from a back: speed, power, very elusive speed, the attitude, he could catch out of the backfield. He knew the offense. He could block well, he pretty much had everything one needed. He had size.

And he came in: I can remember his first scrimmage against us Blackshirts. He takes the ball the first carry and doesn't get too much, but the second carry he gets 40 yards! And we're like, "Hold up. Hold up, who's this punk?" (laughs) And it's two series later and he does it again. The first time scrimmaging with us and he does this. We go, "Okay, this guy can play here," and that's saying a lot considering the running backs that we had there.

Anytime you watch the Florida game or the Miami game you've got to go back to some of those runs that he made: it was pretty to watch. He was just one of those guys who made you look bad in the hole. (laughs) He was a beast. And I keep in touch with Clester and Clinton and Damon a lot, too. They have better memories than me, so between those three they're probably gonna have some crazy stories. (laughs)

End conversation.

Perseverance. Surely we've all seen those familiar, framed office-setting photos of a nature scene or a faceless, athletic individual while below is a positive affirmation of some timeless axiom, something to provide a little inspiration as many go about their hum-drum 9 to 5 in the world of cubicles and windowless offices. Well, if I were to create a print celebrating the concept of perseverance Tony Veland would be my photo's subject. Here's a guy who proved that nightmares are also dreams. But he got through that dark night with the unlikeliest of inspiration: a stranger's letter. With both Tom Osborne and the mentoring Turner Gill at his disposal, who would ever suspect that a heretofore anonymous fan's words of encouragement would turn this young man's life in the most positive of directions? Astounding! There truly is no place like Nebraska, and even though Steve Pederson's (shudder) placement of the "Through these gates pass the greatest fans in college football" at Memorial Stadium's gates may inspire a roll of the eyes for many, perhaps the former A.D. had the Diane Yuetters of the world in mind. I'll give him that much. You can be sure that I will track this lady down if it's the last thing I do.

Tony summarized the reason for the great 60 & 3 in two concepts: the Unity Council and the collective work ethic. The first dealt with thinking as one, which led to their training as one. Pretty succinct, wouldn't you say? By now I think we can pretty much say that the creation of the Unity Council was a stroke of genius of vast dimension, as it not only allowed the coaches to simply coach, but it also raised accountability and gave them an unsurpassed ownership stake. Above even that, the Unity Council was absolutely crucial in creating a bedrock foundation of unity and a leadership dais for dealing with some of the inner, destructive issues during those years: Scotty Baldwin's mental issues and their tragic consequences, Christian Peter's supposed groping of a former Miss Nebraska in a crowded bar (rumors say he may have taken the fall for a teammate) and other (some unsubstantiated) allegations, Lawrence Phillip's highly publicized and hyper-politicized altercation with on-again/off-again girlfriend and Nebraska Basketball student/athlete Kate McEwen, Tyrone Williams' shooting a gun at an alleged Lincolnite gang member's car, and outlandish accusations of robbery/attempted murder against Riley Washington, among others. Dealing with typical issues of 'boys simply being boys' to the most serious in nature (as mentioned above), Unity Council leadership was a weighty burden placed on already taxed young men, but they held the line and learned much from the experience. History will show that a vast majority of them became better men for enduring it, despite national media pundits' painting the program with wholly unfair, ignorant and overzealously misinformed brush strokes.

Another item of note worth addressing was his reference to Coach Osborne's "talking stuff." Now, Tony cleaned up the locker room jargon and sanitized it for the family kitchen table here, but I think it shows the power of the leader they had in Tom Osborne. Here was man vastly devoid of smack talk, of bluster, showiness and bravado, yet the simple voicing of his confident expectation was enough to put these guys over the edge and essentially challenge them to live up to the premise of another season's total domination. Author John Eldridge once wrote that every boy needs to hear these simple words: "You have what it takes," from his father or a father-type figure in order to blossom into true, confident manhood. This was Coach Osborne paraphrasing that same notion.

The last item of note may be a bit nuanced, but it caught my eye and ear nonetheless, and that was Tony's statement of the defensive backfield's being a "supporting cast for the defensive line at that time." For a stellar athlete, a defensive captain and a Unity Council leader to possess the humility to not puff up his chest and point a finger at himself, but instead reveal that they were the 'supporting cast' of the famed Blackshirt Defensive line speaks volumes. Zach Weigert mentioned earlier that the leadership of those teams started on the offensive and defensive lines and then moved in an outward fashion, and Tony here states unequivocally that such was the case. Quite revealing and extremely profound, if you ask me.

Notable quote #2:

Tony Veland on the powerful impact of one Nebraska Football fan: "But she reached me, and the words she had for me changed my life. The words were unreal. She was really a beacon for the Lord trying to reach me, and it kind of opened my eyes to why I was going through what I was going through."

I didn't even know this lady and she wrote me a letter. She was just encouraging me and giving me words of comfort, and for some reason the words that she said really touched me and opened my eyes as to what was going on. Her name was Diane Yeutter.

Tony Veland, previous chapter

As providence would have it, Tony Veland had his Husker Angel's phone number ready at hand when we ended our conversation. I dialed her up from out of the blue to find if this face from the Sea of Red would have the time and/or inclination to share her version of events as it concerned Tony's heaven-sent letter mentioned in the previous chapter. Luckily for us, she kindly obliged. And though you'll never see her name on a roster or in a media guide from that 60 & 3 era, she was there. I officially present to you Nebraska's 12th Man, errr, Woman, of that era: Mrs. Diane Yeutter (rhymes with fighter)…

Diane Yeutter

Question: Hello Diane, I appreciate your willingness to speak to me. Tony Veland brought your name up and mentioned that at one time in his life a letter from you made all the difference; that he found it very encouraging, exhorting, and gave him a proper perspective and mindset going forward. I simply had to hunt you down and find more about the story and the part you played in it.

Diane Yeutter: Well, that's nice of you, Paul. Tony is very special to us to this day. He really is. Our birthdays are two days apart, and my husband and I both love him as a 'spiritual son'.

Q: Before we get going here I must ask, how is your name pronounced?

DY: That's Yeutter. My husband's name is Ed.

Q: From what region does that name originate: Yeutter?

DY: Well, my husband's family was German, so it's a German name. My family was English, so we married the English with the Germans.

Q: Are you a native Nebraskan, born and bred?

DY: Oh, for Pete's sake, yes. My family? We were located in Fremont, Nebraska, which is just a hop, skip and a jump from Lincoln.

And actually, it was my father who would take me to Nebraska Football games when I was five years old or so, so I was born and raised Husker Red. I never knew passion for another team, collegiately, than Nebraska. I remember going to Lincoln, driving in blizzards, and we'd still go to the games. I can also remember in the 1960's when we beat Missouri, and we were sitting in the South end zone. I don't know why I remember it, but we just pounded the flesh out of those Tigers. I just fell in love with the spirit, the fans, the competition of the game, and the noise just thrilled me. And also, during the years my family would watch the traditional Oklahoma-Nebraska game at Thanksgiving and all my family was over. So yeah, I just grew up Red.

And one time Mom and Dad took my brother and I out to eat, Paul, at the Cornhusker Highway Holiday Inn. Well, the entire Nebraska Football team was there. And you have to understand, Paul, this was back in the 60's and at a time when integration was just becoming a common thing. My Mom and Dad looked at Doug, my brother, and I, and said,

"Go over to that table and get these Huskers' autographs." So I had my little napkin and I walked over and I looked at this one player and said, 'Can I have your autograph?' And I remember this like it was yesterday -and he was sitting over there in the booth and he was black- but he blushed. He signed my napkin, and it was Ked Geddes. Ken Geddes. I still have that napkin up in my attic. I never destroyed it. It was Ken Geddes. I don't even remember what position he played, but I was in awe of him. I was in awe of Ken Geddes.

That's the background of the passion from childhood on up. And my father was killed in '73, and in '75 was when I went to college. Then my mother came down to Tau Kappa Epsilon, the TKE house in Lincoln, and she became a TKE House Mom. She had me down for any game I wanted to come to for nine years. I can remember mom had one of the TKE's in her house who was a center and he was second string, and one time my mom said to him, "You know, you could be first string center for probably about any other team in the nation." And he replied back, "Who wants to be number one on the depth chart when you can be number two for the number one team in the nation?" I'll always remember hearing that. It was pretty neat. So a passion for the Huskers and a passion for football was bred into me.

Q: Where did you attend college?

DY: I went to Kearney State before it was UN-K. I got my teacher's degree there. As a matter of fact, after my freshman year I went to UNL to make application and talk with the Dean of Education with my mom. The three of us were having a conversation -and I wanted to transfer to be close to my Husker football team- and my mom said I needed to go back to Kearney because they had an excellent teachers program. So I went back to Kearney and graduated from there. I wanted to relocate so I could be near my football team, (laughs) but I was turned away.

Q: So you ended up in Lexington, Nebraska somehow?

DY: Thirty-one years ago. Thirty-two this coming fall. I made application and became a school teacher and I've been here for that long. It's been a wonderful challenge, a great opportunity here, and we actually teach to around nineteen different nationalities here in town. I teach the best grade of all: the second grade.

Q: So where did the letter-writing come in? When did it start? What was the impetus?

DY: Paul, when my husband and I were first married we wanted children. And we went through twelve years of eight miscarriages, major surgeries for me, minor surgeries, and it was in '92 or '93 that the dream abruptly came to a stop because I had major surgery and almost died. I was hemorrhaging to death and had two ectopic pregnancies and almost bled to death, but as I was walking out of the surgeon's office I looked up and said, 'Lord, you must have a plan for me. You don't want me home yet, so whatever you want me to do, I'll do.' That autumn, Paul, I don't know if I can explain it any other way, I just... I felt like it was a divine appointment from the Lord to write Tony Veland.

Q: Tony specifically?

DY: Yes, and it was something that I had heard, that he had wanted to be quarterback and that he'd broke his collarbone and they were making a position change on him from quarterback to defensive back. And something inside of me had compassion. We had just come off of twelve years of desperately trying to have children and our dream had died, just as Tony's had died of being quarterback in what was to be the one of the greatest eras in college football history, but it wasn't to be.

So Tony had a dream that was lost and we could identify. And I remember praying to the Lord and asking him what scripture he'd like me to share with this young man. And Paul, He took me right to it: James 1:2-4, "Count it all joy when you fall into divers trials and temptations, for the trying of your faith shall produce patience. And patience has its perfect work. Because you shall then become complete and whole." That's what I sent to Tony. And I said, 'Lord, I'm uncomfortable writing this to him. I don't know him. He might think I'm a religious cuckoo.' There were a lot of things going through my mind, but I knew that I was to send it.

Tony told you his response, and that young man wrote us back. He wrote a hand-written letter and then we wrote him back and he wrote us back. Tony even became involved in my second grade classes, becoming a Big Brother. They would write him letters and he would write them back. I always had Tony's back in prayer. There hasn't been a long period of time where I haven't prayed for that young man, so I think of Tony as if he were my son.

I have a notebook that is four inches thick of letters that we have written people during that time. We also wrote the team as a whole. We wrote the team many letters for many years; just notes of encouragement and hope and inspiration from the Lord, encouraging each player, each coach to recognize that God has them on earth and has a plan and purpose for their life, and at this time of life it is to influence the children of Nebraska, since the eyes of the children were on them.

Q: So Tony's was the very first letter you wrote?

DY: Yes, Tony was the very first.

Q: Amazing. And how long a drive is it from Lincoln to Lexington?

DY: Oh, about two hours and fifteen minutes. It's just a hop, skip and a jump.

Q: Pretty much a straight shot down I-80?

DY: Right, and what might be interesting to you is that my husband and I wrote other letters to players and have gotten to know them. Patrick Kagbongo has been in our home several times and we've followed him up in Canada. Willie Amos, we wrote him letters. Willie and I still write. Jeff Hemje, we still write back and forth on facebook. And he even invited us to his wedding. We've just developed great relationships with these boys, these players, and we've actually gotten spiritual sons, so we are richly blessed. And my husband, he was a former football player for the Kearney State Antelopes, too. I'm getting off track here, but when Patrick Kabongo walked into the doorframe of our home he filled it! Not only filled it with his size, but he filled it with his heart. That boy is just a remarkable kid. We've had a lot of fun.

And there's another young man, Tony Ortiz. We also wrote him. And whenever I would write players letters I always prayed and I wrote scripture because I felt the Lord has something very special for individuals. So Tony Ortiz, I can remember writing him and telling him where we sat in the end zone -because we had season tickets for many years until Callahan and Steve Pederson came in- but Tony Ortiz, I told him the exact section we were sitting in, and he'd come by and wave his hands. Not to say, "Hello. Hi," but waving them and lifting his arms up as if to say, "Louder! Louder!!" And I remember one time waiting outside the door where family and friends waited after the game and we saw Tony Ortiz and I said, 'Tony Ortiz?' And I said, 'We're the people who wrote you the letters,' and just told him how much we appreciated and loved him for the young man he was. And the intensity of his eyes? I'll never forget it. He looked me in the eye and said, "Don't you ever stop writing me!" I was like, 'You got it!' (laughs)

But it was really interesting, because you usually think of football players when you are a youngster as one thing: big, tough dudes. But they all have basic needs as any other human being. And I don't know them, but the Lord knows them, Paul, and he's always given me messages for certain players. Now, was it for every player? Oh, probably not. Were there some players who were turned off by it? Probably so. But the point was that was our ministry, and we knew that the Lord was leading us to write these letters, so that's a snippet of the letter writing.

Q: "God's word will not return void"?

DY: Amen. He is just remarkable. It's such a pleasure now getting on facebook. And Tony Ortiz has a job interview soon, so we prayed for him for a second interview. It just kind of cool, Paul, being able to see these young men. And we also wrote Mike Minter and Mike Rucker. And Mike Rucker's mom used to write us Christmas letters, and then when Martin Rucker, Sr. became a Congressman or Senator from Missouri, he and I used to e-mail back and forth. Ross Pilkington's parents, we've written back and forth, too.

And I have to tell you -and this is rather sad- my father was killed in 1973 in a very tragic way on the night of my brother's high school graduation, very tragic, in a twelve car pileup. I can remember -and there are any number of reasons why one would cry- but I remember crying to my mother, 'Now who is going to take me to the Nebraska football games? I'll never go to another Nebraska football game as long as I live.' It makes me cry.(pause) Excuse me… but it reminds me of the time I spent with my father, (crying) and my childhood, thanks to my parents. So writing my letters and loving these boys, it's like I'm giving back to my Mom and Dad, too.

Q: I'm sure those early father/daughter outings mean a lot to you.

DY: Oh dear, yes. My father's Godly perception that all men are created equal and stand equal at the foot of the cross was lived out. As a child I witnessed my father's applause of the player's effort and never heard him criticize play selection or use derogatory comments when the game didn't go well. Being part of the Big Red family is about understanding three life truths: 1) you belong to a family, 2) you are valued and accepted for who you are, and 3) success is attained when each family member does his job and does it well. When a person experiences these three life necessities: a sense of belonging, being valued, and being successful as a Husker you begin to understand why Nebraska Football is the state's passion and why Nebraskans drive hundreds of miles to attend Saturday's Big Red Family Reunion.

Q: So, are you season ticket holders once more now? Or are you on the waiting list?

DY: We are no longer season ticket holders, and that's probably a little bit of my doing. I was so disgruntled and upset with what was happening and didn't see an end to Callahan's reign that I just said, 'It's lost everything. It's lost its joy.' (Though we were still writing players at that time, though) Well anyway, my husband probably regrets it even more, because I find it easier to go with the flow.

And when Bo Pelini was hired, that February I was diagnosed with breast cancer and I had to have surgery; one breast removed because it was pretty well filled. And I don't want to cry again here, but my husband, here's what he did: I was dismissed from the hospital on the day of Bo Pelini's first spring game and wanted to go to the game soooo badly, but I'd just gotten out from major surgery and could not go. But my husband said, "Honey, I'll drive over the bridge (going past the stadium)." He rolled down my window for me and I could hear the band playing, I could see the crowd waving their arms and screaming, and I was crying like a baby. And it was that moment that I knew I was witnessing the part of a new era.

That broke my heart. I couldn't even go to last year's Spring Game because I had to have my other breast removed. Thank goodness it was not cancer that time. Breast cancer and then a hysterectomy kept me away, as well as chemo that first summer, so I haven't been part of the new era as much as I'd wanted to be, but I haven't had the health to be.

Q: Wow, and do you guys ever have the chance to pick up a spare ticket and make it to a game here and there?

DY: Yes, my husband's sister, through their business here in town, they have tickets and they are very generous. They often split it between a lot of people, but this year I will be healthy enough: "I will be healthy enough. I will be healthy enough." No ifs, ands, or buts about it, and I will go to the Spring game! I have no other boobs to remove! (laughs) So I want to be there, definitely.

Q: What do you think when people say that Nebraska football is a state religion? What is your reaction?

DY: To be very honest, there are some people who treat it as a god. I do believe that there are. I really believe there are probably some people who might consider Nebraska Football that high of a pedestal experience. I really do. There are the realists who understand that it's a game. And it is a big business in Nebraska. But it's a game and it's a game of a group of diverse young men from all walks of life coming together under the umbrella of a coaching staff who cares about them, who has passion for them.

And right now I'm specifically speaking of Bo Pelini, but Tom Osborne and Frank Solich would have certainly fit under that umbrella, too. They come together, they come to Lincoln belonging to one family and then they recognize that Nebraska football is not a religion, but that Nebraska football is a family. And head coaches are the head of the family, Tom Osborne's the head of the family, and the players are our sons and, I hope not our daughters. (laughs) But they are Nebraska's sons. It doesn't matter who they are or where they come from or their ability, they are 'our boys.' And that's what I love about Nebraska football, I consider those players our boys.

Q: Whether native or adopted, they're still sons?

DY: Exactly.

Q: It kind of parallels the early Christians, where you originally had only the Jews, then it clefted off to the Ethiopian, the Word spreading through Corinth and the major trade routes, picking up believers and disciples along the way. And they'd be willing to give their life for it…

DY: Yes, and just as a sidebar -as a Christian, divorce breaks my heart - but as a Nebraska fan, the divorce from Callahan made my heart glad. (laughs) So long, sucker! (laughs) But you know what, I have to tell you, Paul, I believe that we as Nebraska fans enjoyed dominance for so many years, so many decades, and we knew that we knew that we knew that our family was close, we knew that our boys knew how to play to the best of their ability. Were they all blue-chippers? Big red boys always don't have to be blue-chippers, they're red–chippers! And the coaches always knew how to pull the best out of them.

But during the time of Callahan and Pederson that changed and we lost that family feeling, that old loving feeling. We lost that. And I think we lost that magnitude and the intimacy and the purpose of the program, which is a bunch of guys getting together to become family, a diverse population coming together to become one family. But in some respects I think it was —I think in a way, that era of horridity that we experienced as fans?- as we look back it could have weakened us and destroyed us, but what it did was remind of us of who we are: and we are family. It's not about trophies, it's not about all the plaques, it's about the process of 'becoming.' And we lost that. But now we have it back with this staff and these players. The players, I believe, had it under Callahan. Callahan, he was an outsider looking in and couldn't be part of the family, but the tough times we went through has made us, set us up for an even bigger family again.

Q: Speaking of family, anything about those years in the '90's stick out to you from a fan's standpoint? A game? A play?

DY: Oh yeah, there's a game.(laughs) My husband and I had the pleasure of also being good friends with Phil Ellis and his uncle and aunt, Shirley and Ron Zimba, we went up with his uncle and aunt to the Michigan State game. And this was when Lawrence Phillips was just a young man and Tony Banks was their quarterback, right? Well, we dominated them as the game went on, we really did a fine job.

But I really liked the Michigan State kids' effort, and that was Nick Saban's first coaching job out of the pros, but what really torqued me was when we were on the way to the airport listening to the radio after the game, Nick Saban said on the radio, "We played like a bunch of boys. Nebraska played like men. That's the difference in the ballgame." And he was angry. And I remember thinking to myself, 'You jerk! You don't criticize the players.' So I remember, I wrote the Michigan State Athletic Director and I told him exactly what Nick Saban said. I wrote him, 'He is not a good coach. Good coaches do not criticize their players publicly, demeaning them and calling them names and comparing them to other teams in the manner that he did. He needs to be reprimanded. And I don't ever want to hear that type of talk from any coach again.' I never heard back from him. (laughs)

But my favorite memory was going to the Tostitos Fiesta Bowl game. We followed the boys on down to Phoenix and it was absolutely a phenomenal experience. We were there against Florida, of course, and we happened to see the Florida players come out and stick their thumbs in their ears and wiggle their fingers at the players. I remember being so angry at those players. And I was looking around and their fans were going just crazy, "Fun & gun! Fun & Gun!" And I wanted to tell them off, but our players did it for me. And the arrogance of the Florida players on the sidelines before the game, they were humbled and humiliated by the third quarter, and I looked around for the Florida fans and they were gone. I don't ever remember being more proud of our Husker players, and having Christian Peter actually running so hard and fast, running to the end zone without running out of steam? That was incredible. And Tommie Frazier's run, the most impressive touchdown run in football history. Those boys played with one heart, one mind, one focus. The just kicked butt every game. (laughs)

Q: So what do you think football means to the state's people? Why are they so gaga over the game?

DY: I think it is the tradition. I used to write this to the players: "Every Saturday Nebraska has a family reunion." That's what it's all about: getting together with family, watching as family and beating up another family. (laughs) When those opposing teams come in they are not our enemy, they are our guest. They come to our home, our house, our dining table. They should be treated with the utmost respect, but it's a Big Red family reunion.

Q: A good, old–fashioned football contest, in other words?

DY: Yep.

Q: Well, if you want my take on it, my spiel on the psychology/sociology of Nebraska Football -and I live in Southern California, now, and it's a little bit of a different place- but I've said that there are a few differences that most Nebraskans don't realize, and one thing they take for granted is that they are an extremely hardy bunch. It takes a special devotion, ambition, perseverance, a drive, more than anything, to withstand the weather. Here in Southern California weather is just something that you pay attention to as far as deciding whether to wear a long sleeve or short sleeved shirt that day or if you should grab a coat as you head out the door, but in Nebraska weather can kill you. Literally snuff out your very life! Weather often comes at you sideways or vertically, and sometimes both.

Furthermore, Nebraska Football harkens back to work ethic, to family, like you've shared. And every fall Saturday you've got a playing out of the culture of Nebraska, where they say, "We're going to give it our best shot after the preparation and take on all the hurdles in our way," much like a farmer who plants a crop, fertilizes it, nurtures it. And when fall comes around he's in a big hurry to harvest it or he might lose it. There is a sense of urgency, looking for the payoff, reaping the reward, or he might lose a good portion of it. And all that timing -the weather, the preparation- that's what makes good crops as well as football players. I think that way of living and thinking is physically manifested on a Saturday afternoon in Memorial Stadium.

And the Midwestern way of life may not be the fanciest, the most glittery, may not always be glorified in the papers of the media capitals, but our way of life works. It simply works. It's functional and it's, for the most part, self-sufficient. And it's a celebration of simple, hardworking, independent people. And I don't know if the figure is still correct, but they used to say that the American farmer feeds about 144 people per year -and they don't get a lot of kudos for it- but it's the one time of year, a fall Saturday, where this way of life is validated and manifested and comes to life on a national stage. Anyway, that's my take on it at present.

DY: Well, I think you have it right. And I thank Bob Devaney, his mindset where he got it all started, and Tom Osborne: those gentlemen were the root of everything.

And let me tell you something, there is another player who stands out to me: David Seizys. In fact, I wrote this to him on facebook -and we haven't talked much about it here - but there's a factor that really stands out, and that's faith in the Lord Jesus Christ. There is a faith, and that's because of Tom Osborne, Ron Brown -there's just some major God-guys hanging around- and Ron Brown is one. And I tell you, I remember David Seizys: he was the first player in my memory to excite the crowd, to wave up and down to get them excited. And then, to find out that he just loved the Lord? That blessed me. And another memory I have, I loved the 1990's prayers after the games. I would hang around and wait for not only the Husker players, but for opposing players, Paul, for them to gather after this 'game' to give glory to God, whoever won or lost.

The second thing I love about Husker games is that after every single game, win or lose, when that opposing team goes into its locker room we applaud and cheer them on. We were at the game when Texas came to our home for that real tough game. Ricky Williams was running that night and he was ready to break that rushing record. He broke it on our field, and when he did that entire stadium stood and applauded him. I remember that, and even Mack Brown made a comment about it afterwards, that he couldn't believe the kindness and generosity of our fans. Basically, we're just good-hearted people.

Q: There is no place like Nebraska?

DY: There's nothing like it.

End conversation.

'Saturday's Big Red Family Reunion' was how Diane put it. Kind of makes you want to print up some special, red t-shirts for the occasion and show up for the fun, doesn't it? (Especially if you've got a zealous Husker Cousin like Diane Yeutter seated next to you) Well, they've been doing it like this every Lincoln football Saturday since November 3rd of 1962 when 36,501 packed the edifice erected five years post-World War I in honor of its fallen sons. Etched in stone on the eastern pillars of the Great Plains' version of Rome's Coliseum are the words: "In Commemoration of the men of Nebraska who served and fell in the Nations War" and "Their Lives they held their countrys trust; They kept its faith; They died its heroes." Men young and old still remove their caps at the presentation of the colors, the mass of red respectfully and humbly sings the national anthem in reverent tones, and Boy Scouts still display a spirit of servanthood and duty in chaperoning lost fans and old ladies to their proper seats. This is the heart of America, where style is overwhelmed by substance and where family devotion is valued and exemplified as tangibly as any Norman Rockwell canvas has shown.

Now, don't get me wrong, Nebraska has its fair share of scalawags, ne'er do wells, liars and cheats, too. You can take that to the bank. But inside this grand Memorial Stadium (still growing and enlarging and metamorphosing as time progresses) a spiritual and psychological disinfecting takes place. It's difficult to describe, to put into words. It's as if every sort of schism and bent is checked at the gate, and inside the limestone-colored bowl you happen upon one perfect, singularly spectacular and unified mass of humanity willing its boys to victory. Honestly, it sends shivers up my spine just thinking about it. The sounds of the Pride of all Nebraska: The Cornhusker Marching Band, as the drum line knocks out its cadence, and then the whole covey breaks into Hail Varsity, then Mr. Touchdown USA, then Come a Runnin' Boys until assembling for the Tunnel Walk and the human causeway for the players' jubilant pre-battlefield entrance. There are smells: Runzas and popcorn and hotdogs and Valentino's pizza slices, not to mention the stench of grilled, burnt bratwurst and a few spilt beers as some clumsy tailgater traipses into the seat-scape. But moreover, it's the sights: red, red, everywhere red! Your blood pressure and perhaps even your temperature jumps a notch or two, the anticipation, the emotion, the sensation of Husker Nation readying itself to explode into the 600 Stadium Drive atmosphere. Ah, Husker Game Day! If you can get a hold of a ticket, that is.

Notable quote #2:
Husker fan Diane Yeutter on Nebraska's affinity for the team: "It doesn't matter who they are or where they come from or their ability, they are 'our boys.' And that's what I love about Nebraska football, I consider those players our boys."

A (family is a) moving, changing collection of objects constantly in motion... Every individual is growing, changing, developing, or declining – intellectually, emotionally, spiritually, physically, psychologically. No two years, two months, or no two days is there the exact same blend of mix within the family...

Edith Schaeffer, *What is a Family?*

"Change is good, but I'd rather have dollar bills." I'm not sure who first coined the phrase, but who could argue with its logic. My good friend and cohort Curt Thompson of Blair showed up as a walk-on member of the strength staff (much like myself and many, many others) and climbed both vertically and horizontally within the program for a number of years, experiencing myriad change every step of the way. He adapted. And he grew. From the Devaney Sports Center weightroom to the West Stadium Strength Complex to the South Stadium Football Offices, Curt had a chance to see and work with all the bells & whistles, the nuts and bolts, the legends and louts from every angle. If you want to get a feel for some of the behind-the-scenes action during that era, Curt is your man...

Notable quote #1:
"The second, third, fourth teamers were encouraging the first teamers. They'd want to get ahead so they could go in there and play. And the first teamers? They'd encourage the heck out of the younger guys playing. So there was great team chemistry."

Curt Thompson

Question: Hey Curt, you were from Blair, right?

Curt Thompson: Yes, I joined the strength staff in my sophomore year in college, which would have been the fall of '88. I worked down at the Bob Devaney Sports Center with Bryan Bailey.

Q: Oh yeah, I think that was my first year over at West Stadium with football...

CT: Yeah, so that created an opening. So I joined on there working under Bailey.

Q: And how did that happen?

CT: Well, in high school I worked at an automobile dealership in Blair called Vinton Motors. Bob Vinton was a Wheel Club member and he provided a car to Boyd, and Bob introduced me to Boyd and kind of opened the door for me.

Q: And you wanted to be a strength coach?

CT: At the time I didn't, it was more just something to do. I kind of enjoyed it and started out as a business major, and after that first year I switched over and got that degree in Exercise Science.

Q: So bring me back to the first time you met Boyd. Do you recall?

CT: I remember it was back in the old West Stadium, before the new expansion and before what they have today. But meeting Linda Ybarra, she intimidated me that first day.

Q: She intimidated all the new guys!

CT: Yeah, she did. She let you know who runs the roost. And I met Boyd and you could tell he kind of had a pretty big ego, but he was very respectful and very straight forward.

Boyd was always very straight forward. We went to his second floor office, which overlooked the weight room.

Q: And you got sent over to the Devaney Sports Center to work under Bryan Bailey…

CT: Definitely a way to start the career, as you know. Bryan, he was definitely and exercise-aholic. He just got up in the morning and ran and worked out all day and worked out at night.

Very dedicated to athletes. I don't think you'd find another strength coach in America more dedicated to athletes. And whether it was a guy starting on the team or the 3rd or 4th string player, he was definitely there for the athletes. He was from Arnold, Nebraska. Maybe 5'6" tall, red hair, 145 lbs., just ripped. He'd just eat the craziest stuff. One time he was eating lettuce salad with Barbeque sauce on it for dressing, and this was when he had the training table available to him.

Q: I called him the 'mad scientist'…

CT: Yeah, that's a good name. Because he would make up the goofiest exercises and he just loved to torture people. He loved to give 'em pain.

Q: You know what's surprising Curt, I ask the players who stood out to them or impacted them behind the scenes and a large majority say it was Bryan Bailey.

CT: I can believe that. Even after these guys were in the NFL or NBA they always came back in the offseason and wanted to work with Bailey. Every one of them did.

Q: So you're over at the Devaney Sports Center working with everybody from gymnasts to swimmers to wrestlers to tracksters to basketball players, when did you move to West Stadium and football?

CT: '91, maybe. I was over there a couple years, so maybe '91 or '92.

Q: So you probably wanted to work with football just as badly as everybody else, right?

CT: Yeah, that's what to expect. And you wanted to work with Boyd, because at that time people were hiring his assistants left and right. Most guys didn't even have their degrees and people would want to hire them away.

Q: Any recollections of your being thrown into that atmosphere?

CT: It was intimidating. Just the size of that weight room over there at the stadium compared to that little room over at the Devaney Sports Center? And you used to have maybe 15 guys from the basketball team being in the room, then the sheer number of football players, 190 guys, being in the West Stadium weight room was a bit overwhelming. It was like an assembly line. Like during the season, everybody is in and it's just crazy for a half hour, 45 minutes…

Q: "Hey! Hey, new guy! Sign my card! I did my squats! Sign my lifting card!" (laughs)

CT: Exactly. And you're the new guy, so obviously they try to single you out and get you to sign their card so they can get out of there. And you're still learning you can't watch all of them at the same time, so they'd try to get out of there as fast as they can so they can go eat. (laughs)

Q: So you're part of the strength staff, still a student assistant, still making peanuts, and then it seems Boyd decided there was a niche for you and he kind of had you doing some computer stuff, didn't he?

CT: Yeah, when they hired me full-time it was Coordinator of Performance Education. That's when the internet was just becoming popular, so it was starting up the Husker Power website, developing some relationships with high schools, creating programs, I went around the area and gave talks, had different coaches who'd come in and you'd teach them techniques and drills, and then we did this line of Husker Power gear and mail-order workouts.

Q: So when did you get your degree?

CT: It was May of '92, and in August of '94 I got a Masters Degree in Education Administration.

Q: And if I recall, you did a study on pre-pubescent strength training, right?

CT: Yeah, I did a paper on that, and then I did my Masters on three different weight programs and how they affected speed, strength, and explosiveness. One was the Metabolic Power Circuit, another was just a regular Monday/Thursday/Tuesday/Friday workout and then maybe an inseason program. I know I've got those papers some place. Some 6-inch three-ring binder. I can't throw it away, but I haven't looked at it for 15 years, either. (laughs)

Q: So somewhere along the line you made a move over to the football offices then, didn't you?

CT: Yeah, during the summer of, it might have been 1996, that summer I got a job offer to go to Colgate out in New York and I told Boyd about it. And he kind of asked me, "What do you want to do? Do you want to be a strength coach or more administration?" At that time I was leaning to do more administration. So Boyd went in to Steve Pederson, who was Director of Football Operations, and they came to an agreement that I would work with the strength staff in the morning and then help out Steve and his assistant Pat Logsdon in the other part of the day.

And at that early time I was doing all sorts of tasks: going through phone records and piddly stuff in the office over there. I was going through phone records and I said, 'Boy, there's an awful lot of calls to Pittsburgh.' And I had over a two inch stack of phone records that I'd gone through, and I was going to Steve and saying, 'What are all these Pittsburgh calls?' (Well, he was talking to Pitt about the athletic director position, and that's why he needed some help because he was getting ready to move out there.) So I was there at the right time in the right spot.

Q: How long did you work with Pederson?

CT: Oh, probably, maybe four months. Because he might have taken off at the middle of the season or late season. He went to Pitt and they promoted Pat Logsdon, and I kept working for Pat. And then she hired me for her assistant.

Q: Why were you going through phone records in the first place?

CT: Just going through them, the football records, for any numbers that seemed to come up and see if a coach is calling a recruit more than once a week. That's not allowed. Anything suspicious there, compliance stuff, self-policing.

Q: Ever run into anything that sent up a red flag?

CT: No, they played very straight.

Q: So you were Assistant to the Director of Football Operations. What happens then?

CT: My main duty was team travel. I didn't do the contractual part, but getting in contact with the hotel on our away games, getting the contacts for buses to transport us -no airline contracts, the University Business Office did that- the seating assignments on the plane, the room assignments in the hotel, itineraries, which Coach Osborne had final say over.

Q: Did you have a lot of contact with Coach Osborne?

CT: Most of it was with Pat. The football staff had a meeting every day at 7a.m. and she'd pass things through him. I did have contact with him, not on a daily or a consistent basis, though. I went to a few meetings.

Q: Anything about them stick out?

CT: They were boring.(laughs) A strength staff member, Boyd usually, was always there and they went over who didn't lift. And Doak was in there to give the injury report, and Pat would do any items she had, so they were only in there for 15 minutes most mornings. I didn't go to maybe just a handful of them. And other duties I had there was on-campus recruiting, when official visits took place I'd set things up so they could see Academic Counseling, see Boyd, see the Training Staff, have a tour of the locker room, the equipment room, would work with the Cornhusker Hotel on getting the room and checking them in, setting the dinners up or have Misty's cater meals or getting reservations at restaurants.

Q: What was the biggest challenge for you in doing the job?

CT: Recruiting changes. You know, I'd have stuff set up and Saturday morning would come and they'd want to change something, wanted to give a recruit some extra sleep because he was coming in from Hawaii, having to redo his schedule so he'd fit in with other guys visiting. Toniu Fonoti and guys like that.

Q: Were there any quirky assignments or strange things about the job?

CT: You know, one of the things that stands out, we were down in Kansas for a night game and we had a shoe contract with adidas. And for pregame warmups Coach Osborne had a red jacket on, and it was last year's team jacket. So they do the pregame warm-ups and they're coming in before the game and doing their last minute deals and Coach Osborne's talking to them, and the adidas rep and Pat both want me to go up to Coach Osborne and ask him to switch his raincoat to this year's model. And I was, 'Oh man, you've got to be kidding me.' So I went up to Coach and asked him to change his rain jacket. And he was very cordial, and he did.

And another quirky thing that I just hated doing was that Tunnel Walk. I just hated it. They wanted it so they'd play the tunnel music and then when you get to the point when you'd see the doors open the team was in the tunnel and they'd start to walk out. And that was like 60 seconds or so after the tunnel walk music and video starts. So you'd have to time that, because you never wanted it where the door would open up and have the tunnel empty. So I had to start this Tunnel Walk while the players are still in there with the captains talking and when they say that pregame prayer. (And you never know how long those captains are going to talk.) So you have to guess on when the captains are going to be done and finish with their prayer and tell Jeff Schmall in Husker Vision to start the music, and hoping they'll be done in a minute.

And if they'd come out there early, then you'd have to tell them to wait. If it's a big game, everybody's ready to go, 'Wait ten more seconds! Ten more seconds!' They're ready to rip off some heads and you have to tell them to wait ten seconds.

Q: How long did you do that?

CT: That was from '97 to 2000. I left right before the season, August of 2001.

Q: I would suppose every year you got a little better at guessing when it was gonna go down?

CT: Yeah, a little bit better. But then again, they changed the thing around every year, so it was always exciting to deal with. Those are the quirky things. Home football Saturdays are always nice, but you're like, 'Arrgh, I just hate that part!' Everything after that was great, but you wake up football Saturday and you're just dreading that. I hated the Tunnel Walk. That was stressful for me.

Q: (laughs) I've heard there are some businessmen who start every day at their desk by bringing up YouTube to get 'psyched up' for the day with the Tunnel Walk...

CT: Well, good. (laughs)

Q: As I recall, when you were coaching there was a bit of a schism among the staff when you were either 'in the loop' or 'out of the loop'. A lot of designs, of master plans. We called you 'The Loopers'....And there was that nickname for Steve Pederson, "Stinky Pete."

CT: (laughs) I remember that! The offensive lineman, Jon Pederson, was the original 'Stinky Pete.' (laughs)

Q: When you were coaching, wasn't each strength coach overseeing a certain segment of the team? His own group of guys?

CT: Yeah, mine was the defensive backs. And I didn't get to work with Coach Darlington a whole lot, because during winter conditioning they could only be there for just a little bit, at that point in time. It was toward the end where they could do some specific drills, and during the summer time they couldn't be there at all. I think before the winter conditioning started we might have gone and talked to the coaches and seen what his ideas for each guy where, what they needed to improve on or concentrate on.

Q: What names stand out to you from those days, those groups?

CT: Barron Miles, he stands out. Such a great guy, hard worker. Great leader. Wasn't very vocal. And you know what, a lot of those guys weren't very vocal. Sure, you had the Peter brothers, but so many of the guys just did it instead of talking about it. Tyrone Williams, he was a decent worker, a pretty good worker. He'd do a drill, if he was supposed to run 40 yards in the summer he might run 30. He was really gifted. Mike Minter, he was a great leader of that group and worked hard. Just work ethic, leading by example, he'd run the full 40 yards. Eric Warfield was very talented. When he ran he was just fluid when he moved, effortless. Wistrom and Peter, also, they didn't have a lot of talk and cockiness, but they had a swagger and confidence. That was the difference. Not just a lot of talk, but they challenged everybody else to pick it up a notch by their efforts.

Q: You were on the coaching staff of what many consider to be the greatest college football team of all time. What, more than anything, stands out to you about those teams of that era?

CT: You know, I think that those '94 and '95 teams, the things that stand out are Tommie Frazier and Brook Berringer. Tommie was just a great option quarterback and great athlete, I don't think we would have won those national championships without him. On the other hand, Brook was just as talented a quarterback, but a different type of quarterback. And those two guys got along so well in my view, you didn't hear of any animosity between those two guys, and especially with Brook. He could've been upset. Especially nowadays, if you're not the starter the players want to take off and leave the place to be the starter elsewhere, be the man. But at that time you never heard him talk to the press of him being the starter, about how he should be number one. I think that team, a big part of that team there was not feuding about that position. And that was a pretty important position. Everybody knows those two were the best guys and they were neck and neck. They did the same things but they did them differently, and you saw it the previous year in the Orange Bowl.

Q: Miami had to practice for two quarterbacks…

CT: And they both did well. In '95 the work ethic, all those guys, the defense, the Blackshirts, it kind of started in the '93 Orange Bowl with 1:16, and during that summer conditioning was where it started. On days before summer conditioning Randy Gobel and I would go up to the scoreboard and we'd start the music. They'd have music playing during the workouts, any old music -and we didn't do it a lot- but he'd put the music on those new speakers and he put 1:16 on the scoreboard in summer conditioning before that '94 season as a reminder. And they got a taste of it in '94 when we won, and it just carried over to '95.

Q: Anything stand out to you as far as a change in the attitude, a change in the mindset among the players?

CT: I know that the Citrus Bowl wasn't a whole lot of fun. I wasn't at it but I watched it on TV, where we got it handed to us. Then the next year we went to the Orange Bowl and got beat like 22-0 and that wasn't a whole lot of fun, either. I was pretty new back in '91 and didn't know what kind of work ethic those guys had -are they big and slow or lean and fast?- but it seemed when I went over to West Stadium that year everybody had those black t-shirts with white letters that said 'UNITY' on them. And it seemed we really focused more on hang cleans and power cleans and those stupid snatch squats, and got all those power racks. We really taught that hang clean where we were trying to become a little more explosive and quicker. So I guess in that strength part of it we were developing more explosiveness.

It seemed like John Parrella and Kevin Raemakers were always in there, those guys were constantly in there, and then Christian Peter came in and Jason did, and Grant, so there was a pretty good succession of, "This is the way we do it," and it got passed down through them. Because Parrella and Raemakers, they didn't let guys slide, they were leaders off the field. Terry Connealy was. Terry was the nicest guy you could see off the field, but a soon as he was on the field you wouldn't want to be near him. He was a monster. And the Peter brothers, they'd make everybody accountable, it didn't matter if it was offense or defense.

In the weight room, you could really see those guys' leadership during that Metabolic Power Circuit. I mean, that thing was tough. And you'd get sick if you did it correctly, that thing was tough. I don't know how many times I'd get sick and throw up, just puke. I remember going back into the kitchen and feeling like absolute crap, then you'd throw up and finally feel great. I mean, those guys are out there in the middle of the workout, in between sets, and we had trash cans all around that thing because guys were puking. Now, some were out of shape, but some of it was because guys were pushing everybody so hard. Just working hard. That thing kicked everybody's ass. I don't know, do they still do that?

Q: I don't know. I still do.

CT: You do? I did it about a year ago for a little bit. It's just the intensity. You know, when you see your leaders doing that? Your captains pushing themselves that hard? It rubs off on the younger guys. Leading by example.

Q: Any thoughts of Coach Osborne?

CT: Very calm, cool, collected. Respected. You can just see that. I think everybody worked so hard because everybody respected him so much, because of his knowledge, his demeanor, how he treated everyone. He treated everyone fairly. The coaches had respect for him. They'd put in so much time, even with their families. I think they did that out of respect for him. Players had tremendous respect for him. And many of them came to Nebraska because they wanted to play for him. He had a stature to him. I'm having a hard time describing him, but you're in awe of him when you see him just because you know of the accomplishments that he had at the time.

Q: Any other staff members stand out to you?

CT: I guess I've got two. Coach McBride, he could get his defensive players to run through fire for him, the same way. Those guys respected him and they'd do anything for him. That was Charlie. I got along well with Charlie. I still get a Christmas card from Charlie, down in Arizona. But he would, especially when you talk to him one on one, it seems like he really cared, he really did. He wanted to know what you were feeling, what you were saying. He just wasn't trying to get you gone so he could do something else. He loved his players in a tough way, because on the field he would get in their face and yell at them, then five seconds later he was over it and had his arm around their neck, just loving them. They'd run through fire for him.

And I think Boyd, he was very driven. He had great vision. I think Boyd would have made a great athletic director. He was always thinking of the future, what we needed to be bigger and better. He could schmooze with anybody.

Q: So your last year was 2001. What was it that urged you to move on to other things?

CT: When I was working in the football office...and a lot of fans think football is August until the bowl game. Well, it's not. It's seven days a week and it's eleven months out of the year with summer camps in June. You've got football that you're preparing for, starting from Sunday through Saturday. In the offseason you've got recruiting. You've got cards mailed out to all the high schools in the country. You're getting the cards back, sending out questionnaires, getting the questionnaires back and entering those. They'd write down their top juniors, sophomores, seniors, start keeping an eye on them, get them into your database, start mailing them. Start identifying top recruits.

It's seven days a week, even January through May, and you're there on Sunday morning at 8 o'clock and you have Coach walks by your door, looks in and doesn't even say 'hello', doesn't really give a shit if you're there or not -You're like, 'You know, I don't need this. I have a wife at home, we're getting ready to start a family.'- if somebody doesn't have any respect for what I do for them. And that was Coach Solich.

Q: You felt a little unappreciated?

CT: Yeah, and you'd see him in the hallway and you'd say 'Hi', and he wouldn't say 'Hi' back, so you felt unappreciated. And I think Coach Solich changed a little bit when he got the head job. And I don't want to make it like I'm bitter about it, I'm way past that. But starting a family and being gone that much, I wouldn't have wanted it, been able to do it. I think it was Coach Solich's first head coaching position and he wanted to know what everybody was doing, all facets of it: strength and conditioning, training room, nutrition, operations. Everything Coach Osborne did -you know, he'd let Boyd do his thing, he'd let George Sullivan do this thing, he'd let Football Operations do their thing. He didn't want to know what they were doing 24/7 as long as everybody did their job- where Coach Solich would agonize over the itinerary and change something. And you'd be, 'You know what, you've got other things to worry about.'

Q: Imagine the pressure following Coach Osborne?

CT: Yeah, and it was even bigger than when Coach Osborne took over for Devaney. And Frank had it then, twelve years ago. Personality-wise, with me and Frank? I think a lot of it was that we just never got along.

Q: What about working with Pat Logsdon?

CT: It was a very good relationship. It was the type of thing where she'd look over the layout of the plane and she'd look over your shoulder and keep her eye on things, but she gave me a task, trusted me to do it and went on. She would probably secure the plane contracts, she'd sign off on the hotel contracts, personnel issues, because at that time she was in charge of the video guys, the secretaries, myself. She was on the Senior Staff with Bill Byrne as well, dealing with Chris Anderson in Sports Information, ticket office stuff, if the coaches had any issues with tickets or parking. She's Head Women's Administrator now.

Q: Any other personalities of the time stand out to you?

CT: You know, the strength staff, I think we had a pretty good mix. Boyd, it's no secret he had a pretty big ego. It kind of got pumped up by everyone else, and he had that big screen above the lifting platform in the weight room. Remember Keith Jackson and his intro where he said, "And this is the reason these guys are so big! Boyd Epley and his weight program." So he'd kind of get fueled that way, but Boyd was very good. He was kind of the same way, he'd kind of let you do your thing. He was a little more 'thumbs on'. Remember those weekly staff meetings? It seemed like we had them all the time. But he let Mike (Arthur) do the program, he didn't really have a hand in that. Mike and Bryan Bailey would develop the program. Same with you. You'd do basketball and all the other Olympic sports for the University and do whatever you'd want -I guess as long as Mike was okay with it- which kind of got frustrating at times, I'm sure. But Boyd, he always liked being out front and the center of attention. Mike, he was a little bit more laid back in his office, Randy (Gobel) was more little bit of the mix in between. You, you were a very outgoing personality. Then we had Kevin Coleman, John Archer...

Q: The 'feeder pig' from Arkansas?

CT: The feeder pig! (laughs) I thought we got along pretty well as a staff together. We did a lot of things as a staff together. We'd go out nights every once in awhile, mountain biking, running. Remember that one time you and I and Bailey went out after workouts and we did the 'One Bourbon, One Scotch, One Beer?' It might have been Iguana's, right?

Q: I'll never forget that night. Stumbling down O Street looking for my car. (laughs)

CT: I hear that. (laughs) Yeah, and Buck (Dave) Ellis, too. Bailey, he was always there for the athletes. We'd get pissed at him because you're supposed to close the weight room at 6, 7 o'clock and he's still got somebody in there, working with them. You'd be trying to get everyone out and here would be Bailey. And if you didn't get them out they couldn't get to showers in time, and then they would be late for the training table, so those people would be mad at you because we kept them so late.

I think Dave Ellis had a big impact as far as turning around everybody's nutrition. I'm also thinking about it, and Bill Byrne had a huge impact because he developed this master plan, the skyboxes, which was impressive to recruits. We'd take recruits up there. It just made the stadium go from an old stadium to something that's pretty nice. And we were one of the first teams to have instant replay boards and the big screens. It's just so hard to pin one thing down.

Jack Stark, I think, had a huge impact when him and Coach Osborne developed the Unity Council, made the players accountable to one another where they kind of policed themselves, where you didn't really have the coach being the bad guy. It was where you didn't want to let down your peers.

Q: So, in essence, the boys don't just dress in red and white on Saturdays and go out there and kick somebody's ass on Saturday? There's a whole lot that goes on behind that?

CT: Yeah, there is. And there are a lot of other things, a lot most people probably don't realize. Dave Ellis and I would travel out the day before the games and make sure everything was set up at the site as far as food and meeting rooms go. Make sure the meeting rooms were consistent, so everywhere we traveled to it was kind of the same in the meeting rooms far as the setup goes, so they're not walking into a meeting room that was different every time. We'd tell the hotel how he wanted the food prepared or how the buffet line was to be set up.

Q: What about December? That was a crazy month getting ready for the bowl game, no?

CT: Oh yeah, it was a lot of hours. You know, you'd get to work at 7 in the morning and work all day until maybe 2 in the morning. You do this for a couple of weeks to get prepared for the 7 or 10 days down at the bowl game.

And then my Mom, at one point, offered to come down and clean my house for me. And I told her thanks, but not to do it, 'There's no need, because I'm not home enough to make it dirty.' (laughs) Some long nights trying to get bowl games and the official recruiting squared away. Back then, the month of December you were doing double duty.

It was a fun experience. I had two unique jobs down there that were fun. At times it was fun and at times it wasn't, but there were more good times than bad.

Q: What would you say was most fun?

CT: This may sound stupid, but it's the plane rides back from the game. That seemed to be a good place: everybody being on the plane, we'd just completed our goal, we'd gotten the victory, it was just the relief that everything was done, you had a couple hours to relax a little bit. It didn't matter if you got home at 2 or 3 in the morning, it was nice to get some sleep. And then you'd get back at it the next day, then you've got to start again.

Q: Any goofy stuff going on? Kid's acting crazy on the plane?

CT: Oh, every now and then we'd be getting ready to land and a bunch of the guys would start throwing pillows back and forth at each other. So Coach Osborne would have to get on the loudspeaker and say not to do it and make sure everybody takes care of themselves and one another that night.

Q: Did you ever run into any stumbling blocks in your travels? Quirky inconveniences, chicanery behind the scenes?

CT: We didn't have many fire alarms pulled, nothing like that. (laughs)

Q: And during the game, you were on the sidelines, right?

CT: Yeah, I was on the sidelines. Two times stand out to me about those sideline moments: One was down in Missouri and that play with the kick and then Davison caught it. And the other one was when Trev dislocated his elbow the last game and he was running off just screaming. I'm like, 'What the heck?' And then you look down at his elbow and see it. So that stands out.

There's more sideline things going on… you'd see the O-line eating hotdogs on the sideline in the 4th quarter because they're not playing anymore. Dave Ellis had this 4-wheeler, his wagon train, where he'd bring all his water and stuff out. Well, some guys would drink so much water that instead of going to the locker room he'd kind of fold those trunks up, so they'd kind of pee in there in this makeshift moat so the crowd wouldn't see them. (laughs) Just little things where Ellis always had hot chicken broth and cocoa out there in those cold games. A lot of people probably didn't realize that.

Q: So you're probably trying to keep the guys who weren't playing away from it so the guys who were could consume some? (laughs)

CT: Yep. And every game, everybody was encouraging everybody. The second, third, fourth teamers were encouraging the first teamers. They'd want to get ahead so they could go in there and play. And the first teamers? They'd encourage the heck out of the younger guys playing. So there was great team chemistry, I thought.

But you think about the different big games, each meant something. I thought those Orange Bowl games were special and neat, just watching those. A huge stadium, which seemed a lot bigger than Memorial Stadium. The Tempe ones were very nice. When the games came, that was the finale for me. You'd work all up just for that. In the bowl games there was so much effort, as far as Pat's and my job in Football Operations.

I think it was that last game, the '97 season, the '98 Orange Bowl against Tennessee. We were there maybe two weeks and I didn't step foot on the beach until after the game. And we stayed on Miami Beach! (laughs) So once the game came you were like, 'This is it, we're relaxing tomorrow.' San Diego was the same trip, the same way. Actually, Mindy and I, we and Dave Ellis went maybe two days ahead on that one. (laughs) I remember down there for the Fiesta Bowl and we were setting up at Scottsdale Community College one night before the team comes in, and Dave's got this wagon train and we're unloading the semi, just the two of us. Well, the wagon train, that 4-wheeler and two or three wagons behind it on wheels -that he hauled all those 5 gallon jugs of water and stuff on the sidelines– well, it starts rolling and it's dark out, and this wagon train goes off the ramp and falls on top of him, lands on his ankle. He's got water in it and power bars and all kinds of crap and he's pinned underneath it, and I'm trying to lift this thing because he was pinned underneath it. You know, if he was there all by himself, he'd probably still be there!

And I don't know if the average fan knows it or realizes, but every year we'd load up half of our huge weight room into the semi-trailer and drive all that stuff down to the bowl site and unload it. It would be freaking cold out putting that stuff in the semi!

Q: And you'd just be finished up with finals and all that stress, and then you'd be up right away at like 5 in the morning and loading the semi, just freezing your butt off under Memorial Stadium as we completely disassembled the strength complex...

CT: Yeah, and some of the older, lazier strength coaches would show up late and point a finger and let you do the heavy work, and then they'd end up disappearing somehow. (laughs)

Q: Yeah, Boyd would be there for a little bit, then he'd be gone. Mike Arthur would mysteriously disappear. Bryan Bailey would always have an athlete come in for a workout. (laughs)

CT: You know, pulling up to Notre Dame one time, we couldn't even get all the way up to the stadium because all the Nebraska fans were in the way. So we ended up walking through a tunnel of Nebraska fans. I'll never forget that. That was a great moment.

Q: I remember going to that game in South Bend. There were a lot of PO'd Notre Dame fans at that game, rude as hell because so many Nebraskans took over the stadium. They were not happy. I lost a little respect for Notre Dame fans that day by the way they reacted. But hey, it was a W.

CT: Yep, a W is good.

Q: Any guys from that era stand out?

CT: Yeah, Lawrence. He was a nice guy. I remember one time down at the Orange Bowl I was walking around with my two nephews and we encountered three of the guys and I said hello to them. And Lawrence, one of the three, was the only one who said 'Hi' back. I thought he was a great guy, a really nice guy on the field, in the weight room, in the football offices.

Q: What did you usually end up doing during practice?

CT: When I was on the coaching staff I went out there during warm-ups and stretched the guys. Don't you remember? When you were a student you'd have to be in the weight room when the other guys like Boyd and Kelvin Clark and Randy Gobel would go The Knolls and play nine. (laughs) But you knew the kickers would come in. Actually, during practice is when I'd go for a run or workout a bit, and during the season it was just, 'Get ready to sign cards.' Watch a lot of sets and sign cards. Make sure your pen has a lot of ink in it.

Q: Exactly. So what would you say you were most proud of during your time there?

CT: Oh gosh, I guess a couple different things. On the selfish side of it, I'm not sure what year it was, but Boyd came up with the Heiser Award, which the first year Ken Williams and I got, which was named after Dr. Tom Heiser, who was paralyzed in a boogie board accident in Hawaii and overcame a lot after that. And myself and Ken were the first recipients of it.

And secondly, I'm just proud of being a part of those years down there. I spent 13 years meeting a lot of tremendous people: athletes, coaches, staff. And you know, helping guys. That's probably the number one thing, helping guys who really wanted to work and get better. That was the job you and I were in. They came to us because they wanted to get better, because they wanted to play and beat whatever opponent they had. Most of that was their will and their drive to excel and be the best they could, and they came to us to use some of our expertise and 'push', I guess. We would push them, make them do a little bit extra, a little bit more to get better. I didn't do anything down there, I was just a guy who signed a card. But somebody had to do it. I didn't win the game for them. It was the athletes who did it. There was a good group of athletes down there at that time.

Q: Anything you took away from it that has made you a better man, made you better in the business world?

CT: I think my biggest influence was Boyd. I had the most contact with Boyd. When I quit down there, I made sure I went down to Boyd on my last day and thanked him for everything he'd done for me. You know, a lot of people don't necessarily like Boyd, but I did. And there's types for everybody, but he gave me a chance as a skinny little kid out of high school and saw my potential and helped me along, his belief in me and his skills. He was very organized. He wasn't a procrastinator. He went down that list every week or so and he made you accountable. He had a great vision, and then he gave you autonomy. He had a way he wanted the final result, but he let you figure how to get there. He let you do the job that needed to be done.

And do you remember the mailboxes we had back in the strength office? Do you remember that sign that Boyd had up on the wall there? It said, "The great ones adjust." I've always remembered that. You know, when you're building houses like I do now, the buyer always wants some last second changes. Some folks let it get to them and they get frustrated, but I always just tell myself, "The great ones adjust." And that makes all the difference.

End conversation.

Curt covered a lot of ground there, but one thing that struck me was his mention of some key names and their multi-faceted leadership from those years: Grant Wistrom and Jason Peter, John Parrella and Kevin Raemakers, Terry Connealy, Barron Miles, Mike Minter. All defenders. Which makes me wonder just what it was about the Blackshirts' effect both during training and off the field, as well. Let's face it, defensive football players are often noted as being a tad bit off-kilter and just a little to the left of center, if you catch my drift, and I can't help but suppose that its leader Charlie McBride had a little something to do with that. Perhaps we'll find out later when I corral him for a conversation. Before we continue on, I think it's important to share how glad I was to have gotten a glimpse of Curt's work behind the curtains. I was a part of this machinery for some years and even I am still baffled and amazed at all of the toil and man hours that made the Big Red Machine go. There were so many names and faces who added their own unique brand of input, and hopefully I'll be able to expose more of them before we're through with the journey. Some might say, "Just talk to more players and coaches. They are the ones who made it go." Well, you might be right to think that, but remember that each and every player and coach had daily interaction with some of these people, individuals who contributed greatly to the unity of the department and the family-concept that was so prevalent during that era. I guess a more succinct way of saying it would be, "Everyone matters. There are no unimportant people."

Notable quote #2:
Curt Thompson on the Nebraska Football machinery: "A lot of fans think football is August until the bowl game. Well, it's not. It's seven days a week and it's eleven months out of the year."

A University should be a place of light, of liberty, and of learning.
Benjamin Disraeli, Speech to the British House of Commons, March 11, 1873

The University of Nebraska leads the nation's Division 1 colleges and universities with 65 CoSIDA First-Team Academic All-American football selections. These classroom All-American selections are made by the College Sports Information Directors of America, with the process going back to Nebraska's first in 1952. Of this impressive number, Dennis Leblanc has had the pleasure of assisting and guiding 33 of them (as of this printing). That's not just a coincidence, folks. Where there's smoke there's fire, and Dennis has been known to light a few under some young men's rear ends over the years. A confident, soft-spoken guy who carries a helluva big stick, he is the second half of the dynamic duo in Nebraska's Academic Study Center along with Keith Zimmer, who we spoke with earlier. Let's get Dennis's perspective, which I am certain will be an interesting one at that.

Notable quote #1:
"National Championships are great, and they're great to celebrate. And that's what you're shooting for when the season starts. But we all know that in those days you could go undefeated and not win the national championship, so it doesn't mean the season was a failure."

Dennis Leblanc

Question: Hello Dennis, your name comes up with great regularity when I ask a lot of former players to name someone who meant a lot to them as a Cornhusker athlete. I hope you're honored by that.

Dennis Leblanc: Well yeah, sometimes you wonder if you're creating more enemies than accomplishing things with those guys, (laughs) because our job sometimes is not the most glamorous part of it, because you're trying to get people to do things that they don't get a lot of praise for.

Q: I understand. So first question: tell me, where did you grow up?

DL: I grew up in Clifton, Kansas, north central Kansas about 20 miles east of Concordia. Just about two hours from Lincoln.

Q: How did you end up in Lincoln?

DL: Well, I was working on my Masters Degree at Wichita State University in 1982 and I had to do an internship, and I thought that I'd like to be an athletic director someday. And I'd read an article that Bob Devaney and Deloss Dodds were considered to be two of the top athletic directors in the United States and knew that Lincoln was not that far away. I thought it made more sense financially to move to Lincoln and such. I was a track athlete in college at a small school called Bethany College in Lynchburg, Kansas and so I was very interested in track. I came up and visited with Gary Pepin at the time and asked him if he had anything available and he said, "We'd love to have you come work." And I found out later that he didn't pay anything. (laughs) But I also found out later in my career just to have an opportunity to work in the athletic department at Nebraska was worth more than any payment I could have received. So that's how I got to Nebraska. I worked in the track & field office and finished up my Masters Degree, and then moved over into the Academic Center in 1987.

Q: And how did that occur?

DL: Well, there was a position that came open. I was handling the recruiting for track & field at that time and I decided that I really didn't want to stay in coaching and recruitment and have to travel like that, and this position came open. It was a godsend for me as far as athletics, but working with student-athletes in a different way. And I never really thought of being on the academic side until this position came open.

So I visited with Al Papik, who was a former track coach at Doane College plus football coach. And I got his advice. He said, "I think it would be something that would be a good fit for you. Why don't you apply and see what happens." So I threw my name in the hat and that was history.

Q: So that was in 1987. Was that when Dr. Ursula Walsh had left to work for the NCAA?

DL: She actually left in, maybe, 1985. Al Papik took over, so in '87 when I came over here to visit with him, Al had moved into the compliance area, which was a new position. The NCAA was just kind of telling schools they had to be compliant with the rules, so Al moved into that area. Al hired Roger Grooters to take over the Academic Center. So it really became Ursula, then Al, then Roger. And Roger left in 1993.

Q: Roger went to Florida State, right?

DL: Yes. So he left in '93 and at that time I had the opportunity to take over as interim, and eventually got the position.

Q: So what is your official title now, Dennis?

DL: Senior Associate Athletic Director. I oversee the Academic Center, which is still what I am most involved with on a daily basis. I still operate very much the same way I did in the past, but I also supervise the compliance area. I supervise Josh White in that area.

Q: Do you recall your first impressions of the football program? I suppose you had some 'easing in' with track…

DL: Probably my first thought of Nebraska football -and I'm trying to remember when I came here in '82- I actually worked some combined time as an intern with promotion and fundraising for women's athletics and with the track program. And my office, per se, was working out of Joyce Johnson's office, and her office was right next door to Bob Devaney. So, being from Kansas, I'd read about Bob Devaney and I guess I didn't know he was such a legend, and until you actually move to Nebraska you don't really understand it. So when I'd see him in the mornings, that was my first thoughts about Nebraska football, was having that office just around the corner from his. What an interesting and great man.

I remember taking a track recruit into him one time (laughs) and he said to the athlete, "Where else are you looking to go to school other than Nebraska?" And the young man said, "Kansas." And Bob said, "What he hell are you looking at them for?! They're not any good in track." Only Bob Devaney could get away with something like that. (laughs) And then, you know, that year was the year that Turner Gill was the quarterback and Mike Rozier and, of course, Irving Fryar. And I don't know if you remember that poster, the Scoring Explosion, I remember that fall I took it upstairs and somebody got signatures from all those guys and I took it back and gave it to a young boy in my hometown. So anyway, that was my first idea of remembering getting to know Nebraska football.

Q: Any recollections of the first time meeting Coach Osborne?

DL: Well, I tell you what, I'd probably walked by him before, but to tell the truth, the first meeting was interviewing for the academic job in 1987. I had an interview with him and he was asking questions of why I wanted to get out of track & field and move into this direction. And I don't remember what I told him, my eyes were probably as big as quarters because I was sitting there talking to Tom Osborne. But you could just feel the respect for him wherever you went in the Athletic Department and the state of Nebraska. I knew that if I was going to take this job that there was a huge obligation to the program, to the student-athletes and to the University of Nebraska, to make sure that I served the student-athletes with integrity and loyalty, and in a way that, sometimes they might not always like what I was telling them. But I always had their best interests in mind.

Q: In retrospect, years later they probably appreciate you a little more, right? Your rigor and discipline and oversight on their behalf?

DL: Yeah, and you don't realize that until you've had somebody leave and maybe after a while they come back and they say, "You know Dennis, I'm sorry I was such a knucklehead when I was here," you know? (laughs) And that's actually what's made it fun, to know now that there were maybe some guys at the time you didn't really think liked you a whole lot - and they probably didn't- but as they matured and grew up they understood what we were all trying to do.

And I'm not just talking about myself, I'm talking about everybody who was involved in the program. The one thing I always tell people when they ask me about Tom Osborne, the one thing I remember was he'd always have a meeting at the beginning of the year and have everybody together and talk about needing to be on the same page and working on the ultimate goal of developing these young men, that championships aren't the most important: "If the championships come, that's great." I remember looking around that room and seeing George Sullivan and Boyd Epley, all the people of Academics, Sports Information. What he was telling us is, "Everybody in this room has your job, and it doesn't matter if you're the academic person or the assistant strength coach, you have your job and it's a very important part of the entire operation. And we cannot do this without everybody in this room. So don't worry about what everybody else is doing. If they need help, take care of them, but if you're doing your job everything else will take care of itself." You know, don't worry about who's going on a trip or who's getting this, just do your job. So you felt as if... and you were, you were an important part of it. Not that you needed that to be able to come to work every day, but that was the enjoyable part about working in athletics, because every year it kind of starts over and you have goals you set for yourself in your job, your department has goals, and it's fun to strive for those. There are very few places you can feel that in your work beyond athletics.

Q: Because every year starts anew, a fresh start to see if you measure up. What goals did you have set for yourself, for the Academic Counseling department?

DL: Well, Keith Zimmer and I have looked back on this some, and the goals have really changed over the years. Early on, our goals were to develop a respect for the student-athletes' academic performance on the University of Nebraska campus. So when people talked about Nebraska student-athletes they would say, "That's a great group of students over there," and I think a lot of that has been accomplished. And I'm not saying it's the work of Keith and I, it's the entire department. It's developing the entire culture within Nebraska Athletics, so if a new coach comes here in any sport they realize, "Wow, this academic thing is very important here."

And the students, as well, when you're really dealing with student-athletes -and I'm mainly dealing with just the sport of football- they come to you in three different categories: One, where they come to you and they're focused on staying eligible. Two, you have the ones who are focused on getting a degree (but maybe that's where it ends, they don't understand anything beyond that.) And three, you have the athletes who understand they're gonna get a degree and then get the skills to go out and get a job when they're done.

My job, and Keith's job, is to move the individuals of the one group into group two, and the two's into group three. So you get them into the phase where they understand graduating is important, and then you move them to the phase where, "Not only am I gonna get my degree", but "..the world is not gonna just hand me things when I walk out with my diploma, I'm gonna need some skills when I leave here." And that's really where Keith has taken the Life Skills area to another level.

Q: So, is it fun to work with the athletes in any of those three areas?

DL: Absolutely. And some? You may get them in the eligibility phase and only get them to the graduation phase by the time they leave here. And maybe you're continually working with them after they've left Nebraska.

You know, through the process they finally realize five years out, they realize that "football isn't going to be a 15 year career for me. I have to be able to capitalize on all the skills I learned through athletics to be able to get out there and compete for a job." There are so many things that are learned through a sport that can be applied in the workplace and can make athletes outstanding employees.

Q: What methods did you use to get these athletes to change and mature in their mindset?

DL: Well, every one of them is different, so you really have to get to know them. So that's a process. Sometimes I wish I could get to know them more personally, but what it takes to motivate one individual is similar to coaching. What works for one might not work for the next kid. And it's very important to me to have a staff that is made up of individuals who will have the ability to reach different people. Maybe if I can't reach someone Keith Zimmer or Alvin Banks or a number of others can.

Q: How many folks were under your supervision?

DL: When I started in '93, and it's hard to remember, Keith and I and Sonya Varnell and Trina Kudlacek, that might have been in it. And then we had an intern, and then our staff grew over the years.

Q: Working with all of the sports, you guys had your plates full…

DL: Yeah, and just like anybody in athletics, I really try to approach my job -because I grew up in the track office watching Gary Pepin operate who, like all great head coaches, have similar characteristics in that they're very focused on what they're doing- they're able to see into the future of what things need to happen and they're able to work backwards from that ultimate goal and determine the steps along the way to see that. So I saw Coach Pepin operate like that, and then having the opportunity watch Coach Osborne work, watching him more directly. You really try to operate this area like a coach would, in that you did not want to leave a stone unturned as far as making sure you had all your bases covered.

Q: What kind of hours would you put in Dennis?

DL: Oh, I don't know. More than I'd want to admit, probably. (laughs)

Q: Surely more than you were paid for, eh? (laughs)

DL: Yeah. But again, I'm not saying that was just me, that's the way everybody operated. Boyd Epley, Chris Anderson, all those people? We put in a lot of hours. I know I didn't put in as many as the coaches did, but you know, we put in a lot of hours.

We're very involved in recruiting as well, and especially now, one of the things that stands out in recruiting is the academic part of it. That's what sells a parent, when they visit here and realize their son or daughter is going to get a great education along with competing, and that means a lot to them. I think a lot of people who come here from outside the state are very pleasantly surprised at what they're gonna be able to experience academically.

Q: Where are you when game time arrives?

DL: Game time? I'm in the stands. In the stands with my family.

Back in those times we had -and still do, a more scaled-down version- but we had a Guest Coaches Program at that time. We really started that back in the late 80's. At that time, on every Saturday Keith Zimmer and I would host two to four faculty members for a home game. We would start out and they'd get to sit in on the meeting with the coaches out at the Kellogg Center on Saturday morning. They'd be in the big team meeting with Coach Osborne when he talked to the entire team and then we'd split up and go into the position meetings, and Coach Osborne would let the faculty members go to any position meeting that they wanted.

Q: Even Charlie McBride's?!

DL: Oh Yeah.(laughs) And of course, in those days, many times they wanted to stay in the quarterback meetings with Turner and Tommie and Brook, so there were times when it was Tom Osborne, Turner Gill, Brook Berringer, Tommie Frazier, Matt Turman and three or four professors. (laughs) And Coach Osborne would say, "Here's what our first play is going to be," and, "Here's what we're going to try to accomplish with this." And even though they went through and covered everything, everything was so calm... and we were getting ready to play Oklahoma and Colorado and we're all sitting in there. There were times when I'd be, 'Wow, this in unbelievable. This is something I can't even believe I'm getting to sit in here,' you know?

Q: The ultimate fly-on-the-wall type of situation?

DL: Yeah. And it's not something you really talk about with anybody, because you knew that was sacred, to keep that in that room. But the faculty members felt like such a part of it.

I think that's where Coach Osborne did such a wonderful job leading the program. He made everybody feel a part of it. So when you won a national championship or somebody graduated, everybody felt a part of it. I'm not just talking about the national championship, I'm talking about when somebody graduated when nobody felt they would, all sorts of people felt a part of that because they'd surrounded the young man the 4-5 years he was there. But the Guest Coaches thing was a fun thing, and we'd bring them down into the stadium and give them a tour: they'd sit in the recruiting luncheon with the recruits, and the coaches would come in there and talk again.

And 30-45 minutes before kickoff, when Coach Osborne would come out of the locker room, Keith and I would have the guest coaches out on the field and Coach Osborne would go right over to the sideline and take two or three minutes and get his picture taken with them on the field. A lot of people don't know that he did all that. And then after the game they would go to the press conference, and he'd always come in and shake their hand, win or lose. So these people got to see it. And I forgot to mention at the beginning, they had the team breakfast with the players over at the Kellogg Center on East Campus, too. So they would see it from the breakfast in the morning to the press conference after the game.

Q: Wow, do you recall any comments from the faculty members?

DL: Not so many comments. I know that I have file full of letters that people have sent through the years, and they say it was such an unbelievable experience. I think they were always extremely impressed with how the operation operated. That goes back to everything from the student manager who had all the rolls of tape out in preparation for the players getting taped, to the preparation for the meal, to how calm the coaches were, and how five hours from the point they were visiting with the coaches, these coaches were going to be on national television being scrutinized for everything they did, and how they were so calm and taking time to sit down and visit with them. I think what people were always so impressed with was the way everything operated and how calm everybody was. Now, I'm sure internally maybe everybody was not, but it was how calm they seemed to be on the exterior.

Q: That's pretty neat, Dennis. Even I didn't know that existed. And speaking of, is there any memorable player or experience worth reflecting on from those years?

DL: I think some of the most memorable are the ones that maybe, while they were here, caused me the most headaches. (laughs)

Q: Kevin Raemakers? (laughs)

DL: Well, Kevin stands out. Maybe not so much for that, but Kevin was a guy that -and it was well publicized at the time, when he didn't qualify with his grades out of high school- and I got permission from the Big 8 Office at the time. I got permission to get Kevin to move into my basement of the house I'd just bought to prepare him to retake the ACT test again. And I don't know if you could get permission to do something like that now, but he did that. And so, then Kevin took the ACT again and got the score he needed and the rest is history.

But I think Jason and Christian Peter are two that stand out, you know? A lot of laughs. Keith and I talk about some stories from the past and chuckle sometimes. I guess there are just so many guys, a lot of great memories. And Kevin, he's a great friend. He's one of those guys, on his recruiting visit he looked you right in the eyes and said, "Hey I'm pretty good out on the field, but when it comes to this classroom stuff I'm not very good." And then to go on and graduate in 4 years and his last year being named Academic All-Big 8 at the time? And go on and supervise how many people he supervises now? He probably already told you, but the guy is doing great, has a beautiful family and he's been very successful. All the things he learned in football he carried over into the workplace.

Q: And as far as carryover, what are some of the main points that football athletes carry over into the working world?

DL: I think the main thing is the teamwork aspect of it. When you watch a football game and you see 11 players line up and they're all from absolutely totally different backgrounds and their goal on that play is to move the football down that field, and every guy has their responsibility. You have the offensive lineman who's not going to get a lot of glory, and there are many jobs that are performed every day where you do the work and somebody else gets the glory for it. And that unit operating together as one, you don't get that very many places except in athletics.

And you know, there's an award handed out every year called The Top 8 Award, and it goes to 8 student-athletes in the United States and represents what we really want athletes to be: perfection in the classroom, in their sport, and in the community, and Nebraska has had 16 of those people win that. It's considered to be the Heisman of Academics. Stanford has had 13 people win it, UCLA is there with 10, and out of the 1,400 schools there's only three schools that have had more than ten, the three I just named.

When Payton Manning won that award his senior year (and I hate to have this as an example because he's from Tennessee) (laughs), but he said something to the effect of, "It would have been a lot easier for me to go to college and just play football. And on the reverse side of that, it would have been a lot easier to just go to college and not play football. But I wouldn't be the person I am today if I'd not done both." And I think that defines college athletes a lot of the time, because they make sacrifices when they're an athlete, you know?

For instance, maybe instead of ending up with a 3.6 GPA maybe they would have had a 3.8 if they wouldn't have had to spend all the hours they did in athletics. And on the reverse side, maybe they would have been able to be a better football player if they wouldn't have had to worry about school.(laughs) But they recognize on both sides of it, they would not have been as complete a person if they hadn't done both. I'm truly convinced that if Kevin Raemakers wouldn't have been a football player he wouldn't be where he is today. That's a part of who he was, but the part where he benefited the most from his football days wasn't going on and playing in the NFL, it was the transferring of all those skills he learned as a football player: teamwork, loyalty, respect, belief, some of those things you mentioned earlier. He wouldn't be the employee he is today without that, and he learned that through Nebraska football. And I think you would find many people out there who would say the exact same thing.

Q: The Lord works in mysterious ways, eh?

DL: That's exactly right. And that's the reason I believe in Nebraska so much. I came to Nebraska in '83 and I truly have no desire to work anywhere else. It's a special place. Football is the main cog, but what people are fooled a little bit through that process, is what results from that. When it's all over, yeah, maybe somebody wins the Heisman Trophy or Outland Trophy or rushing title or whatever, but when it's all said and done you've created better citizens who've created unbelievable relationships. And when they come back they talk about national championships, but not as much as they talk about relationships.

You know, I can remember on Valentine's Day one time, my wife had sent me a big box of chocolates. And I'd gone to some meeting, and when I came back to my office the blinds were closed and my door was shut.(laughs) I opened the door and Christian and Jason Peter were sitting in my office with their feet up on my desk and they'd eaten half of the chocolate, thrown the paper around my office. And they said, "Hey Pencil Neck, what's up?" (They always called me Pencil Neck) And there are so many stories like that. So anyway, it's been a fun ride, and it's great to have Coach Osborne around here again.

Q: Do you recall anything from the '93 to the '97 years? Do you recall any cultural or organizational changes as far as the players' mindsets of the time?

DL: Well, I think the talent level went way up. I guess that's the main thing that I would say. I think it was probably a process, and there are things you learn every year from the one before. Coach Osborne was always doing things to tweak the program.

And although we won championships in those years, Paul, I guess I look at it a little bit differently. I really feel that all those years were championships years. I look at it a little differently. Sometimes people only think it was a success if you won the championship, but I think there was a process of getting to those years, other years where things had happened, maybe something with a certain individual that made it a championship year. And some people might say, "Well, that's what an Academic guy would say." (laughs) But looking at the entire process of leading up to those years in Coach Osborne's career, although we won championships in '94, '95, & '97, there were a lot of success stories in other ways, as well. And Kevin Raemakers was one of those young men. Kevin never won a national championship. Trev Alberts, either. Those guys were laying the foundation work for years to come after that, but what I wouldn't want to do is take away from teams that didn't win national championships. They were still very successful as far as how I look at it.

Q: Wonderful perspective, Dennis. Thought-provoking. It sure changes my perspective a little bit.

DL: I think that's where Coach Osborne revealed a great perspective on it in his book 'More than Winning'. When it was all said and done, there were all the other things you're getting from it, because you're going to go on and those things will help you in your life after you leave Nebraska.

I would like to think that Nebraska football is more than winning national championships. I see it as more than just that. National Championships are great, and they're great to celebrate, and that's what you're shooting for when the season starts, but we all know that those days you could go undefeated and not win the national championship, so it doesn't mean the season was a failure. And I would probably, when you visit with Coach Osborne, there were probably some teams he coached that didn't win national championships that meant just as much or more than those teams who did. And there are some coaches out there that are just so focused on the national championship that they lose sight of what you really want to accomplish with 150 young men, because now it is all about winning the national championship in the public's eye. But when intercollegiate sport was started over 100 years ago it was to provide extracurricular activity where somebody is able to learn other things, and I would like to think that Nebraska has still stayed focused on that throughout the entire department.

Q: Last question, Dennis. How many total athletes do you serve there at a time?

DL: We have around 550. It's around 150-160 football players.

Q: You've got your hands full, my friend.

DL: It's a lot of fun. We have a lot of great help. It's been a fun thing for our family. We have a lot of fond memories of bowl trips and places we've been able to go.

Q: A different Santa Claus every bowl game Christmas Dinner in the team hotel, right?

DL: You've got it. And it's been wonderful for my kids to grow up around as diverse a community as you're going to find in Lincoln, Nebraska. I've always felt that I've learned way more from the athletes that I've worked with than I could ever pass on to them because they come from so many different backgrounds, whether it's someone from South Africa or someone from inner city L.A. or someone from Wahoo, Nebraska. What a blessing to be able to work every day at Memorial Stadium and have an opportunity to work with these young men and women from all over the world and have my family have an opportunity to be around them. You cannot find a laboratory like that anywhere.

Q: Well, thanks Dennis, for all your time and for all the new and valuable perspectives you've brought in our time together here.

DL: Well, I think that through this process you do Coach Osborne justice. It's way more than the national championships; that's who he is, and you don't want to lose perspective of that. And I'm not saying you have, but he's defined by more than those seasons in the '90's. That's always something worth remembering.

End conversation.

Holy National Championship rings, that sure put a different spin on things, didn't it? Dennis made a number of points that really hit home, possibly the most profound being his notion that non-National Championship years were in no way a failure. He's made me rethink my measuring stick somewhat, though I must admit that my fascination with the 60 & 3 era isn't only the fact that they tallied such a fantastic win/loss record, but that they also had a guy like Dennis pushing them toward earning their degrees all the while. (A conference-leading number of them put on the mortar board and walked across the dais to receive their diplomas, too.)

Dennis also brought up the Guest Coaches Program on home football weekends. What a stroke of genius! Not only for its educational and entertainment value to the professoriat, but for the goodwill it engendered to an often otherwise ambivalent and at times an even hostile sect on the campus. I don't mean to go off on a rant here, but we all know that one of the greatest bastions of liberalism and the entitlement mindset in America is on the college campus, possessing a heavily laden socialist ideology that more often than not flies directly in the face of the game and spectre of the sport of football: handouts & entitlements for merely existing versus rewards for proving fit for top competition, pacifism vs. a war-like activity, anti-capitalist/Marxist ideals vs. a million dollar money generator, diversity for diversity's sake vs. the need for purely athletic, young males regardless of race. Perhaps I'm over-generalizing a bit here, but trust me, I had my share of run-ins with some envious and outright anti-Athletic Department instructors in my day.

Notable quote #2:
Dennis Leblanc on the Nebraska Football program's aims: "When it's all over, yeah, maybe somebody wins the Heisman Trophy or Outland Trophy or rushing title or whatever, but when it's all said and done you've created better citizens who've created unbelievable relationships."

Sport, that wrinkled Care derides, and Laughter, holding both his sides.
Come, and trip it, as you go, on the light fantastic toe.

John Milton, L'Allegro

Have you ever wondered what it might feel like to be trampled by a raging & rampaging Miura bull on the stone streets of Pamplona, Spain? Had you been a Husker opponent in the mid-90's and tried to stop running back Clinton Childs (a bull in his own right from the streets of Omaha) you would have done well to suffer the punishment without having to spend ten hours flying in coach back to the U.S. Then again, a restful return trip of the same duration may have put you in good stead to recovery. Nebraska's backs under the tutelage of Frank Solich always were some of the fastest, toughest, meanest SOB's this side of the fifty, as they not only refused to run out of bounds, but were notorious for those jaw-busting rips of the free-arm.

In the course of setting up conversations for this project I've had the most difficult time finding a day and time to accommodate Coach Solich, and the last time we spoke he was smack dab in the middle of a winter's drive to Cincinnati in blizzard conditions with a bad cell phone connection. His being a college head coach, who knows when or if we'll ever meet up, so I'm trying to get a feel both for him and his disciples at every turn. Let's hear what Clinton, the hotstepper, reveals as we proceed full speed ahead.

Notable quote #1:
"We were told in the huddle that we had to run a certain play and we had the confidence that the big guys up front could get it done."

Clinton Childs

Scholarship recruit, Running Back, Omaha, Nebraska (North)
Where are they now? Omaha, Nebraska, Mentor/Coach

Question: It's great talking to you again, Clinton. So what are you doing these days?

Clinton Childs: I did security at my old high school, Omaha North. I was doing that probably about 7 years. Working with the kids, that's my forte. I was coaching football for 11 years and coached wrestling for 8 years, too.

Q: You were a wrestler in high school, right?

CC: Oh yeah, that was my first love.

Q: Really? Do you wish you could have gotten a little mat time at Nebraska?

CC: Oh yeah, I would have loved it. I went in and worked out with them a few times. Actually, Tim Neumann recruited me to wrestle down there.

Q: And how did you make the decision to play football, then?

CC: Well, at the time there wasn't any money to be made in wrestling. There was in football.

Q: Any family?

CC: Yes, I'm married now, have a little baby girl who'll be two next month. My wife's name is Loretta and my daughter's name in Sania. She's definitely got Daddy wrapped around her little finger.

Q: They'll turn a hard man soft, won't they? I thought I wanted a boy, but I wouldn't trade mine for any boy in the world.

CC: That's exactly what I tell people.

Q: So your first fall camp, what year was that?

CC: 1993. I was actually a Proposition 48 coming out of high school. My grade point average was fine, but my ACT score was something that I kind of wasn't taking serious at the time. So from the time of my senior year in high school to my freshman year in college, I had a lot of maturing to do and got it accomplished and went on to have a fairly decent career down in Lincoln.

Q: I spoke with Dennis and Zim recently...

CC: Yeah, I liked both of those guys, Keith Zimmer and Dennis Leblanc. They were good guys, they were a huge part of what the university stood for. Academically, there were a lot of great guys around the system, the academic side. The trainers, Doak Ostergard, he worked really well with all of us and tried to keep us healthy. If I had to name some of my favorite people down there, Doak comes to mind, and Bryan Bailey is probably my all-time favorite.

Q: Tell me why, Clinton.

CC: You know, as we all knew Bryan, he was probably a hundred-sixty-some pounds with a bag of nickels in his pocket. Bryan Bailey? It didn't matter what time in the morning it was, Bryan would get up and he would work out with whoever asked him to. You know, Bryan, by the end of the day, would probably have literally -and this is no joke- probably 10 workouts in over the course of the day.

Q: He typified the term 'over-training'?

CC: Still today, if you look at Bryan Bailey and the techniques he used to get people prepared, Bryan was the guy who would not let you get tired, because his whole thing was, "Do you know how many times I have to workout today? I'm still going, and I'm still waiting to go workout with you, so let's see what we can do."

Bryan was also responsible for working with a lot of guys when their careers were over, for the NFL scouts and stuff like that. Bryan, he specifically pulled 'em to the side and got some things out of them that were needed to get them a legitimate look in the NFL. I haven't spoken to Bryan in awhile. I actually went out to the USC/UCLA football game a few years ago and I hung out with Bryan a little bit at the stadium, sat and chatted with him. I just wanted to make sure I touched base with him. There's no doubt about the type of impact Bryan has on the young men's lives while they're playing college football, and even after their careers. If you look at the type of guys he's worked with, Calvin Jones, Lawrence Phillips, myself, Damon Benning? And then he leaves Nebraska and he gets the same results out of guys like Reggie Bush and LenDale White and those type of guys. That is a true credit to Bryan and how well he gets people to respond to what it is he's trying to get out of them.

Q: There'll never be another like him, Clinton.

CC: Never.

Q: Do you recall your first days on campus?

CC: My first days on campus were about finally really having to step up and becoming a young man, a lot of growing up taking place coming out of high school. And also having a level head. In high school football my head coach was Herman Colvin, and the things, the way that he pushed me to get things done, he was very much like a huge father figure to me and he still is the same way to me today, but just the maturity standpoint is probably one of the biggest things that I can recall. Because like I said, coming out of high school I probably had one of the best high school careers in state history, and when I completed my career I was the #2 all-time leading rusher in Class A's history. And I was only 22 yards behind Calvin Jones.

Q: Hey buddy, that's pretty slim bragging rights there for Calvin...

CC: (laughs) We had a pretty good style of offense where we ran a featured back in the running game, and it gave me a look not only from Nebraska but from schools all around the country.

Q: That being said, if not for Nebraska what would have been your second choice back then?

CC: Well, I never heard from USC. I got a letter from the University of Washington and I was being heavily recruited by the University of Miami. They actually didn't offer James Stewart a scholarship until they found out I wasn't going to sign with them.

Q: Was Miami recruiting Abdul Muhammad about the same time?

CC: He was a year ahead of me, but I think they did. And that's funny you bring Abdul's name up. Myself and Abdul now share an office together. We just started last week as the Gang Intervention Coordinators at the North Omaha Boys and Girls Club.

Q: Congratulations, Clinton. I'm sure you'll have a major impact on a lot of kid's lives?

CC: Well, that's the goal, trying to be an asset to the community I came from and have the same type of impact that my high school football coach had on me.

Q: Did you know many people on campus when you got there to Lincoln?

CC: Tony Veland and I, we played at rival high schools and we knew each other throughout our high school careers. And I knew Tony had already gone to Nebraska. I knew Erick Strickland and Andre Woolridge with basketball. I knew Clester Johnson. There were actually a lot of guys. Cory Schlesinger, I knew him from all throughout high school. He was also a wrestler.

Q: Did you guys butt heads very often?

CC: No, we were in different weight classes. But I knew Cory, we used to sit around wrestling tournaments, always sat around to chit-chat and things like that. So there were quite a few guys that I already knew.

Q: Make's the transition a little easier knowing that many guys, eh? And Coach Solich was your position coach, what can you tell me about Frank?

CC: Very intense, very intense. In my eyes, to this day still, he was one of the better coaches around back then. He knew his stuff. I felt really comfortable with things that he had us doing, learned a lot. Actually, all the running backs that I coached here in Omaha at the different camps and things, I basically taught them all the things that Frank taught us.

Q: Any key points of his coaching doctrine that were just hammered into your head?

CC: Oh yeah, one of the things you can always look at, the types of running backs that he had coached, your Mike Roziers, your Scotty Baldwins, myself, Calvin, Lawrence, everyone was pretty effective. And everyone learned under the same system. I'd say he coached everyone the same, so he was actually really easy to communicate with. I have nothing but good things to say about Coach Solich and the way he cared for his players And he definitely had your back.

Q: Any special drills that stand out?

CC: Well, he had a drill where he'd literally stand 5-6 yards away from us and he'd actually throw balls at us as fast as he could. You'd think he was a pitcher for the Minnesota Twins as fast as he was throwing the ball, he threw them so hard. That's one of the drills that sticks out in my head. We had a balance drill that we did. Three-step cut was one of the drills, one of my favorite drills. Just teaching how to change direction, it was just amazing how these guys come into college football and they're already so talented and how much you still learned under him.

Q: I take it you were pretty natural runner, then Coach Solich just gets to molding and tweaking you?

CC: Oh yeah, he did a great job at that. That is one of the biggest things that really sticks out in my mind, how much you could learn when you're coming into college, from high school. When you have guys that come in that are high school All-American and then make them that much better, that is a true tip of the hat to that guy, for being able to enhance your ability as player.

Q: When you say he was intense, how was he intense? He wasn't screamer, was he?

CC: Oh yeah, he had a lot of the same qualities that Coach Osborne had as far as talking with the kids and stuff like that, but he was so different, as well. He was not afraid to bring his 5'6" frame -or however tall he is- into your face and tell you about whatever it is. As soon as he'd get done whipping your butt he'd turn around and slap you on the ass and tell you, "Good job," too.

That's one of the things that a lot of people miss in coaching, too, telling the young man 'good job' after you're done screaming at him, as well. We had a lot of fun. Individual meeting rooms, he was just one of those guys that was pretty easy to get along with. He'd done a good job with keeping everybody's ego down when you had to deal with so many different talents in our room. At one point he had Calvin Jones in the room, he had Clinton Childs in the room, Damon Benning in the room, Lawrence Phillips in the room. Those are all quality running backs and he did a hell of a job at keeping everybody happy.

Q: How would you say he did that, Clinton?

CC: Years of experience. I'm sure what he had going on, I would probably say that was the most talented group of running backs that he ever had. He also dealt with the Roger Craigs and the Mike Roziers at the same time, but we had 4, 5 guys deep who actually rushed for over 7 yards a carry.

Q: What was it like playing behind the Pipeline?

CC: It was a bond between us, such a big trust there with everyone knowing their job and getting things done. We were told in the huddle that we had to run a certain play and we had the confidence that the big guys up front could get it done. You had Brenden Stai, Zach Weigert, Rob Zatechka and those guys, all those guys. We knew that everyone knew what their assignment was and we had total faith in those guys getting their job done.

Q: Who recruited you out of high school?

CC: It was Dave Gillespie, who was the Recruiting Coordinator at the time. And Dan Young was responsible for recruiting Omaha. It was a fun time, just having different coaches from different colleges actually coming down to visit the home, speaking with my mother, speaking with my grandmother.

My grandmother was a die-hard Tom Osborne fan. I think if it weren't for my mom and my grandmother being able to watch me play, maybe I would have ventured out and played football elsewhere. It was the impression Coach Osborne had made on my grandmother that made it comfortable for me to go down there and that she'd be able to see me play.

And one way I've always described Tom Osborne to everyone? His demeanor is exactly what you see on TV, is exactly what you get in person. You get so many different people who can turn on the switch and they're completely different people from talking to them in person compared to television, they can put on a front, but he was exactly the same all the time. Guys were pretty much gonna tell you what you wanted to hear in the recruiting area, too: "You can come in next year and be our starting running back." That's just one of the things they use as a recruiting tool, and I looked at the big picture.

A cousin of mine had me looking, and I almost went to Kansas. He had me looking at it in a way. Tony Sands was a running back and they started to turn the corner to get good, and he was on his way out and I knew that I hadn't passed my ACT and that I was probably going to be a Prop 48 so I would have to sit my freshman year (which was his senior year), so I probably could have stepped in and been the starter right away, as soon as that one year was over.

Q: Well, I'm glad you came to Lincoln, Clinton.

CC: (laughs) I've heard that before.

Q: Any other coaches stand out to you?

CC: Well, if you want to talk about it from a religious standpoint, Ron Brown was really good at not pressing the issue on you as far as religion goes, but his thing was, "If there is a god that you believe in, make sure you worship that god and be true to yourself and be true to the god that you believe in." Ron Brown, as we all know, is a very, very strong Christian man. I respect him for that. Religion is a huge thing for me and my family, and it always has been.

Turner Gill had a major impact on a lot of things, as one of the younger coaches, and he related to a lot of the young men -coming from Texas- and showed them the ropes. I developed a real good relationship with Turner. Another great guy.

Q: You know, I used to have lunch with Turner and Ron. It was one of the best half hours you could spend at the training table. Upstanding gentlemen, right?

CC: Well, I'm a firm believer in the way they lived their lives. Look at Turner Gill now, all the work he's put in. And a lot of people say it's unfortunate he didn't get the head job down in Lincoln, but I'm a firm believer that God has a plan for everyone. I'm really happy for Turner and his accomplishments. It's about how being loyal to people and being true to yourself can take you a long way.

Q: Clinton, what was your last game?

CC: The Fiesta Bowl versus Florida.

Q: That's a heck of a way to go out.

CC: Oh, yeah. Heck, yeah! My last game for Nebraska. I played in the '96 Hula Bowl that year over in Hawaii, too. It just goes to show you what Frank Solich did with his running backs, you know?

Q: Anything special stand out to you as to why Nebraska was so dominant in that time?

CC: Trusting and believing in each other. It all goes back to the factor of how the offensive line did their job, and it was the same way on the other side of the ball with Charlie McBride. The type of fire he brought to those guys, he was a mastermind defensive coordinator. Everyone believed in it. It was a very, very, very bad taste in our mouth against Florida State, when we got robbed against Florida State.

From the time that we came back from that game, what was it 18-16 or something like that? We had that score in Memorial Stadium every day we worked out. 1:16 on the clock, which was a huge reminder of how close we were to getting that done, and there was no way we were ever going to fail.

Q: What about that game stands out to you?

CC: I think as a whole, as an entire team, we believed we were the real national champions that year. We had these t-shirts made up which said, "Unity-Belief-Respect", and we had those t-shirts and we knew that there was no way we were going to leave it in the hands of referees or whomever to finalize our statement for that next year. We just knew that we were all going to come together, and we came together and everyone had the same goal and everyone worked together. We didn't hardly have guys gone out of town over the course of that summer. Everyone stayed in Lincoln so we could get that job done.

Q: A player in your position, looking back, what would you say you sacrificed to play at that level?

CC: Well, it was always a dream of mine that I had, I actually wanted to wrestle in the 1996 Olympic Games. And like I said, I was being recruited. The guy who's now the head coach of the US Olympic team, Zeke Jones was recruiting me to come and wrestle at Bloomberg College out there. I pretty much had to make a choice, because I was a two time All-American in football, a blue chip, and I was actually ranked #8 in the country in wrestling my senior year. I didn't even go wrestle in the national tournament then. I wrestled as a sophomore in the largest national tournament there is, I placed my sophomore year and my junior year. So I was a three time high school All-American at wrestling. Still to this day, I think I'm the only 2 sport All-American that Omaha North ever had.

Q: Wow, that's pretty impressive.

CC: Like I said, that's my first love. I remember sitting at the high school national wrestling tournament, remember sitting there with Tolly Thompson. We were good friends.

Q: You know, I was the wrestling strength coach. I always thought Tolly would have made a decent defensive end.

CC: Tolly was a heck of an athlete, man. He was actually pretty damn good at football in high school, as well. He was from Cedar Falls, Iowa.

Q: Hey, that's Trev's hometown…

CC: Yeah, and it's great to see Trev at Omaha now. I hope to get over there someday to sit down and talk to him and see how he's doing.

Q: Do you have an all-time favorite or most memorable play?

CC: The fastest touchdown in Nebraska History.

Q: Tell me about it. Refresh my memory.

CC: Arizona State game, it was the only game I started down in Lincoln, when I knew that I was gonna get the starting nod. It let me know the coaches had faith in my abilities. I was pretty excited about it. (In all actuality, I thought I could have started some of the football games, and that's one thing I look back on. I knew I could have started anywhere else in the country and gotten a better opportunity, but I had a great time down there and good things came from it.) When I knew I was gonna start that Arizona State game, I wanted to show the 76,000 people in the stands I was capable of getting the job done.

Q: Describe the play to me...

CC: Well, throughout the course of the year we pretty much knew what the first play of the game was gonna be on maybe Thursday. I don't remember exactly what the play was called, but it was a handoff to the outside left. A good friend of mine still to this day, Jeff Makovicka, is joined up at fullback and he makes a great block out there on the edge. He's one of those guys where you knew the job was gonna get it done if you were playing behind him, just an outstanding blocker out there. And we had the wide receivers out on the blocks, and once I turned the corner it was just wide open.

And later on you see yourself on SportsCenter just for a brief moment, and I'm sitting there at home later on that day and watching that and seeing all the other great plays going on around the country in college football, and here I am among the best college athletes in America and I'm right here on SportsCenter. And come to find out it was the fastest time in Nebraska history. It was my senior year. Very first offensive play of the game, the first snap.

Q: Most memorable game, Clinton?

CC: It would definitely be that Arizona State game. First start of my career. And I had to come out. It was kind of bittersweet, because I only played a quarter and a half, had 12 or 13 carries for 143 yards and 2 touchdowns. I got hurt midway through the second quarter, sprained my MCL. I still remember the exact feeling, when I took a helmet to the knee by one of the Arizona State players, and when I felt it I thought I'd blown my knee out and my season was over.

Q: Favorite game that stands out to you?

CC: Playing Colorado was actually a pretty good game. I scored a touchdown in that game, and playing in Oklahoma, too, a big time rival back then. I would say the first national championship we won was probably one of the most memorable, the first title in many years.

Q: Any special recollections of that night in Miami stand out to you?

CC: Well, I tell you what, if you ever find any film on it and you go back and look at the beginning of the game and how confident all of us were going into that football game, it was so intense at the beginning of the broadcast, how focused everyone was. We knew there was no doubt in our minds that we were gonna be the best team on the football field that night.

Q: From the opening kickoff it seemed like you guys were literally trying to kill each other...

CC: Well, if you think about Nebraska's offense, you probably have the best two teams in the country that played that night. The University of Miami and the group of guys they had on their defense: Sapp ,Lewis, Rohan Marley playing that game, they had a really good defense. The reason I say it was pretty sweet is the simple fact the University of Miami was recruiting me as hard as they were and they knew who I was, and also they had James Stewart, which earlier in this conversation I told you that they didn't offer him until after I'd committed to Nebraska. And for us to beat them and be a running back at Nebraska, it kind of showed the difference.

Q: Where did you get most of your playing time that night?

CC: Kickoff returns and a little bit at running back. I actually had some ankle injuries that slowed me up that year. I want to say I rolled one of my ankles down at practice down there.

Q: Any one play from that night in particular frozen in your memory?

CC: The safety Dwayne Harris got in the back of the end zone. It kind of solidified things that we had taken over.

Q: Any favorite practice story, Clinton?

CC: Abdul and I were talking about that today. We were talking about how the number one offense would go against the number one defense in the goal line stand situation, and how the defensive guys -they don't want to admit it- but we were pretty much having our way with the number one defense at the time. And I was in, and it ended up being the last play of that goal line series… I'm coming at it like it's the same outside zone play and Abdul and I and some of the offensive guys swear up and down that Coach Steele -it's funny- Coach Steele gave Ed Stewart the call, where to meet at.

It was so intense. It was live, one-on-one, heads up. It was probably one of the hardest and loudest collisions in Memorial Stadium history, period. Neither one of us bent or broke. I didn't score on that play. Ed Stewart felt the hit. I felt the hit. We both kind of laughed and laid there a little bit (laughs) and got up. It was an exciting time for both the offense and the defense. We got up and patted each other on the helmet, "Nice play." And the impact of the hit was so loud (because there was no one in there) that it echoed throughout the entire stadium.

Q: Any good friends you keep in touch with to this day?

CC: I keep in touch with Lawrence. About a month ago Lawrence Phillips sent me a letter. Lawrence and I had probably one of the best relationships, still to this day, one of my best friends. I'd drive home from Lincoln to Omaha and Lawrence would already be sitting in my Mom's apartment. She'd be making us dinner and he'd be laughing because he'd seen me pull up. He'd always be sitting on the couch and watching television, talking to my mom, and he'd already have lunch or dinner in his body already. Mom and Lawrence were pretty amazing, and she knew Lawrence came from California and how we felt about one another, with our friendship, and she kind of took him under her wing and treated him like she treated my brothers.

Q: You always had a tattoo, right? It was huge! What did it say?

CC: It said 'Outkast.'

Q: You still got that?

CC: Oh yeah, it wasn't one of those that you could wash off after awhile.

Q: (laughs) It wasn't a tattoo from the bottom of a CrackerJack box, huh?

CC: Actually, Lawrence and I both got those, both had them tatted across our stomach. He got 'Outlaw' and I got 'Outkast.'

To be honest with you, it's how the trend got started. And if you look around now everybody has a tattoo.

Q: Even the Queen of England probably has a tattoo by now, Clinton. (laughs) What are you the most proud of, being a Husker player?

CC: I would have to say it would be two undefeated seasons, going 25 and O, being the team everybody was gunning for and not able to knock off of the pedestal, that would probably be one of the proudest things.

Q: And what do you think you've taken away from those days and applied to your daily life that makes a difference?

CC: Well, especially being from probably the toughest community in the entire state, being born and raised here in North Omaha, living in North Omaha my whole life and working in North Omaha now, just trying to influence some of the youth within this community, just to let them know that the gang violence and the robbing and the stealing and all the criminal society, to let them know there are other avenues. Even if they are from a broken home or single parent home, let them know there are ways to get out: athletics, education, that there are ways to where you can be successful being from North Omaha.

Q: Anything you wish you could do differently or do over?

CC: I don't know. I'm pretty sure there are things everybody looks back on and wishes they did a little differently. But that's one of the things I try to leave in God's hands, learning that from my mom, that everything happens for a reason. I'm pretty sure there are some things that I could have been done a little bit different, but I try to live my life in a way that you don't do things that you're gonna regret later on in life, whatever they may be. I want to do things the right way instead of having to look back in life and wishing I hadn't.

Q: A clear conscience leaves no regrets?

CC: Well, at least that's what they say. (laughs)

End conversation.

"When my mother was pregnant with me, she told me later, a party of hooded Klu Klux Klan riders galloped up to our home in Omaha, Nebraska, one night. Surrounding the house, brandishing their shotguns and rifles, they shouted for my father to come out. My mother went to the front door and opened it..." Malcolm Little, later to be known as Malcolm X, arrived in the world on May 19th, 1925 at Omaha's University Hospital, and his story echoes a refrain of the hard streets of North Omaha to this day. Though the KKK is now old history in Nebraska climes, the mean streets and rough & tumble neighborhoods still turn out young men of considerable mettle. Thus was Clinton. Far from being a violent individual, when the ball was in his grasp he was nonetheless hell-bent on scoring by any means necessary: be it over, under or through a man.

The one thing that really stood out to me from this conversation was the absolute full and implicit trust the running backs had in their blockers up front. We often take such faith for granted when we think of offensive team play, but believe me when I say that this isn't always the case. Not only were the original Pipeline and later versions extra-proficient at mowing down obstructionist defenders, but they were just as nasty and determined as those cradling the ball. Time and again you'll see very talented backs dancing around behind the line of scrimmage hoping to catch a glimpse of daylight while simultaneously looking for an escape route from sure pulverization. That never happened with these teams. Rarely ever. That's what a heartfelt trust and sure faith will do for an organization of unified individuals.

Notable quote #2:
Clinton Childs on the full-tilt practices: "Neither one of us bent or broke. Ed Stewart felt the hit. I felt the hit. We both kind of laughed and laid there a little bit (laughs) and got up. We got up and patted each other on the helmet, "Nice play.""

It was better, he thought, to fail in attempting exquisite things than to succeed in the department of the utterly contemptible.

Arthur Machen, *The Hill of Dreams*

I'm not sure who first coined the phrase 'speed kills,' but if it's true, then the Huskers possessed serial killers galore. One man behind the development of the 60 & 3 team speed was Strength & Conditioning Coach and Crofton, Nebraska native Randy Gobel. A multi-talented individual, Randy was an integral cog in the machine as he delved into the depths of running biomechanics in the early nineties for pointers worth passing on to the student/athletes. The payoff was a faster, more efficient athlete who got from point A to B with the swiftest of ease for dramatic impact. From the smaller, shiftier backs to the big tractors in the trenches, road gear was only a millisecond away after partaking of this man's tutelage. Let's hear from Randy, a coach who embraced the process from start to finish line as the boys in red set the green fields ablaze.

Notable quote #1:

"That was another thing that made Nebraska pretty special, the amount of peer pressure and leadership we had was huge. And that comes from having fifth year seniors who'd been through all that stuff."

Randy Gobel

Question: Hey Randy, good to talk to you once more. So what is your position nowadays at the university?

Randy Gobel: I'm Assistant Director of Athletic Facilities, Director of the Devaney Sports Center. It keeps me busy.

Q: Things coming full circle from all the time you spent with some of the Olympic Sports back in the day?

RG: Yeah, we get to talking and I tell them I remember when I was the basketball strength coach when Danny Nee first got there. I was there when Moe Iba was there, too, but Moe didn't have any of his guys work out. (laughs)

Q: So tell me about the road you took to joining the Husker staff. You were from Crofton, right?

RG: Yeah, from Crofton. Summertimes I worked up at Lewis & Clark Lake up by Yankton, South Dakota, and I met a guy from Falls City, Nebraska up there and we got to be friends. And there were two other guys from Falls City who were working for Boyd at the time, one who was Tom Wilson. I met those guys and got to know them when I came to Lincoln to do my student teaching during college and I got to be pretty good friends with them. One day I was tired of teaching and I talked to Tim and Tom Wilson and said, 'What you do sounds interesting.' And they said, "If you want to try, go talk to Boyd." So I went in one day and talked to Boyd and said, 'I think I want to be a strength coach.' That's how I got started.

Q: Any idea what year that would have been?

RG: Would have been somewhere in the spring of 1980. I finished college in Lincoln and then started in the fall of '81... actually started working there before that, but worked with the athletes the fall of 1981.

Q: So you got your degree at Nebraska and decided to get into coaching then?

RG: Actually, I got my degree in Kearney and came to Lincoln to do my student teaching. I finished up some classes at the University to transfer over, and that's how I got my degree.

Q: Do you recall the first meeting with Boyd?

RG: Yeah, I went in and introduced myself and he said two things, "You're too old and you're too small to be a strength coach." I said, 'What!? I'm not even out of college yet.' He said, "We're looking for people who are freshmen, sophomores. You're gonna need to have money right away," and all these things. And he goes, "Tell you what, you go back and think about it and you write me a letter explaining to me what you can do for this program." And I went and sat down and got kind of miffed about his attitude and said, 'I can do anything, et cetera...' My degree was Industrial Education and he happened to be looking for somebody who could evaluate equipment, because he had a contract with AMF American designing lifting equipment, and my mechanical background was exactly what he was looking for.

Q: So despite being 'too old and too small' you got the job. Maybe being 'too smart' made up for it?

RG: (laughs) I don't know about that! Some days I'm not so sure I'm so smart.

Q: Or too good-looking then, maybe? (laughs)

RG: Well, yeah. That goes without saying.(laughs) I remember the first testing day in the fall for the varsity like it was yesterday. It was out on the outdoor track and they ran 40's, a vertical jump, agility, and they ran something like the timed mile separated by two minutes' rest.

Q: Was that the day Harry Grimminger puked into his cupped hands and then swallowed it up before the coaches noticed how out of shape he was?

RG: Actually, no. That was way before Harry. Gosh, what was that kid's name? Big old middle guard, I can see his face but I can't remember his name. Boyd actually ran behind him and pushed him so he'd make his time…

Q: Sort of 'wind-aided', eh?

RG: Yeah, Boyd-aided. (laughs) It was on the outdoor track.

Q: Boy, 'ol Boyd must not have been such a hard ass back in those early years. I can't imagine him doing that in the '90's.

RG: Well, I think if the kid wouldn't have made his time Osborne would have brought the hammer down on Boyd for not getting him in shape.(laughs)

Q: I'd love to have a picture of that.

RG: Wish I could remember the guy's name. But to start out I was working in the north field house weight room supervising the bench press. At that time we had a weight room in the south stadium, also, where they did the circuit. So the linemen would come to the north stadium and do the heavy lifting there, and the quarterbacks and running backs and receivers would go to the south stadium and do the circuit after practice.

Q: Things changed considerably over the course of the next 10 years, huh?

RG: Yes. Actually, they were in the process of putting together the West Stadium Strength Complex at the time. During the day we worked in there building lifting platforms and painting and whatever else, so when I first started the original one was not done, but they had the money to get the remodeling done.

Q: So you played a part in building the first West Stadium Strength Complex?

RG: Yeah, and then '92 was when we did the renovation and the addition.

Q: So you're doing the bench press station in north stadium with the linemen, any names or guys stick out for you from those years?

RG: Mike Mandelko, Henry Waechter, some of those guys were still around. It's been a long, long time ago.

Q: So you started climbing the rungs as various guys left the program to become strength coaches elsewhere?

RG: Yeah, the Wilson boys both left. One went to Iowa State and one went to Las Vegas. Then we got moved into west stadium and I was in charge of the circuit training at that point.

Q: Mr. Circuit, huh? I'm sure the players loved you. (sarcasm)

RG: No, as a matter of fact, Turner Gill tried to kick my ass one time. (laughs) He'd had some back spasms or something and he came in to lift and didn't want to do his lifting. And he did the hip sled and complained to coach that he got hurt in the weight room. And I got death threats that he wasn't going to be able to play that weekend, which he did anyway. Speaking of some players, Jimmy and Toby Williams were both playing back then.

Q: Man, you jumped right into some really great football years.

RG: Yes, my first bowl game was the lost national championship game against Miami in '84.

Q: And when you first joined the football program, what stood out to you as to how the organization was set up, how it functioned?

RG: Just the number of players. So many players on the team. I remember watching a lot of Coach Osborne's practices and how he ran practice: nobody ever stood around, everybody was always getting reps. He had 4 stations going and people were always constantly doing things.

Boyd's organization in the strength department and the number of people he had working with those players was something that changed a lot over the years, though. A lot of the tweaks happened by Mike Arthur. Mike was really the guy behind the program. Boyd was the motivator and pushed strength coaches to come up with new things. Not that he didn't do a lot of strength coaching, but Mike was that go-to person when you start talking about the programs.

Q: He's the non-descript guy in the lab coat behind the curtain doing his thing, right? What else?

RG: I have a lot of recollections of Coach Devaney of those days. The weight room had an electronic door lock and we were trying to keep people out of the weight room because we didn't want people to see what we were doing. It was the largest weight room in the world at that time and Coach Devaney had a couple buddies who wanted to get in and see the weight room, and they were denied because we didn't know who they were. So he called Boyd, and said, "Boyd, I want these two guys to get in. And they are gonna be there at 1 o'clock." Well, Boyd waited around for them for about a half hour the next day and they never showed up, so he went out for stretching or whatever. And sure enough, they show up late and they didn't get in again. (laughs) And we wouldn't let them in. They were mad and went back to Coach Devaney. So Coach Devaney calls the office and I end up picking up the phone (and I don't know if you want to put this down), but he said ,"Who is this?" and I said my name. And he said, "You tell that sonuvabitch you work for I want to talk to him." (laughs) So Boyd shows up a little while later and says, "Did anybody call?" And I said, 'Yeah, Coach Devaney called. You might want to call him back.'

Q: Did they ever get in?

RG: Actually, I don't know. Coach called them up and chewed them out for not being on time! (laughs)

Q: Any impressions of the finish of that '90 season and Boyd pounding his fist on the meeting room's table? Do you recall that?

RG: Yeah, I do. I think it was a turning point in which Nebraska could have gone backwards. We had a group of athletes who weren't very dedicated. There was tons of attitude on the team and I think a lot of things happened, and it wasn't all in the strength area. But in the strength area we made a lot of changes at that point, with the research that Mike was doing.

And I think the coaches looked at their recruiting, too. They decided they weren't recruiting the right kind of kids. They'd gotten into this national media-foray type of player and I think they went back to looking for kids that were Nebraska-type kids: hard working kids who maybe weren't the most talented in the world, but they had potential. That's what I remember from that whole thing.

That and the strength program, we put together radical things where we didn't need to run so much and we looked at the energy systems football players used and became more sport-specific. And to Coach Osborne's credit -it was a big change to him and his coaches- and they were open to it and they listened and they gave it a chance. And it really made a big difference. You could tell within a couple of years that our team was just a different team in the way they trained and the way they finished games. Part of that was the kids and how hard they worked, and the kind of training we did was much better.

A thing that happened, also, with the strength program, was that we had enough full-time people that we were able to handle just about every position. One guy for the fullbacks and the I-backs, a full-time person for the offensive line, one for the defensive line, and each of the full-time people had a student assistant to help. We gave the kids what they needed during the offseason, not just some generic running to make you feel like you were in shape, but we did stuff that actually helped you as a football player. All those things where defensive linemen need to react on sight to the ball as opposed to an offensive lineman who was listening to a snap count. A defensive back does a lot of backpedaling and turning around, whereas an offensive back is running forward and changing directions laterally, so we became really specific with our workout routines. I think that made a big difference. The whole country went to that after the success that we had.

And we used scientific principles, we looked at physiology and what happened in the different energy systems based on the amount of work-to-rest ratios that an athlete did, and we made it real specific to what we were doing. It was stuff published in textbooks and scientific journals and we brought it into real-life training and made it come together with what we were doing.

Q: What segment of the team was your responsibility, Randy?

RG: Typically, I worked with the quarterbacks, running backs, and then some with the defensive backs quite a bit there, too. Usually it was the smaller, fast guys.

Q: Any recollections of specific players from that time stand out to you?

RG: Oh man, there's so many of them. Clinton Childs, to me, was one of the best athletes we ever had at Nebraska. He just had a tremendous amount of physical ability. And another good thing about Clinton was that he kept other guys in line because he was such a tough kid. From Omaha, him and his brothers were tough guys, he was one to keep Lawrence Phillips in check during his playing days. He'd want to do something and Clinton would say, "Hey, quit screwing around! Get in there and do it!"

And that was another thing that made Nebraska pretty special, the amount of peer pressure and leadership we had was huge. And that comes from having fifth year seniors who'd been through all that stuff. It was probably one of the major things that was the big difference for Nebraska. And you can tell these last years before Pelini, we didn't have those redshirt guys. Coaches can't do it all, so you need those kind of guys. We had attitudes where it was, "Nebraska's not the end for me. I'm going to the NFL." And now? I think now we're coming back to where some say, "Nebraska is the end for me." It's what you strive for. And that makes a difference there, too.

Q: Your name keeps popping up when it comes to the 1:16 on the stadium clock during that summer of '94.

RG: Yeah, in January of 1994 we got pretty close to winning the national championship and there was the 1:16 left on the clock and we were leading and we were beating Florida State, and we got beat in a minute sixteen seconds.

And Boyd pointed that out. Boyd, being his motivational self, every day, he decided, we were going to put 1:16 on the clock, so at the end of the workouts we would do an extra 1:16 of work. So I crawled up the steps to the press box twice a day, (laughs) every day, turned on the clock, put a minute-sixteen on it, and then went back up the to shut the clock off afterwards, all summer long.

Q: You probably had 'buns of steel' after all the stairs you climbed that summer. (laughs)

RG: It paid off. (laughs)

Q: Any memorable game on the sidelines stands out to you more than another?

RG: Obviously the Orange Bowl against Miami stands out. It was huge. Huge, just because we finally got there. I remember standing on the sideline of the Orange Bowl the day before the game (and I had met Lee Corso before in Lincoln, because they'd been there to do a couple of games) and Corso was standing there while the team was practicing and we started talking. He said, "Do you think you guys have a chance?" And I said, 'Oh yeah. We're gonna win this.' And he says, "Oh, really. Why?" And I said, 'Because these guys love each other.' And he goes, "Oh, really?" I remember that conversation with him very well because it was kind of a bold statement. Because Miami had everything. They hadn't been beaten in the Orange Bowl for a long time and they were pretty talented, and we had a bunch of farm boys and just hard workers where you looked at them and went, "Boy, they don't look very athletic. But the kids can play, you know?" And that was a huge deal, because that's what Nebraska was about. Just a bunch of hardworking guys and a few pretty talented athletes to fill in the gaps there, and away we went.

Q: Tell me about the field there. Was it sandy like it was in the '84 orange bowl? I remember Jeff Smith just kicking up sand while running in that game!

RG: Yeah, it was pretty much painted, green sand.

Q: Do you think that affected our guys in those games?

RG: I don't think so. Somebody tried to write a story and made a big deal out of nothing. A lot of it was that we played against the warm weather schools in the warm weather. Before (we had) the Cook Pavilion we were trying to work out in a little crackerjack box or outside in the elements, so that made a big difference.

Q: You know, The Boston Celtics always had the pink visitor's locker room and the old parquet floor with the dead spots, and Notre Dame always had the natural grass that was grown very high and thick-like, so I wanted to know if that Orange Bowl field had any unique qualities.

RG: No, I think it was reporters trying to make a bigger deal of it than anything else.

Q: And funny sideline moments stand out to you?

RG: There was an official named Scott Cook who I knew pretty well, and he was one of the officiating crew that gave Colorado that 5th down. He was from York, Nebraska and I got to be friends with him. And sometimes on the sidelines between plays I'd go out and give him some crap loud enough for the players to hear on the sideline, and he'd go over to me and threaten to kick me out of the game and all. And that would get the players fired up. (laughs) It was all joking. It would freak the players out, because if I would have gotten a flag Coach Osborne would have kicked me out. (laughs)

Q: Were you a "Get Back" Coach?

RG: Oh, yeah. I was the '"Get Back" Coach for a loooong time.

Q: Any memorable occasions?

RG: Not really, it was just hard to keep the players back because they were so anxious to get in and play. Everybody wanted to get in there and do their part. They were pretty controlled, not a lot going on. Other than players grabbing jugs and towels and stuff and trying to go to the bathroom on the sidelines, not really. (laughs)

Q: Any away games, fields or fans where the TV cameras didn't effectively show the environments as they truly were? Anything stand out?

RG: The worst ever was Penn State. Their fans were horrendous. Never, ever have I been around the fans after a game where they came and… they had no crowd control for one thing. Our players were getting pushed around. They were getting cussed at and screamed at. It was the closest to people getting hit that I've ever seen. LSU fans, even after we beat the crap out of them, they were still drunk in the hotel, screaming "Tiger Bait!" to us afterwards. I don't know if they even knew what happened at the game.

And then, of course, there was the Kansas State idiot coaches screaming at our coaches after the game when they finally beat us that one year after 50 years or whatever. They were horrible. One of the Stoops brothers, the one that's down in Arizona, he walked up to Coach Dan Young afterwards and said, "You're a fucking loser!" I was like, 'Excuse me? You win once after losing something like 50 years in a row, and you call *us* losers?'

Some of the best ones were our so-called worst enemies: Oklahoma. Some of the best people and the best friends I had were the strength coaches at Oklahoma back when Barry Switzer was there. We had a great time with them. They respected us, we respected them. We'd get together and party before the game. It was easier to take it from those people because they knew how to win and they had some class, whereas some of these others didn't.

Q: Anything about the other coaches from that time?

RG: My favorite story is about Charlie McBride. We're getting ready to play Oklahoma back when they were beating us in the early '80's… '80 or '81. Myself and Jerry Schmidt and somebody else were walking up the sideline and Charlie McBride was leaning against the sideline fence at practice, and we're running a kickoff return. They did a throwback pass and one of the guys asked Charlie if we were going to run that in the game against Oklahoma (and our coaches were a little uptight, mind you) and Charlie turns and looks at us. He spits, and then he says, "I don't f@@@ing know what the f##'s going on because nobody f***ing tells me what the f###'s happening!" (laughs) Why don't you go ahead and put that in your book? (laughs) We all kind of decided that we didn't talk to Charlie unless Charlie wanted to talk to us. (laughs)

I can remember Charlie taking Jason Wiltz and Steve Warren and grabbing them both by the facemasks and pulling them over and telling them, "You two are f***in' worthless! And when you're out of here ten years from now and you don't have a job and you're worthless? You're gonna remember, because I told you that you were worthless!" (laughs)

Q: And ten minutes later he was hugging them, right?

RG: Oh yeah, and they both loved him. They come back and visit him. I got to be good friends with Charlie as the years went along, and we get to see each other and chit-chat now and then.

Q: Most memorable or favorite game? Favorite player?

RG: There's a lot of them. The Florida game, watching Tommie Frazier was real special, too, another one of those games where no one thought we had a chance. I talked to Frank Solich before the game and I asked him how he thought we were gonna do and he says, "We've got a plan." And I go, 'Yeah? What is it?' And he goes, "Well, we've been watching them and we think they're a little soft. We figure if we can come out and smash them in the mouth, they're not gonna like it too much." And that's exactly what we did.

And once I think about it, my favorite player of all-time was probably Mike Rozier. To this day, Mike is still a happy guy. I just loved seeing him and he was so much fun to be around. I can remember him, he'd have the whole huddle laughing when we were playing Oklahoma, he'd come into the weight room and just be hilarious. He was such a tremendously talented guy, physically, but he always had that happy attitude. I still tell people he was probably my favorite player. Him and John Parrella. John was a great guy, too. They were wild, but they were wild in a good way, they kept things fun for everybody, too. They worked extremely hard.

Q: Any memorable off-field stuff? Bowl trips?

RG: Yeah, there's a lot I can't talk about. (laughs) One that comes up was the Sugar Bowl in 1986, maybe? Being relatively low on the totem pole on the staff, they had a New Years Eve Party for all the bigger shots, and they left myself and a bunch of student managers and others with nothing to do. Well, it got close to midnight there and we got into the hospitality room, so we called room service and ordered some champagne -Dom Perignon from 1958 (because that's when my birthday was), and when the guys brought the bottles of champagne up I scribbled 'Mickey Holmes' (who was the President of the Sugar bowl

Committee, because I knew his name) on the ticket. So we hurried up and partied before everybody else got back after midnight. (laughs)

Q: Did anything ever come of that? (laughing)

RG: Nope.

Q: Now Randy, were you one of those guys who drove the semi-truck down to the bowl game with the weights?

RG: Yeah, I got my truck drivers license and everything. And to get that I had to drive to Kenosha, Wisconsin and deliver some fruit juice and some other things. (laughs) The first trip I took, the truck driver had been on the road to Chicago and he didn't have enough rest (there was a huge ice storm, maybe 1983, and we left early for the bowl game and I rode with him and another guy) and we had ice clear through Kentucky. And we finally dropped off the one trucker in Atlanta, and there was another guy who was supposed to drive. Him and I took off down into Florida, and after I had slept in there for awhile I woke up… and the truck driver's head was nodding off and he was falling asleep! So I said, 'I know I can drive this thing if you get me started.'

So he pulled over and started getting me through the gears, and then he laid and down and slept. We were going down the Florida Turnpike and he slept for about 4 hours. Well, he woke up and crawled onto the passenger seat, and just then a Winnebago cuts right in front of us. And he says, "F### that sonuvabitch!" So I pull out and he says, "Okay, speed up. And when your back wheels of the trailer get right next to this guy, just turn the wheel a little bit and watch what happens." Well, turning the wheel a bit causes the trailer to swerve about 6 or 7 feet both ways, and when I did that the Winnebago pulled over onto the side of the road. And the guy goes, "That'll teach him!" (laughs) And that's how I learned to drive a semi.

Q: (laughing) Now, the smaller, skill position players you worked with… any guys stick out as far as their attitude, leadership, mindset?

RG: Wow, there were so many over the years. Both Tommie and Brook were great guys, you know? Tommie wasn't sometimes the most popular guy because he was pretty demanding, but he'd never demand anything less than what he would do himself. Brook was the quietter guy, but would push himself just as hard. Damon Benning, Lawrence Phillips, the Makovickas were hard working guys. So many of them just did what you asked of them. They'd run through a wall for you. Matt Turman, a good guy, worked hard and gave it all he had. They were all a lot of good buddies. There were some great defensive backs, too.

There were so many of them that were just awesome to work for. They pushed themselves, they pushed the linemen. They'd step up and challenge the linemen to anything, anytime. It went both ways, so that was pretty cool. And some of the guys who didn't see the field worked their butts off just as hard as anybody else. I wish I could remember some of their names, they stand out to me, I need to get a roster and look at some names.

Q: Anything about recruiting stand out?

RG: Well, Boyd being Mr. Show Business and Mr. Promoter always made it a big deal for the kids with the recruiting demonstrations before the games on Saturday. It was really cool, because that's where I really got to know Kenny Walker. And there was a tight end, Sheldon Jackson, who painted his fingernails. Sheldon did a great job in those demonstrations. He'd come in with his fingernails painted sometimes, in front of the whole recruiting class and parents and everyone watching.

And that's actually how we got the money for the weight room expansion in '91 or so. George and Dan Cook came to the weight room and wanted to see the demonstration so Boyd let them come in, didn't know who they were and started talking to them and the Husker Power Club people and how we were trying to raise money, and that's how they got hooked up with the Cooks and got that all started.

Q: Anything else special about those years, those players, their unity?

RG: I always tell people about Coach Osborne's philosophy. And it was really true when we won the first national championship, because in some ways it was the worst letdown of my life: because it didn't change. Yeah, it was fun we won it all that night, it was a big party. And the next day and getting back to Lincoln was exciting. But two days later we're back in a meeting talking about winter conditioning and what we're gonna do about this and that for next year. That's how it was, and he talked about that.

And I even try to convey this to my son and his teams: it's the competition all the way through. That's what it was really about. And you start to think about it, every week and how exciting it was, the questions of: "Are we going to win? How are we going to win? How much are we going to win by?" That was the truly exciting part of all that. Each day, each week, the competition and getting ready for it. More so -yeah, the championship game was exciting- but leading up to that was so awesome, a whole year's worth of stuff that was just so exciting and so intense that it was way more important than the actual championship game.

Q: I suppose it's like your child walking for the first time. Sure it's nice, but the real exciting part is seeing them slowly grow, day by day, leading up to that moment?

RG: Yeah, holding their hands and watching them teeter around that furniture and those type of things. Then you get to the first steps and then you're, 'Well, that's over with.'(laughs)

Q: Anyone behind the scenes that you feel played a big role in those '90's era teams?

RG: I don't know if it was any one person. It was moreover the whole Performance Team that Boyd put together. He did a great job putting a lot of that together and he pushed hard -which made some people mad- but when you put together nutrition and psychology and strength & conditioning and the football coaches and everything, it made for a strong team, combined with a strong team of players. And I shouldn't forget academics, because those people had a big part of it, too. It was a huge team of people.

Q: Do you ever break your rings out? Do you have a favorite?

RG: Yeah, I break them out now and then. I think the first one -with the #1 on the top from '94- is my favorite. I have a collection of all the rings and the watches I've gotten since I've been here. There's a lot of them. And to tell you, there were so many guys over the years, so many guys that worked so hard and were such great guys: Pat Englebert, Jim Scott, Terry Connealy, Clinton Childs, all those guys. They worked hard and they gave everything they had. There were so many guys like that over the years. A lot of them.

End conversation.

Guys like Randy Gobel will never go out of style. Why? Because seeing through the Nebraskan work ethic, the love of the teaching, the development process, the big games and final tallies, the rings and trophies, he's a person who simply cares about people. This strength coach truly, humbly, deeply had a heart for every kid down there on the turf sweating away in the humid, summer heat while he trudged up stair upon stair upon stair to set the infamous minute-sixteen clock to countdown mode that champion-building summer of '94.

What stuck out to me the most from our conversation was his "we put together radical things …and we looked at the energy systems football players used and became more sport-specific." In hindsight, it doesn't take a genius to realize that you don't drive a top fuel dragster along Route 66's 2,448 mile stretch, much like you don't train a lineman or defensive back to develop only straight line speed over long distances. Football, if you strip it of the glitz, is a game of short, intense bursts of acceleration followed by rapid deceleration and a change of direction, then followed by another short, intense burst of acceleration followed by… well, you get the picture. Plus, every briefly timed play is followed by a prolonged rest period until the next snap. Taking these football-specific facts into account, each and every training routine each and every training day was focused on only those aspects of the game that would be replicated during actual competition. It developed muscle memory and explosiveness that soon became second nature, providing the players with the ability to expend full effort every play knowing that their bodies would be fully primed for the next one after. Confidence skyrocketed as a result. Wasn't it Vince Lombardi who said, "Fatigue makes cowards of us all"? These boys were at their physical peak, so you'd be hard-pressed to find a Cornhusker in those days backing down from Saturday's skirmishes in cowardice.

Notable quote #2:
Randy Gobel on the evolution of Nebraska's offseason training: "And to Coach Osborne's credit -it was a big change to him and his coaches- and they were open to it and they listened and they gave it a chance. And it really made a big difference. You could tell within a couple of years that our team was just a different team in the way they trained and the way they finished games."

The harvest of old age is the recollection and abundance of blessings previously secured.

Maruc Tullius Cicero, *De Senectute*

When the Kansas-Nebraska Act of 1854 opened up the conjoined territories to settlement it allowed the new settlers to determine whether the states would be admitted to the union as either "free" or "slave." The arrangement in the southern half of the equation begot the term "Bleeding Kansas," as violence followed the birthing of America's present day heartland. A future generation's son by the name of Ryan Held decided that the educational opportunities both in the classroom and on the field were simply too rich and promising to pass up, despite the promise of blood and bruises, so he left the Sunflower State and headed north to the city of Lincoln and the state of his forerunners. Trust me when I tell you, this should be an interesting conversation and one that you surely don't want to gloss over, as it dares to expose a practical depth and a breadth of football knowledge as wide as the rolling plains themselves. Let's catch up with Ryan Held.

Notable Quote #1:
"The thing that set it apart, also, was that this behavior was done in scrimmages: the cut-blocking, the physicality. In practice. And not many programs do that. You can't just turn it on on game day, you have to do that all the time."

Ryan Held

Walk-on, Split End, Overland Park, Kansas (Blue Valley North)
Where are they now? Highland, Kansas, Coach

Question: So Ryan, where have you been and what have you been up to?

Ryan Held: Well, for the last four years I was in Weatherford, Oklahoma. Head Football Coach at Southwest Oklahoma and the previous three was at Oklahoma Panhandle State, which is in Goodwell, OK. But now I'm Head Coach at Highland Community College here in Highland, Kansas. And do you remember Peru State in Peru, Nebraska? I was up there as Head Coach in 2001.

Q: Wow, you've had quite a football career.

RH: For a young guy I've experienced a lot. We turned the two worst programs in the state of Oklahoma around and had winning seasons. It was a lot of hell going through it, but we found a way to get it done. It was interesting, to say the least. (laughs)

Q: You were from Kansas originally, right?

RH: Yes. Well, my whole life I loved Nebraska. My grandparents lived in Bellevue and growing up we'd go up there for the holidays. I'd always had a love for Nebraska, and my senior year I led the state of Kansas in receiving. I was a possession–type guy, not a speed guy, and I sent my film to Coach Ron Brown -who was the receivers coach at the time- and they offered me to come up and take an official visit and offered me an walk-on opportunity, and that was a dream come true to me. You remember how walk-ons were treated just like scholarship guys? So that was obviously very appealing to play for the team you love.

And I had a chance baseball-wise back then, with Coach John Sanders, the baseball coach, and baseball was a pretty good sport, as well, and he said I had a chance to try to play there as well, though I never did take him up on that. But I figured, "Hey, it's only three hours away from my home, so why not do it?"

Q: When was your first year on campus?

RH: The fall of '93, a freshman from Overland Park, Kansas and Blue Valley North high school.

Q: Original impressions?

RH: Well, I can remember my freshman year was the last year they allowed freshman two-a-days, so we were there maybe a week before the varsity would show up, and they got us out there and put us through some pretty intense practices. And there were only two outside wide receivers -Jeff Lake and I- so we had to run about every play at practice. (laughs) And the only play we got off was the power set, the power I. It was the only play we got off during two-a-days.

I just remember being there and I can remember Lawrence Phillips, a guy I was wowed with, being a special player. I remember, Paul, my first varsity practice they put the freshman against the Blackshirts. For my first practice I'm out against Barron Miles and Tyrone Williams, and you talk about a rude awakening? The game sped up like I'd never seen before. Being a 160 lb. freshman wide receiver, it was an eye-opening experience, but it was a deal where you lived with it.

There were some good days and bad days, Paul. I remember my redshirt year my aunt passed away, so I went to her funeral, and then 4 days later my Mom's dad died, so I went to two funerals in less than a week. So you're redshirting and getting your butt kicked on scout team and you're a little homesick, but the bottom line was that you're playing at arguably the best program in America, so you had to make the best of it and fight through it. And it made you stronger.

You know, you have a girlfriend back home and she's calling you. And I'm like, 'What am I doing? I've got all these freshman girls here on campus and I'm dealing with a girl back home?' (laughs) We all make poor decisions, and that ended and I got smart and began messing with the Nebraska girls. (laughs) It was good, though, you realized what it was going to take, just the work ethic and philosophy of what the program was built upon, and that was what I really enjoyed. And to be honest with you, Paul, the reason I went to Nebraska -a lot of guys go there because they want to eventually play in the NFL, and I knew in a hundred years that I wasn't going to be a great player, I was going to be the typical Nebraska football player that was a walk-on and that I was going to do whatever it took to help the football team, whether it's on scout team, one's or two's or whatever- but I knew I wanted be a coach, so it was an unbelievable opportunity to be a sponge and learn from the best. Guys were there for the NFL, but it was an opportunity for me to learn from the best. And sometimes there might be guys potentially dozing off in meetings, but for me I made sure I paid attention because I might pick up one detail that someday might help me.

Q: When did you decide you wanted to be a coach, Ryan?

RH: I knew when I was a little kid that I wanted to be the guy that wanted bad programs. I tell you what, when Bill Snyder took over Kansas State, that was everything I wanted to do someday. And I love building organizations. I used to take baseball cards when I was 8 years old and I'd put them together like a general manager of a team. Joe Horst was my roommate and he was from Wood River (and Scott Frost eventually transferred back- and they were teammates in high school), another walk-on. I really had a bunch of us walk-ons hung out together a lot in addition to a bunch of scholarship guys, too. We had a common bond that way. Brenden Holbien and Chris Dishman from Cozad, those guys were great.

Q: So Ron Brown was your position coach, how would you describe him?

RH: Well, Ron Brown, first of all, is an unbelievable person, a Christian man of faith and just a guy that would never let you settle for mediocrity, always trying. There was never a second during practice where he wasn't trying to get the tight ends, the receivers better. He was very detail-oriented and expected the best, did what he said he was going to do.

And he's back there now because of those type of characteristics and qualities that it takes to be an outstanding position coach, because he had a chance to go to Florida State. Bobby Bowden wanted him, the NFL and Tony Dungy wanted him. You can't teach that, it's just ingrained in the person. I learned so much from Ron Brown. I would take certain things from meetings and practice habits when I was coaching my team, different drills. All those things.

Q: What mannerisms of his coaching really stick with you?

RH: Really, the stressing of physical play. The receiving corps at Nebraska stood alone in college football, was just known as the all-around type of receivers in the United States because of the work ethic, the physicality, the cut-blocking, all the things that you have to be an unselfish, hard working guy that didn't care about credit. You were going to do whatever it took to spring that block and enable the running back to go all the way, and you know, a lot of times prima donna receivers don't like to do that stuff. If you look at my teams offensively, with the wide receivers we stressed the cut-blocking and all those things.

There were other things, but that was a big thing I took away. And what it is, the thing that set Nebraska apart back then was the philosophy of the physicality of winning that began in the 4th quarter. It was a learned behavior. It was tough in practice. Everybody believed in it from the strength staff to the coaching staff to the tutors in academics, everybody believed in it. It was tough from the moment you walked in to the moment you left, and there was no going against it, and thing that was nice was that you would see success in it and you could believe in it. Sometimes if you don't see it you don't believe in it. But you would see it, and it would make you believe more and more and more. It's not something that happens overnight, it's something that's taught. And it happened over time. It's the same philosophy as the military, they taught a philosophy as to how they were to go about things, and it was the same at Nebraska. You see a lot of programs going up and down and left and right, they don't have that type of philosophy they can hang their hat on. That's why there's turnover and not success in the system.

Q: How long do you think it took the typical player to fully buy into this mindset?

RH: Well, what I look at, Paul, there weren't many freshmen that really played at Nebraska. What did most kids do? Most of them redshirted, maybe they played some special teams or backup duty. A lot of kids didn't play 'til maybe their sophomore or junior year and sometimes their senior year.

And the thing that set it apart, also, was that this behavior was done in scrimmages, the cut-blocking, the physicality. In practice. And not many programs do that. You can't just turn it on on gameday, you have to do that all the time. It went into spring football, the Tuesday and Wednesday full pad practices. And the thing about it, with all the walk-ons and the kids that were in the program, when you've got 145 guys out there you can get a lot of reps in practice, and that allows you to train your body and the motor skills and techniques that they wanted you to do because you were doing it over and over and over. The offensive linemen, they came in 6'5" 240 and by the time they're seniors they're 6'6" 300 and they've done this thing a million times. They don't have to think, they just play. That's what it's all about, that's why it was very successful.

Q: What about Coach Osborne?

RH: He's like John Wayne. Big, tall, 6'3", 6'4" guy. When he walks in everybody shuts their mouth. It's obviously his history and what he did in the past, instant respect. Obviously he was very consistent, too. He explained why we do things. He said, "We're not gonna be a team that throws it 60 times a game because the state of Nebraska in November might be freaking 20 below zero, so this is why we have to do what we do." It doesn't take a brain surgeon to figure out what was right.

I remember this, (and he came in on Monday, and we always had 8 or 9 new offensive plays that week) we're getting ready to play Colorado and he drew up a formation and he said, "Guys, we're gonna line up like this the first play of the game. They're gonna line up just like this, and we're gonna score a touchdown." Well, we lined up like that, Paul, the first play of the game we ran it and it was a 75 yard touchdown, Ahman Green at the University of Colorado. So what he drew up earlier in the week? It was exactly what they did. We were never out-prepared. Everything that he said, they did. And maybe a tinker here or there, but for the most part we were always well prepared and had a lot of meeting time and we were never left with any surprises.

Q: What about other coaches?

RH: Obviously, Charlie McBride, he speaks for himself, just how intense and smart he really was. He was probably, when you look at defensive coordinators in college football, he has to go down as one of the top ten of all time. Unbelievable how he could think ahead and prepare the Blackshirts on a day-to-day basis.

And he came in one day to the meeting room and just absolutely went ballistic at the whole team, the whole football team. I'll never forget, it might have been '94 when we didn't play as well against Wyoming, and I think he just came in that Monday or whatever it was and went absolutely ballistic. And ever since then it was just a turning point. Normally the coordinators didn't talk to the whole football team, it was just Coach Osborne, but he took the stage and just ripped everybody's ass. It was awesome! (laughs)

Q: Can you describe how he would go ballistic?

RH: It was all of the above: spit flying, tobacco juice, he'd go off on some tangents. If he talked, you better keep your mouth shut. Nobody moved an inch. If you moved an inch everybody thought it was over, it was unbelievable.

Q: What would you say your greatest contribution was?

RH: You know, my main contribution was: I redshirted, I was on scout team my freshman year (the year that Tommie Frazier had the clots in '94). I moved to scout team quarterback to help the team and I remember I was 4-time Scout Team Player of the Week because I just got out there and busted my ass to help out as scout team quarterback. That was probably my best accomplishment. For me to get that award 4 times in an 11 game season, that was something.

Again, I wasn't even a guy that played a whole lot. I got a little bit of time here and there, but behind the scenes, just like a lot of guys who helped prepare the Blackshirts every day and just be a team player, man, I was not in it for myself. I was in it to help whatever way I could, whatever role I was given. You've got to have guys like myself and my roommates who didn't care who got the credit. Like that old saying by Ronald Reagan: "You'd be amazed what can be accomplished when you don't worry about who gets the credit." And that's how that program was built. There were a lot of guys like that on scout team that might have gotten one play in their career, Paul, and it was well worth it. And most kids would have quit and said 'forget it' and went out on O Street on Friday night, but they believed what was going on, and the friendships and camaraderie that you get from it? Matter of fact, Aaron Taylor just 'facebook'd' me tonight before you called and asked me how things were and if I was ever going to get back into coaching. Here's Aaron Taylor, the Outland Trophy winner and here's Ryan Held, the walk-on wide receiver, and we're still in contact.

Q: Do you recall the first time suiting up and running onto the field?

RH: It would have been the year after my redshirt, in '94. I just remember there'd be some days like Tuesday and Wednesday practice and you're getting your butt kicked every day, and you're, 'Oh, my goodness.' But then when you run out onto that field on Saturday it takes all that away, Paul. When you see the fans and the excitement and the energy level of the stadium and just being able to run through the band and hear 'Hail Varsity', it's just, you get goose bumps. There's no better deal. That was just a special deal for me, just being on that sideline and seeing all the great players that were playing, you know what I mean?

And the thing is, just like what Coach Osborne would put up on the board -for me, personally?- I would like to sit there and watch it all unfold. I got a kick out of that. Here it goes, 'Boom!' I'd stand there around the quarterbacks writing down the plays and I'd want to know what play was coming and wanted to know, 'Okay, what play is coming? Where should we run it?' And I was always thinking ahead and trying to figure out, 'Okay, what would I do here?' And then watch Coach Osborne call a play and set up things down the road.

Q: What did you get your degree in, Ryan?

RH: Well, I was in Teachers College, and then going into my senior year I switched to Community Health so I could graduate early, so I could go the University of Tennessee and be a graduate football coach instead of coming back to school in the fall and missing that opportunity.

And I don't know if you know, Paul, but I was part of the three national championships at Nebraska, and then in '98 I went to Tennessee and we won the national championship, beating Florida State, so I actually have 4 National Championship rings.

Q: Can you tell me what it was like preparing to play Nebraska?

RH: It was a nightmare. (laughs) There were so many things you had to stop, that Nebraska did offensively. You had to stop the fullback, stop the outside power game, you've got to stop the option game, you've got to stop the bootleg. When you're on the other side there are so many things, you can't believe what you have to prepare for. And you just couldn't simulate it in practice. Teams just couldn't simulate what we did in practice. Coach Osborne, absolutely, was the true inventor, there's no question that a lot of different stuff we did helped evolve the spread offense. If Coach was still coaching, he'd be doing some of those things, obviously.

Q: So you redshirted your first year in '93 and spent 5 years at Nebraska, were you playing your senior year or were you an assistant?

RH: Yeah, halfway through my junior year I hooked my shoulder, so I gave up my senior year to be an undergrad football coach and getting a medical scholarship. My senior year I was actually a coach… well, half my junior year and my senior year. My senior year I was an undergrad coach with Coach Solich and the running backs.

Q: Anything stand out from that time?

RH: Well, you go from player mode to being in meetings and really getting behind the scenes and stuff, and that was just great to be able to watch the film more in depth and hear what the coaches were saying, all those things that helped prepare for an upcoming game. I felt I learned even that much more, obviously, going into those 6 a.m. staff meetings.

You know, Coach Osborne would always do one of those moments where they would take a bible verse and say it and relate it to what was going on at that time, which I thought was awesome. Not many staffs do that: bring spirituality, Christianity, into the mix. And that was the thing, Paul, going back to Ron Brown and talking to Turner Gill and all those things. You know everybody always talks about that separation of church and state, but whether or not you were religious or not, you respected it. It was just awesome, because you felt good about everything about the organization. There wasn't negativity.

Obviously we had issues -every program does- but Saturday morning there was chapel and mass, and that kind of stuff I think is very important. And I adopted it in my coaching when I coached, I gave that as an option in my organizations, as well.

Q: Working under Coach Solich, any reflections about the man?

RH: Well, he's a bulldog, you know? He's a feisty guy. He's a really good football coach and I respect him a lot. He was a great recruiter, worked hard, earned his stripes, it's too bad the whole situation how he got ousted, I think. I respect him a lot, he's a great coach.

And Turner Gill? I knew Turner Gill was going to be an unbelievable coach. With his work ethic, his spirituality, how he treats people, philosophy… and that was another thing with Coach Osborne: how you treat people. Whether it's the custodian, whether it's the secretary, the walk-on kid from wherever? You look at all those things and in any successful organization the top guy knows everybody in the organization, because everybody had a role. Whether it's the guy taking the trash out or the secretary answering phones, everybody had a role. And he knew everybody's name, and that goes a long way when you look at championships and successful business, for any organization, I believe.

Q: And in those film sessions, what stands out to you?

RH: Well, just listening to them watching the opponent, watching the defense of the other teams, their philosophy, how the other team would line up on defense and "Here's how we were going to attack it." Everybody was just on the same page and it was, "They're gonna line up here, so here's how we're gonna attack 'em this way. Oh, and look what they do on this set. We can attack 'em here." You know, Paul, football is the closest thing to a military operation. It really is, attacking, it's the closest thing to military warfare. And you get in there and look at it, and you're preparing for a football battle and you're in there and, "How are we gonna attack these people and what are their weaknesses?"

And then when I got better and was learning everything, I'd be right on the same page and right there along with them, because you just did it over and over and over. And you saw so much film it was just ingrained in your mind.

Q: And I suppose so many of those guys had been together for so long, I'm sure they often began to think alike and almost didn't even have to speak, they just gave a wink or a nod and each knew what the other was thinking, too? Like they had their own special language?

RH: Absolutely. And that was another thing: continuity and camaraderie, that goes a long way. I'm trying to think, Coach Steele might have left during my era and we brought in Nelson Barnes, there wasn't much turnover. And Dave Gillespie came in, and you add all that up and Milt Tenopir and Dan Young, they had such an unbelievable system, we could out-scheme anybody in America because they'd done it so long. And then you get on out on the game field and see what the other team is doing? Just the ability to make adjustments at halftime and during the game and get the guys aside and go, "Okay, they're running this against this, so we're running this." And if you don't have a system like we had and the program like we had, you can't do those things.

Q: Take me back to when you were in the coaching position. Where were you during the games?

RH: Let's see... actually I was on the field. My job during that time was to (along with Graduate Assistants Mike Grant one year and Chad Stanley another), would tell me what the defense was for each play that we ran, and I would draw up the formation and draw in the defense, and then those cards I would give to Coach Osborne and he would go to the quarterbacks and show them, "When we do this, they do this..."

Now, in the NFL, Paul, they take pictures. You watch on the sideline, they've got those cameras, but we would draw it up and that's how we would make adjustments. And he'd call all the quarterbacks, Tommie Frazier, "Hey, we ran One Right 41 Sprint, we probably should have gone 49 Sprint." That's how we made those adjustments in the game and really helped us to be successful.

Q: So tell me, you're on the sideline versus Tennessee and it's the last game you know you're gonna be a Husker. What was that like?

RH: Well, it was special knowing I was gonna be on the coaching staff of Coach Osborne's last game and last season as Head Coach. Not many people can say that. That was just a special deal to be a part of it, whether you were player or coach. That will go down in the history books. And you always want to be a part of history, somehow, and you want to make sure it's positive. (laughs) That was a great deal. Obviously, it was a sad, sad situation with him retiring, but it happened for a reason and I was just happy to be a part of it.

Q: What was your all-time favorite game?

RH: The Miami game in '94. What I can remember is looking out and seeing Warren Sapp. We had this function and we went to a sea aquarium or something, and both teams got together and Warren Sapp was so arrogant and walking around thinking he was the greatest thing since sliced bread, and I can remember him in that 4th quarter sitting on his knees gasping for air. I just remember how we talked about wearing them out and just winning the game in the 4th quarter. And I think it's on a shirt or a picture, somebody's got it, it was him and Ray Lewis and some of those guys out of gas. I just remember that was my favorite game, because we could never beat Miami. They would always beat us in the Orange Bowl down there, and to beat them on their home turf was awesome.

Q: Anything else about that that bowl game stick out to you?

RH: Well, I just remember that old Orange Bowl, it had those old metal seats. And it was so loud in there, you know? It just had a mystique about it. I have to give Miami credit, it was tough to win down there. It was so old, and the announcer was the same guy, they had a heck of a thing going. The odds were against us. We were supposed to get their locker room because they weren't supposed to have their own, old locker room, and somehow they complained about it and we just said, "Screw it. We'll take the visitor's locker room and they can have their old locker", and there we go.

Q: Now tell me, how did you hook up with Tennessee after '97?

RH: We had beaten Florida in '95, so the Tennessee coaches came up and became friends with the Nebraska coaches. Well, I had Dan Young call those guys at Tennessee and say, "Hey, we've got a guy who wants to be a G.A." So I went down there and worked my butt off in the fall, and when David Cutcliffe left to become head coach for Old Miss he took the G.A. with him, so they hired me for the bowl game. So it's all about connections, who you know. So Nebraska coaches called Tennessee and that's how I got my opportunity.

It was the Florida State game, the national championship game, it was my first game as a graduate assistant coach and it was my main job to get personnel from Florida State. I was on offense before that and then I had to become a defensive guy now. I wanted to be a well-rounded guy, so I switched over to defense. I knew offense, but anyway I had to tell the defensive coordinator within 8 seconds what the personnel was in the game: how many running backs, how many tight ends, how many receivers. So my first game as a coach -like a main coach, in my mind- was in the national championship game and we ended up beating Florida State for the National Championship. And then, Paul, you look at the next year in '99, you know who we played? Nebraska that year, in the Fiesta Bowl!

Q: Oh man, I forgot about that!

RH: Now Nebraska beat us, and do you know what they made me do, Paul? You remember I'd played a little quarterback? Well, I had to go there for Tennessee during scout teams and play quarterback, because I was the only guy that knew how to do the correct steps. Now, I wasn't Eric Crouch, obviously. (laughs) But I was out there on the scout team playing quarterback, and that's probably why we lost. Because I was way out of shape and couldn't get it done, but at least I did the right footwork and everything. I did that for a majority of the time.

Q: Sounds like you're mirroring John Gruden's ascent in the coaching ranks, G.A.-ing at Tennessee, coaching at one team, then mirroring the old team as scout team quarterback in preparation for the Buccaneers winning the Super Bowl. I'm sensing flashes of upcoming greatness for you here…

RH: Well, it would be nice to have the chance to win in the big show some day. I'm only 34, so I'm not done yet.

Q: And that NU-Tennessee Fiesta Bowl game, wasn't it a Bobby Newcombe punt return that broke that game open?

RH: Yeah, it did. It was a 96 and a 99 yard drive that ended up really being the difference in the game, actually. We didn't play horrible, it was really a closer game, a play here or a play there and it might have been different. We did some good things, but there were two or three plays that broke our back.

Q: Let me ask you: differentiating Nebraska's organization from Tennessee's, anything stand out as far as likenesses, differences at that championship level?

RH: Well, the biggest difference was the walk-on program. Tennessee didn't believe in the walk-on program like the Nebraska team did. It was more about the scholarship kids. That year we had 9 guys drafted in the first two rounds. We should have won the national championship, talent-wise. To have 9 guys drafted in the first two rounds was unbelievable. A lot of guys, I think, were thinking about the NFL, and I think they came back a little fat and happy and weren't giving it their all like we did in '98 and beat Florida State. We ended up losing a couple games we shouldn't have.

That's why it's so tough to consistently win championships. You think you can just show up the next year and it happens, but it doesn't work that way. But the biggest difference was the walk-ons, and Tennessee was more into the prestigious, high profile recruits. But Nebraska was more into recruiting players that fit the system. So we never had recruiting classes ranked, but we won championships because we'd take guys like Joel Makovicka, a guy who the University of Florida wouldn't take in a hundred years, but was an unbelievable fullback for Nebraska. Does that make sense? We'd take kids that fit our system, and that was another reason we were successful, because we weren't into what a kid was ranked.

That's what happened to Bill Callahan. He was more into the top players in the country instead of finding the right players to fit his style. That's why you can have the #1 ranked class in the country, but that doesn't mean you'll win a national championship. Bill Callahan, at the end of the day, his deal was that philosophy and he didn't embrace the walk-on program like he should've. That really hurt him, I think. That's just my two cents.

Q: Any memorable practice occasions stand out to you?

RH: I remember it was when we were getting ready of the University of Oklahoma in '95 (we won 38-0 I think) Tommie's last game before the Heisman Trophy announcement. It was a Tuesday or Wednesday practice, it was cold, cloudy, night practice, and I just remember it was ones versus ones. And I just remember the offensive line and defensive line -maybe a defensive lineman got cut-blocked or whatever- but it was just a big old brawl. I'll never forget it. We had to stop practice.

There was always a ruckus, but this was a bad one. It was bad. I just remember that practice because it was so intense. We wanted to have another undefeated season and it was just a lot of intensity. We were playing Oklahoma, a big rival, and it was just a meltdown. I'll never forget that. And it was at the end of practice and everybody was just kind of watching. It got a little ugly. It was unbelievable.

Q: Anybody behind the scenes make a big impact, stand out to you?

RH: Mike Arthur. Boyd Epley was tremendous and gets a lot of credit, but Mike did a lot of research. And I believe, it's my understanding, he just prepared and found a lot of different cutting-edge things that not many people knew about. He didn't get a lot of credit, but just worked his butt off behind the scenes.

George Sullivan, too. It was great to have Sully. I'll never forget, it was probably my freshman or sophomore year and I dove for a ball, and one of the guy's cleats rolled up on my hand and ripped off three layers of skin and I'm over there bleeding and everything. Sully taped it up and, "Aw, hell, get back in there!" He didn't blink an eye, just taped it down, taped it up and said, "Come in after practice." That was all it took.

And Duke LaRue was a good guy, he was down in that freshman locker room. He was a guy who was down there, as a guy you could talk to and lean your head on if you had a tough day. He'd be taping you and have a soothing personality and help you through some things. He was great, as well.

Q: You talked earlier about the Tennessee guys getting a little fat and sassy and losing their edge, but we never seemed to do that. Any idea how that intensity was maintained?

RH: I don't think the coaches really let us. And the players didn't either. We had great leaders. Any great football program has great senior leadership, and teams that will consistently win have great leadership.

And Paul, I call it 'institutional control'. The coaches did their part, but if a guy missed a summer workout, there were guys ripping people's asses, "Why did you miss the summer workout?!" It's like a player's prison (and that's a bad analogy), but year in and year out the players ran their own institution. The players would not allow it to get fat and happy because you know when you're successful you want to keep being successful, and you knew that everybody was going to be gunning for you. It was the other team's Super Bowl, so the only team that stands out that we got truly upset was that Arizona State game down there. We were prepared, we had a week off before that game, we'd just pounded Michigan State, and we'd beaten Arizona State like 80-0 the year before, and then that week we had an average week of practice and they beat our ass. That's the only time during that era that we got upset.

And we got beat by Texas, but they were a pretty talented team with Priest Holmes and those guys. But the Arizona State game we kind of rested on our laurels and thought we could just show up and win because of the previous year's outcome. The week before the coaches kept saying, "Guys, this is a different team. Guys, they're gonna play." And we didn't listen. That was the only time I felt we didn't listen to the coaches and rested on our laurels.

Q: Now I have to ask you, any perks or privileges to being a Nebraska Football player apart from the other students?

RH: Just having (the) girls liking you if you're on the football team and all the typical stuff that happened on any campus. The perks, obviously: going to bowl games. While everybody was home we'd be in beautiful places, but just to put Nebraska on your resume was the biggest perk. Having Tom Osborne and Turner Gill and Ron Brown on your resume, that's the big perk to me. Someone else may say something different, but for me that was the big perk because you can't pay for that, you know? You can't pay for Tom Osborne to call and recommend you to get you a job.

Q: And speaking of that turnaround, what was it that you took from your time at Nebraska that helped with that turnaround?

RH: Work ethic and coming up with a philosophy and believing something. When we went in to Panhandle State we told kids, "You're going to be part of the biggest turnaround in NCAA history." It was a belief. Our kids believed in that and we had back to back winning seasons for the first time in 20 years there, and we turned it around in a place.... I could sit there and tell you about that place, that's a book in itself. It was unbelievable. But the work ethic and all those things, they just paid off. My Offensive Coordinator was Chad Stanley, he was with me the whole way in these turnarounds, and our practice schedule was the same as what we did at Nebraska. We tried to do the same things in a lot of different aspects at the worst program in America... and it worked for us.

Q: Anything we haven't touched on that set Nebraska apart those years?

RH: Boy, I just don't know if there will never be a five year era that can really match that many wins and championships. Just think, Paul, we were one field goal away from beating Florida State for a national championship. If we beat Texas in the Big 12 we play for another one. We could have almost won another one and played for another one in a five year period. That's unbelievable. I don't think it will ever be matched.

I will leave you with this: that '95 team was arguably the best college football team -team- ever assembled. In terms of having to stop us on offense and how good our defense was, I don't think anybody today or back in the day would ever have beaten us. That's what I think. I was a part of that football team.

End conversation.

In mid-conversation with Ryan, the first item that became apparent to me was that the 60 & 3 system was replicate-able, producing success at other schools as he and his sidekick Chad Stanley carried the HuskerMethod torch. Knowing this gives me hope that others might see some promise in the way the organization was run and that this book may perhaps enable them to glean some wisdom & insights for their own particular program. If this is you, reader, I wish you success. And I encourage you to read on, because it only gets better.

Of secondary note, it was very revealing to catch a glimpse of Ryan's teenage mindset as to the benefits of latching onto the system and learning its ins and outs from both an athlete's as well as a student's perspective, especially knowing that pro ball would not likely be a part of his future. Surely some naysayers and doubters down in Kansas thought he may have made a mistake in attending Nebraska, for he never became a game day star in his time. But he was a team star nonetheless, and that should never be forgotten. Why do I say this? Because his primary, profoundly meaningful contribution took place out of sight of the crowds as he weekly donned the mannerisms and talents of the likes of opponents Chad May, Jeff Handy, Kordell Stewart, Asheiki Preston, Todd Doxzon, Garrick McGee and Frank Costa, to name a few. To be named Scout Team Player of the Week four times in one season on a championship team of nearly 160 players is the Nebraska scout team equivalent of a Top-Secret Heisman Trophy. There were moments of scout team glory, something that shouldn't be dismissed.

Finally, there was his reference to the term 'institutional control,' and player leadership: "The coaches did their part, but if a guy missed a summer workout there were guys ripping people's asses." Now, (depending on which camp you reside in) one can go two ways with this: the negative angle would be to cast dark shadows and aspersions of a bullying, coercive, haranguing mood about the team, whereas the positive spin would entail a manly accountability and support structure dedicated to living as one's brother's keeper. However you label it, if results are what they intended, it was peer pressure at its very finest.

Notable quote #2:
Ryan Held on the Husker player experience: "It was tough from the moment you walked in to the moment you left, and there was no going against. And the thing that was nice was that you would see success in it and you could believe in it."

WANTED

Young, skinny, wiry fellows not over eighteen.

Must be expert riders, willing to risk death daily.

Orphans preferred. Wages $25 per week.

-Pony Express job advertisement, 1860

Although it lasted for only nineteen month's duration from April 1860 to November 1861, the historic and venerable Pony Express consisted of relays of mail-carrying men on horseback covering 2,000 miles of trail at breakneck speed, oftentimes traveling 250 miles in a day to and fro between California and Missouri. Its trail was a short stretch from the town of Lebanon, Kansas -a straight shot south of Red Cloud, Nebraska on Highway 281- and home to Chad Stanley, another fine example of the good crop of Kansas boys who contributed to the Husker's bountiful harvest of 1991's recruiting class.

This kid had giddyup and more in his satchel, having played a part in the great Smith Center Redmen high school football tradition. Later a player-cum-coach tag-team partner to Ryan Held (from the previous chapter), he still exudes a warm and engaging Midwestern persona, eyes lighting up at the mere talk of football, its strategy and lore. Though his pay was considerably less than even an Express rider back in the day, this non-scholarship walk-on reaped considerable capital in the kNowledge gained from his experience on Lincoln's campus. Let's listen in on Chad's gallop through those memorable 60 & 3 days and a quarter score more…

Notable quote#1:

"Tom was playing chess while everybody else was playing checkers. Tom was just always two or three steps ahead of everybody. All the converstions on the headphones, "If they do this we'll do that." He was just way ahead of the defensive coordinator."

Chad Stanley

Walk-on, Fullback, Lebanon, Kansas (Smith Center)
Where are they now? Kechi, Kansas, Upper Management

Question: You grew up south of the border in Kansas, right?

Chad Stanley: I'm from a little town in north central Kansas called Lebanon, Kansas. It couldn't be more in the center of the United States. As a matter of fact, the exact geographic center is 3 miles south of our house.

And Lebanon didn't have a high school. Smith Center was the high school. They had their kind of a football dynasty in the state of Kansas, so I was pretty blessed.

Q: You know, as a kid, whenever the weather would get nasty and inclement it seemed the TV weatherman was always mentioning Smith Center, Kansas.

CS: Oh yeah, in Lincoln there with Ken Siemek? Yeah, he always brings up Smith Center. They had the nation's longest winning streak in high school football. Quite a dynasty: they've won 67 in a row. I was kind of lucky, Paul, even before I got to Tom I had a great staff, a legendary one in high school.

Q: How did you end up at Nebraska?

CS: Well, it was kind of unique back then. My dad was a K-State grad. My uncles -neither of whom graduated from Nebraska- they were big Nebraska fans when I was growing up. (That was before Bill Snyder got to Kansas State. They weren't very good at football.) And when I was a child, from age 10 through 17, we went to a lot of games at Nebraska. We maybe missed only two or three home games in that span. We got all the Nebraska TV stations and knew all about Coach Osborne and respected him.

I went to the camps and I got to know the coaches really well, had some Division 1 scholarship offers. But like a lot of kids, a walk-on deal at Nebraska back then was better than getting a scholarship from half of Division 1 because you were treated so well, with a quality program. Financially, it wasn't as good, but the experience of being part of a championship program is what drew me to Nebraska.

Q: What position did you play?

CS: I played fullback. Played for Frank Solich.

Q: Your recollections of Coach Solich?

CS: Coach Solich? I will always remember him as the best running back coach in college football. He was tremendously detailed and a tough guy. When he played he wasn't a real big guy, but to this day he still lifts weights and he's stacked up. You can just see that he's a tough guy. And he instilled that in all of us players. We fought for every inch on the football field. There was no running out of bounds, as you know. Great technician, just a tremendous running backs coach. Also a tremendous coordinator up in the box during games. One thing he doesn't get enough credit for during the Tom Osborne era was when he was up in the box offering suggestions to Coach Osborne, which I got to see firsthand as a coach. He was really a good x's and o's guy up in the box. And they had some good box coaches; they could really disect a defense from up there, and he was very good at that. That's what I remember about Coach Solich.

Of course, we all know what a tough, tough transition that was to follow a legend. And he did a good job. He'll go down under-rated as a head coach in Nebraska history, but as head coach his winning percentage speaks for itself.

Q: Years from now people will look at the record & his firing and say, "What the hell were they thinking?"

CS: Exactly. It was an embarrassment, frankly. And I was very involved then as a GA. It's bad for the sport when a guy who wins over seventy-five percent of his games gets fired.

Q: When was your first fall camp?

CS: That class of '91, which was an interesting class. If you remember back then -of course you were there, Paul- that was coming off some seasons in '89 & '90 that were a little disappointing. There was a little strife, where the direction of the program was going (even though it was consistent with 9-3 every year), but Tom really made some changes that year we arrived: they started recruiting more southern athletes, they went to a 4-3 defense, and there was a higher caliber athlete started showing up from that fall forward.

And that was the class that I came in with Brook Berringer, who was my best friend in college there. We were roommates together, both from Kansas coming in together. Brook was a scholarship quarterback. There was Tony Veland, Clester Johnson, Brett Popplewell, some of those guys. That class of '91, it's funny, we'd sit around as a class. And we were just young bucks, you know? And I remember some of the leaders of that class like Aaron Graham, who were super-confident and saying, "In our career here we're gonna win 4 conference championships and a couple national championships." I remember guys saying that. Guys talk when they're young, and gosh darn, during our careers that exact thing happened.

And some of us weren't super contributors. I was never a starter or anything, but I was a contributor and went on to coach and stuff. But that was a special class. I'm really proud of coming in that year. It was happenstance and a blessing, but it kind of picked up to a different level starting in 1991.

Q: Did you know Brook before you arrived at the University?

CS: I had heard of Brook. In the state of Kansas there aren't a tremendous amount of seniors from the state who go to Division 1 football every year. Maybe 15 or so. I'd never met him, but when I signed my papers to walk on I called him after I heard this tall, gangly quarterback from Goodland, Kansas was going to Nebraska, and we became friends thereafter.

Actually, do you remember the trainer Duke LaRue? He used to call us "The Kansas Bus." He always used to say, "Here comes the Kansas Bus!" Brook really was a tremendous player, grew to be a big, young man through the strength staff and you guys. He could move, he could run and throw. I guess the Broncos told his mother they were gonna draft him that weekend he died in the plane crash. But we had a good time there.

Q: What stuck out about your first days on campus?

CS: Just kind of the guys I've mentioned. At my position you had Chris Norris, Jeff Makovicka, of course I knew Brook, and then there was Aaron Graham and Steve Ott in that class. Brett Popplewell joined us from Australia: very athletic guy, very underrated. Then you had Tony Veland. And this big pro wrestler guy, "Who's the pro wrestler-looking guy? Christian Peter?"

Christian deserves a lot of credit in changing the culture to a championship culture. That guy was a total competitor. He was a Charlie McBride guy, I'm telling you. The intensity level in practice going from the Peter brothers right up to Grant Wistrom? It was high when I got there. You had the Trev Alberts' of the world. There were good Blackshirt defenses, but hey, they grew to be *great* Blackshirt defenses. There were Doug Colman and Phil Ellis in my class, and I know I'm leaving some guys out, but we were a tight-knit class. It was a big class, back when you could sign 30 scholarship players, and Nebraska had a one up on the game because they'd bring 25 of us walk-ons, and out of a class that size you're gonna have some guys.

Q: Some guys may fall to injury or get lost along the way…

CS: It was brilliant what Coach Devaney and Coach Osborne devised, because as everyone knows, the population of Nebraska being one million and a half and its proximity to population centers, you had to do that.

Q: A numbers game in many respects?

CS: Bring in the numbers, get them in a good system and certain players are gonna pan out, and that way you cover your attrition. And there was attrition, but you had a solid base of guys at the end.

Q: What was it like for you? I assume you were in the North locker room with all the other freshman at first, right?

CS: Yeah, North locker room. And it was surreal those first meetings when Coach Osborne steps into that room. This was back when the freshman reported early. Of course, the rules kept changing (back then you had the 105 rule), but back then all of us freshman reported early. Walk-ons and scholarship guys, you're learning plays, it was a whirlwind. When Tom Osborne steps in the room it was a little surreal, like Clint Eastwood walks into the room from the Old West or something.

Q: That's so funny you say that. I think the older they get they're starting to resemble one another. Wouldn't it be great if a guy put together a movie about Coach Osborne's life and had Eastwood in the starring role?

CS: They do.(laughs) Kind of that look when they're looking into the sun… the High Plains Drifter look. They look smart and they look competitive, and they look like they're ready to eat you. (laughs)

From the first meeting on it was just crazy, because there are no pro teams in Nebraska and you go to the mall and every fan there knows who I am. A walk-on guy that's gonna redshirt that year and not gonna play, and everybody knows who you are. So it's a shock, because here you are under a legend, and then it's rock star status for you everywhere in Lincoln.

Q: Were there any perks to this rock star status?

CS: Sure there was. It opened so many doors for you. It's such a tight-knit community, and if you're a football player in the state it just opened doors for you. You might get to visit some needy kids at the hospital, or just things that the average student didn't get to do. It was just a blessing.

Q: So you're in that first meeting. Anything catch you off-guard?

CS: You knew it was special in how detailed it was and how much they threw at you the first few days. I came from a high school where we ran the wishbone and it was two or three plays you run to the right and two or three plays you run to the left and just dominate them. But this was so detailed. I remember that first week with Coach Solich going over the steps, "This is how you lateral step toward the guard," everything was so precise, all the main points.

And you look around the room, Paul, (the big adjustment to me was not the thinking part), but you get around all these great players from coast to coast? The speed of these guys! It was just a whirlwind. I was a tailback in high school, so I'm arcing out as a fullback to block these linebackers -and in high school it's no problem- but these guys, they go from sideline to sideline and it's a blur! And George Darlington has the safeties all lining up 10-15 yards deep, so they're in the backfield in a heartbeat! It was a different deal.

Q: High school on nitrous oxide, huh?

CS: The speed was incredible. They recruited a lot of kids who could run.

Q: How did Coach Solich teach toughness?

CS: He just instilled it in us by the way he carried himself. I mean, he was a tough guy. He was a caring guy, don't get me wrong, but he was a tough guy, like I said. Here was a guy in stature, maybe 5'7" 155 lbs., and he had Popeye forearms.

I remember the very first day we went out there in just helmets, no shells or half pads or anything. We're doing ISO blocks, and he wanted us to punch each other in the sternum. Chris Norris and I were paired up and about knocking the wind out of each other, we thought he was crazy. But there was a method to all the little things, you learn quick. Of course, I came from a physical program and knew this, but there was a difference between being injured and hurt. And Coach Solich expected you to go out there and practice hurt. Not injured, but hurt.

And you loved the way he would show the old tapes of Rozier and Rathman. We battled for every inch on the football field; you did not go out of bounds unless it was right before the half or a time-saving situation.

Q: The 'quit' isn't in you?

CS: We took it to defenders. People feared Nebraska backs because we were gonna do the lift drill and punch them in the sternum. I loved the story of Tom Rathman they used to tell, when he'd done the lift drill on an Oklahoma linebacker and broke his jaw. Just by doing the lift drill right into his chin! And Coach Solich was good at that, in instilling that toughness.

Q: I recall that old NFL video clip of Roger Craig running against the Rams and just driving and pushing and striving forward, high knees punishing those poor guys relentlessly for his yards...

CS: Yep, and I think Coach Solich was taught by Mike Corgan. And he was a tough guy, too. Frank was the freshman coach for awhile, and I think it was just passed on down the line. He was a character. I didn't meet Corgan, but I've heard the stories of him. When I went to coaching I heard stories about him. He was a tough guy.

Q: So you were a fullback. How long did you play then? The full four years?

CS: I played from '91 to '94 and actually could have played in '95, but Paul, I had a couple knee injuries: tore my ACL and MCL one year, and tore my MCL again. And you knew I wasn't ever a starter and wanted to coach, so I just jumped into it a year early as an assistant under Frank there and learned a lot. Got to be a student assistant on the '95 team.

Q: You can say you coached for the greatest college football team of all time...

CS: Yeah, no doubt, because that was an incredible year in a lot of aspects.

One thing I'll never forget from that year was the mood in the locker room before the Florida game. I have never seen nor will probably see again a more sure outcome in the pregame, even in the hotel. Just in the faces and the attitude and the determination. That was an organization that not only knew it was going to win a national championship, but decisively. That game was decided before it was ever kicked off. It was just an incredible mood.

Q: What contributed to that mood?

CS: Just the confidence that was built. Obviously, we'd won the national title the year before, and this team was putting up mind-boggling stats and stayed relatively healthy, because that year Tommie got to play all year. Now, we dealt with some of the off-field stuff that year, losing Lawrence Phillips, but as far as health? We, especially on defense, we stayed pretty darn healthy. So you had two waves of players who played in the NFL: not just the first team defensively, but the second team played in the NFL eventually.

Q: I think it was Bryan Bailey who once pointed this out to me, but do you recall that '95 spring practice when the second team actually beat the first team in the spring game?

CS: I always said, if people could have seen some of our Wednesday practices before Saturday -especially for that Oklahoma game- it was about the best game in the nation, I promise. Especially the goal line drill, because it was the ones versus twos and twos versus ones. We had the best talent in the nation on both sides of the ball two deep in the same program. Probably a lot like Bryan sees at USC now. Very similar.

Q: He actually tells those guys at USC that they couldn't hold a candle to those Husker teams. He readily admits that they have the talent but they're not as tough.

CS: There's too much to do out there in California. There really is. They're not as focused.

Q: Too many blondes, too much silicone…

CS: Too much Hollywood! (laughs)

Q: So you make the switch to coaching and probably spent time on the sideline and up in the press box during games?

CS: That first year as a student coach was very interesting, because I got to go up into the end zone during the games with the Graduate Assistant Coaches. It was with Mike Grant on offense and drawing the defenses during the game that would eventually get in front of Coach Osborne, so it was a really important job. Mike would watch the fronts and the 'backers and I might watch the secondary, and Tom would base his play calling off these drawings, so they had to be accurate.

I'll never forget, my first game ever as a coach was down at Stillwater, Oklahoma. A Thursday night game. (It was the debut of Terrell Farley, what a great player that guy was.) But we had these kids running down these cards to Coach Osborne, we'd get the spacing of the defense and everything. So I learned a lot of x's and o's that first year. I knew them as a player, but even as a student coach it picks up a whole other level; kind of a mentoring of me, being a young padawan, a young apprentice in '95. We had such a great offense and people were throwing the kitchen sink at us to stop us. I got to see a lot of junk on defense.

Q: Do you recall the most creative effort?

CS: Washington State played us the toughest that year. I think the final was 35-21. They had some good players, but they ran a bunch of line stunts and stuff that we hadn't worked on and it kind of messed up our option game. 35 points was still a good output, but we didn't score 70 like we had been, and everybody was disappointed in the locker room.(laughs)

It was always a challenge to face the Stoops brothers at K-State, they were pretty good defensive guys, we hadn't played them that year very well. Through those years we would beat them every time, but they were good coaches. It was a good challenge, they were very sound.

Q: So you're up in the end zone with Mike Grant…

CS: Yeah, and I did some work on the field in '95, too. And in '96 I kind of worked in the recruiting office and the film office, I was kind of waiting in the wings until Mike Grant was done with his GA shift and take over for him. So I'd do some administrative things and helped out in the office.

And in '97 through '99 I was a Grad Assistant with both Tom Osborne and Frank Solich, I was right in the heart of it during the transition and Tom's last year, winning it all for Tom. So I was there a long time. I was there for a decade, during the heart of the whole thing, '91 through 2000 both as player and coach.

Q: So, looking back on it, what do you think really contributed -aside from the talent being one thing, because some other teams in America had talent, too- but what played a major part from your freshman year to your senior year?

CS: I think that some of the fringe things that Nebraska did so well was cutting edge. Obviously, as you experienced yourself, Boyd had a cutting-edge strength program. It was ahead of the game in the '80's and through the '90's, revolutionary in the early '90's. I believe we had a head up on everyone else in the strength and conditioning part of it. We developed players from really good athletes to great athletes.

We had the walk-on program that gave us a leg up, and the continuity of the coaching staff can't be underestimated. Tom was a unique guy to be able to blend a lot of personalities together. You know the guys: there were some different guys from different lifestyles and liked different things. Of course, we all do. And of course coaches have egos, we all do. To blend all that together into a common theme of teamwork and exceptional coaching? And back then it wasn't like today where coordinators were bolting for a head job, and they felt loyal to Nebraska. And quite frankly, part of that run being a coordinator at Nebraska was better than being a head coach at most places. And they were paid well and were supported -not like now- but back then Tom did what he could for them and kept them.

And I think along with keeping the coaches together, keeping the system together, they had that academic program with Keith Zimmer and Dennis Leblanc and all that. And the training table was second to none. Just all the fringe things, they all played a part in creating a championship atmosphere. It wasn't just football. We wanted to have the most academic All-Americans, we wanted to set strength records. It was constantly creating a culture of achievers. And when you're creating a culture of achievers among a group of young men you can accomplish great things. That was the Devaney/Osborne program they created, and it really morphed itself in the '90's when they recruited some athletes from Florida and Texas and Louisiana, beating the southern schools on athletes, becoming a national recruiting power and getting the type of speed in there, with the type of offense we ran, a multi-purpose quarterback.

There won't be another decade like it in college football. I don't the think the NCAA would allow it. There's a lot more parity -some schools like USC and Oklahoma- but you can't do it, the scholarship limits, with Title IX and the budgets, it's tougher now. It really is.

Q: Can you delve a little more into the staff dynamic in the meetings?

CS: That was an education for a young man who was only 25-27 years old. I consider these guys to be legends. I have already talked about Frank, how good he was as an assistant head coach, then there was Turner Gill and Ron Brown on the offensive staff. Does God make a finer man than those two? They're beautiful human beings, men of faith, they know the game, they're charismatic. They oozed character. And I sat by those two every day and learned from them. I was actually under Ron's tutelage coaching the tight ends. I got to spend a lot of time with him grading film and getting to know him. Tremendous position coaches who had interests outside of football. They were balanced.

And because I worked with the tight ends I often got to work with the offensive line and Milt Tenopir and Dan Young a lot, too. Milt Tenopir, we kind of called him the 'social chair' of the coaching staff. He really had a gift. Ron Brown said it best in one of the morning bible studies where he was talking about the gifts that they possessed, and Milt Tenopir really had a gift of making high school coaches and outside people feel warm and welcome in our program. He was really a social guy. A tremendous offensive line coach: there's never been a finer one in college football. Tremendous technician, and again, game planning every week. I'm telling you what, Tom is brilliant, but a lot of that stuff? A lot of the ideas from the inside were Milt's. I'm telling you, Milt could look at the grease board and really dissect a defense. In that interior box -the ball between your five or six against their seven or eight- how you could dissect and beat them? Milt was really good at that.

Dan Young helped on offense, of course, and he did a great job of running our summer camps. The joke about Dan was that he recruited the best athletes on the team at punter.(laughs) Here we had one year, the #1 pick in the Major League draft was our kicker and punter, Darin Erstad! And then he's got Bill Lafluer who can do a 360 degree dunk from the baseline on the basketball court. And then later on he recruits Kyle Larsen, who threw the shot put 60 feet in the State of Nebraska high school track meet. So Dan had a tremendous gift for spotting those athletes. Kris Brown in the NFL, Josh Brown, a skinny kid from Oklahoma who comes up. That's the funny thing about that decade, we used to joke, "Even our kickers and punters were better athletes than other team's safeties." I mean, the kickers and punter sometimes on Thursdays would have their touch football games, and they were more athletic than most teams' secondaries!

Just the great dynamic on the offensive staff, Tom was really involved with that. Tom was playing chess while everybody else was playing checkers. Tom was just always two or three steps ahead of everybody. All the conversations on the headphones, "If they do this we'll do that." He was just way ahead of the defensive coordinator. It wasn't just better players, it was strategy.

Especially on defense. You had some characters on defense. I just loved Charlie McBride and George Darlington. They were always getting after each other at the meetings. It was like two old wizards going after each other, it was comical. Charlie was just a classic. He was perfect for Nebraska football and encompassed what Nebraska football should be. He loved the kids; no one loved their kids more than Charlie McBride. He'd hug them around the neck, pray with them before the game, cry with them when they'd graduated. This guy loved his players and they loved him. There was a respect there.

And George Darlington, he was just a classic. He was a good box guy up in the press box. George could come up with 40,000 different coverages, seriously. In fact, George's brain sometimes would work too fast for what we were doing. He was such a genius on the board, he was almost ahead of the college coaches. Tom would have to reign him in, because the guy could x and o. He'd come up with more creative things on the greaseboard -and remember, Paul, we only had 20 hours per week to learn the stuff- so Tom had to reign him in now and then.

Some different defensive end coaches? Tony Samuel was such a good technician and coach, he had so many guys go to the NFL. I remember working with Tony in a football camp once; I was amazed at how good a technician he was on using your hands, a good teacher. And after Tony we got a coach from the University of Texas, Nelson Barnes. He became a good friend of mine, a jovial guy. He did a really good job caring about the kids.

The linebacker position? I got to experience both Kevin Steele and Craig Bohl. Kevin Steele, the old southern drawl and intense guy (you didn't know how to take Kevin when you were a young guy). He'd kind of do the old coaching/hazing thing on the players when you were young, but he was a guy of faith, tough guy, great technician teaching linebackers. He left to take another spot and Craig Bohl took his place, and Craig was a former walk-on and native Nebraskan, and did a good job later on.

I tell you what, Paul, what a staff. And here I was the youngest guy on the staff. And here's Jon Bostick, my officemate, was the defensive GA. Jon was a few years older than I. Funny,

Jon was a receiver when he played, but he was on the defensive side of the ball under George.

And I have to say something about Jon. We're good friends. Jon Bostick is one of the best coaches I've ever been around. If a Division 1 program handed me the keys tomorrow Jon Bostick and Ryan Held would be the first guys I would call. Jon, when I was coaching with him? I thought he was a fine coach, a good talent evaluator. What was cool, Paul, when we were assistants, they kind of let us run the walk-on program. I went full circle, because I got recruited as a walk-on, played as a walk-on, and now they're giving us film and letting us pretty much evaluate potential walk-ons and giving them the thumbs up or the thumbs down. They let Jon and I take all the tapes and call the coaches. It was kind of our own little deal, they let us run with it. Dan Young was in charge, but the experience at talent evaluation was incredible. But like I said, Tom blended all those egos and all the coaching staff's different personalities into one theme, and it worked. It just worked.

Q: Any notable disagreements? Anybody get hot under the collar?

CS: There was, like any staff or organization that's competitive and exchanges ideas. Sure, there were some heated staff meetings. So many funny things happened. We'd spend so much time together.

I'll never forget one morning -and we had those morning bible studies. A couple funny stories I'll tell you about staff meetings: we look over and hear this buzzing noise, and here is George shaving over there. (laughs) George must have been running a little late, and here in the bible study we hear this noise and look over and here George has this electric razor, whiskers flying up and everywhere. It was classic. Ron Brown and Turner Gill, when they talk about it, they cry from laughing so hard. And George didn't think anything of it. And Tom kind of gives him a look like only Tom can, gave George a look, "George, *what* are you doing?" (laughs)

I'll tell you another one on me. We had this big, long, round staff table, and at the head of the table was the end of the room... and Tom would *never* sit there. So they kind of put me at the head of the table. (laughs) Tom would always sit in the middle. And it happened back then, with that decade, it was the beginning of the use of computers (and some of those guys were kind of leery about using them), and that's when the internet was really starting to come into play in our society. I'm the young buck and I know how to operate a computer, so Coach Osborne asks me to bring up the Tennessee roster on the computer. So I'm at the head of the table and we're doing our bible study and we had the internet in there at the time, and Tom told me since I was the research guy, "Why don't you pull up their depth chart and we'll go over it after the bible study?" (And back then, if you remember, things would download kind of slowly.) Well, we're right in the middle of our prayer, Paul, and as I download the Tennessee website it says, "Rockytop will begin playing in 5..4..3..2.." (laughs) Here I am, frantically trying to push every button I could find and nothing was stopping it! And all of a sudden, in the *middle* of the prayer? It blasted: "Nah nah nah nah, nananhannana..!" the Rocky Top Tennessee theme song. (laughs) We were praying and it was just *blaring* Rockytop! That was quite a laugh, they got quite a laugh out of it. Here Tom's praying...(laughs)

And I'd be remiss if I didn't bring up the film guys: Brian Mohnsen, Bryan Carpenter, Dave Finn and those guys. They did such a great job. Then we eventually got HuskerVision, Jeff Schmall and those guys. MaryLyn was the secretary and then Joni; just the stability, the support staff, Director of Football Ops. Dave Gillespie, and then Al Papik and Chris

Anderson and Curt Thompson and Pat Logsdon? We had a good strength staff, too. It was just a well-rounded, well-oiled machine for a decade. I saw a lot for ten years.

Q: Let me ask you, Chad, what was it like making that transition from player to coach?

CS: It was little tough that first year as a student-coach, because some of my peers were still playing; that caused some friction that first year. It was tough for them to view me as the coach, because Frank would give me drills to do as a coach.

And I'll never forget this, a little story: you know the coaches would go out recruiting some Thursdays and Fridays in the fall and we'd have practice with Tom and a few assistants there. Well, one time Frank went back to New Jersey to recruit some guys and he gave me a list of drills to give these guys. And you know, they're banged up and sore -I knew what that was like- and they were grumbling. But Frank gave them to me to do them, and someone said, "Shut up! Chad's going to be the coach today and we're going to do the drills." And do you know who it was? It was Lawrence Phillips. It just shut everybody up and they went through the drills. And I've never forgotten that.

And of all the issues and trouble and different things that Lawrence experienced in his life, until that one incident he was a tremendous practice player. He was a warrior.

Another quick Lawrence story: the year I blew my knee they were having a little bit of hazing and stuff in the locker room. They were doing some stuff and I had my crutches, but that didn't stop them. They'd get you in the shower and grab you and haze you pretty good. It wasn't bad -not that bad - but they were gonna grab my crutches and take hold of me, and Lawrence stood there and said, "No one's touching him." And that was the end of it, nobody grabbed me or anything. I'll never forget that. He put a stop to it. That's the Lawrence I remember. He was a warrior and a good teammate, he really was.

But getting back to your question: it was a hard transition, but after that you've created a little bit of separation as you started getting older than some of the guys (because the guys you played with were gone), then the players started respecting you. And by the time I was 27 yrs old there? By the time I left you had a lot of respect from the players and you were kind of a veteran then.

Q: You were one of the wise, old geezers by then?

CS: I was on the Jedi Council. (laughs)

Q: Do you remember the first game you played in?

CS: Yeah, I do: it was against UCLA. It was a nationally televised game and at home there, and we just drilled them. We really drilled them. It was one of those games where at the end everyone's trying to stand around Coach Osborne to get in. And we go in and call a play, and Brook was in with me. We got into the game at the same time, so that was kind of cool. And I got to carry the ball against UCLA: it was a fullback dive and I got maybe 3 yards. So it was really cool to be out there and gain some game time.

And that was another positive about being in a program like Nebraska, because even if you were young and not first or second on the depth chart, you knew you were going to play in the games. Because we were thumping people so bad everybody got to play. That was a bonus then, too.

And you know, one of the things about the coaching: I'll never forget '97, the year Tom announced when was gonna retire, the extra effort that staff put in to win that title for him.

I'll never forget that. We worked a little longer, we worked a little later. Not that every T wasn't crossed and every I dotted than before, but it was extra effort to get Tom that title.

Q: Was that a year long effort, or just the title game there?

CS: I think once he announced it there in November.

It actually came as a shock. Once he announced it there were a few games there. And the Tennessee game? There was just a tremendous effort from that staff to win it for Tom. And it took a lot of that to win it for Tom, because it took a lot of that from the players and coaches.

The '97 team was very good, don't get me wrong, but not as dominant as the other ones. We got that lucky bounce-kicked ball against Missouri- there were things that were divine, no doubt about it.

And I'll never forget the transition from Tom to Frank. I picked up Frank Solich at the airport when he was gonna be named head coach. Tom had announced it, and I'll never forget picking Frank up. I said, 'Are you ready for this?' And he said, "I'm gonna need all your help." (laughs) We knew the task of, the weight going onto a guy following a legend. Obviously, the knowledge was there, the experience, but to get the keys turned over to you there? That was quite a big deal. And the expectations at Nebraska are second to none. Just the transition was interesting.

Q: Was there some staff grumbling, a schism?

CS: I think everyone all along thought it was gonna be Frank just because Frank had been named Assistant Head Coach before. I think Frank went after that K-State job but Bill Snyder got it, went after the Kansas job, the Minnesota job. He was being sought after in college football, no doubt about it, and everyone on the staff thought he was the natural next guy.

Among the fan base you always heard if it should be this guy or that guy. There's no right answer when you follow Tom. There were so many good choices after that, you could have named about anybody. It was an interesting transition, and then in the end the new administration thought it wasn't good enough. That's too bad, I guess 80% is not good enough.

Q: As a player, do you have a most memorable game?

CS: I didn't play in it, but my favorite has to be Tom winning his first title there down in Miami. That was really the last game I was a player. I didn't get to play in that game, but it was my last as a player. All the hard work, all those years, all those close calls for Tom, back in '84 against the Canes and all that, the out of bounds stuff with Penn State in '82, and with Oklahoma, getting so close so many times. The year before with Florida State. It was just like a big weight lifted off the program. It finally happened, and to be the team there with a stadium half full of Husker fans down in the Orange Bowl? Half the fans were Nebraskans.

And I still remember to this day, the people grabbing grass off the field as mementos. It wasn't even like it was a game, but more like a battlefield, and all the honor that goes with that. And the locker room afterward? Just the release that was going on there.

And there were some other ones there, Paul, that some people probably forget about, but we had some of the first night games ever on ESPN in '93. If you remember, back to back Saturdays we had KU and Colorado. And that stadium literally shook on those night games because, of course, the students and fans had all day to get lubed up. I'll just never forget those two night games in '93 when we started to really become a Top 3 power. Not just a Top 20 power, but a national power. When we scored 50 points on these two top-rated teams, I'll just never forget the stadium and how it actually shook.

Q: Was one of those night games versus Colorado, was it snowing or something?

CS: It was pretty cold, and if you remember earlier in the game Trev Alberts had a safety and Travis Hill picked one off for an interception for a touchdown, they were just hammering Koy Detmer. That's back when Nebraska/Colorado was a pretty heated thing back then. It wasn't a respect rivalry like Oklahoma/Nebraska. It was kind of chippy back then, (laughs) there wasn't a lot of 'like' between the two programs back then.

Q: And speaking of that Miami game again, any other things stand out to you being on that sideline, pregame, postgame?

CS: Well, I probably have the same recollection a lot of the fans do, in that I was absolutely shocked that these south Florida athletes and that heat like they were used to, they were on their knees sucking gas in the 4th quarter. We all remember Warren Sapp on his knees sucking air. Warren Sapp had an awesome first half, and then Brenden Stai and those guys trapping him -even though they were well conditioned and great athletes- but we'd never been down in that heat.

Q: If you remember, as soon as a play was over it seemed the offensive line were actually sprinting to the line of scrimmage to get the ball snapped again...

CS: Yeah, and just the feeling on the sideline as it's transpiring, realizing that we're finally gonna get this done, after all those close calls, like the year before against Florida State: we kind of had a miracle drive to get it down there but Byron's field goal was just wide. And knowing they were to run out of gas?

But how vintage was it to beat them with a fullback play and Cory Schlesinger? Now *that's* Nebraska football. It wasn't a 4-wide post pattern, it wasn't even an option play, it was a fullback trap! And that statement was Tom Osborne-football there.

Q: With Matt Shaw and Abdul Muhammad throwing the biggest blocks of their lives on that play?

CS: Yeah, and how about Ron Brown's Mighty Mites out there that decade? Unselfish guys that were feared. We'd go into the stadium and the secondary would just fear these little ninjas out there. They were like assassins. Seriously! They wanted people-knockdowns! You'd hear Ron Brown talk about knockdowns; they'd go for 10 a game, that was just unheard of!

I remember seeing some All-Big 12 safeties -I remember one from KU- he was just laughing at our sideline. It wasn't a mocking laugh, it was a funny laugh like, "You guys are just *killing* me." It was almost to the point where he asked us to call off the dogs.

And another thing: against Tennessee in that national championship game in '97? I remember Leonard Little, their All-American linebacker, I remember him actually walking over to Charlie McBride in the 4th quarter and he said, "Call off the dogs, Coach. Call off the dogs," I'll never forget that. Tennessee had had enough. I saw him say it.

Q: And as a coach, any most favorite game?

CS: It was cool once I got to be a GA because I got to go up to the box. Then I was in charge of the drawing and had to get the cards to Coach Osborne or Coach Solich. It was neat to see, especially when we got to see the development of a young, eventual Heisman Trophy winner: a young Eric Crouch. He was just coming onto the scene in my last years there. It was neat to watch from the box, the defensive alignment, because you knew the way they'd line up sometimes. You'd say in the headphones, 'This is gonna be touchdown.' And it would be. It was amazing. From that high up you could tell the alignment and the way they were going to block it, you just knew. It was neat being up there and being with Milt and those guys and see a play and see what we'd work on in practice, and you knew Eric was gonna score. You knew they didn't have enough people for the angles to catch him, the way our set was lined up.

One play I'll never forget was at Iowa. Remember that year Eric Crouch ran over their safety at the goal line? That was a super-hot day. Their press box facilities aren't very good and we're all crowded into one on like the 10-yard line. And we had some bigger coaches, so it was pretty full-on sweating on that day, we were just crammed in there. But Eric running over that safety was a good one. It was a great time.

Q: Any memorable practice occasions?

CS: I got one for you, this could be practice –slash- summer camp story. You probably remember… in fact, we had a little nickname for Coach Osborne. We called him "Charlton Heston-Moses" behind his back. He wasn't afraid of lightning. I remember Ron Brown telling me, "Now, you watch out for Coach. He's not afraid of lightning. He'll just keep on rolling." I remember one time (and you might remember this practice, Paul), stretching and whatever, there was a squall line of thunderstorms came into Lincoln there. And of course, Moose and Carp, the video guys, were up on this big lift getting ready to film practice, and we'd heard of this severe thunderstorm warning for Lancaster County. And Tom was like, "Nah, let's keep going." And I'm not kidding you, Paul, there must have been a straight line of wind hit at about 70 miles per hour and lightning is just hitting everywhere around those big light poles… and of course Tom wants to keep practicing, keep going! Eventually some of the assistants and some of the players start making their way toward the locker room. (laughs) It was like being on top of a mountain, with lightning crashing everywhere. Those guys up on these lifts? I was like, 'My gosh, either they're gonna get blown over or struck by lighting.' Lightning didn't scare Coach Osborne.

And one time during a summer camp we were doing quarterback drills, throwing out of the end zone, and we were near the goalposts (those things were metal back then). And I had one of my buddies up from Smith Center coaching, they were doing 5 step drops, and all of a sudden a lightning bolt hits the press box! And I'm not kidding you, Coach Osborne didn't even hesitate. Without blinking an eye Coach Osborne just claps his hands and squinted like he does and said, "Okay, boys, lets just move this drill out a little ways from the goalposts." He kept going! He kept going after lightning had hit the press box. (laughs)

Q: Now, there's a man secure in the knowledge of his salvation…

CS: That's why we called him "Moses," like the Ten Commandments. I can just see him holding up his clipboard and getting struck.

There was another one: this is in the early '90's and Ryan Held likes to tell this one. You know they used to put these trash cans around Memorial Stadium there on a Friday or something? Well, nobody had cleaned them out. And for some reason there happened to be a ton of bees around Memorial Stadium that day. It was like a sweats practice on Thursday or Friday, and all of a sudden there were guys running around acting odd and everything… because these bees were getting into guys' helmets! And it was just annoying Tom to death, because he wanted to stay on track, and he kept saying, "C'mon guys, don't pay attention to those bees! Just stand still!" I remember Clester Johson saying, "I ain't standing still!" (laughs)

Q: Any memorable off-field stuff worthy of repeating?

CS: Well, you know, Coach Osborne you know -it's funny, he seems so stern to the public- but he could really hold his head back and laugh. Ryan Held? I'll tell this at his expense, but one summer Ryan was working for Coach Solich as his Undergrad Coach, and I was the GA so he kind of worked under me. And he had a girl he was dating and he kinda got dumped. Well, Ryan came to a couple of meetings looking like he hadn't shaved or even maybe showered. And Ryan was sitting across the table from Coach Osborne (and he was maybe thirty seconds late and looked all disheveled and kind of rough), and Tom looked at him and said, "Ryan, what's wrong?", as Tom can. And Ryan just looked him straight in the eye and said, "Got dumped, Coach." And I tell you what, that tickled Tom, and he threw his head back and he must have chuckled for a whole five minutes. And here's poor Ryan, heartbroken, and Tom Osborne threw his head back and laughed. He thought that was the funniest thing: just the way Ryan said, "Got dumped, Coach." They obviously knew Ryan was having a hard time, but it kind of made everyone loosen up. (laughs)

Q: Can you give me more info about Carp and Moose and the roles they played for the coaches?

CS: Yeah, I got to spend a lot of time with them later in my career. Earlier in my career Bryan Carpenter helped out with coaching a little bit sometimes, and he got to coach me a little bit, worked with him in some summer camps. And later in '96 when I was helping out in the recruiting office and the film office I got to spend some time with Moose and Carp. Great guys. They knew the game, that's what helped them as a film crew. They had played there, they knew the game, they each knew what they wanted on each side of the ball.

Carp was the offensive film guy and Moose was the film guy for Charlie McBride and the defense. They knew what the coaches wanted, they knew what to look for. They cut up the films appropriately, and that was a pretty big deal. I mean, when you get these films in in real time and you're preparing for the next game it's obviously a time crunch, and they need to be dissected and chopped down and spliced. And these two guys, (Bryan) Carp (Carpenter) and (Brian) Moose (Mohnsen)? Because they had played the game and knew the coaches and they'd played for the coaches they weren't just a couple of film guys who came in. They knew the game and I think that sped up that process, Paul, at least two-fold. They were guys who could just help out administratively: summer camps, you name it. They filled needs and were a great film crew. How many guys have been a film guy for awhile and now they're a Division 1 assistant? That says something about Moose, there.

Q: I'm thinking that must have been a great education from both scheme and talent evaluation standpoints?

CS: Oh sure. And quite frankly, we all wanted to be full-time assistants there. There's only so many slots, but those two could have been full-time assistants. Bryan Carpenter knew the game, he was an excellent fullback himself, a Kansas guy himself. They loved to ride motorcycles together and they were a big part of the social aspect, too, keeping things loose. They were an integral part. I spent a lot of time back there as a GA, film and how it was cut up, and it was interesting to see the new technology we got in.

That was something, too, the new film breakdown machines, how the technology really revolutionized during those ten years, how we used computers to splice all the film. Then dvd's became a part of it. It was pretty amazing.

Q: Now, correct me if I'm wrong, but did the NCAA put some limits on what we could do with the film portion of the game?

CS: I don't know if they did on the film end of it. What's funny is the coaching staff size -as far as what could be designated as coaches and what could be designated as recruiters-really shrunk during that decade. When I arrived in '91 Carp was kind of being a coach and Gerry Gdowski was helping out, and they had a coaching staff of like 15 to 20 guys. And by the time I left, it was just the full-timers and me and Jon and some student assistants. But it was just 12 adults and that was it. You had twelve adults responsible for 150 guys.

Q: Who else was with you as a student assistant then?

CS: We had Chad Young, he was a defensive back from Omaha. Damon Schmadeke, Merritt Nelson from Fremont, they were some of the guys that were student assistants along with me.

Q: Tell me a little more about Brook. It hurts me not to be able to interview him for this…

CS: Yeah, what a special human being in my life. I mean, we were a couple of kids grew up in rural Kansas areas and liked to fish and hunt and had that in common. Just kind of went through a lot together as roommates. Especially that first year as college freshman do: all the anxieties and fears and changes going on in your life, and we got to share those. And you know Brook had lost his father when we was young, and we used to stay up late and talk about that. My family, when the Berringers weren't around, kind of took him under their wing a bit. When they weren't around, I took Brook home for Easter one time.

He was a tremendous person, he taught me a lot. We were really close and had tons of things in common coming from Kansas. It was a heartbreaker, because in college he was my best friend, no doubt about it. He lived life to the fullest, because he was always on the go doing things. He was a pilot, he liked to hunt and fish, he was great in the community going to schools and such, talking to kids. He was a competitor and he was a great teammate to everybody. Most schools? If he'd have gone to a Kansas or Kansas State he would've started for 3 years.

He didn't get to play a whole lot, and he backed up a legend, Tommie Frazier, during his tenure there. But he stuck with it and he really… the type of quarterback he was? Probably, to be honest with you he would have fit another system better -but he was mobile enough to do Tom's offense, no doubt about it. Great thrower, very accurate passer, strong arm, a Tom Brady-type. He was gonna be a third or fourth round pick.

He was so skinny when he pulled up as a freshman. He pulled up in a Mustang, and Brook always drove in such a hurry, like his hair was on fire. (laughs) He was late to the first dorm meeting, he slid up sideways going 70 coming in from the I-80. He was 190 then and by the time he left he was 230 lbs. He was a man. But a good student, a smart guy. He was gonna be a pilot someday, and as the outpouring of grief and support showed, he kind of epitomized what was good about Midwestern life and character and hard work and what a Nebraska football player should represent, down to its core. Not just football, but off the field, as well, being a good student and all. He was kind of like Clark Kent back then. He was larger than life.

Q: You know what's funny, Chad? A few years after the accident I'm sitting on a cross country flight and I notice this gal on the asile seat is looking at me kind of oddly. I'm wearing my '95 National Championship ring at the time and she says to me, "I've seen that ring before." And I said, 'Really? Are you sure?' (Because at the time I was flying out of San Diego and on to Dallas) And she said, "Yeah, you went to Nebraska." Surprised, I replied to her, 'How'd you know that?!' And she said, "I'm Brook Berringer's sister." It was Nicole, I believe, and she had this beautiful little baby girl next to her in the middle seat between us. And she said, "Her name is Brooke." I almost cried a tear when I heard it, seeing that beautiful little girl with the same name. It was touching.

CS: It really reverberated around college football for awhile. He was really popular among the College Game Day crew when they came around. And we all became really good friends with Mark Miller and Sawyer Brown and they wrote a song about it and it was really a legendary deal. And Paul, his death, because he was such a person of faith? We'd heard about the outpouring of people who were reevaluating their lives. (Because Husker football can kind of become a religion in and of itself) It made a lot of people look back and realize there's more to life than this.

Q: But a great life, nonetheless. And I'm not sure if you've heard the story, but Kyle Orton, the old Purdue quarterback who played for the Bears and the Broncos and KC, I guess he wore number 18 because he was such a huge fan of Brook. Did you know that?

CS: Yeah, I was thinking about that when he went to the Broncos. It's kind of neat in a way, it's almost like it was Brook out there.

Q: What about anyone else behind the scenes who you feel had a big influence on the teams of those years, who've never gotten their due?

CS: I know one guy who needs some due: it's Jack Stark. Not a lot of people back then had a sports psychologist. It's kind of touchy-feely to what you'd consider warrior-men.

When they started that Unity Council and I got there in '91, there was actually some racial tensions on the field. It wasn't bad, but it wasn't good. It wasn't positive toward the chemistry of the team, but once they started that Unity Council and Jack counseled these players? This was about the time we started seeing a lot of guys from some broken homes and some bad backgrounds and didn't have any family, and Jack kind of took them under his wing and counseled them through college and talked them through their problems. And we could go to him about anything.

He deserves a lot of credit during that run, and in fact I became close to Jack and served on the Unity Council and helped ramp that up when I was the GA. That was really neat, and Jack knew enough about sports, had been around enough sports -and not to paint all psychologists with a broad brush- but he wasn't the typical psychologist. He 'got' the athlete, and could deal with that ego and bring 'em down to real people. He's a special guy that the fans may not remember.

Another guy who played an integral part and we were all close with was the cook at the training table, Art. Art, we always said, could pick a boot up off the highway and barbecue it and make it taste good. Art was always good with the players. It wasn't just good food, he was good with the players, good for morale. You might have had a tough practice or tough game, and Art was always smiling. The players were always respectful towards Art and he understood the importance of that food part, the nutrition part, the strength and conditioning and all that, he made it good, simple. Him and Dave Ellis working together, just a tremendous job. They had a knack for finding championship people. There were a few drifting through in the ten years who didn't cut it, but I couldn't even name them, they weren't there very long. (laughs)

And of course, the strength guys: Bryan Bailey and Randy Gobel and you? Great people, great technicians. We were taught the right technique, and we didn't know we were pushed. But you guys were real, too. It wasn't like Sports Illustrated portrayed us: just some factory.

And even though there were broad strokes to the program, it was individualized, too. I didn't have the same workout as Jason Peter. It was unique.

Q: If you could pin something down that you're most proud of during your time there, what would it be?

CS: Probably the thing I'm most proud of is just being there a decade, a part of something so special, so unique. Championships and making so many friends and gaining so much knowledge, getting a couple degrees out of there, Paul, a Bachelors Degree and a Masters Degree.

I always wanted to walk out those big red doors… it's different now, but remember those big red doors at South Stadium? Well, I always said, 'When I walk out of those doors for the final time, I want to do it with my head high and say, 'I did it all, accomplished all I could." And I wasn't a great ballplayer or anything, but I feel like I maximized my opportunity there as a player and being on Coach Osborne's last staff. That was a special thing. And the main thing is that you can call a guy like Tom Osborne your friend, now. He was a legend that first meeting and, in the end when you walk out the doors, he's your friend.

Q: Your last game coaching there?

CS: That would have been against Tennessee in the 2000 Fiesta Bowl after the '99 season. And Ryan Held and I were on opposite sides, because he was at Tennessee then.

And we could see each other. During the game he was one box over, so we could see each other during the game. And we had a bet: at the end of the game the other one would come out of the box and give the other his fitted cap. I thought, 'Your cap's cool.' (He had a fitted Tennessee cap.) And he never said a word after the game: He had John Chavis behind him and the other coaches coming out of their press box -they weren't too happy- and he just reached out his cap and gave it right to me. (laughs) So I got his brand new, fitted bowl cap. I still have it, from the 2000 Fiesta Bowl.

Q: And then where'd you go?

CS: Well, 2000 I was around there that next season. They indicated there may be an opening for me, so I hung around and helped run the recruiting department, breaking down film, doing some administrative things, help with Pat Logsdon, helped organized the recruiting girls who showed the families around, I worked with them.

Q: Oh, you poor guy…

CS: Yeah, what a tough job. And then Ryan Held got a job at Peru State, and that's when I started to see the friction between the athletic department: of course that would have been Steve and Coach Solich. And when the AD and your head coach don't get along and you're the youngest guy on the staff? When the music stops you're not gonna have a chair to sit on. I could kind of see the crack in the foundation even though there were a couple of seasons before all that happened. But I didn't want to be without a job, so I went with Ryan and we had a great time coaching at Peru State.

Q: I can imagine. It would be a shame to see all that knowledge go to waste and not be shared with the kids out there…

CS: I know. And it's funny, being 36 years old I recently got together with a local high school staff on the greaseboard putting some defenses up, and all those mentoring sessions from Osborne and the coaches -the Tenopirs, the Browns, the Gills, McBrides- all come back to you. You can share this knowledge and it's applicable to you today. You can help win football games. It will be eternal, as far as football knowledge. I always tell people there was nothing special about me, I was just a sponge for a decade. I just soaked it all up and I can complete a sentence and I can transfer knowledge. And that's what I'm doing with the young kids again.

Q: Is there one overriding philosophy that you carry with you from those days?

CS: Well, and this kind of comes from my Smith Center background. The game of football today has changed so much, it's almost become basketball on grass, everyone's out in space. It's pretty soft football, from what I grew up with. And Barry Switzer even says it down here where I live, "You can still run the offenses of the Switzer era, the Tom Osborne era." And Smith Center still runs it. They're 67 and 0, it's just not as sexy to these kids. You can still run them, but it takes a special toughness to run these offenses. And I think if you can get a group of kids to believe in them and run them in 21st century life, it will teach them more than some of this other stuff. I almost feel like it's gone to "Hollywood football".

I feel that Nebraska football taught you real life. It was toughness. It was 'only the best survive.' I think you can still do that today with kids, they need that more than ever. I just feel like our society, especially young men, it's soft. They've only grown up with affluence. And with the world changing it's a perfect time to teach some of these young men the values that I learned at Nebraska. And I've got to say, Paul, it's been great taking a walk down memory lane. I could do this for hours.

End conversation.

If only I had more hours with each and every one of these people, it still would never be enough. This far into our journey it's really hitting home to me that the Scarlet Brotherhood will only die when they do, and that what we had there in the bowels of Memorial Stadium will live on well after our souls are loosed for the heavenly realm (His second-coming notwithstanding). Also, I've arrived at a place of belief that I no longer see myself as less than adequate for this task, because my long-standing relationship with these people has enabled a comfortable ease of conversation and trust, allowing them to reveal more of themselves and their experiences than they might normally would a stranger piecing this chronicle together. Due to this fact, you are truly getting at the heart and the emotion of the subject, unplugged and unfiltered. In the same vein, I hope you that also feel as if you're getting the straight stuff and not some buttered-up, built-up or puffed up load of contrived nostalgia. Remember when I mentioned authenticity at our journey's start? It still holds true, and I hope you find great comfort in this fact.

There was so much to digest from this conversation, but I'll highlight a few subjects that I feel are most key. One was Chad's mentioning of the technology and rather craftsman-like use of it, "They cut up the films appropriately, and that was a pretty big deal… these two guys, Carp and Moose… they knew the game and I think that sped up that process… at least two-fold." Call me a tech-dweeb, but the use of digital video played an enormous role in allowing an already accomplished coaching staff hum along at warp speed while everyone else in their field was crawling with film projectors in dark rooms. This makes me want to add Bryan Carpenter and Brian Mohnsen to my list of must-have interviews. I'll have to seek them out and track them down, somehow, for I think they have a story or two to tell about the part technology played.

The other piece that stood out was his lumping all of the little things together and linking them into the achievement-oriented culture of the time, "Just all the fringe things, they all played a part in creating a championship atmosphere. It wasn't just football. We wanted to have the most Academic All-Americans, we wanted to set strength records. It was constantly creating a Culture of Achievers." Think about that for a second. Remember how Ryan Held previously mentioned that practicing mid-week at full-tilt led to success because one can't just 'turn it on' on game day? Well, I think the same applied to all aspects of the program, now that Chad mentioned it, because it fostered a constant, never-ending loop of improving efforts, of dispelling contentment, of continuing to reach for the highest rungs in life's ladder. In this spirit, I believe former UNL philosophy professor Hartley Burr Alexander hit it right on the head when he penned Southwest Memorial Stadium's cryptic and infamous verse: "Not the Victory but the action: Not the goal but the game: In the deed the glory." Glory be!

Notable quote #2:
Chad Stanley on playing opportunities: "And that was another positive about being in a program like Nebraska, because even if you were young and not first or second on the depth chart, you knew you were going to play in the games. Because we were thumping people so bad everybody got to play."

Great hopes make great men.

Thomas Fuller

Heading southbound on two-lane Nebraska Highway 14 on an early summer day, airborne Plains cottonwood seeds can be seen wafting past your windshield just a mile before you cross the Beaver Creek bridge and curve past the old train tracks and into the county seat of Albion. On this stretch of asphalt roadway the east ditch's crown of bromegrass crests a barbed-wire fence and the hill flashes onlookers with acre upon acre of cornrows. It's there where you'll notice a longstanding roadsign: Farmers Mutual Insurance Company of Nebraska. Schmadeke Inc. Insurance & Real Estate. Low Cost, Dependable Insurance.

Which brings us to the Schmadeke twins. Damon and Darren Schmadeke (rhymes with 'Let it be'), were both low cost (sic), dependable young men, much like their father's insurance offerings, as both walked-onto the team and steadfastly refused to ever quit the task of contributing to the quest for a Husker championship. One survived the trial and finished his career in pads, whereas the other's body never quite made the grade, so he later assumed an undergrad coaching position and a sideline polo shirt. Some could (though many couldn't) distinguish between the two, so just to be safe you always greeted them in passing with a, "Hey, Schmads." Let's get to differentiating between these two young Boone County speedsters, piggybacked here one after the other.

Notable quote #1:
"I think we learned a lot from the '92 Iowa State game when we lost 19-10 over in Ames. It was an embarrassment, something we were never going to let happen again. I remember Coach McBride at the time -in '93 and '94- he would reference that periodically. And all he would have to say was, "Remember Iowa State.""

Darren Schmadeke

Walk-on, Cornerback, Albion, Nebraska
Where are they now? Trenton, Missouri, Sales

Question: Hey Darren, I'm trying to remember your first fall camp..

Darren Schmadeke: It was '91 when I was a freshman. I grew up going to Nebraska football games since I was 6-7 years old. My grandparents had tickets in the family for well over 50 years, they sat in the west stadium and at one point had twelve seats in a row. Over the years they sold them off, but it was amazing. Growing up going to Husker games? I was a fan all my life. And also, we went to the Big Red Football Schools; went there before my freshman, sophomore, junior and senior years in high school. And I think that really helped me and my brother get our names out to the coaches, for them to ask us to walk-on at that time.

Q: Who ended up inviting you to walk-on?

DS: It was Turner Gill. February of 1991 on the phone, he's the one who officially asked us to walk-on. I'll never forget that night.

Q: Was it a little bit of a surprise? Were you expecting it?

DS: I think we were, but it was one of those things where you just didn't believe until it actually happened. And we had no idea who was calling. No idea. So it really was quite a surprise. We were very excited. And the way it was presented in a letter afterwards? It was kind of like a gentlemen's agreement. That's kind of really what it was. I was just glad that we had the opportunity to do that.

Q: So you and your brother were pretty determined that you wanted to be Huskers early on?

DS: Yes, and I think a big part of that was the influence of football at a young age from my parents and grandparents being long-term Husker fans. I would classify it as the 'classic Husker fan' if you really dig into true Husker fans, as you pass these tickets down the family tree. I remember getting in the car and driving two hours from Albion, Nebraska to Lincoln, making a day trip out of it, and always driving home late after the game. It was something I always looked forward to.

My grandmother, she never missed a game. I remember taking her to her last game before she passed away. I remember she was 82, and I remember it was her last game. And she died when she was 83 -didn't make it to the next season in 2003- you could just see the tears in her eyes as she was leaving the stadium and probably knowing she wouldn't ever be back again, because she'd been going to games for close to 50 years. And you look at that: that's the true Nebraska fan. I still look back at that today when I go.

I actually use my great uncle's tickets. My great uncle Lloyd Schmadeke played baseball for Nebraska back in the 30's and he's had tickets forever. And he's 93 now and can't go, so I use his tickets now and then. Still tough as a tack, he just can't get up the steps and go to the games but he enjoys that I get to take my kids and continue the tradition.

Q: Some of the guys talk about not knowing a soul when they arrived, but you were a special situation because your brother came with you…

DS: Yeah, that was unique, and I do have some close friends. When we first moved there and went to school I lived in Harper Dorms and roomed with Steve Ott out of Henderson. Steve and I became good friends and are still good friends to this day. I see him periodically when I head up to the Omaha area, and I was good friends with Steve Volin. We're all good friends. That's funny, because I was cleaning out my office closet and found a picture of us three at picture day during my sophomore year, of us standing out on the field. Just looking at it makes me realize how young we looked and how much hair I had. (laughs)

And Christian Peter was on the same floor as my brother, but two doors down. He roomed with Ken Bello from New Jersey. I'll never forget, the second semester Christian Peter was voted Harper 10 Floor President. And you could imagine what that was like. I'm not gonna say any more than that. All I'll say is that he called the shots. (laughs)

Q: It must have been a banana republic!

DS: Exactly. What he said was the law, and you can only imagine what went down on that floor. (laughs)

Q: So when you finally arrived on campus and got into the swing of things, what stood out to you the most?

DS: You know, when you come from a small town in Nebraska like a lot of Huskers, you come out of there and you get asked to walk-on you're kind of the big fish in a small pond at that point, and then you realize you're really a small fish in a big pond when you get with some of your classmates and the great players who get recruited in on national scholarships, talent-wise. That, for me, made me realize what I was associated with. This was big time.

That was the biggest thing for me, along with that first game. I remember when we played the first night game my freshman year. Of course I didn't play, but I was a walk-on and I got to suit up, and we played Washington. You remember that game? Steve Emtman was with Washington at that time, and seeing him and doing the tunnel walk and walking out into the stadium for the first time? At that time 76,000 to 78,000 screaming fans all in red was amazing just being on the sidelines. That was something being on national television, just putting it to reality, something I'd seen on TV over the years. I'll never forget that first night game. There was one of the Huard brothers and Napolean Kauffman. That was a good team.

Q: Was that when freshmen still reported a week early to camp?

DS: Yes, that was true, we did. I don't really remember a lot about that week, but they were really trying to get us prepared for the three-a-day practices. You know, that's something that I think every football player dreaded, no matter how many years you were there. I remember working out at home and running up and down the hills and lifting weights trying to get prepared for it. I was not going to show up for training camp not in shape in any way or form. Granted, I could have been in a little better shape, but I was running and trying to get in shape the best I could, and that really helped me with some of the endurance and the two-three hour practices we had.

I think overall, looking at that my freshman year, I remember at that time the walk-on program was quite big at the time. And it was amazing that every practice was filmed. You had Moose and Carp up on the scaffolding, and I remember we had enough players that we could have four different games/scrimmages going on at one time. (laughs) And I was thinking, 'They're watching every move you make out here.' And obviously that's what they did, and the meeting the day after we'd watch the film. And we'd watch the game film of the upcoming team that week and we'd review every step. You had to take five steps on post square-ins, and if you were a wingback or split end and if you took four, they knew it. I was amazed at the detail, the precision they had at running the routes correctly.

Q: What position did you play, Darren?

DS: Well, I was under Coach Ron Brown first. My redshirt freshman and my true freshman season I was a wingback/receiver under Coach Ron Brown, and then I transitioned to a cornerback under Coach Darlington my sophomore, junior and senior year.

Q: Tell me about Coach Brown.

DS: Coach Brown is a class act individual all the way around. I'll never forget him, he was always one of the coaches who took pride in doing little mini-drills after practice. He took pride in being the last group to come off the field. We'd typically run little routes and have defensive backs cover you, or as receivers we'd cover guys and try to use alligator arms in catching the ball and then stripping it out of them. He was always throwing balls at us, it seemed like. But that taught me something -because you know, you pick up a lot of things you use later in life– he taught what it took in order to be great. He always said that you had to do the little things. I'll never forget that, "The little things that you do in life will pay off. This is why we're here today. And everyone else is gone in the locker room and showered up and we're still working, because I want your guys to be the best you can be, the best blockers or what have you." One thing at the time.

We weren't throwing a lot at that time and he took a lot of pride in his role in pulling his fair share of the weight for the team in training & coaching excellent blockers with the split ends, wingbacks, et cetera. That's something, because if you look through the years you see our success with running the ball was because we've always been very good at having receivers who could block downfield.

Q: Any special techniques you receivers used in blocking downfield? Any the average fan wouldn't realize?

DS: You know, that's a great question. Basically, he'd emphasize us practicing it. And that's one thing from those times: other schools didn't really put the emphasis and the focus on practicing to be good blockers downfield. That's one thing he really stressed, "To have these I-backs breaking 50, 60, 80 yard runs, this is what we need to have." It was something that, at the time, a lot of the receivers in that group realized that we weren't going to be the J.J. Stokes receivers, because we weren't throwing that much, but we knew our role was very, very important in contributing to the success of the team, and blocking downfield was it. He talked about "the defensive backs and the linebackers are the ones who are going to be catching the running back, and we've got to be doing our part," and if we weren't and we reviewed that in the film the next day we were called to the mat on it, "Either you hit them too low or hit them too high." That's something I remember about him.

He was a big Christian. I think he was part of the Fellowship of Christian Athletes. He was very similar to Coach Osborne: I never heard him say a curse word, ever. Coach Osborne was that way, as well. I think Osborne's worst words were 'dadgumit.' You looked to him as a coach, a mentor, a leader. Coach Brown was incredible. He really became kind of a mini-father figure with that position for a lot of receivers. Coach Ron Brown really cared about you as an individual.

And something I remember, after each game he'd go to the 50 yard line and begin a circle and say a prayer thanking the Lord. And that's something, too, that a lot of players really were looking at the spiritual side of their lives.

Q: Were any particular teammates more inspiring or better leaders?

DS: I would say, at the time looking up to David Seizys, he was two years older than me at the time. He was a true leader. Coach Brown really liked him, as well. He was a walk-on and eventually earned a scholarship.

Tyrone Hughes was there, he was big. Tyrone Legette was on the defensive side, running routes against him. Toby Wright as well, he was a safety at the time. It's something that, overall, everybody in the group was really nice, and it was something that I'll never forget. I really enjoyed the time under Coach Brown.

And I want to tell you a story, which I think is pretty funny: at the time we were doing one-on-one drills where I was on the receiver's side and we would run routes. (I never really had great hands at catching the ball, okay?) I was a running back in high school and I never really was thrown the ball that much, but I remember I'd get a little nervous with Coach Osborne standing there and watching with Mike Grant or another one of the quarterbacks throwing to us as one of the defensive backs would cover us. Well, I'd always get nervous for that, for whatever reason, and sometimes I'd drop the ball or whatever. One time during practice -and this was my second season as a wingback- Coach Brown pulled me aside and said, "You know Darren, I'd like to make a suggestion to you and kind of get your thoughts on this, but it might be a good move," and he told me, "Darren, the thing is… you've got hands like feet." (laughs) I'll never forget that! "I think I'd like to propose to you that you move over to the defensive side and be a cornerback." And I kind of looked at him and said, 'I thought you'd never ask.' (laughs) So that's really the transition of when I went over to the defensive side, and that was really a much better fit and role for me. I was much happier swatting the ball versus catching the ball and I got to play a lot more and everything. I'm glad that he as a coach recognized that and switched me over.

Q: "Hands like feet", huh?

DS: Yeah, that's what he said. I'll never forget that.(laughs)

Q: And you weren't greatly offended! That's the beauty of it…

DS: Yeah, I didn't argue with him. (laughs) It was like, 'Okay.' It was funny, and then we went from there and I transitioned under Coach Darlington for the next three years.

Q: Tell me about George Darlington?

DS: Coach Darlington? Great guy. He always had a big -at the beginning of the year in the fall when we were reporting- he'd have us out at his house. He lived out east of Lincoln on a nice little acreage. He'd have all the defensive backs out once a year for a cookout/grill out. We'd play video games, have his pool table, met is family, his daughter, his wife.

And Coach Darlington was always a big Snapple guy. He used to drink a lot of Snapple at the time. I'll never forget that. He'd have a case of it, a case or two in his office all the time, he'd just drink that like nothing else. I'll always remember that. But we had a lot of fun with him. He was very good at reviewing game film, as well. We watched a lot of game film in his office, watching game film and critiquing routes as well. Very meticulous, very good at giving technique and suggestions. He was a little different person than Coach Brown, a little more down-to-business, per se. I learned a lot from him, as well. He'd been under Coach Osborne there for quite some time, and I had a chance to get in to play a few times for home games.

My sophomore year, I remember playing against UCLA and I covered J.J. Stokes at one time; I knocked a pass out of his hands or knocked him out of bounds. It was my highlight of that game, was covering J.J. Stokes. He went on to become a great professional athlete. And I did letter my sophomore year, so I lettered three years in a row up through my senior year. My junior year I played a lot more, I traveled every game my junior and senior year. There was one game I didn't make it -I think it was Oklahoma State- but after that I was backing up behind Tyrone Williams and Michael Booker. I was the backup between those two and got to be on the travel roster, the top 60. I believe they only took sixty players, if I recall, to the away games.

And I worked kickoff and punt returns. I think against Pacific, a small college out of California my junior year, I got in to play the later part of the first quarter and played the second, third and fourth quarter. I'll never forget walking out after the game and I heard the radio announcer mention that "Darren Schmadeke had 9 tackles and led the team in tackles as a defensive back." I don't know if that's a good thing or not, but good for me. (laughs) Typically it's the linebackers. But the next week I got presented a nice little plaque from George Darlington as Defensive Back of the Game, and it had a nice little quote on there about character. It was fun playing in front of the home crowd and getting a bunch of tackles in that game.

And looking into that junior year we end up going 13-0 and going to the Orange Bowl. We went to the Orange Bowl four years in a row, counting my redshirt year, and then my senior year we played in the Fiesta Bowl and beat Florida. That was pretty good. And I remember the three years, my sophomore, junior and senior years we were 36-1, losing to Florida State and Charlie Ward. It was just one of those games. We had it, and I don't blame Byron for missing it at all. We shouldn't have been in that position, from my line of thinking. After that game? I remember even spring ball, on the clock would say 1:16. We had it won at that time and then lost it, and we used that as a reminder of where we were, how close we were.

I remember Tommie Frazier at the time basically being such a huge motivator. Him and Christian Peter. They were two of the real prominent motivators of the team. When we came into my junior year -the '94 season, Osborne's first championship season- it just seemed that we were destined to win every game. It was expected. The confidence level? I've never seen it higher. We just knew we had to perform every week, one game at a time, to get that perfect record. Looking back I'm just in awe that we were able to do that. Just the confidence in the teammates and mentors, the captains at the time. Their leadership was pivotal in our success that year, as well as the following year. And they expected everybody —everybody- to raise their level of play. Even the backups and walk-ons, they all played their part in special teams. Everybody played at a higher level because we knew our teammates were counting on us and we were gonna win the national championship that year.

Q: When you say 'a greater effort', how would you typify that?

DS: Everybody was so focused on the end result of going to the Orange Bowl and winning a national championship, they took every practice seriously, every game seriously. I think we learned a lot from the '92 Iowa State game when we lost 19-10 over in Ames, one of Tommie Frazier's first or second games when he started playing a lot. We'd never lost to Iowa State. It was an embarrassment, something we were never going to let happen again. I remember Coach McBride, at the time -in '93 and '94- he would reference that periodically. And all he would have to say was, "Remember Iowa State." That's all that needed to be said, and we never forgot that. That's one game that we overlooked and were just not prepared and mentally ready to play at the top of our game. And I think it shocked everybody. It was a real eye-opener, a pivotal turning point for our teammates to see what we had to do and take care of our business each and every week and not to look over any team that we play. Because any team could knock us off, and if you had one loss that could ruin the whole season and the possibility of a national championship game. It even happens today, you trip up in your championship game and things fall apart.

Q: And Coach Osborne?

DS: One thing I'll say about him: a class act individual. A very strong Christian, somebody who I have a lot of respect for. I remember first seeing him when I was probably in junior high, he came to our school for a speaking engagement and one thing about him (a lot of players probably say this), he had such conduct and such respect, everybody respected him, all levels of the players. I remember sitting in the meeting room, the tiered room with all the meeting chairs, and everybody would be laughing and joking and teasing with the guys, but when Osborne would walk in at 2 o'clock for the meetings it was complete silence. You could almost hear a pin drop. I don't ever remember him having to say, "Okay guys, can you hold it down again?" When he walked into the room we knew it was business, the attention was on him and he had the floor. That really sums it up.

Being that he had a Doctorate in Psychology, he really had an amazing ability to adapt and really get to know each individual player on a personal basis. And I'll say this, he would really take pride in studying the new freshman coming in and getting to know them as they moved up the ladder of the team, knowing everybody by first name. And out of all the coaches - Darlington, Brown, Steele, all those guys, my nickname in college was "Schmad"- But Coach Osborne was about the only coach who could differentiate between myself and my twin brother, Damon, and he always called me 'Darren.' He always called me by my first name. He had an amazing ability to really get to know people by first name.

I remember a lot of times you'd see him down the hallway and he'd actally stop and talk to you. He'd say, "Hey, Darren, how are you doing? How is school going for you? Doing well in your classes?" Really personal things like that. I was really shocked he'd ask that. That meant a lot. Basically, he really showed he cared about me as an individual and being a contributor to the team no matter what my role was. It made you feel special. It really did.

Q: Any other coaches stand out to you?

DS: I would say Coach McBride. I'll never forget him, the Defensive Coordinator and D-line Coach. He'd always meet with the D-line in the shower stalls. I was never really a part of that, but he would always talk to us. And I'll never forget some of the quotes, but a lot of times he'd say to us individually, "Each one of you guys have your mom, your dad, your uncles, your aunts, your grandparents sitting in the stadium today. We do not want to let K-State or Colorado or whoever we were playing come into our house and beat us. It's actually an embarrassment to you and especially your family members who love you, who are out in the stadium rooting for you today. I just want you to thinking about that." Basically, we've got to be prepared. We prepared all week. You're gonna play well, but don't let these guys come in and embarrass you in front of your family. I'll never forget that, it was something else.

I remember him also saying, "The quarterback? I want you guys to be all over him like Jack the Bear." (laughs) I don't know why he said that -Jack the Bear- but I'll never forget it. Kind of funny. (laughs) I tell you one thing with him, I had a lot of respect for him. He was kind of intimidating a little bit with his presence, but very confident, and he had a whole lot of respect from the defensive team. Very intense. You didn't want to cross paths with Coach McBride.

Another person I'll talk about, too, is Kevin Steele. He was the linebackers coach, and if I recall I think he played for Johnny Majors at Tennesseee, I think. But he was very, very intense. I remember him almost kind of like a drill sergeant getting in front of the linebackers: Terwilliger, Phil Ellis, Ed Stewart, those guys. He'd get right in your face, an inch from your face and scream at you from the top of his lungs. I tell you, he'd correct you when you were wrong, but he'd be your best friend and back you to the hilt when you were in trouble and what else. You just kind of had to learn to work and operate with him. That's just my view from the side, but everybody saw and noticed it. One of the things I'll never forget, when he moved on and I was watching the game and he was in the face of Kevin Greene, the pro linebacker, and was yelling at him, and I think Kevin Greene got mad and yelled back and grabbed him or something. And it's just my interpretation, but maybe that was a sign for him that maybe he should get back into the college game. (laughs) But he was a neat guy, he really was. Intense, in-your-face kind of guy, a drill sergeant.

Q: From '91 to your senior year of '95, how would you say the team dynamic changed, if at all?

DS: We were basically 9-2, 9-3 my redshirt freshman and true freshman year, and honestly, we were satisfied at that time with winning the 9 games. You know, Coach Osborne won nine games in a row for over 25 years and never won less than that, and we were just kind of continuing on the tradition, but there was something that was missing, not having won the big one.

Looking back, that's where I think honestly having the players come in like a Tyrone Williams, a Tommie Frazier, Christian Peter, those kind of guys right there were the ones to kind of put it together and said, "We're taking it to the next level and we're winning every game." That group of players, I would say in general, those were the ones who really stick out and made it happen our junior and senior year when we were undefeated back to back national champions. It was basically about having no doubts, our confidence level was raised. And they had the presence to raise the confidence factor of every member of the team to play to the best of their ability each and every play of every game we had. Losing was not even a thought in our minds, not even a speck of a thought in our minds. We knew going into these games that we were going to win. We just had to execute and do what we did in practice, study our films, take our tests. You know, we had to get 90 or 95% on our test each week for who we played, and we knew what we had to do.

And being a part of it, I could see it evolving as we went through. I think that was the biggest thing looking at it from the 10,000 foot view. I just think we were satisfied with those nine win seasons my first few years, and some of those guys who came in decided we were going to take it to the next level and raised the bar. We had some superior athletes, changed up some of the defensive schemes, went faster by putting some of the outside backers... the Ed Stewarts', Jamel Williams', Terrell Farley, those guys were extremely fast. And we were so strong at the running back positions, and finally put together an incredible defense and amazing offensive records, racking up 400-500 yards per game those years. Looking at it now, it's been on ESPN's Top Teams of All Time -the '95 season- and it's interesting to look around and compare it to other teams. It's always at the top every year.

Q: Do you have a favorite game you played in that stands out to you?

DS: I would say it was probably my senior year when we played Missouri in Lincoln. We beat them like 55-0, I believe. It was a blowout. I was a left cornerback and the backup quarterback for Missouri at the time -I was in Cover 9 and basically was kind of backpedaling into the end zone- and the guy threw a pass. And the receiver was not around and I got an interception in the end zone to preserve the shutout. They were getting ready to score and we held them. That's probably one of them.

There's one other one that pops up. It was my junior year that '94 season when we played West Virginia in the Kickoff Classic and Keith Jackson, the announcer for ABC, "Whoa, Nelly!" that guy was doing the play calling. We beat them pretty well that game, and I was in at left cornerback and they threw like a 5-7 yard out, and I remember kind of on purpose jumping the wide receiver and ended up tackling him before the ball got there. I remember Keith Jackson saying, "Darren Schmadeke" -the legendary Keith Jackson said my name in a play- "Darren Schmadeke had him locked up, zipped up, and in his back pocket before the ball got there." And we got the penalty, but it was the right thing to do because they didn't score. We held them. I look back at that and it ended up working out pretty good. I remember, 'I've got to hit this guy, I can't let him score.' (laughs)

Q: And as far as the bowl games, anything really stand out to you there?

DS: I would say probably the first year winning it in '94 in the Orange Bowl. What stands out to to me was the emotion in the locker room after the game. Reality had hit us. We really couldn't believe it, beating Miami in the Orange Bowl on their home turf. 24-17 was the score and having the players realize that we made history, we were 13-0 and national champions and all the hard work paid off. And it was just kind of a great relief to see it was over with, and then kind of a great joy to be part of Osborne's first national championship. I know he was just as excited as we were.

And you just can't beat beating Miami in the Orange Bowl on their home turf. That was part of it. And we were on top. That was great, really a phenomenal time.

Q: Darren, I would suspect most guys, after finally reaching that spot, most people would sit back and lose a little bit of fire and not have as much of it the next year. How would you say we dealt with that, from a player's perspective?

DS: That's a great question. I would say overall we worked really hard from the '93 season where we had that Florida State loss by two points and just said that it wasn't going to happen again. We got so close, but we dropped the ball, didn't get it done. We saw what it took to be national champions. We lost some players, but we had some good backups that were filling in the holes. We still had Christian Peter, we had Tommie Frazier back, Tyrone Williams, we had some great offensive linemen with Stai and Weigert, but we had some other players that stepped in: Steve Ott started, Aaron Graham those two or three years, Eric Anderson at right tackle, it was something that we really just wanted to continue it on. We knew what we had and we wanted to repeat again.

And honestly, we looked at it going into that '95 season that we were not going to lose again. We were playing very well, blowing people out. I remember on the defensive side we had goals, a little laminated sheet of the goals for the '95 season. I remember some of the goals of the defense was to keep the total yardage to 285 yards or under for the opponent. Another goal also was to have three turnovers per game, so those were little things to look at. And of course, we were averaging close to 500 yards or so on offense, so if we could keep the opponent under 285 (and a lot of times we held them to 250 or 225 total yards) which, "Hey, if you keep them off the field and you get yards, they can't score." And we had the running game and used the time clock, so that was an advantage, too, because of time of possession. Those are things that really stick out.

We were on the high point my junior and senior year, and it was business as usual. We had t-shirts made up that said, "Business as Usual." The previous years were, "We Refuse To Lose," then it was, "Unfinished Business," then it was, "Business As Usual," if I recall correctly. Looking back at that, realizing what we accomplished? At the time I didn't realize just how significant it was. I knew it was good, but as time has gone on and I've gotten kind of older and looking back, it truly is amazing what we accomplished at the time. It is just so rare to see teams go 25-0 over two years, 36-1 over three years. We dominated the 90's. We really did, and when you look at what Coach Osborne did with never winning less than 9 wins a season, that's just something.

And me coming from a small town, I played a lot more than I ever thought I would, as a Nebraska walk-on. And to be associated with that caliber of people? Those guys, it was fun watching all those guys we played with play in the pros for the years, too. That was neat seeing that. It really taught me a lot of things about life: the fact that you never give up. I was on the scout team for two years and that second year it was kind of wearing on me. I had thoughts of quitting the team, but I was the kind of person who could not live with myself if I quit the team, and in my mind that just wasn't an option. And I've got 9 football rings: the '92, '93, '94, '95 Big 8 championships and 2 national championship rings from '94 and '95, and my Letterman rings. It's really kind of a neat thing to show off to friends and family.

Q: Any memorable practices?

DS: Yeah, probably some things I couldn't tell you. (laughs) I'll just say one thing: there were some interesting practices that some of the different positions had at initiating freshman. Especially the defensive line, that was probably the worst.

Q: 'The Girthing?'

DS: Yeah!(laughs) Just seeing that, I was glad I wasn't part of them. I remember a lot of the defensive line picking a lot on Mike Rucker. Christian Peter and them, a lot of them picked on Mike Rucker, who ended up being an incredible player and amazing athlete. He took it so well, he really did. Of course, when he got older it didn't happen. (laughs)

I always remember after practice Coach Osborne running around Memorial Field, doing his three miles alone in the stadium. Overall, the practices were really well organized, every move we made was filmed, it was a complete practice. We had meetings at 2 p.m., were always dressed and out to the field by three-thirty, practice from 3:30 to 5:30-5:45, lift weights for another half hour, then we'd shower, go eat, and then study hall. So there was a full, full day. I remember thinking about that. We didn't have time for extra-curricular activity because we were exhausted after a hard day's practice. And then you had class the next morning at 8 o'clock.

Q: And Darren, what would you say to those who might say, "You football players, you have it made. Everything is given to you and you're pampered?"

DS: That's a good question. I think overall they may have that perception that we had it all. We had a nice weight room, nice locker room, you'd get to eat prime rib on the special occasions at the training table, but I don't think they realize the time commitment involved: the practices, the studying, the classes, the meetings, the quizzes, the preparation behind it to make it happen to become champions. There was a lot of effort and time put into it, a lot of training.

Those coaches on the football team? When it's football season those coaches are working around the clock. Of course, my brother was an Undergraduate Assistant Coach (he played for two years and got hurt and became a coach), and I remember him going in on Sundays at 8 a.m. and sometimes not coming home until 6 or 8 at night. He would make cue cards for the scout team to run that coming week, of the teams we would play. He'd draw all of them up. He'd work 8 or 10 hours on Sunday, that was his deal as an Undergraduate Assistant Coach. Granted, there were a lot of good things that were provided to us, but the football team brought in a lot of revenue for the University, and today it covers a lot of other sports like swimming, diving, whatever else, helps to finance them. And it's something I'm sure will always continue to be big.

Some people from out of the state ask me, "Why is football so big?" Well, there are no other big teams. You've got corn, you've got cattle, and you've got Nebraska Football. It's an agricultural state and we've traditionally been a great team over the years, and people from way out west in Scottsbluff or Chadron that would make the 4-5 hours trip every week to go the games, packing I-80? Those are Cornhusker fans. Then you have fans like my grandmother, going to the games for over 50 years, and she was 82 and was bound and determined to go to as many games as she could until her last day. I remember her walking out of the stadium with tears in her eyes knowing she wouldn't see it again. I'll always remember that. She was a huge supporter, a true die hard. Something I enjoyed, playing for her. And I'm introducing my kids to it now. They're a little scared of Lil' Red, but they'll get used to him.

Q: Would you point out a certain person behind the scenes who played a huge role?

DS: Many different people were a big part of it. There are a couple: Sully was a big part of it, and Doak, as well, back then. Different people. Those people were really pivotal in providing the best care for injuries and rehabilitation and getting guys back on board, and then on the training table side.

And also, I remember Keith Zimmer with mandatory study hall for true freshman, which I think is a fantastic thing. In high school you didn't have to study much, but there you do. It was setting up tutors, all of that. Then we had such a high degree of graduates and Academic All-Americans over the years. It's hard to say any one, because everybody kind of pulled their fair share.

Another coach a lot of players really liked was Dan Young, a lot of people had a lot of respect for him. He grew up in the small town of Primrose, just a short ways from Albion and Petersburg.

So it's tough for me to pick any one person. Coach Osborne was just really good at getting great people to work underneath him. Everybody had their own unique ability, all very focused and dedicated to the players and would give the shirt off their back to you. We spent a lot of time together over the years in practices, meetings, traveling, I have a lot of fond memories. I'm really glad looking at it from being a Nebraska kid, to dreaming and playing for them. I actually did it. I had some offers at some other schools I could have taken, but it wasn't about that for me. I knew where I wanted to go and I knew where I belonged. I wanted to be a part of the Nebraska Football team. It's something that -the timing of it, I have to thank my parents for that- but the timing of it was perfect for those championship teams. (laughs) I have no regrets. I'm glad to have associated with the coaches, the staff and the players, and it's really helped me with my career. Helped me get my first job, just letting them know during the interview that I was a walk-on and had to pay my own way and be dedicated and be a part of the team. That kind of conveyed to them that I'd be a good worker.

Q: The value of determination and sacrifice…

DS: Hard work, and realizing that it's the little things in life you have to do to make a difference, some things that are very true today. You don't go long in life just doing the status quo, you have to make it happen, you want to be a leader and take charge. That's something that allies to my personal life and my career right now.

Q: Anything I haven't brought up that you think set those teams apart from others of their day? Any grand revelation we haven't touched upon?

DS: I'm gonna have to really go back to looking at some of the players. The two that really stick out in my mind as being pivotal to the confidence and leadership of the program were Tommie Frazier and Christian Peter, those two guys. Tommie was on the offensive side and Christian was on the defensive side.

A funny story I'll tell you about Christian Peter: we were playing Michigan State, it was in East Lansing. And right before the game Coach Devaney was there (because he'd coached at Michigan State years before, I believe), and he was gonna give us a pep talk. And typically the coaches leave the room and the captains get up and give us a pep talk and fire us up. Of course, Devaney was a little older at the time and he ended up speaking to us, but it was one of those things where Christian and the captains were doing their thing, getting riled up. And I remember Christian grabbed this clock off the wall in the locker room and breaks it over his head, and he cut himself and he was bleeding down his face, and he just kept on going and talking about, "We're going to beat these guys!" He almost looked like a WWF wrestler, blood was coming down and it didn't even phase him, the plastic on the front part of the clock broke on his face and cut him. He threw the clock in the trash can, put his helmet on his head and away we go. That locker room was going crazy after that, it was funny.

Overall -to answer your question- the type of people, the caliber of people on the coaching staff with Coach Osborne: we believed in each other, we cared about each other, and we knew what we had to do to take care of business. We were extremely unified as a team, took one game at a time to win every game, and that's what we did. It really never, honestly, crossed our mind that junior and senior year at all, of losing. I really believe that if you believe and have confidence in yourself that you're going to win. You're going to win. And if you think that way and prepare that way, that's what's going to happen. If you're the other guy who is a little wishy-washy and goes into things with that attitude, you might lose. But being focused and driven and knowing what the end goal is, that's what you keep focused on, that prize, that championship trophy, for us. And Tommie and Christian stood out to me from the players perspective, getting everybody to jump on the boat and saying "We're gonna beat everybody one game at a time." They were incredible about rallying the whole team from freshmen to seniors, believing that we were unbeatable. And honestly, that's exactly how it was. Losing was never an option.

Q: I haven't heard much about Tommie's motivation and leadership. Any examples come to mind?

DS: Christian was a lot more vocal than Tommie. Tommie would say some fiery things, but he was more of a silent, confident leader. My impression of him, how he carried himself? Basically his confidence in watching him operate with this offensive line, he had the trust and the belief in his offensive line to block for him like they should. He was very motivated and competitive -not as vocal as some- but there was something about him. Just in looking at him and watching him operate, he had an incredible amount of confidence about it, and I think it carried on to other offensive players on the team. We knew that when Tommie was behind the center, we knew we were going to win.

The same thing with Brook. We had confidence with him. And I'll never forget the day he passed away in the plane accident and all of us going to his funeral was quite a deal. But overall, just looking at those two guys from my perspective, Tommie being the quarterback, the leader on offense and producing 500-plus yards or whatever it was. When Tommie was on the field everybody raised their level of play two notches, to the highest degree they could. There are other players, too, but those two really stand out to me, their presence on the field, 'I can't let these guys down. I have to do my part. I have to be focused and follow through on the tackle, make sure I catch all the balls thrown to me.' That's my interpretation.

End conversation.

Darren's reminding us of the mantra "Remember Iowa State" makes me wonder if every champion needs to at some time or another go through a crushing loss, a humbling & pivotally embarrassing experience to drive him or her in future endeavors."It was a real eye-opener, a pivotal turning point for our teammates to see what we had to do and take care of our business each and every week and not to look over any team that we play." Funny how he brought that up out of the blue, but I think the '93 team and thereafter benefitted greatly from that '92 defeat at the hands of the lowly Cyclones in Ames. Revolutionary patriot Thomas Paine once penned, "What we obtain too cheaply, we esteem too lightly; 'tis dearness only that gives everything its value." That's common sense.

   Also, it was the first time somebody specifically pointed out both Tommie Frazier and Christian Peter as being catalysts for leadership. I find it interesting to note that whereas Christian was both physically and vocally motivating, Tommie predominantly led with his fierce determination and minimal talk. (Numerous attempts to contact Tommie Frazier for an interview were not answered. Christian Peter, on the other hand, availed himself after a year of contact, and we'll hear from him later on in this endeavor.) In other words, I surmise that there's more than one way to skin a cat -to use an old colloquialism- and that a group of student/athletes as large as the one Nebraska possessed was diverse enough to need and benefit from a variety of peer leadership examples. Next, on to brother Damon...

Notable quote #2:
Darren Schmadeke on quarterback Tommie Frazier: "When Tommie was on the field everybody raised their level of play two notches, to the highest degree they could."

Harry Arms

Stricken while at work in a house at Springfield, Nebr., Harry Arms, 54, said to have been Nebraska's only one-armed paperhanger, died Tuesday. He lost his arm in a shooting accident when a youth. He had followed the paperhanging trade for more than ten years.

Newspaper Obituary, Gretna Breeze, May 27, 1938,
courtesy Nebraska State Historical Society

For a long spell of those years there was a sizeable, engaging, and downright agreeable fellow by the name of Don Daugherty who patrolled the hallways and entrance gate to the Bob Devaney Sports Center. On an almost daily morning basis we'd greet each other something very much in this manner:

Paul: *"Good mornin! How's life treatin' ya'?"*

Don: *"I'm busier than a one-legged man in a butt-kickin' contest!*

Then on we'd go about our ways.

Having already spoken to Darren, one of the "Schmadeke boys," now we come to Damon, who could very easily empathize with both Mr. Dougherty and the late Mr. Arms above. Damon had a busier five years than most and saw life from both sides of the fence, having a great appreciation for the process no matter which side of the ball he was on. Keep an ear out for his unique insight as to what made the whole thing go…

Notable quote #1:

"I think it comes down to those film guys: Bryan Carpenter and Brian 'Moose' Mohnsen did a lot of stuff and never did get much credit… If we didn't have that we weren't gonna be ready in preparing for the team. What they would do is break it down and slice and dice that tape."

Damon Schmadeke

Walk-on, I-Back, Albion, Nebraska
Where are they now? Rolla, Missouri, Sales

Question: You had a unique experience playing and coaching at Nebraska, right Damon?

Damon Schmadeke: I played for three years and then I was an undergrad assistant coach in those '94 and '95 seasons. It was fun to see both sides of the ball, I tell you that.

Q: Obviously you already knew someone there, your twin brother, but was there anyone else?

DS: We'd competed a lot in track so we kind of knew some guys. And the Makovickas? I didn't know them until I was there, we were both walk-ons. And Chad Stanley, I got along with Chad very well. I guess you kind of hung out with, more so, the running backs, the fullbacks, what I was doing. You're in meetings, in practice, sometimes in the same classes and all that, study hall, that first year. But it was sure an interesting year, how busy we were from freshman study hall to football to weightlifting, it was just, 'Where do we go now?'

Q: Not, "Where do I want to go?", but "Where do I have to go?" (laughs)

DS: Yeah, you'd get back to your dorm at 9:30 or ten at night and you'd just be exhausted. Then back at the grind again. I guess when you're at that age with all of the energy, that's what you can do. It was a great experience.

Q: Do you recall your initial thoughts of the organization, the program?

DS: It was hard for me to believe I was here and actually going through fall camp for real. It was real-time: guys were bigger, stronger, faster than you thought, coming out of high school. That tends to be an eye opener for most people. Going through all the testing skills: the 40 yard dash, the 300 yard shuttle was always a killer. (laughs) Just the experience of saying, 'I've got myself here. I have some work to do. They mean business.' When it comes down to it, with football and school and the structure, the honor of being in the presence of Tom Osborne was sure a great thrill.

Q: Anything stand out to you about Coach Osborne from the start?

DS: He was thorough. He knew you by name the first day you were there and he would call you by name. And the amount of players that were under him, with the walk-ons and the scholarship players? I just thought it was very neat that he could remember everybody's name pretty much; he'd acknowledge you as he walked by you, and that would assure you that you weren't just a number.

When you started off you'd have tape on the front of your helmet with your name on it (until he can kind of get to know you), especially being new people. That's a challenge, but once you sit on the coaching side like I did, you just know every player on that team. You know the depth chart and who was moving up and who was slipping back at every position. So I could see over time, throughout the year, how he would get to know every person. You'd look up at the whiteboard and see the running back depth and the quarterback depth and move people around based on position and first team, second team, third team.

Q: Do you recall times that you moved up or moved down and what that did for your psyche?

DS: Well, I started out at I-back, you know, and to me just being there was a thrill. I just knew I needed to do my best and focus on working hard at practice each day and studying hard. But I guess it didn't really bother me that I wasn't a starter. I was 4th string my freshman and sophomore year and I sure would have liked to move up, but the talent level there was very high. You just had to do the best you could.

Q: Can you bring up any names of the guys you were competing against?

DS: I competed with Jeff Makovicka at that position, then Jeff got switched to fullback, and Chad Stanley was always a fullback, Clinton Childs, Damon Benning. Damon was a year younger than me. With those guys -all those guys- it pushed everybody each day to do better and better and better with that type of talent.

Q: What about Frank Solich?

DS: What I liked about Coach Solich was that when we went through the plays and if you didn't run it to the exact place where he wanted you -either outside shoulder of the tackle or the inside shoulder- he was very precise on his routes and the techniques, of running down hill and catching that option. Fine-tuning that option? He was a master at that. When you'd get that ball you wanted to be going downhill when you crossed that line of scrimmage. He was a very good coach and I enjoyed playing for him and working with him as a coach.

I always remember Coach Solich saying that when you ran the ball you had to "speed through the hole." He wanted us to accelerate through the line of scrimmage on each play, but he was very precise on where he wanted the route to be on the play call. But "speed through the hole' was something he really repeated all the time. I sure learned a lot of things, a lot of techniques, compared to what I knew at the high school level. At the high school level you just run over people, but at the college level you had to put your shoulder down, make them move, run over them, drive through their chest and not take the brunt of hits that you did in high school. You wanted to deliver the punishment and not take the punishment, let's put it that way.

Q: I heard somewhere that Tom Rathman once broke an Oklahoma guy's jaw?

DS: Yeah, I heard about that. That's one of the things Coach Solich wanted to infuse in us running backs: "You guys do the punishment to the people. Don't take it. Take your fist and drive through their sternum. Then pop your fist through and drive through them." Cory Schlesinger, too, he was good at that. Everybody called him "Blockhead." He would hit you so hard and it wouldn't phase him. I would be, 'Wow, that was a hit! Are you okay?' And he'd be, "Oh, I'm fine." (laughs) Cory could sure hit hard. Very tough player. A tough kid.

Q: What brought you to coaching with Coach Solich?

DS: Well, when we were recruited Coach Turner Gill asked us to walk-on back there in high school, both Darren and myself. Coach Osborne told us if we came here and something would happen -if we got hurt, like blow a knee or a back or whatever- that they would take care of us on a medical hardship. Well, I had a stress fracture in my L5 vertebrae and Dr. Pat Clare said, "You better just take a rest, because you don't want to mess your back up anymore." So I had a discussion with Coach Osborne and he wanted me to come on and be an undergrad assistant coach for the last two years of my 5 years there at Nebraska. It was an honor to do that.

Q: Did that come out of the blue for you?

DS: I wasn't really expecting it. And I was hoping my injury would get better but obviously it didn't, and there was nothing really that they could do. They were shooting my back up with Cortisone, the sacro-iliac joint, and I was getting stim and ultrasound on my back in the training room, and it just came to a point where my body just locked up in the lower back and said, "You can't be doing this." My back just needed a break, so I figured I didn't want to mess myself up for the rest of my life, so 'I'll stop.'

Q: How's the back now?

DS: Fine. (laughs) Fine, no knee problems, no nothing. I got through football with no long term injuries. That's a good thing. (laughs)

Q: Other coaches stand out to you?

DS: Dan Young, he was the kicker's coach, from Primrose, Nebraska (and we're from Albion). We sure got a kick out of him and the dry sense of humor that he had. A lot of people would like to imitate a lot of things he would say. Steve Ott was really good at doing impressions of him. He was a great guy.

Then Charlie McBride, he would get in your face if you did something wrong, he had such a good command of the defense. Each week running plays into them? He'd be intimidating, because if you didn't run the right play he would tell you. (laughs) A lot of people respected him and he got the defense ready for game days.

Q: Do you recall the first game you played?

DS: I'm trying to think. I don't remember the exact first game I got in, but I remember the game I ran the ball was against Oklahoma State in Lincoln. I got a pitch and nothing big, maybe a five or six yard gain after getting the pitch, and got tackled out of bounds. But for me that was a thrill to run the ball. I didn't get in a ton when I was a freshman and sophomore, but I'd get in on kickoffs and stuff when we were blowing them out. I also got to go to the Tokyo Coca-Cola Bowl because Derek Brown got injured down in Norman, Oklahoma. I didn't travel because I was fourth string. It was Derek Brown, Calvin Jones and Jeff Makovicka, then myself. Then I'm sitting at home watching the game and I saw Derek got injured and I said, 'Uh oh, I guess I'd better get my passport ready,' because Derek was out with a shoulder injury and I got to go to Tokyo, Japan and play Kansas State over there.

Q: Any memories of that game?

DS: Well, I think the whole memory of that thing was the travel over there and how long it was: a 14 hour flight and all the guys playing cards. And sitting on that plane? They put the small guys between the offensive linemen -I had to sit between Brenden Stai and Zach Weigert- like a sandwich meat between those two guys on one of the Japan Airlines 747's. (laughs) We flew from Kansas City to Vancouver, British Columbia, and then from Vancouver to Tokyo.

Q: I have a feeling you didn't get to use the arm rests...

DS: No, I would get up and walk around. That was the longest flight I'd ever been on. You were going stir crazy after that long.

Q: I heard there was a memorable off-field incident that trip. Remember anything about that?

DS: Yeah, I don't know the specifics, but it was something like John Parrella, Kevin Ramaekers or somebody. Somebody got into a fight with a professional WWF wrestler in a bar, and they had to wear sunglasses on to the plane home so Coach Osborne wouldn't see the black eye. I can't remember exactly who that was, but maybe it was an offensive linemen? I can't recall who it was. (laughs) They wore sunglasses on the plane.

I remember going out in Tokyo and not being a part of that, but being around and heard that went on. I don't know what happened, but the bars there, you had to go upstairs to get a drink. Everything was vertical in that town. You ordered McDonalds on the first floor but you had to go upstairs to eat it. It was a great trip and great experience; we got to do a little bit of sightseeing and stuff. We were over there for 6, 7 or 8 days in December of 92'. It was a long flight to go play at the equivalent of Manhattan, Kansas I tell you that.(laughs) We won that game and I got in in the 4th quarter there, where Tony Veland was the quarterback and I got in a couple of plays there towards the end. It was fun to get in that game.

And it was funny, when you walked into the stadium there were either red pompoms or purple pompoms sitting in the seats, so that's the team they were supposed to cheer for. So wherever people sat, that's the team they cheered for. They were going, "Rah-rah, who's Nebraska? Rah-rah, who's K-State?" (laughs) But they were great.

Q: That would have been a long flight back had it been a loss...

DS: Yeah, K-State had to be on the right side of the plane and Nebraska had to be on the left side of the plane. They had us on the same plane, split us on the left side and right side of the plane. I know in the back they were all rolling dice. I didn't get into that. (laughs)

Q: Rigggght, Damon. It's okay to fess up now, I don't think they'll drag you in front of the Unity Council for gambling... (laughs) So then you made the switch over to the coaching side of things. What sticks out from that?

DS: I think the first meeting that I sat in… sitting in the meeting room with all the coaches, we would discuss the players. And it would blow me away each Monday with how much the coaches knew about what the players did that past weekend. They were like, "Did you hear about this guy…?" I was like, 'How do they know this stuff?' If you sneezed, they knew. (laughs) They know more than you think they know: if you're in trouble with school or skipping class or failing a class. They were very involved in that, which I think was very good, because Coach Osborne would talk to the players and maybe straighten them out a bit and get 'em back on track to where they needed to be, if they're slipping up or messing around.

Q: One thing you never heard was the term, "Lack of institutional control", huh?

DS: Yeah, it was really interesting to sit in there and hear what they would know about you and how much they knew about you: off-field and on-field issues, girl issues, classes, I think that was just the way Coach Osborne was. He was always looking out for your best interests and making you a man.

Q: Sure, he made a promise to the mothers and fathers during recruiting…

DS: He really did, and he tried to do that with everybody the best he could. He did a great job. That was the first thing that surprised me when I sat in some of those meetings. That, and we watched a lot of film.

Q: Share a 'fly on the wall' moment from those sessions…

DS: Let me think. Well, Coach Darlington would always pipe up and say a few things. He'd speak his mind and go on a few times sometimes. And some of the other coaches wouldn't always agree, but he'd always put his two cents in.

I think Coach Osborne kind of ran the meetings, and a lot of people bounced their ideas off him or what. But whatever Coach Osborne decided, that's what we did. They all did their work together as a cohesive group and brainstormed. And the amount of film we watched? I'd be there for 10 hours on Sunday breaking down film for Monday's practice.

Q: Was that after Moose and Carp had already broken it down?

DS: Well, yeah. They'd be breaking it down late Saturday and even early into Sunday morning. Then we'd be watching tapes (and they had all of us undergrad assistants), I'd be drawing the play card, the routes, draw the formations on the right and turn it over and draw it on the left, with colors for pass play or run play. And we'd draw these cards based on down and distance: 20 yards and under, third and long, and he would have every play broken down into what formation they would run, and we'd run each one of the plays to the defense based on them.

And then we'd have the numbers of the star players of the opponents like Oklahoma State or Colorado, we'd have that player on the field wearing that jersey so they could see where that player was going to be. We ran the offense -teams three and four- against the one and two defense; that was our job to coordinate the three and four offense to run that week's plays against the one and two defense. That's what we did.

It sure was a lot of work, just amazing that you can watch that much film and you can almost call the play when seeing some formation. And that's how Coach Osborne would see some formation and maybe make some adjustments to Charlie, and then Charlie would see that and make some adjustments, and then we'd make some interception and surprise these guys.

Q: Do you ever recall saying to yourself, "Wow, these opponents are good!" or the like?

DS: When I sat up versus KU. We were down at Lawrence, Kansas and Mike Grant and myself were sitting in the end zone. We would chart the defensive front of the Kansas Jayhawks versus Nebraska's offense. We'd chart the defensive front and if there was any slants or blitzes based on our offensive fronts. So then after each series we'd have a runner run those down to Coach Osborne so he could see the formations from the way we saw it in the end zone, from the goal posts where we were sitting. So sitting at that angle you could see the defense and then you could see our offense go into a formation, and you could almost call a touchdown before it happened by seeing it from that angle. You could see by the way they lined up, 'Oh boy, this guy is gonna be wide open.' And it was, with that option pass and the tight end streaking down the line and no one covering him.

Q: Like those times when a Mark Gilman just standing in the end zone, wide open?

DS: Yeah, you could see a big play before it happened, based on that.

Q: So you're just kind of giddy sitting there, just waiting for it to go down? Knowing that you and maybe thirty other people knew what's gonna transpire there in the next few seconds among the 78,000+ people who have no clue about what's going to take place?

DS: Yeah, because we'd have the headphones on, too. Sometimes we'd be upstairs or in the north end zone for home games and we'd have the headphones on, so I could hear the play being called, and then I'd watch us line up and then the other team's defense would line up and I'd go, 'Oh, this is going to work.'

And then you'd hear the coaches go back and forth, too, making these comments. And you could see that they could see the same thing that we could see, because you have the guys up top talking to the guys down there. You would hear, "That guy's cheating up over here, he's biting, he's biting. Let's go to this, we're gonna get him and then trip him up and… TOUCHDOWN!" I think that was neat seeing some of that stuff fall into place, and you knew you were one of the few people in the stadium who could see that.

Q: Any fond recollection of those games?

DS: I remember Lamar Thomas was one of the Miami receivers who was very proud of himself. I don't know if you knew about him; he was #36, one of their hotshot wide receivers, and he would come out of the tunnel with the smoke and he would run around the whole Orange Bowl field and kind of taunt people, like the Nebraska fans, and run by us saying this and that. I think a lot of the Nebraska players saw that and kind of got motivated, defensive-wise. It was like, "Okay, we're gonna bring it."

And I think in the '95 season it would be Lawrence Phillips out there in Tempe just tearing it up on the field, having almost the game of his life. It was unbelievable just watching him, he had an impressive game as a running back, such a talented individual. Those couple plays kind of stood out to me, because I went to four Orange Bowls and one Fiesta Bowl in my five years there. It would have been nice to go to the Sugar and the Rose, like they have in the BCS now, but those were the ones we were hooked into. I've got 4 Orange Bowl rings and one Fiesta Bowl ring from my time there.

Q: Any off-field stuff stand out?

DS: I think the most memorable event (and you'll likely hear this from a lot of players): We were at the Sheraton Bell Harbour -that's where we stayed when we played Miami- and right before we left to get on the buses where they have the Miami-Dade Motorcade Police (when they take our three or four buses over to Joe Robbie Stadium or whatever you call it), but one of the audio-visual guys, they put together this video of the '94 season: highlights of offensive plays and defensive hits throughout the whole season, and they put it to Phil Collins' 'In the Air Tonight'. (singing) "I can feel it coming in the air tonight..." That was like a five minute video right before we left the hotel and got on the bus to leave for that game. That tape there? I don't think any of the players will forget that, how motivating that was, and it fired up the players and coaches to get out there on the field and believe in ourselves to go and beat the Hurricanes. That was an awesome tape to music that they played to motivate us in closing the meeting up, before we got on the bus and went to the game. It kind of gives you chills, watching all the hits, and I think everybody walked out of there like they were on a different level, as a team.

Q: So tell me, any recollections of the actual Florida game, which was your last game, right?

DS: Yeah, Florida with Danny Wuerffel and Steve Spurrier, that was my last game. I think the preparation going into that game, Coach Osborne kept the players in very good shape. Everybody was running gassers and not slacking. I think after that Colorado game (we didn't have a Big 8 Championship game), there were three or four weeks between that game and finals and all, but for those weeks we never let down on conditioning. It showed in that game, just hammering it to those guys in the third and fourth quarter, that we weren't out of shape at all. I just remember looking over at the sideline at Steve Spurrier taking off his hat that he always wore and just, "What are we doing here?" I thought that was the best thing, him just shaking his head when we started scoring and scoring and scoring, and seeing the Florida fans start leaving Sun Devil Stadium. (laughs) They were like, "This is embarrassing." (laughs) It was just like, not even a game.

But I think that the Nebraska team -just like '94- they believed in themselves and "if everybody does their job, don't worry if we get down." I think that's one thing that Coach Osborne kept with his players: we never got into a panic situation. Whether we were down by seven or down by ten, "Let's just focus on what we have to do and everybody do their job, and we'll be alright." He talked in such a calm nature, and he would say that: "We need to get back to the basics and everybody execute the play and you do your job. Everybody do their job and we're gonna be fine." And that's how he was, very calm.

And talking it through for people? Even if some people were frustrated because they missed a block or missed a run or dropped a ball -you know what I mean?- he would be very encouraging, "You're going to get that next time," and not be down on a player. He was going to point something out if something wasn't done right -if you didn't know the play or ran the wrong way- but I think it was his calm nature of talking with players that would not belittle you. He'd say, "Let's work on this and you'll do better next time," and that's the way you learn.

Q: Do you recall any humorous moments with the coaches?

DS: I know that the defensive line would always do some nasty, disgusting stuff for birthdays: the Girth. That was something where pretty much everybody would be off the field when that was going on. (laughs) It was something with the D-Line; they would do the nastiest stuff you'd ever want to know. (laughs) Birthdays or initiation, or somebody got a Blackshirt or a yellow shirt, or whatever, but they had some interesting stuff went on with that.

Then you think of Coach Osborne and when he'd get mad. You knew he was really upset when he'd say 'Dadgumit', and that would be about as bad as it would get.

Q: I think one time he said 'Judas Priest.'

DS: Yes, I believe that. That was pushing it for him. When he'd raise his voice and say dadgumit, you knew he meant business. (laughs) That's as bad as somebody's four letter words right and left, but he'd never do that. Other coaches would, but not him.

Q: Charlie was pretty salty...

DS: Yeah, and Coach Darlington could be, too. But I think Charlie keeping the defense in line? You kind of have to be pretty stern with people. Everybody knew he meant business and you need to get back to what you need to do.

Q: So from the time you were a freshman to your last game there, can you recall a change in the mindset, the tenor, the atmosphere of Nebraska football? I know there were a lot of constants, but do any changes stick out to you?

DS: I think when we came in in '90 Nebraska had this stigma of "Coach Osborne could not win the big one." We'd get in these big games in the Orange Bowl, but I think that as we worked each year and improved each year into that '94 season, it had something to do with the morale of the coaching staff as well as the quarterbacks with Tommie Frazier and Brook Berringer and the confidence those two guys had. Just working with them and with the other players, they had a sense of control as to what was going on and what we were going to do.

Remember those t-shirts we had made? Unfinished Business t-shirts? Just the '94 and '95 seasons, the way we approached each game, took one game at a time, didn't look ahead to the next, everybody focused and executed to a level that other people couldn't keep up with us. If you believe in yourself like that? That's something that's hard to explain to somebody. But when you get everybody believing that we're going to win this game and we're gonna do it, it would happen.

It was interesting how that came through my last two years there, being a coach and being part of that team, as well, I think the self-confidence level we had at that time was something that a lot of other teams were never even close to having. Or they'd thought about it, but it wouldn't all come together.

Q: That self-confidence, would that be a result of 'X'? And if so, what would that 'X' be?

DS: I would just have to say that the coaches coming together... and everybody working toward one goal and doing their job and going to the highest possible level each time, every play, run that like it's your last play of the game.

Q: Was that preached?

DS: I don't think that was preached. Coach Osborne could have said that, but everybody played at that high level, and when we'd go through practice on Tuesdays and Wednesdays it was full contact, full pads. We'd be hitting those people like it was game day. We wouldn't take them to the ground, but having that aggression -especially the defense taking the hits during the week like that- you don't lose that knack of hitting that you would if you weren't doing that type of stuff.

Q: Like the Callahan teams? They weren't hitting during the week.

DS: If you're not doing that time after time and you have too much time in between? Maybe in the NFL you can get away with it, but I don't think in college you can. That's my two cents on that: you've gotta have the 'hit', because you can't just run through it each time. If you try to do it on game day you'll get clobbered.

Q: It's my thought that college kids easily to lose focus. What approach contributed to limiting mental letdowns?

DS: I really think it had to do with the seniors on each team, and the captains who would get up and talk to the people and set the direction each week in the meetings. And we had the Unity Council, too, who would get up and say a few things. The upperclassmen were doing that, but the real thing would be the captains who would set the tone, and when those guys would say something it would be, "How high do you want me to jump?" The captains really dialed everybody in and broke it down by each game: what our goal was and what we wanted to get accomplished and how we were going to get there. And our goal was to get back to that national championship game every year -that was on the front of everybody's mind each game- and I think the leadership we had really helped pull the guys together and keep everyone focused.

Q: Any particular captain saying any particular thing to the team?

DS: Let's see, was Phil Ellis a captain? Christian Peter, Tony Veland, Zach Weigert, Mark Gilman? I can't remember. I think Christian and maybe Tony Veland or Phil or Mark. But those guys? Wow. Christian would sure give a motivating talk. He had that East Coast swagger that sure brought some aggression. (laughs) I roomed right next to him my freshman year in Harper Hall, you know. (laughs)

Q: Was he actually voted dorm floor president one time?

DS: Yeah, he was Harper Ten Floor President my freshman year. I was right next door to him with a freshman walk-on kicker from Wyoming.

Q: It must not have been easy sharing a common wall with Christian?

DS: He'd do about anything he'd want: grill steaks in his room, have girls in his room. He'd make me drive him to the grocery store to get food because he didn't have a car. (laughs) It would be 10 at night and he'd say, "Let's go to the grocery store. I need to get some food." (laughs) I'd just say, 'Okay.'

Q: How would you describe Christian in those days?

DS: Christian, at that time: "never cross him." And you were upfront and honest with him and did what he wanted to do, because come practice time he could put it to you. (laughs) He was a very strong guy and he did what he wanted to do.

Q: Where do you think he got his motivation, not being a native Nebraskan?

DS: I really don't know. Christian was in a league of his own compared to Jason. Jason was a very talented player, too, but Christian had a side… when it was game-face time he had a game face. He was in a zone, that's how he played. I think that's what some of those defensive linemen have to do: put your mindset in a different zone. And he would do it. He was an animal.

Q: What do you think set these teams apart from others of their day?

DS: I think the walk-on program that Nebraska had, for sure. At that time, guys like myself and the Makovickas and the guys that come in and just worked their tails off to become a starter. I think it's motivating in itself, because it's going to drive and challenge those starters and the scholarship athletes, it's going to push them to perform their best, too. When you have these guys fighting for their lives, living and dying and growing up Nebraska football fans, you're going to have some talented players, and I think we had a lot of talented walk-ons who contributed to that team, gave their all to challenge the scholarship athletes. It made us a better team.

Some of these guys coming up the ranks were surprising people sometimes. But those type of guys -those second and third stringers- when you need relief for the starter? Man, they'd be ready to go in there and you wouldn't even know the starter was out, sometimes. I think the depth that we had at every position… if somebody had to go out you didn't even know that they were out. They wouldn't know there was a sub in. (laughs)

Q: Which reminds me of the Miami game: Ed Stewart was out lame near the end of the first half and, if I recall, Clint Brown was in there and he made a few plays…

DS: Seriously. And another thing, too, was switching the defense from the 5-2 that we did in the early '90's to the 4-3, when we got speed at the linebacker position. These guys were just blazing fast. That changed this team.

Q: Your being a practice player and seeing it Tuesday, Wednesday and Thursday from your freshman to your third year, could you tell a difference as far as speed went?

DS: Oh, yeah. When we got recruited in '91 (and Darren and I were sprinters in high school), when they were recruiting us they said, "We've got to recruit speed at every position." And I remember back in the day when we were in high school and going to the games and seeing the linebackers, they were huge! They were 6'3' and 250 and they were huge, but they couldn't run like the Ed Stewarts, the Doug Colman's, the Phil Ellis's.

Then you get into the defensive backs, the Toby Wrights'. Some of those guys could just fly! Increasing the speed at these positions, I think, improved us as a team, and people were in shock because of how fast we were at each position in those years when we made that switch.

Q: Darren, what would you say was your most valuable contribution?

DS: I would say two things: the contribution of being on second team offense my first few years backing up the starters and supporting morale -which was a good thing- and the second part was running the scout teams for those '94 and '95 teams and helping Coach Solich, getting the team ready to play upcoming opponents on Saturday. It was a lot of time that went into it, but it was all worth it. Everybody was chipping in to do that, and you can't do that with one or two individuals with the time and film breakdown. We wanted our defense -every play and every position that our guys would run?- it was our job to give them the best picture possible, to coordinate that 3rd and 4th string offense to do that. And they did.

Q: Would there be any one person behind the scenes who never got their due?

DS: That's a hard one. I think it comes down to those film guys: Carpenter and Moose. The behind the scenes stuff they did? They don't get the credit, the public wouldn't know: filming our practices day in and day out, getting the tapes ready for coaches to review, exchanging tapes with the opposition. And sometimes, you know, we would have to sometimes go to opposing teams to get tapes, and not the team we were playing sometimes, too. I think it took a little creativity to get it from different teams. And I liked Bryan Carpenter a lot because he played there and sometimes he'd help us out with that position.

But Bryan Carpenter and Brian 'Moose' Mohnsen did a lot of stuff and never did get much credit. A lot of people won't realize how much work they put into that. If we didn't have that we weren't gonna be ready in preparing for the team. What they would do is break it down and slice and dice that tape.

And the training staff, too, the nights and weekends they would put in. Jerry Weber and Jack Nickolite and those guys, they worked on me quite a bit. (laughs)

Q: Any memorable training room experiences?

DS: I think the one that was interesting to me -I had a subluxed separation of my shoulder. I got tackled and kind of drilled into that hard turf before we got the better turf -and I had to do some really odd stretches with my shoulder on all these different moves with that rubberband-type device, that was a killer. And another thing was putting your ankle into that ice cold tub, where you could barely stand it and you were about to go crazy. (laughs) That was a nail-biter sometimes, dunking your ankle up to your calf in that ice cold metal… whatever they called that thing. Some guys would sit and submerse themselves in that. It was like a cattle tank. They've improved things dramatically since we've been there, but that was funny.

Q: Anything you wish you would have done differently?

DS: I wish I wouldn't have gotten injured and played the whole five years like my brother did, but you have to play with the cards you're dealt with. I was fortunate to be on the team and still coaching as a part of that team, because it would have driven me nuts to have gone to regular school and not been on the team. It would have driven me crazy. I wish that I would not have had the injury and continued to play that '94 and '95 season and do what I could.

And seeing both sides of the ball? That -to me?- there's not that many players/coaches can experience what I experienced, seeing both while I was there.

Q: As a summation, what did you take away from that experience?

DS: I just think that coming out of college and having Coach Osborne's mentality of working hard every day and doing your job right, you're going to be successful. That's how I've carried on in my career, too. When I have a task: be very focused, get it done, exceed expectations, and strive for better the next day. The hard work ethic and the time we put in, being very structured and time-organized, it's really ingrained in you how you should function as an adult.

End conversation.

I had already figured they'd be in the mix somehow, but it's now an absolute necessity that we hear from 'Moose' Mohnsen and/or 'Carp' Carpenter, the video guys. We've heard their names more than once, and as I go along I'm beginning to find points from earlier interviews validated and repeated, which is a nice thing to see. In a roundabout way I guess these many conversations are serving as default fact-checkers, ensuring that what was often previously out of reach of the average fan (or at the least, in the shadows) is now being exposed to light and expanded upon by repeat members.

   If one could pick another golden kernel of insight from Damon's conversation it would be his remembrance of the mid-week practices' intensity: "We'd go through practice on Tuesdays and Wednesdays it was full contact, full pads. We'd be hitting those people like it was game day…" In other words, running like red heifers on Wednesdays didn't translate well to blood-lusting Black Angus bulls on Saturdays. (We Husker fans saw what that type of philosophy can do for a unit even as revered as the Blackshirts in those Callahan/Cosgrove years) The coaches as a whole held no quarter when it came to physicality, no matter the day of the week. And were opposing staffs of the more skittish mindset, I can see how their players' spirits could have been easily broken and bloodied come the typical third or fourth quarter of that 60 & 3 era's Nebraska teams.

Notable quote #2:
Damon Schmadeke on the benefits of the walk-on program: "…it's going to drive and challenge those starters and the scholarship athletes, it's going to push them to perform their best, too. When you have these guys fighting for their lives, living and dying and growing up Nebraska football fans, you're going to have some talented players, and I think we had a lot of talented walk-ons who contributed to that team, gave their all to challenge the scholarship athletes. It made us a better team."

The difficult we do immediately. The impossible takes a little longer.
Motto of the U.S. Army Corps of Engineers during World War II

Doctor Who, the long running BBC television program about a mysterious time- and space-traveling adventurer who finds himself in the most outlandish of spots and predicaments, always managed his way out of a scrum. Always. With a run of over 25 years, many actors have played the role, very much like the role of Certified Athletic Trainer at the University of Nebraska. Already we've been introduced to one former trainer in Doak Ostergard, and now we happen upon three other 'good doctor'-types, each with their very own personalities, temperaments, methods, and insights when it comes to the long, limping walk down Cornhusker Memory Lane. If I didn't get the point across earlier, you have to know that without these guys -*these guys*- the team doesn't get on the field. Period. At least not a healthy team anyway, because it's a long season of bruises, strains, pulls, and sprains.

The strength of the training room lineup, here we happen upon Jack Nickolite in the batter's box, with George "Sully" Sullivan on deck and Jerry "Webex" Weber in the hole, a literal Healer's Row to paraphrase the '27 Yankees. So grab a comfy bleacher seat, a cold brew and a box of Cracker Jacks as these fellas take their cuts…and fix 'em up lickety split, as usual.

Notable quote #1:
"He never wavered. He knew the best way to run a football program on the collegiate level. And this isn't the easiest place to recruit players, but he knew it could be done here and he kept after it and he had great teams."

Jack Nickolite

Question: What got you involved in sports medicine, Jack?

Jack Nickolite: Well, what got me interested the most? I had always had interest in medicine and always loved sports, so the combination of the two was what got me there.

I didn't have major for awhile. I was in general studies and then got into sports medicine and biologic sciences, health education, and physical education. Then from there I got interested in sports medicine.

Q: How did you first begin working with the training room?

JN: Well, one of the classes we would try to take was the athletic training class. And Jerry Weber taught it, so that was probably the most influential thing that happened to me as far as getting involved in athletic training.

Q: In what way?

JN: Well, it was the material. The material and taking care of athletes. Jerry Weber was a very good teacher.

Q: So the class is over and you go in to somebody and say, "I want to be an athletic trainer"?

JN: There were some specific guidelines as far as getting involved in it, and you talked with George Sullivan and Jerry Weber, and Dennis Seely was the director at that time, and then Glen Johnson was involved, too. So you talked to those people and they gave you some general direction. I started working some volunteer hours in the training room (which were required), and the rest is history.

Q: What year did you start?

JN: I believe it was about '79, and the biggest thing was the size of the people. The size of the athletes. It was big back then, but they aren't even comparable to today. Back then there were guys like Kenny Brown, Richard Berns the running back (who was a real good player), Junior Miller. I still see him every once in awhile. He's every bit as great a guy now as he was back then.

Q: So you're a student trainer working for free and putting your hours in, what was your next step?

JN: Well, by the time you were junior or senior you'd get a chance to work in the training room and there was some reimbursement for your hours, so that was nice because it helped with your tuition and going to school.

Q: Were you tasked with working with a certain team?

JN: Well, my first assigned sport was men's basketball. Before then we'd put some time in with all sports teams and rotate.

Q: So you're on track and it comes time to graduate. Then what happens?

JN: Then I became a Graduate Assistant. I think that was around '81. At that time most of the weight room people got their Masters degrees, as well as most people in the training room in collegiate settings. So I did that.

Q: So you get your Masters. Then who did you work with? Any football duty?

JN: Sure. I worked with football and basketball, and had a lot of responsibilities at the Bob Devaney Sports Center training room.

Q: Do you recall any specific games back then? Any moments stand out to you?

JN: If you're talking about success on the field, I remember the losses more than the wins.

Q: Any stand out more than another?

JN: Losing to Oklahoma a few times, and losing one year to Penn State and losing to Florida State. That was a tough schedule.

Q: Were you traveling with the team to Penn State and that scandalous out of bounds call in '82?

JN: I sure was, though I was too far away to see it. That was a huge loss. We had a heck of a team, and there was also a bounced pass in the end zone that was called a touchdown!

Q: Do you recall meeting Coach Osborne for the first time?

JN: Well, he'd come down into the training room quite frequently. He'd usually hunt down George (Sullivan). Tom always had a presence, an aura. And it was usually very positive, as you recall yourself. I think probably because he treated people as fairly as anyone could treat anyone. Tom was friendly, cordial, and very fair to everyone he's ever met. He was always very honest and forthright.

Q: Any recollections of any other coaches of the time?

JN: Oh yes, Tom had a great staff. It was a huge asset, too. He had a few coaches that were left over from Coach Devaney's staff: people like Jim Ross. Jim Ross was an administrator as I got to know him, but what a great guy he was. Then he had Cletus Fischer who was an absolutely great coach, a fellow Nebraskan, had coached in high school. He coached at St.

Edward and St. Ben's in Columbus, and then I think at Holy Name in Omaha, and then coached at Nebraska. Then, also, Mike Corgan was on the staff.

Q: I hear he was a real character…

JN: He was a great coach and a great guy. And the thing about those guys is that players absolutely loved them. They had the respect of the players.

Q: How you do you think they earned that?

JN: Well, their longevity and their confidence. And then as new coaches arrived and -I don't want to say developed, as they matured further- guys became great coaches on Tom's staff, guys that Tom hired on. Like Charlie McBride.

Q: What sticks out about Charlie?

JN: Charlie was a great motivator. He could motivate a team and he could give some great talks. He knew the game of football and he knew how to get kids to play it.

Q: What about when Turner Gill joined the staff?

JN: Turner arrived as a player in about 80'ish. When he arrived as a player, just watching him on the practice field and the way he carried himself? You knew he was a great athlete, destined to be a great quarterback and a great team leader. Then he comes back as a coach and he's probably gonna be as every bit as good a coach as he was a player.

Q: So, when did you become a full-time staff member?

JN: I believe it was about '83. I worked with men's basketball and football primarily, as much football as I could early in the season and then as basketball got under way I did a little less because of basketball responsibilities. But it was good, because you got to work with two teams, got to know more guys and travel and do all the rest, what with my taking care of the basketball team, too.

Q: For the uninitiated, what was it like going to the bowl game as a trainer? Is it a vacation or the usual hard work?

JN: Well, if you're in a different city and you're in a hotel things are really close together, so it's easy to get around as far as getting up, going to breakfast, taping and going to the practice field. Sometimes the practice field was a ways away, a few miles, but for the most part things were close together. And so, time management was pretty good.

They were fun days just like working a regular day in the training room when you were back home. Coach Osborne tried to keep a routine schedule, if you will, but he tried to give the players some time to have fun, too. But we'd be taping and giving treatments and practice pretty much like a regular day.

Q: Can you describe a regular day for an athletic trainer?

JN: Well, with football it's usually getting to the early meeting, talking to the coaches somewhere between 6:30 and 7 in the morning, telling them about injured players and their progress, and then usually from the meeting time to about noon was involved with treatments to the injured athletes, treatments and rehabilitation as they came in between classes. Lunch, and taping for an hour an half or two, then another short meeting giving us some time for rehab or catching up on any paperwork you had to do, cover practice from 3 to 5 p.m., treatments for an hour or so, then Dr. Clare and Dr. Dugas or Dr. Strassberger would come in and see the injured athletes and usually get done any time between 6:30 and 8 o'clock. That was usually our day.

Q: What did you guys usually do during practice?

JN: Usually watching practice, watching the guys who were coming back from injuries, being out there in case someone is injured out there on the field, in case they're hurt.

Q: Speaking of the field, do you remember Bill Shepherd?

JN: You know, probably the greatest groundskeeper of all time. And a great guy. I remember one morning I was going to the stadium and we were gonna work out early in the morning, and it get there and I see this guy and I see somebody else in the old north fieldhouse (there was some construction going on the field house and I thought they must have been some construction people), and then old Bill Shepherd comes walking up out of the basement at north stadium and I say, 'Bill, who are those two guys over there?' He said, "They're trying to break in over there!" So I go call Campus Police! (laughs) Anyway, after all was said and done, he ran one of those guys down into the pit of the old fieldhouse and cornered him and made him sit there in a chair. And when he got up to call the Campus Police the guy jumped out of his chair and ran out the side door... ran over the railroad tracks and jumped a fence and he lost track of him. (laughs)

Q: Cornered him down in the pit, huh? (laughs) Was that when you and I used to work out at 5 in the morning before the athletes showed up to start the day?

JN: Yeah, that was it. It was eventful.

Q: Didn't Shep always have that polka dot or striped cap?

JN: Polka dot. Kind of an old engineer's cap like they used to wear on the railroad. (laughs)

Q: What was your least favorite sideline moment or stadium to visit?

JN: I would say, without a doubt, the University of Iowa. You know what, I was there once and never wanted to go back, and I never had to. We played 'em once there and never again in my career did I have an opportunity to go there, and I was glad we didn't go.

Q: What made it so distasteful?

JN: I would probably say the fans. Just the fans. That was an unpleasant experience as far as the fans. There probably isn't a close second of all the places I've traveled to.

Q: Compared to Colorado, even?

JN: Colorado, they had their spectators that were obnoxious, if you will, but Iowa had a whole lot more. From the minute we got there to the minute we left it didn't change. Always somebody with wisecracks, just wise remarks. There was probably a lot of frustration behind that, being a fan of Iowa football and just not having a lot of success. Your next door neighbor's probably got the best program in the nation for 15-20 years, and they're stuck watching Iowa football. Just a lot of frustration coming out that day.

Q: Have you heard that joke about the Iowa fan and his dog? There's a fellow visiting his friend in Iowa and a Hawkeye game is on TV: Iowa kicks a field goal and the dog does a backflip, howls and dances around on his hind legs in a circle. Well, the visitor is pretty impressed, as you can imagine. Then, a half hour later Iowa kicks another field goal and the dog once more does a backflip, howls and dances in a circle. So the visitor then says to his Iowa buddy, "Wow! That's a pretty neat dog! Tell me, what does he do when they score a touchdown?" The Iowa guy replies, "I don't know, I've only had him for three years."

JN: (laughs) So there you have it!

Q: So Jack, do you have any special players who stand out to you? In particular, those '90's players?

JN: You know, all the guys were really, I guess what you would call 'stars.' Every single one of those guys were great leaders. The Peter brothers, Tomich on defense, all those guys, and then offensively, Tommie Frazier, Mike Grant the Field General, they were great players. We had a lot of them.

Q: Did you develop any special relationships with these guys in any way?

JN: Well, the thing I always tried to do was treat all the players the same. Whether they were a walk-on and maybe not going to see a lot of action ever, or maybe a superstar, I wanted to give them the same opportunity as far as getting them ready or keeping them healthy.

Q: Did that come from you internally or was it something that was encouraged?

JN: That's pretty much the way Tom treated them, and that's pretty much the way George Sullivan always did it. I never questioned it and always felt that's the way it should be, and I never strayed from it. That's the way it should be. You'd get your crowd of regular guys who came to you for treatment and training and everything else. They kind of feel comfortable with somebody and confident, because you can't take care of every single one of them all the time. But I think that with Jerry and George and I, the players had good confidence in us. We had great doctors. If you don't have great doctors it's hard to take care of those players.

Q: Who? Can you give me names?

JN: When I was there you had Tom Heiser and Pat Clare. You even go back to Chuck Newman, they were great doctors. They knew how to keep a football team on the field, they can help you get those guys with the minor injuries or even the serious guys who require surgery, they help get them back on the field.

Q: You work with Drs. Heiser and Clare these days, don't you?

JN: Yep, and they both played in their day, too. Tommy played in the early to mid 70's and Pat Clare played in the early 60's, I believe. Pretty good players and pretty good students. And Scott Strassberger was a good student and a very good player from like '82 to '85 or so.

Q: So let's say it's the early 90's, we're winning 9 games year, but it seemed like that bowl hump was just a hard thing to overcome, and next thing you know in '93 we gave Florida State everything they could handle and more. Anything from those years ring true to you as far as differing from other teams previous?

JN: Well, there was a swagger, if you will. Very confident. Swagger, confidence and leadership. Those teams practiced very, very hard and very intense offensively and defensively, too.

Q: Had that intensity been previously lacking?

JN: It was always there, but when you had a very talented bunch who were that intense and that focused and that driven, it's just hard for them not to be successful. And they believed in the entire system: the coaching, the philosophy, the weight room, the medical aspects of the training room, and also the educational aspects.

Q: What do you think contributed to that?

JN: I think it developed over a long period of time. Coach Devaney and Coach Osborne believed in that philosophy, which was very grounded. I think that as it developed and as Tom got more and more of the talented athletes that he wanted, it was gonna be a success. And it was because Tom never wavered from the things that he believed in.

Q: Such as…?

JN: He never wavered. His philosophy on the football field, his philosophy on getting an education for each one of those kids, spiritual aspects, too. He never wavered. He knew the best way to run a football program on the collegiate level. And this isn't the easiest place to recruit players, but he knew it could be done here and he kept after it and he had great teams.

The other thing about Tom: he was very, very competitive on a national level even when he didn't have as much talent as other teams did. And he beat a lot of those programs that had better athletes, maybe more pro prospects than he had.

Q: Was it preparation? How did he do it?

JN: Tom? He was driven. I think he was driven in his profession, driven to be the best. I don't think that winning was ever his most important goal, but more 'how you got there.' But he knew that if you did it right you'd be successful, and he knew if you did it right long enough you'd win national championships, that all those things would come.

And of course, he's very spiritual. He has great faith. His faith was probably much more important to him than profession, and those kids were very important to him; all those athletes and making them the best they could be. Tom knew how to make them great athletes, and he knew that was going to be by coaching and their development on the field & in the weight room, he knew it was very important. Boyd got that started on the home front. That was super important to our program; we were ahead of the rest of the country in the development of players for a very, very long time. That was critical to the development of Nebraska football, without a doubt. The people who came out of Nebraska and made it a special place -including Boyd and Tom and even George Sullivan- that was a milestone in collegiate athletics.

Q: All very visionary names there, Jack. How did it happen that we had so many visionaries, most of them native Nebraskans? What do you think that could be attributed to? Making do with what you have? Perseverance? A distraction-less creativity?

JN: I think that's definitely a part of it. It's good to have people from your own state, because they want to achieve a lot of the same goals, and their work ethic. The work ethic here in Nebraska is pretty darn strong.

Q: And as far as the training program, were you guys leaders, advancing anything in special ways?

JN: You know, guys like George Sullivan and Kenny Rose were pioneers in athletic training. Kenny Rose was a doctor who did a lot of sports medicine along with Samuel Fuenning. George was one of the first athletic trainers and did a lot for the athletic training profession.

And Paul Schneider, he was a very motivational trainer. I got the chance to work with him for a couple years, and those people were pretty outstanding people; not just good in their profession, but getting to know them and the great people they were. Strong personalities, and the kind of people Tom knew could do a good job, just keeping people in the position if they were pretty good at it. Tom is a good judge of talent and character.

Q: To be a good judge of it you must have it yourself, right?

JN: In his case, there's no doubt about it. Because you have George (who now has the George Sullivan Training Room, the new training facility, named after him in his honor), and you had Jerry Weber, too. Jerry is a great guy, too. Jerry was very multi-faceted and has worked a long time in the training room.

Q: Heck, he taught you! How old is that guy?

JN: He's gotta be in his early 50's, I think. (laughs) One of the things I took from him when I was there, was trying to get along with and trying to work well with other departments.

Q: That was trying at times, no?

JN: It wasn't for me. I've always felt -especially the training room and the weight room- I think it's a must that they work together, work in unison. I would say that all the weight coaches I worked with, we had a good relationship and did things well together.

Q: Heck, you had to. Because sometimes the kids would try to play us off each other, right?

JN: Just like kids try to play parents off one another. It's important to present a unified front for the student-athletes to benefit, right?

Q: You've got it. And do you have a favorite game?

JN: I don't think I have favorite game. I'd say they were all memorable and I enjoyed every single one of them. It's the opportunity, it's about the opportunity.

Q: All those times going down to Miami and the Orange Bowl, did you guys actually get sick of going down there so often?

JN: No, I liked going to Miami because that was usually where the Big 8 Conference Champion went. The goal was always to go to Miami, so if we went there we knew we had a pretty good year. Miami was very good to Nebraska, because Nebraska won national championships there with Bob and with Tom. They probably got a little tired of us being down there all the time -us and Oklahoma- but that goes with the territory.

Q: In your view, was that a pretty tough atmosphere to be in?

JN: Yeah it was, especially if you were playing a Florida school or playing a nearby ACC school because they'd pack the stadium and make it like a home game for them, so it made it pretty tough. They were sold out, so it made it just like a home team.

Q: I heard for the '95 national championship game versus Miami that Coach Osborne capitulated and actually allowed Miami have its own locker room for the game..

JN: I'm not sure, but that was a very memorable game because it was so up and down. They played well and there was some things happened that didn't turn out so great, but we had a marvelous finish and came out in the end.

Q: Those years you were dealing with Tommie and his blood clots & Brook with his collapsed lung… any memories about that?

JN: I worked pretty closely with Tommie Frazier his entire career there at the university. Tommie's a great athlete and a great guy, and with his blood clot, that was tough. And then Brook stepped in and played very, very well and had injuries. The collapsed lung, that was kind of touchy and it was dangerous, but trying to keep his lung in good shape and trying to keep him on the field at the same time, it was day by day.

But Brook played very well, and in the end Tommie came back and played in the bowl game, too. It was tough for those two quarterbacks because they went through major injuries that year, and at the end kind of shared some playing time in that Orange Bowl. But maybe sharing time in the Orange Bowl was one of the major reasons we won that game, because they didn't know who to prepare for. And Tommie was very fresh in that 4th quarter.

Q: That's when Tommie and Warren Sapp had their special little conversation, wasn't it?

JN: Yeah, I remember Tommie talking about that. If I recall Sapp said something to the effect of, "Hey Tommie, where've you been all game?"

Q: And I believe Tommie answered back, "Hey fat-ass, it's not where I've been. It's where I'm going!" (laughs)

JN: Exactly. (laughs) But that was a great atmosphere. And you know, we played at Penn State back then, that was really a great football atmosphere. Of course, nearly all the games with Nebraska were that way, back when both Oklahoma and Nebraska were very competitive and played every year for the Big 8 Championship. That NU/OU game was always an incredible atmosphere.

Q: What stands out to you about the field in Norman?

JN: It's a stadium where the sideline bleachers are a whole lot closer than they are in Lincoln, not a lot of room on that sideline. So when a guy gets thrown into the sideline -it's not as close as it is in Oklahoma State- we had a guy once get hit out of bounds and slide into the bleacher and really had a nasty laceration of his leg in the Oklahoma game. That was Mickey Joseph, and that was because those bleachers are pretty close to the sideline. But that was a good place to play because of the atmosphere and tradition there. Barry Switzer brought a lot to the table there at Oklahoma. A great guy. And as a coach? College football lost a great one when he left college football, I'll tell you that.

Q: Any memorable off field occurrences?

JN: I just remember the '95 team had some off the field incidents that were tough on everybody. They were a lot of fun to be with, but there were some distractions.

Q: Why do you suppose that? Just typical college kids? The fishbowl atmosphere in Lincoln?

JN: I think some of both. But at the same time, every college athlete, every athlete high school, college or pro, they're in the limelight, and you get a couple of guys that do things late at night, you're gonna read about it the next day. That's part of the deal.

Q: Were you usually in the locker room pre-game?

JN: Yes, it just depends. Sometimes there are a few things you need to do just before a game: taping, bracing, preparation, just whatever needs to be done.

Q: Any special locker room moment stand out to you?

JN: Absolutely. Coach Osborne's pregame talks, I enjoyed listening to them. Tom didn't give a lot of rah-rah speeches before the games. But more than that, the morning before the game and the night before the game when he addressed the team, he instilled confidence. He told them how they were going to play and told them what to expect, and they were very well prepared.

Q: Eliminating the unknown upped the confidence level so much more?

JN: I think so. Tom set very realistic goals. He didn't like a lot of secrets, I'll tell you that.

Q: In what regard do you say that?

JN: Tom would address the football team and how they needed to prepare and what they needed to do. And then the football team goes out and does exactly what Tom tells them to do. But on the other side, Tom also told them what the opposing team was going to do, and so if the opposing team did something very well our guys were prepared for it: they knew how to take it and not be discouraged because of it.

And unbelievably enough, I'd be listening to Tom on the radio as I was driving home from the game and, sure enough, he'd tell the radio people almost the exact same thing he told the football team.

Q: Any memorable pregame speeches stand out to you in particular?

JN: I think against Florida State -we were beaten in that Orange Bowl- and he told them to play like champions. And they really did. That was the standout.

Q: Did you ever have occasion to listen to Charlie's pre-game speeches?

JN: No, mostly Charlie's halftime speeches. Mostly because the training room -we had a big taping area where Charlie would address the defense- I heard some pretty motivational things there. Charlie told them to get after it. His guys really appreciated that.

Q: Anything about his style, his tenor, his mood, certain choices of words?

JN: Charlie was "no clichés", but he said the right things in the right way and in the right manner. And he would say it loud and intense and he meant business, and he was right.

Q: So, at one point you decided to go to PA school. When was your last year with the Athletic Department before joining Nebraska Orthopaedic?

JN: I worked with the university up to the summer of '97. And then left to work with Scott Strassberger out at Nebraska Orthopaedic. I just wanted to do something a little different that would improve my skills as a clinician. I believe, like a lot of people, you're either getting better or you're getting worse, never plateaued. So I wanted to get better at the things that I do.

Q: Continually challenging yourself?

JN: Yeah, I wanted to learn a little bit more, and I knew there were some things out there orthopaedically I could get a grasp of and also allow me more family time.

Q: Well said, Jack. So is there anything else we haven't touched upon that played a part in the success of Nebraska football, specifically those 90's teams?

JN: I think it was the caliber of players we had, their character.

And I would also say the people in the athletic department: guys like you and Bailey and Boyd and that staff, Dennis and all those people over in academics, and the coaching staff, the administration. Just go down the list.

Q: Anybody in particular stand out to you, who you had the utmost admiration for?

JN: Pat Clare. He is a great team physician. It takes a heck of a team physician to keep a team on the football field. You're doing things this year to set yourself up for next year coaching-wise. Same thing goes when an athlete gets hurt, but you're getting him ready for next year…and you're trying to patch them up and get them ready for next week. He is very good at that. At Nebraska there was not a lot of pressure as far as getting somebody on the football field, at least with athletic medicine. Tom was very astute on athletic injuries. We got them back when it was safe, but as quickly as we could.

Q: Hey, is former O-lineman Steve Volin with you guys now?

JN: Yes, he's with us. He's a great addition. He's a spine specialist and he's been with us for a little over two years. I believe he's our fourth Cornhusker Football graduate in our office.

Q: That's great to hear. And by the way, are you staying in shape? Remember we used to have those 5 a.m. workouts and then we'd head across the street to the old Denny's for a Grand Slam, over by the old Big Red Shop?

JN: Remember that day we walked in and Bryan Bailey was hanging upside down from that squat rack? (laughs) Geez to Pete! It was like, 'What are you doing up there?' I mean, come on! (laughs)

Q: Bryan was either crazy, creative or both.

JN: You know, Bryan's a good guy and he took care of some players and they loved it. Boy, I tell you, that guy? He's a good guy, too. He's something else. You could always count on him. He fired up Doak pretty bad. (laughs)

Q: What was the dynamic there between those two?

JN: I think that if a guy just went to work with Bryan Bailey instead of fighting with Bryan Bailey you'd get a whole lot more done. Don't you think? (laughs)

And I must say, George (Sullivan) did a lot in the development of the pregame meal, now that I think of it. Him and Dr. Kenny Rose. And they were big in the use of nutritional drinks: liquid pregame meals, like a can of Nutriment, those type of things. That is still a very good approach as far as pregame meals. The liquid pregame meal, it's something you can still use instead of a hard meal, if you will. It's a good, sound approach.

Q: Here's a quirky question: what is the oddest injury you ever encountered? Any come to mind?

JN: I've heard about all of them. (laughs) We had a guy on the basketball court and he was from another country in Latin America somewhere, and Moe Iba was running windsprints. And this guy laid down on the basketball court and started pounding his heart, and he said, "My heart's going ba-boom ba-boom ba-boom!", and he refused to run any further. And I told him, 'I'll take you over to see Dr. Fuenning.' And he got up and ran to the dorms.(laughs) Screwball. His name was Victor Ciccone.

End conversation.

I have great admiration for Jack for a number of reasons, the first of which remains his dedication to the health of all walks of human life, student/athletes included. The second is that he was a great workout partner for a number of years, and third is that he was a pleasure to work with. For a time there was an uneasy truce between the Strength Staff and the Athletic Training Staff as to methods, modalities, and which personnel should be conducting rehabilitation for a wide array of slightly injured players. The issue causing most tension was the use of the squat exercise and its effect on knee joint integrity, if I recall. (Team Doctors were eventually called upon to weigh in on the situation, and with their blessing the squat exercise remained part of the regimen) Jack was able to see through that fog quite clearly and find a way to work as a unified staff, a trait for which I commend him.

His reverence and respect are only second to his knowledge of Coach Tom Osborne's ways, for Jack spent a number of years within the program and even on the periphery in these latter times. It was refreshing and inspiring to hear him say about Tom Osborne, "He never wavered. He knew the best way to run a football program on the collegiate level. And this isn't the easiest place to recruit players, but he knew it could be done here and he kept after it and he had great teams." I am absolutely convinced that without the relentless, dogged adherence to bedrock Christian principles, foundational ethics and a steadfast prairie pioneer's resolve, Tom Osborne would have never achieved such outright leadership greatness, much less his many teams' stellar accomplishments. In never wavering from the cause of nurturing and guiding those many young men about educational pursuits, football perfection, and dealing with life's resultant struggles, his system would have been a mere mish-mash of brutish collisions, mangled psyches, and meaningless highlight reels. But it was otherwise, as the 60 & 3 era attests, due to the system Jack Nickolite referred to: Coaching excellence, a Power Offense philosophy, use of the weight room, the medical/training staff, myriad educational aspects, and even the spiritual element.

Notable quote #2:

Jack Nickolite on Tom Osborne's public/private persona: "Unbelievably enough, I'd be listening to Tom on the radio as I was driving home from the game and, sure enough, he'd tell the radio people almost the exact same thing he told the football team."

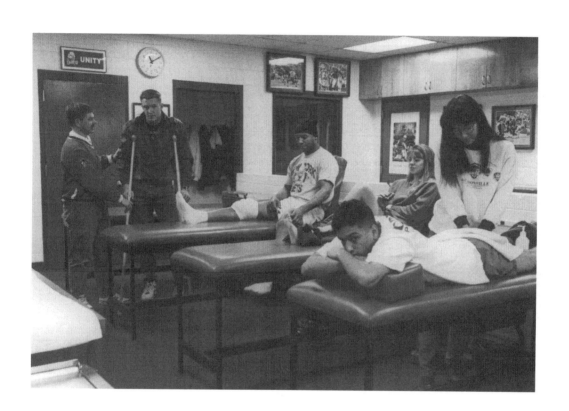

1966: At the University of Florida, Dr. Robert Cade and Dr. Dana Shires create Gatorade for the university's football team, the Gators.

1966/1967: Dr. Cade comes to an agreement with Stokely-Van Camp, Inc.(S-VC) to produce the already patented product.

1967: The Gators begin to officially drink Gatorade. They beat Georgia Tech for their first Orange Bowl title. The Tech coach is asked why his team lost: "We didn't have Gatorade. That made the difference."

1968: Sports Illustrated writes: "Famous athletic teams rave over a cloudy, lime-green liquid with some strange attributes and an unfamiliar taste."

1969: The Kansas City Chiefs begin to drink Gatorade, which they attribute to their Super Bowl title of that year.

1970: Elvis Presley drinks Gatorade on stage, taking a sip between songs and saying, "This is Gatorade -- in case you want to aid your gator."

1973: S-VC and Dr. Cade settle a lawsuit with the University of Florida. The university claims they own the rights to the Gatorade formula. From that day on, the University receives well over $80 million in royalties.

Gatorade Timeline, courtesy of Twoop.com

We now encounter the Ruby of Rockville, Nebraska: George Sullivan, Nebraska Athletic Trainer Emeritus. Why the precious gemstone of a moniker, you might ask? Well, it's only fitting if you know a little Nebraska history:

You see, there was another notorious George born in late March, 1915, out of Butte, Nebraska. Born George Wagner, most pro wrestling aficionados of the 1940's and 50's might recognize his more popularized name: Gorgeous George, the Human Orchid. (known for his luxurious blond locks) Acting every bit over-the-top by conjuring up an incredibly flamboyant ring persona, he packed the house wherever he journeyed and alone had a remarkably grandiose effect on the future public personas of boxer Muhammad Ali and singer/performer James Brown. George Sullivan, more popularly referred to as "Sully," played things a little more low-key but had just the same degree of effect on many of Husker student/athletes through the years. To wit, just as we all know about Kool-Aid's being invented in Hastings, Nebraska, you should know that Gatorade had its own Nebraska-based origins. What's that you say? Wasn't it formulated in Florida, as the timeline above points out? Hogwash! Here's the real story from a man who had a hand in it, literally stirring the sauce. In my mind, the drink should forever be known as Huskerade. Here's George Sullivan.

Notable quote #1:
"There was not just one who was the sole leader. It was tough to pick a captain, because they were all captains."

George Sullivan

Question: Thanks again for making yourself available, George. Like I said, your name comes up quite often as to the effect you had on the organization and the kids and getting your due. And hey, I hear you have a training room named after you now. Is that true?

George Sullivan: Yes, Tom come back and named the training room after me. It really happened when we were at the other end of the stadium over at the South Stadium Office building, old 'Dollar Bill' (Byrne), the old A.D. -to get me to retire- (laughs) so he got to building this new training room. And the Touchdown Club, bless their souls, they named a scholarship after me.

Q: That is awesome, George!

GS: It really was. I kind of spun on my heels there for ten days. People were congratulating me and I couldn't believe that it had happened. I think about a half-million dollars got put into that thing.

Q: You must have rifled through the couch cushions for some spare change to contribute to that fund, eh? (laughs)

GS: They must think I won the big jackpot and contributed to it. (laughs)

Q: So George, what year did you retire from the University?

GS: Well, I retired in '97. Really, I shouldn't say that completely, I really retired as head of the whole caboodle in '94 and I just did half-time so that they could -they needed money at the time to continue, and they wanted to revamp the medical thing, and there was no way they were gonna hire Weber until we got our way - so Tom thought it would be a good deal if he retired, too, but only if I retired. (laughs) So he blessed me by naming the training room after me after he got to be A.D.

Q: So we have Osborne Field and the Sullivan Training Room, huh?

GS: That's right. That's right. (laughs) We had to keep it going. You did hear, though, that the Regents yesterday extended his contract so he can go as long as he wants to now?

Q: I heard that. I'm a big fan of HuskerMax.com, so I keep up to date with the goings on in Lincoln. Things are always changing, eh George?

GS: There's always time for change. (laughs)

Q: Where did you grow up?

GS: I grew up in the little town of Rockville, Nebraska. But during the war years they closed the school down because of a teacher shortage and I went to Loup City High School and I became a Red Raider there.

Q: My college roommate was from Loup City: Lance Kaiser. His Dad was a teacher there.

GS: He sure was: Lonnie Kaiser. I'll be darned.

Q: And we used to go fishing out there…

GS: Sherman Lake! I had a cabin out there for 28 years.

Q: So what road did you travel to end up at the University?

GS: Well, I was in the service and played some football overseas on a couple teams right at the end of the war and came back. I was in the Army and we were over in Germany. Went into France and north into Germany, but I didn't see any real first class action. It was right toward the tail end. So I went to go to the University here and I went out for football. And we just didn't have very good teams… and I was even worse. And I was up on the table getting taped by Blain Rightout, the trainer at that time, and he says, "Are you sure you want to go out there?" And I said, 'I don't have any other druthers, do I?' (Of course, we didn't have scholarships in those days, we had jobs if we wanted them) "Well", he says, "I need some help." I said, 'Hand me the scissors.' And damned if he didn't do it! So I cut the tape off. And he says, "Well, you have enough tape on you... I think you understand how to do this." (laughs)

I went along with it. I was in Engineering at that time, and I switched over to Physical Education and the sciences and went to Physical Therapy school. And they came over to Iowa where I was taking my Physical Therapy school and -Paul Schnieder was the head trainer at that time- and they wanted me to come back over and head up the student health and physical therapy department and the football program. So I did it. That was in '53 and I've been there ever since.

Q: What year were you playing football?

GS: That would have been '47, '48 and the first part of '49.

Q: So joined on at the university. Who was the coach during those years?

GS: Bill Glassford. I played under him and then I came back and worked under him. He wanted somebody other than Paul Schneider.

Q: And the advances athletic training has made since your early beginnings?

GS: Oh, fantastic. Really fantastic advances! From the time I became a trainer, there couldn't have been more than 6 or 7 physical therapists in the field of training at that time. (All the trainers had double-duty at that time: they were track coaches and baseball coaches and equipment managers, so they didn't really have a background in sciences at that time.) Nebraska kind of became the leader of advancement and Dr. Sam Fuenning, who managed student health, was the promoter of many things, promoting student health. He was one of the first to become a member of the Athletic Trainers Association. Sam Fuenning was an innovator of health care for young people.

Q: I remember Doc Fuenning. So all of a sudden this guy, Devaney, walks through the door...

GS: First, we had Bill Jennings. When Glassford left they hired Elliot, then Jennings, then Bob Devaney arrived. Bill Jennings had really recruited quite a class, so Bob had a real good bunch of athletes when he came in. Both speed and size, that was that early 60's bunch and those guys became very, very close knit. Prior to that it was mostly old veterans; they liked the game, but they were more concerned about their families, so it was no big situation to them.

Q: So then in '73 Coach Devaney hangs 'em up and decides to hand things over to Coach Osborne. You were the head trainer at that time?

GS: I was the head football trainer at the time. They didn't give me the head trainer over the total department until about the time they built the Bob Devaney Sports Center, and then Schnitz went over there with Jim Ross. And I was seeing all the players over at Student Health, anyway. And I was fortunate enough to have a real good bunch of students and assistants: Roger Long, a former baseball player, Jack Nickolite, if you remember him, Jack was a tremendous kid, and we got him into Physicians Assistant and Doc Clare swiped him from me. He was too darn good. (laughs) Jerry Weber, we brought him back, he's been here over thirty years now.

Q: Jack was telling me about one of his first athletic training classes, that Jerry was teaching it...

GS: Yeah, he taught a full-time class. We just had a one hour thing with PE before. I had it and Jerry taught it a little bit, and so did Roger Long, and we put in a full curriculum.

Q: And the rest is history, huh? And speaking of Dr. Clare, he was a player too, right?

GS: Yes, he was in the early sixties. He was a good running back for us. His dad had a business out on Cornhusker Highway, but we talked him into coming back to us.

Q: So, fast forward to Coach Osborne taking the reigns. You had the 70's, 80's and then the nineties, and from my recollections (I joined the athletic department in 1987 as a student assistant) it seems to me that the football team, once we hit the mid-90's, something happened as far as team cohesiveness. What stands out to you?

GS: I think it really kind of gelled and everything came together. All of the staff that were working for Tom, especially, were good teachers. If they fell off on anything at all, it might have been that they had so many good friends around the country, and all those good friends were telling them a few good stories about how a good a recruit might be. But if they hadn't have been such good teachers I don't think we would have been as strong in that overall department.

Q: So it's not just that fact that we possessed great, hard-working athletes, it was that the staff also did such a wonderful job coaching them up?

GS: Exactly.

Q: What were your first impressions of Coach Osborne, meeting him as a young Grad Assistant?

GS: He's changed a lot. He was really kind of a meek person, in a way, he wasn't able to really jump out and jump on things. But he could read right off the bat... you could see that he could read a person's values and their mind. And if they accepted him they were 100% his. It was like they were his kids, his sons.

Q: A pretty quick study in and a judge of character?

GS: Exactly. Bob picked that up right away, too, and took him along with him. And Bob had some guys with him from way back: Jim Ross was with him even in high school up in Michigan. One coached basketball and the other coached football and they were assistants to each other. Jim was more of a First Sergeant, and Bob thought everybody was great people. Jim could handle coaches and everything else. He was one of the only, really, assistant athletic directors.

Q: So Coach Osborne as a young assistant, a pretty quiet fella?

GS: He was the kind of a person who wouldn't just jump up over something. You needed something drastic to get him going, not like Mike Corgan would. I guarantee you, Mike Corgan was different. He believed in making a person's nose snotty or putting it on 'em. He was very intense.

Q: I hear stories of his spunk and his pluck...

GS: Oh yeah, all of his players loved him, though. He'd have some of the damnedest things for them, and they still talk about him when they get together. And I tell you what, I don't know why it makes me think of him all the time, but he'd keep it away from Bob: him smoking his pipe. He'd try and sneak a little puff on the sidelines when they'd have a break -look and see if Bob was watching him- and he'd sneak the pipe back in his pocket. That is, until it caught fire one time. (laughs) He was so intent on what he would do: he was a great cook, gardener and all that type of thing, and he was a great winemaker. He had 'The House of Corgan' labels on his wine.

Q: A self-sufficient, modern day Renaissance man, eh?

GS: Oh yeah, but that old nose was tough. You didn't cross him.

Q: Do you suppose Coach Solich picked up a thing or two from him?

GS: Oh, definitely. (laughs) He tried but he was too small. (laughs) No, just kidding, he really listened to him. He thought he was a really great innovator of plays and that whole deal. Frank really learned a lot from him.

Q: In essence, George, you had a great view of Coach Osborne's growing into his Head Coach-ship?

GS: Oh, I think so. Just following him and seeing his ability and leadership, and his thoughts and his relationships with the professors and so forth, how he wanted his kids to have the grades and everything? He filled a lot of shoes there by himself before he became head coach.

Q: He was Johnny Rodger's shadow for awhile there, wasn't he?

GS: Oh, yeah. (laughs) He was taken by surprise when Bob put him onto that case. Bob was really the one that was the old Chief of Police, so to say, and handled it all with expertise.

Q: Your witnessing Coach Osborne's growth throughout the years, anything stand out as to major hurdles that he may have overcome?

GS: Oh, especially in the conditioning program, he was very, very instrumental. That was one of the things Roger Long and I started, because all coaches didn't believe in any kind of weights. And Bob let me go down and buy out a health store that went kaput downtown, with the University Purchasing Agent. We went down and made bids at the sale, and the same time, very soon after that Boyd Epley was sent over to me. And after a little tough time right at first (because he thought he wanted to be body-beautiful and oil up his body and show off) we got it squared away. And we were lucky enough to have Bob Brown there about that same time, and Bob moved the weights. He would work those things over. And Boyd would see that, and what little bit of weights we had got bigger and bigger and bigger, so we got more room and Boyd built a well-known program around the country and everybody wanted to come in and copy it.

Q: I spoke with Boyd and he has a lot of respect for you, George.

GS: Well, bless his buttons. He and I would get in a few arguments when I'd tell him I didn't want him to do things because I didn't think that's what we needed -like when a knee got hurt because of squats- because we didn't think that was what everybody needed. I was on him pretty big and had a few discussions, but they were good ones.

Q: I remember there were always a few guys on staff who you didn't want to make angry: Coach Osborne, Charlie McBride, Milt Tenopir and George Sullivan. You didn't want any of those guys on your bad side...

GS: (laughs) They all would laugh (the coaches,) because at the Dining Hall they didn't have much control over things and I guess they left it to me because I ran the whole thing. And when I started slapping even the girls on the back of the neck? They thought that was pretty tough.

Q: George, that's so funny! I was talking to a former player a week or so ago and they mentioned how you would quietly sneak into the training table area and spot some athlete eating at the dinner table with his cap on… and you'd scare the living hell out of them with a quick slap on the back of the neck! (laughs) Then every head in the room would be on a swivel and they'd rapid-fire rip their own caps off and throw them to the floor!(laughs)

GS: That's the way I was brought up. If I'd have walked in the house and kept my cap on, my mother was right there to give me a good whack on the fanny. I thought it was probably better not to whack these guys on the fanny, so I did it on the neck there, instead. (laughs)

Q: And from what I understand, you had quite a bit to do with the concept of the pregame meal…

GS: Well, we put it together and it was on a national basis with the American Medical Association, and they had a big display going around to all the meetings about how Dr. Rose and Dr. Fuenning put together a liquid pregame meal. And fact of the matter, I took the liquid pregame meal to the Pan-American Games in Sao Paulo, Brazil. The Kramer Company made drinks for us and it really went over big. And I forget how many more gold medals we'd won in those Pan-American Games than we'd ever won and have done since. That was in about '63, because in '64 were the Olympics, it was usually a year before them.

Q: I swear somewhere along the road someone said Gatorade was actually invented at Nebraska?

GS: Well, we *know* it was.

That was another thing. The doctor in Omaha -the head of the Neurological Department- was giving a lecture down here on sports. And we had a program going for the coaches where we put something together for hydrating these kids and we gave it to the coaches. So we put it together, (and all we had to do was use what they call a 'normal saline' in it, only took a tablespoon of salt to a gallon of water). Well, we're playing in the Orange Bowl against Auburn and the doctor at Florida was at that game and he came over to the sidelines and asked the kids, got into the backside of the sidelines, "What are your trainers doing there?" and they said, "You can talk to George." And so they hollered and called me over here to talk to this guy and I told him and he says, "I never heard of such a thing!"

Well, it wasn't long before he went back and his trainer was calling me, and he says, "What were you using?" And I said, 'Saltwater.' And he says, "We'll never get our kids to drink that." I said, 'Well, throw some Kool-Aid into it..' And he says, "What do you call it?" And I says, "HuskerAid." (laughs) What you never heard later, the doctor was sued by the Gators for using the name Gatorade, and they settled for $50,000. And he sold out to Stokely-Van Camp and received a 5 figure retainer fee for the rest of his life. We got nothing out of it. I talked to Gatorade and Gatorade knows the history. But of course, we never did use it. We were doing it for the kids, but this sucker goes out and makes a million dollars, you know?

Q: And Kool-Aid was also invented in Nebraska, right?

GS: That was invented in Hastings, Nebraska. It was a big thing going in TomOsborne-ville. I think it's funny two famous things came out of Hastings, Nebraska: Tom Osborne and Kool-Aid. (laughs)

Q: Any fond recollections of the assistant coaches? Any unique personalities?

GS: I think it was strictly the togetherness and cohesiveness of the whole group there. They were so good to me that there's not one of them I can't say they weren't nice. There were times some charlatan would want to do something odd with them, like inserts in shoes, and padding and taping situations (there's always somebody trying to get a coach to sign on with them or something), but they had enough respect to come see me if it was one of those things. In the treatment of a knee or fixing of an ankle? I'd just as soon listen to what some mothers had to say about getting a guy better than some of those guys. Jarvis Redwine's mother, when he got hurt down in Missouri that time, she called me and told me how to treat the thing, and I thought, "Oh my gosh, how's that possible?" But I did it anyway. I dipped that sack, dipped it in vinegar and did what she told me and wrapped that thing up, and I'll be danged, he didn't have any swelling the next day. (laughs) It's a matter of listening at the right time and doing it then. (laughs)

Q: Anything in particular about the 90's teams stands out to you about that era, the personalities…

GS: That group is still real close today, that group of players. It was the closeness of the group as a whole.

And there again, the Florida State game… and I forget who was holding the ball for that last second field goal at the time… David Seizys! There should have been a penalty. They just smeared him. And the officials ran off the field like they didn't see it. It should have been a defensive penalty. And so we should have won that Florida State Orange Bowl game. And Bobby Bowden was confronted on that and he wouldn't talk about it. He was just like old Joe Paterno and that little square out of bounds in '82. So Tom was really ruped a couple times there.

Q: I had a chance to talk to David Seizys and he does recall getting wiped out…

GS: That was bad, bad news. And Tom just kept right on coaching at that time; he was going right down the line and it didn't phase him. He didn't holler about it. Well, he didn't have a chance… because they were off the field already, you know?

Q: And George, could you run me through a typical day as the head trainer at the University of Nebraska? What were your days like?

GS: Usually I'd be down there for treatments at 7 o'clock in the morning so I could get 'em off to class. We'd treat all types of sports. What really kind of changed things, and what changed a lot of policy was when Title 9 came in and we had to let the girls in the training room over here, so consequently that changed the total situation. So we'd get them off to their classes and they'd come back early for another treatment.

During football season we'd start taping at 2 o'clock and tape 'til 3 o'clock, whenever they were going to have their meetings. They'd have their meetings up there in the football offices, and we'd go up to the field and watch them very closely with hydration and if anybody goes down, bring 'em back in at 5 o'clock and start treatment and hold the ones for Dr. Clare and his staff. They'd come down to see 'em and I'd always leave. Jerry was so good at staying on and seeing the final one with the doctors. I'd finally leave about 6:30 and he'd probably get out of there at 7 p.m. It was usually a twelve hour day, and that was six days a week. And then Sunday mornings, we would have a little workout and see all the injuries from 10 to twelve noon.

Q: Nonstop, eh? Not just a job, it was a lifestyle?

GS: It was a lifestyle.

Last night on public television they had the great Big Bands of the fifties, my wife and I were sitting enjoying that. And I forget the name of this one song. My wife said, "That's probably because you were still down to work!" I shouldn't have brought that up. (laughs)

Q: You were in the vacuum known as the Nebraska Athletic Department, huh?

GS: It was a ring around the rosy.

And computers changed things a lot and you had to be more cognizant of record-keeping and so forth. It was hard to find time to write down all the John Does, but my time when the computers came around and it changed things, it was good. But by the same token, if it wouldn't have helped out the athlete or young person later in life, we made sure we wouldn't be treating stuff like that.

Q: Speaking of the players of the 90's, do any of them stand out in particular for you?

GS: I suppose when Frost came back to us, because I knew his dad so well; Larry was one of my athletes. He was over at Malcolm and he lived right next to Paul Schnieder in those days, so when Frosty came back to us (he had some problems, a little different throwing motion, and we tried to straighten that out, but we went back to his original delivery because he was still pretty good with that), but I used to do a lot of shoulder treatments on that. I think he'll do very well coaching. He's been brought up with it all his life.

Q: Do you have a most memorable or favorite game as a trainer at Nebraska?

GS: I would still have to say the Game of the Century stood out the most. That was the most fascinating game. You knew we had those tear-away jerseys at that time, and all the changing of the jerseys. And the old McCook Flash, Jeff Kinney? My gosh, how many times we had to change jerseys on that guy! Him and Johnny, it was something to behold. I thought we were going to run out of 'em, to the point that we were going to have to use plain practice jerseys. (laughs) We could sometimes go through five or six on those backs in a game. If they'd get torn so very much the official would tell us to get them changed, you know?

As far as tough injuries, Mickey Joseph at the Oklahoma game when he got his leg lacerated on the aluminum bench on their sideline, their trainer jumped right in and helped me out, he had pressure on that thing. I forget how many stitches he had to have. Many stitches. And right after that happened, his quarterback broke his leg out on that field. Both of us lost our quarterbacks in the first five minutes of that game.

Q: The athletic training community was pretty tight knit no matter what color of shirt you were wearing, eh?

GS: Yes. And as a matter of fact -in the old days, the minor sports?- when the track teams would come up I'd take care of their track teams for them when the coach was watching his budget. But the only time we'd be all together was when we were together for a football game.

Q: That would be very rare nowadays, huh?

GS: They're like the assistant coaches now: they just hate one another. (laughs) That's one thing about Charlie. Charlie McBride and Milt Tenopir, those guys were always with the other coaches. Consequently, how many clinics were they invited to talk at, you know? So the coaches, that used to not be.

Bob (Devaney)? That's probably why he was asked to go everyplace around. He just liked everybody, even the Bear. That's the way he was and that's how Tom was, but we had coaches down through the years who wouldn't do something like that, you know?

Q: What in particular stands out about the Game of the Century?

GS: Just that fact that we were always going back and forth. And kind of like Don Bryant said, he came down on the sideline and he said, "We've got to get this game over with, I'm gonna have a heart attack! I can't stay up in the stands!" (laughs) There was just more action than you'd see in most games, and both sides were so determined to really win that game.

Q: If you ask me, that '94 Orange Bowl against Florida State holds a very close second place.

GS: I would say that, too. Very much so. And I guess the 1971 National Championship game, here we were standing there winning the National Championship, it was unbelievable. Unbelievable. You just go to the hotel and everybody was just so exuberant and so forth, I don't know if anybody ever went to bed. You didn't get back to the hotel until about 11:30 or midnight, but everybody just kept on going and singing. And I heard "Go Big Red" that night for so long, I never could get it out of my head, like a ringing in the ears.

Q: Anything stand out to you as to Coach Osborne's last game, that Tennessee game?

GS: That was really unbelievable how those kids were playing their hearts out for him. Tennessee just couldn't believe what was happening to them. Both sides of the line, those kids were just playing tremendous. You just never thought we could have prepared for that game that well.

Q: And what was your last game as a full-time trainer?

GS: Actually in '94. The Miami game.

Q: What stands out about that game?

GS: I guess I wasn't even thinking about it, that that was going to be it. (Because I was going to stay on and work until '97.) Jerry had been doing so much with the management thing and building a new training room, I guess it didn't even seem that anything major was really happening.

But I remember there against Miami, with Warren Sapp, he kept mouthing off at the time and I kept hollering at him. (I shouldn't have been doing it.) (laughs) He was so funny in that he kept running back along the sideline after he'd make a good hit downfield. He said, "How'd you like that one, Doc?" I said, 'That was out of bounds, you rat!' (laughs) He just laughed. Later on I was down to Tampa one time and he says, "Weren't you the Doc for Nebraska when we played?" I said, 'I was. And you cheated!' He laughed so hard. He was a great guy.

Q: So he remembered you by sight?

GS: He remembered me. Yes, he did. (laughs)

Q: Any memorable off-field occurrence for you?

GS: Oh golly, that is a good question. I guess there were so many, many, many good things in the Devaney and Osborne era, how could you put them all together? And they were all so good to the family. I had a good life is all I can say.

Q: Any memorable practices stand out to you?

GS: I guess, I kind of remember we bought a couple of new pieces of equipment that Corgan had them running through, and he had them diving over a cart, acting as if it was a goal line stand and the backs diving over the top. That was the time with Jeff Kinney and that bunch, he had them doing that: two of them came up in a row with their shoulders hurt a little bit. That was the only time I saw Bob really come out and get after his coaches. He said, "Let's cut that dadgum drill out!" (laughs) That was a memorable time, because I could just see the look on all the coaches faces, because here's Bob hollering at him, you know? It was a little too risky.

Q: Anybody behind the scenes who you feel had a huge part in those teams? Someone who most folks wouldn't realize their contributions?

GS: I would really think way back to Sam Fuenning and what he did at the University of Nebraska for all those students; building the student health center for the students and the program for athletic medicine and all that. I thought they should have named the student health center after him. He started the School of Health, he was the first president of that. That's never been recognized and it really surprised me. He did so much for the students: his innovations for cold remedies and the students coming in and getting checked out, the overall health of students. He and Kenny Rose developed a chair that we would do an electrocardiogram in the giving of physicals. When I heard my name was going on the training room, I thought, 'Dang, and Sam didn't even get his name on the student health center.'

Q: So what is it like to walk down into the training room with your name on it?

GS: Well, the students all run over and turn the light on so I can see it. (laughs) It's real nice. I really don't know the athletes anymore, being as I don't work on them directly. But I can hear them talking in the background when I'm around there, and the kids say, "That's him, the guy whose name is up on the wall."

Q: I'm sure the guys have quite a few stories about 'Ol Sully, being that you're an honored individual now. I recall my first few years on the staff there, where for some reason or other I'd go over to Bill Sheppard's shop area when 'ol Tom 'Trainwreck' Novak would be hanging out there with him. In retrospect, I wish I would have gotten to talk with Trainwreck a little more and gotten to know him better…

GS: Yeah, that's another thing. Bill Sheppard, he deserves some recognition for all he did there and all the time he put in. He'd always show up down there at 5 o'clock in the morning and he'd go home and cook dinner at 3:30 (because his wife didn't like to cook) and then he'd come back down and close up the place. But how many hours the guy put in down there! And if you needed a picture framed, why he'd build it. He did everything. Everything from the minor things to going out there and scooping the snow during the Kansas State game.

But the tough thing about Bill, which I hate most of all, was all those years with the blowers down in the stadium. After the games he'd make sure all that trash and stuff was finally pushed down the aisles and down below to be cleaned up, and all those years with those blowers he got to so he could hardly hear anymore, even if he was standing right in front of you. He'd read your lips, more or less. He was a fantastic young man. I remember when he first came on and the guy who he worked for -the name eludes me now- but Bill used to work out there on East Campus at the Ag College handling those big Holstein bulls as a fifteen year old, for crying out loud.

Q: He seemed like a farmer in the city, what with his tanned, weathered face and that polka dotted cap he'd always wear. It was like his section of land was Memorial Stadium. Old Shep, working his ground…

GS: Around Thanksgiving he'd often cook up a whole meal for all the campus maintenance guys and they'd gather over there and sit and eat with him, too. (laughs)

Q: What was it like in South Stadium at that time with the Equipment guys right next door to you?

GS: We always worked so doggone close. If we had a new piece of equipment we'd go down and see them and show it to them. They had no qualms about buying a special shoulder pad, or if I could draw a design -something to protect the ribs or something- they knew exactly what equipment guy to call to make the thing, and we'd have it in there the next day. They just did a tremendous job.

Q: So you ended up fabricating a lot of your own stuff, huh?

GS: Oh yes, especially shoulder pads or rib pads, braces and stuff. There's a couple things on the market a company named after me, for crying out loud, like the 'Sully Shoulder Wrap.' That was my design of taping. Doak Ostergard took it and talked the companies into putting my name on it. That, and the groin wrap and a hamstring wrap, that's been a real popular thing. It's been popular for rugby in Europe. I guess they don't believe in surgery at all over there. (laughs) They use a ton of those shoulder wraps.

Q: Everybody's got their own Sully, huh?

GS: Yep, everybody has their buddy named Sully. (laughs) But here we were doing that kind of thing in the early days. Like I said, Gatorade -really Huskerade- we did for the athletes, we just never did garnish all the goodies with those big contracts.

Fact of the matter, I was in the group that designed the first football shoes for Nike, too. Nike was just a track outfit, and Nike wanted us to use their football shoes they designed. And I didn't like them: we were getting more sprained ankles. So they picked out a bunch of trainers from around the country and we all met in Massachusetts and that's where they designed the things. That's where we designed the very first football shoe for them that was worth something. It would have been the late '70's, early '80's.

Q: I remember those early 80's teams and those white Nike hightops for the turf. They were very popular.

GS: Yes, very popular. Then all of those outfits made a move to have them made in China, for crying out loud.

Q: As a summary, George, your last few years in the 90s' there: any other lasting impressions or comments about the teams themselves worth noting?

GS: I think those early 90's with the Connealy's and all those guys, they stuck together to the Nth degree, and they were just fun to be around. (And they were kind enough to include me in a lot of things.) I guess (the neck slapping) there was one of the things I'm popular for, because they were a bunch who liked to wear caps all the time. (laughs) The togetherness of those teams was remarkable. There was not hatred or big squabblings, even from the lowest, meek guy to the biggest loudmouth. If they thought something was happening they settled it themselves. It was a togetherness that was really developed.

Q: That's the difference between a group of football players and a team of football players.

GS: And there was not just one who was the sole leader. It was tough to pick a captain, because they were all captains.

Q: Amen, George. Amen. Thanks so much for your time.

GS: It was a delight. You take care.

End conversation.

What a trip. I just love 'ol Sully. It was never a dull moment with him in the room, especially with oftentimes pointed commentary backed by his years of experience. Wasn't it Solomon who said "There's nothing new under the sun"? Well, wise old George had the same worldview, as the guy practically invented modern day Athletic Training.

Do you want to know the most precious bit of info I gleaned from this conversation? It's this: Out of all the teams Sully had known over a span of five decades, he mentioned the 60 & 3 era as having a most particularly strong bond: "They stuck together to the Nth degree… The togetherness of those teams was remarkable. There was not hatred or big squabblings, even from the lowest, meekest guy to the biggest loudmouth… It was a togetherness that was really developed." Though it's almost cliché, a true sense of 'family' existed, for we all know that you can pick your friends, but your family you're stuck with, for good or ill. The fact that many incoming classes hardly knew each other until they arrived on campus, I guess the setup could have been described as resembling a family of siblings: each waiting to find who the new kid is, and then welcoming him with open arms to the dinner table, the dirt playground out back, brotherly advice and encouragement, you name it.

Notable quote #2:
George Sullivan remembering long-time Nebraska Groundskeeper Bill "Shep" Shepard: "He deserves some recognition for all he did there and all the time he put in. He'd always show up down there at 5 o'clock in the morning… how many hours the guy put in down there! … He did everything… He was a fantastic young man."

We have not lost faith, but we have transferred it from God to the medical profession.
George Bernard Shaw

Bringing it all together for the full-time Athletic Training staff of the 60 & 3 era, we finish with the one man still standing in the training room this very day, recent National Athletic Trainers Association Hall of Famer Jerry Weber. After first hearing from the Gothenburg Dane, Doak Ostergard, some chapters ago, it's a bit odd that I hadn't yet touched on the genesis of this wonderfully odd game that has our rapt attention and oftentimes grotesquely skewed affections in the first place: the sport of American Football. I do so because -in a roundabout way- it started with the Danish.

The story goes that after England finally defeated the occupying Dane Army in the year 1042 an Englishman thereafter happened to unearth a Danish soldier's skull, which he then proceeded to kick around his field just for giggles. Surprisingly, it quickly became all the rage, as other landowners swiftly began digging up their own "headballs," as they became known.

Soon though, the rigidity of a skeletonized human melon became too painful for the delicate feet of the local populace, so they quickly reverted to the use of inflated cow bladders instead. The next great advance was to place one of these "footballs" half the distance between two neighboring towns, whereafter the townfolk to first kick the ball first into the others' town square was declared the winner.

Flash forward then, to 1869, where a mutated version of the sport a little closer to present day football first took place between Rutgers and Princeton. I'm not sure what the final score was, or who even won that contest, but suffice to say, it caught on like a prairie fire. And almost exactly 100 years to the day of that first game, a son of the Western Nebraska grasslands joined the staff as a greenhorn trainer: our very own Jerry Weber. Let's hear from our man, "Webex," a training machine spanning a career of "headballs" and the calamity they've wrought on young mens' bodies and spirits.

Notable quote #1:
"It isn't just the X's and O's and getting the A's and B's. There's a spiritual element to it. There's an element of leadership and mentorship."

Jerry Weber

Question: So tell me, Jerry, first off: where did you grow up?

Jerry Weber: Sydney, Nebraska.

Q: Out west. Past Ole's Big Game Bar in Paxton…?

JW: Even way past that. About a hundred miles west of there. A long way from Lincoln, Nebraska.

Q: So how did you end up joining the staff there in Lincoln?

JW: Well, I was not athletic at all in high school; I was not an athlete. One of the coaches, Harold Chaffee (who ended up being the Wesleyan Head Coach for years there), and Duke Osterday, they asked me if I'd like to be a student manager in high school. And there was a company in Olathe, Kansas called Kramers Sports Medicine, they had a student course you could take. They'd send you the stuff, you'd study it and you'd take a test: how to tape an athlete, how to take care of wounds and injuries and whatever. Just a very rudimentary level. And I took that course.

And then Tom Ernst, who was the football coach after that (He had played down here at the University. He was from Columbus, Nebraska, State Athlete of The Year at one time), he knew Paul Schneider and George Sullivan and called and said, "I've got a kid I think would be good to work with you guys." So Paul said, "Send him down here." That would have been the summer of 1969.

I stopped in and met Paul. Paul was doing basketball camp and it was hot in the Coliseum, and he was sweaty and he said, "Yeah, I think you'll be fine. Be here at such and such a date." And that was it. (laughs) So I started as a student athletic trainer here in 1969 and was here 5 years as an undergrad, and George and Roger Long were both Athletic Trainers and Physical Therapists. (At one point in my early career I thought I wanted to be a doctor, but after the time there and being a training room rat and hanging out with those guys and seeing this was going to become a passion of mine, I decided to go to Physical Therapy school, because I saw that as the best pathway to eventually get a job here.) So I did that and was in the Med Center PT program and graduated in '76 and went to Western Illinois University for a year. And every year Duke LaRue would bring in a young PT to be the staff physical therapist in the Health Center in the mornings, and then at 4 p.m. you'd come to the athletics and work with the kids. And the thing that was nice, they paid you a salary. And then they also paid for me to go to school and get my Masters.

So it was ideal: I worked with football, traveled with football, wrestling, track and baseball... travelled quite a bit with baseball. Then Paul Schnieder, who was a lifelong smoker, he got emphysema and then he moved over to the Devaney Sports Center with Jim Ross, so they asked me to come back. And I've been around her for forty years. So my career path was very fortunate.

Q: What's your title right now, Jerry?

JW: I'm the Head Athletic Trainer, Physical Therapist and Associate Athletic Director for Athletic Medicine.

Q: Wow, sounds like you have a lot on your plate...

JW: Yeah, I do, but it's kind of the point where we have demands on athletes all year long now. And the size of the program with the teams and sports we have? We have a fairly large staff. And I've been able to hire really, really good people. And that's the key to any success, hiring people to do a good job and make you look good.

We have a full-time football staff, which we started in the mid-90's that we kind of organized when George retired. And I became Head Athletic Trainer and we decided to hire a full-time head football athletic trainer, because the demands of that sport require you to devote your whole time to that. You can't do that if you're also going to be looking over and seeing how the other teams are doing. So we split up those duties and it's worked out really well. Some athletic trainers are full-time with certain sports, and I oversee them and work with a number of sports, yet.

Q: Was gymnastics always something you did?

JW: Yes, men's gymnastics, and of course, women's gymnastics, because when I got here in 1977 most of the sports like football had priority, and basketball, and we had maybe a part-time female assistant and that all grew when I first came here. The model around the country was the head athletic trainer and then an assistant. And the head ATC was in charge of football year long, the assistant worked football yearlong until the bowl game, after the bowl game he traveled with men's basketball. So we did that, and then we had students with the other sports.

So I did that for my first four or five years until the demands of rehab just got to be too much. We had a good student, our first graduate assistant in Jack Nickolite, we hired him as men's basketball athletic trainer. So that's kind of grown along those lines ever since.

Q: Wow, amazing how that's changed from even a dozen years ago. And you've been there a full forty years now in some capacity?

JW: Well, forty years as of yesterday. You just take some personal pride and accomplishment to be in one place that long, and hopefully I've contributed. But you just don't think about it, you know? It's really unusual for somebody in my profession. I'm a dinosaur, there are very few young people in their thirties or forties that will have a career like I've had at one place. You get burned out or bounced around, you just can't handle the stress, and sometimes you go into a different profession or do it part-time. So it's been quite a run.

Q: Now, most of the fans reading this may not realize how time-intensive being an athletic trainer is. What has kept you going strong?

JW: Just the day to day interaction with the athletes. We're in a position, where we see a young man or young woman, 17 or 18 years old, and a lot are very mature, a lot of them aren't. A lot just don't have a lot of life down yet, you see them grow from a boy or girl into a man or woman those four, five years they're here. It's that maturation process and the interactions. Some people ask me, "Isn't it boring doing the same thing every day, taping ankles over and over, etc?" And I don't think of it that way. Every day is a challenge. You never know what's going to come up. You think you're cruising along and all of a sudden something comes up that you haven't seen or somebody else hasn't seen, and maybe you have the answer. So it's just the day to day interaction with the athletes that I enjoy.

Q: Now, my focus for this book is the arc the program took in that 1990's era. And speaking of that, who stands out to you as far as personalities?

JW: Well, there were an awful lot of them, obviously. I wish I had the media guides from those years. I have people come up to me all the time and they go, "Hey Jerry, it's good to see you, you're looking great. Remember me?" And I go 'No.' (laughs) I say, 'Okay, you've got to help me. When did you graduate?' I'll have to think about who else was around then, because after awhile it all runs together.

But some kids you really remember from that era. It sounds weird, but Byron Bennett was one really special kid. Byron was a kicker (and I hate to say this, and a few of them aren't) but most kickers are a little goofy, you know? (laughs) Them, and pole vaulters and divers. They have a specific talent, they're individualist and they're really on an island. And you have to understand them, because often times you're either gonna be the hero or the goat. And Byron had all those things happen to him. As a freshman or sophomore at practice with that old Astroturf they were practicing field goals or extra points and there was a fumbled placement. He picked it up and scrambled for the goal line, turned his knee, and he tears his ACL. So here you go: a young kicker trying to prove his worth and tears his ACL, so he had to go through all that rehab. So I got to know Byron very well after that. And he came back and became a very successful kicker for us, and of course, he's unfortunately known for the miss at the Florida State game...

Q: Among the many 'makes'...

JW: Yeah. Many, many makes. He probably saved a bunch of games, but a lot of people remember Byron for missing that field goal, and it's unfortunate. So kids like that stand out. When we played at the Cotton Bowl a few years ago he came down to the field at a practice and he came up and said hi, and we even corresponded for a year or so after that.

You get little notes from some kids sometimes. They say, "I want you to know you were special to me, etc." And Byron did that. He was special. Another kid who was special to a lot of people, and me in particular, was Brook Berringer: his personality and character. He was always kind of an underdog guy. I always kind of hung with the underdogs a little bit. Not that you paid them any more attention, but you appreciated them a little more. Kind of like the walk-ons. But he was always in the shadow of the other quarterbacks he played with. He was hurt, had the lung injuries, and just ended up fighting back through those chest injuries and was a key element to getting us to that '95 Orange Bowl. That whole time, just a quality kid who never complained about anything, was really well grounded, had lost his father early in life. So some of those kids.

There were so many kids who, as you get older, you tend to be a bit of a father figure for some kids, and I think I helped fill that role a little bit; just somebody to confide to and ask questions about things. And you feel good about the answers that you give those kids, because you'd like to think that you're helping them grow up. But Brook was really special: he'd be respectful, had a great work ethic. And his legend grew when he was killed in the plane wreck. That was a devastating time for everybody. It was a rough time.

I can't remember when Jake Young played, but he was a special player, too. Great athlete, really smart, always a great sense of humor. A smart ass, basically. You get close to kids because you spend more time with them when they get injured; sometimes 3 hours a day when they get injured, so you really get a chance to know them more. Some kids, for some reason, you turn around and they're sitting in your office, and you say, 'What are you doing here?' And they say, "I just wanted to stop by and see what's going on." And they want to get to know you better, which is fine, and you become their 'guy', which is fine. And that's another thing that's special about this profession. Because a lot of times you can't get that close to people and they to you, so it's pretty special when you're here all day long. They appreciate when you're gonna be here and available to them all the time.

Q: Matt Turman said that you were his 'guy'…

JW: We all had our guys, and we still do. Regardless of who is on staff or if you come in and out of football. That's what I do now, I'm helping these guys with some things but I don't make football decisions. I take guys and, even though I'm not the head football guy, they vegetate towards you…(laughs)..gravitate towards you. And Matt was one of those who did that. There are a lot of them.

Matt was a good guy. I remember he got hurt, he was just easy to get along with. And you had no expectation when he got here: undersized kid from a small town in Nebraska. Good athlete. Not a great athlete, but a smart kid. And especially when Brook and Tommie got hurt, that Kansas State game? He really did a great job. It's good to hear some of those kids remember you and are kind enough to mention you once in awhile.

Q: Well, a lot of them say that you were really special to the whole organization and that you were one of the wizards behind the curtain…

JW: You know, to a certain extent that's a good way to put it. We are behind the curtain. We're behind the scenes and that's fine, we're not hired to be out there. And we do some things that you weren't specifically hired to do for them, but you do, because we care for them. And if you're an athletic trainer or a strength coach or whatever kind of advisor. And often something special clicks, and it's my job to make sure I do see that happens a bit.

I'm sure there are a lot of people in this profession that don't want that relationship. They either don't have the personality or are scared by it, or some just embrace it. But I think you have to as a part of this profession. I tell our young student assistants that, 'Hey, you have to treat our athletes better than that. You don't have to be their best buddy and their comrade and feeling sorry for them, but you have to be their friend.' And a lot of people, I don't think they get that sometimes. And, of course, that's another reason they don't stay in this profession. They need to be some kind of an ally to the kids.

Q: That being said, is there something about being a Nebraskan which speaks to that? Was there something to that when Coach Osborne was the head coach?

JW: I think it goes back all the way to Coach Devaney. Seriously, you look at his ethic when he came in and developed a culture here. It was one of the underdogs that all of a sudden became the top dog, because Nebraska certainly was the underdog in the early 40's and 50's and 60's until he got here. He created a sense of wellness for the state, and I think everybody in the state took hold of that. It became pretty apparent that was what was expected. And I think your Midwest attitudes -conservative and family values- they are really important. I think it's really easy for them to wash over to this system, and certainly Coach Osborne exemplified that.

He surrounded himself with great coaches and great people. He certainly led the way, set the tone as far as how you're supposed to treat people. It isn't just the X's and O's and getting the A's and B's. There's a spiritual element to it. There's an element of leadership and mentorship. His whole thing is mentorship, you know. I guess that's one thing we could all certainly use. I look at my career as being a lifelong mentoring system, where you like to lead by example, and think that kids look up to you and appreciate you because you treat them right and you show them the right way to do it.

They'll come in and tell you what they did last weekend. And they have these stories, "Oh man, I did this and I did that.." And I say, 'Wait a minute. You had a good time and that was cool, but what did you learn from that?' And they say, "Oh yeah. Man, I ain't going to do that again...." I try to emphasize some of those things. And then, of course, they go back and do it again and then you hear about it. And I go to them, 'Hey, I thought we talked about that?' And they go, "Yeah, I know. I just…" And I say, 'Hey, well here's what you do: Don't hang out with them or do this..' And the ones who do listen to you? They come back around and say, "You know what? You were right. I was screwing up back then." There's so many, Paul. I could go on and on if I had a roster in front of me.

Q: You talked about Coach Osborne and his mentoring. Could you expound upon his leadership coming from the top down? Anything that was unique, original, special about his particular brand of leadership?

JW: I think Coach Osborne was -and I don't think this was intentional- I think it's just the way he lives his life: He always led by example. There's never any question about his faith and his belief system. He never really forced that down on people, but it was very apparent that he felt it was strong in athletes' lives and he would live his by example, would show that. He would also point it out, "Guys, take this anyway you want to, but there are certain things that you need to guide you in life. What you have to ask yourself is, "Is this the right way to do it or the wrong way to do it?"" Another way he put it was, "Could you tell your Grandmother what you did last night?" Things like that. And it would kind of get their attention.

But he was also smart, he surrounded himself with really good people. And at some point he also -because of the people he worked with- he never had to be the bad guy. He could be, but usually he led with his expectations. And if you hadn't met the expectations there would be consequences, but he never had to drop the hammer. But Charlie McBride would certainly drop the hammer, and Frank Solich would drop the hammer, or Jack Pierce, whoever it was. And it wasn't like they carried the message of, "Coach Osborne says you're screwing up." It was more like it was coming straight from the man, "Hey, you're screwing up! And you know it. And we don't -the total worldwide we- don't appreciate that or we don't expect that. Our expectations of you are higher." He was able to do that, and a lot of people can't get that across to their staffs and their athletes, and I don't know how he did that. I'll never figure it out, but he still does it today in leadership. He certainly will drop the hammer, because I think his role as an athletic director is a little different, because you have to be a little more forceful. I think he was just able to get his ideas across very subtly, sometimes. He could be direct, but it was usually innuendo or subtlety. And if you didn't get it, there was somebody next to you who was gonna get it and figure it out for you. I think that was just his strength. Quiet leadership.

And I know the man's brilliant, so I don't think it was all totally unintentional, either. He understands what works and what doesn't work. He's able to get peoples' attention and get you to understand goals. He's a genius.

Q: Any recollections about Charlie or Frank, like you were saying?

JW: Charlie was probably, in that group of coaches, kind of the roughest edge of any of them: verbally, vocally, physically. I've seen him on his tiptoes and scream at a guy face to face, whether it was Christian or Jason or Grant or Tomich, any of those guys. He would dress you down. But the next moment he'd have his arm on their shoulder telling them they did this and this right, and "cut the other crap out" again. (laughs) But the guys loved him. Talk to any of those guys. He was like total love/hate relationship sometimes. It was kind of fun, almost like seeing him go into an act sometimes. He knew what buttons he could press and what buttons he couldn't press on others, and he would press them all. I think he really did have a little bit of an act he would go into. (laughs) Frank wasn't quite like that at all. Frank was more into the teaching aspect of it. Charlie was a great teacher, but he went about it a little differently.

Frank had a great rapport with the athletes and was really an athlete's coach. I think he was. He really was empathetic with the athletes. He would really listen to them, he liked to hear their story and he'd help them work through any problems they had. And as far as a coach, he was a great technician. They appreciated that and understood. He really didn't have a Napoleon complex like some guys his size would. The power he had, that could turn very negative, but he never did.

Q: Anyone else on that staff?

JW: Turner, especially, he was one of my athletes. Then his hardship and problems with his foot and leg, and he overcame that and became a superstar and is probably still the most beloved quarterback we've ever had here. A Christian, quiet demeanor, never brash, a total leader by example. Turner was a great technician, just a great comrade and friend to his athletes. There was a great love there. I think he picked a few things up from Coach Osborne: his faith and belief in human nature, and he did that when he was an assistant coach and athlete.

Q: Do you have a shining moment in your career?

JW: Oh, wow. I guess, for me, it would be a bunch of kids who overcame terrible injuries to go play, and without your help they never would have overcome some of those problems. A lot of them, no one will even remember their names. They came back and did a great job. They never played in the pros and they're not out on the wall of All-Americans even. It's just that accomplishment in being a vital part of getting that kid back to being a healthy athlete.

Q: Any memorable road trip or bowl game stands out to you most?

JW: It's kind of weird, but it's the one where we got our butt kicked. It was the Citrus Bowl. Because it was kind of a turning point, that season and that bowl was a turning point in Coach Osborne's career, I think. We were not very good, they out-athleted us, they just did some things. That's when Tom figured if we wanted to compete with the Georgia Techs, the Miami's, the Florida State's, we have to change how we recruit, how we play on defense and how we do certain things.

And he did it. And that's not easy to do when you've been playing a certain way and doing a certain thing for years and years and years. That sounds weird, but it became a very emotional game. At halftime Tom made the comment that, "I may not be here next year. You guys can't play like this…" And all of a sudden you're thinking, "Uh oh, he's retiring."

And other bowls, other trips? The '99 Fiesta Bowl, that was very memorable. Eric Crouch was a sophomore, we just lit 'em up, and we'd lost to Texas earlier that year: Correll Buckhalter going across the goal line, he tried to extend it across the goal line and instead fumbles, so instead of being up and going away with the win they got the ball back and marched down the field. And then we came back and kicked Tennessee's butt in that bowl game. We were probably the best team in the country at the end of that season, and it kicked Eric's career off. He was a great athlete and a great player.

Obviously, there's the '97 win when Scott Frost took us to the national championship against Peyton Manning. Our defense just swarmed and picked them apart. And Joel Makovicka running? But I'm not a memory guy or a highlight guy, really. I just can't do that. If I could, I'd be writing this book instead of you. (laughs)

Q: Any memorable practice occasions?

JW: Well, I remember there were some scrimmages we had. We'd go live on Tuesdays or Wednesday, and there'd be the plays on the goal line. You just held your breath because you knew somebody was going to get hurt. Actually, Phil Ellis did break his hand one time during those tiffs. You remember those. And Jason or Christian would end up fighting somebody, throwing a punch at somebody. It was just a different time.

I know back in '78 or '79 we had a defensive coordinator, Lance Van Zandt, he was crazy, he was nuts. He was mean. He practically killed Andy Means. (Andy's now head coach at Millard South) He'd have a drill -and he was a defensive backfield coach- he had this drill where the kids would stand straight up with their hands to their sides and be a tackling dummy, and guys would run full speed into them, Bang!, and hit them under the chin. Well, after about two neck injuries, George runs out there and gets in Lance's face and, "What the hell's going on?! This bullshit has to stop!…" and Tom comes over and he's, "What's going on here, guys?" And George and Van Zant were toe to toe over it. And they stopped doing it, it was stupid. Lance thought it was funny, but it was just stupid. There are so many other things that go on, but that's one thing I remember.

Q: Did you ever find yourself, as a trainer, cringing at the kids playing and hoping to heaven they don't get hurt, like a protective mother?

JW: A little bit. To a point you are. I'm still amazed to this day, as much men's athletics I've watched over the years, that some guys didn't get seriously hurt every play. You look at a play and you go, 'How did that guy just get run over there and just pop right up? How did you get hit by four linebackers and you're only a 185 lb. running back or receiver, and you pop up and throw the ball back in their face?' It just amazes me, the size and speed of these kids is just scary anymore. Hopefully the equipment is caught up to the athleticism on both sides of the ball and allows them to get away with it.

But you do it often. You get immune to it, after seeing it. The biggest change for me is when I travel with football in the fall and then you change gears and travel with men's gymnastic and baseball, an entirely different level of violence. And yes, there's some danger of risk in gymnastics, but not like football. Especially my first ten or fifteen years, then I'd come back to Spring Football and go, 'Whoa!' That brings you back to reality right away that it's an entirely different sport.

Q: I think it was old running backs coach Mike Corgan who was quoted as saying, "Football is a nasty game played by nasty boys."

JW: Yeah, surely. And Mike Corgan, he was a character. And Frank was one of his guys. Frank picked up Mike's work ethic and his ability to work with his athletes, as well.

Q: In summary, Jerry, is there anything else from those years that stands out to you?

JS: There was never any doubt, never any question if we were going to win a game. You never went in to the game thinking, "Boy, I hope we play well. I hope we have a chance in this game." Even that 7-7 season with Frank, we never felt that way.

I don't remember that kind of a feeling until Callahan's second year and kids were questioning themselves. Even in Frank's season there, we were just out-manned. I hate to say it, but we had poor quarterback play that season. I hate to say it.

But it was an attitude that you carried. It was a swagger. That's what most people call that. There was never any doubt. The teams we were playing knew they were gonna get their butt kicked. There was no mercy. We weren't going to go out there and hurt anybody, but we were gonna be better than you and physically pound on you all game long on offense and defense.

And we're getting that back with Bo and his staff. It's back. I remember the last season of Bill Callahan -and Paul, I'd never heard this, never in twenty five years- but kids would come in and you'd hear, "Well, what do you think? Do we have a chance this week against Kansas State?" or "How bad do you think Missouri's going to beat us?" I heard that and I was, "What the fuck did you just say?! Don't you ever say that again! Son, did you really just say that?! There's never any doubt in your mind whether we are gonna win or lose!" They just weren't sure. They didn't know if they could do it. They just had some bad mentoring going on. It was amazing.

Before that, it was just Nebraska. That's the way it was. When you came here you learned real fast from the upperclassmen and the coaches that anything else was unacceptable. In all sports. We kind of lost that, "We have to go out there with a look in our eye." I think it was just a reputation. Bob Devaney established it, Tom kept it going, Frank had it going there. Nebraska was Nebraska. You put that uniform on and you became invincible. You'd see that all the time. The greatest guys in the world off the field were guys like Grant Wistrom and Jared Tomich and Bret Clark and some of those guys, George Andrews. But you put a uniform on them and you wouldn't want to be close to them, they became different people. They really did. Terry Connealy could be like that, too. Even Schlesinger. Cory could be great, but he was like that, too. Just great guys who worked their butts off and never took a day off or a play off, you know? A lot of kids nowadays don't get that concept.

Q: Do you think that ties into the Nebraskan, the Midwestern work ethic?

JW: Absolutely. And the other thing that's starting to get going again is the walk-on program. You'd get kids in here from the east coast, from the South, from California and Texas, great athletes who worked hard, but they'd never worked that hard. And they'd get here and there'd be some little kid from Mullen, Nebraska trying to kick your ass every day in practice.

And they would go, "Wait a minute, don't you understand? I'm so and so from some place or other." And those kids would go, "F*&# you! I want your job. I'm gonna make you better." And they did, because it was for Nebraska. At that time, most of the guys were playing for Nebraska, they weren't playing at Nebraska. This was the ultimate. This was the best. And whatever came after that was the cherry on top of the sundae. And that's back again. Unless you've got a program where you have your pick of the top five athletes every year like USC, Texas, those schools, you have to work and develop kids. Both Bob and Tom knew how to develop talent. You start with some raw talent and you work with them, and in a few years those kids are gonna be great players.

End conversation.

Straight talk from a Sandhiller is what you got here, folks. Can you imagine the influence Jerry's had for forty-plus years there in the Husker training room? It's real world toughness combined with tender-hearted, healing hands, the kind of pioneer spirit that got our forefathers through a wagon-load of killer winters, droughts, endemics and the like. It's that fighting Nebraska spirit manifested via the sport of football; It's spit, it's spunk, and it's survival instinct all distilled daily during stim treatments and stretches and ice baths and tape jobs. That's a real Hall of Famer, and I absolutely love it!

Funny, but these trainers hardly ever talked about some great fix-up they managed to perform, some miracle-cure that saved the day and got the All-American back on the field for Saturday's big showdown. Instead, they speak mostly about the Nebraska Football attitude, the culture, the relationships and friendships nurtured, their mentoring capacities fully capitalized upon. Trainers walk a very fine line, because they don't want to seem as if they are coddling a student/athlete and encouraging a pity party, but instead are firm in their positive-minded pursuit of engaging the kids while the oftentimes painful healing process takes place. One thing I think many of us take for granted are those times when a young athlete experiences a major injury and how delicate a spot they are placed in when that happens. For some, it's the first time in their young lives that their body has not been able to answer the call to action. It's a severe emotional blow to find that one's physical faculties have failed them, yet the trainers find a way to lead them through it and perhaps emerge from the experience better human beings, more appreciative of their athletic talents and the opportunities presented.

I guess if there were two precious items of note to take away from our time with Jerry Weber, they would have to be the concepts of role-modeling and of change. Starting at the top, you can see how Coach Osborne and every staff member on down the flowchart were thoroughly cognizant that eyes were always upon them. Were they always angels? Heck no, but the student/athletes witnessed how certain personalities with distinctly unique temperaments blended with the mentoring/teaching function, giving the place a unique educational flavor and experience all its own.

As for change, I'd like to think that Jerry's statement of Coach Osborne deciding that, "we have to change how we recruit, how we play on defense and how we do certain things. And he did it. And that's not easy to do when you've been playing a certain way and doing a certain thing for years and years and years." This may be me out on a limb here, but I have a feeling that Coach Osborne and the rest of the staff went out on a limb and decided to go for broke, all or nothing, with the changes they affected after that 1990 season. If you recall, many were calling for the collective staff's head on a platter, wanted to run them out of town in exchange for some flamboyant "name coach" out there who would accomplish the grand feat of a big time bowl game win. (You know who you are) In hindsight, I believe history should give us pause the next time some coach doesn't seem to be measuring up, for they are oftentimes most close to the grandest of victory when suffering the most heart-wrenching of defeats.

Notable quote #2:
Jerry Weber talking about the mindset of that day: " "We have to go out there with a look in our eye." I think it was just a reputation. Bob Devaney established it, Tom kept it going, Frank had it going there. Nebraska was Nebraska. You put that uniform on and you became invincible. You'd see that all the time."

If you don't invest very much, then defeat doesn't hurt very much and winning isn't very exciting.

Dick Vermeil, Football Coach of the Year at the High School, Junior College, NCAA Division I and Professional Football levels.

Nebraska is the second-ranked beef-producing state in America, so it's only right that it had its own particular version of a Philly Steak Sandwich on staff, epitomized by a Philadelphian who capitalized on the assistance of a coaching legend's favor to garner a role during that 60 & 3 era. Now back east and coaching in the Ivies, Clayton Carlin still retains the taste of his Nebraska experience and relishes its lessons and people, perpetuating its wholehearted positivity and welcoming embrace. Let's hear from one of the younger kids on those days' coaching block with a very unique tie-in to the making of Husker History.

Notable quote #1:
"They all had the same goals and same vision, and they treated me and treated everybody with nothing but class and integrity… the players, they impacted me greatly, being so coachable. And no egos there, either. Just great kids."

Clayton Carlin

Question: Hey Clayton, it's been a long time! I was watching some old film the other day and saw you roaming the Nebraska sidelines and figured I just had to get a hold of you for this book…

Clayton Carlin: (Laughs) I'm sure I looked a lot younger than than I do now, some 15 years ago now.

Q: So you're married with kids? The whole works?

CC: Married with 5 children and a sixth on the way. I met my wife in Nebraska. She's from Oakland, Nebraska. Yeah, it made those three years that much better. (laughs) We've been married a little over 11 years.

Q: With as hard as they worked you GA's, how did you find the time to find a wife?

CC: (laughs) You're not kidding, Paul. I'm still trying to figure it out. (laughs) It's the truth. She's just unbelievable. She's incredibly patient and supportive. A good girl to be married to in this crazy profession.

Q: You grew up in Philly, right?

CC: Right outside Philadelphia. A suburb outside of Philadelphia, Pennsylvania.

Q: What road did you follow to become a GA at the University of Nebraska, then?

CC: Well, here's exactly what I did: I was a high school coach for 5 years, Paul, and I coached at a Division 3 school, Delaware Valley College, which is in Doylestown, Pennyslvania, again, right outside of Philadelphia.

Then I got an opportunity to come to Nebraska. And I got it! I caught a big break because of Dick Vermeil. My father works for the Philadelphia Eagles, and Coach Vermeil was coach of the Eagles when I was growing up. I was able to get to know him and he was very helpful to me earlier in my career. Still is today. At that time he was broadcasting and doing different games around the country and dropping my resume at different places. He dropped it off with Coach Osborne and I came in for an interview… and a month later I was moving to Lincoln.

Q: What did your father do for the Eagles?

CC: He's the Director of Ticket Operations. He's been there, my gosh, for over 45 years. There was a three year stint there when he was out. Remember the old United States Football League?

Q: Dude, I absolutely loved that league! The old USFL!

CC: Yeah, he left the Eagles to go with the Philadelphia franchise and was with them as the Vice President of Business Operations and Ticket Operations.

Q: The Philadelphia Stars! They had Kelvin Bryant at running back, Chuck Fusina..

CC: You got it, Chuck Fusina was the quarterback. Irv Eatman… there were some really great players there.

Q: I loved the Breakers teams. They had first dibs on all the former Nebraska players…

CC: They were great to watch. (laughs)

Q: So, going back to Coach Vermeil, I guess that old saying rings true: It's not what you know, but who you know?

CC: Oh yeah, no doubt. You get an opportunity to get it done and you have to hold your own when it happens.

Q: So you interviewed and then somebody gives you a call to come and join Nebraska?

CC: Yeah, that's exactly how it worked. I packed up and moved out there and the rest is history. Absolutely three wonderful, magical years.

Q: Did they tell you on site? On campus?

CC: They didn't tell me while I was there. It was another day or couple of days when Coach Osborne called me. They flew me out there and I visited with George Darlington and some other coaches. It was before the National Championship game versus Florida State.

Q: Really?

CC: It was before that game, so it was in December sometime. And I joined right after that game.

Q: So you spend the majority of your life back East, and then you show up in Nebraska. First impressions?

CC: Well, I would have to say, Paul, just the people. The people and the coaches there on staff, everybody involved with the football program was just so wonderful, they all had the same goals and same vision, and they treated me and treated everybody with nothing but class and integrity. That's what I'll always remember, how accepting everybody was. I just moved out there and didn't know a soul. George Darlington there, a wonderful man, and Charlie McBride and Tony Samuel? They were just great. And my first year there, it was Kevin Steele and then Craig Bohl. And then Frank Solich and Milt and Dan, Ron and Turner, it was all wonderful and, obviously, because of Coach Osborne. I remember the people being so gracious and so accepting and so helpful.

Q: Any recollections of that helpfulness?

CC: Yeah, there were no egos involved. You were a graduate assistant, but I tell you what, you were just treated very well. You had to work hard, obviously, and do some tough things, but everybody just treated you with nothing but the utmost respect day in and day out.

Q: You worked as the GA with the DB's and Coach Darlington, if I'm correct. What can you tell me about being a Graduate Assistant that most fans likely wouldn't be aware of?

CC: Well, I'll tell you what, I think Nebraska at that time was a unique place. I don't know if it is anymore, being a GA there, but at that time -because of George and Charlie- you got a chance to coach, too. You had to do the film breakdown and drawing the cards and prepare things but George had no problem: one day he took the safeties and I took the corners, and the next day vice versa. It was one of those deals where they'd give you as much responsibility as you can handle. That's what made it a unique place, and I grew as a coach there.

Q: What kind of impact did the coaching staff have on you, as far as your coaching methods and the leadership style that you use now?

CC: Well, certainly Coach Osborne had an impact. Just how he treated people and how he was always the same day in and day out. I learned from him to keep things on an even keel. There was no, there was very little difference that you could sense in his demeanor whether it was the start of spring practice or right before the national championship game. His demeanor day in and day out certainly impacted me. Just because of the man that he was, and how everybody there, Paul, had no egos, same goals, same vision. No one had any hidden agendas. They just really worked well together. Everybody impacted me, spiritually the way I was impacted. And Tony Samuel was very good to me, working side by side. Just the influence of a lot of people.

Q: When people ask you about Coach Osborne, of course they know the name but not so much the man, how do you describe him?

CC: Well, I don't know if there's words out there. I just tell people everywhere I've been that I still use a tremendous amount of things I learned from him. There are things I bring up in staff meetings here at Cornell. When we as a staff have to deal with a situation, I'll say, 'Well, here's how Tom Osborne would have approached it this way or handled it that way.' He had a heavy influence on me as a coach. What better way to describe my respect for him than that?

Q: So you showed up in the spring of '94, right?

CC: Yeah, January of '94. My first season was the first national championship when we beat the University of Miami. The second season was the Florida national championship game. And the third season, my final, was that game against Virginia Tech.

Q: That last year was the big flu game where Texas caught us at a weak moment?

CC: Yeah, they sure did. I remember it like it was yesterday. They ran a play action pass in the Alamodome and we bunched 'em all in in a two-tight formation, 4th and 1, and they snuck the tight end out and hit a long pass on us, you know.

Q: You can't get all the bounces, can you?

CC: No, you can't. (laughs)

Q: Now, I heard you had a connection with the Miami quarterback, Frank Costa…

CC: Well yeah, I was Frank's high school head coach at St. Joe's Prep School (where I also went to), in Philadelphia. Frank's junior and senior year I was his head coach. So we met again in the national championship game there. It was quite a story.

Q: I suppose you played a uniquely crucial role in the preparation for that game?

CC: I don't know if I did. I didn't have much more to offer than what we saw on film. I remember at that time just talking more about how we could just rattle him with some blitzes and different things like that, just talking about the type of young man he was, because they were so intelligent in what they were doing. But we did hit him quite a bit. He took some shots. I contributed whatever I could, so it was an interesting time.

Q: So here's a kid you're very proud of, and a few years later you're on the opposite sideline trying to get into his head...

CC: Yeah, it's funny how things like that happen. He's a great kid. Doing well to this day, married and has a couple kids and is in the financial services field in New Jersey.

Q: You keep in touch with him much?

CC: I do. I haven't talked to him recently, but we exchange e-mails and I know he's doing well.

Q: And let me ask you, some of the athletes you were working with, who stands out to you among that group?

CC: Gosh, there were as couple, but the first young man that comes to mind is Mike Minter, just the type of young man he was and the type of player who practiced hard every day. And he overcame some adversity too, Paul, because he missed the first national championship season with a knee injury, but he came back the following year. Certainly, Barron Miles stands out as a guy that would just go 100 miles an hour. Just a very smart kind of guy who just loved playing, was very helpful to the younger players coming in. I remember Tony Veland, who was a quiet kid but who practiced hard. All those kids were just so great to be around and coach. Those three stand out.

Of course, you had Phil Ellis (a linebacker who was a Nebraska kid and had a good career), Grant Wistrom and Jared Tomich and the Peter brothers. And they practiced as hard as they played. They only knew one gear, and that was top gear.

Q: Any particular practice event stand out in your mind from those days?

CC: Nothing in particular. Just the intensity and how hard those teams practiced every single day throughout the year. That stood out to me. It was a continual thing.

Q: Speaking of that top gear, was it the coaches pushing the concept, the players themselves, or a combination of the two?

CC: It was a combination. The coaches did a great job and the players completely bought in and respected all the coaches. There wasn't a deal there in my three years, Paul, I don't know of anybody ever raising their voice. And that stems from the top, too..

Q: Even Charlie MCBride?! Come on!

CC: Okay, maybe Charlie once or twice, (laughs) over three years... (laughs) But I just think there was such a great -you talk about team- and the whole organization just worked together and there was great mutual respect from coaches to players, and players to coaches and staff. They just went hard all the time.

Q: Did that unity come as a shock you?

CC: No, I can't say that it shocked me. It was certainly impressive and something I still look back on to this day and just marvel at how it all came together. I can't say that it shocked me because, again, because of Coach Osborne and how he handled things and treated players and coaches and got everybody moving in the same direction.

Q: Can you take me into some staff meetings? What was the dynamic there?

CC: Well, it actually worked very smoothly. Coach Osborne at that time pretty much spent all his time on offense, and defensively at that time you had Charlie and Tony and George and you had Kevin and then you had Craig. We would watch film together. And Charlie and George would focus a lot on the run game along with Craig, and then George and I the passing game. It just flowed so smoothly. You'd watch all the cutups together on Sunday night and Monday and Monday night and start putting ideas together on the board, and that game plan would pretty much be finalized by the time you hit the field on Tuesday. It just flowed so smoothly because of the people like Charlie and Tony and George being such great leaders. There was no egos. None, in no way, shape or form.

Q: You've made a few stops. Is that a little of out of the ordinary?

CC: It certainly was unique in a high pressure, high intensity atmosphere like that. I've been fortunate, the places I've been, it's worked pretty well. But you hear of different places and different staffs and the dynamic is otherwise. I would tell people how smoothly it flowed at Nebraska. And listen, every now and then there was a differing opinion, but when the final hammer was put down they left that room on the same page.

Q: Now, during the games George Darlington was up in the press box, right?

CC: George was up in the press box along with Tony Samuel, and down on the field was myself, Charlie, and either Kevin or Craig the last two years. Charlie would signal in the front and I would signal in the coverages.

Q: Take me into the dynamic between you and George talking amongst yourselves and your handling of things on the sideline....

CC: You know, again, it's a high intensity thing. You only have so much time. Most of the time we would see the same things, although from up above you could see things a whole lot better, that's for sure. You know, after each series coaches would talk and any adjustments that had to be made in the secondary, we'd go over with the guys on the board, and Charlie and Craig would handle things with their guys.

Q: Correct me if I'm wrong, but I've always been of the opinion that Moose Mohnsen and Bryan Carpenter running films, did they make things much easier on the coaches for the game prep?

CC: No question. Those guys did a fantastic job. Great guys. And of course, Moose is coaching now. So I run into him every now and then. But you're right, those guys would work hard and work late into the night. Incredible preparation, everything was always ready and on time and clean and made the coaches job that much more efficient each year.

Q: What are you most proud of about your time there?

CC: That's a tough one. There are so many things. I'm grateful for my three years there, the relationships I was able to establish. To be around those guys, they impacted me deeply. Tom Osborne with what he'd done on the field, Paul, but even more important was what he did off the field, the kind of impact he had on his staff, his players and the state of

Nebraska. He impacted me greatly. I'm very proud of the relationships I have with George and Tony Samuel, who I talk to frequently. And I talk to Turner. And I met my wife there, so that's part of it, too. Funny how the good Lord works sometimes! (laughs)

Q: You've got a gal who understands football!

CC: I sure do. I'm so appreciative of those three years there. And the players? They impacted me greatly, being so coachable. And no egos there, either. It was a pleasure to be around the Minters' and the Miles' and the Velands'. Just great kids.

Q: And the unity. Is there anything about the confidence, the swagger, the belief you try to inculcate into your own players now?

CC: You know, the one thing I try to share with my players -thinking back to those years- was really just how hard those guys worked.

And certainly the unity (and we have a Leadership Council here at Cornell.) The great thing about the Unity Council at Nebraska was: one, you gave the players a voice, and number two, you were teaching them how to be leaders, also. Sometimes we take for granted that kids with a certain status or a senior, that automatically they know how to be a leader. And these days -with all the kids and the things going on in their lives- you get to teach them how to be leaders. That's what I took from the Unity Council and how it was implemented. I tell my players today about that.

And one other thing I try to impress upon my guys here is the practice tempo. You've got to practice 100 miles per hour. I say, 'Guys, listen. Back in Nebraska we had to get them to gear down, because they were going so hard and so fast all the time.' The tempo, that's the thing that stood out.

Q: Is it difficult to get kids these days to practice at that tempo?

CC: I don't know. I don't think it is. You just constantly have to stay on it in a positive way and constantly reach them. And because of working with Coach Osborne, I'm not a yeller and a screamer. You just constantly have to not take anything for granted, you constantly have to be looking for ways to push them and motivate them to get them to practice. Especially here at Cornell University where they're getting pounded academically all day. When they walk into the football building it's football time.

Q: How is that Leadership Council working for you guys?

CC: We just put it in place, Paul, just this past February. We didn't have it in place up 'til now, and it's something I kind of nudged my head coach on over the years and thought it would be a good idea, and we finally put it in place. We haven't had it in place for the season, but they've done a fantastic thing with it thus far.

Q: I had a chance to talk to Dr. Jack Stark recently, and it's amazing the effect it had on those guys, the peer pressure in a positive way...

CC: No doubt, no doubt...

Q: Now, when it came to recruiting, were you involved in that?

CC: At that time GA's were not allowed to go on the road, so I was on campus in the office, evaluating film, and helped on the weekends. But we weren't allowed to go on the road at that time.

Q: Any one particular game stand out to you from any other?

CC: Well, I would have to say that first national championship game against Miami. Being part of Coach Osborne's first national championship, that game certainly stands out.

And probably the very, very first game was against West Virginia in the Kickoff Classic in the Meadowlands. That meant a lot to me, too. I certainly remember that one, too. I had family there. My parents were at that game and some of my family.

And beating Florida as badly as we did stands out, too. But the locker room after that Miami game? Just the release of emotions was something special. It was crazy in there for a long time. The release of emotion -I remember the players, obviously being very happy and joyful and emotional. Not only Coach Osborne, who'd been there a long time, but Charlie, Milt, Dan, Tony, they'd been there a long time, too.

Q: I'm a firm believer that most people, when they achieve a certain level, they start to cruise and take it easy and rest on their laurels. What do you think made the kids come back even better and stronger the next year in 1995?

CC: I think it was their incredible work ethic and incredible desire to succeed, to stay hungry. And again, even though the coaching staff was very happy -the next day, Paul, I remember on the plane the next morning, there was the big celebrations there at the Devaney Sports Center, and then everybody went about their way- honest to goodness, the next day after the celebration we were in the office at 8 a.m. having a recruiting meeting. It was business as usual. And that was Coach Osborne, an astounding influence, never getting too high or too low. Less than 36 hours later we were in there having a recruiting meeting.

Q: You didn't stay around Miami Beach drinking mai-tai's, eh?

CC: No. (laughs) It was all on an even keel. There was no emotional rollercoaster. I think that had had a lot to do with it.

Q: Can you tell me more about Charlie McBride or Coach Darlington?

CC: With George -and I worked very closely with him- he's a very, very smart football coach. A very solid man who treated me very well and leaves no stone unturned. Very prepared, a ton of x and o knowledge, and treated the players well.

Charlie, he was probably the 'Mr. Intensity' of the group. But the thing that stood out to me, Charlie treated me great from the first minute I met him. And again, everybody did. And those players loved Charlie and would go through a brick wall for him. Those players, Grant and Jared and Christian and Jason, they knew that Charlie loved 'em. That's where he had a very good player-coach relationship with his players, that really stood out to me.

Q: How did the players know of this love for them? How was it displayed?

CC: It's probably because he pushed them hard, particularly the defensive line. He would push them hard, but he was a guy who knew you could push them hard and push them hard, but you better be sure you give them a hug. I remember him saying that one time when we were sitting around. You push them -and it didn't matter who it was, a scout team kid or Christian Peter or Grant Wistrom- they don't care how much you know until they know how much you care. There was a great mutual respect there with Charlie and all the players, not just the D-line. They knew just by daily actions and what he would do for them off the field, how much he was there for them.

Q: What kind of off-field stuff?

CC: Anything. They just knew Charlie was in their corner, as a reference for a job or picking up the phone and calling someone for a shot in the NFL. They just knew they could come to him and he would pick up the phone for them.

Q: Any other things stand out to you as far as your coaching, things you gleaned from those days that you find yourself always using?

CC: Philosophically, one of the things I still carry with me is: you don't need to try to make the game confusing. You don't need to reinvent the wheel. You have to let the players play. Charlie and Tony were big advocates of that. Less is more. If you wanted to play fast you better not burden them down mentally.

And one other thing even more important than the x's and o's, it is the trust and relationship part of it, and mutual respect between the coaches and players. Nobody really ever raised their voice, except Charlie a few times, over the years. The ultimate thing, I think, was the great relationships there and the total trust between players and coaches. I think those are the main points there that mattered. It's great reminiscing about those years, I tell you.

End conversation.

As we continue on like prospectors making our way up the trickle of a promising mountain stream, it feels like we've traded in our smallish pan for a massive sluice because the golden nuggets keep appearing left and right, validating that we're on the right path. One of those priceless finds was Clayton's knowledge about his former high school pupil, University of Miami's starting quarterback Frank Costa. I have a sneaking suspicion that he downplayed his accumulated personal insight about the kid, myself, and had a few precious tidbits for the Blackshirts in preparation for that pivotal first National Championship game. We all know the Hurricanes had the benefits of their home stadium, home locker room, home climate and, for all intents and purposes, the home crowd, but getting into young Costa's head had to be the Huskers' ace in the hole. What made it all the more providential was the fact that the '94 team actually yearned to meet up once more in the championship contest with Florida State, and not Miami U. As for the Carlin/Costa connection, I guess sometimes a guy just gets a little lucky in his hiring practices, eh?

Coach Carlin sure drove the point home about the level of professionalism and welcoming arms as he joined the Nebraska Football family, by both coaching staff and the players. Notice his comments about the lack of player egos and how they were such joys to teach, "And the players? They impacted me greatly, being so coachable. And no egos there, either. It was a pleasure to be around the Minters' and the Miles' and the Velands'. Just great kids." You don't' get that very often. But from Clayton's recall, as well as that of my own, it's surprisingly true that most every individual ego within the organization was suppressed, or at the least, willingly subjugated for the betterment of the team. I believe it was former U.S. President Ronald Reagan who said, "You can accomplish much if you don't care who gets the credit." I equate ego with a tendency to seek attention and personal glorification, and for the most part they players never seemed too concerned with drawing attention to themselves aside from their on-field performance. How refreshing.

Notable quote #2:
Clayton Carlin on the Husker practice tempo: "Back in Nebraska we had to get them to gear down, because they were going so hard and so fast all the time. The tempo, that's the thing that stood out."

Fletcher Christian: [to Captain Bligh] *But I assure you, sir, that the execution of my duties is entirely unaffected by my private opinion of you.*
Charles Nordhoff and James Norman Hall with Charles Lederer, *Mutiny on the Bounty*

We now happen upon another in a long line of good guys who populated the Memorial Stadium environs of those days: linebacker Doug Colman. You heard from Jerry Weber earlier how sometimes you find yourself 'latching onto' a guy for some reason or another, whether it be his underdog status, his disposition, his unique plight, et cetera. Well, I always held Doug in kind regard, for he was a hard worker, had a very friendly and even-keeled temperament, and found himself many times in Linebackers Coach Kevin Steele's doghouse (along with a few others, I might add). A Lincoln preacher once sermonized that, "Sometimes you've got to know what you don't believe in in order to know what you do." To put it frankly, Doug found enlightenment from both sides of the coin during his time as an undergraduate and can presently say that the troubles served him well. I tackled him while he was serving a term as the Huskers' defensive quality coach before he was spirited away for a full-time coaching position down in Louisiana, then to South Carolina.

Notable quote #1:
(Coach Osborne said)"The media is calling us "The Miami of the Midwest." And it hurt him so bad that they were thinking… that people considered us at the time, (to be) like Miami, convicts and all, you know? We didn't want to be associated with anything like that. I remember his eyes tearing up. I remember my eyes tearing up. I just wanted to go out and wreck somebody."

Doug Colman

Scholarship recruit, Linebacker, Ventnor, New Jersey (Ocean City)
Where are they now? Conway, South Carolina, Coach

Question: Hey Doug, thanks for your time.

Doug Colman: No problem, we've been pretty full-on already here. There's a lot of young kids and a lot of teaching going on, that aspect of it.

Q: Do you like that aspect of coaching?

DC: Absolutely.

Q: I have to say, before I called you I was watching an old video highlight on YouTube and I couldn't help but laugh about that Florida game where you and Christian were playing 'hot potato' for awhile there as you guys ran down the field..taking that supposed Danny Wuerffel fumble back down the field for a touchdown…

DC: I should have taken it from him, but I knew there wasn't anybody else around. So, no problem.

Q: You come from a line of coaches, don't you?

Doug: Yeah, my dad was a high school coach and track coach. And he also was an NFL player, too. He played nine years in the NFL.

Q: So you being a player in college and then going to the pros, did you already have a unique perspective about that experience?

DC: Not really. To tell you the truth, when I was growing up I really didn't realize the significance of my father playing pro football. He retired and started coaching when I was three. And I started playing football when I was 7, and the only reason I started playing football was because all my friends were doing it and I didn't want to be left out of the crowd.

I had no idea of the significance of what my father did until my friends started coming around with football cards to sign. They'd give them to me at school and I'd give it to my dad for him to sign, and I'd bring them back to school the next day and give it to them. I was kind of like, 'Wow, why does he want this?' (laughs)

Q: Did you ever have any connection with Clayton Carlin, with his dad's working for the Eagles for some years?

DC: He's at Cornell now, correct? He used to recruit New Jersey when I was playing high school there and he'd be looking at guys. There was a kid he wanted who ended up at Delaware as a wide receiver. The guy was the quarterback of our state championship team, he actually walked on and became starting wide receiver this year.

Q: You coached a state championship team back there, right?

DC: Yeah. My first year out of football, 2001. I had just gotten married and just bought a house. Actually, the day we're settling in the house I'd just gotten released from the Jets. I wasn't sure if I was done with football and all that, in my head. I'd just gotten that, and we're going to settle on the house, and the day we went to sign the final papers was 9/11 and the first plane goes into the World Trade Center.

So that was going on, and things are all kind of discombobulated and I'm thinking, 'Boy, if I was up in New York right now and my wife, who is kind of new to that area, what would she be thinking? And would I even be able to call her on the cell phone while all this was going on?' You know? And as we're signing the papers the second plane went in. So a lot of things happened: my father had a real bad injury to his knee and had surgery and got a real bad case of staph infection. We weren't sure how that was going to turn out with him. And he was actually coaching freshman football at the time. I wasn't even thinking of getting into coaching. I was training, and at that time I took over and was coaching his freshman football team. It was my first coaching gig.

Q: After being a player for some time, how did that come to you? Did you have to work at it or did it just come naturally?

DC: My major was Physical Education. I completed my student teaching and so on, so for me it was kind of natural. My dad was a teacher, my sister is a teacher, my aunts and uncle, and my wife's a teacher, so everything was kind of natural.

Q: Where did you meet your wife?

DC: I met her my senior year at Nebraska. She's from Silver Creek. Now it's Twin Rivers High School.

Q: So '91 was your first year. What do you remember about that first day?

DC: I remember I came in and we had to do our heights and weights and our physicals and stuff, and I remember jumping into a truck with Christian Peter, Ken Bello and Barron Miles. I'm not sure who was all there in the truck, but we had four guys from New Jersey join the team that year. We headed over to the Medical Center and we did our physicals at that time.

Q: You didn't know any of those guys previous to that, did you?

DC: No, I didn't know anybody. I came to Nebraska with my mind mainly focused on football. I had dreams of playing in the NFL and, realistically, it was more about going to a place, a football factory, and maximize what I could do as a player. And that's what I thought at the time, just being honest with you.

Q: And saying that, Doug, you seemed to have a change of mind or a change of heart further down the road?

DC: Yeah, absolutely! As time went on, one, I realized that I wasn't always in control of my own destiny and that other people were -when things started to feel like they were out of my hands- and times I thought I was playing better than other people and so on. I wasn't getting a shot and all that and I said, 'You know what, I'm just gonna leave things as they are and work as hard as I can at this point, and then hopefully get my opportunity and hopefully get noticed.'

At that point my heart kind of turned. My focus went away from 'Me, me, me, me, and what can this place do for me?' to more about 'What can I do to help this team?' And my focus got turned to, 'Hey, what can we do to win a national championship?' So we were more of team-oriented thing. I started looking at these guys coming into Nebraska - especially the kids who gave up scholarships to Kansas State and Iowa State and Kansas just to walk-on at Nebraska- and I figured, 'They gave up so much to come out here.' And it starts to kind of wear on your heart a little bit and I kind of, you know, felt myself feeling like, 'Hey, there's something bigger than me here.' And the group of guys that we had at the time kind of started to boil at that time.

We had a lot of close games and basically topped off in '93 when we lost the national championship to Florida State. And even that, it was like that game was fixed, you know? It was one of those things where I think we really, truly felt the powers that be were thinking, "Hey, it's Bobby Bowden. It's time he won a national championship" and that type of thing. If you go back and look at that film you can just see how many blown calls there were in that game that really affected the outcome.

But that '93 game, all those guys? I always felt terrible about them because people always want to talk about the '94, '95, '97 teams, about the national championships. But all that time leading up -I especially felt this way, from my freshman year on- those '91 guys, '92 guys, and '93 guys, they were the ones that kind of started getting everything going again and really started getting that team atmosphere and getting everybody to commit. Those workouts in the summer time? I can remember those workouts after '93; we all made a commitment to each other that we were all going to really work hard in the offseason and get ourselves together here. And we had that opportunity, which for me was phenomenal to go play in the Kickoff Classic back home in New Jersey. And that first game, that kind of set the tempo. People didn't know what to expect from us, and we just went out there and completely dominated West Virginia.

Q: You were Big 8 Defensive Player of the Week for that game, if I recall?

DC: Yeah, I was up for it, but I don't think I got it. They gave it to somebody else because - I remember Kevin Steele, my linebacker coach came up and said,- "This other kid was a senior, so they gave it to him instead." (laughs)

Q: From one coach to another coach, what would you say about or describe Coach Kevin Steele? How you gelled or didn't gel? How was that dynamic?

DC: Wow. (short silence) I'll say I learned a lot from him. I learned a lot about myself and a lot about people.

I think it's really affected the way I coach. I've had a lot of good coaches in my time and I've had a lot of bad coaches in my time. I hope to emulate the good ones, but I also understand what the bad ones do. And I know people have different relationships with the same people. I didn't learn a lot as far as technique that I applied that made me a better player (though some stuff I was able to use in the NFL). I had Steele up to my junior year and had Craig Bohl my senior year.

Q: How was that change?

DC: (laughs) Not any better. It was hard for me during that time, but I think it really made the difference in knowing who to surround myself with, get involved with. In the end, what really helped me out -even a coach deciding what kind of guys I need on my staff and the best way to win- the negative things that happen to you through sports, actually in the long run, can be positive. It does make you realize, "Do you really want it that bad?" And if you really want something that bad you're gonna want to stick it out. And for me, I stuck it out and in the long run it worked out for me.

For me, I had that opportunity and went on and started doing the high school thing after the pros, and my next job after the freshman job was the assistant coaching job at a high school called Oak Crest. It was a big high school, it was a mixed group of kids as far as ethnic groups and I worked with another great group of guys. But we had a head coach who would not listen to any of his assistants, but decided how we were going to do things each week. We'd meet and meet and meet and discuss things, but it always came back to nobody else having a say in anything we did. And we didn't win too many games. The following year I actually got hired as the Head Football Coach, and I interviewed all the assistants from the old staff and only ended up bringing one guy back, and had him coach the freshman team. And then I accumulated guys that I knew were good character guys who were good teachers and didn't have a whole lot of knowledge, but we put together a system that really worked for us.

Historically, the team I coached for would win four or five games a year, and that first year we actually went to the second round of the state playoffs. It was the first time the school ever went to state playoffs and it was the first time they'd ever won a playoff game. The second year we went again to the playoffs, won our first conference championship in school history, and ended up losing in the first round. The third year we won the conference again and then went to the state championship, which we lost in triple overtime.

Lessons even came with that, of course. My kids? We had a great football team but had a kid fumble going into the end zone and we ended up missing an extra point one time -so there were some extra things that we could control that we didn't. I actually went back and related the story to them about our '93 championship game and how we should have won that thing and how, in turn, for the younger guys coming up, how we could learn what it felt like to lose the big one like that. And how we, as players, didn't want to have it happen again that way in '94. We were relentless. That whole game against Miami it was nonstop. Nonstop to the very end, to find who was going to win that game. We just out-played them. We were better conditioned than them.

Anyway, the following year the high school went to the state championship again, and we were playing the same team that we lost to the year before. (Now, the year before we were a much better football team than the team we were playing.) Well, this particular year we were playing a team that was a much better football team than we were. So we get the ball with two minutes left in the game and we march the ball down seventy-six yards in two minutes, and with fifteen seconds left in the game ended up winning the championship.

Q: Incredible!

DC: Then I coached for the Amsterdam Admirals for a season, so I was over in the Netherlands for two months and at Tampa for a month for training camp.

And then I got the opportunity here at Nebraska. I was at the Coaches Convention and started looking into further jobs and Coach Osborne was being honored at a dinner, and I was walking by and saw Coach McBride and his wife, and he says, "Have you seen Coach Osborne, yet?" And I said, 'No.' And he says, "Go go in back there. Nobody will bother you." Well, you had to have a credential to go to this party, and as I'm walking in the door I run into a guy who was the D-line coach at Syracuse at the time, and he recruits my area in New Jersey and I'd often try to help him out with guys from the area, and he says, "Hey, do you want to come in?" So I walked in, and there were all sorts of head coaches from around the country and I talked to Coach Osborne, and he said that some intern positions may become available and if I was interested. I told him that absolutely I was. I sent my resume in and got a call back and went in and talked to them a little bit. It didn't feel much like an interview, more of a conversation where they were trying to convince me to come out here. (laughs)

So I had other jobs on the table at the time, but my heart felt like it wanted to go back to this place and make it better, and I want to get them off the doormat and get things going again. And that's why I came back.

The other big, impacting thing that happened to me, that turned me over to coming back and coaching is this: in thinking back on my first year of coaching the freshman football team my wife came to one of my games and we ended up beating a team we probably shouldn't have beat -that we hadn't beaten in a long time- and the kids were all excited and I was real excited. And my wife came down to the field after the game and I said, 'What do you think?!' And she said, "I think you look like a big gorilla jumping up and down the sideline." (laughs) And I say, 'What?' She said, "It was embarrassing. You were jumping up and running up and down the sidelines yelling at the referees. I was embarrassed." That kind of really hit me, and I started thinking back to how reserved Coach Osborne was (not that I'm ever as reserved as he is), and now I try to emulate a lot of that "What would Coach Osborne do in this situation?"-type thing. Just being able to have that to fall back on and relate back to that and actually apply it to your coaching style, it's always great to have a mentor like that. In the end, it really helped out my coaching and allowed me to stay calm in tough situations and even, to this point, allowed me to make the right decisions a lot of the time.

And when Harvey Perlman got up in front of the media and announced Coach Osborne as the Athletic Director, Coach got up in front of the press and started telling some stories. And he actually said that in all the time, of all the guys that he's coached his entire career as the head coach -and even as an assistant coach- that he'd coached a lot of talent and great guys, but he told a story about a player that he met on an airplane when he was flying on a trip from Detroit to Lincoln, and the guy started to say how much his heart changed because of the type of guys that were there, because of the walk-on program and these guys were giving up scholarships and going to this place and what that meant and how it changed his mindset to a team-oriented philosophy, and he said my name. He said, "Doug Colman was a linebacker we recruited out of New Jersey, and all these things really hit me hard," he said. And I started thinking about that. Of all the people's names he could have said, mine was the one he mentioned. For me, that hit me so hard. I just got triggered back into, 'I need to get back to that place and get something going.' Before that I even had the intern job come up and positions start rolling in a little bit, but I met a lot of those guys on Bo's staff and a lot of them were previously high school coaches. Carl Pelini, Tim Beck, all those guys started in high school like I did and they worked their way in. So I was excited to get things going again.

Q: What effect did Coach McBride have on you as a player and coach?

DC: Coach McBride, his whole persona was intimidating early on. You're coming in and you're worried about him sticking his foot up your ass and you wanted to do everything right. He was definitely a 'tough love' guy. He'd love you once you gained respect and everything else, and even after. As long as he thought you were giving it all, he loved you. And you didn't even have to be a starter.

Even to this day, he's still close to all those guys. It was a different time, there was some 'old school' coaching during that time as far as 'get all up in your face and yell at you', but he was the guy who, right after practice he'd put his arm around you. That was one of the things you'd appreciate. The thing you didn't like was when a guy yelled at you and didn't tell you why they were yelling at you, who didn't explain why they were yelling at you and ignored you. Those are the ones that you always had to watch out for.

Q: So much so that it affects your psyche after awhile, right?

DC: Absolutely. You get to the point of, 'What's wrong with me? What's wrong with me? Why does he think I'm so bad? Am I really that bad?' You go through these things and, honestly, a lot of people have gone through those things for years and it just comes to a point when you say, 'Wait a second. I'm not the one that's wrong here. This is the guy who's messed up. It's not me.' And a lot of guys went through that, too. But again, I don't look back and say, 'Why, why, why?' It's more about everything being a learning experience for me and it allowed me to really try to treat people the right way.

Q: Any other coaches stand out to you from those days?

DC: Everybody had their quirks about them. I really appreciated Ron Brown. Number one, here he is a wide receiver coach, worked with the tight ends and receivers and just what he was able to get those guys to do? We didn't always have #1 recruit wide receivers. We had transition guys who were quarterbacks or walk-ons -like Jon Vedral- and their dream was to be on that football field, and he'd get them to be relentless guys, just non-stop hitting guys and blocking guys, our wide receivers were so damned physical. People were scared to play us because they were worried about getting cut by these guys, you know? I really respected what he did, what he stood for.

It was always a big kick for me where somebody'd be cursing or something and Coach Brown would be the first one to stare over at them like, "What are you doing? What are you doing?" You know the type of profanity that goes on in colleges sports from players now; it just didn't happen in front of the coaches when I played. You did not want to curse in front of Coach Osborne and you did not want to curse in front of Coach Brown.

And now, being able to be on the staff, for me it's a pretty awesome thing, too. To walk down the hall and have somebody like Coach Brown call you 'Coach', too, "Hey, Coach!" The other thing that blows me away is sitting over at the lunch table and here Coach Osborne puts his tray down next to you and sits next to you and starts talking to you. I never had a 'come up and talk to you' relationship with Coach Osborne. My relationship was kind of one where you just had so much respect for him. It was almost kind of intimidating, you know? Where you didn't want to bother him with any of your problems, because you felt like your problems weren't worth bringing to him. Not that he wasn't available. He was more available than anyone, you know? I think it was more out of respect for him not to bother him. And he was never the type of guy that wasn't approachable, but I saw him as this 'figure' during that time.

I can't remember, it might have been '91 or '92 and you were there at the time, but I think it was after the Scotty Baldwin thing where Coach Osborne actually called a team meeting and he came up all teary-eyed and said, "The media is calling us 'The Miami of the Midwest'". And it hurt him so bad that they were thinking, that people considered us at the time -like Miami- convicts and all, you know? We didn't want to be associated with anything like that. I remember his eyes tearing up. I remember my eyes tearing up. I just wanted to go out and wreck somebody now, because of the way he felt. And that's what good coaches do. They know you're big guys, but at the same time you play emotionally and you want to do things for those people, too. That's the way a lot of guys felt when we played.

Q: Speaking of wrecking somebody, Doug, I think it was the fourth quarter against Miami and you had just the sweetest tackle against their fullback, James Stewart. How did you guys operate back there? How much was emotion, how much was reaction? What was the linebacking corps' mindset.

DC: After that tackle? Put it this way: after that tackle I didn't get up and jump around, nobody got up and jumped around on me. That's how tired we were at that point, where it was just about preserving our energy. It was that kind of thing, and we ended up in the fourth quarter and it helped to decide that game.

But one thing about our linebacking corps: we were very, very close. And when things were wrong, when things didn't go right for us, we really came together. As a group of guys we came together. They were a great support system at the time, from my freshman year on. You had guys go through the same things you were going through, and it was really good to have those guys around.

And it was great in the respect that you talk about leadership? When you talk about those teams? You passed it on. You were always trying to groom the guys. You got groomed, and then you were getting the young guys ready for the time they were seniors, so they were ready to take over. That's one other difference I see in college football now, I don't know exactly how many teams have done that, but it really seemed like: you pay your dues, you work your tail off, and this is usually what happens to you in the end. It's usually good things for you. We were that way, it was really a good group of guys.

Q: Who groomed you and the guys in your class?

DC: Coming in my freshman year, I was really close to Mike Anderson, to Troy Branch. Mike Petko was part of that group, but he was kind of an oddball. (laughs) I'm friends with the guys now and he's a different guy, but he was one of those guys that really tried to take it to you. Troy is from New Jersey, and Mike Anderson was my host when I first got out there. Phil Ellis played with me. Those other guys that would come up, the younger guys like Jon Hesse, Ryan Terwilliger, Matt Penland, who's now our team chaplain and his younger brother Aaron Penland, we were all really close.

Q: And some of the guys you passed things on to?

DC: I'd say John Hesse and Terwilliger. Jay Foreman coming in at that time. And that went on for awhile. I think it was something that happened and continued during Solich's time.

And somewhere along the way, I don't know if they lost their focus on exactly why they were here… or kids may have thought too much about the NFL or what. That may be the original reason why you're coming to a place, but that shouldn't be the final reason while you're there. And like I said before, the whole experience changed me as a player and a person.

Q: Looking back, what would you say is the greatest benefit from your time as a player?

DC: I'd tell you 'my wife.' (laughs) Because, again, I didn't meet somebody who was the same as me. I met a woman of higher standards and higher morals than I had, but again, those are all changes for the good, you know? I tell you what, I learned a lot.

I'll tell you this, I took what we did here at Nebraska -from the strength program to the way things were run to the practice organizational things- and applied it to a high school program that never really had a history of winning, and we had great success. You could almost say we had instant success. Even that first year, we lost a couple of close games we should have won, and kids believed in it. I just got back from New Jersey a few days ago and I saw a kid who I coached in high school. They're all in college now, and basically, they come back and tell me the same thing, "Coach, what you taught us is more advanced than what we're doing now. What you did in strength training is more advanced than what we're doing now." They're Division 3, but it's the time you put in and the guys you hire.

And I say it jokingly, but I mean it: you have to brainwash them. You have to brainwash them that, "this is the way it's supposed to be done." I'd say, 'I walked away from Nebraska and had five conference championships, two national championships, got the opportunity to play professional football,' and I had a great platform to come back and get kids to believe in that. And the next step is to get coaches to believe in it, and then the next step is to get the parents to believe in it. And the last step is to get the administration to believe in it." (laughs) The administration part of it, in the end that's what gave me kind of the sour taste in my mouth about the high school thing. I felt bad about leaving, I probably could have done that for awhile and been happy and not have gotten this bug to coach at a higher level. But it got to a point where I was just busting my tail and doing all these things I could do and trying to help the school out, and everybody wanted to know, "Why are you doing this or that? What are you supposed to get out of it?" And I'm like, 'I just want this to be the most special high school in the area. I want this to be the best it can possibly be.' And not everybody plays the game that way.

Q: They're not used to pushing to be the absolute best because they're willing to settle? Willing to hanker down into that comfort zone rather than be vulnerable to failure by pushing the envelope?

DC: Yeah. For me, I don't want to be around those people. Because in the end, it's a horrible place to be. Whenever you don't surround yourself with people who want to be the best at what they do and when you're not in control as to who is on your team, it's a horrible thing. It's a horrible feeling.

And again, in comparison here I was able to be coached by one of the winningest coaches in all of college football, and probably the most respected. And I say that because one of these last Coaches Conventions they had Coach Osborne and Coach Joe Paterno up on the stage, and basically Coach Paterno was cracking jokes and people were laughing. And Coach Osborne is up there, sincere with an occasional tear in his eye as he's talking about things, to the point where he stole the crowd. Joe Paterno was seeing some of the things Coach Osborne did, the way he managed things, and Joe Paterno said he was going to go home and apply what Coach Osborne said to his team. So here's a guy who's likely the winningest coach of all time and he's saying that Coach Osborne has a better idea than he does? For me, I can honestly say he's probably the most respected coach at this point in history. I take a lot of pride in being able to say I played there at Nebraska.

And another thing: there was a thing in the NFL -when your college team plays another teammate's college?- there's a friendly wager of something like $100 bucks. And it doesn't matter if it's like a MAC school against a Big 12 or a Big 10 school, you're still gonna place that $100 bet. It's funny, there were weeks when Nebraska was playing some other guy's team... and nobody would lip off to me about their team playing Nebraska because they didn't want to lose that bet. (laughs) No lie, I didn't bet once. Not once. And I didn't bet anybody or go after them to force a bet either, because we were Nebraska and we dominated everybody. That's what my thought process was: 'It's no fair to them, we're just that much better.' And then to see where Nebraska was at (after the Pederson/Callahan years), in my mind it was like, 'Wow!' It was hard to come to grips where you just didn't believe it got to the point it was, because that wasn't the way it was supposed to be.

Q: Unity, Belief, Respect, huh?

DC: Absolutely. And I believe Nebraska can make it happen again, because Nebraska is a special place. Everybody in Nebraska looks forward to Nebraska football. There aren't many places can say that. Everybody has a lot of love for the program, and there isn't a whole lot of people that hate Nebraska around the country because they respect them for who they have at the helm and the way they play.

Q: Doug, that's why I'm titling the book "No Place like Nebraska." Because I think there's a special dynamic, a unity that makes those teams achieve more than anybody gives them credit for. And they have that fighting, pioneer spirit.

DC: I couldn't agree with you more, because I say it all the time when I do speaking engagements and stuff. I say, 'Look, we give so much homage to the '94 and '95 teams for the championships they won, but I feel horrible, absolutely horrible for those guys on the '93 team.' I honest to God do. I say that that game was taken away from us. And if you talked to Coach Osborne about this, I'll bet he'd say there were 4 games in his entire career where they took it away from him. And that '93 team and the Orange Bowl loss to Florida State was completely manipulated by the refs.

It's just a shame, because at the time when we went to school it was "Coach Osborne can't win the big game." And then all of a sudden here's the first national championship and then the following year in '95 we steamroll everybody, and then he's the guy who they say "He's a win at all costs coach." And that's one thing I never enjoyed about that, either, you instantly get to that point and then everybody gangs up on you because you're successful.

Q: It's like, "Make up your mind!" I think the national media just jumped on him about the Lawrence Phillips thing with preconceived notions, not knowing what in the hell they were talking about...

DC: Right. And if you remember, we had 4 guys, five guys! We had Damon Benning, Clinton Childs, Ahman Greeen, James Sims. Sims! Sims would be starting at most schools at running back. And you put him in at the end of the game versus the University of Florida? He almost scores if he doesn't trip on his first carry. And then we just down the ball (to end the game). It was crazy.

And here's the philosophy, what I believe was Coach Osborne's philosophy. (I don't know if it is or if he's ever said it this way, but my philosophy is this: 'You give a kid every opportunity he needs to succeed until he starts doing things that are gonna affect the guys around him.' Once he starts affecting the team, then you've got to get rid of him. That's the thing. If you've got kids who have issues or problems, hey, you need to work with those kids and try to straighten them out. And it's your job to do that. But when he starts doing things that are affecting the guys around him, attitude, bringing them down the wrong road, where you know these aren't changeable habits that you can change in this kid, it's time to hit the road. That's how I approached coaching high school and that's how I would approach business. If guys aren't doing what they're supposed to do, you have to get rid of them. And in business I'd probably have a shorter fuse. But of course, in business you aren't dealing with kids so much. But you expect them to abide by and do what they're supposed to do. That's why you shouldn't get me talking about this kind of stuff. I get to walking around and get all worked up about it.

Q: Aw, it's good for you, man. You're a born coach, Doug. You need to get some exercise and jump up and down like a gorilla every now and then, despite what your wife says...(laughs)

DC: And I'll have a heart attack when I'm 45! (laughs)

End conversation.

"Hey, there's something bigger than me here." I'll bet that if I were to ask every single student-athlete of those 60 & 3 seasons if Doug's quote rang true to their own experience, every one of them would concur. It was quite refreshing to hear of his change of heart and how it completely altered his approach to football, as well as life and leadership. It's already been pounded into our heads ad infinitum, but I still find it amazing the myriad ways Nebraska walk-ons contributed to the character and influence on those teams. I hope you don't discount their interviews here as lesser than, either, for their points are just as valid as the more prominent stars of those days.

Before the Unity Council ever was gathered, there was first the small group I've chosen to label the "Unity 'Backers." What am I talking about here? Well, the linebacking group of the day had an extremely tight bond within its own little confines due to the nature of their position coach Kevin Steele's maddening and often de-spiriting ways. (Coach Steele did not answer requests for this project to refute this claim) The more recent, eclectic addition to the ranks of the Husker Coaching staff in 1989, this fellow was -how do I put this?- unique. Yeah, that's the word. Unique. Often a complete antithesis to the mien of a Tom Osborne - but a technician unequaled all the same- there was no love lost between most of the linebackers and their master of those days. To put it bluntly, you didn't play for Kevin Steele as much as you survived Kevin Steele. And in order to outlast the man and maintain a shred of composure, of dignity and the fight to press on, these guys leaned heavily on each other as they daily bore the brunt of sometimes brutal, demeaning, and somewhat unfair treatment from their tutor. I suspect that it was his Southern charm during recruiting that ultimately won him the job (he landed Tommie Frazier). Regardless, the brotherhood and unity of those linebackers was a small test run, a forerunner to the Council of future days, and these guys proved how a unified front could outlast and defeat most any foe, within or without.

Notable quote #2:
Doug Colman on brotherhood and shared suffering: "But one thing about our linebacking corps: we were very, very close. And when things were wrong, when things didn't go right for us, we really came together. As a group of guys we came together. They were a great support system at the time..."

On the trail of another man, the biographer must put up with finding himself at every turn; any biography uneasily shelters an autobiography within it.

Paul Murray Kendall

For any journey other than the usual neighborhood streets and thoroughfares of daily life we typically face a choice of the oft traveled highway for speediness' sake or alternately kicking up a plume of dirt on the rolling, graveled backroads for a bit of adventure and a chance at whimsy. As you are well aware, for this trip into the Why and How of the 60 & 3 era I've chosen to turn off of the more beaten path a time or two, sometimes to interject an unknown figure, others to reintroduce you to individuals hidden or long forgotten, and still yet a few who I felt might hold a more colorful, revealing, or excessively insightful viewpoint to the collection of our acquired kNowledge. In this particular case I found myself taking a pit stop at a figurative roadside convenience store embodied in sportswriter Mike Babcock.

A living, breathing vault of Husker lore and the man many consider the preeminent biographer of Tom Osborne -especially through his 1996 work *Heart of a Husker*- Mike has spent a majority of his adult life covering Nebraska Football for both the Lincoln Journal-Star, Huskers Illustrated, and finally Hail Varsity in these latter years. You should know that beat writers are a contrast in styles and personalities, sometimes playing the cheerleader and 'homer,' others the mocking jester or even the muckraking radical. The key, it appears, is walking the fine line in choosing what info goes to print and what is not quite fit for public consumption (or at best, maybe to be divulged years long gone when less harm is done to relationships and/or reputations). If successful organizations are -as some suggest- driven from the top down, I wanted to gain a view from a man with access and years as an insider at the top, yet also detached enough to look at Husker Football from outside the sphere. (I say this as a check against myself, just in case my own personal experience has been too close to the situation and might find me lacking objectivity) Here is just the man for the occasion, Mike Babcock...

Notable quote #1:
"...I remember one of those earlier Orange Bowls when Nebraska played Miami and the Coaches Luncheon after that, and (Tom Osborne) said, "Maybe the game has passed me by.""

Mike Babcock

Question: So, Mike, It sounds like you're pretty busy at the moment with announcing Legion baseball there in Lincoln..

Mike Babcock: Yes, they have a hard time finding volunteers. So I guess the bottom line is I'm available rather than good. And it pays well: nothing. (laughs) My wife has to be pretty understanding when tournament time comes, because it's pretty much every night.

Q: It's amazing: the more a guy is around sports, the more you find that everyone's wife has to be pretty understanding, no matter what you do.

MB: Yeah, and when I was at the newspaper, The Journal-Star, like any reporter who covers the beat (obviously, it's a lot harder on the coaches with the recruiting and everything they do), but there are some similarities in a minor way with the travel demands and such. For example, when Nebraska was going to a bowl game for 35-some consecutive seasons, you're gone during the holidays every year. You can just kind of figure on that.

And the way we'd do it at the newspaper was we'd be there a week before the bowl, as well, so you'd often spend Christmas Eve and New Year's Eve on the road.

Q: Did you ever take your family along on those trips?

MB: You know, it became a function of whether or not you could afford it. I remember once as a family we went to the Fiesta Bowl together, and after the bowl game we went on to Disneyland. But typically, not. It was kind of an expense thing, that was the bottom line. (laughs)

Q: Well, again Mike, I appreciate your time in talking a little about those '90's years and giving me your unique perspective from your position covering the beat for the Lincoln Journal-Star. I've spoken to many and varied people thus far, from Al Papik to Trev Alberts, from Boyd Epley to the Schmadeke brothers...

MB: Oh yeah, Darren and Damon Schmadeke, those guys were both walk-ons from... I can't remember the town off the top of my head, but yeah, I remember those two guys.

Q: And I speak with Coach Osborne next week before things really get super-busy for him...

MB: Yeah, that's important. He has his own book coming out, Beyond the Final Score. It is kind of his views and experiences post-football. I heard him talking about it. The way I heard about it was when the publisher called me and said Tom wanted to quote some things from the Heart of a Husker book and they needed permission to do that, so that's when I first heard about the book.

And I don't mind at all. When I did that book I said that the only way I would do it was if Tom was okay with it. And the publisher said, "That's okay, you're not going to interview him. It's just going to be about him." And I said, 'Well, I understand that. But personally, I won't do the book unless, a) Tom is aware that I'm doing it, and b) he is comfortable with me doing it.' And so they said, "Well okay, we'll contact Tom and make sure he's okay with it." So two weeks went by and I called 'em up and said, 'Have you talked to Tom? I'd like to get started on this.' And they said, "You go ahead and get started on it. We'll contact him and we're sure that he'll be okay with it." And I was, 'How about I just call and ask him?', and I talked about 10 minutes with him and he said, "Yeah, that's fine. I don't have any problem with your doing the book. We've known each other for awhile." So I told the publisher I would do it, and actually had several players who said the same thing as I did: they'd do it "if Tom was okay with it."

Q: Where did you grow up and what got you into sportswriting?

MB: Well, I was born in Beatrice but I grew up in York, forty miles down the line. My first year of school I went to York College there in town because I could afford to do that. I wanted to go to the University but I could afford to go to York College because I got an academic scholarship. I'd hoped to play basketball and ended up playing a semester of basketball and played baseball in the spring. My second year I transferred to the University of Nebraska, and my folks moved to southern California in the summer of '67, and as soon as they moved I was a non-resident in Nebraska and I just couldn't afford the tuition, so I went to California with my folks. And after nine months out there you established residency, so I got my undergraduate from Chico State in English and then I came back to Nebraska and went to graduate school and got my Masters Degree in English and started out teaching at a community college in Illinois for seven years.

When I was teaching at the community college I hooked onto a newspaper there in town (I always wanted to be a newspaper guy, but I didn't want to be a journalism major because sports was my only interest in it). So I was teaching and worked half-time for the newspaper; one of those guys who calls up coaches after a Friday night and writes up little deals. Then they assigned me a high school beat: Champaign Central High School. So I went to football, basketball games, volleyball, and Saturdays I did locker room stories at the home games at the University of Illinois. And they always gave me the visiting locker room, so it was Michigan, Ohio State and that sort of thing. A friend of mine who worked for the Champaign-Urbana Courier (which is no longer), he was from Hebron, Nebraska and his name was Lou Engel, and he said there was an opening at the Lincoln Journal-Star and said, "I'm gonna apply for it. You ought to apply for it, too. Why not try?" And I tell you, Paul, if I could have live anywhere I wanted, it would be in Nebraska. And if I could live -and I thought this at the time- I thought, 'If I could do anything I wanted to do, it would be to work for the Lincoln paper and live in Lincoln, Nebraska.' So applied for the job sight unseen, and they hired a guy from either Florida or Louisiana and he was here for two days and didn't like Lincoln and left.(laughs) So they called and told me I was their first choice, but I knew I was their second choice. (laughs) They said, "Are you interested in this thing?" I said, 'Yeah!' At my own expense I came back to interview and they said they'd pay me mileage (but they never did). (laughs)

And they gave me the Nebraska beat. This guy took off and opened up the job on the Husker beat, so I went from basically covering the high school beat half-time and working full-time as a teacher in the community college to working full-time on the Husker beat. I started on August 5th and four weeks after Nebraska opened the '78 season against Alabama in Birmingham.

And my journalism background? My high school journalism teacher was great, that's where I really learned a lot about it in high school. When I was at Chico State I think I had a couple of courses like "African-Americans in Cinema." (laughs) Maybe thinking I'd be a film critic. (laughs)

Q: Thumbs up, thumbs down, huh?

MB: (laughs) Yeah. I was a little unrealistic in my expectations, but that's what I thought at the time, you know? I always felt I could do anything I wanted to do, but if ever possible I'd be a sportswriter and were I to live anywhere it would be in Nebraska.

Q: So after spending some time out in California and then Illinois, Nebraska was still close to your heart?

MB: Oh yes, and to some extent my parents were the same way. We moved there in '67 and my father hated it in California. He wanted to come back. It was probably a tougher thing on him that it was on me. But I felt that I was probably going to come back at some point and if I were ever going to retire (which I probably wouldn't), but if I were ever to retire I just can't imagine myself leaving Nebraska. I don't know if that's a character flaw or what, but Nebraska is where I always figured was my home. I'm probably a 'Nebraska hick' to some. (laughs)

Q: So let me ask you: those early nineties years building up to the Florida State, Miami, & Florida national championship games, as a sportswriter what was your main aim? Was it to inform, to entertain, to set policy? How did you envision the main gist of your role as writer?

MB: I'll probably make this sound like I was more organized or had a clearer sense than what I did…

A couple things I learned early on -and I might have known this even before I got back to Nebraska- but during the early years when I got here, when I took the job in 1978, it was like most people would perceive that job as, "Oh my gosh, this guy has the opportunity to sit in the press box every game and watch this stuff. It's just a great deal, everybody would want to do that." But if they knew more they would change their mind about it. Because when the game is over with you have to sit there and put together an article and they're out partying.

And let me preface this by saying one other thing: my uncle was the Equipment Manager at the university. I don't have the exact year, but early on when Tom was the coach. His name was Gibb, and Gibb was basically a retired farmer. My dad's family was up near the North Loup-Scotia area and when he finally retired they moved to Lincoln, and I think he started as assistant groundskeeper with Bill Sheppard. I knew Shep really well, Walt Johnson, Glenn Abbott, all those guys. (When Gibb stepped aside Glenn replaced him) But I can remember when Nebraska, I believe it was while I was a sophomore at the university - which would have been in '67 or '68, in the fall of 67 when I was a sophomore- Nebraska put the N on the helmet for the first time. I can remember the first semester. (I lived in the second floor of my uncle's house -he lived right across the train tracks there on Y Street). There wasn't any room in the dorms so I lived with my aunt and uncle for probably the first half of the first semester and then moved into temporary housing in Abel Hall.) But I remember my uncle going into the locker in the field house there and taking all the helmets out and putting the strips on them and placing the N's on the side. So I always had a little bit of an insight into it since my uncle was there. And it was a big deal to be around there. When they'd collect the shirts, ones the guys didn't pick up or threw on the floor, he'd wash them and he always had a bin full of those things. And I had a Colorado Buffaloes t-shirt that somebody had left there. (laughs) But I had a tenuous connection there.

Q: So one could say that, in certain respects, that Mike Babcock was partly responsible for putting the infamous N on the Husker helmets?

MB: My recollection was that we may have cleaned them or something, but I just remember taking them out of the lockers and putting some N's on them.

(And you know, the N's were initially a little bit smaller. There was a sequence there: first they were smaller, then they were bigger. So I think they played around with it for awhile.)

But back to your original question? My aim was never to set policy. And I believe this to some extent: you're almost an entertainment writer more than anything. Because the newspaper during football season always sold more copies than at any other time of the year, and I don't think that probably changed the thinking that appealed to me most about the job. And I still maintain this, because I've done it for more than thirty years, but my interest has never really been the outcome of any games: the thing that's kept me doing this is the people involved. I was impressed and interested in the people involved in this project that is Nebraska Athletics.

I loved those things, because you're dealing with people. Football has more interest overall with people in the state, but volleyball athletes, track and field athletes, golfers, whatever, it's the people that make it interesting. The good thing about football, I guess, when you have 150-180 guys on the football team you've got that many stories. You could talk to Darren Schmadeke and get a good story from him just as easily as getting a good story from

Jarvis Redwine. So that's what's always driven me to do it. It's the people. To some extent, I guess, that's the appeal of it, completely, for me.

The other thing I learned, also, is that no matter how much you think you know about it, there's somebody out there reading the newspaper who thinks they know more about it than you do. Now, it might not be that many people, but there's always somebody out there who knows more about what you're writing about than you do. Newspaper writers are generalists more than anything. I know a little about a lot of things and I have access to things other people don't have access to. For example, when Nebraska had the Lincoln Parents program you could interview Turner Gill and you had access to him and you were around practice every day, but obviously Bill Wright knew more about him than you do, because he's the Lincoln parent. The same way with coaches. You can talk to them on a regular basis but maybe Charlie McBride goes down to the Tam O'Shanter and he's got some drinking buddies down there and they know more about what's going on than you do. So there's a certain humility you have to have about it, I think. Because there's always the danger of being a sports writer -when you're covering something that people are so passionate about- that somehow you're important. Professional wrestlers call it a 'rub.' You get known, you get a 'rub' by associating yourself with somebody well known, like when they have WrestleMania they have Pete Rose come in to be the special timekeeper for something like that.

Q: (laughs) Ha! I guess I'm the classic case of the 'rub' for you, then. I was at that very WrestleMania in Philadelphia, Mike! I actually met Pete Rose there and shared a locker room with him, got him dressed up in the San Diego Chicken's costume for that event! I was the manager/producer for the San Diego Chicken for a half-dozen years after I left Nebraska. (laughs)

MB: Is that right!? (laughs) Then you understand then. Another thing that always fascinated me was professional wrestling, even since I was a kid.

Q: Hey, mind if I tell you a story about that?

MB: Sure, I love to hear about pro wrestling…

Q: Well, here it is '98 or '99, The WWF's Wrestlemania is in the Spectrum in Philadelphia and it's supposed to be the biggest payday ever in Pay-Per-View history, right? And we get out of this limo at the WWF Hotel, me and the Chicken -this little 5'5" Greek guy- we step out of this super-freighter-sized limousine and there's a massive crowd ranging from kids to grandmas, everybody, waiting for a brush with the performers, the wrestelers. They're pressing up to the car as it pulls curbside and peering in to see what famous, larger than life personality is behind the tinted windows, and in a split-second the door is opened and the poor saps are just dumbstruck trying to figure out just who the heck these two clowns are, me and the Chicken without his suit on. (laughs) They fully expected The Rock or Stone Cold Steve Austin to get out of the limo, right? It was the greatest anti-climactic occasion I've ever been involved in. I think their brains shorted out. They just stood with their autograph pens… and stared. (laughs)

So anyway, we make our way into the Spectrum and a WWF representative takes us to our dressing room. And there are wrestlers backstage, everywhere, a virtual Hall of Fame of pro wrestling just milling about and chewing the fat, guards down. And they've got this little old grandma-type sitting back stage at a sewing machine placed in a corner completely surrounded by trunk after trunk filled to the brim with fabrics and you name it. And here are these big, hulking wrestlers and stringy-haired, steroid-enhanced freaks asking her to sew this & that on their costumes to give 'em more color, more flair, you name it, right?

Anyway, there are video cameras and production booths and black drapes and scaffolding all over the place, and we're led to our dressing room. And the door's already open as we walk in to enter. Well, as I make my way through the door I notice some run-of-the-mill horse race is playing on the dressing room television, and as I look down to my left there on the couch is Pete Rose -engrossed, just completely mesmerized and totally locked-in- to this horse race on TV! I thought to myself, 'Nah, Pete's not a betting man.' (laughs) As you probably recall, later that night one of the wrestlers rips the Chicken's head off on live Wrestlemania TV, only to find it's Pete Rose in the suit! (laughs)

MB: (laughs) No, I don't think Pete Rose had a betting problem. (laughs) It was obvious. That Prince Valiant haircut? He didn't have any betting problem. (laughs) That's why the WrestleMania, that's why they always had those celebrities, and the Pete Rose thing would rub off on the WWF.

And I think the newspaper reporters and TV guys to a lesser extent, you start to think that what you cover is so important to people, you start thinking you're important. It's one of the few perks you get working for a newspaper, because it doesn't pay that well. If your ego gets stroked that way, I guess it's not a bad thing. But you have to pay attention to it to some extent because people are not interested in you. You're just the guy who has access to things that other people don't have.

I'll give you a quick story about that: I do this Big Red Wrap-up thing on TV about once a season. They have me on there -there was times I'd be on there twice- but once or twice in 52 weeks I'm on there, and Nebraska's at the Alamo Bowl game. (And I love the Alamo and have been there multiple times) And I'm walking through the Alamo on a Friday afternoon and there's people everywhere, and some lady walks up to me and says, "Hey, you're on Big Red Wrap-up" and she looks at this group of people and says, "Hey, he's on Big Red Wrap-up", and she's from Sydney or some place out west. Now, what does that say? I've worked at a newspaper for seventeen-some years and I probably get more recognition by being on Big Red Wrap-up on TV once per year than for 17 years at the newspaper. But what that shows you is that if you're associated with Nebraska football it gets you recognition.

Now, I haven't worked at the Journal Star since 1995 and I'll still go in the grocery store today and people will say, "How are things at the Journal-Star?" (laughs) And I'll say, 'Well, they're great.'(Because I do maintain great contact with those people) And they say, "We really enjoy reading your stuff in the newspaper." And I haven't written in there since '95, but that's just the association when you're a sportswriter-journalist. You have to keep it in perspective: It's not about you. People don't think you're important because of anything intrinsically, it's because of the program.

And one other thing I've learned that applies to sports coverage is that you don't realize how much power you have when you put things in print. You're always going to affect somebody.

Q: Any column you ever wish you could take back?

MB: The things I always wished I could take back was usually just poor editing or mistakes, a poor job of writing things on my part. I got to the point where I spent a lot of time on it. (I was never good with deadlines and I'd always push it to the end.) I always re-read it and polished things, which you're not supposed to do. But the thing that just killed me were the mistakes, the factual or grammatical. So it got to the point where I'd write the story and work as hard on it as I could, but once it got into the paper I wouldn't read it because I didn't want to see my mistakes.

But I don't think I ever wrote anything I regretted. I remember one day after practice when Tom had his little meeting with reporters. We got done with the interview and as we're walking away Tom stopped me and said there was something in the paper the previous day. He said, "It wasn't a big deal, but you misquoted what I said there." I'm not sure if I misquoted him, but from that point on I recorded every interview. I bought a tape recorder and recorded it. Not because that I wished to turn around and say, 'No, I didn't misquote you,' but because I wanted to make sure that I did have it right.

Q: Which also revealed to you that Coach Osborne read the newspaper… (laughing)

MB: Right. (laughs) Right! I think Tom was always aware of it, and I had tremendous respect for Tom from the beginning and I was never very comfortable around him because of the respect I had for him.

And this was the worst moment for me: I was two weeks into my working at the paper, and about two weeks into it Nebraska had a scrimmage, the last major scrimmage before the Alabama game. And Coach Osborne got all the players together in the south end zone and kind of recalled what he saw during the scrimmage and he said to the defense, "Hey, you guys played pretty good defense. If you play defense that way Alabama will be lucky to score more than a touchdown or two against you guys." He was that impressed.

So the next day I write a story about the scrimmage and I include that in the story. So they go down to Alabama and they get beat 20-3 (and I believe Alabama was national champions in '78). But anyway, the Extra Point Club the Monday after that, which I believe was at Miller & Paine, and Tom Osborne is there and he talks about the opening game against Alabama, and they have a Grad Assistant go and give a scouting report about the next game (which I believe was against Hawaii), and then they have an assistant coach come in to finish off the luncheon with some game film. (Well, I was sent over there to cover it for the Journal so it would have something in the afternoon edition -which they thought was news- so you had to really listen to all the stuff and really hustle and get back and type up a quick story on the thing.) Well, anyway, I'm listening to Tom and listen to the Grad Assistant give the scouting report, and George Darlington is supposed to show film on the Alabama game and give comments on it.

And George gets up and says, "I'm not going to show this film 'til a certain sportswriter leaves." And I'm looking around to see if there's any other sportswriters there. And there isn't. (laughs) It's a bit of an uncomfortable silence there, and I can't leave because I have to stay to write the story. And maybe it was me, but it seemed like it was the longest, most uncomfortable silence. Then George says, "Okay, I'll show it as long as long as a certain sportswriter doesn't quote anything I say," which was a reference back to my quoting Tom. So George's implication was that I costed them the Alabama game by quoting Tom on the deal.

So here I'd been on the job for about a month and I thought I'd already done something that Kansas State, Kansas and Oklahoma State never did, which is beat a Tom Osborne-coached team. And I'd only been on the job for a month! So Tom is 255-49-3, and one of those losses is my responsibility. I thought my job was gone for sure. Then that day after practice Tom asked if he could talk to me for a minute after questions. He took me aside and told me, "My policy on practice is that reporters can watch practice, they just can't report on anything they see or hear. And if you see something or hear something you can ask me about it and I'll either answer your question or not, but that's the policy we have. And you're kind of new on the job, but that's just our policy on the thing." So Tom was very gracious about it and understood.

And about two days later Lance VanZant, the defensive coordinator, wanted to see me in his office. He was a crusty old guy. I thought he was going to jump all over me, but he said, "You're new on the job and you're gonna occasionally write things that are gonna make people unhappy. I just want to encourage you to ignore it and do what you think is right." That was just a great response on both parts.

The impact you have? You really have to be careful what you write. And I wrote columns for awhile, too, my columns ended up being more feature-ish and less technical. It always seemed the less you knew about a subject the better off you were. And I don't see the world very much in black and white, I see mostly gray and it's all point-of-view. I probably wasn't a great reporter in some respect. I never tried to tell people what their job was, and I would never have wanted to have been a columnist while Bill Callahan was a coach that last year there. Short of some really criminal behavior, he's a coach, he's a person. He might not be the perfect person for that situation, but I never saw myself trying to tell people how they ought to do things.

Q: So Mike, let me ask you, in putting together that book Heart of a Husker -you'd been around Coach Osborne since '78- was there anything new that was revealed to you about how he ran things, his style, his character? Something that surprised you?

MB: My reaction is to say 'no, not really.' I guess the thing that was most impressive to me was that people were able to characterize him. And what I understood about him? They were able to express it in better ways.

I'll give you an example: Kevin Steele told me that Tom's success in part -and in large part- was that Tom had the ability to make everybody in the organization, when he was dealing with them, to make them feel like they were the most important person to the success of that organization: whether you were a secretary or an assistant equipment manager or whatever. When Tom came to you and you talked he had the ability to make you think that you were important and the success of the organization depended on you doing your job in a positive and effective way.

And I think that Tom's ability, his relationships with people who worked for him by and large helped define his success. There's no question about Tom's understanding of x's and o's. People always said that if any head coach could coach from the press box it would be Tom, because he had the strategy, the understanding of offensive football in particular, such an understanding that he could do it from there. And player after player would say, "Well, I won't do this interview unless he's okay with it." And one former player, who preferred to be nameless, there was one road game at Kansas or Kansas State where Nebraska always took a bus. Well, afterward if the players wanted to go home with their parents, they could. So he said that Tom said, "Well, that's fine," thinking that he was going to back with his parents. He said that he told Tom that he was going back with his parents... but he didn't. He stayed with his buddies and they went out on the town. So the kid said he'd gone out and had a good time with his friends. Not that they got into any trouble and got drunk or hauled into jail or anything like that, just that they had a good time out on the town. To this day Tom didn't know that he did that, and to this day he does not want Tom to know that. And we're talking 20-plus years later. And the reason he wouldn't is because he didn't want him to know so Tom wouldn't feel like he'd let him down. Now, what does that say about the relationship and the respect a player has for him some 20 years later? That's the kind of relationship-building that went on.

And whether it was directly stated or the implication, they played hard because they didn't want to let Tom down. They didn't want to disappoint him. When they won that national championship, it was most important to them that they did it for Tom, that they won that national championship for himYou've talked to Trev, I'm sure, about that '94 national championship game against Florida State where Byron Bennett couldn't get that kick through at the end there, and Trev said that in the locker room that Tom's first inclination was to walk over to him in the locker room and apologize that they weren't table to get him and the seniors the national championship.

And you know, the Lawrence Phillips thing? Tom still gets nailed on that from a lot of people. And, from the beginning, Nebraska didn't need Lawrence Phillips. He was a great player, no question. If Lawrence Philips had been a social sociopath or whatever... he could have been the greatest running back ever at Nebraska, and he had that ability. But they didn't need him in that national championship game. They had Ahman Green, they had a great team. Tommie Frazier. They would have won that game without him and they did so without him during the year, anyway. But Tom looked at Lawrence Phillips and I really think he thought that the only way of salvaging him was to let him play football and to put that out there for him. And if people didn't believe that, why did Tom suspend Terrell Farley down the stretch in '96? If they wouldn't have suspended Terrell Farley I think they would have won three in a row. If he'd not been suspended they would have had an outside rush versus Texas down there in the Big 12 Championship.

And Tom always felt that he was one bad season from them running him out of there, I think. They would have maybe given him two seasons, but he understood that. And that's kind of what drove him. But understanding that, he didn't compromise his principles with Lawrence Phillips. There was a reason he did those things.

Q: Lastly, what do you think the national media failed to grasp when it came to the Nebraska/Lawrence Phillips issue? When they piled on and tried to bring us down, so to speak?

MB: Well, it was that. And I think the fact that Nebraska is a low population state. You know everybody, where they go, "Look at Nebraska. All they have is football and it's the only thing they have." And I think that's a positive. Anytime you can have something for people to rally around and have some enthusiasm about, something special in their life? Nebraska football was that to them. I think the national media looked at that with disdain, because "that's all they have." But I'm not a great one to answer that, because I want to live here, anyway. (laughs) My view of things is distorted.

But when Tom went for two in '84 -here's the good thing- when Tom went for two instead of just kicking the extra point and going for the tie. He played to win against Miami in the Orange Bowl, and they lost 31-30. I think a lot of national media? Tom got a lot of respect for that. And when the Lawrence Phillips thing came up eleven years later a lot of people bailed out nationally and said that "it's all about winning." And Bernie Goldberg was here with the cameras and all and caught him coming out of a news conference. That was bush league as far as I'm concerned.

I just think that people to some extent don't understand what it's like to live in Nebraska. I mean, I don't understand what it's like to live in Michigan or Ohio. So maybe it's just like that with the Ohio State fans or the Michigan fans; I don't know because I don't live there. There are things you don't understand about other places, but what makes Nebraska unique is the thing some people don't understand. How do you get 300 consecutive sell-outs since 1962, you know?

And I remember one of those earlier Orange Bowls when Nebraska played Miami and the Coaches Luncheon after that, and (Tom Osborne) said, "Maybe the game has passed me by." He wasn't looking to step down or anything, but he was mulling over the possibility out loud, you know? People were bitching about he wasn't throwing the ball enough, but those were great Miami teams. But you don't have 25 years of success that he had and eleven years under Bob as an assistant, and that doesn't happen without a pretty good system in place. And I don't know if the national media understood it or even wanted to understand it. And like I said earlier, sometimes when you're a columnist, it's easier to be a columnist and have an opinion the less you know about things."The less you know, the better off you are" kind of thing. Oftentimes they just want to deal in stereotypes, "the N on the side of the helmet stands for Knowledge," that kind of cheap stuff.

Q: And it all started with Mike Babcock, the man who put the 'N for knowledge' on the Husker's helmets? (laughs)

MB: Yeah. That's my recollection, anyway. (laughs)

End conversation.

After getting to know Mike one might say he is a 'homer,' not that there's anything wrong with that. He doesn't beat around the bush, acting a pompous boor and lecturing with turned up nose as if elevated above 'the dirty-collared, uninformed bourgeois' he serves and entertains, and I can respect him for that.

I'm glad we had a chance to delve into his personal opinions and understanding of the press and the role they played during that era, because while the Huskers became nationwide media darlings after winning it all that '94 season they soon became media demons in '95, (a la "We want Barabus!") when Lawrence Phillip's indiscretion garnered a multitude of nationwide headlines and opinion columns, sports sections and otherwise. This was back when the internet and sharing online opinion was just a faint notion, so the sportswriters of the day held greater sway in fomenting public outrage and opinion. Some spewed ignorant, broad-brushed falsehoods, stereotypes, hyperbole and venom of the most crude and rapacious manner. Much were prime examples of capricious, opportunistic perversion of journalistic integrity. Many names come to mind, but one such ignorant and opinionated bloviator -thinking himself above the fray of tattered humanity and the "win at all costs, football lovin', criminal enabling, cornhusking hicks" was Chicago Sun-Times columnist Jay Mariotti. Among others, this magnificent, middle-aged tool penned a column for the January 3rd, 1996 edition of the Sun-Times titled, *"Nebraska's Title Tainted by Phillips' Participation."* (Feel free to google it and the words "Jay Marriotti Decrying Domestic Violence" and feast your eyes)

As for Lawrence? Foregoing a convenient college exit and early payday during that ugly span of the '95 season, the 20 year old instead bore down and followed a rigorous routine of therapy, counseling and study, earning the privilege of that bowl game's reinstatement. Living in semi-sequester and public shunning, if Hester Prynn's capital A was the Scarlet Letter, Lawrence's jersey numeral 1 was its equivalent as the Scarlet Number. Seeking these days to remain in the background for a day of eventual correctional release, he wished only to share this short, personal statement:

"Thank you to all the Husker fans who supported us before, during and after those great seasons we had. Thank you to the Husker fans who support me now when I need it more than ever. And to those Husker fans who feel they cannot support me any longer, I apologize for letting them down."

That's an honest, apologetic and refreshingly heartfelt message. I can respect Lawrence for that. And we would all do right to wish him well, for I believe his future has potential to be brighter than his past and present.

Notable quote #2:
Mike Babcock on the power of the printed word: "I don't know if the national media understood it or even wanted to understand it ... it's easier to be a columnist and have an opinion the less you know about things... Oftentimes they just want to deal in stereotypes, "the N on the side of the helmet stands for Knowledge," that kind of cheap stuff."

In addition to all the engineering and business courses, I also studied four years of psychology and abnormal psychology ....I'm not being facetious when I say that these were probably the most valuable courses of my college career.

Lee Iacocca, *Iacocca: An Autobiography*, with William Novak

When histories are written, men are most often defined by their successes, their failures, and to a lesser extent the choices made in arriving at those destinations. Such is the personage of Thomas William Osborne. A man of action, words, and deep introspection, he's been a moral compass, a study in leadership styles, a Christian model, and a surrogate father for over a generation of Nebraskans.

In my mind, his defining moment will forever be that "Forget the polls, we're going for the win" two-point conversion call on January 2nd, 1984. What I find most peculiar and providential about that fateful night is the quirky coincidence of his name's monogram: T.W.O., as if he was destined for that precariously illuminating situation long before history had run its course.

A man described by outsiders as stoic, insular, overly private, ethically challenged and even morally bankrupt on one occasion, I and many, many other individuals know reality to be just the opposite, as experience and interaction have revealed a bedrock strength of meekness, humility and intellect. His inspiring aura often makes you want to gather together and accomplish something larger than you could merely do by yourself, to strive to be a better man at everything in life. To quote former trainer Jack Nickolite, "If I were a quarter the man that he is, I'd be twice the man that I am." Let that sink in, then listen in on this brief conversation with someone I'll forever know as 'Coach,' as we pull the curtain back on the man, his mindset and some rationale for his methods.

Notable quote #1:
"A lot of times if you look behind the behavior you'll begin to understand more. And I think, as a result, many times we got maximum effort out of players because they felt that they were important, that we cared about them as people. We were certainly interested in winning football games, but were even more concerned with their general welfare."

Tom Osborne

Question: Good morning Coach. I appreciate your making some time for me. If you don't mind, I have a few questions.

Tom Osborne: That would be fine.

Q: Well, for starters I re-read your book 'Faith in the Game' last night, and it made me curious... how did your Doctorate in Educational Psychology help you as a football coach?

TO: Well, I think it helped me to realize that sometimes behavior wasn't always caused by what it appeared to be on the surface. Sometimes people say, "He's just lazy" or "This person is trying to show their independence" or "This person is just stubborn," and you realize that a lot of people don't really want to behave in ways that are destructive or obstructive. And you realize that usually behavior is caused by a reason. And that maybe caused me to listen a little bit more and fly off the handle less; instead of telling people what to do, trying to listen a little bit more for what is behind the behavior.

That didn't mean I was trying to psychoanalyze every player; I wasn't doing that. But I just realized that maybe a player was playing poorly, but if you sat down and listened to him you found out his grandmother was dying, for instance, and his grandmother was the one who raised him. And so a lot of times if you look behind the behavior you'll begin to understand more. And I think, as a result, many times we got maximum effort out of players because they felt that they were important, that we cared about them as people. We were certainly interested in winning football games, but were even more concerned with their general welfare.

Q: It always seemed like you were a very good listener. Was that something you had to work on?

TO: Well, to some degree. But as I said, I think that realizing that if you listen you can oftentimes understand people better. And one of the greatest needs people have is to feel understood. Even though you may not be able to fix the problem, if a player felt that I at least tried to understand him, understood where he was coming from, it made a difference. It seemed to fire them up to play to the best of their ability.

Q: Did you have any coaching role models or people you wanted to emulate when you first got into the business?

TO: I think the person in the coaching profession who's had the most important influence on me was someone I never really saw coach in person: it was John Wooden.

But I read a lot of what he wrote, talked to him on the phone a few times and have met him a couple of times, and I was always quite interested in his approach to coaching. I thought, philosophically, we were fairly similarly aligned. One thing that John emphasized is 'the process,' how you do things was more important than the final outcome. And if you did things well enough and often enough over a long enough time period then hopefully the outcome would be good. But he never talked about winning, never focused on winning: "Focus on how you put your socks on, how you bend your knees when you shoot a free throw, how you dribble, the techniques of passing," the process that you go through every day to get better.

Q: You seemed to have a lot in common with a lot of basketball coaches. Is there any rhyme or reason to that? Are you an inherent basketball fan?

TO: No, I played basketball. I played basketball in high school and college, but football was my first love. I just happened to find a guy like John Wooden was probably the person in coaching who seemed to align philosophically with me better than anybody else. Although I certainly have been a close friend and admirer of Bobby Bowden, Bo Schembechler. I saw things in Bo that I liked, and Joe Paterno to some degree, but John Wooden would be the one who had the most influence.

Q: Was there one great, important lesson you learned or experienced as a player that you were able to bring into your coaching? Which made you a better coach?

TO: Oh, I think maybe when I went to the National Football League. I was an 18th round draft pick, as I recall. At that time there were thirty rounds. There were thirty rookies that came in plus another 20 or 30 free agents. And I think there were 36 spots on the team at that time, and there were 36 veterans. So the odds of my hanging around were just about zero, coming from a small college.

But I found that perseverance, you know, just hanging in there and going to practice the next day, working hard, I saw guys eliminate themselves. The #1 draft pick got homesick and got on a bus one night and left camp. One other guy dropped out. Somebody would get hurt and you realized that perseverance is really critical to any kind of endeavor.

Q: In your book you said that he actually asked you for a ride to the bus station. You were more than willing to oblige him, eh? (laughs)

TO: Yeah, I drove him down there. He was a guy I knew. He was a friend. He just had really made up his mind he was leaving so I drove him down.

Q: I have to tell you, Coach, in talking to all of these former players they've spoken about the Unity Council and the empowerment it brought, but they also infer or mention the love that existed in the program. Love and caring for one another was absolutely pervasive. Any comment on that?

TO: Well, we certainly tried to put players first and let them know that whether they were a first team player or fourth team player, that we cared about them as individuals. And I guess you show that in various ways. I tried to spend some time down in the weight room every day after practice and I talked to five or six guys maybe for three or four minutes each. And by the end of the season I'd talked to most everybody several times and knew a little bit about their family, what was going on academically, wouldn't let them play if they didn't perform academically, let them know their education was placed above football, that their health was important. Obviously, we never tried to play a player that the medical staff said wasn't ready to play, and so I think by showing concern in various ways by listening to them and getting to know them personally, that they felt cared for. And I think that was important.

And I think that when the coaches care about you that you're a little more apt to care about the program, about other players. And so I think that overall the chemistry really came together very well.

Q: You probably know it already, but a wonderful brotherhood still remains from those days in the '80's and '90's. And one thing that seems to shock so many of the players was your ability to remember so many people's names, their family members' names. I have to know, how do you do it?

TO: Well, of course, when you go out to recruit them you meet all these players' families. And I guess what's important to you... you remember what's important to you. It was always important to me.

And I think that, of course, spending time either at the training table or the weight room talking to them personally, you'd get a little better chance to pick up on their personal life and their family and how things were going. And that was always important.

Q: I believe you said that you came to knowledge of a saving faith in Christ at 20 years of age, is that right?

TO: Yeah. Nineteen or twenty, uh huh.

Q: How did that come about? Can you tell me?

TO: Well, I had grown up in a Christian home and had always gone to church and Sunday School, and so it wasn't that I was without faith. But I guess that most people, as they are growing up their faith tends to be second-hand faith -the faith of your parents- and at some point you have to decide, really, what your faith is.

So I went to a Fellowship of Christian Athletes conference out in Estes Park, Colorado in 1957, and at that point I guess I heard Christianity expressed and explained in a little different way than what I'd heard in church, and then I saw the vitality and the virility to Christianity, the realization that this was something that was very demanding, that might require you to even sacrifice your life if you're going to be faithful. And I guess I heard it expressed and articulated by people I could relate to, other athletes, a number of professional athletes. There were a number of players from Oklahoma and LSU and other schools that I could admire. So anyways, it was during that week sometime that I made a spiritual commitment that I never turned away from.

Q: You talk about a demanding faith. Going throughout your personal history it seems you've enjoyed taking on very demanding things, that you are very competitive. What was the genesis of that competitive spirit?

TO: Oh, I really don't know. I've never seen myself as someone who's terribly competitive, but I guess anyone who's in coaching probably has a competitive streak. And of course, I was involved in athletics from an early age and I played 'em all: football, baseball, basketball, and track. So I've been in a lot of competitive situations. But I can't tell you exactly where that comes from; it's something that I've always enjoyed, the competition.

Q: Some people love competing to prove something to themselves, sometimes to prove something to others, or maybe a combination of the two. What drove you?

TO: I don't know. I know that my Dad being overseas during World War Two and returned when I was about 9 or 10 years old, I knew that athletics was important to him and wanted to get to know him better and gain his approval, so I'm sure some of my athletic competitive nature in competition may have had to do somewhat with my Dad.

Still, it's something that you either have it or you don't. Some kids just naturally like to compete and challenge themselves and some people don't. I always found that it's something that was appealing to me, to test myself in competition.

Q: You said football was your first love. What was it about the game of football that made you really cling to it?

TO: Well, I enjoyed the contact. Some people didn't like scrimmages; I always liked scrimmages, I always liked games. And even though I was not built like many football players -I guess I was relatively slender- but I still liked the contact of it. So I just enjoyed the game. And as time went on I began to enjoy the strategy of it more, and I believe I even called my own plays in high school and most of my years in college I called the plays.

Q: I talked to Al Papik recently and he talked about coaching against you when you were a college player. I told him I would love to see some of that game film. (laughs) Now, society doesn't necessarily esteem or promote the necessity of support from spouses today. Can you tell me the ways your wife Nancy best supported you?

TO: Well, Nancy is somebody who was very encouraging, to do whatever I, whatever we thought was best, and was a great coach's wife. Because there are times when there are three kids and the coach is absent. Sometimes the PTA meetings, sometimes the games -I went to every one I could- but there were times during the season that I couldn't. And she shouldered that burden and did a great job and also always had a good attitude.

You know, sometimes when the press was on you or things weren't going well, she still maintained a good balance, and I thought that was always very helpful to not come home to more criticism or problems than what you were already dealing with. So that was helpful to have someone like Nancy. She was a great coach's wife and has been great over so many years.

Q: Can you tell me: how did you know that you were fully prepared for a game? Was there ever an occasion in that process when you said to yourself, "Okay, I've put my study in. I've fully prepared. As a staff we've put our time in and feel secure about things now"?

TO: Well, we would go through a certain process: The game film would be broken down on our opponent the week before the week we played them, so we'd get all the game film in and Graduate Assistants and various people would chart offense, defense, and have a computer printout for us on Sunday afternoon. We'd get started on it, and then we would do certain things throughout the week: we'd have a quarterback audible sheet, alter our pass patterns if we were going to change anything. They were always done by Monday. We'd always have the computer printout in regard to tendencies and we'd put a game plan together and practice schedule and on and on. But you still never knew for sure. You might occasionally.

Because of the style of offense we ran, we'd come out and first series we'd find out they were lined up on defense with something they'd never shown all year, that we hadn't worked on at all that week, because there was no way to anticipate it. But we had enough experience as a staff and had enough institutional knowledge to draw on that we could think about maybe what we had done when something like that had happened four years before, five years before. So I think we were a staff that was able to adjust during a game quite well. Sometimes people get locked into a game plan and they're gonna stick with that game plan no matter what; sometimes the game plan goes out the window that first two or three minutes and you're gonna adjust.

Q: Any particular games come to mind as far as that happening?

TO: Well, I can remember one time we played Kansas up here and they basically came up in an 8-man front and they essentially were challenging us to run wide, and so we did some things and eventually we figured out some ways to pick it apart: some trap plays and a few passes.

And when we played Tennessee that last game I coached, I think they had eleven people within 3 or 4 yards of the line of scrimmage that first series and just stuffed the run. I think we threw four straight passes the next series and completed every one of them, and they backed off and we ate 'em up. We might have had close to six hundred yards that game. My feeling is if they'd stayed with what they had originally lined up in they'd have given us a harder time, but they got taken out of it when we hit the passes.

So that's just the way it was. There were times when people played pretty vanilla and played the way you had practiced & what you had expected, and there were times when they just felt we were so good on offense or defense they figured they might as well roll the dice and come up with something that we'd never seen before.

Q: And let me ask you, is there anyone behind the scenes who you feel played a truly integral part in what you were able to accomplish, someone who's never fully gotten their due?

TO: Well, over the years I think Boyd Epley was important because he really brought to the forefront the importance of strength training and offseason conditioning. Boyd was always, I thought, ahead of the curve a little bit. When people were emphasizing just power lifting, he began to get into explosiveness and quickness and agility and those kinds of things, so I thought he always helped provide us with an advantage.

Jack Stark in those later years was helpful in helping formulate the idea of the Unity Council and some of those things that worked.

But there was no one person or one thing. A lot of it was the players themselves. They had a lot of pride in what they were doing and forced things internally. They had a pretty strong sense of ownership of the program and they didn't want to have anyone stand in their way to be successful, so they just didn't tolerate people who'd deliberately not be with the program.

Q: They'd taken some things off of your plate, so internal control wasn't bogging you down every day?

TO: Uh-huh.

Q: And I have to ask, do you have any memorable or comical moments that make you giggle to this day?

TO: Well, I thought we tried to have a fair bit of fun playing football. It wasn't all strictly business. I remember Christian Peter and I threw our trainer Doak Ostergard into the pool down at the Fiesta Bowl one year, and a few things like that that happened that were kind of interesting, kind of fun.

Q: And if one were to invest in a time machine, is there anything you wish you had the chance to do over again? Tweak? Change? Do differently with the knowledge you have now?

TO: Well, I think that probably my leadership style evolved and changed over the years, which is natural. The more you do something the more you reflect on it, and probably I was a little bit different coach and leader in the '90's and '80's than I was in the '70's. When I started out in 1973 I was 35 years old and there was a lot of pressure to come somewhere close to what Bob Devaney had done. And Bob had set the bar very high, so there was a natural tendency to focus on performance and winning, and I think as time went on I focused more and more on the process. I probably got better at listening to people and understanding people better. But that's just sort of a natural evolvement over time, I think.

Q: Have you found any time for fishing lately?

TO: Yeah, I still get away. I try to go. In the summer I get away for a couple weeks for a couple days to do some fishing. But that's just about to end here. Once August starts you can't do a whole lot of that.

Q: If I recall, one of your favorite spots is up near Merritt Reservoir by Valentine, right?

TO: Yeah, although I haven't been up there for about 4 years. But I do fish some on the Snake River up there below Merritt Dam, that's pretty good.

Q: I have to know, do you still rise early in the morning for prayer, meditation and scriptures?

TO: Yeah, when I was coaching our meetings always started at 7, so I'd get up at 5:30. Now I probably get up about 6 and do the same thing. But, yeah, I start my day that way.

Q: Do you have a favorite Bible verse, a scripture verse that you latched onto and always held a little closer than most?

TO: Well, yeah, I had several. But one I come back to quite a bit is Second Timothy 1:7, that says, "for God has not given us a spirit of timidity, but of power and love and self discipline." I think that probably is something that's fairly appropriate to an athletic arena. And Hebrews 12:1-2, "Surrounded as we are by so great a crowd of witnesses, let us cast aside every hindrance and the sin that so easily entangles and run with perseverance the race set before us, keeping your eyes fixed on Jesus Christ, the Author and Perfector of our faith." That's another favorite of mine.

Q: That Second Timothy verse is one my favorites, also. Last question, Coach: it's about the concept of emotional intelligence. You never designated someone else to be a full-fledged offensive coordinator, but rather took that on in addition to all of the other head coaching hats you wore. Were you purposefully cognizant of all those tasks from the outset and did you have to work on developing the capability to do so, or did you always possess the ability to take on a lot of roles simultaneously and perform them well?

TO: Well, I did them all one at a time. (laughs) I never tried to do them all at the same time. I guess I wasn't really flipping a page in my mind thinking about emotional intelligence from one thing to another, I just did the best I could with whatever I was doing and one thing led to another. So I don't know, it's just something that sort of evolved over time.

Q: Well, I have to tell you, you have no idea how I appreciate the giving of your time... and I just want to let you know you had a profound impact on my life. I owe you a great debt of gratitude.

TO: Well, thank you. That's quite a compliment. I wish you well with the book and hope it goes well.

End conversation.

Our conversation took place just as Nebraska began to entertain serious thoughts about moving on to the Big 10 Conference, so Tom's scheduling allotment for talk meant a great deal to me. I felt guilty for even requesting a few minutes of his time, but he graciously asked his secretary Anne Hackbart to work me into his day. I wished it had gone on longer, but he had more important issues to deal with than a former strength staffer trying to dissect him and his former teams over a long distance telephone line.

In my feeble attempt at dissection both the humility and the honesty with which he answered my queries spoke volumes. It wasn't a fake, 'aw shucks' humility, either, for he spoke matter-of-factly and gave thoughtful pause to each question I brought up. I found it very refreshing when he flat out answered with an "I don't know" more than once, too. The honesty is endearing, if not quotable.

And if you must know, Tom Osborne's humor can border on the dry to slightly sarcastic side. Sadly, this conversation didn't allow for it to shine through as I would have liked. Perhaps that's why so many outsiders over the years have had a difficult time getting a fix on him, for he's an acquired taste, becoming all the more revealing the longer you're with the guy.

Additionally, I hope you noted that his primary emphasis was more about the players' general welfare rather than perpetuating the dominance of Nebraska Football, his status as a top-tier coach, winning just for the sake of winning, or any number of selfish, egotistical reasons. He's always had a unique -and I think proper- perspective about Nebraska Football through the years, once speaking of it degradingly as *"this thing we have concocted for ourselves."* (Which makes me chuckle)

Of secondary note, it was classic 'Tom Osborne' when he shared one of the reasons for the 60 & 3 era's success: "A lot of it was the players themselves. They had a lot of pride in what they were doing and forced things internally. They had a pretty strong sense of ownership of the program and they didn't want to have anyone stand in their way to be successful, so they just didn't tolerate people who'd deliberately not be with the program."

He reminds me of the Plutarch's biographical sketch of Roman consul General Gaius Marius (157 BC – 86 BC) who, throwing off the entrance requirement of only land-holding men into the pre-Caesarian Roman armies, he *"at once proceeded to levy soldiers, contrary both to law and custom, enlisting slaves and poor people; whereas former commanders never accepted of such."* In other words, General Marius had a deep appreciation for the 'walk-ons' of his day as did Coach Osborne in his.

I was somewhat surprised, though, to hear his opinion of the nature of the human competitive streak when he mentioned, "it's something that you either have it or you don't. Some kids just naturally like to compete and challenge themselves and some people don't." For such an education-oriented, nurture-minded man -and a Doctor of Psychology to boot- his 'nature over nurture' position statement caught me off guard. Perhaps that explains why he was never a 'rah-rah coach,' because in his mind the game of football -offensive football at least- is more about execution and less about motivation. By recruiting athletes with a pre-existent competitive nature there would be no need to pump them up into a pre-game frenzy, as it was already an inherent article by his mind's standard. A follow-up question I wish I'd asked is: "How were you best able to identify the great competitors from the ones only moderately so?" Then again, who's to say what type or degree of competitor is best for athletic achievement, anyhow? Could a win-at-all-costs student/athlete be the one you want on the team? Maybe, maybe not. Perhaps you'd want a player more concerned with the process than the end result -one whose competitive nature was dialed down just a notch- maybe they're the ones to covet most? I don't know. I look forward to gaining a deeper understanding as we continue on with player interviews.

Last off, I couldn't help but notice a parallel to scripture verse Matthew 5:37: *"Let your yes be yes, and your no be no…"* He talked about his making a *"commitment that I never turned away from."* From this simple turn of phrase at the end of that sentence you grasp that he places great value in honoring commitments. None more so than the one he made to each and every recruit whose living room he visited, because Tom Osborne always promised a kid's parents two things and two things only: that the young man would receive a quality education and that he would be given an opportunity to compete. I don't recall him ever turning away from those commitments in his score and five years as leader of Nebraska Football.

Notable quote #2:

Tom Osborne on his longtime staff of coaching assistants: "We had enough experience as a staff and had enough institutional knowledge to draw on that we could think about maybe what we had done when something like that had happened four years before, five years before. So I think we were a staff that was able to adjust during a game quite well."

You have to play this game like somebody just hit your mother with a two-by-four.

Dan Birdwell

When most folks hear the name 'Cory Schlesinger' they recall the vision of a muscled, dirtied and grass-stained number 40 tumbling for six points into a Miami end zone on his way to snuffing out the last vestiges of Hurricane pride.

As for me? That's apt. But even more ingrained in my mind are the sights of numerous scraped, scarred and smashed facemasks, as if the kid had taken a barreling Peterbilt truck head-on and won the duel. If evolution exists as a viable scientific theory, then the kid from Duncan was custom-created and morphed to fill the illustrious and all-important role as a Husker fullback to start that 60 & 3 era. You hear about guys willing to run through a brick wall? That's all good and well, but a more daunting task was running up against Cory Schlesinger and surviving the encounter. Strap it on tight and keep your head on a swivel, 'cause here's Cory...

Notable quote #1:
"It was almost like a drug of wanting to improve and get better. And that was the one place to do it, because you could see the progression of getting stronger and getting faster, you just keep wanting more and more of it."

Cory Schlesinger

Scholarship recruit, Fullback, Duncan, Nebraska (Columbus)
Where are they now? Dearborn, Michigan, Teacher/Coach

Question: So, you're living in Michigan now? How's that treating you?

Cory Schlesinger: We lived there, but I always came back to Nebraska to train. When I was playing for Detroit it was always six months there and six months here. We were living there and then I got my teaching job, so it's kind of nice to have my summers off, I guess, get some things done around the house and not going to the club since I'm not playing so much anymore.

Q: I spoke with Bryan Bailey last night and he misses seeing you and training you.

CS: Yeah, I know it. I tell you what, I give him credit all the time. He did an outstanding job with me. The great thing about Bryan was, every offseason with the Lions I'd say, 'Listen Bryan, this is what I need to get done: I need to get stronger doing this. Or more flexibility doing that', and he would fix it for me. My body would be brand new every season entering training camp and people would be, "What the world have you been doing?! You're just tearing people up!" And I'd go, 'Well, this Bryan Bailey guy, you know? He's the one that did it for me.'

Q: A skinny, little redheaded guy in Lincoln, Nebraska, huh?

CS: That's right! (laughs) He's so hard to get a hold of. And the USC guys that I played with, who got drafted by the Lions? They would go, "He's the best strength coach we've ever had." And I'd go 'Obviously!' Mr. Steve Pederson, the idiot, I don't know why in the world they would ever get rid of Bryan.

Q: Lord only knows, Cory. Lord only knows. So you're from a little town outside of Columbus, right?

CS: Duncan, Nebraska. When I was there it was 410 people. Now it's probably 365. It's 8 miles from Columbus. They used to have an elementary school there, and I went to junior high and high school in Columbus. They recently closed the elementary school, too, so now everybody's gonna leave there.

Q: In addition to football, you were a pretty decent wrestler, weren't you?

CS: Yeah, not too bad. I was a two-time state champion at 189 lbs. and I weighed about 185. (laughs) It was good because I never had to diet my last two years. (Though I wouldn't eat in front of my other wrestling teammates who were dieting; I tried to watch myself a little bit.) I had to diet my sophomore year and that was not fun at all.

Q: I talked to Clinton Childs a few weeks ago. Did you ever wrestle Clinton?

CS: Yeah, I beat him up pretty good. I think. (laughs)

Q: Clinton was pretty good in his own right, wasn't he?

CS: Yeah, I think he got to the finals his senior year but he got beat by another Columbus guy.

Q: That was your freshman year at Nebraska, right?

CS: Yeah, and for me it was a little bit different coming in, because it was the last year for Freshman Football. So we kind of had our own coaching staff and players, where we were in the north locker room all kind of by ourselves. They had the varsity and everybody else on the other side of the stadium in the south locker room, so we kind of had our own little group of trainers and everything. It was kind of like an all-star football team on that side because we were the best of the high school guys, and some guys from the other states there that were some scholarships, a lot of walk-ons. Our own little group.

That was some really good times. I'm glad I had the opportunity to play freshman football. It was kind of the beginning of your career, because you kind of knew the next year you were gonna redshirt. And going out playing on Friday afternoons was a blast; playing those little junior colleges, schools from Iowa and Air Force, too. I can't think of some of the other schools. Iowa Snow? I don't even know what the other teams were, but it was a lot of fun playing on Friday afternoons.

Q: Now, do you think you freshmen being there together in the north stadium, do you think that developed some cohesiveness that would not otherwise have occurred had you been thrown in with the varsity right away?

CS: Well, when I first started there were so many players. There were eleven fullbacks, I remember. I counted them: Eleven fullbacks. Eleven for one position! I remember thinking, 'How in the world am I going to get up there and start playing?' Then I realized after I played with the guys and watched them compared to what I was doing out there, I figured, 'Okay, I'll weed through them pretty fast.' I was the starter for the freshman football team and did pretty well, I guess.

Then after freshman season was done I got an opportunity to go up and practice and run cards against the varsity with the scout team, which was a lot of fun, too. It was November and getting cold out, and I'm doing the run drill and doing isolation blocks on Mike Petko and Pat Tyrance. I remember those guys. Hitting those guys, they would literally pick me up off the ground. Especially if you had the ball, they would pick you up. It was just amazing. You asked what I remember when I first got started, that's the one thing I remember, those guys hitting you, but you'd literally come off the ground and be, 'Geez, I can hardly imagine what it's gonna be like playing football with those guys,' you know? But I got a lot of respect from those varsity guys because I'd go after them: 'I'm not gonna slow down, I'm still gonna try to hit you.' I know I hurt Mike Petko's shoulder before the bowl game. He had to put his arm in a sling for that game and maybe had surgery after that, but I'm pretty sure it was me that did it. (laughs) Those were good times there.

Q: So obviously, practicing with the big boys provided you your first experiences with Coach Solich. Any comments on that?

CS: We really didn't work a lot with him yet, because we would kind of go down and do our scout team stuff, we'd help with the cards and stuff. I remember sitting in the meetings a lot with Coach Solich, and even my redshirt year, you did a lot of bag work and held bags and stuff like that. We were kind of like pretending we were linebackers and things like that. He was coaching us, but he wasn't really coaching us yet, because he was worried about his first stringers. And my running back coach was Turner Gill, actually, my freshman year. It was Turner Gill.

Q: What sticks out about Turner from those days?

CS: I remember his calves. (laughs) I don't know why, but he had some big old calves.

I just remember his personality. He was kind of like the rest of those coaches about precision and doing things right and "we'll do it until we get it done right." That's one of the things that makes a winning organization, doing the little things and doing them right.

Q: Repetition, repetition?

CS: Exactly. The option. We had a whole option drill and that's why no one could stop us in the option. We could run on the short side of the field and they could put all eleven guys over there and run at you and we'd still get yards on you. We were just masters of it. That's because we did it so often, which was great for us.

Q: Find one thing and decide you're going to be the best in the world at it, right?

CS: That's right. And we were.

Q: And I'd be remiss if I didn't ask you, how many years did you block for Barry Sanders in Detroit?

CS: Four years.

Q: I'm guessing it was a little different than your time at Nebraska because of all the moving around and improvising Barry did?

CS: It was very difficult. (laughing) I mean, it was to the point where you were going to get your SAM linebacker and he's hauling tail on the other side of the field and Barry is doing his own thing, he's not going to follow you. On the other hand, Barry could make my bad block look great (laughs) because he could out-juke them when no one was blocking, let alone having a fullback in front of him putting a block on. It was, 'What is this guy gonna do?' I remember talking to other guys I played with who then played against him and they were, "What can you do to prepare for Barry? There's nothing you can do!" (laughs) Of course, it helps that we had three great receivers out there, so when they'd bring all eleven guys up we'd just dump it right over them to the receivers. It's too bad we did not get to the Super Bowl with that team. I don't know how we didn't because we had a lot of weapons over there.

Q: Did you guys have Scott Mitchell at quarterback then?

CS: Yes, we did.

Q: I tell you what, Cory, the most beautiful pass I've ever seen in Memorial Stadium was a 50-60 yard touchdown rainbow that he threw when he and the University of Utah came and visited us in the late 80's/early 90's. It was a thing of beauty. What a talented guy he was. But as far as blocking for Barry, was it coached to you that one should continuously block until the whistle blows?

CS: Basically. It was taught to the linemen, too. You just go until the whistle blows, because Barry would run laterally. He probably ran fifty yards laterally and still had a twenty yard gain. And he really went about 79 yards on a play, but only got 10 yards, you know? That's how he played. He was the only player that I've ever seen who could fill away stadiums. Some of these away stadiums, they were rarely packed, but when we came to town there would be a ton of Barry jerseys in the crowd and the place would be packed. That was the cool part. And also, everybody watched. You know, usually if the other team's offense is out there, the defensive guys are on the sideline looking at photos or sitting on the bench, but when Barry would play the other team's offense would be standing there on the sideline watching the game, too. Watching to see what he was gonna do. We all stood there and we'd watch him to see what he was gonna do. Everybody's jaw would just drop every time, too.

Q: Cory, did you guys ever talk about him wanting to play for Nebraska coming out of high school?

CS: I can't say that we ever did. No. I don't think. I think he came for a visit to Nebraska, but was he from Oklahoma, anyway?

Q: He was from Wichita, Kansas and he was a good friend of former Husker I-back Jeff Smith. The story goes that Charlie McBride recruited him and Barry desperately wanted to be a Husker, but Coach Osborne said that we already had a small running back coming in that year, Johnny Rodgers' son Terry, and that we didn't want two small running backs in the same recruiting class.

CS: (laughing) That was a big mistake.

Q: I was there for the Oklahoma State game when Barry was a sophomore and he was lighting us up on special teams, and Charlie goes over to Coach Osborne on the sidelines and says, "Hey Tom, that's the one we passed on." And Coach Osborne says with a grimace, "Uh-huh, I see that." (laughs) So, back on track here, tell me about your first year or two at Nebraska. What about the organization itself stood out?

CS: One of the things I do remember about playing there, and I think why we were so good, was there were fights between the offensive linemen and defensive linemen. And it wasn't fighting because they were mad at each other, it was fights because somebody wasn't trying hard enough. And I remember going, 'Wow, I've never seen a fight because they were, "You're slacking! You're not going hard enough!"' They pushed the other guy to get better, also, because it's gonna help the whole team out. That was like the most amazing thing I ever saw. It was like, 'Wow, I've never been yelled at by my own teammate for not playing hard enough during practice.' It was definitely the reason we were better, was because of that reason. Those guys made each other accountable to play like they were going to play in the game on Saturday: 'Practice like you were going to play.' And that's what we did, we battled every day in practice.

Q: Do you recall any specific guys would call another out a lot?

CS: I really can't. I just remember it happening. Maybe Raemakers or someone like that. I can definitely see him or someone like that, he sticks out. (laughs) And we just did a radio show together for Jerry Murtaugh's Legends Radio Show. That was pretty cool talking to him again.

Q: What could you tell me about Coach Solich?

CS: Well, what I liked about him? For being a smaller in stature he was very intense. He could definitely get very intense. That's one thing I remember. He was like a little pit bull, just 'switch' on you and very intense at times. Then again, he was very personable and you could talk to him. But he was about the details, and that's what always made us better as running backs: blocking, running the ball, making sure the ball's in the right hand. And that's what made our running game so strong, how we became such good running backs. And I'll always remember him saying, "We will be the leaders of this team by the way we practice. We will finish out every play, and other guys on the team will be like, "Wow! Look at these running backs. We have to keep up with these running backs." We don't have to say anything, it's just by our actions. When we're practicing and playing games we'll be the leaders that bring the team along." And I definitely believe that was true, because our running game was strong. Our line and people blocking for us? They believed in us and wanted us to succeed.

"And we're gonna go back and congratulate them, also." That's one thing I remember, too, "When we do score we're gonna go back and congratulate our offensive linemen, because they're the ones who got us in there -and the wide receivers and the tight ends- because without them we're not getting into the end zone."

Q: So Frank was always fighting the 'I'm an All-star, pretty-boy-kind of thinking' and instead created a sense that 'We're all in this together-kind of thing'?

CS: Yep. But then again, "We will be the guys where they go, "Wow, look at how hard they're working. I'm going to work just as hard as those guys so we don't let them down.""" And that's what we did every day in practice, and that's why he talked about that.

And we always had this thing we did pre-game. We would always do this little blocking drill, isolation blocks and pass pro. We kind of got after each other pretty good, (laughs) and that's why our blocking was so good. And we would always go to the 50 yard line and do these drills in front of all those linebackers of the other team as a way of showing, "This is what's coming at you during the game, so you better be ready." (laughs)

Q: You're trying to put a little fear in the guys from the other team?

CS: Yeah, and we were all very good, our pad leverage and everything. You'd hear that 'thud', that hit, and it would sound so nice every time. I guarantee, if you ever hunt any of those guys down, those linebackers, if you ever got an opportunity to interview those guys and ask, "Did you ever remember seeing those guys doing that?" And I used to, before game time? I'm going even harder.

Q: So your freshman year, that was the fall of '90 when we lost to Georgia Tech in the Citrus Bowl, right?

CS: That was against Bobby Ross, and those guys ended up being my coaches later on in Detroit. The special team coaches would always give me a hard time, and I was, 'Hey, I wasn't even in that game. I was a freshman.' (laughs)

Q: Some have thought that was a low point of sorts, not as much team morale or team unity that year…

CS: Well, honestly, my freshman year I was just surviving, too. I didn't really get a full gist of the unity and all that stuff. I was just out there trying to bang helmets and show the coaches I could do this.

Q: It seems to me when that the Unity Council got implemented, a lot of people seemed to think that built some unity within the team and got everybody focused. Would you agree?

CS: I definitely agree, because you do not want to let down your peers. You're more like, 'if your coach yells at you you're going to blow them off, but if you have a council of your peers go, "Why did you not make it to class on time? Why are you not doing this? Why are you not doing that?" That's a little bit harder than having a coach or a counselor say that.' When you've got guys out there that you're playing with, fighting with every day out there on the field? When they say, "You need to be accountable, because we need you out there." Even outside the classroom, that really drove the team together. So the Unity Council started and I think everything started picking up after that.

Q: The motto 'Unity, Belief, Respect', did that mean anything to you?

CS: Yeah, I think so. That was pushed a lot. And you hung out with your classmates, but I think it came about earning the respect from the older players from what you did on the field. Other guys were saying, "Man, you're hitting hard!" And that felt good. And I don't want to sound like a wimp or anything, but I remember at first thinking, 'Man this is big time football, can I handle this?' At first I was a little bit timid, but then after awhile I figured, 'I can do this. I'm going to do this.'

And also, the Unity Council was also good for school because you don't want to have to come in there saying, 'Well, I failed this class' or something like that. So you definitely wanted to make sure that your grades were up. And it took me a couple of years to figure out what I wanted to do with myself, too. It was just a good cause and a great thing because you don't want to let down your teammates, and that's the Council, those are the people you have to talk to, that's who you answered to. I don't think I ever had to go in front of them. I was a part of the Unity Council, but I don't recall ever having to go in front of them. (laughs)

Q: What are you most proud of?

CS: What am I proud of? Of course, just our success. I mean, being undefeated, having people want to implement the Cornhusker tradition, the program, and trying to study it: "What are you guys doing that is so great? And how do they do this all the time?" That's the cool thing. People, the coaching clinics, there were hundreds of coaches there. And the football camps? All these kids wanted to come to the football camps and participate because they wanted to get better. And the state, the support and how they all rallied around the team at the time? And game time, there was no better feeling than playing in front of over 76,000 people and they're all wearing red. It's a feeling that you just can't get anywhere. I mean, Detroit in the NFL was good, a pretty good place, they're definitely football fans there, too. But I tell you what, the support you got there at Nebraska was amazing.

Q: What was your favorite part of gameday?

CS: Well, I'll give you my first experience of game day: It was my sophomore year and we used to practice out in the stadium all the time and it was so big and empty, and game day came and that place felt so small. It was like, 'Is this thing the same field we're on during the week?' Because there are people around the whole stadium. It felt so small out there, it was almost claustrophobic. It was just awesome. I loved the feeling and high you get from the fans who are cheering you on and encouraging you. There's no better feeling than that. I was a goosebump when I walked out there. You were like, 'Look at this. The sea of red.' You always heard about that 'Sea of Red', but when you're out there in the middle of the field and experience it, there is no better feeling. Other than the opponents, though. (laughs)

Q: Do you recall ever being at an opponent's stadium and thinking, 'Wow, this is a tough place to play'?

CS: Not really, because we just had a swagger about it: "We are gonna come to your stadium and we're gonna give it to 'ya." The one place I do remember; it was pretty amazing when we played Washington. I think it was my sophomore year and we were both in the top 5 and this was a big game for us, and that had to be probably the loudest stadium I ever played in. They would always let both teams come out of the tunnel together, but they wouldn't let us do it. Because everybody was just so ready to go, it was too intense in the hallway there. They let them come out first and we came after them, but it was one of the loudest games I ever played in.

Q: What was your shining moment, where it all came together and summarized your playing time there?

CS: I know everybody has heard this story before, but I still have to say it -not a real shining moment, really- but the championship game kind of summarized my whole college career. On the opening kickoff return -and we had a pretty good kickoff return team and pretty good front line- and a guy came through there and I just blasted him, knocked him out cold. You just knew, when something like that happens it's gonna be a good game. (laughs) That game summarized the whole season for us. I was basically a blocker (and honestly, it happened my freshman year, I knocked out one of my own teammates in practice), it was like a goal line play and I knocked him out. And I figured, 'Okay, I can do this.' I don't want to say his name and rub it in, though. (laughs)

Q: Everyone probably brings up your first touchdown run in the Orange Bowl on that 36 or 38 Trap, with 'ol number 40 rambling across the goal line in the Orange Bowl...

CS: It was a great opportunity. And that play was put in only for that game. Never ran it all year long, and during the bowl practices it was a play that worked all the time. And when they called it, in my head I knew it was going to be a touchdown. I just knew it.

Q: Was that 9 yards out?

CS: It was 14 yards.

Q: Who called the play? Did a receiver run the play in?

CS: A receiver ran in with the play and Tommie Frazier called it up, and I was like, 'Holy smokes, I'm gonna score!' I just knew it.

Q: At that moment you were thinking, "I'm gonna score," was there a also little guy on your other shoulder saying, "Do not screw this up!!"?

CS: No. The confidence was there. There was nobody telling me that.

Q: Did the rest of your teammates feel the same thing? The confidence?

CS: I don't know. (laughs) I hope that they had confidence in me. We only practiced the play during the Orange Bowl practices.

Q: Coach Osborne could always come up with new wrinkles, eh? And is there anything you wish you could do over or better or differently?

CS: No, not really. I trained hard, I was Lifter of the Year. And that was voted on by my teammates, so I did the right thing there. I graduated, I did the right thing there. I played all-out every game, so there was no regrets about anything.

Q: A wonderful feeling, eh? No regrets?

CS: Yeah, knowing you left everything on the field? That's something that, when you're done, you can say, 'I gave it all.' There's no better feeling than that.

Q: That's a beautiful thing to say. Many people live with regret and say, 'Woulda, coulda, shoulda,' but to leave it all out there like that does wonderful things for your soul...

CS: It does. You do not want to have that happen, and you're gonna be living with it forever. And I know now there are probably players out there who do live with that and say, "Why didn't I leave it all out there?"

Q: What drove you and motivated you in the weight room?

CS: I never even dreamt of getting that award. I guess my teammates saw me differently, they saw how hard I worked in the weight room and how hard I ran in winter conditioning. It was almost like a drug of wanting to improve and get better. And that was the one place to do it, because you could see the progression of getting stronger and getting faster, you just keep wanting more and more of it. It also helped that we had a great strength staff. That's another thing, they knew how to get the best out of us, and we were just performing at that level. The crew that was there, Randy Gobel, Bryan Bailey, Mike Arthur and, of course, Boyd, those guys really stuck out to me. To me, Boyd knew what we needed to do. He just had that personality of, "I'm gonna get the best guys in there to make us the best program." And he wasn't out there really coaching us, but he knew how to get the best guys to get us to be the best, and that is what I remember.

I remember talking to him on my official visit. I guess it was out in that trailer, while they were re-doing the weight room, and he was asking me how much I do on this lift or that. And I didn't even have any numbers, I was kind of making them up off the top of my head; I didn't know, really. (laughs) But he was just like, "This is what we'll want you to do. This is what you'll become and this is how fast you'll become," and I was like, 'Really? Well, yeah! This is great!'(laughs)

Q: He shined some headlights down the road and gave you a vision of the plans he had in mind for you?

CS: Yes, he basically had a plan. He knew and had confidence in his staff and his program. He knew, "Hey, if you do 225, we'll have you doing 345 in no time." He just knew his program was successful and it would work to improve all his players. And I don't know if he saw the frame I had and, "You'll get some meat on that body easily. And it's going to be dense, and when you hit somebody it's just going to be a thud." But he had the vision. He had the vision and he knew how to share it.

Q: Boyd was always a good salesman, Cory. And he said it in such a confident way that you couldn't help but believe him, right?

CS: Oh yeah. It wasn't, "What do you want to get?" It was like, "This is how you're gonna do. You're gonna do this and this, and this is how fast you're gonna be." And it was like,

'Wow,' and you believed it. And then you went out there and it became, 'I'm gonna prove it.'

Q: Do you recall the very first game you played in?

CS: Yeah, it was my sophomore year, and like I said, going out in front of the 'Sea of Red'. That was probably my first game out there. It was just how small the stadium felt my first game day. I don't remember if I played or who we played at all. I just wanted to go hit somebody. (laughs)

Q: Sounds like a typical fullback. (laughs) Can you explain the perverse joy and gratification it gave you to blow somebody up like you guys did?

CS: The most satisfying thing was the things that no one else saw. That you knew it happened and that guy you hit knew it happened, but no one else saw it, because they all looked at the running back or whomever. No one saw what actually happened, but it was my block that got him open, and it was my block that that linebacker is gonna remember. And he knows it's going to come again and again and again. (laughs)

Q: And speaking of 'again and again and again', anything about that Miami game stand out to you about those guys?

CS: No, not really. I just remember the confidence we had. There was no one that had doubts. It was just the confidence we had in Coach Osborne and each other, and just the way we looked at each other and were like, "Man, we're just gonna do this." No one had their head down and no one looked nervous. It was just, "We're gonna go do this! Let's bring that trophy back and let's not stop!" The confidence was there at halftime. We were down, but we were excited to go out there and play. That's just the feeling that we had, and how everyone looked in the locker room: "Let's just go out there and play and win this game." That's the one thing that stuck out the most: the look in everyone's eyes that we were going to finish it. The Unfinished Business.

Q: What did the '94 Orange Bowl do for you? Any recollections of that game?

CS: I don't think anybody really gave us a chance in that game, and we went out there and proved that we could do it.

Actually, I almost hate to say it, but that was the beginning. It was almost better that we lost that game. I hate to say that, because the guys that were seniors missed out on the opportunity that we had. But the guys the next year? I remember during training camp it was just like, "Man, we are ready to go." It was just amazing how the confidence was. People were practicing hard and not really joking. Almost joking, but it was like, "Let's get back to the huddle and do it again. Let's do that again." I remember standing in the huddle outside that end zone thinking, 'Wow, this is the year. Everything is in place. The Unfinished Business...it's time to finish that thing.'

Q: That game gave you guys a lot of confidence in knowing that you could finish it, that you had what it took?

CS: Yeah, definitely. It took us to the point that we knew we were going to take it home.

Q: Do you think we got hosed in that Florida State game with some calls?

CS: Oh, probably. Yeah. We looked at it again. We got hosed. But you know what? We should not have even allowed it to get that close anyway. That was our mentality: "Don't let the referees decide the game. We should go out there and destroy them. They shouldn't even make it that close."

Q: And what about the Offensive linemen? I'm sure you have some things to say about those guys, being a blocker yourself?

CS: Oh definitely. We're just glorified linemen, I guess. We're linemen in the backfield. Especially when you go to Detroit your first year, definitely didn't touch the ball there.

Q: And what about your running mates?

CS: All my running backs where great guys, there's no one I could ever say I liked better than the others. We had a group of guys that just worked great together. They supported one another and they made each other accountable and they worked hard. And Lawrence Philips, he was a great guy to block for. Even in practice, he would give you that confidence and tell you 'good job' when you made a good play. In practice even. He and I were so in touch with each other. He knew what I was going to do. He had the confidence, "I know what Cory's going to do here." He knew I was gonna do my job. The trust.

I remember looking back on Scott Baldwin… I don't know if anyone has brought up his name. I remember him, he was a stud. I tell you what, I loved watching him run the ball. I remember one time on a kickoff return, he was in the front line and turned around and just lit this guy up. I saw that and I'm like, 'That's Nebraska football! That's what I want to get to! The point where I can hit somebody and knock them backwards like he did!" He was a good character. I hated to see how everything turned out for him. I would have loved to see how he performed.

Q: Who behind the scenes played a huge role for you or the team?

CS: The strength staff, definitely.

Q: And Coach Osborne, how would you say he affected you as a person and a player?

CS: Well, what I liked about him: if you did see him in the hallway he'd always be sure to acknowledge you. But he'd never ask you about football, he'd ask you about school. Now, you had to make sure your grades were up, so when he did ask that, you had a good report. (laughs) You knew he was probably going to ask you about school, and that's very important for these college students. You don't want to say, "Oh, I'm not doing very well." (laughing)

Q: And looking back on it, almost 20 years removed, what do you treasure most?

CS: That's a good question. Just the unity, the chemistry that we had together. Even when we had scout team guys, they just knew their job was to run the card right and simulate what's going to happen during the game. And I know there were a few hits out there, game–ready stuff, which is only gonna make us better. You practice like you're gonna play in the game, and those guys had to sit there and endure the hits. And sometimes they gave them, too, which is also gonna make you better.

Q: Any most memorable practice?

CS: Every day! Someone was doing something every day in practice. Those fights were always fun, but I tried to avoid them because they were too tiring.

And you didn't want to run stadium steps. That's true.

Q: So if someone gave you a football team to start from scratch, what would you fall back on?

CS: Being a coach who's not two-faced, I guess. A coach that believes in you, a coach that, if you have a beef with him, he says, "Bring it to me." He'd never downgrade you behind your back. It gets around, players aren't dummies. They know what's said in meetings, but when you have a coach who truly believes in you and is gonna fight for you? That's a man you want to play for.

Q: Was that preached, spoken verbally? Or did it just sense it?

CS: It was just how the guys in front of you practiced. You did not want to let them down, and you learned from the best, the older guys that were practicing hard. And the guys that weren't? They usually got weeded out. They didn't make it their whole college career. They didn't hang with the guys who wanted to be the best. The guys who won the national championship were the best and they did what they were supposed to do. That's what it comes down to: do what you're supposed to do. You've got a job, just do it. Don't make an excuse or try to fake your way through it. Do what you're supposed to do.

Q: So when you finally left the university and got drafted by Detroit, was there any one thing you missed more than another?

CS: Well, not really. My five years? I was ready to move on. My opportunity came and I had a ring, and I wanted to see how I would do at the next level. There were no regrets and it was time to move on to the next level. My time at Nebraska really prepared me for the next twelve.

Q: Wow, twelve years in the pros. That's quite a career, man.

CS: Yep. 2006 was my last year. It was hard to hang it up, but your body at the same time was going, "Yeah, you're not doing what you used to do." (laughs) That's kind of the hard part: you want to do it, but your body's not doing it.

Q: Thanks so much, Cory. Any last comments?

CS: I would say that the Husker fans are an amazing group of people. When you talk to other players that played in Memorial Stadium, they really loved playing there. It was just a great experience. Even after the game, no one spit on them or threw things at them. Even when they got smoked, they were, "Hey, good job out there today." That is Nebraska football."We're gonna give you a licking, but we're going to pick you up and say 'good job." I've heard from several players that we had the best fans. And I would say that they prepared me not only for life after college football, they also formed me for life after football.

Q: And hey, what about Tommie? Any special comment about him?

CS: No. Not really.

Q: (laughs) And what about the Kansas State game when Matt Turman started?

CS: (laughing) It didn't matter who the quarterback was that day: we were going to run the ball and do what we were going to do. We knew the coaches prepared him. We went out there and did the job. We had to step it up a notch and do what we had to do. And we did. Our game plan changed a little bit. It was, "Alright, we have four plays to run. We're going to run them all game!"

End conversation.

"Those guys made each other accountable to play like they were going to play in the game on Saturday.'Practice like you were going to play.' And that's what we did, we battled every day in practice." No eloquency here, as Cory took us behind the scenes and into the minds of the bruisers laying the licks for paths of glory. There was a tough-minded, rugged individualism in the Husker fullbacks, and they reveled in it. So did we. Who among the fanatics of the day didn't relish the vision of these hybrid behemoths tearing downfield open-throttle on a surprise trap play, ball crushingly cradled, blowing up linebackers and dragging DB's along like mere piss ants on a pig? "..other guys on the team will be like, 'Wow! Look at these running backs. We have to keep up with these running backs.' We don't have to say anything, it's just by our actions." Attitude and good ol' work ethic hammered into their heads by Frank Solich, they rarely disappointed.

By and large the most home-grown of the position groupings, the Nebraska fullbacks' exploits made them fan cult favorites. Other than Clinton Childs from Omaha (1995 population 681,000) and Chris Norris of Papillion (~22,000), the rest hailed from tiny, rural burgs like Duncan (~410), Brainard (~747), Battle Creek(~1,600), Fullerton(~1,500) and Clearwater/Elgin(~380/806). With determination and purpose, they were weightroom denizens: "It was almost like a drug of wanting to improve and get better. And that was the one place to do it, because you could see the progression of getting stronger and getting faster, you just keep wanting more and more of it." It transferred well out onto the field, too, "That's what it comes down to: Do what you're supposed to do. You've got a job, just do it."

As for team concept, it was refreshing to hear Coach Solich's championing unity by way of his, "When we do score we're gonna go back and congratulate our offensive linemen, because they're the ones who got us in there -and the wide receivers and the tight ends- because without them we're not getting into the end zone." The 'Unity, Belief, & Respect' mantra was lived out in celebration.

Notable quote #2:
Cory Schlesinger on fan sportsmanship: "Husker fans are an amazing group of people. When you talk to other players that played in Memorial Stadium, they really loved playing there... I've heard from several players that we had the best fans."

Our entry song started playing, our fans erupted and the stage was set.
Miami's players looked around in a daze. After all, this was their home stadium.
"You aren't supposed to upstage our entrance." The 60 minutes of football that
followed was a thing of beauty. My linemen performed at their best. They were
relentless. They pounded away on every single play.

Milt Tenopir, *The Assembly Line*

Have you ever heard the exploits of the Knights of the Order of St. John? This small, unrelenting cadre of Middle Ages warrior/princes saved all of Europe from Moslem conquest and, by many accounts, the world. Scorned as 'archaic relics of the past' by the divided European nations of the time, this small band on the island of Rhodes, the gateway to the European continent, took on the powerful Persian armies of Mehmet, the Sultan of the Ottomans, and prevailed despite gargantuan odds against.

Rick Joyner in *Leadership, Management* writes, "(brilliant)Mehmet was also a conqueror at heart who fashioned himself after Alexander the Great. He marched on the great city of Constantinople, and conquered it. He then set his sights on the rest of Europe." But first he had to do something about this irritating little brotherhood, a band of "annoying knights who continued to plunder his shipping and supply lines. In 1480 Mehmet sent his most able generals with an army of 70,000 men to subdue the 600 knights and 1,500 to 2,000 militia at Rhodes. The Grand Master of the Order was a Frenchman named D' Aubusson...a remarkable leader of men who had with great foresight prepared his knights for the siege" that would one day come. After the first wave of the Sultan's troops were repulsed (with great casualties, I might add) they "began another general bombardment that would hurl over a thousand cannonballs a day at the city continuously for several weeks." (emphasis mine) Another assault was made, where "the knights contested every acre of ground, for which the Turks paid dearly...In hand to hand combat, over burning rubble, through choking smoke and fire, in possibly the worst hell that men could create for themselves on earth, the Turks continued to throw themselves against the knights." Humiliated as their advances were met with greater cost than they could bear, the finest fighters of the Ottoman Empire fled, while "Rhodean sharpshooters on the walls poured deadly fire into them," mustering enough strength to chase the attackers all the way back to their base of operations."To the astonishment of the entire world, the Order of St. John had not only survived- they had prevailed. All of Europe celebrated. All of Islam was enraged."
(Excerpted from: *Leadership, The Power of a Creative Life* (formerly titled *Leadership, Management and the Five Essentials* copyright 1990) by Rick Joyner. Copyright 2001 by MorningStar Publications and Ministries. Used by permission.)

Which brings us to Milt Tenopir, a lion of a man 500 years removed but yet of like-spirit with the Grand Master D' Aubusson. With a penchant for churning out All-American linemen like combines do corn-filled grain wagons, this great leader/teacher experienced perhaps his grandest achievement in the way 1995's pupils not only replaced four of the great 'Pipeline 5' of '94, but succeeded in obliterating any morsel of doubt as to their fitness for the task. Defenses gave them everything they had and more, but come the end of the day it was still "Business As Usual." Listen in on our short, but succinct, repartee with Milt Tenopir...

Notable quotes #1:

"They were aggressive football players and our whole offense was built around them. We were a physical football team and that all started with the kids up front. They took challenge to that and it was important to them to let the other guys get out there in the fourth quarter, and that was what we'd do."

Milt Tenopir

Q: Thanks so much for your time, Milt. I know you've got a softball game coming up in a few minutes so I'll try to be quick. So what year did you first join the staff?

MT: It was 1974. I actually worked with the freshman the first year. I worked with the linebackers under Monte Kiffin and the following spring of '75 I worked with the offensive line on the freshman team.

And the next fall I worked freshman offensive line and I think I went to the varsity in '76 or some place in there, and I got to work with the offensive line.

Q: As a player, were you an O-lineman?

MT: No, I was a quarterback.

Q: Really? At what school?

MT: A little school in Kansas. Sterling College, down in Kansas.

Q: So how did you gravitate toward line play then?

MT: Well, I coached high school ball for 12 years as a head coach, and that was the most critical area, so I took that upon myself. You didn't often have an opportunity to pick the coaches on your staff: you had the English teacher and some other teacher that wanted to help coach football, but I took the line because of the criticalness of that particular area, and coached the line ever since I got out of college. I had a fairly good understanding of it playing quarterback, but I coached that offensive line in high school and it just worked out that I continued to do that.

Q: You always had a special group of guys, and a person never had to worry about Milt's boys. What made those guys unique? Was there a special mindset you preached?

MT: Well, there's always a special mindset to those kids up front. I think I earned those kids respect and at the same time I could -after the fact, after practice and all of that- I could still be their bud and have good friendships with them off the field, as well. But the kids just played hard for us.

I never tried to coach out of fear. If a kid earned the number one spot, he was number one. He was there for a reason, through fall camp and spring ball. They just played hard for me and never had to worry about getting demoted and all that. We just had a good relationship with them, we shared things inside and outside of football. My biggest concern all the way through -whether they were first or third or fourth team- I just tried to make sure they understood their role on the football team. You're only gonna have five starters, but everybody else had to play an integral part in preparing for the next game. So they understood their role and that was the big thing that helped them accomplish what they did.

Q: As far as guys knowing their roles, how did you get that message across? Were some of them kicking against the goads? How did you get them to play their role and accept it?

MT: Well, you get 29 practices in the fall and you get 15 or 20 at that time in the spring. And if a kid makes it through all that and grades out the best, you're gonna have those five starters.

But your big deal was to make that third and fourth teamer feel like he was a part of it in helping prep the defense when they were on scout team and what have you, treating them all the same. It didn't make a difference if you were scholarship or walk-on, they just knew that if they worked their butt off hard enough and long enough that they'd eventually get some playing time. And, of course, it's changed -that time has changed- their whole scope of things has changed and the walk-on program was diminished, and part of that was because of no more freshman programs and that type of thing.

And you were working with a lot of numbers: we'd have 32 or 33 linemen because we were in 4 different team work stations every night at practice. We needed bodies, you know? So our job was to impress the importance of those kids that had to run the scout team against the defense, and they bought into it. And, of course, every opportunity we got, if they had a chance to get in -an opportunity to clean up a game and play a few downs- that was gravy for them. And they lived and died Nebraska football their whole lives, whether they were scholarship or not. They were just tickled to death. And we took care of them, we didn't put them down or make the starters ride the bus and the other kids walk. They were treated the same and they all knew that we loved them as well as we did the scholarship guys, whether they were starters or non-starters.

Q: So would you say some of the guys just naturally had a nasty bent to them? Stai, Weigert, those guys?

MT: Those kids had a little moxie about them, you know. Of course, that was needed for our offense: we played a very physical game and it was a challenge for those kids, all of them.

Those two that you mentioned there are two great examples. They got a thrill just knocking somebody on their can and watching them roll, you know? It was just part of the nature of what we were trying to do offensively, and that was to try to physically out-handle you. It didn't make any difference to us whether they were 6'5" or 6'1", but what we did played into the hands of the kids we had. They were aggressive football players and our whole offense was built around them. It didn't center around the receiver or center around the quarterback, necessarily (even though it's nice to have a good quarterback, that's fine). But we were a physical football team and that all started with the kids up front. They took challenge to that and it was important to them to let the other guys get out there in the fourth quarter, and that was what we'd do.

Q: Hit the defense on the chin hard enough and knock them on their backside, and sooner or later they'll get tired of it and give up?

MT: We did enough of that. You've got to interview Warren Sapp. He got his ass kicked good by us. (chuckles)

Q: Great idea Milt, I might just do that! (Warren Sapp did not respond to interview requests) And let me ask you: if you were back on the field today coaching, would you find yourself repeating the same lines over and over again?

MT: Well, I didn't have any catchphrases or anything like that. They knew what they had to get done and we knew what we had to do to win a football game. You know, whether it's first and ten or fourth and one, they knew they had to get their ass in gear and get going.

And we'd get into some big games, so to speak, and won three national championships, and all I'd tell them was, 'You handled things so far, all you have to do is do it one more time. And that's doing what you did.' In bowl games? We dominated in those national championship games not necessarily doing battle on the scoreboard. But as far as physically dominating? That's what we were all about. Those kids took the word 'dominate' to heart. They knew what the heck that meant. It wasn't just a quote, saying we were gonna dominate them. They did it.

Q: Funny you say that word –dominate- Milt. Brenden Stai gave me a copy of that drawing of the O-linemen that had the word 'Dominate' on it. I believe it was a freshman that drew it up for you guys…

MT: Oh yeah, I'll tell you who that was in a minute, a kid from down in the Houston area. I've got the original pencil drawing in my basement. This kid brought me a pencil drawing - I had it on the wall in my office- it was Mike Van Cleave!

Q: And Coach Osborne, what effect did he have on how you went about coaching and teaching?

MT: Well, he let me do it. (laughs) Tom was very good at that. He let us -I did the run schemes in the late 70's on and we'd tweak things that would work and what have you- and Tom gave us free wheel at that. We tried to tweak things and execute things and change up schemes weekly, depending on what defense we were looking at, but Tom just gave us free wheel of that and let us go.

We never did punish our linemen, as far as having a problem with beating them up, hopefully not in practice. Sometimes things would get physical. I worried about their health like everybody worries about a running back or a quarterback, you know? But Tom pretty well gave us free wheel about what we wanted to get done and let us do it. And that was the thing that was important about him: he let us coach. And that's what I respect most about him.

Q: What about Charlie McBride coaching the opposing side? You guys used to have some fun little go-arounds during the one-on-ones down there in The Pit, didn't you?

MT: Charlie and I, we used to bark at each other. We strapped on the helmets one time there. He accused us of holding during our one-on-one drills and I accused them of doing some different things, too. We strapped on the helmets a couple times to no avail. Neither one of us were fit to do anything. (laughs) But it made for a good story. (laughs)

Q: Do you a have a favorite game that sticks out to you?

MT: Probably the one that sticks out most was Kansas State the year we didn't have Tommie and Brook was hurt. Matt Turman was the quarterback and we ran 22 or 23 isolations at the end and we won the game 17-6, but I felt that game was won by my guys up front; just lined up and hammered their butt. Never ran an option the whole game because of the health of our quarterbacks, even though they gave us every opportunity to run one. They challenged us to run an option with the 7- and 8-man fronts they were doing. But that game sticks out the most as the most gratifying, because I felt the offensive line left it all out on the field that day.

Q: The way you coached the guys and the way they played was pretty much smash-mouth. Would you say that reflected your personality, straightforward and all?

MT: I wasn't a 'rant and rave' or hollering guy, but I loved the physicalness of the game and those guys knew that. They'd get more of a thrill from knocking someone on their can than most guys would catching a touchdown pass. (laughs)

Q: Thanks for your time, Coach. Any last comments that reflect on what made your offensive linemen unique in their day or the way you went about things?

MT: We did the same thing year in and year out. We just happened to have kids who could dominate every week.

You know, in the 90's and the early 80's was exceptional, but in the 90's we just had the athletes who could do anything that we asked of them and were probably more physical than anybody we faced. They were something. Pretty special. I still keep in touch with those guys. Just got back from fishing with a few guys, Zach and Eric Weigert. Brenden Stai and Aaron Graham, sometimes, too. We keep in touch. We've built good relationships over the years.

End conversation.

Milt had to take off for a promised appointment, but in this small block of time we heard a few basics about the Nebraska O-Line mindset. There was a great synergy among the group and their coaches (Coach Dan Young included), and he reiterated the one word that summarized the intent of their mission: Dominate."Those kids took the word 'dominate' to heart. They knew what the heck that meant. It wasn't just a quote, saying we were gonna dominate them. They did it."

This one item in particular stood out: "(the offense) didn't center around the receiver or … the quarterback, necessarily…we were a physical football team and that all started with the kids up front." In retrospect, Milt's right one hundred percent. Our thoughts typically go to the quarterbacks or the running backs of those Husker offenses, but even that array of talents proves futile without the bruisers up front doing their work. Sure, Tommie Frazier is hailed as one of the greatest college quarterbacks of all time, but recall that he played in only 5 of the twelve games en route to achieving the '94 national championship. Quarterback Brook Berringer? Five games. Matt Turman? About two. And freshman Monte Christo brought up the rear with a few scattered minutes, too. What does this tell us? It speaks of that first, amazing injury-racked '94 championship year's offensive hopes pinned exclusively on the Pancake Patrol. And though they may not have won any Mr. Universe contests, they were far from doughboys. It was muscle and spit and sweat and guts… but desire above all.

Search on Amazon.com for Milt's magnum opus, *The Assembly Line*, and you'd be shocked to find the least expensive used edition available has an implausible asking price in the $69 range. Why? Because it's pure gold, baby. Any offense intent on excelling at the inside zone, outside zone, counter and trap plays of Nebraska Football dominance of the day knows this as its bible, and that's Gospel truth.

The gospel account of Mark 12:31 states, *"The second (great commandment) is this, Thou shalt love thy neighbor as thyself. There is none other commandment greater than these."* In this particular case, brotherly love meant opening up opportunities for their fellow linemen deeper down on the depth chart to get some playing time, too: "..it was important to them to let the other guys get out there in the fourth quarter, and that was what we'd do." Hallelujah, that's brotherly love exemplified!

Notable quote #2:
Milt Tenopir on breaking spirits: "We dominated in those national championship games not necessarily doing battle on the scoreboard. But as far as *physically* dominating? That's what we were all about. Those kids took the word 'dominate' to heart."

I don't agree with everything they report, but in general find (reporters) to be people who do their homework and try to be fair. I can honestly say that there are very few sports reporters, local or national, that I don't like and get along with reasonably well.

Tom Osborne, *On Solid Ground*

"The longest way round is usually the shortest way home, and the one truly reliable shortcut in writing is to choose words that are strong and surefooted to carry readers on their way" say Strunk & White in 1935's classic *The Elements of Style*. Carrying readers on their way at the Omaha World-Herald for a good 30 plus years is Lee Barfknecht, another scribe known for his ever-present finger on the pulse of Nebraska Athletics. We shared quite a few bus trips over the years down to Kansas City for the annual Big 8 Conference Basketball Tournament and I've always respected his warm manner, his probing intellect, and his prose of substance.

As you can surmise from our time with Mike Babcock earlier, I feel it's necessary to provide a little background on these guys for greater depth of understanding into not only the viewpoint from which they wrote, but also their mind's eye back when they were simply young fans of Husker Football, too. Strong and surefooted the Husker beat writers had to be, because fans near and far hung on their every word. Surely you've heard the old riddle about the three colors of every newspaper, right? If not, here's the answer: They're black and white and read all over. Well, Lee was all over the Big Red, so let's see if he has something worthy for our 60 & 3 journey's Why and How.

Notable quote #1:
"There were guys who were very straight-laced and religious and there were other guys on the staff who liked to go out and have a good time. You had some loud guys and some quiet guys, and you had some big story-tellers and some other guys who just kind of did things by example."

Lee Barfknecht

Question: Hey Lee, how are you doing?

Lee Barfknecht: Good. It's a little early out on your end of the world, isn't it?

Q: Well, what do they say, "The early bird gets the interview?" Or something like that.

LB: There you go. (laughs)

Q: And life, in general, is treating you well?

LB: Not too bad. I'm healthy and employed. That's about all I ask for anymore. (laughs)

Q: For this project I'm seeking insight into all aspects of the 90's Husker football teams, so I wanted to get your impressions, ideas, insights and opinions, especially since you were always on the periphery. So tell me, I recall you used to follow along with the basketball team at the time, too. Were you perpetually doing double-duty?

LB: Yeah, I covered both football and basketball, so there was a little bit of crossover; pretty much going full blast from the start of August until the end of March, so that's how I liked it.

Q: Where did you grow up?

LB: I grew up in Superior, Nebraska, a small town near the Kansas border in central Nebraska. I got a Regents Scholarship to go the University of Nebraska and went to

Journalism School there and had an internship at the World-Herald my last summer of college, and when I graduated they hired me. And it's been 30 years since.

Q: Did you originally want to be a sportswriter?

LB: My Dad passed away when I was 8 years old and my mom took a job at the weekly newspaper in town, and at the end of the school day when I couldn't find a football or basketball game to get into I'd go down to the newspaper shop and hang around 'til she got off work. I guess I kind of got 'ink in my blood' that way, I guess. That's kind of how I got started.

Q: Did you always see yourself as wanting to be sportswriter?

LB: Not necessarily. I'd always read the sports page growing up and, you know, paid attention to the guys who wrote at the World-Herald and the Journal-Star. I don't know that I necessarily wanted to be a sportswriter, but I knew I was interested in the business. And it dove-tailed with my interests that way, so it kind of led in that direction.

Q: What year did you first start working for the World-Herald?

LB: My summer internship was the summer of '79, and my actual first day of work was the first of January, 1980.

Q: Wow, you jumped right into some pretty good years of Nebraska football, then?

LB: Yeah. (laughs) That's for sure.

Q: Any peculiar experiences when you first started covering the beat?

LB: You know, I was just kind of getting used to the rhythm and the routine. Coach Osborne and his staff were great people to work with.

And we'd occasionally bump heads with things I'd write that they didn't want me to find out or write about, but at the end of the day it was all done cordially and was a good business relationship. And there were times we had to agree to disagree, but it was never a problem. People just did their work and we respected each other for what each other had to do, so that was the best part of it.

Q: You studied in Lincoln. Did you do anything for the Daily Nebraskan at that time?

LB: Yeah, I worked for the Daily Nebraskan for two years, did a little football and basketball and a little bit of everything. I worked in the sports department of the Daily Nebraskan.

Q: You said that sometimes you'd butt heads. Any particular situations you recall?

LB: Oh, I remember. You know, in the late 80's there was a lot of talk about Coach Osborne, getting criticism about his offense being behind the times or being kind of stodgy and running too much, and after one of the bowl games there were some of the players that were kind of grumbling about it. I quoted them anonymously and Coach Osborne didn't like that very well, and he wrote me a letter and let me know that.

Q: Wrote you a letter?

LB: Oh yeah, (laughs) I've got a couple envelopes full of correspondence we've had through the years. And like I said, there were times we had to agree to disagree on certain things and he had certain things he wanted to get across and I had things I wanted to get across. That's kind of the give-and-take of the business.

Q: So, it's 1991: bring me up to speed after the first dozen years of covering the beat. Any changes or metamorphoses coming about during that time that caught your eye heading into those wonderful 90's seasons?

LB: Probably in the 80's, I don't know if there was anything that really struck me of any consequence, but when you examine the period from '90 to '93, I think that's when they really evaluated what they were doing. I think the thing that was clear to me was that Coach Osborne and his staff were ready to honestly evaluate their program and see what they were doing. I mean, they were still winning 9 games a year, but they weren't playing at the upper level of the top ten teams. They were struggling a little bit and the speed issue was clearly going on: they looked at their recruiting, they looked at the style of play, the teams they were playing, they looked at their practices.

When Kevin Steele came on I think he may have had a hand in convincing Coach Osborne to maybe have more ones versus ones in practice. I think that helped set a different tempo. They looked at every single thing they were doing. Even though this was a veteran staff and they had year after year after year success, they weren't afraid to go back and honestly look at what they were doing. The result was that you go on deeper into the 90's and you could tell it was a valuable process for them.

Q: Indeed. Any articles written that you wish you could have taken back?

LB: Oh, sure... (pause) you know, I don't know. It is the speed of daily journalism: you do the best you can with the information you have at the time. And if you find out something more later? You go back to that and revisit that.

And you always think you could write -when you have time to go back you figure there's something you could have written better if you could have done one more interview or something like that, and you always try to be fast- but the first thing you try to do is be accurate and fair. And if you adhere to those principles, you just go on about your business.

Q: Now, am I correct in assuming the World-Herald has the largest circulation of any newspaper in Nebraska?

LB: Yeah, clearly. Our circulation actually is larger than all the newspapers in the state combined.

Q: Looking at how you perceived your job, what would you say your aim was? To entertain? Inform? Set policy? What sway do you feel you've held?

LB: Well, the baseline part of my job as the football beat writer was to be the fans' representative inside the program. The people who have intense interest in Nebraska football can go to the games but they couldn't go to practice and they couldn't know the players and be around the coaches, and a lot of times I tried to put myself in the fans' shoes.

Like, if they were leaving the game? If there were 4 buddies leaving the game and driving home they'd be talking about the game, saying, "I wonder why they did that?" or "Did you see that?" I tried to think in those terms and tried to answer those questions for the readers. I think that's as clearly as I can state what my purpose was. You tried to break news, you tried to explain things, tried to put things in context, just tried to basically answer those questions people might have about the program.

Q: And the average fan, what would you say is or was the biggest misconception about Nebraska football? Any glaring ones?

LB: You know, sometimes the interest is so intense and there's a certain percentage of people that are just blindly loyal to it. And it wasn't like we were going around prying open doors and looking for dirt, but at the same time if there was something -an issue going on with the program- we tried to honestly address it and let people know that every organization has it's warts, that not everything is perfect.

And you'd get some nasty letters (and now e-mails and things like that). If you write some story that isn't glowingly positive about the program they say that you're trying to tear it down. But that was never the issue: we were just trying to cover what we saw. And I think, all in all, the Nebraska football fan is a highly educated fan and really knows and pays attention to what is going on.

Q: From your perspective how would you say the outside media, the national media was? Did they have a decent grasp or a rather poor grasp of the program, specifically pointing to the Lawrence Philips years?

LB: You know, I don't think you can generalize. I think it boiled down to the individual person who was writing for whatever organization that came in.

But in the same way, I wouldn't want to be painted with a wide brush like that. I wouldn't want to paint with a widespread swath about what was or wasn't going on. There were some national writers who came into Lincoln, did their homework, talked to the right people and did excellent work. There were other people that didn't do their job or didn't do it in the way I would have done it, and therefore came up with what I thought were stories that weren't as complete or as accurate as they should have been. I think it just came down to the person who was doing it.

Q: So do you have a favorite interview or postgame moment that stands out to you?

LB: Wow, let's see. There's so much, it's hard to pluck one out. After games, always talking to guys like Broderick Thomas or Johnny Mitchell or the Peter brothers, those guys were great. They always spoke their mind and had things to say.

And really, the high intensity games when the Colorado/Nebraska series was heating up, they were interesting times. The Nebraska/Oklahoma series, too. Not just one. It's kind of hard to nail one down.

Q: And obviously, when it's game time you were up in the press box?

LB: Right.

Q: Was there ever a time during a game when you weren't up in the press box?

LB: No, that was our office away from home.

Q: Do you have a game that was extra-special to you?

LB: You know, I'd have to say that whole '93 season when they took on the motto, "Refuse to Lose." You know, it wasn't the most talented team Nebraska ever had -talent-wise, by any means- but it just seemed like it was that group of guys that was gonna take the program and said, "Look, we're gonna change things a little bit." That was the year they changed the defense a little bit and the guys just kind of bonded, and I think that was a real turning point-season. And even though they lost the bowl game I think the way they lost the game to Florida State that year set the stage for their run the next 5 years. It showed and proved to those guys that the things they were doing were the right things to be really good. And it gave them the hunger to go on and prove that Nebraska football was back among the elite. I guess if I have a soft spot in my heart for any team, it's that '93 team.

Q: I've got to tell you, I was just getting out of my diapers in the '70 and '71 years, but I have to say the Florida State '94 game had all the elements to be the greatest college football game ever..

LB: You could make that argument. I won't disagree with you on that. I know some people would argue with you, but I understand where you're coming from. That was an amazing game, you know, Nebraska being such a huge underdog.

I remember in the press box that night, the national media was talking about how Florida State was going to win by 4 or 5 touchdowns. They were thinking they were just wasting their time being there and all that. I think that season, and especially that game, was the jumping off point for Nebraska joining and getting back into the elite.

Q: Any names stand out to you from that team?

LB: You know, Trev Alberts was clearly quite a leader on that team. Some of the guys that didn't have the big names, guys that you don't hear about too much? Troy Branch was on that team and Kevin Raemakers was involved there, and clearly Tommie Frazier early in his career had become a force on the team by then, you know? It was just a bunch of guys that had that look in their eye: "We've been kicked around a little bit and we're not going to take it anymore." They took it upon themselves to really energize the program.

Q: Any particular visiting press box location other than that game stand out to you? I know you're supposed to be neutral in the press box, but was there ever any occasion where that didn't prove to be the case?

LB: As far as other media people? No, it's a professional atmosphere up there in the press box, it's an office space up there. There's no cheering in the press box. Those are Football Writers Association rules. People who are involved? If they are up there cheering they get warned once. And if they do it again they get escorted out of the building. People I have known who've come up to visit the press box during a game, they say they hate it because they say it's quiet. People are working. You might be conversing with your fellow employees about what you're working on, but it's not a raucus atmosphere. It's a quiet place of business and that's how it's supposed to be in the press box.

Q: Did you ever find yourself quietly, internally, hoping or cheering for a touchdown?

LB: Oh, now, no, no, no....

Q: How does a guy do that? I mean, you probably grew up a fan. How can you not secretly root for the team?

LB: Well, you're trained to do that in Journalism School. You just cannot do that. You don't root for the team you're covering and you don't root against any other team you don't cover. You just sit there and quietly analyze the game.

Q: You just kind of bite your lip and glue your butt to your seat?

LB: It's not even that. You just know going in that that's part of the deal. If you're not willing to do that, you don't get the privilege of getting the job of covering major college football or basketball. You just have to divorce yourself from any of those feelings, and you just cover it like a news event.

Q: Wow, I'm thinking if that was me it would have been tough to do, Lee.

LB: Hey, small-town Nebraska kid? You grew up listening to games and stuff, but that's part of what you learn when you go through Journalism School. Nebraska has one of the highest rated journalism schools in the country year after year after year. I had great instructors, and you learned the right way to do things.

Q: What places the Nebraska journalism school so high on the list?

LB: Well, the Dean used to be a guy named Neale Copple. Neale really set the tone for having a nationally renowned program that was based on good, old-fashioned journalism: working hard and getting the facts straight and being fair. There was just a tenor that was set and carried out by the instructors. It was just a good, solid baseline program that taught you the right way to do things.

Q: Is there a special sportswriter code or a credo to live by?

LB: I don't know that there's really anything about the way you really set yourself apart as a sportswriter. I think you just consider yourself a professional journalist. You try to be fast, but the first thing you do is: number one, be accurate, and number two, be fair, and you proceed from there.

Q: So, fast and accurate…

LB: Well, accuracy is number one, fair is number two. And then if you're fast and first that's great. (laughs) You've got to get the story right or it's no good.

Q: Sounds just like the game of football: it helps to be fast but accuracy matters most. (laughs) Going beyond Coach Osborne, what about the other fellows on the coaching staff?

LB: If you're trying to put it in the context of a business book, you really think it was a credit to Coach Osborne that he knew it was important to have different personalities on his staff. And clearly there were. I mean, there were guys who were very straight-laced and religious and there were other guys on the staff who liked to go out and have a good time. You had some loud guys and some quiet guys and you had some big story-tellers and some other guys who just kind of did things by example.

And I think that's a real key to any organization like that: that you have varied people yet they can all blend their strengths and they could work together. Those guys? All those guys were memorable people. The stuff that Turner Gill brought to the table and Charlie McBride brought to the table and Milt Tenopir? Everybody had different strengths and different elements yet they all came together, they got along and they produced a quality product. The thing that sticks out to me was that Coach Osborne recognized the need to have different people and then blended them together to have a strong staff.

Q: Now, you attended some practices. Any practice occasion that stands out to you from those days?

LB: You know, just the organization and the fact they used to have -one of the unsung things that made Nebraska football good was having four practice stations running plays on four different stations every day- the repetition really helped the players progress. Football is a game of repetition and you have to run those plays over and over again to get proficient.

And I think that's where the walk-on program comes in. You had to have those guys to fill out the roster and have enough people to do that, to have a full-blown practice situation like they wanted it. You know, there were times Charlie was yelling at people or occasions when Coach Osborne would raise his voice (that would definitely get people's attention, because he didn't do that very often). (laughs) Other than that, football practice is football practice.

Q: About Coach Osborne, in retrospect, how would you sum up the man and his leadership qualities and the ship he ran?

LB: Well, I think it's clear from the results: he was a very effective leader and principled man, and did things according to the plan he'd set up. It's hard to question the results. He always championed the student-athlete. He really cared about the players who went through his program. I'm not sure you could always say that about every other head coach you come across.

But looking at it from a 30 year lens you could see it was about the kids for him and that he was a very good teacher and coach. That's what it was always about: it was about the kids. That was always number one for him. And even as athletic director, I think he still enjoys interacting with the athletes and having a good experience with the student-athlete during their college experience.

Q: Do you still interview and interact with him?

LB: Oh, yeah. And it's apparent that he's very happy being back and involved. And I think he's felt there were things that needed to be corrected after the Steve Pederson years, and he wanted Bo involved in getting those things fixed and turned around. There's days he looks ten years younger just being back, involved and being on the ship. So I think he enjoys it.

Q: And during the Lawrence Phillips -I'll call it a debacle- anything about that moment in time stand out to you from that '95 season?

LB: Just, I think the shock of them going to Michigan State that day and Lawrence had a great game and Nebraska was the number one team in the country and Nebraska was rolling along, and to find out the details the next day as to what happened? I think it was just a jolt to everybody. I'm not sure what can be said, it was just a bad situation. Lawrence is in jail and has continued to have problems in life after that so I guess we saw the beginning of it, and I'm not sure what else there is to say.

I guess my thought was, 'I wanted to cover football. I didn't want to cover courts and the legal system and things like that.' That doesn't mean we didn't do that because that was part of the job, but I clearly would have preferred writing about the game and things on the team. I didn't want to write about things going on in the courtrooms. And the facts of his case are what they are and that's the way it is.

Q: Have you ever been on the Heisman Voting Committee? Any thoughts about Tommie not winning it?

LB: Yeah, I was. And I thought clearly that he should have won. I voted him first that year, and I don't understand why the Heisman voting isn't done until after the bowl games. He would have been the winner if that was the case, but he's not the first guy that situation's happened to him. Vince Young for Texas in '05 finished second in the balloting and he would have been number one, clearly. But that's a part of the process.

Q: Is there any provincialism going on?

LB: No, that's a misnomer, because the votes are split geographically equally around the country. There's always this talk about the East Coast bias with voting and polls and all that, but the votes are distributed around the country, so there really can't be an East Coast bias because they don't have more votes.

Q: Thanks for pointing that out, Lee. And I have to ask, was there anyone behind the scenes who you think played a big part but never got their due? Anyone stand out?

LB: You know, we covered the program so extensively, I think we wrote a story about just about everyone who ever worked there. (laughs) I'm sure there are, but nobody really comes to mind right off the top of my head.

The coaches' secretaries were clearly great people and did a lot of work behind the scenes, but I don't know if I can tell you of anybody who just pops to mind. Mary Lyn was always great, she had a great sense of humor and was wonderful under stress. There were times when Mary Lyn and I had to get a meeting because Coach Osborne wanted to see me about something or I wanted to see Coach Osborne about something, so she was great to work with.

Q: How often would you need these meetings?

LB: Well, it just depended on what was going on. (laughs) It was just if special issues came up and I wanted to talk to him about them or if he had an issue with me and wanted to see me, we'd get together. We had good lines of communication. So it's just like any kind of business relationship: just deal openly and honestly. I think that's the best way to operate.

Q: You felt that you always had Coach's respect and attention?

LB: Well, I tried to conduct myself in a professional way and had been in the business a long time and received some recognition for my work, so I think he respected the work that we did. I hope he did. We sure respected him and his work, so I think that was a two-way street.

Q: And in closing, about those 90's years, anything else stand out to you as to what made it special?

LB: Well, I just think that the fact that some of the slippage that they had in '90 and '91, it caused them to go back and look at everything they were doing. From recruiting to scheduling to the way they practiced to nutrition and weightlifting, everything. They went back and that's what every good organization does. If you have slump in your sales or a slump in your production, you go back and you take a good look at what you do and try to fix it and make it better and consult with other people in their business and look at how they do things. And clearly, the results, the 60 and 3 record over a five year period, it's clear they did things the right way.

End conversation.

Back in a Sunday, August 30th, 2009 edition of the World-Herald's College Football Preview, Lee wrote about one of the keys to Nebraska's 90's Football success in his article titled '*NU walk-on program succeeds as quantity brings quality, unity*':

"*So how do you explain the walk-on program's success? What's the "real" secret?*

Hard work and commitment.

Not the sexy answer you were looking for?

Tough."

Like I said, Lee's writing was always insightful, as well as succinct.

The most interesting tidbit I heard was his mention of the myriad personalities of the football coaches: the curious mix of counselors, characters, carousers and Christians. It was a mixed bag. Were there conflicts? Sure. Was there convergence and divergence of philosophy? Sure. Was there eventual consensus, though? Thrice I say sure. Some of these fellows even rubbed their share of players the wrong way, but for each example there was evidence of another standing in the gap and having a positive and profound effect on the kid. Teamwork, in a word. Unity among diversity. Pretty sharp fellow, that Osborne, for assembling such a crew.

The Lord only knows if I'll have a chance to confirm it (Kevin Steele did not answer requests for this project) but it was the first I'd heard of Steele's influence on "convincing Coach Osborne to maybe have more ones versus ones in practice." Lee added, "I think that helped set a different tempo." That's an understatement. To end many a practice the number one offense was pitted against the number one defense: a goal line stand. Can you imagine the egos, the pride, the pressure, the prowling and prodding, to shut the other guys down and hold bragging rights, if only for a day? Some championship games aren't this intense. Maybe that's why the Huskers had so much confidence in themselves and performed so well in those big games, as they'd already survived the many skirmishes amongst one another.

And, oh yes, you can bet I'll be tracking down Mary Lyn Wininger, Coach Osborne's secretary during those times. Thanks for the great lead, Lee.

Notable quote #2:
Lee Barfknecht on turning the corner to greatness: "It was just a bunch of guys that had that look in their eye: "We've been kicked around a little bit and we're not going to take it anymore." They took it upon themselves to really energize the program."

It is in games that many men discover their paradise.

Robert Lynd

As you wend your through a vast sea of wildflowers, switchgrass & big bluestem, past the windmills and scattered clusters of Black Angus on the gently undulating plains of western Nebraska's Grant County, you'll come upon the tiny township of Hyannis, a wee burg on the hinterland prairie. The county seat with a population of 287, if you luck upon its red brick courthouse on a Tuesday or Wednesday afternoon you'll partake of the rare chance to view the local museum's world class barbed-wire collection and John Wayne's saddle from the 1969 movie *True Grit*. Sharing the same determination, fortitude and reserve of character acted out in the span of The Duke's cowboy film career, Terry Connealy followed the Loup River eastward to Lincoln and enjoyed the thrill of a lifetime.

In the defensive huddle during the waning moments of 1995's crushing victory over the Miami Hurricanes, a fellow Blackshirt said, "Let's everybody meet at the quarterback." And doing just that moments later set off a celebration for the ages. Terry therafter described the victory as "My best day on earth." From tiny Hyannis to college football heaven, let's hear what Terry has to share about the exhaustive effort leading to his apogee of ecstasy, his personal pigskin promised land.

Notable quote #1:
"You sucked it up and you went harder than you thought you could go, and it's things like that that you remember. You don't really realize how far you can push yourself until you do it… But you survive, and you find out you can push yourself a lot harder than you think you can… (that loss) hurt too much that we weren't going to let it happen again."

Terry Connealy

Scholarship recruit, Defensive Tackle, Hyannis, Nebraska
Where are they now? Omaha, Nebraska, Banking

Question: Hey Terry, thanks for making the time for me. So what are you doing nowadays?

Terry Connealy: For the last 8 years I've worked for Wells Fargo and, actually, I kind of cover the western half of the country for a division of their mortgage company called Private Mortgage Banking. We are the division of Wells Fargo Home Mortgage that focuses on lending to the affluent client. It's pretty fun. A pretty neat group, to say the least.

Q: How did you get hooked up with Wells Fargo?

TC: It's kind of a funny story. Prior to working for Wells Fargo I was in the financial services business and I was selling stocks, bonds, and mutual funds, setting up 401K's, and I got a call from a gentleman from Wells Fargo that had actually been referred to me by Doak(Ostergard). Probably the only reason I returned his call was because he dropped Doak's name in there. (laughs) 9 months later I joined Wells Fargo, and I look back and it's been a wonderful move. Great company, couldn't be happier.

Q: Last time we talked you mentioned you'd read Jim Collins' book 'Good to Great', so would you say that Wells Fargo is still running the same type of operation as was highlighted in the book?

TC: I really would. And it's been awhile since I've read Good to Great, but it uses Wells Fargo a lot as a company that's gone from good to great. Nothing's really changed; a very consistent company. Leadership at the top is very consistent, very modest, and we continue to just keep doing things as we have before. A lot of consistency in the company.

Q: Sounds like you're describing Nebraska Football of your playing days.

TC: Yeah, and I really do think there's a lot of similarities. I look back at my time at Nebraska and the obviously fantastic leadership: consistency in the leadership and in the way we approached things.

And probably the other thing: there is just a great work ethic. Nothing is going to be given to you; you have to go out there and earn it. And earn it every day. And if you do that, everything will fall into place.

Q: I'm thinking you're a pretty blessed guy going from Nebraska football to an organization like that, but in the meantime where did you go?

TC: Right. After I graduated from Nebraska after the Orange Bowl? Obviously I thought I'd better at least see if I could play in the NFL, see if I could get a chance or opportunity. I played in the Senior Bowl and then continued to work out. And I didn't get drafted, but I ended up a having offers from several NFL teams right after the draft and actually went to camp with the New York Jets. I went to their mini-camps and some of their training camp and got cut there, and ended up getting signed by the Packers. So I spent a little time in Green Bay before I realized I was in over my head. I didn't have the talent and the size to compete at that level, especially the Packers.

It was something. At the time it was certainly difficult, but I don't have any regrets. I knew that it was probably a long shot for me to play in the NFL just because trying to play noseguard/defensive tackle at 265-270 lbs. was a reach, but I also knew that if I didn't give it a try I'd probably always regret it and always wonder if I could have. I gave it a try and found out pretty quickly that it wasn't going to be for me, but no regrets.

Q: Was there one major thing that signaled to you that it wasn't to be?

TC: Well, when I chose the team to sign with, I think I had offers from 10 or 12 teams. I chose the Jets, quite honestly, because the Jets were one of the poorer teams in the league and didn't have a ton of depth and a lot of guys really sticking out there. If it's a long shot to making the team you don't want to go the the Super Bowl champions and try to get on their defensive line, so I went to New York. And actually with the Jets, I thought I had a pretty good chance to make the team, and if I didn't make the team, to at least get on their practice squad. And then it kind of turned out I got caught in a numbers game: some guy had been holding out. They had to sign this guy and they had to make room, and I was the guy to get let go.

But when I got to Green Baby and the NFC Central, Reggie White was there. And I was the smallest defensive lineman/tackle by probably 35-40 lbs. and just was probably not big enough to play defensive tackle/noseguard. I would hold my own a couple plays, but I just wasn't big enough and I just wasn't fast enough to be out there on the defensive end spot. So I realized pretty quickly that I just didn't have the physical makeup to be playing for the Packers.

Q: Is their fan base as rabid as Nebraska's?

TC: You know, I will always be a Green Bay Packers fan after my experience there. When I went to New York it was pretty evident at the time why they were the worst team in the NFL. (laughs) Just the atmpsphere there, how it felt around camp and how the coaches interacted? And then you went to Green Bay and it was the polar opposite.

It really did remind me of Nebraska. That fan base was fantastic, the coaches seemed like they really had a vested interest, that you were more than just a number to them, that they cared about you. There were just a ton of similarities between the Packers and the Huskers. And it's funny, but the next year or two years later, a lot of the same coaches and same players that were in camp? The Packers went on and won the Super Bowl. I wasn't surprised at all, there were a ton of similarities between there and Nebraska.

Q: What was the most telling?

TC: To me the most telling thing from a player's perspective was the coaches and the leadership. Mike Holmgren was the head coach and just a good guy that sincerely cared about you, actually knew who you were. When I was with the Jets none of the coaches knew who you were, you were just whatever number was on your jersey. Then all of a sudden I got to Green Bay and I was an undrafted free agent and had already been cut by one team, and Coach Holmgren makes it a point to come up and introduce himself when I get to camp. Just very impressive. And when I decided to leave camp they came and spent some time with me and thanked me and wished me luck. I think the biggest similarity was just the way the coaches treated the players with respect, the caring. Obviously, I have didn't have that much experience -that's my only experience- but from what I've heard and read that's certainly not the norm, I don't think. Yeah, you're gettng paid to play the game and it's your job and it's a business, but I don't think it's a coincidence the successful people in the NFL have something special there.

Q: Let me ask you: coming from Hyannis, did you play 8-man or 11-man football?

TC: I played 8-man. Where are you from? Where did you go to high school?

Q: A little town called Petersburg. Pretty close to Albion.

TC: Was that the #41 on the license plate?

Q: No, that was #23. I think #41 was York county's number, if I recall, about halfway to Lincoln from my hometown.(laughing) What position did you play in 8-man ball, Terry?

TC: The only position I didn't play my senior year was quarterback. (laughs) I was primarily on offense at tight end or a tackle being eligible for a pass, and then my senior year we had some kids get hurt so I literally ended up playing fullback, I-back, longsnapper, kicked off. And then on defense my senior year I was primarily a linebacker, but I played some defensive end. You played it. (laughs)

Q: Kind of like a day on the farm? You go where you're needed most?

TC: Yeah, that's exactly right. We only had -I forget how many kids we had out for football- but we didn't have enough kids to do a full-scale scrimmage, so we had to do half-line scrimmages, you know? From the center to the right. So you started from the center and you ran the play with those people on the right for that particulaur play, (laughs) because you didn't have enough to go 8 on 8. (laughs)

Q: And if you did, it was usually against 105 lb. freshmen, right?

TC: Yep. It didn't really do you any good. (laughs)I absolutely loved playing 8-man football. Arthur played 6-man and some other schools around us did, but we never played any 6-man games. And the beautiful thing about 8-man is that it's 3 less guys and a smaller field, but really the rules are the same. You're just playing a smaller version of 11-man.

Q: Exactly, you just hope your linemen have better hands in case you throw a center-eligible pass to them...

TC: Yeah, right. I never played an 11-man game until the Shrine Bowl after my senior year of high school.

Q: Were you concerned about the adjustment to the eleven man game?

TC: You know, a little bit. I remember going to camp for the Shrine Bowl before the freshman year of college and it being just a little bit different in trying to learn your assignments -you've got a couple extra guys out there and the like- but for the most part you were doing the same thing. It wasn't that big a deal.

It was a much bigger transition when I went from that to camp at Nebraska a few weeks later. I never had any idea that there was so much technique to being a defensive lineman. In high school playing 8-man football, at the time I was one of the biggest and fastest guys, and you just kind of played by instinct. You knew what you were supposed to do, and then you get down to Nebraska playing the defensive line and Coach McBride is talking about "a 6-inch step here followed by a twelve-inch step there and your hands are here." (laughs) My head was swimming. Truly, I never knew that there was that much technique to being a defensive tackle or a noseguard.

Q: Even the bull rush has a technique to it?

TC: Yes, and you found that out real quick when you started two-a-days.

Q: Did you get recruited as a defensive lineman, Terry?

TC: You know, really, when they recruited me they didn't exactly know where I was gonna go. I'd gone down to the football camp at Nebraska the summer year before my senior year of high school football and, gosh, they moved me around and put me over with Coach Brown at the tight ends, they put me down with Charlie at the D-line, and I think I even worked with the linebackers. So when they recruited me it was kind of between a tight end and defensive tackle. And Charlie evidently said, "I want him on the defensive line," and that was the only position I ever played, was noseguard and defensive tackle. I wasn't 100% sure when I got recruited where I was gonna end up.

Q: You were recruited as an 'athlete', per se?

TC: I would say that's a stretch. (laughs) I'd like to say that was the case, but I was destined to be a defensive lineman.

Q: (laughing) So your freshman year was the fall of '90 or 91?

TC: That was '90. I redshirted my first year. They still had the freshman team actually; the last year they had the freshman football team, but I didn't play on it. So at that time they still brought in 100 freshmen and there were probably 15 or 18 of us that redshirted, and the rest of the guys that came in that year played on the freshman team.

Q: Take me back to your first day or two on campus, what stuck out to you?

TC: Oh, yeah, it was so different from where I had come from, obviously, just the whole experience. The first class I ever sat in on was at the auditorium in Love Library. And I don't know how big it was, but I remember thinking, 'There's more people in this class than in my entire hometown!' (laughs) There probably was. I'm guessing that auditorium seated 400 people, but it was a little different.

But as far as the football, in Hyannis? Just a wonderful experience. I had a fantastic coach my junior and senior year: Chris Krause. And he's coaching in Hyannis even today. A wonderful coach. And we had an assistant, Bob Waldman, those were our two coaches, and you get to Nebraska and, gosh, you've got three Grad Assistant coaches and specialists and the like.

Obviously, it was different for me to be a defensive tackle and a noseguard, and you went to your own meetings for noseguard before practice, just with your position, and the structure of the practice. It was a well-oiled machine and you could tell that from the second you even started the recruiting process, "Here's where you are supposed to be, here's what you do, here's how we run things." And if you did what you were supposed to do and worked hard, it set you up for successs. The road map was laid out for you, what you needed to do.

Q: Just plug you in and let your work ethic and perseverance take over?

TC: Yeah, that's it. And the thing is, the guys that had been in the program? You followed them. They were leaders and they knew what was expected. And even the though the coaches obviously played a huge role in it, it was the upperclassmen, the role they played trickled down to you, and it's amazing the consistency. We were very, very fortunate.

And I look back and I can't remember -the whole time I was there, Paul- any change in the assistant coaches. Turner Gill came on, but I don't think anybody left. Right? I think Coach Osborne was coaching the quarterbacks. Maybe there was a change in the rules where they were allowed to bring another coach on, but I can't think of anything other than the GA's rolling through and the like. You had Steele at linebacker, George in the secondary, you had Tony at defensive ends, you had Charlie at tackle, you had Ron Brown and Milt and Dan and Osborne and Solich, and then you brought Turner in. So my recruiting class, I don't think we had a single turnover in the assistant coach ranks.

Now, after I graduated, I think the next year maybe Tony left and Kevin left, but truly I was there for a 5 year period and unless memory fails me, the leadership in that team did not change a bit.

Q: Speaking of leadership, from your freshman year to your senior year it seemed to me there was a change in the mindset of the team. Would you agree with that?

TC: Well, from the players leadership or coaches leadership, or maybe both.

When I got there we had it on the defensive line. We had some great leaders that were team captains, a friend to this day: Pat Englebert. Pat led by example and did all the right things and the like.

But I think before I arrived, or maybe my freshman year, they instituted the Unity Council and I think that that was probably kind of a turning point, my best guess is that the Unity Council really did bring the team together. All of a sudden you have not only the coaches who were leading the team, but then you've got the players monitoring themselves and assessing penalties. There's nothing more motivational than when your peers are telling you you're screwing up and you better straighten out, right? That means a lot more coming from your peers than the coaches, which is what you'd expect. When it comes from your own classmates and the guys you're playing with, I think that that was probably a real turning point in bringing the team together and building unity. Certainly, you pull that many guys together, 23 or so guys, not everybody is going to get along, but there was a mutual respect and a sense that we're all there for the same goal and "Here's what we've got to do to achieve it."

Q: Speaking of goals, it seems earlier on there wasn't as much of a focus on winning the national championship than there was in later years. Does that ring a bell? Do you recall the first time it was spoken outwardly, "Hey, our goal is the national championship"?

TC: I remember early on in camp we would be in an all-team meeting, we would sit in there and would put down that year's goals on the whiteboard, and they would get each position and each game goal. You'd have this many yards per rush and all that, but I can remember 'Winning the Big 8' at that time, 'Winning the bowl game', but really Coach always kind of had the philosophy that you take care of those steps along the way, the things you can control, not the things you can't.

And the mindset was, "You can't always control winning the national championship, because that's up to the voters." At that time there was no mathematical poll to get you in there, so at that time we didn't really put that as a goal, because the theory and the concept was if you achieved all the goals, that's gonna come, the fruits of your labor, right? That was kind of the underlying fact: you knew that if you took care of business you were gonna have an opportunity to compete for a national championship.

Q: Tell me about Charlie McBride.

TC: (laughs) Charlie is on my speed dial right now. Coach McBride and Coach Osborne are two of the best guys and role models that I've ever had besides my own father. Coach McBride was the most genuine guy you would ever meet. You might not always like the feedback you got, but you learned that you don't take it personal, that he's doing it to make you a better person or a better football player.

On the flip side he'd be the first guy on your tail if you screwed up, but he'd be the first guy to congratulate you, too, if you did the right thing. He'd be the first over there giving you a hug, too. But Coach McBride, coming in as a true freshman? He's a pretty intimidating figure to go through two-a-days with. I wondered what the heck I got myself into. (laughs)

Q: Did Charlie have any frequent sayings?

TC: (laughs) I can always remember him shouting across the practice field, "Connealy, if you got any slower your heart would stop!"

Q: (laughs) Was that just with you? Or others, too?

TC: I think it was with more people than me, but I was maybe slower than most, so I probably heard it more often than anyone else. If you were having a bad day and he didn't think you were putting out, he'd ask you if you heart was "pumping kool-aid or blood?"

Q: You know that Kool-Aid was invented in Nebraska?

TC: Yeah. And he had several other phrases that I can't mention. (laughs)

The first year and a half, two years I was there my typical conversations with Coach McBride were, 'Yes sir', 'No sir', and 'Okay, sir.' (laughs) But oh, my goodness, the best defensive line coach. I can't imagine there being a better defensive line coach as far as knowing football, as far as knowing technique, just a brilliant guy. One of my best friends to this day. We talk several times a year and when he gets back we try to get together. He's the best.

Q: How would you contrast Coach McBride's style with Coach Osborne's?

TC: I think there was something there, the defensive mentality. I've always said I think a good defensive coordinator has got to have a screw loose. You've got to be fiery, you've got to be intense. And offensive players and offensive coaching? Certainly adrenaline and effort and everything will get you a long ways, but I think it probably gets you farther on the defensive side. Pure hustle, pure heart, pure determination will probably make up for some technique errors and some strategy errors, if you've got eleven guys flying to the ball.

Coach always used to say, "If you screw up, you screw up going 110 miles an hour." If you screwed up going half-speed he was really gonna get exasperated, but if you're screwing up 100 miles an hour you could make up for it. Charlie was really intense in practice. You saw it, he could get in a guy's grill and chew a guy's tail and spit and swear, and you didn't want to be on the other end of that tirade. And certainly, I saw some of the offensive coaches do that, but certainly not to the extent that Charlie and some of the defensive coaches would.

Q: Say, I was watching video of the Miami game the other night, and I swear at the end of that game I actually saw you do a spin move…

TC: (hearty laugh) Which Charlie hated! Paul, I figured I only had about 4 snaps left as a Husker, and if I was going to pull it out, that was going to be the time. (laughs)

Q: And if I'm correct, I believe you and about 2 other guys converged on Frank Costa, the quarterback at that time…

TC: Yeah. And Charlie did, he hated when you did that. I can remember him saying, "Dammit guys, if you're gonna do that you better make a play." If you don't, you might not be in the game too much longer.

And I can remember, I'd been setting the guy up for the longest time and I thought, 'Well, now or never. I've got nothing to lose.' Thank goodness it worked out! (laughs)

Q: I'm also thinking that the Miami guys, their offensive linemen, were taught that 'Nebraska guys don't spin."

TC: It's a deal where you've been kind of setting a guy up for a play like that. Occasionally, you lull them into the situation where they haven't seen it all game, and if you do pull it out you better make it work.

Q: Terry, who was the first person you befriended when you arrived on campus?

TC: Paul, I was very fortunate to have a wonderful bunch of guys that I came into the program with in my recruiting class. It's really hard to pick one guy out. And even to this day, those guys are still my best friends, the guys I played ball with. And not just my class, but other guys in the program. When I came on campus we all bonded pretty quickly, a bunch of us, and maintained those friendships and have still done so. The one consistent guy that I lived with, Jason Pesterfield, I lived with Pesty for 4 out of the 5 years I was in college.

Q: He was from Oklahoma, right?

TC: Yep, Paul's Valley, Oklahoma. We still keep in touch. He lives in Dallas now and we talk and see each other several times a year.

Q: Corey Dixon is down in that area too. I guess he's keeping very busy with his daughters, who happen to be pretty talented at soccer. They must have their dad's wheels…

TC: Man, that's a name I haven't heard recently. That doesn't surprise me. Corey had some pretty good weels. I can see some pretty good soccer players coming out of that.

Q: As for a mindset, an attitude, as inspiration… what drove you?

TC: You know, I think it's something that I was fortunate, Paul, that that was instilled in me by my parents. But to take it a step further, when I got to Nebraska that was instilled in you by Coach McBride and by the upperclassmen. I can always kind of remember a pride factor among the defensive linemen, that "You're never going to be outworked. Whatever it takes, you're gonna work harder and do this and that." It just seemed like it kind of trickled down. I learned it from the Kenny Walkers and the Pat Engleberts and the John Parrellas. It's something that, after I was gone it was the Peter brothers, it was just something that we had a lot of pride in, the defensive line, that we weren't going to be outworked. It came from Coach Osborne and Coach McBride and we were fortunate to have a bunch of guys that bought into it and truly tried to live it.

Q: Did playing with Kenny Walker leave any impression upon you?

TC: (laughs) Kenny was a fifth year senior when I came in as a freshman, so I was Kenny's blocking dummy my whole redshirt year. So Kenny left many impressions on me, mostly black and blue bruises. (laughs) Here's a guy that had an interpreter with him so that he could understand what was going on and had to get his defensive calls by hand signals and all that, and it really had an impression on me. Here this guy is deaf, is a fantastic football player, and nobody works harder. If anybody could make an excuse it would have been Kenny, and I never heard him make an excuse. It really was pretty inspirational to see a guy that had that handicap be such a great teammate, a great player. But Kenny was a guy that nobody outworked him. He was a pretty special guy.

Q: I ask that question to maybe find if there was something that was a part of your early learning and inspired you to carry it into later years. Who knows, maybe it made the system better, made the coaches rethink what they were doing, etc.

TC: Yeah. You know, I think there were a couple things I was the beneficiary of, Paul, and one of those was when Coach Osborne and Coach McBride decided to make the switch full-time from the old 50 defense to the 4-3. My first three years, my redshirt year and then as a freshman I played just a little bit, we were pretty much exclusively a 50 defense at that point. We would run in what we called the Dime Defense occasionally on passing downs, but maybe that was, I'm guessing 10-15% of the plays? The majority of the time we were in the 50 defense.

My third year, when I was a sophomore, I was on the first string Dime Defense and we would start the game in the 50. Every game we started in the 50 and as the season went on we ended up playing -it switched- the dime defense 90% of the games. Oftentimes we'd only be in the 50 the first 4 plays and bring in the dime and play the rest. We figured out we could stop the run with the dime just as good as we could the 50 with all that speed on the field.

We kind of got to a point where we were the read and react defense at some times (which the 50 was a little bit), then we got into an attacking defense and all of a sudden we had some guys on the defensive side of the ball with speed at every position. At the linebacker spot you had Ed Stewart, Doug Colman, Phil Ellis, Mike Anderson, these guys could all run. And all of a sudden, I'd like to say there was some profound thing that I did or was instilled, but that wasn't the case.

I think a lot of that credit has to go to Coach Osborne and Coach McBride for evolving and being willing to kind of step out of the mold. We were in the Big 8 and you thought you had to run the 50 defense to stop the run, and they stuck their neck out and decided to play a 4-3 defense in a running conference, and it turned out it worked pretty well.

Q: Coach Darlington said about the same thing, how he used to chart the efficiency of the various defenses and how the dime package was just as successful as the 50. I wonder if his talks with Charlie might have helped that change along.

TC: It was an evolution all of a sudden. I don't think my junior year we hardly even put the 50 defense in. We had a few wrinkles for some things, but it almost went exclusively to the 4-3 my last two years there.

Q: Do you have a favorite play or favorite moment?

TC: You know what, that's kind of a tough question because there are so many. It was really special to me, playing for Nebraska had been my dream and I was fortunate enough to live it and be there at a time when there were a lot of great players coming together.

Obviously the play in the Orange Bowl at the end of the game where I sacked the quarterback, that's the one that sticks out because that was the culmination of 5 years of hard work at the end of the national championship game, and the timing was great, but there were a lot of great memories there. It seems like you almost remember the plays where you were unsuccesssful more than the plays where you were successful, the plays when you got beat or did something wrong and it costed you. That sticks in my mind as much as the good plays…

Q: The plays where you took a twelve inch step with one foot and six inch step with the wrong foot and were out of position?

TC: Yeah, and then I had to hear about it in meetings on Monday. You might spend a lot more time on those the next week in practice than you did the successful plays.

Q: Any memorable off-field occasions worth sharing?

TC: (laughs) The 'worth sharing' is the tough part there. All kinds of great off-field memories. Gosh, you didn't just spend your days on the practice field. These were the guys you lived with and did things with.

Some of my favorite times were in summer school, because you'd get up and go to class for three or four hours and you were usually living with a bunch of guys in the summer. You'd go work out together in the summer. It was just a lot of fun because you got to spend so much time together and you only had like three hours of class. You got to work out and run together.

A lot of the camaraderie and work ethic and everything were formed after my junior year when we lost the Orange Bowl to Florida State: that next summer was so wonderful. That's when it all came together, at the end of every practice we'd put the 1:16 back up on the clock, and we were that close. You sucked it up and you went harder than you thought you could go, and it's things like that that you remember. You don't really realize how far you can push yourself until you do it. You remember thinking, 'Gosh, I don't know if I can do it.' But you survive, and you find out you can push yourself a lot harder than you think you can. Just the summer workouts, it was great. We made a lot of improvement between my junior and senior year that summer. It was just fun to see the determination and work ethic that everybody brought to it. It's easy to say, in hindsight, that we knew we weren't going to lose the next year. It hurt too much that we weren't going to let it happen again.

Q: Any practice stories worth recalling?

TC: Oh boy, there's a lot that come to mind. I'm trying to think of an appropriate one (laughs) where somebody doesn't get in trouble. I don't want to throw anybody under the bus.

Q: I ask that question and usually get a lot of nervous giggles on that, Terry. Even 15 years later they still don't want to call out their teammates…

TC: (laughs) Some of the funniest ones –well, not necessarily funniest- I remember when the offensive line and the defensive line, at that time the O-line would be over in the pit. We'd be over in the Schulte Fieldhouse and then at the end of team work, once or twice a week we'd all get together and do live one-on-ones -run blocking or pass blocking- and they used to get intense. About once a week or so there would just be a knock-down, drag-out fight between the O-line and the D-line, and Charlie and Milt certainly wouldn't jump in to break it up. They let you work things out on your own.

And you look back? Those were some of my best friends and here you'd be trying to knock their block off. There were some funny stuff used to happen, it was just so intense. It was a lot of fun.

Q: That's where the true combat capabilities were being forged, so to speak?

TC: Yeah, you better bring it 100% because the other guy was going to. You were playing for pride. You didn't want to be the guy who lost the most battles consistently, because you'd hear about it. (laughs)

Q: And speaking of pride, what would you say you are most proud of from your time there as a student-athlete?

TC: You know, probably the thing I'm most proud of was that I had the opportunity to be on Coach Osborne's first National Championship team. Growing up in the 70's and 80's, we were so close several times where we lost one ballgame throughout the year and it cost us the national title and you go for two and we don't make it. We'd just been so close, and it was very rewarding to be on Coach Osborne's first National Championship team. It probably didn't mean nearly as much to Coach Osborne as it did to the rest of us because that's the kind of guy he is, but the rest of us felt like we helped get the monkey off his back a little bit.

Q: Did it?

TC: I think so. Gosh, it's really kind of crazy how we were so close. So close. So close for two decades and then all of a sudden in the '93 season we were within a 1:16, and then from that point on Nebraska had a 3 or 4 year run that is gonna be hard to ever match. You go undefeated in '94, you go undefeated in '95, you skip a year in '96 and go undefeated in '97. All of a sudden you just kind of turn into a juggernaut.

Q: I'm trying to get into the nuts and bolts behind that juggernaut…

TC: It didn't just happen. To me it didn't change dramatically to make it happen: it was tweaks here and there along the way. Because certainly in the 1982 and '83 seasons when we lost to Penn State and Miami, we were good enough to win the national championship. We were a bad call against Penn State from winning two straight titles, that's the honest truth. If those two plays happened differently in the early 80's Coach Osborne's got 5 national championships.

So they didn't have to make dramatic changes. I think it was just a culmination and tweaking, refining things: the Unity Council bringing the team tighter together to really work towards unified goals. But nothing was really that badly broken that all of a sudden things just got fixed and we start winning national titles. We'd been pretty good the whole time.

Q: Was there anyone behind the scnes who never go their due for what they did for the program? Can you single anybody out?

TC: Paul, there were so many people behind the scenes there who worked so selflessly.

Think about it. Think about the team that you worked with. Think about yourself, think about Bryan Bailey, think about Mike Arthur. I could have had a class and needed to meet one of you guys at 5 every morning to get my workout in and someone would have been, "Absolutely. I'll meet you there." There were so many selfless people that had your best interests in mind.

Think of Dennis Leblanc, Keith Zimmer. Those guys worked harder than anybody, do whatever it takes. If you weren't successful as a Nebraska football player it certainly wasn't because people were not willing to help you, because the support staff was just unbelievable. And I think that's probably a pretty rare occurrence. I know it is. Because the brief time I was at camp in the NFL? You'd think everybody had the same college expereince as I had: you loved your head coach, you loved your position coach, it was such a great experience. But it was amazing how many guys you sat down with from big time conferences and big time programs that had a crummy college experience and couldn't wait to get out of there.

And gosh, the training staff: Doak and Jerry Weber and Sully. Whatever fit into your schedule, they were there to help you. There were just so many people willing to step up to the plate to make you successful. And I'm sure I missed some people. That's not my intention, because you look back and, you know, the older you get the more you appreciate it. At the time, like I said, you thought that was the status quo, that everybody had that support staff and that team behind us. And then you find out that's pretty special. At the time I'm sure I took that for granted. Or I'd be thinking, 'Geez, what a pain in the ass Paul Koch is for making me get on the treadmill,' but that wasn't the case..

Q: Or do an extra set of Hang Cleans because it wasn't technically perfect?

TC: Exactly! (laughs) But you look back and it's pretty amazing how we were all pulling in the same direction for the same goal by pulling different levers, but certainly it all helped push us in the right direction.

Q: I've got to ask: do you remember the slogans, "Unity, Belief, Respect", "We Refuse to Lose" & "Unfinished Business"? Did the mottos ever mean much to you?

TC: Yeah, it did. Some more than others. The one that I think captured the team's mentality and detemination was the year, "We Refuse to Lose." I can just kind of remember that that was the mantra there, where you're going into a tough spot and you just felt like failure was not an option. You just did whatever it took to not to lose, but to win. I think that really took on a life of its own, especially that next year with "Unfinished Business." To me those two were really kind of tied together and almost went into one, because, unfortunately, we had some unfinished business. But we took care of it.

Q: Well, if you ask me, that '94 Florida State game, we didn't get beat. We may have lost, but we didn't get beat…

TC: We beat them everywhere but the scoreboard. And that happens. You could have pouted about it and sulked and the like and it wouldn't have made any difference, or you just could have decided you could have done better next year. We fortunately had a bunch of guys that did the latter and got back there.

The guys that I feel badly for is that bunch of seniors in 1993, because they deserved to have the national title. We deserved to have the national title that year, but it just didn't work out. That kind of goes back to an earlier question about setting goals for the national championship. Well, that was kind of out of our control. We played good enough to win in, but we didn't.

Q: Whathave you gained most from your experience at Nebraska? How do you think that made you a better man?

TC: You know, the whole experience? You always hear the old clichés about athletics and how it carries over to life after athletics? But to me, Paul, it's really not a cliche. All the things we've talked about the last hour as far as leadership, not taking shortcuts, working hard, being able to handle adversity. Because obviously, in football not everything goes your way, and what are you gonna do when that happens?

And as corny as that sounds, it's the same with life after football. Life's not fair: you've got adversity, you've got to work hard, things aren't going to fall in your lap. Just the determination and the work ethic that my whole experience taught me there.

You find that if you have those characteristics and you do them and you work hard at it, that generally things turn out okay. And it doesn't happen by accident. To me it's really something that I was fortunate enough to be plugged into a program and a bunch of people who taught me that, and hopefully I'm carrying it on and doing it in my day to day life now. And it's certainly helping me.

Q: Do you think having a guy like you in an organization, is there any rubbing off onto the others who haven't had that previous experience?

TC: I certainly think there can be. I was very fortunate to join an organization that had a lot of those same characteristics. And I was fortunate enough to find that. But if you weren't fortunate you'd think that would rub off, because if you do all those things your chances of being successful certainly increase. So yes, I think that would rub off on co-workers in the organization.

Q: Well Terry, I appreciate the time you've given me here.

TC: Oh Paul, I enjoyed it. I haven't relived the glory days or had to think about a lot of that stuff for a long time. It brings back a flood of really great memories. I enjoyed it.

Q: I'm always under the impression that you guys are bugged incessantly to sit down and relive the old days?

TC: Not so much. (laughs) Obviously, the older you get the less hair you have, and gray hair arrives and people don't recognize you.

And you know, I'm more than fine with that, but I think I probably speak for a lot of guys you've spoken to, as well, a lot of guys have kind of sacred memories. Sometimes you don't just want to share it with anybody else. If you share them with somebody else who wasn't there and didn't to through it, it's just hard to understand.

Q: You've had to swallow some of the same dirt,the same grass, the mutual sweat to fully understand it?

TC: Yeah, you have to have a bar to measure it against, probably. I have more of these conversations when we get together with old teammates, and the guys that even came before us with Charlie and all that, swap stories.

Q: When it comes to Charlie, he was supposedly a great motivator. What was his key?

TC: You know, the thing that Coach McBride taught you from the second you sat in on his first meeting was that you had to play for each other and you had to play for the people around you that you loved: your teammates and your family. It was so true, and I can remember him giving his psyche-up speech, and he used to do it the night before the game. And I didn't know if anybody could sleep, Paul, so he changed it and started to do it the morning before the game.

And it grew from just the defensive line to the whole defense, and then pretty much everybody was in there and he's giving his psyche-up speech, and it was unbelievable. I don't think there was any key to it, it was just so genuine. It was what he had preached his entire coaching career. He didn't have to change anything. He just spoke from the heart. Man, I think back and I wish somebody had a tape recorder in there, because they were unbelievable. You felt like you could have walked out of that auditorium and ran through a wall.

Q: Sometimes in life a person needs a speech like that to start the day...

TC: You do. (laughs)

End conversation.

Listening to Terry makes me want to take on a brick wall somewhere just now. I wonder if anyone ever had the presence of mind to record some of Charlie McBride's speeches? If so, I'd like to package 'em up and sell them. We'd make a killing! I hope to talk with Charlie in the coming weeks. That is, if I can get the nerve up to do it, because you didn't want to mess with ol' Charlie, I tell you. He was one intimidating cat. Hopefully retirement has softened him up a little. That's my hope.

I thought it was pretty neat how Terry tied in the sense of community, the fan support, and the genuine caring of the Nebraska and Green Bay Packer coaching staffs as they both achieved great things in those years. It makes me wonder why some staffs out there try other methods to attain the same goal, usually failing. And tying into the Unity, Belief, Respect theme of the early 90's around Memorial Stadium and vicinity, notice how that word came up once more: Respect."I think the biggest similarity was just the way the coaches treated the players with respect, the caring." As these boys matured into young men it seemed that rather than wishing to be merely liked or admired by their coaches and peers, they came to seek out respect more than anything. It was not easily or quickly given, as Terry spoke of the first few fearful years of Coach McBride's tutelage: "Nothing is going to be given to you. You have to go out there and earn it. And earn it every day."

It was also pleasing to hear of Terry's honor and awe for Kenny Walker, "If anybody could make an excuse it would have been Kenny, and I never heard him make an excuse. It really was pretty inspirational to see a guy that had that handicap be such a great teammate, a great player. But Kenny was a guy that nobody outworked him. He was a pretty special guy." Call me a nut out on a limb, but I think this interview pretty much solidifies the extent to which previous year's upperclassmen affected these guys. It's one thing to watch some All-American cruising along on talent alone during his swan song of a season, but it's another to see him working, sweating, grinding, churning, striving for the brass ring each and every day, whether the stands are full with fans or not. Ralph Waldo Emerson once said, "In every man there is something wherein I may learn of him, and in that I am his pupil." Terry was, in that sense, an observant student in the buildup to the 60 & 3.

Finally, I believe it gave us an insight into the mindset of the yearning for excellence, of the refusal for complacency, of continuously reaching for grander accomplishments when Terry mentioned his most glaring memories of the time: "It seems like you almost remember the plays where you were unsuccesssful more than the plays where you were successful, the plays when you got beat or did something wrong and it costed you. That sticks in my mind as much as the good plays…" One word we rarely hear the players use is that of regret, come to think of it. But in this case, I can see where in not wanting to disappoint one's teammates or fail to bring honor to one's family, you'd want to have the perfect, mistake-free, dominate-your-opponent game each time out.

Notable quote #2:
Terry Connealy on the process leading to the 60 & 3: "…the thing that Coach McBride taught you from the second you sat in on his first meeting was that you had to play for each other and you had to play for the people around you that you loved: your teammates and your family."

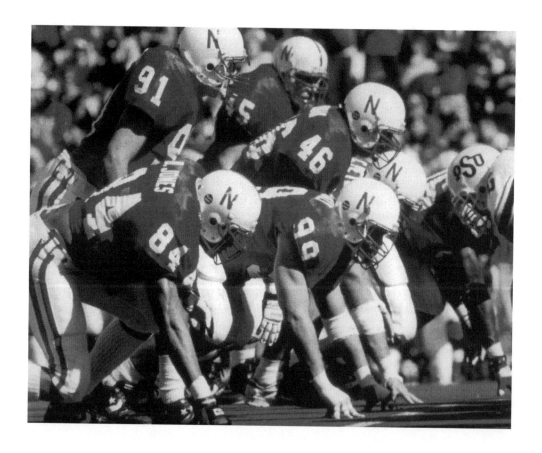

Sharing the limelight may mean working behind the scenes – in effect, not getting any "light" at all. Team players... handle a myriad of other things required for accomplishment of a team's task.

Glenn M. Parker, *Team Players and Teamwork,* 2008
(This material reproduced with permission of John Wiley & Sons, Inc.)

I've enjoyed every one of our conversations so far, but the one you're about to read is uniquely significant. Why? Well, I'm of the opinion that Tom Osborne is one of the more humble fellows you'll ever run across, which means that he's quite hesitant to talk about himself. Sure, he'll talk about his approach to life or his line of reasoning as to why he made choices in his career and such, but to really know the man, the leader, the visionary? It might be of benefit to ask someone who knows him in a more intimate way, someone who's spent many a day and year working for and with and alongside him.

Which brings us to his longtime secretary, Mary Lyn Wininger. Self-effacing and quite humble in her own right, Mary Lyn was a force in the coaches' offices, especially when it came to maneuvering and maintaining some sanity among the busied offensive staff of the day. Tag-teaming with Joni Duff (who handled the duties for the defensive staff), their assistance, wisdom, surefire stability and ever-present availability made the whole place hum.

Notable quote #1:
"...he cared about each one, whether it be the ones who were in trouble or the ones that weren't. He would try to be there for that person... I thought that really meant something, about making a difference for just that one. It says something about him."

Mary Lyn Wininger

Question: Thanks for making time for me, Mary Lyn.

Mary Lyn Wininger: You've gotten me fired up, Paul. I hear you're talking to all of these players and it brings back so many good memories. I hear you're trying to get ahold of the Peter brothers and the Mackovickas, too.

I remember one time -I think it was Jeff- his little brother was playing baseball against my son's team and the other team was winning by a very large margin. I saw Jeff there at the game and said, 'You know, it would be cool if you'd go to our dugout and just say 'hi' or something, because you're a bit of a celebrity around here, you know?' So he goes over to our dugout -my son's dugout- and gives them this little pep talk. Well, my son Thomas gets up and hits a grand slam and they won the game! (laughs) It was like, 'Oh, my gosh! It motivated them so much.' I laughed about that.'I don't think he will be doing that again.' It really motivated them, and all the players were like, "That was so cool!"

Q: It seems the concepts of "unity & caring" were very motivational for the football the program. Did you sense that, too?

MLW: Oh, definitely. And it started from Tom. He loved those players. Those were his kids and he would do anything for them. And in turn, those players would do anything for Tom.

Definitely. That was there and was very evident in all the battles he had to go through, whether it be trying to fight NCAA rules to Ernie Chambers. (laughs) The battles we had to fight… Ernie's heart was in the right place and he wanted to pay the athletes, but we couldn't: "It's an NCAA violation to do this. And it's the law, so that wouldn't work." Just funny little things like that.

But Tom, not only for the players but for the staff, he had such a strong faith. I guess that's what impressed me, as well, trying to be the father figure and still living his faith and living by example. People truly loved him. I learned so much from him and the program.

Q: So let me ask you, Mary Lyn, are you an original Nebraska girl?

MLW: Yep, I'm a Nebraska girl and I grew up in Auburn, Nebraska, which is where the Kelsay boys were from.

And I hate to tell this story, but I went to school at Johnson-Brock and my Basketball Coach was Jackie Kelsay, the mother of Chad and Chris. My senior year she was pregnant - and you know, I didn't quite keep track of that kind of thing- and she comes in to the football office one day and she brings Chad in… and here she was pregnant with Chad when I was in high school! And, oh my gosh, it made me feel really old. (laughs) Chad and I were really close and we really bonded, especially with the ties to Auburn. But I went to school at the university and had actually worked at the College of Agriculture.

Q: Over on East Campus?

MLW: Yes, I actually got an Associates Degree and felt like two years of school was enough, and went out to East Campus to work for the School of Agriculture. I had this not-too-exciting job. But anyway, one of my friends called and said, "Hey, there's an opening in the football office and it's Assistant to the Head Football Coach," but nobody she knew could apply because you had to know shorthand (which is no longer used anymore).

But that's how I got the job: because I knew shorthand. So on the last day that it was open they kind of dared me, because I'm like, 'I'm not looking for another job. What would my boss say?' and all this stuff. And they were, "You've got to at least try." So I put my name in and they called me the next day, to call me in for an interview. So I did, and just like that they offered me the job!

And then I had to go tell my boss, of course. And if it would have been anybody else they would have been mad, but they were like, "Oh, since you're gonna go work for Tom, alright." So they understood, so that was kind of cool. It was spread across campus; the whole university just had so much respect for him.

Q: What were you doing on East Campus?

MLW: I was working for the Dean of the College of Agriculture. It was entry level and I did a lot of computer input and worked with students and stuff like that. It was okay, but I was stuck in the back room doing computer input, which wasn't real exciting. But then I was presented with this great opportunity, so it was better than what I was doing.

Q: I can imagine you were probably stuffed in front of one of those old Apple2e's with a green screen and 3.5" floppy disks and all…

MLW: (laughs) Exactly! Yeah, that's what it was.

Q: Sounds like my first job at the Devaney Sports Center weightroom.

MLW: That's how you started?

Q: Yep, working under Bryan Bailey over there.

MLW: Do you still talk to him now?

Q: Oh yes, about every few weeks we talk. And by the way, he said to tell you 'hello.' He's still the workaholic that he always was.

MLW: I knew that. I'll bet those players at USC love him to death. Bryan and I were really close. I'll bet he hasn't gotten married yet, either. He was always working so hard, he never found time to find a wife. (laughs)

Q: So the job interview, were there any coaches in there for the interview?

MLW: It was just Tom. And I didn't even really have time to think about it, because it was such a whirlwind: "Can you come in?" I think they actually called that morning and I went in that afternoon for the interview. I'll always remember: I didn't have time to worry about what to wear because I didn't have time to change. I'll always remember going in there.

And when I walked out after they'd given me the job, Dave Rimington was sitting there at the time and he teased, "It's just your red hair that did it." (laughs) I'd like to think it was more than the red hair, but that was always his comment.

Q: Dave was a redhead, too, right?

MLW: He was, and then Tom, too. It was like there was this red-headed thing going on. But he was the only one in the interview, coaching-wise. I interviewed with some of the staff people that were there.

Q: So what year was this?

MLW: It was in '83 before the season started. My first season working there was Turner Gill and Irving Fryar and their senior year, so we went all season without losing and then in the bowl game, you know, we went for two and didn't make it. Yeah, that was my first year.

Q: So did you have a chance to get broken in before the games started?

MLW: I actually started in January. I got started before spring ball and all that, it must have been in January of that year. Dave Rimington was still around at that time.

Q: Do you recall your first day working there? Any peculiar happenings or impressions of how things operated?

MLW: The first days I worked there it was kind of odd, because it was recruiting season, so the coaches were gone a lot. It was really, at first, very intimidating, because you think about it: a little gal coming from Auburn, Nebraska and working for Coach Osborne.

And he dictated a bunch of letters, and I'm sitting there taking shorthand. And I don't know if you've done shorthand before, but you really have to concentrate on what you're writing, and my mind was like, 'Oh, my gosh! I'm in here with Coach Osborne'-type of thing. (laughs) So it was really hard to concentrate on what I was supposed to be writing because I was so in awe.

And he'd be there for a day and then recruit all week, and then he'd come in on Friday and we'd have recruiting visits that weekend and stuff. So I just remember it was so frantic until I really got to know him. And he's human like all of us, a super guy. But it was just the whole thought of, 'Oh, my gosh, this is really my job! I'm supposed to answer his phone and type his correspondence.' It was intimidating.

Q: Did you call him 'Tom'?

MLW: Yeah, I did.

Q: Did it take awhile to get accustomed to that?

MLW: Well, actually it didn't. And this is probably bad -because everybody teaches their kids "Mr. this and Mrs. that"- but down in small-town Nebraska you called everybody by their first name. Mom and Dad were farmers and we didn't do much of the high society things, calling people Mister and such, and when he said, "Call me Tom," I was like, 'Okay,' because he gave me permission to do it.

I didn't just start calling him 'Tom.' He could tell I wasn't quite sure and he said, "Just call me Tom." So I did. When I think about it now, he probably deserved so much more than that. But knowing him as a person, he wasn't like that. He wanted to just be 'Tom.'

Q: Forget the titles?

MLW: He wasn't into titles. I always remember when I was typing this one book. I typed 'On Solid Ground' for him, and it was the second book he wrote. The first book I was involved with, but not as much as the second book. The second book he'd give me these little audiotapes and I'd type them up and work on editing them and such. Then I'd send them to Gordon Thiesen (who also was a former player) and then he would edit it as well, and we kind of worked together on it.

And I'll always remember Gordon coming in at the end -and in the foreword part Tom said, "I want to thank my Secretary, MaryLyn Wininger." And Gordon said, "Are you sure you want to put the word 'Secretary' there?" And the look on Tom's face was like, "Well, what else would I call her?" Titles are nothing to him, no 'Administrative Assistant' or that kind of thing, he didn't get wrapped up in that part of it.

Q: Some puffed up name, like the term 'custodial engineer' referring to a janitor?

MLW: Exactly. You know, he just respected you for how you did and you didn't have to have a big title to impress him. That wasn't a big deal to him. He was just a down to earth person, which I respected. But I just remember that conversation, he was like, "What's wrong with the word 'Secretary'?" (laughs)

Q: What time did you usually begin your workday?

MLW: It was usually 8 o'clock in the morning and sometimes we had summer hours, 7:30-ish or whatever. And then it always wasn't a regular end of the day at a certain time. If there was work to be done you did it. You did it, and that happened a lot with football and the different seasons, but you enjoyed it. It was the coaches who stayed so many hours above and beyond what we did as a staff. We really couldn't complain, because look what they did. It was, 'Okay, I can do this.' But it was fun.

And one thing I appreciated, too, was the openness of it. I remember that we were allowed to go over and lift weights in the weightroom, in the "Weenie Lane," we called it. (laughs) It was the room in the back that had the little weights, and we always felt special because we felt they were for us, where we'd take all the weights off and just lift the bar. We felt it was our own little room where we would come and work out.

Q: That's too funny. So let's say it's in-season: what about those in-season days? Were there not enough hours in the day to get everything done?

MLW: There were a lot of days like that, but you made it happen. Because I did the offense. Joni Duff did defense and I did offense, because Tom was the Offensive Coordinator. I did, basically, like everyday we'd have a practice schedule. And for two-a-days the coaches would all go in and decide what they were going to be doing. (And they started out with a chalkboard and they ended up with the greaseboard) But anyway, they would write the offense up and the defensive coaches would come in and write the defenses up there. And then myself and Joni would go in there with our laptops and would type them and then we'd print them out for practices and stuff. I got to do that and I got to be involved in putting together the offensive playbook, too. Not that I designed any plays.(laughs)

Q: Come on, Mary Lyn, you were the brains behind the Fumblerooskie all this time. Admit it! (laughs)

MLW: I wish I could take credit for that. (laughs) No, I didn't, but it was fun just to be part of it, because I knew the computer program. They would do the drawings and I would take it and put it in the computer with the little plays and which way they could block and run and the description of the play and stuff like that. So you always felt like you were a part of it. I loved to be behind the scenes, because I'm not a person who likes to get up and do public speaking. Interviews were very hard for me, so don't put anything 'dorky' in the book, okay? (laughs)

And the progam we used to draw the plays up was, I think, called 'Playmaker.'

Q: Like AutoCAD for football?

MLW: Something like that. And back in the 90's people didn't use computers that much, especially the guys like Tom there. He was so busy trying to design plays. He'd be working on plays, probably sitting at a restaurant and drawing x's an o's on a napkin, and he'd bring them back to me. He didn't have to bother with that. He was the genius behind the plays and I just felt honored that I could be part of it, you know, and put it in the playbook.

Q: You would actually get napkins from him?

MLW: Well, I didn't get them at that point, but I did see him doodling. If you ever looked at his deskpad after he was talking on the phone or doing interviews or whatever, there would always be plays on his pad. It just makes sense: he lived and breathed football.

Q: And not to besmirch his reputation, but I always had the feeling that Coach Osborne, if he had his druthers, he wouldn't even have done media interviews, no? It always seemed as if press conferences and that type of thing were just so far down on his priority list. Would that be true?

MLW: Well, yeah. And that was probably the case just because he felt like he could spend his time better coaching the team, which is what his job was. And when you look at it that way, he's expected to come up with results and have a great team, and for him to do that you need to be drawing plays, you need to be with your coaches trying to figure out what works and what doesn't, what players are here and who you need to recruit. There are so many things a coach has to think about.

Q: It's not just those three hours on the sideline on Saturday…

MLW: Definitely not.

Q: The older I get, Mary Lyn, the more apparent it becomes to me that to be at the apex of one's profession, like that coaching staff was, you have to have an almost obsessiveness that is beyond most people's rational thought. Including yourself, I hope this book exposes just how dedicated everyone was to achieve that dominance.

MLW: But I'm such a small little part of that, though. It took a bunch of small, little parts to make it what it was, when you look at it that way.

I even remember they did that documentary thing about Tom and they interviewed the janitor, and Tom had a way of making the janitor feel important. He would talk to them on the way in and out, he just had a way of making everybody feel like part of the team. And I think that's why he was so successful, because I would have done anything that he had asked, just to try to make it work, you know? Whether it be working hours upon hours, but I think everybody felt that way. The players respected him so much.

Q: Did you sense a servanthood-type of mindset and a selflessness exhibited by Tom in these kids' lives?

MLW: Yes, exactly. And it was all in a positive way. I just remember he told us the story once about somebody walking along an ocean beach -and I can't remember it exactly- but a story about all these tiny sea creatures washing up on the sand, like a crab or something like that, and the guy would pick some up one by one and throw them back in. But there were thousands of them along the seashore! And somebody asked the man, "Why do you do this? There are so many of them. Why would it make a difference?" And the man said, "Well, it means all the difference for this one." I've thought about that so often, because he cared about each one, whether it be the ones who were in trouble or the ones that weren't. He would try to be there for that person. And maybe it's an endless thing, but if he can help this one here and that one there, you know? I thought that really meant something, about making a difference for just that one. It says something about him.

Q: And I'm sure along with that mindset came the frustration of going into the living rooms of some kids throughout the years, kids who were in abhorrent conditions like the nastier, drug- and gang-infested, inner-city environments, and seeing how you could completely turn some kid's life around by persuading him to come to a place like Nebraska, only to lose them to another school that may not have had that type of fostering attitude. Do you think that made those 'fish that got away' occasions that much more painful to him on a personal level?

MLW: Yeah, because you feel like you could be there for them. And he was involved in the Fellowship of Christian Athletes and we'd do so many chapel services, like every time we went to a bowl game that was one of his focuses: a church service on Sunday for the players and the families.

And before each game we would arrange to have chapel service either the morning of the game or the night before, depending on what time the game was, but he definitely tried to instill in them a solid foundation going forward. So he not only taught them football, and the academics come from football, but also show them how important God was in his life and that kind of thing. I always respected him for that, too.

Q: Which brings me to this question: From the first day you worked for Coach Osborne to the last, how would you say he rubbed off on you? Did he rub off on you?

MLW: Oh yeah! I learned so much from him. Just by watching him, he was such a good example in all aspects of what he did.

Q: Any one, specific thing stand out?

MLW: One thing: not only was he a hard worker (which is a great thing to learn, because I do think I learned that a lot from him, and to this day I work hard at what I do. I think a lot of that comes from that), but he took time. And I'll always appreciate that. You know, Thomas, my son, he was born on Tom's birthday, February 23rd.

Q: Is it any coincidence his name is Thomas? (laughs)

MLW: No, and that's the whole thing! There was an article in the paper, this big writeup with my picture in the paper. An Omaha writer, I can't remember who was the ornery one behind that -it might have been Lee Barfknecht- but Thomas's great grandfather is Thomas Wininger, and we planned on naming a son Thomas, anyway, and his due date was the 13th of February. Well, anyway, the morning of the 23rd, that day I was going to take a fruit salad to work for Tom for his birthday, because we would always celebrate birthdays (and he ate healthy). Everybody usually brought cake and everything but I was going to bring something healthy, and that morning I realized I wasn't going to make it to work. I was like, 'Oh no, of all days!' I'll always remember riding on the way to the hospital to give birth and saying, 'Well, can we stop by the stadium football office to drop the fruit salad off?' (laughs) Like, 'Will Tom be able to eat?' (laughs)

Of course, I didn't get to do that because I had to get to the hospital. But then Tom and Nancy came that night to the hospital and visited with us on his birthday. And it just meant a lot to me that he would take time out to do something like that. And later he took Thomas fishing and different things like that that I really appreciated, because he wouldn't have had to have done that. That will always mean a lot for my kids, that he took the time to notice them and come and talk to them.

Q: I was going to ask what it was like having two children along with the calamity involved with the job? Did you take a few weeks' maternity leave or something?

MLW: Yeah, I took the normal six weeks like we could. And I'm sure I came in during that time and did a little work or something, but it almost made you feel guilty to take time off. And I guess I didn't like that part of it. Tom always kind of joked, "Why do you need six weeks?" (laughs) He used to joke about that.

Q: Kind of like, "Coach, you pop out a football and see if you can come back the next day?" (laughs)

MLW: Exactly. Because you never missed work. Nobody ever seemed to be sick on the coaching staff, because they were always there. I don't ever remember, other than the time Tom had his open heart surgery he did take a little time off, but not a lot. They just always seemed to be there.

And one time I looked at the days I'd missed, other than giving birth to my two childrern, and I think it was 3 days in the last 5 years. And Tom remarked about me not being there, and I thought about it for while and came to the realization, 'Aw, he missed me. (laughs) He really does want me there!'

Q: I'm sure one day of your not being around slowed him down immensely. And I have to say, you were speaking of his propensity to spend time with so many people earlier, which reminds me of a gentleman I know: Alan Roth out in El Cajon, CA, who owned a muffler shop. One day Alan presented me a letter that he'd received from Coach Osborne just a few weeks after the '94 Orange Bowl loss to Florida State, and in the letter he shared a thank you for the support and how the team played very well but somehow wasn't able to gain the victory, and how he thought the upcoming year's team could be a pretty good team, too. Well, it just occurred to me that you were probably the person who typed that letter from Tom's dictation and sent it! (laughs) Did he always have such an open door policy with fans like he did the players?

MLW: He probably responded to the gentleman's letter, you're right. Tom answered those letters, whether it be fan mail or whatever. For the most part we attempted -we tried to answer the correspondence that came in, and some of them obviously were form letters-but it was from him and he would dictate them and I'd type them and send them out. But he felt like that was important. And it is.

You know, the fans were so important to that program, even moreso than I realized at the time. But that was part of my job: an enjoyable part of my job was to protect him, and a way of doing that would be when sometimes people would come to the offices with little kids I'd say to them, 'Would you like to go see the field?' and I'd take them down there and take a football and they'd throw it around. And just the look on their faces?! I'd even have people come up years later and say, "Remember when you took my son down there?" And I did that so often (and you don't always remember all of them), but I'd sometimes say, 'Yeah.' But I remember taking people down there and it was good public relations for the program... and at the same time was able to allow time for Tom to do his work.

It was kind of the way of making the fans feel like they were a part of it, too. They were able to come up, and we had the National Championship trophys there right outside of Tom's office, and they could walk up and look at the trophies. It was probably too open. (laughs) I've never seen another football office like that. I'd go visit other football offices if I'd go traveling, going in to see what it was like, looking at their setup and trying to get ideas and such. But anyway, these people could come up and just be part of it, and I think that's why we have such awesome fans, because they truly feel like it's their team, that they're a part of it. And they are. Tom has a way of making everybody feel like they are part of the team, like they each have a part to play.

Q: Now, I asked if he rubbed off on you. I have to know if you think you rubbed off on him at all?

MLW: Oh, I doubt it. (laughs) I don't know if there was anything I could have taught him.

Q: When I recently interviewed him I asked him how he had improved from his early coaching days to his latter ones and his answer was that he'd become a better listener.

MLW: I think he did learn, but not that he learned that from me. That's interesting he would say that, because I could see that. That makes sense.

Q: I left the question very open-ended for him, too, because he could have talked about the evolution of the spread offense, about some x's and o's type of thing, but it was his listening skills that he felt the strongest about. I was extremely taken with his answer.

MLW: And he had to do that. I always remember one of those things that I still use to this day -because of the people I work with at my job now- and it was his, "There is always this side of the story and then the other person's side of the story, and the truth is somewhere in between those two." And he would say that a lot. He would do a lot of research to get to the bottom of whatever he was working on. He'd repeat that: "The truth is somewhere in between the two." He did a lot of sorting out of things now and then, with Lawrence and Riley and Tyrone, too.

Q: Were those times really hard on him?

MLW: They were very hard on him, because he cared about them as people and not necessarily as football players, but as a friend. He genuinely cared about each player. And to see somebody struggle like that? It's hard, because you try to do what you can but sometimes it's beyond your control. I don't know the best way to word that, but I just want to get across that he definitely cared about each person and was always trying to make them a better person.

That's what was so frustrating with the media. It was frustrating to watch what the media would do. They would take little bits and pieces and then it wasn't always factual, and when people pick up a paper they just assume that it's all correct, and sometimes those stories didn't come across as they really were.

Q: That's very interesting you would say that, Mary Lyn, because it was later on in my education that I finally came to the realization that just because something is in a book doesn't necessarily mean that it's true. (laughs) That was an epiphany for me. I guess I was a little naïve to think that anything in print was somehow vetted or verified to be of a truthful nature, you know?

MLW: And a lot of people don't realize that. And until you really see that, it's an eye-opening thing. Those players would do something that any other college person would do and not get in trouble for it and not get brought up, but they were in a fishbowl and they had to always set a good example. They were always expected to do that. And for college students, you've got to admire them for what they had to go through.

Q: Do you think some of these players often felt pressure because of that, at a mere 17-20 years of age?

MLW: They kind of knew that was expected of them, because if you are an athlete you have all these kids that look up to you, and if you're recruited you kind of know that that's what you have to do.

But yet, you're a college-aged student. And I don't want it to come across the wrong way, but you do have all the kids that look up to you and the notoriety, as well. So that's what they knew was expected of them.

Q: In other words, you may get a better seat in a local restaurant, but the flipside is that everybody is going to be watching your every move while you're in that seat, huh?

MLW: Yeah…

Q: And they'll be watching to see if you're a good tipper, too! (laughs)

MLW:(laughs) Exactly. Or coming up and asking for your autograph.

Q: Just when you have a mouthful of Valentino's Pizza or something?

MLW: Yeah. It always amazed me. You know, Tom used to take us out for Secretary's Day and that kind of thing, and people would just kind of stare at you. He'd be sitting there with this table of people who worked for him and they'd come up and ask for an autograph as we were sitting there eating. And he'd just sign it and smile. He was just used to it.

Q: Where would you go to eat on occasions like that?

MLW: Oh, it would depend. Different places. We would try different places downtown. He'd usually ask us where we wanted to go and we'd pick different places. It was always something with halfway healthy food if we wanted him to eat with us. Just a variety of places. He was always good about that kind of thing.

Q: I was going to ask: did you ever need to kind of be his fail-safe so he didn't forget wedding anniversaries, birthdays, things like that?

MLW: I kept a calendar. (laughs) We'll put it that way: we had a calendar. Say no more. (laughs)

Q: And obviously, you were probably a guardian in seeing some nasty mail and that type of stuff arrive, too, right?

MLW: Yeah, unfortunately. But surprisingly, even after that first year I worked there and he went for two? Well, they had those Postal Service baskets, I don't know why but they called them 'FREDS' or something like that. They would bring in one of those every day – completely full- I don't know how many days after that game, and that's how much mail we would get. And out of those (and I tried to keep track: I'd take it home at night and I'd open them as I was sitting at home, just because there was so much mail! To open it took forever!), but out of those there was probably one in two hundred to three hundred letters that would be negative. All the other ones of those would be positive: "We would have done the same thing. We admire your decision." And so there wasn't a lot of negative mail, which was interesting, too.

Q: I have to say, Mary Lyn, I was a freshman in high school and I was profoundly affected by that two point attempt.

MLW: Really?

Q: Yes, I think many people in the state of Nebraska learned a lesson from that historic play call. It made me realize that it's always about more than winning: you're there for a purpose, you put it all on the line, you have to be willing to take chances and stick to your guns, your principles. Maybe it was just me, but I think that had a profound effect on my worldview and goal-setting and personal accountability.

MLW: Yeah, and I think it did a lot of people. It made you sit back and think, 'Hey, we could tie this and win the national champimship that year.' But it is more than that. Hopefully that touched more lives. That's interesting you say that.

Q: Let me tell you, after I left the University I traveled the United States extensively with the Famous San Diego Chicken and I'd run into people from all walks of life -even those who knew next to little about college football- but whenever folks found out I was from Nebraska they would bring up Coach Osborne and his going for two and how much respect they had for him doing that."Oh, Nebraska? Tom Osborne. That's the guy who went for two." And they'd say it with reverence and respect and an admiration. That was a great moment in television history, in Nebraska history, if you ask me.

MLW: And then he never regretted it. Even though we didn't make it, he came out later and said, "I would still have done the same thing."

Q: And what, twelve years later, finally, in that same end zone going for two and tying it up and then beating Miami? A dozen years of clawing to make it a success, you know? Which brings me to ask: do you have a favorite game?

MLW: Well, I went to all the home games.

And gosh, it would have started in '91, I guess it was, the first year my daughter was born was the first year that they started taking the staff along to bowl games. Before that I heard that the players' wives and stuff would sometimes type the practice schedules and they would kick in and come. And finally the staff needed to go, as well, because we have these practice schedules and we'd have all that stuff we needed to do. So from that year on we got to be part of the team. We got to be on the team plane and got to bring our families, and we set up an office. So we got to go to all the bowl games.

Q: Do you have a most memorable road trip?

MLW: I probably liked the Phoenix one, the Fiesta Bowl we won after the '95 season. It would have been Christian Peter and those guys.

I remember my folks came to that game. They live in Auburn and they caught a ride out there to the Fiesta Bowl and got to go to the game. And a lot of the players go home directly from the bowl game and then there are empty seats on the plane, so I brought my folks back on the team plane. And that was always just so special to me. My mom and dad had never flown before.

But anyway, when we came back it was just amazing, because there were all these people lined up on the streets from the airport to the Devaney Center! It was just amazing the number of people who turned out for that, and the look on my parents' face taking a part in all of that? And then going to the Devaney Center and being totally full of people? Some people were turned away and they were standing outside because they couldn't even get into the Devaney Center. My son Thomas was pretty young, and I'll always remember Christian Peter was so excited, he picked him up and my mom took his picture. And to this day we have this huge picture of Christian Peter holding Thomas. And they both were just smiling! It was so cool. So that is probably my favorite. There were a lot of them. But the whole thing? That whole trip just worked out so well.

Q: That leads me to ask if there were any players you got to know better than others, who stand out to you from those days?

MLW: There are a lot of them that stand out, especially the ones who would take time to stop by.

One who was very special to me, (and I have a daughter named Brooke and a son named Thomas- so when Tommie and Brook were quarterbacks that year, you know, that was always kind of neat) I remember Brook always used to come in my office and I'd have a Rock station on my radio, and he'd always come in and turn it to Country.(laughs) I'd go,'Brook!'(laughs) It was just his thing. He liked country and he would always mess with my radio. And now, to this day, I like Country. And I can give him credit for that. (laughs) So that's kind of cool.

And I don't mean for this book to be about me, though, because it's about the players. But I remember that bowl game because I have pictures of Brooke with Brook and Thomas with Tommie. I just always thought that was kind of neat. Brook was awesome and his family was so awesome, and that was such a tragic thing.

Q: I'd moved out here to San Diego only about a month before the plane crash happened, Mary Lyn, and I arrived home and turned on ESPN and saw the news. I recall just sitting there all alone on my couch, dumbstruck. I just sat and cried.

MLW: That whole thing with having the FCA Banquet that night and the poster of a little kid wearing a number 18 jersey? (Because that was Brook's number.) It was unfortunate. He was always special.

But there are so many, I couldn't even start to name them all: The Peter boys, the Makovicka boys and the Kelsays, and it goes back to the Stan Parkers. And I still talk to Mike Rozier. Sometimes he'll just call out of the blue if he's gonna be in town. It's just fun.

Q: Mike was kind of a joker, no?

MLW: Oh yeah, he was the ornery one. He would park in the parking spaces he wasn't supposed to.

Q: Coach Osborne's space?

MLW: I can't remember. One time he parked in Tom's space or Bob Devaney's, but he would always park where he wasn't supposed to and he'd come up in the office and he'd smile. (laughs) Mike was so ornery. And to watch all those guys together was something.

And I know there's always talk about the Scoring Explosion, but another one was Neil Harris, who also played that year. And he came down from Lincoln to Brooke's graduation in May, I guess it was. And he just always kind of kept in touch. He coached Brooke in basketball when we lived in Lincoln and Brooke played on the select team for him, and he'd always had a special affinity for Brooke and followed her and her volleyball team's success. And I just thought that was so cool that Neil Harris would come down here to the graduation party, so it is kind of like a family. You keep in touch with those guys, it's awesome.

Q: Like most any family, I'm sure there were some days the coaches didn't quite get along with each other all the time. Where there ever any coaches who took losses harder than others?

MLW: Well, you always wished for a win, because it made the next week happier. It's always easier. (laughs)

Q: Could you tell before the Oklahoma game? Was it usually a different kind of a week, from your perspective?

MLW: I think the coaches tried to make each game just another game, because that's so important for the players. If there was (there probably was a little bit), but they definitely tried to hide that. But the whole thing is the consistency and keeping things going each week the same way to get into a routine.

Q: Keep things on an even keel and in a groove, so to speak?

MLW: You'd very seldom hear the coaches raising their voice, and if they did the player deserved it. (laughs) A few 'dadgummits' from Tom, but not very many. But they deserved it when there was a dadgumit.

Q: Anything other than a dadgumit?

MLW: Oh, no. That was all. It was no cursing or anything, at least from Tom's perspective. That's what I would hear, because I was in the office by him there.

Q: Was there another secretary who assisted the other offensive coaches?

MLW: I assisted the offensive staff and Joni Duff would take the general calls and assist the defensive staff. She did the equivalent of what I did for offense. She did the defensive practice schedules, the defensive notebook and game plan and all that stuff, as well.

Q: Were you happy you worked for offense rather than the defensive end of it? In talking to Terry Connealy, he mentioned that to be a defensive coach it helped to have a screw loose...

MLW: (laughs) Yeah, I'm very glad I worked for offense. (laughs) I got along with the defensive coaches, too, though.

Q: Any personalities stick out to you? As far as being unique people?

MLW: I actually started working there at around the same time Frank did. When he started as the freshman coach we worked closely, since he ran the football school. He was the head person and I did the bookwork, so Frank and I kind of went through it and assisted at the same time. And I totally admire him, as well, and Tom picked him for a reason. He deserves respect, too. Tom picked him. Tom knew so much about football, and Frank did an awesome job the years he was there. He needs to get a little recognition and I appreciate that Bo's given him that.

Q: When was your last year there?

MLW: Frank got fired and then I worked with Bo during that bowl game, and then they hired Bill. So I worked with Bill through spring ball and through football school and stuff like that, and then I ended up I couldn't do a full football season. But now I'm happy that they're all back, so I want to forget those years. Tom's back and Bo's back, so I'm happy again.

Q: Well, Mary Lyn, I am so thankful that you've given me your time. We've spent more than an hour here.

MLW: Wow! Have we been on that long? I just wish to say, please make this whole book be about the players and what's important, okay?

Q: Sure thing. And I probably told you this earlier, but I always ask the players and coaches to give me the name of somebody who did a tremendous job behind the scenes, and your name was brought up, so I simply had to profile you. It was an off-the-record interview so I can't divulge the individual, but he mentioned you and Joni specifically. So I'm very appreciative of your time and your service, Mary Lyn. Do you have any parting shots before we end our time here?

MLW: Just to never lose sight of your goals. That's one thing that Coach Osborne really taught me: every week they would set goals. And they'd go over them every week whether they made them or not, marking them either black or red.

And his faith? That's everything. Just don't lose faith in what you're trying to accomplish in the end. Never lose that focus.

End conversation.

"Never lose that focus." Funny, but from Mary Lyn's interview you get the feeling that the main focus wasn't entirely on football. It's almost as if Coach Osborne was using his position as springboard to serving as a guardian, caretaker, father, mentor-like figure to as many young men as humanly possible and, "Oh, by the way, let's prepare to win some football games while we're at it." I find this extremely admirable and very motivational, as it provided the entire athletic department staff with a greater sense of purpose. Even if you won 'em all, what does that matter if you didn't win the kids' hearts and set them on life's way?

Mary Lyn's retelling of Tom's parable about each individual human being's worthiness kind of summed it up for me, too, when the man questioned, *""Why do you do this? There are so many of them. Why would it make a difference?"* And the man said, *"Well, it means all the difference for this one."* ...I thought that really meant something, about making a difference for just that one. It says something about him.""* When you think of Kevin Ramaekers from his earlier interview, about Tommie Frazier, about Brook Berringer, about Riley Washington, Tyrone Williams, Christian Peter, Lawrence Phillips, Scottie Baldwin and hundreds more, Tom Osborne valued every person and the worth they possessed beyond the realm of any football field. That's what made him a coach and a leader rather than an egomaniac and tyrant, which happens to many a high profile college coach. It also made him lean heavily on his faith in Jesus Christ. He needed that faith during 1995, and then some.

Notable quote #2:

Mary Lyn Wininger on Tom Osborne's inclusionary leadership: "He just had a way of making everybody feel like part of the team. And I think that's why he was so successful."

National Champions
1970
1971

Big 8 Conference Champions
1963	1978
1964	1981
1965	1982
1966	1983
1969	1984
1970	1988
1971	1991
1972	1992
1975	1993

Orange Bowl
1955	1982
1964	1983
1966	1984
1971	1989
1972	1992
1973	1993
1979	1994

Cotton Bowl
1965
1974
1980

Sugar Bowl
1967
1974
1985
1987

Fiesta Bowl
1975
1986
1988
1990

Sun Bowl
1969
1980

Rose Bowl
1941

Astro-Bluebonnet Bowl
1976

Liberty Bowl
1977

Citrus Bowl
1991

March 11, 1994

Allan Roth
Valley Muffler Shop
533 W. Main St.
El Cajon, CA 92020

Dear Allan:

    Thanks so much for writing. I am sorry I am slow in responding, but I am just getting to my correspondence after the recruiting season.

    We were pleased with the effort put forth by our players, but we were disappointed with the outcome of the game.

    We should have a good team next year and hope very much that you continue to support our team.

Best wishes,

Tom

Tom Osborne
Head Football Coach

mlw

UNIVERSITY OF NEBRASKA
NEBRASKA FOOTBALL, 217 South Stadium, P.O. Box 880125, Lincoln, Nebraska 68588-0125   TOLL FREE: 800-6BIGRED

FAX 402/472-8877
402/472-3116

Be a yardstick of quality. Some people aren't used to an environment where excellence is expected.

Steve Jobs

In his '99 travel tome *The Distance to the Moon*, James Morgan writes, "The Nebraska plains pack a cumulative power... and I knew that if the sun were out today the heat would already be unbearable. Nebraska in summer is like living in perpetual noon... The trains, Union Pacific, kept rumbling by -I counted six of them in less than an hour- and each little town I passed through (Lexington, Cozad, Gothenburg) had its own tin-roofed elevator by the tracks." I liked his descriptive choice of words, especially the 'cumulative power' part. They bring to mind the brunt opposing defenders took after successive series' against the cumulative power of those 60 & 3 offensive lines.

One of the diesels steadfastly churning up the turf yard by green yard was guard Chris Dishman, the Cozad Collosus. Joining his teammates on many a sticky, sultry, summer afternoon workout in the perpetual noon of a Lincoln steambath, he laid down track and rolled into history as a punishing piston on one of the most dominant rushing lines in college history, the '95 edition of the Pipeline, and spent some years doing the same in the NFL ranks. Let's catch up with 'Dish' now.

Notable quote #1:
"Trying to pace yourself was not an option. You always pushed yourself to the limit that you think your body couldn't take it anymore, and then you pushed it a little bit further. That's what I learned from those guys. We would run a practice and that was 120-some plays. Basically two games."

Chris Dishman

Scholarship recruit, Offensive Tackle, Cozad, Nebraska
Where are they now? Garland, Nebraska, Financial Advisor/Coach

Question: Hey Dish, when was your freshman year at Nebraska?

Chris Dishman: My first year was '92.

Q: Did you know many guys when you first arrived on campus?

CD: Yeah, I knew Brendan Holbein, who was my teammate in high school. Ryan Terwilliger was from Grant, Nebraska out west, and Jeff Ogard. And I'd played with Damon Benning and Clinton Childs and those guys in the Shrine Bowl, but other than that it was just showing up to camp.

Q: You and Brendan were in the same high school class?

CD: Yeah, we were team captains. We were the State High School Champions in Class B.

Q: So you aleady knew a little success, eh?

CD: Yeah, we played pretty well. I think he was the all-time leading rusher in the state of Nebraska for a few years. He averaged almost 3,000 yards his senior year.

Q: Running behind you, I take it?

CD: We actually had a pretty decent line in Cozad. We had a couple guys: one went to Wyoming, another to a smaller school in Nebraska. So three of us went on to play college football.

Q: So it's your first day of fall camp. What stood out to you most?

CD: You know, it was run like a business. You basically showed up and you knew what to expect and they mapped it out. Pretty cut and dried as to what was going to happen. It wasn't like high school where you just kind of show up and you kind of figure it out over time. Everything was written down and done to a schedule. I remember it was a smooth transition when you looked at the schedule and you knew what was going to happen next.

Q: Were you on the last freshman team?

CD: Well, yes and no. Actually, when I was a redshirt freshman I was still rotating with Lance Lundberg and Zach Weigert at the tackle position with the ones, so I actually didn't make it down to the scout teams. I redshirted that year, but for some reason Coach Tenopir kept me up there to run with the big boys. I always remember looking across the field and seeing all my friends and roommates getting their butts kicked on the scout team. (laughs) And here I'm sitting on my helmet across the field from them. (laughing)

With Lundberg and Weigert and Zatehcka? They never wanted breaks, so I just had to basically sit on my helmet. And when they said they needed a blow for water I just jumped in there for one play before they came back.

Q: Was it a pretty easy transition for you stepping up to the next level, then?

CD: I don't know if it was an easy transition. But with football, the x's and o's always seemed pretty easy to me. And that helped me out when I went to the pros, too. It wasn't that I was so much more physically gifted than anybody: it was that I mentally understood the game, the concepts behind the plays, the philosophy of what they wanted to get done. I think that's what helped me out, I guess.

And it was kind of a complex system with all the shifts and motions that Osborne did. It was complex to a point, I guess. Once you got it it was so simple, you know? But learning it at first? People don't understand all the complex shifts and motions and what Coach Osborne was trying to get accomplished when he was doing that.

Q: Have you had a chance to read Coach Tenopir's book?

CD: No, I haven't read that.

Q: I told him a few weeks ago that I was going to do a little homework by reading his book in advance of our interview, and the cheapest I could find one online was $90. Which tells me that the coaches who own it consider it pure gold since they're not reselling it very cheaply, you know what I mean?

CD: Right! It was very efficient. From the blocking schemes to the fullback to the I-back to what everybody did, everyone in the whole system had a part and they had it broken down in detail to what each one individual had to get done to make the play work.

It just showed what kind of assistant coaches Coach Osborne had, too. They were all part of that whole process; we'd work on our individual position drills first and then we'd put our product together on the fields when we'd come together, and it would all work so well. Even though we'd be working on the same plays apart from each other up to that point - working on different aspects of the same play- things seemed to work out. It was pretty cool when it all came together.

Q: So Chris, you went to Arizona to play pro ball, right?

CD: Yes. I played seven years in Arizona and one year with the Rams.

Q: What about Coach Young and Coach Tenopir? What would you say about their teaching and coaching methods?

CD: I just remember the times that we spent with them: Coach Tenopir was more of a fiery guy and Coach Young was more of a laid back kind of coach. Coach Tenopir'd get so riled up right before gametime... he'd get so pumped up right before the Saturday speech right before the game, and we'd be ready to run through a wall for him. He wouldn't share a whole lot of emotion, he was more of a stern kind of guy. But you knew when he wanted to get something accomplished: his voice would start cracking and he'd have that chew sticking out of his lip. (laughs) What I remember most about Coach Tenopir was the Saturday morning meetings over in the Nebraska Center and all the O-line was in their own room, and he'd get up to give us a motivational speech. He always got us fired up to go play and kick some heads in.

Q: Do you recall how the typical speech would go?

CD: You know, that's the bad part. I try to think back and just remember the feeling. I don't remember the words he used or anything like that, I just remember the feeling in the room and the dead silence among us and all of that. I probably got hit in the head too many times. (laughing) I talk to some of the guys and they remember everything, and here I don't even remember the plays sometimes.

Q: A lot of guys compare and contrast Milt and Charlie McBride. Would you say that Milt was like the offensive 'Charlie,' so to speak? He'd get a little more fired up than most?

CD: Oh yeah. Those two were the ringleaders when we went down to the pit. Down there in the pit where we did the one-on-one blocks and stuff like that? Those guys were the instigators. They knew there were gonna be fights that broke out there and they knew Coach Osborne wasn't going to be down there. It was pretty much 'anything goes' down there.

Q: Pure, unadulterated combat?

CD: Oh, definitely. It was combat. And I don't know if this is true, but I heard the coaches even used to bet with each other about who would get into the first fight. It would be a six pack or a roll of chew. (laughs)

Q: I'm thinking they were putting their bets on Christian Peter?

CD: They bet on Christian and Jason! (laughs)

Q: In your early years, who would you usually go against in practice?

CD: My early years, I remember the first time I did one-on-ones in practice it was against Trev Alberts. Right away, right out of the gate, my first one-on-one. I had a run block on him and actually came off and actually stood him up and got him right there at the line of scrimmage. I got the best of him.

And then Charlie just ripped into him and they told me to get back on the O-line, and "We're gonna do it over again." And the first thing that hit the ground was the back of my helmet. He just ran right through me the next time. That was my introduction to one-on-ones. I got him the first time, but the second time wasn't so good.

Q: There wasn't much time to gloat over your victories down there in the pit, eh?

CD: No, not at all. You win some and you lose some. (laughs)

Q: Now, was Coach Samuel down there because Trev was?

CD: Oh yeah, Coach Samuel was down there."Hey, Chief." (laughs)

Q: What about Coach Dan Young, where did he fit in the mix?

CD: He was kind of our Passing Coordinator for Nebraska and when we were in our prime I think we threw 20 times the whole year, so the passing game wasn't a big focus.

But I remember vividly the meetings when Coach Young would say stuff in there. His passing technique went like, "This isn't AT&T. You don't have to reach out and touch somebody." (laughs) He'd make comments like that, and then if we had to pick up a linebacker he'd say stuff like, "It's like the free spot in Bingo. If you want to take him, take him. If you don't want to take him, don't take him." (laughs) That was like his passing techniques to us. It was kind of funny. Things like that stick out in my head.

Coming from Nebraska and going on to the NFL, the passing technique that we learned at Nebraska was totally different than what you learned in the NFL. (laughs) But we didn't have to pass block because if you're getting 6 yards a play on the ground with a carry, why would you think about throwing it?

Q: And even if we did it was usually play action, so it wasn't like the pocket was getting pressured on a 7-step drop?

CD: Exactly. It was more like an option pass.

Q: What about your interactions with Coach Osborne?

CD: You know Coach Osborne still -as old as I get?- is still the same guy. He still has the same respect factor, the dad factor. It's kind of weird, you know, how you don't want to get out of line. I'm 35-36 years old now, and he's still so high on a pedestal. Whenever I see him I still get nervous to talk to him. It's like,'Hey Coach.' Like he's gonna scold me for something, you know? (laughs) It's kind of weird that way. You have so much respect for him that you don't want to say the wrong thing or do the wrong thing.

It was that way when I played, too. I always respected all the coaches with the most respect I could. Even Tenopir's the same with me. Coach Osborne a lot more so -because I was with Coach Tenopir every single day- but Coach Osborne was the head guy. He gets all the respect he deserved and he put up with a lot of stuff when we were playing, you know? And now he's still like a father figure to a lot of us.

Q: So '96, was that your last year?

CD: Yep, '96 was my last year.

Q: Tell me about your arrival.Aany of the starters &/or leaders have an impact on you?

CD: When I was a freshman Coach Tenopir always said to "watch the older guys in front of you and they'll show you the way." I had Will Shields there, Jim Scott, Kenny Mehlin, Lance Lundberg and Zach Weigert. That first 5 were starting then; they were pretty good leaders, especially watching Will. Will was never the vocal leader but more the silent guy, does everything right and actually does it to a perfection that none of us could really achieve. He was so good at what he did, and that's probably why he played 13 years in the Pro Bowl.

But you learned from them. You learned from the guys who were older and you tried to style yourself after how they practiced, how they put their effort in. Like what I said earlier: when I was supposed to be giving them breaks they never wanted to come out, they never wanted to miss something. They were perfectionists to the point that they never wanted to take breaks, ever. So I would be sitting there on my helmet, and when they wanted one it was just one to get a drink of water and they were back in there the next play. (laughs)

That's something that stuck with me through the NFL and everything I've done, 'I don't want to come out of the game. I want to make sure I'm in there.' And if I'd push my body to a point where you're just dead, that's when you felt you've actually accomplished something. Trying to pace yourself was not an option. You always pushed yourself to the limit that you think your body couldn't take it anymore, and then you pushed it a little bit further. That's what I learned from those guys.

We would run a practice and that was 120-some plays. Basically two games. I think we would have 30 plays at each station, so it was like almost 150-ish plays each practice. And they'd take probably 98% of them. (laughs) I'd get maybe one or two plays and they just wanted to push through the whole thing. And it wasn't like Coach Tenopir wanted a regular rotation either, he'd just say, "Give those guys a blow." And they never wanted to to give anybody a blow.

And I think I took that mindset to the next level. When I'd gone to the Senior Bowl and the NFL everybody was like, "What's the rotation?" And I was like, 'Rotation? Just give me a break when you need to give me a break,' you know? And they were like, "What do you mean?" And I was like, 'I'll just go until you want me to come out.' Seeing that work ethic? When I got to the NFL it made me realize those guys at Nebraska took things to a different level.

Q: Was it ever spoken about?

CD: I think it was just something you picked up on. I remember vividly in the Senior Bowl, and guys were asking coaches for the rotations. I remember saying, 'I don't need a rotation. Just tell me where you want me to be.' I just went from right guard to right tackle to left guard to left tackle, and they kind of moved me around. Jim Hanifan was with the Rams and with Washington when they used to be 'The Hogs' and he coached me in the Senior Bowl, and he'd look at me and go, "Don't you ever need a break?" And I'd say, 'No.' And he'd just kind of shake his head. (laughs)

Q: When you got to that next level what stood out or revealed to you that Nebraska had been a little different, a little special?

CD: It was more physical at Nebraska. The practices were a lot more physical. They try to save everybody's body in the pros. When I was first a rookie I was more like, 'Why don't we just take them to the ground?' You know? And the older and older I'd get the more I liked that rule. (laughs) By the time my eighth year rolled around it was like, 'Don't touch me, rookie.' (laughs) Because you know the older you get the more you didn't want anyone touching you.

But coming from Nebraska where we went full contact and took people to the ground -we cut our defensive linemen and we cut linebackers at full speed- we did things that normal teams don't do in practice. We basically practiced like it was a game tempo every day. Heck, we even went full pads on short yardage situations, in full pads some Thursdays. Days where some people thought it was like a walk-through? We would go 'live' on those days, too. It was just a different mentality and a different way to prepare, and I think it did well for us.

And interestingly, it needs to be done that way in college. You have to go 'live', you have to practice fast. The kids at my high school, they don't know the difference between tempo, being where you need to be, working on your technique. High school kids are just like,

"Hey, we had prom three months ago, we need to know how to hit." They're not able to just turn it on on Saturdays, so we practiced game speed all the time.

Q: For the uninitiated, what is a cut-block?

CD: A cut-block is running full speed and basically putting your shoulder right into someone's kneecap and trying to take them down. When we ran a lot of option we were always trying to get to the corner, get to the outside, so we'd try to take on that linebacker. And a lot of times when you tried to take them on high they'd juke you and throw you out of the way because they were more athletic than you. So basically you take all the 'jukiness' out of them by putting a shoulder into their kneecap. Either they're gonna blow their knee or they're gonna fall down on top of you.

Q: You took advantage of their desire for self-preservation?

CD: Yeah, they'd have to definitely think twice about what they were going to do when they played against us, you know?

Q: Was that pretty distinct to Nebraska at that time or did a lot of teams do that?

CD: Yeah, we cut-blocked a lot at Nebraska. Even on the line of scrimmage we cut blocked. With the option the more people you get on the ground the less people they have to catch the running back. That was our philosophy. We didn't always say they were pancake blocks as much as they were knockdown blocks, because we're not actually trying to literally drive them back and knock them on their backs, we just wanted them on the ground so there was a lesser chance they could put a hand on our ballcarrier. You know, we'd cut people at the line of scrimmage because a lot of plays we'd try to get to the corner and use our speed with our I-back and quarterback, to get out to the corner and make things happen out in space.

Q: I'm trying to recall: were you in there for Tommie's long 75 yard touchdown run against Florida?

CD: You know, I was actually off on that play. I was in and then Adam Treu came in. (Me and Adam would do spells.) I would start at left tackle and then go to left guard, and then Aaron Taylor moved to center. We kind of had a little rotation going there that year, which was weird. But I was actually out on that series. He went down the right side on that run.

Q: I was watching that the other night and there were so many different numbered jerseys flying around on that play. I had a hard time figuring out who was in on it.

CD: I think it was Aaron Graham at center, Aaron Taylor at left guard, Adam Treu at left tackle, Steve Ott at right guard, and Eric Anderson at right tackle.

Q: What was it like for you the year after Weigert, Stai, Wilks and Rob Zatechka left?

CD: The line left. The original Pipeline? They left. They laid a good foundation for us and they were just of a different build. A lot of them were tall. Zach and Brenden and Rob and all those guys were 6'4", 6'5" bodies, all taller than the next group of us coming in, and everybody thought that was going to be the big question mark, "There was no way we could match up to what just left." We kind of took that as a chip on our shoulder.

We knew we were probably a little more athletic than those guys, but we were smaller and we weren't as big and long. We were just short, basically looked like little cookie-cutters as far as body-style, we were just little blocks. (laughs) We knew our body style was more matched to the style of football we played and that would work. We cut-blocked and we were able to get out on a linebacker quicker.

After that first game where everything was going well -and I remember me and Aaron Taylor, we were talking before that first game, the Arizona State game, and we had to make sure that people realized that even though the old Pipeline left we weren't going to let this thing fall off- we had something like 630 yards that game or something like that.

Q: And Chris, is it your belief that the '95 team was one of the best college football teams of all time?

CD: Yeah, at the time I probably wouldn't have said that, but the older I get? You know what they say, "The older you get the better you were?" (laughs) Looking back and realizing how each game we would go in and just dominate in every aspect of the game, it's just unheard of now. The parity in college football is right here, everybody's the same, but for some reason the stars lined up and we were blessed with Tommie as our quarterback. We had three deep at running back with Ahman and Lawrence and Damon Benning. We had a bunch of ankle biters out there at receiver that were probably better blockers than we were: Brendan Holbien and John Vedral. I think they had more blocks than we did. They'd line up out there and they knew their role on the team. They weren't going to catch a pass and they bought into it, and they just beat the crap out of the other teams' defensive backs. We were gonna run the ball and just come right at you, and everybody bought into it.

And defensively, with Jason and Christian and the linebackers with Terrell Farley and Phil Ellis -Phil Ellis might be the best middle linebacker I've ever played against- even with the pros, I think. Phil was probably one of the hardest hitters and most athletic middle linebackers I've played against. I think if he would have went to the NFL he would have played a long time. He was so much quicker going downhill and he could hit.

Q: Wow, that's quite a compliment.

CD: It's true.

Q: And tell me about the offseasons. After '94 happened, I suppose most teams kind of sit back, relax and get a little lazy, but what do you think made you guys push so hard for the '95 season?

CD: I think the foundation was set when we first got there. Everybody worked hard. Just because we didn't win that '93 game.

And we were in that game. We had our chances. When Byron Bennett missed wide left we were so close to winning the championship that year, but I think the work ethic those guys instilled in us from the get go.. when we won in '94 it was a great feeling, but like Coach Osborne said, "In a couple of weeks we're gonna start up again." The train kept on moving, you just got back on your saddle. You didn't gloat in what you did, you went to work. And I had two years left and I wanted to make the best of those two years. But the people that came before us? The tradition, the work ethic they instilled in us? You don't settle for just winning one big game, you win them all.

Q: Any upperclassmen have a real big impression on you as to their intensity and dedication?

CD: Everybody. Stai and Weigert and Rob Zatechka and Joel Wilks, all those guys made an impression on me. They pushed themselves, even in the offseason, going through drills. The intensity was where you'd push yourself to a level as hard as you could.

I remember lifting, when we'd do circuits in the morning. Us linemen would go around 6 or 7 in the morning. I remember we'd do the circuit lifting and there was twelve or thirteen trash cans there, and I probably puked in every single one of them. You pushed yourself to exhaustion and throw up and then keep going. They put trash cans out there for a reason and pretty well knew people were gonna puke, and that's what we did. A lot of people don't know how to push themselves to where everything is coming back up, but that's just an example of our work ethic.

Q: Was that the old Metabolic Power Circuit you're talking about?

CD: Yep. (laughs)

Q: Is there a most memorable play, a favorite?

CD: I think the favorite for me was my sophomore year. We were playing Miami in the first national championship game. Pretty much the whole year I got in scrub duty when the game was out of hand, when we were winning by so much, but for some reason in that Miami game it was the first or second quarter and I guess Coach Tenopir wanted to say something to Rob and I heard, "Dishman, get in." And I'm like, 'Are you kidding me? This is a national championship game and we're down. It's not like we're up by 50 here.' (laughs) So I remember going in and that whole series we went down -and I think it was my first play and I had to pull off a countersweep, and I pull to the right and I'm playing left tackle (and that was the time when they moved Brenden Stai over to left guard from right guard)- so it's a countersweep call. And Aaron Graham doesn't step flat enough to get Warren Sapp, and I'm in my mid-pull step and Warren just ear-holes me and drives me back and throws Lawrence Phillips on the ground for like a six yard loss. It was my fist time getting in to play in a primetime situation and I'm like, 'Are you kidding me!?' You know? 'Jesus, I just got embarrassed on TV!' Coach Tenopir let me in the game for that series where we went down and drove and scored in the corner there, and I think we were down 10 to 7 at that point, now. It was the drive that actually meant something during that game. That was the most memorable series I ever remember being in.

Q: I remember that play, too, the one for the loss.

CD: (laughs) Sapp just ran right through me. And the bad thing is, when Aaron comes back he goes, "Oh man, I'm sorry. I stepped too high." And I was like, 'I don't give a shit! (laughs) Step down and get your guy. It makes me look like a jerk!' (laughs) This guy missed the block while I'm pulling and, 'I'm not even supposed to touch that guy!' (laughs) I could envision them making the highlight tape and, "See how he just ran through Chris Dishman?" And I'm like, 'I'm not even supposed to block that guy, and everybody thinks that he ran right through me. Oh, my God.'

Q: Sapp was a pretty special player, no?

CD: Yeah, he was the real deal. I got a chance to play against him a lot in the pros, too. He was a heck of a three technique defensive tackle. Wasn't much of a defensive end, but he was pretty good at defensive tackle.

Q: Did you ever talk to him?

CD: No, not really. In the pros you don't really talk to a whole lot of players. The ones in your division, maybe you talk to a little more. People think it's trash talk and whatever, but it's usually more like, "Hey, how's your family doing? How are the kids?" You know?

It was our job. We'd try as hard as we could, but when the play was done? When it was over? It was back to the huddle. It's just like going to work. People don't realize it was just like an office job to us. I think the only person who really talked a whole lot of smack in the NFL was John Randle. He just did it to talk. He didn't talk smack, he just talked to hear himself talk. (laughs)

Q: Did you ever line up against other Huskers during your time in the pros?

CD: Oh yeah, I went against Parrella and Wistrom and Jared. I went against them all. Parrella was tough. Wistrom and Jared played outside -they played defensive end and I played guard- but in third down situations they'd move in a little. It was pretty fun going against them. We'd talk smack, and they'd get the best of you and you'd get the best of them. You just tried to win more than you'd lose.

Q: Just like the old days, huh?

CD: I went against Christian a lot, too, because we played the Giants in our division. So I went against him twice a year, too. (laughs) It was fun.

Q: And Chris, any memorable off-field incidents?

CD: Off-field occurrence…hmmm. Ones that I can talk about, huh? (laughs) I don't want to throw anybody under the bus. There were so many good memories about college, I can't think of any right off the bat.

Q: Protecting the innocent?

CD: Yeah. (laughs)

And a lot of people during their college years went out and partied and everything. But I went and had a daughter my junior year. My wife -who was my girlfriend at the time- gave birth to our daughter in June, so my senior year I basically didn't eat at the training table because I had my daughter at home with the babysitter. And I'd come home and make dinner for the babysitter, so basically my whole senior year I was pretty involved there. From 20 to 21 years old was a hard age: I didn't go out and party or anything like that because I had a pregnant wife and then a daughter. I lived with my wife and never went out after my daughter was born.

Q: You were a full-time football player, full-time student and full-time dad?

CD: Yeah, pretty much. Most people have those college years where they rip and roar and have all these wild stories, but I pretty much stayed home. That was just me. I guess I had an option, but I chose not to and that was my life and I loved it.

Q: That's the best part, Chris: Loving it.

CD: Yep, wouldn't change it for anything.

Q: Any memorable practice stories?

CD: I remember (laughs) the most memorable was late in the season and I think Aaron Graham made All-American. And Christian was just getting in his grill about it, talking, "You ain't All-American. You suck!" Just going on and on. And we get in a short yardage situation and it was one-on-ones, and Christian just ran over Aaron Graham and was talking smack the whole time. And Aaron Graham comes back to the huddle just screaming, "Let's kill 'em!" I remember that instant we were full go.

And we end up having about two more plays and it was getting really physical, and that was one time where Coach Osborne actually cut us off. He was afraid somebody was going to get hurt. We were going for blood and they were going for blood. No longer was it Nebraska against Nebraska, it was Nebraska against the enemy. (laughs) It was good against evil. I just remember Coach Osborne calling that up and then basically just shutting down practice. At the very end it was like, "That's enough. We're done." It was late in the season, so it had to be against Colorado or Kansas or one of those late games in the season. I can't remember who we were getting ready for. It was under the lights, so it must have been Colorado and we were practicing late at night for some reason. I just remember it was a foggy day and you could see your breath, and I just remember Christian talking smack and Aaron coming back to the huddle all pissed off and just spitting out of his facemask, "Let's kill 'em!" He was so worked up you could hardly understand a damn thing he said, which almost made you want to laugh. (laughs)

Q: What are you the most proud of?

CD: Most proud of? You know, being part of that '95 team, I guess. I think just being able to say that you were on probably the greatest team ever to play the game. Looking back now? If you look at the stats and everything, we were pretty salty. You didn't look at it that way when you played, but I think the closest game we played was like 14 points against Wyoming. They got their points and it really wasn't a game, but that was considered the closest game that year. I don't know, I just think being a part of that was probably my greatest accomplishment there at Nebraska.

Also, being named a team captain for the '96 team, that was an honor. Just knowing that tradition of the captains who came before you, who they were; being voted by your peers to be captain was a great honor.

Q: Were you one of those guys who got the flu the week before that inaugural Big 12 Championship/Texas game?

CD: No, I didn't get the flu, but like 13 of them did. I remember the '95 year against Kansas -which was back-to-back night games- because during the Colorado week I came down with walking pneumonia. I had a week and a half to prepare for that Thanksgiving game. And I remember I lost 25 lbs. and had to go the hospital and get put on a respirator thing, and got to come in and play against Colorado that week. So I didn't get the flu like everbody got after that game, I already had pneumonia for the previous game. (laughs)

It was walking pneumonia or something like that. I went in for treatment every day. I went in to see Dr. Albers and those guys and said, 'Man, I feel great! I just jumped in a cold shower and broke the fever. I feel great!' And they were like, "You just broke one and you feel great?" And they took my temperature and it was 104, still. (laughs) And the whole time I was, 'Now I feel great!' (laughs)

Q: It beat the heck out of 106 degrees, right?

CD: Yeah, I felt like a million bucks because I just 'broke it.' I felt awesome. (laughs)

Q: Maybe you guys on the O-line had more pain tolerance than most folks?

CD: I don't know, but anytime you've got fevers, they suck. I just remember being so miserable I couldn't even get out of bed.

Q: Any thoughts on the backs you guys were blocking for?

CD: Tommie was all business in the huddle. He wanted to score on every play. He was very, very serious. His demeanor was his demeanor, that was Tommie. Some people might call it a negative knock on him because he was that way, and he didn't really build the great friendships off the field because of the way he was on the field. He made it clear he was there to play football and not be friend, but that's just the way Tommie was. But I never wanted a different quarterback in the huddle, because Tommie wanted to score on every play. He let it be known that if you missed a block, he'd tell you. If he did something wrong he was the first one to admit that he did it wrong. It wasn't like he was all blame and no responsibility. If he missed the pitch he'd say, "My fault, guys." That was just Tommie.

As for Lawerence, he didn't say much on the field. He just ran like the wind blows. Ahman was such a low runner. When Ahman came in he was a freshman at the time. I just remember the way he'd run, so crouched over and so low to the ground. Clinton was more of a.. kind of looked like a wet dog on tile when he ran. (laughs) He was just all over the place. It was just a lot of movement, it was not compact by any means. Clinton was just all over, but he moved fast. It was just the way he ran. Damon was more shifty, he was more of a bouncer. When he'd get to a hole he'd try to jump out of it. He didn't have that straight ahead burst of speed, but he was very good side to side, laterally. I think, overall, Lawrence had it all. He had the speed, the side to side, he was a compact runner, he could run with power. Ahman had straight-ahead speed, straight-ahead flat-out speed and power, his lateral movement I didn't think was that well. Damon was good laterally and didn't have that straight-ahead power. And Clinton was so stocky and so muscular he'd look like he was just straining to run. His mechanics were all off. (laughs)

Q: Any remembrances of Brook?

CD: Yeah, I remember playing with him the whole time. Looking back, he reminds me a lot of Marc Bulger who was with the Rams. His demeanor? Like Bulger is a real calm, quiet guy. Bulger had ice in his veins, and that's kind of how Brook was. Brook wasn't your typical option quarterback, but he's gonna step in there and he was gonna do it, do the best he could.

It was kind of an eery feeling when I went to the Rams and was in the huddle with Bulger the first time. I was like, 'Man, this is like Brook being here.' It was kind of weird. It was 10-12 years after the fact of Brook being gone, and when he'd talk and the way he'd act in the huddle reminded me of Brook. So it was kind of cool bringing my memory back to him. He was a silent leader. He definitely wasn't a vocal leader -rah-rah or anything like that- but a great teammate. He knew his role on the team, stepped in there. I know it probably had to eat him alive, because when Tommie was back and he went from winning all the games to standing there. He never complained, that was just Brook.

Q: Anything from those days you wish you could do over or do differently?

CD: Do differently? Not much. I don't live with any regrets. I think if you live that way you just beat yourself up over what you should have done the first time. I couldn't have asked for a better college experience, when you go back to those national championships. My senior class lost three games, we were like 47-3. You can't take that back. The friendships I built over the years are lifelong, lasting friendships. I wouldn't take anything back. Coach Osborne and Coach Tenopir were like fathers to me, and they made that college experience one of the best. I wish everybody would experience what we experienced.

Q: Coach Tenopir had that yearly party, right?

CD: Yep, after spring ball. He would break out the sausages and steaks. For a couple years we had both O-line and D-line, and then they kinda got out of hand. (laughs) We'd be lining up in the front yard and things like that. We couldn't do it anymore. It was a good old time.

Q: Can you tell me, was there anybody behind the scenes who played a huge role for you or the team, who never got their due?

CD: Bryan Bailey. I think if you look at people that he really helped, he helped the O-line out a lot, he helped our training. He'd do a lot. He was one guy.

Trainer-wise? Doak. Doak was always there. I don't know if he'd really get you back on the field, I guess. He was just one of those guys who was super-nice. Doak had always been Doak.

I think anybody on that staff, they all played a huge role for us. The marketing people all the way down to the trainers and weightroom, everybody played their role and they all contributed to our success.

Dr. Stark, he actually helped me out a lot. I was going through a lot of different things: I'm having a baby when I'm 21, I was still with my wife. I don't know, just a lot of pressure, I guess. Trying to go to school, trying to raise a kid, 'How am I gonna do this?' That kind of stuff. Dr. Stark? He did a lot for me. I went in and met with him (not all the time), but we'd talk and he'd help me through it. Looking back, it was a lot of pressure for me having to raise a daughter.

Buck Ellis, too, he probably loved the linemen because we were so out of shape. (laughs) We pretty much gave him job security.

Q: Well Chris, thanks for answering all my questions. Is there anything we haven't touched on that made a difference between success and failure?

CD: The only thing is: tradition was such a key for us. Coming from small town Nebraska, I never expected to play at Nebraska. When I got a scholarship I still never expected to play there. I thought it was too big, out of my reach. To run out of the tunnel was basically all I ever wanted to do, to feel the electricity of the fans. Even when I got a scholarship, I still, in my mind, thought, 'I'm never gonna play here. I just want to run out on the field with these guys.' (laughs) And so, the tradition was upheld so high for me as a kid growing up, putting Coach Osborne up onto this pedestal. It was so surreal. I think the first time when I went against Trev Alberts on those one-on-ones I realized, 'I might be able to play.' That's when my mentality started to change and I figured if I could compete with the best ones, I surely could make a name here and play. It was a really surreal moment and I was just happy to be there.

The tradition there at Nebraska, that's what it's built on. That's what makes the Big Red go, just doing it for the people who came before you, playing your best because they played that way. Just because you're a true freshman now, you had to wait your turn. That's where it came down to learning from those senior leaders. I'm not saying that if you're a freshman you can't play, but there are few freshmen who can pull it off and do it. They haven't taken the hits, haven't sweated out on that field to earn the right to play. And if they are, that pretty much means you aren't working hard enough if you're a senior, junior or sophomore.

And again, Bryan Bailey meant a lot us offensive linemen. He'd work out with us in the winter conditioning. We were his group. He'd stretch us and help us do ropes in those summer workouts. He was always there for us.

Q: What made him special, Chris?

CD: He was a kid from Arnold, Nebraska, which is back where I'm from, you know? I knew he was from Arnold, Nebraska when I was coming down here. You know, when you're from small-town Nebraska and you have someone that's nearby at Nebraska people are like, "Bryan Bailey is from Arnold, Nebraska." I didn't know who he was when I first got there.

And if he could do anything to be on that field, Bryan would have been on that field playing football. But God didn't bless him to be an offensive lineman.'Cause at the time he ran with us offensive linemen; he had the same demeanor as us. He was just like an offensive lineman, just in a little person's body. (laughs) He definitely did a lot for us on the offensive line.

End conversation.

Three things stuck out from this time spent with Dish, and one of them would have to be his mention of the work ethic displayed by his forerunners on the O-line, "they never wanted breaks." You've gotta know that Chris showed up on campus as a 6' 4" 300 pound freshman. I'm sure Coaches Tenopir and Young were salivating about throwing him into the mix, but the poor fellow was soon subjected to the equivalent of two daily sessions of film study: first in the meeting room and second watching on the field. Nutritionist Dave Ellis mentioned the coaches' amazement at the conditioning levels the boys operated at, and Chris's sharing confirms it. Man, what a lucky kid to be able to learn from the likes of Will Shields and Zach Weigert and Brenden Stai, et al, as an understudy.

Staying with this line of thought, I surmise that this initial lack of practice work became for him a lesson in redeeming the time, creating a sense of urgency for the moments when he finally got in there for a spell. And this sense of the precious nature of playtime access stayed with him for quite some time, did you notice? Because he took it all the way to the pro ranks. I would like to think that this sense of urgency permeated the culture there, enabling the process by motivating each player to go all-out at all times, "We basically practiced like it was a game tempo every day. Heck, we even went full pads on short yardage situations, in full pads some Thursdays. Days where some people thought it was like a walk-through, those days we would go 'live' on those days, too. It was just a different mentality and a different way to prepare, and I think it did well for us." Quite well, I might add.

Then you had the "chip on our shoulder" comment about the '95 offensive line. If you must know, the phrase 'chip on your shoulder' is a unique American idiom from the 1700's when, instead of starting a fight and playing the part of unlawful aggressor, a young man would place a woodchip on his shoulder and dare another to knock it off. The opponent's doing so then constituted an act of aggression, whereby the chip-holder could then swing away in an act of 'self defense.' In short, these guys eagerly anticipated the opportunity to show their capabilities and put to shame any mention of their supposed lack of skills in comparison to '94's Pipeline; 'cause they were itchin' for a fight. Peculiar, isn't it? How the questioning of their capabilities placed these student/athletes on a motivational spree for all of college football history.

Notable quote #2:
Chris Dishman on Husker Football legacy: "The people that came before us? The tradition, the work ethic they instilled in us? You don't settle for just winning one big game, you win them all."

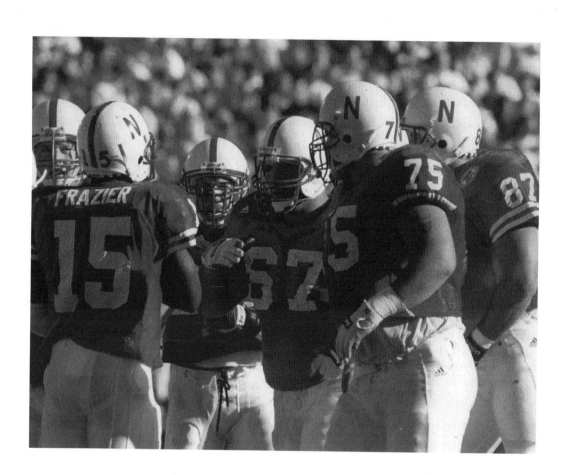

In the land of the blind, the one-eyed man is king.

H. Ross Perot

History is engorged with fatal lapses. Lapses of judgement, of character, of vision, of clarity of foresight, of action, inaction, even overreaction. Any reasonable and objective individual viewing Corey Dixon -the speedy, Smurf-ish Texan wearing jersey number 2 and sweeping, skirting, sprinting, sliding by and slipping into the Orange Bowl endzone on his 71 yard punt return for a Husker touchdown, knows whereof I speak. Over the years many eyes (you too?) have beheld TV replay upon replay of his fantastically furious heroics in that '94 Florida State Orange Bowl bout, and still to this day shake their heads in disbelief. Why? Because to the naked eye not one example of an illegal block has ever been found, lending reason to believe that his spectacular return's performance should never have been nullified. That heart-wrenching loss shouldn't be pinned only on Byron's final field goal try, but in the officiating crew's refusal to award Corey his hard-earned romp for 6 points, a crucial Husker lead, and accompanying glory. Not even a one-eyed man could argue that. Let's reacquaint ourselves with the hero who wasn't to be, Corey Dixon.

Notable quote #1:
"I think the offense and defense started to get a little bit closer, too. And we had an incident over there in Tokyo where the team became one, fighting against some wrestlers."

Corey Dixon

Scholarship recruit, Split End, Dallas, Texas (Hillcrest)
Where are they now? Dallas, Texas, Entrepreneur

Question: Hey Corey, I hear you have two daughters who are pretty good soccer players?

Corey Dixon: Yeah, two. 14 and 11 years old. And they both wear Number 2. (laughs)

Q: So you had your first daughter two years out of school?

CD: Actually, when I finished up in '94. She was born in '94. She was born in Atlanta when I was with the Falcons. I went as a free agent.

Q: How was that experience?

CD: It was a beautiful experience. I loved the situation we were in as far as the Run & Shoot, especially with me being a small and speedy guy as a receiver. You'd get some situations where we'd need four or five receivers out there at the same time, so that was something you looked forward to.

I was in Atlanta two years and I played in the CFL for a little while and then I played with Barcelona of the World League. After that I kind of fell out of love for it. My mom was diagnosed with cancer, and then you go through politics of the NFL and you learn it is not just about the game anymore: it's a business, the adaptation to that with agents and money and endorsements. It was like, 'Wow, it's not fun anymore.' (laughs) The money was good, the limelight was nice, and if I were to do that over again I wouldn't pass it up for the world.

Q: How did you end up in Dallas?

CD: I was born in Dallas. Born and raised right out of Dallas, Texas.

Q: So it was only natural you went back home?

CD: Atlanta was like my second home and I loved Atlanta. It was a nice city, but like they say, "There's no place like home." (laughs)

Q: What are you doing as a vocation?

CD: I still have a production company. We produce a lot of records, put on shows. Like now I'm doing some work for the Steve Harvey Morning Show and I have graphic design company, as well. I have a production company and a graphic design company, and during tax season I have a tax company that we run here in Dallas, as well.

Q: Man, you could take over a whole city block! Fill up a whole strip mall all by yourself. (laughing)

CD: Yeah, you know, you've got to keep busy. It's kind of like football, you get paid for sixteen weeks and then the offseason happens and you have to find your niche to take up the free time.

Q: Well, let me ask you, how did you end up at Nebraska?

CD: Growing up I was always a running back, one of the top running backs to come out of Texas. And I remember Nebraska being the powerhouse it was when I was growing up. I wore red and white growing up and there was always the Nebraska/Oklahoma rivalry. And my freshman year of high school I told my coach, "If I can't get to Nebraska from here, I need to go somewhere else," and coach told me it would be up to me.

I tell you, Coach Osborne and Ron Brown and Jack Pierce recruited me pretty heavily and it actually came true.

Q: What did your family and friends think about your Nebraska fascination?

CD: First, with me growing up and talking about it, it was, "Yeah, right." I think a lot of people I knew growing up knew that I would go somewhere, but not go that far from home to play ball. So when I made the commitment at that time -my mom wanted me to go to Texas because it wasn't too far, and my father wanted me to go to Oklahoma State- but they wouldn't tell me until after I made that commitment. But Nebraska was my dream, and once I made that move we created a lot of fans right here in my family. Right up to this day they're die-hard Nebraska fans.

Q: Did you have any favorite players?

CD: Watching TV, I used to love to watch the way Steve Taylor walked from the huddle. When they'd break from the huddle Steve Taylor would take his time to walk to the line of scrimmage to call a play. And I liked Turner Gill, who was from Fort Worth. And Irving Fryar and Roger Craig were the guys I watched; I used to always do the high knee action from watching him. Quite a few guys come out of Nebraska I used to look up to. And then closer in to age bracket? When I got older Dana Brinson was a guy I would watch and say, 'Yeah, I can go up there and do what he's doing.'

Q: So Corey, what was your first year on campus?

CD: My first year was 1990. That was my class.

My first day on campus, my parents drove me up. Two-a-days was up, and me not being away from home for the first time? I tell you what, it was probably one of the hardest days in my life, seeing my family leave me 11 hours away from home and not able to look back and see my mom and them leave. I was trying to hold the tears in. I think I had to go off somewhere and just let it all go.

Q: I'm sure they were doing the same in the car, huh?

CD: All except for my sister. I think she was smiling. (laughs) She had the house to herself now.

Q: Do you remember any first impressions of the program?

CD: You know, I think when I came to Lincoln it was kind of like you or me growing up here where the Cowboys are America's Team. When you were in Lincoln and you were a football player you were a celebrity. When I'd walk around it was 'autograph time', learning how to be in front of the cameras. It was like you always wanted to carry a nice demeanor/leadership-mentality about it, because you never knew who was watching you. And me being from the South, I learned how to speak a little more fluently, because I'd seen myself one time on camera and I tell you what, I said, 'I sound too country.' I needed to change that, so when I'd leave school to come home and visit all my friends and family they would say, "You sound all proper now!" And I'd say, 'I sound educated.' (laughs)

Q: Do you recall the first friends you made on the team?

CD: My first buddy -we're still close to this day- was Sedric Collins. Jack Pierce, he recruited us both, and Sedric -being from Slidell, Louisiana- me and him would talk in the summertime before we even got up to campus. When we got up to campus we pretty much knew each other and that made the transition that much smoother. Sedric was my roommate, too.

Q: Anything peculiar or different about the Nebraska people in general, compared to Texas?

CD: I think -city-wise?- Lincoln at the time was more of a college town, and the people kind of looked at you and recognized you, everybody treated me nicely and respected me and looked after me. It made me grow up and get used to living in the limelight a little bit.

Q: Were you expecting to be at running back right away or go straight to the receiving corps?

CD: Well, I went in as a running back. Tom would always throw at me: "Wingback is a good position for you." And I was always like, 'Nah, I'm a running back, Coach. I'm a running back.' So my first scrimmage in the stadium -I think we had Pat Tyrance and Mike Petko at linebackers, and Reggie Cooper was sitting back there at the safety spot- well, Leodis Flowers was in the running back spot and I was the next running back to go in. But then Leodis took a handoff and Pat Tyrance hit him so hard! The hardest hit I'd ever seen in college football. Then T.O. had the next play for me to run in and I stood back and said, 'Nah, I'm not quite ready, Coach.' (laughs) They hit hard, I tell you. And I think that was the time I made the decision to play wingback. I said, 'Yeah, they're hitting.'

Q: Did you work with Coach Solich then, as a running back?

CD: I worked with him at the beginning, but I made the transition over to wingback and I got to work with Ron Brown ASAP. I was with Nate Turner and Tyrone Hughes real quick.

Q: What about Coach Brown? What made him special?

CD: Coach Brown? He believed in you, he was honest with you, and he'd make you become a workaholic. He was the type of guy that's gonna make you be at practice thirty minutes before practice and then work forty-five minutes after practice, catching 100 balls after practice. I do that every day when I'm coaching. I tell the young guys today, 'At least catch a hundred balls a day if you want to have good hands.' Coach Brown was a workaholic, and whatever your craft was -I don't care what it was, whether it was blocking, catching, running routes, learning the audibles, learning to read defenses- that's what he programmed you to do. He made it seem like school in meetings and you'd get graded after every game. You had to make good grades in order to play, and I'm talking about grades on the football field.

Q: How did you usually grade out?

CD: Some games we'd make a mistake (and a lot of the fans that watched really don't see what we see once we're in the film room with running routes and blocking assignments and making the right reads). It limits your mistakes. That was something good. I can't watch football, to this day, without grading players on the field. (laughs) I'll watch Terrell Owens come off the line of scrimmage and I'm like, 'Oh, T.O., wait 'til you get in the meeting. What kind of route was that!?' (laughs)

Q: Would the benefit be that you always knew whether you were improving/declining?

CD: You'd know if you were improving because you started to limit your mistakes and you began to know everything that you was supposed to do. If you made bad grades you knew something was wrong. And I was the type of one that didn't want to sit down, I wanted to be on the field.

Q: Nothing worse than standing on the sidelines, eh?

CD: Yeah, 'Don't even bring me out, Coach. I need the ball.'

Q: Did you notice a positive aspect to the coaching? Rather than negative?

CD: I'd never seen any negativity from our staff. The program was an A-type program. I'm talking about Tom all the way down to every assistant coach to the players. There was nothing negative. I'd hear things from other schools and I wondered how that could be, because I'd never witnessed anything negative in our program.

Q: Any other coaches stand out to you?

CD: Tom Osborne: the way he was, his demeanor and his character. I always said that places have pretty much the mentality that the coach has. He had a lot of patience, which helped you become humble and patient.

Coach Steele was a hardnosed guy that believed in you and wanted you to get after it. He made you aggressive offensively. We had a lot of coaches -even Turner Gill when he got there and started coaching- I liked what he had to offer to us. All the coaches had a lot to share, especially if you were a good player. You just had a lot of respect for all the coaches who knew who you were and believed in what you could to. That helped with the positive turn right there.

Q: Any special occasions with Coach Osborne stand out to you?

CD: You know, we were playing Oklahoma in Norman and I was getting ready to run a play, and the defensive back -I'm coming off of the line of scrimmage, I'm blocking him- and he says something about my Mom. He says, "Your mom looks like something or other," you know? And the next play I went out there and didn't even do what I was supposed to do and I went directly for that defensive back. I was throwing punches and everything. And a referee threw a flag and said if I didn't calm down they were gonna throw me out. T.O. looked at me and said, "Is everything okay?" And I said I was fine.

So after the game we were the last guys in the locker room and T.O. and me were the last guys in the showers. And Coach asked me what was wrong with me. And I told him that player said something about my momma and I had to get him. And he asked me if I did a good job of getting him, and I told him I felt pretty good about what I did. And he was like, "Okay, as long as it's out of your system we can go on from there." (laughs) I was like, 'I'll take that.' I wasn't in trouble after that.

Q: Where were you the next New Years after you'd graduated, when the Huskers played Miami in Miami?

CD: Oh, I was in Atlanta with a group of guys: a couple guys that had played at Miami. We had made some wagers (and we were always the underdog all the time), so we'd talk a lot of noise. We sat and watched the game and we were talking on the phone, too, over at a Falcons teammate's house. Those guys playing in that first national champion game were guys I came in with, because I didn't redshirt: Ed Stewart and all those guys. I played four years and I was done, but wish I would have redshirted and played another year, though.

Q: Now, I have to be honest with you Corey, I have watched that Florida State game in its entirety more times than most sane people should admit, and I think that was one of the top 5 college football games ever played.

CD: To this day, I get nervous if I see it again. I haven't watched it in about 5 years. I get nervous watching that punt return because I know in my head that they called it back. But it's an unanswerable question of, 'What if they didn't?' and, 'What if they hadn't given William Floyd that touchdown?' It bugs me to this day. I don't even have the game on DVD. I'd like to get a copy of it.

Q: I actually have a copy. It's the NBC telecast with Dick Enberg and Bob Trumpy and has O.J. Simpson doing on the sideline reporting. And I have to say, had that last second field goal gone through, I think Cory Dixon's name would have forever been linked in Husker history as one of the grittiest performances ever. You played a heck of a game...

CD: Yeah, I was always looking forward to speedy-type games. I remember back when 'Rocket' Raghib Ismail returned a punt one time and I remember saying, 'I want to do that one day,' and that opportunity actually came and it didn't count.

Q: Do people ask you about that play and the phantom clip?

CD: Yeah, I always get that question. I still haven't seen that clip. And even some players say they haven't seen the clip.

I was talking to a Florida State fan about a year ago and they said we really won that game. I said, 'That's understandable, but we still didn't get to take home the awards.' They said that's always talked about and it's an unforgettable game and that I always made the Florida State fans nervous when they kicked it off to me. On that last kickoff return I wanted the ball, but they kicked it off to Barron Miles. He grabbed it, but I was calling for it. It was the heat of the moment and I wanted to be the guy to make that play. That runs in my head to this day, 'What if I would have caught that ball? What could I have made happen?' You know?

Q: Can you recall the one you ran back? What was going through your mind as you crossed the goal line?

CD: It was just excitement! The first thing that crossed my mind was my mom. Then all my friends just watching (being excited because we were the underdogs in the national championship game, and how that's not supposed to happen), and then taking the punt return to the house and seeing that flag out there was a heartbreaker. And they couldn't find the clip, it was a mystery clip. The other touchdowns that I had in other games were nice, but that was a special one.

Q: Speaking of other games, do you have anything more memorable?

CD: I think the Colorado game out in Boulder, that touchdown catch against those guys. I had a real exciting game against them returning punts and receiving that game.

Also, in Tokyo I had a nice, beautiful catch over there in Japan. But overall, every year against Florida State? Both years I had a decent game against them.

Q: Were they the fastest team you'd played?

CD: Yeah, they were the fastest: them and Miami. Playing them in the bowl games was tough, with their speed and all, but what motivated you was that you're the underdog and the world is against you saying you can't beat them, you know?

I remember interviewing with the guys from ESPN, Craig James and Mike Tirico. Craig James would always tease me saying we weren't even gonna be able to stay on the field with Florida State. I tell you, in the 4th quarter during a TV timeout we were in the huddle and the Florida State defense was just on their knees. I was like 'Okay, boys, we got these guys. We got them now, they're tired.' Just being the underdog motivated me. Then the showing we put out? We couldn't ask for nothing better than that. I actually have an MVP trophy from the Orange Bowl right now, here in my living room.

Q: Do you have a most memorable off-field occurrence?

CD: My college career? That experience was fun. If I were talking to any youthful person thinking about going to college today, I'd say, 'Go to college, because that's a beautiful time of your life.' There were so many moments… And becoming a man? Being able to get the degree? And the system they have there and graduating in 4 years? I didn't go to college even thinking I was gonna be able to graduate. (laughs) But once I get there in the system, in the program, they were like, "You have to graduate." And once that gets in your system? I guarantee you we had a lot of graduates.

And I tell you what, once I got back to Texas and had a chance to share it with other people, I inspired other people to go back to school and get their degree. Walking across that stage was something. I learned a lot and made a lot of friends, and we still talk today. Lincoln was good to me, and they tell me now that it's even better than what it was.

Q: Lincoln has grown up a bit in the last decade and a half…

CD: Yeah, I need to take my kids up to see it. The last time my daughters were there was when my youngest was two or three years old. There's nothing like it, seeing that Sea of Red out there on the field, it was something.

Q: Do you ever have the occasion to meet any of the guys to watch the games together in any sports bars?

CD: You know, years ago I used to get invited by the Texans for Nebraska group to watch the game. And I would go do autographs and there would be 500-plus in there wearing nothing but red, and it would be just as loud. (laughs) And I thought, 'Wow, to be in a bar and these people are going crazy about Nebraska?' It's something.

Q: What was your shining moment?

CD: Being on the field that Florida State game, especially playing for the national championship. What game could be bigger in college? That was a great moment for me.

And the fans, the kids? There was a foundation where they'd have a wish list and they would want to meet you. And to meet some of those kids that put you on a wish list, you'd never assume that kids would want to do that, you know? I mean, they wanted to meet me?! To meet me! That's amazing. Of all the people in the world, a sick kid wants to meet me. I think I still have a t-shirt that a kid drew me. It had a picture of me running the ball on the front of this t-shirt. I'll always remember that being special.

Q: Now, from your freshman year to your senior year some changes took place within the team. From your perspective, do you recall anything special happening?

CD: I think the transition from my freshman year, I think what Nebraska had more was power. And from my sophomore year to my junior year, I think we started developing a little more finesse and speed.

I think that kind of changed how we approached the game and we started to do a little bit more. And with Tommie starting as a freshman the year before, we were able to make some adjustments.

I think the offense and defense started to get a little bit closer, too. And we had an incident over there in Tokyo where the team became one, fighting against some wrestlers. And there were the Blackshirts, but we as an offense wanted to come up with something and we came together and got closer. I think that was our time, that moment.

Q: Do you recall the Unity Council?

CD: When someone got into trouble we had to bring that issue in front of everybody. I remember when Mike Petko and the rest of the guys my freshman year, they got that together and all. And once we became upperclassmen the younger guys respected us.

We had a pretty good mentality. We wouldn't allow guys to do nothing wrong because we respected Coach Brown a lot, respected T.O. If someone was getting out of line we'd say something about it. We had to represent ourselves and get guys straightened out if they were doing anything that wasn't proper.

Q: Would there be one person behind the scenes who you recall contributing a lot? Someone many fans might not have been aware of?

CD: I'm gonna say Bryan Bailey. Bryan was the kind of guy that pushed you to be the best you could be in the weightroom and definitely turned me into a different player as far as my body, my strength. I know it was Boyd Epley's program, but there was something about Bryan that would make you go out and do something that you normally wouldn't do, that he pushed you to do. Bryan was strong and he was a small guy, but the way he talked to you and believed in you? It put a lot of things in your head to go out there and be the best you could be. And it's because he had to get you ready, because in that weightroom it was something serious.

And also, Doak. Because you know, if you're hurt Doak would take you through the pain. He made it to where you didn't want to be in the training room, rubbing something out of your hamstring. (laughs)

Q: So what was it like being in the huddle with Tommie running the show?

CD: Tommie had a voice that was so small. He had a real serious voice. Depending on the situation we were in, we were all serious and focused, and we knew with Tommie handling the guys that anything was possible: if it was a pass play we knew it could turn into a running play, so we never knew what was going to happen. So when we'd leave the huddle we just made sure to do exactly what we were supposed to do: we were trying to get the ball into the end zone. We were serious about it.

Q: And what about the mottos?

CD: I remember, "A team that can't be beat won't be beat." I had it printed up. I was trying to share it with my kids the other day. That was part of the team prayer. Vernon Powell brought that to the team. He used to say it every game. He learned it from high school and brought it to Lincoln.

Q: Any recollections of pregame speeches standing out?

CD: Every game required a different speech. We were going off of how we felt that game, depending on who we were playing. Coach Brown would give us some good speeches. They would definitely motivate us to grow from boys to men. I can't recall any certain speech, but it was about the opportunities we were given: some might see them again and some might not, so we had to play the game like it was our last. Sometimes Coach Brown would get so deep and motivate you and you'd be so anxious that you'd get teary-eyed.

Q: Did you read Coach Brown's first book?

CD: I remember that book.

Q: We used to pass it among the younger strength staff. For a time there it was a dare to read that first chapter about the late offensive line recruit Victor Stachmus out of Oklahoma, who died of leukemia before he ever set foot on campus. The challenge was to read that first chapter and not cry.

CD: Coach Brown could bring it out of you, man. He could bring you to tears. To this day, Coach Brown made me a different person. I reached out to him again when he first joined the staff again. I saw him when they were on the road to Baylor and the Cotton Bowl, and I'm gonna make a trip back to see the stadium again soon.

Q: And how often were your parents able to see you play at Nebraska?

CD: My mom, I don't think she missed a single game. They drove up a lot. My family would come up as much as they could.

The sad thing? My last home game against Oklahoma it was iced over so she wasn't able to drive up. My mom cried and I was sad about it, but she was able to watch me on TV.

Q: What was it like shaking Coach Osborne's hand and running out of the tunnel for that last time?

CD: It had a little bit of everything. Just being your last game with T.O. and the last home game was a sad moment. You wished you could wind the tape back and give yourself another two years. It was a happy/sad moment. You were excited because we were getting ready to play Oklahoma, but at the same time you were saying, 'This is it!' You'd get teary eyed, but it was exciting.

Q: What do you value most from your experience as a Nebraska student-athlete?

CD: I think just being able to live up to your expectations as a man. Being there, you had people that had certain expectations of you that you had to honor within yourself and not be selfish. You had to carry the weight of saying, 'I've got to play for me, but then I still have to deliver a lot to satisfy the team.' You had to take those things into consideration and become humble. It wasn't just about Corey Dixon, it was about doing it for the rest of these guys. It's like when you do something wonderful and you do something great, you dedicate those moments to your teammates. You learned to share a lot with those who are on the battleground with you. That created a bond because you know what those guys have gone through. That's what you miss, playing with those guys.

Q: Any comments about some of the walk-ons who hardly ever got on the field?

CD: I can't recall the names at this particular time, but I tell you, it's amazing to see that as a senior: these guys are walking on and they're scout team guys… and then two years later you see them being starters. That's amazing to me. It just takes hard work and dedication. All of a sudden it's two years later and I'm watching Nebraska on TV and they're starters.

I remember one guy I know who honored his assignment, and that was Lance Gray. Lance was known to be the wedge-buster. For him to go down on the kickoff and bust a wedge like he would, that's amazing. Because those guys would literally get up and fall back down dizzy, probably from a concussion. (laughs) Lance had that down. He was something else.

End conversation.

Coach Ron Brown didn't respond to my requests for this project, as he just made the switch to running backs coach at the University of Nebraska at that time, having his hands more than full."He believed in you, he was honest with you, and he'd make you become a workaholic" was Corey's summation of his coaching. Now, Ron wasn't the prototypical 'receivers' coach' you'd find in most college offenses or the professional ranks, but instead was something of a mini-offensive line coach, by all intents. Sure, his disciples caught a pass now and again, but it was their scrappy, dogged, punishing downfield blocking they were most known for. And when the ball was put to flight? The pressure was on. Because it was a rare occurrence compared to most, and not one to be taken lightly, "…it was about the opportunities we were given. Some might see them again and some might not, so we had to play the game like it was our last." And if anyone could tug at your heartstrings, it was this man."Sometimes Coach Brown would get so deep and motivate you and you'd be so anxious that you'd get teary-eyed." Read his book, 'I Can' and have some tissues nearby, just in case.

Maybe you've tired of the recurring 'sour grapes' refrain over the '94 Florida State loss, but after all the time, all the energy, all the effort, the years of striving to finally hit the heights of an Orange Bowl victory, to see success literally snatched from those youngsters' grasp by a bogus penalty makes my heart ache. To this day. Like the '82 Penn State game's officiating, perhaps it's just a bitter pill I'll never swallow, volleying back and forth in my mouth instead despite the distaste. Danny Nee once said in a basketball halftime speech, "Life is not easy and life is not fair. Once you accept these statements as truth, life becomes tolerable." I agree with him and can tolerate the poor calls by fallible human beings, but that still doesn't make the hurt go away for these guys.

Before we move on, it's important to note how Corey again mentioned the Husker/Pro Wrestler fight that took place in Tokyo, Japan: "And we had an incident over there in Tokyo where the team became one, fighting against some wrestlers." I'm not aware of the number of players who were in the fray, but it absolutely astounds me how a quick scrum or two could have such a profound bonding effect on those guys (though it could have potentially given the University a black eye). (pun intended)

Notable quote #2:
Corey Dixon on the walk-on spirit: "…these guys are walking on and they're scout team guys… and then two years later you see them being starters. That's amazing to me. It just takes hard work and dedication."

Football is easy if you're crazy as hell.

Vincent 'Bo' Jackson

Taxonomically speaking, football players are positioned among a unique species of the genus known as humankind. The naked eye's understanding of them is often belied by a kinetic inertia, whereas -in reality- their casual walking gait hides an accelerant powderkeg, their commonplace posture concealing a furled synapse of fury. Psychologically speaking, one could posit that footballers are a constrained amalgam of split-personalities due to the fact you'd never know such a vicious hitter stood in your midst unless he strapped on the pads and unhinged some poor sap's vertebral column before the next whistle. From personal recollection, time and again I've beheld hellacious, savage and brutally violent turf-roaming monsters who only hours earlier gave one the impression of a lackadaisical, mild mannered & bookish Clark Kent-type. But don't for a second let the eyeglasses fool you; it's as if the scent of trampled grass or the staccato pop of a lone shoulder pad had the power to unleash, to snap a trip-wire, to trigger the fatal release of an inner madman upon an unsuspecting and altogether soon-to-be-maimed opponent.

Just the same, one is quite often unable to tell the studs from the duds by physical traits alone. Sure, you might find a chiseled Adonis in the lineup on rare occasion, but for the most part footballers are blocky, utilitarian fellows of pedestrian proportion, inhabiting garden-variety physiques save for one tell-tale give-away: a larger than average backside. The entire pelvic region's musculature is their engine house of speed and the base of all power for the accelerating and sprinting, the stopping and starting, the pushing and shoving, the planting and leveraging. In truth, the Cornhuskers of that day were craftsmen whose delicate and intricately knit tool -their bodies- they held intensely intimate. Conversely -and in defiance of this fact- they more than often punished this precious tool with indifference of abandon. It's a paradox, to be sure.

What's remains for a coaching staff is to then meld eleven of such kind into one simultaneous organism of efficiency, churning the chaos into collusion, the singularity into synergy, and plotting a course by harnessing the Shetlands, Clydesdales, mustangs and thoroughbreds to the same wagon and then riding it... riding it hard to a mid-winter's finish. It took a master's touch to accomplish this annual run repeatedly.

Omahan Vershan Jackson habitually fought his way through the sideline crowd for a front row seat and a partaking of the controlled, calculated and unusually calm master strokes of that collaboration's maestro: Dr. Tom Osborne. And aside from the baccalaureate he garnered on graduation day, Vershan also earned his PhD in Football by doing the rounds and shadowing the Doctor himself, up close and personal, on every game day's sideline. Let's listen to Vershan's impressions gained and the wisdom imparted during that 60 & 3 era...

Notable quote #1:
"Our practices were tougher than games. A lot of people don't know that. They think Coach Osborne was a soft spoken, great guy, but when we put the pads on it was blood and sweat. He worked us hard."

Vershan Jackson

Scholarship recruit, Omaha, Nebraska (South)
Where are they now? Lincoln, Nebraska, Coach/Administrator

Question: Hey Vershan, I hear you're doing a little coaching. Is that right?

Vershan Jackson: I'll always be coaching. People always would kid around with me about me standing next to Coach Osborne all the time and trying to get on TV when I was younger. And they were partly right. (laughs) But the other part was I wanted to know what was going on, what play he was calling, what he was doing and all that; figuring out what he wanted to do.

Q: What did you pick up from standing next to Coach Osborne all the time, then?

VJ: The way he carried himself on the field, his play-calling. He had a lot of the plays he called memorized and he would just put a complete game together... and the adjustments that he would make on the fly? I don't know if there is another coach that made the type of adjustments that Coach Osborne made during the game.

His calm, cool demeanor? But there were also times when we needed a good talking to. I remember the Missouri game he told us, "Just keep playing, keep fighting." Like the Miami game, that halftime speech, too. He said, "We're gonna keep hitting them in their mouth and they're gonna break." And that actually happened.

You even take Coach Osborne in practice: our practices were tougher than games. A lot of people don't know that. They think Coach Osborne was a soft spoken, great guy, but when we put the pads on it was blood and sweat. He worked us hard.

Q: So you're with the Nebraska Football Academy?

VJ: Well, I was working recruiting as an intern at the University and an opportunity came along to be Director of the Nebraska Football Academy, which is a year-round football academy at the Abbott Sports Complex. We're really trying to build the fundamentals into these kids and put that football spirit back in the kids again, and I have a lot of former Huskers as coaches.

We do all sports combines: 3 or 4 of those with 500 kids where we basically test the kid from 5 years old on up to 18. The pro agility, the 40, the vertical jump, we teach them how to do the different events the correct way. If they make it to the NFL Combine they'll know how to do that correctly. We have football camps in Lincoln, Omaha, Grand Island, and Mitchell, Nebraska, which is about 10 miles from Scottsbluff. We're putting together former Huskers to go out and really show and get football inspired back into the state of Nebraska back to when I was growing up. With video games and all that we kind of get away from going outside and playing a pickup game of football with your buddies, because back when I was growing up we were always outside doing stuff and staying active. Now with the video game era a lot of kids are couch potatoes. We want to steal some of that time away from the video games and the TV and get the football going again in the state of Nebraska, because you've got to have your recruits coming from the state of Nebraska. When I came out we had about 8 or 9 guys, and recently they had only two one year. Getting football revitalized in Nebraska is our goal.

Q: Any other names helping out that I might be familiar with?

VJ: Octavious McFarlin and Jamel Williams. We've had Tommie Frazier, Dwayne Harris, Riley Washington, Matt Hoskinson, and some of the younger guys, Terrance Nunn, Armando Murillo. I talked Terrance Nunn into giving football one more chance at the next level and told him to give me 6 weeks, and he just had a great game for the Patriots last Sunday.

Q: Wow, Vershan. Sounds to me like you're a modern-day hybrid of Coach Osborne, Boyd Epley and Ron Brown.

VJ: I would agree with that. (laughs)

Q: So what year was your first fall camp in Lincoln?

VJ: It was '93. That might have been the first year without freshman football.

And you know what? I played in the Shrine Bowl and ended up hurting my ankle in that game, so when I first walked out there at the university I had crutches. It really broke me in quick, too, because I can't remember if it was (Kevin) Ramaekers or Christian Peter, but he basically said to me, "This ain't South High School. This is the big leagues now." They kind of let me know real quick, if you get hurt people will be looking at you. They didn't want any excuses for getting hurt, and I needed to be out there: "Hey buddy, you ain't gonna get no love from us. Get out here on the field."

Q: You probably got to know Doak or Jerry or George right away?

VJ: When I first came in Doak was in the freshman locker room. My whole career Doak taped me. (I went to Jerry once or twice.) Once you get a trainer that you liked and they taped you you would kind of stick with them, so me and Doak became friends real quick.

Stuff would happen over the weekend. It was funny, Doak would ask me about certain things and I'd be, 'Doak, how in the world do you know what kind of things happened over the weekend? Are you an investigator of some kind?' Doak's always been a good guy and one I missed the most, as far as training goes. George Sullivan, he was such a hard-nosed guy, but he was a loving guy, too. George would ask you a question: "Are you hurt or are you injured?" If you were injured then you sit out, and if you're hurt then you go back in there.

Q: Now, you spent some time between fullback and tight end, didn't you?

VJ: Right. I tell you what -for the record?- Coach Solich is the best running backs coach, ever. I learned so many techniques and so much from Coach Solich: from how to run the ball, how to carry the ball, how to block people, just being a better running back in general. He was awesome, and it was always physical between the backs. I enjoyed my two years of playing fullback.

I remember in '95 we were loaded. You had Makovicka, Clinton Childs had just moved over, you had Brian Schuster. You had a host of fullbacks and I was sitting there probably about 4th or 5th on the depth chart (and they only took two fullbacks on the travel team), and I was tired of waiting and wanted to play. And they came to me and said, "Hey, we're low at tight end. Would you like to make that move?" And I thought, 'Would I rather be at home and on scout team or do I want to play a little bit?' And I made the decision: I wanted to play.

On scout team I played all over the place: running back, wide receiver, tight end. From watching the film I think they got an idea of what I could do at all the positions. I used to always tell Joel Makovicka, 'For you I moved to tight end or you might not have seen the field until after I'd left.' (laughs)

Q: So you joined Ron Brown's group…

VJ: Went over to ol' Coach Brown. The change in pace was that you had to go from running the ball by getting the ball in the backfield to having to go 50 yards downfield and trying to catch the football.

I remember the first time trying to switch in that spring practice. I was always a pretty good route runner and I could get open. Well, we ran a bootleg and I'm wiiiiiide open and about

40 yards downfield. Brook threw the ball and I'm by myself for a sure touchdown… and the ball hit me on top of the head. (laughs) I couldn't catch a cold when I first got there at tight end. And that same scrimmage? Everything is the same and we're going the opposite way and I'm wide open again, running downfield, and Brook, again, throws the ball, and I'm along the sideline running past the defense and I can hear Christian Peter yell out, "He's nooooot gonna catch iiiiiiiittttt….!" And, of course, I drop the ball again. (laughs)

Adjusting to catching deep balls was the toughest part because it was something I never did before. Coach Brown did a good job right after that and got my eyes checked. I was out there with no contacts and couldn't see a lick, but he got me contacts and everything became a little clearer to me.

Q: All of a sudden you start seeing the thread and the grain of the ball?

VJ: Right.

Q: So you developed some tender hands after awhile?

VJ: Coach Brown is a great coach: he knows exactly what you needed to do to be better. Especially tight ends; catching a hundred balls, catching tennis balls, catching the X on the ball, catching balls on the pole. It all worked out in time.

Q: "Catching balls on the pole"?

VJ: We had the poles, where you had to sit down and lean into the goal post so your arms are around the goal posts. And we caught balls like that. Every Thursday we'd have to catch hot balls from Coach Brown. At one point I had the record where I think I dropped 15 or 16 straight. It was where he was 5 yards away and he's bringing the heat; it's a low ball and he's bringing the absolute heat on you. He did a great job of teaching how to catch the ball and secure the ball.

Q: Not just catching the perfect passes, right?

VJ: *Any* pass. Bad balls. Tipped balls.

Q: Tell me more about Coach Brown, his methods…

VJ: Coach Brown is so consistent. I have a chance to watch him coach now. He's the same now that he was 10-15 years ago. His mindset was for us to outwork everybody out there on the field. And when you have a coach that pushes you to be great? He pushed us to be perfectionists, to play hard every single snap. When we made mistakes he would definitely correct those mistakes, but also wanted us to show him that we learned what he taught us on the football field, when the lights were on. He always wanted us to pay attention to details, to be great, great, great blockers, technique wizards.

And playing tight end at 6', 245 lbs. I had to go against Grant Wistrom and Jared Tomich and Dwayne Harris and even, at times ,Trev Alberts. He knew that for me -especially because I was undersized at tight end- that I would have to be a great technician when it came to blocking, getting my hands into a guy's chest first, driving my legs, keeping my head up, all those different things. Coach Brown, he stayed on top of them.

Q: Did coming from the fullback position help in that regard?

VJ: I think scout team helped me, because on scout team you were playing multiple positions.

And our scout team had been kind of picked by Aaron Penland as being one of the best scout teams ever. We challenged the Blackshirts. All bets were off. The Blackshirts back then? It was like they were in gameday mode any time the scout team was out there. They'd take shots at you, they didn't let up. They'd try to take your head off if they could. We took pride in that, "We are the group getting this defense ready to play and we need to play 100 miles an hour."

And I think on scout team, that's where I learned I could play tight end, because I'd have to line up at tight end at times and block those guys. So my time at fullback definitely helped me, but being on scout team and going against guys that are Blackshirts in that era? You'd either get beat up every day in practice and washed out or you're gonna step up to the plate and get some courage and heat in you and learn how to fight.

Q: Any memorable practices stand out to you going against those guys?

VJ: My most memorable practice was '95. It was a bye week. We were getting ready to play Oklahoma. Normal practice schedule with the exception that we had a scrimmage on Friday: ones against ones, twos against twos. That was the most physical practice that I've ever been a part of. You had Jamel Williams and Clinton Childs: they had one of the most ferocious hits ever in practice. It stopped practice, that's how hard they hit. It was like two battering rams hitting up against each other. You could hear it echo all the way to the top of Memorial Stadium. It was the most aggressive, fireworks everywhere. It was just hitting, hitting, hitting.

Then we went goal line situations. I think it was Ed Stewart and Clinton Childs. Clinton, again. And Ed stopped Clinton cold on the goal line and it was just wild. That's probably my most memorable practice. It was so, so physical. And it was competitive.

Q: And a week later didn't we shut out Oklahoma 37-0?

VJ: Yes, a week later. We did the things that we did to football teams in that era because we practiced harder than anybody else. Our practices were harder than the games. Once we got to the game it was easy. A lot of us couldn't believe how easy it was come game time because we went against each other so much, and now it was time to set that aggression off on someone who had absolutely nothing to do with us. It was like a bunch of wild dogs out there. It was fun. It was a great time.

And at practice there was always that mystique of, "We don't lose at Nebraska. Losing is not an option." That's how we felt. In my five years our career record was 60 wins, three losses, and three national championships. Our mindset was, "We refuse to lose." And we had to practice hard in order to achieve that.

Q: Wow, so you have three rings. Do you ever break them out?

VJ: No. You get a little older and you don't necessarily like having people come up to you asking this and that. I kind of outgrew that about 7 or 8 years ago. (laughs) It was good to get those rings, but once you get older you know that the hardware is always good but it's what in your heart that people need to understand. It means more what's in my heart than what's on my fingers.

Q: As far as saying what's in your heart, what did you take away from those days?

VJ: In order to be the best you have to outwork all the rest. And that's in sports, life and school.

When we played at Nebraska in that era? Number 1 was that we had a lot of athletes, and number 2? We were smart football players. Across the board -of course, you had a couple knuckleheads in there- but across the board Coach Osborne recruited smart guys. Guys were smart, but they were also physical.

You know, football is a tough sport. With some of the vanilla offenses we see in football in this era, you have to get back to understanding that football is a physical sport and you want the other teams to know that you were the most physical team that they ever played against. When you go out there and express that dominance against an opponent and hit them in the mouth every single play -play after play after play after play- it's gonna demoralize them. They'll eventually break. When you do things in practice, you do things at 110%.

And you can't take away a guy's heart. You've got to have heart when you play football, you've got to be physical and pay attention to detail. And I think that's what Coach Osborne was about. As far as teaching how to pay attention to detail, how to be physical, how to love our teammates and play for each other, how to play for your family, play for the coaches, play for the greatest fans in America? You put all those things together and that's why you have championships. Everybody of the same accord, on the same page, thinking the same thing, going the same way. And when you have 124 guys thinking that same way -from scout team to the starter to the Blackshirts- you've got a well-oiled machine.

Q: What do you think got everybody focused in that same direction?

VJ: Not only the coaches, who were of one mind as far as being physical and all that, but as players we had coaches out on the field: player-coaches. Players who would get up in your face when you made mistakes, players that would light you up when you made a mistake, players that would be there when you found success.

We pushed ourselves as players at Nebraska. You have to take that on yourself. It can't just be the coaches that push you. You have to put in the extra work yourself and push yourself, doing extra fieldwork. I can remember, I was up for Lifter of the Year in '96 and, of course, Jared Tomich won it, and I was second place.

And going into '97? That summer we didn't have coaches out there pushing us. We pushed each other. We said, "Hey, look, if you're loafing, are you a part of this thing or not? If you are, we expect you to get up there and work just as hard as everybody else that's working hard." We got in their face. I was a team captain in '97 along with Aaron Taylor and Grant Wistrom and Jason Peter. So we really were all about making sure that everyone knew that we were gonna work hard and we expected everybody else to work just as hard as we worked.

Q: Speaking earlier of the necessity of physicality, what team do you have the most respect for in holding up as well as they did versus Nebraska?

VJ: There were two teams in '94: Wyoming and Washington State. I have awesome respect for those two teams in '94, because they came into Lincoln and they gave us a fight. We hit them in the mouth but they didn't lay down, they hit us right back in the mouth. Those were the two most physical games that I've ever been a part of.

But if you talk about consistency and we get back into the Big 8/Big 12? And this is gonna shock you, but the team that we would beat the smoke out of, but they would not lay down, was Missouri. We would beat 'em up and beat 'em up, but those guys at Missouri always came to fight. And even though they were always out-manned, out-gunned and out-matched, they came to fight. Over the long haul I have a lot of respect for Missouri because they wouldn't back down. They couldn't beat us but they didn't back down.

Q: What is your most memorable play?

VJ: Talking about my own play I was in on? Gosh, there are so many. I think it probably would be one of the many touchdown runs. I was a pretty good blocker. I loved the blocking and running aspect, but I think my most memorable play would probably be the Iowa State game when I caught my second touchdown pass, about a 30-yarder. My eyes were huge! It was my junior year and I'm having the game of my life, almost 100 yards receiving and two touchdowns (I should have had three but I slipped down on one).

But my most memorable play would be the '95 Kansas game. I was just starting to get some action at tight end, having just moved. And Mark Gilman got hurt, so here comes young Vershan Jackson fresh out of the water having to bring plays in. (That's another reason I love to coach, because I was one of the guys having to bring plays in and having to regurgitate it back to the quarterback.) Anyway, they were giving us fits in Kansas that year. The first half of the game and I'm in there playing and we're battling. And I don't remember what the score was at that point, but we drove it all the way down. And this is right after halftime in the third quarter. And we always had this audible: t he play was 44 Dive on the goal line. And Tommie's in the game and he audibles, "44 52", and I'm on the right side and I'm thinking,'44, 52. 44, 52. Is that me?!' It's just a quick tight end release turnaround. (Keep in mind, we're on the one yard line.) So I'm thinking to myself -when he calls '52' I look over at Tommie- and I'm like, 'Oh my goodness, he's calling 52. This is me. This is my chance to score a touchdown. Don't drop the ball. Look the ball in. Get off the line.' I'm thinking all these things. And I end up with one catch, one yard, one touchdown. That was my first touchdown. I always tell Tommie, 'I appreciate you getting me my first touchdown.' And that was my most memorable play because it came at a time of adversity. The score may have been 7 to 7 at the time and we went on to win. I don't remember the final score, but it was my first touchdown and first reception.

Q: Running plays in and standing next to Coach Osborne all the time, what kind of working dynamic was going on between Tommie and Brook and Coach Osborne? Was it like three brains operating perfectly on the same wavelength?

VJ: Definitely. Let me just say this -Coach Osborne may disagree, but I don't think he will- 50% of the plays were called by Tommie, Brook and our quarterbacks on the field by way of audibles. 50% of the time when coach sent the plays in the quarterback could audible or call, "Opposite." They were like coaches on the field, they were mini-Osbornes.

Q: 'Opposite', that's when they tapped a hand on the helmet to change the play call, right?

VJ: You know it.

Q: Adam Treu informed me that it was a way to run the same play, but simply in the opposite direction. Were there ever times when you missed a call?

VJ: The same game, that Kansas game. Of course this was a televised game, and I believe 47 Dive was the play. It was maybe Tight Right 47 Dive.

But it's on TV, and I run it in and tell Tommie the play. And we get up on the line of scrimmage and Tommie is looking like, "Something's not right. Something's not right." And you kind of just see him call the timeout... and you can hear him do it on the TV. When I got home all my family and friends were like, "You messed up, didn't you?" I was like, 'Why'd you say that?' They said, "We could hear Tommie say, "Vershan, you brought in the wrong play!" (laughs) I was like, 'Oh, my gosh!' When I got to the sideline Coach Osborne was, "What play did you call?" (laughs) That was one time where I definitely brought in the wrong play.

Q: By the time you entered the huddle from the sideline you completely forgot the play?

VJ: I might have said the wrong thing that one time, but after that I never forgot a play. If he told me what play it was I never forgot it after that. If you forgot it a couple two or three times you'd find yourself sitting on the bench. And to win three national championships in four years is proof that we didn't forget very often. (laughs)

Q: Since there were only three games lost, which one of those stands out to you the most?

VJ: All three of them.

Because you take Florida State my freshman year: we should have won that game. And we fought and fought and fought and we came up a little short, but I think that game gave us... it almost was like blood in the water and we were sharks. We understood at that point that we could play with anybody in the country, because here was this Florida State team that was supposed to blow us out, and here we are hanging and fighting and biting and clawing. And at the end of the day there were some controversial calls in that game that could have went the other way and I think the game would have turned out differently.

The second game that sticks out is Arizona State. I think that was a wakeup call in '96 where we went back out there to the desert again. We were going against Jake 'the Snake' Plummer and we didn't play very well on offense, and the defense played pretty good. We gave them two safeties; offensively we just couldn't get it going. Scott Frost was in his first year trying to get it going, but to bounce back and win the rest of the games the way we did?

And I think that Texas game is the game that really sticks out. And not to make any excuses, but we had a lot of guys that were really sick that week and had the flu going around, but losing that game after losing early? And here we would have been in another national championship game. You go back to that game and relive it in your mind and you say, 'We left a lot on the field that game.' To win that game would have put us back in the Sugar Bowl and the national championship game where, technically speaking, had things gone our way, my five years at Nebraska we could have played for the title for 5 straight years. All we had to do was win that Texas game and we would have been back in the National Championship game.

Q: That's amazing! For 5 straight years in college football to be at that level, that's something special...

VJ: There's not too many guys who can say they went 60-3. You've got Grant Wistrom and Octavious McFarlin, who played as freshmen in '94: those two guys probably have one of the best career records of anybody in college football at 49-2. These guys didn't lose too often, and two of the games they lost was in the same year. It's amazing.

Q: And not to talk down about it, but Nebraska of all places, Vershan! It's not like it's a social and entertainment mecca, it's not glamorous, it's not a vacation destination or anything like that...

VJ: Yeah, where are you going to go? The Henry Doorly Zoo? Maybe the College World Series or some hunting? But I think the one thing you do see in Nebraska is football. I'd always wanted to play for Nebraska. I've been a Nebraska fan since I was 5 years old. I sold lemonade at the games.

Q: Really?

VJ: Oh yeah, I sold lemonade as a young man at the games. I would sell as many racks as I could the first half so I could sit the second half and watch the games. We had a great run, and at the end of the day it boiled down to us playing for each other, loving each other, and working out with everybody else.

Q: Now, I've got to go back to the lemonade thing. I suppose by halftime you were a pretty sticky kid after spilling lemonade all over yourself?

VJ: I was pretty good at what I did, so I didn't spill too much lemonade on me. (laughs)

Q: So how did you get the job?

VJ: Well, Johnny Rodgers and Robert Faulkner had started a lemonade deal. And Faulkner (who coached football at Flanagan, which was right down the street from my house and we'd always go up to Flanagan for track practice and stuff like that), of course he would employ some of us inner city kids to make some money and sell lemonade. We didn't make a ton of money, but we had a rack of 25 lemonades. Sell the whole rack and I think you got three bucks. (One lemonade was almost three dollars!) (laughs) It wasn't a glorious job but it kept us employed. It kept Nebraska football in front of us and we got to see the games for free, so you wouldn't trade that for anything in the world.

Q: I'm sure your legs the next day were dead tired from walking those stadium steps?

VJ: No, not really. Like I said, there was a reason I played at Nebraska: I was one of those kids who had a lot of energy and the stadium steps never bothered me at all. It was a good time.

Q: Now, you went to the pros after school was over?

VJ: First I went to Seattle, then Kansas City. It's so funny, because all three of my years I always walked into the situation where we had a new coach: Dennis Erickson just got the coaching job at Seattle. And then when I went to Kansas City Gunther Cunningham just took over.

Q: Playing for Erickson, did he ever bring up the fact that you guys beat his Miami team?

VJ: He didn't really say too much about that. He always said that us Nebraska guys were strong guys, but he never dabbled much into that.

Q: Was there a particular type of athlete they recruited, any special parameters Nebraska was looking for in those days?

VJ: You want to recruit a kid who plays with heart. Football players? It's not about the size or how big they are. It's not the size of the dog... it's about the size of the fight in the dog. And I think you want to get a guy that will fight, that has a big heart and is not scared to run through a brick wall, a guy who has a high motor and runs all over the place. That's the type of guy to go recruit because that's the type of guy who's gonna give 110% and then some. Guys who are leaders and not followers.

Q: So do you have any funny, memorable off-field occurrences?

VJ: I can tell you a funny on-field occurrence.

It's my senior year and we're playing at Baylor. A young Joe Walker is our return guy and it's opening kickoff and everybody's excited. I'm all juiced up, and here Joe comes and he's breaking out and I'm excited and jumping up because he looks like he's going to take it to the house. And the ref is backing up and running down the sideline... and I don't realize that I've stepped over the sideline and I'm on the field! And I'm jumping up and down, and all of a sudden the ref comes out of nowhere. And he's just about to turn around. And the second he turns around I just 'rock and roll' him; I give him a shot that lifted him right up off the ground.

And before he hits the ground, the flag is coming out. I was like, 'Oh, my God! I am in so much trouble!' Of course, I ran back away and he gave us a flag for sideline interference. And you could tell the ref was angry and Coach Osborne is still looking around like, "What happened? What happened?" We get into the locker room after the game and he says, "Who ran into that ref?" Of course, me being me, there's no way I'm gonna fess up. (laughs) So here it is on Monday and we have our film session, and what does he do? The first thing he shows us is that play. He must have rewound it twenty times. And they laughed. After I did it you see me just try to sneak off. I didn't want to get caught. We laugh about it to this day. You just see me as plain as day knock that ref down and just run over to the back of the sideline by the bench and just sit down. (laughs)

Q: The film doesn't lie! (laughs)

VJ: Right! I should have known they were gonna catch me on film. I figured it was better they catch me on film on Monday than during the game.

Q: So who do you think played crucial role behind the scenes?

VJ: When I think about guys I think about Dennis Leblanc: him keeping us eligible, him keeping us graduating. There's a reason Nebraska leads all its member schools in graduation rates among its athletes. You've got to take your hat off to Dennis Leblanc because that guy kept us eligible, he kept us going, let us know when we were messing up in school. He kept tutors on us. He just kept an eye on us when you talk about school work. That so important, because we weren't just athletes, we were student-athletes. He sees the educational pieces and how important that is. He was always great at making sure you understood the position you put yourself in.

Another guy who doesn't get a lot of exposure and gratitude is Bryan Bailey, who worked for our strength staff and works for USC now. There's a reason why USC is a dominant team, and I assure you Brian Bailey is a key part of that. If you wanted to get some extra work in the weight room he always had a workout for you, he always pushed you whether you were running or lifting weights. Bryan Bailey pushed us and gave us techniques that you couldn't pay for. A lot of crazy stuff.

Q: Did you sometimes wonder, "Is this guy for real?"

VJ: There was times. Not a lot, but there was times. (laughs)

Q: So is there anything I haven't touched on that you feel made a difference for those great Nebraska teams?

VJ: Like I said before: you've got to work hard, you've got to prepare hard, and you've got to play hard. And you've got to play with heart. When you do that you're tough to beat. When you play with heart and know what you're doing and go 110% you're a tough team to beat.

End conversation.

I especially appreciated Vershan's mention of the weaning and winnowing process, revealing those who could hack the punishing long haul and remain with the group through the oft-inflicted scout team battering, *"..you'd either get beat up every day in practice and (get) washed out or you're gonna step up to the plate and get some courage and heat in you and learn how to fight."* We've heard of the fighting: In pads, out of pads, perhaps even behind locker room doors. Like a secret society, a club or fraternal order, they had their ritual 'beating in' through a series of two-a-day efforts and season-long one-on-one run-ins under the watchful eye of staff, peer and press. Only the strong survived, only the undaunted endured. The men who speak on these pages passed that crucible, conquering trauma, cowardice and self-doubt at just about every turn, yet persevered. We owe them honor if only for that.

Notable quote #2:

Vershan Jackson on the model team-concept: "That's what Coach Osborne was about. As far as teaching how to pay attention to detail, how to be physical, how to love our teammates and play for each other, how to play for your family, play for the coaches, play for the greatest fans in America? You put all those things together and that's why you have championships."

Each of us has an inner voice that speaks of the gold in our shadow. It is the voice of our secret, hidden self- our most authentic self in many ways...

John R. O'Neil, *The Paradox of Success*

As Nebraska was hitting its unified stride in 1993, a cherubic freshman from Wichita Falls, Texas -whom no one else had coveted- was quietly learning the ropes as a redshirt offensive lineman. The only non-native Nebraskan starter on the '97 National Championship team's offense, Aaron Taylor first emerged as a cog on the fabled '95 team's O-line. Perceived as too small by other college coaches, Milt Tenopir told him, "I don't care how high you are. I care about the size of your heart." (*"Then Osborne Said to Rozier..."*, Steve Richardson) With a heart of gold and a reservoir of culled wisdom, I'm looking forward to a rousing and revealing tabletalk with this multi-faceted jewel of a man... who now calls himself a Nebraskan.

Notable quote #1:
"The coaches didn't have to get on you when you blew a play because you were already riding yourself and you expected more than what they were expecting of you, so it was almost a self-governing of the practices and the teams those days. The players were harder on themselves than the coaches could ever be to them."

Aaron Taylor

Scholarship recruit, Offensive Guard, Wichita Falls, Texas (Rider)
Where are they now? Omaha, Nebraska, Management

Question: Hey, Aaron. Thanks so much for making time to talk.

Aaron Taylor: No problem, Paul. I think one of the things I learned from the college days was the leadership abilites I developed and used then. They definitely transfer into the business world.

Q: In what way?

AT: Oh, I would say just the ability to lead, to create a coalition, to have a calming effect, to give directives and have someone believe in you, and to also make yourself a part of a team. And that was a big thing, Paul.

And you know this, but back in the '90's the team atmosphere was something that I don't think has been replicated. I think they're on the right track right now, but '93 to '97, my senior year? There was such camaraderie among us. There were some great athletes, but no one person was greater than the team.

Q: That calming effect: would you have gotten some of that from Coach Tenopir or Young or Osborne?

AT: I would say, number one, on the offensive side of the ball you have to have a little more control of your emotion, and the second and third thing would come from Coach Osborne and Milt Tenopir. They both had a fire to them -and I think we all saw it- but it was a controlled fire in their belly, and when it needed to be unleashed they could unleash it.

But there were awesome control mechanisms in there, you know? The difference between the offensive side of the ball and the defensive side of the ball was just dramatic. Look at the way Charlie McBride handled himself on the sideline versus the way an offensive coach did. On the defensive side you have to play with a lot more emotion, more conviction, more adrenaline, if you will. On the offensive side there it has to be a little more controlled and in spurts.

Q: More cerebral, more technical?

AT: Exactly. I remember vividly how some emotions would get out of control and I would completely botch the play. And if I botched the play that usually meant we didn't have a play for many yards, so it has to be a little more controlled fury.

A prime example: I remember like it was yesterday, the Missouri game in 1997, when we were down and we needed to drive almost 70 yards to score a touchdown and put it into overtime. We called a timeout and all went over to the sideline and Osborne was just standing there -just cool, calm and collected. The Missouri fans? It was so loud. It was unbelievable the atmosphere there, and so much tension. And here we had a minute and something like 40 seconds to drive 70 yards and put the game into overtime… and we go over to the sidelines, and he just looked at us all and said, "Well, here's what we're gonna do. We're gonna run 32 and 38 option pass." And here he's just cool, calm and collected, and we all just had adrenaline flowing out of our pores. And he was, "Linemen, you get a good block. Scott, make a good throw. Receivers, catch the ball and get out of bounds. Let's go." And it was that calm tone. And here you've got eleven men on the field who are just ready to go out and take someone's heads off and go down and score. And just with that kind of little pep talk and calm manner he was able to take you and bring you down a notch from being out of control to, "Hey, the guys are still fired up. They're gonna go out there and do their job. They'll be fine if they go out there and do their job." Little did we know Shevin Wiggins would kick that ball to Matt Davison.

Q: Were you so embroiled in blocking on that play that you missed seeing 'the catch?'

AT: You know, as far as 'the kick': I had a guy that I was engaged with on their defensive line (and usually when a pass is thrown the defensive line kind of lets down their guard a little bit), and when my defensive linemen did that I turned and looked at the play and saw the kick go up.

And actually? I thought that Shevin had caught the ball, first. And then next I see the ball go up in the air. I saw Davison running and then I couldn't see anything after that. Then all of a sudden I see him standing up with his hands in the air! And it was an eternity looking over at the ref, waiting for him to signal a touchdown. Just an absolutely awesome feeling. And you could just feel the air sucked out of the stadium. Absolutely amazing.

Q: The other day I was talking to Vershan and he mentioned that he really respected Missouri because they always came to fight. Would you say the same thing?

AT: I would say the same thing. They had a pretty good crop of talent down there that kind of reminded you of a 'mini-me', like a mini-Nebraska. They weren't quite to our level, but they ran the same type of offense and they had the same type of kids that worked hard and battled all game long, and they would just get in your face and they wouldn't stop. They weren't the most physical or the most talented group of guys that we played against year in and year out, but I think they did a pretty good job of giving us a run for our money every single year.

I would have to say, Paul -and this sounds so weird- but the toughest games that I had were against Oklahoma. And we were running through Oklahoma big time, if you remember, 70-something to 20, in the mid-90s; the Schnellenberger years we were just killing them. But man, I tell you what, the next day or the day after that you felt like you just went through a battle. They didn't really give up, but man they were physical. They were that way, also, a lot like us. I don't know why it was Oklahoma, but for me that was always a tough game. But they always had pretty good interior talent, too...

Q: Any one guy you went against who you developed great respect for?

AT: I would say it would be someone from our own team: Jason Peter. I really feel that way. Just from the aspect that Jason was such a great, well-rounded player: he didn't have a chink in his armor whatsoever. He worked extremely hard to stay at 280-285 lbs. and he worked his tail off on the football field. And I tell you what, just his repertoire of being strong, being fast, being quick, being a knowledgeable football player always made it difficult for me as an offensive lineman; by far the best at developing me as a player -going against him- than anything I was involved in in athletics. There wasn't a day in the 5 years we were there that I didn't go against him and butt helmets.

Q: Would you agree that practices were twice as hard as the games?

AT: Oh yeah. When we had the likes of Trev Alberts, Terry Connealy, Christian Peter, Jason Peter, Grant Wistrom, Chad Kelsay, Mike Anderson, Phil Ellis? I could just go on and on and on. You were going against those guys day in and day out, and then you go to a game against the likes of an Iowa State or a Missouri or a Baylor? There's no one you're gonna play that's better than the teammates you were going against for 5 days before the game. It just developed you so much, and that's why it's so crucial and critical to have good talent and good depth across the board in a program.'Cause if you can simulate game experience in a practice? Whenever we walked into a ball game we knew that we had already faced our toughest opponents. And that was our teammates earlier that week.

Q: Gives you quite a bit of confidence then?

AT: Oh yeah, you'd step on the field on Saturday and never felt like you were gonna lose. Saturday was a cake walk. It was an easy deal on Saturday.

Q: So Aaron, was '93 your freshman year?

AT: That was the first year on campus. I redshirted in '93 and then I backed up Joel Wilks in '94, and then '95 I started at left guard ('cause Wilks was done in '95), and then I moved over to center in '96. Aaron Graham had graduated -and I don't know if you remember Josh Heskew at all. He wasn't quite ready to play, a year and a half earlier had an ACL or shoulder surgery- and we didn't have anybody else really ready to take over for him at center. And then Adam Treu came in and played left tackle and Dishman moved down to left guard.

And then in '97 I moved back to left guard, which was actually what I wanted to do. Center was probably my most natural position where I could have stayed longer in the NFL if I'd wanted to, but whenever you're running an offense like Nebraska's the guards were so critical to the play developing and the play succeeding... you were always pulling and always the lead man on the block, and that was something I loved and cherished. And I wanted to get back and get my nose into the play, if you know what I mean? I didn't want to be the second or third option. I wanted to be the guy leading the play, so that's why I moved back to guard my senior year.

Q: You wanted to be the 'tip of the spear', so to speak?

AT: Exactly. Part of the thing is -just like any athlete will tell you- you want to be the guy that's out front leading. (Most would say that, at least.) You want to be the guy that has the pressure on his shoulders. And it was almost a challenge to yourself: 'Can I get it done?

Can I be the spearhead of making the play break or is it gonna fail?' To me, that's the truest test of an athlete: who wants to show up and perform? And that was what I wanted. I wanted that pressure on me. If the play was going to break it was going to break off me.

Q: Were you always that way? In high school, too?

AT: No, I wasn't. Because my dad was retired Air Force, right? I spent two years over in Germany so I played soccer throughout all my adolescent years all the way up to high school. I came into high school and really my freshman year was my first year to play ball. And the way it worked for me? I was still learning the game and when I came to Nebraska I was a really raw talent. And being raw and never going against talent as good as it was at Nebraska? I wouldn't say my confidence was completely shot, but I had some doubts in my ability. And you know as well as I do, whenever you have doubts you have tentativeness. And that's the way I was for my first almost two years.

My confidence really didn't start gaining and developing until I started my sophomore year, the '95 season. And I tell you who did a good job of fostering that, telling me I was a good ballplayer and telling me I could do a lot of things? That was Aaron Graham. That was his senior year in '95. He was from Texas. We gelled really well, and I could always look at myself as an Aaron Graham. I thought I was a better athlete than him but I didn't have the technique, the confidence, all those types of things, but as a senior and as a leader he did a good job of fostering that in me. And when he left it was almost as if he was saying to me, "Okay, it's yours now."

Q: How did he foster that? Encouraging words?

AT: Numerous ways. It was by example, there was no one who worked harder. That encouraged you and showed you how to do things on the field.

The next way was verbally, you know, and Aaron Graham is such a super guy. Just talking to you, getting you excited about the whole program in general, all the way down to the offensive line, and then down to you. It wasn't just about you, it wasn't just about the offensive line. It was about everything. He did such a good job of building that, but verbally and showing it by his leadership skills, he did it both ways.

Q: What stood out most when you first arrived on campus?

AT: I don't want to say anything surprised me, but what stood out the most was the family atmosphere. It was the camaraderie amongst the guys and the coaches.

As I said earlier, there was no one individual that stood above the team. And if you did there were other athletes that were as good as you and they let you know that you weren't 'The Man', you know? (laughs) If you take a look at it, imagine all the guys that came through there, all those guys I mentioned on the defense, earlier. You had Barron Miles and Tony Veland, too. You had Ahman, you had Lawrence. (Lawrence was kind of out there on his own) (laughs) You had Rob Zatechka, Brenden Stai, Aaron Graham. You take a look at all those guys. You never had one star, you had a bunch of stars. And what that did? Everybody just kind of came together and was on the same level.

And just the family atmosphere? I can remember sitting right there in Coach Tenopir's office one time and Coach Tenopir is just hammering on Freddy Pollack. He's just hammering on Fred. And Fred was kind of one of the headcases and was a hell of an athletic talent and was strong and fast -but would struggle a little bit- and Tenopir was riding him for blowing a play in practice. And I could see Fred started getting pretty aggravated, so I spoke up and said, 'Coach, that was my fault. I gave him the wrong call and that's why he did what the did.' (Knowing damn well that I didn't do it) (laughs) But the thing is, I'm covering his ass and I fully expected him to cover my ass the next time I blow a play. (laughs) But that's the thing: Tenopir turned his anger at me for a minute or two. And that was fine.'I'll take the heat off of Fred.' And Fred realized it and he was thankful for that and he reciprocated. And that's the way it was for everyone. The thing is, if Fred blew that play again he knew I was gonna jump down his throat and 'I wasn't gonna take the heat for ya', you know what I mean?

It was even that way in practice, Paul, where the coaches didn't have to get on you when you blew a play because you were already riding yourself and you expected more than what they were expecting of you. So it was almost a self-governing of the practices and the teams those days. The players were harder on themselves than the coaches could ever be to them.

Q: How do you think that was, Aaron? I'd think that human nature typically leads a person to coast here and there and not necessarily hold oneself to a higher standard on such a consistent basis?

AT: I think that you had to recruit the right kind of kid. I really do. Were we talented? Yes, we were. Were we more talentd than a Florida, Florida State, Texas back in those days? Were we better than them, person by person? No, we weren't. I think it's recruiting the right kind of kid. I really do.

We were all good guys, we all had a lot of fun, but we also knew what it took to succeed and were willing to do it. I think it's more the type of person you recruited rather than just athletic ability alone. A prime example? Look at the Callahan years. Callahan fan or not, he had some pretty darn good talent that came in but just never really developed it. It was never that same feeling that was there as when we were winning. I don't think there was ever a more ballyhooed recruit than there was with Harrison Beck and with Marlin Lucky at running back. And here we'd go out and we're winning with a walk-on from Wahoo down at K-State, playing a top 15 team in the nation. (laughs)

Q: Do you remember much of that day?

AT: Oh yeah. That was '94 and I was the second string behind Joel Wilks and I was 19 years old and still kind of learning the game of football. (laughs) And Paul, I tell you what, it was kind of one of those days where it was in the mid-50's, so it wasn't real cold and it wasn't real warm. And the stadium was electric!

And really the only person I knew fairly well was Chris Dishman, so I just remember my heart sinking when Brenden Stai broke his ankle during that game. And at that time I believe Bryan Pruitt went in. I think it was Bryan Pruitt, he went in and replaced Brenden Stai, and Dishman looks over at me and says, "You know Aaron, if either one of the guards needs a rest you're going in." And I just kind of looked at him and go, 'Huh?!' I knew I was a backup, but I never looked at it like that. (And I never really stretched much before the game, I wasn't ready at all.)

And quite honestly, Paul, just mentally I wasn't prepared to play either guard position. I was still so young that I just knew my position of left guard and left guard only. So I remember my heart rate racing the whole game as far as the score, as far as the emotions of the game, I was completely lost in it. (laughs) I was just sitting there just trying to concentrate on those two guys not getting hurt and me not having to go in because I didn't want to screw it up in such a big game. (laughs) Of course, my sophomore to senior year? I would have wanted to go in any time, but that was my redshirt freshman year.

And I remember this like it happened twenty minutes ago: Chad May was the quarterback back then, and him moaning and groaning after the game. And I remember Christian running off the field and had his left hand wrapped around his right index finger about halfway down, so you only saw half of his right index finger. He's grinning, and he said, "I had my finger this far in his f***ing eye! I had my finger this far in his f***ing eye!" (laughs) And I'm 19 years old -so it's really my first game or two traveling, so everything is new to me- and I'm looking at him going, 'What in the hell is going on?' (laughs) It was just a great experience and we ended up beating them pretty good. What a great day. It was a learning experience on so many different levels. I didn't even play, but what a learning experience.

Q: Tell me a little about Milt. His techniques, his demeanor, his methods?

AT: Oh, simplicity. Simplicity. We had a pretty technical offense even though it all kind of looked the same, but Coach Tenopir probably did the best job of instilling confidence in you. Keeping it simple, but expecting perfection.

That's one of the things I loved about him: in the five years I was there he never changed the way we blocked technically. Never. So what you did was, for 5 years you did the same thing day in and day out. And the only way to get better at anything in life is just repetition. So when you're sitting there and doing that for 5 straight years there's only one way to go, and that was up. He never changed his coaching technique, never changed his philosophy, and never changed his blocking techniques.

And to me, that's a recipe for success: Do one thing and do it well. I was telling a guy the other day, we were talking about the local high school football team and I said, 'They have twenty different plays that they block twenty different ways. We had twenty different plays that we blocked two ways. If it was an outside play we blocked it one way and if it was an inside play we blocked it a different way.' And they stayed the same. (Now, I'm just talking interior offensive line, I'm not talking fullbacks or tight ends or receivers, because you've got motion and different formations and those things.) But for us, if it was an outside play and it was Ahman Green or Lawrence Phillips going right we blocked it one way, and if it was an inside play between the tackles we blocked it another way, and we did that for five years. And we did that so well, because that's all you do.

Q: And the defenders knew you were going to do it!

AT: Absolutely, and that's the beautiful thing about Tenopir's blocking schemes, because they knew exactly what was coming at 'em. And a lot of times, Paul, I would point on the ground to the defensive tackle and I'd say, 'Dish, we have him back to number 32, linebacker.' So you're sitting here telling that you're gonna double-team this tackle and you're gonna take him back to the linebacker behind him. But the thing is, if you're technically sound and you do your job that you were taught, it doesn't matter what they do or if they hear you; you have a way to combat it and get the job done. It doesn't matter if the linebacker stunts or if the defensive tackle slants, if you did the job that you were taught you weren't gonna lose.

Q: That must have been demoralizing to the defense?

AT: Yeah, (laughs) it was great for us. But the thing is, you just couldn't screw it up. Because if you did, the play's gonna fall apart. But I tell you what, what a deal.

Q: And Coach Dan Young?

AT: Probably one of the most fun coaches I've been around. You know his attitude. He was a very good coach for us, knew the plays just as well as anyone there, technnically sound.

Coach Young was probably the lighter side of the two. I remember really young in my career it was Coach Young that came down and talked to me and was trying to get me to be more aggressive and not passive. That was Coach Young more on a personal level versus a coach level, which I enjoyed. You could joke with Coach Young a lot more. And gosh, I don't want to make that sound bad -because you could also talk with Tenopir- but it was different, you know what I mean? I want to say a 'players coach,' but in a different way. I'm having a real tough time saying it, but you couldn't have Coach Tenopir without Coach Young and you couldn't have Coach Young without Coach Tenopir.

Q: Kind of like Batman and Robin, eh?

AT: (laughs) Exactly. You can't have one without the other.

Q: The question is, who is Batman and who is Robin?

AT: Coach Young would have to be Robin, wouldn't he? I don't think Tenopir would settle for anything less than Batman. (laughs)

Q: What about the different personalities on staff?

AT: Oh boy, where do you start? Of course, you go to Osborne: cool, calm, collected. One of the things I loved and respected about him was that it didn't matter if you were an All-American athlete or a walk-on from Harvard, Nebraska, he appreciated the work that you gave him, he knew you personally, he knew your family and he just had a genuine interest in all of that. He would talk to me about my family down in Texas: "Has your dad retired from the Air Force yet?" And down to the walk-on from North Platte: "How is your dad doing, your mom doing? How's school going?"

I remember being in the NFL and talking to a couple players from Florida State and one guy from Penn State about their coaches. And the guys from Penn State? Paterno didn't know them, he would sit up in the tower at practice and say, "Hey number 54! You need to be doing this…" And there was a receiver from Florida State and I asked him, 'How much interaction did you have with Coach Bowden?' And he said, "Oh, about 15 minutes or so." And I said, '15 minutes a day, or what?' and he was, "No, no. That was my whole career." Can you believe that?

Osborne knew every single player he had, every staff member he had. He was a coach. He wasn't a figurehead, he was a coach. And to me that's the biggest compliment he could have. He knew all about the receiver on the right side of the field all the way across to the receiver on the left side of the field. He knew what they were supposed to do, how they were supposed to accomplish it, and the techiniques involved with all that. And if Coach Tenopir was busy coaching somewhere else I could turn to Coach Osborne and say, 'Hey Coach, on this play I've got a three technique. Am I supposed to get the middle linebacker or the backside linebacker?' and he would literally walk me through the steps of what I was supposed to do. And in meetings I could turn around and ask that question of Coach Tenopir and it was the exact same way that Coach Osborne taught me. That's the beauty of it: everything was consistent from top to bottom.

Q: Unity of one mind?

AT: That's exactly right. So you had him, then you had Coach Solich… I loved Coach Solich, you know? Running Backs coach and Assistant Head Coach. Fiery. He'd get on people, yet he was also a lot of fun. I loved working with him. Us offensive linemen? We kept telling him he could be an offensive lineman because he was as short as us. (laughs) We had a lot of fun with him.

I remember Turner Gill just being a mini-Coach Osborne. I loved the way he worked: he had great respect among the players, but he was still willing to be a player's coach, if you will. You could just see him developing as a coach. He'd be running across the field and pitching it to Frazier and Berringer and Frost, playing catch with those guys, throwing balls to receivers. But yet, had a very good understanding of the game. And I could do the same thing that I did with Coach Tenopir and Osborne: I could ask Turner what I needed to do on a play and he'd know and he'd teach you.

Coach Brown? Same way but kind of your spiritual guy, a little bit more of your upbeat 'rah-rah.' I've never seen a more fiery Christian than him.

Q: The Apostle Paul might have given him a run for the money…(laughs)

AT: (laughing) All the coaches, top to bottom, had their own personal style, but they had one common goal and they all knew what they were doing from top to bottom. Crazy deal.

Q: Looking across to the other side of the field, what can you tell me about the defensive coaches?

AT: I tell you what, I would have loved to play for Coach Charlie McBride. I think he was about as fiery a coach as I've ever seen. I think he was very technically sound.

I loved the fact that the defensive side of the staff was so aggressive. Everybody from Darlington (who was pretty aggressive in his techiniques), and you had Coach Samuel and Nelson Barnes, you had Coach Bohl and Kevin Steele. How about that nutjob? He was awesome. And Coach Bohl? Great assistant. Not so much coordinator, but a great assistant.

So you had a good group of coaches over there that was just relentless and aggressive, and they did a hell of a job of coaching these guys up. I never really got fully involved in their meetings or any of that kid of stuff, but you always had admiration for them because they had their guys ready -be it practice or game time- all the time.

Q: I heard that sometimes non-defensive players would try to sneak over and listen to Charlie give his pregame speech.

AT: Sometimes you didn't have to sneak over, you could hear it coming out of the showers. (laughing) But I tell you what, those guys came out of that shower pregame speech just absolutely fired up, which was awesome. It would have been a fun time playing for those guys. It really would have.

Q: Was there anything else that set those teams apart from others in history?

AT: I would just say what strikes me the most was the group of players that we had was so tight, the coaches that we had were so tight. There was respect amongst everybody, there was really no one person that was trying to be bigger than the system. And everything from -this is just crazy- everything from the coaching staff to the administration to the trainers to the academic staff with Leblanc and Zimmer to the weight staff, there was really no one trying to show anyone up or think that they were the end all, say all. And it just fostered great communication, great commitment, a great work ethic that created a synergy. The synergy that created? You're going to accomplish much more than what that group should normally accomplish, you know what I mean? With everyone on board and no one's trying to be the star and you're willing to make sacrifices for you and your teammate or whatever situation? You make those sacrifices for the betterment of the team and you're gonna do nothing but just flourish.

I look back to those days and I think about it, and what strikes me more than anything is just that right there. And one of the difficult things was -as I moved into my professional career- that's the most difficult thing I've had to deal with: you know that if you're a Realtor and if you're trying to sell a home you've got another agent who'll try to backstab you to get that 3.5% cut. Or whatever. When I was in sales it was the same way. To me? 'I'll take the cut and you take the cut, it doesn't matter as long as we're making the company money, we'll all get rewarded in the end. Let's quit trying to jump ahead and be the star and be the greedy person.' Boy, when I joined the corporate world that stuck out. I had a hard time adjusting to that. I really did.

Q: Gave you a better appreciation for the concept of 'teamwork?'

AT: Absolutely. I remember sitting down and talking to Jack Stark about it. We actually got a group together to talk about it, and it's called a Level 5 Leadership Group. Basically, Paul, I just had some trouble taking what I learned and what worked so damn well in college and moving into the professional world. And not that you necessarily didn't expect that, but when you have a bunch of employees working for the same goal and then you've got two or three rogue guys? It can botch the whole damned thing. And that's what was disappointing coming from the background I came from and seeing how it worked and developed and was just an awesome deal. Boy, you get one or two bad apples and you can see how it can fall apart pretty quickly.

Q: Do you recall any bad apples while you were playing? Some that had to be brought into line?

AT: No, not really. You had your guys and a few that were lazier... or you could take the Lawrence Philiips case, for example. Osborne wanted him off the team and that was the deal. I remember being part of that Unity Council and sitting right there and discussing Lawrence Phillips. And Osborne said, "Guys, I'm kicking him off the team. He's gonna have to get this counselling. If you want him off the team he's off the team for good."

And this is why I admire the man so much, because he took a lot of heat for the deal: "If you want him off the team, he's off the team. If you want him back on the team I need some rules and regulations that you want out of him on top of what I'm gonna make him do, and this is what I'm going make him do: X,Y,Z." And he ended up saying, "If he misses anything I require him to do, he's done. Let me know what you decide." He left and we sat there and talked about it with Jack Stark in the room. We said that he had to show up and go to the counseling deal, do all of Osborne's stuff, and we put restrictions on him: if he missed a class he was done, if he missed a workout he was done, if he missed his running for the next two months or however many months he was gone. But that was the deal. Osborne let us decide the punishment and then when he'd come back and play. I mean, ultimately, Osborne's going to be responsible because he's the head coach, but he was willing to take the heat and be the front man for what the group decided.

Q: The point you make is that the media made it out like it was all due to Coach Osborne's impirious decision rather than bearing heavily on you and your fellow Unity Councilmembers' shoulders?

AT: Right. And whether it was a little wheel or the big wheel in a big, intricate clock, unless we were all functioning as one it wasn't going to work.

Q: Do you have a favorite game?

AT: I would have to say the Florida game would have to be, but there were so many. Probably the Florida game, just because we weren't expected to win and we go down there and every single player for Nebraska was excited, they all did a hellacious job from the defensive line to the linebackers to the defensive secondary to the offensive line to the receivers to Tommie and Ahman and Lawrence and all those guys. Every single guy had just an awesome game.

It was just so much fun, because we weren't supposed to be playing with them at all. And the next thing you know every single guy shows up and perfoms and it's 62-24 or whatever the score was, you know what I mean? We went from being nobodies who shouldn't even belong on the same field to absolutely crushing these guys. Just the feeling of it all, because we knew what we did in '94 and then to replicate it in '95? Because we were so close in '93, the 'Unfinished Business' in '94 and then it didn't seem like we got the respect in '95, you know? After having two good, solid years you go into that Florida game in '95 without that respect, and just to cememt it like that and go, 'Boom, this is us, boys! Deal with it. We're a damn good football team. Give us some respect!'

Q: Going back to the Florida State game after '93, were you in sitting the stands with the rest of the redshirts for that game?

AT: I was in the stands.

Q: Anything stick out to you about that game?

AT: Just the emotion and what a weird feeling it is being a member of the crowd. Being a member of the crowd yet being a part of the team and knowing a little bit more about what's going on than the normal fan. You had highs and lows. I remember having the feeling, 'Yes, we're gonna win the championship.' And then the next minute having that feeling of, 'Oh, we're losing.' Then, 'Hey, we're gonna win again.' Just that whole thing. And just the emotions the last quarter, the ups and downs.

And quite honestly? The last thing I remember about it was, 'Damn, the game's over. How are we gonna get to the bus?' (laughs) You remember where that old Orange Bowl stadium was: just a shit hole. And halfway scary whenever you walked out, you know? 'How do we get back to the hotel?' (laughs) What a deal.

Q: Did you have a favorite site you liked playing at?

AT: I've got a couple. I liked playing in Missouri because the fans were so damn passionate and that was always a good game. So I liked that as far as fan-wise.

As far as stadium-wise, I really enjoyed Colorado. I always thought that was such a beautiful stadium in Boulder. I really did. Iowa State was like going to a high school stadium. It was a glorified high school stadium, but it was still fun to play in because it kind of brought you back to your past. Other than that, Kansas and Kansas State were really nothing.

Q: Did you have a place you hated going into?

AT: Yeah, I usually didn't like going into K-State. Those guys? They were so arrogant. From the fans all the way down to the players, I just didn't enjoy that. Also, it was fun to just pound them and go about your way. (laughs) Everybody from the announcer to the fans was talking trash about you, not really having a respect for you, your coaches, your history. They were just building history there with Bill Snyder and they wanted to sit there and degrade us and talk about us? 'C'mon guys, you guys are doing a good job of trying to build yourself as a program, there's no need to try and tear us down in the process. Have some respect.'

Q: Was there much smack talking out on the field?

AT: Not really. I get that question a lot. They'd talk trash to you, but we never really got talked to whole lot. It's awful difficult to talk trash whenever you're getting your ass kicked. (laughs)

Q: Maybe right before that first snap, but after that things changed, huh?

AT: Right. And that was the thing, too: Tenopir always taught that you always get the first lick in. Always put that doubt in their mind first.

Q: Are there any favorite practice stories?

AT: I would say, yeah: Jason Peter and I. It was our sophomore year, the spring of 1995, and we were doing a lot of one-on-ones now because the Pipeline had left and there were a bunch of new guys on the offensive line. And the defensive line was gearing up for a change, so we were doing a lot of one-on-ones in the pit. Jason makes a move on me and I, in turn, combatted that and absolutely stopped him, just handed it to him. Well, he gets mad because he's trying to do the best he can. So I, in my mind, am going, 'Man, I just stuck him! Hell of a deal! good job.' Well, the next thing you know, he tees off and he punches me. Well, I'm young and I'm still trying to prove myself, so I turn around and I punch him back. Next thing I know the fight's on. It seemed like an eternity before it got separated. So we end up getting separated and emotions were high for the rest of the session. Well, when we go to team practice right after that we all have to walk through the same door to the field into the stadium, and Jason and I ended up walking next to each other. And he looks at me. (pause) And then he goes, "That was a good one, huh?" I go, 'It wasn't too bad.' And then I go, 'Don't you think we could've not fought as long? I'm shot for the rest of practice.' Then he said the same thing, "When we fight next time, let's just not fight for so long." (laughs)

So that's what it was: a spur of the moment thing. We both needed to 'create a personality' if you will, show our coaches, show our teammates that we weren't going to back down, that we cared, that we had a passion, those kind of things. Yet, in turn, when it was time to get together and work for a common cause with each other we were willing to work shoulder to shoulder, hand in hand, and do it together.

Q: It's just occurred to me: do you think maybe it was by design that Coach McBride and Coach Tenopir let you guys have at it down in the pit during the week so that maybe you wouldn't go off on an opponent come Saturday and draw a penalty?

AT: I'm glad you brought that up, because it wasn't just them.

I can remember this vividly: on the field, when there would be a little scuffle on the field and Coach Osborne saw it? He would turn around and walk away for about 20 seconds and watch someone else on the field, then he'd turn around and go, "Hey, hey, hey! What are you guys doing!?" like he was completely oblivious. (laughs) Then he'd make the guys go run, knowing damn well he saw every bit of it. And that's exactly what you talked about: they would let you go and let you get fired up and let you get it out of your system and kind of do that deal. They'd condone it.

Q: You think the fights during the week prevented some dumb penalties on Saturday?

AT: Yeah, I think so. It let you get it out of your system. There was just so much testosterone flowing around there.

And not only that, but to instill some toughness. There's a reality to that, too, that you have to be tough to play the ballgame, and they wanted to make sure that guys were ready and willing to stick up for each other. A lot of times it was sticking up for each other, and you're the one joining in the fight for somebody else. I think there were just a lot of different variables that went into why they let it happen. They didn't just let it happen, but they kind of let it go on for a little bit longer than it needed to. (laughs)

Q: Any memorable off-field stuff?

AT: You know, the thing that I remember the most -that I'm the most fond of- is that everyone got along. Everyone got along really well. When practice ended and we'd go back to the locker room and get showered up, then we still hung out and played cards, BS'd forever. There were times it wasn't 'til 8:30, 9 o'clock we were actually just getting out of the stadium, from just hanging out with guys when you're there from 1 o'clock to 9 o'clock with someone, sometimes 10 if you're in the study hall, too. You have nothing but fondness. They become a family, they became a brother. You know what that person's feeling, what gets 'em going, what makes 'em depressed, you become their best friend, their brother.

Q: And I've got to ask you, Tommie wasn't the most social guy, was he?

AT: Oh, not at all.

Q: But that was just Tommie, right?

AT: That was just Tommie, exactly right. Tommie was social on his own terms, but it wasn't an arrogance. There was a little bit of arrogance -because we all have it- but there wasn't really any disrespect. There was so much pressure on Tommie that we all kind of understood it.

Not the most sociable guy, but he was a hell of a leader and he expected perfection out of everyone. I remember being in the huddle with him -and I was just a young pup- and it didn't matter who you were, he would ride you. But the beautiful thing about Tommie, when the game was on the line? When you had third or fourth down and a yard or two to go? He was willing to put that pressure upon himself and make the play and show you he could get it done, and that's why he expected excellence out of you. A hell of a leader. Not the most sociable guy; I never hung out with him.

Looking back on it, that was one of the things I remember about Tommie: he wasn't afraid to speak up and let you know what he felt and what he expected out of you. But you knew what you were going to get out of him each and every time he needed to step up and a play had to be made. And there was no failing, he would just do it. So it became the sort of thing where you were, 'If he'd do it and he's gonna ride my ass, I better do it.'

Q: Recollections of Brook Berringer?

AT: Brook? Just a great guy. In the locker room? Great personality. Him and I liked to do a lot of the same stuff: hunt and fish and do the outdoor things. Gosh, just sitting at the training table with us just BS-ing after we ate, a group of guys.

What I remember about his playing was that everytime he came into the ballgame it seems like we always went down and scored. Always. Whether that was the case or not, it's just what my perception was. A great leader, but a different type of leadership. He was more one of the guys, but still expected a lot out of you. And the big thing I admire about him was where he was second string and stuck in a tough situation. He never let it get him down and never let if affect his ability to go out and perform.

Q: Character?

AT: Character. That's exactly right. And that's a tough thing to do. And he not only did it, he exceeded it.

Q: You had Frosty for a quarterback, too…

AT: And I had Frosty, who I think was actually the best option quarterback we ever had. I don't think he was the best, say, quarterback or best talent or anything like that, but as far as running the option I don't think there was anyone better than Scott Frost.

And the reason I say that? He was tough, he was big, he was strong, and he knew exactly… hey, there were many times Scott Frost would get blown up or deliver a blow, but he knew how to run that option so well that he would take it right to the pitch man. A lot of times Tommie Frazier would rely on his athletic ability instead of pitching it out to Calvin Jones or Lawrence or whomoever, he would take it on himself. He might break a big play or not, but Scott Frost would actually run the play out like it was designed. So it's just a real interesting thing that I felt made him the better option quarterback. Not necessarily the most athletic quarterback or the best breakaway quarterback -like an Eric Crouch- or as dynamic a player as Tommie Frazier was, but as a straight option quarterback I don't think there was anyone better.

And tough! Just tough as nails. There were times I would pick him up off the ground and he was seeing stars. And the receiver -whether it was Lance Brown or Jeff Lake or somebody- would run in the play, they would actually have to call the play in the huddle and Scott would just give the snap count. And I remember thinking, 'How the hell is he going to run this next play?! He's out of it!' And he'd do the same damn thing. Just absolutely amazing, Paul. You just go, 'Wow!'

Q: Who would you spotlight as playing a key role behind the scenes? Someone who never got their due for what they contributed?

AT: Well, that's easy: Bryan Bailey. That's an easy one for me.

Q: Why?

AT: Just my perception of Bailey? God, I wish he was still here, big time. He was always there. Always there. Whether you came at six o'clock in the morning or stayed 'til 8 at night, he was always there. And you might have a different perception because you worked with him side by side. But as a player? He was always there, he was always willing to listen to you bitch or moan. He was always pushing you to get better in the weightroom. There was no one else I worked out with. I don't know why, and it was just kind of a weird deal. I didn't work with (Kevin) Coleman or anybody else, or Big John Archer. (Where the hell's Archer at anyway? He was always a pretty good cat.) I don't know, but I always worked out with Bailey. He always had something quirky or -I call it innovative- that he was working on. So he got you out of the boredom that can be working out and shook it up but still remained true to the core principles of what we were trying to do, trying to accomplish.

And I think he had the trust of a lot of players. And that was really important. He wasn't the head strength coach that you had to stay away from, he wasn't the head coach that you had to stay away from, he could be one of the guys that you go to to talk about your family, how bad practice sucks or any of those things. He'd sit there and listen to you, but yet he'd still make you, in some roundabout way, get a good workout in when you didn't want to.

Q: He was punishingly accessible?

AT: Yeah, there you go. (laughs)

Q: It surprises me, Aaron, how many times I hear Bryan's name. I'm lucky to count him as a great friend, so it's nice to hear how you guys appreciated him.

AT: Yeah, and Boyd was in his own little world. Even though I like Boyd, he was in his own little universe. And that's another thing, how many little dynamics were there in that whole strength staff. You had you, Mike Arthur, Randy Gobel, John Archer, Kevin Coleman…

Q: And this skinny little redheaded guy from Arnold, Nebraska coming up with the craziest, most outlandish things to do, right? And the next thing you know you're running without that 'hitch in your giddyup', right?

AT: What a deal. So many different dynamics, but there was still a common work ethic for a common cause.

Q: And hey, come to think of it, you earned a spot on the Record Platform, right? Didn't you hold the Performance Index record for 10 yard dash?

AT: Yeah, 10 yard dash, hang cleans, and I think I was up there for squats, too.

Q: Well, is there anything else to touch upon that really made Nebraska special during those days?

AT: Well, in conclusion, I would say it was really the fans that made it what it was all about. There's nothing better than playing in front of Nebraska fans; whether it was the expectation of winning or just the great history of the excitement of gameday. And here we are over 300 sellouts, and it's just because of the great fans. And I tell you what, I love this Pelini.

Q: He's got a good measure of Charlie McBride in him, don't you think?

AT: Oh yeah. But watch him develop, because I also think that he's getting some Osborne in him. It's kind of interesting to watch because I love his fire and all that, but I kind of hope he calms down a little bit, (laughs) just because I grew up with Osborne and all that. (Coach Osborne) is fiery, but it's a calm fieryness.

End conversation.

I have one question for starters: Who made who? Was it Jason Peter who made Aaron Taylor the best of his class or did Aaron Taylor first draw out in Jason Peter the same effect? Can you imagine the number of reps and rips and bruises and battles between the two throughout those five college years? Talk about symbiosis; it was steel sharpening steel. I plan to track down Jason for his viewpoint too, and am giddy about hearing his take on the great 60 & 3.

Aaron made a great point that I hadn't previously thought of: the numbers of stellar talent had a smoothing effect throughout the program, leading to no one 'superstar' to cannibalize the hype, the public's focus, never allowing one overriding ego to run amuck -to the detriment of team unity. They were their own built-in system of checks and balances, *"You take a look at all those guys, you never had one star. You had a bunch of stars. And what that did, everybody just kind of came together and was on the same level."* On the other end of the spectrum, with that came the home-grown walk-ons and scout team scrubs pushing everyone from the depths, resulting in a pressure-cooker environment where every man was constantly looking over his shoulder, pushing himself to seek constant improvement and expend full effort, along with the unified culture, *".. it just fostered great communication, great commitment, a great work ethic that created a synergy. The synergy that created, you're going to accomplish much more than what that group should normally accomplish.*" The one main point here, the key that cannot be missed if you are wanting an early answer to the great Why and How of the 60 & 3 is this: Competition led to respect. Respect led to synergy. Synergy led to team-wide perseverance. Perseverance led to victories.

Thereby endeth today's lesson. Class is dismissed.

Notable quote #2:
Aaron Taylor on gaining the crucial physical/psychological edge: "Tenopir always taught that you always get the first lick in. Always put that doubt in their mind first."

You'll find the road is long and rough, with soft spots far apart,
Where only those can make the grade who have the Uphill Heart.
And when they stop you with a thud or halt you with a crack,
Let Courage call the signals as you keep on coming back.
                                    Grantland Rice, *Alumunus Football*

Seventeen miles north of York, Nebraska on US Highway 81 lies the town of Stromsburg, birthplace of William J. Froelich (1901-1980), the first chairman of the Federal Deposit Insurance Corporation (FDIC) in 1933, but more notoriously known as the 1931 co-prosecutor of Prohibition gangster Al Capone. Meting out justice and providing stability for a troubled populace in that short, tumultuous span of the nation's history, we now come upon upon another local from the area who levied a slightly different brand of prairie justice on the Blackshirts' offensive foes of the early 90's. Bruce Moore was one of Charlie McBride and his defensive staff's pack of punishers, exhibiting speedy displays of athleticism, doling out severe sanctions and ferocious fines on the enemy scofflaws palming the pigskin. Let's hear his story and how he contributed to the great mix of the 60 & 3's student-athletes, uphill hearts every one of them.

Notable quote #1:
"Kids want to be pushed and kids want to be challenged, but (the coaches) also need to know there's gotta be a balance and that you're human, and you're gonna need a pat on the back sometimes."

Bruce Moore

Walk-on, Outside Linebacker, York, Nebraska
Where are they now? Gretna, Nebraska, Coach

Question: So what was your first year on Lincoln's campus, Bruce?

Bruce Moore: It was in the fall of '89.

Q: So your last game playing was the…

BM: The two point loss to Florida State.

Q: A heartbreaker to say the least. Moving on to your first few days on campus, what is most memorable?

BM: Well, I actually went home for a day. Making the jump from high school -where you're pretty much bigger than most other people- and being a walk-on from a small town, then you get down to the University? I graduated college with Kevin Raemakers and Lance Lundberg and those people, so those guys were huge when I came in. And here I'm 6'7" and probably about 210 lbs. -if I'm lucky- and those guys show up weighing around 250-260.

And when you practice wearing only sweat clothes in high school nobody touches each other. If you do so, the coaches will rip you a new one. But you get to the University and it's basically full contact, almost; guy's trying to earn their job the first week. I had my shoulders beat up and my hands were swollen and I was like, 'What in the world am I doing?' So I went to talk to Coach Osborne and I'm like, 'I'm struggling.' (Because you have to make new friends and all that process, and I was pretty isolated) That was a huge jump, and I hadn't really expected that side of things to affect me that much, so I went home and slept for about a day (laughs) and got caught up, talked to my Dad and things. I think the biggest thing is you wanted to make sure you were doing it for all the right reasons and not because of the other people's expectations.

And then I went back the next day with a clear conscience, so that was kind of the biggest thing: adjusting to the atmosphere, the pace of practice, the totally new environment that you get thrown into. You get a new dorm room and a guy you've never met before. And the roommate I had was from North Platte and he had a mohawk and he liked to party all the time. He was a wild man. And it wasn't like I was some angel coming out of high school, but he partied a lot more than I was used to. (laughs) It was a totally different environment for me to get used to, but after that little bit of going through that it was all downhill from there.

I had a good freshman year and got my feet moving, and then you go through your redshirt season and you learn to practice and things start to slow down for you. And then I lettered every year after that.

Q: Anybody stand out? Anyone you started bonding with?

BM: The guys on the defensive line, obviously, were huge influences. Kevin (Raemakers) was on the freshman team and I got to know him, and there were a couple other guys on the freshman squad. Gerald Irons was on that freshman squad, Greg Fletcher at defensive end. You started getting that camaraderie built up just being on that side of the ball. Matt Penland, who's down at the University with his ministry now. You had Darren Williams and Troy Branch, Mike Anderson at linebacker and Chris Demuth was an offensive lineman from Seward. Zeke Cisco, Jeff Lindquist (who transferred to Wesleyan after his first year or so). So there are just some names that I remember getting to know right away.

Freshman year seemed like kind of a blur, because you're trying to do all the school work and get all that taken care of. Then you have the coaches. Steve Stanard was our freshman defensive line coach, and that's kind of how I ended up coaching later at Wesleyan, knowing him from that situation. A lot of different people helped you get your feet on the ground, I suppose.

Q: So you're on the freshman team your first year and redshirted your second year. What was it like when you first start having contact with Charlie McBride?

BM: Scary. Like hearing horror stories and stuff like that, (laughs) because you'd hear so many rumors from people. The upperclassmen, they'd want to put the fear of God in you, almost, telling all these crazy stories. And that first spring practice when they introduce you to stuff? That first spring was probably my most memorable spring with Coach McBride, and I didn't make a lot of major mistakes because I picked up the schemes very fast from a mental standpoint.

Physically? Trying to put on weight was probably my biggest issue. But Kevin Ramaekers - we were on the grass fields and Kevin was trying to figure out goal line technique and Coach McBride was trying to explain to him what an Inside Eye Technique was for the noseguard position -and Kevin, for some reason, that day could not get that thing figured out. You know, his outside eye was on the offensive guard's inside eye and he was just not getting it, and McBride just went off on him one day. He was just yelling at him and screaming at him, "You take your foot and you put it…" And I remember him stomping on his foot where he was supposed to put his foot at, you know? (laughs) And Kevin was just standing there and you could just see the looks in everybody else's eyes saying, "Please don't let me screw up next?" That was the first major 'McBride Freakout' type of thing, and after that you were so puckered up trying to make sure you didn't make a mistake and get Charlie to yell at you.

Q: That wasn't the same day where Charlie ended up throwing his tobacco, was it?

BM: No, I think that might have been the next year. I remember he had that big, nasty, ugly green football that he had painted green. Anyway, he painted this football green -and Kenny Walker couldn't hear, obviously- and Kenny took off and did the wrong technique and McBride couldn't get him stopped, so he just picked up this ball and just drilled Kenny in the numbers. And Kenny was, "What!?" It was pretty funny.

But I remember that day he threw his tobacco at Kevin. I don't recall what it was, but McBride just started walking away after that and we didn't know what was going on: 'Are we done for the day or what?', you know? And he ended up walking over to Kevin Steele and got a new dip of tobacco from him and came back. (laughs)

Q: Did having Kenny Walker in your group rub off on you guys in any way?

BM: Kenny was such a gifted athlete and he worked so hard. And everybody had their different little things they contributed, too: You had Joe Sims during that time period and he was so laid back, you had Kent Wells and you had no idea what he was gonna do. At the end of my freshman year we were allowed to come up and practice with the varsity, and when you get up there with those guys -it was Mike Murray, Kent Wells, Ray Valladao and that group, they were just crazy. Those guys just weren't right in the head, you know?

But that whole culture, that was your indoctrination to the Blackshirts. Those guys wouldn't let you forget that they were the first team guys and that they were wearing those Blackshirts for a reason. When you were in practice and you weren't going to step up in practice they'd throw you down and let you know, "Hey, if you're not going to bring it, then you're gonna get taken." So that was kind of a, "Hey, this is how we practice. When we go, we go hard." You had that old-school pecking order kind of thing, but it also makes sure you learn the ropes the right way.

And McBride made sure that when you worked, you worked hard. And then there were times, he'd slip in times where you were able to sit there and let your hair down and just stop practice, and everybody would stand there together and he'd tell jokes and stories about the good old days, about guys that he coached and stupid things they'd done and what have you. He always had a good sense of when people were at their edge. He always wanted to keep you nervous and keep you moving and made sure you never got totally comfortable, but he also was good at realizing when you needed to have a diversion of some kind, make sure you knew that he was still human, that he still cared about you as a person.

I remember one of the first times that I had a good one-on-one session. (You remember Chris Zyzda on the offensive line? I had a good bullrush on Chris Zyzda one day. And you go through that process and you learn that you don't brag about it, because that could be you the next day.) But anyway, I kept it on the down low and didn't really say much about it. And the guys pat you on the back during film work that next day, but after it was over he pulled me back in and told me, "You did a real nice job there." He didn't do it in public, and he'd always say, "I'm gonna kick you in the butt when you need to be kicked in the butt, but I'm gonna hug you next and let you know what it's all about." I think there was a lot of those type of things, that you understand that kids want to be pushed and kids want to be challenged, but they also need to know there's gotta be a balance, and that you're human and you're gonna need a pat on the back sometimes. You just can't be fire and brimstone all the time.

I see that with Bo Pelini now. But sometimes when they know there are people down there they're on their better behavior. (laughs) Charlie never worried about his behavior when there were people around, but I bet Bo has a little bit of a sense of that because of the position he is in. (laughs)

Q: Your first week, when you went to Coach Osborne you said you... "weren't really sure if this is for me"?

BM: Yeah, right after like a week of practice. I think it was a Thursday. I got up that morning and had my car packed and got over to the stadium and sat down with Coach McBride, and he took me over to Coach Osborne and we chatted for a long time. He said I was welcomed to take some time and think about it, and he said, "I'll be honest with you, most people who take this route don't come back." And I just told him, 'I need to think about where I'm at and what it is.' And I drove back home about 45 minutes away, walked in the door, and mom and dad were away at the time. Dad was working and mom, I didn't know where she was at. I don't even remember what time I got back at the house, but I just laid down on the couch and slept 'til like 2 or 3 in the afternoon. I just passed out because I was so beat up and tired. We talked for about an hour that night and had dinner, and I turned around and the next morning I went back.

And they took me back without saying a word. That was the nice thing: they accepted you right back and I didn't hear anything from the players or anything. Nobody questioned where I was at for a day or so. That was the most comforting thing, they allowed you to do what they allowed you to do and they didn't hold it against you, you know?

Q: Can you imagine being one of those guys who's fifteen-hundred miles away from home and dealing with homesickness, also?

BM: I can't, because I was only an hour away. And what Coach Osborne and Coach McBride said -it really had nothing to do with friendships and high school kids, because I knew they were all gone- because they reiterated, "You know, it's not gonna be like it was back home, like it used to be. High school is over and people have moved on. It's just gonna be a different atmosphere." Knowing that you could just jump in a car and be home in an hour? Boy.

When I left high school I was close to taking a scholarship offer from Wyoming. They had offered me a scholarship for a long period of time and recruiting visits got kind of tied up and didn't pan out... and Paul Roach I think, was the coach at that time. Anyway, I chose to walk-on and signed the letter and those type of things, and I understood after my redshirt year and with playing time I would get a scholarship. On the dime team is when I started playing my sophomore year.

Q: So, looking back to your freshman and redshirt freshman year -when you'd gotten a better feel of what was going on- can you then jump ahead to your senior year and reflect on the changes that took place for you, personally?

BM: Personally, you do a lot of growing up. Things slow down the longer you're at practice and you get a better idea of what it is you're supposed to be doing. Obviously, you get physically stronger, you get to know a little more about Charlie McBride and what his expectations are, the technique that he drills into you.

I mean, one of the things I learned about and makes a huge difference in some coaches is the attention to the little details. McBride was just a monster on technique, "Your foot has to be here, your hand has to be here, you're foot has to be here, your hand has to be here." He drilled those little, tiny things over and over and over, and it takes awhile for you to learn those skills where they become a natural thing and you stop thinking about it and you get to lose those bad habits you picked up in high school. So you just kind of learned the process and learned the details, those kinds of things helped a great deal.

As for the team dynamic? It's kind of interesting to think about that process, because we had some good teams as we went through those years. We had Gerry Gdowski as quarterback and they played very well but they couldn't quite get over the hump, still playing the 5-2 defense, still had that old mentality. There for awhile we were still playing against Oklahoma's wishbone, Iowa State still ran the option, triple option, Colorado was still running the half-bone, Missouri still had kind of a wishy-washy identity, so that defense still worked for the most part.

Playing some of those Big 8 schools it was always fun. And then we'd get to the bowl game and we'd run into a team that was a multiple-offense and was more balanced and that 5-2 defense would struggle a great deal, because it was such a change in kind of a mentality and sort of a process. So you go through those Keithen McCant years and we went through a process and played Washington and stuff at home when they had the national championship run. I think from that point the transition started -defensively, anyway- as well as the team identity.

The offense? Osborne really had a pretty multiple offense at the time depending on the type of quarterback he had, and I think slowly from Keithen McCant's year to making that transition to Tommie Frazier where Mike Grant was kind of around for a few games in '92. After the Washington game I think Tommie really started getting more of a grasp of what he was trying to do, and then by that Missouri game he pretty much had taken over that year as a true freshman. The offense, obviously, then was being a little bit more molded, but I remember seeing a little more shotgun. That started being developed and Osborne started moving that in, and the shotgun had the spread stuff to spread the field, and Osborne started running the option out of the spread. You look at that spread option package that everybody's running now, and Coach Osborne was doing that back in '91 or '92 already.

Q: And nobody will ever give him credit for it, you know?

BM: Of course they won't. Because nobody thought that, "Hey, this is a good thing."

And then at that point the defense started doing a lot of dime work and that's how I got on the field. We were doing more nickel and dime situations, and that's where we started doing more of a 4-man front. And Kenny Walker kind of got his start in that process, really, where he was playing defensive tackle in more of that nickel situation against teams like Washington and some of those people that had more of a spread offense. And as we went through the year in '92 we started running more and more dime, and the coaches were leaning towards that.

And my senior year they made that big jump. I went to the defensive end position. It was one of those things where you always wish you had another year, (laughs) because they made that transition after four years and things went really well in '93, defensively. I think we made a lot of jumps in statistics and played real well defensively, especially that last game against Florida State when people didn't think we had much of a chance. It's just the change in that thought process of 'how we were going to attack?' kind of thing. You need to give Coach Osborne and all that staff credit there, because they didn't just sit on their laurels; they kept looking for a combination of something that would move us forward.

Q: Going to rush end in the dime package, did you start working with Coach Samuel?

BM: Yeah, after the spring we started making that transition. I started out playing both: I'd be with Coach McBride in meetings and those kind of things for a period of time, then I'd go over and play rush end. I started out playing both, so I'd go over and play defensive line in passing situations -third down and that kind of thing- and then I would go back and play rush end and those kinds of things, and after awhile things just kind of gradually diminished. It was hard to jump back and forth from a continuity standpoint because the defensive line -you guys work together, you're running stunts and those kind of things- and then to come back over and do it for a little while but not full-time, when you're trying to learn a different position. And I just didn't pick it up as well as I think they wanted me to, so I ended up playing mainly rush end.

Q: So Chief, tell me about Coach Samuel.

BM: Yeah, (laughs) "Chief, how's it going?" Utterly different coaching style, so much more laid back. He was interesting, because you'd go through McBride's technique stuff -and you knew that if you didn't grade at least 90% or better on Charlie's stuff, you wouldn't play. His phrase was, "You won't see the green grass of Memorial Stadium."

And when you go over to Coach Samuel the technique really was so watered down, it wasn't near as driven as, "You've got to step here, put your hand here, do this..." It was a couple of things he taught over and over, and then the rest of it was really kind of freelancing, almost. My first scrimmage I graded like a 94% or something like that and I was, 'How can this be? I haven't played this position, ever.' With McBride 90-92% was the highest grade I'd ever gotten, because you step one foot in the wrong way and he'd give you a negative grade, so I had to adjust to not being as regimented as McBride did it. It was much more laid back.

You had a lot of personalities there: Trev Alberts, Jerad Hickman was a sophomore there. He ended up being my roommate and stuff. David Leader, and Dante Jones was real young, Dwayne Harris was real young. But they were young, free spirits. I remember Jared Tomich, because he was a defensive tackle with me for McBride, and he moved over and played defensive end, so he was still developing a little at that point. So you kind of think back to the guys you played with and how they played in the NFL in some point in time, and it was a pretty talented group across the board, that they made the transition with.

Q: And talking with Coach Samuel, do you recall him telling you it was up to you to 'make the play?'

BM: That's what I meant by more of a 'freelance' kind of thing. He taught... the drill I can remember doing a million times was the fullback cutback to boot. You just made sure that you never gave up contain and you always knew what your basic responsibility was, and after that it was up to you to find a way to beat that offensive tackle. His main philosophy was: you were basically doing a bullrush or speedrush on every play like it's a pass, and then you just react to it.

Basically you were just flying as hard as you can go to the ball and trying to make the play on the other side of the line of scrimmage. The previous defense we were just pretty much trying to read and just kind of stay on the line of scrimmage the whole time. This one? We're pressing it three yards deep and trying to put as much pressure on the quarterback as we could through that process. I just remember drilling over and over again, "Front side play, front side play" and then just being aware of trying to find the fullback. I think every single practice we drilled bootleg, bootleg, bootleg, just so that you never got burned. And the misdirection stuff? You're going as hard as you can but you're watching for the misdirection keys or unbalanced or anything different that they'd throw at you. But like I said: technique-wise, it was so simple. It allowed you to do a lot of that stuff.

Q: Do you think Coach Samuel's philosophy was that you could make up for lack of technique with more effort, greater intensity?

BM: You know, I think so. But it really lent itself to being a little more athletic. I think that I was kind of a hybrid: I felt better when I could engage somebody, because that's how I trained all the time. (laughs) It's one of those things where you almost wished you were gonna play front side, and play front side defense and take the tight end where they were at. I would have been a lot more comfortable letting the other guys come off the edge sometimes. It's a totally different thing playing out in air and forcing the issue rather than having a guy out in front of you that will take you to the play. But like I said, it just took a while and I felt pretty good about it after I got three or four games into the year. And then I had a groin pull and got a little dinged up.

Q: Do you recall significant organizational changes from your freshman to your senior year?

BM: I think winning the national championship was always there in our mind, because the Big 8 championhsip was always something that we expected to be in the running for every year. You know, you had three seasons every year: you had the 3 or 4 non-conference games, then you had the Big 8 season, and then you had the bowl game. And if you won the Big 8 then you knew you were going to be in the running for a national title.

When I was growing up that was always something you expected Nebraska to have a shot at it, and I think that bigger expectation of really taking this to the next level began when Coach Osborne created the Unity Council. I think things changed dynamically on the team at that point. I mentioned there was the senior pecking order based on your experience and how much confidence you had and a lot of things. That was there, definitely, when you went into McBride's office and things: the seniors got the front seat, the juniors got the next seat, and all the way to the freshman getting the back of his room. It was one of those things where every year you just expected to move up.

I remember getting my Blackshirt the same year with Raemakers and Terry Connealy and we were all sitting in the front row, so you kind of had that old order. I always remember the days of Ray Valladao, Kent Wells, Mike Murray and those guys, where you almost had a little fear of the upperclassmen. But with the Unity Council? By the time we got to our senior year, and with Tommie along as a freshman and Will Shields playing a little bit as a freshman, we went through a transition. I really felt like our senior year everybody was kind of on the same level at that point. Then again, I was a senior that year so maybe my perception was off, but rather than seniors looking down I think it was more of everybody looking on the same level as guys, now. I think it really helped to solidify a lot of things. When guys sat down to eat it was more guys in a group rather than the clique there used to be. And I think the way it was previously kind of kept guys from trusting each other on the field as much, too. It was nothing real overt that would come out, but every little thing kind of stacked up as you go through the process.

But guys were handling our discipline and stuff more than the coaches, who drove us in practice. You had guys that were standing up, John Parrella and those guys really driving the practice tempo. If guys wouldn't play hard you kind of took care of that in the old fashioned way: in practice. You had less coaches and more driving people to do it, and it started being more and more player-driven.

Q: Do you think the coaches appreciated that, the disciplining being out of their hands? They were then able to focus more on coaching, teaching, encouraging and less on disciplining the meatheads?

BM: I would think so. One of the best things I learned about that situation is that you can give a lot of speeches that will affect the first five or ten minutes of the ballgame, but after those first two series you don't remember anything that was said in the locker room and you have to actually play. So if you're not self-motivated to go out there and take care of business? It doesn't matter how great of a pregame speech a coach can throw out there, all that's gonna help you for is probably the first two or three plays. After that a team's got to play on its own merits.

So when a team takes ownership of themselves and they're self-motivated -that practiced habit of confidence, of taking over things- I think it really carries over into games. That confidence level of knowing, 'I can handle it. I can take care of things.' You're not really relying on the coaches so much to take care of stuff, because they obviously don't play the game for you. They're on the sidelines giving you the plays, but you still have to handle the situation out there on the field.

Q: Tell me little more about the Unity Council.

BM: They chose representatives and they went through that every year: one guy for each position or something like that, four or five offensive and defensive guys. And they sat with Osborne and there were disciplinary actions. I remember before the Orange Bowl game my senior year when Lawrence Phillips kind of first started having a few issues here and there, missing practices and such. I remember he sat out the first half of the Orange Bowl. (Coach Osborne) sat down with us and asked us what our thoughts were, what we thought we should do in that situation, because he'd skipped a couple practices and had been slowly working into Calvin Jones' place that year. And when Calvin Jones came back versus Colorado that end of the year, I'm sure that frustrated Lawrence. And stability-wise and maturity-wise, I'm sure that had something to do with Lawrence at that point, and it was something that would come into play again in later years.

Q: You usually hung around for the summer workouts. Do you recall anything special about the summer before your senior year, that year you guys put together in '93?

BM: You know, it's one of those things where it all starts in the spring. I remember you people on the strength staff and the coaches. After you finish your bowl game, how you're going to play next fall starts with the offseason conditioning. And one thing I recall, a major change there, was the focus on training how to run properly, the bag work and running technique, becoming more efficient with your running style. You have a lot of guys come in and they're big and physical and strong, but if they're not in track or a sprinter, most of the time nobody ever taught you how to run. Especially someone from a small school, where if you could run they'd let you do it because you had the ability to do it, but otherwise nobody really taught you, you know? And I know that my 40 time and my agility time, I never went through more gains than that year when we went through that process. But I think it all goes back to Coach Osborne and the staff saying, "We need to get faster and increase our team speed", and they really dived in with that. I don't know who developed that -whether it was Randy Gobel and all that stuff that spring- we did a lot of Olympic weight training and stuff. And I remember Boyd came up with that circuit.

Q: The Metabolic Power Cicruit?

BM: Yeah, that really started my senior year and they did that for a couple years. I hated that thing.

Q: You became very intimate with the puke buckets?

BM: Yeah, you just made sure you didn't eat or drink anything before you came in. And it took you twenty minutes to recover after it was over. You go through my education there and look at the way we did weight training, and you really get to understand the metabolic threshold.

They made little changes all the way through. And it wasn't just one specific area. I think it was a commitment, and I think it was starting right away after that Citrus Bowl. We had a number of top draft picks that year with Bruce Pickens and Kenny Walker and all those guys that were drafted in the first and second round and stuff. That was a very talented group of guys, and to lose like we did those last couple games of the year (granted, we did lose our quarterback), but the Unity Council came after that and there was a different emphasis in how Coach Osborne approached the team.

Q: Change in what manner? A changed way of pursuing objectives?

BM: Like I said, just the little things, where we were not doing the same routine. Coach Osborne was a very habitual human being, with the particular routines, and he still maintained a lot of that. I mean, I could be away from practice and then come back two years later and know what we were going to do next in practice again, you know: "We're gonna do kicking drills, we're gonna do this, and then this is what we're gonna do next."

Q: As a player did that drive you a little crazy? Did you wish every now and then to visit the unfamiliar, or did you prefer not deviating from the norm?

BM: I know everybody has their different likes, but me personally? I think change is good. Because it gives you a different perspective, it shakes things up a little. Doing it differently from a weight training principle, for example, you have to mix it up every once in awhile or otherwise your body gets flat. So I really think that process really kind of pumped a lot of life into people.

Then also, like I said, the recruiting they brought in really started to develop and pay off, and the change in the schemes and bringing in more speed and that kind of stuff really started to develop, and we saw the benefits of that. And if guys could see that and trust that and put the results on the table, it really helps to move forward.

Q: Any favorite or memorable play stand out to you?

BM: Well, I scored as a defensive lineman. And I think any defensive lineman dreams of touching a football in a game and getting to score. (laughs) I intercepted a screen pass against Arizona State my junior year and took it back.

But getting that first Blackshirt, too. I remember when Coach Osborne, when I met him and was able to get my scholarship, too: you signing your scholarship papers after beginning as a walk-on is a huge thing. There are a ton of things you go through to get there, and playing as a Blackshirt and going through that process and being a part of that group of guys, the camaraderie of those guys… It's always good to see those people, you know? It's always nice to get back every once in awhile and know those relationships are there, those are the big lessons I got from it.

Everybody would love to have the national championships and the rings, you know, but I would never trade the process or even the loss that we took to Florida State in that championship game, because it taught me that: you can't leave something on the field, you can't make mistakes, you have to make sure you go as hard as you can to finish. And we made enough mistakes in that Orange Bowl to lose us the game. No matter what anybody wants to say about the officials, we had a lot of opportunities to take care of some things here and there, and enough things compounded that gave Florida State a big enough window to pull it out.

Q: Which brings me to this: is there any particiuar game stands out to you more than the others?

BM: I would say that one. It's not my favorite one because of how it ended: we felt like we were in pretty much control for most of the game, and then that last two or three minutes of that game where we went down, we went up, and we had that chance with the field goal at the end? It was just an emotional rollercoaster. You just weren't sure quite how to handle it. You knew the coaches were proud of you, you knew you gave everything you had during the game, and you knew that on the field we played pound for pound as good or better than them for the most part, but we just made a few more mistakes down the stretch and it costed us.

But from a personal standpoint, how it affects my life? I think it really shaped a lot of things, that you have to make sure you do it on the field. You can't point at officials, you can't do all those kinds of things, because none of that stuff you have any control over.

Q: Anything else about that Florida State game stand out to you, about the preparation, the mindset going in?

BM: Yeah, I think that was our turning point. I really do. I think that was the game that proved to everybody on the national stage that we had arrived. So many years we played it was 22-0 with Miami, the Georgia Tech loss, and we got in those big games and we didn't compete very well.

I remember my first bowl game, the Citrus Bowl, and Georgia Tech was there. I was a redshirt and it was my first experience, so there were so many distractions, but I just remember feeling real disappointed the whole game.

But it was my sophomore year, we were just in awe when we saw Miami play that year. That was that '92 Miami team and we lost 22 to nothing, and they were so fast, with their defense and their coverage units. You stood there on the sideline and thought, 'My gosh, they are fast!' They were just relentless. And I think we kind of said, "That's where we need to be."

And you look at that Florida State game: we went through that process. And you heard all the hype about Charlie Ward, and I think a lot of it was that lack of respect that people still had for us not winning a bowl game, yada, yada, yada. And you remember that little twist they had right at the end of the season there? Where Notre Dame was going to be who we were going to play because they beat Florida State, and they looked like they were going to play us? And I remember practicing -some practices before all that finished up- and I remember preparing for Jerome Bettis because he was still on the Notre Dame team at that time. And then they go and lose to Boston College a week or two later and that just totally changed the whole perspective of going down to Florida again and playing a Florida team. I think that really threw us for a twist, mentally, because here we were finally going down to Florida and playing a bowl game against a team from the Midwest, a different team, somebody more of our style, kind of a smash-mouth kind of a thing.

Q: Exactly.

BM: And then we go back and face that same old nemesis we'd been seeing for years, again.

Q: I hear you, Bruce. Do you have any memorable practice moments?

BM: Well, we were watching the Husker Century program on TV the other night and they had a clip of McBride and this noseguard, I forget his name -he had made it up to second string behind Englebert and just had this big old bucket head (laughs)- well, I saw this guy and remember how he was running one time, and Coach McBride said, "Boogs, if you get any slower your heart is gonna stop." And I think the biggest thing was his personality, Charlie McBride's personality. He had so many one-liners, that tinge of sarcasm he used all the time, you know? Another one was, "I don't think that guy is smart enough to put his hands down if he fell." (laughs) Another one was, "You're running around like you're smashing grapes," when you weren't really getting any place on the line: "You're running around like you're Jack the Bear." I don't know how many times people heard that one.'Whoever the heck this Jack guy is, I don't know, but you knew that wasn't a guy you wanted to be near.' (laughs)

The time the linebackers kind of rebelled on Coach Steele and wore shirts to a meeting where they said, "My name is Ed, too." (laughs) So those little things that happened in camp that you really didn't take too much stock in at the time, but it was those little things that stand out when you reminisce about the place and what made it special. And you talk about those little interactions when you meet up with the guys, too. It's not so much the games. It's not like the guys will say, "Hey, do you remember when we lost to Florida State by two and we lost national title?," you know? (laughs)

Q: Any memorable off-field stuff? I remember you wore a baseball cap now and then. Did George Sullivan ever catch you with a cap on at the training table and give you a slap upside the back of the head?

BM: Oh, I don't know how many times I got slapped. You learned after a couple of years and getting slapped. (laughs) Jerry Weber and those guys, I remember hanging out with them over at the training room at the other side. You had your favorites. Certain rituals some guys would go through and have to get taped by the same guy every day. Doak, he started taping a lot of our hands, the defensive lines'. He would lace the fingers and a lot of guys went through that process.

And then a bunch of us -I think it started with John Parrella that year- John Parrella, Terry Connealy, myself, and Kevin Ramaekers used to go to Dick Olson. It was the Straight Edge Barber Shop downtown, and everybody would get their hair cut by Dick. I remember the guys in the locker room, probably one of the stupidest things the guys had done -remember that year they shaved their heads?- I don't remember who it was, maybe it was Ernie Beler, I think he used to be the 'haircut guy' for a lot of the black guys and would shave their heads in the lockers there. It seemed there was always somebody getting their hair cut. Well, they shaved their heads and they nicked them. And I remember Kevin and those guys, Christian Peter, just sitting there in the chair with all the nicks on their head and bleeding down their heads. You'd just look at them and shake your head and go, 'Something isn't right about some of these guys.' (laughs) I never shaved my head. I wasn't gonna go that far. I said, "I'll look stupid: a tall, skinny guy with a bald head is not gonna be impressive at all." (laughs)

Q: You always had a pretty high and tight one, didn't you? A buzzcut?

BM: I always had a tight buzzcut when I played, because I didn't want to deal with hair in my helmet. And that's why I talked about Dick Olson, he always gave me the flat top, that military-style, Marine-style haircut.

Q: So is there anyone behind the scenes that most fans wouldn't know about? Anyone special who played a major role in the process?

BM: My goodness, there so many people when you think about all the little things people did. I remember Bryan Bailey. He was kind of a sadist at the time. He would always take guys and take a special interest in people and try to motivate them to train, so he'd grab you and, "Hey, let's go workout today." And he'd train you and just kick your ass. So he hung out with guys and did some of those things from a training standpoint. He went out of his way to do a lot of stuff.

And also with Doak, I always felt bad about how he was treated when all that went down in the transition there, but I remember one summer I was having trouble gaining weight and he got me a bunch of Sustacal to try to gain some weight.

Q: That was before Dave Ellis came on, I believe?

BM: We started working with a lady from Omaha, but she was more focused on Lance Lundberg and trying to keep him from hitting 300, you know? (laughs) I just remember I got put on a 6,000 calorie diet my junior year in spring ball and I ate 6,000 calories for a month and gained only 5 pounds. I was like, 'That isn't right,' you know? Lundberg just *looked* at a hamburger and gained fifteen pounds, you know? And all I gain is five pounds? Geez!

Q: (laughs) Well, anything we haven't touched upon? Anything to sum things up?

BM: When it came to change, the biggest thing I remember was the change of the mentality from the schemes standpoint, where the coaches really stepped it up and went through that process of making solid changes, visible changes, rather than continuing to do what they'd been doing a long time. But I think that work ethic and ownership the players took on, you really had the sense that they were going to work harder. And the talent? Those guys that came in behind us -Terry Connealy and that group- those special people came along. And you just don't get that very often.

End conversation.

Already having spoken to & about Tom Osborne and delving into what made him a unique personality, coach and leader, Bruce has piqued my interest about our upcoming conversation with Charlie McBride. You've no idea how filled I am with giddy excitement - as well as a juxtaposed sense of anxious dread- because Charlie could scare lightning back into a thundercloud. Then again, he could also be as warm and fuzzy as fur on a bunny's backside when he wanted. To summarize Coach McBride's perceptive abilities, Bruce mentioned that, 'He always had a good sense of when people were at their edge…was good at realizing when you needed to have a diversion of some kind, make sure you knew that he was still human, that he still cared about you as a person." That last part made all the difference in the world to the kids. And then to hear how Rush Ends coach Tony Samuel was almost the polar opposite of Charlie, I find it very telling how you just can't pigeon-hole too heavily with stereotypes, but that we should keep an open mind as we go through this process.

As far as pushing physical limits in the weightroom, the Metabolic Power Circuit -a uniquely challenging lifting routine- was devised to spur the body's natural increase of the testosterone hormone, enabling muscle growth and its key offshoot: power. Youngsters are often fond of pushing the envelope, testing the limits of their athleticism, competing to discover how they measure up to and against their peers, and this twice weekly routine gave them all they could handle. Hellish organized labor is what it was, but its effect was pure heaven, as they weekly came face to face with the heights of their willpower, strength, pain and endurance. The thanks go to Boyd Epley, Mike Arthur and Bryan Bailey -and Penn State University researcher William J. Kraemer and. Funny thing was, Penn State at the time had primarily a roomful of fixed movement weight machines -the kind you might allow unsupervised adolescents to lift with- while Nebraska made plentiful use of free weight barbells, dumbbells, and the explosive, ground-based Olympic lifts. To sum it up, here's the math: sweat + pain + nausea + rest = muscle. And muscle x motivation = victory.

The last subject worth highlighting was Bruce's mention of the mental toil of knowing that almost every year they had to go down to sweaty, sticky, steamy, stinky Miami to play a Florida-based team in the Big 8 Champion-designated Orange Bowl. Man, just hearing the words 'Orange Bowl' brings on a rush of memories at once triumphant and distasteful, exuberant and wincing. Can you imagine how these student-athletes were so looking forward to playing a like-kind team down there for once -Notre Dame, perhaps- only to watch the Golden Domers rust out come season's end? And then who were they saddled with? Florida State once again, a repeat of the previous year's contest, *"I think that really threw us for a twist, mentally."* You can say that again.

Notable quote #2:
Bruce Moore on the bonding taking place off the field: "When guys sat down to eat it was more guys in a group rather than the clique there used to be. And I think the way it was previously kind of kept guys from trusting each other on the field as much, too. It was nothing real overt that would come out, but every little thing kind of stacked up as you go through the process."

I like to believe that my best hits border on felonious assault.

Jack Tatum

Born to a prostitute mother and pimp father in Austin, Texas in 1928, Dick "Night Train" Lane was ditched into a back alley dumpster a few short months later, an infant left to die a most hideous death. By God's graces he was salvaged from sure demise by a passing widow. Later adopted by this same Ella Lane, Dick was raised to take on whatever the rough and tumble world could throw at him. After high school he somehow found his way to collegiate football in extreme western Nebraska at Scottsbluff Junior College, where the motto was and still is, simply, "The place to be." Going across the middle was not the place to be for opposing receivers, though, as this most vicious of defensive backs was almost single-handedly responsible for the outlaw of face-masking and the clothesline-tackle, a practice known during his NFL days as the "Night Train Necktie." Goading quarterbacks into ill-advised throws by giving the impression of playing too far off a receiver, he set an NFL season record of 14 interceptions as a rookie cornerback in 1952 for the Los Angeles Rams. Later inducted into the NFL Hall of Fame, he was one of football's more unique characters and talents.

Which brings us to John Reece, though a far cry as to his own family history, was a Texan who matriculated to eastern Nebraska in hopes of making something of a football splash in his own right. A talent of great proportion from the outset, he was a calculating ball-hawk and a skilled supervisor of the Blackshirt backfield. Also a character in his own right, he too made his mark in the pros as a Ram, albeit in St. Louis after their move from Los Angeles in 1995. I urge you to get comfortable in your seat for this one, as catching up with John is sure to be a smash hit.

Notable quote #1:
"One thing about Nebraska, they were never gonna put you on the field if you weren't ready, because they didn't want to embarrass yourself, the program or your family."

John Reece
Scholarship recruit, Cornerback/Safety, Houston, Texas (Jersey Village)
Where are they now? Lantana, Texas, Sales/Management

Question: So John, how did you end up at the University of Nebraska?

John Reece: It was really kind of strange, because I was out of Houston and I was a Top 40 prospect. It was me and a guy by the name of Patrick Bates -I don't know if you remember him or not- he was a big old safety. I was a little faster than he was. I was 6' 1" and about 195, he was like 6' 3" and about 230. And I came out and ran a 4.3 out of high school and he ran like a 4.38, and he was a specimen, man, a big old kid. We were the number one and two safeties coming out that year, so we were a real good defensive class.

So it boiled down to my top two picks, and at that time the Southwest Conference was in shambles, so I knew I didn't want to play in Texas and the Southwest Conference. My two dream teams had been Nebraska and UCLA. I always had this desire to move out west because of the weather, for one thing, and as a defensive back playing in the Pac 10 I was going to see a lot of action because most of those teams threw the ball. So it came down basically to me and Patrick for Nebraska and UCLA. And the same weekend I was visiting Nebraska he was out visiting UCLA (and I didn't hear how all of this shook out until a long time after), so me and my dad flew up to Nebraska and we went and talked to Coach

Osborne. And the guy I was rooming with on that recruiting trip was Billy Wade out of Texas, a tight end. And he'd broken is leg or something three or four games into that high school season and he couldn't play, so he comes hobbling out of Coach Osborne's office and he's on Cloud 9 and says, "Man, I think they have one more scholarship left. So if they want to give you one, you better take it." So I walk in there thinking, 'I'm gonna be offered a scholarship. This is great! I'll get the last one.' So me and my dad sit down and we do the formalities and talk to Coach Osborne and he goes, "Well John, I'm holding a scholarship for a guy who's out at UCLA right now taking a visit, so I really don't have a scholarship unless he decides not to come here." And I said, 'I know who that is.' (laughs)

And it was funny, because I was supposed to go to UCLA the next week, and the day before I was to fly out to Nebraska I got a call from the UCLA defensive coach who was recruiting me and he said, "I need you to commit right now. There's one scholarship left. It's yours if you want it. Commit right now and you can have it." And I said, 'I can't. I haven't seen your campus. I haven't met any of your players. I'm going to Nebraska this week and I'll be out there at UCLA next week, can you hold it?' And he goes, "No. If you don't accept right now on this phone call then forget it. You can't come." So I turned him down. It was sad, because my mom had just paid 400 bucks for a plane ticket and there was nothing the NCAA could do about it. She was upset and called Coach Donahue at UCLA and he said, "Hey, let me talk to this one guy." But they really never called me back.

So here are my top two prospects and they just flew out the damn window, (laughs) because, you know, I just spent the weekend at Nebraska. And I was, 'Why *wouldn't* a guy like to come here? It's great!' And Tom said, "Here's what I'll do: If you're interested in coming here I'll call you tonight. What time does your plane arrive home?" And I was like, 'Oh, we'll probably be home at 10 o'clock.' So he said, "I'll call you at ten o'clock and tell you whether or not you have a scholarship."

And so at 10 p.m. -on the nose- he called and he said, "I don't know if you've heard or read by now, but Patrick has decided to go to UCLA, so the scholarship is yours if you want it." And I said, 'I'll take it under one condition.' And he said, "What's that?" and I said, 'I'm not going to come up there to redshirt. I want to play.' And he laughed. He goes, "Well, John, we normally don't do that up here, particulary on the defensive side." So I said, 'Well, those are my conditions. I'll take the scholarship, but I want to you to seriously consider me as a top prospect and I want to be on varsity next year.' And he said, "Well, you'll have to work your butt off, I'll tell you that. I'll give you that. You come up here in great shape and you learn the system and we'll see."

So Paul, I worked my ass off. Really did. George Darlington, the defensive backs coach at the time, sent me some basic formations and defenses they had, so when I stepped on campus I had a pretty good understanding of what the defense was trying to accomplish. And free safety was where I thought I was going in at -and we captain the whole defense- there's a lot of calls and check calls you have to make, formations you have to know and all that stuff. So when I got there it was, honestly, there just wasn't enough time in training camp to really learn all of it, so they had me at corner and at dime back and some other places. So midway through camp Tom came to me and kind of shook his head and said, "John, I don't know what I'm going to do with you yet." And I said, 'Well, I told you on the phone, 'I didn't come up here to redshirt." (laughs) And he said again, "Well, I don't know what I'm going to do with you." And I said, 'Let's see how it goes this scrimmage and base your decision off of that.' And he says, "Great." So I had a really good scrimmage.

And it's funny, the first day the varsity was practicing I was standing outside our dorm room talking to the other freshmen on the team and one of the assistant coaches pulls up and says, "What the hell are you doing?" I said, 'What do you mean?' He said, "You're on varsity. Let's go!" (laughs) So I jumped in the car and went on over and I'm like, 'Yeahhh!' It was a good ride. It was me and Will Shields, we were two freshmen who made the traveling squad that year.

Q: What year was that?

JR: It was August of '89.

Q: So you show up that first day on campus, anything in particular stand out to you?

JR: It was all so surreal at the time. The varsity was all into their routine and all that. It was funny -because you know the walk-on program was so huge- so I walk in and, honestly, there was only a handful of us with color there, (laughs) which was no big deal for me. My high school was 70% caucasian and all my friends were different races, so I never had an issue with it, but I was just intrigued by how many guys would actually pass up opportunities to go elsewhere just to walk-on there.

The first day? The one thing that did stand out, there was over 100 guys there that turned out for the freshman team, and as the days went on through two-a-days -and I'm from Texas and it's a hundred degrees in the shade in the summer, so it wasn't that big of a deal- but to see the numbers dwindle each day? And I think we ended up with like twenty guys. My numbers may be off, but it seems there were a ton of guys that first day of practice, but as the week went on the numbers were less and less and less.

And we had guys from all over the nation there and we had a couple of receivers that did real well and were pretty quick, and it got to a point that anytime we did one-on-one drills or something and one of those guys got up there, most of the guys on our defense would look over to me and say, "Okay, John, you go in and cover those guys." (laughs) They just weren't used to that speed.

I still remember going out for my first practice with the varsity. That was awesome. With high school you walk in and you're kind of the top dog, and then at Nebraska the first guy I saw getting dressed and take the field was Pat Tryance at linebacker. And I remember looking at him and saying to myself, 'That guy is a grown man!' (laughs) Pat was huge, man. He came out and had this little spandex and no shirt on and I was, 'Damn, this guy is like Arnold Schwarzenegger! That's a linebacker! That's a middle backer!' You know what I mean? Big old guy, deep voice. It was like I was playing with my dad or something. (laughs) I'm 18 and barely have any facial hair; this was big-time football. But I was there to compete, so it was pretty cool.

Q: Any guys you first befriended from the start?

JR: You know, one of the guys who really took me under his wing was Curtis Cotton. I don't know why, but we ended up competing for the nickel back position that year and then ended up giving it to me mid-season, but he was just a guy that took me under his wing and showed me the ropes. He invited me over to his house and showed me the ropes, and he roomed with A-Train, LeAndre Anderson, defensive tackle. Those guys were roommates and they'd take me over to their place on the weekends. We didn't have training table on Sunday, so we'd go over and they'd have meals and stuff prepared and we'd sit and read and watch Sunday football together, it was cool. You weren't out there on your own.

Q: Curtis Cotton. He had that high haircut for awhile, didn't he?

JR: Yeah, he had that big old high-top fade haircut. (laughs) If you see him now, he's bald-headed. His hair started falling out so he cut it all off. (laughs) But talk about a physical specimen! Oh, my God! And he was pretty strong. We had a really good weight program out of high school; I squatted with John Parrella and most of our defensive linemen. I squatted with Curtis and we'd do bench press and stuff, so that's one of the things we had in common. So it was just kind of a natural fit for a relationship. We weren't competing directly as safeties; he was at strong safety and I was at corner, but that toss-up position there for the dimebacker, nickel backer, we did compete a little bit. But it was fun. We helped each other out.

Q: Coach Darlington: tell me more about him and what the meant to you?

JR: He was always good to me. He really was. I have no complaints about George.

He was a little brash. I think he rubbed me way, way wrong after the '94 Orange Bowl. We played our lights out and, quite honestly, after going through the films -and I've gone through the film year after year after year- it was a tough loss losing that championship to Florida State. It was the first time we'd played for it in a while.

And my freshman class, we always said that we wanted to be the ones to give Tom his first title, and I honestly saw comfort from my teammates' words that night, because I had the toughest position on the field. That there was a time I had a rough outing. We had Lo Brinkley, who was a defensive back -and he and George really didn't see eye to eye on a lot of things. It actually worked out to where we made a rover-type position, so him and Ernie Beler shared that job. Well, Lorenzo was more of a corner, he was quick and he'd get his hands on receivers and he's quick at blitzing, but he broke his arm like the third or fourth play of the game, so he was out. Ernie, he was more of a true strong safety-type and wasn't real quick on his feet, so he really didn't get a whole lot of jersey on the guys that he was covering- so I'm covering these guys 10 yards out, middle of the field, he's got a two-way go. And George's philosophy was, "Okay, if you just don't fall of the cliff when the ball is snapped, you should be able to cover this guy." And I'm standing still while Kez McCorvey's coming full speed at me, (laughs) to give the blitz time to get to Charlie Ward. So we're trying to make everything look the same and disguise it and all, and it was a tough position.

And I was up for the challenge, but apparently I didn't play as well as he thought I should play. And at the end of the game me and Toby Wright are standing in the locker room crying and Toby walked off for a second, and George grabbed him and said, "Hey, you know what? You played a great game is what you did. And I think we could have won the game had we gotten better free safety play." That's the type of guy George was, kind of brash, and whatever was on the top of his mind was what was coming out, "I'll think about what I said later." And I knew kind of how to deal with that, but most guys he would rub the wrong way.

Q: A few guys have made comments that they and George didn't see eye to eye. Was that a common theme with a lot of you defensive backs?

JR: Well, it was tough. Because the guy never played defensive back in football. He was a lacrosse player, and everything he knew was all book knowledge. His philosophy was, "If the guy runs a 4 nothing and you run a 4.5, you should be able to cover him as long as you get your hand on him." And I was like, 'Yeah, and I could probably cover him for a couple of seconds, but after that the guy's gonna run by me.' (laughs) Sooner or later the laws of physics are gonna take over, right?

He was really good at x's and o's, but the one thing that killed me -and it used to drive me crazy- was that we got really good at playing bump and run. We had some really good bump and run corners (me being one of them), and we would get to the damn bowl game and he would back us all off 6 or 8 yards. And it just sent that message to those Florida teams -and I remember we got beat 27-14 or something in '93 in that Orange Bowl and the following year was a rematch and I remember going out for picture day that day- and some of their receivers came in and were talking, and they just flat-out asked us, "Why do you guys play bump and run on everybody until you get to us?" And we go, "What do you mean?" And they go, "Well, you just send the message that you're afraid of us." And I go, 'We're not afraid of you. We're just trying to make everything look the same.' And they were like, "Well, it looks like you guys are afraid of us, so you guys are giving us the edge every year you come down here." And that just stuck out to me, because every big game we had, be it Colorado when they had Westbrook and Charles Johnson, we played the hell out of them. And what really killed us that game was we backed off and we still beat them like 65-7 or something like that. And Coach Darlington was like, "See, it works." And I'm like, 'It worked against them because it's freezing cold out here! (laughs) We get down to Florida they're gonna have the edge.' Nothing pleased me more than to watch them the next year against Miami because they bumped and ran. They really did. And they won! And it was like, 'Kudos to us!' I felt like, in talking to those those guys that won it, they looked back at us and go, "Man, we never would have won it if not for the leadership you guys provided and seeing what you guys went through." They practiced an extra 1:16 in memory of us that year before. And I was just happy to see Tom win one the next year. He certainly deserved one.

Q: So you were playing in the pros that next year, right?

JR: Yes, I was.

Q: Do you recall watching that Miami game? Do you remember where you were?

JR: I was actually at my parents' house. The NFL season had just ended and I was talking to Toby Wright at that time. We were watching the game and he was in Arizona and I was in Texas, and we were on the phone the whole game just talking about different plays, the fact that they were being aggressive this time. It was about time! (laughs) 'Why didn't we do that when we were playing?' (laughing)

Q: So you came in August of '89 and played your last game in January of '94. Can you put your finger on a transition that went on there during that span of time?

JR: You know, I played my freshman year and blew my knee out, so I redshirted my sophomore year, and that season was a horrid season. We got beat by Oklahoma -got thrashed by Oklahoma- and I'm sitting home at Thanksgiving because I couldn't travel. I'm sitting home and just wanted to beat the TV up. We got thrashed like 52 to something. They went to the Citrus Bowl and got thrashed by Georgia Tech, and I think we went 9-4, maybe? We lost to Colorado -got schooled in Colorado- lost in Washington to start the year off, lost to Oklahoma and lost the bowl game. All horrible losses. The public around there was really upset with Tom. We had gone 9-2 my first year and then went through that year, and then coming back my redshirt sophomore season I think we went 9-3 or 9-2, and there was just an uproar.

People thought that Tom was just outdated and it was time to move on. And he made a decision and created the Unity Council at the time, kind of a governing board. I think that two players from each position group were voted on. I think they had to be juniors or seniors, upperclassmen. They were kind of the governing board. Tom wasn't, quote unquote, the 'bad guy' anymore. One thing about him: when he said he was gonna do something he did it, you know? And he told us from the start, "It's gonna be your team.

I'm gonna come to you guys when there's tough decisions to be made. And we'll make them together." I remember him coming to us and saying, "I'm tired of losing these bowl games. We used to recruit for a certain type of athlete and not go into certain neighborhoods. I think for us to compete at a level you guys want to compete at and a level we want to compete at and win national titles, we're gonna have to go into those areas and after those guys, who are gonna be able to academically live up to our standards." Basically, he just came to us for our permission. And everybody was like, "Yeah, go for it!' That recruiting season we brought in Tommie Frazier and the rest is history, you know? (laughs) But for him to come to us and ask us our opinion and we were like, "Hey, it's your team." And he was like, "No, it's our team." And for him to come to us, that really won a bunch of guys over.

Q: He handed you bona fide ownership of the team?

JR: Yeah, he did. There was a player in question going into that last game for us, getting ready to play in the national title game where one of the running backs got in trouble, Lawrence missed curfew or something. And Tom's whole policy was, "You miss, you're out." And it turns out Calvin Jones tweaked his ankle in practice and didn't feel like he was gonna be 100% for that game -and we really didn't have any experienced running backs for that game- and Tom came to us and said, "I've always been a man of my word, and told Lawrence that he wasn't going to start and he's not going to start. And I don't know if we're going to get him in or not. It just depends on how Calvin feels. And I wanted to come to you guys and it's your call. If you say that he can't play, then he can't play, but this is a pretty tough game and we're gonna need all the men we can get. He's healthy. We don't know how long Calvin's going to be healthy." And we all got together and said, "Well, he can't start. We agree to that. If we can wait until the second half or whatever it's gonna be, to kind of teach him a lesson," knowing Calvin can't carry the whole load, that we were gonna need somebody back there to carry the ball. But we got the point across. So he brought Lawrence in and we all talked to him and made the decision at that point of, "Okay, if we need you, you'll play. If not, you aren't gonna play." And he ended up playing and he rushed for 100 yards and a touchdown, so it's kind of one of those things where if it wasn't that big of a game he doesn't play, but hey, this is what we all worked for, so we needed him to play. And he was probably the greatest running back I ever saw in my life, man, up close and personal.

Q: Really?

JR: Yeah. Talent up the wazoo. Just incredible. Incredible. And I was the one that recruited him! (laughs) Well, he was George's prospect, and during recruiting season the upperclassmen would have to host recruits. I remember George called me in there Friday morning and said, "I need to talk to you", and he put on some filmwork of Lawrence in high school and I was, 'Who is this kid!?', and he was, "Well, this is who I want you to show around this weekend. He's kind of fragile. He comes from a broken home. Don't take him partying. Just hang out with him and talk to him about the university. Hopefully we can sign him." So that's what we did. Me and Toby took him to our place and we sat and had meals and we just kind of talked about goals.

And I told him flat-out, 'I've seen you on film. You've got more natural talent than I've seen around here in a long time. If you keep your nose clean you'll win the Heisman and everything else.' And I don't know, we left and he didn't have the leadership there, and I think at one point they got so successful they felt they were untouchable with some things. I can't recall Tom ever telling a guy to go to the NFL before finishing his schoolwork, but Lawrence had been in such shambles that it was just time for him to go.

Q: I hate to get off track here, but what was your first impression of Lawrence?

JR: I thought he was a great kid. A great kid. I still do. It's just unfortunate, there may be some type of imbalance there that may need to be addressed. He was just an outstanding kid. He was really quiet. That was the shocker to me and Toby, when we heard about what happened, because he was always the quiet jokester, to me. When I heard all the horror stories of about what went on I was, 'There's no way.'

Q: So after the Florida State game you got drafted by the Rams?

JR: I actually got drafted by the Arizona Cardinals. (laughs) I kid with people all the time that I left heaven and I got sent to hell. (laughs) Me and Buddy Ryan, man, we just didn't get along. He drafted a guy by the name of Perry Carter out of Southern Miss, so he drafted the guy two picks ahead of me. He was like the 111th pick and I was the 113th pick. So he had those picks back to back. We played the same position: we played corner. We were both pretty big, fast guys. And it turns out I had a pretty good sports agent at the time; he had a lot of Cowboys. And we had talked ahead of time going into mini-camp, "Don't talk contract. Let me talk contract. Here's a number that we're gonna start at and here's probably what we're gonna get." And we left it at that. And I remember after mini-camp Perry and his agent were on the phone with me and his agent says, "Perry just told me he signed for a little bit of money." And I go, "What do you mean?" And Perry goes, "Yeah, he just got me this much..." And I told him, 'Dude, you got screwed! We should have gotten a hundred grand more..' I said, '...why'd you do that?' And he goes, "Well, they told my agent they're out of money and yada, yada, yada, and all that." So I called my agent and he's like, "What?!" So he called them and the (Cardinals) played this game like, "Well, we can't pay more than we paid Perry because we picked him two picks ahead of you." So I held out of training camp for one day, (laughs) which was totally stupid for a fourth round pick. Not something a fourth round pick wants to do, you know? So I get back up there and he's giving me the cold shoulder, and it just wasn't a good fit at all.

Then they come to me and say, "You know, there were a lot of teams that were interested in you before we drafted you." And I was, 'Oh great, just send me someplace. I don't care.' So I ended up going to Kansas City. It was great, man, with Joe Montana and Derrick Thomas. I got to hang out with Derrick a lot. For some reason he took me under his wing. It was fun, a great team, great camraderie, great teammates, great coach in Marty Schottenhiemer, back in the Midwest where I was comfortable with things. And as it turns out they had a bunch of running backs get hurt going into the 10th week. And I was on the developmental squad, so they needed to bring in some running backs and I got axed. And then I got picked up by the Raiders. I finished the season with the Raiders, signed back with Kansas City in January or February, and before I could pack up all my stuff and move back to Kansas City they signed James Hasty, Brian Washington, Ronnie Lott, A.J. Johnson, all these guys that had years in the league, (laughs) All-Pro's and they all walk in with million dollar bonuses. So I go from being #2 on the depth chart to #5 overnight and I go, 'There's no way.' So I ended up working my ass off during that offseason program and I ended up getting married that June and go to camp in July, get all situated and wake up the next morning with a phone call from Marty Schottenmhiemer saying they're gonna let me go. And I go, 'You're not even gonna let me compete?' And he was like, "I just signed too many guys. I'm sorry. You know I like you as a player, but there's other guys we're paying a lot of money, so we'll roll the dice and just see where we end up."

And it's funny, because my wife was the Entertainment Coordinator for the Rams and also one of the Rams cheerleaders, and they knew we were getting married and it was at that time the Rams had moved to St. Louis. So while I was in Kansas City going to practice they were flying her back because she was helping them get their cheerleading outfit started out there. So during the week she'd fly out there and on the weekends she'd fly back home. Then the special teams coach I had with the Raiders, Steve Ortmeier, got the General Managers job with the St. Louis Rams. So I'm getting released and I call her, and Debbie Polan, the recruiting person, walked by the desk and talks to my wife, "Hey, when you see John tell him hello." And she goes, "Well, you're not going to believe this, but I just got off the phone with him and they just let him go." So she's like, "What?! Well, where is he?" So she goes and talks to Ortmeier and he says, "Yeah, we want him." So they got me on the next plane to St. Louis, went to the training camp, ended up making the team and signed a two year contract with them. So it all worked out in the end, but man, it was stressful. A stressful time. (laughs)

Q: A nice time to be a newlywed, right?

JR: Yeah, exactly.

Q: John, how did you meet your wife?

JR: Oh, it gets better. Do you remember that trip we took to Tokyo to play Kansas State? Yeah, she danced for Long Beach State's Competitive Dance Team, so they got invited over there. They won the national title the year before. Florida State's Dance Team was over there cheering for us and Cal State-Long Beach was cheering for Kansas State, but they were staying at our hotel.

And you remember Kareem Moss? He was begging me one night to go out on the town. I always had this thing where I didn't want to go out before the games. (And if we went out for a bit later after the game that was okay, but I didn't want to go out on nights before the game) So we're sitting in the lobby of that hotel and my wife comes walking down, and Kareem is just begging me to go out. I said, 'Dude, you know I don't go out. I'm not going out.' And he's like, "C'mon! We're in Tokyo! Let's go see the city, let's have a beer and we'll be back before midnight. Let's go." And I'm kind of eye-balling her the whole time as she's getting her money exchanged for yen and not really paying any attention to him while he's giving me his sales pitch… and he notices that I'm staring at her. So he turns and goes, "Hey! Are you going out?" And she says, "Yes, I'm going out with my friends." And he says, "See, she's going out!" So I made my mind up then that I was gonna go out. (laughs)

And it was so funny, because here's a shot in the dark, right: we're in Tokyo, Japan and I see this girl walk across the lobby and I knew she was probably from Cal State-Long Beach. We ended up jumping in a cab: me, Kareem and Tyrone Hughes, and going down to some area the guys told us about. We get out of the cab and this guy, about 6' 9" comes out - blonde hair, blue eyes- and he goes, "Hey, you guys are Americans?" We're like, "Yeah, we are." And he goes, "Come up! I just opened up a new club upstairs. We've got great music. I'll buy you guys a beer." So we go upstairs and lo and behold her and her friends are all sitting there and I go, 'Okay, this is fate.' We sit down -Tyrone, Kareem and I- and they get up and start dancing. And she walked over to our table and says, "Hey, how are you doing?" And I'm like, 'Hey, I'm great.' (laughs) So we talked and talked for most of the night and just really hit it off.

Talk about long distance relationships. For about a year and a half, talking back and forth, long distance phone bills, trying to get to know each other. And we were married two years later.

Q: So that was the latter part of your junior year and your whole senior year?

JR: Yeah, that's the story.

Q: So while your teammates are getting into fights with professional wrestlers you're meeting pretty dancing girls…

JR: Oh man, you brought back my memory now. Dude! I met her that Wednesday and then we played. It was weird, our timing was all screwed up. It was like Friday there and Saturday over here -or the other way around- but that night we all went out kind of as a group and she went out with me, and we end up at the same place we were before. And getting off the elevator at the hotel I see David White getting pummeled by these two big ol' guys. So John Parrella, before the elevator closed, just punched one of the guys in the nose. We'd won the Big 8 the year before and he had his ring on and just lacerated the guy's face.

What started it all was one of the linebackers from Kansas State was talking trash to these guys. So as he's getting off the elevator he says something to David, who just happens to be on the elevator with the guy, and he gets stuck on the elevator. And these guys think they're together, so these guys just start pounding on him. As it turns out, we ended up meeting them downstairs at the bottom floor of this place and all hell broke loose. Elbows were flying. It was crazy. I forgot all about that. They closed David's eye, though. They did a pretty good job on him.

Q: Was David the one who wore sunglasses on the flight home?

JR: Yeah, we got back and Tom was like, "David, come up here and take those glasses off. (laughs) I understand you guys were fighting." And we're like, "Coach, it wasn't us. It was a guy from Kansas State. He started it. We saw these guys beating up our teammate and we all jumped in." Tom understood. He said, "I told you guys I don't like you guys going out drinking and that other stuff." It was really innocent. We were all gonna meet up at the same place. Some of the guys from Kansas State were pretty cool, but apparently this guy had a chip on his shoulder. Old memories. (laughs)

Q: So tell me, what about your moving to Nebraska stands out to you, such as the team mindset or the walk-ons?

JR: It gave me a greater appreciation for the place. I'll always hold Nebraska in high regard. I always watched the Oklahoma- Nebraska game. You dream of playing for a program like that growing up. I never realized in my wildest dreams that dream would actually come true.

I befriended a guy in a class that I had, his name was Shad. He's from Norfolk and he took me home one weekend, "I'm gonna take you to Norfolk." And I'm like, 'No problem.' And he was going back because he was the prom king the year before, to crown the new guy, and I go walking in, and it was right after the Fiesta Bowl. So I walk in with all my Fiesta Bowl stuff on into this gym and I'm like the only guy colored in the place. (laughs) And everybody knew who I was and it was, "Hey, how you doing?" It brought it full circle for me. This was their life to these people: the program. It was just cool, because I was never treated unfairly. Nobody ever made crazy comments to us.

I was talking to Kevin Raemakers and Toby a few months ago, and the more I'm away from it the more I appreciate what went on there. We were treated like kings, man. Aside from me having kids and everything nowadays, those are the best times of my life.

Q: Wow, Norfolk, Nebraska. You know John, I grew up about 45 miles away from there, and as a kid Norfolk was the 'big city' for me. (laughs) It was a 45 minute drive from my hometown to the Norfolk, and at the time it was the nearest place a person could get McDonald's french fries…

JR: (laughs) That is hilarious. Hey, what was the place with those..what were they called? Runza's? The food place? My mom and dad still talk about that place, and my sister, too. They had the best swiss mushroom hamburger and fries! I was talking to my sisters a month ago, man, and they always used to get dragged along to all the games, right? And I said, 'I know that was tough on you.' And they go, "No, we had a great time. Those people were wonderful. I loved that Runza place. When we pulled into Lincoln there, mom always said, "Okay, we've got to get a Runza before we go to the hotel." (laughs) "And on the way back they would stop and get something for the ride home." I said, 'I never knew you guys liked that place. That was my favorite, too.' (laughs)

Q: You know John, if we were smart we'd both buy the California franchise rights. We'd make a killing.

JR: Oh man, I tell you what. I was telling my wife the other day, "We go back, I'm gonna take you there. You'll understand." Especially on a cold night, right?

Q: Bingo, my friend. Say, does any favorite game stand out to you?

JR: They were all special. All special to me. One game that does stand out was coming back my junior year and breaking back into the starting lineup. Colorado had been kicking our tails for so many years. And a lot of the games we got screwed out of. Beating their butt the ways we beat 'em then, and beating Oklahoma, as well.

And winning the Big 8 was awesome. The whole season my senior year was just magical. We'd coined the phrase, "Refuse To Lose" one day. And lo and behold we go 11 and 0 going into the bowl game, and that just seemed like that was going to be our year. We got over the hump and we were going to win the national title. We were two points shy, but that was just a magical season. And not necessarily any game in particular, but what I miss about it is the camaraderie. That year, in particular, we did everything together. We had a cookout at different guys' houses every weekend. We didn't have any cliques. We hung out together, we studied together, we went to movies together. We did everything together as a team. It was special. And I think that's what the young guys picked up on from us and carried that over in the back to back championship years. We all hung out together. If we saw each other today we'd probably be like we never left the place. I hadn't talked to Kevin Raemakers since I'd left until just a few months ago and it was like I'd been with the guy the whole time.

Q: How did you end up talking to Kevin?

JR: Somehow Doak was trying to put a reunion or something together. We always talked about that '94 class coming back and some of those guys have always said, "Hey, if it weren't for you guys we never would have won it." So we were seeing if we could set that up through Doak, and Toby was talking to Doak. Then he called Raemakers and he called me and three—way'd me in. Toby was like, "Hey John, who was the craziest guy the whole time you were there? Give me his name!" And I'm like, 'Ramaekers.' And here Kevin breaks in on the phone just busting up laughing. (laughs) It was a great time. Those type of relationships we had those days? You can't buy them. I miss those guys.

Q: Did you ever have the chance, while you were in the pros, to sit down with other guys and talk about your college experiences?

JR: You know what was funny, when I was with the Raiders Tom Rathman and Jamie Williams were still on the squad. (laughs) When I first arrived I was just amazed, because here Rathman walks in and goes, "Hey Husker, how are you doing?" I'm like, 'It's Tom

Rathman!' And Jamie Williams was the same way. Knowing me and knowing they'd signed a guy from Nebraska, it was kind of cool.

Q: Did they have any good Coach Solich or good Coach Osborne stories?

JR: None I could share. (laughs)

Q: I think Rathman used to cut his own hair in those days…

JR: Yeah, he did. And it looked like it, too. (laughs) But what great guys, him and Jamie. Great guys, man. Typical Nebraska guys.

Q: Any favorite practice stories?

JR: I've got one funny story. Do you remember Big Twinkie, offensive lineman Doug Wadell?

Q: Twink! King of the Airdynes!

JR: We were sitting on the sideline and Doug, he'd always run scout teams for us. And he'd always get everybody so fired up, he was so damned funny.

And they were running a sweep where he had to pull, and I remember Reggie Cooper was our strong safety. Well, Twinkie saw the card beforehand and he was talking trash to Reggie, "You watch out. I'm gonna get you! I'm coming after you!" And Reggie was like, "Alright Twinkie, you better leave me alone. You better leave me alone." So he pulls full steam and he's sprinting, and he comes around the side and Cooper lit his ass up. Bam! Just knocked him on his ass. And something went wrong on the play, so Coach McBride was like, "Run it again!" So Twink gets all fired up: "You got me this time. But I'm coming back. I'm gonna get you good this time!" And Reggie was, "I told you, Twink. Leave me alone." So they snap the ball and Twinkie comes around full steam again and it looked like a damned replay. He hit him in the same place again, dropped him in the same place. Everybody on the sideline lost it, man. (laughs) Old Twink picked the wrong guy to mess with. Reggie Cooper was physical, the most physical safety I've been around.

Q: Did you room with Toby Wright?

JR: Yeah, we were roommates.

Q: Well, I was talking to Lorenzo a while ago and he said that Toby really brought a level of physicality to the defensive backfield…

JR: Yeah, by far. And I don't say that just because he was my roommate and my best friend.

There's two guys that George had me recruit. And there were two guys he had me watch film on. It was Lawrence and Toby. George and me had a great relationship. I used to get razzed all the time, "Oh, you're the Coach's pet." For some reason he really didn't mess with me. He'd call me up 7 in the morning, "Hey, I want to show you this guy. I've got film for you." And so I'm watching this film and Toby's just lighting everybody up. It was just like a highlight reel for a strong safety. Every hit was a textbook hit: form tackles, driving them in the chest, driving them, just running through them, playing with this ferocity like he was just mad at the world. I was like, 'Who the hell is this kid?' and George was like, "I'm bringing him up here tonight. I want you to spend some time with him. Derek Brown is going to be his host. I told Derek to find you wherever you are so you can talk to him. So talk to this guy." Derek actually ended up dropping him off at my place and we hung out most of the night, and I told him, 'We have a need for a safety, big time. We need somebody like you who's physical, who can change the attitude of this defense. We've got to get more aggressive.' He decided to come out and it was just amazing.

That Tokyo trip was so special to me because it was kind of Toby's coming out party. He had two or three sacks against Kansas State, I met my wife and had a really good game. I look back on that, and it solidified friendships between him and I and Kareem, Ed Stewart and some other guys.

That trip was so special, but Toby, he was unreal. And he had a knack for just getting to the football and making stuff happen. He and George had a really difficult time. Toby was a guy where you just wanted to open it up and let him go. To give him a whole bunch of assignments or have him think about where his feet were going before the snap of the ball and all that? I was like, 'Hey, just line him up and let him go.' It was kind of my job there. It was difficult because I was actually rated pretty high as a corner going into my senior year and we get into the Kansas State game and Troy Dumas, who was a hell of a young safety, he and George were really butting heads one game and Troy blew an assignment, and I look up and we're behind 14-0 at home. And George called me on the intercom from the press box and says, "How much safety do you know?" And I go, 'Coach, I know the package.' And he says, "You go tell Troy that you're going in at safety." And I said, 'No, you tell Troy that I'm going in a safety and I'll tell Tyrone Williams to get prepared to go in at corner.' I thought it was just going to be for that game, but it ended up remaining that way for the rest of the season. But anyhow, it worked out. You do what you've got to do to benefit the team. Me and Toby were a great combination at safety. I was able to get everybody lined up and just get in the right defense and calm everybody down back there. Tyrone was a hell of a corner. It was a shame keeping him on the bench, so it all worked out.

Q: And then Troy moved to linebacker...

JR: Where he probably should have been. Troy was another guy that was good going straight ahead and covering the H-back, your tight end, but really didn't have the hips to play safety the way we needed to play, doing a bunch of covering. That's not a knock against Troy, but he was just better suited at that linebacker position.

Q: Watching film from those days, he would hurt people!

JR: Oh yeah, he's a big old backer, man. Big old kid. They thought he was going to be another Steve Atwater, but he just didn't have the hip movement. A little stiff in the hips, but he should have been put a little closer to the line of scrimmage for starters. He didn't have any business being ten yards off the ball. You wanted him 3 to 5 yards off of the ball where he could go in and get physical. That was an attribute of his. The same thing with Toby. Only Toby could cover, good hips and everything. He was just a good football player.

Q: Watching the Florida State game the other night, I never felt so bad as I did when Toby bumps into that receiver when they make that pass to the endzone, when the ball was supposedly thrown out of reach...

JR: I had a dream about that the other night, too. That game haunts me, I swear. I had an interception. I had an interception -I actually had two that game- but on one of them I think Dante Jones was supposed to go outside or inside but he gave away his position a little too early, and so I had the guy there.

And Charlie Ward was just -he pissed me off- (laughs) he saw me twice at the very last possible second, twice before making a decision. On both of those passes he lobbed the ball up and I broke on the ball early and the receiver broke his route. Dante came underneath and the back got him, Charlie flushed out to the right and actually ended up beating the tackle and getting there the last minute to beat him there to affect the throw, but I think if he'd have stayed outside we had him. When we got to the locker room George was just livid, "John had an interception if you'd just stay outside!" He was yelling at Dante and going off. And that second play, Toby? He was there. He was there, and I got a little greedy and I jumped too early. I saw it and I was scoring and was gonna run 90 yards for a touchdown, right? And he saw me, last second, and he just threw it out of the endzone. He totally panicked a little bit, because he was obviously in pressure time, we were up and we're winning and we don't want to give up a damn touchdown. We can't let them in the endzone, so Toby did the right thing: just tackled his ass. I don't think he was aware. If he had actually looked up he would have seen the ball was going out of the endzone. Had I not gotten so damn greedy early on I might have had a pick and it would have been over with. So maybe George was right. (laughs) I gotta go back. That haunts me. Maybe George was right about that...

Q: Hey, you live by the sword and you die by the sword, right?

JR: You could cut the tension with a knife. Me and Toby for four quarters… we're both sitting on the sidelines just bawling like babies, because we just wanted to win that game so damned bad. Everybody was playing their hearts out and nobody wanted to make a mistake, but you still wanted to give it 100%. It was just one of those games, man, just wasn't meant for us to win it. We had so many bad calls that game. And we weren't ones to really harp on that, but I truly, in my heart, felt like we'd beat those guys up and down that field.

And Bobby Bowden was out there and said, "We didn't play that well tonight…" and I was like, 'No, you got your asses handed to you tonight. We just had an extra opponent out there on the field.' (laughs)

Q: We didn't get beat, we simply ran out of time that night, John. That's my take on it…

JR: Oh, that's a tough one. That one still hurts...

Q: That's the hard part for me, talking to some of you guys who weren't able to slap that national champ ring on your finger, you know what I mean?

JR: It was bittersweet watching the guys the next two years win it. Me and Zo (Lorenzo Brinkley) used to sit around and replay that damned Florida State game over and over. It was like, "Why are we torturing ourselves over this? We did everything we could possibly do." And to this day, I bought that whole series and I have that game and I'm still just …AARGGGGH… biting my lip everytime I watch it. (laughs)

Q: Hey, you later played alongside Toby for the Rams, didn't you?

JR: Yeah, I did. He came into his own, man, he was a beast. That was my second or third year with the Rams. He had an All-Pro season, led the team in interceptions, 100+ tackles, just playing football, being the guy that he was. It was a pleasure to watch.

Q: So I have to ask you, was there anyone behind the scenes that the average fan may not know about, someone who should be spotlighted for their efforts from the time you were there?

JR: I know: I always, always, always loved Bryan Bailey, because Bailey rehabbed my knee. He kicked my ass. But you know what, he told me ahead of time, "Bring a towel with you when you come in here, so you can put it in your mouth. Because we're gonna do this right.

Tom told me he wanted you back to as good as you were, but I'm gonna bring you back better than you were. So we're gonna go to work." He kicked my ass for about a year.

It was a long rehab, it was tough for me after reaching a certain status. I didn't know if I was gonna come back the same way, I was a young college guy with a whole bunch of hormones and attitudes and away from home. And things went on with my family, had a couple deaths in the family that were tough. Bryan helped me tremendously. We'd just go, and I stopped asking how long we were gonna run; we'd just run. And I would just talk to him, and he'd talk and he'd listen. He was instrumental. He and Mike Arthur, I think those guys did a lot of work behind the scenes that went unrecognized. Boyd got a lot of credit. And I talked to Boyd a couple of months ago and he's doing that national strength coach deal, but Bryan was awesome.

And Bryan Bailey, he did such a tremendous job rehabbing my knee that I got a higher rating on my surgically repaired knee than most guys were getting on their non-surgical knees at the Pro Combine. And Tom Heisier was the doctor that did my knee. It was the last one he did before he broke his neck. He went out surfing right after he did my knee and came off a boogie board and landed wrong. That was tough.

Charlie McBride, too. I always loved Charlie McBride. That was one guy who could get me fired up before every game. He just knew what to say, when to say it and how to say it. He would get us playing for teammates who were injured, playing for such and such family member, you know, whether they had a sickness or death in that family. We'd leave that locker room literally crying, ready to kill for each other. (laughs) I always held him in high regard. Him and Kevin Steele, great regard.

Q: Anybody else?

JR: Tommie was just a great quarterback. Incredible quarterback. We never could have made it as far as we did without him. I thought he had such character and such leadership at such a young age. And one thing about Nebraska, they were never gonna put you on the field if you weren't ready, because they didn't want to embarrass you, the program or your family. So when Tommie made the travel squad we knew he was gonna be special. But I don't think anybody had any idea of just how special he was going to be. Just the patience, the intelligence, the leadership ability at such a young age, the composure, that talent level. If there was ever a guy, I thought him and Jamelle Holloway were two of the best option quarterbacks I'd ever seen in my life, just incredible. Quiet, understated, never in trouble. Just a good kid.

Q: Tommie was all business, wasn't he?

JR: Yeah, he was. When he stepped on the field, we knew. Big jokester. Funny kid. But a hell of a football player.

Q: Well, John, I could bother you for another hour's worth of questions. (laughs)

JR: One thing I've got to mention… the other day we talked about that book 'Good to Great' and character and all that. Well, they used to bring in the high school students during summer camp. And so a lot of us would go out there and they have the guys doing all sorts of stuff -and Kevin Steele was a great coach, but he was really one of those high energy personalities, always on the go- and I remember one time he kind of slipped and let out some profanities around these high school students. And I remember Tom going, "Hey Kevin, come here!" And he said this in front of everybody, he said, "I don't ever want to hear you talk to a guy like that. You can get your point across without talking to a guy like that." And Kevin said, "Okay, Coach. I'm sorry." And Tom was, "No, there's no need to apologize. Just make sure it doesn't happen again." And that's the type of guy that he is: he lived it. We all knew that he was a faithful guy to Christ and I have such an appreciation for him that I don't think I really had when I was there. It's grown over the years. And I look back on it, and he really was teaching us to be men.

And I think that's something that goes understated. Because there were a lot of guys there who didn't have both parents in the house, they didn't have a father. A lot of guys, if you look down deep and you really admit it, they'll say, "He was like a father to me." There was a lot more than being a head coach, man. He was... he was somebody you could count on. If he gave you his word on something, he was gonna do it. And it was awesome. I hated to piss him off by going to play baseball, but, oh well. (laughs)

Q: When did you play baseball?

JR: I played the summer before my senior season. I got drafted by the Braves and got a call from the Braves scout. The White Sox had just given up my rights because they drafted me out of high school. A guy named Brian Kohlsheen, a native Nebraskan, he was a huge Tom Osborne fan, so he worked me out and I had a pretty good workout for him. Well, I drove home and talked to my parents and they said, "Well, whatever you want to do, go ahead and do it." So I actually signed the contract then and I actually had to give up my scholarship, which was no big deal because they were going to pay for the rest of school and all that.

And I never consulted Tom. It didn't, in my wildest dreams, cross my mind that I should consult Tom. It was just the excitement of being able to play another additional sport, accomplish some childhood dreams. And when I go back to camp I guess word got out that this guy was working me out, and I hadn't told anybody that I'd signed with them yet. So Tom called this meeting -and I felt so bad, because this guy walks in and he's like, "Oh my god, it's Tom Osborne." He holds him in such reverence, "Oh, this is Tom Osborne!"- he goes, "Coach Osborne, how are you doing? I'm a long-time fan…" And Coach Osborne looks at him and he goes, "How dare you come onto my campus and try to recruit one of our players!" And I go, 'Oh man, the mood is not the way that I thought it was going to be.' (laughs) I figured I'd gently tell him that I was gonna play baseball for the summer, and it got pretty heated. And I finally said, 'You know what, let's cut through all this crap. I've already signed with them.' And Tom looked at me and said, "The conversation is done." He got up and he walked out.

And I remember talking to Toby when I got back to the apartment. He called Coach McBride and Charlie said, "Tom told me. I saw him leaving the locker room." And then I spoke with Coach Osborne and said, 'What's the deal. What's your problem?' And he said, "You signed and you didn't even ask me." And I said, 'I have a dad. My dad is in Houston.' And he goes, "That's fine, but I'm having a tough time deciding whether or not I'm gonna let you play football for me next year." And I went, 'What?!' (laughs) And we were going back and forth for a little while and I told him, 'You won't win a game without me.' And he said, "Are you that confident?" And I said, 'Yeah, because you've got a young secondary back there and I'm the only guy coming back with experience.' So we kind of left it at that. Later on Toby called Coach McBride and Coach McBride said, "You know what, things got heated. Tom's not going to kick him off the team. He's probably going to come back with something John's gonna have to do, so he better be ready for it. He'll calm down and it'll blow over. Just tell him to have fun playing baseball and don't get hurt and come back ready to play." So I went home and Tom called me before I was to leave on the plane for Atlanta. And he said, "I guess we both said some things we didn't mean. Okay, here's the deal: you're coming back and I want you to play corner, and I want you coming back at 185 lbs. Anything above 185 and you will not play." And I said, 'That's it?' and he said, "Yup. And by the way, learn how to hit a curve ball." (laughs)

So I get there and Bruce Benedict is our coach -and I'm a long-time Atlanta fan, so I knew who Bruce was- and Bruce grew up in Omaha, right? So he's a huge Osborne fan. So I caught him trucking on the field the first day and he's walking around with his chest all stuck out and he looks at me and he goes, "Guess who I talked to today?" And I said, 'Judging by the size of your chest and how far it's sticking out, you probably talked to my head coach.' (laughs) And he goes, "Oh yeah, I've been a fan of Nebraska for years and I always wanted to talk to him. So you made one of my childhood dreams come true." It was pretty cool. He goes, "He told me not to let you get too big out here lifting weights, and he told me that you better come back in shape and I better not hurt you. He needs you next year." It was cool. We ironed everything out.

When I got back he called me into the office and I stepped on the scales at exactly 185 that day. He said, "Well, you're a man of your word." And I said, 'Yeah, you're a man of your word, too.' There was mutual respect that day, so it was cool. I've got so many stories. I'm Mr. Nebraska.

Q: So you were in single A, high Rookie Ball?

JR: Yeah, I was in high A. I hadn't picked up a bat in like 3 and one half years. So it was, honestly, like learning how to play baseball all over again. A lot of talent, but a lot of bus trips.

It was weird, because we were treated like kings in Division 1 football, and here I am on these cheesy, crappy buses. I would get up in the morning and do football drills and things like that and then go to the baseball fields. So many days were like 6 in the morning to 11 o'clock at night.

Q: Hanging around the clubhouse eating fried chicken, going to Denny's..

JR: And the Waffle House.

Q: Dude! That's what I loved about the South. I had the Waffle House menu memorized!

JR: That was my one vice. I would eat a waffle, but everything else was grilled chicken salad and everything for the summer. I knew I had to come back in shape.

Q: What team were you assigned to?

JR: I was with the Danville Braves. Appalachian League.

Q: There you go! I was racking my brain trying to think of the name of that team. We swallowed some of the same dirt from those fields, only different years.

JR: Really?

Q: Oh yeah, I'd passed through just about every minor league park in America when I was doing the minor league circuit with the Chickenman. And I have to tell you, Waffle House to me is like Runza to you. I've witnessed more, heard more, done more crazy things in Waffle Houses throughout the South than you would ever believe, John. (laughs) From Amarillo, Texas to Chattanooga, Tennessee to Daytona, Florida...

JR: (laughs) You're serious? Get outta here! That was my one vice.

I got too big up top lifting for football, and by the time I got things straightened out and got to hitting I had to go back and play football. And I had the draft coming up the next year, but it was fun while it lasted. As far as doing things in life I was able to check that box off, but the minors were brutal.

Q: Dealing with all those crazy Dominicans on the roster?

JR: Yeah, that was three quarters of our team! Funny, I was sitting here a couple years ago and I was watching an Angels game on TV, and the relief pitcher comes on and it's Esteban Yan! And I'd been telling my wife all these stories about these guys, because they were some funny characters; some of the things they would say and their broken-English and stuff. And his whole thing was, "Yacky-yacky," and he'd make this sign with his thumb like he was masturbating or something."Yacky-yacky." Those were the only words he knew. And here he is on TV and comes to the mound and I'm just busting up! (laughs) My wife comes in and says, "What are you watching?!" And I'm, 'It's Esteban!' And she goes, "Oh, the 'yacky-yacky' guy?" (laughs)

Q: (laughing) Well, John, it's about both of our bedtimes, but thank you so much for your evening on the phone. I forget how fun it was working with and being around you guys.

JR: It was great. I had a good time rehashing some of these old memories.

End conversation.

A master storyteller with a steel bear-trap of a memory, John took us back to the precise time in history that turned the tide for future Husker fortunes. Some things change and some things stay the same, and it could be honestly and accurately said that every season's team had as one of its main goals the winning of the final bowl game that would give Tom Osborne his first National Championship. It's a shame John isn't able to claim that proud honor today, but you as well as I know that he had a grand hand in making it happen. It still bothers him. Remember, his 'Arrrggh', earlier? That's evidence of a man's frustration for ever so closely missing the making of football history, eternal bragging rights and all.

John took us into the most private of team discussions, behind closed doors and into an almost sacred inner sanctum, allowing us to listen in on the turning point, the nexus, the critical juncture of where Nebraska's recruiting mentality was headed when he spoke of Coach Osborne's, "I'm tired of losing these bowl games. We used to recruit for a certain type of athlete and not go into certain neighborhoods. I think for us to compete at a level you guys want to compete at and a level we want to compete at and win national titles, we're gonna have to go into those areas and after those guys who are gonna be able to academically live up to our standards." What I find quite enlightening and truly astounding is the fact that the Nebraska coaching staff, in every sense of the word, was actually asking the student-athletes' permission to begin recruiting in some of the more questionable social demographics and locales of America, intimating that taking a chance on some of them would also be taking a chance on the refininement and revisement of the image of Nebraska Football, for good or possible ill. And their answer was? "Yeah, go for it!" This meant their newfound team ownership also came with a potentially profound task of exhibiting greater organizational stewardship, peer leadership, and brotherhood as they helped steer the ship. As we all know, times came when the ride was less than smooth sailing: "We were like, "Hey, it's your team." And he was like, "No, it's our team.""

"As it turns out...." John said, "we ended up meeting (the pro wrestlers) downstairs at the bottom floor of this place and all hell broke loose." I've been thinking about these fights we've heard about, and despite their rather unsavory and uncivil nature of dispute resolution, I've arrived at a place where I believe it should be mandatory -almost a necessity- to place a group of young men in a physical confrontation to test their mettle without the benefit of a structured play call: without referees, without rules, and allow them to sink or swim, bloody or be bloodied, to bond or fracture as a consequence. I'm not here to say what they did was wrong or what they did was right on these occasions, but we do know that many of these young men have given us every indication to believe that the off-field fisticuffs played a most positive part in making those great 60 & 3 teams what they were. Remember Dave Ellis', "Warriors, Paulie. Warriors…" earlier? Don't mess with Nebraska.

Notable quote #2:
John Reece on a young Tommie Frazier: "Incredible quarterback. We never could have made it as far as we did without him. I thought he had such character and such leadership at such a young age... Just the patience, the intelligence, the leadership ability at such a young age, the composure, that talent level."

Please continue to:

No Place Like Nebraska: Anatomy of an Era, Volume 2

:Appendix/Attachments

WASHINGTON STATE
SEPTEMBER 30, 1995

DEFENSIVE SPECIAL TEAMS

KICK-OFF COVERAGE

L5	L4	L3	L2	L1	KICKER	R1	R2	R3	R4	R5
FULLMAN	WARFIELD	MACFARLIN	KELSAY	HESSE	BROWN	PENLAND	LEGATE	WILLIAMS	STOKES	T. WILLIAMS
DENNIS	VELAND	JO.MKVKA	JO. MAKOVKA	KELSAY	REITZLAFF	COLMAN	RUCKER	FARLEY	BOOKER	FULLMAN
BENES	ELAHAK	SCHMADEKE	SKODA	V.JACKSON	KOSCH	TOLINE		HOGREEE	ROBERTS	WALTHER

DEFINITE ON-SIDE KICK

F1	F2	F3	F4
CHEATHAM	FARLEY	ARNOLD	BOOKER

B1	B2
WARFIELD	MINTER

S1	S2	S3	SS
DENNIS	STOKES	MCFARLIN	WILLIAMS

(C. JOHNSON)

BAT TEAM (X PT. FG BLOCK)

Position	Starter	Backup
RC	FARLEY	STOKES
RUSH	WISTROM	RUCKER
TACKLE	J. PETER	JENKINS
NOSE	C. PETER	SALTZMAN
TACKLE	OGARD	SALTSMAN
SAM	FOREMAN	WILLIAMS
F/S	WARFIELD	MINTER
ROV	MINTER	MCFARLIN
WILL	TERWILLIGER	PENLAND
MIKE	COLEMAN	HESSE
C	WILLIAMS	BOOKER

SPECIAL FORCES (PUNT RETURN)

(B) (B)
(E) (T) (G) (C) (G) (T) (E)

LR	LOB	LIB	N	RIB	ROB	RR
WARFIELD	BOOKER	J. WILLIAMS	KELSAY	PENLAND	RUCKER	FARLEY
DENNIS	TOMICH	KELSAY		POREMAN	WISTROM	STOKES

LC	PP	RM	RC
MCFARLIN	CHEATHAM	BAUL	MINTER
SCHMADEKE	FULLMAN	FULLMAN	LEGATE

Huskers

OFFENSIVE PRACTICE SCHEDULE
Tuesday - October 3, 1995

NEW OFFENSE
52-58
PRO RT 42 CS FL REV LT PASS

Time	Activity
3:30 - 3:40	Stretch
3:40 - 3:45	Spec
3:45 - 4:00	Group - 3:55 - 4:00 1 on 1
4:00 - 4:20	Full Team Skeleton & GL
4:20 - 4:25	Break
4:25 - 4:35	Option
4:35 - 4:45	Kick - Separate

I	SPD	DEF
4:45 - 5:00	1 - 3	2 - 4	3 - 4 - 1 - 2
5:00 - 5:15	2 - 3	1 - 4	3 - 4 - 1 - 2

Time	Activity
5:15 - 5:25	K.O.
5:25 - 5:45	Run, Throw, Lift

SPD

PRO LT
48 CS FL REV RT PASS FL MOT (H SHADE 8)
PRO RT
SHIFT F 42 CS BOOT LT (H OV 5)
49 OS P 9 SLNT & C PROT (H SHADE 9)
44 ISO P 9 REL (UNDER 5)
53 9 P & C IB DRAG (BEAR MIKE BEAR RT 1 F)
TIGHT RT
11 OPT P 1 SLNT & GO TB PROT ('')
46 ISO P 2 REL (H SHADE SAM BINGO 8)
47 DRAW P 1 CB (OVER LT WIDE SAM BUMP TOM PLUG 1 F)
47 DIVE P 8 DEL FLAT FL MOT (H SHADE WILL BINGO 8)
OPEN LT
SHIFT 11 OPT P (H OV 5)
57 8 CROSS IB DRAG (BEAR MIKE BEAR LT 1 F)
19 OPT P 9 HOOK & GO (UNDER SAM BINGO 2)
ACE
47 DRAW P 9 PIVOT PROT√(H SHADE SAM RT 9)
99 HITCH & GO DUMMY AUD (UND SAM LT BLITZ 2)
42 CS FL REV LT (UND SAM LT 9)
43 DRAW P 2 OUT PROT√(WIDE BLITZ 2)
SG
79 DBL SCRN (WIDE BLITZ 2)
36 IB TRAP√(H SHADE 11 ROB)
79 AUD (UND SAM RT AND FOLD BLITZ 1 F)
71 D.T.O. (OVER SAM LT AND FOLD TIM PLUG NOSE)
POWER LT
11 OPT P WB FLAG PROT SM (50 4 EYE 5-3 3 DEEP ZONE)
F 48 CS BOOT RT TB (" ")
SPD LT
SHIFT 43 DIVE P 8 DEL FLAT (H SHADE WILL WIDE 9)
ACE TRIPS LT
39 SPNT PASS (UNDER SAM RT 4)
47 DRAW P 9 DEL PROT (WIDE BLITZ 2)

GL

POWER RT
44 ISO (60 GL)
41 OS√(49) (60 GL LC FIRE)
41 P√(41) (RED EAG PSY)
11 B√(19) (60 PSYCHO)
32 OPT√(38) (RED EAG 2)
44 ISO P 8 DEL FLAT (60 GL)
*58 (60 PSYCHO)
41 OS PASS 2 CROSS (60 GL)
F 48 CS BOOT RT GL WBM (60 GL)
41 P√(49) (RED EAG 2 SAF LEFT)
41 OS√(41) (RED EAG PSY SAF MID)
TIGHT LT
16 SMASH (60 GL)
19 B√(11) (60 GL SS FIRE RT)
38 OPT√(32) (60 GL)
*52 (RED EAG PSYCHO)

I
PRO LT
47 T TRAP (UND 5)
38 ROLL FL MOT (BEAR 1 LB, PLUG RT 1 F)
38 TRAP SEAL FL MOT (H SH 5)
SHIFT 48 CS SEAL FL MOT (UND 5)
43 DRAW (H OV STG SAM BUMP WILL SUB 1 F)
*48 CT (H OV STG SAM BUMP TE 8)
56 DRAW (H OV STG 11 R)
36 T√(36) (H SH STG 5)
41 OS√(41) (H SH STG SAM BUMP TE 11 R)
42 BOUNCE (UNDER WILL PLUG 1 F)
48 CS FL REV RT FL MOT (UND 5)
OPEN RT
42 CS√(42) (H SH SUB 11 R)
54 DRAW√(56) (UND SAM RT FOLD 11 R)
41 OS√(49) (UND SAM LT BINGO 11 R)
41 P√(41) (H OV SAM LT SUB 1 F)
34 T√(34) (H SH 11 R)
42 BOUNCE√(48) (UND SAM LT FOLD 11 R)
11 DIVE√(11) (UND SAM LT FOLD 9)
TIGHT RT
32 T√(H OV STG 11 R)
32 ROLL√(H OV STG SAM BUMP 11 R)
44 ISO√(H SH STG SAM BUMP M/W TOM PLUG 2)
49 P FL MOT (H SH STG M/W TIM PLUG 2)
ACE
41 OS√(H SH STG SAM RT 8)
*42 CT (H SH SAM RT WIDE BLITZ 8)
SG
48 IB SP LT√(H SH SAM LT W/S FOLD 9)
PRO RT
43 TT (UND 5)
47 DR (H OV STG 5)

OPTION
PRO LT
*19 B (H SH WIDE BLITZ 1 F)
*11 B (BEAR 2 LLB PLUG)
38 OPT SEAL FL MOT (BEAR 2)
19 WALL√(H OV STG 8)
41 SPNT (BEAR 1 FR ONE LB PLUG LT 3 GAP)
OPEN LT
49 SPNT√(H SH WIDE BLITZ 1 F)
19 WALL√(11) (H OV STG 11 R)
*19 B (DE 1 F)
ACE
39 SPNT√(H OV STG SAM RT STEM BEAR 1 F)
31 SPNT SEAL√(H SH SAM LT 2, 9 TECHS)
SPD LT
31 SPNT√(UND 11 R)
SG
39 SPNT√(UND SAM LT FOLD 11 R)
POWER LT
38 OPT√(32) (H SH LT SAM BINGO M/W TORN RC FIRE)

FT SKELETON
OPEN RT 71 2 UNDER (H POWER 9 PI)
SPD LT SHIFT 79 AUD (DIME) (H OV STG NOSE 9 PI)
SG 71 DBL DEL (DIME) (HUSK POW 9 FOOL PI)
ACE 47 DRAW P 9 PIVOT PROT√(H H 4 PI)
SPD RT SHIFT SG 79 8 FIN PROT (MB NOSE 2 SPEC)
PRO LT *57 AUD (SINGLE SWITCH 1 FR)
ACE 71 DBL SCRN (OV BUB 0)
OPEN LT 57 8 POST IB FLAT (HUSK GO 4 PI)
SG 47 DRAW P IB CH (DIME) (HUSK 9 TUFF FULLY PI)
OPEN RT 91 (DIME HUSK OV STG NOSE 11 R)
ACE TRIPS LT 47 DRAW P X WHEEL (HUSK 4 PI)
SG 42 IB SP RT√(DIME BUZZ SAW)

	TONY	GEORGE	CLAYTON	CRAIG	CHARLIE
Meet	2:00				
3:30	STRETCH	STRETCH	STRETCH	STRETCH	STRETCH
3:40 Spec	Ropes-Bags Take Ons	Red Cone Tackling		Warm-up	Warm-up Agil.-FW
3:45	Z Tech Scramble Block Cutback to Boot	Cut Drills		Tackle Boots Cover 9	Tackle Fumble
	Dbl Team Work the Combinations				Down-G T Bub/Ov
G	Mix In Pass Read with TE or OT Blocking	Slot Trips 96 1 TO/2 Hk/3Flat 1 2 3 TO			Dwn & G N-Off Ctr Swp
R		Smash 3 Post 1 Under 2 & 3 TO			
O	Sams Man to Man Drill Trail Tech				Pass Rush Big Bags
U	Wall Call				
P 3:55	Bubble - TE Runs Pick Calls Run Color Checks	1 on 1	1 on 1		

Team Defense   Date 10/3/95

4:00	Full Team Skeleton ①️ v s. 1, ②️ vs. 2 - Switch at 10 Min.
4:20	Break
4:25	Blitzes & Adjustments
4:35	Kicking-->

TEAMWORK

4:45	①️ - 3	②️ - 4	
5:00 T E	②️ - 3	①️ - 4	
5:15 A M	Kick-offs		
5:25	Run, Throw, Lift----	------------------------>	
5:45			

Defense Red Zone

Date 10/3/95

	#	D/D	H	FORM	PLAY	FRONT	COV	CK
-16	1	1-10	R	Ace	IDB12B 1	Husker	Pan	
-13	2	2-13	R	Ace	QDBLBBL	Husker		
-12	3	2-11	R	Ace	IDB4150A			
-12	4	2-11	L	Ace	IDB4150A			
-8	5	2-8	L	AT Rt Mot NB's	QDB18BB1	Hk Ov Stg		
-3	6	1-3	L	Ace	QDBZBBZ	Hk Ov Stg	Zone	
-32	7	2-9	R	Sg NB's Lt	DDB0550H	H Husk	4 PI	
	8	2-14	M	PT Rt	DDB15N1	Husker	4 PI	RR
	9	3-11	R	PT Lt	IDBH7B4	Husker	9	Steal
	10	3-6	M	Sg Duce STNB;s	DDBA0020	Hk	11 Rob	Blue
	11	3-10	R	PT Lt	IDB1101	Hk	9 PI	
	12	1-10	R	IB Mot Ace Trips Lt	IDB11B41	Single Blitz	1 Fr	
BLACK	13			REPEAT 1-6				
	14							
	15							
	16							
	17							
	18							
DIME	19	3-6	M	Mot PT NB's	IDB2151U	Husker	4	Grn/Org
	20		RM	Double Shift PT NB's	IDB14B10	H Husker	4 PI	RR
	21	2-5	M	PT Lt	QDBLLBL	H	4 F PI	
	22	1-10	R	PT NB's	IDB11B11	H	9 PI	
	23							
	24							
	25							
	26							
	27							
	28							
	29							
	30							

Defense   Blitz   Date   10/3/95

		D/D	H	FORM	PLAY		FRONT	COV	CK
D T η #1	1	2-9	L	Ace	IDB-0225A	1	Und Bub Torn	Y 1 Fr Y	
	2	3-6	L	Ace Trips Rt	SDP-NNBBB	2	Und Bub Torn	Y 1 Fr Y	
	3	2-9	R	Y Mot/PT Lt	IDB-12BLB	3	Mid Blitz Cross	2 Spec	
	4	2-11	R	Ace	QDB-LBBLB	4	Mid Blitz M/W	2 Spec	
	5	3-6	M	Ace	IDB-N88NG	5	Buzz Saw	2 Buzz	
D η #2	6	3-4	L	Dbls Wide East	QDB-LB0LB	6	Buzz Saw	2 Buzz	
	7	2-9	L	Dbls Wide East	IDB-0420B	7	Mid Blitz 2 Cross	2 Spec	
	8	3-10	R	Ace Trips Lt	QDB-H40BG	8	Mid Blitz M/W	2 Spec	
3 5 SHIRTS	9	2-8	R	Y Mot/PT Lt	QDB-L207B	9	Wide Blitz Swap	2	
	10	3-6	L	Ace	33 Draw	10	Black	2 Blk	
	11	2-9	M	PT Lt	IDB-1UNHW	11	Sub Blitz X	X 11 Sub	
	12	3-5	L	H Mot/ Ace Trips Rt	IB Screen	12	Und Bub Torn	Y 1 Fr Y	
	13	2-6	M	Ace Trips NB's	QDB-N8B21	13	Black	2 Blk	
GOLD	14	2-9	M	Ace	39 Option	14	Black	2 Blk	
SHIRTS	15	3-4	R	Nr I Pro Lt	SDP-HG0B	15	Wide Blitz	2	
	16	2-7	L	Dbls Wide East Lt	WBP-5B20B	16	Sub Blitz Jet	11 Sub	
DIME #1	17	2-8	L	Ace	SBP-5021B	17	Und Bub Torn	Y 1 Fr Y	
	18	2-6	M	Ace	SBP-0520B	18	Buzz Saw	2 Buzz	
	19	3-5	R	I Pro Rt	19 Spt Opt	19	Wide Blitz	2	
	20					20			
	21					21			
	22					22			
	23					23			
	24					24			
	25					25			
	26					26			
	27					27			
	28					28			
	29					29			
	30					30			

Notes

Notes

Notes

Notes